The ACA ENCYCLOPEDIA of COUNSELING

AMERICAN COUNSELING ASSOCIATION
5999 Stevenson Avenue
Alexandria, VA 22304
www.counseling.org

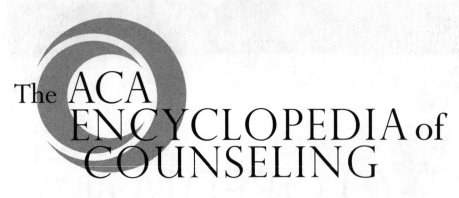

The ACA ENCYCLOPEDIA of COUNSELING

10 9 8 7 6 5 4 3 2 1

AMERICAN COUNSELING ASSOCIATION
5999 Stevenson Avenue
Alexandria, VA 22304

DIRECTOR OF PUBLICATIONS
Carolyn C. Baker

PRODUCTION MANAGER
Bonny E. Gaston

EDITORIAL ASSISTANT
Catherine A. Brumley

COPY EDITOR
Judith O. Johnson

Cover and text design by Bonny E. Gaston

LIBRARY OF CONGRESS CATALOGING-IN-PUBLICATION DATA

The ACA encyclopedia of counseling / American Counseling Association, with contributors.
    p. cm.
  Includes bibliographical references and indexes.
  ISBN 978-1-55620-288-9 (alk. paper)
 1. Counseling—Encyclopedias. I. American Counseling Association.

BF636.54.A23 2008
158'.303—dc22

2008029382

DEDICATION

This effort is dedicated to The One: the Giver of energy, passion, and understanding;
Who makes life worth living and endeavors worth pursuing and accomplishing;
the Teacher of love and forgiveness.

—B. T. E.

CONTENTS

PREFACE

The ACA Encyclopedia of Counseling serves as a comprehensive yet easy-to-use resource for students, practitioners, educators, and researchers in the professional counseling disciplines. It includes more than 400 entries based on the Council for Accreditation of Counseling and Related Educational Programs' (CACREP) eight core areas outlined in its 2009 Standards (see the CACREP Web site). Specifically, traditional and emerging issues in professional counseling disciplines have been selected and presented as entries based on the following CACREP core areas:

- **Professional Orientation and Ethical Practice.** Professional functioning topics that include history and philosophy of the counseling profession, counselor roles and responsibilities, ethical and legal concerns, professional advocacy, professional organizations, and professional credentialing
- **Social and Cultural Diversity.** Multicultural relationship concepts that include awareness, knowledge, and skills related to working in a diverse counseling relationship and increasing cultural self-awareness; historical and contemporary trends that characterize the United States as a pluralistic society; social activism in counseling settings, local schools, and communities as well as in larger social, political, and legal systems
- **Human Growth and Development.** An understanding of human processes and development in individual, familial, cultural, and community contexts, including the following topics: cognitive and personality development; the influence of crisis and trauma on human behavior; psychopathology, addictions, and situational factors that affect normal and abnormal behavior; and the facilitation of wellness models for human processes
- **Career Development.** Career and other life development topics that include career theories; career decision-making process; job placement and labor market information; career assessment; and the integration of career, leisure, family, and cultural roles in individuals' lives
- **Helping Relationships.** The counseling process in a multicultural context, including topics such as the integration of the counseling philosophy in counseling goals, interviewing and counseling skills, differential responses for crisis and emergency situations with clients and communities, consultation, and counseling theories

- **Group Work.** Components of group process and outcome that are both theoretical and experiential and include topics such as group dynamics, group theories, group leadership skills, group methods, curative factors, and group member roles
- **Assessment.** An understanding of individual and group assessment and evaluation in a multicultural context that involves concepts such as history of assessment; assessment types and purposes; statistical concepts; validity and reliability; and social, ethical, and legal issues in assessment and evaluation
- **Research and Program Evaluation.** An overview of research methodological and statistical concepts, including program evaluation and needs assessment; qualitative, quantitative, single-case, and outcome designs; and professional, social, and cultural rationale for increasing research practice in professional counseling settings

The entries collectively provide substantial information about each of these areas to assist in the preparation and continued education of various CACREP professional counseling degree programs, including clinical mental health counseling; career counseling; school counseling, college counseling, and student development; addiction counseling; and marriage, couple, and family counseling.

The ACA Encyclopedia of Counseling was created to fill a void in the professional counseling literature by offering a sole resource that presents and integrates material from the CACREP eight core areas for the reader in a scholarly yet understandable manner. The editors undertook the development of *The ACA Encyclopedia of Counseling* to offer the reader an optimal number of entries that adequately cover the core areas, provide foundational as well as recent literature about a particular topic, and include professional counseling examples in many entries to illustrate complex concepts. Although there are several documents and texts in the professional counseling literature that speak to these CACREP core areas individually, no document or text to date has provided information on as many professional counseling topics as this one. This book goes beyond simply defining counseling concepts to making the material come alive for readers and connecting the material to their practice, teaching, supervisory, and research endeavors.

The final list of entries for this book was selected from reviewing seminal documents and texts used in a variety of professional counseling-degree programs, identifying keywords and themes among these sources in a rigorous manner, and undergoing several iterations of expanding and collapsing topics as necessary.

The *Encyclopedia* entries included in this book are presented in alphabetical order to make finding information quicker and more efficient. Each *Encyclopedia* entry contains essential information for a particular topic, with boldfaced terms indicating a topic to which the reader should attend. References to other entries in the *Encyclopedia* appear in many entries to direct the reader to other places in the text that a topic or subtopic is discussed in more detail. Furthermore, readers can investigate additional resources provided at the end of entries for more information about the counseling topic.

■ Citing Encyclopedia Entries

Entries should be cited according to the style of the *Publication Manual of the American Psychological Association,* using the chapter in an edited book format and giving appropriate credit to the entry author or authors and listing the American Counseling Association as the book editor, such as:

> Hays, D. G. (2009). Trustworthiness in qualitative research. In American Counseling Association (Ed.), *The ACA encyclopedia of counseling* (pp. 555–556). Alexandria, VA: American Counseling Association.

Please note that the editors volunteered thousands of hours to accomplish the production of this work and received no remuneration in any form, nor was any scholarly credit sought. The editors considered this project a gift to the profession and sincerely hope that it fulfills the stated purpose of enhancing preservice and continuing education for professional counselors, students, supervisors, and counselor educators.

■ Selection of Content Editors

The work of soliciting, revising, and finalizing more than 400 submissions from approximately 400 authors in less than 1 year requires hard work, team work, and connections. As the General Editor, I handpicked the content editors for their demonstrated competence, work ethic, collegial disposition, and professional connections in the counseling world. I have worked with each of these editors in the past, and each has demonstrated extraordinary competence, excellence, and professionalism. Each content editor donated several hundred hours and brought years of scholarly achievement and vital expertise to this project. The counseling profession owes them a deep debt of gratitude.

■ Contributors to the Book

Individual contributors of entries to *The ACA Encyclopedia of Counseling* were either invited by editors or participated in an initial self-nomination process. Contributors were selected or approved in collaboration among area content editors and the General Editor. Contributors' entries were submitted and processed through a tiered peer review, whereby a contributor submitted an entry to the relevant content editor or editors for a CACREP core area for an initial review. Subsequent communications with the Associate General Editor and General Editor resulted in multiple revisions of each entry. Ordinarily, contributions were reviewed by at least three peer reviewers and, at times, by as many as five peer reviewers. This approach to reviewing each entry allowed an optimal, thorough evaluation from multiple perspectives to ensure that an entry was addressing a particular topic in an accurate, relevant, and comprehensive manner.

ACKNOWEDGMENTS

The editors thank Lacey Wallace and Katie Tasch, graduate assistants extraordinaire, for their tireless assistance with the coordination of numerous tasks involved in preparation of the original manuscript. All of the contributing authors are to be commended for lending their expertise in the various topical areas. Carolyn C. Baker of the American Counseling Association has been wonderfully responsive and supportive. Her production staff included Judith O. Johnson, Susan Wilmoth, Bonny E. Gaston, and Catherine A. Brumley.

ABOUT THE EDITORS

◼ General Editor

Bradley T. Erford, PhD, NCC, LCPC, LPC, LP, LSP, is a professor in the school counseling program of the Education Specialties Department in the School of Education at Loyola University Maryland. He is the recipient of the American Counseling Association (ACA) Research Award, ACA Arthur A. Hitchcock Distinguished Professional Service Award, ACA Professional Development Award, and ACA Carl D. Perkins Government Relations Award. He was also inducted as an ACA Fellow. In addition, he has received the Association for Assessment in Counseling and Education (AACE) AACE/*MECD* Research Award, AACE Exemplary Practices Award, AACE President's Special Merit Award, the Association for Counselor Education and Supervision's Robert O. Stripling Award for Excellence in Standards, Maryland Association for Counseling and Development (MACD) Maryland Counselor of the Year, MACD Counselor Advocacy Award, MACD Professional Development Award, and MACD Counselor Visibility Award. He is the editor of seven texts: *Transforming the School Counseling Profession* (1st & 2nd eds.; 2003 & 2007, Merrill Prentice Hall); *Professional School Counseling: A Handbook of Principles, Programs and Practices* (1st & 2nd eds.; 2004 & 2008, PRO-ED); *Assessment for Counselors* (2007, Houghton Mifflin/Lahaska Press); *Research and Evaluation in Counseling* (2008, Houghton Mifflin/Lahaska Press); and *The Counselor's Guide to Clinical, Personality and Behavioral Assessment* (2005, Houghton Mifflin/Lahaska Press). He is also the author of two more books: *Educational Applications of the WISC-IV* (2006, Western Psychological Services) and *Group Activities: Firing Up for Performance* (2007, Pearson Merrill Prentice Hall). His research specialization falls primarily in development and technical analysis of psychoeducational tests and has resulted in the publication of several dozen refereed journal articles, several dozen book chapters, and eight published tests. He is a member of the ACA Governing Council and the ACA 20/20 Visioning Committee. He is past president, past treasurer, and past member-at-large for publications of AACE; past chair and parliamentarian of the ACA Southern Region; past chair of ACA's Task Force on High Stakes Testing; past chair of ACA's Standards for Test Users Task Force; past chair of ACA's Interprofessional Committee; past chair of the ACA Public Awareness and Support Committee (cochair of the national awards subcommittee); chair of the convention and past chair of the Screening Assessment Instruments Committee for AACE; past president of the Maryland Association for Counseling and Development; past president of the Maryland Association for Measurement and Evaluation; past president of the Maryland Association for Counselor Education and Supervision; and past president of the Maryland Association for Mental Health Counselors. He is also an editorial board member of the *Journal of Counseling & Development* and an ad hoc reviewer for *Counselor Education and Supervision, Measurement and Evaluation in Counseling and Development,* and *Educational and Psychological Measurement*. Dr. Erford has been a faculty member at Loyola since 1993 and is a Licensed Clinical Professional Counselor, Licensed Professional Counselor, National Certified Counselor, Licensed Psychologist, and Licensed School Psychologist. Prior to arriving at Loyola, Dr. Erford was a school psychologist/counselor in the Chesterfield County, Virginia, Public Schools. He maintains a private practice specializing in assessment and treatment of children and adolescents. A graduate of The University of Virginia (PhD), Bucknell University (MA), and Grove City College (BS), he teaches courses in Testing and Measurement, Psycho-Educational Assessment, Lifespan Development, Research and Evaluation in Counseling, School Counseling, Counseling Techniques, and Stress Management.

Associate General Editor and Research Content Area Editor

Danica G. Hays, PhD, LPC, NCC, is an assistant professor in the Department of Educational Leadership and Counseling at Old Dominion University. She received her doctorate in counselor education and practice from Georgia State University. She is the recipient of the American Counseling Association (ACA) Research Award and the Glen E. Hubele National Graduate Student Award. In addition, she has received the Association for Assessment in Counseling and Education (AACE) *MECD* Research Award, AACE President's Special Merit Award, Association for Counselor Education and Supervision (ACES) Outstanding Graduate Student Leadership Award, Chi Sigma Iota International (CSI) Outstanding Doctoral Student Award, and CSI Fellow. Dr. Hays's professional service includes AACE member-at-large for membership, AACE member-at-large for publications, AACE secretary, Southern Association for Counselor Education and Supervision cochair of the Multicultural Interest Network, and the ACES supervision task force. She also serves as an editorial board member of the *Counselor Education and Supervision* journal and an ad hoc reviewer for the *Measurement and Evaluation in Counseling and Development* journal. Dr. Hays's research interests include qualitative methodology, assessment and diagnosis, trauma and gender issues, and multicultural and social justice concerns in counselor preparation and community mental health. She has published numerous refereed journal articles and book chapters. She is coeditor of an upcoming text, *Developing Multicultural Counseling: A Systems Approach* (Pearson Merrill Prentice Hall). She has been a faculty member at Old Dominion University since 2006 and has prior teaching experience at the University of New Orleans, Argosy University–Atlanta, and Georgia State University. Her primary teaching responsibilities are master's- and doctoral-level research methods courses, assessment, and doctoral supervision.

Social and Cultural Foundations Content Editor

Catherine Y. Chang, PhD, LPC, NCC, is an associate professor and program coordinator of the counselor education and practice doctoral program in the Department of Counseling and Psychological Services at Georgia State University. She received her doctorate in counselor education from The University of North Carolina at Greensboro. She is the recipient of the American Counseling Association (ACA) Research Award, the ACA Counselor Educator Advocacy Award, the Association for Assessment in Counseling and Education (AACE) *MECD* Research Award, and the Pre-Tenure Counselor Educator Award from the Southern Association for Counselor Education and Supervi-

sion (SACES). She serves on the editorial boards for *Counselor Education and Supervision* and the *Measurement and Evaluation in Counseling and Development* journals. Dr. Chang's professional service includes president-elect of Chi Sigma Iota International (CSI), treasurer of CSI, past member-at-large for awards and past secretary for AACE, chairperson for the Association for Counselor Education and Supervision Committee on Social Justice and Human Rights, and chairperson for SACES Multicultural Counseling Interest Network. Her research interests include multicultural counseling and supervision, Asian and Korean concerns, and multicultural issues in assessment. Dr. Chang has been a faculty member at Georgia State University since 2000, and her primary teaching responsibilities include practicum/internship, appraisal, supervision of supervision, and counseling seminar. She is a Licensed Professional Counselor in Georgia and a National Certified Counselor.

Human Growth and Development Content Coeditor

Darcie Davis-Gage, PhD, LPC, is an assistant professor in the Department of Educational Leadership, Counseling, and Postsecondary Education at the University of Northern Iowa. She received her BA in psychology from Loras College in Dubuque, Iowa, and both her master's degree and specialist in counseling degree from Pittsburg State University in Pittsburg, Kansas. She completed her doctorate in counselor education from the University of Iowa. She holds a counseling license for the state of Missouri. Dr. Davis-Gage is an active member of the American Counseling Association and the Association for Counselor Education and Supervision. Currently, she serves on the executive board of the Iowa Mental Health Counseling Association and is president of the Iowa Association for Counselor Education and Supervision. Dr. Davis-Gage's research interests are in the areas of group counseling, clinical supervision, and diversity issues related to counselor education and practice. She recently authored a book chapter in *Counseling Children and Adolescents* (4th ed.; 2008, Love) and coauthored book chapters in *Group Work in the School* (2009, Pearson Merrill Prentice Hall). Her teaching interests are in the areas of group counseling, psychopathology and diagnosis, multicultural counseling, and mental health practicum and internship. Dr. Davis-Gage worked as a counselor for 10 years in a variety of mental health settings. During her internship as a master's-degree student, she worked with geriatric clients in a partial hospitalization program conducting various counseling and psychoeducational groups. After graduating, she accepted a counseling position at the Lafayette House, a women's mental health agency, that provided individual, group, and family counseling to women and children affected by substance abuse, domestic violence, and sexual abuse. She also facilitated group treatment for men who were charged with domestic assault. Following her work at the Lafayette House, she was the counselor and coordinator of outreach at Missouri Southern State University (MSSU). While at MSSU, she developed and implemented individual and group counseling services and programs designed to address the mental health needs of the students. In addition, while working at Lafayette House and MSSU, she had a small private practice. While working on her doctorate, she worked as an academic counselor for 1st-year students. In this setting, she helped students adjust to university life and choose courses and majors and helped connect them to various university resources.

Helping Relationships Content Area Editor

Samuel T. Gladding, PhD, NCC, CCMHC, is the chair of and a professor in the Department of Counseling at Wake Forest University. His academic degrees are from Wake Forest (BA, MAEd), Yale University (MA), and The University of North Carolina at Greensboro (PhD). In addition to his current position at Wake Forest University, he has served as assistant to the president for special projects (1990–1997) and associate provost (1997–2007) at the university. He has taken students abroad to study in Vienna, Austria, and to work with Mother Teresa in Calcutta, India. He has also served as a disaster relief worker with the American Red Cross both in New York and at Virginia Tech. In addition, Dr. Gladding has done work with universities, associations, and agencies in Malaysia, Australia, South Africa, and Sweden. Prior to his arrival at Wake Forest University, Dr. Gladding held academic appointments at the University of Alabama at Birmingham (1984–1990) and Fairfield University (1981–1984) in Connecticut. He has been a clinician at a mental health center, a captain in the U.S. Army, and an instructor of psychology at a community college. He has served as president of the American Counseling Association (ACA; 2004–2005), the Association for Counselor Education and Supervision (ACES; 1996–1997), the Association for Specialists in Group Work (ASGW; 1994–1995), and Chi Sigma Iota (CSI; 1989–1990). He is the former editor of *Journal for Specialists in Group Work* and has also published widely (30 books, 40 refereed journal articles, 20 book chapters, 50 poems). In 1997, Dr. Gladding was cited as being in the top 1% of contributors to the flagship journal of ACA, the *Journal of Counseling & Development*. Dr. Gladding is the recipient of numerous honors including being named an ACA Fellow and ASGW Fellow. He is also the recipient of the Gilbert and Kathleen Wrenn Award for a Humanitarian & Caring Person (ACA Counselor of the Year); the Bridgebuilder Award from the ACA Foundation; the Humanitarian Award from the Association for Spiritual, Ethical, and Religious Values in Counseling; the Lifetime Achievement Award from the Association for Creativity in Counseling; the Eminent Career Award from ASGW; the Professional Leadership Award from ACES; the Academy

of Leaders for Excellence designation from CSI; the Thomas J. Sweeney Professional Leadership Award from CSI; the Outstanding Service Award from the National Association for Poetry Therapy; the Joseph W. and Lucille U. Hollis Outstanding Publication Award from the Counseling Association for Humanistic Education and Development; and the Ella Stephens Barrett Leadership Award from the North Carolina Counseling Association. Dr. Gladding is a National Certified Counselor, a Certified Clinical Mental Health Counselor, and a Licensed Professional Counselor in North Carolina. He continues to practice as a counselor in Winston-Salem, North Carolina, with CareNet of the Triad. He is also active in civic affairs and has served as president of Leadership Winston-Salem.

Assessment Content Area Coeditor

Brian A. Glaser, PhD, received his doctorate from Indiana State University. He is a professor in the Department of Counseling and Human Development Services at The University of Georgia. He is on the faculties of the community counseling program, the counseling psychology program, and marriage and family certificate program. Dr. Glaser received his BS and MS degrees from Bradley University. He worked for several years as a master's-level psychologist in state hospitals in Illinois before returning for doctoral training. He was a temporary assistant professor at Indiana State University for 1 year before arriving at The University of Georgia in 1990. He is codirector of the Juvenile Counseling and Assessment Program and Gaining Insight into Relationships for Lifelong Success(JCAP/GIRLS), which are collaborative instruction/research/service projects among the Georgia Department of Juvenile Justice, the College of Education, and the Clarke County Juvenile Court. The International Association of Addictions and Offender Counselors named JCAP/GIRLS 2005 Program of the Year. He is active in the Association for Assessment in Counseling and Education (president 2005–2006), the International Association of Addictions and Offender Counseling (IAAOC), and the American Association of Marriage and Family Therapy. His principal areas of interest are appraisal, conduct-disordered youth, and juvenile offenders. He received the 2003 Association for Assessment in Counseling Research Award and was recently named *Journal of Addictions & Offender Counseling's* third most prolific scholarly author and contributor from 1999 to 2004. In 2006, he received the Addictions and Offender Counseling Educator Excellence Award from IAAOC.

Career Development and Assessment Content Areas Coeditor

David A. Jepsen, PhD, is professor emeritus in the Department of Counseling, Rehabilitation and Student Development at the University of Iowa (UI). He first joined the American Personnel and Guidance Association and the National Vocational Guidance Association (NVGA) in 1960 and a few years later joined the American School Counselor Association and the Association for Counselor Education and Supervision and was a charter member of the Association for Measurement and Evaluation in Guidance, now named Association for Assessment in Counseling and Education (AACE). After serving on a NVGA committee and on the *Vocational Guidance Quarterly* (*VGQ;* later renamed *The Career Development Quarterly*) editorial board, he was selected as *VGQ* editor for two 3-year terms. This was followed by election as president of the National Career Development Association (NCDA) and serving a 3-year term on the American Association for Counseling and Development (AACD) Governing Council and 1 year on the AACD executive committee. In the 1990s, he served on a few American Counseling Association (ACA) committees and journal editorial boards. In 2002, he was elected to the executive committee of the Association for Assessment in Counseling (now AACE). After receiving an MS degree in counseling and guidance from the University of Wisconsin–Madison (UW), in 1963, he was a counselor in Wisconsin public schools and UW laboratories for the next 7 years. He earned a PhD from UW in 1970 in counseling and guidance and became a counselor educator at UI, where he worked continuously, except for a brief time at the University of Maryland, College Park, until retirement in 2005. He is very proud of many former students who have made their own contributions to the counseling profession and to ACA and its divisions. Through contacts in professional associations and with professionals who graduated from UI, he has presented papers, workshops, and lectures in Japan, Taiwan, Portugal, Spain, Canada, Great Britain, and Ireland. Longevity and loyalty within universities and professional associations have brought public recognition in the form of awards. He is especially proud of the NCDA Eminent Career Award (1995), election as a charter member of the Iowa Academy of Education (1996), the UI College of Education Teaching Award (1999), and the ACA Extended Research Award (2006). He is both an NCDA Fellow (2000) and an ACA Fellow (2007). Early in his career, he overlearned the value of sound scholarship to a profession and measures his own successes in terms of the quality of scholarly work produced and frequency with which it is used by fellow professionals. Over the past 4 decades, he has authored about 80 published articles and book chapters for counselor and counselor educator audiences.

■ Professional Identity and Ethics Content Area Coeditor

Lynn E. Linde, EdD, NCC, is the director of Clinical Programs for the school counseling program in the Educational Specialties Department at Loyola University Maryland. She is an American Counseling Association (ACA) Fellow and a recipient of the ACA Counselor Educator Advocacy Award, the ACA Carl Perkins Government Relations Award, the Association for Counselor Education and Supervision (ACES) Distinguished Professional Service Award for Supervision, and the Southern ACES Award for Outstanding Program Supervision. In addition, she has received the Maryland Association for Counseling and Development (MACD) Advocacy Award, The MACD President's Award for Outstanding Contribution to the Profession, the MACD Legislative Award, the MACD Professional Development Award, and the MACD Counselor Visibility Award. She also received two (Maryland) Governor's Citations, one for her work in youth suicide prevention and the other for service to the profession; the Maryland State Board of Education recognition for service to the profession; and several other local awards. She is currently the president-elect of ACA and cochair of the ACA Ethics Committee, the Southern Region representative to the 20/20 Visioning Committee, and a subcommittee chair and the secretary for the Professional Counseling Fund. She is a past ACA Governing Council representative, past chair of ACA Southern Region, past member of the ACA Finance Committee, ACA PPL Committee, ACA Blue Ribbon Task Force, and Governing Council liaison to the High Stakes Testing Committee. She is also the past president of MACD. Her area of expertise is ethical, legal, and professional issues for school counselors. She has authored or coauthored five chapters in textbooks and has conducted numerous workshops on these topics. She has been a clinical faculty member at Loyola since 2004 and teaches clinical classes, Professional Issues and Ethics, and Theories of Counseling. Prior to joining Loyola full-time, she was the chief of the Student Services and Alternative Programs Branch at the Maryland State Department of Education. She holds a doctorate in counseling and an MA in school counseling from The George Washington University and a BA in psychology from Clark University.

■ Career Development Content Area Coeditor

Spencer G. Niles, PhD, is professor and department head for Counselor Education, Counseling Psychology, and Rehabilitation Services at The Pennsylvania State University. Previously, he served as professor and assistant dean of the Curry School of Education at The University of Virginia and as a senior career counselor at Penn State University Career Services. He is the recipient of the National Career Development Association's (NCDA) Eminent Career Award (2007), the American Counseling Association's (ACA) David Brooks Distinguished Mentor Award (2003), the ACA Extended Research Award (2004), and the University of British Columbia Noted Scholar Award (2001) and is an NCDA Fellow (2002) and an ACA Fellow (2007). Within NCDA, Dr. Niles has served in roles such as president (2004), North Atlantic Region trustee (2005), trustee-at-large (1996–1999), editor of *The Career Development Quarterly* (1998–2003), chair of the Public Policy and Career Development Council (2006–present), cochair of the Long Range Planning Committee (2001–2002), and Research Awards Committee (1993–present). Dr. Niles has also served as U.S. national correspondent to the International Association for Educational and Vocational Guidance and is on the editorial board for the *International Journal for Educational and Vocational Guidance*. He is the editor of the *Journal of Counseling & Development* and has authored or coauthored approximately 90 publications and delivered more than 85 presentations on career development theory and practice. He is an honorary member of the Japanese Career Development Association (2003), honorary member of the Italian Association for Educational and Vocational Guidance (2005), and a lifetime honorary member of the Ohio Career Development Association (2003).

■ Human Growth and Development Content Area Coeditor

Ann Vernon, PhD, NCC, LMHC, is professor emeritus at the University of Northern Iowa where she served as professor and coordinator of the school and mental health counseling programs for many years. During her tenure there, she taught courses related to counseling children and adolescents, counseling skills and theory, and practicum and internship in school counseling. Dr. Vernon has published numerous books, including *Developmental Assessment and Intervention With Children and Adolescents* (1993, American Counseling Association); *Assessment and Intervention With Children and Adolescents: Developmental and Multicultural Considerations* (2nd ed., 2005, American Counseling Association) with Roberto Clemente; *What Works When With Children and Adolescents: A Handbook of Individual Counseling Techniques* (2004, Research Press); *Thinking, Feeling, Behaving: An Emotional Education Curriculum for Children* (2006, Research Press); *Thinking, Feeling, Behaving: An Emotional Education Curriculum for Adolescents* (2006, Research Press); and *The Passport Program: A Journey Through Development* (Grades 1–5, Grades 6–8, Grades 9–12; 1998, Research Press). She is the editor of *Counseling Children and Adolescents* (4th ed., in press, Love). In addition, she is the sole author of more than 30 book chapters dealing primarily with counseling children and adolescents, developmental counseling, and applications of rational emotive behavior therapy (REBT) with children and adolescents as well as numerous journal articles on a variety of topics. Dr. Vernon is the recipient of The Regents Award for Faculty Excellence, the Association for Counselor Education and Supervision (ACES) Professional Service Award, the Outstanding Contributions Award for Improving the Status of

School Counseling (Iowa), the University of Northern Iowa College of Education Service Award, The University of Iowa Outstanding Alumni Award, and the Iowa School Counselor Lifetime Contribution Award. She has served as president of North Central ACES, the Iowa Counseling Association, and the Iowa School Counselor Association and as cochair of the ACES Women's Interest and Mentoring Network. She developed and continues to coordinate the ACES women's retreats and has been a member or chair of numerous professional committees, including the ACA Restructuring Task Force, as well as a member of several editorial boards. Dr. Vernon is vice president of the Albert Ellis Board of Trustees and is considered one of the few leading experts on applications of REBT with children and adolescents. She currently conducts REBT training programs in Romania at the University of Oradea, the RINO Mental Health Center in Amsterdam, and throughout Australia for the Australian Center for Cognitive-Behavioral Therapy. For many years, she has been an active presenter throughout the United States, Canada, and South America and offers workshops on a variety of topics related to counseling children and developing comprehensive school counseling programs. Until last year when she moved to Arizona, she maintained a private practice in Iowa where she specialized in working with children, adolescents, and parents.

■ Group Work Content Area Editor

F. Robert Wilson, PhD, LPCC, NCC, ACS, is a professor of counseling at the University of Cincinnati with over 30 years experience in counseling and counselor education. He is a Fellow of the American Counseling Association (ACA) and Association for Specialists in Group Work (ASGW) and has been the recipient of the American Mental Health Counselors Association Public and Community Service Award for advocacy for the counseling profession, the Association for Assessment in Counseling and Education's President's Special Merit Award for service to the community of specialists in measurement and assessment, and the Ohio Counseling Association's Susan J. Sears Counselor of the Year Award for leadership in the provision of services to homeless and indigent individuals with serious mental illness. He has been an active professional leader with service as a member of the Governing Council of ACA, president of the Association for Assessment in Counseling (AAC; now the Association for Assessment in Counseling and Education), treasurer of AAC, vice president of the Council for Accreditation of Counseling and Related Educational Programs, and member of the governing board for the Ohio Mental Health Counselors Association. His research and clinical interests include service to indigent and homeless people with mental illnesses; assessment, problem identification, and diagnosis; and individual and group treatment modalities with emphasis on ecological psychotherapy and evidence-based practices. For over 10 years he has served as cochair of the ASGW Training Standards Committee. In that capacity, he has conducted research on group work training, receiving the *Journal for Specialists in Group Work* Outstanding Article Award for a study of counseling program compliance with national training standards, and he has coauthored the 2000 revision of the ASGW Training Standards. Recently, he published a coauthored instrument for assessing the degree to which examinees value and feel confident in their ability to enact the core group work skills articulated by the ASGW Training Standards. He has coauthored two books and more than 50 articles and book chapters. He has made more than 100 presentations at meetings of regional, national, and international scholarly conferences. He coordinates the University of Cincinnati's master's-degree program in mental health counseling and has teaching responsibilities in the master's, certificate, and doctoral programs. He supervises beginning and advanced master's-degree interns and teaches courses in clinical mental health counseling, group work, and legal and ethical practice in counseling. He also provides pro bono clinical mental health counseling services at an ecologically grounded, multidisciplinary health resource clinic that serves inner-city indigent and homeless individuals with serious and chronic mental illness. He received his doctorate from Michigan State University and postdoctoral training in Gestalt therapy from the Cincinnati Gestalt Institute. He is independently licensed to practice counseling and provide supervision in both the State of Ohio and the Commonwealth of Kentucky and is a National Certified Counselor and an Approved Clinical Supervisor.

ABOUT THE AUTHORS

Angela J. Adams completed a PhD in counseling psychology at the University of Missouri–Columbia and an MBA in strategic leadership at Amberton University. She is a core faculty member at Capella University and consultant for Dauphin Consulting, specializing in training and consultation in executive coaching, strategic leadership, organizational change management, and diversity training.

Debra L. Ainbinder, PhD, LPC, NCC, ACS, is director of the Graduate Program in Applied Psychology at Lynn University in Boca Raton, Florida. She currently teaches and supervises students in undergraduate and graduate education. Research activities and interests include work in clinical supervision, family interventions' impact on drinking behaviors, and counseling interventions in the postmodern and expressive therapies.

Hunter D. Alessi, PhD, LPC, is a graduate of the University of New Orleans. She is a professor in the Department of Counseling and Human Development at Southeastern Louisiana University in Hammond, Louisiana. She teaches Introduction to Diagnosis and Treatment of Mental Disorders, Career Counseling and Information Services, and Community Counseling Internship. Her research includes helping individuals with problems such as substance abuse, sexual abuse, and trichotillomania.

Carrie Alexander-Albritton, NCC, LPC, is completing her doctoral degree at Idaho State University in counselor education and counseling, specializing in mental health counseling with core foci in human growth and development and research and program evaluation. Her research interests include women and parenting in higher education, mentoring, substance abuse, quantitative and qualitative research, and assessment and diagnosis.

Leah Jean Alviar, PhD, LPC, completed her doctoral study at the University of the Incarnate Word and is currently an assistant professor and director of field experience in the education department at Our Lady of the Lake University in San Antonio. Her research interests include qualitative methodology, multicultural and leadership studies, special education issues in counseling preparation, and school counseling program effectiveness.

Julie R. Ancis, PhD, is a professor in the Department of Counseling and Psychological Services at Georgia State University. She has written extensively in the area of multicultural issues, and her most recent books include *Culturally Responsive Interventions: Innovative Approaches to Working With Diverse Populations* and *The Complete Women's Psychotherapy Treatment Planner.*

Lauren Aponte is a graduate student in the school counseling program at Monmouth University and has an interest in working with Latin American clients and families.

Leslie Flint Armeniox, PhD, LPC, ADTR, completed her doctoral study at The University of North Carolina at Greensboro and currently teaches at Guilford College and Capella University. She also has a private practice at the Center for Creative Counseling in Greensboro, North Carolina. She is a member of the Academy of Registered Dance Therapists and specializes in dance/movement therapy and the use of creative arts in counseling.

Jesus (Jesse) Aros, PhD, is the director of counseling and disability services at Texas A&M International University. He is also the founding director of the Blossoming Rose Foundation of Aztlan. In addition, he has been an administrator, senior faculty, and psychologist in both the Eastern and Western hemispheres and writes on a variety of issues of importance to the *mestizo* and about indigenous identity, psychometrics, and human development in the Americas and the Pacific Rim.

Jennifer Ascolese is a graduate student in the school counseling program at Monmouth University and a research assistant. She works at a local agency for children with disabilities.

Rita A. Baker, MEd, is the assistant director of Career Services at Davidson College. She completed her graduate work at the University of North Carolina at Charlotte (UNCC), where she was also the senior assistant director of UNCC's University Career Center and, prior to that, the associate director of the Career and Personal Counseling Service in Charlotte, North Carolina. Her interests include career counseling issues with students in higher education and women's issues as they relate to career choice and vocation.

Richard S. Balkin, PhD, LPC-S, NCC, is an assistant professor at Texas A&M University–Commerce with primary teaching responsibilities in research methods and clinical course work. His research interests include counseling outcomes, program evaluation, counseling adolescents, and cross-cultural concerns in counseling.

Amy E. Baranek, MA, is a doctoral student in school psychology at The University of Southern Mississippi. She received an MA degree in clinical psychology at Minnesota State University. Her research interests include behavioral therapy for children with disruptive behavior disorders and developmental disabilities.

Phillip W. Barbee, PhD, LPC, completed his doctoral studies in counselor education at the University of New Mexico. He currently is an assistant professor at the University of Texas at El Paso. He teaches courses in counseling ethics, school counseling, research, and internship. His research interests include service learning in counselor preparation programs, school counselor roles and duties, and multicultural training experiences and attitudes of counseling students.

Jason J. Barr, PhD, received his doctorate in applied developmental psychology from Fordham University and is an assistant professor in the educational counseling program at Monmouth University, teaching courses in developmental and educational psychology. His areas of interest are in cognitive and moral development, with a specific focus on the development of empathy and perspective-taking in adolescents and applied interests in school culture and moral education.

Mary L. Bartlett, PhD, LPC-CS, NCC, CFLE, is a counselor educator at the University of Montevallo, Alabama; a counseling supervisor; an educator in family life matters; and a professional counselor with experience in the United States and Europe. She began her career with the U.S. Department of Defense. Her area of research is suicide, and she is an authorized trainer for the American Association of Suicidology and the Suicide Prevention Resource Center.

Alan Basham, PhD, is a counselor educator at Eastern Washington University, where he teaches in CACREP School Counseling and Mental Health Counseling programs. He is past-president of the Washington Counseling Association and the Association for Spiritual, Ethical and Religious Values in Counseling, a division of the American Counseling Association (ACA). He has written invited chapters in several texts, coauthored a volume on leadership ethics and teamwork, drafted ACA's Code of Leadership, and contributed to ACA's position papers on High Stakes Testing and Test User Qualifications. He is especially interested in integrating spirituality into the counseling process and in applying Native American perspectives.

George R. Beals, PhD, LPC, completed his doctoral studies at Mississippi State University in counselor education. He is currently in private practice in Starkville, Mississippi, and an adjunct lecturer in the Department of Counselor Education, Education Psychology, and Special Education at Mississippi State University.

Robinder P. Bedi, PhD, completed his doctoral degree at the University of British Columbia and currently is an assistant professor in the Department of Educational Psychology and Leadership Studies at the University of Victoria. He teaches courses in assessment, career counseling, substance abuse counseling, and counselor skills. His counseling practice has included providing career and vocational rehabilitation assessments in university counseling centers and medical centers and in an independent practice setting.

Debra Behrens, PhD, is a career counselor at the University of California, Berkeley, working with graduate students and postdoctoral fellows. She was a professor at California State University, teaching in the master's-degree counseling program. Her scholarly research and publications are focused on multicultural counseling, career development, and counselor supervision.

Andrew Benesh is a doctoral student in the Department of Educational Leadership and Counseling at Sam Houston State University. He is pursuing a PhD in counselor education.

Phyllis Benjamin is a doctoral student in community counseling at Mississippi State University.

Elisabeth Bennett, PhD, earned a doctorate in counseling psychology from the University of Utah in 1994. She is an associate professor in the Counselor Education Department at Gonzaga University, where she directs the Community Counseling Master of Arts program accredited by the Council for Accreditation of Counseling and Related Educational Programs. Primary teaching responsibilities include clinical courses and assessment.

Debra E. Berens, MS, CRC, CCM, CLCP, has a master's degree in rehabilitation counseling from Georgia State University, where she is currently a doctoral student in counselor education and practice with a cognate in rehabilitation and disability issues. She has been a practicing rehabilitation counselor since 1989 and maintains a private practice that specializes in catastrophic disability consulting and development of life care plans for children and adults with a disability. She served a 5-year term as a commissioner to the National Commission on Rehabilitation Counselor Certification and currently is editor-in-chief of the *Journal of Life Care Planning.* Her research interests include the impact of traumatic brain injury and other catastrophic injuries on adults and children, disability and the aging process, and rehabilitation ethics, among others.

David J. Bergen, PhD, LPC, NCC, completed his doctoral study at The University of North Carolina at Greensboro and is currently associate professor and chair of the Human Relations, Sociology, and Nonprofit Studies Department at High Point University in High Point, North Carolina. His research interests include leadership development, job satisfaction, job engagement, organizational commitment, and experiential learning.

Christine Suniti Bhat, PhD, is an assistant professor at Ohio University. She has experience as a counseling practitioner in India and Australia and holds advanced degrees in psychology from both countries. Her current research interests include bullying and cyberbullying, early practice issues for students of counseling, group interventions, and multicultural issues in counselor supervision.

Sara Bicard, PhD, BCBA, completed doctoral work at The Ohio State University and is currently an assistant professor in the Department of Special Education at the University of Memphis. Primary teaching responsibilities and research interests include instructional strategies for students with disabilities and applied behavior analysis.

Kacie M. Blalock, PhD, CRC, completed her doctoral study at the University of Wisconsin–Madison and currently is an assistant professor in the Department of Human Development and Services at North Carolina A&T State University, with primary teaching responsibilities in rehabilitation counseling courses. Her research interests include vocational rehabilitation, multicultural counseling, and psychosocial aspects of disability.

L. Shane Blasko, PhD, NCC, received her doctorate in counseling psychology from Georgia State University. Her clinical and research specialties include trauma, health psychology, and gender issues.

Carol L. Bobby is the executive director of the Council for Accreditation of Counseling and Related Educational Programs. She received her doctoral degree in counselor education and supervision from the University of Florida in 1986. She is a Licensed Professional Counselor in the Commonwealth of Virginia and a National Certified Counselor. In addition to holding these two credentials, she maintains membership in the American Counseling Association, the Association for Counselor Education and Supervision, and Chi Sigma Iota (the international honor society for counseling).

Annette P. Bohannon, EdD, LPC, NCC, completed her doctoral study at Auburn University and is employed by the Alabama Department of Education, Prevention & Support Section. Her research interests include school stressors, effective evaluation in school counseling, drug prevention efforts in schools, use of groups for career counseling, geriatrics counseling, pet-assisted therapy, creativity in counseling, and crisis-response counseling.

L. DiAnne Borders, PhD, LPC, NCC, ACS, is the Burlington Industries Excellence Professor and chair of the counseling program at The University of North Carolina at Greensboro, where she teaches a doctoral course in clinical supervision and supervises supervisors-in-training. Coauthor of *The New Handbook of Counseling Supervision* (with Lori L. Brown) and numerous empirical studies of the supervision process, she has conducted supervisor training workshops throughout the United States and internationally.

Kristi Bracchitta, PhD, completed her doctoral study at Fordham University in the area of applied developmental psychology and is currently an assistant professor at the College of Mount Saint Vincent in Riverdale, New York. Her research interests include relationships with individuals with disabilities and injury prevention in children and adolescents.

Loretta J. Bradley, PhD, LPC, NCC, completed her doctoral study at Purdue University and currently is a Paul Whitfield Horn Professor and coordinator of the counselor education program at Texas Tech University. Her research interests include advocacy, counselor supervision, ethics, gender issues, leadership, social justice, and outcome research.

Claudia Brasfield, MS, CRC, NCC, has a master's degree in rehabilitation counseling and is currently completing the counseling psychology doctoral program at Georgia State University. She has over 12 years of clinical and research experience with a specialization in women's issues, disability issues, and stress management.

Wanda P. Briggs, PhD, LPC, NCC, completed her doctoral study at the University of North Carolina at Charlotte and is an assistant professor in the counseling and development program at Winthrop University with primary teaching responsibility in core and community counseling courses. Her research interests include cross-cultural empathy development, diagnosis and medical crisis counseling, and multicultural concerns in counselor preparation and community counseling.

Lindsey M. Brooks is a doctoral student in counseling psychology at Lehigh University. She received her bachelor's degree in psychology and women's studies from Chatham College. Throughout her undergraduate and graduate career, she has gained a variety of clinical, research and advocacy experiences with lesbian, gay, bisexual, transgender, and questioning individuals (LGBTQ). Her current research interests include bisexual identity development, multicultural and LGBTQ counseling competency, and the intersection of sexual and other cultural identities.

Susanna Capri Posey Brooks, MA. LPC, NCC, completed her master's degree at New Orleans Baptist Theological Seminary and is currently a doctoral student at Mississippi State University (MSU) and a graduate teaching assistant at MSU.

E. Claire Brown, MS, LPC, NCC, is pursuing her doctoral degree at Mississippi State University. She recently opened her own private practice in Meridian, Mississippi. She specializes in physical, mental, and emotional trauma and posttraumatic stress disorder.

Nina W. Brown, EdD, received her doctorate from The College of William and Mary and is currently a professor and Eminent Scholar at Old Dominion University and a Fellow of the American Group Psychotherapy Association (AGPA). She is a board member and cochair of the Membership Committee for AGPA; a member of the Publications Committee for the American Counseling Association (ACA); a member of the editorial board for the *Journal of Specialists in Group Work* and the *Journal of Counseling & Development;* a member of the test panel for the American Association of State Credentialing Boards; and a member of the National Counselor Examination review, item writing, and job analysis committees for the National Board for Certified Counselors. Her major research and scholarship areas are group counseling and narcissism, and she is the author of 16 books.

Shawn T. Bubany, MS, completed a master's degree in counseling psychology at the University of Kansas and is currently working toward his doctorate in psychology at the University of Minnesota. His research interests span the areas of vocational and occupational health psychology.

Matthew Buckley, EdD, LPC, NCC, is professor and chair for the Division of Counselor Education and Psychology at Delta State University.

S. Kent Butler Jr., PhD, holds a doctorate in educational psychology, with a concentration in counseling psychology, from the University of Connecticut. He has diverse experiences in counseling and teaching in Connecticut, Texas, and Missouri and recently joined the faculty at the University of Central Florida as an associate professor. Previously, he was on the faculty at the University of Missouri–St. Louis where he was the Division of Counseling and Family Therapy's director of the School Counseling Program, director of the Counseling Clinic, and faculty adviser to the local chapter of Chi Sigma Iota. He also served as the principal investigator, on a Substance Abuse and Mental Health Services Administration Earmark Grant: University of Missouri, Division of Counseling and Family Therapy—Drug Free Family Initiative. His research and academic interests lie in the areas of multicultural, group, and school counseling.

Nancy G. Calley, PhD, LPC, is an associate professor and chair of the Department of Counseling and Addiction Studies at the University of Detroit Mercy and the clinical director of Spectrum Human Services, Inc., & Affiliated Companies. She primarily teaches counseling theories, multicultural counseling, and diagnosis in counseling and coordinates the counseling internship program. Her publications and research include juvenile sex offender treatment, clinical program development in juvenile justice programs, and practical application of ethics in counseling.

Edward P. Cannon, PhD, LMFT, LPC, completed his doctoral study at The College of William and Mary and is an assistant professor in the Department of Counsel-ing at Marymount University. His research interests include promotion of cultural competence and moral development in counselor trainees and issues of diversity in community mental health.

Kristi B. Cannon, PhD, NCC, LPC intern, completed her doctoral degree in counselor education and supervision at St. Mary's University in San Antonio. She was the lab instructor for the doctoral-level statistics course at St. Mary's University and she teaches graduate-level research methods as an adjunct professor at Our Lady of the Lake University. Her research interests include neurofeedback, relational aggression and relational competence in adolescent girls, and gender issues.

Peggy K. Cantey, MS, completed her master's degree in counseling and guidance at Jacksonville State University and is currently a professional school counselor in the Fairfax County (Virginia) Public Schools, adjunct professor at George Mason University, and instructor at Fairfax County Public Schools Professional Learning Academy.

Li Cao, PhD, completed his doctoral study at McGill University and currently is an associate professor in the Counseling and Educational Psychology Department at the University of West Georgia, with primary teaching responsibilities in research methods, educational psychology, and developmental psychology courses. His research interests include research methods, program evaluation, metacognition, and self-regulated learning.

Jessica A. Carboni graduated with a BS from The Pennsylvania State University and is a graduate student in the PhD program for school psychology at Georgia State University.

Barbara L. Carlozzi, PhD, completed her doctoral study at Oklahoma State University and currently is an assistant professor there in the School of Applied Health and Educational Psychology. Her research interests include human development, particularly Robert Kegan's theory of constructive developmentalism; resilience; and expressive writing.

Laurie A. Carlson, PhD, NCC, NCSC, completed her doctoral study at the University of Arkansas and currently is an associate professor in the counseling and career development program at Colorado State University with primary teaching responsibilities in school counseling, assessment, and research courses. Her research interests include school counseling and climate; counseling children; and lesbian, gay, bisexual, and transgender youth.

David M. Carscaddon, PhD, LPC, completed his doctoral studies at the University of South Carolina and is currently a professor in the School of Psychology and Counseling at Gardner-Webb University. His research interests include philosophical issues in counseling, how cognitive sets affect the counseling relationship, and forensics.

David J. Carter, PhD, is an associate professor in counselor education from the University of Nebraska at Omaha. His research and teaching agenda includes diagnosis, tests and measurements, and theories. He is a past president of the Nebraska Counseling Association and editorial board member of the *Sufundi Journal.*

Laura Baylot Casey, PhD, LPC, NCC, NCSP, completed doctoral work at Mississippi State University and is currently an assistant professor in the Department of Special Education at the University of Memphis. Primary teaching responsibilities and research interests include assessments (behavioral and academic) and applied behavior analysis.

Craig S. Cashwell, PhD, LPC, NCC, ACS, is a professor in the Department of Counseling and Educational Development at The University of North Carolina at Greensboro. His research and teaching interests are primarily in the area of integrating spirituality into counseling.

Veronica Castro, PhD, LPC, completed her doctoral course work in counselor education at Texas A&M University at Corpus Christi and is an assistant professor in the counseling and guidance program at The University of Texas–Pan American. Her areas of expertise, research interests, and teaching responsibilities include courses in school counseling, personal and social development, human growth and development, methods and techniques of counseling, and multicultural counseling.

Marion L. Cavallaro, PhD, LPC, NCC, completed her doctoral study at The Ohio State University and is an associate professor and clinical coordinator in the Department of Counselor Education at The College of New Jersey with primary teaching responsibilities in counseling theory and techniques, career counseling, practicum and internship, and clinical supervision. Her research interests include career counseling, gender issues, and counseling supervision.

Cynthia K. Chandler, EdD, LPC, LMFT, completed her doctoral study at Texas Tech University and is currently a professor in the counseling program at the University of North Texas (UNT). She is the founder and director of the UNT Center for Animal Assisted Therapy and teaches a graduate course on animal-assisted therapy.

Kananur V. Chandras, PhD, NCC, LPC, has been a counselor educator for the last 35 years. He taught in India, Canada, and the United States. He has published 10 books and a number of articles in refereed journals. He serves as an editorial board member of two national counseling journals. His research interests are multicultural counseling, research, online learning, at-risk students, school violence, and other counseling-related topics.

Sunil V. Chandras, CHT, is a student who has served on many committees and presented at American Counseling Association and American Mental Health Counselors Association conferences. His interests are in multicultural counseling, counselor education preparation, research, and psychopathology.

Michael P. Chaney, PhD, LPC, NCC, completed his doctoral studies at Georgia State University and is an assistant professor in the counseling department at Oakland University. His research interests include addictions, sexual behavior and the Internet, HIV/AIDS prevention, sexual orientation/gender identity development, social justice, and advocacy in counseling.

Catherine Y. Chang, PhD, LPC, NCC, is an associate professor in the Department of Counseling and Psychological Services at Georgia State University. Her research interests include multicultural issues in counselor education and supervision, racial identity development, privilege and oppression issues, and Asian American and Korean American issues in counseling.

James R. "Jamey" Cheek, PhD, LPC-S, NCC, NCSC, is currently a faculty member at the University of Houston–Clear Lake, maintains a small private supervision practice, and serves as a consultant and trainer with the Council on Alcohol and Drugs–Houston. He has extensive experience in counseling and working with people through trauma, crisis, resiliency, and burnout, including extensive service during the September 11, 2001, World Trade Center disaster, where he served as the assistant director of recovery for the American Red Cross and as the coordinator of counseling for Houston-area school children and families directly affected by the hurricanes Katrina and Rita.

Stuart F. Chen-Hayes, PhD, is associate professor of Counselor Education/School Counseling at Lehman College of the City University of New York and a consultant with The Education Trust's National Center for Transforming School Counseling. He is a past president of Counselors for Social Justice; an editorial board member of *Professional School Counseling* and the *Journal of Lesbian, Bisexual, Gay, and Transgender Issues in Counseling;* and specializes in school, social justice, and sexuality counseling and counselor education.

Julia S. Chibbaro, PhD, LPC, NCC, completed her doctoral work at the University of South Carolina and is an assistant professor in the Counseling and Educational Psychology Department at the University of West Georgia with primary teaching responsibilities in school counseling. Her research interests include advocacy, ethics, spirituality and religiosity, concerns in counselor preparation, and resiliency of children.

Rebecca Christensen received her MA and MEd in psychological counseling from Teachers College, Columbia University, and is a career counselor at the University of California, Berkeley. Her research interests include career counseling issues and inventions with underrepresented college students; college student development; and access, retention, and success in higher education.

Teresa M. Christensen, PhD, LPC, NCC, RPT-S, completed her doctoral studies at Idaho State University and is an associate professor of counselor education at Old Dominion University, with primary teaching responsibilities in play therapy, counseling children and adolescents, group work, and supervision. Her research interests include play therapy, group counseling, child abuse, supervision, and new counselors' experiences in study-abroad programs.

Dawnette L. Cigrand, MA, completed her masters' degree at the University of Iowa in school counseling and is a doctoral student in counselor education at the University of Iowa. She has been a practicing school counselor in rural Iowa since 1998 and continues to work with and research special populations such as students with autism spectrum disorders and exceptional students with multiple handicapping conditions.

Deb Cohen, PhD, earned a Master of Health Science degree in biostatistics from Johns Hopkins University before completing her doctoral study in clinical psychology at the University of Delaware. She is a psychologist and assistant director at the University of Delaware's Center for Counseling and Student Development.

Angela D. Coker, PhD, LPC, NCC, completed her doctoral study at The Union Institute & University and is currently an assistant professor of Counseling and Family Therapy at the University of Missouri–St. Louis. As a researcher, she examines the intersections of race, gender, and class, with specific focus on the counseling needs and experiences of African American women.

James Colangelo, PsyD, received his doctorate from Southern California University for Professional Studies. He is currently an assistant professor in the school counseling and mental health counseling programs and the program coordinator of the Mental Health Counseling Program at Long Island University, C.W. Post Campus. His primary teaching responsibilities include assessment and intervention strategies in mental health counseling, clinical practicum, and supervision. His research interests include recovered memories, adult survivors of sexual abuse, and sex therapy. He is also a Licensed Mental Health Counselor and a Licensed Marriage and Family Therapist in New York State.

Karesha (Kaye) Williams Cole, PhD, NCC, is the cofounder and director of educational services for The Cole Group, LLC, and an adjunct professor in the School of Human Services at Capella University. She received her BA in sociology, MEd in K–12 school counseling, and EdS in counselor education from the University of South Carolina. She received her PhD in counselor education with a cognate in sports psychology from the University of Iowa. Her research interests include counseling high school and college student athletes, multiculturalism in schools, sports counseling, and school counseling related issues.

Don C. Combs, EdD, LPCC, NCC, CCMHC, completed his doctorate at New Mexico State University and is an associate professor and coordinator of the counselor education program at the University of Texas at El Paso. He has primary teaching responsibilities in the clinical sequence. His research interests include grief and bereavement issues and the male grieving process as experienced in a group setting.

Dana L. Comstock, PhD, is a professor of counseling and chair of the Department of Counseling and Human Services at St. Mary's University, San Antonio. She is the editor of *Diversity and Development: Critical Contexts That Shape Our Lives and Relationships* (2004, Wadsworth Brooks/Cole).

Morgan Brooks Conway, PhD, NCC, completed her doctoral study at the University of New Orleans and is currently an assistant professor of mental health and school counseling, as well as director of the school counseling program, at Niagara University. Her primary teaching responsibilities include psychopathology and diagnosis courses as well as practica and internships in mental health and school counseling. Her research interests include adult children of divorce, personality disorders, and issues in school and college mental health.

Robert K. Conyne, PhD, is a charter member, past president, and Fellow of the Association for Specialists in Group Work (ASGW). He served as editor of the *Journal for Specialists in Group Work* for two terms and represented ASGW on the board of the Council for Accreditation of Counseling and Related Educational Programs. He chaired the ASGW Professional Training Standards Committee when the concept of "group work" was differentiated. He is a Licensed Clinical Counselor, psychologist, National Certified Counselor, and Approved Clinical Supervisor.

Phyliss Cooke, PhD, is adjunct faculty in the School of Psychology at Capella University, specializing in the applied behavioral sciences in the workplace. She is a registered organization development consultant with the OD Institute and former dean of the University Associates Laboratory Education Intern Program.

Ernie Cowger, PhD, LPC, LMFT, NCC, psychologist, completed his doctoral study at The University of Georgia and is currently an associate professor at Louisiana Tech University, Barksdale Air Force Base, Louisiana, with primary teaching responsibilities in the clinical courses of group, techniques of counseling, practicum, and internship. His research interests include mental health counseling, career, clinical supervision, and couples and families.

Hugh C. Crethar, PhD, is an assistant professor in the school counseling program of the Department of Educational Psychology at the University of Arizona and the 2007–2008 president of Counselors for Social Justice. His research interests include the promotion of multicultural and advocacy competence in the field of counseling; effective curricular approaches of school counselors; and school counselors as academic leaders, change agents, and advocates.

Jeri L. Crowell, EdD, NCC, LPC, completed her doctoral studies at the University of Cincinnati and currently works as an assistant professor at Fort Valley State University in Fort Valley, Georgia, in the school counseling and mental health counseling programs. Her research interests include qualitative methodology, ecological counseling (particularly as applied to educational settings), group work training, gender and multicultural issues, assessment and interventions for at-risk students, and counselor advocacy training and practice.

Carol A. Dahir, EdD, is associate professor in counselor education at the New York Institute of Technology. She is the coauthor of *Sharing the Vision: The National Standards for School Counseling Programs* (1997) and also has coauthored *The Transformed School Counselor* (2006) and *School Counselor Accountability: A Measure of Student Success* (2nd ed., 2007) with Carolyn Stone. She writes extensively about school counseling improvement, transformed school counseling, and accountability in textbooks, journals, and publications and presents at professional development venues across the United States.

Elaine Weir Daidone, MEd, CRC, completed her master's degree at The Pennsylvania State University and currently is an associate professor in the Department of Counseling and Career Services at Middlesex County College, New Jersey, where she works as the counselor for students with disabilities. She is past president of the New Jersey Association on Higher Education and Disability.

Darlene Daneker, PhD, received her doctorate from The University of North Carolina at Greensboro in counseling and counselor education. She works at Marshall University as an assistant professor in the Counseling Department. Her research interests include ethics, gender identity, and grief and trauma in human development.

Charlotte Daughhetee, PhD, LPC, LMFT, is an associate professor of counseling and foundations at the University of Montevallo in the Department of Counseling, Leadership and Foundations. Her research interests include evaluation of counselor trainees, counselor program evaluation, and the career-long continuing competency of counselors.

Becky R. Davenport, PhD, LMFT, is an assistant professor at St. Mary's University in San Antonio. She is the program director for the marriage and family therapy programs in the Department of Counseling and Human Services and teaches several doctoral research methods and statistics courses.

Tamara E. Davis, EdD, EdS, is an associate professor of psychology at Marymount University in Arlington, Virginia. She teaches a career counseling course and other graduate courses for students in the school counseling (K–12) and community counseling programs.

Telsie A. Davis is clinical supervisor of the Southside Behavioral Lifestyle Enrichment Center of Southside Medical Center, Inc., in Atlanta, Georgia, and a doctoral student in the Department of Counseling and Psychological Services at Georgia State University. Her research and clinical interests include women's issues in therapy and multicultural and gender-sensitive counseling.

Darcie Davis-Gage, PhD, LPC, completed her doctoral studies at the University of Iowa and is currently an assistant professor in the Department of Educational Leadership, Counseling, and Postsecondary Education at the University of Northern Iowa. Her research interests are in the areas of clinical supervision, intimate partner violence, social class, and feminist pedagogy.

Gregory A. Dawson, PhD, completed his doctoral work at Ohio University in 1982 and is currently assistant professor of counseling and psychology at the Troy University, Orlando, Florida, site. His primary teaching responsibilities are research methods, psychopathology, diagnosis, and treatment planning in the clinical mental health counseling program. His research interests include adult learning and psychological issues affecting heart disease patients.

Laura A. Dean, PhD, is an assistant professor in the college student affairs administration graduate programs at The University of Georgia. After receiving her doctorate at The University of North Carolina at Greensboro, she worked as a college counselor and senior student affairs officer in several small colleges. She served as a graduate student on the American Association for Counseling and Development organizing committee for the American College Counseling Association (ACCA), is an ACCA past president, and represents ACCA on the Council for the Advancement of Standards in Higher Education.

Karen M. Decker, MEd, LAC, completed her master's degree in counseling at William Paterson University and is currently a clinical faculty member in the counseling services program there. She is also a certified school counselor specializing in middle school students.

Scott L. Decker, PhD, graduated from Ball State University with a doctorate in school psychology and specialized in neuropsychology. After completing his degree, he consulted on the development of several popular intelligence measures including the Stanford–Binet Intelligence Scales–Fifth Edition and the Woodcock–Johnson III. In addition, he is a coauthor of the Bender-Gestalt II. He currently is an assistant professor at Georgia State University where he teaches courses and conducts research in cognitive and neuropsychological assessment.

Suzanne Degges-White, PhD, LMHC, LPC-NC, completed her doctoral studies at The University of North Carolina at Greensboro and is an associate professor in counseling and development at Purdue University Calumet. Her research interests include women's wellness over the life span, women's midlife transitions, and the intersection of societal expectations and women's experiences of adult development and aging.

David A. DeLambo, PhD, CRC, is an assistant professor in the Department of Rehabilitation and Counseling at the University of Wisconsin–Stout. His expertise and interests are in rehabilitation counselor preparation and multicultural counseling.

Janice L. DeLucia-Waack, PhD, is an associate professor in the Department of Counseling, School, and Educational Psychology at the University at Buffalo, State University of New York. She is the former editor of the *Journal for Specialists in Group Work* and is a Fellow in the Association for Specialists in Group Work (ASGW) and American Psychological Association (APA) Division 49: Group Psychology and Group Psychotherapy. She is author or coauthor of six books, past secretary of APA Division 49, and past president of ASGW. She is also a group cofacilitator in the DVD available from the American Counseling Association: *Leading Groups With Adolescents.*

Michael P. Demask, PhD, LMHC, NCC, CAP, holds the rank of professor at the Hazelden Graduate School of Addiction Studies in Center City, Minnesota. His teaching responsibilities include ethics, multicultural issues, and clinical supervision. His research interests are currently focused on improving learning outcomes for graduate students in a variety of classroom settings.

Melissa Deroche-Philpot, LPC, LMFT, is a counselor at the Arkansas State Hospital and has experience as a clinician in both outpatient and inpatient facilities, as well as in residential group homes. Her clinical and research interests involve adult survivors of childhood trauma, adjustment to disability, and ethical issues in Web-based counseling.

Faith Deveaux, PhD, NCC, has a master of arts degree in counselor education and a doctorate in counseling psychology from New York University. She is the chair of the Department of Counseling, Leadership, Literacy, and Special Education and coordinator of the Graduate Program in Counselor Education at Lehman College of the City University of New York. Her research areas include the impact of family and culture on individual functioning and the integration of aesthetic education into the preparation of professional school counselors and their appreciation of multiple perspectives.

James M. Devlin, MA, is a doctoral student in counselor education at Texas A&M University–Corpus Christi. He is the editorial assistant for *The Family Journal* and is president of the Counselor Education Research Consortium at Texas A&M University–Corpus Christi. His research interests include counseling research identity, couples counseling, therapeutic alliance and multicultural considerations, supervision model development, and counseling trends.

Joyce A. DeVoss, PhD, LP, NCC, is currently an associate professor and coordinator of the school counseling program in the Department of Educational Psychology at Northern Arizona University at Tucson. Her areas of expertise include school counselor preparation, leadership, and advocacy; child and adolescent counseling; solution-focused counseling; and Adlerian counseling.

Ginger L. Dickson, PhD, NCC, received her doctorate from The University of Iowa and is currently an assistant professor in the counseling program at the University of Texas at El Paso. Her research interests include multicultural education, counselor training, diversity issues, and social justice concerns.

Bryan J. Dik, PhD, completed his doctoral study at the University of Minnesota and currently is an assistant professor in the counseling psychology program at Colorado State University. His scholarly interests include person–environment fit theories of career development, measurement of vocational interests, and basic and applied research on calling and vocation.

Andrea Dixon, PhD, LAC, NCC, is an assistant professor in the school counseling and mental health counseling programs at the University of Florida, with primary teaching responsibilities in counseling techniques and school counseling. Her research interests include mattering and meaning and their place in the counseling relationship, school counselors' work climate, racial/ethnic and gender identity in adolescence, Native American issues, and multicultural and social justice concerns in counseling and counselor preparation.

Fallon K. Dodson, MEd, received her undergraduate degree in psychology from The College of William and Mary and her master's degree in education/school counseling from Cambridge College. She is a school counselor for Charlottesville High School in Charlottesville, Virginia.

Colette T. Dollarhide, EdD, NCC, LPC, ASC, completed her doctoral study at the University of Nevada, Reno and is a visiting professor at The Ohio State University, teaching general counseling skills and specialty courses in the school counseling program. Her research interests include professional identity; leadership; creativity; supervision; counselor education; and issues in school counseling, a professional area in which she has also written two textbooks.

José F. Domene, PhD, completed a doctorate in measurement, evaluation and research methodology at the University of British Columbia and is an assistant professor in the Counselling Psychology program at Trinity Western University, in Langley, British Columbia,

Canada. His primary teaching responsibilities are in statistics and research methods. His research interests include career development, family relationships, and qualitative methodology.

Katherine Dooley, PhD, LPC, CRC, NCC, ACS, is a professor of counseling at Mississippi State University, where she is coordinator of the doctoral program in counseling. She teaches courses in chemical and sexual addiction, pharmacology and diagnosis, and counseling supervision with research interests in chemical and sexual addiction and counseling supervision.

Sondra R. Dowdle, MS, completed her master's degree in community counseling and is currently pursuing her doctoral studies at Mississippi State University.

Thelma Duffey, PhD, is professor of counseling and director of the Counseling Program at the University of Texas at San Antonio and maintains a clinical counseling practice. She is founding president of the Association for Creativity in Counseling, a division of the American Counseling Association (ACA), and editor of the *Journal of Creativity in Mental Health.* She received the Professional Development Award from ACA and the Counseling Innovation and Vision Award from the Association for Counselor Education and Supervision.

Brad Dufrene, PhD, is an assistant professor in the Department of Psychology at The University of Southern Mississippi. He received his doctorate in school psychology from Mississippi State University. His research interests include school and clinical applied behavior analysis and direct assessment and intervention for academic problems.

Roxane L. Dufrene, PhD, LPC, LMFT, NCC, completed her doctoral study at Mississippi State University and currently is an assistant professor in the Educational Leadership, Counseling and Foundations Department at the University of New Orleans with primary teaching responsibilities in doctoral counseling courses. Her research interests include assessment, crisis counseling, ethics, and research.

Cass Dykeman, PhD, NCC, NCSC, MAC, completed his master's in school counseling at the University of Washington and his doctorate in counselor education at The University of Virginia. He is an associate professor in the Department of Teacher and Counselor Education at Oregon State University. His research interests include addiction counseling and psychopharmacology.

Beverly E. Eanes, RN, PhD, LCPC, NCC, has a BSN from Johns Hopkins University and master's degrees in maternal/child health and in community counseling from the University of Maryland and completed her doctoral study at Loyola University Maryland. She is an affiliate faculty member in the Pastoral Counseling Department of Loyola University Maryland, where she was formerly the clinical director. Her interests are family and community health, crisis intervention, and multicultural and aging issues in counseling. She has done research in the areas of pain perception and grief and loss.

Laura T. Easter, PhD, completed her doctoral study at The University of Virginia, where she continues as an adjunct instructor. Her research interests include psychosocial group support and issues concerning families with twins and higher order multiples.

Susan H. Eaves, PhD, LPC, NCC, completed her doctoral degree in counselor education at Mississippi State University and is a behavioral specialist at Weems Children and Youth. In addition, she serves as graduate adjunct faculty with experience teaching courses in sexuality, human development, group techniques, statistics, and personality. Her research interests include empirically based counseling, personality disorders, research methodology, and sexual relationship behaviors as they relate to gender, attachment, and self-worth.

Lennis G. Echterling, PhD, received his doctorate from Purdue University and is professor and director of Counseling Psychology at James Madison University. Along with his colleagues, he has written books on crisis intervention, brief counseling, community counseling, and counselor education.

Daniel Eckstein, PhD, LPC, is currently associate professor in the Department of Educational Leadership and Counseling at Sam Houston State University. He is a past president of the North American Society of Adlerian Psychology. His research interests include encouragement, reframing, changes in early recollections as a measure of counselor efficacy, and birth order correlations with personality.

Donna Eckstein, PhD, completed doctoral work at the United States International University and is an adjunct faculty member at Capella University with the Harold Abel School of Psychology and associate professor with Continuing Education for Older Adults at San Diego Community College. Research interests include life span development, health and sport psychology, and online education.

Grafton T. Eliason, EdD, LPC, NCC, is an assistant professor in the Department of Counselor Education and Services at California University of Pennsylvania. He has published on the topics of death, dying, and spirituality and has a special interest in existential philosophy and religion. He received his doctorate in counselor education and supervision from Duquesne University, and he is an ordained Presbyterian minister.

Cyrus Marcellus Ellis, PhD, completed his doctoral study at The University of Virginia and is an associate professor in the counseling program at Governors State University with primary teaching responsibilities in the community counseling sequence. His research interests include self-concept development, addiction and recovery, race-based information, social justice, and social and cultural foundations.

Lori Ellison, PhD, LPC, LMFT, is a practicing counselor, adjunct instructor at Texas A&M–Commerce, and a graduate of Texas A&M–Commerce's counselor education program. Her research interests include ethics, spirituality in counseling, college counseling, student development, and counselor supervision.

Christopher Engle is a professional counselor in Ohio and a doctoral student at the University of Cincinnati. He specializes in mental health work with homeless individuals and nursing home residents and is interested in research applying group work to these and other underserved populations.

Robert Eschenauer, PhD, LMHC, NCC, completed his doctoral study at St. John's University, where he is an assistant professor and director of the counselor education program.

Kathy M. Evans, PhD, NCC, completed her doctoral study at The Pennsylvania State University and is currently an associate professor in counselor education at the University of South Carolina where she teaches in the entry and doctoral-level programs. Her research and writing have been devoted to counseling marginalized groups. Her publications address multicultural and career counseling, feminist therapy, racial identity, and counseling African Americans.

Danyell Facteau is a graduate student in the counseling program at Old Dominion University. Her clinical interests include addictions, group counseling, and multicultural issues.

Stephanie I. Falke, MS, is currently finishing her PhD at Loma Linda University. She is in her doctoral internship at MFI Recovery Center, working in women's residential and adolescent intensive outpatient programs, and she also teaches in Loma Linda University's School of Nursing. Primary research interests include training and supervision, trauma and attachment, and gender and social justice issues.

Kevin A. Fall, PhD, LPC, LMFT, NCC, is chair and associate professor of the Department of Counseling at Loyola University New Orleans. He is the author of several books and articles on theory, group work, domestic violence, and ethics.

Mardi Kay Fallon, MEd, LSW, PCC, is a doctoral candidate at the University of Cincinnati. She works as a mental health therapist in a community mental health center in Cincinnati, Ohio. She is currently specializing in work with reactive attachment disorder and helping preschool children become socially and emotionally ready for kindergarten.

Leigh Falls, EdS, LPC-S, NCC, is a counselor and a doctoral student in counselor education and supervision at Sam Houston State University. Her research interests are school counselor burnout, school counselor accountability, developmental trajectories of adolescent sex offenders, the effects of trauma on school performance, and social justice issues.

Marie Faubert, EdD, CSJ, is a professor at the University of Saint Thomas, Houston, in the School of Education. She is an authority on multicultural counseling and director of the counselor education program.

Mary Fawcett, PhD, LPC, NCC, completed her doctoral study at the University of South Carolina and is currently an associate professor in the counselor education department at Winona State University with primary teaching responsibilities in life-span development, career development, and theories courses. She is a past president of the Minnesota Counseling Association and received the Minnesota School Counselors Association's Postsecondary School Counselor of the Year award. Her research interests include multicultural career counseling and school counseling.

R. Charles Fawcett, MSEd, NCC, is a doctoral candidate at The University of Virginia. His research interests include testing and assessment, integrating spirituality in counseling, and gender issues. He is the coauthor of the textbook, *Essentials of Testing and Assessment: A Practical Guide for Counselors, Social Workers, and Psychologists.*

Lane Fischer, PhD, completed his doctoral studies in educational psychology at the University of Minnesota. He serves on the faculty in counseling psychology and special education at Brigham Young University. His teaching and research focus on psychometrics and psychological assessment.

Trey Fitch, PhD, LPC, NCC, completed his doctorate at Texas A&M University–Commerce and currently is an assistant professor in psychology at the University of Cincinnati —Clermont College with primary teaching responsibilities in human development and general psychology. His research interests include counseling adolescents, counselor supervision, and school counselor performance.

Lea R. Flowers, PhD, LPC, NCC, completed her doctoral study at the University of New Orleans and is an assistant professor in the counselor education program at Georgia State University. Her research interests include ethics and leadership, group work, socialization, women's developmental and career issues across the life span, and advocacy for special populations in school settings.

Linda H. Foster, PhD, NCC, NCSC, LPC, completed her doctoral work at Mississippi State University and is an assistant professor in the agency counseling program and clinical coordinator at the University of Alabama at Birmingham. She currently serves on the Board of Directors of the National Board for Certified Counselors and has a keen research interest in standards, certification, and professional identity. Other research interests include research methods, supervision, assessment and test construction, and cinematherapy.

Robyn Fraser-Settoon is a doctoral student and teaching assistant in the counselor education program at Mississippi State University with an emphasis on rehabilitation counseling. Her research interests include concerns about SSRI/SSNI effects on individuals and use of the mapping process in counseling.

Daniel C. Frigo, PhD, is a graduate of Washington University in St. Louis. He has taught at the graduate level for 16 years and has 19 years of private practice experience. He is an associate professor at the Hazelden Graduate School of Addiction Studies.

Carol S. Froehlich completed her MEd in speech pathology at The University of Georgia and her MS in counseling at Georgia State University. She is currently a professional school counselor in the Fairfax County Public Schools (Virginia), adjunct professor at George Mason University, and instructor at Fairfax County Public Schools Professional Learning Academy.

Susan Furr, PhD, is an associate professor in counseling at the University of North Carolina at Charlotte. Her teaching interests include a specialized course in psychoeducational groups. Other teaching and research interests include grief and loss counseling, crisis counseling, and instructional theory in counselor education.

Michael T. Garrett, PhD, is associate professor in the Department of Counselor Education at the University of Florida. He completed his doctoral work in counselor education at The University of North Carolina at Greensboro. His current teaching responsibilities are in developmental counseling, introduction to counseling, and supervision. His research interests include counseling Native Americans, multicultural counseling and supervision, multicultural group work, narrative analysis of oral traditions, counselor self-care, group work with children and adolescents, spirituality in counseling, wellness, and indigenous spiritual traditions as healing.

Wangui Gathua is an international student pursuing her doctoral degree in counselor education at the University of Iowa. Her research interests include HIV/AIDS in Kenya and empowering the girl child in Kenya.

Sally Gelardin, EdD, NCC, DCC, received her doctorate in international and multicultural education. She teaches certificate and continuing education unit programs for counselors and career practitioners and has created several online and blended-learning courses. She is the creator of the Job Juggler's Lifelong Employability Program and Entrepreneur Kits for career professionals and entrepreneurs.

Lawrence H. Gerstein, PhD, is professor of psychology and director of the Center of Peace and Conflict Studies at Ball State University. He is also the director of the doctoral program in counseling psychology at Ball State University. His expertise is in community, peace, and family psychology; consultation; and research methodology. He earned his doctorate in counseling and social psychology from The University of Georgia.

Donna M. Gibson, PhD, LPC/I, NCC, completed her doctorate in counseling and counselor education at The University of North Carolina at Greensboro and is an assistant professor in the counselor education programs at the University of South Carolina. She has served as member-at-large for membership and president of the Association for Assessment in Counseling and Education. Her research interests include pedagogical issues in teaching assessment, K–12 career assessment, leadership in school counseling and counselor education, and relational/cultural theory.

Ann Shanks Glauser, PhD, received her doctorate from The University of Georgia in counseling and human development services and is an associate professor in the Division of Academic Enhancement at The University of Georgia and a licensed professional counselor. She has published on topics related to client-centered counseling, multicultural counseling and training, and teaching from a developmental perspective.

Joshua M. Gold, PhD, NCC, completed his doctoral study at Kent State University and is an associate professor in the counselor education program at the University of South Carolina with primary teaching responsibilities in the family counseling and doctoral programs. His current research interests include assessment, spirituality, and client resistance.

Rebecca M. Goldberg, EdS, NCC, is a doctoral fellow in mental health counseling at the University of Florida. She has taught interpersonal communication skills to undergraduates and veterinary graduate students; supervises graduate counseling students throughout clinical experiences; and has research interests in women's issues, self-esteem, the media, and relational aggression.

Angel Cole Golson, MS, NCC, is a doctoral student in the community counseling program at Mississippi State University and a counselor for Behavioral Services LLC. She specializes in the development and implementation of early intervention strategies, functional behavioral assessment, and training teachers in behavior management protocols. She provides services to the pregnant women enrolled in the Head Start early intervention program.

Emiliano Gonzalez, PhD, is an associate professor at the University of Saint Thomas, Houston, in the School of Education. He is an authority on multicultural populations and working with English-language learners. He works extensively with counselors who will be counseling English-language learners.

Jane Goodman, PhD, is a professor emerita of counseling at Oakland University in Rochester, Michigan. She was the 2001–2002 president of the American Counseling Association and is a past president of the National Career Development Association. She is the author of many articles and book chapters, primarily in the area of transitions and the career development of adults.

Donald F. Graves, MA, is an instructor at The Sage Colleges in Troy and Albany, New York. He is a doctoral candidate in cognitive psychology at the University at Albany, State University of New York. His research interests include visual perception and human memory.

Eric J. Green, PhD, LCPC, LMFT, RPT-S, completed his doctoral study at the University of New Orleans and is an assistant professor in the counselor education program at Johns Hopkins University, with primary teaching responsibilities in school counseling courses. His research interests include the effectiveness of play therapy in elementary school counseling programs, Jungian analytical play therapy with children affected by trauma and/or natural disasters, and closing the achievement gap for disenfranchised children through advocacy.

Peter J. Green, PhD, completed his doctoral study at the University of Iowa and is currently an associate professor and chair of the Psychology Department at Barton College. His primary teaching responsibilities include introduction to psychology, social psychology, and health psychology. His research interests include risky behaviors among college students, including alcohol and unsafe sex; violence in intimate relationships; and scholarship on the teaching of psychology.

Bianca M. Gregory, MEd, completed graduate work at Cambridge College. Her research interests include female adolescent sex offenders, children who self-harm and self-mutilate, and gender identity disorders in children. She serves on the executive board of the Virginia School Counselor Association as vice-president-elect–student.

Charles F. Gressard, PhD, NCC, LPC, MAC, LMFT, LSATP, is a counselor educator at The College of William and Mary, and prior to that he was at The University of Virginia. His primary areas of interest are substance abuse counseling and ethics, and he has served on the Virginia licensure board and the American Counseling Association Ethics Committee; as chair of the National Board for Certified Counselors; and, most recently, on the 2009 Council for Accreditation of Counseling and Related Educational Programs Standards Revision Committee.

Cullen T. Grinnan, PhD, LPC, NCC, completed his doctoral study in counselor education and supervision at St. Mary's University in San Antonio. He is currently a member of the Education Department faculty at Our Lady of the Lake University, and his research interests include the effective modalities for school counselor preparation in distance learning programs, mental heath trauma treatment, and development and implementation of educational best practices in laboratory school environments.

Lorraine J. Guth, PhD, LPC, NCC, completed her doctoral study at Indiana University and currently is a professor in the Department of Counseling at Indiana University of Pennsylvania. She serves as the Awards Committee cochair for the Association for Specialists in Group Work, and her research interests include group work, diversity, sexuality, and technology.

Norman C. Gysbers, PhD, completed his doctoral study at the University of Michigan and is currently professor with distinction in the Department of Educational, School, and Counseling Psychology at the University of Missouri–Columbia. His teaching and research interests are in career development; career counseling; and school guidance and counseling program development, management, and evaluation.

Sally M. Hage, PhD, LPC, LP, is a member of the *Journal for Specialists in Group Work* editorial board and coauthor of the *Best Practice Guidelines on Prevention Practice, Research, Training, and Social Advocacy for Psychologists* (2007). She is an assistant professor at Teachers College, Columbia University, Department of Counseling and Clinical Psychology. Her research interests include prevention, group work, spirituality and counseling, and multicultural psychology.

W. Bryce Hagedorn, PhD, LMHC, NCC, MAC, completed his doctoral work at The University of North Carolina at Greensboro and is an assistant professor and clinic director in the Counselor Education Program at the University of Central Florida. He is a current board member of the Council for Accreditation of Counseling and Related Educational Programs and editor of the *Journal of Addictions & Offender Counseling* and remains very active with the International Association of Addictions and Offender Counselors and the Association for Spiritual, Ethical, and Religious Values in Counseling. His research areas include addictive disorders (and those they affect), spirituality and counseling, clinician self-care, and wellness.

Kimberly R. Hall, PhD, LPC, NCSC, is an assistant professor in the Department of Counseling, Educational Psychology, and Special Education at Mississippi State University with primary teaching responsibilities in the school counseling program. Her research interests include problem-based learning, school counselor accountability, and gender issues in the educational environment.

Stephanie F. Hall, PhD, LPC, completed her doctoral study at the University of New Orleans and is an assistant professor of counseling at Eastern Kentucky University. Her research interests include teaching preparation of counselor educators, multicultural and social justice issues, advocacy for the counseling profession, and the professional identity development of counselors.

Tonya R. Hammer, MA, LPC, is a doctoral student at St. Mary's University. Her research interests include incorporation of relational cultural theory into career counseling, the use of film in counseling, and the impact of humiliation and shame on violence in relationships.

Cheree Hammond, MS, EdS, is a doctoral student at The University of Virginia. Her teaching and research interests include multicultural counseling competencies, social justice issues, psychopathology (particularly Asperger's syndrome and high-functioning autism), and counselor training.

Marie S. Hammond, PhD, LPC, NCC, LPC, completed her doctoral studies at the University of Missouri–Columbia. She is currently an assistant professor in the counseling psychology program at Tennessee State University with primary teaching responsibilities in vocational psychology, program evaluation, and statistics. Her research interests include vocational identity development, the career development of people of color, and personality.

Mary D. Hancock, PhD, completed her doctoral study at Indiana University in Bloomington and is an assistant professor in the Department of Counseling and Educational Psychology at the University of West Georgia. Her primary teaching responsibilities include human development and research methods courses. Research interests include religiosity/spirituality and risky behaviors in adolescents, adolescent health and well-being, self-efficacy, and program evaluation.

Edward J. Hanna, MS, is a social services liaison for Maximizing Adolescent Potentials at the University of Pittsburgh. He received his master's degree in counseling psychology from Chatham University. He is a Certified School Counselor (K–12) in Pennsylvania and works with students in Pittsburgh and Fox Chapel area schools. He also works with at-risk children through the Youth Advocacy Program as a mobile therapist. Other interests include writing and performing music with a message for the Peace Bus, Communities in Action for Peace.

Jo-Ida C. Hansen, PhD, earned her doctorate in psychology from the University of Minnesota. She is a professor of psychology at the University of Minnesota and directs the Center for Interest Measurement Research and the Vocational Assessment Clinic. She has received the American Counseling Association's Extended Research Award for her work in interest measurement and the Society of Counseling Psychology's Leona

Tyler Award and has served as editor of *Measurement and Evaluation in Counseling and Development* and the *Journal of Counseling Psychology*.

Christine Harrington, PhD, completed her doctoral degree at Lehigh University and is an assistant professor in the Department of Counseling and Career Services at Middlesex County College in New Jersey. Psychiatric and learning disabilities are her area of expertise, and she has presented on these topics at conferences.

Veronica Renee Harrison is currently a doctoral student at Mississippi State University in the College of Education. Her major area of study is vocational rehabilitation.

Paul B. Hastings, PhD, earned his doctoral degree in counseling at Washington State University and is an associate professor at Gonzaga University, where he serves as the chair of the Counselor Education Department. Primary teaching responsibilities include clinical courses and research and statistics.

Sarah L. Hastings, PhD, is an assistant professor in the psychology department at Radford University. Her research interests include gender issues, relationships, self-compassion, and professional training and practice.

John Hawkins, EdS, LPC, NCC, NCSC, is a doctoral student in counseling at Mississippi State University, a school counselor at the Mississippi School of the Arts, and a therapist in private practice. His research interests include counseling applications of the internal family systems model, religion and spirituality in counseling, and uses of technology in school counseling.

Richard L. Hayes, PhD, is professor and dean of the College of Education at the University of South Alabama. He has authored more than 90 publications in four languages and made more than 100 presentations at international and national meetings of professional associations on topics related to education and counseling psychology since 1990. He is a Fellow in both the Association for Specialists in Group Work (ASGW) and the American Psychological Association and was recognized for the excellence of his scholarly and professional contributions by the American Counseling Association, the Association for Moral Education, ASGW, and the Association for Humanistic Education and Development.

Danica G. Hays, PhD, LPC, NCC, is an assistant professor in the mental health counseling program at Old Dominion University, with primary teaching responsibilities in research methods courses. Her research interests include qualitative methodology, assessment and diagnosis, trauma and gender issues, and multicultural and social justice concerns in counselor preparation and community mental health.

April K. Heiselt, PhD, is an assistant professor in the Department of Counseling, Educational Psychology, and Special Education and the service-learning coordinator for the Global Leadership Programs at Mississippi State University. Her teaching emphasis is in student affairs in higher education, and her research interests include qualitative methodology, student leadership, and service-learning.

Richard C. Henriksen Jr., PhD, LPC, NCC, ACS, completed his doctoral study at Texas A&M University–Commerce and is an associate professor in the Department of Educational Leadership and Counseling at Sam Houston State University. His research interests include multiple heritage identity development, multicultural and diversity issues in counseling, multicultural pedagogy in counselor preparation, community mental health with an emphasis on substance dependence and substance abuse, and group counseling.

Nicole R. Hill, PhD, LPC, is an associate professor in the Department of Counseling at Idaho State University. Her scholarly and research interests include play therapy, mental health counseling, working with children and adolescents, multicultural counseling competencies, professional development of faculty and graduate students, and outcome research.

Sin-Wan Bianca Ho, BA, is a doctoral student in the University of Southern Mississippi counseling psychology program. She also serves as the cochair of the Asian American Psychological Association, Division of Student. Her primary research interests involve parenting, parent–child relationships, and cross-cultural studies in these related areas. Other research interests include ethics and self-efficacy and career decision making in high school students in a cross-cultural context.

Rachel M. Hoffman, MSEd, PC, is a doctoral student in the counseling and human development services program at Kent State University. Her clinical experience has focused on helping children and families in crisis situations, and she currently works as a counselor at a child and adolescent inpatient psychiatric unit.

Thomas H. Hohenshil, PhD, LPC, is professor emeritus of counselor education at Virginia Tech, and his primary teaching responsibilities have been in the areas of assessment and diagnosis and doctoral intern supervision. He has published more than 120 professional articles in the areas of assessment and diagnosis and the use of technology in counseling. He was the recipient of the American Counseling Association's 2005 Arthur A. Hitchcock Distinguished Professional Service Award.

Janice Miner Holden, EdD, LPC-S, LMFT, NCC, is a professor in the counseling program at the University of North Texas. Her research interests include transpersonal counseling theory and practice with specific emphasis on near-death experiences, after-death communication, and Ken Wilber's integral psychology.

Alicia M. Homrich, PhD, is associate professor and chair of the Graduate Studies in Counseling Program at Rollins College in Winter Park, Florida. She began her

involvement with the Association for Specialists in Group Work (ASGW) in 1995 while a student at The University of Georgia. She has remained active in ASGW through committee work and as newsletter editor and was named a Fellow in 2007.

Pei-Hsuan Hsieh, PhD, received her doctorate in educational psychology from the University of Texas at Austin and is an assistant professor at The University of Texas at San Antonio. Her primary teaching responsibilities include psychological learning theories. Her research interests include student retention, achievement, self-efficacy beliefs, attribution, and goal orientation.

J. Duncan Hubbell, MEd, received his bachelor's degree from The University of Virginia and his master's degree from Old Dominion University. He is the special education department chair for Northside Middle School in Norfolk, Virginia. He is also an adjunct instructor at Old Dominion University with teaching responsibilities in special education law and method courses.

Rosemarie Scotti Hughes, PhD, LPC, LMFT, NCC, NCSC, is dean of the School of Psychology and Counseling at Regent University. Her interests include women's issues, disability issues, and spirituality in counseling.

Rosalie R. Hydock, PhD, LP, completed her doctoral study at Capella University and is currently in private practice in Scottsdale, Arizona. Her research interests include late midlife development, multicultural and gender issues, goal setting and subjective well-being, and the use of positive psychology in counseling and coaching.

Farah A. Ibrahim, PhD, LP, completed her doctorate at The Pennsylvania State University and is currently a professor of counseling psychology and counselor education at the University of Colorado at Denver and Health Sciences Center. She is a Fellow of the American Psychological Association and past president of Counselors for Social Justice and the Connecticut Association for Multicultural Counseling and Development. Her research focus is on culturally competent and effective counseling.

Elliott Ingersoll is a professional clinical counselor, psychologist, and life coach who resides in Kent, Ohio. He is one of a handful of people who has completed the advanced certification in measuring ego development offered by Cook-Greuter & Associates. He also works as a counselor educator at Cleveland State University.

Arpana G. Inman, PhD, completed her doctoral study at Temple University and is an assistant professor in the counseling psychology program at Lehigh University. Her research interests include qualitative methodology; issues related to gender, sexuality, ethnicity, race, and the intersections of these identities; and the integration of multiculturalism and social justice into the field of counseling psychology.

Lisa R. Jackson-Cherry, PhD, LCPC, NCC, ACS, NCSC, completed her doctoral study at The University of South Carolina and is currently the department chair and associate professor in the Department of Counseling at Marymount University with primary teaching responsibilities in clinical supervision and crisis intervention. Her research areas include ethical and legal issues in counseling supervision, crisis intervention and risk assessment, and treating mental health issues of the military and their families during deployment and reintegration. She is also a member of the Maryland Board of Professional Counselors and Therapists.

Sachin Jain, PhD, completed his doctoral degree in counselor education at the University of Wyoming and is a counselor educator at the University of Idaho.

Shari-ann H. James, PhD, completed her doctoral study at The University of Georgia and currently is a staff psychologist at the University of Central Florida's Counseling Center. Her professional interests include multicultural issues, international students, relationship concerns, developmental issues, and training and supervision.

Gregory R. Janson, PhD, CFLE, PCC-S, completed his doctoral studies at Ohio University and is an associate professor of child and family studies at Ohio University. His research interests include trauma; emotional abuse; and gay, lesbian, bisexual, transgender, intersex, and questioning issues.

Renée N. Jefferson, PhD, MSIO, MLIS, completed her doctoral studies at the University of Iowa and is currently an associate professor in the School of Education, College of Graduate and Professional Studies, at The Citadel with primary teaching responsibilities in research methods and applied measurement courses. Her research interests include quantitative and qualitative methodologies, educational testing, virtual learning, and information literacy in higher education.

Stephen W. Johnson, PhD, LPC, LMFT, completed his doctorate at the University of Nebraska and is currently an associate professor in the counseling program at the University of Texas at El Paso, with primary teaching responsibilities in marriage and family therapy courses. His research interests include counselor preparation and supervision, parent–child relationships and academic achievement, and counselor efficacy.

Sharon Blackwell Jones, PhD, NCC, completed her doctoral studies at The Pennsylvania State University in counseling psychology and is currently a full-time lecturer in the Department of Counseling and Human Development Services at The University of Georgia. Her primary teaching responsibilities and research interests include multicultural training and social justice issues in school settings, counseling psychology, and counselor education.

Joseph P. Jordan, PhD, NCC, MAC, LPC, LCAS, CCS, completed his doctorate at The University of North Carolina at Greensboro and is currently the ethics officer and director of corporate projects for the National Board for Certified Counselors. His research and professional practice interests include ethics, substance abuse competencies in the field of professional counseling, co-occurring disorders, credentialing issues for substance abuse professionals, and juvenile justice interventions with youth abusing alcohol and other drugs.

Gerald A. Juhnke, EdD, LPC, NCC, MAC, CCAS, ACS, is a professor and the director of the counselor education and supervision doctoral program at The University of Texas at San Antonio. He is the past president of the Association for Assessment in Counseling and the International Association for Addictions and Offender Counseling and is the former editor-in-chief of *The Journal of Addictions & Offender Counseling*. His three research strands of addictions, suicide, and family counseling coalesce into his research on life-threatening behaviors research.

Carol J. Kaffenberger, PhD, is an associate professor at George Mason University in Fairfax, Virginia, and program coordinator of the Counseling and Development program. She is a consultant for the National Center for the Transformation of School Counseling, has held several leadership positions in Virginia, and is the American School Counselor Association Counselor Educator vice-president, 2007–2009.

Jeanmarie Keim, PhD, LP, completed her doctoral study at Arizona State University and currently teaches in the counselor education program at the University of New Mexico. Her primary teaching responsibilities are in group work, group counseling and psychotherapy, group practicum, and the diagnosis and treatment of mental disorders. Her research interests include factors affecting career achievement, stress, burnout, vicarious trauma, and workplace violence in relation to career longevity.

Kathleen Kellum, MEd, is completing her doctoral study at the University of Iowa and was an instructor for career guidance and job placement. Her research interests include counseling supervision/consultation, group work, career development, and development of international counseling.

Virginia A. Kelly, PhD, LPC, NCC, is an associate professor in the Counselor Education Department at Fairfield University with primary teaching responsibilities in research methods courses. Her research interests include addictions and the application and assessment of wilderness-based approaches to counseling.

Maureen C. Kenny, PhD, NCC, is an associate professor and director of the counselor education program at Florida International University in Miami, Florida, with primary teaching responsibilities in the mental health counseling program. She is the principal investigator on a funded project, Keeping Kids Safe, which examines sexual abuse prevention in minority populations. Her other research interests include child abuse reporting, counselor preparation, and multicultural counseling concerns.

Carolyn W. Kern, PhD, LPC, NCC, completed her doctoral degree at Oklahoma State University and is an associate professor and clinic director in the counseling program at the University of North Texas with primary teaching responsibilities in adolescents, college students, and clinical course including counselor supervision. Her research includes crisis intervention, college students, and supervision.

Margaret King, EdD, completed her doctoral studies at the University of Massachusetts, Amherst. She is professor of early childhood teacher education at Ohio University. Her research interests are appropriate educational practices for young men and the social, emotional environments of schools.

Lauren M. Klein, MEd, NCC, is a professional high school counselor in Ridgewood, New Jersey. She has a master's degree in education in school counseling from Loyola College in Maryland and is a National Certified Counselor who is currently pursuing her license in professional counseling at Montclair State University. She assists students in Grades 9–12 throughout the college application process.

Victoria Kress, PhD, LPCC-S, is the counseling program coordinator at Youngstown State University. She has over 15 years of experience working in clinical settings, has coauthored a book, and has published numerous refereed articles on topics such as self-injurious behavior, the *Diagnostic and Statistical Manual of Mental Disorders,* sexual abuse and trauma, and strength-based counseling approaches.

Richard P. Lanthier, PhD, completed his doctoral work in developmental psychology at the University of Denver and is associate professor of human development at George Washington University, with primary teaching responsibilities in child, adolescent, and life span development. His research interests include social and personality development in adolescents and young adults.

Michael G. Laurent, PhD, received a doctoral degree from the University of Southern California, where he also completed a certificate in gender studies. He is both a licensed psychologist and licensed marriage and family therapist in California. He is currently a full-time professor at California State University, Northridge, where his primary teaching and research areas include multicultural counseling, gender issues, group theory, psychopathology (advanced behavioral disorders), and graduate-level practicum and fieldwork experiences.

George R. Leddick, PhD, NCC, CCMHC, completed his doctoral study at Purdue University and has worked as a counselor educator for more than 25 years. A Fellow of the Association for Specialists in Group Work, he served as its president in 2004. He was a member of the American Counseling Association's (ACA) Council of Presidents and Regional Chairs from 2002–2004 and served on the ACA Governing Council from 2006–2008. Research interests include group work, psychotherapy supervision, and organizational consultation.

Robin Wilbourn Lee, PhD, LPC, NCC, is an associate professor in the professional counseling program at Middle Tennessee State University. She received her doctoral degree in counselor education and supervision from Mississippi State University. Her research interests include counselor training issues, ethical and legal issues, counseling supervision, gender issues, and generational characteristics.

W. Vanessa Lee, BA, is currently working toward her doctorate in psychology at the University of Minnesota. Her research interests include career development, career counseling, and multicultural diversity in vocational psychology.

Wanda M. L. Lee, PhD, Licensed Psychologist, completed her doctoral study at the University of Oregon and currently is the associate dean, College of Health & Human Services, at San Francisco State University. She is also a professor of counseling, with former primary teaching responsibilities in multicultural counseling and clinical practicum courses. Her research interests include multicultural issues in counseling and counselor preparation. She has published on the topics of counseling biracial girls, multicultural competency in faculty hiring, ethnic and gender issues in assessment, and counseling effectiveness with Asian Americans and has written a textbook on multicultural counseling.

Erin H. Leff is an attorney, retired school psychologist, and mediator who has worked in special education for more than 30 years. She earned an MS in educational psychology from the University of Wisconsin–Madison and a JD from Rutgers–Camden. Currently, she is deputy special master in the federal district court case regarding special education in the Baltimore (Maryland) City Public Schools.

Elsa Soto Leggett, PhD, LPC-S, CSC, completed her doctoral study at Texas A&M University–Corpus Christi and is an assistant professor of counseling at Texas Southern University in Houston. Her research interests include the professional identity and roles of school counselors, counseling children and adolescents, attachment theory, and solution-focused counseling.

Matthew Lemberger, PhD, received his doctoral degree from the University of South Carolina and is an assistant professor and school counseling program coordinator for the Division of Counseling and Family Therapy at the University of Missouri–Saint Louis. His research areas include school counseling and academic achievement, urban education and the achievement gap, counselor education and supervision, and Adlerian psychology.

Jan C. Lemon, LPC, NBSC, is currently enrolled in the counselor education doctoral program at Mississippi State University. She is the senior counselor at Florence High School in Florence, Mississippi. Her research interests include educational ethics, psychological constructs in successful teaching methods, and accountability for school counselors.

Mark Lepore, EdD, obtained a doctorate in counselor education and supervision at Duquesne University. He holds an MA from Duquesne University and an MSW from West Virginia University. He also has a clinical social work license and five education certifications. He has worked as a school counselor and is an assistant professor of counseling psychology at Chatham University in Pittsburgh, Pennsylvania. He has worked extensively in the field of trauma and grief and loss counseling and is a mental health trainer for the American Red Cross and a supervisor for National Disaster Response, having volunteered for assignments after the terrorist attack of September 11, 2001, Hurricane Katrina, and many other disasters.

Melanie E. Leuty is a doctoral student in counseling psychology at the University of Minnesota. Her research interests include changes in work values, the use of vocational interest assessments, and predictors of career choice. She was the recipient of a Society for Vocational Psychology ACT travel award.

Lisa Lopez Levers, PhD, LPCC (OH), LPC (PA), CRC, NCC, completed her doctorate at Kent State University. She is an associate professor of counselor education and supervision at Duquesne University. She teaches doctoral-level courses in qualitative methodology, counselor supervision, and instructional design. Her master's-level courses focus on developmental issues, trauma, and diversity. Her intellectual project revolves around marginalized populations, marked by various qualitative inquiries into psychiatric disability, indigenous healing, effects of trauma on human development, the Rwandan genocide, cultural aspects of HIV/AIDS in sub-Saharan Africa, and the plight of vulnerable children in sub-Saharan Africa.

Carol A. Lewis, PhD, completed her doctoral work at the University of Mississippi and is assistant professor of counseling and psychology at the Troy University, Pensacola, Florida, site. Her primary teaching responsibilities are theories of counseling, facilitation skills, practicum, and internship. Her research interests include adult learning and child and adolescent development.

Rolla E. Lewis, EdD, NCC, is associate professor and coordinator of the school counseling program in the College of Education and Allied Studies at California State University, East Bay. His research interests include constructing university–community collabo-

rations, action research in school counseling, social justice in higher education, the use of structured narratives as reflective instruments, and appreciative inquiry in evaluating program effectiveness.

Todd F. Lewis, PhD, LPC, NCC, is assistant professor and coordinator of the community counseling track at The University of North Carolina at Greensboro. His theoretical and research interests include Adlerian theory and its application to substance-related problems; older adolescent drinking behavior; motivational, existential, and postmodern approaches to counseling; and multivariate analysis and design in counseling research.

Chi-Sing Li, PhD LPC-S, LMFT, is an assistant professor in the Department of Educational Leadership and Counseling at Sam Houston State University. His doctorate is in counselor education, and he is currently the coordinator of the counseling internship and teaches Cross-Cultural Issues in Counseling. His research interests include distance learning and online education, crisis intervention, and multicultural counseling.

Ben K. Lim, PhD, LMFT, is an associate professor of marital and family therapy at Bethel Seminary San Diego, Bethel University. He is a clinical member and approved supervisor of the American Association for Marriage and Family Therapy and has a private practice at LifeSpring Center, San Diego. His teaching, research, writings, and counseling have focused on cross-cultural issues, the self of the therapist, and spirituality.

Soh-Leong Lim, PhD, LMFT, and AAMFT Approved Supervisor, is an assistant professor in the marriage and family therapy program at San Diego State University, with primary teaching responsibilities in multicultural counseling courses and family therapy supervision. Her research interests include best practices in marriage and family therapy, intergenerational relationships in immigrant and refugee families, and mental health service delivery to underserved populations.

Yu-Fen Lin, MA, LPCI, is a doctoral fellow in the department of Educational Leadership and Counseling at Sam Houston State University. Her research interests include feminist theology and counseling, domestic violence, self-esteem issues of women, and cross-cultural issues.

Morgan Litchfield, BS, completed her bachelor's degree in educational psychology at Mississippi State University (MSU). She is currently a master's-degree candidate in the community counseling program at MSU's Meridian campus. In addition to her studies in community mental health, she is also interested in testing and assessment.

John M. Littrell, EdD, is professor and program coordinator of the counseling and career development program at Colorado State University. He specializes in brief, solution-focused counseling (*Brief Counseling in Action,* 1998) and school counseling (*Portrait and*

Model of a School Counselor with J. Peterson, 2005). Research interests include brief counseling and qualitative research; teaching responsibilities include foundations of counseling, counseling theories, practicum, and brief counseling.

Hanoch Livneh, PhD, CRC, NCC, is a professor and the coordinator of the rehabilitation counseling program at Portland State University, Portland, Oregon. He obtained his graduate degree at the University of Wisconsin–Madison in rehabilitation counseling psychology.

Gabriel I. Lomas, PhD, is an assistant professor at the University of Houston–Clear Lake. He has substantial experience with school counseling, play therapy, and the assessment of individuals with disabilities, especially those who are deaf and hard-of-hearing. He is the current coeditor of the *Journal of the American Deafness and Rehabilitation Association.* He maintains a private practice in Houston that aims to provide culturally affirmative mental health services to deaf people.

Eugenie Joan Looby, PhD, LPC, NCC, completed her doctoral studies at The University of Georgia and is a professor in the community counseling program at Mississippi State University with primary teaching responsibilities in multicultural issues, counseling theories, sexual abuse, community counseling clinical practice, and life-span development. Her research interests include diversity, spirituality, eating disorders and body image concerns among African American women, and sexual abuse. She is the coauthor of *Multicultural Counseling: Context, Theory and Practice, and Competence.*

Melissa Luke, PhD, LMHC, NCC, ACS, is an assistant professor and coordinator of the school counseling program at Syracuse University. Her research interests include clinical supervision of school counselors-in-training; comprehensive, developmental school counseling program implementation; and school counselors' role in social action through systemic change.

Rachel E. Crook Lyon, PhD, completed her doctoral study at the University of Maryland, College Park and currently is an assistant professor in the counseling psychology program at Brigham Young University, with primary teaching responsibilities in supervision, career theories, and consultation. Her research interests include supervisory training, dream work in counseling, and multiculturalism and spirituality.

Kathryn C. MacCluskie, PhD, completed her doctorate in counseling psychology at West Virginia University and is currently at Cleveland State University, where she is the coordinator of the counselor education programs. She teaches a variety of skill-based courses, such as counseling techniques and internship, and her research interests are in skill acquisition among counselor trainees.

Sandy Magnuson, PhD, is an associate professor of counselor education at the University of Northern Colorado. Couples counseling, school counseling, play therapy, and supervision are her areas of specialty. Her research has focused on counselors' growth across the professional life span.

José M. Maldonado, PhD, NCC, is an assistant professor and director of the school counseling program at Monmouth University. He has over 10 years of professional experience as a mental health clinician and middle and high school counselor in several school districts. He has worked extensively with families in urban environments focusing on multicultural counseling and therapeutic techniques.

Coretta J. Mallery is a doctoral student in counseling at the George Washington University. Her research interests are in adolescent development, delinquency, and social processes.

Krista M. Malott, PhD, NCC, is an assistant professor at Villanova University, with research interests in multicultural counseling, multicultural instruction, and ethnic identity development.

Matthew A. Malouf is a doctoral student in counseling psychology at Lehigh University. He received his bachelor's degree in psychology with a minor in women, gender, and sexuality from Johns Hopkins University. He has been involved in sexuality advocacy and outreach through his work as a staff member in several higher education offices devoted to multiculturalism and social justice. His current research interests include nonbinary sexual and ethnic identities, intersections of multiple identities, and disorders of sex development and related counseling competencies.

Eric D. Manley, PhD, LPCA, completed his doctoral studies at the University of Memphis and is currently a staff counselor at the Counseling and Testing Center of Western Kentucky University. His research interests include gay, lesbian, bisexual, transgender, and questioning issues; career counseling; and couples.

David F. March, PhD, LMHC, CAP, NCC, completed his doctoral study at the University of Central Florida and is an assistant professor in the Department of Counselor Education at Stetson University in DeLand, Florida. He also maintains a part-time private practice in Winter Park, Florida, providing individual, group, couples, and family therapy. His research interests include self-disclosure in counselor training, characteristics of counselor education, professional identity, addictions and addiction treatment, group work, the supervisory working alliance, and the therapeutic relationship. He currently serves as the chapter faculty adviser to the Alpha Omicron chapter of Chi Sigma Iota (CSI) and is the southern regional chapter facilitator for CSI.

Jennifer L. Marshall, PhD, CCBT, LPC, NCC, completed her doctorate at Texas A&M University–Commerce and currently is an assistant professor in psychology at the University of Cincinnati–Raymond Walters College, with primary teaching responsibilities in human development, crisis intervention, and abnormal psychology. Her research interests are eating issues and counseling groups for adolescents and college students.

J. Barry Mascari, EdD, LPC, NCC, received his doctoral degree at Argosy University/Sarasota and is an assistant professor in the Counselor Education Department at Kean University in New Jersey. He was president of the American Association of State Counseling Boards in 2006–2007. Research interests include counselor licensing issues, such as violation patterns, and school counselor intervention programs.

Kimberly L. Mason, PhD, NCC, completed her doctoral study at the University of New Orleans and is an assistant professor in the community agency and school counseling program at Cleveland State University, with primary teaching responsibilities in school counseling courses. Her research interests include school counseling issues, bullying, cyberbullying, Internet safety, standards-based counseling programs in schools, and school counseling preparation.

Michael J. Mason, PhD, completed his doctorate at Oregon State University and completed a National Institute of Mental Health postdoctoral research fellowship at Johns Hopkins University, School of Public Health, in child and adolescent mental health. His research focuses on understanding the social ecology of urban youth and high-risk behaviors such as substance use through using individual, social network, and geographic analytical approaches.

Wanda C. McCarthy, PhD, completed her doctoral studies in personality and social psychology at the University of Pittsburgh. She is currently an assistant professor of psychology at the University of Cincinnati–Clermont College. Her research interests include social power and intimate partner violence, workplace violence, burnout, and chemophobia.

Kristi McCaskill, MEd, NCC, NCSC, completed her master's-degree program at the University of North Carolina at Chapel Hill and currently is the counseling advocacy coordinator at the National Board for Certified Counselors. Previously, she worked as a middle school counselor for nearly 10 years.

Vivian J. McCollum, PhD, is an associate professor at Albany State University, where she is the coordinator of the counseling program. Her areas of emphasis are school counseling, multicultural counseling, trauma, and advocacy. She is a past president of Counselors for Social Justice.

Mary E. McCormac, PhD, NCC, NBCT, completed her doctoral work at St. Louis University. She is an elementary school counselor and adjunct professor at Marymount University in Arlington, Virginia.

Patricia J. McDivitt, vice-resident, Test Development, Data Recognition Corporation, has had over 20 years of test development experience, including overseeing the development of criterion-referenced assessments for statewide standards-based programs. In addition to her experience developing assessments, she recently served as president of the Association for Assessment in Counseling, a division of the American Counseling Association. She also serves as a member of the Joint Committee on Standards for Educational Evaluation.

Kelly A. McDonnell, PhD, completed her doctoral study at Indiana University and currently is an associate professor and director of the Center for Counseling and Psychological Services in the Department of Counselor Education and Counseling Psychology at Western Michigan University. She serves as the Awards Committee cochair for the Association for Specialists in Group Work, and her professional interests include counseling process and outcome, group work and group leader development, supervision, and domestic violence.

Adriana G. McEachern, PhD, NCC, NCRC, LMHC, completed her doctorate at the University of Florida and is a counselor educator at Florida International University. Her research interests include child abuse, emotional maltreatment, counseling exceptional students, and career development. She is the past chair of the American Counseling Association Southern Region and past president of the Florida Counseling Association.

William P. McFarland, EdD, NCC, LCPC, completed his doctorate at Indiana University of Pennsylvania and is currently a professor in the Counselor Education Department at Western Illinois University, with primary teaching responsibilities in assessment techniques, career development, and school counseling. His research interests include the career development of diverse populations, the impact of comprehensive school counseling programs, and the use of technology for training counselor education students.

Jason M. McGlothlin, PhD, PCC-S, is an associate professor in the counseling and human development services program at Kent State University. He completed his doctoral degree in counselor education and supervision at Ohio University. His primary research interests include the prevention of suicide and the assessment and treatment of suicidal clients.

Bill McHenry, PhD, NCC, LPC, completed his doctoral study at The University of South Dakota and currently is an assistant professor in the Counseling and College Student Personnel Department at Shippensburg University of Pennsylvania. His research interests include therapeutic techniques, qualitative research, school counselor roles and responsibilities, and diversity.

Jim McHenry, EdD, NCC, LPC, CRC, completed his doctoral work at George Washington University. He taught counseling (school mental health, rehabilitation, college student personnel) at Edinboro University of Pennsylvania for 32 years and is professor emeritus.

Amy L. McLeod, EdS, LPC, NCC, is a doctoral student in the counselor education and practice program at Georgia State University. Her research interests include multicultural issues in counselor education and supervision, assessment and diagnosis, women's issues, and crisis and trauma counseling.

Niloufer M. Merchant, EdD, NCC, LP, completed her doctoral study at the University of Cincinnati and currently is professor and department chair in the Community Psychology Department at St. Cloud State University. Her teaching responsibilities include courses in multicultural and group counseling and other clinical courses in the community counseling program. Her research interests include qualitative methodology, racial identity development, and multicultural group work. She is actively involved in the community with social justice, women's, and multicultural issues.

Tammi F. Milliken, PhD, NCC, is an assistant professor in the Educational Leadership and Counseling Department at Old Dominion University. Her research interests include developmental theory and application, adult development and learning, ethics, multicultural competence, and critical issues in human services.

Casey A. Barrio Minton, PhD, NCC, completed her doctoral study at The University of North Carolina at Greensboro and is an assistant professor of counseling at the University of North Texas. She teaches courses in community counseling, diagnosis and treatment planning, cultural diversity, and counseling skills. Her research interests include crisis intervention, developmental counseling and therapy, and counselor preparation for diagnosis and treatment planning.

Brian J. Mistler received his master's degree in conflict resolution and international peace studies from the University of Bradford, United Kingdom. He has trained and worked at the Gestalt Center of Gainesville, Florida, since 2003. Current research interests include humor, parables, epistemology, work with minority (especially Muslim) populations, Sufism, organizational leadership and second-order change, analogical reasoning, cybernetics, and multivalent logic.

Robika Modak is a doctoral student in counselor education at Mississippi State University. She is employed as a middle school counselor in Starkville, Mississippi.

Nykeisha Moore completed her master's degree at South Carolina State University and is pursuing her doctoral

degree in rehabilitation counselor education at the University of Iowa. Her research interests include posttraumatic stress disorder, aging population, rehabilitation closures, and crisis interventions in higher education.

Rachel N. Moore is completing a master's degree in counseling, with an emphasis in school counseling, from Old Dominion University. Her research interests include multicultural competency issues and K–12 prevention programming, specifically related to diversity and tolerance training and substance abuse education.

Gayle Morse, PhD, is an assistant professor at The Sage Colleges in Troy and Albany, New York. She is a licensed psychologist who conducts research in the areas of cultural identity, environmental toxins, and risk factors for psychopathology.

Rochelle C. Moss, PhD, LPC, received her doctorate from the University of Arkansas and has worked at the University of Mississippi and Texas A&M–Commerce. She is currently employed as an assistant professor in the Counselor, Adult and Rehabilitation Education Department at the University of Arkansas at Little Rock, where her research interests include school counseling concerns, women's developmental issues, and effective strategies for counseling adolescents.

Suzanne D. Mudge, PhD, LPC, NCC, received her doctoral degree in counselor education and supervision from St. Mary's University and is currently an assistant professor and chair of the Education Department at Our Lady of the Lake University, with primary teaching responsibilities in school counseling courses. Her research interests include emotion assessment, burnout, and professional identity development.

Nyaradzo Mvududu, EdD, is an assistant professor in the curriculum and instruction program at Seattle Pacific University, with primary teaching responsibilities in research methods courses. Her research interests include issues in statistics education and multicultural concerns in teacher preparation.

Jane E. Myers, PhD, NCC, NCGC, LPC, completed her doctorate in counselor education at the University of Florida and is a professor in the Department of Counseling and Educational Development at The University of North Carolina at Greensboro. Her research interests include wellness and assessment as well as developmental counseling and counselor education. She is the coauthor of both theoretical and evidence-based models of wellness and associated assessment instruments.

Sylvia C. Nassar-McMillan, PhD, LPC, NCC, ACS, is a counselor educator at North Carolina State University and a licensed counselor and clinical supervisor. She has an active research agenda in areas of multicultural diversity and is experienced in assessing issues related to career, gender, and ethnic identity development and psychological well-being, particularly among Arab Americans.

Margaret M. Nauta, PhD, completed her doctoral degree in counseling psychology at Iowa State University. She is currently an associate professor in the psychology department at Illinois State University where she is affiliated with the clinical-counseling psychology master's-degree program. Her primary teaching responsibilities include introductory psychology and graduate courses related to counseling. Her research interests are in the area of career development.

Judith A. Nelson, PhD, earned her doctoral degree in human services from Capella University and is currently an assistant professor in the counseling program at Sam Houston State University with primary responsibilities in marriage and family therapy and school counseling courses. Her research interests include mixed methods research, schoolwide cultural competence issues, and the meaning of commitment in partner relationships.

Ed Neukrug, EdD, NCC, LPC, LP, is professor of counseling and teaches in the master's and doctoral programs at Old Dominion University. He has written numerous texts in the field, including *The World of the Counselor, Essentials of Testing and Assessment,* and *Skills and Tools for Today's Counselors and Psychotherapists.*

Mark D. Newmeyer, EdD, is an adjunct assistant professor in the University of Cincinnati's counseling program and cochair on the Association for Specialists in Group Work Professional Standards Committee. His clinical and research interests include group work, addictive behaviors, prevention, and ecological theory.

Nancy Nishimura, EdD, NCC, completed her doctoral study at The University of Alabama–Tuscaloosa and currently is an associate professor in the counselor education program at The University of Memphis, with primary teaching responsibilities in clinical skills and multicultural counseling courses. Her research interests include multicultural counseling issues and spirituality in counselor education.

Amy Nitza, PhD, is an assistant professor of counseling and counselor education in the School of Education at Indiana University–Purdue University Fort Wayne. She is the producer of a group training DVD, *Leading Groups With Adolescents;* coauthor of a group workbook; editor of the newsletter of the Association for Specialists in Group Work; and the author of several journal articles on group topics. Her research interests include the use of psychoeducational groups for prevention and therapeutic factors in groups for children and adolescents.

Brigid M. Noonan, PhD, LMHC, NCC, ACS, completed her doctoral study at the University of Maryland College Park and is associate professor and chair in the Department of Counselor Education at Stetson University. Her research interests include substance abuse, advocacy within the counselor education field, competency devel-

opment of counselors-in-training, social justice issues in diverse populations, and career development.

Ken Norem, PhD, is a counselor educator who has taught in six university programs and held offices in four branches of the American Counseling Association. His specialty interests include counselor identity and pride, family counseling, school counseling, and supervision.

Rosanne Nunnery, MS, NCC, LPC, received her master's degree from Mississippi State University. She has worked as a counselor in various areas, including domestic violence, community mental health as a children's therapist and supervisor, inpatient therapy, intensive outpatient therapy, and therapy groups for adolescents at a residential facility and is in private practice at Psychology Associates, LLC, in Meridian, Mississippi. She is currently a doctoral student in counselor education at Mississippi State University. Her research interests include resiliency, child abuse and domestic violence, and anxiety.

Aaron H. Oberman, PhD, NCC, completed his doctoral studies in counselor education at The University of Tennessee, Knoxville. He is currently an assistant professor of school counseling at The Citadel, primarily teaching career counseling and fieldwork courses. His research interests include job satisfaction, supervision, and school counselor training and development.

Kathryn A. Oden, PhD, LPC, completed her doctoral study at the University of North Texas and is currently an assistant professor in the counseling program at Texas A & M University–Commerce with primary teaching responsibilities in clinical courses. Her research interests include the role of forgiveness in the therapeutic process, the impact of the core condition of acceptance on the counselor, and the concept of inner peace.

Kimberly B. Oliver, BA, graduated with a bachelor's degree in psychology from Georgia State University, where she is a graduate student in the PhD program for school psychology.

Leslie W. O'Ryan, EdD, NCC, LCPC, completed her doctoral study at the University of South Dakota and is an associate professor in the Counselor Education Department at Western Illinois University, with primary teaching responsibilities in counseling across the life span, addictions, and career development. Her research interests include aging and spirituality, qualitative inquiry into career development of diverse populations, and adult development.

Sherlon P. Pack-Brown, PhD, LPCC-S, completed her doctoral study at the University of Toledo and is a professor in the mental health and school counseling program at Bowling Green State University, with primary teaching responsibilities in theory, group, practicum, and diversity courses. Her research interests include diversity competencies in counseling and education and multicultural and social justice concerns in counselor preparation, diversity competent group work, and ethics in a multicultural context.

Betsy J. Page, EdD, LPCC, NCC, completed her doctoral study at the University of Maine and is currently an associate professor in the counseling and human development services program at Kent State University, with primary teaching responsibilities in the group and supervision courses. Her research interests include group leadership skills, supervisor identity development, and assessment.

Pamela O. Paisley, EdD, LPC, NCC, is a professor and program coordinator at The University of Georgia. Previously, she was a counselor educator at Appalachian State University and a school counselor in public schools in North Carolina. Her research and clinical interests include collaborative action research, school counseling, human development, and the use of expressive and creative arts in counseling. She is committed to principles of social justice and is active in related initiatives at the local, state, and national levels.

Charles D. Palmer, PhD, is an associate professor and clinical coordinator in the Department of Counselor Education, Educational Psychology, and Special Education at Mississippi State University. He is the president of the National Rehabilitation Counseling Association.

Tina R. Paone, PhD, LPC, NCC, is an assistant professor at Monmouth University. Her research interests include multicultural school counseling, group activity therapy, school counseling, and play therapy.

Stephen Parker, PhD, is a graduate of Emory University and professor in the School of Psychology and Counseling at Regent University, with primary teaching responsibilities in counseling and personality theories and human development. His research interests include spiritual and religious development and the interface of theological and psychological theories of the person.

Robert H. Pate Jr., PhD, LPC, NCC, completed his doctoral studies at The University of North Carolina at Chapel Hill and is currently the William Clay Parrish Jr. Professor of Education in the counselor education program at The University of Virginia Curry School of Education. His primary professional interests are life and career planning, ethical and legal aspects of counseling, and client spirituality and counseling. He is a past chair of the National Board for Certified Counselors and a recipient of the Thomas J. Sweeney Award from Chi Sigma Iota.

John Patrick, DEd, LPC, NCC, CRC, completed his doctoral studies at The Pennsylvania State University and is an associate professor in the counselor education program at California University of Pennsylvania, with primary teaching responsibilities in career counseling and counseling skills and techniques. His research interests include career counseling, counselor preparation, and college counseling.

Matthew J. Paylo, PhD, a recent graduate from the University of Virginia's counselor education program, is currently the mental health director at Fluvanna's Correctional Center for Women.

Cheyenne Pease-Carter, MS, is currently a doctoral student in the counselor education program at the University of North Texas. Her primary research interests include counselor preparation, grief, ethics, and animal-assisted therapy.

Dale-Elizabeth Pehrsson, EdD, C-LPC-S, NCC, ACS, DCC, is an associate professor for counselor education at the University of Nevada Las Vegas, with primary responsibilities for coordinating the PhD program in counselor education. Her clinical and research interests include play, art, and story counseling interventions across generational and cultural contexts. She is a registered play therapist supervisor and current clinical editor for *Play Therapy™*.

Paul R. Peluso, PhD, LMHC, LMFT, is assistant professor and program coordinator of the mental health counseling program at Florida Atlantic University. His theoretical and research interests include Adlerian counseling and psychotherapy, family and couples development, parenting, and attachment theory.

Debra A. Pender, PhD, LCPC, NCC, ACS, completed her doctoral studies at Southern Illinois University–Carbondale and is an assistant professor at Northern Illinois University, with primary teaching responsibilities in doctoral research, mental health, crisis intervention, and individual and group practicum. She is cochair of the Association for Specialists in Group Work Professional Standards Committee and a recipient of the Peg Carroll Award.

Jennifer L. Pepperell, PhD, NCC, LPC, completed her doctoral study at Oregon State University in counselor education and supervision and is an assistant professor at Minnesota State University, Mankato. Her research interests include qualitative methods from a feminist perspective, issues related to adolescent girls' development, giftedness, school counseling, gender issues, and training methods of child and adolescent counselors.

Dilani Perera-Diltz, PhD, completed her doctoral degree at The University of Toledo and is an assistant professor in the community agency and school counseling programs at Cleveland State University. She is a licensed Professional Clinical Counselor, a Licensed Independent Chemical Dependency Counselor, and a licensed school counselor. Her current research interests include substance abuse, trauma, supervision, and school counselor role and duties.

Jean Sunde Peterson, PhD, LMHC, NCC, is an associate professor and coordinator of the school counseling program at Purdue University. Her main research interest is the social and emotional development of high-ability students, particularly of understudied or underidentified gifted populations.

Yegan Pillay, PhD, PCC-S, is an assistant professor in counseling and higher education at Ohio University with primary teaching responsibilities in clinical counseling courses. He is a past president of the South East Ohio Counseling Association. His research interests include multicultural issues, racial/cultural/ethnic identity development, storytelling and narrative therapy, psychological health, secondary trauma, and HIV/AIDS counseling.

Mark Pope, EdD, is a professor and chair of the Division of Counseling and Family Therapy at the University of Missouri–Saint Louis. His primary area of interest and research is in multicultural career counseling, especially gay/lesbian, Native American, and Asian career development issues. He has written on the history and development of professional counseling in the United States and other countries, violence in the schools, and Native American traditional healing. He is a past president of the American Counseling Association and National Career Development Association.

Tarrell Awe Agahe Portman, PhD, LMHC, NCC, is an associate professor at the University of Iowa and coordinator of the counselor education and supervision program. Her research focuses on attribution theory as it interacts with counseling in the areas of counselor development (supervision and consultation), multiculturalism (disenfranchised populations, particularly American Indian women), and school counseling reform (programs and practice).

Elizabeth A. Prosek, MSEd, is a doctoral student at Old Dominion University and is a supportive living counselor for the seriously mentally ill and mentally retarded at the Norfolk Community Services Board. Her research interests include program evaluation and assessment, diagnosis, and gender/trauma issues.

Jake J. Protivnak, PhD, PCC-S, LSC, NCC, completed his doctoral work at Ohio University and currently is an assistant professor in the counseling program at Youngstown State University, with primary teaching responsibilities in school counseling courses. His research interests include school counseling, career counseling, and professional identity and development of counselors.

Steve Rainey, PhD, is an assistant professor of counselor education at Kent State University. He teaches courses on counseling adolescents and school counseling that focus on ethics related to school-age clients. He is an active member of professional organizations at the national, state, and local levels and has made several presentations that include ethical issues related to school-age clients.

Mary-Jeanne Raleigh, MEd, MA, NCC, LCMHC, is a doctoral student in environmental studies at Antioch University, New England. Her research interests include the development of coping skills throughout the life span, the use of restorative natural environments for the treatment of anxiety, and the influence of nature contact on child development. She is currently the director of health services/assistant director of counseling services at New England College (NEC), an adjunct faculty member of the mental health counseling program at NEC, and a nationally recognized speaker on the use of natural restorative environments in therapy.

Timothy D. Rambo, PhD, LPC, completed his doctoral studies at The University of Virginia. He is a school counselor at Charlottesville High School, Charlottesville, Virginia. His professional and research interests include adolescent depression, adjustment disorders, clinical supervision, and collaboration between school and community counselors.

MaryLou Ramsey, EdD, LPC, NCC, NCSC, ACS, completed her doctoral study at Fairleigh Dickinson University and is a professor in and coordinator of the school counseling program in the Department of Counselor Education at The College of New Jersey, with primary teaching responsibilities in multicultural counseling and clinical supervision. Her scholarly achievements include numerous refereed publications and more than 100 professional conference and workshop presentations, many of which are devoted to multicultural counselor education and training, clinical supervision, ethical challenges in multicultural counseling and counselor education, and scholarly productivity in counselor education.

James D. Raper is a college counselor and doctoral student in counselor education at Syracuse University. His research is focused on educating students and practitioners in effective suicide assessment.

Lynn S. Rapin, PhD, cowrote the *ASGW Best Practice Guidelines* and the *ASGW Professional Standards for the Training of Group Workers*. She is a private practitioner and an adjunct associate professor of counseling at the University of Cincinnati. She served as president of the Association for Specialists in Group Work and president of the American Psychological Association Division 49, Group Psychology and Group Psychotherapy. She is a consultant to health, social service, and education organizations and an active scholar and presenter in the areas of best practice and ethics in group work and program development and evaluation.

Scott Rasmus, PhD, LPCC, IMFT, NCC, is a former assistant professor at Delta State University, where he taught a course in testing and assessment for counseling students. He is employed by Lifespan, Inc., of Hamilton, Ohio; is a member of the Association for Assessment in Counseling and Education; and has research interests in the areas of statistics and outcome measurement.

Manivong Ratts, PhD, NCC, completed his doctoral degree at Oregon State University in counselor education and supervision and is an assistant professor in the Department of Counseling and School Psychology at Seattle University. His research is in the area of social justice, advocacy, developing Safe Space Training programs, and implementation of the American Counseling Association advocacy competencies in counselor education.

Nabiha Rawdah, BA, is a graduate student in counseling psychology at the University of Victoria. Her professional interests include career and life planning, and she has provided career-related workshops at the University of Victoria counseling center while on practicum.

David M. Reile, PhD, is a licensed psychologist, National Certified Career Counselor, and Master Career Counselor with 20 years of education and experience in career planning and psychological consultation. His experience has been applied in organizational development and consultation as well as management of counselors and career development projects in a variety of settings. He is also a faculty associate in the master's-degree Pastoral Counseling Program at Loyola University Maryland and chair of the Ethics Committee of the National Career Development Association.

Melanie Reinersman, MA, completed her master's degree at the University of Illinois, Urbana-Champaign. After 10 years in career services in higher education, she is now a self-employed consultant, offering career counseling and Web site editing. She is editor of *Career Convergence,* the Web magazine of the National Career Development Association.

Theodore P. Remley Jr., JD, PhD, NCC, LPC, LMFT, is professor of counseling, holds the Batten Chair in Counseling, and is the graduate program director of counseling at Old Dominion University. He is a former executive director of the American Counseling Association and is an author and presenter in the area of legal and ethical issues in counseling.

Edina L. Renfro-Michel, PhD, NCC, completed her doctoral study at Mississippi State University and is currently an assistant professor in the counselor education program at Montclair State University. Her research interests include child and adult attachment, attachment and counseling supervision, and the use of technology in counselor education.

Glenda P. Reynolds, EdD, NCC, received her doctorate in counselor education from The University of Alabama. She is an associate professor in the counseling program at Auburn University Montgomery. Her areas of research interest are international persons, children, and self-esteem.

Richard J. Ricard, PhD, is professor of counseling and educational psychology at Texas A&M University– Corpus Christi. He received his doctoral degree from Harvard University in developmental psychology. His research interests lie primarily in the application of psychological principles to educational settings and program evaluation in counseling and social service entities. He is particularly interested in the evaluation of programming efforts that address the needs of students considered "at risk" for academic failure. He is a member of the Texas Counseling Association, American Counseling Association, and American Evaluation Association.

Kimberly A. M. Richards, PhD, NCC, SACC, completed her doctoral study at Oregon State University and is currently a principal investigator for the HIV/AIDS Counseling and Education Research Group. In addition, she is a behavioral scientist on attachment from Comforce to the Centers for Disease Control Zimbabwe office as a technical adviser for HIV/AIDS Behavior Change. Her professional interests include research epistemology, psychological experiences of HIV/ AIDS counselors when counseling HIV/AIDS clients, behavior change as related to HIV/AIDS, multiracial/ ethnic/cultural identity development, and the impact of oppression/colonialism in Southern Africa on identity development.

Laura R. Ritchie, MA, is a doctoral candidate in counselor education and supervision at the University of North Carolina at Charlotte. She has a master's degree in marriage and family therapy. Currently, she is an adjunct professor in the human development and psychological counseling program at Appalachian State University. Her research interests include study of the effectiveness of experiential therapy models, sexual minority counseling issues, women's issues in counseling, multicultural counseling, substance abuse counseling issues, and clinical supervision.

Martin H. Ritchie, EdD, LPC, NCC, completed his doctoral studies at The University of Virginia and is professor and coordinator of school counseling at the University of Toledo. His research interests include school counselor accountability, legal and ethical issues, and group and peer influences.

Maria T. Riva, PhD, completed her doctoral study at the University of Pittsburgh and is a professor in the counseling psychology program at the University of Denver, with teaching responsibilities in group counseling, adolescent development, supervision, and practicum. Her research interests include group leadership, group supervision, and group dynamics. She is a past president of the Association for Specialists in Group Work (ASGW) and an ASGW Fellow and has written many articles on teaching group leadership, selection of group members, effective leadership, and group supervision practices.

Leila F. Roach, PhD, LMHC, LMFT, NCC, completed her master's degree in human development at Vanderbilt University and her doctoral study at the University of

Central Florida and is currently an assistant professor in the Department of Counselor Education at Stetson University, with primary teaching responsibilities in human development, family systems, theories, group, and human relations methods and skills. Her research interests include counselor development and wellness in counselor preparation and community mental health settings.

Gail K. Roaten, PhD, LPC-S, CSC, completed her doctorate in counselor education at Texas A&M University–Corpus Christi and is an assistant professor in professional counseling in the Department of Educational Administration and Psychological Services at Texas State University–San Marcos, where she is the school counseling program coordinator. She teaches school counseling, counseling adolescents, and development through the life span, and her research interests include professional identity issues related to school counselors as well as effective interventions with children in schools.

Chester R. Robinson, PhD, earned his doctorate from The University of North Carolina at Greensboro and is an associate professor of counseling at Texas A&M University–Commerce. He maintains a record of dedicated professional service, particularly in the Texas Counseling Association.

E. H. Mike Robinson III, PhD, NCC, is professor of counselor education and the Robert N. Heitzelman Eminent Scholar Chair for the study of greed and altruism at the University of Central Florida. He currently serves as the director of doctoral programs.

Kim H. Rodriguez, PhD, LMHC, GCDF, completed her doctoral study at the Union Institute & University and is an assistant professor in the school counseling and mental health counseling programs at Long Island University with primary teaching responsibilities in clinical practicum and supervision. She worked as a school counselor for 13 years, and her research interests include the professional development and training of school counselors, as well as children from addictive families, eating disorders, and body image disturbances.

Patrick J. Rottinghaus, PhD, completed his doctoral study at Iowa State University and is an assistant professor in the counseling psychology program and director of the Career Development and Resource Clinic at Southern Illinois University–Carbondale. His research examines numerous aspects of career development and assessment, including vocational interests, personality, and self-efficacy. He teaches courses in adult development, psychological assessment, positive psychology, and counseling practicum; serves on the editorial board for the *Journal of Career Development* and as an ad hoc reviewer for several journals; and chairs the Research Committee for the National Career Development Association.

Chadwick Royal, PhD, NCC, LPC, completed his doctoral work at North Carolina State University and is currently an assistant professor in the Department of Counselor Education at North Carolina Central University. He is the coordinator of the career counseling program, which is one of only eight career counseling programs accredited by the Council for Accreditation of Counseling and Related Educational Programs in the United States. He teaches classes in introductory and advanced career counseling, human growth and development, consultation, and family counseling. His research interests include the use of technology in counseling and counselor education.

Daniel R. Russell is pursuing a master's degree in college counseling at Mississippi State University. His interests include spirituality and anxiety.

Carmen F. Salazar, PhD, NCC, completed her doctoral study at the University of New Mexico and is currently an associate professor in the Department of Counseling at Texas A&M University–Commerce. Her research interests include gender, diversity, and social justice concerns in counseling and counselor education and qualitative methodology. She is active in the Association for Specialists in Group Work (ASGW) and has served as a cochair of the ASGW Human Rights and Diversity Committee since 2003.

Carol Z. A. Salisbury, PhD, LGPC, is a graduate of the Pastoral Counseling Department at Loyola University Maryland. Her research focuses on the use of anger as a positive, healthy emotion.

Jeff L. Samide, EdD, LPC, has over 30 years experience in working with individuals, groups, and families. He regularly consults with private organizations, governmental agencies, and schools regarding a wide variety of issues, including sexual assault, domestic violence, and substance abuse. He currently teaches school and community counseling at California University of Pennsylvania and maintains a general counseling practice in Indiana, Pennsylvania.

Daya Singh Sandhu, EdD, NCC, NCCC, NCSC, LPCC, is distinguished professor of research, Fulbright Senior Research Scholar, and former chairperson of the Department of Educational & Counseling Psychology at the University of Louisville. His research interests include multicultural counseling, school counseling, and the role of spirituality in counseling and psychotherapy. He has coauthored or coedited 12 textbooks, 60 book chapters, and more than 50 refereed articles. He has been recognized as one of the 12 pioneers in multicultural counseling.

David P. Sarnoff, PhD, ABPP, earned his BA in mathematics from Harvard University and his PhD in counseling psychology from the University of Kentucky. He currently is a core faculty member in the counseling psychology specialization at Capella

University and in private practice in Charleston, South Carolina.

Mark L. Savickas, PhD, is professor and chair in the Department of Behavioral Sciences at the Northeastern Ohio Universities College of Medicine and a Fellow of the American Counseling Association.

Jennifer Savitz-Smith, PhD, LPC-S, is a counselor in private practice in Columbia, South Carolina. Her practice is diverse and includes children, families, and individuals. Specific clinical interests include abuse issues across the life span, family issues of divorce and separation, and women's issues.

Kristin Schaefer-Schiumo, PhD, completed her doctoral study at Fordham University and is an associate professor in the school counseling and mental health counseling programs at Long Island University, C.W. Post Campus, with primary teaching responsibilities in clinical practicum and supervision. Her research interests include qualitative methodology, the biopsychosocial bases of behavior, and the ethical and legal issues pertaining to advising students who are inappropriate for mental health counseling programs for nonacademic (emotional, social, behavioral) reasons.

Megan Scharett, EdM, is a doctoral student in counselor education at the University of Florida. She completed her master's-degree training in school counseling at the University of Buffalo. Her research interests include identity development and academic achievement in adolescents, innovative approaches in school counseling, emotional competence, and mattering.

Gibson Scheid, PhD, is a career counselor who helps individuals redesign their careers through her counseling practice, writing, and teaching activities.

Travis W. Schermer, MSCP, completed his master's degree at Chatham College in Pittsburgh and is currently working on his PhD in counselor education at Kent State University. He has worked as a senior research associate at Western Psychiatric Institute and Clinic, Pittsburgh, Pennsylvania.

Lynn Schlossberger, MA, LPC, is a mental health counselor with Family Service of Greater Baton Rouge, a nonprofit agency, where she works within the Title IV Program, serving HIV positive women, children, youth, and their families. Her practice includes individual, family, and group counseling with HIV-positive clients as well as trauma work with evacuees of Hurricane Katrina. She completed her studies at Louisiana State University.

Lewis Z. Schlosser, PhD, completed his doctoral study at the University of Maryland and is an assistant professor of counseling psychology at Seton Hall University. He teaches graduate courses in counseling skills, adult psychopathology, psychological assessment, and research methods. Using both quantitative and qualitative methods, he has research interests in many areas, including advising and mentoring relationships and multicultural counseling; the latter area includes Jewish issues; religious climate; and the intersection of race, religion, and ethnicity.

Mark B. Scholl, PhD, LMHC, NCC, completed his doctorate at The University of North Carolina at Greensboro and is an assistant professor in the Department of Counseling and Development at Long Island University. He is the editor of the *Journal of Humanistic Counseling, Education and Development,* and his research interests include client counseling preferences, factors influencing client attitudes toward and continuation in counseling, college student persistence, and uses of the expressive arts in counseling.

Valerie L. Schwiebert, PhD, LPC, NCC, NCGC, CRC, completed her doctoral study at the University of Florida and is a professor of counseling at Western Carolina University, with primary teaching responsibilities in community counseling. Her research interests include gender issues, adult development and aging, mentoring, assessment, and diagnosis.

Alan M. "Woody" Schwitzer, PhD, is a licensed clinical psychologist and associate professor of educational leadership and counseling at Old Dominion University. He is editor of the *Journal of College Counseling.* His professional and research interests focus on college student development; adjustment, learning, and counseling; and diagnosis and treatment planning.

David A. Scott, PhD, LPC, NCC, completed his doctoral study at North Carolina State University and is currently the community counseling program coordinator and assistant professor at Clemson University, with primary teaching responsibilities in community counseling. His research interests include at-risk youth, community counseling, and racial identity development.

Kerry E. Sebera, PhD, PCC, completed her doctoral work at Ohio University and is an assistant professor in the Counseling and Educational Psychology Department at the University of West Georgia. Her professional interests include leadership in counseling, best treatment practices with children, psychosocial aspects of cerebral palsy in children, school counseling, and training and supervision of counselors.

William E. Sedlacek, PhD, is emeritus professor of education at the University of Maryland. His latest book is *Beyond the Big Test: Noncognitive Assessment in Higher Education,* and his research areas include racism, sexism, diversity, college admissions, scholarship selection, advising, and employee selection. He has received research awards from the American Counseling Association, the American College Personnel Association, and the National Association for College Admission Counseling.

James N. Sells, PhD, is professor of counseling and director of the PhD program in counselor education and supervision at Regent University. His primary research interests are in relational conflict resolution, forgiveness/reconciliation, international applications of counseling, and supervision. He maintains a private practice specializing in marriage and family issues and conflict resolution.

Alia Sheikh, PhD, NCC, completed her doctorate at the George Washington University and is currently an assistant professor in the clinical psychology program at Newcastle University in England. She has a special interest in clinical and research aspects of trauma as well as in reflective practice in education.

Kimber Shelton, MS, is a counseling psychology doctoral candidate at The University of Georgia. She completed her master's degree in mental health counseling at Niagara University. Her research interests include racial and gender microaggressions and increasing minority populations' use of mental health services.

Carl J. Sheperis, PhD, NCC, LPC, is an associate professor in community counseling at Mississippi State University. He specializes in the assessment and treatment of behavioral and developmental issues in early childhood. In addition to his role as a professor, he is the clinical director of Behavioral Services LLC, a company that provides behavioral services to children, parents, and teachers associated with Head Start programs. Behavioral Services also provides assessment and intervention services to all pregnant women enrolled in the Head Start early intervention program across 13 counties in Mississippi.

Jocelyn Sherman, PhD, OP, is an adjunct at Capella and Argosy Universities as well as Alvernia College and the University of Phoenix. An author and collaborator with religious communities, she focuses on instruction of brief therapeutic methods within multicultural approaches. She is the founder of Spirit of Hope, a nonprofit organization supplying reading and school materials to children in Africa. Her primary teaching responsibilities include psychology and counseling courses.

Nancy E. Sherman, PhD, NCC, LCPC, ACS, completed doctoral study at The Ohio State University and is a professor in the human development counseling program at Bradley University and director of the Counseling Research and Training Clinic. She teaches appraisal of the individual, counseling and aging, and prepracticum. She is a Fulbright Scholar and has served as president of Chi Sigma Iota.

S. Alan Silliker, EdD, LMHC, completed his doctoral study at Boston College and is an associate professor in the counselor education program at St. Bonaventure University. His teaching responsibilities include career counseling, techniques of counseling, and school coun-

seling internship supervision courses. His research interests are job-getting strategies, extracurricular activity participation, the promotion of students' academic success by school counselors, and the use of WebCT as a teaching aid.

Laura R. Simpson, PhD, LPC, NCC, ACS, is an assistant professor of counselor education at Delta State University, where her teaching responsibilities include social and cultural foundations, crisis intervention, psychodiagnostics, general internship, spirituality in counseling, and substance abuse counseling. A mental health clinician for 15 years prior to moving into academia, her primary areas of research interest include counselor wellness and secondary trauma, spirituality, crisis response, cultural diversity, and supervision.

Robert Sindylek, NCC, LPC, has experience working as a counselor in a variety of settings, including the K–12 public school sector, community college, and university level. He maintains licensure/certification as a National Certified Counselor, Texas Licensed Professional Counselor, and Texas School Counselor. In addition, he teaches Assessment Issues in Counseling and Career Development & Counseling at Texas A&M, Galveston.

Anneliese A. Singh, PhD, LPC, NCC, completed her doctoral study at Georgia State University and is an assistant professor in the Counseling and Human Development Services Department at The University of Georgia with primary teaching responsibilities in the school counseling program. Her research and clinical interests are in multicultural and social justice, focusing on qualitative methodology with historically marginalized groups (e.g., people of color; lesbian, gay, bisexual, transgender, intersex, and questioning individuals; immigrants), and empowerment interventions with trauma survivors. She works locally and nationally in the movement to end child sexual abuse.

Christopher A. Sink, PhD, NCC, LMHC, is professor and chair of school counseling at Seattle Pacific University. His research interests primarily involve issues related to research and statistical methods, psychoeducational assessment, comprehensive school counseling, and spiritual and communitarian approaches to education.

Eva D. Sloan, MA, NCC, LPC-Intern, is a doctoral student at St. Mary's University in San Antonio. Her research interests include the study of posttraumatic stress disorder in children, the use of neurofeedback, and the use and impact of play therapy.

Marty Slyter, PhD, LPC, LMHC, NCC, completed her doctoral study at the University of Northern Colorado and is an assistant professor in the mental health and school counseling programs at Eastern Washington University with primary teaching responsibilities in professional school counseling courses. Her research interests include counseling gifted youth, women's issues, the role of existential counseling in modern society, and counselor self-care.

Allison Smith, MEd, NCC, completed her master's degree at The University of Georgia and is a doctoral student in the Department of Counseling and Human Development Services at The University of Georgia. Her primary research interests include defining multicultural competency, cultural competency and awareness development in undergraduate students, and assessment of racial identity.

Carol Klose Smith, PhD, LPC, NCC, completed her doctoral study at the University of Iowa and is an assistant professor in the counselor education program at Winona State University. Her research interests include interpersonal violence, group therapy, social class concerns in counselor education, and academic transitions focusing on stress and coping among adolescents.

Carol M. Smith, PhD, MACE, LPC, NCC, completed her doctorate at Kent State University and is an adjunct professor of counseling at Marshall University Graduate College and at Liberty University in Lynchburg, with primary teaching responsibilities in clinical skills. Her areas of research interests include end-of-life care, theodicy, and biomedical ethics. She specializes in grief, loss, and trauma counseling.

Lydia B. Smith, MA, NCC, received her master's degree in counseling from the University of North Carolina at Charlotte, where she is completing her PhD in counseling. Her research interests include issues related to people who are elderly, evidence-based therapy for clients diagnosed with early dementia, and multicultural and ageism concerns in counselor preparation and community mental health.

Timothy B. Smith, PhD, is a professor of counseling psychology at Brigham Young University. His research interests include multicultural counseling and spirituality/religion.

Brent M. Snow, PhD, has been a professor and chair of the Department of Counseling and Educational Psychology at the University of West Georgia since 1992. He was previously a faculty member at Oklahoma State University for 13 years and also a faculty member at the University of Idaho, where he also completed his doctorate.

Shawn L. Spurgeon, PhD, LPC, NCC, completed his doctoral studies at The University of North Carolina at Greensboro and is an assistant professor in mental health counseling program at The University of Tennessee at Knoxville. His primary teaching responsibilities include clinical counseling skills and research methods courses. His research interests include resistance in the counselor–client interaction, African American males and development throughout the life span, gender issues in supervision, and resilience and cohesion in foster children and foster families.

Donna S. Starkey, PhD, LPC, NCC, is an assistant professor of counselor education at Delta State University, where she teaches community counseling courses, including ethics. She is a long-time, active member of the counseling profession and a regular presenter at the state and national levels in the field of counseling ethics and the client–counselor relationship.

A. Renee Staton, PhD, LPC, NCC, completed her doctoral work at The University of Virginia and is currently an associate professor in the counseling psychology program at James Madison University. Her research interests include multicultural counseling, socioeconomic class in counseling, and women's issues.

Alan E. Stewart, PhD, is an associate professor in the Department of Counseling and Human Development at The University of Georgia. His research interests include the psychology of weather and climate, death and loss, and Adlerian individual psychology.

Joseph A. Stewart-Sicking, EdD, completed his doctoral studies at the University of Cincinnati and is an assistant professor in the graduate programs in pastoral counseling at Loyola University Maryland, with teaching responsibilities in counseling theory and research methods. His research interests include spiritual practices and personal transformation, research methods in the social sciences, and engaging faith communities in community counseling.

Julie Strentzsch, MA, LPC, CART, is currently working to complete her doctorate in counseling education and supervision at St. Mary's University in San Antonio and is working as a graduate assistant to the department as well as providing counseling services to adjudicated youth and their families. She is a member of Chi Sigma Iota and currently serves as the University chapter's secretary. Her research areas include education, trauma, gender issues, neuroscience, and multicultural and social justice concerns as they relate to the practice of community counseling.

Daniel L. Stroud, MEd, is a doctoral candidate at the University of New Mexico. His research interests include relationships between childhood memories of receiving corrective feedback and perceptions of receiving corrective feedback in counselors-in-training and group work best practices.

Jannette Sturm-Mexic, PhD, LPC, LMFT, Registered Play Therapist, completed her doctoral study at the University of New Orleans and is an assistant professor and program coordinator for the counseling program at Xavier University of Louisiana. Her research interests include family therapy and counselor development and supervision. She also has a private practice in New Orleans, helping individuals and families recover from the emotional impact of Hurricane Katrina.

Chandra R. Sumlin-Brown, EdS, LPC, NCC, completed her specialist degree at Mississippi State University and is a Psychologist I at East Mississippi State Hospital. Her research interests include body image and self-efficacy. Counseling interests include multicultural counseling and group and individual counseling.

Joffrey S. Suprina, PhD, LPC, NCC, AHT, is assistant professor at Argosy University–Atlanta and a case manager at the Ridgeview Institute and runs a private practice. He is a Safe Zone trainer as well as cofounder and past president of Counseling and Psychological Services–Association for Gay, Lesbian, and Bisexuals in Counseling at Georgia State University. His research areas of interest include wellness; lesbian, gay, bisexual, and transgender issues; addiction; and spirituality.

Lynn E. Swaner, EdD, LMHC, NCC, ACS, completed her doctoral study at Teachers College, Columbia University and currently is an assistant professor in the Department of Counseling and Development at C.W. Post Campus of Long Island University, with teaching responsibilities in mental health and school counseling programs. Her research interests include substance abuse and depression in college, graduate student learning and development, spirituality in counseling, and mixed methods research.

Thomas J. Sweeney, PhD, LPCC, completed his doctoral work at The Ohio State University and is professor emeritus at Ohio University in counselor education. His clinical and scholarly interests have been in Adlerian counseling, career counseling, group work, and consultation. His professional interests have been advocacy for professional counselors and those whom they serve.

Luellyn Switzer, MS, is a community counseling doctoral candidate in the Department of Counseling, Educational Psychology and Special Education, Mississippi State University. She did her thesis research in the area of early maladaptive schemas and risky sexual behavior. Her doctoral research is in the area of eating disorders.

Brian J. Taber, PhD, is an assistant professor of counseling and the director of the Adult Career Counseling Center at Oakland University. His research interests are career development and vocational assessment.

Angelia Taylor, MEd, EdS, is a doctoral candidate and lecturer in educational psychology at Mississippi State University. She has a master's degree in education, with an emphasis in gifted studies, from Mississippi University for Women and EdS in counseling from Mississippi State University. Her research interests include the identification process for individuals who are gifted or have learning disabilities, the psychometric properties of identification instruments for selection of students for gifted and remedial programs, and the social/emotional development and counseling needs of individuals who are identified as gifted or learning disabled.

Rivers S. Taylor Jr., MEd, is the director of school counseling at Blair Middle School in Norfolk, Virginia. He received his undergraduate degree in business and mathematics from Norfolk State University and his master's degree in school counseling from Norfolk State University.

Sandra K. Terneus, PhD, NCC, LMFT, completed her doctoral study at Southern Illinois University–Carbondale and currently is an associate professor in the Department of Counseling and Psychology at Tennessee Tech University, with primary teaching responsibilities in group counseling, abnormal psychology, and supervision. Her research interests include childhood disorders, mood disorders, trauma and gender issues, multicultural holistic healing, group dynamics, and training concerns in counselor preparation.

Suzy R. Thomas, PhD, completed her doctoral study in educational psychology at the University of California, Davis, and is currently an associate professor in the graduate counseling program in the School of Education at Saint Mary's College of California. She teaches Law, Ethics, & Values; Group Theory & Practice; and several courses in the school counseling specialization. Her research focuses on mentoring and ongoing professional development, collaboration and collaborative action research, and school counseling reform.

Siu-Man Raymond Ting, PhD, LPC, NCC, CDFI, obtained his doctorate in counselor education from the University of Iowa and currently is an associate professor and assistant department head in the counselor education program at North Carolina State University, with primary teaching responsibilities in college counseling and career counseling. His research interests include college student development, international applications of Holland's theory, and assessment and evaluation.

Taunya Marie Tinsley, PhD, NCC, LPC, is an assistant professor in the Department of Counselor Education at California University of Pennsylvania. Her interdisciplinary research areas of interests include youth, adolescent, and adult development through sports; sports counseling; multicultural issues in counseling; and multicultural training and development. She completed her requirements and graduated with her PhD from Duquesne University's executive doctoral program in counselor education and supervision. She received her MA degree in higher education administration and college student development from the University of Iowa. She also holds a BA in business administration from Augsburg College.

Shelly Prochaska Trent, SPHR, is the southeast regional manager for the Society for Human Resource Management (SHRM). Prior to joining the staff of SHRM, she worked in government human resources and for universities in career services and business/industry training. She is certified as a Senior Professional in Human Resources and obtained her master of public administration degree with an emphasis in human resources. She is a PhD candidate at the University of Louisville in human resources development and career counseling.

Cindy M. Trevino, MA, LPC-Intern, NCC, is completing her doctoral study at St. Mary's University in San Antonio. Her research interests include chronic pain, and her professional interest includes rehabilitation counseling.

Barbara C. Trolley, PhD, CRC, is a licensed psychologist and associate professor in the Counselor Education program at St. Bonaventure University and cofounder and codirector of the School of Education Counseling Clinic. She is the founder and editor of the *New York State School Counseling Journal* and author of two books. Her research interests include cyberbullying, special education, youth wellness issues, and grief.

Karen Tsukada, PhD, completed her doctoral study at The Ohio State University in counseling psychology. She currently works at the Center for Counseling and Student Development at the University of Delaware and is a part-time assistant professor in the Department of Individual and Family Studies.

Sherri Lou Turner, PhD, completed her doctoral study at the University of Missouri–Columbia. She is an associate professor in the counseling and student personnel psychology program at the University of Minnesota, with primary teaching responsibilities in assessment, career development, and psychological disorders of adolescents and adults. Her primary research interests include the educational and career development of inner-city and minority youth and counseling strategies for Native American people.

Robert I. Urofsky, PhD, completed his doctoral study at The University of Virginia and is assistant professor and school counseling program coordinator at Clemson University. His research interests include ethics in counseling, school counseling, and the role of school counselors in school reform.

Sandra I. Valente, PhD, LADC, completed her doctoral studies at the University of Connecticut and is an associate professor of psychology at Naugatuck Valley Community College, where she teaches for the Psychology Department and is coordinator of the Drug and Alcohol Recovery Counseling Program. She also works as an addictions counselor in private practice.

Brian Van Brunt, EdD, LCMHC, completed his doctoral study at the University of Sarasota/Argosy and is the director of the Counseling and Testing Center at Western Kentucky University. He is active in the Association for University and College Counseling Center Directors, American Counseling Association, and the American College Counseling Association. His research interests include counselor training and education, ethics, assessment and evaluation, and the revitalization of the Thematic Apperception Test.

Linwood G. Vereen, PhD, LPC, NCC, is an assistant professor at Idaho State University and has teaching responsibilities in social and cultural foundations, group counseling techniques, counseling practicum and internship, supervision, and mental health counseling. His research interests are in multicultural counseling, social justice, humor in counseling, group work, and counseling student athletes.

Jennifer Douglas Vidas, PhD, LCPC, NCC, completed her doctorate in counseling at George Washington University. Her research interests include counselor education and supervision, especially in the area of cognitive complexity and its relationship to counselor development.

Carrie A. Wachter, PhD, completed her doctoral degree at The University of North Carolina at Greensboro and is an assistant professor in the counseling and development program at Purdue University, with primary teaching responsibilities in preparation of school counselors. Her research areas include crisis and crisis intervention, collaboration between professional school counselors and other mental health and educational personnel, and counselor education and supervision.

Jacqueline A. Walsh, PhD, LPC, NCC, completed her doctoral studies at Kent State University. She is an associate professor in the Counselor Education Department at California University of Pennsylvania. Her interests include family counseling, group work, use of technology in counseling, and professional counselor identity.

Donald E. Ward, PhD, LCPC, NCC, ACS, completed his doctorate at Purdue University and is professor and chair of the Counseling Committee in the Department of Psychology and Counseling at Pittsburg State University, with primary teaching responsibilities and interests in group work, theories of counseling and psychotherapy, and community counseling professional orientation courses. He is a self-study reviewer and past executive board vice-chair for the Council for Accreditation of Counseling and Related Educational Programs and past editor of the *Journal for Specialists in Group Work.*

Cheryl B. Warner, PhD, is an assistant professor in counselor education of the Eugene T. Moore School of Education at Clemson University. Her research interests include ethnic identity development across the life span, multicultural competency in helping professionals, and multicultural counseling and supervision. She earned an MEd in community counseling and completed her doctoral study in counseling psychology at The University of Georgia.

Laurae Wartinger, PhD, NCC, completed her doctoral study at Ohio University and is the director of the professional school counseling program at the Sage Graduate School. Her primary teaching responsibilities are in research methods courses, group counseling, and practicum. Her research interests include school counselor supervision and childhood and adolescent bereavement.

Joshua C. Watson, PhD, LPC, NCC, ACS, completed his doctoral study at The University of North Carolina at Greensboro and is an assistant professor in the counselor education program at Mississippi State University–Meridian with primary teaching responsibilities in assessment and educational statistics courses. His research interests include counseling student athletes, wellness, and counselor training issues.

T. Steuart Watson, PhD, is professor and chair of educational psychology at Miami University and is coeditor of the *Journal of Evidence-Based Practices for Schools*. His clinical and research interests include applied behavior analysis, direct behavioral consultation, behavioral treatment of habits/tics, functional behavioral assessment, the effects of extrinsic reinforcement on internal motivation, and using olfactory stimuli to enhance learning.

Tonya S. Watson, PhD, completed her doctoral degree in school psychology at Mississippi State University and is a visiting assistant professor in family studies at Miami University. Her primary teaching responsibilities include child development and parenting. Her research interests include school-based consultation, applied behavior analysis, and examining the effects of olfactory stimuli on memory and learning.

Richard E. Watts, PhD, LPC-S, is professor and director of the Center for Research and Doctoral Studies at Sam Houston State University. His primary teaching responsibilities are in doctoral counselor education courses. His theoretical and research interests include Adlerian, cognitive, and constructivist approaches to individual, group, and couple and family counseling; counselor supervision and counselor efficacy; ethical and legal issues; play therapy; and multicultural issues, including religious and spirituality issues in counseling.

Jane Webber, PhD, is an assistant professor and clinical director of the Counseling and School Counseling Programs at Seton Hall University, with research interests in adolescent multimodal counseling, school counseling programs, and trauma counseling. She is a former chair of the American Counseling Association (ACA) Public Awareness and Support Committee and the ACA Foundation.

Joseph D. Wehrman, PhD, LPC, NCC, completed his doctorate in counselor education at The University of South Dakota and his master's degree in applied behavior analysis at St. Cloud State University. He is an assistant professor in the Division of Counselor Education at The Citadel. His research interests include technology and counseling, counseling services for children and adolescents, and mental health services for victims of trauma.

Daniel J. Weigel, PhD, LPC, LADC, NCC, CCMHC, MAC, completed his doctoral studies at Idaho State University and is currently an associate professor and coordi-

nator of the community counseling program at Southeastern Oklahoma State University. His research interests include prescription opioid addiction and treatment, counseling licensure portability, and rural mental health practice.

Kelly L. Wester, PhD, NCC, LPC, completed her doctoral degree at Kent State University and is an assistant professor in the Counseling and Educational Development program at The University of North Carolina at Greensboro. Her primary teaching responsibilities include research methods courses, theories, and internship and practicum supervision. Her research interests include research integrity, research self-efficacy, self-injurious behaviors, professional identity of counselors, and gender issues.

Amy Wickstrom, LMFT, is a licensed marriage and family therapist and registered play therapist. She completed her master's degree at Bethel Seminary and is completing her PhD at Loma Linda University. Her practice, San Diego Center for Play Therapy, is dedicated to research and clinical practice with children and their families.

V. Van Wiesner III, PhD, MBA, LPC, NCC, CCMHC, is an assistant professor at Sam Houston State University, with primary teaching responsibilities in methods of research, diagnosis, and counseling practicum. His research interests include redecision therapy, existential life positions, mechanisms of change, the use of metaphors and hypnosis in psychotherapy, personality disorders, statistics, interdisciplinary connections (e.g., physics), and spirituality.

Marsha I. Wiggins, PhD, LPC, LMFT, NCC, completed her doctoral study at the University of Florida and is a professor in the counseling psychology and counselor education program at the University of Colorado at Denver & Health Sciences Center. Her teaching and research focus on couple and family issues, multiculturalism, and diversity. She published a book on spirituality and counseling, *Integrating Religion and Spirituality Into Counseling: A Comprehensive Approach*.

S. Allen Wilcoxon, PhD, is professor and coordinator of counselor education at The University of Alabama. His specialty interests are in supervision, ethical decision making, and educational pedagogy.

Angela Williams, MEd, is a doctoral candidate who completed her master's degree at Norfolk State University. She is the dean of students and 504 case manager for Blair Middle School in Norfolk, Virginia. Her primary responsibilities include monitoring student behavior, reviewing Section 504 plans annually, and ensuring students that have Section 504 plans are receiving accommodations.

George T. Williams, EdD, is professor and coordinator of counselor education programs at the School of Education, The Citadel Graduate College. He is past president of the South Carolina Counseling Association.

He has held former full-time counselor education faculty appointments at California State University, Fullerton; University of New Orleans; and the University of Minnesota–Duluth. He earned his BA and MEd degrees at Kutztown University of Pennsylvania and his doctorate in counselor education at the University of Cincinnati. He is a licensed psychologist in California and Minnesota. He has practiced as a certified elementary and secondary school counselor, college counselor, counselor educator, counselor supervisor, and psychologist.

Denise Williams-Patterson, MEd, has been in public education as a teacher and specialist for more than a decade. She received her undergraduate degree from Norfolk State University, master of education degree from Regent University, and a Certificate of Advanced Graduate Studies from Cambridge College.

Deborah M. Wilson, EdD, LPC, NCC, CADC, completed her doctoral studies at Texas Southern University and is an assistant professor in the counseling and psychology program at Troy University's Augusta, Georgia, site. Her primary teaching responsibilities are professional orientation and ethics, counseling theories, community counseling, and supervision. Her research interests include ethics, African American issues in counseling and mental health, and social justice.

F. Robert Wilson, PhD, a professor of counseling in the Division of Human Services at the University of Cincinnati, is now in his 30th year of service. His teaching and research interests include assessment in counseling, ecologically grounded mental health counseling, group work, and the clinical training of counselors. He is professionally active, having served as president and treasurer of the Association for Assessment in Counseling and Education (AACE); a member of the Governing Council for the American Counseling Association; the vice chair for the Council for Accreditation of Counseling and Related Educational Programs; and a member of the editorial board for several professional journals, most notably, AACE's journal, *Measurement and Evaluation in Counseling and Development*.

Ashlea R. Worrell, MA, CRC, is a doctoral student in counselor education and supervision, with concentrations in rehabilitation, neurofeedback, play therapy, and relational cultural theory at St. Mary's University. Her research and clinical interests include body dysmorphic disorder, eating disorders, and self-injury.

Darren A. Wozny, PhD, completed his doctorate in human development and family studies, with specialization in marriage and family therapy, at Iowa State University and is an assistant professor of counselor education at Mississippi State University–Meridian Campus, with primary teaching responsibilities in family counseling theories, cultural foundations, developmental counseling, legal and ethical issues, and counseling the suicidal client. He is the principal investigator and project

director of the Mississippi State University–Meridian Campus Suicide Prevention Program (sponsored in part by a 3-year Substance Abuse and Mental Health Services Administration grant).

Bonnie M. Wright, PhD, completed her doctoral study at The University of Georgia and is currently dean of the School of Psychology and Counseling at Gardner-Webb University. Her primary teaching responsibilities include experimental psychology, life-span development, general psychology, and the history of psychology. Her research interests include issues related to cautiousness, program evaluation, and aging.

Robert E. Wubbolding, EdD, is the director of the Center for Reality Therapy in Cincinnati, Ohio; director of training for the William Glasser Institute; and professor emeritus of Xavier University. A former elementary and high school counselor and adult basic education instructor, he is the author of 10 books on reality therapy, including *Reality Therapy for the 21st Century*. He has taught reality therapy in North America, Asia, Europe, and the Middle East and has received the Marvin Rammelsberg Award, the Herman Peters Award, the Mary Corre Foster Award, and an award as the outstanding alumnus of the University of Cincinnati, College of Education.

J. Scott Young, PhD, NCC, LPC, is a professor in the Department of Counseling, Educational Psychology and Special Education at Mississippi State University, where he also serves as the clinical director of the Counseling and School Psychology Laboratory. He has been a practicing counselor in private practice, agencies, or hospitals for over 15 years. His leadership in the field of counseling includes service as president of the Association for Spiritual, Ethical, and Religious Values in Counseling and as a member of the Governing Council for the American Counseling Association.

Mark A. Young, PhD, LPC, NCC, completed his doctorate at Idaho State University and currently is an assistant professor in the mental health counseling program at Eastern Washington University. His teaching and research interests are in couples and family counseling, supervision, and professional development.

Mark E. Young, PhD, is professor of counselor education at the University of Central Florida and codirector of the College of Education's Marriage and Family Therapy Institute. He is the author of *Learning the Art of Helping* and other counseling texts.

Adam P. Zagelbaum, PhD, NCC, completed his doctoral work at Ball State University and is an assistant professor in the counseling program at Sonoma State University, with primary teaching responsibilities in school counseling courses. His research interests include conflict management, career decision-making issues for children and adolescents, and mentoring issues for young professionals.

Carlos P. Zalaquett, PhD, is an associate professor, coordinator of the community/mental health counseling specialization, and coordinator of the graduate certificate in mental health counseling in the counseling education program at the University of South Florida. He teaches the study of mental disorders and the internship in community mental health agencies courses. His research focuses on the areas of mental disorders, academic performance of diverse students, and Latina/Latino college success.

Shuangmei Zhou (Christine), MEd, is a Chinese international student currently working toward her doctorate in counseling psychology at the University of Minnesota. She received her master's degree in education from Texas Christian University. Her research interests include cross-cultural adjustment of expatriates, use of assessment instruments cross-culturally, adapting and modifying psychotherapy cross-culturally, and vocational and occupational health psychology issues.

Katherine Ziff, PhD, is interim executive assistant to the provost for institutional equity at Ohio University and an adjunct assistant professor in the counselor education program. Her areas of research include the history of psychiatry and the visual arts and counseling. Her doctoral study was completed at Ohio University and her master's degree was earned at Wake Forest University.

Jolie Ziomek-Daigle, PhD, is an assistant professor and coordinates the practicum and internship field experiences for the school counseling program at The University of Georgia. Her research interests include the clinical development of school counseling graduate students and training students to counsel children and adolescents.

Accountability in Counseling

Counselor **accountability** is defined as a method of providing evaluative information on the effectiveness and efficiency of counseling services to **stakeholders** (e.g., clients, students, parents, teachers, supervisors, administrators, other counselors, funding sources, and community members; Studer & Sommer, 2000). Although assessing the impact of various social and educational programs has been emphasized for several decades, in recent years accountability in counseling has been one of the most emphasized issues in the professional literature. As funding sources become scarcer and stakeholders become more results oriented, counselors are being asked to demonstrate clearly the effectiveness of their interventions. Managed care has demanded that counselors be able to measure and document treatment progress and effectiveness in order to gain preapproval for sessions and be reimbursed for services. The American School Counselor Association (ASCA; 2005) National Model reinforces the importance of data-driven programs focused on improved school success for students. Counselors have been working to identify evidenced-based treatments or empirically supported treatments to best serve the needs of clients and to satisfy the needs of payers for improved outcome data for clients. Finally, demonstrating effectiveness in well-defined, measurable terms is included in the counselor education standards for the Council for Accreditation of Counseling and Related Educational Programs (2009) as well as in the ethical standards of the American Counseling Association (2005) and ASCA. Clearly, accountability as a counselor in today's world is imperative at the individual, local, state, and national levels.

To measure effectiveness, professional counselors may use outcome assessments such as a reduction in symptoms or changes in client behavior, clinical ratings, client self-assessments, and satisfaction inventories. External stakeholders, peers, and supervisors may also be asked to measure counselor effectiveness through formal evaluations. In addition to evaluation on a case-by-case basis, professional counselors can use program evaluation as a part of accountability to study how programs are meeting the needs of the school and/or community, share program outcomes, and make improvements to services.

Accountability Bridge Counseling Program Evaluation Model

The accountability bridge model (Coker, Astramovich, & Hoskins, 2006; see Figure 1) can be used by professional

Figure 1. Accountability Bridge Counseling Program Evaluation Model

Note. From *VISTAS: Compelling Perspectives on Counseling 2006* (p. 208), edited by G. R. Walz, J. C. Bleuer, R. K. Yep, 2006, Alexandria, VA: American Counseling Association. Copyright 2006 by the American Counseling Association.

counselors to plan, deliver, and assess services. The model comprises two recurring cycles: the counseling program evaluation cycle and the counseling context evaluation cycle. The **counseling program evaluation cycle** incorporates program planning and implementation, planned interventions, monitoring of progress, and refining the program. Counselors first complete needs assessments and identify objectives to plan and develop services. Outcomes assessments, such as pretests and posttests, performance indicators, and observable data, are also identified. Next, counselors begin delivering the actual services and programs and use preliminary data and feedback to make adjustments. During the outcomes assessment stage, final data are collected and analyzed to evaluate the services and programs. Once the data are analyzed, counselors communicate the program outcomes to key stakeholders who have an investment in the success of the clients or programs, and the **counseling context evaluation cycle** begins. Professional counselors then obtain feedback from these stakeholders to use, along with the data collected, in strategic planning for future interventions.

Accountability is an ongoing responsibility of professional counselors. Through the use of empirical studies and action research, counselors can plan more effective interventions and demonstrate to others the impact counselors have on the lives of others.

Contributed by Kerry E. Sebera, University of West Georgia, Carrollton, GA

References

American Counseling Association. (2005). *ACA code of ethics*. Alexandria, VA: Author.

American School Counselor Association. (2005). *The ASCA National Model: A framework for school counseling programs.* Alexandria, VA: Author.

Coker, J. K., Astramovich, R. L., & Hoskins, W. J. (2006). Introducing the accountability bridge model: A program evaluation framework for school counselors. *VISTAS 2006,* Article 46. Retrieved May 1, 2007, from http://www.counselingoutfitters.com/vistas/vistas06/vistas06.46.pdf

Council for Accreditation of Counseling and Related Educational Programs. (2009). *CACREP accreditation manual* (3rd ed.). Alexandria, VA: Author.

Studer, J. R., & Sommer, J. A. (2000). The professional school counselor and accountability. *NASSP Bulletin, 84,* 93–99.

Additional Resources

Brott, P. E. (2006). Counselor education accountability: Training the effective professional school counselor. *Professional School Counseling, 10,* 179–188.

Education Trust's National Center for Transforming School Counseling Web site: http://www2.edtrust.org/EdTrust/Transforming+School+Counseling/main

Granello, D. H., & Granello, P. F. (2001). *Counseling outcome research: Making practical choices for real-world applications.* (ERIC Document Reproduction Service No. ED 457437)

University of Massachusetts Amherst Center for School Counseling Outcome Research Web site: http://www.umass.edu/schoolcounseling/

Whiston, S. C. (1996). Accountability through action research: Research methods for practitioners. *Journal of Counseling & Development, 74,* 616–623.

Accreditation

Accreditation is a term used to define a quality-assurance review process whereby individuals, schools, or other organizations are deemed to meet a set of standards. Accreditation processes are used by a variety of professions. In education, however, accreditation holds specific meaning. The *American Heritage Dictionary* (2000) defined accreditation as the act of accrediting or the state of being accredited, especially the granting of approval to an institution of learning by an official review board after the school has met specific requirements. In this definition, accreditation pertains to the review of a school, college, or university against specified criteria that outline what is deemed necessary for the provision of a quality education to students. The institution must demonstrate that the criteria or standards are being met in order for accredited status to be granted.

There are many benefits of accreditation to institutions. Accreditation stimulates self-evaluation and self-directed improvement. It provides ongoing external peer consultation and a system of accountability. In addition, accreditation enhances the reputation of an institution and the programs it offers. Students and the public also benefit, because accreditation ensures a threshold for measuring quality, allows for access to federal funding and student loans, and eases the transfer of credits between institutions.

In the United States, there are two major types of accreditation: institutional and specialized. **Institutional accreditation** is an overall review of the curricular offerings and operations at a school, college, or university. **Specialized accreditation** differs from institutional accreditation because it focuses on programs in a particular field of study, such as medicine, law, or counseling. Regardless of whether the focus of accreditation is on the overall institution or on specific programs, higher education accreditation in the United States represents a unique process of voluntary, nongovernmental reviews, in contrast with the mandated, government-sponsored Ministry of Education review processes found in many other countries around the world.

The counseling profession offers a specialized accreditation process for its master's- and doctoral-degree preparation programs through the Council for Accreditation of Counseling and Related Educational Programs (CACREP). CACREP (2009) defines the term *accreditation* as follows:

> **ACCREDITATION**—a system for recognizing educational institutions and professional programs affiliated with those institutions for a level of quality performance and integrity based on review against a specific set of published criteria or standards. The process includes (1) the submission of a self-study document that demonstrates how standards are being met, (2) an on-site review by a selected group of peers, and (3) a decision by an independent board or commission that either grants or denies accredited status based on how well the standards are being met. (p. 57)

The three basic steps of the process included in CACREP's definition of accreditation are considered standard by almost all higher education accrediting organizations. It is important to note, however, that the process does not end when accreditation is accomplished; institutions and programs must periodically undergo additional reviews against organizations' standards in order to remain accredited.

Although accrediting agencies that offer quality-assurance review processes for higher education institutions and programs in the United States are usually private nonprofit organizations, legitimate agencies submit to an external recognition process to verify that good accreditation practice is being followed. Accrediting agencies may be recognized by either the Council for Higher Education Accreditation and/or the U.S. Department of Education. The Department of Education's recognition process is restricted to accrediting agencies that are Title IV gatekeepers for federal funding.

Contributed by Carol L. Bobby, CACREP, Alexandria, VA

References

American Heritage® Dictionary of the English Language (4th ed.). (2000). Retrieved June 25, 2007, from www.bartleby.com/61/

Council for Accreditation of Counseling and Related Educational Programs. (2009). *CACREP accreditation manual: 2009 standards* (3rd ed.). Alexandria, VA: Author.

Additional Resources

Council for Accreditation of Counseling and Related Educational Programs Web site: http://www.cacrep.org

Council for Higher Education Accreditation Web site: http://www.chea.org

U.S. Department of Education Web site: http://www.ed.gov/admins/finaid/accred/index.html

◼ Achievement Tests

Achievement tests are designed to assess the knowledge, understanding, and skills a person acquires as a result of instruction, training, or life experience. As such, they are most frequently used in educational settings and can range from a teacher-made, criterion-referenced test to a commercial norm-referenced instrument. **Criterion-referenced tests** focus assessment on specific knowledge or competencies (e.g., the content of a particular course or lesson), and the scores on these types of tests are compared with some standard of performance for interpretation purposes. They are often used to set a minimum criterion or cutoff score for screening or decision purposes. **Norm-referenced assessments,** on the other hand, are designed so that the performance of an individual student can be compared with the performance of a reference group of students who are the same age or grade. This reference group can be a representative sample of the national population of students the same age or grade (i.e., national norms) or a representative sample of the local population of similar students (i.e., local norms). Norm-referenced assessments yield standardized scores. Standardized scores, such as T scores and stanines, are preferred because they lend themselves to comparisons across other tests and samples of test takers. Nonstandardized scores, such as percentile ranks and age-equivalent or grade-equivalent scores, are easy to understand but must be interpreted cautiously because they do not lend themselves to comparisons across other tests and samples of test takers. In general, use of developmental scores, such as age-equivalent or grade-equivalent scores, should be avoided; if used, the scores should be carefully applied according to the instructions in the examiner's manual.

Commercial norm-referenced achievement tests usually assess multiple academic skill areas (e.g., reading, mathematics, language arts, science, social studies) across a number of grade levels (e.g., kindergarten through 12th grade). In addition, these tests must be administered, scored, and interpreted in a standardized manner, as specified in the examiner's manual, in order for their results to be valid. These batteries can be used to give educators and other stakeholders (e.g., parents, teachers, community leaders) information regarding the extent to which students have acquired information and skills, thus providing accountability data for use in evaluating programs. In addition, the results of these tests can be used to measure students' academic growth over time and to help identify students who are struggling with the curriculum (low achievers) as well as identify those students who are excelling in academic performance (high achievers).

Most achievement tests are designed to be given to groups of students and can be administered by classroom teachers. Other achievement tests are designed to be given to individual students; these usually require the test administrator to have some specialized training to administer and interpret these scores properly. Achievement tests may differ from each other in terms of the depth of the material they cover. **Survey achievement tests** cover material from multiple sources of information and, as a result, do not cover any particular topic in great depth. They may only contain one or two items on a particular skill, whereas a **diagnostic achievement test** would contain more items on a particular skill because its purpose is to examine a skill or competency in depth and provide information regarding a student's particular strengths and weaknesses in an area. There are also special **criterion-referenced tests** that specify the **minimum level of skills** that must be attained in order to move from one level or grade to the next. These achievement tests are the ones used in what has been termed **high-stakes testing.** Table 1 contains a sample of the frequently used achievement tests.

Contributed by Robert Eschenauer,
St. John's University, Jamaica, NY

Table 1. Examples of Commonly Used Achievement Tests

Group Administered Instruments	Individually Administered Instruments
	Survey achievement batteries
Gates-MacGinitie Reading Test (GMRT 4)[a]	Basic Academic Skills Individual Screener (BASIS)[a]
Iowa Tests of Basic Skills (ITBS)[a, b]	Kaufman Test of Educational Achievement–Normative Update (KTEA-NU)[a]
Iowa Tests of Educational Development (ITED)[a, b]	Peabody Individual Achievement Test–Revised–Normative Update (PIAT-R-NU)[a]
Iowa Early Learning Inventory (IELI)[a]	Test of Mathematical Abilities (TOMA-2)[a]
Metropolitan Achievement Tests (MAT8)[a]	Wide Range Achievement Test 4 (WRAT 4)[a]
Stanford Achievement Tests (SAT)[a, b, c, d]	Woodcock–Johnson: Tests of Achievement–III (WJ-III)[a]
Terra Nova Tests[a]	Wechsler Individual Achievement Test II (WIAT-II)[a]
	Diagnostic achievement tests
Stanford Diagnostic Reading Test (SDRT 4)[a]	Gray Oral Reading Test (GORT 4)[a]
Stanford Diagnostic Mathematics Test (SDMT 4)[a]	Key Math–Revised/Normative Update (Key Math-R/NU)[a]
	Test of Adult Basic Education (TABE 9/10)[a, c]
	Test of Language Development–3 (TOLD 3)[a]
	Test of Written Language–3 (TOWL 3)[a]
	Test of Written Spelling–4 (TOWS 4)[a]
	Woodcock Reading Mastery Tests–Revised Normative Update (WRMT-R/NU)[a]

[a]Norm-referenced test. [b]Criterion-reference test. [c]Spanish version available. [d]Braille and large type editions and also a special edition available for assessing individuals who are deaf and hearing impaired with norms from Gallaudet Research Institute.

Additional Resources

Hood, A. B., & Johnson, R. W. (2007). *Assessment in counseling: A guide to the use of psychological assessment procedures* (4th ed.). Alexandria, VA: American Counseling Association.

Reynolds, C. R., Livingston, R. B., & Willson, V. (2006). *Measurement and assessment in education.* Boston: Pearson Education.

Salvia, J., Ysseldyke, J. E., & Bolt, S. (2007). *Assessment in special and inclusive education* (10th ed.). Boston: Houghton Mifflin.

Action Research

Action research is a type of disciplined inquiry designed to address a specific problem through a cyclical process of planning, action, and reflection. The problem is identified and acted on by those most directly involved in the situation. Participant involvement in both the identification of the problem and the action taken is one of the central premises of action research. The methodology emerged as a process for providing real-world solutions to social problems. Originating in the work of Kurt Lewin, this type of research seeks to enhance or improve social systems, organizations, and individual or group performance. Examples of action research can be found in social justice initiatives as well as in industrial organizations, community development projects, and education.

Action research meets specific criteria (Breakwell, Hammond, Fife-Schaw, & Smith, 2006). Action research (a) is educative; (b) deals with individuals as members of social groups; (c) is problem focused, context specific, and future oriented; (d) involves a change intervention; and (e) aims at improvement. The researcher is centrally and directly involved in identifying the issue of concern, determining the intervention to address or improve the issue, evaluating the outcomes, and refocusing the action based on the evaluation.

Practitioners from a variety of disciplines, including counseling and education, use action research to improve both the knowledge bases and practices of their specialties. Although less sophisticated than traditional methods of research, action research can include both qualitative and quantitative approaches. Typically, the process involves members of a community or organization in (a) selecting a focus, (b) collecting data, (c) analyzing and interpreting data, (d) determining and taking action, (e) reflecting on outcomes, and (f) either continuing or modifying the intervention. In sum, action-oriented research is typically focused on specific, participant-identified situations and immediate applications and seeks to improve the quality of programs, services, and interactions.

An example of action research in counseling is seen in the work of an elementary school counselor who, in collaboration with the school leadership team and faculty, identified attendance as a significant concern at her school. These educators gathered and analyzed schoolwide baseline data, reviewed the professional literature to determine appropriate strategies to address the problem, and implemented a variety of interventions relevant to their collective goals. An attendance policy was changed, a schoolwide incentive program was begun, relevant materials were presented through brochures for parents and on bulletin boards throughout the school, and a target group was identified that included students who had been chronically absent the previous year. The school counselor worked with the target students individually and in small groups as well, assigning them school or community mentors. At the end of the year, the educators reflected on the outcomes, which included significant increases in attendance for the target group as well as the school meeting Adequate Yearly Progress goals for all subgroups. All of the attendance initiatives were continued the following year.

Contributed by Pamela O. Paisley,
The University of Georgia, Athens, GA

Reference

Breakwell, G. M., Hammond, S., Fife-Schaw, C., & Smith, J. A. (2006). *Research methods in psychology* (3rd ed.). London: Sage.

Additional Resources

Glanz, J. (1998). *Action research: An educational leader's guide to school improvement.* Norwood, MA: Christopher-Gordon.

McNiff, J., & Whitehead, J. (2003). *Action research: Principles & practice.* London: Routledge.

Reason, P., & Bradbury, H. (Eds.). (2007). *The SAGE handbook of action research: Participative inquiry* (2nd ed.). Thousand Oaks, CA: Sage.

Addiction Counseling

Addiction is a preoccupation with and a dependence on a drug or process, resulting in increased tolerance, withdrawal, and repeated patterns of relapse. Addictions can be subdivided into substance and process addictions. Substance addictions include abuse and dependence on licit and illicit drugs (e.g., alcohol, tobacco, benzodiazepines, methamphetamine, opiates, cannabis, amphetamines, caffeine, sedatives, hypnotics, phencyclidine, hallucinogens). Substances may be either legal or illegal and are used for the purposes of altering the individual's functioning or level of consciousness (e.g., increased pleasure; reduction of physiological, psychic, and emotional pain; relaxation; stimulation; and socialization). **Substance abuse** is the use of a drug, in a manner not medically justified, for its physiological or psychological effects, and this use causes problems in the user's life. Examples include taking more than the prescribed amount of a medicine, such as Xanax, or "having a drink" to calm down. **Substance dependence** involves tolerance, withdrawal, and persistent or unsuccessful attempts to cut down or control use of the drug. Impairment in one or more of the following areas of functioning is present: social, familial, financial, legal, health, education, and employment. Examples of substance dependence include the individual who uses needles to inject heroin and falls asleep ("nods off") while caring for his or her children at home or the alcoholic who goes to the bar for another drink immediately after getting out of jail for a driving-while-intoxicated offense. Two primary differences between abuse and addiction are **tolerance,** or the need to take more of the substance to achieve the same physiological or psychological effect, and **withdrawal,** which occurs when the drug is taken away. Individuals who abuse drugs and alcohol may experience negative effects with their families or in their work and have legal problems, but they have not yet increased the amount of their use to the point that withdrawal occurs when they stop using.

Process addictions involve behavioral compulsions with the purpose of altering consciousness, such as seeking a euphoric state. Process addictions can also lead to tolerance and withdrawal symptoms and include compulsions around food (e.g., eating large amounts of food at one sitting, then inducing vomiting afterward), sex (e.g., a married individual seeking sexual encounters with a prostitute on a nightly basis), gambling (e.g., going to the casino and losing house or car gambling), and "surfing" the Internet (e.g., spending hours viewing Internet pages, resulting in neglect of family members).

The role of a professional involved in **addiction counseling** is to reduce the negative effects of substance abuse or dependence and to stop the use of the substance. Addiction counselors provide education about the nature and progression of addiction; teach relapse prevention strategies; encourage coping skills; and, in the process, use a variety of counseling techniques to bring about change. Individuals enter counseling to achieve abstinence, prevent relapse, or participate in harm reduction approaches. The harm reduction approach recognizes drug use as a health problem, for example, the transmission of AIDS through sharing needles, and emphasizes reducing the problems and health risks associated with drug use. Addiction counselors can be viewed as teachers, coaches, or advocates, depending on the stage of the client's treatment. Addiction counselors encourage participation in 12-step programs and coordinate referrals for medical, psychiatric, vocational, and other services as needed by the client.

Characteristics of effective addiction counselors include strong interpersonal skills, warmth, consistency, empathy, cultural sensitivity, ability to maintain boundaries, and a capacity for seeing that clients with substance use disorders are capable of growth. One characteristic found among many addiction counselors is previous personal or familial experience with an addiction. As a result, addictions counselors are encouraged to have at least 1 year or more of sobriety prior to engaging in addiction counseling. It is also assumed that counselors will have an understanding of the benefits of pharmacological agents in treating particular substance use disorders, such as opiate, alcohol, and cocaine addictions.

Traditional treatment may occur in a variety of settings: inpatient residential placements to address detoxification and psychiatric and medical management and residential settings that provide structured daily activities, including morning meditation, educational activities, Alcoholics Anonymous (AA) and Narcotics Anonymous (NA) meet-

ings, recreational activities, a family component, and group and individual counseling. Counseling may also occur in less structured outpatient settings such as partial hospital programs, intensive outpatient programs, and relapse prevention programs. Individual and group counseling may also be provided in freestanding outpatient clinics and private practice settings.

Assessment

Addiction assessment involves determining the client's readiness for treatment, level of care, eminent crises, and need for detoxification or psychological stabilization. Often, the counseling process begins during the initial session with a biopsychosocial evaluation in which information is gathered about the client's presenting problem and family, educational, social, employment, spiritual, ethnic, cultural, medical, psychological, and legal history. Professional counselors must be culturally competent throughout all steps of the intake and treatment process by taking into account a client's cultural, ethnic, and socioeconomic context.

Presence of a co-occurring disorder may also become evident during the initial evaluation. A co-occurring disorder is a condition of having both a psychiatric disorder and chemical dependency (i.e., **dual diagnosis**). Counseling individuals with co-occurring disorders involves providing education about the nature and progression of the mental illness; interaction of the mental illness with the addiction; pharmacological treatment; and collaboration with other mental health providers such as psychiatrists, medical facilities, and family members.

Domestic violence often occurs among those who abuse or are addicted to substances. It may be necessary to ensure the safety of clients and their family members and to refer the perpetrator to a domestic violence program during the assessment phase. Addiction counselors must recognize whether presenting problems fall within their area of expertise and refer when necessary, such as in cases when counselors do not have the training to treat specific disorders such as a gambling addiction or an eating disorder.

Physiological and Psychological Factors Involved in Addiction

There are numerous, confounding causes of alcoholism and drug addiction. No one model of causality addresses all of the reasons for a user's behavior. Models that address physiological factors include tension reduction, self-medication, disease/genetic, and neurological models. Tension reduction models suggest that individuals have an innate desire to reduce pain, feelings of fear and anxiety, and stress and that the use of drugs reduces tension and produces pleasurable effects. The self-medication perspective suggests that drug use occurs for specific desired effects. These include reducing negative emotional states, increasing positive emotional states, reducing pain, increasing or decreasing stimulation, changing a person's perception of the world, and stimulating the senses. The disease model views addiction as a disease because it meets the criteria of (a) a known etiology; (b) the presence of symptoms that worsen over time; and (c) progression of the condition, leading to dependence, physical symptoms, and eventual death. Research has also found that genetic factors may predispose individuals toward developing an addiction such as alcoholism. From a neurobiological perspective, addiction is associated with the brain reward centers. Use of drugs stimulates pleasurable feelings to the extent that the using behavior is repeated until tolerance develops and more of the drug is needed to achieve the same effect. Ongoing use of drugs results in alteration of neural communication, which has the potential to cause profound changes in brain chemistry.

Psychological factors of alcoholism and drug addiction include the personality trait and behavioral perspectives. There are specific personality traits and disorders associated with addiction. Common traits include anxiety; high emotionality; low frustration tolerance; difficulties with expression of or handling anger; compulsiveness; and feelings of isolation, low self-esteem, and poor self-concept. Personality disorders that correlate highly with substance use disorders include narcissistic, antisocial, and borderline personality disorders. Behavioral factors include early conditioning and reinforcement patterns. One factor associated with continued use is the pleasure and euphoric recall of the initial drug-using experience. Any behavior that is followed by a reinforcer is more likely to be repeated; hence, drug use occurs again and again until the body develops tolerance. When withdrawal symptoms occur, individuals again use drugs to avoid these unpleasant feelings and negative physiological responses.

Counseling Approaches and Techniques

Addiction professionals may use an extensive array of treatment approaches across different settings. Motivation enhancement therapy, cognitive-behavioral therapy, family therapy and interventions, behavior therapy, harm reduction, brief solution-focused therapy, group counseling, 12-step programs, holistic methods, and relapse prevention are commonly used counseling approaches that research has demonstrated have efficacy. Approaches specific to addiction counseling are discussed in the following paragraphs.

Harm Reduction Approach

The harm reduction approach helps minimize the dangers of drug use while teaching skills to stop or reduce substance-using behavior. Clients help themselves by gradually decreasing substance use from regular, daily use to managed, reduced use of drugs and alcohol. This approach attempts to break through denial, reduce resistance to treatment, decrease violence and mortality rates, promote family stability, address employment problems, and prevent spread of infectious diseases. Harm reduction promotes abstinence as an ultimate goal and does not condone drug use. It emphasizes that there are individuals who are going to use drugs and alcohol regardless of the consequences. Examples of harm reduction strategies include needle exchange programs, smoking cessation/reduction programs, and controlled drinking programming.

12-Step Programs

Individuals can participate in **12-step programs** such as AA, Cocaine Anonymous, or NA without intervention by counselors, or participation can be a component of residential or outpatient treatment programs or individual counseling. The only requirement for participation in these types of programs is a desire to stop drinking and/or abusing drugs. Addiction counselors provide education about AA, help individuals obtain a sponsor, and encourage working through the 12 steps. The 12 steps provide a spiritual basis to help clients find meaning in their lives and represent a pathway to recovery for anyone addicted to drugs or alcohol. AA programs can serve a transitional role while clients internalize more normalized daily routine patterns and coping strategies. Newcomers to AA are encouraged to attend 90 meetings in 90 days ("90 in 90"), which leads to their relying on the individuals in these meetings for support and acceptance. The environment and "anonymity" provide safety and security and promote bonding, thereby meeting the belonging and attachment needs of the individual. Self-help groups for process addictions, such as Gamblers Anonymous, Sex Addicts Anonymous, and Eating Addictions Anonymous, also exist. Some self-help groups that are not spiritually based include Smart Recovery, Rational Recovery, and Women for Sobriety.

Relapse Prevention

In addiction treatment, relapse prevention is an ongoing process and needs to be addressed as a component of the counseling process throughout treatment. Relapses provide the counselor and client with opportunities to learn about specific factors leading to substance abuse. Professional counselors help clients to identify triggers and cues to high-risk situations that can lead to using behavior and to develop problem-solving strategies that incorporate resistance to using, refusal skills, and healthy life-style changes and routines. Clarification of issues, feelings, and events preceding the relapse helps individuals develop awareness of the stimulus cues that need to be avoided in the future.

Pharmacological Treatment

Several pharmacological agents are effective in reducing cravings and overall use of substances, particularly if used in conjunction with psychotherapy. Naltrexone, methadone, levo-alpha acetyl methadol, and buprenorphine are effective in reducing cravings and overall opiate use. Disulfuram and acamprosate are effective in reducing alcohol cravings. Research studies are evaluating the use of topiramate, baclofen, and modafenil to decrease cocaine cravings and usage.

Addiction Treatment Outcome Research

Years of research have yielded several evidence-based approaches in drug addiction treatment. Successful treatment usually involves multiple treatment episodes or extended participation in a program for 3 to 6 months or longer. Effective treatment addresses familial, social, community, economic, and personal factors that may pose continued risk factors for engaging in drug use. For individuals with co-occurring disorders, both the addiction and psychiatric disorder should be addressed concurrently and incorporated into the treatment plan. Treatment should address harmful behaviors associated with drug use, such as use of needles and unprotected sexual behavior, that may put the individual or others at risk. Behavioral treatment, use of medication-assisted treatment, cognitive-behavioral therapy, motivational interviewing, and harm-reduction strategies are all treatments effective with addictive disorders. Finally, community reinforcement is also a scientifically based approach that involves connecting individuals with other agencies, such as health services, employment training, case management, and family services, while they are receiving individual and group counseling services from the addiction treatment center.

In summary, the addiction field continues to progress, with advances in brain research, use of pharmacological agents to reduce cravings, and counseling techniques individualized to each client's needs and presenting problems. Future considerations include a need to integrate mental health and addiction and medical treatment, including the use of pharmacological agents to address the craving for drugs, into a collaborative effort so that all areas of a client's life can be addressed within one treatment setting and plan.

Contributed by Sandra I. Valente,
Naugatuck Valley Community College,
Waterbury, CT

Additional Resources

Coombs, R. H., & Howatt, W. A. (2005). *The addiction counselor's desk reference.* Hoboken, NJ: Wiley.

Frances, R. J., Miller, S. I., & Mack, A. H. (Eds.). (2005). *Clinical textbook of addictive disorders* (3rd ed.). New York: Guilford Press.

Staussner, S. L. A. (2004). *Clinical work with substance-abusing clients* (2nd ed.). New York: Guilford Press.

■Adjustment Disorders

The predominant feature of a diagnosable adjustment disorder according to the *Diagnostic and Statistical Manual of Mental Disorders* (4th ed., text rev; *DSM-IV-TR;* American Psychiatric Association [APA], 2000), is a psychoemotional response to an identifiable life situation or stressor that causes clinically significant distress or impairment in a person's social or occupational functioning or in a person's ability to fulfill other important life roles. Normally expected adjustment experiences, culturally expected reactions to life events, and developmental or age-appropriate changes that affect adjustment but do not result in clinically significant distress or impairment often share similarities with diagnosable adjustment disorders; however, they typically do not warrant a mental disorder diagnosis. Furthermore, competent diagnosis of adjustment disorders requires an understanding of the variations in the presentation of symptoms that can result from individual differences due to such common demographics as age, gender, ethnocultural background, religious affiliation, socioeconomic status, or nation of origin.

Specifically, the primary characteristic of a diagnosable adjustment disorder according to *DSM-IV-TR* (APA, 2000) criteria is the development of clinically significant emotional or behavioral symptoms in response to a recognizable life stressor that occur within 3 months of the stressor's onset. In the diagnosis, clinical significance includes substantial distress that is in excess of what is usually expected when exposed to the stressor or impairment in social or occupational functioning. A diagnosis of adjustment disorder is not made when another *DSM-IV-TR* diagnosis describes the individual's symptoms better, when the symptoms are simply an exacerbation of another preexisting disorder during times of stress, when symptoms last more than 6 months after the stressor has subsided, or in the case of bereavement.

There are several types of adjustment disorders (APA, 2000). **Adjustment disorder with depressed mood** indicates that the most important adjustment symptoms are low mood, tearfulness, and hopelessness. Likewise, **adjustment disorder with anxiety** indicates that the most important adjustment symptoms are anxiety features such as worry, nervousness, and agitation. In children, fears of being separated from important attachment figures can occur. **Adjustment disorder with disturbance of conduct** indicates that some of the main symptoms are behaviors that violate the rights of others or violate age-appropriate social or legal norms. Examples are clinically significant adjustment concerns such as truancy, reckless driving, fighting, or defaulting on legal obligations. **Adjustment disorder with mixed anxiety and depressed mood** indicates the presence of a combination of anxiety symptoms and low mood. **Adjustment disorder with mixed disturbance of emotions and conduct** indicates that both emotional features and disturbed conduct predominate. In the diagnosis, other clinically significant adjustment responses—such as social withdrawal, work or school problems, and physical symptoms—are described by **adjustment disorder unspecified.** When a diagnosis of adjustment disorder is made using the *DSM-IV-TR* diagnostic system, the exact stressor to which the individual is adjusting may be indicated on Axis IV, where psychosocial and environmental problems are presented.

Contributed by
Alan M. "Woody" Schwitzer,
Old Dominion University, Norfolk, VA

Reference

American Psychiatric Association. (2000). *Diagnostic and statistical manual of mental disorders* (4th ed., text rev.). Washington, DC: Author.

Additional Resources

Neukrug, E., & Schwitzer, A. (2006). *Skills and tools for today's counselors and psychotherapists: From natural helping to professional counseling.* Belmont, CA: Thomson Brooks/Cole.

Seligman, L. (2004). *Diagnosis and treatment planning* (3rd ed.). New York: Plenum Press.

Adolescents, Counseling

Adolescence refers to the transitional period between childhood and adulthood that occurs between roughly ages 10 and 20 years. Counseling adolescents requires a solid knowledge base in adolescent development. Adolescents experience biological, social, cognitive, and emotional changes. Biologically, adolescents are dealing with hormonal changes that influence thinking patterns and emotions. Their bodies are physically changing, and self-concept is affected. Socially, for many adolescents, the peer group is a major influence. Interactions with peers are critical during adolescent development. Adolescents have a strong need for social belonging and recognition. They define their own identities within the social setting in relation to their peer group. Adolescence is a time of paradoxical behavior that encompasses self-expression and independence via conformity to some peer group, which results in taking on the mannerisms, speech, and dress of that group. Cognitive abilities are transitioning from concrete operations to formal operations. Emotionally, adolescents are constantly exploring and struggling with their self-awareness and self-confidence.

Many adolescents are able to navigate through developmental stages in a progressive pattern, and these adolescents become mentally healthy adults without needing counseling intervention during their adolescent years. Adolescents who have difficulty mastering Erik Erikson's stages of psychosocial development, "industry v. inferiority" (e.g., develops talents and abilities, achieves competence, finds place in the world) and "identity v. role confusion" (e.g., develops identity, self-acceptance, and independence), can benefit from counseling interventions. Mastery of these developmental stages can be affected in either positive or negative ways by the social influences of parents and peers.

Common Issues Among Adolescents

Due to a variety of factors, many adolescents deal with mental health, physical, social, and spiritual challenges that interfere with healthy developmental maturation. Some common issues during the adolescent years that are related to mental health include eating disorders, substance use, depression, violent behavior, anxiety, and unsafe sexual activities. Although the symptoms of eating disorders are known to originate primarily in adolescence, research on the frequency of eating disorders among adolescents is surprisingly limited. Many believe that the magnitude of this problem is seriously underestimated. As of 2002, 56% of ninth-grade girls and 28% of ninth-grade boys reported binge eating or engaging in one or more of the following to lose or control weight: fasting or skipping meals, taking diet pills or laxatives, inducing vomiting, or smoking cigarettes (Walsh & Cameron, 2005). In 2001, almost two thirds of female high school students and one third of male students were trying to lose weight. It is estimated that as many as 0.5% of American teenage girls have anorexia nervosa, 1%

to 5% have bulimia nervosa, and up to 10% of all cases of eating disorders occur in boys (Walsh & Cameron, 2005).

Regarding substance abuse, in 2000 the annual prevalence rates for high school seniors were marijuana (37%), amphetamines (11%), cocaine (5%), LSD (7%), and inhalants (6%; McNeece & DiNitto, 2005). Alcohol use remained prevalent, with just over half (52%) of 8th-graders and the majority of 10th-graders (71%) and 12th-graders (80%) having tried alcohol at least once (McNeece & DiNitto, 2005).

Depression in adolescents is viewed as a significant problem that affects approximately 30% of the adolescent population (Lewinsohn, Hops, Roberts, Seeley, & Andrews, 1993). One in 5 youth reported a minimum of one episode of major depression by the age of 18 years.

The decade from 1983 to 1993 has been described as a "violence epidemic" (Cook & Laub, 1998). The rate of violent crime committed by youth rose by 1,000%. There has been a slight but steady decline in violent crime among adolescents since this time. However, even though the rate of arrests of youthful offenders has declined, confidential self-reports indicate that the rate of potentially lethal acts of violence has remained unchanged (U.S. Department of Health and Human Services, 2001).

On any given day, from 3% to 5% of children and adolescents in the United States have some type of anxiety disorder (American Psychiatric Association, 2000). Without treatment, an anxiety disorder can interfere with the ability to carry out everyday tasks, succeed in school, or make and keep friends. Also, it may simply cause great distress that takes away the enjoyment of life.

Sexual activity among adolescents has steadily increased over the past 30 years, and present-day adolescents are engaging in sexual intercourse at much younger ages. Surveys have revealed that 76% of women and 80% of men have experienced sexual intercourse before the age of 20, and only 56.8% of those sexually active students reported using a condom during last coitus (Blake & Bentov, 2001).

Physical issues can manifest in several ways. Some adolescents mature physically early and others late. Both present unique problems to an adolescent wanting to fit in and belong with the peer group. Some adolescents deal with chronic health issues that serve as isolating barriers to feeling accepted and valued by peers.

Socially, an adolescent's view of self is influenced by self-perceived personal success or failure experiences; interactions with others; perceived evaluations by significant others; and feelings of self-respect, approval, worth, and esteem. Spiritually, adolescents are trying to find their place in the world. Many are idealistic and actively pursue making a difference in the local and international communities. Others struggle in finding meaning and purpose.

Counseling Implications

Counseling adolescents also requires a solid knowledge base in adolescent cultural and gender differences. Understanding the cultural and gender developmental context is imperative in understanding each adolescent's worldview.

Developmentally, adolescents are becoming more cognizant of their sexual identity. It is usually during this stage of development that heterosexual, gay, lesbian, and bisexual youth are coming to terms and dealing with their sexual or gender identity issues. The professional counselor also needs to be aware of the adolescent's religious orientation; ethnic, cultural, and racial background; economic class standing; and the influences of the family of origin. It is important to be aware that varied cultures have different definitions of the adolescent life stage, how adolescents should appropriately act, and the deciding factors that determine when adolescents reach adulthood.

Before beginning the counseling process, professional counselors first need to have a basic understanding of the systems approach to counseling. In order to help adolescents best, the professional counselor must look at the systems that influence adolescents mentally, physically, socially, and spiritually. Examples of systems that influence adolescents are families, schools, sports organizations, churches, peer groups, and clubs. In using the systems approach, it can be quite advantageous to have more than one treatment provider (e.g., drug/alcohol specialist, mental health therapist, professional school counselor, medical doctor, pastor, family counselor).

Second, professional counselors need to have a basic understanding of the counseling theories and techniques used most effectively with adolescents. Cognitive-behavioral theories and techniques are commonly used for a wide variety of adolescent counseling issues such as eating disorders, depression, anxiety, and low self-esteem. Examples of other theories and techniques commonly used are solution-focused/brief theories, reality (choice) theory, Adlerian approach, social skills training, bibliotherapy, and art therapies (art, music, dance, and drama). Solution-focused counseling has been effective in working with resistant adolescents. An integrative approach to treatment appears to be the first choice for many professional counselors. The integrative approach takes a holistic approach to match treatment approaches with each adolescent's needs.

Contributed by Marty Slyter,
Eastern Washington University,
Cheney, WA

References

American Psychiatric Association. (2000). *Diagnostic and statistical manual of mental disorders* (4th ed., text rev.). Washington, DC: Author.

Blake, B. J., & Bentov, L. (2001). Geographical mapping of unmarried teen births and selected sociodemographic variables. *Public Health Nursing, 18,* 33–39.

Cook, P., & Laub, J. H. (1998). The unprecedented epidemic in youth violence. In M. Yonry & M. H. Moore (Eds.), *Youth violence, crime and justice: A review of research* (Vol. 24, pp. 27–64). Chicago: University of Chicago Press.

Lewinsohn, P. M., Hops, H., Roberts, R. E., Seeley, J. R., & Andrews, J. A. (1993). Adolescent psychopathology: I. Prevalence and incidence of depression and other *DSM-III-R* disorders in high school students. *Journal of Abnormal Psychology, 102,* 133–144.

McNeece, C. A., & DiNitto, D. (2005). *Chemical dependency: A systems approach* (3rd ed.). Upper Saddle River, NJ: Pearson Education.

U.S. Department of Health and Human Services. (2001). *Youth violence: A report of the surgeon general.* Rockville, MD: U.S. Department of Health and Human Services, Centers for Disease Control and Prevention, National Center for Injury Prevention and Control, Substance Abuse and Mental Health Services Administration, Center for Mental Health Services, and National Institutes of Health, National Institute of Mental Health.

Walsh, B. T., & Cameron, V. L. (2005). *If your adolescent has an eating disorder: An essential resource for parents.* New York: Oxford University Press.

Additional Resources

Erk, R. E. (2004). *Counseling treatment for children and adolescents with DSM-IV-TR disorders.* Upper Saddle River, NJ: Merrill/Prentice Hall.

Sklare, G. B. (2005). *Brief counseling that works: A solution-focused approach for school counselors and administrators* (2nd ed.). Thousand Oaks, CA: Corwin.

Vernon, A. (2002). *What works when with children and adolescents: A handbook of individual counseling techniques.* Champaign, IL: Research Press.

Adult Learning

Research into **adult learning** has been scant until fairly recently. Psychology and education have focused primarily on how animals and children learn rather than focusing on how adults learn. Cattell (1971) suggested that fluid intelligence, after peaking in an individual's 20s, begins to decline, whereas crystallized intelligence gradually and steadily increases until about age 65 years. **Fluid intelligence** includes such things as problem solving, pattern recognition, and skill learning. **Crystallized intelligence** correlates with skills and abilities, which depend on knowledge but, more important, on experience. Cattell (1987) claimed that these two types of intelligence operated independently of each other, whereas Cavanaugh and Blanchard-Fields (2006) have suggested the interdependence of fluid and crystallized intelligence. In essence, it is not that adults learn substantially differently than children do but that adults use their experience and knowledge, which may take longer in processing, rather than relying on specific skills.

Recent brain research suggests that fluid intelligence involves brain systems that are related to attention and short-term memory. These systems include the dorsolateral prefrontal cortex and the anterior cingulated cortex as well as other systems involved in attention and short-term memory. In contrast, crystallized intelligence involves brain regions that process storage and retrieval of long-term memories. This brain region includes the hippocampus. Lee, Lyoo, Kim, Jang, and Lee (2005) reported that the decline in fluid intelligence was most likely due to local atrophy of the right cerebellum. Lack of practice and not using skills acquired while in school as well as changes in the brain attributed to age may account for this decline (Cavanaugh & Blanchard-Fields, 2006).

Andragogy, which implies that children and adults learn differently, is a concept introduced into the United States by Malcolm Knowles (Knowles, Holton, & Swanson, 2005). Knowles et al. developed an adult learning model that identifies six core principles that apply to all adult learning situations: (a) the need to know why, what, and how; (b) self-concept of the adult learner; (c) prior experience of the adult learner; (d) readiness to learn; (e) orientation to learning; and (f) motivation to learn. Other issues that affect these principles include goals and purpose of learning; subject matter and situational differences; and societal, institutional, and individual growth. This model of adult learning is a process model rather than a content model. Traditional educational institutions most often use content models. Content models suggest that children and adults learn best by reading, lecture, and rote memory via visual and auditory mechanisms. Pedagogy is a content model of learning. Content models tend to be passive and dependent, focusing on what to learn. The process model of adult learning is concerned with providing the resources and procedures necessary for learning rather than teaching specific skills and content organization. Knowles et al. described adult learners as having a problem-centered or learner-centered orientation. Adults want to learn to fulfill an immediate need in the present. This immediate learning need requires engaging and motivating teaching methods designed to accomplish multiple goals based on what the learner needs to learn. This model appears to key into the theory that crystallized intelligence increases over the lifetime and it is the learning model most often used in the United States by teaching institutions focused on adult learners.

Merriam, Caffarella, and Baumgartner (2007) suggested five major theories of adult learning. Behaviorists examine objectives, accountability, performance improvement, and skill development. Humanist theorists holistically define andragogy, self-directed learning, cognitive development, and transformational learning. Cognitivists stress learning how to learn, social role presence, and memory as it relates to age. Social cognitive theorists are oriented toward socialization, self-directed learning, locus of control, and mentoring. Constructivist theory focuses on experiential learning, transformational learning, reflective practice, and situated learning.

Assessing learning styles of adults is a practical way to move from theory of adult learning to the practice of teaching adults the way they learn most efficiently. Honigsfeld and Dunn (2006) defined **learning style** as "the way each individual begins to concentrate on, process, internalize, and retain new and difficult information" (p. 15). Their learning style model is a matrix of five stimulus strands and 20 elements. The stimulus strands include environmental effects such as sound, light, temperature, seating design; emotional effects such as motivation, persistence, responsibility, structure; sociological effects such as working alone, in pairs, with a team, with authority, or varied; physiological effects such as perceptual strengths (i.e., visual, auditory, tactual and/or kinesthetic); time of day energy patterns, need for

mobility, need for intake as in food or drink; and psychological effects such as global or analytic, reflective or impulsive, and hemisphericity (i.e. right or left brain processing). They suggested that when adult learners were aware of their individual learning styles, they could study new and difficult information through their primary modalities, making the learning process more efficient.

Lovelace's (2005) article, "Meta-Analysis of Experimental Research Based on the Dunn and Dunn Model," indicates instruction that methodologically addresses student learning style preferences raises achievement levels as well as improves attitude toward learning. With increasing numbers of nontraditional students enrolling in postsecondary institutions, it is incumbent on educators to address teaching adult students from a process model rather than from a purely content model. Assessing the learning styles of adult learners in order to tailor instructional methods can affect adult learner outcomes. Current studies, constructs, and theories in adult learning suggest that further research should focus on learning styles and learning context, taking into account both instructors and fellow learners (Merriam et al., 2007).

Contributed by Gregory A. Dawson,
Troy University, Orlando, FL
and Carol A. Lewis,
Troy University, Pensacola, FL

References

Cattell, R. B. (1971). *Abilities: Their structure growth and action.* New York: Houghton Mifflin.

Cattell, R. B. (1987). *Intelligence: Its structures, growth, and action.* New York: Elsevier.

Cavanaugh, J. C., & Blanchard-Fields, F. (2006). *Adult development and aging* (5th ed.). Belmont CA: Wadsworth/ Thomson Learning.

Honigsfeld, A., & Dunn, R. (2006). Learning style characteristics of adult learners. *The Kappa Gamma Delta Bulletin, 72,* 15.

Knowles, M. S., Holton, E. F., & Swanson, R. A. (2005). *The adult learner* (6th ed.). New York: Elsevier.

Lee, J., Lyoo, I., Kim, S., Jang, H., & Lee, D. (2005). Intellect declines in healthy elderly subjects and cerebellum. *Psychiatry and Clinical Neurosciences, 59,* 45–51.

Lovelace, M. K. (2005). Meta-analysis of experimental research based on the Dunn and Dunn model. *Journal of Educational Research, 98,* 176–182.

Merriam, S., Caffarella, R., & Baumgartner, L. (2007). *Learning in adulthood: A comprehensive guide* (3rd ed.). San Francisco: Wiley.

Additional Resource

Dunn, R., & Griggs, S. A. (Eds.). (2000). *Practical approaches to using learning styles in higher education.* Westport, CT: Bergin & Garvey.

▌Advocacy Counseling

Advocacy counseling involves professional practices to sustain and advance the counseling profession, such as advocating for public policy change, counselor licensure, and rights of counselors. An advocacy orientation involves not only systemic interventions but also the implementation of empowerment strategies for clients. Three levels of advocacy have been identified by the American Counseling Association's (ACA) Task Force on Advocacy Competencies and are available on ACA's Web site. Levels included are the client/student level, the school community level, and the larger public level. Each level is composed of both direct and indirect interventions that an advocacy-oriented counselor should embrace. Implicit in advocacy counseling is its impact on client services and clients' general psychological, social, and economic well-being (see Social Justice in Counseling).

Promoting the profession in a public arena encourages both the growth and understanding of professional counseling. This is often accomplished through collaboration with existing professional associations, such as ACA. An example used to promote the profession of counseling, Public Awareness Ideas and Strategies for Professional Counselors, can be found on ACA's Web site. A spectrum of suggestions for promotional purposes ranges from delivering speeches to working with the media. Activities may include, but are not limited to, networking with community-based organizations for legislative agendas; providing advocacy training at local, regional, and national conferences; and promoting goals of the professional association. Because advocacy efforts promote change, the advocacy activities of professional counselors and professional advocates are frequently connected. For example, professional counselors in community-based agencies and schools may work with professional advocates to support legislative policy changes. Such policies may affect clients' access to services, thereby directly affecting the work of professional counselors at the community level.

The competencies required for successful advocacy are similar to those required for successful counseling. These skills include effective listening; sensitivity to the needs of others; and the ability to adequately assess presenting problems or needs, define goals, implement effective interventions, and evaluate outcomes. Because of this similarity, professional counselors simply need to be trained to apply their current skills in a different area of practice.

The new millennium has brought a change in the conceptualization of the role of traditional counseling, and it is now more focused on the alleviation and removal of barriers that prevent clients from obtaining needed services. In this role, professional counselors may face issues surrounding the practice of counseling, such as managed care, as well as societal issues involving their clients. Possessing knowledge of resources, parameters, legalities, dispute resolution mechanisms, and systems change is necessary for successful counseling and advocacy efforts. The need for professional counselors as advocates will continue to grow. Societal issues, such as multicultural and ethnic groups obtaining needed services, children needing protection from abuse and neglect, and persons with severe and persistent mental illnesses receiving proper care and medications, create problems that are not easily eradicated. It is not possible to know the problems that future advocates will face; however, it is

certain that advocacy counseling and professional advocacy will continue to evolve and define the role of the professional counselor.

Contributed by Julia S. Chibbaro,
University of West Georgia, Carrollton, GA

Additional Resources

Advocacy Institute Web site: http://www.advocacy.org
American Counseling Association Web site: http://www.counseling.org
Community Tool Box Web site: http://ctb.ku.edu
Patrick, P. K. (2007). *Contemporary issues in counseling.* Boston: Pearson Education.

African Americans, Counseling

Although they have been referred to by many different names (e.g., colored, Negro, Black), **African American** is the most often used term to describe Americans of African descent. The term typically is used to describe individuals who are the descendents of Africans who were enslaved in the United States, but it may also describe any U.S. citizen with African ancestry.

At 36.6 million people, African Americans represent 12.8% of the U.S. population, making them the second largest ethnic minority group in the country (U.S. Census Bureau, 2000). Of the African American population, 60% lived in 10 states and the Southern states still have the highest concentration of African Americans in their populations. In addition, 80% of African American adults were high school graduates, 17% had at least a bachelor's degree, and the median income for African Americans was $30,200. Although these figures appear to be positive for African Americans, it should also be noted that all education and income levels fell significantly below those for White Americans during the same time period. African Americans continued to be overrepresented among the poor (26% had incomes below the poverty line) and employed in low-paying service occupations. Unfortunately, figures like these cannot be completely explained by factors within the African American population itself. These figures most likely represent the legacy of slavery and subsequent racial discrimination.

Because only 8% of persons of African descent are foreign born (U.S. Census Bureau, 2000), it is likely that most professional counselors will encounter clients born in the United States who have vicarious as well as personal knowledge of the United States' long history of oppression of its people. It is important that professional counselors gain knowledge of the history and traditions of African Americans—not only of how discrimination and racism have affected this population over the years but also of the traditions and practices that contributed to their survival under such adverse conditions. The cultural factors of most importance for professional counselors to become familiar with include the African American Vernacular English (AAVE), the African American concept of family, racial socialization, the Black church, and racial identity.

After Africans were brought to the United States as slaves, they learned to communicate with their owners and with one another by using a mixture of their original languages and the English they were expected to understand but not to read or write. One of the results of this language adaptation is the AAVE—a dialect that often has been maligned as poor Standard English.

Similarly, the African American concept of family is a carryover from Western African roots. In this concept, the family includes extended family members (e.g., uncles, aunts, cousins, grandparents) and may even include close family friends. Not only do African Americans broadly define family, family tasks are also broadly assigned. Tasks are less likely to be gender specific but tend to be aimed toward enhancing family functions. That being said, the growth of the African American middle class has resulted in more families adopting the dominant White cultural values of the nuclear family.

Racial socialization is the process by which children are taught the truths about their cultural group and are desensitized to the racism, prejudice, and discrimination they will encounter throughout their lives. This process is necessary to foster high self-esteem in African American children. During racial socialization, children learn about their African heritage and the bravery of their ancestors. They also learn that racism exists but that they should pick their battles and use family support and faith in God to overcome the hurts of racism and discrimination.

Christianity and faith are important values for many African Americans. Equally important is their commitment to the Black church. The **Black church** refers to all denominations of Christian African American churches. The Black church is where most African Americans find strength, renewal, support, and refuge from the daily microaggresions they experience in society, where they continue to be oppressed.

Discrimination and oppression are also influential in developing a positive racial identity. Racial identity attitudes can range from hatred, rejection, and nonacceptance of an individual's own racial group to acceptance not only of his or her own group but also of other groups. Individuals' racial identity can be influenced by their personal and vicarious experiences and the sociopolitical context in which they live. It can affect the way individuals feel about themselves, the way they act toward those in their own and other groups, and their overall psychological health.

African Americans and Mental Health

African Americans are less likely to seek help for mental illnesses, more likely to leave treatment prematurely, and more likely to receive emergency psychological treatment than are White Americans (Office of the Surgeon General, 1999). There are several reasons cited for these facts. Mental health institutions have not been kind to African Americans in many ways, including overdiagnosing severe mental illnesses such as schizophrenia but underdiagnosing more common illnesses such as depression and anxiety. In addition, there are cultural taboos against psychological treat-

ment, in general, and against 'telling your business to White folk," specifically. African Americans are more inclined to seek help from family and friends and their primary physician over seeking help from professional counselors, psychologists, and psychiatrists (Evans & George, 2008; Leong, Wagner, & Tata, 1995; Office of the Surgeon General, 1999).

In fact, mental illness is viewed so negatively that individuals who seek help are stigmatized for doing so (Nikerson, Helms, & Terrell, 1994). It is no wonder that African Americans are almost half as likely as Whites to use mental health services of any kind (Swartz et al., 1998). Although it is believed that African Americans are more likely to use a family doctor, there is no empirical evidence they seek such help more than do other racial groups (Office of the Surgeon General, 1999).

To be able to counsel the members of this group effectively, professional counselors must (a) develop an awareness of their own biases and prejudices, (b) gain knowledge of the African American history and culture, and (c) perfect skills for adapting counseling theories and styles to best meet the needs of their African American clients.

Although slavery no longer exists in the United States, unfortunately its legacy is the lingering racism that endures today. Professional counselors must sincerely question their own beliefs about African Americans to discover whether or not they may be taking part in one of many subtle forms of racism. Some of the attitudes and beliefs that professional counselors should explore include the following:

1. Feeling resentment when issues of slavery are discussed,
2. Believing that it is beneficial to African Americans to ignore racial differences,
3. Feeling overwhelmed when asked to learn about the history and culture of African Americans,
4. Believing that affirmative action hurts Whites, and
5. Feeling helpless to do anything about racism or racists.

If professional counselors determine that racism is a problem for them, they should take steps to overcome these racist beliefs before they can effectively counsel African Americans. Even professional counselors who determine that they have overcome racist attitudes should remember that to be effective, they must (a) appreciate African American vernacular and communication styles; (b) use racial identity stages to help African Americans develop a positive racial identity; (c) appreciate the importance of spirituality and the Black church; (d) understand the African American concept of family, parental practices, and gender roles; and (e) understand how African Americans socialize their children to survive the racial challenges they will encounter.

Professional counselors will find that developing skills for counseling African Americans is complicated by the fact that there is no typical African American client, even though many African Americans share a common history and culture. That said, when clients need assistance in overcoming oppression,

African Americans from most backgrounds may benefit from approaching counseling from an Afrocentric perspective, including spirituality, history, kinship, and community.

Professional counselors must communicate with African Americans by being flexible in their own communication styles while understanding and appreciating African American styles of communication such as AAVE. In addition, professional counselors need to expand their notions of informed consent to include familiarization with the counseling process. Most important, professional counselors need to know when and how they should intervene when institutional and personal forms of racism interfere with client growth. There are no hard and fast rules for counseling African Americans. Above all, professional counselors with African American clients need to become comfortable with the culture of their clients and honestly address their own biases and prejudices.

Contributed by Kathy M. Evans,
University of South Carolina, Columbia, SC

References

Evans, K., & George, R. (2008) African Americans. In G. McAuliffe & Associates (Eds.), *Culturally alert counseling: A comprehensive introduction* (pp. 146–187). Thousand Oaks, CA: Sage.

Leong, F. T. L., Wagner, N. S., & Tata, S. P. (1995). Racial and ethnic variations in help-seeking attitudes. In J. G. Ponterotto, J. M. Casas, L. A. Suzuki, & C. M. Alexander (Eds.), *Handbook of multicultural counseling* (pp. 415–438). Thousand Oaks, CA: Sage.

Nikerson, K. J., Helms, J. E., & Terrell, F. (1994). Cultural mistrust, opinions about mental illness, and Black students' attitudes toward seeking psychological help from White counselors. *Journal of Counseling Psychology, 41,* 378–385.

Office of the Surgeon General. (1999). *Mental health: A report of the Surgeon General.* Retrieved October 19, 2007, from http://mentalhealth.samhsa.gov/cre/ch3.asp

Swartz, M. S., Wagner, H. R., Swanson, J. W., Burns, B. J., George, L. K., & Padgett, D. K. (1998). Comparing use of public and private mental health services: The enduring barriers of race and age. *Community Mental Health Journal, 34,* 133–144.

U. S. Census Bureau. (2000). *Census 2000 demographic profile highlights.* Retrieved December 31, 2007, from http://factfinder.census.gov/servlet/SAFFIteratedFacts?_event=&geo_id=01000US&_geoContext=01000US&_street=&_county=&_cityTown=&_state=&_zip=&_lang=en&_sse=on&ActiveGeoDiv=&_useEV=&pctxt=fph&pgsl=010&_submenuId=factsheet_2&ds_name=DEC_2000_SAFF&_ci_nbr=005&qr_name=DEC_2000_SAFF_R1010&reg=DEC_2000_SAFF_R1010%3A005&_keyword=&_industry=

Additional Resources

Dovidio, J. F., Kawakami, K., & Gaertner, S. L. (2000). Reducing contemporary prejudice: Combating explicit and implicit bias at the individual and intergroup level. In S. Oskamp (Ed.), *Reducing prejudice and discrimination* (pp. 137–164). Mahwah, NJ: Erlbaum.

Koch, L. M., Gross, A. M., & Kolts, R. (2001) Attitudes toward Black English and code switching. *Journal of Black Psychology, 27,* 29–42.

Levine, M. L. (1996) *African Americans and civil rights: From 1619 to the present.* Phoenix, AZ: Oryx Press.

Ridley, C. R. (1995). *Overcoming unintentional racism in counseling and therapy: A practitioner's guide to intentional intervention.* Thousand Oaks, CA: Sage.

▧ Aggression, Violence, and Microaggression

Aggression is any behavior directed at an individual or group with the intention of causing harm. Aggression can be expressed verbally, physically, and relationally. **Verbal aggression** involves saying hurtful and demeaning words or phrases to another individual. **Physical aggression** involves a physical act toward an individual causing bodily harm. **Relational aggression** happens within group relationships and involves demeaning and dishonest tactics to damage social standing within the group. Aggression is distinct from assertiveness. **Assertiveness** is a communication style that professional counselors help clients learn so they can express aggression in a way that is respectful of others while maintaining their rights. Aggression is generally impulsive and is in response to a hurtful act that has resulted in a feeling of humiliation. An example of a subtle form of both verbal aggression and **relational aggression** is known as cyberbullying. The dilemma with **cyberbullying** is that taunts once expressed only verbally are now written and sent through instant messaging to a wide network of "cyber friends." Once the message is sent, there is no longer any control over what happens to the words. The messages can be printed, resent, and saved to use in continually shaming and humiliating the victim. Although aggression is universal, it is important to note that the way aggression is expressed can differ by gender and culture. For example, in general, men tend to express their aggression physically whereas women use more verbal forms of aggressive behavior.

Violence is aggression with extreme harm as its intent. Individuals who commit violent acts do so either impulsively or with forethought, but they do so with the intention of inflicting extreme harm on their victim. Anger interwoven with feelings of shame and humiliation is believed to lead to acts of violence. The intensity of expressed violence parallels the intensity of shame and humiliation felt. Gilligan (1996) discussed that

> one of the integral reasons someone commits violence is an intense feeling of shame that could be called humiliation, which is felt in the absence of other emotions like love. The feelings of shame stimulate rage and in the absence of other feelings like love or guilt allow the individual to express their violent thoughts . . . the way people regain their "power" in situations where they feel impotent (shamed and humiliated) is to turn to violence. (pp. 113–114)

Hartling (2007) posited that there is a pathway to violence that begins with shame and ends with violence. This chain of events begins with a humiliating act that causes an individual to feel social pain, which is the perception of psychological distance from others in society. This social pain increases anger and decreases self-awareness, which in turn increases self-defeating behaviors and decreases the ability to regulate the self. Understanding this power dynamic and the disconnection from feelings of worth may help provide insight to prevent further national and global tragedies. As professional counselors become more aware of the effects of social pain in national and global society, they can work to assist individuals who feel socially excluded to find a way that does not lead to violence to express themselves.

Microaggression is a term coined by Chester Pierce in the 1970s to explain the many sudden and disheartening acts that happen to women and people of color. Today, this term has been extended to describe any person or group that feels powerless or disenfranchised. Microaggressions are experienced as small acts of racism (or any other ism) that are cumulative and accumulate throughout the day. These little things add up until the victim of the microaggression explodes. Many acts of microaggression are invisible and can be intentional or unintentional. An example of a micro-aggressive assault is a woman of color walking into a salon and only seeing pictures of hairstyles featuring White women. An example of an intentional microaggression is telling an individual of Asian descent who was born in the United States that he or she speaks English well. Yvonne Jenkins (2007) indicated that a lifetime of these microaggressions can affect people if not interrupted or checked. This implies that the effects of microaggressions are cumulative and draining, and this type of assault, if not addressed, can lead to continued cultural breakdowns in society. Specifically, acts of microaggression allow people of privilege to stay in a "power-over" dynamic as a way of attempting to keep those who feel disenfranchised or invisible silenced.

Shame, Humiliation, and Anger

To understand aggression, violence, and microaggression better, it is necessary to define the feelings of shame and humiliation and their link with anger. **Shame** can be associated with the internalized belief that one is not worthy of relationship with others, whereas **humiliation** is associated with the belief that one's actions in relation to others indicate one is less worthy than others in the group. Linder (2006) eloquently discussed the linguistic meaning of humiliation. She discussed how the root of humiliation is "humus," which means earth or ground. The suffix "-ate" means to cause; therefore, humiliation means to cause movement to the ground. This same theme can be found throughout other languages, and, universally, humiliation is spatially associated with a downward movement. Understanding this concept can give a visual representation of how individuals move toward aggression, violence, and microaggression when linking the anger response to feelings of shame and humiliation.

Professional counselors see expressions of aggression, violence, and microaggression everyday and see how these expressions cause clients to disconnect from pain and hurt. Understanding what is behind these behaviors is important in promoting growth, fostering relationships based on mutuality, and providing opportunities for reconnection. Ultimately, it is the professional counselor's and client's responsibility to understand the differences between aggression, violence, and microaggression and to understand how each is displayed in a multicultural world. Models that professional counselors can use to assist clients to work through culturally based aggression and violence include relational cultural theory, anger resolution therapy, and addictions models of therapy. The use of these types of models will help professional counselors and other mental health professionals assist both victims and perpetrators to find ways to move away from shaming and humiliating thoughts and feelings, begin the long road to healing, and once again finding a connection with society.

Contributed by Julie Strentzsch and
Dana L. Comstock,
St. Mary's University, San Antonio, TX

References

Gilligan, J. (1996). *Violence: Reflections on a national epidemic.* New York: Vintage Books.

Hartling, L. (2007). *Humiliation: Real pain, a pathway to violence* [Preliminary draft]. Retrieved August 15, 2007, from humiliationstudies.org.

Jenkins, Y. (2007, October). *Transforming shame and humiliation: Walking toward our talk.* Paper presented at a meeting sponsored by the Jean Baker Miller Institute, Boston.

Linder, E. (2006). *Making enemies: Humiliation and international conflict.* Portsmouth, NH: Greenwood.

Additional Resources

Human Dignity and Humiliation Studies Web site: http://www.humiliationstudies.org

Jean Baker Miller Training Institute Web site: http://www.jbmti.org

Aging Theories

Two earlier theories of aging are disengagement theory and activity theory. **Disengagement theory** (Cumming, Henry, & Damianopoulos, 1961) is defined as "an inevitable process in which many of the relationships between a person and other members of society are severed, and those remaining are altered in quality" (p. 211). The nine postulates describing the process of disengagement are presented in the following list.

- Postulate 1: Although individuals differ, the expectation of death is universal, and decrement of ability is probable. Therefore a mutual severing of ties will take place between a person and others in society. (Cumming et al., 1961, p. 211)

- Postulate 2: Because interactions create and reaffirm norms, a reduction in the number or variety of interactions leads to an increased freedom from the control of the norms governing everyday behavior. Consequently, once begun, disengagement becomes a circular, or self-perpetuating, process. (Cumming et al., 1961, p. 211)

- Postulate 3: Because the central role of men in American society is instrumental, and the central role of women is socio-emotional, the process of disengagement will differ between men and women. (Cumming et al., 1961, p. 212)
- Postulate 4: The life cycle of the individual is punctuated by ego changes. For example, aging is usually accompanied by decrements in knowledge and skill. At the same time, success in an industrialized society is based on knowledge and skill, and age-grading is a mechanism used to insure that the young are sufficiently well trained to assume authority and the old are retired before they lose skill. Disengagement in America may be initiated by either the individual because of ego changes or by the society because of organizational imperatives, or by both simultaneously. (Cumming et al., 1961, p. 213)
- Postulate 5: When both the individual and society are ready for disengagement, completed disengagement results. When neither are ready, continuing engagement results. When the individual is ready and society is not, a disjunction between the expectations of the individual and of the members of his social systems results, but usually engagement continues. When society is ready and the individual is not, the result of the disjunction is usually disengagement. [Cumming et al., 1961, p. 214)
- Postulate 6: Because the abandonment of life's central roles (i.e., work for men, marriage and family for women) results in a dramatically reduced social life space, it will result in crisis and loss of morale unless different roles, appropriate to the disengaged state, are available. [Cumming et al., 1961, p. 215)
- Postulate 7: (a) If the individual becomes sharply aware of the shortness of life and the scarcity of the time remaining to him, and if he perceives his life space as decreasing, and if his available ego energy is lessened, then readiness for disengagement has begun. (b) The needs of a rational-legal occupational system in an affluent society, the nature of the nuclear family, and the differential death rate lead to society's giving echelons of people its permission to disengage. (Cumming et al., 1961, pp. 216–217)
- Postulate 8: The reductions in interaction and the loss of central roles result in a shift in the quality of relationship in the remaining roles. There is a wider choice of relational rewards, and a shift from vertical solidarities to horizontal ones. (Cumming et al., 1961, p. 217)

- Postulate 9: Disengagement is a culture-free concept, but the form it takes will always be culture-bound. (Cumming et al., 1961, p. 218)

For a full discussion, including the corollaries to the postulates, see Cumming et al., 1961.

An example is a man who is now 70 years old. Because he is retired, he has given up one of his primary responsibilities of adulthood (i.e., work). He is still involved in church activities and spends his weekends reading, gardening, and visiting grown children and grandchildren. Disengagement theory focuses on the gradually shrinking number of roles now played.

Activity theory, by contrast, focuses on life satisfaction being related to the activities in which the adult is involved. **Activity theory** is the idea that adults who are older should remain as involved in their world as they desire. Optimal aging is staying active and resisting the loss of social roles (Havighurst, Neugarten, & Tobin, 1968). Activity theory would consider it important that the man in the previous example be as active and involved in the world as he wants to remain. Any roles that are lost between middle age and old age may be replaced with substitutes. A very active older adult might continue to work past the traditional retirement benchmark of age 65 years. An active retired adult, for example, might take classes at a local community college, take up a new hobby, or volunteer through a social service organization.

Havighurst (1963) compared activity theory and disengagement theory by interviewing older adults up to seven times each between 1956 and 1962. The results of the study were mixed. There was evidence of a decline in activities and involvement with aging, which indicates disengagement. The results also indicated a moderate correlation between contentment and activity level, which is support for activity theory. The author concluded that neither theory is sufficient to account for the fact that older adults regret the change of activity in their lives but accept the change as a part of aging. Older adults do, however, retain their sense of self-worth and life satisfaction.

Newer theories of aging include the **life span model of successful aging** (Schultz & Heckhausen, 1996) and the **selective optimization with compensation** theory (Baltes & Baltes, 1990). These theories are variations on the idea that people change their goals as they age. An example is the case of a woman who, at age 35 years, still likes to jog and play racquetball. Fifteen years later she may change her sports due to injuries, but she still remains active. Another example is a 30-year-old manager of a busy restaurant who works 40–50 hours a week. At age 45, she may revise her position and hire an assistant manager to take some of the strain off of her due to physical changes and family demands. At age 60, she may make someone else the manager but stay busy overseeing the business at a different level.

Baltes and Baltes (1990) discussed these changes in terms of selective optimization and compensation. The adult selects which activities are important (e.g., jogging). If an adult can no longer engage in certain activities, then these activities will be changed. Choosing an activity is **selection.** Maintaining the ability is **optimization.** Changing an individual's exercise strategy from jogging to walking is described as **compensation.**

Schultz and Heckhausen (1996) discussed changes in terms of primary and secondary control. **Primary control** involves an adult engaging in preferred activities, such as jogging. The adult is exerting control over the immediate external environment. What happens if the individual is injured? **Secondary control** is about the cognitive process that allows the adult to consider options and to decide to change direction and accept walking as an acceptable alternative to jogging.

Porfeli (2003) described the theories of Schultz and Heckhausen (1996) and Baltes and Baltes (1990) and then showed that the theories work together in discussing the choices of an adult client. Selective optimization is used with primary control, and compensation is used with secondary control.

Ouwehand, de Ridder, and Bensing (2007) described the Baltes and Baltes (1990) model as the leading model and suggested that proactive coping is an important additional strategy to the idea of selective optimization with compensation. Proactive coping helps to bolster the resources necessary for a person to cope with changes so that disengagement is delayed. Gignac, Cott, and Badley (2002) applied the process of selective optimization with compensation to adults with osteoarthritis. A survey was devised to assess coping in terms of selection, optimization, and compensation. In this application, selection referred to restricting or limiting an activity, such as walking. Optimization refers to coping in terms of trying to avoid pain and resting. Compensation refers to a person modifying or switching activities. The survey was given to 248 adults with osteoarthritis. The results showed that most adults reported all three types of coping but that compensation occurred most often (selection, 20.4%, optimization, 31.3%, compensation, 48.3%). The Baltes and Baltes theory has also been applied to industrial-organizational psychology (Baltes & Dickson, 2001). As a metatheory, it is flexible enough to cover conflict between work and family, leadership, and functioning at the organizational level.

The main ideas that make up activity theory and disengagement theory have evolved over time to give interesting perspectives for aging in the technologically more complex 21st century. The current era includes more complex roles and choices for men and women in terms of work, social opportunities, and family.

Contributed by Bonnie M. Wright,
Gardner-Webb University,
Boiling Springs, NC

References

Baltes, P. B., & Baltes, M. M. (1990). Psychological perspectives on successful aging: The model of selective optimization with compensation. In P. B. Baltes & M. M. Baltes (Eds.), *Successful aging: Perspective from the behavioral sciences* (pp. 1–34). Cambridge, United Kingdom: Cambridge University Press.

Baltes, B. B., & Dickson, M. W. (2001). Using life-span models in industrial-organizational psychology: The theory of selective optimization with compensation. *Applied Developmental Science, 5,* 51–62.

Cumming, E., Henry, W. E., & Damianopoulos, W. (1961). A formal statement of disengagement theory. In E. Cumming & W. E. Henry (Eds.), *Growing old: The process of disengagement* (pp. 210–218). New York: Basic Books.

Gignac, M. A. M., Cott, C., & Badley, E. M. (2002). Adaptation to disability: Applying selective optimization with compensation to the behavior of older adults with osteoarthritis. *Psychology & Aging, 17,* 520–524.

Havighurst, R. J. (1963). Successful aging. In R. Williams, C. Tibbitts, & W. Donahue (Eds.), *Processes of aging* (Vol. 1, pp. 299–320). New York: Atherton Press.

Havighurst, R. J., Neugarten, B., & Tobin, S. (1968). Disengagement and patterns of aging. In B. Neugarten (Ed.), *Middle age and aging: A reader in social psychology* (pp. 161–172). Chicago: The University of Chicago Press.

Ouwehand, C., de Ridder, D. T. D., & Bensing, J. M. (2007). A review of successful aging models: Proposing proactive coping as an important additional strategy. *Clinical Psychology Review, 27,* 873–884.

Porfeli, E. J. (2003). Designing lives and empowering clients: The case of Sue. *The Career Development Quarterly, 51,* 300–305.

Schultz, R., & Heckhausen, J. (1996). A life span model of successful aging. *American Psychologist, 51,* 702–714.

Additional Resources

Bjorklund, B. R., & Bee, H. L. (2008). *The journey of adulthood* (6th ed.). Upper Saddle River, NJ: Pearson/ Prentice Hall.

Moody, H. R. (2006). *Aging: Concepts and controversies* (5th ed.). Thousand Oaks, CA: Pine Forge Press.

■ American Association of State Counseling Boards

The **American Association of State Counseling Boards (AASCB)** is made up of representatives from legally established bodies that regulate the practice of counseling. It serves as a forum for board members concerning counselor licensing and regulation, test development, and standards for licensing. Eligible voting delegates represent counselor licensing boards from the states, Puerto Rico, the Virgin Islands, and Guam. Nonvoting members include counseling organizational affiliates and individual members. AASCB holds an annual conference, publishes an electronic newsletter at least twice a year, and maintains a Web site with information about licensing and links to licensing boards.

Prior to AASCB's founding, the counselor licensing movement began in Virginia, which in 1976 became the first state to license counselors, followed by only two other states (Alabama and Arkansas) by 1979. Counselor licensing momentum built with Texas (1981) and Idaho (1982), and by 1987 nine other states successfully passed licensing laws and created the climate for AASCB's founding.

Organizational History

On April 19, 1986, Willie Jackson, chair of the Licensing Committee of the American Association for Counseling and Development (AACD; now known as the American Counseling Association [ACA]), directed a discussion on the possible formation of an association of state counselor licensing boards be held at the convention in Los Angeles, California. The steering committee, chaired by Ted Remley, met with representatives of nine state counselor licensing boards and set October 12–13, 1986, for a bylaws convention in Kansas City, Missouri (AACD, 1986). At that meeting, the 21 delegates present adopted bylaws, and at 2:43 p.m. on October 21, 1986, AASCB was born, with Remley elected the first president (AACD, 1986). Members initiated a discussion of licensing reciprocity, with differences among state requirements cited as a roadblock. Required credit hours ranged from 30 (Alabama) to 60 (Virginia; AACD, 1986).

Approximately 50 people attended the first annual convention of AASCB in Charleston, South Carolina, March 20–22, 1987, where Remley was appointed unpaid executive director for 1 year (AASCB, 1988). By that time, 24 states had adopted counselor licensing laws.

Important AASCB Historical Events

AASCB faced a number of critical issues in its development, paralleling the growth of the counseling profession and the licensing movement. These issues included nonuniform standards, management, testing, commissions, and license portability.

The Problem of Standards: Summits on Credentialing and Unity of the Profession

Although ACA's licensing model set the number of credits required to qualify at 60, the Council for Accreditation of Counseling and Related Educational Programs developed different standards. The first national certifying body for counselors, the National Academy of Certified Clinical Mental Health Counselors, offered its own exam and certification. The National Board for Certified Counselors (NBCC) followed with the National Counselor Certification and the National Counselor Examination (NCE). Later, NBCC assumed responsibility for the National Clinical Mental Health Counselor Examination (NCMHE) that is still used by some states as their licensing exam, although most states still use the NCE.

Concerned with the diversity of standards, AASCB began meeting with counseling organizations to develop a Counseling Credentialing Summit (B. Bertram, personal communication, March 31, 1989). Although a proposal was developed and funding sought, the idea died after two meetings when the ACA Foundation did not accept a proposal to fund the project and the various counseling entities were not willing to fund their own delegates' participation.

Research on the wide diversity of licensing standards among the states (Mascari, 2004) led the AASCB presidential team to approach Samuel Gladding, ACA president, and professional staff with their concern about counselor identity. After a subsequent meeting, ACA and AASCB agreed to hold a summit addressing counselor identity and licensing-related issues critical to the health of the profession. The summit was named "20/20: A Vision for the Future of Counseling."

Management

A series of volunteer executive directors managed AASCB until 2001 when the executive committee hired NBCC through its affiliate, the Center for Credentialing Education, to provide day-to-day management. NBCC continued its management until August 2006, when the executive committee invited proposals from interested organizations and hired ACA as its management company.

Testing

In February 1990, after AASCB sought proposals for development of a test that would improve portability chances through the use of a common test, NBCC was awarded a contract that designated the **NCE** as the recommended standard. Currently, AASCB promotes a two-test protocol and recommends that the NCE be passed prior to beginning to accrue hours of experience and that the **NCMHCE,** formerly the Certified Clinical Mental Health Counselor exam, be passed prior to issuing a counselor license. Only a few states have moved to this two-test protocol.

Commissions

Originally called committees, **commissions** are the heart of AASCB's activities, addressing critical issues at the annual meeting. The first major committee outcome was supervision, when AASCB endorsed the Association for Counselor Education and Supervision document, *Standards for Counseling Supervisors,* as a guide for developing state boards' rules and regulations for counselor supervision (AASCB, 1992).

License Portability and National Credentials Registry

At the 2004 annual meeting, AASCB adopted the portability proposal creating the **National Credentials Registry (NCR).** Jan McMillan of Virginia was appointed to chair the NCR and lead a committee to assist states to adapt or change regulations to accept portability.

Current Licensing Issues Needing Resolution

AASCB's commissions are continuing to work on the following issues critical to counselor licensing and portability.

- What common title will be used for licensing?
- What is the common number of credits that will be required for licensing?
- What common examination or examinations (two tiers) will be required?
- What common number of hours or years of experience will be required for licensing?
- What credentials and/or training will be required for supervising counselors seeking licensure?
- Will licensed professional counselors achieve nationwide portability in the near future?

Contributed by J. Barry Mascari,
Kean University, Union, NJ

References

American Association for Counseling and Development. (1986). *Minutes of the annual meeting.* Alexandria, VA: Author.

American Association of State Counseling Boards. (1988). *Minutes of the state counselor licensing board meeting.* Washington, DC: Author.

American Association of State Counseling Boards. (1992). *Minutes of the state counselor licensing board meeting.* Washington, DC: Author.

Mascari, J. B. (2004). *The relationship between counselor licensing standards & violations: A mixed methodological review.* UMI Dissertation Services/Proquest No. 3148764.

Additional Resource

American Association of State Counseling Boards Web site: http://www.aascb.org

◼ American College Counseling Association

The **American College Counseling Association (ACCA),** a division of the American Counseling Association (ACA), was created for individuals who identify professionally as counselors who work in higher education with the purpose of fostering students' development. This combined focus on professional identity, a specific work setting, and student development as a foundation for college counseling is a distinctive characteristic of ACCA. From its founding in 1991, ACCA has sought to include professionals across various functional areas and institution types, and because of its commitment to the development of students, it has involved graduate students in significant ways.

ACCA is governed by a nine-person elected executive council, and one of three member-at-large positions is reserved for a graduate student; all other offices and committees of ACCA are open to graduate students as well. ACCA also has a strong commitment to diversity and social justice, as reflected in the ACCA Diversity Statement adopted in 2000 (ACCA, 2001). The mission of ACCA reflects the commitment to include a wide range of professionals and to support their work in multiple ways

ACCA was created in response to the disaffiliation of the American College Personnel Association (ACPA), a former division of ACA, to ensure a continued place within ACA (then the American Association for Counseling and Development) for those working in colleges and universities. ACPA's decision reflected the "intent to serve those with a primary identity in student affairs. Consequently, individuals working in higher education who had a primary professional identity in counseling had to reevaluate their professional affiliations" (Davis, 1998, p. 7). When it became clear that the disaffiliation would occur, then AACD president Jane Myers appointed an organizing committee, chaired by Mark E. "Gene" Meadows of Auburn University, to develop plans for a new division to meet the needs of counseling professionals in higher education. Because of the legal and organizational challenges that became apparent through the situation with ACPA, ACCA was developed as a division that was not incorporated separately from AACD, making the legal relationship between the two different from that of other divisions at the time. In less than a year from its creation, ACCA had met all requirements to move from organizational affiliate status to an approved division status in 1992. Gene Meadows served as the first president of ACCA, and membership had grown to approximately 2,000 during that time.

Since its inception, ACCA has grown into a strong and active organization. *Visions,* the organization's newsletter, is published three times per year and is now disseminated electronically. The *Journal of College Counseling* was initiated in 1998 and has developed a strong reputation as a scholarly, peer-reviewed journal with a practitioner focus. The ACCA-L electronic mailing list, open to anyone interested in college counseling, provides an electronic forum for discussion of issues, sharing of practices, posting of positions, and seeking of referrals, especially for college students traveling home for the summer or moving because of graduation or transfer. Since 2002, ACCA has also sponsored a biennial national conference, cohosted with one of its state divisions, in addition to its annual business meeting and other activities held at the ACA conference. Other professional development opportunities include 23 state divisions, public policy and legislation activities, online courses providing continuing education units, research grants, professional awards, and emerging leader grants to support graduate student participation at ACA and ACCA conferences.

One of the major sustained initiatives within ACCA has been advocacy for college counseling. In an era of outsourcing and budget constraints in higher education, and with much of the work of college counselors being behind the scenes, there is a need to educate the general public, students, parents, and administrators about the value of counseling services on college campuses. ACCA in 2001 published the second edition of the *College Counseling Advocacy Booklet* to support members in their advocacy efforts. As an association, ACCA also advocates actively for professional standards and accreditation, especially through membership in the Council for the Advancement of Standards in Higher Education and connection with the International Association of Counseling Services.

Contributed by Laura A. Dean,
The University of Georgia, Athens, GA

References

American College Counseling Association. (2001). *College counseling advocacy booklet* (2nd ed.). Retrieved June 17, 2008, from http://www.google.com/search?hl=en&safe=active&q=College+Counseling+Advocacy+Booklet+ACCA&btnG=Search

Davis, D. C. (1998). The American College Counseling Association: A historical view. *Journal of College Counseling, 1,* 7–9.

Additional Resources

American College Counseling Association archives: National Student Affairs archives, Bowling Green State University: http://www.bgsu.edu/colleges/library/cac/nsaaintro.html

American College Counseling Association Web site: www. collegecounseling.org

Davis, D. C., & Humphrey, K. M. (Eds.). (2000). *College counseling: Issues and strategies for a new millennium.* Alexandria, VA: American Counseling Association.

Dean, L. A., & Meadows, M. E. (1995). College counseling: Union and intersection. *Journal of Counseling & Development, 74,* 139–142.

▪ American Counseling Association

The **American Counseling Association (ACA)** is the world's largest professional association dedicated to the needs and interests of practicing counselors. At the time this volume was published, ACA's membership was more than 40,000 individuals. ACA members are counselors employed in a variety of work settings, including schools, community mental health centers, private practices, colleges and universities, rehabilitation agencies, government agencies, addictions treatment centers, career centers, and a number of other work environments.

Headquartered in Alexandria, Virginia, just outside Washington, DC, ACA promotes public confidence and trust in the counseling profession so that professionals can further assist their clients and students in dealing with the challenges life presents. ACA serves professional counselors in the United States and at least 50 other countries and is associated with a comprehensive network of 19 divisions and 56 branches (states or other territorial entities).

The divisions of ACA enhance professional identity and are organized around specific interest and practice areas to satisfy the diverse needs of the counseling community. The 19 divisions are Association for Assessment in Counseling and Education (AACE); Association for Adult Development and Aging (AADA); Association for Creativity in Counseling (ACC); American College Counseling Association (ACCA); Association for Counselors and Educators in Government (ACEG); Association for Counselor Education and Supervision (ACES); Association for Lesbian, Gay, Bisexual and Transgender Issues in Counseling (ALGBTIC); Association for Multicultural Counseling and Development (AMCD); American Mental Health Counselors Association (AMHCA); American Rehabilitation Counseling Association (ARCA); American School Counselor Association (ASCA); Association for Spiritual, Ethical, and Religious Values in Counseling (ASERVIC); Association for Specialists in Group Work (ASGW); Counseling Association for Humanistic Education and Development (C-AHEAD); Counselors for Social Justice (CSJ); International Association of Addictions and Offender Counselors (IAAOC); International Association of Marriage and Family Counselors (IAMFC); National Career Development Association (NCDA); and National Employment Counseling Association (NECA).

History

In 1952, four independent associations held a joint convention in Los Angeles, California, and created the American Personnel and Guidance Association (APGA), which was the organizational forerunner to ACA. The groups that joined to form APGA were the National Vocational Guidance Association, the National Association of Guidance and Counselor Trainers, the Student Personnel Association for Teacher Education, and the American College Personnel Association. These associations joined forces with the visionary hope that together they could accomplish more for the counseling profession than any of the groups could alone. In 1983, APGA changed its name to the American Association for Counseling and Development. On July 1, 1992, the association changed its name to the American Counseling Association to reflect the common bond among association members and to reinforce their unity of purpose.

Organizational Partners

ACA collaborates with the following corporate and related organizations to enhance member services:

1. **Council for Accreditation of Counseling and Related Educational Programs.** This independent council was created in 1981 to accredit the counseling profession's graduate-level preparation programs (see Council for Accreditation of Counseling and Related Educational Programs).

2. **Chi Sigma Iota.** The official honor society of the counseling profession, Chi Sigma Iota is an independent membership organization that recognizes outstanding individual contributions to the profession and excellence in educational achievement (see Chi Sigma Iota).

3. **National Board for Certified Counselors (NBCC).** The NBCC is an independent, nonprofit, voluntary, nongovernmental corporation established to advance the credentialing of professional counselors (see National Board for Certified Counselors).

4. **ACA Insurance Trust, Inc. (ACAIT).** ACAIT is an independent corporation promoting and administering quality insurance coverage and services at competitive rates for ACA members and groups in the human development professions.

5. **American Counseling Association Foundation (ACAF).** Created in 1979, ACAF enhances the counseling profession by focusing its mission in many areas, such as encouraging the next generation of counselors, honoring outstanding educators and practitioners, publishing on cutting-edge topics, reaching out to elementary age children through the Growing Happy and Confident Kids project, and most recently aiding fellow counselors who had been affected by Hurricanes Katrina and Rita by creating the Counselors Care Fund.

Major Foci and Initiatives

ACA provides leadership to the counseling field through a number of efforts. Key services and programs include the following:

- **Publications and research.** ACA publishes a variety of journals, books, monographs, DVDs/videos, and other materials that support the work of professional counselors. All members receive the *Journal of Counseling & Development,* which is the flagship journal of ACA, and the monthly newsletter, *Counseling Today.*
- **Public policy and legislation efforts.** ACA employs full-time staff members who conduct coordinated efforts on Capitol Hill to encourage the passage of legislation that supports the counseling profession. Furthermore, ACA offers training and support for counselors wishing to have an impact on public policy at the state or national level.
- **State licensure.** ACA provides leadership and support to counselors in state-level efforts to obtain licensure and other legislated privileges for counselors.
- **Ethics.** ACA (2005) published the *ACA Code of Ethics* that is used by counselors across the nation and beyond to guide them regarding standards of practice and client care. The ACA ethical code is a hallmark of professionalization, assisting counselors in providing quality services.
- **National leadership.** ACA holds a national conference annually, bringing together thousands of counselors for training and collaboration. Recognized as the largest, oldest, and most visible association in the counseling field, ACA serves as the public face of the counseling profession, thereby serving as a guidepost for counseling professionals, their clients, and other interested parties throughout the United States and beyond.

Contributed by J. Scott Young,
Mississippi State University,
Starkville, MS

Reference

American Counseling Association. (2005). *ACA code of ethics.* Alexandria, VA: Author.

ACA Code of Ethics

The first American Counseling Association (ACA; then the American Personnel and Guidance Association) *ethics code* was initiated by Donald Super and approved in 1961. The association acknowledged that to be a recognized profession, counselors needed ethical standards. The ethics code was revised periodically, beginning in 1974 and again in 1981, 1988, 1995, and 2005. Revisions were necessary to reflect the realities of current practice and to address new issues in counseling and practice areas. The current version (ACA, 2005) retained the basic eight-section structure of the previous code but infused diversity issues throughout; added information about end-of-life issues, selecting interventions,

and ending one's practice; and replaced the concept of dual relationships with the concepts of beneficial and harmful relationships. The 2005 *ACA Code of Ethics* prohibits sexual relationships with clients for 5 years, an extension from the previous 2 years, and extends the prohibition to partners and members of the client's family. An entire new section on technology applications, including Internet counseling and telephone counseling, was added, as were mandates about the diagnosis of mental disorders. An in-depth guideline regarding relationships with colleagues, employers, and employees and guidelines for forensic evaluation are among the new and expanded provisions. In addition, each section begins with an introduction, and the Standards of Practice from the 1995 *Code of Ethics and Standards of Practice* were incorporated into the body of the 2005 *Code.*

The 2005 *ACA Code of Ethics* may be downloaded from the ACA Web site. ACA states that the *Code* serves five main purposes:

1. The *Code* clarifies the nature of ethical responsibilities held in common by its members.
2. The *Code* reinforces the association's mission.
3. Best practices in counseling are defined by guiding principles.
4. The *Code* helps guide ACA members in decision making to best serve constituents while promoting professional values.
5. The *Code* offers structure for dealing with professional complaints and inquiries concerning ACA members.

The *ACA Code of Ethics* addresses the responsibilities of counselors toward their clients, colleagues, workplace, and themselves by describing the aspirational standards for a counselor's conduct. The code is divided into eight primary areas, each of which addresses the responsibilities and standards for that area. Section A focuses on the counseling relationship and the counselor's responsibilities toward the client to foster growth and the development of healthy relationships. Topics covered in Section A are welfare of those served by counselors, including primary responsibilities, records, counseling plans, support network involvement, and employment needs. Additional topics include informed consent in the counseling relationship, including types of information needed, development and cultural sensitivity, and the inability to give consent. Other areas covered in this section are clients served by others and avoiding harm and imposing values. Roles and relationships with clients, individuals, groups, and institutions and society are reviewed, as well as group work, end-of-life care, and fees and bartering. Termination and referral and technological applications round out this section. This section encourages professionals to pursue client-centered approaches by challenging counselors to support their clients' growth and development in ways that contribute to the forming of healthy relationships.

Section B covers confidentiality, privileged communication, and privacy. Important issues include respecting clients' rights, exceptions to confidentiality, sharing information with others (including groups and families), working with clients lacking capacity to give informed consent, records, and consultation. These areas underscore the value of trust in the counseling relationship and the special nature of the relationship between the counselor and client. The professional counselor is reminded to foster a collaborative partnership with clients while adhering to professional boundaries in a culturally appropriate manner.

Section C covers professional responsibility. Included in this area are professional competence, advertising and soliciting clients, professional qualifications, public responsibility, and responsibility to other professionals. Professional counselors are reminded of their responsibilities to the public and should use evidence-based approaches and practices. Professional counselors are additionally reminded of their duty to themselves to exercise self-care in order to meet the rigors of their professional responsibilities.

Section D encapsulates the issues related to relationships with other professionals and their impact on the counseling relationship. Guidelines regarding relationships with colleagues, employers, and employees are included as well as consultation issues. Professional counselors need to understand the necessity of appropriate relationships with colleagues and value interactions with multidisciplinary professionals as a way to serve clients better.

Section E covers evaluation, assessment, and interpretation. This section addresses the appropriate use and administration of assessments, the competence of the assessor, and the use of assessment data. Guidelines are also outlined for informed consent, releasing outcome data to other professionals, and diagnosis of mental health disorders. Issues of instrument selection, conditions of assessment administration, multicultural/diversity scoring and interpretation, assessment security, obsolete assessments, outdated results, assessment construction, and forensic evaluations complete this section. This section promotes the value of counselors using culturally appropriate assessment and evaluation tools.

Section F addresses supervision, training, and teaching. Counselor supervision and the welfare of the client and counselor supervision, competence, supervisory relationships, and supervision responsibilities are addressed. This section also includes guidelines on counseling supervision, remediation, and endorsement. The area of counselor educator responsibilities, student welfare, student responsibilities, and evaluation and remediation of students' issues follow. This area concerns information regarding roles and relationships between counselor educators and students and multicultural/diversity competence in counselor education and other programs. Professional counselors must value fairness and honesty in their interactions with supervisees and other students while maintaining appropriate professional boundaries.

Section G addresses research and publication. Areas covered include research responsibilities, rights of research participants, and relationships with research participants. This section concludes with ethical guidelines for reporting results and publication ethics. These guidelines encourage counselors to contribute to the development of the field while minimizing bias and respecting diversity.

Section H addresses a process for resolving ethical issues. This last section informs members about standards and the law and addresses suspected violations and cooperation with ethics committees. Ethics codes, in general, are not proactive in that they do not instruct counselors on what to do in the event of a particular situation. This limitation does not diminish the value of the codes, however, because ethics codes should be consulted to guide the professional counselor through the ethical decision-making process. Counselors use an appropriate decision-making model when resolving ethical dilemmas, and this practice supports a legal, ethical, and moral standard for their discipline. Professional counselors continue to engage in professional development throughout their career.

Contributed by Michael P. Demask,
Hazelden Graduate School of
Addiction Studies, Center City, MN

References

American Counseling Association. (1995). *Code of ethics and standards of practice.* Alexandria, VA: Author.
American Counseling Association. (2005). *ACA code of ethics.* Alexandria, VA: Author.

Additional Resources

American Counseling Association Web site: www.counseling.org
Corey, G., Corey, M. S., & Callahan, P. (2007). *Issues and ethics in the helping professions* (7th ed.). Belmont, CA: Brooks/Cole.
Martinez, J., Lescicki, S., & Andersen, S. (Eds.). (2007). *Codes of ethics of the helping professions* (3rd ed.). Pacific Grove, CA: Brooks/Cole.
Wheeler, A. M., & Bertam, B. (2008). *The counselor and the law: A guide to legal and ethical practice* (5th ed.). Alexandria, VA: American Counseling Association.

■ American Mental Health Counselors Association

In the 1970s, professionals working as mental health counselors lacked a clear sense of identity. They did not have a professional organization to champion their efforts to be recognized as a legitimate, distinct profession within the counseling field. At that time, there were a large number of individuals who (a) were trained at either the master's or doctoral level; (b) worked in community agencies, community mental health, or private practice settings; (c) were delivering services very similar to those provided by the established groups of psychiatry, psychology, and social work; and (d) felt they had no professional home (Smith & Robinson, 1995). It was in this climate that the **American Mental Health Counselors Association (AMHCA),** founded by James Messina and Nancy Spisso of the Escambia County Mental Health Center, Florida, and a division of the American Counseling Association (ACA), was born in May 1976. Other early leaders who played a significant role in the birth of this organization included Gary Seiler and Jim Hiett, as well as Ed Anderson and his Wisconsin colleagues (Weikel, 1985, 1994).

The uniqueness and importance of this association were apparent in several ways. The initial priorities included (a) instituting licensure laws for mental health counselors in those states that did not yet have them; (b) obtaining third-party payments from health insurance plans for services rendered by mental health counselors; (c) defining private practice standards for mental health counselors; (d) acquiring "full parity" for mental health counselors with other providers of mental health services (e.g., psychiatrists, clinical psychologists, psychiatric social workers, psychiatric nurses); and (e) allowing for the provision of treatment to special populations, such as individuals who were elderly or mentally retarded (Hershenson & Power, 1987; Weikel, 1985).

AMHCA Contributions

The contributions made by the AMHCA through its history have greatly affected the development of mental health counseling as a distinct and nationally recognized profession on several levels. One early and noteworthy effort was the development of the Blueprint for the Mental Health Counseling Profession. In 1978, that historic document led to the formation of the **National Academy of Certified Clinical Mental Health Counselors (NACCMHC).** The role of that organization was twofold: (a) to certify counselors nationally in the new specialty of mental health counseling and (b) to address the lack of counselor licensure at that time (Weikel, 1994). The NACCMHC managed the credentialing of Certified Clinical Mental Health Counselors (CCMHCs) from July 1979 to July 1993. In 1993, the NACCMHC affiliated with the National Board for Certified Counselors (NBCC) and the Association for Counselor Education and Supervision, and the CCMHC credential was transferred to NBCC management (NBCC, 2007).

AMHCA also played a critical role in the formulation of accreditation standards for mental health counseling programs, eventually adopted by the Council for Accreditation of Counseling and Related Educational Programs (CACREP). In 1981, CACREP had been established as an independent, incorporated body to accredit counselor education programs and to revise training standards. The significant AMHCA players in the development of training standards for mental health counselors during those early years were Jim Messina, Gary Seiler, Robert Stripling, Edward Beck, and David Brooks. By 1987, their diligent and comprehensive efforts resulted in the AMHCA board of directors accepting the comprehensive training standards for mental health counselors that required mental health counseling training programs to include at least 60 semester credit hours and a minimum of 1,000 hours of clinical instruction. CACREP accepted and incorporated, with some modifications, AMHCA's document on standards, establishing a new and separate mental health counseling track. AMHCA also promoted specialty accreditation within the broader mental health counseling area, including marriage/couples and family counseling. CACREP also eventually adopted specialty standards for marriage and family counselors that were similar to those

proposed by AMHCA in the mid-1980s (Seiler, Brooks, & Beck, 1987; Smith & Robinson, 1995).

From its inception, obtaining licensure laws for mental health counselors was a major priority for AMHCA. At the time of its incorporation in 1976, only Virginia had passed a counselor licensure law. By 1989, counselors were licensed in 28 states; received benefits from the Civilian Health and Medical Program of the Uniformed Services; and were recognized by the National Institute of Mental Health, other federal agencies, the U.S. Congress, and several private insurance carriers. By 1991, 15 years after its inception, AMHCA had achieved mental health counselor national certification, licensure in 36 states, and standards for accreditation of training programs (Fong & Sherrard, 1991; Weikel & Palmo, 1989). Presently, Licensed Mental Health Counselors, also referred to as Licensed Professional Counselors, number 80,000 strong in the United States and are recognized as licensed practitioners in 49 states, the District of Columbia, and Puerto Rico (AMHCA, 2004).

The publications developed by the AMHCA in late 1978 and early 1979 also helped to establish a distinct professional identity for mental health counselors. Under the initial leadership of Colleen Haffner and Janet (Asher) Anderson, the *AMHCA News,* now the *AMHCA Advocate,* was devoted to the communication of professional news. The *American Mental Health Counselors Association Journal,* now the *Journal of Mental Health Counseling (JMHC),* was committed to supporting the accumulation of scholarly literature for the profession. Slightly more than 12,000 people received *JMHC* by 1989, making it the second highest circulated counseling journal at the time. Furthermore, *JMHC* had become a rather selective periodical, with only 25% of the more than 100-plus manuscripts submitted yearly being accepted for publication (Gerstein, 1989; Weikel, 1994). Today, *JMHC* is an influential peer-reviewed, scholarly journal devoted to addressing issues significant in the field of mental health counseling from both research (experimental) and clinical (practice) perspectives.

AMHCA's Mission

Currently, AMHCA's ongoing mission is to promote and enhance the mental health counseling profession through licensing, advocacy, education, and professional development. Virginia Moore (personal communication, February 17, 2007) of AMHCA's national office stated,

> the long-term vision statement is to be the national organization representing licensed mental health counselors and state chapters, with consistent standards of education, training, licensing, practice, advocacy and ethics. Our goals are to provide the best services possible to our members, state chapters and consumers. We support our student members through grants and the funding of a student committee. We work to provide a variety of quality member benefits and services. We will continue our legislative work for licensure in all 50 states and for equality with other professional mental health providers.

AMHCA has always encouraged and supported legislative activities at the federal, state, and local levels affecting all aspects of the mental health counseling profession. This organization continues to recognize that strong support and legislative advocacy can result in the inclusion of mental health counselors in federal health care programs. AMHCA actively participates in advocacy efforts through advocating in the U.S. Congress for recognition of mental health counselors as providers in such federal programs as Medicare and Medicaid. A recent success of such efforts was realized with the passage of federal legislation establishing licensed professional counselors as mental health specialists within the Department of Veterans Affairs (VA) health care system. AMHCA executive director and chief executive officer Mark Hamilton said,

> The inclusion of licensed mental health counselors by the VA, and the quality of services they provide, will make it easier for those who served our nation and who are in need of mental health services to get the health care they need. Passage of this legislation could not have been achieved without the long-time collaborative efforts of AMHCA and ACA. (Barstow, 2007, p. 16)

Contributed by James Colangelo and Kristin Schaefer-Schiumo, Long Island University, C.W. Post Campus, Long Island, NY

References

American Mental Health Counselors Association. (2004). Hawaii becomes 48th state to license mental health counselors. *The Advocate, 27*(8), 12.

Barstow, S. (2007). Counselors claim major victory. *Counseling Today, 49*(7), 1, 16.

Fong, M. L., & Sherrard, P. A. D. (1991). Mental health counselor training: Directions for the 1990s. *Journal of Mental Health Counseling, 13,* 167–171.

Gerstein, L. H. (1989). The *Journal of Mental Health Counseling*: A tenth anniversary and a new beginning. *Journal of Mental Health Counseling, 11,* 3–5.

Hershenson, D. B., & Power, P. W. (1987). *Mental health counseling: Theory and practice.* New York: Pergamon Press.

National Board for Certified Counselors. (2007). *Statistics.* Retrieved March 20, 2008, from http://www.nbcc.org/stats

Seiler, G., Brooks, D. K., & Beck, E. S. (1987). Training standards of the American Mental Health Counselors Association: History, rationale, and implications. *Journal of Mental Health Counseling, 9,* 199–205.

Smith, H. B., & Robinson, G. P. (1995). Mental health counseling: Past, present, and future. *Journal of Counseling & Development, 74,* 158–161.

Weikel, W. J. (1985). The American Mental Health Counselors Association. *Journal of Counseling & Development, 63,* 457–460.

Weikel, W. J. (1994). A brief history of the American Mental Health Counselors Association. *AMHCA Leader Handbook.* Retrieved January 10, 2007, from http://www.amhca.org

Weikel, W. J., & Palmo, A. J. (1989). The evolution and practice of mental health counseling. *Journal of Mental Health Counseling, 11,* 7–25.

Additional Resource

Weikel, W. J. (1996). The mental health counselors association. In W. J. Weikel & A. J. Palmo (Eds.), *Foundations of mental health counseling* (2nd ed., pp. 30–37). Springfield, IL: Thomas.

■ American Rehabilitation Counseling Association

The **American Rehabilitation Counseling Association (ARCA)** is an organization focused on improving and enriching the lives of people with disabilities. ARCA also attends to the quality of the field of rehabilitation counseling and works to increase public awareness of rehabilitation counseling. A division of the American Counseling Association, ARCA recently celebrated its 50th anniversary and is one of several rehabilitation counseling organizations in the profession. With approximately 800 members, the organization consists of practitioners, educators, and students working in different areas such as educational, federal, private, and nonprofit settings.

ARCA is active in outreach and education to help increase access and opportunities for people with disabilities. One way ARCA has been involved is through legislative activities. Not only did ARCA support the Americans With Disabilities Act, but ARCA members were also involved in the drive to establish the standard in the field for rehabilitation counselors. Through the reauthorizing of the Rehabilitation Act, the definition of a Certified Rehabilitation Counselor (CRC) was established. ARCA also helped to create the Council on Rehabilitation Education, which decides what training is required for the CRC.

ARCA contributed to establishing a code of ethics in 1987 and adopted a scope of practice for rehabilitation counselors in 1994. ARCA initiated student chapters of the organization in 1994 and recently began offering liability insurance to rehabilitation counselors. Throughout the history of ARCA, there have been attempts to connect or combine ARCA with the National Rehabilitation Counseling Association. Although this has been unsuccessful so far, the two organizations still collaborate informally.

In keeping with the goal to educate and promote, ARCA publishes the academic journal, *Rehabilitation Counseling Bulletin,* and a quarterly newsletter, *The ARCA News,* which focuses on current issues in the organization. ARCA continues to focus on maintaining the excellence of the rehabilitation counseling profession, increasing public awareness of rehabilitation counseling, and addressing new issues in the field. In its efforts to improve the lives of people with disabilities, ARCA strives toward the ultimate goal of enhancing the development of people with disabilities throughout their lives by eliminating physical and attitudinal barriers.

Contributed by Karen Tsukada,
University of Delaware, Newark, DE

Additional Resources

Peterson, D., Hautamaki, J., & Hershenson, D. (2006). Reflections on our past and prospects for our future: A survey of the members of the American Rehabilitation Counseling Association. *Rehabilitation Counseling Bulletin, 50*(1), 4–13.

American Rehabilitation Counseling Association Web site: http://www.arcaweb.org/

American School Counselor Association

The **American School Counselor Association (ASCA),** a division of the American Counseling Association (ACA), is dedicated to the support and ongoing professional development of professional school counselors. ASCA consists of a large group of people, more than 20,000 globally, with similar objectives. ASCA holds a conference each year that includes an annual meeting and a variety of educational sessions covering many topical issues affecting professional school counselors from the elementary to the university levels.

The mission of ASCA is to represent professional school counselors and school counselor educators and to promote professionalism and high ethical standards of practice. A goal of ASCA is to increase the ability of students to achieve academic, personal/social, and career success and to enhance the image and viability of the school counseling profession through professional development, collaboration, professional interest networks, and a host of supportive resources. System change and advocacy are important aspects of improvement of the delivery of services to consumers. The *ASCA National Model* is an example of attempts to standardize and elevate the excellent work done by professional school counselors.

ASCA promotes research and evaluation through publications, including the journal *Professional School Counseling* and the ASCA *School Counselor* magazine. Other high-profile initiatives include the promotion of National School Counseling Week.

Contributed by Mark Lepore,
Chatham University, Pittsburgh, PA

Additional Resources

American School Counselor Association Web site: http://www.schoolcounselor.org

American Counseling Association Web site: http://www.counseling.org

ASCA National Model Web site: http://www.schoolcounselor.org/content.asp?contentid=134

Animal Assisted Therapy

Animal assisted therapy (AAT) is the integration of qualified animals as therapeutic agents in the counseling process.

AAT uses the relationship between people and animals to provide therapeutic services for persons in need. It is used as an adjunct to counseling, whereby the client's interaction with a therapy animal facilitates or contributes to the client's healing and development. Three levels of human assessment are required for AAT: (a) client screening for appropriateness of AAT, (b) documentation of the type and impact of client–therapy animal interactions, and (c) evaluation of the contribution of AAT toward therapeutic goals. The most common therapy animals are dogs and horses. Other common therapy animals are cats, rabbits, birds, hamsters, and gerbils. Less common therapy animals include aquarium fish, dolphins, farm animals, llamas, camels, and elephants.

The discovery of therapeutic benefits of AAT in mental health was first credited to child psychologist Boris Levinson. Levinson found he could make significant progress with a particular disturbed child only when his dog Jingles was present in therapy sessions. He later found that many children who were withdrawn and noncommunicative would interact positively with the dog. Much of Levinson's work with Jingles is documented in his book *Pet-Oriented Child Psychotherapy* (1969).

AAT techniques can be as simple as inviting a client to pet or hold a therapy animal or as complex as teaching a client to care for or train an animal. Victims of trauma often find comfort in holding or petting a therapy animal. Clients who are socially inhibited can learn to communicate more effectively by initially communicating with a therapy animal. Clients with low self-esteem can build self-confidence by commanding a therapy dog to perform obedience skills and tricks or by establishing competency as a rider with a therapy horse. Horses and dogs are especially effective at therapy work because they are socially inclined; that is, they are herd and pack animals that desire to be with humans, and they are very adept at responding to social cues. Therapy horses and dogs give immediate feedback to a client about the client's current attitude and behavior. At the same time, a client often finds it easier to trust a therapy dog or horse than humans because the animals are honest about how they feel and do not judge persons for what they have done or experienced outside of the relationship with the animal. Because the client–therapy animal relationship is vital to the effect of AAT on the client, a counselor encourages and reflects client–therapy animal interactions that are of therapeutic significance and assists the client in generalizing experiences with a therapy animal to better understanding self and others. Some commonly observed benefits of AAT include the following:

- A client may have an increased motivation to participate in counseling out of a desire to spend time with a therapy animal. This is especially the case for children and resistant clients.
- A client may receive healing nurturance and affection through physical contact with a therapy animal. Several research studies have demonstrated a relationship between interaction with a therapy animal and psychophysiological gains.

- A therapy animal may shift a client's focus away from disabling pain, thereby enabling the client to gain greater benefits from counseling. This has been demonstrated for clients with psychiatric disorders and trauma victims.
- A client may experience unconditional acceptance from a therapy animal, thereby facilitating a greater sense of safety and trust in the therapeutic relationship.
- A client may be able to form a more trusting relationship with a professional counselor if the client observes that the counselor has a positive relationship with a therapy animal.
- A client may be able to achieve goals not otherwise possible without the assistance of a therapy animal. Interactions with a therapy animal can mimic life challenges and growth opportunities in a less threatening and more entertaining atmosphere.

AAT may be applied as directive or nondirective, structured or unstructured interventions. It can be effectively practiced in group, individual, and couple or family formats. It is appropriate for all age and ethnic groups; however, sensitivity to differing individual and multicultural attitudes toward animals must be maintained. Clients with certain animal phobias may not be appropriate for AAT, and precautions for clients with allergies to animals must be taken. Clients with aggressive tendencies or with abusive histories toward animals should not be allowed to participate in AAT, or they should be allowed to participate only under strict supervision. All AAT must be practiced with the safety and welfare of both humans and animals in mind.

Professional counselors who work with a therapy animal should receive proper training in AAT assessment and techniques. Qualification as an AAT team is achieved by successful completion of AAT training by the human therapist and a standardized evaluation of the human–animal therapy team. In order to pass the evaluation, animals must be healthy and well-groomed, well-behaved, friendly and sociable, nonaggressive, nonfearful; where appropriate, they must respond to species-specific commands, such as obedience commands for dogs and riding or pulling commands for horses.

Professional training and certification in AAT is available through national organizations such as Delta Society, Therapy Dogs International, Equine Assisted Growth and Learning Association (EAGALA) and the EAGALA subdivision Equine Facilitated Mental Health Association, and the North American Riding for the Handicapped Association.

Contributed by Cynthia K. Chandler,
University of North Texas, Denton, TX

Reference

Levinson, B. M. (1969). *Pet-oriented child psychotherapy.* Springfield, IL: Thomas.

Additional Resources

Chandler, C. K. (2005). *Animal assisted therapy in counseling.* New York: Routledge/Taylor & Francis.

Fine, A. H. (Ed.). (2000). *Animal-assisted therapy: Theoretical foundations and guidelines for practice.* San Diego, CA: Academic Press.

Levinson, B. M., & Mallon, G. P. (1997). *Pet-oriented child psychotherapy* (2nd ed.). Springfield, IL: Thomas.

Anxiety Disorders

The predominant feature shared by all of the diagnosable **anxiety disorders** appearing in the *Diagnostic and Statistical Manual of Mental Disorders* (4th ed., text rev.; *DSM-IV-TR;* American Psychiatric Association [APA], 2000) is the presence of panic, increased arousal, excessive worry, or other signs of anxiety that cause clinically significant distress or impairment in a person's social or occupational functioning or in his or her ability to fulfill other important life roles. Normal life experiences, culturally expected reactions, and developmental or age-appropriate changes that cause anxiety, but do not result in clinically significant distress or impairment, typically do not warrant an anxiety disorder diagnosis. For example, normal worry about important life situations, occasional periods of life stress, and situational nervousness often share similarities with diagnosable anxiety disorders; however, these expectable reactions typically do not warrant a mental disorder diagnosis. Furthermore, competent diagnosis of anxiety disorders requires an understanding of variations in symptom presentation that can result from individual differences due to such common demographics as age, gender, ethnocultural background, religious affiliation, socioeconomic status, or nation of origin.

The following variety of anxiety disorders are included in this class of diagnoses: panic disorder without agoraphobia, panic disorder with agoraphobia, and agoraphobia without a history of panic disorder; specific phobia and social phobia; obsessive-compulsive disorder; posttraumatic stress disorder, and acute stress disorder; generalized anxiety disorder; and anxiety disorder due to a general medical condition, substance-induced anxiety disorder, and anxiety disorder not otherwise specified.

The first of two primary characteristics of **panic disorder without agoraphobia** is the presence of recurring, unexpected panic attacks. The features of a panic attack include a specific, brief time period of about 10 minutes during which the person experiences uncomfortably intense fear or panic, along with several of the following symptoms: pounding heart or accelerated heart rate, sweating, trembling, breathing difficulty, chest pain or choking feelings, nausea, lightheadedness or dizziness, feeling of unreality or detachment from surroundings, fear of losing control or becoming crazy, fear of imminent death, numbness or tingling, or chills or hot flashes (APA, 2000). The second primary characteristic of panic disorder without agoraphobia is a period of 1 month or more after a panic attack during which the person worries persistently about having future panic attacks; worries about losing control, becoming crazy, experiencing a heart attack, or another consequence of having panic attacks; or substantially changes behavior related to the attacks. If the panic attacks are better accounted for by another anxiety disorder or another diagnosable mental disorder, a diagnosis of panic disorder is not normally made.

The primary characteristic of **agoraphobia without history of panic disorder** is the presence of agoraphobia. The features of agoraphobia include anxiety about being in places or situations from which it might be difficult to escape or embarrassing to leave should a panic attack or panic-like symptoms occur and avoidance of these places or situations or endurance of them with great distress (APA, 2000). Examples of situations that often cause distress and, therefore, are avoided by individuals experiencing agoraphobia include being in a crowd or standing in a line; traveling by automobile, bus, or train; being on a bridge or in a tunnel; or being outside of home. Enduring such situations sometimes requires the presence of a companion. If the agoraphobic symptoms are better accounted for by another anxiety disorder or another diagnosable mental disorder, a diagnosis of agoraphobia is not normally made. **Panic disorder with agoraphobia** describes a situation in which recurrent, unexpected panic attacks occur and are followed by at least 1 month of consequences as described for panic disorder, agoraphobia is also present, and the symptoms are not better accounted for by another anxiety disorder or other mental disorder.

Specific phobia and social phobia are narrowly focused anxiety disorders (APA, 2000). The primary characteristic of **specific phobia** is a persistent, clinically significant fear that is excessive or unreasonable, brought on by the anticipation of or presence of a specific event, situation, or object in the environment. Clinically significant fears of dogs, elevators, heights, and receiving an injection are examples. The primary characteristics of **social phobia** include persistent, clinically significant fear of one or more social or performance situations in which the individual feels under scrutiny by others and fears exhibiting anxiety symptoms or acting in some other way that will be embarrassing or humiliating and having panic-attack-like reactions when exposed to the feared social situation. Avoidance of or anxiety during the feared social situations causes clinically significant distress or interferes with functioning. In adults, there is awareness that the fear is excessive or unreasonable. Symptom variations occurring in children and adolescents are outlined in the *DSM-IV-TR* (APA, 2000) for both specific and social phobias.

The primary characteristics of **obsessive-compulsive disorder** are the presence of obsessions, compulsions, or both; the obsessions or compulsions cause clinically significant distress, are very time consuming (e.g., require more than 1 hour daily), or interfere with social or occupational functioning or the ability to fulfill other important life roles; and in adults, awareness that the obsessions or compulsions are excessive or unreasonable (APA, 2000). Some individuals experience obsessive-compulsive disorder with poor insight, indicating difficulty recognizing the symptoms as excessive or unreasonable. When another mental disorder better describes the obsessions or compulsions, that diagnosis is used instead; examples are trichotillomania, characterized by compulsive hair pulling, and eating disorders, characterized in part by obsessions related to food and body weight.

Posttraumatic stress disorder (PTSD) and acute stress disorder both occur in response to trauma. The primary characteristics of PTSD are exposure to a traumatic event, persistent re-experience of the event, general numbing of responsiveness and persistent avoidance of stimuli related to the trauma, and increased arousal (APA, 2000). To warrant a diagnosis of PTSD, symptoms must be present for a least 1 month and cause clinically significant distress or impairment. The disorder may occur at any time after the trauma. In the diagnosis, trauma includes any event in which there is actual or threatened serious injury; death; and danger to one's or another person's physical integrity (as in the case of sexual assault) and in which the person reacted with helplessness, horror, or extreme fear. According to the diagnosis, exposure requires that a person experience, witness, or be confronted by the traumatic event. For example, a child who witnesses physical abuse of a parent, but is not the victim of physical abuse herself or himself, meets the criteria. Symptoms of re-experiencing the trauma may include recurrent distressing recollections, frightening dreams, the illusion the event is recurring, and psychological or physiological hyperreactivity to cues of the event. Avoidance symptoms may include avoiding associated thoughts, feelings, or conversations; avoiding activities, places, or people; diminished interest and restricted affect; and other means of avoidance. Increased arousal symptoms include sleep difficulties, anger, concentration problems, and hypervigilance or heightened startle reactions. **Acute stress disorder** describes onset of characteristic posttraumatic symptoms within 1 month after exposure to an extreme trauma and may be described as potentially leading to PTSD.

Generalized anxiety disorder is characterized by a period of at least 6 months during which the person experiences excessive worry or undue anxiety about multiple life events or situations at a level that causes clinically significant distress or interferes with social or occupational functioning or other important life roles; has difficulty controlling the worry; and experiences several characteristic symptoms, such as restlessness, fatigue, difficulty thinking or concentrating, irritability, muscle tension, and sleep difficulty (APA, 2000). As with obsessive-compulsive disorder, when another mental disorder better describes the worries and anxiety, that diagnosis is used instead; examples are separation anxiety, characterized by worry of being away from home, and anorexia nervosa, characterized by worry of gaining weight. Generalized anxiety disorder also is distinguished from expectable worry about life problems.

The remaining anxiety disorders indicate mood symptoms that are due to the direct physiological effects of a physical medical condition, as is the case with **anxiety disorder due to general medical condition,** or are due to intoxication, withdrawal, or the consequences of problematic substance use, as in the case with **substance-induced anxiety disorder.** Examples include anxiety symptoms due to hyperthyroidism (general medical condition) and anxiety symptoms due to caffeine intoxication (substance induced). The final diagnosis among the anxiety disorders, **anxiety disorder not otherwise specified,** describes situations in which an individual experiences clinically significant anxiety symptoms that do not meet the criteria for any other anxiety disorder and are not better captured by any other mental disorder diagnosis.

Contributed by
Alan M. "Woody" Schwitzer,
Old Dominion University, Norfolk, VA

Reference

American Psychiatric Association. (2000). *Diagnostic and statistical manual of mental disorders* (4th ed., text rev.). Washington, DC: Author.

Additional Resources

Neukrug, E., & Schwitzer, A. (2006). *Skills and tools for today's counselors and psychotherapists: From natural helping to professional counseling.* Belmont, CA: Thomson Brooks/Cole.

Seligman, L. (2004). *Diagnosis and treatment planning* (3rd ed.). New York: Plenum Press.

Aptitude Testing

Aptitude testing is a subset of ability testing, otherwise known as assessment in the cognitive realm. Aptitude testing attempts to measure an individual's aptitude, or what a person is capable of learning; thus, the assessment of aptitude is an attempt to predict how well an individual may do in the future. An individual has aptitude in a number of realms, and aptitude testing has been used to assess an individual's aptitude in a variety of these areas, including the assessment of intelligence through the use of intelligence tests, learning in schools through the use of cognitive ability tests, and ability to do well in vocations through the use of special or multiple aptitude tests.

Intelligence Tests

Intelligence tests measure a broad range of intellectual ability and provide an assessment of an individual's aptitude in the area of overall cognitive functioning. Because the definition of intelligence has varied greatly over the years, some controversy exists over what to measure. The more traditional models, such as those of Spearman and Vernon, assume there is a "g factor" that underlies the development of intelligence as well as specific factors that address specific types of learning (e.g., musical ability, logical reasoning). In addition, scholars like Cattell assumed that intelligence was both genetic and learned and that there was a high heritability factor for the genetic portion of intelligence. More recently, scholars like Sternberg and Gardner have criticized these more traditional conceptions of intelligence and have suggested that in assessing intelligence other areas such as creativity, musical ability, kinesthetic ability, and interpersonal ability, to name a few, should be assessed (see Intelligence; Intelligence Testing).

The more traditional and widely used intelligence tests rely on the more traditional definitions of aptitude and are often used to assess for mental retardation, giftedness, learning disabilities, and general cognitive functioning. These kinds of intelligence tests are almost always given one-on-one by a well-trained examiner who generally has taken an advanced course in the assessment of intelligence. Intelligence tests tend to provide a number of subtests that assess for a broad range of intellectual functioning, and these subtests can be subsequently subdivided to assess for possible learning disabilities. For instance, many intelligence tests offer assessment of verbal intelligence, nonverbal intelligence, memory, attention span, comprehension, sequencing ability, and attention to detail. Some personality factors can also be assessed by observing how the individual approaches the assessment process. Some of the more popular intelligence tests today are the Stanford–Binet, the Wechsler intelligence tests, and the Kaufman Assessment Battery for Children (see Intelligence Testing).

Cognitive Ability Tests

Cognitive ability tests assess aptitude in the area of ability to do well in school and make predictions about the future, such as how an individual might do in future grades, college, and graduate school. They are different from achievement tests, which tend to be content specific (e.g., science, social studies), in that they tend to assess broad areas of cognitive ability, such as verbal ability, math ability, and analytical ability. Although often given in a group format to large numbers of students (e.g., a whole grade), some cognitive ability tests are given individually, especially when a student may have a learning problem. The accuracy of the assessment is increased through a one-on-one administration. Although group-administered tests of cognitive ability can generally be given by a responsible individual who may not have advanced training in assessment (e.g., a teacher), individually administered cognitive ability tests are often given by highly trained examiners who have extensive knowledge of learning disabilities.

Unlike the results of achievement tests, the results of K–12 cognitive ability tests are often analyzed by professionals who are trained in assessment techniques, and the results are used to devise instructional strategies for teachers. Students who score higher on cognitive ability tests (e.g., overall ability to do well in school) compared with their scores on achievement tests (e.g., specific learning at grade level) may be struggling with learning disabilities, problems at home, poor teaching, lack of motivation, or other variables that cause them not to be able to focus on grade-level learning. Two of the more common K–12 cognitive ability tests are the Otis-Lennon School Ability Test and the Cognitive Ability Test.

College or graduate school entrance examinations of cognitive ability are used to make predictions about how well an individual will do in postsecondary education, and they do predict about as well as high school or college grades and predict better than most other forms of assessment. College or graduate school entrance examinations are used along with a variety of other predictors (e.g., interviews, essays, extracurricular activities) when making important decisions, such as acceptance for college or graduate school. The SAT and the ACT are two cognitive ability tests that predict how well individuals do in college. The Graduate Record Examination, Miller Analogy Test, Law School Aptitude Test, and Medical College Admission Test are cognitive ability tests that predict how well potential graduate students might do.

Multiple Aptitude Tests

Multiple aptitude tests measure a number of distinct and homogenous aspects of ability and are generally used to predict aptitude in a variety of occupations. They are distinct from cognitive ability tests because of the wide variety of areas they measure (often eight or nine areas) and because they focus mostly on vocational assessment (e.g., mechanical ability, clerical ability, spatial ability, and so forth). To refine these tests, factor analysis is used to ensure that the varying subtests assessed are pure, that is, that each subtest is measuring a separate area of ability. The Armed Services Vocational Aptitude Battery (ASVAB) is the most widely used multiple aptitude test battery and is given at no cost by the military in many high schools. It consists of eight tests, including General Science, Arithmetic Reasoning, Word Knowledge, Paragraph Comprehension, Mathematics Knowledge, Electronics Information, Auto Shop Information, and Mechanical Comprehension. The Differential Aptitude Tests measure aptitudes for students from Grades 7–12, has similar subtests to those on the ASVAB, and includes a career interest inventory to cross-reference aptitude and interests for use in career counseling.

Individual or Special Aptitude Tests

Individual or special aptitude tests measure one clearly defined homogenous area of ability and are used to make predictions about ability in specific vocations. They are particularly useful when an individual is interested in pursuing a specific occupation or when decisions are being made by organizations or schools about an individual's ability to do well in a specific area. Dozens of such tests exist, the following being somewhat of a representative sample: The Clerical Test Battery, the U.S. Postal Service's 470 Battery Exam, Wiesen's Test of Mechanical Aptitude, and the Music Aptitude Profile.

Important information to consider when selecting a specific aptitude test includes the purpose of the test, the author(s) of the tests, the test publisher, the length of the test, the cost of the test, and test worthiness (e.g., validity, reliability, practicality, and cross-cultural fairness).

Contributed by Ed Neukrug,
Old Dominion University, Norfolk, VA

Additional Resources

Drummond, R. J. (2004). *Appraisal procedures for counselors and other helping professionals* (5th ed.). Upper Saddle River, NJ: Pearson.

Neisser, U., Boodoo, G., Bouchard, T. J., Jr., Boykin, A. W., Brody, N., Ceci, S. J., et al. (1996). Intelligence: Knowns and unknowns. *American Psychologist, 52,* 77–101.

Neukrug, E. S., & Fawcett, R. C. (2006). *Essentials of testing and assessment: A practical guide for counselors, social workers, and psychologists.* Belmont, CA: Brooks/Cole.

Spearman, C. (1970). *The abilities of man.* New York: AMS Press. (Original work published in 1932)

■ Arab Americans, Counseling

Arab Americans are individuals whose ancestry is from the Arab Middle East, also known as the League of Arab States. The League is made up of 22 countries spanning Asia and North Africa. It is important to note that the geographic region often referred to as the Middle East includes many non-Arab countries and peoples (e.g., Turkey, Afghanistan). Most, but not all, Arab League States are Arabic speaking. The Arab Middle East encompasses many religious faiths, but it is predominantly Muslim.

Demographics

Arab Americans are diverse in country of origin, religion, language, and other characteristics. Within the overall Arab American population, approximately 40% of individuals self-identify as Lebanese, whereas another 20% self-identify as Arab. Approximately 12% self-identify as Egyptian, and another 12% as Syrian. Smaller groups of Arab Americans self-identify as Palestinian, Moroccan, Iraqi, or Other Arab (Arab American Institute, 2008).

The **Arab American Institute,** a leading advocacy group for Arab Americans and their issues, estimates the overall population of Arab Americans in the United States is at least 3 million. Although the U.S. census definition for Arab Americans has changed numerous times over the course of U.S. immigration history, Arab Americans today are classified as White despite how individuals themselves might self-define. This phenomenon has contributed to inaccuracies in official census counts for this group of Americans. Approximately 10 to 15 cities around the United States have substantial, close-knit Arab American communities, or enclaves, that are rich in Arabic heritage and tradition, with Detroit, Los Angeles, Chicago, New York, and Houston being among the leading cities in this regard. Most U.S. cities, however, have identifiable Arab American communities, some with their own community centers, mosques or churches, and restaurants.

Although the majority of Arabs in the Middle East practice Islam, only about one quarter of Arab Americans are Muslim, with another quarter being Orthodox Christian and approximately 35% self-identifying as Catholic. Compared with other ethnic groups, the Arab American community is composed of younger and more foreign-born individuals and families. They tend to represent higher education and income levels than the national averages.

Immigration History

Arab Americans have emigrated from the Arab Middle East in four separate waves. The first of these occurred during the turn of the 20th century, paralleling the immigration of many other ethnic groups in search of economic opportunity. In addition, many of these Arab immigrants hoped to escape the Ottoman Empire, which was an Islamic, or Muslim, regime. This group was predominantly Christian; uneducated; and largely from Palestine, Syria, and Jordan. The members of this group created the foundation of the mercantile trade in many present-day Arab enclaves and quickly embraced the values and traditions of their new lives in the United States.

The second and third waves primarily comprised educated Muslims. Palestinians, Egyptians, Syrians, Jordanians, Iraqis, Lebanese, and Yemeni individuals and families came to the United States, mostly due to dissatisfaction with sociopolitical issues in their native countries. These immigrants became assimilated both professionally and economically while frequently maintaining the cultural traditions and values of their countries of origin.

Most recently, since the early 1990s, the fourth wave has primarily consisted of refugees from Iraq. Like other refugee groups, these individuals and families experience multiple acculturation stressors and traumas. In addition, these refugees maintain strong homeland ties with the hope of possibly returning there someday.

Cultural Values

Although the majority of Arab Americans are non-Muslim, the traditions and values of Arab and Muslim cultures are intertwined. In general, Arab Americans place a high value on their respective religious faiths and traditions. For Muslims in particular, Islamic traditions are those most recognized. Islam, the predominant religion within the Arab Middle East, is a religion with beginnings between the 7th and 10th centuries CE. The **Prophet Muhammed,** according to Muslim faith, was a messenger of God. These messages are stated in the **Qur'an,** the holy book of Islam. The Qur'an represents a continuation of the Bible's Old and New Testaments, with its messages founded upon those of Judaism and Christianity. The **Five Pillars,** or Islamic traditions, include a belief in Allah, or God; five daily worship periods; fasting during the holy month of Ramadan; charitable donations for economic justice causes; and a once-in-a-lifetime journey to Mecca, the Islamic holy city.

In addition to important holidays celebrated in the United States, such as Thanksgiving, Christian Arab Americans are likely to commemorate traditional Christian holidays as well as additional Christian traditions from their countries of origin. Many Muslim Arab Americans also celebrate Eid al-Fitr and Eid al-Adha, which mark the end of the holy month of Ramadan and the end of the pilgrimage to Mecca, respectively. In addition, important values include accountability to God, both fate and self-responsibility, global unity, racial equality, peace, and social harmony. Outside the spiritual or religious area, values of collectivist, extended family; educational and economic achievement; and civic engagement are held by Arab Americans overall.

Current Events

Historically, the Arab Middle East has had troubled relationships with the United States and other Western countries.

Chronologically, the Crusades, the Ottoman Empire, the Palestine–Israel conflict, and the Iraq wars have served to perpetuate the notion that Arab Americans pose a threat to U.S. interests. Arab American advocacy groups work to combat the stereotypical and inaccurate images of Arabs as terrorists and as individuals intending harm to all Americans that are often depicted in the media and other places. Legal issues, particularly around immigration quotas and restrictions, have historically been problematic for Arab Americans.

According to advocacy groups, the most salient current issues for Arab American communities in the United States are the Palestine–Israel conflict, the war with Iraq, and profiling and civil liberties violations. In particular, the latter two issues, having been triggered by the tragic attack on the World Trade Center buildings in New York City on September 11, 2001, seem to have also resulted in the regeneration of an immigration quota for individuals characterized as being Middle Eastern.

Counseling Issues

Like individuals from other ethnic backgrounds, Arab Americans as a group have many resiliencies as well as risks. Particularly in the post–"9/11" climate, anxiety and depression may be more prevalent among this population. Mental health concerns tend to be experienced and reported as physical ailments rather than psychological ones, and, therefore, medical treatment is more likely to be sought than counseling services. As with other groups, there is still a stigma attached to the idea of psychological treatment. In addition, even within counseling services, a medical model may sometimes prove most effective, wherein the practitioner is the expert who provides concrete advice and guidance.

To facilitate culturally competent counseling, mental health practitioners should attempt to learn about their clients' backgrounds in terms of demographic issues such as gender, age, religion, and sexual orientation, as well as educational level and socioeconomic status. Status of residency or citizenship, length of time in the United States, at-home spoken language, and country of origin also represent important information.

Because of the backlash after the events of September 11, 2001, exploring clients' discrimination experiences and history is important in assessing levels of immigration trauma, even for later generations of Arab American immigrants. In this context, ethnic identity development will often come into play in counseling situations. For example, stereotyping through popular media sources, educational texts, and so on may affect an individual's level of ethnic identity development as an Arab American as well as an American in general. For more recent immigrants, particularly refugees, depression, anxiety, and even posttraumatic stress disorder may be more prevalent and may be heightened by experiences with discrimination and profiling.

Effective counseling is most likely to occur if these risks and resiliencies are fully explored. Cognitive-behavioral and problem-solving strategies, such as solution-focused counseling, have been reported by Arab American counselors as more effective than insight-based approaches, such as psychodynamic counseling and therapy. A benevolent authority role, such as may be the case in a medical practitioner model, also seems to be well received by Arab American clients.

Contributed by
Sylvia C. Nassar-McMillan,
North Carolina State University,
Raleigh, NC

Reference

Arab American Institute. (2008). *Demographics.* Retrieved August 19, 2008, from http://www.aaiusa.org/Arab-Americans/22/demographics

Additional Resources

Arab American Institute Web site: http://www.aaiusa.org/
Council on Islamic Education Web site: http://www.cie.org/
Dwairy, M. (2006). *Counseling and psychotherapy with Arabs and Muslims: A culturally sensitive approach.* New York: Teachers College Press.

Asian Americans, Counseling

Several questions are important to address when considering the topic of counseling Asian Americans. First, who makes up this population? Second, what are some of the shared values of Asian Americans? Third, what are some of the presenting problems encountered by this group? Last, how do these values affect Asian Americans' willingness to seek counseling, the type of counseling that may be more effective with this population, and the meshing of counselor and client worldviews?

Demographics

Asian Americans are the second (or first if grouped with Pacific Islanders) fastest growing ethnic minority group in the United States. Chinese, Japanese, Filipinos, Indochinese, Indians, Vietnamese, and Koreans are examples of some of the groups that are considered Asian Americans, but more than 40 disparate cultural groups are represented in this broad classification. There is diversity in their language, cultural and religious practices, history of and reasons for immigration to the United States, degree of identification with the mainstream American culture and their own culture (i.e., ethnic identity and level of acculturation), socioeconomic status, political and financial backgrounds, and residential setting of their countries of origin (i.e., rural, suburban, urban). It is important that professional counselors, while understanding the shared generalities of Asian American culture, not perceive clients from this group as homogeneous. Use of a "cookie cutter" mold to categorize Asian Americans will continue to foster stereotypes and misconceptions and ignore the uniqueness of the culture and individuality of each client.

Values

The values discussed here are general considerations and may not apply to every Asian American. **Filial piety** relates to parental respect and family interdependence, loyalty, dependence, and trust. Individual achievements are attributed to family accomplishments, and individual failures are perceived as shame to the family. For example, the success of a student in school is seen as successful parenting. Conversely, school failure can be associated with family shame. It is important for Asian Americans to "save face" and protect the family name; therefore, problems may be minimized or hidden to avoid stigmatization. **Community** (collectivism) supersedes the individual (individualism). Respect for and deference to elders and living with and importance of extended family prevail. **Hierarchy** and **authority** are evident and to be respected. Fathers remain particularly important figures in this patriarchal society. The importance of self-control, emphasis on nonverbal communication, and emotional circumspection are often stressed, as are exhibiting poise and calmness in times of highly emotional distress and modesty in one's accomplishments. These tendencies, along with a focus on compliance and conformity, help to maintain familial harmony. The emphasis on educational and occupational success has already been addressed. Shame, guilt, and threats may be used to obtain compliance from family members. Although Asian Americans belong to a variety of religious orientations (e.g., Buddhist, Islam, Hindu), ancestral worship is a key factor across many of these beliefs. One of the main issues professional counselors must wrestle with in counseling Asian Americans is that of the delicate balance of respecting Eastern values while addressing Western values as advocates of social and behavioral change.

Presenting Problems

Asian Americans face problems that all people experience. The **model minority myth** is an especially significant problem for this group. This myth creates the image that all Asian Americans emphasize high standards and are academically gifted, multitalented, and free of emotional and psychological problems. This perception leads to many counseling concerns, including anxiety and stigma regarding help seeking and insufficient access to needed services and support for those with lower education levels and socioeconomic statuses. Such positive biases also appear to minimize the existence of racism and associated prejudices.

In addition, Asian Americans may experience issues specific to their history. For example, due to biases and misunderstandings, Asian Americans have been subject to being placed in concentration camps, being denied rights, and experiencing cultural oppression and shock. For example, after the attack on Pearl Harbor in 1941, many Japanese Americans lost their homes, possessions, and jobs and were sent to internment camps. Korean Americans have struggled with language barriers and job discrimination. Many medical professionals of Korean heritage, although allowed to immigrate to the United States, have had their training and credentials denied, leaving them underemployed and running family-owned businesses. There have also been incidents of hate crimes (e.g., the killing of five Southeast Asian children in California) and racial profiling (e.g., the assumption that a Taiwanese American scientist was a Chinese spy).

Asian youth, specifically, may feel higher levels of distress from peer discrimination. Asian American students have been threatened, called racially insulting names, and excluded from activities. Depression, withdrawn behavior, and social isolation are common among these youth, as well as poorer self-images, inadequate social support, peer conflict, and dislike of school. In addition, because academic achievement and education are highly valued in the Asian culture, stress from the pressure to succeed and the stigma and shame of failure may be evident in Asian American youth.

The concepts of ethnic identity, acculturation, and assimilation are also important factors to consider in the counseling process. **Ethnic identity** refers to the values, behaviors, and expectations associated with a shared ancestry or genealogy and involves recognition by others as a distinct group. **Acculturation** is the modification of a group or individual as a result of contact with a different group. Although raised with traditional values and worldviews, there is adaptation to the customs and values of the mainstream culture in order to function. **Assimilation** involves identification with the values, behaviors, and expectations of the mainstream culture.

Individuals with high ethnic identity but who have minimally assimilated into the mainstream culture often are recent immigrants and elders in the cultural group. There may be little contact with the dominant culture and difficulty adjusting to "new ways." In regard to the acculturation process, stress may occur in the form of psychological, somatic, and social difficulties. For example, teens may be caught between their desire to "fit in" with their peers and the American culture and their loyalty to their parents and culture of origin. Individuals who become fully assimilated into the mainstream culture may abandon the richness of their cultures of origin and be ostracized by their families for abandoning their roots. It is possible to be high assimilated while maintaining high ethnic identity, called **bicultural adaptation.** Americanized versions of ethnic identities may evolve.

Counseling Use and Considerations

Numerous reasons exist to explain why Asian Americans underutilize counseling services. Language barriers may exist, and there may be a lack of knowledge about community resources and how to access them. Additional reasons include stigma around mental illness and the pressure to keep personal problems private in order to not shame the family and to avoid abandonment. Due to religious beliefs, some Asian Americans perceive that mental health and mental illness concerns may be "fixed" by supernatural powers and prescriptions for right conduct and beliefs. Psychology and counseling may be misunderstood and discouraged. "Thinking" about something can be seen as the cause of problems; introspection is not valued as a norm. Self-disclosure is seen as "immaturity," and a focus on affective intensity may be seen as unnecessary. Somatization of problems frequently occurs as a more acceptable means of expression, with a focus on medical and academic problems rather than on psychological ones. All of these factors can also lead to a higher drop-out rate in counseling. Clearly, a number of consider-

ations should be addressed when providing counseling to Asian Americans:

- Awareness of own biases and assumptions;
- Balance of knowledge of Asian American culture with a respect for individual diversity;
- Provision of linguistically relevant services;
- Professional counselor disclosure of credentials and training as perceived authority figures and experts;
- Consideration of a hierarchical counseling structure rather than egalitarian;
- Development of ways for parents to interact in a hierarchical manner with school administrators while not disengaging out of respect for this authority structure;
- Problem formulation and treatment goal specification embedded in a social and cultural context;
- Use of counseling approaches that are more problem-focused, concrete, directive, and task-immediacy oriented rather than open-ended and self-directed;
- Integration of an education approach with inclusion of homework assignments, focus on small steps, and acknowledgement of positive changes;
- Focus on somatic and academic issues as a way to build rapport with clients and focus on more psychologically oriented issues;
- Emphasis on receptivity and listening and support versus dynamic treatment and requirement of immediate verbal expression;
- Awareness of nonverbal differences, such as lack of eye contact being a sign of respect;
- Inclusion of and respect for family involvement and patriarchy as relevant;
- Avoidance of confrontation of parents to minimize blame;
- Acknowledgement of parental good intentions and efforts;
- Redirection away from shame and guilt to strength and skills;
- Avoidance of ignorance, minimization, and challenging of family value orientations;
- Assessment, acknowledgement of, and balance between the degree of monocultural (traditional versus assimilation) and bicultural (acculturation) identification among family members;
- Assessment and acknowledgement of ethnic identity development issues;
- A balance between cultural value orientations, such as interdependence, with realities of living in the Western world and developmental emphasis on individuation, so that clients may live successfully in both worlds.

Contributed by Barbara C. Trolley,
St. Bonaventure University,
St. Bonaventure, NY

Additional Resources

Comprehensive Literature Web site: http://www.janet.org/ janet_soc_services/ja_healthbiblio_mental.html

Barreto, R., & Segal, S. (2005). Use of mental health services by Asian Americans. *Psychiatric Services, 56,* 746–748.

Kurasaki, K., Okazaki, S., & Sue, S. (2002). *Asian American mental health assessment: Theories and methods.* New York: Kluwer Academic/Plenum.

Lee, E. (1997). *Working with Asian Americans: A guide for clinicians.* New York: Guilford Press.

Assertiveness Training

Assertiveness training involves the development of the specific skills that underlie assertive behavior. Some of the more familiar goals of assertiveness training have been to promote equality in human relationships, act in one's own best interests, stand up for oneself, express feelings honestly and comfortably, exercise personal rights, and acknowledge and respect the rights of others. There has been a shift in emphasis, however, in the past 30 years. The "me" generation has encouraged an emphasis on an individual's personal views and preferences; "I think," "I want," "I need," "you should," "you will," "you must," are all commonly overheard in families and places of work. Assertiveness has become aggressiveness in behavior and in attitude in many cases.

One of the most basic skills taught in assertiveness training is to be able to maintain a focus on a personal objective while communicating effectively with someone who is equally assertive but who has a different objective. Professional counselors will be dealing with clients whose personal behavior may be sufficiently assertive but who lack the understanding or the communication skills to be able to interact effectively with people who are equally assertive. When that is the problem, the professional counselor's ability to demonstrate one of the most basic concepts, the continuum of responses that range from nonassertive to assertive to aggressive, becomes an effective tool. That means that counselors must be comfortable in both confronting their clients and in providing support to them. This ability is the essence of assertive communication. Modeling the combination of confrontation and support in coaching interventions is what ultimately enables clients to acquire the communication skills to understand and resolve their problems.

Regardless of how specifically defined a person's goals are stated, they always involve these two main components: reducing anxiety (an internal component) and exhibiting effective interpersonal behavior (an external component). One of the basic concepts presented in most assertiveness training is an individual's personal rights. Typically, the list of rights includes the right to be treated with respect and the right to be appreciated or valued as a human being.

In most assertiveness training, time is spent on trying to identify the "causes" of a person's anxiety or inability to speak up or respond effectively to others. The individual hears "he or she made me feel _____," as if external factors cause his or her feelings. The most effective assertiveness training is based on the counselor helping clients accept that no one can "make" them feel a certain way.

The essence of assertiveness training involves identifying patterns of ineffective thinking and behaving, reframing those beliefs, and establishing new behavioral responses. One strategy that counselors can use to help clarify a client's specific vulnerability is to identify whether clients have the most trouble behaving effectively with family and friends or with strangers. A second important element is to discover whether a client is most troubled in situations that involve approaching or making requests of others or responding to the initiation of interaction or saying no to others' requests. Patterns within this 2 x 2 grid can be a starting point to explore the internal dialogue that results in client anxiety. Once the counselor has helped the client identify the situational factors that are most troublesome, the work can begin to decode the self-talk and explore more effective responses to the requirements of the situation.

The acronym **DESC** (pronounced desk) abbreviates the four key phrases: *D*escribe, *E*xpress, *S*pecify, *C*onsequences. To use DESC, a client objectively describes the behavior that he or she finds offensive to the person whom the client believes is trying to put him or her down, expresses how he or she feels about that behavior, specifies how he or she would like to see that behavior changed, and spells out the consequences of such a change. An example is a client who related an incident that has upset her and wants to learn how to respond effectively to it. A friend called her on the phone and immediately attacked in a loud voice saying,

> You know that I hate it when you make me wait for you to reply to my messages. I called you several hours ago and you ignored me. You are always doing that to me and I'm sick of it! It is rude and hurtful.

A suggested assertive response would be

> OK, I understand that you are upset, and if I had ignored your call that would have been rude. The fact is that I didn't receive the message. Being shouted at and accused of something I didn't do is upsetting to me. Unless you are willing to calm down so that we can discuss what happened in a more respectful tone, I am going to hang up. I value our friendship, and if I have been guilty of disappointing you, I do want to discuss that, but not until we are both able to do that more calmly.

Contributed by Phyliss Cooke,
Capella University, Minneapolis, MN,
and Daniel Eckstein,
Sam Houston State University,
Huntsville, TX

Additional Resources

Alberti, A., & Emmons, M. (2001). *Your perfect right.* Atascadero, CA: Impact.

Bishop, S. (2006). *Develop your assertiveness.* Philadelphia: Thompson-Shore.

Bower, S. (1991). *Asserting yourself.* Reading, MA: Addison Wesley.

Assessment, Key Ethical Issues

Assessment involves the collection and evaluation of data using a normative standard or a set of criteria, which can involve tests, inventories, interviews, or behavior observations, among other methods. Individual state licensing regulations, legal statutes, and professional associations, such as the American Counseling Association (ACA), have jurisdiction over the assessment practices of counselors. Ethical issues can arise with respect to assessment. Section E: "Evaluation, Assessment, and Interpretation" in ACA's (2005) *ACA Code of Ethics* provides a framework to discuss key ethical issues in assessment. This discussion includes the following key ethical issues: (a) counselors' competence to conduct assessments, (b) informed consent of clients and release of information, (c) diagnosis of mental health disorders, (d) selection and use of assessment methods, (e) conditions in which assessments are conducted, (f) diversity issues and clients, (g) interpretation and communication of results, and (h) forensic evaluations.

Competence of Counselors

According to Welfel (1998), "possessing a particular graduate degree is not in itself proof of competence" (p. 226) for a counselor to conduct assessments. Assessment competencies may vary depending on the length of training, the educational background, and the particular area of assessment practice of a counselor. For example, competence in statistics and measurement should include a counselor's ability to understand and use concepts such as validity, reliability, norms, and descriptive data of assessment methods, thereby making supervised practical experience of counselors important. Competence and professional judgment also include a counselor's ability to study and carefully review the available instruments and related research and the strengths, limitations, and applications of manuals and assessment materials for a specific client situation (ACA, 2005). Considerable professional competence and expertise are needed to select the most appropriate assessment methods from the many available methods and instruments, understand what they measure, be aware of the purpose and proper administration of the assessment, and accurately interpret the findings.

Informed Consent and Release of Information

Another key ethical issue related to assessment is informed consent of clients. Prior to the assessment procedures, professional counselors have a responsibility to inform clients, in a language that they understand, about the nature and purpose of the assessment, length of time required, any special requirements and conditions, and any cost (Fair Access to Coalition on Testing, n.d.). Counselors also must respect a client's privacy and never transfer assessment results to another person without the client's permission or transfer results to anyone not qualified to receive the results.

Diagnosis of Mental Health Disorders

Professional counselors use assessment methods to diagnose mental disorders of clients properly. Counselors should be sensitive, however, to the fact that "some clients do not understand the stigma that might be associated with being diagnosed with an emotional or mental disorder" (Remley & Herlihy, 2001, p. 215). Counselors should also inform clients of the impact that a mental health diagnosis may have on them. For example, society in general continues to view mental health disorders negatively.

Selection and Use of Assessment Methods

Professional counselors' selection of tests and other assessment measures is important to the assessment process. Counselors must avoid using outdated or obsolete assessment methods. The choice of the assessment methods to be used is crucial to a meaningful outcome for clients. Professional counselors must be cautious when selecting and using assessment methods that do not have norms on special populations or culturally diverse clients. For example, tests that do not have norms appropriate to a particular client require a counselor's knowledge of how to adapt the methods used to the unique circumstances of that client without jeopardizing the validity of the results. In a situation in which clients are referred to another assessment professional, counselors are required to provide complete information about the client to assist in the assessment.

Conditions of the Assessment

Professional counselors must provide an appropriate assessment environment and tell clients what conditions will occur during the assessment process. The assessment procedures used should be based on the same standardization that was used when the original assessment procedures were conducted. For example, if assessment procedures were standardized in a controlled environment and conducted individually, assessment procedures used by counselors with their clients should be conducted in the same way, if possible. In situations where those conditions are not possible, the professional counselor should inform clients of the possible effects that changes in the assessment procedures may have on the results.

Diversity Issues and Clients

Professional counselors must be cautious when using assessment methods with culturally diverse clients and recognize the effects that age, culture, disability, gender, race, religion, sexual orientation, and socioeconomic status may have on the process of the assessment and the results (Remley & Herlihy, 2001). For example, when counselors use tests, they need to be knowledgeable about the characteristics of the norm group and recognize the limitations of tests with other populations. Another issue related to diversity of clients is that counselors should also examine tests used for content bias. Test items that are content based may refer to individual experiences that are not familiar to certain groups of individuals. Also, tests may include ambiguity of test items. For example, when using multiple choice items and more than one alternative to a multiple choice item can be successfully defended as the correct answer, responding to an item can be frustrating and affect the assessment results (see Multicultural Assessment Standards).

Professional counselors also need to be alert to the laws that affect assessment and practices. The Americans With Disabilities Act, Public Law 101-336, is a civil rights law that prohibits discrimination on the basis of a disability. When assessing clients with disabilities, counselors may have to provide assessment materials in alternative formats or make other adjustments to methods as an accommodation for clients. For example, a client who is deaf will need verbal instructions in a written format or through the use of a sign language interpreter. The Civil Rights Act and Equal Opportunity Employment Act, Public Law 82-352, prohibits employment discrimination on the basis of race, color, religion, sex, national origin, or disability. Again, accommodations needed by clients for employment assessment methods should be made by counselors. The Individuals With Disabilities Education Improvement Act (IDEA) addresses the way students are evaluated and educated with regard to special education and mandates that all children with suspected handicaps be identified through the use of assessment methods, regardless of severity of their handicap. Professional counselors who are part of the team for the Individualized Education Program for students must follow all of the guidelines set by IDEA. When counselors assess children, assessment methods must be conducted in a student's native language. The Family Education Rights and Privacy Act requires that parents and eligible students be given access to school records and that students' and parents' privacy rights be protected by limiting access to students' records. Counselors working with students have a responsibility to allow students and parents access to students' records and to respect students' and parents' privacy rights.

Interpretation and Communication of Results

One of the most demanding areas of the assessment process is the interpretation of assessment results. When interpreting results, it is important to recognize any concerns regarding the validity and reliability of the assessment methods used in addition to the limitations of the assessment methods. Counselors should understand their responsibilities when asked to make inferences on the basis of assessment results. Communication of results to clients is also important. Clients have a right to receive information and feedback about results. Counselors should communicate with clients in a manner that is as positive and nonjudgmental as possible (Fair Access to Coalition on Testing, n.d.). It is important to be thorough without overwhelming clients, while making sure clients understand what is being explained. Face-to-face communication is needed whether the assessment was done individually or by commercial computerized services. This allows counselors to discuss limitations of tests and the assessment process.

Forensic Evaluation

One of the newer areas of Section E of the *Code* (ACA, 2005) is **forensic evaluation.** Professional counselors who are forensic evaluators should base their evaluations on spe-

cialized knowledge and professional opinions and provide objective findings of their forensic evaluations. Counselors are responsible for providing comprehensive, timely, accurate evaluations with defensible conclusions, while also providing any limits to their evaluation reports. Professional counselors should inform clients that their role is clearly evaluative in nature. Counselors as forensic evaluators cannot evaluate their present or previous clients.

Contributed by Roxane L. Dufrene,
University of New Orleans,
New Orleans, LA

References

American Counseling Association. (2005). *ACA code of ethics*. Alexandria, VA: Author.

Fair Access to Coalition on Testing. (n.d.). *Model testing practices*. Retrieved March 21, 2007, from http://www. fairaccess.org/model/testingpractices

Remley, T. P., & Herlihy, B. (2001). *Ethical, legal, and professional issues in counseling*. Upper Saddle River, NJ: Prentice Hall.

Welfel, E. R. (1998). *Ethics in counseling and psychotherapy: Standards, research, and emerging issues*. Pacific Grove, CA: Brooks/Cole.

■ Assessment, Key Historical Events in

Credit for the earliest testing is often given to the ancient Chinese. Starting around 2,200 BCE, civil service examinations for government positions were administered to applicants in hundreds of small huts (DuBois, 1970). The examinations were grueling and could last for days. Much later, Jean Esquirol (1772–1840) used language development (forerunner to verbal IQ testing) to categorize patients by intelligence in French mental asylums. He argued that mental retardation or "idiocy" was not a mental illness (Esquirol, 1838). Shortly afterward, Edouard Sequin (1812–1880) developed the form board, a predecessor to performance IQ testing, to assist individuals with mental retardation by improving motor skills (DuBois, 1970). The form board has objects that are placed through corresponding shaped holes. Sir Francis Galton (1809–1882), Charles Darwin's cousin, believed that grip strength was associated with intelligence. His pursuit of the relationship between these two constructs led to the development of the correlation coefficient. A little later, Wilhelm Wundt (1832–1920) developed one of the first psychological laboratories, where he measured reaction times. One of his students, James McKeen Cattell (1860–1944) applied statistical concepts to test mental functioning, which led him to coin the term *mental test* (Watson, 1968).

Development of Ability Testing

In 1904, Alfred Binet (1857–1911) was commissioned by the Paris Ministry of Public Education to develop an intelligence test to assist in identifying and placing students who were "sub-normal" (Watson, 1968). Shortly afterward, a professor from Stanford University, Lewis Terman

(1877–1956), gave Binet's instrument to hundreds of children in the Stanford area. After analyzing the normative data, Terman made modifications to the instrument, which eventually became the Stanford–Binet Intelligence Test, with a subsequent version still in use today (Minton, 1988). Terman is also credited with early use of the concept of **intelligence quotient (IQ)**. Although it is calculated differently today, Terman used the individual's mental age divided by chronological age, which was then multiplied by 100, called a **ratio IQ.** For example, a child who is 10 years old and scores at the level of an 8-year-old would have a ratio IQ of 80 (8/10 = .80 x 100 = 80). Although the Stanford–Binet may be the most famous historical intelligence test, the Wechsler scales are the most widely used today. David Wechsler (1896–1981), after beginning his career as an Army psychological examiner, developed the Wechsler-Bellevue intelligence scale in 1939 with the help of colleagues. Today there are three different Wechsler Intelligence scales for three different age groups. The use of individualized ability testing, however, is not always practical.

The onset of World War I created a need for large-scale ability testing to assist the military in properly placing new recruits. The president of the American Psychological Association, Robert Yerkes, was selected as chairperson of a committee to develop a group abilities measurement for the U.S. Department of Defense (Geisinger, 2000). Yerkes requested Terman, as well as other famous psychologists, to assist in the process. In less than 4 months, the committee created the **Army Alpha,** which was administered to 1.7 million recruits in the next 2 years (Haney, 1981). Many of the recruits, however, were unable to read or speak English. Consequently, a language-free version was developed, known as the **Army Beta.** The directions were given in pantomime, and recruits were asked to complete tasks such as mazes and form boards.

Group ability tests continued to be developed and privatized during the early and mid-1900s. After World War II, the Educational Testing Service, with influence from the president of Harvard University, James Bryant Conant, developed the **Scholastic Aptitude Test.** Conant believed such an instrument would provide opportunities for underprivileged students to obtain a higher education and help create a classless society. With an ironic twist, contemporary critics and opponents of standardized testing argue it has done the opposite (Frontline, 1999).

As student populations continued to rise across the country, the need for large-scale achievement tests grew. One of the first of these was the Stanford Achievement Test, developed by Edward Thorndike in 1923. During the 1930s, similar tests, such as the Iowa Test of Basic Skills and the Metropolitan Achievement Test, were created. Analogous to these efforts, personality tests were also developed.

Development of Personality Testing

Interest and vocational inventories, objective personality measurement, and projective personality assessment began to blossom during the early 20th century. J. B. Miner (1922) developed the first formal interest inventory that was given to large groups of high school students to assist them in determining potential occupations. A few years later, **Edward Strong** (1926) and his colleagues created the Strong Vocational Interest Blank. After numerous revisions, the Strong Interest Inventory is still one of the most well-known and widely used career assessment tools.

Objective personality assessment was needed to screen military recruits for mental health issues during World War I, which led to the development of the Woodworth's Personal Data Sheet. Considered the forefather of modern-day personality inventories, respondents answered a series of 116 *yes* or *no* questions, which assisted in the detection of mental illness (DuBois, 1970). In 1942, **Hathaway and McKinley** created the **Minnesota Multiphasic Personality Inventory (MMPI).** The first version was normed by providing inpatients and their relatives index cards with statements about themselves. Participants were asked to place the cards into piles of either *yes, no,* or *I don't know.* The second version, MMPI-II, is the most widely used diagnostic personality test today. Also during the 1940s, Katherine Briggs and her daughter Isabel Briggs began to develop an instrument based on the work of Carl Jung's psychological types, which eventually became the **Myers–Briggs Type Indicator (MBTI).** Unlike instruments such as the MMPI and **Millon Clinical Multiaxial Inventory,** the MBTI was created to assess normal or nonpathological personality variables. The Briggs's goal of helping people better understand themselves and avoid conflict may have been realized, considering more than 2 million people take the inventory annually (Quenk, 2000). Not all personality measurement is done with paper and pencil.

Projective techniques use visual stimuli to tap into the unconscious mind to understand the individual better. One of the first to do this was a student of Carl Jung's, **Herman Rorschach** (1884–1922). He splattered ink onto pieces of paper, which he folded in half to create mirror images on each side. His 10 original ink blots, developed in 1921 and referred to as the **Rorschach Inkblot Test,** was the Number 1 assessment in clinical practice in 1959 (Sundberg, 1961) and is still in use today. Another famous projective instrument was developed in 1938 by **Henry Murray** and his colleagues: the **Thematic Apperception Test.** Other projective instruments that were developed in this era that are still in use today are the Bender Visual-Motor Gestalt Test and the House-Tree-Person (see Personality Tests).

Looking toward the future, it appears testing and assessment will likely play an expanding role in the field of counseling. Accountability has been, and will continue to become, an even more important emphasis for both mental health and school counselors. The demand for evidence-based practices by governmental agencies, school districts, and health care providers is creating a surge in the areas of assessment and research. The counselors of tomorrow may find themselves administering additional instruments and collecting, analyzing, and evaluating more data in an effort to justify resources and improve counseling effectiveness.

Contributed by R. Charles Fawcett,
University of Virginia,
Charlottesville, VA

References

DuBois, P. (1970). *A history of psychological testing.* Boston: Allyn & Bacon.

Esquirol, J. (1838). *Des maladies mentales considerees sous les rapports medical, hygienique, et medico-legal* [On mental diseases considered in medical, hygienic, and medico-legal terms]. Paris: Bailliere.

Frontline. (1999). *Secrets of the SATs.* Retrieved, November 21, 2003, from http://www.pbs.org/wgbh/pages/frontline/shows/sats/etc/script.html

Geisinger, K. (2000). Psychological testing at the end of the millennium: A brief historical review. *Professional Psychology: Research and Practice, 31,* 117–119.

Haney, W. (1981). Validity, vaudeville, and values: A short history of social concerns over standardized testing. *American Psychologist, 36,* 1021–1033.

Miner, J. (1922). An aid to the analysis of vocational interest. *Journal of Educational Research, 5,* 311–323.

Minton, H. (1988). *Lewis M. Terman: Pioneer in psychological testing.* New York: New York University Press.

Quenk, N. (2000). *Essentials of Myers–Briggs Type Indicator assessment.* New York: Wiley.

Strong, E. (1926). An interest test for personnel managers. *Journal of Personnel Research, 5,* 194–203.

Sundberg, N. (1961). The practice of psychological testing in clinical services in the United States. *American Psychologist, 16,* 79–83.

Watson, R. (1968). *The great psychologists from Aristotle to Freud.* Philadelphia: Lippincott.

Additional Resource

Kaplan, R. M., & Saccuzzo, D. P. (2001). *Psychological testing: Principles, applications, and issues* (5th ed.). Pacific Grove, CA: Brooks/Cole.

∎ Assessment, Key Legal Issues in

The field of assessment is guided in part by law that requires certain actions and cautions be taken by counselors who are educated and trained and who conduct assessment in the specialties of education or employment or in the general practice of counseling. The following is a synopsis of selected key legal findings counselors must know to navigate successfully and legally through the maze of assessment.

Public Law

Laws result from bills that successfully pass Congress and are signed into action by the president. Some laws require committees (regulatory bodies) to develop regulations delimiting the processes by which the law will be fulfilled. These regulations are considered like law but can be altered by later decisions by regulatory bodies. The following are laws or regulations resulting from legislative action that affect the entire United States. State laws further govern the assessment actions of counselors in specific states. Professional counselors must be cognizant of, and adhere to, both federal and state laws and regulations governing assessment.

Title VII of the Civil Rights Act of 1964, amended in 1972, 1978, and 1991, outlaws employment discrimination based on race, color, religion, gender, pregnancy, or national origin. Professional counselors must ensure that assessment materials used in job placement or wage setting is free of bias against any protected group and that they have educated employers in the appropriate use of job-related assessment materials.

The **Tower Amendment to the Equal Employment Act of 1966** allows professional counselors who are assisting an employer to use ability tests that are developed to fairly assess knowledge or skill required by a job so long as there is no discrimination based on race.

The **Age Discrimination in Employment Act of 1967, Equal Pay Act of 1967, and Vietnam Era Veterans Readjustment Act of 1974** outlaw discrimination against people who are 40 years or older, gender-based pay, and status as a veteran of the Vietnam War.

The **Family Educational Rights and Privacy Act of 1974** aims to ensure confidentiality by limiting access to student records (including assessment materials/results) by others, yet secures the rights of parents to examine their children's records, including test scores and other assessment results. Thus, professional counselors must protect student confidentiality and test security, yet provide necessary information to parents or guardians when sought.

Public Law 94-142: Education of all Handicapped Children Act of 1975 requires written, informed consent from parents (in the parents' native language) for valid assessment of students' aptitude and achievement levels by a trained professional in order to identify exceptional needs and develop individual education plans for each exceptional child to ensure reduced disparity in educational opportunities in the least restrictive setting between exceptional and nonexceptional children. Professional counselors help to ensure that assessment of a child leads to accurate and appropriate identification of, and plan for, a child's educational needs.

Public Law 99-457: Amendment to the Education for Handicapped Children Act of 1975 extends Public Law 94-142 by extending the right to a free and appropriate education to all children who are 3 years or older and encouraging states to develop early intervention for those children with disabilities as well as individualized family service plans for all involved families.

Public Law 98-524: The Vocational Education Act of 1984 assists underserved individuals (i.e., those disadvantaged or handicapped, those entering nontraditional occupations, adults needing training or retraining, single parents or homemakers, those with insufficient language ability, and those incarcerated) in vocational education programs by mandating vocational assessment, support, transitional services, and counseling for individuals identified as handicapped or economically or academically disadvantaged. Professional counselors must ensure that vocational assessment and educational plans are conducted for such individuals who are disadvantaged as described.

Public Law 101-476: Education of the Handicapped Act of 1990 (later named Individuals With Disabilities Education Act) ensures transition for students with disabilities from school to vocational rehabilitation, employment, post-secondary education, or adult services. This act allows parents access to all pertinent records regarding the identification, evaluation, and educational placement of their children as well as the opportunity to gain independent educational evaluation of their children. Professional counselors provide educational evaluation and ensure that relevant assessment materials are available to parents to assist students with disabilities in transitioning to posteducational positions.

Public Law 101-336: Americans With Disabilities Act of 1990 extends civil rights laws to people with disabilities, making professional counselors responsible for selecting and administering tests that are pertinent to the job to ensure accurate assessment of aptitude and achievement or other factors without confounding results with an individual's sensory, manual, or speaking difficulties.

Health Insurance Portability and Accountability Act of 1996 secures client privacy and requires that all clients receive information regarding any disclosure of their information, including electronic delivery between providers, health care plans, employers, and clients themselves. Furthermore, the client's right regarding the dissemination of his or her information and reporting laws that may supersede those rights must be made clear to the client.

Public Law 107-110: No Child Left Behind Act of 2001 contains four education reform principles: (a) stronger accountability (e.g., all students expected to meet state-established standards in mathematics and reading as measured by a state testing system that meets federal requirements), (b) increased flexibility and local control, (c) varied parent options, and (d) implementation of proven teaching methods. There is an increased focus on the responsibility of school counselors to assist in providing optimal learning environments for all students.

Court Decisions

Legal guidelines are also created by judicial interpretations that are given as the basis of court decisions. The following are important court decisions rendered on cases pertaining to assessment in counseling. It is important to note that the decisions of various judges can differ. In such cases, the latter decision is sometimes the benchmark, whereas at other times, the earlier decisions serve as the standard. In some cases, confusion remains, and further litigation, including appeals of the original judicial decision, serves to clarify the pressing assessment issue.

Larry P. v. Riles **(1974, 1979, 1984)** ruled that schools had used inappropriate assessment measures for placing children in programs for the educable mentally retarded, thus disadvantaging African American students. Counselors assessing children must provide written documentation with statistics demonstrating nondiscriminatory and valid assessment tools.

Parents in Action on Special Education (PASE) v. Hannon **(1980)** was an Illinois ruling opposite to *Larry P. v. Riles* (California). Professional counselors must be clear about the most recent and predominant case rulings, because conclusions may differ, given individual judicial interpretation,

regardless of the similarities between cases. In addition to remaining current in the assessment literature, counselors should regularly consult to determine best practices in assessment.

Marshall v. Georgia featured a decision that also opposed the *Larry P. v. Riles* decision in that the court allowed schools to use tests to determine which classroom assignment would produce the best outcome for the students, thus shifting the focus from testing to what would best benefit students. This resulted in attention to curriculum-based assessment as opposed to intelligence testing. This case further demonstrates the need for counselors to be thoughtful in selection of tests, because court decisions sometimes contradict other decisions made regarding similar cases.

Diana v. California State Board of Education **(1973/1979)** was an out-of-court agreement that made schools responsible to test students both in their first language and in English and to limit verbal sections of test administration. Professional counselors must ensure that the examinee is able to understand instructions and testing materials by providing testing information in the client's primary language.

Debra P. v. Turlington **(1979, 1981, 1983, 1984)** ruled that the school system was responsible to show that material covered in tests used for granting high school diplomas had actually been taught to students. Professional counselors involved in assessment practices to determine education proficiencies must ensure that the test is valid and covered only materials students were taught.

Sharif v. New York State Educational Department **(1989)** ruled that New York could not use Scholastic Aptitude Test (SAT) scores alone in determining scholarship awards. Thus, professional counselors involved in assessment to determine awards for students may not rely on SAT scores alone.

United States v. Georgia Power **(1973)** made note of the possibility of differential validity (i.e., that tests may work better in one population than another). Thus, professional counselors must ensure reliability and validity of testing materials.

Griggs v. Duke Power Company **(1971)** set up a two-step process in which a plaintiff must demonstrate discrimination has occurred (adverse impact), whereas the employer must show hiring procedures were job related and a reasonable measure of job performance. Professional counselors involved in assessment used for hiring employees must ensure that tools used are job related.

Washington v. Davis **(1976)** determined that a selection rule was appropriately used despite evidence of adverse impact because the test was a good predictor of the final marks in a program and therefore a logical criterion measure. Professional counselors may use tests that are good predictors despite evidence of adverse impact. This ruling differs from others; therefore, counselors should use great care and ensure that tests used for such matters are necessary and yield valid and reliable scores.

Bakke v. California **(1978)** ruled that professional schools would end use of the quota system for minority group admissions. Professional counselors involved in assessment for admissions may not promote the use of a quota system that reverse discriminates.

Golden Rule Insurance Company v. Richard L. Mathias **(1980)** was an out-of-court agreement that the testing company would revise its criteria for selecting items for an examination so that there was not a difference in success rates of more than 15% between African Americans and Caucasians. As a result, professional counselors must ensure testing materials do not discriminate against protected classes.

Contreras v. City of Los Angeles **(1981)** ruled that employers could meet their burden by demonstrating that assessment methods were professionally acceptable, effective predictors of job success or significantly correlated with important work behaviors relevant to the job. Professional counselors must ensure that assessment methods do not discriminate and are job related.

Watson v. Fort Worth Bank and Trust **(1988)** diverged from *Griggs v. Duke Power Company* by indicating that employment-testing procedures for supervisory promotion can be more subjective. This decision widened the option for counselors by allowing greater subjectivity when testing to determine best fit for supervisory promotion.

Wards Cove Packing Co. v. Antonio **(1989)** ruled that the plaintiff needed to make clear discriminatory problems with job-selection procedures by demonstrating that instruments used for job placement were not job related. This case put the onus of responsibility of determining a lack of fit of assessment on the plaintiff rather than on the assessing counselor.

Although not all counselors practice in the specialties of educational or employment assessment, it is important to understand the laws and court cases that govern such activities. The American Counseling Association's (ACA; 2005) ethics standards note the importance of keeping abreast of both the historical and current legal issues by following the professional literature and published texts that guide assessment in counseling.

Contributed by Elisabeth D. Bennett
and Paul B. Hastings,
Gonzaga University, Seattle, WA

Reference

American Counseling Association. (2005). *ACA code of ethics*. Alexandria, VA: Author.

Additional Resource

Drummond, R. J., & Jones, D. J. (2006). *Assessment procedures for counselors and helping professionals*. Upper Saddle River, NJ: Pearson Merrill Prentice Hall.

Assessment Purposes

Assessment in counseling is the systematic process of gathering information to help professional counselors and clients make decisions about the client. Information can be gathered through observation of behavior, product analysis (e.g., transcript, sample of writing, goal statement), interview (e.g., structured, semistructured, unstructured), and/or standardized instruments (e.g., Minnesota Multiphasic Personality Inventory).

Assessment in counseling can be used for diagnosis, placement, admission, selection, and outcome. An assessment is conducted to determine whether a client needs services. Information is gathered to unravel personality structures and detect the presence of symptoms of a mental condition. Furthermore, a client's strengths and weaknesses are ascertained during this process. The purpose of such an assessment is to **diagnose,** which in turn would assist in client conceptualization and **treatment planning.** An accurate diagnosis is the key to effective treatment. A diagnosis can be made through an in-depth interview or in combination with standardized testing. Although some clinicians may prefer not to use testing for diagnostic determination, test reports provide a second opinion, or a confirmation of diagnostic conclusions arrived through observation and interview. In addition, the interpreted data and the process of doing so may provide both the client and the professional counselor an alternative or deeper understanding of the client's strengths and weaknesses that were not obvious through observation or the interview process. A diagnosis based on a thorough and valid assessment is essential for insurance reimbursement through managed care and for liability management.

Once a client is determined as suitable for services, then further assessment is necessary to determine the type of services or **placement** appropriate for the client. Sometimes, placement is determined based on the least restrictive environment, and, at other times, placement is determined based on the most effective treatment option. For instance, a professional school counselor may compare intelligence test results with classroom observations and product analysis to determine what type of educational placement is appropriate for a student. An agency counselor may gather information to determine what level (e.g., inpatient, residential, partial hospitalization, intensive outpatient, group counseling, or individual counseling) of placement is effective to maximize benefit of treatment at minimal cost. Appropriate placement in clinical practice facilitates insurance reimbursement.

Assessment is also used to determine **admission** to a program. For instance, the results of aptitude testing (e.g., SAT) are used as an indicator of future academic performance in determining admission to programs. Assessment is also conducted for **selection.** For instance, certain professions (e.g., police force) require that a person complete a psychological evaluation or assessment, including a battery of tests, as part of the hiring process. Information pertaining to the person's personality structure, strengths, weaknesses, and aspirations are assessed in determining suitability for the tasks and endurance required for the position.

Assessment also functions as a method to gather **outcome data.** Assessing outcome could be conducted as formative or summative evaluation. **Formative evaluation** provides information about the process of counseling and is useful to provide feedback to the client on progress as well as to monitor treatment effectiveness. **Summative evaluation** provides information on the end product. For instance, in a clinical setting, summative evaluation would be conducted to determine either short-term or long-term reduction of symptoms. In a business setting, summative evaluation would determine the appropriateness of selection for employment on the basis of assessment data. Both forms of evaluation are valuable for accountability.

Contributed by Dilani Perera-Diltz,
Cleveland State University,
Cleveland, OH

Additional Resource

Meehl, P. E. (1954). *Clinical versus statistical prediction: A theoretical analysis and a review of the evidence.* Minneapolis: University of Minnesota Press.

■ Assessment Terminology in Counseling

Assessment in counseling can be defined as the process of evaluating the soundness of a client's functioning and the resulting report that translates accumulated data into statements of relative strength or limitation of the characteristic(s) measured. Assessment involves the professional review, selection, and administration of tests or evaluation instruments or use of interviews or behavioral observations (among other techniques) to gather information about the characteristics of persons and make decisions about the diagnosis, treatment, and possible counseling outcomes. Assessment focuses on client strengths and growing edges, as well as on areas of challenge or weakness for clients. Assessment is also used to gather data to make decisions about classification, selection, placement, diagnosis, or intervention. Several concepts are related to assessment, including appraisal, measurement, evaluation, and interpretation.

Assessment, the professional term currently used by the Council for Accreditation of Counseling and Related Educational Programs in place of the term *appraisal,* is the use of methods or processes to gather data about, or evidence of, human behavior, thus determining the dimensions of an attribute or trait to better identify those human behaviors that facilitate or impede optimal functioning in specific life areas. **Measurement** in counseling is a process of defining specific characteristics or behavioral expressions of human attributes or characteristics, predicated on the hypothesis that all human traits and characteristics can be defined and quantified. In addition, measurement is based in a belief that all human traits and characteristics are present, to some extent, in all people. It is the distinct display or deficit in specific traits or characteristics in specific situations that contribute to or maintain individual or systemic strength, normalcy, or deficiency. **Interpretation** is the act of stating the meaning or usefulness of behavioral data by comparing the results from one individual to either a representative sample or to the professional counselor's professional judgment (i.e., criterion based on previous experience, theory, or statistical model) regarding client functioning. **Evaluation** involves the process of applying judgments to or making decisions based on the results of measurement. Evaluations can be designed to measure and assess the individual's growth, adjustment, or achievement or an intervention's effectiveness in facilitating identified and intended client change.

Types of Assessments

In counseling, assessment is ordinarily conducted using tests, interviews, observations, or other instruments. Each of these types of assessment will be addressed in other entries in this encyclopedia in greater depth. The remainder of this entry focuses on various methods for categorizing tests and other forms of assessment that have been discussed in the literature. Such categorizations, or typologies, include power and speed tests, standardized and nonstandardized tests, individual and group tests, maximal and typical performance tests, and objective and subjective tests

The distinction between power tests and speed tests focuses on the difficulty level of the items in the assessment instrument and whether time allowed for item completion is a factor. A **power test** measures how well items of varying difficulty can be answered correctly regardless of the time it takes to do so. Power test questions vary in the degree of complexity and demand for responder comprehension. The results of a power test demonstrate the level of content difficulty that the test taker has mastered. At times, more credit may be earned for the correct response to a more difficult question. A **speed test** offers many easy questions, but the response time is strictly limited and measured as a component of performance. Therefore, although hypothetically all test takers could answer every question correctly, the time limit also provides a measure of response rate or how quickly the test taker can understand the question and select the correct answer. Both power and speed tests are designed to prevent test takers from attaining perfect scores so that differences between test takers can be established.

Standardized tests differ from nonstandardized tests in important ways. **Standardized testing** procedures are developed in accordance with professional standards and ensure that item content, administration, and scoring remain stable across clients. This type of test has been administered to differing samples from the population the test claims to represent. Ordinarily, norms have been established from these samples, and perhaps levels of functioning or pathology have been calculated by comparing healthy samples or dysfunctional samples to obtain some numerical distinction in the presence or absence of the measured characteristic. Standardized tests always offer fixed instructions for administering and scoring. **Nonstandardized** tests provide flexibility and accommodation in terms of test administration and call on the examiner's judgment to make sense of the data. Examples are fill-in-the-blank and some projective personality tests. This type of test does not allow for comparison between test takers or comparing the scores of an individual who takes the test at differing times.

The distinction between group-administered and individually administered tests is another important consideration. **Individual tests** are administered to one individual at a time, and **group tests** can be administered to more than one test taker at a time. Individual tests can account for factors that might influence performance (e.g., reading level, anxiety, fatigue) and permit the examiner to closely observe the test taker under standardized conditions, providing additional safeguards or accuracy. Group tests are usually multiple choice tests, are more objective, and have better established norms. Group tests simplify the examiner's role by directing the examiner to distribute and then collect the test at a specified time.

The categories of maximal performance tests and typical performance tests are based on the intent of the testing procedure. A **maximal performance test** provides information about the test taker's "best" possible performance (i.e., what the person can do when conditions are maximized), whereas a **typical performance test** yields data about the test taker's usual performance. Achievement or certain aptitude tests could be categorized as measures of maximal performance, whereas a personality, interest, or other aptitude measures may be seen as inventories of typical performance.

An **objective test** is a style of test in which the testing procedures and scoring are established for the purposes of consistent administration, tabulation of results, and interpretation of data. **Subjective tests,** in comparison, offer more open-ended data collection (e.g., essay, extended response) leading to a more flexible scoring system, which may reflect the judgment of the scorer rather than the data.

Contributed by Joshua M. Gold,
University of South Carolina,
Columbia, SC

Additional Resources

Erford, B. T. (Ed.). (2006). *Counselor's guide to clinical, personality and behavioral assessment.* Boston: Houghton Mifflin/Lahaska Press.

Erford, B. T. (Ed.). (2007). *Assessment for counselors.* Boston: Houghton Mifflin/Lahaska Press.

Hood, A. B., & Johnson, R. W. (2007). *Assessment in counseling: A guide to the use of psychological assessment procedures* (4th ed.). Alexandria, VA: American Counseling Association.

■ Assimilation and Acculturation

Assimilation (often called **cultural assimilation**) refers to the process by which racial/ethnic minorities or immigrants gradually adopt the customs and attitudes and cultural and social norms of the prevailing culture. For example, when new immigrants arrive, immersion or absorption into the established or larger community into which they move often occurs, generally based on the expectation of the dominant culture. This presumes a loss of many characteristics that make the newcomers different. Although the terms *assimilation, cultural assimilation,* and *acculturation* are often used interchangeably in texts and research and are used interchangeably in this discussion, it should be noted that there are differences in the meanings of the terms.

Assimilation can be defined in terms of behavioral assimilation or structural assimilation. **Behavioral assimilation** refers to interactions among culturally diverse groups through friendships or intermarriage within various settings (e.g., community, school, work). Behavioral assimilation is theoretically a process that is gradual and consistent and is based on mutual respect and acceptance of cultural differ-

ences. The validity of this theory, in terms of mutual respect and acceptance of differences, is often the subject of debate when factors such as stereotyping related to race, class, and religion are taken into consideration.

Structural assimilation refers to the legal safeguards afforded to various groups that are based on laws enacted to ensure equality among groups. The 1964 civil rights legislation, which ensures the equal rights of African Americans, women, and other minority groups, and ongoing legislation concerning the Hispanic population are examples of structural assimilation. Several metaphors have been developed to explain what occurs when different cultures come into continuous direct contact with each other and the subsequent changes in the original cultural patterns of either or both groups that usually occur. These include the melting pot, the salad bowl, and the mosaic. The **melting pot** phenomenon is an acceptable way of describing how homogeneous societies develop, in which different cultures, religions, or larger communities blend and to an extent lose their distinct identities. This phenomenon was proposed by the playwright Israel Zangwill, and the term dates back to the early 1900s when Europeans began mass immigration to the United States. The movie *The Gangs of New York* (Grimaldi, Weinstein, & Scorsese, 2002) and writings detailing the history of Europeans who immigrated to the United States during this period are excellent examples of the melting pot phenomenon. Although these groups have fully assimilated into American culture, they still maintain many of the indigenous customs and traditions of their home countries. Although the melting pot phenomenon is sometimes equated with cultural assimilation, the two are not necessarily the same. For example, although the melting pot may imply the melting of cultures and intermarriage of various ethnicities, assimilation often occurs without intermarriage. Many have criticized the theory of the melting pot as both unrealistic and racist because it focuses on the Western heritage and excludes non-European immigrants (Laubeová, 2000).

The **salad bowl** concept, another term used when discussing assimilation, suggests that the many different cultures of U.S. residents combine like a salad. In the salad bowl model, various American cultures are combined but do not merge into a single homogenous culture; each culture keeps its own distinct qualities. For example, an African does not take on traits of Caucasians just by being placed adjacent to Caucasians. This idea proposes a society of many individuals and the preservation of culture; *salad bowl* is a more politically correct term than the term *melting pot,* which suggests that ethnic groups do not preserve their cultures.

The **cultural mosaic** suggests that various cultures coexist, each maintaining its unique differences. John Murray Gibbon introduced the term (from a multicultural perspective) in his 1938 book *Canadian Mosaic.* As the title indicates, the focus is on the multiplicity of cultures in Canada. The significance of the idea of the mosaic is that cultures coexist, maintaining their ethnic and cultural values, unlike the American idea of the melting pot that suggests a blending or melting of cultures into the dominant culture. Regardless of the terms used to describe the extent or degree to which various groups assimilate into a given society or social system, the process has social and psychological implications.

Terms often used to describe social and psychological issues experienced during the assimilation process are *acculturative stress* and *culture shock*. **Acculturative stress** refers to the psychological, somatic, and social difficulties that may accompany acculturation processes. In Freudian terms, "psychic conflict" may arise from conflicting cultural norms. Acculturative stress is a fundamental psychological force in acculturative processes. Immigrants who have strong indigenous roots in their home countries and who have established cultural beliefs and values that often conflict with American cultural values may experience extreme acculturative stress during the process of assimilation. This may or may not lead to what is known as culture shock.

Culture shock is a term used to describe the physical and emotional discomfort an individual or group may experience during the acculturation process. Culture shock, which usually happens early in the acculturation process, occurs in stages and either can be ongoing or appear only at certain times. Although culture adjustment takes place every time a person moves to another country, culture shock usually subsides when the individual becomes more familiar with the environment. An individual's state of mental health, personality type, past experiences, socioeconomic status, educational level, or other factors may contribute to the duration and effects of culture shock.

Numerous opinions, theories, and psychosocial scales of measurement have been developed over the years to address issues related to assimilation and acculturation. Opinions and theories serve to address issues related to the immigration and assimilation issues, and scales of measurement allow researchers and practitioners to quantify assimilation and acculturation and are relevant across fields of study.

Cultural Assimilation Theories

One of the earliest and most prominent theories is the **Anglo-conformity theory.** The crux of this theory was the complete renunciation of the immigrant's ancestral culture in favor of the behavior and values of the Anglo-Saxon core group. Maintaining English language and English-oriented cultural patterns as dominant and standard in American life is a key factor in this theory. This ideology has received consistent support in federal policies throughout U.S. history. The Anglo-conformity theory in part supports the belief that the persistence of ethnic cultures, ethnic and racial communities, and foreign languages in English-speaking entities (e.g., schools, communities) should be aggressively discouraged. An excellent example of this line of thought is evident in the ongoing debate of English as a second language in American public school systems.

The cycle of race relations theory, introduced in the early 1900s by Park (1950), focuses on four cycles of assimilation: contact, competition, accommodation, and assimilation. Parks proposed that contact through exploration occurred initially; followed by economic competition (e.g., housing, jobs); followed by accommodation; and, finally, assimilation. The **six orders of interracial contact,** introduced by Banton (1967) in the mid-1960s, assert that there are six phases of racial assimilation that progress from minimal contact between racial groups to increased contact and integration of cultural values.

The **Suinn–Lew Asian self-identity measurement model** suggests three dimensions in acculturation. A person may be entirely assimilated, such as when an Asian completely identifies as part of the dominant Western culture, called "Western identified" or "assimilated." Another person may retain identity with his or her ethnic heritage and refuse total integration with the Western society, called "Asian identified." A third may assume the cultural characteristics of both cultures, denying neither, called "bicultural" (Suinn, Ahuna, & Khoo, 1992).

The **Berry (1997) cross-cultural model of acculturation,** also called **Berry's fourfold model,** suggests a two-dimensional model with four options based on a person's desire to have positive relations with other groups in society and the desire to maintain his or her heritage. In this model, a person or group may chose to integrate or assimilate into the larger culture or choose separation or marginalization. The model suggests that a person can "adopt" a combination of alternative attitudes related to heritage and the dominant culture. Other models or theories exist, and all have in common the various psychological and social characteristics inherent in the assimilation process. Regardless of the acculturation framework, the following factors affect an individual's level of acculturation: gender, age, length of stay, parent culture, host culture, education, social status, migration motivation, and expectation.

These and other theories exist in an attempt to explain the process of assimilation and acculturation and to account for the various aspects of a society (positive and negative) that are inherent in the process of assimilation and acculturation in terms of natural resources; economics; and, many times, resistance by members of the dominant culture. The ongoing debate about the current laws addressing immigration of Hispanics into the United States is an excellent example of these theories in action.

To determine how well a particular group is able to assimilate into a particular society and to identify areas that may be of interest or concern in the process (e.g., language, preferences, adjustment issues, barriers) requires various measures to determine the level or the extent of acculturation that has been developed.

Measures of Acculturation

One well-known scale of acculturation is the **African American Acculturation Scale.** This assessment measure determines the level or extent of assimilation and acculturation of African Americans primarily in American society. It is a 74-item scale that has shown good initial score validity (Klonoff & Landrine, 2000). The scale is made up of eight theorized dimensions of African American culture. These dimensions are (a) traditional African American religious beliefs and practices, (b) traditional African American family structure and practices, (c) traditional African American socialization, (d) preparation and consumption of traditional foods, (e) preference for African American things, (f) interracial attitudes, (g) superstitions, and (h) traditional African American health beliefs and practices. These subscales and the full scale score demonstrated high internal consistency.

The **Suinn–Lew Asian Self-Identity Acculturation (SL-ASIA) scale** (Suinn et al., 1992) is an instrument developed to assess the level of acculturation of Asian Americans. The SL-ASIA scale is a 21-item measure of acculturation, intended mainly for use with respondents of East Asian backgrounds in the United States. Items assess a respondent's reported language abilities and preferences, ethnic self-identity, friendship choices, food preferences, generational status and migration history, cultural and entertainment preferences, and reported ethnic interactions. As indicated, this scale suggests that assimilation can take on three dimensions that may include total assimilation, maintenance of cultural heritage, or the adaptation of various characteristics from the dominant culture while maintaining an individual's own cultural characteristics.

Other scales include the Minority–Majority Relations Scale, the Bicultural Acculturation Scale, the Acculturation Scale for Vietnamese Adolescents, and the Acculturation Rating Scale for Mexican Americans–Short Form. The Antioch University New England, located in Keene, New Hampshire, has a comprehensive online Multicultural Center that includes information on these tests and other topics of interest in the area of acculturation and assimilation.

Research Findings and Acculturation

Information derived from the administration of the various instruments used to measure a particular group's level of assimilation or ability to assimilate can provide professional counselors with important information that can assist in understanding and explaining to clients who immigrate what they might be experiencing. The Rating Scale for Mexican Americans–II developed by Cuellar, Arnold, and Maldonado (1995) is used to measure cultural orientation toward the Mexican culture (i.e., Mexican and Mexican American) and Anglo culture (e.g., White non-Hispanic) across various measures and across generations. Some findings revealed that older Mexican men who immigrate, followed by older Mexican American men, experienced higher rates of depression than did younger Mexican American men. Employment, education, and other conditions were cited as factors that might be considered when working with this group. Another finding was that Mexican women experienced depression more often than did Mexican men. Nguyen, Messe, and Stollak (1999), using the Acculturation Scale for Vietnamese Adolescents, examined the association between acculturation and adjustment of Vietnamese youth living in Anglo-American communities by exploring levels of distress, depression, self-esteem, and interpersonal relationships. It is interesting that they found these youth experienced positive outcomes related to acculturation within the larger culture but experienced some levels of distress in interpersonal rela-

tions with family. One recommendation was further investigation into the social contextual aspect of this particular group. A common research finding is that economics, education, employment, and interracial attitudes often stand out as possible mitigating factors, which could have an impact on the mental health and well-being of clients from an acculturative perspective. Research is available on practically every ethnic group and can provide professional counselors working with clients from a different cultural background valuable information to assist in diagnosis and treatment planning.

To what extent an individual or group assimilates into a given society is important and has far-reaching implications on the well-being of the individual, the community, and society as a whole. An individual's or group's ability to assimilate successfully can affect mental health or mental illness and harmony and disharmony within societies.

Cultural Assimilation and Implications for Professional Counselors

Understanding the assimilation process, the psychological implications inherent in the process, and the theories and assessment tools available that help to explain the process can assist professional counselors in better diagnosing and treating clients from a different cultural background. An example is the case of a professional counselor working with an elderly Hispanic man who recently immigrated to be closer to his children. The children have been in America for many years. Reports are that the client is experiencing symptoms of anger or depression. The professional counselor's knowledge and understanding of the various tools available to assist in examining beliefs and values and the level of assimilation can prove invaluable in working with the client and his family

Given the ongoing debates and criticisms that abound about the ability of one group or another group to assimilate fully into a particular society and given the global nature of the society in which people live, it is essential that professional counselors have knowledge about the processes of assimilation and acculturation.

Contributed by Deborah M. Wilson,
Troy University, Augusta, GA

References

Banton, M. (1967). *Race relations.* London: Tavistock.

Berry, J. W. (1997). Immigration, acculturation, and adaptation. *Applied Psychology: An International Review, 46,* 5–34.

Cuellar, I., Arnold, B., & Maldonado, R. (1995). Acculturation rating scale for Mexican Americans–II: A revision of the original ARSMA scale. *Hispanic Journal of Behavioral Sciences, 17,* 275–304.

Gibbon, J. M. (1938). *Canadian mosaic: The making of a northern nation.* Toronto, Ontario, Canada: McClelland & Stewart.

Grimaldi, A., Weinstein, H. (Producers), & Scorsese, M. (Director). (2002). *Gangs of New York* [Motion picture]. United States: Miramax Films.

Klonoff, E. A., & Landrine, H. (2000). Revising and improving the African American Acculturation Scale. *Journal of Black Psychology, 26,* 235–261.

Laubeová, L. (2000). *Melting pot vs. ethnic stew.* Retrieved November 3, 2005, from http://www.tolerance.cz/courses/texts/melting.htm

Nguyen, H. H., Messe, L. A., & Stollak, G. E. (1999). Toward a more complex understanding of acculturation and adjustment: Cultural involvement and psychosocial functioning in Vietnamese youth. *Journal of Cross-Cultural Psychology, 30,* 5–31.

Park, R. E. (1950). *Race and culture.* New York: Free Press.

Suinn, R. M., Ahuna, C., & Khoo, G. (1992). The *Suinn-Lew Asian self-identity acculturation psychosocial measures for Asian Americans: Tools for practice and research.* Retrieved October 25, 2007, from http://www.columbia.edu/cu/ssw/projects/pmap

Additional Resources

Dion, K. L. (1966). *2.0 Acculturation and immigration: Social psychological perspectives.* Retrieved October 25, 2007, from http://canada.metropolis.net/research-policy/litreviews/tylr_rev/tylr_rev-05.html

Sue, D., & Sue, D. W. (2007). *Counseling the culturally diverse: Theory and practice* (5th ed.). New York: Wiley.

Association for Adult Development and Aging

The **Association for Adult Development and Aging (AADA),** chartered in 1986, is a division of the American Counseling Association (ACA) that serves a membership dedicated to meeting the counseling needs of adults across the life span through advocacy for adult clients and skill enhancement of counselors who work with adults. There are approximately a dozen state and regional chapters of this organization across the United States. The goals of AADA emphasize the healthy development of individuals from the end of adolescence through the end of life. The mission of AADA is fourfold: (a) improvement of the skills and competence of ACA members for working with adults; (b) expansion of professional work opportunities in adult development and aging; (c) promotion of the lifelong development and well-being of adults; and (d) promotion of standards for professional preparation for counselors of adults across the life span. One of AADA's key initiatives is the development of guidelines for counselors to use in assisting adults across the life span.

Since its establishment, chartered under the leadership of Jane Myers as first president, AADA has thrived under leaders who have spearheaded efforts to promote awareness of the unique needs of the adult and aging populations. Many of the past leaders of this organization have held leadership offices in ACA. Active involvement of these individuals at the national level has served to bring greater focus to the counseling needs of adults who face a variety of changes in their physical, psychosocial, and cognitive development throughout the life span.

In an effort to highlight the importance of adult development, AADA selects an outstanding research project by one of its members and presents an award acknowledging the researcher's achievement at the ACA annual convention. *Adultspan* is the journal of AADA and is published biannually. This journal provides an important outlet for researchers and theoreticians who address issues related to adulthood and aging, because it is the only journal under the umbrella of ACA that specifically addresses the needs of this population. This division provides sponsorship for miniconferences held in collaboration with regional or state chapters, with typically one to two conferences scheduled each year. These conferences encourage networking among existing members as well as increase involvement of new members at the local level. The *Adultspan Newsletter* is published quarterly and provides members with information about organizational leadership activities and local chapter activities and informative articles.

Contributed by Suzanne Degges-White,
Purdue University Calumet,
Calumet, IN

Additional Resource

Association for Adult Development and Aging Web site: http://www.aadaweb.org/

Association for Assessment in Counseling and Education

Chartered as the seventh division of the American Counseling Association (ACA), the **Association for Assessment in Counseling and Education (AACE)** and its mission are integral to the identity of all professional counselors and the missions of all divisions within ACA. Historically, the primary mission of AACE has been to provide leadership, advice, and counsel on matters related to **measurement** and **evaluation** in counseling and development. Recently, the mission of the division has expanded to offering support in investigating evidenced-based practices and other research projects in the profession. In providing direction in assessment and research practices, AACE has identified the importance of these practices in the repertoire of skills professional counselors use on a daily basis.

When it was chartered in 1965, AACE was known as the **Association for Measurement and Evaluation in Guidance.** It has undergone several name changes, with the most recent name change in 2003 (formerly the Association for Assessment in Counseling). The founding president in 1965 was Harold Seashore, and AACE has flourished and expanded its scope of professional influence and leadership. Leaders of AACE have consisted of assessment and evaluation professionals from the private sector, K–12 public education, and counselor educators from colleges and university settings.

Since its inception, AACE and many of its individual members have assumed national leadership roles in promoting responsible use of measurement instruments and have been part of major groups engaged in the development of standards for measurement and evaluation, including the position statement on the *Responsibilities of Users of Standardized Tests* (now in its 3rd ed.); the Joint Committee on Standards for Educational Evaluation's statement of standards for evaluation of educational programs, projects, and materials; the Joint Committee on Testing Practices, AACE's and American School Counselor Association's Competencies in Assessment and Evaluation for School Counselors; AACE/International Association of Addictions and Offender Counselors Standards for Assessment in Substance Abuse Counseling; ACA's Position Statement on High-Stakes Testing; and ACA's Standards for Qualifications of Test Users.

Over the last 30 years, AACE has published numerous monographs and books. AACE's journal, *Measurement and Evaluation in Counseling and Development,* is highly respected in the fields of counseling and education. AACE's annual national assessment conference provides opportunities for counseling and assessment/research professionals and students to educate others and exchange ideas. In addition, AACE members are updated via the division's newsletter, *NewsNotes,* and electronic newsletter, *Newsbytes.* AACE also recognizes the research efforts of professionals and students by providing funded research awards that are distributed at the ACA annual convention.

AACE has expanded its focus and mission and continues to strive to meet the needs of its members and constituents. By addressing the current needs of the profession and promoting the practices of assessment and research in counseling and education, AACE strives to stimulate research and development in order to disseminate results that will promote better communication between the producers of that research and the consumers who will practice using the results.

Contributed by Donna M. Gibson,
University of South Carolina,
Columbia, SC

Additional Resources

Association for Assessment in Counseling and Education Web site: http://www.theaaceonline.com
Information on *Measurement and Evaluation in Counseling and Development:* http://www.counseling.org/Publications/Journals.aspx

Association for Counselor Education and Supervision

The **Association for Counselor Education and Supervision (ACES)** is a division of the American Counseling Association (ACA). Founded in 1952 as the National Association of Guidance and Counselor Trainers, this organization has evolved into a professional association focused on the training and professional development of counselor educators and supervisors. Membership in ACES requires ACA membership.

As a professional association, ACES offers members involved in counselor education and counselor supervision a forum for professional dialogue and professional growth. These goals can be realized through involvement in the

national association as well as in one of the five regional divisions of ACES, one of the state divisions of ACES, or through one of the many specialized committees of the organization. As advocates for change and legislative recognition for education and supervision initiatives in the counseling field, ACES, through its membership, continues to advance the mission of ACA through advancement of research and counseling services. These services have included research grants focused on counselor education and supervision issues, journal presentations on special concerns in the field, promotion of graduate student professional development, and ongoing discussions of appropriate training and supervision standards.

ACES provides training opportunities, encourages relevant research and publication activities, and offers guidelines for professional standards and accreditation processes, as outlined in its vision statement. As an organization, ACES provides member feedback to the Council for Accreditation of Counseling and Related Educational Programs and offers members the most current information on training standards and policies related to accreditation. This has included dissemination of competencies in all fields related to counseling, executive council endorsement of training and professional development initiatives, and conventions and publications whose themes have focused on the most relevant issues in the counseling field (e.g., social justice, social advocacy).

ACES offers a biennial national convention focused on the professional enhancement of counselor educators and supervisors. The conventions provide forums for the organization to set forth the most crucial issues facing counselor educators and supervisors. On alternating years, each region coordinates a specialized biennial conference for its region with an education, training, and networking orientation. The ACES journal, *Counselor Education and Supervision,* is published quarterly. This journal includes theory, research, and practice for this specialty. The *Ethical Guidelines for Counseling Supervisors* was written and adopted by ACES (1993) and addresses specific concerns related to unique challenges for counselor educators and supervisors. These guidelines are in conjunction with ACA (2005) ethical standards but provide for the additional responsibilities of the specialization. ACES also publishes a quarterly newsletter, *The Spectrum.*

Contributed by Debra L. Ainbinder,
Lynn University, Boca Raton, FL

References

American Counseling Association. (2005). *ACA code of ethics.* Alexandria, VA: Author.
Association for Counselor Education and Supervision. (1993). *Ethical guidelines for counseling supervisors.* Retrieved June 19, 2008, from www.acesonline.net/ethical_guidelines.asp

Additional Resource

Association for Counselor Education and Supervision Web site: http://www.acesonline.net

Association for Counselors and Educators in Government

Formed in 1978 as the Military Educators and Counseling Association, the **Association for Counselors and Educators in Government (ACEG)** is a division of the American Counseling Association (ACA) and provides counseling and educational professionals who work in government or military settings a network for professional contacts, assistance, and guidance. ACEG seeks to provide its members with assistance necessary to ensure that counseling and educational services provided to those in government and the military are of the highest caliber possible. ACEG's membership consists of counseling and educational professionals who wish to share their experiences, expertise, and training with other professionals who may find themselves providing services in direct support of military operations, embassy and consulate posts, and diplomatic missions worldwide and includes military personnel, civilian employees, and government contractors. The *ACEG Report,* published three times a year, provides association members with information and contacts that span a broad range of counseling, education, and personal assistance matters. The association holds a 1-day professional development institute in conjunction with the annual ACA conference. Key events in ACEG's history include the assumption of its charter under ACA in 1984 and the name change to its current form in 1994. ACEG offers online continuing education programs to serve the professional development needs of its members regardless of their location in the world and provides a sense of professional community to those who may be serving in widely dispersed locations.

Contributed by Mary L. Bartlett,
University of Montevallo, Montevallo, AL

Additional Resources

American Counseling Association Web site: http://www.counseling.org/AboutUs/DivisionsBranchesAndRegions/TP/Divisions/CT2.aspx

Association for Counselors and Educators in Government Web site: http://www.dantes.doded.mil/dantes_web/organizations/aceg/index.htm

Association for Creativity in Counseling

The **Association for Creativity in Counseling (ACC)** became the American Counseling Association's (ACA) 19th division in September 2004. The group that spearheaded the effort to develop this division moved to establish a division that focused on creativity, diversity, and relational development within ACA. The steering committee, chaired by Thelma Duffey, included Stella Kerl-McClain, JoLynne Reynolds, Drema Albin, Colleen Connolly, and Christopher Brown and many students, most notably Gene Ashlock and Richard Simmons.

A primary objective in forming ACC was to create an inclusive forum for counselors and counseling students to explore unique and diverse approaches to counseling and counselor education. ACC's mission includes (a) promoting greater awareness, advocacy, and understanding of creativity among members of the counseling profession and related helping fields; (b) advancing creative, diverse, and relational approaches to services; (c) identifying conditions that enhance creativity in the work and lives of counselors, clients, and communities; and (d) using counseling skills, programs, and efforts to preserve, protect, and promote such creativity. The committee intentionally chose to use the word *creativity* because it is a broad term that encourages diversity in its membership of the association. The committee chose the word *counseling* because it reflects the association's professional identity and promotes the efforts of the professional organization. More specifically, the committee hoped the membership would include counselors and other mental health professionals working from a wide range of professional perspectives that value creative, relational, and complementary therapies.

ACC members include mental health and community agency counselors, private practitioners, counselor educators, school counselors, students, retired counselors, psychologists, and professionals new to the counseling field. Some ACC members also hold licensure or certification in the creative arts, including art therapists, music therapists, play therapists, and dance therapists, or other advanced specialties in creative and complementary therapies such as eye movement desensitization and reprocessing, hypnosis, and emotional freedom technique, to name a few.

Maintaining this relational perspective and focus on diversity is fundamental to the mission of ACC. In that vein, its flagship journal, ***Journal of Creativity in Mental Health,*** is designed to serve as a multidisciplinary, consolidated reference source for academics and practitioners and to examine the benefits and practical applications of using creative approaches to help deepen personal insight and build growth-fostering relationships.

In addition, one benefit that the ACC leadership initiated on behalf of its membership was structuring ACC's collaboration with the already existing Dr. Lesley Jones Creativity in Psychotherapy Conference, led by members of the steering committee and John Garcia. The conference was designed to create a forum where counselors and counselor educators could celebrate their passion for the creative and a place where music, the media, art, theater, poetry, storytelling, and other creative processes could be explored. The vision of ACC's founding leadership was that the conference, which had established roots in Texas, could serve the membership of ACC. ACC held its first conference in 2005 and has plans to hold future conferences. ACC also disseminates an annual newsletter, scheduled for release in March of each year.

Contributed by Thelma Duffey,
University of Texas at San Antonio,
San Antonio, TX

Additional Resources

Association for Creativity in Counseling Web site: www.aca-acc.org

Duffey, T. (2006). Birthing an organization: Creativity, counseling, and mental health practice. *Paradigm, 11*(4), 7–8. (see www.onlineparadigm.com)

Duffey, T. (2006/2007). Promoting relational competencies in counselor education through creativity and relational-cultural theory. *Journal of Creativity in Mental Health, 2*(1), 49–64.

Duffey, T., & Kerl-McClain, S. (2006/2007). The history of the Association of Creativity in Counseling. *Journal of Creativity in Mental Health, 2*(3), 61–70.

■ Association for Lesbian, Gay, Bisexual, and Transgender Issues in Counseling

Although begun in 1975, the **Association for Lesbian, Gay, Bisexual, and Transgender Issues in Counseling (ALGBTIC)** did not become an official division of the American Counseling Association (ACA) until 1997. Those 22 years involved numerous individuals providing peer education and advocating for increased visibility of sexual minority issues in the counseling profession. From its humble beginnings as The Gay Caucus founded by Joe Norton, the name has changed several times to better exemplify the expanded focus and mission of the organization and to promote inclusion of heterosexual allies. The change from the Association of Gay, Lesbian, and Bisexual Issues in Counseling (AGLBIC) to the Association for Lesbian, Gay, Bisexual, and Transgender Issues in Counseling (ALGBTIC) was made in 2007 to denote an inclusion of transgender issues and advocacy against sexism. Although the American Psychiatric Association removed homosexuality as a mental disorder in 1974, many counselors still lack full acceptance of or respect for gay, lesbian, bisexual, and transgendered individuals and their unique issues.

ALGBTIC has persistently expanded its programs and resources for counseling professionals. A number of important historical events merit mentioning. The first ALGBTIC exhibit booth at an ACA conference was established in 1986. The first Day of Learning at an ACA conference was held in 1996. The first state-affiliated offices were founded in 1998 in North Carolina and Kentucky and since then have expanded into six states. The Competencies for Counseling Gay, Lesbian, Bisexual, and Transgendered (LGBT) Clients were developed in 1997 and approved by ACA in 2004. The first University Affiliated Group was founded at Georgia State University in 2003. The first affiliated journal *(The Journal of LGBT Issues in Counseling)* was published in 2005. ALGBTIC sponsored a wedding of lesbian and gay couples at the 2006 ACA conference in Montreal, Canada.

The mission of ALGBTIC includes the recognition of both the individual and societal confluence of race, ethnicity, class, gender, sexual orientation, ability, age, spiritual or religious belief system, and indigenous heritage in order (a) to promote greater awareness and understanding of LGBT issues among members of the counseling profession and related helping occupations; (b) to improve standards and delivery of counseling services provided to LGBT clients and communities; (c) to identify conditions that create barriers to the human growth and development of LGBT clients and communities and to use counseling skills, programs, and efforts to preserve, protect, and promote such development; (d) to develop, implement, and foster interest in counseling-related charitable, scientific, and educational programs designed to further the human growth and development of LGBT clients and communities; (e) to secure equality of treatment, advancement, qualifications, and status of LGBT members of the counseling profession and related helping occupations; and (f) to publish a journal and other scientific, educational, and professional materials with the purpose of raising the standards of practice for all who work with LGBT clients and communities in the counseling profession and related helping occupations.

Membership in ALGBTIC is open to any counseling student or counselor and includes opportunities for networking, service, advocacy, education, and awards. For additional history, information, and resources such as the competencies for counseling LGBT clients (translated into five languages), an extensive bibliography, journal information, and a therapist listing in addition to membership information, explore the division's Web site.

Contributed by Joffrey S. Suprina,
Argosy University–Atlanta, Atlanta, GA

Reference

Association for Lesbian, Gay, Bisexual, and Transgender Issues in Counseling. (1997). *Competencies for counseling gay, lesbian, bisexual, and transgendered (GLBT) clients.* Retrieved June 20, 2008, from http://www.algbtic.org/resources/competencies.html

Additional Resources

Association for Lesbian, Gay, Bisexual, and Transgender Issues in Counseling Web site: http://www.aglbtic.org

Logan, C. R., & Barret, R. (2005). Counseling competencies for sexual minority clients. *Journal of LGBT Issues in Counseling, 1,* 3–22.

■ Association for Multicultural Counseling and Development

The Association for Non-White Concerns (ANWC) was founded in 1972 as a division of the American Personnel and Guidance Association (APGA), which is now known as the American Counseling Association (ACA). In 1985, ANWC made a change to its name and became the **Association for Multicultural Counseling and Development (AMCD),** which also entailed changes to its organizational structure and mission. The journey to becoming a division of APGA began in the late 1960s under the leadership of founder Samuel H. Johnson. The vision of the founders paved the way for people of color and other disenfranchised helping professionals to be embraced as viable leaders within the ranks of ACA and opened the door to multiculturalism becoming the fourth force in counseling.

AMCD endorses a greater consciousness and appreciation of multicultural therapeutic practices and of the impact of cultural and ethnic differentiation among counseling and helping professionals and strives to advance the standard of care and delivery of counseling and development services. AMCD members are committed to the eradication of conditions that generate obstacles impeding the growth and well-being of individuals from all cultural and ethnic groups.

Another critical endeavor of AMCD is the fostering and development of interest in altruistic, professional, and scientific programs intended to further the welfare of ethnic groups, with the goals of securing equality of treatment for all humankind, enriching life experiences, and improving the circumstances of individuals of every culture and ethnic grouping through the practice of counseling and development.

AMCD members are challenged to provide leadership, engage in scholarly research, and increase the multicultural knowledge base, competency, and preparedness of counseling professionals. To this end, AMCD publishes an award-winning refereed quarterly journal, the *Journal of Multicultural Counseling and Development,* that includes practice-based multicultural processes, outcome research, and case studies. AMCD also provides supplementary scientific, educational, and professional development resources, such as leadership and crisis management materials. AMCD periodically publishes a newsletter, *The Multicultural Counselor.*

AMCD is probably best known for one widely cited policy document. A landmark 1992 article by Sue, Arredondo, and McDavis, titled "Multicultural Counseling Competencies and Standards: A Call to the Profession," drew from the work of AMCD's Professional Standards Committee, under the leadership of then president Thomas A. Parham. This article has had a profound historic effect on the counseling profession. The work opened the door to significant academic curriculum changes that have transformed the counseling profession as a whole and provided a firm platform to further enhance the multicultural awareness, knowledge, and skills of a diverse body of helping professionals for years to come. According to a statement on AMCD Online (2008), the AMCD Multicultural Counseling Competencies represent "a benchmark for the counseling profession and the American Counseling Association, these competencies are a manifestation of the universality of multiculturalism as a construct that reflects and affects our personal and professional lives."

Contributed by S. Kent Butler Jr.,
University of Central Florida, Orlando, FL

References

AMCD Online. (2008). Retrieved June 20, 2008, from http://www.bgsu.edu/colleges/edhd/programs/AMCD/Prof-Standards.html

Sue, D. W., Arredondo, P., & McDavis, R. J. (1992). Multicultural counseling competencies and standards: A call to the profession. *Journal of Counseling & Development, 70,* 477–486.

Additional Resources

Arredondo, P., Toporek, R., Brown, S., Jones, J., Locke, D. C., Sanchez, J., et al. (1996). *Operationalization of the multicultural counseling competencies.* Alexandria, VA: Association for Multicultural Counseling and Development.

Association for Multicultural Counseling and Development Web site: http://www.amcdaca.org/amcd/whatisamcd.cfm

Journal of Multicultural Counseling and Development Web site: http://www.multiculturalcenter.org/jmcd/

Multicultural Counseling Competencies Web page: http://eric.ed.gov/ERICWebPortal/custom/portlets/recordDetails/detailmini.jsp?_nfpb=true&_&ERICExtSearch_SearchValue_0=EJ445488&ERICExtSearch_SearchType_0=eric_accno&accno=EJ445488

Association for Specialists in Group Work

The purpose of the **Association for Specialists in Group Work (ASGW),** a division of the American Counseling Association (ACA), is to establish standards for professional and ethical practice, to support research and the dissemination of knowledge, and to provide professional leadership in the field of group work. ASGW seeks to extend counseling through the use of group process and to provide a forum for examining innovative and creative concepts in group work. In addition, ASGW seeks to foster diversity and dignity in groups, and the members of ASGW seek to be models of effective group practice.

Prominent on the ASGW Web site are documents that have been disseminated in texts published around the world. For example, in 1983 ASGW published ethical standards for use by group leaders. Having been revised three times since then, they now appear on the Web site as ASGW Best Practices (ASGW, 2008). In 1990, ASGW published professional training standards that distinguished between core competencies and the four group specialty areas: group counseling, group therapy, group guidance, and organizational groups. In 1999, ASGW was the first organization to establish diversity competencies for group leaders.

The Journal for Specialists in Group Work, which has been published continuously since 1975, is indexed or abstracted by 16 organizations, including Educational Resources Information Center, PsycINFO, and MasterFILE FullTEXT. ASGW members receive a copy of each current journal edition; the members-only section of the Web site allows access to an online version of the journal.

In addition to a quarterly journal, ASGW publishes paper and online versions of a newsletter, *The Groupworker,* containing additional practitioner columns and news about the organization's training opportunities, conferences, and graduate student scholarships. The Web site also contains a pamphlet: *What Every Counselor Must Know About Groups,* available for free download.

Along with providing financial support to graduate student members assisting at national conferences, ASGW has three named scholarships. The Peg Carroll Scholarship honors Marguerite "Peg" Carroll, a pioneer in group work and former ASGW president. This $2,000 award is given annually to support the study of group work and the understanding of group dynamics. The Vicki E. Bowman Outstanding Graduate Student Scholarship is a $250 annual award dedicated to the late Vicki Bowman and is awarded to persons who, like her, demonstrated great character and integrity, involvement in the study and practice of group work, and leadership and support roles among fellow graduate students. The Barbara Gazda Scholarship honors the late partner of ASGW's first president, George Gazda. Two $200 scholarships are available to support students and/or new professionals who are attending the biannual ASGW national conference.

The ASGW national conference is held biannually in January or February of even-numbered years. The 3-day event features internationally renowned group experts and includes preconference full- and half-day workshops, plus numerous 1 hour interest sessions. Conference presentations are juried, and the call for programs is posted on the ASGW Web site approximately 6 months prior to the event. Locations vary for the convenience of members. In addition to the ASGW national conference, every year ASGW sponsors programs as part of the ACA annual conference.

ASGW has several levels of membership, including professional, regular, new professional, graduate student, and retired. The latter two pay reduced dues. Although many people are members of both ASGW and ACA, membership in the latter is not required of ASGW members. All levels of membership have voting rights. Low membership dues are attributable to the proceeds from ASGW videos and DVD sales. Visual examples of a variety of groups are available for sale via the ACA online store; annual profits from ASGW productions typically have equaled the amount generated through membership dues.

ASGW was incorporated on December 12, 1973, by George M. Gazda, Jack A. Duncan, and Charles L. Lewis. The first board of directors included Fannie R. Cooley, Jack A. Duncan, George M. Gazda, Kevin E. Geoffroy, Merle M. Ohlsen, and Barbara B. Varenhorst. George Gazda was elected the first president of ASGW. On November 12, 1973, he sent the ASGW bylaws and a list of 267 charter members to ACA executive director, Joe McDonough, who validated 220 as members of ACA, and ASGW became a division of ACA (then known as the American Personnel and Guidance Association). In only 10 years, the membership of ASGW swelled to more than 7,000, making it the largest professional organization for group leaders in the world.

One of ASGW's charges is to recognize and promote the understanding of group process and practice. Each year ASGW honors individuals who have made significant contributions to the field. Recognitions of merit include the Group Work Practice Award, Professional Advancement Award, President's Distinguished Service Award, and the most coveted Eminent Career Award. The latter is not necessarily granted each year; it is only given when a nominee's lifetime achievements are deemed exemplary.

In 1986, ASGW initiated a Fellows program to recognize people who have made extraordinary contributions to group work practice and/or research. An ASGW Fellow cannot self-nominate, and there are years in which no awards are given. Only ASGW Fellows are eligible to nominate candidates. Résumés and letters of support are generated for the

following year; fellows then debate and vote on the candidates. Selections are approved by the ASGW executive board, and recipients are introduced by the president at the annual awards ceremony. Inductees are also invited to give their perspective on the state of the art of group work during the Fellows Symposium, an event held during the ACA annual conference and open to the public. When ACA initiated its own Fellows program in 2004, three of the first four ACA Fellows were ASGW Fellows.

Contributed by George R. Leddick,
Association for Specialists in Group Work,
Campbell, TX

References

Association for Specialists in Group Work. (1983). *ASGW professional standards for group counseling.* Alexandria, VA: Author.

Association for Specialists in Group Work. (1990). *Professional standards for the training of group workers.* Alexandria, VA: Author.

Association for Specialists in Group Work. (1999). ASGW principles for diversity-competent group workers. *Journal for Specialists in Group Work, 24,* 7–14.

Association for Specialists in Group Work. (2008). *ASGW best practices.* Retrieved June 20, 2008, from http://www.asgw.org

Additional Resource

Association for Specialists in Group Work Web site: www.asgw.org

Association for Spiritual, Ethical, and Religious Values in Counseling

In the Archdiocese of New York in 1951, a Catholic Guidance Council was formed to support and encourage counseling and guidance in the diocesan parochial schools. In order to facilitate national contact between the increasing numbers of diocesan councils, the National Conference of Guidance Councils was formed in 1958. Many of those involved in the diocesan councils were active in the move to create a national Catholic guidance organization within the American Personnel and Guidance Association (APGA). They met at the APGA convention in Chicago in 1955 and called themselves Catholic Counselors in APGA. This group of Catholic counselors met annually at the APGA convention until 1973.

In 1961, a formal connection between the National Conference of Guidance Councils and Catholic Counselors in APGA was established as the National Catholic Guidance Conference (NCGC). A constitution and bylaws were written, and the conference was to be held simultaneously with the APGA convention. In 1973, the executive director of NCGC, Willis Bartlett, and the president of NCGC, James Lee, applied to APGA for division status, which was granted in 1974 at the APGA convention in New Orleans, Louisiana.

Robert Doyle, one of the original members of Catholic Counselors in APGA; Willis Bartlett, then president of

NCGC; and James Lee, past president of NCGC, met at the 1977 Dallas, Texas, APGA convention to propose new directions and a new name for the organization: the Association for Religious and Values Issues in Counseling (ARVIC). The name change went into effect the following fall.

In 1993, at the American Counseling Association convention in Minneapolis, Minnesota, the ARVIC board of directors passed the motion to expand the focus of the division and to rename it the **Association for Spiritual, Ethical, and Religious Values in Counseling (ASERVIC).**

ASERVIC grew to a membership greater than 4,000 counselors of varied religious and spiritual backgrounds and beliefs. Its Catholic roots have been a source of strength over the years as well as a challenge for those who pushed for a broader perspective for counselors committed to spirituality and its place in the therapeutic enterprise.

One of the major contributions of ASERVIC to the counseling field has been the development of the Spiritual Competencies that emerged as the result of the Summit on Spirituality held in Belmont, North Carolina, in October 1995. Mary Thomas Burke and Judy Miranti conceived the notion of a summit on spirituality whose purpose was to discuss how to infuse spirituality into the counseling process. Participants in the Summit on Spirituality determined that

> In order to be competent to help clients address the spiritual dimension of their lives, a counselor needs to be able to: 1) explain the relationship between religion and spirituality, including similarities and differences, 2) describe religious and spiritual beliefs and practices in a cultural context, 3) engage in self-exploration of his/her religious and spiritual beliefs in order to increase sensitivity, understanding and acceptance of his/her belief system, 4) describe one's religious and/or spiritual belief system and explain various models of religious/spiritual development across the lifespan, 5) demonstrate sensitivity to and acceptance of a variety of religious and/or spiritual expressions in the client's communication, 6) identify the limits of one's understanding of a client's spiritual expression, and demonstrate appropriate referral skills and general possible referral sources, 7) assess the relevance of the spiritual domains in the client's therapeutic issues, 8) be sensitive to and respectful of the spiritual themes in the counseling process as befits each client's expressed preference, and 9) use a client's spiritual beliefs in the pursuit of the client's therapeutic goals as befits the client's expressed preference. (Burke, 1998, p. 2)

ASERVIC has a Web site where ASERVIC'S newsletter, *INTERACTION,* can be found. ASERVIC also publishes the journal *Counseling and Values.* ASERVIC is committed to the spiritual competencies and hosted its first national conference focused on spirituality and counseling in June 2008.

Contributed by Marsha I. Wiggins,
University of Colorado Denver,
Denver, CO

Reference

Burke, M. T. (1998, Winter). From the chair. *The CACREP Connection*, p. 2.

Additional Resources

Association for Spiritual, Ethical, and Religious Values in Counseling Web site: www.aservic.org

Miller, G. (1999). The development of the spiritual focus in counseling and counselor education. *Journal of Counseling & Development, 77,* 498–501.

Attachment

Attachment is an emotional bond that one person forms with a specific person that endures over time. Much of early attachment theory was written by John Bowlby (1969), who attempted to understand the distress experienced by infants who had been separated from their parents. Bowlby observed that separated infants would go to varying lengths to either prevent separation from their parents or to reestablish proximity to an inaccessible parent. Bowlby believed that these attachment behaviors were adaptive responses to separation from a primary attachment figure. An **attachment figure** is someone who provides support, protection, and care. The behaviors used by an individual (i.e., his or her attachment behavioral system) are gradually designed through countless interactions to regulate proximity to an attachment figure.

The **attachment behavioral system** asks the following fundamental question: Is the attachment figure nearby, accessible, and attentive? If the individual perceives the answer to this question is "yes," he or she feels loved, secure, and confident and, behaviorally, is likely to explore his or her environment, interact with others, and be sociable. If, however, the individual perceives the answer to this question is "no," the individual experiences anxiety and, behaviorally, is likely to exhibit attachment behaviors ranging from simple visual searching on the low extreme to active following and vocal signaling on the other. These behaviors continue until either the individual is able to reestablish a desirable level of physical or psychological proximity to the attachment figure or until the individual wears down, as may happen in the context of a prolonged separation or loss. In such cases, the individual experiences despair, depression, and eventual detachment.

Although Bowlby believed that the basic dynamics described here captured the normative dynamics of the attachment behavioral system, he recognized that there are individual differences in the way children appraise the accessibility of the attachment figure and how they regulate their attachment behavior in response to a threat. However, it was only when his colleague, Mary Ainsworth (1968), began to systematically study infant–parent separations that a formal understanding of these individual differences was articulated. Ainsworth developed a technique called the strange situation, a laboratory for studying infant–parent attachment. In the strange situation, 12-month-old infants and their parents were brought to the laboratory and systematically separated and reunited. In the strange situation, most children behaved in the way implied by Bowlby: They became upset when the parents left the room, but when they returned, children actively sought the parents and were easily comforted by them. Children who exhibit this pattern of behavior are often called **secure.** Other children were ill at ease initially, and upon separation, they became extremely distressed. When reunited with their parents, these children had a difficult time being soothed and often exhibited conflicting behaviors that suggested they wanted to be comforted but that they also wanted to punish the parents for leaving. These children are often called **anxious-resistant.** The third pattern of attachment that Ainsworth and her colleagues documented is called **avoidant.** Avoidant children do not appear too distressed by the separation, and upon reunion, actively avoid seeking contact with their parent, sometimes turning their attention to play objects on the laboratory floor.

Although Bowlby was primarily focused on understanding the nature of the infant–caregiver relationship, he believed that attachment characterized human experience from the cradle to the grave. It was not until the mid-1980s, however, that researchers began to take seriously the possibility that attachment processes may play out in adulthood. Researchers Cindy Hazan and Phillup Shaver were two of the first researchers to explore Bowlby's ideas in the context of romantic relationships. The emotional bond that develops between adult romantic partners is partly a function of the same motivational system (i.e., the attachment behavioral system) that gives rise to the emotional bond between infants and their caregivers. Proximity to responsive attachment figures provides individuals a safe haven offering comfort and protection and a secure base, a source of confidence and security that makes exploration possible and enhances coping.

Attachment security may also be understood as the degree to which individuals hold positive models of themselves and of others or the degree to which they see themselves as worthy of others' love and affection, feel comfortable with intimacy, are able to depend on others, and see others as accepting and willing to offer help and support when needed. Attachment theorists also believe that models of self and others are internalized from repeated interactions with those who matter most.

A summary of the core principles of attachment theory include the belief that attachment is an innate motivating force and that seeking and maintaining contact with significant others is innate and occurs throughout the life span. Secure dependency complements autonomy, and, from an attachment perspective, there is no such thing as complete independence or overdependency; rather, there is only effective and ineffective dependence. When secure dependence is fostered, it builds autonomy and self-confidence. Secure attachment offers a safe haven and a secure base. The presence of an attachment figure provides comfort and security, whereas perceived inaccessibility creates distress. The secure base offers individuals support from which they can explore their world and most adaptively respond to their environment. Accessibility and emotional responsiveness from the attachment figure are key to building security. Fear and uncertainty activate attachment needs, and when an individual is threatened, attachment needs for comfort and connection become salient and compelling, and attachment behaviors are activated. Attachment to key others is individuals' primary protection against feelings of helplessness and meaningless, and the process of **separation distress** is predictable. If attachment behaviors fail to evoke comforting responsiveness and contact from attachment figures, a predictable process occurs that consists of protest, clinging, depression, and despair, ending eventually in detachment. Attachment involves working models of self and others. These models of self and others come from thousands of interactions and become expectations and biases that are carried forward into new relationships. Isolation and loss are inherently traumatizing. Attachment theory describes and explores the trauma of deprivation, loss, and rejection and the trauma of being abandoned by those whom an individual needs the most and the enormous impact on the individual. These events have a major effect on personality formation and on a person's ability to deal with other stresses in life.

Contributed by Mark A. Young,
Eastern Washington University,
Cheney, WA

References

Ainsworth, M. D. S. (1968). Object relations, dependency, and attachment: A theoretical review of the infant–mother relationship. *Child Development, 40,* 969–1025.

Bowlby, J. (1969). *Attachment and loss: Vol. 1. Attachment.* New York: Basic Books.

Additional Resources

Bowlby, J. (1988). *A secure base: Parent-child attachment and healthy human development.* New York: Basic Books.

Cassidy, J., & Shaver, P. (Eds.). (1999). *Handbook of attachment: Theory, research, and clinical applications.* New York: Guilford Press.

Johnson, S., & Whiffen, V. (Eds.). (2003). *Attachment processes in couple and family therapy.* New York: Guilford Press.

Attention Deficit and Disruptive Behavior Disorders

Disruptive behavior disorders include diagnoses of attention-deficit/hyperactivity disorder (AD/HD), oppositional defiant disorder (ODD), and conduct disorder (CD), each of which is usually diagnosed in childhood. In each case, the behavior must be evaluated in terms of what is developmentally appropriate and clinically significant.

AD/HD

A diagnosis of **AD/HD** is made in three subsets of the disorder: predominately inattentive type, predominately hyperactive-impulsive type, and combined type. **Predominately inattentive type** individuals often have difficulty completing tasks and are easily distracted but may have no trouble focusing on something they enjoy. Inattentive individuals may make careless errors in work or tasks, may have difficulty sustaining attention to tasks for developmentally appropriate amounts of time, may not be able to come to closure or complete tasks, may be poorly organized and misplace items necessary for task completion, or may be easily distracted and forgetful. **Predominately hyperactive-impulsive type** individuals may fidget and squirm, frequently blurt out answers to questions and interrupt others, rush through assignments, and engage in more physical activity than developmentally appropriate. Adults and teens may experience feelings of internal restlessness. Impairing characteristics of the disorder must be observed prior to age 7 years, present in more than one setting, and not be the result of another mental disorder. The behaviors must significantly affect at least two areas of a person's life, such as school, home, or social settings (American Psychiatric Association [APA], 2000).

Studies have shown that the most effective treatments of AD/HD combine medication, behavioral coaching or counseling, school accommodations, and social skills training. Treatment should be highly individualized and coordinated by a physician or trained mental health professional. AD/HD is a lifelong disorder, although many adults learn accommodations and are able to discontinue medication.

ODD

ODD occurs in about 5% to 8% of American children. ODD is more common in younger boys, although prevalence does balance as girls mature. ODD is characterized by a pattern of purposeful uncooperative, defiant, and hostile behavior and, therefore, must be differentiated from normal developmental oppositional behavior. If the behavior is not addressed, it may become a precursor for conduct disorder. Oppositional behavior is not uncommon in preschool children and teenagers. Many people with ODD purposefully irritate and annoy others and respond in an aggressive manner (APA, 2000). Children with ODD frequently refuse to comply with requests, repeatedly lose their tempers, argue, and rarely take any responsibility for the conflicts created. Impairing characteristics of the disorder must be observed prior to age 8 years of age and no later than 13 to 15 years, must be present in more than one setting, and must not be the result of another mental disorder. The duration of these characteristics must be for at least 6 months. Help is often sought when the chronic pattern of behaviors begins to interfere with a child's social, family, and/or academic functioning. Lack of success in establishing and maintaining relationships with adults and peers is consistently observed.

Diagnosis of ODD can be complex and should be made by a qualified mental health professional. A complete evaluation includes a medical examination to rule out any health concerns, developmental and social history, and review of any current medications. Evaluation must also include identification of coexisting disorders. ODD usually does not occur alone. It is commonly seen along with AD/HD, anxiety, learning disabilities, obsessive-compulsive behavior, and mood disorders. Because children with ODD create high

levels of family stress, an analysis of family dynamics should be conducted to determine the underlying patterns of behavior that lay the foundation for the ODD diagnosis and treatment.

Currently, there is no medication specifically designed to treat ODD, and parent education through formal parent training is viewed as the primary treatment approach. Parents should learn strategies to maintain a consistent and structured discipline approach to use with their child that focuses on communication and positive reinforcement. The child may also benefit from individual counseling with the objectives being to teach anger management skills, improve communication and social skills, and teach tolerance and flexibility.

Individuals with ODD are motivated to engage in power struggles and will attempt any action to "push one's buttons." The most effective response is to show little or no reaction. Responding rather than reacting and doing so in a calm manner may at times disengage the potential power struggle. ODD students function best in a caring environment that is well structured with consistent and clearly stated expectations.

CD

CD is usually diagnosed in clients over the age of 10 years who have a persistent pattern of repetitive behavior that violates the basic rights of others or violates the major rules or laws of society at large. CD is more serious and threatening than ordinary adolescent or childhood pranks. Typically, the earlier the diagnostic criteria appear, the worse the prognosis. Approximately 6% of the population may have CD; it is the most frequently diagnosed childhood disorder in inpatient and outpatient mental health facilities. The diagnostic criteria include the presence of three or more qualifying behaviors within the past 12-month period and at least one qualifying behavior within the past 6 months. Qualifying behaviors include **aggression to people and/or animals,** including physical violence or cruelty, using a weapon, stealing while confronting a person, or forcing someone into sexual activity; **deliberate destruction of property,** which may include fire setting, vandalizing automobiles, or other destruction of property; **deceitfulness or theft,** such as breaking into houses or cars, lying for personal gain or to avoid consequences of behavior, shoplifting, or forgery; or **serious violations of rules,** such as defying parents by staying out at night, running away from home overnight, or being persistently truant from school (APA, 2000). Young people diagnosed with CD may have difficulty feeling empathy, remorse, and reading social cues. They often escalate situations because they misinterpret the actions of others. Their behavior causes clinically significant impairment in social, academic, or occupational functioning. Subtypes include childhood-onset and adolescent-onset. **Childhood-onset** is defined by at least one criterion being present prior to age 10 years. Children diagnosed with CD are usually male, engage in physically aggressive behaviors, and have poor peer relationships. They are at greater risk of having their clinical symptoms evolve into antisocial personality disorder when reaching adulthood. High levels of poorly regulated behavior and activity predict a poorer prognosis. If aggression is present at 8 years of age, it may continue into adolescence. Individuals with no characteristics of CD before age 10 years who develop the symptoms prior to about age 16 years are determined to have **adolescent-onset.** Individuals with adolescent-onset type are less likely to be aggressive and tend to have more normal peer relationships than those with childhood-onset. Girls are most likely to fall into this type. Adolescent-onset type clients develop adult antisocial personality disorder less often and are more likely to hold jobs and be contributing members of society.

The causes of CD are thought to be both genetic and environmental. Although the children of parents who had conduct problems themselves often exhibit the disorder, it is also found in children who experience abuse, harsh and punitive parenting, extreme poverty, or have a significant prenatal or birth history. CD is also found to be more prevalent in children whose biological parents have or had other mental disorders, including mood disorder, alcohol dependence, schizophrenia, or AD/HD.

Diagnosis of CD begins with a complete evaluation, including medical history, psychological testing, psychoeducational testing, and neurological exam. The best treatment results occur when the disorder is diagnosed early. There is no single treatment approach that works best, and a combination of therapy, medication, and involvement with community services may provide the best approach. Older children and teenagers with entrenched problems require longer and more intense treatment that may extend until the age of 18 years. Some medications have been found to be minimally effective in treating the symptoms of CD; however, medication alone is not sufficient. Treatment should also include structured and intensive family therapy and skill building in the areas of anger management and reading social cues. In addition, parent management training focusing on communication, structure, routine, and consistent reinforcement is valuable. Treatment should be overseen and coordinated by a trained mental health professional who coordinates with a medical professional for medication management. Not all individuals with a diagnosis of CD become antisocial or criminal. For most children diagnosed with CD, the condition remits by adulthood (APA, 2000). Early detection and committed treatment provide the best chance of recovery.

Despite their challenges, children with disruptive behavior disorders can grow up to be successful, productive members of society. Channeling their positive traits into productive paths; obtaining an early diagnosis; and instigating an individualized treatment plan that includes individual counseling, medication, school accommodations, a structured environment, family counseling, and a team of knowledgeable and caring family members and professionals who are committed to the long-term needs of the individual make the transition most likely.

Contributed by Peggy K. Cantey and Carol S. Froehlich, Fairfax County Public Schools, Fairfax, VA

Reference

American Psychiatric Association. (2000). *Diagnostic and statistical manual of mental disorders* (4th ed., text rev.). Washington, DC: Author.

Additional Resources

Barkley, R., & Benton, C. (1998). *Your defiant child: Eight steps to better behavior*. New York: Guilford Press.

Reif, S. (2005). *How to reach and teach ADD/ADHD children*. San Francisco: Jossey-Bass.

■ Attribution Theory

First developed by Fritz Heider, **attribution theory** is useful for explaining the behaviors and outcomes of self and others. Most individuals have both a need to understand why things occur as they do and a need to control their environment. In an effort to accomplish each of these goals, people assign reasons or **attributes** to events and outcomes in an effort to explain a situation. It is this explanation that attribution researchers are interested in studying, and in doing so, they place considerable importance on an individual's perception of an event rather than on the actual reality of the event. To understand a person's typical attribution style, researchers focus on the attribution dimensions of stability, locus, and control.

A person in the first **dimension of stability** will explain an event or outcome with either stable causes or unstable causes. **Stable causes** are those that are consistent over time and unlikely to change. If a person believes an event was attributable to a stable cause, he or she is also likely to perceive the event as having the same outcome on future occasions. **Unstable causes** are inconsistent and likely to change across time, increasing the likelihood of a different outcome in the future. Using stable attributions to explain negative events can lead to hopelessness, whereas using unstable attributions to explain these same events can foster persistence and hope for the future.

Second, the **dimension of locus** involves internal and external attributions. **Internal attributions** are those that are within the individual. These attributions increase the likelihood that the person will claim direct responsibility for the event or outcome. **External attributions** are those that place responsibility on an outside agent or force for the event. Consistently using internal attributions to explain negative events has been found to lead to a lack of confidence and to an increased likelihood of depression.

Third, the **dimension of control** involves both controllable and uncontrollable attributions. A **controllable attribution** signifies that the person had some control over the event or outcome, whereas an **uncontrollable attribution** implies that the person did not have control. A person who uses controllable attributions to explain negative events is likely to experience guilt, whereas using uncontrollable attributions is likely to elicit shame.

The example of a student who receives a failing grade on a test demonstrates the dimensions of attribution theory. In trying to make sense of his or her failing grade, he or she may ascribe to either internal attributes, such as low motivation to do well, or to external attributes, such as having a teacher who did not cover the test material well enough to understand it. Next, he or she may assign either stable attributes, such as a lack of intelligence, or unstable attributes, such as an upsetting morning the day of the test, to explain the performance. Finally, he or she may credit either controllable attributes, such as not studying long enough, or uncontrollable attributes, such as poorly written test questions, for the poor outcome. It is generally accepted that the attributions an individual ascribes to an event can have an impact on emotional response and motivation level. It is possible to see in the example given that the student who views the failing test grade as a result of low motivation, an upsetting morning, and too little study time and preparation is likely to take responsibility for his or her failure and try harder in the future.

Contributed by Susan H. Eaves,
Mississippi State University,
Starkville, MS

Additional Resources

Heider, F. (1967). *The psychology of interpersonal relations.* Hoboken, NJ: Wiley.

Weiner, B. (1985). An attributional theory of achievement motivation and emotion. *Psychological Review, 92,* 548–573.

Weiner, B. (1986). *An attributional theory of motivation and emotion.* New York: Springer.

Behavioral Assessment

Behavioral assessment is a global term referring to the observation of overt behaviors exhibited by an individual or individuals and then the systematic recording of the behaviors and its antecedents and consequences. Behavioral assessments can be used with multiple populations, including preschool and school-age children, adolescents, and adults. These assessments also can take place in multiple settings, including daycare centers, schools, residential facilities, adult group homes, and assisted living arrangements.

Antecedent identification is useful in determining whether there is a precipitating factor that elicits the behavior. Identifying the **consequences** that follow the behavior is helpful in identifying the types of rewards or punishments that may work to maintain the occurrence of the undesirable behavior. Ultimately, correctly identifying the antecedent and consequence will help the observer understand the behavior in terms of the function of the behavior, or the "why" behind the behavior.

In other words, the behavior is believed to serve a function for the individual in a particular setting, and through the behavioral assessment, the function can be identified. The functions of behavior fall into four categories: attention, escape/avoidance, tangible, and sensory reinforcement (Shapiro, 2004). Therefore, the behavioral assessment is aimed at uncovering whether the individual is performing a behavior in an attempt to receive attention, escape or avoid a task, gain something tangible, or receive personal gratification.

Characteristics of Behavioral Assessments

According to Marsh and Terdal (1988), behavioral assessment has several characteristics. First, behavioral assessment is idiographic and emphasizes the role of current situational influences on the behavior. Second, assessments are data based, with a low level of inference, and the data drive the interventions. Third, data are taken over a series of sessions or class periods and, thus, are ongoing in nature. Finally, behavioral assessments are empirically based in terms of data collection and treatment design.

Phases of Behavioral Assessments

Conducting a behavioral assessment involves four phases (Sterling-Turner, Robinson, & Wilczynski, 2001): a descriptive phase, an interpretive phase, a verification phase, and a treatment implementation phase. The **descriptive phase** is the first phase and involves data collection on the behavior as well as the situational events, such as the antecedents and consequences. Thus, direct and indirect observations take place in this phase. The **interpretive phase** consists of forming a hypothesis about the function of the behavior. The third phase, **verification,** is when the hypothesis or hypotheses are tested through manipulating the environment. This testing of the hypothesis helps ensure that the last phase, treatment implementation, is successful at remediating and/or alleviating the problem behavior or behaviors. Thus, the last phase is **treatment implementation** and monitoring.

Types of Behavioral Assessments: Direct and Indirect

Direct observations include data recording in the natural environment. Direct observations are systematic and use methods of recording behavior in real time (e.g., observational procedures and observational instruments). Examples of observational procedures are narrative, antecedent-behavior-consequence chart, and event and interval recording (partial and whole; Eckert, Dunn, Codding, & Guiney, 2000). Definitions can be found in Table 1. Some observational instruments are Behavioral Observation of Students in Schools, Ecological Behavioral Assessment System, State-Event Classroom Observation Code, and Peer Social Behavior. A brief description of these measures with advantages and disadvantages can be found in Table 2 (Shapiro, 2004).

Indirect methods include activities that assess an individual's behavior through self-report or the use of informants such as parents, teachers, and caretakers. Typically, indirect methods include behavioral interviews, checklists, and rating scales. Examples of **rating scales** used in the school include the following: Behavior Assessment System for Children, Behavior Evaluation Scale, Devereux Behavior Rating Scale–School Form, and the Revised Behavior Problem Checklist (see Rating Scales).

Conducting a behavioral assessment requires an observer to use multiple modes and methods to obtain the data necessary to aid in problem identification. The process begins with the recognition that a child is exhibiting a problem behavior, then proceeds with the observer conducting multiple observations (both direct and indirect) and forming hypotheses, and then ends with a treatment intervention that is specific to the individual case. The behavioral assessment can be a lengthy process, but when appropriately performed, problem behaviors can be decreased and often eliminated.

Contributed by Laura Baylot Casey,
University of Memphis, Memphis, TN

Table 1. Observational Procedures

Measure	Definition
Narrative	Written descriptions of behavior as it occurs in the environment to confirm problems and define problems. Provides topographical and sequential data and assists the observer with future observations. However, it is difficult to actually record all behaviors due to the fast pace of the classroom.
ABC	Recording the target behavior, events that precede the behavior, and events that follow the behavior in a sequential manner. Helpful in identifying plausible functions of behavior. However, it is time-consuming and can be difficult to record antecedents since they occur before the target behavior is witnessed.
Event	Provides a frequency count of the behavior exhibited during a specific time frame but does not yield any information on antecedents or consequences.
Duration	Records the amount of time the behavior occurs from beginning to end and thus provides a time frame for how long a child engages in the target behavior. This does not provide frequency data or give antecedent or consequence information.
Partial interval	Using a recording sheet with predetermined intervals, the observer marks if the behavior occurs at any point during that interval, thereby obtaining a percentage of time engaged in the target behavior. This works well with high frequency behaviors. However, it can yield an overestimate in terms of the target behavior's severity or persistence because the behavior only has to occur to be recorded.
Whole interval	Using a recording sheet with predetermined intervals, the observer marks if the behavior occurs throughout the entire interval. This works well with continuous behaviors such as on-task. However, it can yield an underestimate in terms of the target behavior's severity or persistence because the behavior has to occur during the entire interval.

References

Eckert, T. L., Dunn, E. K., Codding, R. S., & Guiney, K. M. (2000). Self-report: Rating scale measures. In E. S. Shapiro & T. R. Kratochwill (Eds.), *Conducting school-based assessments of child and adolescent behavior* (pp. 150–169). New York: Guilford Press.

Marsh, E. J., & Terdal, L. G. (1988). Behavioral assessment in child and family disturbance. In E. J. Marsh & L. G. Terdal (Eds.), *Behavioral assessment of childhood disorders* (2nd ed., pp. 3–65). New York: Guilford Press.

Shapiro, E. S. (2004). *Academic skills problems: Direct assessment and intervention* (3rd ed.). New York: Guilford Press.

Sterling-Turner, H. E., Robinson, S. L., & Wilczynski, S. M. (2001). Functional assessment of distracting and disruptive behavior in the school setting. *School Psychology Review, 30,* 211–226.

Additional Resources

Doggett, R. A., & Baylot, L. (2004). Conducting functional assessments in general education classroom settings. In T. S. Watson & C. H. Skinner (Eds.), *Encyclopedia of school psychology*. New York: Kluwer.

Shinn, M. R., Walker, H. M., & Stoner, G. (2002). *Interventions for academic and behavior problems II: Preventive and remedial approaches*. Bethesda, MD: National Association of School Psychologists.

■ Behavioral Counseling

When counseling from a behavioral perspective, the counselor's primary emphasis should be the behaviors expressed by the client. In addressing these behaviors, the professional counselor focuses on overt characteristics that can be operationally defined and measured. For example, one client might report difficulty getting out of bed in the morning, whereas another client might report wanting to reduce the number of arguments with her spouse. Throughout the process, the professional counselor can help the client increase desirable behaviors and decrease undesirable behaviors. This entry provides a brief overview of influential figures followed by an introduction to and examples of a variety of behavioral counseling techniques. It is important to note that this is not an exhaustive list of techniques. More behavioral techniques can be found in the suggested readings at the end of this entry.

Behaviorism and Influential Figures

A number of significant figures have created and contributed to the foundational concepts within the behavioral perspective. Among them are **Ivan Pavlov** (classical conditioning), **B. F. Skinner** (operant conditioning), and **Albert Bandura** (social learning theory).

Influenced by Pavlov's concept of classical conditioning, **John B. Watson** (1928) conducted one of the first behavioral studies with a young child named Albert. Watson exposed

Table 2. Observational Instruments

Measure[a]	Purpose	Norms	Advantage	Disadvantage
BOSS	Observations of independent seatwork, small group, or other instructional activities	No, built-in feature for peer comparison	Simple, provides data on academic engaged time	Minimal information about teacher and classroom variables
E-BASS	Observations of traditional and nontraditional classrooms and preschool	No, built-in feature for peer comparison	Computerized data collection system	Requires extensive training
SECOS	Observations of independent seatwork, small group, large group, or other instructional events	Yes	Detailed information on teacher, student, and the interaction	Complex
PSB	Observation of nonacademic settings in elementary grades	Yes	Simple to learn and provides data on nonacademic settings	Not relevant for academic settings

Note. BOSS = Behavioral Observation of Students in Schools; E-BASS = Ecological Behavioral Assessment System; SECOS = State-Event Observation Code; PSB = Peer Social Behavior.
[a]Instruments primarily used with school-age children but can be adapted.

Albert to a white rat while simultaneously striking a hammer on a metal rod, producing a loud noise that created a startle response. After pairing the noise and the white rat several times, Albert elicited a fear response to the rat and later to other furry white objects such as rabbits or fur coats. Although ethical review boards today would not approve such a study, it demonstrated that fears can be conditioned in human beings. Watson originated many of the classic behavioral tenets applied throughout counseling processes today. Watson's study also laid the foundation for much of Joseph Wolpe's work.

Joseph Wolpe (1958) developed the concepts of reciprocal inhibition and systematic desensitization. **Reciprocal inhibition** is based on the belief that a person can experience only one emotional state at a time. For example, anxiety and relaxation are incompatible states. Using this technique, if a client is anxious as a result of a phobia of spiders, the professional counselor would facilitate relaxation exercises to replace the anxiety. The goal of this procedure is to interrupt the less desired state (anxiety) and reduce the relationship or pairing of the conditioned response (anxiety) and the stimulus causing the conditioned response (e.g., a spider).

Wolpe (1958) also developed the therapeutic technique of **systematic desensitization,** a procedure based on reciprocal inhibition, designed to help individuals struggling with extreme fear or anxiety. The desensitization process is conducted in a gradual manner by exposing the client to anxiety-producing stimuli without the resulting anxiety-producing consequences. The process begins with the professional counselor teaching the client relaxation exercises. Next, the counselor elicits detailed information from the client about stimuli that cause anxiety. One way of gathering this information is through the use of a subjective units of discomfort scale. The client lists items in order from least to most anxiety producing and assigns each item a number between 0 and 100. Zero represents complete relaxation and 100 represents great anxiety (Sharf, 2008). Next, while engaging in relaxation exercises, the client is asked to visualize an anxiety-producing stimulus from the list. As the process continues, the goal is to use the relaxation exercises to eventually reduce or eliminate the anxiety.

Examples of Behavioral Techniques

Every behavior is made up of individual stimulus-response elements that take place in a sequence or chain, called a **stimulus-response chain.** Brushing one's teeth can be used as an example. Although this task is often thought of as one behavior, it consists of several individual stimulus-response elements, such as reaching for the toothbrush, then reaching for the toothpaste, then opening the toothpaste container, and so on. The stimulus-response chain only continues if the final response in the chain is reinforcing. With brushing teeth, for example, the result is clean teeth and fresh breath.

A variety of methods can be used to teach stimulus-response chains, including forward chaining, backward chaining, and whole-task method. Assembling a chair can be used as an example to illustrate the different methods. With **forward chaining,** the assembly is broken down into a series of steps that must be followed and accomplished in a specific order. Step 1 must be successfully completed prior to moving on to Step 2, Step 2 prior to moving on to Step 3, and so on. As with forward chaining, **backward chaining** also breaks the assembly down into a series of steps. The difference, however, is that the assembly is accomplished in the opposite order. The last step must be successfully completed prior to moving onto the second-to-last step, the second-to-last step prior to moving on to the third-to-last step, and so on. In **whole-task method,** any process or procedure can be used to reach the end result: the correctly assembled chair. One step is not required to be completed prior to beginning another.

Behavioral rehearsal (also referred to as *rehearsal*) allows the client, through modeling and instruction, to practice and learn a behavior. For example, children in a social skills group listen to a description and observe the group facilitator engaging in the behavior of greeting group members. Next, each group member is given repeated opportunities to practice the behavior. The facilitator observes each attempt, immediately giving specific feedback by correcting incorrect behavior and reinforcing correct behavior. Each group member continues rehearsing the desired behavior until it is demonstrated correctly a few times.

A number of factors should be considered to implement behavioral rehearsal successfully. The environment in which the behavior is practiced should be conducive to learning the desired behavior. Furthermore, the group facilitator should begin with simple behaviors that progressively become more complex to ensure successful performance. For example, after learning to greet one another, group members may learn to sit quietly and listen while another group member talks.

Time-out reduces the likelihood of future incidences of problem behaviors by removing the child from the reinforcing situation or activity for a short time. Time-out can be **exclusionary** (i.e., the child is completely removed from the activity) or **nonexclusionary** (i.e., the child stays in the environment but is removed from the activity). For example, if a child is playing on a playground and destroys another child's sandcastle, the caregiver can remove the child from the activity to a time-out space still on the playground but away from the activity. After a few minutes, the child is allowed to rejoin the activity and plays without further difficulty. This is an example of nonexclusionary time-out.

A number of factors should be considered to implement time-out successfully. A reinforcement method should be used in combination with time-out to allow the child opportunities to increase the desired behavior and be rewarded for doing so. The space used for time-out should completely remove the child from the activity, minimize distractions, and be less appealing than the activity from which the child is removed. The child should not be able to continue the problem behavior while in time-out and should not be interacted with. The child should remain in the time-out space for the entire specified time.

Response cost reduces the likelihood of the incidence of problem behaviors in the future by removing a specified amount of a reinforcer. Although money is commonly used, any reinforcer or privilege can be removed when using this procedure. For example, Johnny receives $5 of allowance money every Saturday. As his weekly chore, Johnny is required to take the garbage out each evening during the week. Johnny's parents let him know that each time he does not complete the chore, a quarter will be removed from his allowance.

A number of factors should be considered to implement the response cost procedure successfully. Similar to time-out, a reinforcement method should be used in combination with response cost to allow the child opportunities to increase the desired behavior and be rewarded for doing so. In addition, the reinforcer and amount that will be removed should be determined in advance and that information shared with the child. The amount removed should be enough to ensure that the problem behavior will decrease; however, its removal must not harm the child. For example, withholding an entire meal would not be appropriate.

Overcorrection reduces the likelihood of incidences of problem behaviors by requiring the child to engage in a consequence that is less favorable than the problem behavior. Commonly, this procedure is used to decrease disruptive or aggressive behavior. There are two types of overcorrection: positive practice and restitution. **Positive practice** requires the child to conduct the corrected behavior for an extended period time. For example, Susan is required to wash the dishes after dinner on Monday. She does not complete the task; therefore, her parents require her to wash the dishes after dinner for the next five evenings. **Restitution** requires the client to restore the environment to a condition better than it was prior to the occurrence of the problem behavior. For example, Susan colors with markers on a wall in her bedroom. As a result, her parents require her to clean all of the walls in her bedroom.

A **behavioral contract** is a written document to which two parties agree. The contract specifies (a) a target behavior, (b) the method used to measure the target behavior, (c) a time interval in which the target behavior must be completed, (d) the consequence (contingent on a specified amount of the target behavior within the identified time interval), and (e) who will make use of the consequence. For example, David and his parents create a behavioral contract outlining David's homework and study obligations during the upcoming school week. David agrees to spend 2 hours completing homework and studying each evening, Monday through Friday. If David does not complete these obligations, the consequence is that he will not be allowed to go to a movie on Saturday. David's parents will make use of the consequence.

Working from a behavioral counseling perspective allows the professional counselor to assist the client by being a teacher, coach, and support system. Overall, behavioral approaches tend to (a) focus on behavior, (b) use a scientific approach to understanding behavior, (c) operate pragmatically to address behavior change, (d) use clearly defined procedures to address behavior, (e) place a significant emphasis on environmental causes of behavior, and (f) avoid using intrapsychic explanations of behavior (Grant & Evans, 1994).

Contributed by Joseph D. Wehrman,
The Citadel, Charleston, SC

References

Grant, L., & Evans, A. (1994). *Principles of behavior analysis*. New York: HarperCollins.
Sharf, R. S. (2008). *Theories of psychotherapy and counseling: Concepts and cases* (4th ed.). Belmont, CA: Thomson.
Watson, J. B. (1928). *The ways of behaviorism.* New York: Harper & Brothers.
Wolpe, J. (1958). *Psychotherapy by reciprocal inhibition.* Stanford, CA: Stanford University Press.

Additional Resources

Miltenberger, R. G. (2004). *Behavior modification: Principles and procedures* (3rd ed.). Belmont, CA: Wadsworth.
Spiegler, M. D., & Guevremont, D. C. (2003). *Contemporary behavior therapy* (4th ed.). Belmont, CA: Wadsworth.

■ Between-Groups Design

A **between-groups design** describes the statistical comparison of two or more different groups of participants who are subjected to different experiences or treatments. A between-groups design is a research design that uses a separate sample for each treatment condition; that is, the participants for each condition are different from one another. Between-groups designs are used in both experimental and quasi-experimental research. In developing a between-groups research project, a counselor would use a random assignment or restricted random assignment process to divide the participants among the various conditions (e.g., treatment and control). Researchers rely on randomization of participants among the treatment groups to control for unmeasured variables, although sometimes the arranging of participants is used to guarantee proportions on certain key variables (e.g., gender, race, socioeconomic status).

Independent variables have different levels. In a between-groups design, each participant is assigned to a different level of the independent variable, and no participant is assigned to more than one level of any independent variable. Thus, each participant is only measured once, and the scores between conditions are independent of each other. For example, a counselor who is interested in the effect of brief therapy on reduction of depressive symptoms might recruit participants for one of three groups (e.g., brief therapy, psychoeducational consultation, and delayed treatment control group). Each participant in the research would complete a pretest and posttest of depressive symptoms. The results of the measures would be compared between the groups.

Types of designs may include two levels of the independent variable (i.e., use an independent t test to determine the difference between the mean of the control and treatment groups or between two treatment groups) and more than two levels of the independent variable (e.g., use a one-way analysis of variance to determine differences between three or more levels of the control group[s] and treatment group[s]).

In experimental research, participants in a between-groups design are randomly assigned to their conditions. In quasi-experimental research, a lack of random assignment can be confounding and a threat to both internal validity (see Internal Validity) and external validity (see External Validity, Threats to). Of course, all threats to internal validity also threaten external validity. Threats to internal validity of between-groups design include assignment bias (how participants were assigned), differential attrition (differential loss of participants), diffusion of treatment (comparison group learns about program from participants), compensatory equalization (demands by participants to be placed in certain treatment conditions), compensatory rivalry (comparison group develops a competitive mind-set with the treatment group), and resentful demoralization (comparison group is aware of treatment being given to other group and becomes demoralized).

Contributed by Chandra R. Sumlin-Brown and Carl J. Sheperis, Mississippi State University, Starkville, MS

Additional Resources

Gravetter, F. J., & Forzano, L. B. (2006). *Research methods for the behavioral sciences* (2nd ed.). Belmont, CA: Wadsworth.

Gravetter, F. J., & Wallnau, L. B. (2007). *Essentials of statistics for the behavioral sciences* (6th ed.). Belmont, CA: Wadsworth.

■ Bias in Assessment

Bias in assessment occurs when an individual or group of individuals is denied the opportunity to demonstrate their true knowledge, skills, thoughts, or feelings on the measured task. Sources of bias in assessment include the design of the test (i.e., test bias); the examinee's approach to taking the test (i.e., response bias); the examiner's technique for giving the test (i.e., examiner bias); the scorer's method of interpreting the results (i.e., interpretive bias); the physical location of the testing (i.e., situational bias); and the systems affecting the administration, interpretation, and use of testing (i.e., ecological bias).

Test Bias

Test bias occurs when the design of the test prevents the examinee from demonstrating knowledge or skills. An example is an Alaska Native child living in rural Alaska where snow machines (snow mobiles) and sled dogs are used for transportation. Asked to identify the missing part on a car door as part of a standard intelligence test, this child might have never seen a car and, therefore, have difficulty identifying the missing part. Although the child may be quite intelligent, her or his IQ test scores may be lowered by the presence of the unfamiliar car; thus, the child is unable to demonstrate her or his true intelligence.

Response Bias

Response bias occurs when something about the examinee prevents him or her from accurately responding to a task. Some people tend to answer *yes* on surveys (i.e., acquiescent

response bias). When presented with a question that generates mixed feelings or for which they have no clear answer, some examinees are more likely to pick *yes*. To address response bias, researchers often design surveys with a mixture of *yes* and *no* correct answers. Thus, a researcher studying problem-solving skills might ask, "Do you act quickly to resolve problems?" and "Do you avoid making decisions as long as possible?" The desired answer for the first question is *yes*, whereas the desired answer for the second question is *no*. If the examinee answered *yes* to both questions, it might suggest a response bias or other problem with the accuracy of the results.

Examiner Bias

When the behavior of the examiner modifies the test administration process, **examiner bias** occurs. When administering standardized intelligence tests to people whom they like, some examiners may ask questions prompting test takers to clarify their answers. Examinees subsequently receive more points for clearer, higher quality answers. The same examiner may provide fewer prompts and apply stricter grading for examinees they do not like, reflecting examiner bias.

Interpretive Bias

Interpretive bias occurs when the examiner's interpretation process provides an unfair advantage or disadvantage to the examinee. When a test taker's response is ambiguous, the examiner might give a bright honor student the "benefit of the doubt," interpreting the answers favorably by assigning higher points. Alternately, when told that an examinee is a troublemaker who consistently struggles academically, the examiner may be more likely to interpret ambiguous information punitively by assigning lower points. Some argue that many standardized IQ tests contain bias that prevents fair interpretation of results for ethnic and cultural minorities. Others say the tests are based on the dominant American culture and provide a good indicator of how minorities function in the dominant culture.

Situational Bias

Situational bias occurs when the people or things in the testing situation fail to provide the needed resources for a category or classification of people to demonstrate their true knowledge, skills, thoughts, or feelings on the measured task. An example is a classroom where the instructor plays music in the background while students complete their assignment. This situation might be biased against the student with attention-deficit/hyperactivity disorder for whom the music provides a barrier to optimal performance on the assigned task.

Ecological Bias

Ecological bias consists of global systems, called the ecology, that affect the group to which the examinee belongs rather than affecting the individual alone. Thus, systems prevent a group or classification of people from demonstrating their true knowledge, skills, thoughts, or feelings on a measured task. For example, some contend that a system that requires racial and ethnic minorities to complete standardized college admissions exams that are not designed for or standardized on the ethnic minority group constitutes ecological bias.

Contributed by Angela J. Adams,
Capella University, Minneapolis, MN

Additional Resources

Kaplan, R. M., & Saccuzzo, D. P. (2004). *Psychological testing: Principles, applications, and issues* (6th ed.). Belmont, CA: Wadsworth.

Lopez, S. J., & Snyder, C. R. (Eds.). (2003). *Positive psychological assessment: A handbook of models and measures.* Washington, DC: American Psychological Association.

Sattler, J. M., & Hoge, R. D. (2006). *Assessment of children: Behavioral, social, and clinical foundations* (5th ed.). La Mesa, CA: Sattler.

■ Biracial/Multiracial Clients, Counseling

The 2000 U.S. census (U.S. Census Bureau, 2000) was the first time respondents had the opportunity to mark more than one racial category to designate their racial heritage. Although governmental recognition has been a recent phenomenon, the reality is individuals whose biological parents are from two or more different racial groups have been a part of the U.S. history since the country's inception. The 2000 census reported that approximately 7 million adults identified themselves as being from two or more racial groups. Moreover, there may be as many as 4.5 million children who are similarly characterized. From all indications, as the number of interracial marriages continues to increase, the number of **biracial/multiracial persons** in the United State will increase. In an attempt to reflect the existing literature, the term *multiracial* is used to describe both biracial and multiracial individuals in this entry.

Racial Identity Development

Identity development is a universal task that everyone undertakes, and racial identity is one component of identity development. There have been numerous theories related to racial identity development in the literature that address a monoracial perspective. Poston (1990) presented a model of biracial identity development to highlight the process by which multiracial persons experience themselves racially. One aspect that sets this model apart from other racial identity models is the recognition that when the challenge to identify with one racial group is posed, no matter which group is chosen, one or more parts of a multiracial person's heritage will be unacknowledged. In other words, it is not an "either/or" proposition; it is more of an "either/and/or" situation. Poston's model has five stages: (a) personal identity, (b) choice of group categorization, (c) enmeshment and denial, (d) appreciation, and (e) integration. The personal identity stage focuses on the young child's world, which is usually made up of family and nurturing members of the community. Here, race is often a secondary factor in the child's day-to-day

existence. In the second stage, choice of group categorization, multiracial individuals are pressured to declare a singular ethnic identity. This often occurs during adolescence when belonging to a group is so important. Many times, physical features and community expectations influence how others view multiracial persons, thus creating external expectations of how multiracial persons "ought" to self-identify and pressure to do so. The third stage of Poston's model is enmeshment and denial. Once the choice of racial group is made, the next step is emersion in the culture of that group. Although this portion of the stage is similar to many other racial identity development models, the latter part of the stage, denial, is unique to multiracial persons. If/when the choice is a single racial group, obviously other aspects of the multiracial person's heritage are ignored. For many multiracial persons, denying important aspects of their personhood can lead to feelings of guilt or dissonance.

Poston's (1990) later statuses, appreciation and integration, mark an internal movement toward developing a racial self-identification according to the culture that resonates with the multiracial person. For some individuals, a monoracial identification fits best. For others, a multiracial identity is their choice. It is important to remember that racial identity is a developmental process; therefore, a multiracial individual may articulate a different racial identity at different points in time.

Interracial Families

One challenge to **interracial families** in which both the mother and father have a monoracial heritage, albeit a different one, is that neither parent has experienced life from the perspective of a multiracial person. Given that one of the tasks of the family is to share cultural values, beliefs, and a sense of identity with the children, how to present multiple cultural perspectives to children often becomes a challenge for parents. Although some parents may choose to highlight only one racial/cultural perspective, more and more parents of interracial children are imparting aspects of all their racial/cultural heritages to their children, with the renewed belief that the children will benefit from being exposed to their diverse racial heritage. The recent availability of literature that includes children's books with stories about multiracial children as well as books for parents who are raising multiracial children provides affirmation and support for families who have previously existed as invisible entities.

Adolescence

For multiracial adolescents, the developmental tasks of increased sense of self through peer interactions may present unique challenges. American society is racialized, and peer groups are often formed along racial lines. The desire to "fit in" may greatly influence how a multiracial adolescent self-identifies; the choice is often made based on gaining entrance into a desired peer group. Physical features can be a factor in determining how smoothly peer acceptance occurs; the more the multiracial adolescent physically resembles the desired peer group, seemingly better the chances for acceptance.

Adulthood

The transition into adulthood affords individuals the opportunity to revisit various aspects of their identity with less emphasis on peer influence. For multiracial persons, developing a racial identity that is internally congruent as opposed to being heavily influenced by outside opinion is a common phenomenon. The choice of a life partner and thoughts of future children often give multiracial adults an opportunity to view themselves racially in terms of family and community.

Recommendation to Professional Counselors

Multiracial persons often describe themselves as strong, open-minded individuals who have experienced the challenges of navigating between the potentially complex worlds of race. They believe that they have spent a great deal of their lives viewing issues from multiple perspectives. As a result, they see themselves as better prepared to live in a diverse society than many of their monoracial counterparts. Professional counselors are recommended to articulate strengths they note as they work with multiracial persons.

Additional recommendations for professional counselors to consider when engaging multiracial clients in counseling include the following:

1. Professional counselors should engage in self-reflection related to their own attitudes about interracial couples and multiracial persons. It is crucial that counselors' attitudes not interfere with their ability to be supportive of multiracial clients.
2. Professional counselors should not assume that the basis of every counseling issue presented by a multiracial client is related to the client's racial heritage.
3. Professional counselors should be aware that racial identity development is a long-term process and that multiracial individuals may change how they racially self-identify at different points in their life.

Contributed by Nancy Nishimura,
The University of Memphis, Memphis, TN

References

Poston, W. S. C. (1990). The biracial identity development model: A needed addition. *Journal of Counseling & Development, 69,* 152–155.

U.S. Census Bureau. (2000). *2000 census.* Retrieved June 21, 2008, from http://www.census.gov/main/www/cen2000.html

Additional Resources

Root, M. P. P. (Ed.). (1996). *The multiracial experience: Racial borders as the new frontier.* Thousand Oaks, CA: Sage.

Root, M. P. P., & Kelley, M. (Eds.). (2003). *Multiracial child resource book: Living complex identities.* Seattle, WA: Mavin Foundation.

Wehrly, B., Kenney, K. R., & Kenney, M. E. (1999). *Counseling multiracial families.* Thousand Oaks, CA: Sage.

Bowen Family Therapy

Murray Bowen (1913–1990) was one of the original researchers in family therapy and a pioneer in the development of family therapy. Using systems theory concepts to explain the complex interactions in the family, Bowen developed a comprehensive theory (1978) of families based on the concept of the family as an emotional unit with interlocking relationships and multigenerational patterns.

Originally trained as a surgeon, Bowen became interested in the field of psychiatry as a result of his experiences in the Army during World War II. At the Menninger Clinic in the late 1940s to early 1950s, Bowen observed the intense interactions between individuals with schizophrenia and their mothers, in which "mother-patient symbiosis" occurred that created such an intense bond that the mother could not differentiate herself from her child. Bowen believed these interactions were a magnified form of the natural process that existed in all relationships.

Bowen's most noted family research began in 1954 at the National Institute of Mental Health, where he initiated a 5-year project to work with families that had a child with schizophrenia. The entire family lived in a hospital ward, thus offering Bowen a unique opportunity to observe the impact of the child's behavior on the family unit and relationships within the family. Once this project ended, Bowen moved to Georgetown University in Washington, DC, and began working with families whose problems were less severe, although what he observed in these families appeared similar to those families struggling with schizophrenia. These clinical experiences led to the development of **Bowen family therapy.**

Bowen's theory is based on two main variables, the degree of anxiety in the family and the degree of integration of self as a result of chronic stress and anxiety. **Integration of self** refers to the ability to be an independent individual with healthy, functioning family relationships and the ability not to absorb the emotional impact of the family unit's anxiety. The goals of Bowen family therapy are to decrease anxiety in the family and increase an individual's integration of self or "I-position." These goals are achieved by first examining patterns of emotional reactions and interlocking relationships. Once the family has an understanding of how these patterns and relationships have negatively affected the family unit and its members, experimenting with new behaviors to help reduce stress and anxiety and increase integration of self begins.

Key Concepts

There are eight interrelated concepts in Bowen family therapy. Three are characteristics of the family, and the other five provide information on emotional aspects of the family. The three family characteristics are differentiation of self; triangles; and the nuclear family emotional processes of marital conflict, dysfunction in one spouse, impairment of one or more children, and emotional distance. The five emotional family aspects are family projection process, multigenerational transmission process, sibling position, emotional cutoff, and societal emotional process.

As in other types of groups, families naturally put pressure on their members to think and emote alike. **Differentiation of self** refers to a person's ability to separate feelings and thoughts from those of others, thus freeing him or her to be able to recognize personal involvement in a problematic familial relationship while still remaining connected to the family. Families with intense interdependence will not be able to adapt to stressful events without increased chronic anxiety, fueling the need for all family members to react in unison. Conversely, differentiated members of a family can make healthy decisions based upon self-needs, not as an emotional response to pressures from the family unit. Hence, one of the goals of Bowen family therapy is to help family members differentiate.

The concept of **family triangles,** or **triangulation,** is a common construct in family therapies. A family triangle consists of a family dyad whose relationship becomes triangulated when a third member joins the relationship to deflect tension in the original two-person relationship. Often the third person is a child, and the push–pull of this position in the triangle can cause emotional distress. Bowen believed that the third member is added to the two-person relationship to help stabilize emotional stress during times of extreme closeness or distance. Eventually, a new family dyad relationship emerges within the triangle, the third person begins to feel like an outsider and reacts to the anxiety of discomfort, and chaos results in the family unit. For example, in an effort to avoid financial discussions with his wife, a husband begins spending a large amount of time with the wife's brother, thus drawing her brother into a family triangle to deflect tension in the parental dyad; as the husband–brother dyad succeeds at avoiding the financial discussions, the wife begins to feel resentful toward her brother and begins to avoid her family's functions.

Bowen theorized two ways in which the marital dyad relationship has an emotional impact on the family unit. Marital conflict causes family tension and results in each spouse focusing on what is wrong with other family members while attempting to control the other spouse. Dysfunction in one spouse occurs when a spouse is pressured into thinking or acting in certain ways, and the pressure results in growing anxiety and dysfunction in thoughts, behaviors, or social interactions.

Family projection process refers to parents projecting their own emotional problems onto a child. Fearing something is wrong with the child, parents focus on the child and eventually interpret the child's behavior as confirmation that there is something wrong, thus justifying the parents treating the child as if something is really wrong. The child then reacts through impaired functioning to relieve the anxiety of parental focus and may become emotionally distant and triangulated in the parental relationship.

Impairment of one or more children can result in the parents focusing their own anxieties on one or more of their children, and parents often develop an idealized or negative view of the child. The child then becomes less differentiated and is, therefore, vulnerable to internalizing family tensions;

the result can affect social functioning, school performance, and even the child's health.

Nuclear family emotional process refers to four primary emotional patterns that can cause anxiety and relationship problems in a family; the four primary emotional patterns are (a) marital conflict, (b) dysfunction in one family member, (c) impairment of one or more children, and (d) emotional distance. The concept of **multigenerational transmission process** is based on the way that the nuclear family emotional process passes from one generation to the next. A Bowen therapist will use a genogram as an effective visual technique to diagram multigenerational family structure, adding nuclear family emotional processes for examination and understanding (see Genogram).

Differentiation of self can be affected by parental expectations that are based on **sibling position.** Similar to the basic concept of birth order in Adlerian theory, Bowen believed that sibling position had an impact on family roles and expectations for both children and their parents. For example, a mother who was the oldest child with two younger brothers might have different expectations of her youngest son than she does of her husband who was the baby of the family. As new children become a part of the family, sibling position must be modified and renegotiated, causing stress and anxiety in the family.

Emotional distance is inherent in the nuclear family emotional processes and connected to the underlying construct of triangulation. The basic concept of emotional distance is exhibited in two ways: A family member distances himself or herself from other members to reduce the intensity of the relationship, although the family member risks becoming too isolated or feeling abandoned, or a family member becomes overly connected to the family unit but is harmed emotionally as the member absorbs too much of the family's anxiety. A common example of emotional distance occurs when an adult child becomes the primary resident caregiver for a parent. As the adult child becomes more involved with maintaining the parent's health, the child becomes less differentiated from the parent and becomes isolated from friends and other family members.

Emotional distance in a family can lead to a family member exhibiting **emotional cutoff,** in which a family member totally severs emotionally from the family or individuals in the family in an attempt to manage unresolved issues. Not only does emotional cutoff result in avoiding the problems in individuals' familial relationships, these individuals risk using new relationships to replace the unresolved family relationships, thus placing too much importance on the new relationships.

The concept of **societal emotional process** examines other influences on the family unit, looking outside the family for cultural messages and other societal norms regarding expectations and behaviors in a family. For example, current U.S. societal norms encourage independence in adolescence that often results in behaviors parents find unacceptable; parents and their teenage children experience anxiety trying to negotiate family values that do not conflict with societal expectations.

Interventions

The Bowen family therapist remains neutral and objective, assuming multiple roles in sessions. Seeking to engage family members in understanding family dynamics, the therapist becomes the lead researcher, asking questions to solicit more information, offering interpretations using the eight Bowen family therapy concepts, and experimenting with new approaches to reduce stress and anxiety in relationships. A **genogram** is used to organize family information, identify triangles, and identify relationship dynamics. **Relationship experiments** give the family opportunities to become aware of existing triangles and to try new interactional processes. **Therapy triangles** temporarily merge the therapist into the family unit, creating triangles designed to reestablish stability in the family. Other interventions used by Bowenian therapists include **multiple family therapy,** in which couples learn by observing the interactions of other couples, and the use of videotaped **displacement stories** selected to teach improved family functioning in a nondefensive way.

As a combination of therapist and coach, the therapist uses paradoxical comments, humor, and serious observations to diffuse or decompress tension and return family members to focused engagement in the therapeutic process. As a **coach,** the Bowenian therapist does not tell clients what to do but does ask questions and makes comments guiding clients toward increased understanding and relationships that are more functional. Bowen encouraged clients to take an **I-position** stance, focused on personal feelings rather than on the actions of another; an example of an I-position is the statement, "I wish you would help out more with the kids" instead of "You always make me take care of everything with the kids."

Contributed by Jannette Sturm-Mexic,
Xavier University of Louisiana,
New Orleans, LA

Reference

Bowen, M. (1978). *Family therapy in clinical practice.* New York: Aronson.

Additional Resources

Bowen Center for the Study of the Family and the Georgetown Family Center's Web site: http://www.thebowencenter.org
Niolon, R. (1999). *Bowenian family therapy.* Retrieved July 12, 2007, from http://www.psychpage.com/learning/library/counseling/bowen.html

Career Adaptability

Because of the volatile nature of the global economy and technological advancements since the latter part of the 20th century, people must adjust to changing contextual circumstances affecting their work lives. This reality underscores the importance of understanding one's self and the world-of-work and adapting career plans accordingly. The term *adapt* comes from the Latin word *adaptare*, meaning "to fit," which invokes numerous career theories that emphasize matching one's self to a suitable position. The **career adaptability** construct extends from a related term, called *career maturity,* which was considered central to understanding career development in **Donald Super's life-span life-space theory.**

Super emphasized the critical importance of considering how clients manage the career development process throughout the life span. In 1979, Super published separate papers with Jennifer Kidd and Edward Knasel to introduce the career adaptability construct, later defined as "readiness to cope with changing work and working conditions" (Super & Knasel, 1981, p. 195). By focusing on the process of coping with complex tasks that are involved in choosing, developing, or managing a career, the incorporation of career adaptability into counseling supplements the traditional assessment of interests, abilities, personality, and work values. Following is a brief overview of Super's career maturity construct, an explanation of why the recent emphasis on adaptability is more appropriate, and the components of career adaptability from Mark Savickas's (2005) recent update and expansion of Super's theory, called career construction theory (see Career Construction Theory). Several constructs related to adaptability are also discussed in the Minnesota theory of work adjustment (TWA; see Person–Environment Fit). Career adaptability emphasizes the coping processes involved in how people manage careers across the life span. On the other hand, adjustment within the context of TWA draws on the individual differences tradition, which emphasizes how fit, or correspondence, between people and their work environments is achieved and maintained, leading to work satisfaction, satisfactoriness, and tenure.

Career Maturity

Super (1955) conceptualized **vocational maturity** (later named *career maturity*) as the ideal of how adolescents approach tasks involved in making vocational and educational choices. The term *career maturity* initially was divided into Vocational Maturity I and Vocational Maturity II. The former relates to identifying whether the person is coping with the tasks that could be expected, given his or her age (and life span theory). The latter focuses on how a person copes with tasks regardless of age. Career maturity is typically understood as the degree to which a person achieves developmental tasks expected by society relative to a person's peers, or Vocational Maturity I. From the developmental perspective, people were thought to advance in an orderly manner, following a predictable sequence over time, culminating in a mature end state.

Super's multidimensional model included planfulness, exploration, decision making, knowledge of the world-of-work, and preferred occupation. Overall, career maturity is composed of two attitudinal dimensions (i.e., attitudes toward career planning and exploration) and two cognitive dimensions (i.e., knowledge of occupations and effective career decision making). These dimensions encompass general factors of effective career choice content and process. The Career Maturity Inventory (CMI; Crites & Savickas, 1996) and the Career Development Inventory (Savickas & Hartung, 1996) have traditionally been used to measure these dimensions. A large body of research indicates that these measures yield construct validity, with scores generally increasing throughout adolescence and as the result of interventions. However, the individualistic nature of career maturity has raised questions regarding the cross-cultural validity and counseling utility of the CMI, in particular. For example, Asian Americans, who typically have a collectivistic orientation, tend to score lower on the CMI, likely due to a more interdependent decisional style. Mature attitudes are theorized to yield the necessary information to make realistic choices. Accordingly, adolescents will make the most mature choices by using sufficient decision-making competence based on the knowledge of career possibilities gained through planful exploration. Super later attempted to refine the construct to address the entire life span and to bridge key segments of his theory (e.g., individual differences, development, self, and context) across the entire life span.

Career Adaptability

Super's earlier emphasis on maturational processes involved in adolescent career development was not as appropriate for understanding factors affecting adults in a less stable era; therefore, he introduced the career adaptability concept, which was later advanced by Savickas who made it a central component of career construction theory. Building on earlier empirical and theoretical work by Super, Knasel, Kidd, and others,

Savickas (1997) asserted that career adaptability should replace career maturity as the central construct related to the segments of Super's theory. Unlike maturity, adaptability ignores references to natural maturation or growth and emphasizes how people develop in response to novel challenges and inherent shifts in a postindustrial economic environment. Savickas (2005) defined career adaptability as "a psychosocial construct that denotes an individual's readiness and resources for coping with current and imminent vocational development tasks, occupational transitions, and personal traumas" (p. 51). Essentially, career adaptability addresses the processes involved in how clients deal with the inherent challenges of navigating complex educational and career transitions within changing psychosocial contexts throughout the life span. Contrary to people drifting or otherwise floundering in their careers, adaptive individuals demonstrate the following four global dimensions of career adaptability:

1. Concern about future work life,
2. Control over career future,
3. Curiosity to explore possibilities for future selves and scenarios, and
4. Confidence to seek career goals.

Professional counselors can inquire about how clients approach and make career decisions to assess for components of career adaptability. Each dimension encompasses a set of more specific attitudes, beliefs, competencies, and affiliated coping behaviors that reflect adaptability. Concern is the most fundamental dimension because it provides a future orientation that increases the awareness necessary to plan careers strategically, control involves assertiveness that fosters decisiveness, curiosity entails experimentation and exploration, and confidence yields persistence and efficacious problem solving. Professional counselors can use this model as a guide for assisting clients in approaching their career decisions wisely and learning coping skills so they are prepared for both expected and unforeseen transitions in the future. Ultimately, these four qualities represent adaptive strategies that enable an individual to maximize fit between an ever-changing self-construal within complex environments. Adaptive individuals are able to implement their self-concepts into careers through increasing their orientation to the future, asserting control over the process, exploring new possibilities, and having the confidence to meet valued goals.

Contributed by Patrick J. Rottinghaus,
Southern Illinois University at Carbondale,
Carbondale, IL

References

Crites, J. O., & Savickas, M. L. (1996). Revision of the Career Maturity Inventory. *Journal of Career Assessment, 4,* 131–138.

Savickas, M. L. (1997). Career adaptability: An integrative construct for life-span, life-space theory. *The Career Development Quarterly, 45,* 247–259.

Savickas, M. L. (2005). The theory and practice of career construction. In S. D. Brown & R. W. Lent (Eds.), *Career*

development and counseling: Putting theory and research to work (pp. 42–70). Hoboken, NJ: Wiley.

Savickas, M. L., & Hartung, P. J. (1996). The Career Development Inventory in review: Psychometric and research findings. *Journal of Career Assessment, 4,* 171–188.

Super, D. E. (1955). The dimensions and measurement of vocational maturity. *Teachers College Record, 57,* 151–163.

Super, D. E., & Kidd, J. M. (1979). Vocational maturity in adulthood: Toward turning a model into a measure. *Journal of Vocational Behavior, 14,* 255–270.

Super, D. E., & Knasel, E. G. (1979). *Specifications for a measure of career adaptability in young adults.* Cambridge, United Kingdom: National Institute for Career Education and Counselling.

Super, D. E., & Knasel, E. G. (1981). Career development in adulthood: Some theoretical problems and a possible solution. *British Journal of Guidance & Counselling, 9,* 194–201.

Additional Resources

Crites, J. O. (1981). *Career counseling: Models, methods, and materials.* New York: McGraw-Hill.

Savickas, M. L. (2001). Toward a comprehensive theory of career development: Dispositions, concerns, and narratives. In F. T. L. Leong & A. Barak (Eds.), *Contemporary models in vocational psychology: A volume in honor of Samuel H. Osipow* (pp. 295–320). Mahwah, NJ: Erlbaum.

■Career Adjustment

Career adjustment is the ability to adapt to a work environment. Several theorists have discussed the relationship between the worker and his or her environment, including Dawis, England, and Lofquist's (1964) theory of work adjustment (TWA); Crites's (1969) work related to vocational adjustment; and Super's (1984) discussion of the worker role. Each of these theorists has shaped the current views of career adjustment.

TWA, more recently known as the **person-environment-correspondence theory** (Lofquist & Dawis, 1984) was developed by Dawis et al. (1964) and describes the relationship between an individual's satisfaction and job performance. First, the individual must bring the skills to perform the required job tasks. Second, the work environment must provide the sources for satisfying the worker needs, and the tasks need to be performed at a satisfactory level. Job satisfaction occurs when these conditions are met for the individual. Job dissatisfaction occurs when the individual does not have the skills or cannot adequately perform the job tasks or the work environment does not present compensation or a safe, comfortable work setting.

Another significant contribution to the understanding of career adjustment is the work of **John Crites** (1969, 1976). His work focused on how the individual joins an organization, works with other employees, and progresses up the career ladder. Crites's (1982) main contribution to career adjustment was the development of the Career Adjustment and Development Inventory to measure factors such as becoming part of the organization, completing job requirements, being dependable, working well with others, and having a future career path. Crites found that successful employees follow a particular pattern by adjusting to the workplace and job tasks, developing adequate relationships with other workers, and looking at future career goals.

The role of work is also important to an individual's quality of life (Super, 1984). Adapting to changes in the workplace, learning different skills, and being aware of sources of stress are some keys strategies that lead to job satisfaction. Being satisfied with his or her work can contribute to an individual's career adjustment.

In summary, the work of Dawis et al. (1964), Crites (1969, 1976), and Super (1984) have made significant contributions to understanding the value of career adjustment. The key to career adjustment is the ability to adjust to the work environment.

Contributed by Aaron H. Oberman,
The Citadel, Charleston, SC

References

Crites, J. (1969). *Vocational psychology: The study of vocational behavior and development.* New York: McGraw-Hill.

Crites, J. (1976). A comprehensive model of career development in early adulthood. *Journal of Vocational Behavior, 9,* 105–108.

Crites, J. (1982). Testing for career adjustment and development. *Training and Development Journal, 36,* 20–24.

Dawis, V., England, G. W., & Lofquist, L. H. (1964). *A theory of work adjustment* (Minnesota Studies in Vocational Rehabilitation Monograph No. 15). Minneapolis: University of Minnesota, Department of Psychology.

Lofquist, L. H., & Dawis, V. (1984). *Essentials of person-environment-correspondence counseling.* Minneapolis: University of Minnesota Press.

Super, D. (1984). Discovering the significance of life roles and potential conflicts. In V. Zunker (Ed.), *Career counseling: A holistic approach* (7th ed., pp. 156–161). Belmont, CA: Thomson Brooks/Cole.

Additional Resources

Dawis, R. V. (1996). The theory of work adjustment and person-environment-correspondence counseling. In D. Brown & L. Brooks (Eds.), *Career choice and development* (3rd ed., pp. 75–120). San Francisco: Jossey-Bass.

Savickas, M. (1993). Career counseling in the postmodern era. *Journal of Cognitive Psychotherapy: An International Quarterly, 7,* 205–215.

■ Career Assessment

Career assessment is a broad process of systematic information gathering using multiple methods to answer career-related questions. A common question addressed in career assessment is, "What career options provide the best fit for this individual?" Many individuals seeking career counseling expect that the professional counselor will administer tests that will unequivocally reveal the individual's ideal career. However, professional counselors and clients take joint responsibility for both the process of career assessment and the conclusions that follow it. To assist individuals with career planning, counselors use a variety of assessment tools to help clients learn about and carefully consider interests, values, personality, academic achievement, aptitudes, career-related beliefs, career development stage, and personal barriers. Career-related testing (i.e., administration of standardized tests and inventories) is just one method of career assessment, and other procedures used include interviewing the individual and significant others, reviewing relevant historical records, and a collection of self-assessment activities such as questionnaires, occupational card-sorting tasks, and self-monitoring.

Methods Used for Career Assessment

There are three common methods used in career assessment: interviewing, testing, and self-assessment activities. **Interviewing** an individual is a key aspect of career assessment. A career assessment interview covers topics such as employment history, academic background, life aspirations, career interests, personal barriers to employment (e.g., disabilities, injuries, mental health issues), and other variables that can have an impact on career planning. Significant others (e.g., spouse, parents) can also be interviewed to provide additional information and for corroboration purposes. Historical records that speak to an individual's academic achievement, abilities, or aptitudes (e.g., school transcripts, job performance evaluations, reference letters) can also be reviewed for relevant information.

Formal testing with career-related standardized instruments plays a large role in most career assessments. Consequently, professional counselors should carefully evaluate the psychometric properties (e.g., reliability, validity, standardization sample, measurement norms) of the instruments that they use in order to confirm the quality of the instrument and its appropriateness for the particular individual's unique characteristics (e.g., gender, age, ethnicity, national origin, language, socioeconomic status, sexual orientation, disability status). Several sources for test reviews and testing guidelines are available to assist with the selection and use of career-relevant instruments, including the online *Mental Measurements Yearbook* (developed by the Buros Institute of Mental Measurements), *Standards for Educational and Psychological Testing* (American Educational Research Association, American Psychological Association, & National Council on Measurement in Education, 1999), the *Responsibilities of Users of Standardized Tests–Third Edition* (Association for Assessment in Counseling and Education, 2003a), Standards for Multicultural Assessment (Association for Assessment in Counseling and Education, 2003b), and *The Counselor's Guide to Career Assessment Instruments* (4th ed.; Kapes & Whitfield, 2002).

Self-assessment involves nonstandardized activities (e.g., questionnaires, self-monitoring, card sorts) that invite and encourage individuals to discover, reflect upon, and report their own interests, values, relevant personality characteristics, academic achievement, aptitudes, stage of career development, career-related thinking, and personal barriers. It is important to recognize that an individual's self-understanding can be restricted due to factors such as low-level cognitive skills (such as self-awareness, abstract thinking, and memory), insufficient or incorrect knowledge about the world-of-work, limited life exposure, environmental barriers (e.g., discrimination), and personal biases (e.g., occupation-related messages internalized from parents without careful scrutiny).

Domains Commonly Assessed

Many career-planning domains need to be carefully considered to determine which occupations provide the best fit for the particular individual. The areas most frequently addressed in career assessment include career interests, values, personality, academic achievement, aptitude, career-related thinking, and stage of career development. As the distinction between career counseling and personal/mental health counseling is becoming blurred, partly because there is increased awareness that a person's career is a highly personal issue that can play a key role in mental health and mental distress (and vice versa), career assessment is increasingly including an examination of an individual's life problems and clinical symptoms. These domains can all be examined using one or more of the several methods already mentioned (i.e., interviewing, record review, standardized testing, and self-assessment techniques).

Interests refer to objects or activities that an individual likes and gets pleasure from, as indicated by the person giving them more attention and time or participating in them. In other words, career interests reveal what an individual is likely to find enjoyable and motivating but do not indicate abilities or the probability of job success or act as direct guides for evaluating a person's behavior and judging the meaningfulness of life and career pursuits. Interests can be classified into three types: explicit (i.e., what an individual states), implicit (i.e., inferred by how an individual spends leisure time), and measured (i.e., determined through testing with standardized inventories and judged in relation to others' interest levels). Some examples of inventories commonly used to assess interests include the Strong Interest Inventory–II, Self-Directed Search (4th ed.), Campbell Interest and Skill Survey, Kuder Occupational Interest Inventory, and Career Assessment Inventory.

Whereas interests indicate what an individual likes to do, **values** delineate what an individual believes is worthwhile and significant. More specifically, values refer to conditions or results an individual finds important and meaningful. Values develop so that individuals can meet their needs in socially desirable ways, but, unlike needs, values are stable influences on behavior whereas needs are more transitory and, if satisfied, may not significantly influence behavior for certain periods of time. For an individual, having an occupation consistent with his or her values is a stronger predictor than career interests, in forecasting how satisfied he or she will be with the chosen occupation. Values can be characterized as **intrinsic** in nature (i.e., the conditions or effects are pleasurable in and of themselves) or **extrinsic** (i.e., the conditions or effects lead to other circumstances that elicit feelings of pleasure and satisfaction). Examples of intrinsic values are job variety, autonomy, and opportunities for self-expression. High income would be an example of an extrinsic value because the reward results from the items and services that can be purchased with the income. Values can also be identified as work specific (e.g., high income, prestige, working in a team environment, job security) or general (e.g., giving back to society, placing high priority on family time). According to some theories, the needs of workers can also be understood as values that workers expect to satisfy on the job. Some examples of inventories commonly used to assess values include the Values Scale (2nd ed.), Survey of Personal Values, Rokeach Values Survey, and Minnesota Importance Questionnaire.

Certain work environments and occupational duties may be more challenging, depending on the inclinations rooted in a person's personality. Consequently, many individuals are motivated to seek a work environment that they experience as suitable based on their personality. In other words, an ideal occupation would fit well with the expression of a person's personality. For example, an individual with a very extraverted personality may find working at home particularly dissatisfying. As another example, a highly conscientious individual who prefers high levels of organization, thoroughness, planning, and self-discipline will likely experience a better fit in a graduate education program compared with another individual who is not detail oriented, who is highly spontaneous and impulsive, and who typically takes a haphazard approach to task completion and satisfying life roles. Some examples of inventories commonly used to assess personality include the California Psychological Inventory, Sixteen Personality Factor Questionnaire, Myers–Briggs Type Indicator, and NEO Personality Inventory–Revised.

Achievement refers to present levels of developed abilities. In career assessment, the assessment of achievement is often centered on academic achievement. Achievement can be assessed in particular subject areas (e.g., mathematics), general academics (i.e., subjects commonly taught in secondary school), or cross-content (e.g., academic skills such as reading comprehension that cut across academic subjects). Certain types of academic achievement are important determinants for success in certain occupations; therefore, an individual's current level of achievement can limit the scope of career exploration for him or her or highlight areas in need of remediation if an individual wishes to pursue a particular career path not in line with current abilities. For example, individuals with an interest in becoming accountants need to be aware of the notable challenges that they may face if they have below-average mathematics abilities. As another example, an individual with an interest in becoming an editor would be more likely to succeed if he or she had strong reading comprehension skills. Some examples of tests commonly used to assess achievement include the Wide Range Achievement Test 3, Stanford Achievement Test (10th ed.), Wechsler Individual Achievement Test (2nd ed.), Woodcock Johnson III Tests of Achievement, and Canadian Adult Achievement Test.

Unlike achievement, which indicates how much an individual has already learned and refers to skills already attained, **aptitude** refers to an individual's ability to acquire specific skills and proficiencies. Aptitude assessment, therefore, seeks to identify activities in which an individual is more (or less) likely to succeed and skills that an individual is more (or less) likely to develop quickly and with minimal effort. For the purposes of career assessment, aptitude is often assessed by examining higher level cognitive abilities or capacities (e.g., verbal intelligence) or integrated physical abilities or capacities (e.g., hand–eye coordination) expected to be important for carrying out tasks or duties associated with certain occupations. Certain types of aptitudes are better suited for certain occupations (e.g., strong hand–eye coordination is beneficial for success in many sports) or for the education/training required for job entry (e.g., ability to learn a large vocabulary and to engage in abstract thinking facilitates success in postsecondary education, a level of education required to become a professional counselor, psychologist, counselor educator, or counseling professor). Some examples of tests commonly used to assess aptitude include the Career Ability Placement Survey, Differential Aptitude Test (5th ed.), Stanford–Binet Intelligence Scales (5th ed.), Graduate Record Examination, and Wechsler Adult Intelligence Scale (3rd ed.).

When planning a career, an individual needs to be aware of her or his level of progression across **theory-based career stages** (often compared with individuals of a similar age) and career-related thinking, because this has implications for whether an individual is ready to select a career path. Depending on the theoretical orientation followed and the particular measurement tool used, individuals may require additional self-awareness or career knowledge before selecting a career path, or they may need to reevaluate personal or familial beliefs that are limiting their career progression. Some examples of measures commonly used to assess theory-based career stages or career-related thinking include the Career Factors Inventory, Career Beliefs Inventory, Career Thoughts Inventory, Career Maturity Inventory, and My Vocational Situation.

Greater consideration is being given to an individual's **personal problems and clinical symptoms** (e.g., excessive marital conflict, inadequate social support, history of abuse, acculturation problems, difficulty controlling anger, excessive impulsivity, feelings of depression, social anxiety, preoccupation with body weight) and how these potential barriers affect occupational choice and career-related decision making. Certain issues may require resolving prior to seeking particular employment or may limit occupational choices. For example, even if an individual has an inventoried interest in working as a bartender, is a very extroverted person, values a fast-paced work environment, and is limited by child care responsibilities in the afternoon, this individual should be cautious about pursuing this occupation if there is a clear personal or family history of alcohol dependence. As another example, an individual with a history of an unre-solved traumatic experience (e.g., due to military combat) whose trauma is easily triggered may need to avoid, at the current time, jobs that involve close contact with other military personnel (e.g., working in a Veterans Affairs office). Some measures commonly used to assess personal problems and clinical symptoms include the Beck Depression Inventory–II, State-Trait Anxiety Inventory, Personality Assessment Inventory, Substance Abuse Subtle Screening Inventory–3, Alcohol Use Disorders Identification Test, and Minnesota Multiphasic Personality Inventory–2. In addition to testing, all of these domains can be assessed by self-assessment techniques. The types of self-assessments are too numerous to list and are constantly being developed because they depend on the creativity of the professional counselor and the individual being assessed. Some examples of self-assessment techniques include (a) writing a work autobiography, (b) list writing (e.g., 10 things an individual would most like to do, top five values, key elements of an individual's personality, 10 skills that an individual believes he or she possesses, top 10 most favorite and least favorite occupations being considered, top five most favorite and least favorite school subjects, top five role models and reasons why, three most significant barriers to success in a particular occupation), (c) card sorting activities (e.g., classifying occupations written on cards into piles indicating like, dislike, or neutral), (d) forced-choice activities (e.g., choosing which of two work values is more important across 10 different work values), (e) rank-ordering activities (e.g., ranking a list of personality descriptors from most to least characteristic), (f) values-clarification activities (e.g., if asked to populate a new island, which 10 occupations should be considered necessary and why), and (g) self-monitoring activities (e.g., keeping track of any career-related self-talk or career-related messages from others for the next week).

In summary, career assessment is the general process of using multiple methods to collect systematic information to help answer career-related questions. Methods used typically include standardized tests and inventories; interviews; record review; and a wide variety of self-assessment activities such as questionnaires, card sorts, self-monitoring, and rank-ordering tasks. Specific areas important to assess as part of a career assessment include interests, values, personality, achievement level, aptitude, level of career development, career-related thinking, personal problems, and clinical symptoms.

Contributed by Robinder P. Bedi and
Nabiha Rawdah, University of Victoria,
Victoria, BC, Canada

References

American Educational Research Association, American Psychological Association, & National Council on Measurement in Education. (1999). *Standards for educational and psychological testing* (3rd ed.). Washington, DC: Author.

Association for Assessment in Counseling and Education. (2003a). *Responsibilities of users of standardized tests* (3rd ed.). Alexandria, VA: Author.

Association for Assessment in Counseling and Education. (2003b). *Standards for multicultural assessment*. Alexandria, VA: Author.

Kapes, J. T., & Whitfield, E. A. (2002). *A counselor's guide to career assessment instruments* (4th ed.). Tulsa, OK: National Career Development Association.

Additional Resource

Zunker, V. G., & Osborn, D. S. (2002). *Using assessment results for career development* (6th ed.). Pacific Grove, CA: Brooks/Cole.

■ Career Conflict: The Janis and Mann Conflict Model of Decision Making

The **Janis and Mann (1977) conflict model of decision making** describes the ways in which people cope with decisional conflicts and proposes processes to improve the quality of making important decisions in life that often have unknown or unanticipated outcomes or consequences. Some of the important life events accounted for in Janis and Mann's writings include marriage, life-style, career, and health decisions. Their primary theoretical assumption is that stress plays a vital role in the quality of the decision made. Stress, then, is perceived as a factor that can lead to "defective" decisions. Two sources of stress suggested by the authors are material/social losses and self/reputation losses.

The authors proposed five alternative methods for coping with stress when making decisions. These methods are termed *coping patterns* in Janis and Mann's model, but consistent with other decision-making models, these methods can also be conceptualized as decision-making styles. The five coping patterns (i.e., decision-making styles) are (a) **unconflicted adherence** (i.e., an individual ignores information about the potential losses for a particular decision), (b) **unconflicted change** (i.e., an individual accepts whatever actions or recommendations are offered without questioning), (c) **defensive avoidance** (i.e., shifting responsibilities to others, procrastinating, or rationalizing; the least objectionable alternatives are used by the decision maker to escape conflict), (d) **hypervigilance** (i.e., the decision maker senses time pressures to make the decision and impulsively picks the solutions that could provide immediate relief from stress; a high level of emotional stress and panic is associated with this pattern), and (e) **vigilance** (i.e., using various methods to weigh the cost/benefits before reaching final decisions). According to Janis and Mann, vigilance is the only coping pattern that produces decisions that are rational and logical.

The conflict model proposes the presence or absence of three antecedent conditions that determine the reliance of an individual on a particular coping pattern. The first determinant is the awareness of serious risks about preferred alternatives, which, if absent, can lead to unconflicted adherence or unconflicted change. The second antecedent is the hope of finding a better alternative. If there is not a better alternative, this will lead to defensive avoidance. The final determinant is the belief that there is adequate time to search and deliberate before a decision is required; when time is not available, a hypervigilant decision style occurs. The absence of these antecedent conditions leads to maladaptive decision-making styles, but the presence of the three conditions leads to a vigilant coping style that is adaptive.

The authors suggested a decisional balance sheet as a tool to help the decision maker analyze alternatives and consequences as well as identify patterns of coping with stress that may be used during the decision-making process. For example, the balance sheet might shed light on whether the decision is being made thoroughly (vigilant style) or is being made in a defective manner (unconflicted change, defensive avoidance, or hypervigilance). The model recommends presenting four categories of consequences on the balance sheet: (a) utilitarian gains and losses for self, (b) utilitarian gains and losses for significant others, (c) self-approval or self-disapproval, and (d) approval or disapproval from significant others. When the decision maker is able to provide positive examples of what would be the consequences of a course of action, then the model predicts positive outcomes. A defective balance sheet shows that there are errors of omission and commission on the sheet, and, therefore, a decision made on this basis will lead to a negative outcome. The decisional balance sheet has been used in research that involves making difficult life decisions. For example, one study (Hanna & Guthrie, 2000) that examined the knowledge and attitudes of diabetic adolescents used questions derived from the balance sheet to learn and evaluate the perceived benefits of and barriers to the self-management of diabetes.

In the career context, the balance sheets have been shown to provide valuable information in determining job satisfaction for an individual and to provide a useful tool for helping someone to make a decision to leave a job if dissatisfied. For example, Janis and Mann (1977) used the balance sheet to conduct systematic interviews of 81 British managers and technical specialists. In the study, the researchers found that many of the participants wanted to find different jobs. One of the participants, thoroughly discussed in the study, was a manager who wrote down numerous "minuses" on his balance sheet; nevertheless his "pluses" outweighed the negatives on the job, and after reviewing his balance sheet, he concluded that he would remain in his job.

Janis and Mann also suggested using the balance sheet with college seniors who have few ideas about what to do after college. They have conducted studies with college seniors and concluded that the balance sheet seemed to be helpful in increasing awareness about potential consequences of decisions and in encouraging the seniors to consider a range of alternatives.

The conflict model of decision making has also been used by counselors in treatment planning and evaluation, especially in short-term counseling settings. In 1982, Janis published a book that described ways to help clients make decisions during treatment and provided examples from weight-reduction programs.

Janis and Mann's model does not explicitly state that it is useful with people from different cultures; however, the authors stated that the motivating factors and coping patterns involved in decision making dealt with difficult decisions in life that were common to everyone. In a cross-cultural study by Mann and colleagues (Mann et al, 1998), no cultural differences regarding life decisions in general were found for the vigilant decision-making style. Nevertheless, some cultural differences in coping patterns were found (Mann et al., 1998). In that study, Asian students were more likely to score higher on avoidant decision-making style than were Western students.

Overall, the evidence from field research on the application of the conflict model of decision making suggests that the propositions of the model provide practical mechanisms to help people make better decisions. The model also stimulates researchable hypotheses about the causes and consequences of decisional stress and decision-making behavior.

Contributed by Jo-Ida C. Hansen and
W. Vanessa Lee, University of Minnesota,
Minneapolis, MN

References

Hanna, K. M., & Guthrie, D. (2000). Adolescents' perceived benefits and barriers related to diabetes self-management–Part 1. *Issues in Comprehensive Pediatric Nursing, 23,* 165–174.

Janis, I. L. (1982). *Counseling on personal decisions: Theory and research on short-term helping relationships.* New Haven, CT: Yale University Press.

Janis, I. L., & Mann, L. (1977). *Decision making: A psychological analysis of conflict, choice, and commitment.* New York: The Free Press.

Mann, L., Radford, M., Burnett, P., Ford, S., Bond, M., Leung, K., et al. (1998). Cross-cultural differences in self-reported decision-making style and confidence. *International Journal of Psychology, 33,* 325–335.

Additional Resource

Mann, L., Burnett, P., Radford, M., & Ford, S. (1997). The Melbourne Decision Making Questionnaire: An instrument for measuring patterns for coping with decisional conflict. *Journal of Behavioral Decision Making, 10,* 1–19.

■ Career Construction Theory

Career construction theory provides an integrative conceptual framework for synthesizing scientific accounts of vocational behavior and for how to use this knowledge in career education and counseling. Accordingly, the theory includes both a model for understanding vocational behavior as well as a method and materials for counselors to use as they assist clients to make vocational choices, adjust to work, and manage their careers. Fundamentally, the theory views work as a context for human development. Proponents of the theory encourage people to design their lives to achieve success and enjoy satisfaction by engaging in work activities that matter to them and to their communities. The theory of career construction and life design seeks to combine diverse models of vocational behavior and career choice into a single, comprehensive model. To accomplish this collaborative ambition, the theory's integrative framework synthesizes three perspectives that deal, in turn, with personality types, developmental tasks, and life themes.

Personality Types

Types conceptualize scientific accounts of individuality in terms of personality. Each individual, in her or his family of origin, creates a personality with which to adapt to the neighborhood, school, and employer. Personality psychology has a long tradition of studying individual differences. Developers of psychological tests, starting during World War I, have used a matching model that fits individual abilities to job requirements and personal interests to occupational rewards. A good fit between person and position leads to success and satisfaction, whereas a poor fit leads to failure and frustration. The current methodology for matching personality to jobs rests on the concept of resemblance. Information is collected on some set of criterion groups, and the deciding person is then tested and matched to the best fitting group.

This matching model has three clever variations for measuring resemblance with interest inventories. The first version, crafted by E. K. Strong, compares an individual to group profiles of individuals who are successful and satisfied in particular occupational fields. The closer the resemblance, the higher the client's score for that occupation. The second variation, crafted by John Holland, combines Spranger's value types with Adler's notion of life-style to formulate ideal prototypes. Holland formulated six vocational personality types called Realistic, Investigative, Artistic, Social, Enterprising, and Conventional. He then used the same taxonomy to type work environments. Most of the popular interest inventories now report six scores that indicate degree of resemblance to each of the six types. Knowing which personality types they resemble, individuals may explore occupations in which their type tends to congregate (see Career Typology). The third version, crafted by Frederic Kuder, is person matching. Using the idea that people do jobs, not occupations, Kuder and his colleague Donald Zytowski created a technology that compares an individual's interest inventory responses to a large group of diverse individuals. Clients then read vocational biographies of 10 individuals whom they most resemble.

Career construction theory uses the idea that personality is a sketch of an individual's reputation and characteristic adaptations. It also agrees that the metaphor of resemblance allows researchers and counselors to understand an individual in terms of similarity to a known group, prototype, or individual. Career construction theory, however, asserts that these traits and types are not scientific discoveries. Instead, the theory emphasizes that the criterion groups used in the matching method are socially constructed metanarratives. This means that Strong constituted his occupational groups, Holland formulated his six prototypes, and Zytowski recruited people and told them how to write their biographies.

Developmental Tasks

Sketches of personality types are drawn using psychological content, such as abilities, interests, and values. The second perspective of career construction theory deals with the psychosocial processes used to cope with developmental tasks. These tasks articulate the social expectation that individuals prepare for and then enter and participate in the work role. Instead of concentrating on how individuals differ from each other, tasks concentrate on how an individual differs from her- or himself across time. In the middle of the 20th century, Donald Super charted these tasks of development and organized them into five stages of career maturation (see Life-Span, Life-Space Career Theory). Career construction theory reconstructs Super's biological and organismic unfolding conception of maturation into a contextual and cultural conception of adaptation and niche making. In stable societies, careers can unfold in a predictable sequence over 30 or more years, and often within one organization. In today's unstable, global economy, preparedness has replaced planfulness and possibility has replaced prediction.

Adaptability in a postmodern world essentially consists of self-regulation in meeting changes occasioned by developmental tasks, occupational transitions, and vocational traumas. Self-regulation means managing limited resources to maximize gains and minimize losses. Various models of self-regulation have been advanced, including Bandura's social learning model of self-efficacy and Baltes's developmental model of selective optimization with compensation. Career construction theory's model of self-regulation relative to social and developmental tasks arises from a synthesis of vocational research viewed through the prism of Erikson's model of psychosocial development. It privileges four self-construction processes named concern, control, curiosity, and confidence. Together, these four syndromes of attitudes, beliefs, and competencies constitute career adaptability. Concern about the future helps individuals look ahead and prepare for what might come next. Control enables individuals to become responsible for shaping themselves and their environments to meet what comes next by using self-discipline, effort, and persistence. Possible selves and alternative scenarios that they might shape are explored when the curious person thinks about self in various situations and roles. These exploration experiences and information-seeking activities produce aspirations and build confidence that the person can actualize choices to implement his or her life design. Deviations in these four processes produce unrealism and apathy. Variations in the processes produce indecision and indecisiveness. Whether on time, off time, or absent, the engagement of personality type with social expectations and developmental task produces a life story. In short, the self's engagement with society writes a script.

Life Themes

The third perspective of career construction theory deals with scripts that glue type to task and self to society. As each personality meets social expectations to prepare for and enter the work role, she or he lives a unique story, one written by her or his attitudes and activities. People evolve a life theme that holds their stories together with continuity and coherence. Career construction theory uses narrative psychology to comprehend stories and highlight their meaning relative to life design. As individuals meet tasks, transitions, and traumas, they make choices that express and extend the theme and its variations. Each decision that they make further narrates the theme in a new "con text" (i.e., in Latin the word *con* means "with"). Individuals tell stories about the self and society that they themselves need to hear because the stories reconfigure the past, support current preferences, and inspire future action.

Career construction theory uses a narrative paradigm for understanding stories, whether in research or in counseling. Literary criticism offers various paradigms for understanding stories. Career construction chooses to use the narrative paradigm, meaning that one can listen to stories to hear the turn of events during which the individual actively masters what she or he has passively suffered. This involves listening for the structure of meaning that patterns the life and the stories that hold it. Concentrating on how an individual turns tension into intention enables the listener to identify the story line of how preoccupation may become occupation.

Counseling for Career Construction and Life Design

By considering type, task and theme, a counselor can understand the complexities of an individual's script for engaging self with society. Narrating back to clients the story themes that hold their lives helps clients clarify what is at stake and enhances the ability to make choices that support their lives and resonate with their spirit. Increasing the "narratability" of this script and making it the best possible account enable the client to clarify what she or he can do (type), should do (task), and may do (theme). Career construction theory provides methods and materials that counselors and researchers can use to help clients engage in autobiographical reasoning as they narrate what matters to them and how they might manifest it in work activities that matter to their families and communities. Thus, meaning-making replaces match-making, and mattering replaces congruence in an information society with a global economy. By witnessing and corroborating the narratives of clients, counselors encourage them to advance further and deeper into the world.

Contributed by Mark L. Savickas,
Northeastern Ohio Universities College
of Medicine, Rootstown, OH

Additional Resources

Savickas, M. L. (2005). The theory and practice of career construction. In R. W. Lent & S. D. Brown (Eds.), *Career development and counseling: Putting theory and research to work* (pp. 42–70). Hoboken, NJ: Wiley.

Savickas, M. L. (2007). Occupational choice. In H. P. Gunz & M. A. Peiperal (Eds.), *Handbook of career studies* (pp. 79–96). Thousand Oaks, CA: Sage.

Career Counseling: Its Nature and Structure

What is career counseling? Is it different from other forms of counseling? Is it the same? Is there overlap? These questions are being asked with increasing frequency today as attempts are being made to clarify this form of counseling. Central to the ongoing discussion about career counseling are three issues. First is the issue of the nature of career counseling. What are its intrinsic characteristics and qualities? Are psychological processes involved? Second is the issue of structure. Does career counseling have structure? If so, what are the configuration, sequence, and interrelationships of the phases involved? Third is the issue of the role of theory in career counseling. What theories are involved? What purposes do theories serve?

The Nature of Career Counseling

Career counseling was one of the foundation stones of the counseling profession. Unfortunately, along the path of history, it became stereotyped and began to be seen as different from other forms of counseling. It was viewed as time limited, devoid of attention to psychological dynamics and processes, and focused mainly on outcomes and methods. Counselors who did career counseling were perceived as active and directive. They used assessments and information. On the other hand, counselors who did personal–emotional counseling were seen as facilitative and exploring because they focused on client–counselor interactions, that is, on the psychological dynamics and processes present in client–counselor interactions.

Contrary to the stereotype, career counseling is counseling just as personal–emotional counseling is counseling because they both possess the same foundational intrinsic characteristics and qualities. Both focus on psychological dynamics and processes and both feature the working alliance. Given the same foundation of intrinsic characteristics and qualities, they do differ in expression at times due to the topics covered and the techniques used, depending on the goals and concerns of clients.

If career counseling is counseling, why is the term *career counseling* used at all? It is used partly because of history. The term is part of the profession's heritage. Precedent alone, however, is not a sufficient reason to continue to use the term *career counseling*. There is another reason—the need to focus attention on client problems dealing with work and career issues that require theoretical conceptions and interventions originating from career development theory, research, and practice. These needed theoretical conceptions and interventions are not usually found in the literature that surrounds other forms of counseling. At the same time, theoretical conceptions and interventions that emerge from and undergird personal–emotional counseling perspectives are not usually found in the literature that surrounds career counseling.

The stereotyped division of counseling into personal–emotional and career types is artificial and cannot stand in practice, because many clients are dealing with multiple personal–emotional and career problems simultaneously. Most life problems cannot be divided into separate career or personal–emotional categories. They are connected and intertwined.

The Structure of Career Counseling

Career counseling can be organized into phases, which can be arranged and sequenced and are interrelated. The six phases are opening, gathering information, understanding/hypothesizing, taking action, goals/plans of action, and evaluating and closing. Central to the career counseling process is the working alliance.

All of the phases of career counseling may occur in one session, but more likely they will unfold over a number of sessions with most clients. Also, although the phases logically follow one another, in actual practice they do not. There often is a back-and-forth flow to career counseling in that it may be necessary to backtrack to earlier phases before moving on again. Sometimes taking action is reached only to realize that other interventions, not anticipated, may be needed, necessitating a return to gathering client information.

Not all clients who seek help want to or need to go through the full process of career counseling. Some may want or need only limited assistance. Other clients, however, may need to be involved in the full process over time but may be resistant to do so. Dealing with resistance may be a first priority in the opening subphase as the working alliance is beginning to be formed. Even if resistance seemingly is handled then, counselors should be aware that it may reoccur again and again, perhaps later in career counseling because some clients struggle with their problems. It is important to remember, for these clients, dealing with reoccurring resistance is part of the psychological dynamics and processes involved in career counseling.

The Role of Theory

Theories developed from conceptions of personality, human growth and development, counseling, and career development provide the foundational knowledge from which practitioners can draw useful concepts to explain client behavior. Theories offer a framework within which client behavior can be examined and hypotheses formed about the possible meanings of that behavior. In turn, this knowledge helps in identifying, understanding, and responding to clients' goals or problems.

Clients often become involved in career counseling because they are in transition, either by their own choice or because of conditions over which they have only limited control or no control at all. Internal thoughts and feelings appear jumbled and confused, at least on the surface. "What should I do?" "In which direction should I go?" "How should I respond to and resolve my problem or achieve my goal?" These are the kinds of questions with which clients may be struggling. Sometimes the questions, let alone any possible answers, are not clearly formed in clients' minds.

How does theory inform practice to help clients deal with these issues? Theory helps identify and interpret client behavior and information. It provides ways to give meaning to the internal thoughts and feelings of clients. That meaning can then be connected to practical strategies for assisting clients in pursuing career goals and resolving problems.

In summary, career counseling is counseling. Client presenting problems often are only a beginning point, and as career counseling unfolds, other problems can and do emerge. Career issues frequently become personal–emotional issues, family issues, and then career issues again, and sometimes they unfold all at once. Psychological stress is often present. Counselors doing career counseling use the same basic counseling interventions as counselors who are doing personal–emotional counseling. Counselors doing career counseling encounter the same psychological dynamics and processes that all counselors encounter in their work with many clients. Client resistance is sometimes present in career counseling as it is in other forms of counseling.

Contributed by Norman C. Gysbers,
University of Missouri–Columbia,
Columbia, MO

Additional Resources

Amundson, N. E., Harris-Bowlsby, J., & Niles, S. G. (2005). *Essential elements of career counseling.* Upper Saddle River, NJ: Pearson.

Gysbers, N. C., Heppner, M. J., & Johnston, J. A. (2003). *Career counseling: Process, issues, and techniques* (2nd ed.). Boston: Allyn & Bacon.

Zunker, V. G. (2006). *Career counseling: A holistic approach.* Belmont, CA: Thomson.

■ Career Decision Making

When deciding to enter a particular career path, many individuals forget that this process takes place over the course a lifetime. Just as clients differ in their approach to solving problems, they also differ in their approach to making career decisions. Many times, clients enter the counseling relationship not realizing that making decisions about a career has a direct impact on their personal lives.

Career decision making is a dynamic and ongoing process in which knowledge about self, values, interests, culture, temperament, financial needs, physical work requirements or limitations, the effects of past experiences, new information, and changes in life situations and environments all intertwine. This process also involves choice, and anytime choice is a factor so is risk. In their work on prospect theory, Tversky and Kahneman (1981) explained that individuals valued gains and losses differently and that they would base their decision on perceived gains rather than on perceived losses. An example is an individual who excels in a career he or she dislikes, then changes to a career he or she has wanted to pursue but loses $15,000 in salary. The individual's perceived gain (e.g., satisfaction and happiness) may outweigh his or her potential loss in salary. The risk for that individual was worth the perceived loss.

Many different paradigms have been developed regarding the decision-making process. The following task approach skills (Krumboltz & Baker, 1973) are important in that process:

1. Recognizing an important decision situation;
2. Defining the decision or task manageably and realistically;
3. Examining and accurately assessing self-observations and worldview generalizations;
4. Generating a wide variety of alternatives;
5. Gathering needed information about the alternatives;
6. Determining which information sources are most reliable, accurate, and relevant;
7. Planning and carrying out the above sequence of decision-making behaviors.

Whether insignificant or long lasting, the decision-making process can take many approaches. Janis and Mann (1977) proposed five stages of decision making: (a) appraising the challenge, (b) surveying alternatives, (c) weighing alternatives, (d) deliberating about commitment, and (e) adhering despite negative feedback. Furthermore, these authors noted that a "good" decision has seven components:

1. Thoroughly canvasses a wide range of alternative courses of action
2. Surveys the full range of objectives to be fulfilled and the values implicated by choice
3. Carefully weighs whatever is known about the costs and risks of negative consequences as well as the positive consequences that could flow from each alternative
4. Intensely searches for new information relevant to further evaluation of the alternatives
5. Correctly assimilates and takes account of any new information or expert judgment to which the individual is exposed, even when the information or judgment does not support the course of action initially preferred
6. Reexamines the positive and negative consequences of all known alternatives, including those originally regarded as unacceptable, before making a final choice
7. Makes detailed provisions for implementing or executing the chosen course of action, with special attention to contingency plans that might be required if various known risks were to materialize (p. 11)

Just as some individuals are ready to make a career decision, others are not. Gati, Krausz, and Osipow (1996) studied career decision-making difficulties and suggested a taxonomy that involves three major areas: (a) lack of motivation to engage in the career decision-making process, (b) general indecisiveness concerning all types of decisions, and (c) dysfunctional beliefs about career decision making. These authors also pointed to two other major categories of difficulty, lack of information and inconsistent information, that may also arise during the actual process of career decision making. In the first, lack of information, four categories are included: (a) lack of knowledge about the steps involved in the process of career decision making, (b) lack of information about the self, (c) lack of information about the various occupations, and (d) lack of information about the ways of obtaining additional information. In the second category of difficulty, inconsistent information, three categories of problems exist with using the information: (a) unreliable information; (b) internal conflicts, which are conflicts within the individual (e.g., contradictory preferences); and (c) external conflicts, which are conflicts involving the opinions of significant others.

Janis and Mann (1977) also offered the following four patterns of defective decision making:

1. **Unconflicted adherence.** The individual denies that there is any risk involved in the course of action taken.
2. **Unconflicted change to new course of action.** The individual denies that any risk is involved in the decision-making process.
3. **Defense avoidance.** The individual gives up looking for a solution by avoiding any painful feelings or anxiety-provoking thought.
4. **Hypervigilance.** As the decision-making process becomes more urgent and time is constrained, the individual becomes emotionally excited.

Assisting the client through the career decision-making process is a crucial element in the counseling relationship. Career counseling helps clients learn what characteristics (e.g., beliefs, skills, values, interests, personality) they possess that will ultimately assist them in creating satisfying lives. This process may require clients to experience new things, which may seem daunting. Supporting the client to self-assess critically, follow up, and follow through are effective techniques in determining the anticipated goals, expectations, and outcomes in relationship to the career and life changes being made.

Contributed by Brigid M. Noonan,
Stetson University, Orlando, FL

References

Gati, I., Krausz, M., & Osipow, S. H. (1996). A taxonomy of difficulties in career decision making. *Journal of Counseling Psychology, 43,* 510–526.

Janis, I., & Mann, L. (1977). *Decision making: A psychological analysis of conflict, choice, and commitment.* New York: Free Press.

Krumboltz, J. D., & Baker, R. D. (1973). Behavioral counseling for vocational decisions. In H. Borow (Ed.), *Career guidance for a new age* (pp. 235–284). Boston: Houghton Mifflin.

Tversky, A., & Kahneman, D. (1981). The framing of decisions and psychology of choice. *Science, 211,* 453–458.

Additional Resources

Bolles, R. N. (2006). *What color is your parachute 2007: A practical manual for job-hunters and career-changers.* Berkeley, CA: Ten Speed Press.

Herr, E. L., & Cramer, S. H. (1992). *Career guidance and counseling through the lifespan: Systematic approaches* (4th ed.). New York: HarperCollins.

Walsh, W. B., & Osipow, S. H. (Eds.). (1988). *Career decision making.* Danvers, MA: Routledge.

■ Career Development, Key Ethical Issues in

To understand some of the key ethical issues in career development today and their effect on the development of the **National Career Development Association's (NCDA; 2007)** *Code of Ethics,* it is important to understand the context of the evolution of ethical issues in career development over the past 100 years. When Frank Parsons, generally regarded as the founder of modern career development in the United States, published his book *Choosing a Vocation* in 1909, he espoused a tripartite theory to help individuals in their job search. For Parsons and many of his contemporaries, all that was necessary for successful outcomes in career counseling was (a) an understanding of a client's individual traits obtained through assessment, (b) a knowledge of the factors needed to become employed in the world-of-work, and (c) the application of "true reasoning" on the part of the counselor to blend the aforementioned traits and factors into a coherent vocational "choice." Obviously, the major ethical issues during Parsons's time would have focused on the expertise of the counselor. If it was the counselor's responsibility to apply "true reasoning" to help in the job or career choice, the counselor truly needed to be the expert. Although assessment and world-of-work issues were a part of the knowledge base of a vocational counselor in the early 1900s, these areas did not come to the forefront until World War II.

As a result of the need for vocational testing and placement in the military, and subsequently in the private sector, career counselors and their psychologist counterparts led the way in developing a variety of career and psychological assessments in the 1940s, 1950s, and 1960s. These assessments dealt with many areas, including an individual's values, interests, skills, and personality. Although the major assessments of this era have been revised and updated over the years, assessments have remained a core component of the work of career counselors, and the ethical issues of this period and beyond have been concerned with the appropriate development, use, and interpretation of assessment results. Research on assessments and the development and use of them spawned a host of ethical concerns as well.

Since the late 1960s, diversity and multiculturalism have gained prominence in the counseling field, including career counseling. Ethical issues that arose incorporated not only the obvious ones of bias in the development, use, and interpretation of assessment results but discrimination in workplace hiring and firing; access to career services; and the need to look holistically at an individual's career development, including the impact of work and family.

Since the late 1990s, professional counselors have seen an integration of the ethics issues of the previous decades with the new ethics issues posed by technology (most notably the Internet), training and credentials, and globalization and the world-of-work. These are the newest ethical issues of today. They can be viewed separately, but in reality they are interconnected.

Technology

Although career counselors have always been at the forefront in their use of technology, whether paper-and-pencil assessments, the telephone, video, or computer-based career guidance programs, the Internet poses new opportunities and challenges. Section F of the NCDA's (2007) *Code* specifically addresses the myriad of ethical issues a career counselor might face in the use of the Internet in the provision of career services. Key issues include informed consent and confidentiality (F.2.f.), maintaining Internet sites (F.5.b.), use of assessment (F.7.), unacceptable behaviors on the Internet (F.9.), and laws and statutes (F.2.d.).

In order to work effectively with clients, professional counselors must be able to determine who their clients are, and clients must be able to know with whom they are working. Career counselors are increasingly working with clients online. In fact, some clients may never meet with their career counselor face-to-face. Section F.2.f. outlines part of the process of establishing informed consent and defining confidentiality and its limits when working with clients on the Internet. In addition, many career counselors have their own Web site or work for organizations that maintain Web sites with career and job search information. Section F.5.b. provides guidelines to career counselors regarding their responsibilities not only to maintain Web sites that provide appropriate content but to link only to Web sites that are ethically responsible in their design and dissemination of information. For example, although some informational resources on a Web site may provide value, other areas of the same Web site may be questionable. In this case, the career counselor may link to the Web site but only with a disclaimer explaining the concerns related to the questionable content. Section E of the NCDA *Code* provides detailed information regarding ethical considerations in evaluation, assessment, and interpretation. However, Section F.7. specifically addresses the online administration of career assessments. Determining whether the psychometric properties of the assessments are in some way altered by online administration, protection of assessment results, and referral to qualified career counselors for face-to-face interpretation of results if needed are among the ethical issues addressed in this section. Section F of the *Code* ends with a prohibition against certain online activities. These include using a false identity, working with clients who will not identify themselves, and anonymously monitoring sites to obtain clients. Finally, Section F.2.d. of the NCDA *Code* stipulates that career counselors must know and abide by all applicable statutes, laws, regulations, and procedures when offering services online that cross state and/or national boundaries. Although this may seem obvious, this is a significant ethical issue and will likely become even more so as career counselors offer more and more services using distance technology (e.g., telephones, Internet).

Training and Credentials

Training and credentialing in career counseling and development continue to evolve. In the 1980s when the National Board for Certified Counselors (NBCC) began issuing specialty credentials for counselors, the National Certified Career Counselor (NCCC) credential was the first. The NCCC credential was retired in 1999. In the late 1990s, NCDA and NBCC introduced the first career practitioner training and credential designed for individuals working in the field of career development who were not trained as counselors. The Career Development Facilitator curriculum and its credential (Global Career Development Facilitator [GCDF]) have grown exponentially over the past 10 years. The Center for Credentialing and Education now administers the GCDF credential, including curriculum review.

The 1990s and beyond have also seen the rise of a new area of career development services in the form of coaching. **Coaches** assist their clients in goal identification and attainment through various activities, including active listening and encouragement. Although coaching tends to be more directive than counseling, the two fields have much in common. Coaches do not necessarily have graduate-level training in psychology or counseling; however, many mental health practitioners have been "re-branding" themselves as coaches. Career counselors have followed this trend and have been marketing themselves as career coaches. Numerous associations and programs, varying in the depth, breadth, and quality of training and supervision, exist to credential career coaches.

With the rise of multiple areas of training and credentialing in career development, however, it is important that clients understand the true nature of the education and experience of the career practitioner serving them. Section G.1.b. of the NCDA *Code* reminds supervisors of the requirement that supervisees inform clients regarding the supervisees' qualifications. In addition, because many NCDA members have advanced education in areas other than counseling, it is important that they represent themselves to clients and the public as possessing the education, qualifications, and credentials related to their practice of career counseling. Section C.4.d. of the NCDA *Code* emphasizes that career professionals are not to imply doctoral-level competence when possessing only a master's degree in counseling or a related field. Even if career professionals have a doctorate in another field, they are not to use the title "doctor" nor refer to themselves as "doctor" in a counseling or career services context when their doctorate is not in counseling or a related field.

Finally, with the expansion of education and training in the career profession, many experienced in the field of career development will find themselves supervising a wide range of individuals. Section G.5.d. of the NCDA *Code* provides guidance to supervisors regarding their endorsement of their supervisees for such things as certification, licensure, employment, or completion of an academic or training program. Supervisors are expected to provide an endorsement or recommendation only when they believe their supervisees are qualified for the endorsement. Conversely, supervisors should not withhold endorsement of qualified supervisees for any reason unrelated to their fitness as a student or professional. This latter admonition is meant to discourage counseling supervisors, including professors, from withholding an endorsement or recommendation simply because they may not like a supervisee or student.

Contributed by David M. Reile,
Career Development Alliance, LLC,
Olney, MD

References

National Career Development Association. (2007). *Code of ethics.* Retrieved June 23, 2008, from http://ncd.org.org/pdf/code_of_ethicsmay-2007.pdf

Parsons, F. (1909). *Choosing a vocation.* Boston: Houghton Mifflin.

Additional Resources

American Counseling Association. (2005) *ACA code of ethics.* Alexandria, VA: Author.

Center for Credentialing & Education. *Ethical standards for global career development facilitators.* Retrieved June 23, 2008, from http://www.cce-global.org/credentials-offered/gcdf_buffer/resources

Herlihy, B., & Corey, G. (Eds.). (2006). *ACA ethical standards casebook* (6th ed.). Alexandria, VA: American Counseling Association.

Mitchell, R. (2007). *Documentation in counseling records* (3rd ed.). Alexandria, VA: American Counseling Association.

■ Career Development, Key Historical Events

The need for career development interventions emerged during the late 1800s as the United States was transforming itself from an agricultural economy to an industrial and manufacturing economy. This shift brought about new occupational opportunities as well as alarming social conditions, such as the expansion of the immigrant population in urban slums, long working hours in sweatshop factories, exploitation of children in the labor force, increasing disparity between the status of the rich and the poor, and labor unrest and violence (Zytowski, 2001). Reform efforts were begun to remediate these conditions. Against this social and economic background, the career development movement was initiated by Frank Parsons, who established the Boston Vocational Bureau in 1908 to offer career counseling services to youth who needed to choose a vocation. In a book written by Parsons and published in 1909 after his death, the term *vocational guidance* first appeared (McDaniels & Gysbers, 1992). The "Parsonian approach" to vocational guidance was described by Parsons (1909) as follows:

> In the wise choice of a vocation there are three broad factors: (1) a clear understanding of yourself, your aptitudes, abilities, interests, ambitions, resources, limitations, and their causes; (2) a knowledge of the requirements and conditions of success, advantages

and disadvantages, compensation, opportunities, and prospects in different lines of work; (3) true reasoning on the relations of these two groups of facts. (p. 5)

This trait and factor approach to vocational guidance was the first model for career counseling and remains influential in career development work. Frank Parsons is considered to be the parent of career counseling. As a result of his efforts, by 1910 approximately 35 cities in the United States had some form of vocational guidance taught in their schools, and the first national conference on vocational guidance occurred in Boston that same year.

Another important factor in the establishment of career counseling in the United States was the founding of influential professional organizations whose mission was to promote vocational guidance nationwide. In 1913, the National Vocational Guidance Association (NVGA) was founded in Grand Rapids, Michigan. The first journal of NVGA was the *Vocational Guidance Bulletin,* which was first published in 1915. As a result of the growth of vocational guidance in the United States, in 1951 NVGA became one of the founding divisions of the American Personnel and Guidance Association (APGA, which later became the American Association for Counseling and Development and then the American Counseling Association). According to Niles and Harris-Bowlsbey (2005), NVGA (which is now the National Career Development Association [NCDA]) is the primary organization for professional career counselors dedicated to improving the quality of services provided by career development practitioners. The NCDA's journal is *The Career Development Quarterly.*

In the early part of the 20th century, laws critical to the expansion of the vocational guidance movement were enacted. The founding of the U.S. Department of Labor in 1913 was followed by the Smith-Hughes Act of 1917, which established secondary school vocational education training. The Vocational Rehabilitation Act became law in 1918, and the Wagner-Peyser Act created the U.S. Employment Service in 1933. In 1939, the U.S. Employment Service created the publication *The Dictionary of Occupational Titles,* which defined 18,000 occupations, and it soon became an important source of career information for people engaged in the process of occupational choice.

As mentioned previously, the goal of the Parsonian approach to career was to facilitate a high degree of fit between the person and an occupation. As an extension to this approach, E. G. Williamson (1939) illustrated a directive process for career counseling in his book *How to Counsel Students: A Manual of Techniques for Clinical Counselors.* In this model, the counselor collected data about the client through interviews and testing, diagnosed the client's problem, and then offered the client alternative courses of action to consider. Williamson conceptualized the career counseling process as consisting of six steps. "These steps are analysis, synthesis, diagnosis, prognosis, counseling (treatment), and follow-up" (p. 57). This classic trait-and-factor approach defined the practice of career counseling for many years, but it was very counselor directed. For example, Niles and Harris-Bowlsbey (2005) summarized this historical approach by saying,

> the counselor is active and directive while the client is relatively passive. . . . It is the counselor's responsibility to take the lead in the collection, integration, and organization of client data . . . the counselor uses these data in conjunction with occupational information to help the client identify a plan of action. (p.16)

During the 1930s and 1940s, the development of career counseling was affected by several major events and conditions. The Great Depression produced a need to help retrain dislocated workers. In response to this need, D. G Paterson, known as a contributor to the Minnesota point of view, extended Parson's earlier work on trait and factor theory by developing special aptitude tests, personality inventories, and other devices. Those methods and assessment assisted career counselors in helping individuals obtain work during the Great Depression (Brown, Brooks, & Associates, 2002). Concurrently, Roosevelt's New Deal (1933–1938) created jobs through public work projects for millions of people who were out of work.

The entry of the United States into World War II in 1941 created a need to select, train, and place individuals into occupational specialties for the armed forces. Coinciding with WWII was the development and expansion of the formal testing movement. In response to the need to assess large numbers of individuals efficiently and accurately for military duty, formal inventories and tests were developed to measure individual traits such as aptitude and intelligence. It was during this time that women began entering the workforce in much larger numbers, finding employment in occupations that had been abandoned by men serving in the armed forces. During this time, expanded testing and placement activities became critical components of career development. The Veterans Administration established career services for returning veterans as well as for disabled veterans. The Servicemen's Readjustment Act (i.e., G.I. Bill) was enacted in 1944 and paid for a veteran's entire education, encouraging many universities across the country to expand enrollment and offer career services to former service members.

The expansion of career development theory and congressional actions contributed to the growth of the career and guidance movement throughout the 1950s and 1960s. In 1951, Ginzberg, Ginsburg, Axelrad, and Herma introduced a broader awareness of occupational choice based on a developmental perspective and the term *occupational choice* emerged as a new career concept. Perhaps the most influential developmental theory was introduced by Donald Super (1951–1990), who emphasized the importance of self-concept in career decision making. At the same time, theorists such as Anne Roe and John Holland introduced career theories based on personality traits.

In 1957, the Soviet Union (USSR) launched the first artificial satellite, Sputnik 1, which marked the beginning of the space race between the United States and the USSR. In order to compete in the space race, the National Defense Education Act (NDEA) was passed in 1958 as a means to strengthen math and science education in the United States. The NDEA had a larger impact on career counseling than did any other single event in career counseling history and to a great extent determined the future of counselor education. NDEA expanded counselor education programs by reimbursing K–12 counselor education programs for developing counselor training institutes and provided stipends for graduate students enrolled in NDEA counseling and guidance institutes (Hoyt, 2001). NDEA also allowed for the development of counselor education institutes throughout the United States, which emphasized helping high school graduates gain admission to institutions of higher education to pursue math and science careers.

During the 1960s and 1970s, career development was increasingly supported by federal and local government funding agencies. The U.S. Department of Education recognized the important role that education played in students' career decision making. As a result, it made career education a national priority and mandated that career education be included in all school curricula. The goals of career education included increased career awareness, expanded career exploration, promotion of values clarification, acquisition of decision-making skills, and development of extensive career preparation for all students K–12. Civil rights legislation in the 1960s (Civil Rights Act of 1964) opened the door to greater employment possibilities for minority individuals and women. Prior legislation had been directed primarily toward career development for White men. The Civil Rights Act of 1964 also reflected a mounting national concern for people who were poor or underprivileged.

Federal legislation, the Manpower Development and Training Act of 1962, created new jobs through training and retraining workers who had become unemployed due to automation and technology. In addition, career education took a step forward when the amendments to the Vocational Act of 1963 provided guidance services for elementary and secondary schools, public community colleges, and technical institutes. As a result, the number of counselor education training programs increased. As the profession of career counseling gained credibility, The National Occupational Information Coordinating Committee (NOICC) was created by Congress in 1976 (Zunker, 2006). The committee later developed the National Career Counseling and Development Guidelines, which provide a framework for creating comprehensive career development programs at the state and local levels (NOICC, 1989). The guidelines focus on three broad areas of development: self-knowledge, educational and occupational exploration, and career planning.

Throughout the time from the 1960s to the 1980s, career theory continued to evolve. The expansion of theory reflected the continued enhancement of the concept of career. It moved from a narrow definition of vocation to a broader and more holistic conceptualization of career. Building on the trait-and-factor framework and the Minnesota model, Dawis and Lofquist (1984) defined work adjustment as a "continuous and dynamic process." In addition, theorists such as Tiedeman and O'Hara; Krumboltz, Mitchell, and Gelatt; Lent, Brown, and Hackett; and Gottfredson increasingly addressed career from a point of view that included factors such as culture, ethnicity, gender, social context, and life events across the life span.

In 1982, the Job Training and Partnership Act and the Carl Perkins Vocational Act served to address the needs of disadvantaged youth, vocational students, and unemployed workers. As a result, career development expanded into business and private enterprise. The National Certified Career Counselor certification was established in 1984 as a means of offering national certification for career counselors. At this time, descriptors such as career guidance and career counseling had almost completely replaced vocation, vocational guidance, and vocational development.

Federal legislation continued to play a key role in career development through programs such as the School-to-Work Opportunities Act in 1994 that supported career counseling as a high priority in secondary education. The Americans With Disabilities Act of 1990 created a further demand for career counseling as individuals with disabilities gained protection from discrimination.

Throughout the 1990s and early 2000s, the field of career development recognized the contextual and constructivist approach to career. Theorists such as Brown, Brooks, and Associates and Savickas proposed a developmental, contextual viewpoint based on the philosophical position of postmodernism. Globalization, advances in technology, increased attention to diversity, changing demographics, continued focus on the school-to-job transition, and multiple life roles have all created a need for continued inquiry and investigation (Pope, 2000). As the dynamic field of career counseling continues to evolve, the profession is being shaped by a vision that emphasizes career counseling for all people across the life span, embraces the development of technological tools that better serve the global workforce, and is based on research that informs and directs public policy.

Contributed by Leslie W. O'Ryan and
William P. McFarland,
Western Illinois University, Moline, IL

References

Brown, D., Brooks, L., & Associates, (2002). *Career choice and development* (3rd ed.). San Francisco: Jossey-Bass.

Dawis, R. V., & Lofquist, L. H. (1984). *A psychological theory of work adjustment: An individual differences model and its application.* Minneapolis: University of Minnesota.

Hoyt, K. B. (2001). A reaction to Mark Pope's "A brief history of career counseling in the United States." *The Career Development Quarterly, 49,* 374.

McDaniels, C. M., & Gysbers, N. C. (1992). *Counseling for career development: Theories, resources, and practice.* San Francisco: Jossey-Bass.

National Occupational Information Coordinating Committee. (1989). *National career development guidelines.* Washington, DC: U.S. Department of Labor.

Niles, S. G., & Harris-Bowlsbey, J. (2005). *Career development in the 21st century.* Upper Saddle River, NJ: Pearson Education.

Parsons, F. (1909). *Choosing a vocation.* Boston: Houghton Mifflin.

Pope, M. (2000). A brief history of career counseling in the United States. *The Career Development Quarterly, 48,* 194–211.

Williamson, E. G. (1939). *How to counsel students: A manual of techniques for clinical counselors.* New York: McGraw-Hill.

Zunker, V. (2006). *Career counseling: A holistic approach.* Belmont, CA: Thomson Brooks/Cole.

Zytowski, D. G. (2001). Frank Parsons and the progressive movement. *The Career Development Quarterly, 50,* 57–65.

Career Development, Key Legal Issues in

In general, legal issues that apply to the broad field of counseling extend to career counselors; however, there are some legal issues that may be particularly pertinent to career counselors. These issues include concerns regarding licensure, role designation and advocacy, distance services, labor laws, and ethical decision making.

Licensure and accurate representation are legal issues for career counselors and career programs. Sometimes licensure laws have loopholes (Isaacson & Brown, 1997) that allow career professionals without graduate degrees to deliver career services. Although the National Career Development Association's (NCDA; 2007) *Code of Ethics* recognizes the role of all career professionals such as career counselors, career coaches, consultants, and facilitators, NCDA maintains that career counselors are obligated to represent their qualifications, credentials, and educational degrees to their clients accurately and only to practice within the scope of their professional competence.

Another legal issue in career counseling relates to role designation and advocacy. The role of the career counselor may change in a working professional relationship as the needs of the client become clearer. When role changes occur (e.g., from counselor to advocate), the client needs to be informed of the different role in which the counselor is acting and how that change may affect the client personally, financially, legally, or therapeutically (NCDA, 2007). Likewise, if a career professional would like to extend services to include advocacy efforts, consent should also be obtained to act in that role, and changes in confidentiality agreements should be communicated.

Distance career services, or services delivered by telephone, the Internet, e-mail and other communication devices, are becoming more common in career counseling. Laws pertaining to the use of these services vary by state, province, and country. Career counselors providing these services need to investigate the federal, state, local, and institutional laws in their locales and the residential areas of their clients to be sure they are in compliance with the law. Special considerations include obtaining informed consent, maintaining confidentiality through cyberspace, and upholding duties to warn and protect. The NCDA's Web site and Kanani and Regehr's (2003) article thoroughly discuss the legal considerations related to this topic.

Career counselors also need to be aware of the laws that protect their clients so that advocacy efforts or appropriate legal referrals can be made when necessary. Legislation like the American With Disabilities Act, the Individual With Disabilities Education Improvement Act, and civil rights laws like Section 504 of the Rehabilitation Act of 1973 may help clients with disabilities in schools or the workplace. There are more than 180 labor laws in the United States, such as the Fair Labor Standards Act, the Occupational Safety and Health Act, and the Family and Medical Leave Act, that are applicable to employers and employees. A summary of the major laws can be found on the U.S. Department of Labor Web site.

Regarding legal issues that pertain to career counselors or their clients, knowledge of the laws and their implications is essential to a sound career counseling practice. When ethical responsibilities conflict with legal ones, career counselors first try to resolve the conflict, but ultimately they must adhere to the law. However, career counselors who face legal issues or dilemmas should always seek legal advice when questions or concerns arise, and they should refer their clients to legal counsel if their clients need legal advice or representation.

Contributed by Dawnette L. Cigrand, University of Iowa, Iowa City, IA

References

Isaacson, L. E., & Brown, D. (1997). *Career information, career counseling, and career development* (6th ed.). Boston: Allyn & Bacon.

Kanani, K., & Regehr, C. (2003). Clinical, ethical, and legal issues in e-therapy. *Families in Society: The Journal of Contemporary Human Services, 84,* 155–162.

National Career Development Association. (2007). *Code of ethics.* Retrieved June 1, 2007, from www.ncda.org

Additional Resources

Sales, B. D., & Miller, M. O. (Eds.). (1996–2007). *Law & mental health professionals series.* Washington, DC: American Psychological Association.

U.S. Department of Labor Web site: http:www.dol.gov/

■ Career Development, Key People in

Many key people have shaped the career development field within the counseling profession. Significant individuals in the beginning of the career development movement include Jessie B. Davis, Meyer Bloomfield, and Frank Leavitt who founded the National Vocational Guidance Association (NVGA), now the National Career Development Association (NCDA; Pope, 2001). Leavitt served as the first president of NVGA in 1913 (NCDA, 2007a). This entry highlights individuals whose contributions continue to have an impact on the training of professional counselors: Norman C. Gysbers, Sunny S. Hansen, Joanne Harris-Bowlsbey, Edwin L. Herr, John L. Holland, Kenneth B. Hoyt, John D. Krumboltz, Frank Parsons, Mark L. Savickas, and Donald E. Super. With the exception of Frank Parsons, all of the following individuals have been recognized for their lifetime of service to the career development field as recipients of the NCDA Eminent Career Award, and all have provided service to the counseling profession through their involvement with the American Counseling Association (ACA).

Norman C. Gysbers, is a curator's professor in the College of Education at the University of Missouri–Columbia, focused his research on several areas of career counseling, including the development of comprehensive developmental school counseling programs. Gysbers's experience includes working as a teacher, school counselor, director of guidance, and member of the U.S. Army (Gysbers, 2006). Following completion of his master's and doctoral degrees from the University of Michigan, Gysbers authored more than 80 articles and 15 books, many on the topic of career counseling in community and school settings. One of his most significant recent publications was the book *Developing and Managing Your School Guidance and Counseling Program* (4th ed.) with Patricia Henderson (Gysbers & Henderson, 2006). This textbook provides school counselors a model for implementing and evaluating school guidance programs. Gysbers served as president of NCDA in 1972–1973 (NCDA, 2007a) and ACA in 1977–1978 (Sheeley, 2002). He also served as editor of both *The Career Development Quarterly* from 1962 to 1970 and *The Journal of Career Development* from 1978 to 2006 (Gysbers, 2006). Gysbers's contributions were recognized by ACA in 1982 when he received the Distinguished Professional Service Award. Gysbers was recognized for his contributions to the field of career development in 1989 as the recipient of the NCDA Eminent Career Award (NCDA, 2007b), the NCDA National Merit Award in 1981, and the President's Award for a Lifelong Commitment to Career Development and the NCDA in 2000.

Sunny S. Hansen, emeritus professor in the Counseling and Student Personnel Psychology Program at the University of Minnesota, focused her research on many areas, including women's career development, holistic life planning, multicultural issues, and developmental career guidance (Skovholt, Hage, Kachgal, & Gama, 2007). Hansen has served as a role model for women balancing work with family life through her work as a teacher and counselor educator and as a pioneer integrating the male-dominated academic environment. Hansen received her doctorate in psychology from the University of Minnesota in 1962 and served there as a faculty member for 45 years. Hansen authored more than 150 publications related to career counseling. Some of Hansen's most significant work include creating BORN FREE, an intervention project to reduce gender stereotyping in both men and women, and developing the integrated life planning theory of career counseling. Hansen's (1997) book, *Integrated Life Planning: Critical Tasks for Career Development and Changing Life Patterns,* provides a discussion of critical tasks for holistic life planning. Hansen served as the president of NCDA in 1985–1986 (NCDA, 2007a) and of

ACA in 1989–1990 (Sheeley, 2002). Hansen was the 1991 recipient of the NCDA Eminent Career Award (NCDA, 2007b) and was recognized as an NCDA Fellow in 2002 and an ACA Fellow in 2005.

Joanne Harris-Bowlsbey has focused her career on endeavors in both academia and in the private sector. Harris-Bowlsbey received her master's degree from the University of Wisconsin and her doctorate in counselor education from Northern Illinois University. She has served as a director of guidance, career counselor, consultant, executive director of ACT Educational Technology Center, and the executive director of the Career Development Leadership Alliance (Harris-Bowlsbey, 2007). Her career in academia has included work as a professor at Northern Illinois University, Western Maryland College, and Loyola University Maryland. Her contributions to career counseling include working to develop computerized vocational information systems (e.g., CVIS, DISCOVER, VISIONS), training Career Development Facilitators internationally, and writing print-based career curriculum (e.g., *Take Hold of Your Future, Realizing the Dream, Focus on Your Future I, II and III*) for high school and college students. One of her most recent publications, *Career Development Interventions in the 21st Century* (Niles & Harris-Bowlsbey, 2004), provides a practical overview of career counseling interventions and focuses on NCDA's Career Counseling Competencies used in counselor education programs. She has been engaged in service to the counseling profession as chair of the ACA Inter-Professional and International Committee and as president of NCDA in 1996–1997 (NCDA, 2007a). Her service to career counseling was recognized in 1999 when she was the recipient of the NCDA Eminent Career Award (NCDA, 2007b).

Edwin L. Herr, distinguished professor emeritus of education at The Pennsylvania State University, has focused his research and service on a number of different career-related areas. Herr has authored almost 300 articles and 30 books that focused on approaches to career guidance in schools, advocacy for professional counseling, connecting mental health and career counseling, and career theory (Niles, 2003). Herr received his master's degree and doctorate in counseling and student personnel administration from Columbia University, Teachers College. He identified Donald Super, the professor of his first course at Teachers College, as contributing significantly to his development. Herr's blue-collar work experience (e.g., dishwasher, jackhammer operator, mail sorter), the variety of positions held in the U.S. Air Force for 16 years, and experience as a school counselor contributed to his understanding and ability to work with a wide range of individuals. Herr served as president of NCDA in 1979–1980 (NCDA, 2007a) and ACA in 1983–1984. Herr's contributions were recognized by ACA in 1979 when he received the Distinguished Professional Service Award (ACA, 2005). He was recognized by ACA in 1990 when he received the Professional Development Award, and he received the Extended Research Award from ACA in 2003 (ACA, 2005). Herr was recognized for his contributions to the field of career development in 1986 as the recipient of the NCDA Eminent Career Award (NCDA, 2007b).

Most recently, Herr was honored as a Fellow by ACA in 2004.

John L. Holland, professor emeritus in the Sociology Department at Johns Hopkins University, was best known for constructing his theory of types and person–environment fit. Holland's theory proposed that most individuals and work environments can be categorized on the basis of their resemblance to the six types: realistic, investigative, artistic, social, enterprising, or conventional. One of his most significant contributions to career development was creating the Self-Directed Search (SDS; Holland, 1994). The SDS is a self-administered and self-scored instrument that provides a list of careers that might be of interest to an individual based on his or her personality. The Strong Interest Inventory (Harmon, Hansen, Borgen, & Hammer, 1994) and the Armed Services Vocational Aptitude Battery (U.S. Department of Defense, 2002) have used Holland's typology in presenting their assessment results. Holland's work experience included military service, employment at the Center for Advanced Study in the Behavioral Sciences, and ACT (Weinrach, 1980). Holland received his bachelor's degree in psychology from the University of Omaha and his master's degree and doctorate from the University of Minnesota. Holland's contribution to the field of career development was recognized through the ACA Research Award in 1960 (ACA, 2005), and he was the recipient of the NCDA Eminent Career Award in 1980 (NCDA, 2007b).

Kenneth B. Hoyt, distinguished professor emeritus of education at Kansas State University, has focused his career on advocating for the counseling profession and career education. Hoyt received his master's degree in counseling and guidance from George Washington University and doctorate in educational psychology from the University of Minnesota (Engen, 2003). During his half century of service to the counseling profession, Hoyt's work experience included school counselor; director of guidance; director of the Office of Career Education in the U.S. Department of Education; and counselor educator at the University of Iowa, University of Maryland, and Kansas State University. Hoyt advocated on the state and national levels for career education and the establishment of school counseling programs and encouraged other counselors to take an active role in advocacy. Hoyt served as the founding editor of *Counselor Education and Supervision,* the journal of the Association for Counselor Education and Supervision (ACES), and over his career authored almost 100 articles and several books, many on career education, including his recent publication, *Counseling for High Skills: Responding to the Career Needs of All Students* (Hoyt & Maxey, 2001). Hoyt served as president of ACA in 1966–1967 (Sheeley, 2002) and of NCDA in 1992–1993 (NCDA, 2007a). Hoyt was recognized for his contributions in 1965 with the first ACES Distinguished Service Award, in 1981 as the recipient of the NCDA Eminent Career Award (NCDA, 2007b), and in 1994 with the Distinguished Professional Service Award from ACA (ACA, 2005).

John D. Krumboltz, professor of education and psychology at Stanford University since 1961, is best known for constructing his **social learning theory of career counseling.**

Krumboltz's theory focuses on helping individuals understand their learning experiences, which, in turn, create beliefs that influence their career preferences or choices. Krumboltz received his bachelor's degree in psychology from Coe College, his master's degree in guidance from Columbia University, and his doctorate in counseling and educational psychology from the University of Minnesota (Krumboltz, 2007). Krumboltz's work experience includes serving as a school counselor and teacher, research psychologist for the U.S. Air Force, and professor of education and psychology at Michigan State University. Krumboltz authored more than 90 articles, many on the topic of career thoughts and beliefs. Krumboltz's contribution to the field of career development was recognized by ACA in 1966 and 1968 as the recipient of the Research Award (ACA, 2005). Krumboltz was the 1994 recipient of the NCDA Eminent Career Award (NCDA, 2007b) and received the ACA Living Legend in Counseling Award in 2004.

Frank Parsons (1854–1908) has been credited as being the "father" of the counseling profession. Parsons developed the **trait-and-factor approach** to vocational counseling. This approach encouraged individuals to develop a clear understanding of themselves and the world-of-work and to use true reasoning to make a choice of vocation. Before becoming a counselor, Parsons studied civil engineering at Cornell University and law in New England (Gummere, 1988). He worked as a laborer at an iron rolling mill, teacher who supervised an art program for a school district, professor at Boston University and Kansas State University, social activist testifying in Washington, and a politician who ran for mayor of Boston. Parsons developed his theory of vocational counseling while providing vocational assessment interviews, counseling, and information to a large population of new immigrants at the Vocations Bureau in the Boston Civic Service House. Parson published 14 books over his career, with his most significant work, *Choosing a Vocation* (Parsons, 1909), published after his death by his colleague Ralph Albertson.

Mark L. Savickas, professor and chair of the Behavioral Sciences Department at Northeastern Ohio University College of Medicine and adjunct professor in the counselor education and supervision program at Kent State University, is best known for his **career construction theory** of vocational development and career counseling. Savickas's theory of career counseling uses a postmodern narrative counseling approach to help individuals identify and reconstruct the story of their lives. Savickas's approach focuses on an individual's personality, the interaction with his or her environment, and the life themes that are created (Savickas, 2005). Savickas received his bachelor's degree in psychology and his master's degree in school psychology from John Carroll University and his doctorate in guidance and counseling from Kent State University (Savickas, 2007). Savickas has authored more than 80 articles, many on the topic of vocational interest, and has served as the editor of the *Journal of Vocational Behavior* since 1999. Savickas was the 1994 recipient of the Outstanding Work Award from NCDA, the 1996 recipient of the NCDA Eminent Career Award, and a

2001 charter Fellow in NCDA. Most recently, Savickas was honored as a Fellow by ACA in 2007.

Donald E. Super (1910–1994) developed the life-span, life-space theory. Super believed that career choice was more than a match of abilities and interests to the world-of-work. He believed that career choice was a developmental process that reflected an individual's self-concept. Super created a theory of five life stages as well as a career rainbow to provide a representation of individual's various life roles. He developed the Work Values Inventory (Super, 1970), Career Development Inventory (Super, Thompson, Lindeman, Jordaan, & Myers, 1981), and the Adult Career Concerns Inventory (Super, Thompson, Lindeman, Myers, & Jordaan, 1986). Super studied economic history at Oxford University and vocational guidance at Columbia University, Teachers College, and obtained his doctorate in education psychology and guidance at Clark University (Savickas, 1994). Super credited his father's occupation as a personnel specialist and his mother's occupation as a writer as significant influences on his career. He identified Harry Dexter Kitson, his doctoral adviser at Teachers College, as a significant mentor. Super authored more than 120 articles, most notably his longitudinal Career Pattern Study on how adolescents develop educational and vocational choices (Super et al., 1957). Super served as the second president of ACA in 1953–1954 and was president of NCDA in 1969–1970 (NCDA, 2007a). Super's contribution to the field of career development was recognized when he received the ACA Research Award in 1961 (ACA, 2005), the NCDA Merit Award in 1963, and the NCDA Eminent Career Award in 1972.

NCDA has recognized one individual annually since 1966 for his or her lifetime achievement in the career development field by conferring the Eminent Career Award. Although not discussed in this entry, the following NCDA Award recipients have also contributed significantly to career development: Anne Roe, Robert Hoppock, Harry D. Kitson, Edward Roeber, Seymour Wolfbein, Roy Anderson, Helen Wood, Blanche Paulson, C. Gilbert Wrenn, Leona Tyler, E. G. Williamson, Henry Borow, David V. Tiedeman, Russell Flanders, Anita M. Mitchell, John O. Crites, John W. Rothney, Nancy Schlossberg, Carl McDaniels, William C. Bingham, Martin R. Katz, Donald Zytowski, David A. Jepsen, Garry R. Walz, Dale Prediger, Samuel Osipow, James P. Sampson, Robert Reardon, Thomas Harrington, Duane Brown, Jane Goodman, and Spencer Niles. The key people discussed in this entry and the NCDA award winners, as well as other professional counselors who focus on career development at the local, state, and national levels, continue to advance the field of career development within the counseling profession.

Contributed by Jake J. Protivnak,
Youngstown State University,
Youngstown, OH

References

American Counseling Association. (2005). Past ACA award winners. Retrieved July 20, 2007, from http://www.counseling.

org/PressRoom/NewsReleases.aspx?AGuid=33e1fa4f-469c-4db4-99fc-19d9ab30a209

Engen, H. B. (2003). Kenneth B. Hoyt. In J. D. West, C. J. Osborn, & D. L. Bubenzer (Eds.), *Leaders and legacies: Contributions to the profession of counseling* (pp. 199–203). New York: Brunner-Routledge.

Gummere, R. M. (1988). The counselor as prophet: Frank Parsons, 1854–1908. *Journal of Counseling & Development, 66,* 402–405.

Gysbers, N. C. (2006). *Vita of Norman C. Gysbers.* Retrieved December 23, 2007, from www.gcdf.com.cn/forum/doc/yjjb.htm#2

Gysbers, N. C., & Henderson, P. (2006). *Developing and managing your school guidance and counseling program* (4th ed.). Alexandria, VA: American Counseling Association.

Hansen, L. S. (1997). *Integrated life planning: Critical tasks for career development and changing life patterns (ILP).* San Francisco: Jossey-Bass.

Harmon, L. W., Hansen, J. C., Borgen, F. H., & Hammer, A. L. (1994). *Strong Interest Inventory applications and technical guide.* Stanford, CA: Stanford University Press.

Harris-Bowlsbey, J. (2007). *Curriculum vita.* Retrieved December 23, 2007, from http://webdev.loyola.edu/dmarco/education/Counseling/CVBowlsbey.pdf

Holland, J. L. (1994). *Self-Directed Search*: *Assessment booklet–Form R* (4th ed.). Lutz, FL: Psychological Assessment Resources.

Hoyt, K. B., & Maxey, J. (2001). *Counseling for high skills: Responding to career needs of all students.* Greensboro, NC: ERIC/CASS.

Krumboltz, J. D. (2007). *Stanford University School of Education.* Retrieved July 17, 2007, from Stanford University Web site: http://ed.stanford.edu/suse/faculty/displayRecord.php?suid=jdk

National Career Development Association. (2007a). *Mission, history, purpose.* Retrieved December 23, 2007, from http://209.235.208.145/cgi-bin/WebSuite/tcsAssnWebSuite.pl?AssnID=NCDA&DBCode=130285&Action=DisplayTemplate&Page=AWS_NCDA2_about_mission.html

National Career Development Association. (2007b). *NCDA Eminent Career Award.* Retrieved December 23, 2007, from http://209.235.208.145/cgi-bin/WebSuite/tcsAssnWebSuite.pl?Action=DisplayNewsDetails&RecordID=807&Sections=&IncludeDropped=1&AssnID=NCDA&DBCode=130285

Niles, S. G. (2003). Edwin L. Herr. In J. D. West, C. J. Osborn, & D. L. Bubenzer (Eds.), *Leaders and legacies: Contributions to the profession of counseling* (pp. 173–181). New York: Brunner-Routledge.

Niles, S. G., & Harris-Bowlsbey, J. (2004). *Career development interventions in the 21st century.* Upper Saddle River, NJ: Merrill Prentice Hall.

Parsons, F. (1909). *Choosing a vocation.* Boston: Houghton Mifflin.

Pope, M. (2001). A brief history of career counseling in the United States. *The Career Development Quarterly, 48,* 194–211.

Savickas, M. L. (1994). Donald Edwin Super: The career of a planful explorer. *The Career Development Quarterly, 43,* 4–24.

Savickas, M. L. (2005). The theory and practice of career construction. In S. D. Brown & R. W. Lent (Eds.), *Career development and counseling: Putting theory and research to work* (pp. 42–70). Hoboken, NJ: Wiley.

Savickas, M. L. (2007). *Curriculum vita.* Retrieved July 17, 2007, from http://chdsw.educ.kent.edu/dr__savickas.htm

Sheeley, V. L. (2002). American Counseling Association: The 50th-year celebration of excellence. *Journal of Counseling & Development, 80,* 387–393.

Skovholt, T. M., Hage, S. M., Kachgal, M. M., & Gama, E. P. (2007). An interview with Sunny Hansen: Pioneer and innovator in counseling and career development. *Journal of Counseling & Development, 85,* 216–226.

Super, D. E. (1970). *The Work Values Inventory.* Boston: Houghton Mifflin.

Super, D. E., Crites, J. O., Hummel, R. C., Moser, H. P., Overstreet, P. L., & Warnath, C. F. (1957). *Vocational development: A framework for research.* New York: Harper & Row.

Super, D. E., Thompson, A. S., Lindeman, R. H., Jordaan, J. P., & Myers, R. A. (1981). *The Career Development Inventory.* Palo Alto, CA: Consulting Psychologists Press.

Super, D. E., Thompson, A. S., Lindeman, R. H., Myers, R. A., & Jordaan, J. P. (1986). *Adult Career Concerns Inventory.* Palo Alto, CA: Consulting Psychologists Press.

U.S. Department of Defense. (2002). *The ASVAB career exploration program, counselor manual.* Retrieved December 23, 2007, from http://www.asvabprogram.com/downloads/asvab_counselor_manual.pdf

Weinrach, S. G. (1980). Have hexagon will travel: An interview with John Holland. *Personnel and Guidance Journal, 58,* 406–414.

Additional Resource

National Career Development Association Web site: http://www.ncda.org

■ Career Interests

Career interests, also known as **vocational interests,** have been a primary focus of vocational psychology research and practice for nearly a century. Career interests are included as a key variable in most models of career choice and development. Career counselors frequently use the assessment of career interests to help clients expand or narrow their occupational options for consideration; ultimately, the purpose of assessing interests is to assist people in identifying an occupation they will likely enjoy doing and find satisfying. Researchers and counselors typically define career interests as preferences for particular life activities and distinguish between expressed, manifest, tested, and inventoried interests, a distinction that was articulated by Donald Super (1949) in his landmark book *Appraising Vocational Interests by Means of Psychological Tests.*

Expressed interests refer to a person's verbal report of preferences (i.e., liking or disliking) for various activities, tasks, or occupations. For example, expressed interests consist of responses to questions such as, "Which occupation would you like to pursue?" This method of assessing interests is simple and direct and assumes that the best way to know something about a person is to ask. The degree of usefulness in asking for a stated preference of an occupation varies with the maturity of the individual answering the question; therefore, issues of developmental readiness are often salient, such as the extent to which the individual is sufficiently prepared to state an occupational preference that is realistic and appropriate. In addition, when stating an occupational preference, a person often moves beyond affective liking and disliking and evaluates a multitude of personal and social factors related to the desirability of various occupational alternatives. Because expressing an occupational interest typically involves considerable deliberation, it is generally an effective predictor of occupational choice.

Manifest interests, sometimes referred to as **evidenced interests,** refer to a person's actual involvement or participation in an activity, task, or occupation. This method of assessing interests consists of observing a person's behavior across different situations and assumes that people tend to participate in activities that they find interesting or satisfying. Because direct observation of a person's activities is often impractical, assessment of manifest interests typically relies on self-report. To accomplish this, two methods have historically been used. The first is the use of an interest diary. In creating the interest diary, a person records her or his activities over a specified period of time. The counselor then analyzes the type of activities engaged in and their frequency of occurrence by creating a graph. In examining the patterns, dominant themes are expected to emerge, suggesting general activity preferences. Another method of assessing manifest interests uses an "interest autobiography." In this type of assessment, a person is asked to reflect on different moments in life such as starting school, last years of high school, and years of occupational activity and record interest-inducing activities and tasks at each developmental stage. As with the interest diary, patterns of interests in activities are expected to emerge; the counselor then summarizes these interest patterns and their continuity over time.

Tested interests refer to interests that are reflected in a person's knowledge of special terminology or information about a particular topic, which can be measured by objective tests of such knowledge. This assessment method infers interest in an occupation, for example, based on the level of accumulated knowledge a person has for characteristics of that occupation. The assumption underlying this approach is that people are motivated to accumulate knowledge of and information about activities, tasks, and occupations in which they have high levels of interest. Because numerous factors other than interests predict performance on such tests (e.g., abilities, past experiences, available opportunities, family and cultural influences) and because of the indirect nature of this approach to assessing interests, it is used less often than other methods of interest measurement.

Inventoried interests refer to scores generated from responses to a comprehensive interest inventory. Such inventories typically assess self-reported likes and dislikes for a broad range of activities, occupations, or people. Item responses are used to calculate scale scores, which often are normed relative to a criterion group, thus providing information about how the individual's pattern of scores compares with the interests of women and men in general or with the interests of individuals employed in specific occupations. This assessment approach is widely used, has been extensively studied, and offers the advantages of a broad sampling of the interest domain and objective scores useful for predicting satisfied pursuit of particular interest areas or occupations. Numerous interest inventories currently are available for researchers and counselors, including the Campbell Interest and Skill Survey, Jackson Vocational Interest Survey, Kuder Occupational Interest Survey, Strong Interest Inventory, and the Vocational Preference Inventory. Generally, between 40% and 60% of people enter an occupation recommended from their results on an interest inventory (Fouad, 1999), although some studies have found "hit rates" as high as 74% (e.g., McArthur, 1954).

Through the assessment of interests, career counselors help clients focus on their occupational alternatives and assist them in identifying occupations for exploration and possible entry. Typically, career counselors use more than one approach to assessing interests. A career counselor may ask what kinds of occupations a client has been considering (expressed interests) or enjoys doing (manifest interests) to supplement and confirm information obtained from more formal assessment results (tested and inventoried interests). Drawing from multiple sources of interest assessment allows a career counselor to identify the overall interest patterns of the client more comprehensively to help him or her identify a satisfying occupation.

Finally, expressed, manifest, tested, and inventoried interests have historically been considered different ways of operationalizing the same underlying construct, namely, career interests. However, some scholars (e.g., Silvia, 2001) have questioned this assumption, pointing to evidence that expressed interests better predict entry into an occupation than do inventoried interests, for example, and that there is often not agreement between expressed and inventoried interests for the same person. This perspective points to a possible distinction between career interests (reflected in inventoried interests) and **career intentions** (reflected in expressed interests). More research is needed to explore possible differences in latent constructs that are measured by expressed, manifest, tested, and inventoried interests.

Contributed by Bryan J. Dik, Colorado State University, Fort Collins, CO, and Brian J. Taber, Oakland University, Oakland, MI

References

Fouad, N. A. (1999). Validity evidence for interest inventories. In M. L. Savickas & A. R. Spokane (Eds.), *Vocational interests: Meaning, measurement, and counseling use* (pp. 193–209). Palo Alto, CA: Davies-Black.

McArthur, C. (1954). Long-term validity of the Strong Interest Test in two subcultures. *Journal of Applied Psychology, 38,* 346–354.

Silvia, P. J. (2001). Expressed and measured vocational interests: Distinctions and definitions. *Journal of Vocational Behavior, 59,* 382–393.

Super, D. E. (1949). *Appraising vocational interests by means of psychological tests.* New York: Harper.

Additional Resources

Crites, J. O., & Taber, B. J. (2002). Appraising adult career capabilities: Ability, interest, and personality. In S. G. Niles (Ed.), *Adult career development: Concepts, issues, and practices* (pp. 121–137). Tulsa, OK: National Career Development Association.

Savickas, M. L. (1999). The psychology of interests. In M. L. Savickas & A. R. Spokane (Eds.), *Vocational interests: Meaning, measurement, and counseling use* (pp. 19–56). Palo Alto, CA: Davies-Black.

Savickas, M. L., & Spokane, A. R. (Eds.). (1999). *Vocational interests: Meaning, measurement, and counseling use.* Palo Alto, CA: Davies-Black.

Career Interventions

A **career intervention** is a deliberate act focused on fostering some aspect of a person's career development that has a direct impact on the career decision-making process (Spokane, 1991). The **career decision-making process,** in turn, requires intuitive and rational processes using numerous problem-solving approaches that challenge clients to explore and expand their potential. Even in the most ideal career counseling situations, there is an element of uncertainty that often leads clients to experience fear and vulnerability. Underlying this vacillation between **decisiveness** and **indecisiveness** is the need for control and certainty (e.g., a high level of self-assuredness in a decision or the attainment of desired financial stability or success). For career counseling to be productive, these inner challenges must be addressed at their core. The ultimate goal of any career intervention is to decrease fear and uncertainty while increasing a sense of self-competence in the work and related personal areas. Specifically, career interventions include career counseling, mentoring, career placement services, coaching, and career education and guidance. Group interventions, career decision making, and life planning are interwoven throughout these processes.

Career counseling is the method by which a professional counselor works collaboratively to help clients identify, cultivate, use, and modify work-related decisions while simultaneously addressing the interaction of work with other life roles (Amundson, Harris-Bowlsbey, & Niles, 2005). **Career counselors** work to assist people in clarifying their career goals, a process that often requires individuals also to define and explore their life goals in general. The **National Career Development Association (NCDA)** offers clear and authoritative guidelines defining the scope of career counseling on its Web site. Although the specific techniques used by career counselors vary, because they are customized to meet the individual needs of each client, the general procedures used are somewhat universal to the field of career counseling. The career counselor establishes rapport, assesses the nature of the problem, sets realistic goals, determines a means of executing or attaining those goals, and appropriately terminates the counseling relationship. The outcomes of effective career counseling include enhanced self-understanding, improved knowledge of one or more occupations, selection of a career, increased certainty about a career choice made prior to counseling, integration of strategies helpful in adjusting to particular work role(s), implementation of approaches for coordinating work roles with other life functions, and enhanced mental health (Brown & Brooks, 1991).

Career guidance is a broad construct that has been traditionally used as the rubric under which all career development interventions were placed. Career guidance programs contain some or all of the following: systematic attempts to dispense career information, activities to enhance self-awareness, career planning classes or individual career counseling, and job placement. The term *career guidance programs* is increasingly being replaced by the term **career development programs** but is still widely used in reference to the career development efforts of counselors working in public schools.

Individual and Group Career Counseling Interventions

Career counseling sessions may be conducted as individual or group meetings that purposefully provide opportunities for enhancing decision-making skills. Various tests or inventories may be administered and interpreted as a means of identifying career opportunities and assessing individual interests, abilities, and strengths. Although each counselor has his or her own professional preferences, some examples of these instruments are the Self-Directed Search; the Strong Interest Inventory; the Differential Aptitude Test; Career Occupational Preference System Interest Inventory, Professional Level; Meyers-Briggs Type Indicator (MBTI); and the Comprehensive Personality Profile. Because self-assessment and exploration activities are foundational to the development of career plans, clients may be encouraged to participate in structured exercises both during the sessions and on their own. Some examples of these exercises are card sorts; checklists of interests, values, or abilities; job shadowing; guided imagery; mock interviews; forced-choice activities; observation of skills being demonstrated; reflective writing assignments; group discussions; and transferable skill activities. Job loss, job-related stress, career transition, and personal conflicts on the job are areas in which career counselors can offer support and encouragement. Individuals experiencing such job-related pressures often experience frustration, anger, anxiety, low self-esteem, and discomfort in familial relationships. Career counselors can assist clients in developing clear-cut objectives and achievable goals while enhancing their communication skills and sense of self-worth.

Mentoring as a career intervention is a developmental process in which a more skilled, experienced person serves as a role model, teacher, and coach for the purpose of promoting the professional career development of a younger, more junior individual. A mentor's job is to establish an interactive relationship, show support and encouragement, and teach and counsel. A favorable mentoring relationship involves patience, trust, and a willingness to challenge others to change old behaviors and learn new information.

Technology

Technology may also be used in pursuit of a fuller understanding of the work world, whether as a means of accessing career and occupational information or teaching job-search strategies. Web sites such as Monster, America's Career InfoNet, and Career Builder provide access to a myriad of job opportunities, whereas sites such as Career Key, Live Career, and University of South Florida's Career Laboratory offer online career assessment tools career counselors can offer for support and practice in communication and interpersonal skills.

Career Placement

Placement services may be used by clients at various points in their career development. The most common **career placement services** available are public agencies, private agencies, school-based services, online placement centers (e.g., Headhunter, Monster, and America's Job Bank), and outplacement services to assist workers whose jobs have been terminated.

Career Coaching

Career coaching uses the expertise of coaches to identify career-related obstacles and devise strategies to develop new skills and maintain newly acquired behaviors. One example of the value of career coaching is when a business uses a **career coach** to demonstrate management's investment in facilitating the career development of employees while assisting the business in identifying talent necessary for its continued success. Although not limited to business and industry, this model serves as a template for coaching in any aspect of a person's life in which motivation, focus, and encouragement are needed. Career coaching can also help people identify opportunities that exist in their work settings as well as prepare for and enter new professions. Bench (2003) suggested that career coaches also helped clients clarify their values, become aware of the choices available to them, set goals, and move toward meeting those goals, paralleling many of the tasks of career counselors. In addition, career coaches may help clients to develop management skills, manage transitions, develop job-search skills and conduct job searches, or simply become more effective in their current jobs. Career coaching is similar to career counseling, in which the ultimate goal is to assist the client in achieving success with work-related dilemmas. Unlike career counseling with its clearly established competencies, educational requirements, and code of ethics, career coach-

ing, however, presently has no specific training or educational requirements.

Career Education

Career education services encompass educational strategies aimed at influencing a person's career development. These services include providing occupational information, incorporating career-related concepts into academic curricula, taking field trips to businesses in various industries, having guest speakers representing various occupations talk about their jobs, offering classes devoted to the study of careers, establishing career internships and apprenticeships, and setting up laboratories that simulate career experiences.

Contributed by Kim H. Rodriguez and Kristin Schaefer-Schiumo, Long Island University, C.W. Post Campus, Long Island, NY

References

Amundson, N. E., Harris-Bowlsbey, J., & Niles, S. G. (2005). *Essential elements of career counseling: Processes and techniques.* Upper Saddle River, NJ: Pearson Education.

Bench, M. (2003). *Career coaching: An insider's guide.* Palo Alto, CA: Davis-Black.

Brown, D., & Brooks, L. (1991). *Career counseling techniques.* Boston: Allyn & Bacon.

Spokane, A. R. (1991). *Career interventions.* Englewood Cliffs, NJ: Prentice Hall.

Additional Resources

America's Career InfoNet: http://www.acinet.org

America's Job Bank Web site: http://www.ajb.org

Brown, D. (2007). *Career information, career counseling, and career development* (9th ed.). Boston: Pearson Education.

Career Builder Web site: http://www.careerbuilder.com

Duggan, M. H., & Jurgens, J. C. (2007). *Career interventions and techniques: A complete guide for human service professionals.* Boston: Pearson Education.

Live Career Web site: www.livecareer.com

Monster Web site: www.monster.com

National Career Development Association Web site: www.ncda.org

University of South Florida Career Laboratory: http://career-resource.coedu.usf.edu/linkcareerlab/careerlab.htm

■ Career Interventions for Children

Choosing a career or an academic or training path leading to a particular career is a process that generally occurs during adolescence or early adulthood; however, the foundation for effective career decision making involves a developmental process beginning in early childhood. Children's awareness of the world-of-work begins before they even enter the school-age years as they gain a basic understanding of what their caretaker(s) do and receive work-related messages from their family and the media (Hartung, Porfeli, & Vondracek, 2005). Effective career planning and decision making necessitates that children and young adolescents engage in a variety of processes, including, but not limited to, becoming aware of the need to plan for their futures, learning about their personal characteristics, identifying occupations that are compatible with their views about themselves, collecting information about occupational alternatives, choosing among occupational alternatives, and acting on their occupational choices (Sears, 2004).

Donald Super (1957), following up on Ginzberg, Ginsburg, Axelrad, and Herma's (1951) proposition of occupational choice as a developmental process, proposed a developmental approach to career development and occupational choice. Building on the five life stages identified by Buehler (1933; i.e., growth, exploration, establishment, maintenance, decline), Super et al. (1957) delineated substages for each stage to describe vocational behavior and development across the life stages. According to Super's (1957) life-span, life-space approach to career development, children are in the growth stage. From age 4 years through approximately age 10 years, children are in the fantasy substage of the growth stage, in which personal needs dominate and children engage in fantasy-based role-playing. During this substage, children seek to expand their self-awareness, learn how different jobs are valued, and develop a sense of competency and satisfaction through their activities (Niles, Trusty, & Mitchell, 2004). Around age 11, children transition into the interest substage of the growth stage, in which their aspirations and activities are based primarily on personal likes (Super et al., 1957). During this substage, children identify those activities they enjoy most and in which they are most interested. They then begin to base their initial career aspirations on these interests (Niles et al., 2004).

Young adolescents around 13 years of age enter into the capacities substage of the growth stage, in which personal abilities and actual job requirements are given more weight in terms of aspirations (Super et al., 1957). These young adolescents seek to gain a better sense of their own abilities and how these abilities may help or interfere with their career aspirations (which up until this point had been based primarily on interests rather than interests and abilities; Niles et al., 2004). Around 15 years of age, they transition into the tentative substage of the exploration stage. At this point, they are considering needs, interests, capacities, values, and opportunities in their vocational aspirations and begin to make and try out tentative choices (Super et al., 1957). These young adolescents seek to clarify their self-concepts further and connect these self-concepts to appropriate work goals and postsecondary plans (Niles et al., 2004). It should be noted that Super (1990) stressed that the ages for the transitions among the stages and substages were very flexible and that there could be a recycling through the stages. For example, a young adolescent entering her or his first job may go through a period of growth in this new experience as well as a period of exploration in relation to the nature and expectations of the new role.

Given the age ranges associated with these early stages, much of an individual's early career development occurs during his or her school years. Prior to this age, children generally receive career-related information in an unstructured and unplanned format. Once a child reaches school age, the process of career development ideally becomes more structured and actively fostered as teachers, counselors, and other educators incorporate learning and awareness activities throughout the school. The majority of career awareness activities at the elementary level consist of classroom guidance activities and whole-school or grade-level activities delivered by teachers, school counselors, career specialists, or community members. These activities are linked to growth stage tasks of developing self-concept and identifying interests. Sample activities include career collages, career speakers, career fairs, and a host of knowledge-of-self activities. In addition, career-related technologies, such as WebQuests or computer-assisted guidance programs, are important because the World Wide Web has become an essential resource for career information. Although schools ideally offer structured career education, parents and other significant adults in the child's and young adolescent's life remain important influences on career decision making.

Ideally, young adolescents enter the middle grades with an expanded self-concept and sense of curiosity relating to connections between interests, academics, and the world-of-work. Educators, counselors, and caretaker(s) seek to assist students entering the capacities substage of the growth stage in furthering knowledge of personal interests, values, skills, abilities, and strengths and weaknesses and how these relate to academic and career choices. School counselors assist the students' career development through the use of a range of interest and aptitude assessments, often in conjunction with computer-assisted guidance programs, to help link knowledge-of-self to academics and careers. Career development activities in the capacities substage focus on fostering students' understanding of their abilities and assisting students in engaging in active exploration that includes more specific information about particular careers. This exploration may include activities such as virtual tours, job shadowing, informational interviews, and volunteering. In the middle grades, academic and career planning activities become increasingly important for students. In many states, middle school students and their caretaker(s), aided by school counselors, develop a formal academic plan that is aligned with preliminary academic and career goals.

The planning that students do late in the middle grades ideally carries over formally and informally to the secondary school setting. Students now seek to gain further clarity in their self-understanding and to refine their personal, academic, and career goals. As students progress through secondary school, they narrow in on specific jobs that most closely align with their interests, values, and aptitudes and determine the appropriate education and training pathways for achieving their goals. School counselors and career educators at this stage continue to engage in the provision of information and individual, small group, and large group planning activities for postsecondary transitions. Activities may include student internships, college and career fairs, service learning, and job skills workshops. School counselors may conduct individual and small group counseling through-out the secondary school years, targeting students who may be experiencing career indecisiveness or experiencing heightened anxiety surrounding the career choices they have made.

Contributed by Robert I. Urofsky,
Clemson University, Clemson, SC

References

Buehler, C. (1933). *Der menschliche lebenslauf als psychologisches problem* [The human course of life as a psychological problem]. Leipzig, Germany: Hirzel.

Ginzberg, E., Ginsburg, S. W., Axelrad, S., & Herma, J. (1951). *Occupational choice: An approach to a general theory.* New York: Columbia University Press.

Hartung, P. J., Porfeli, E. J., & Vondracek, F. W. (2005). Child vocational development: A review and reconsideration. *Journal of Vocational Behavior, 66,* 385–419.

Niles, S. G., Trusty, J., & Mitchell, N. (2004). Fostering positive career development in children and adolescents. In R. Pérusse & G. E. Goodnough (Eds.), *Leadership, advocacy, and direct service strategies for professional school counselors* (pp. 102–124). Belmont, CA: Brooks/Cole.

Sears, S. (2004). Investigating the world of work. In R. Pérusse & G. E. Goodnough (Eds.), *Leadership, advocacy, and direct service strategies for professional school counselors* (pp. 71–101). Belmont, CA: Brooks/Cole.

Super, D. E. (1957). *A psychology of careers.* New York: Harper & Row.

Super, D. E. (1990). A life-span, life-space approach to career development. In D. Brown & L. Brooks (Eds.), *Career choice and development: Applying contemporary theories to practice* (2nd ed., pp. 197–261). San Francisco: Jossey-Bass.

Super, D. E., Crites, J., Hummel, R., Moser, H., Overstreet, P., & Warnath, C. (1957). *Vocational development: A framework for research.* New York: Columbia University Bureau of Publications.

Additional Resources

Harrington, T. F., & Harrigan, T. A. (2006). Practice and research in career counseling and development–2005. *The Career Development Quarterly, 55,* 98–167.

Zunker, V. G. (2002). *Career counseling: Applied concepts of life planning* (6th ed.). Pacific Grove, CA: Brooks/Cole.

Career Salience

Career salience is defined as the level of importance that an individual places on the role of work and career in relationship to other life roles. A more detailed explanation focuses on the three dimensions of career salience: participation, commitment, and value expectation. **Participation** is the act of sharing in the activities of a group of people with similar likes and dislikes. Participation as the behavioral component of career salience denotes spending time and energy in (experiencing) a work role. This participation can be sought after, imposed, or accidental. It is also the condition of sharing beliefs, purpose, and enjoyment that are held in common with others who are in similar roles.

Commitment is the state of sincere steadfastness of purpose. It is the act of binding oneself (intellectually and/or emotionally) to a course of action. In the career context, the emotional aspect of commitment involves the emotional attachment to a job, home, studies, and/or family. **Value expectation** evolves from work experiences and can change over time; it is the satisfaction an individual gains from the vocational choices and actions made over the course of his or her life span. Value expectation differs from general work values because value expectation occurs over the life span and is developed from all the vocational choices the individual has made and his or her actions, not just individual work experiences. These three attributes combine in various ways to create an overall view of career selection, life-style satisfaction, and career identity.

The implication of career salience for counselors is the need to determine at what point clients are in their life-span development of acceptance, assimilation, and evaluation of choice in the work field and to assist them to develop the traits of career salience in accordance with their developmental level. By guiding and encouraging the individual in attaining satisfaction and stability in the career, the client experiences an actual improvement in quality of life. The client–counselor relationship is based on the assessment of the client's qualities, attributes, and personal strengths.

Contributed by Charles D. Palmer,
Robyn Fraser-Settoon, and Angelia Taylor,
Mississippi State University,
Starkville, MS

Additional Resources

Brown, D. (2002). *Career choice and development* (4th ed.). San Francisco: Jossey-Bass.

Fassinger, R. E., Santelbury, K., & Richmond, G. (2004). Career, family, and institutional variables in the work lives of academic women in the chemical sciences. *Journal of Women and Minorities in Engineering, 10,* 297–316.

Career Self-Efficacy

Self-efficacy beliefs are judgments that people make about their abilities to perform specific behaviors (Bandura, 1977, 1986). For example, a student who feels confident about her ability to perform well in a mathematics class is said to have high math self-efficacy. An employee who doubts that he could successfully manage others has low management self-efficacy. Self-efficacy is domain specific, meaning that people have different self-efficacy beliefs for many different types of behaviors.

Self-efficacy beliefs determine whether a person will initiate behaviors, how much effort will be expended, and how long a person will persist when difficulties are encountered (Bandura, 1977, 1986). A student with high counseling self-efficacy is expected to seek opportunities to try new counseling techniques, put forth a great deal of effort in learning those techniques, and continue to try to learn the techniques even if she struggles initially. A student with lower counseling self-efficacy may avoid trying new techniques and, if he does attempt them, would be expected to give up more quickly if his initial efforts are not met with success.

Self-efficacy beliefs are derived from four primary sources: (a) performance accomplishments and failures (e.g., when a person has succeeded or struggled with related tasks in the past), (b) vicarious experiences (e.g., when a person has seen another person succeed or fail on a particular task), (c) verbal persuasion (e.g., when a person has been encouraged or discouraged by feedback from others), and (d) emotional arousal (e.g., when a person associates feelings of excitement or anxiety with engaging in a particular task; Bandura, 1977, 1986). These four sources might raise or lower self-efficacy beliefs, depending on whether they are positive or negative.

Hackett and Betz (1981) first applied the concept of self-efficacy beliefs to career decision making. People tend to consider and pursue careers for which they have high self-efficacy, and they avoid careers for which they have low self-efficacy. Thus, someone with high writing self-efficacy would likely consider careers that involve written expression, whereas someone with low writing self-efficacy would eliminate from consideration careers that involve written communication. Self-efficacy beliefs are also related to performance within a career domain; individuals with high self-efficacy tend to perform at higher levels than do those who have lower levels of self-efficacy. In fact, some research has indicated that self-efficacy may be a stronger predictor of people's career choices and performance than is actual ability.

A specific type of self-efficacy beliefs is **career decision-making self-efficacy,** which refers to the degree to which people feel confident about their abilities to make effective career decisions (Taylor & Betz, 1983). Those with high career decision-making self-efficacy tend to engage in self- and environmental exploration behaviors readily and persist in doing so even when they initially encounter difficulties. Those with low career decision-making self-efficacy tend to avoid engaging in behaviors that would help them make decisions, and they may give up easily when they encounter barriers to career decision making.

It is important to note that although they are usually related, self-efficacy beliefs do not always correspond with actual abilities. Some individuals may underestimate their abilities and thus have unrealistically low self-efficacy beliefs. It is also worth noting that self-efficacy beliefs are malleable. Through interventions designed to enhance performance accomplishments, positive vicarious learning experiences, positive verbal encouragement, and positive emotional arousal, individuals may develop higher levels of self-efficacy beliefs, thereby increasing the number of career areas that they perceive as options.

Contributed by Margaret M. Nauta,
Illinois State University, Normal, IL

References

Bandura, A. (1977). Self-efficacy: Toward a unifying theory of behavioral change. *Psychological Review, 84,* 191–215.

Bandura, A. (1986). *Social foundations of thought and action: A social cognitive theory.* Englewood Cliffs, NJ: Prentice Hall.

Hackett, G., & Betz, N. (1981). A self-efficacy approach to the career development of women. *Journal of Vocational Behavior, 18,* 326–329.

Taylor, K. M., & Betz, N. E. (1983). Application of self-efficacy theory to the understanding and treatment of career indecision. *Journal of Vocational Behavior, 22,* 63–81.

Additional Resources

Betz, N. E. (2004). Self-efficacy: Contributions of self-efficacy theory to career counseling: A personal perspective. *The Career Development Quarterly, 52,* 340–353.

Betz, N. E., & Hackett, G. (2006). Career self-efficacy theory: Back to the future. *Journal of Career Assessment, 14,* 3–11.

Gainor, K. A. (2006). Twenty-five years of self-efficacy in career assessment and practice. *Journal of Career Assessment, 14,* 161–178.

■ Career Transitions, Nancy Schlossberg's Transition Theory Applied to

A **transition** may be defined as an event or nonevent that results in change. An event is a transition when it changes an individual's roles, routines, or assumptions, for example, losing a job, getting a divorce, learning of a serious illness. A nonevent is something that a person expected to happen that did not, for example, getting married, having grandchildren, receiving a promotion. Career transitions follow this same structure. **Schlossberg's 4S model** is a way to analyze an individual's ability and readiness to cope with a transition (Goodman, Schlossberg, & Anderson, 2006) It is based on the premise that there are four variables, the 4Ss described in this entry, that tell more about an individual's experience than do the traditional ways of looking at transitions: age and stage. These four variables are the situation, self, support, and strategies.

The **situation** tells what is happening. Each individual's situation is unique, depending on the context—concurrent events, the trigger, the timing, the individual's previous experiences, and the meaning placed on the transition by the person experiencing it. For example, two women have recently retired. The first retired at age 62, as she had always planned. Her life partner had recently retired, and the two were looking forward to having time together. Past job changes had always gone well for her and she was sure this one would also. She had planned carefully for her financial future and her health was good. The second woman was forced out of her job at age 50. Although she had access to retirement funds, she could not yet collect Social Security and she felt pressured about money. Her husband was still working, at a job he hated, and he was resentful of the fact that she no longer had to go to work. The situation for each of these women is clearly different.

The **self** variable indicates to whom it is happening. Each individual is different in terms of life issues and personality. Demographic characteristics such as socioeconomic status, ethnicity, or gender need to be considered, as do psychological resources such as optimism and self-efficacy or spirituality and resiliency. One example is a man has just lost his job. He has been the sole breadwinner for his family and has always considered providing for them as central to his sense of himself as a man. He believes that bad luck follows him and has no hope that he will be able to find an equivalent job. He feels emasculated and depressed. Another man is in the same situation in that he has also just lost his job; however, he gets a sense of identity and worth from his work with his church, feels confident he will bounce back from this setback, and pursues his job search with expectations of success.

The **support** variable indicates what help is available. Supports and available options vary for each individual. Support can be instrumental or emotional. It includes family and intimate relationships, friends, and the institutions and/or communities of which the people are a part. Support systems help individuals master emotional burdens, share tasks, and provide affirmation and aid. Assessing available support and planning to use available resources or enhance or expand existing systems are good first steps in helping individuals manage transitions. For example, one young woman finishes college and begins her first job search. She has made and maintained good relationships with her professors, took advantage of internship and volunteer opportunities, and worked part-time and summers in settings where she wanted to work after graduation. She also has a close family and a network of friends for emotional support during the job search. She took advantage of the placement office at her college for assistance with her résumé and job interviews. Another young woman took all the required classes in college, made excellent grades, but never got to know any of her professors. She worked her way through school so she was not able to take advantage of volunteer or unpaid internship opportunities. She lived with a sister, but both were very introverted and had few other friends. She had never used the university placement office. It is clear that she has a less well-developed support system than the first student.

The **strategies** variable indicates how the person normally copes with change. There are three basic strategies for managing transitions. The first is to change the situation, the second is to change the meaning of the situation, and the third is to manage the stress accompanying the transition. Imagine a man who has received an unwanted transfer to another work site, out of state. His wife works and does not want to change jobs or move. His parents are elderly, live nearby, and need some assistance with daily living. How might he change the situation? He could speak to his boss and ask for reconsideration, perhaps offering to take a different position within the organization. He could seek another position with another organization. He could convince his wife and parents to move also.

How might he change the meaning of the situation? He could define the move as temporary, planning to retire early or find other ways of making this a short-term experience. He could decide this was a way to explore living in another area, one that he and his wife might want to live in someday. He could decide to use the time after work, previously spent in family activities, to learn a new skill such as cooking or woodworking. He could view the move as part of a career ladder and plan on ways of returning to home in a higher level, better paid position. He might use this time to gain an advanced degree to further his chances of subsequent better jobs.

Finally, how might he manage the stress of the transition? First, he could use the resources identified in his assessment of "self" and "support." Second, he might use traditional stress management techniques such as exercise or relaxation, staying physically healthy, or avoiding unhealthy behaviors. Finally, he might call on his spirituality or his faith.

In summary, there are four determinants of a successful transition: the characteristics of the situation; the internal qualities of the individual, the self; the instrumental and emotional support available; and the strategies available in the individual's repertoire. The counselor and the client can use these four determinants as an assessment process. The model then provides a way to develop coping strategies based on the assets and deficits identified in that assessment.

Contributed by Jane Goodman,
Oakland University, Rochester, MI

Reference

Goodman, J., Schlossberg, N. K., & Anderson, M. L. (2006). *Counseling adults in transition* (3rd ed.). New York: Springer.

■ Career Typology

John Holland developed a **career typology** in his theory of vocational personalities and work environments. His theory operates on four basic assumptions. First, he believed that people develop into different types of personalities as a result of heredity and environment. Interacting with environment and under the influences of genetic inheritances, people tend to develop aptitudes in specific areas. Most people develop modal preferences, leading to the emergence of several typological preferences that consist of realistic, investigative, artistic, social, enterprising, or conventional (**RIASEC**). **Realistic** people like to work with animals, machines, or tools and have good related skills. They value practical items such as plants and animals or items that they can build or make better. **Investigative** people enjoy studying and solving mathematical or scientific problems, and they are precise, scientific, and intellectually oriented. **Artistic** people like to be engaged in creative activities such as art, drama, music, dance, crafts, or creative writing. They are artistic, imaginative, original, and independent. **Social** people prefer helping people through teaching, advising, and serving, and they are good at doing these tasks. They are people oriented, helpful, and friendly, and they value helping people and solving social problems. **Enterprising** people like to lead and persuade people. They enjoy selling items or ideas. They are energetic, ambitious, and sociable. They value success in business, leadership, or politics. **Conventional** people enjoy working with numbers, records, or machines in a systematic, orderly way. They are well organized and good at following a plan. The most important personality type, listed first in Holland's profiled personality's descriptive acronym, is called the dominant personality. The next most important type, listed second, is called secondary personality, and the third most important type is called the tertiary type. For example, a person may be Social-Enterprising-Conventional, or an SEC type. Such a person's Social attributes would be dominant, but he or she would display some attributes of Enterprising and Conventional types.

Second, Holland assumed that there are six models of work environment: realistic, investigative, artistic, social, enterprising, or conventional. Each environment is dominated by a given type of personality. For example, Realistic environments are dominated by Realistic types of people. People of different personality types have different interests, competencies, and dispositions, and they tend to surround themselves with people of similar kinds. Also, there is a person–environment interaction; that is, people change jobs and jobs change people. It is therefore possible to assess the environment in the same way an individual's personality is assessed. Holland believed that individuals search for an environment that fits them. For example, Realistic people seek Realistic environments. Finally, behavior is a function of the interaction between personality and the environment. This means that on the basis of understanding personality types, it is possible to predict an individual's choice of vocation, job changes, vocational achievement, personal competence, and educational and social behavior.

To supplement his basic assumptions, Holland developed some secondary concepts to explain further the relationships among personality, environment, and behavior. **Consistency** refers to the degree of relatedness among a person's modal personality or environment type. For example, the Social and Enterprising types as a pair have a higher degree of relatedness than Realistic and Artistic types. In a hexagonal model (see Figure 1), Holland believed that adjacent types on the hexagon (e.g., Social and Enterprising or Realistic and Conventional) are most consistent, or have compatible interests, personal dispositions, or job duties. Holland believed that the degree of consistency between personality types can affect vocational preference.

Differentiation is the degree to which a person or an environment is well-defined; that is, some people or environments are more clearly defined than others. For example, a gifted person may have multiple personality types of similar importance (i.e., low differentiation) compared with another person who may have a single very strong personality of the Realistic type (i.e., high differentiation). In real terms, through assessment, a highly differentiated profile example is a personality code of SEC, with high scores on Social and comparatively low scores on Enterprising and Conventional.

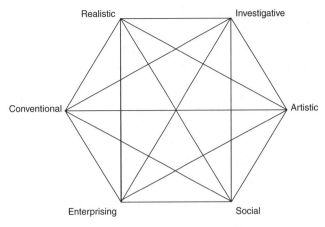

Figure 1. Holland's Hexagonal Model

Note. From "An Empirical Occupational Classification Derived From a Theory of Personality and Intended for Practice and Research" (ACT Research Report No. 29), by J. L. Holland, D. R. Whitney, N. S. Cole, and J. M. Richards Jr., 1969, Iowa City: The American College Testing Program. Copyright 1969 by The American College Testing Program. Reprinted with permission.

Congruence refers to how well personality and environment types match. Holland believed that different personality types require different environments. For example, Social types grow and achieve well in Social environments because such environments provide the opportunities and rewards that match well with Social types' needs. Incongruence refers to a misfit between personality and environment, which may cause job dissatisfaction or burnout.

The Self-Directed Search

John Holland developed the **Self-Directed Search (SDS)** based on his theory of vocational choice. SDS is a self-report inventory that assesses individuals' occupational interests, competencies, and values. It consists of an assessment booklet and the Occupational Finder (personality types arranged by Holland codes and occupations arranged by alphabetical order). The assessment booklets consist of Occupational Daydream Activities (total 66 items; 11 items for each personality type); Competencies (total 66 items; 11 items for each type), Occupations (total 84 types, 14 for each environment type); and Self-Estimates (12 self-estimated work abilities on a scale of 1 to 7, from *low* to *high;* two abilities on each personality type). Users can calculate total scores by adding together the scores on each part. The three highest scores in order become the three-letter Holland code of personality types. From SDS Online, an individual can obtain a list via computer of occupations (and college majors) with codes identical and/or similar to his or her own. After obtaining the personality profile, users may explore the careers they are most likely to find satisfying based on their interests and skills. Users are also encouraged to consider other sources of career information, such as taking additional assessments or obtaining more services from career counselors. SDS may be the most widely used career inventory, has been translated into 25 languages, and has a record of more than 500 related research studies.

SDS has been studied extensively and used widely with students and adults in the United States and throughout the world. Self-scoring errors reported (Holland, Powell, & Fritzsche, 1997) were 3.7% for the first-letter code and 7.5% overall. The SDS manual (Holland et al., 1997) reports internal consistency reliabilities for the summary codes as .86 to .91 for the personality scales ($n = 172$). Test–retest reliabilities over 1 to 4 weeks ranged from .70 to .90. The manual also cites numerous studies that have examined the validity, with the majority of them yielding positive results.

The Vocational Preference Inventory

The Vocational Preference Inventory (VPI; Holland, Daiger, & Power, 1980) was also developed by John Holland and is used by counseling professionals to assess career interests in one-on-one counseling sessions with either students or adults. The VPI consists of a list of 160 occupations. Users rate whether or not each occupation interests or appeals to them. It takes about 15 to 30 minutes to complete the testing. Scores on each scale may range from 0 to 14. Similar to the SDS, the three highest scores in order become the three-letter Holland code of personality types. In addition to the six personality type scales, there are five additional scales: Self-Control, Status, Masculinity/Femininity, Infrequency, and Acquiescence.

The VPI manual summarizes numerous studies that generally support its validity and reliability. For example, the internal consistency (K-R 20) of scores on the VPI scales of the RIASEC types range from .85 to .91 for men and .86 to .91 for women. Test–retest reliabilities are from .61 to .86 for college freshmen. Construct validities of the RIASEC scales related to other interest inventories, such as the Strong Interest Inventory, range from .26 to .69. In general, the concurrent or predictive validity of the VPI interest scales are equal to or exceed those validities of other interest scales (Holland, 1985). Normative data on mostly high school/college students and some adults are provided in the professional manual. In application, professional counselors interpret the client profile and discuss vocational interests and adjustments, life-style, and personal effectiveness.

Contributed by Siu-Man Raymond Ting,
North Carolina State University,
Raleigh, NC

References

Holland, J. L. (1985). *Vocational Preference Inventory: Professional manual.* Odessa, FL: Psychological Assessment Resources.

Holland, J. L., Daiger, D. C., & Power, P. G. (1980). *My vocational situation.* Odessa, FL: Psychological Assessment Resources.

Holland, J. L., Powell, A. B., & Fritzsche, B. A. (1997). *The Self-Directed Search professional user's guide.* Odessa, FL: Psychological Assessment Resources.

Holland, J. L., Whitney, D. R., Cole, N. S., & Richards, J. M., Jr. (1969). *Holland's hexagon* (ACT Research Report No. 29). Iowa City, IA: The American College Testing Program.

Additional Resource

Holland, J. L. (1995). *Making vocational choices* (3rd ed.). Odessa, FL: Psychological Assessment Resources.

■ Case Study

A **case study** is a qualitative research method that explores a bounded system, or **case,** involving an event, setting, process, or an individual or small group of individuals. Case studies are used extensively in social science research, exploring the "how" and "why" questions of contemporary, real-life events for a deeper understanding and description of a particular issue or criterion. In essence, a case study thickly describes the context of a case. A case study may involve a single case or multiple cases (i.e., **collective case study**).

A case may be selected for study based on its uniqueness (i.e., **intrinsic case study**) or its representativeness of an important issue (i.e., **instrumental case study;** Stake, 1995). For example, an investigation of counselors' responses to elementary school children who had been adversely affected by a traumatic event would be an example of an intrinsic case study, whereas exploring mental health treatment processes in a particular residential setting would be an example of an instrumental case study.

Types of Case Studies

Choosing the most appropriate type of case study depends on what type of research question or questions the investigator is posing. There are three types of case studies: explanatory, exploratory, and descriptive (Stake, 1995). If the focus is mainly on "what" questions, an **exploratory case study** may be appropriate. For example, an investigation in a school setting on testing outcomes would explore what it is that influences the results (e.g., what factors contribute to higher test scores?). In a mental health setting, assessing the influences that affect or lead to developing a substance abuse disorder would be an appropriate use of an exploratory case study method. A case study that posits a theory that attempts to explain a certain phenomenon or asks "how" and "why" questions is called an **explanatory case study.** This approach theorizes why a certain phenomenon, event, or process came to exist. Investigating how children's heavy use of video games might lead to increased behavioral disruption and decreased physical activity or why school-age children of lower socioeconomic statuses perform lower than average academically demonstrates potential explanatory case study examples. In a **descriptive case study,** a researcher follows a set of events, people, or a phenomenon over time, describing the characteristics of importance. Following war veterans with posttraumatic stress disorder over time or observing the long-term effects of trauma is an example of descriptive case studies.

Data Analysis

The first step in analyzing a case is defining the scope of that case. Is the case an individual (or individuals), a program, event, process, or a combination of some of these types of bounded systems? Does the inquiry involve a single case or multiple cases? If there are multiple cases, are these found within or among many sites? It is imperative that researchers thoroughly conceptualize the type and number of cases that will be used for data analysis.

Once data are collected about the case or cases, coding or **categorical aggregation** occurs (Creswell, 2006). This involves organizing and segmenting aspects of the case study that are relevant to the research question or questions. For example, in a case study of an after-school program that explores changes in study skills acquisition among at-risk eighth graders, categorical aggregation might involve labeling key categories that address study skills (e.g., time management, test anxiety, dislike of teachers, dislike of science). From these codes or categories, a researcher would then look for patterns among themes and investigate larger issues to make **naturalistic generalizations** (Creswell, 2006). In the study skills case example, some issues that might become apparent during data analysis include a relationship between students' perceived lack of support from teachers and their increased test anxiety. In addition, **within-case analysis** and **cross-case analysis** may occur for inquiries that involve multiple cases. The final step in case study data analysis involves "telling the story" or **embedded analysis**, which involves selecting one aspect of the case in presenting an issue of the bounded system.

Challenges to Case Study Research

Although case studies have been shown to be an effective form of qualitative research, many criticisms have nevertheless arisen. Overall, the greatest lack of support for case studies may come from the perceived lack of rigor in research. Because case study research is nonsystematic, subjective in nature, and not able to be generalized to entire populations, it is has been looked upon as a less desirable form of research and reporting of phenomenon. This may be a result of its reputation as an initial, exploratory form of data collection for another research strategy. Although the specific skills for performing case studies are evolving, case studies are a valuable asset to qualitative research in exploring, explaining, and describing contemporary phenomenon.

Contributed by Rachel N. Moore and
Danica G. Hays, Old Dominion
University, Norfolk, VA

References

Creswell, J. W. (2006). *Qualitative inquiry and research design: Choosing among five traditions* (2nd ed.). Thousand Oaks, CA: Sage.
Stake, R. E. (1995). *The art of case study research.* Thousand Oaks, CA: Sage.

Additional Resources

Creswell, J. W. (2003). *Research design: Qualitative, quantitative, and mixed method approaches* (2nd ed.). Thousand Oaks, CA: Sage.
Yin, R. K. (2003). *Case study research: Design and methods* (3rd ed.). Thousand Oaks, CA: Sage.

Central Tendency

Data sets are not very helpful if people cannot make sense of them. By computing measures of central tendency, a person is better able to understand what is a typical or average score as a starting point for data analysis. **Central tendency** involves computing a mean, median, or mode as a way of describing raw data.

The **mean** is the arithmetic average of a set of scores. The scaling of these scores must be either ratio (e.g., height) or interval (e.g., standard scores, Celsius). It is calculated by adding the values in the data set and dividing by the total number of values. For example, the mean of the data set 7, 2, 4, 5, & 2 is 4.0. Because mean is an average of all values, it can be affected by outliers or extremes in the data set. **Outliers** can skew the results so that the mean is not the best representation of the data set's central tendency. For example, if a score of 20 is added to the data set 7, 2, 4, 5, & 2, the new mean would be 6.67 (i.e., $40 \div 6 = 6.67$).

The **median,** or the middlemost value in a data set, is computed by arranging data in ascending or descending order, with the value that falls in the middle identified as the median value. For example, the median of the data set 7, 2, 4, 5, & 2 is 4.0. If there is an even number of scores, then the middle point will actually be the midpoint between the two middlemost numbers. For example, if a score of 20 is added to the data set 7, 2, 4, 5, & 2, the median is the midpoint of 4 and 5, or 4.5. It is important to note that the median is not influenced as dramatically as the mean in the presence of outliers. Also, the median may be the better statistic to use if trying to find the typical person, particularly when there are extremes in interval data. In addition, a median may be used as a measure of central tendency when the data are ordinal (rank order) in nature.

The **mode** is the value occurring most frequently in a data set. This would be an appropriate statistic to use if dealing with nominal or categorical data (e.g., gender, ethnicity) or ordinal data (e.g., rank order). For example, if people were asked what type of dog they have, the mode would be the answer given most often.

Contributed by Leigh Falls,
Sam Houston State University,
Huntsville, TX

Additional Resources

Holcomb, Z. C. (2004). *Interpreting basic statistics* (4th ed.). Glendale, CA: Pryczak.
Salkind, N. J. (2003). *Statistics for people who (think they) hate statistics.* London: Sage.

Certified Rehabilitation Counselors

Certified Rehabilitation Counselors (CRCs) work with individuals who are dealing with the personal, social, and vocational effects of disabilities. CRCs counsel people with disabilities resulting from birth defects, illness (both physical and mental), disease, accidents, or stress (as defined in the Rehabilitation Act of 1973 and the 1998 Amendments to the Rehabilitation Act, as well as in the Americans with

Disabilities Act of 1990) in order for them to achieve their personal, career, and independent-living goals. CRCs also evaluate individuals for eligibility to receive services. They assess the strengths and limitations of individuals; provide personal and vocational counseling; and arrange for medical care, assistive technology, vocational training, and job placement as necessary. CRCs often interview individuals with disabilities and, when appropriate, their significant others. In addition, CRCs evaluate school, medical, and psychological reports and confer and plan with physicians, psychologists, occupational and physical therapists, and employers to determine the functional capabilities and skills of the individual. In collaboration with the individual with a disability, the CRC will develop an individualized written rehabilitation program that often includes educational and/or vocational training to help the person develop job skills. CRCs also work toward increasing the client's capacity to live independently. CRCs are often found in private practice, various types of rehabilitation facilities, universities, schools, government agencies, insurance companies, and other organizations in which people are being treated for congenital and/or acquired disabilities with the goal of becoming employable or returning to work (U.S. Department of Labor, Bureau of Labor Statistics, 2006).

The Commission on Rehabilitation Counselor Certification (CRCC) grants certification to counselors who meet educational and work experience requirements and have passed an examination indicating that they possess the competencies and skills to become a CRC (CRCC, 2007). To become certified, rehabilitation counselors usually must graduate from an accredited graduate-level educational program, complete an internship, and pass a written examination. Certification requirements vary according to an applicant's educational history. Employment experience, for example, is required for those with a counseling degree in a specialty other than rehabilitation. After meeting these requirements, candidates are designated CRCs. To maintain their certification, counselors must successfully retake the certification exam or complete 100 credit hours of acceptable continuing education every 5 years (CRCC, 2007).

Contributed by John Patrick,
California University of Pennsylvania,
California, PA

References

Commission on Rehabilitation Counselor Certification. (2007). *CRCC certification guide.* Retrieved July 2, 2007, from http://www.crccertification.com/pages/10certification2.html

U.S. Department of Labor, Bureau of Labor Statistics. (2006, August 4). *Occupational outlook handbook, 2006-07: Counselors.* Retrieved July 2, 2007, from http://www.bls.gov/oco/ocos067.htm

Additional Resource

Rubin, S., & Roessler, R. T. (2000). *Foundations of the vocational rehabilitation process* (5th ed.). Austin, TX: PRO-ED.

■ Chi Sigma Iota, The Counseling Academic and Professional Honor Society International

Chi Sigma Iota (CSI), the Counseling Academic and Professional Honor Society International, was officially established January 1, 1985, following several months of planning by representatives of the counselor education program at Ohio University and leaders in the U.S. counseling profession. The impetus for forming an international honor society in counseling was a desire to provide recognition for outstanding academic achievement as well as outstanding service within the counseling profession. The formation of CSI was seen as an avenue to provide a much-needed link between students, educators, practitioners, and administrators in various counseling settings who identified themselves as professional counselors first and foremost.

In 1988, Rho Chi Sigma, the national rehabilitation counseling and services honor society, initiated negotiations concerning unification with CSI. Rho Chi Sigma was formally merged into CSI in March 1989. This was a landmark move to unify rehabilitation counselors with the mainstream of the counseling profession.

By 2008, the total membership of CSI was over 55,000 individuals who had been honored and recognized publicly for their excellence as students and practitioners of professional counseling. Through more than 260 chapters in the United States and abroad, they were invited to join not only to be recognized but also to serve as leaders and contributors to the growth and excellence of their profession. Chapters in other countries include those where U.S. university programs exist (Europe and Japan) or where U.S. programs have been emulated (most notably the Philippines). As professional counseling increasingly becomes more international, CSI's presence will also become more international.

Purpose

Although the scope of the Society is international, its focus is the personal and professional development of its individual members. CSI is committed to upholding the high standards of its members. The purposes of CSI, International, as noted in Article I of the bylaws, are "To promote scholarship, research, professionalism, and excellence in counseling, and to recognize high attainment in the pursuit of academic and clinical excellence in the profession of counseling."

Organization

The goals of CSI are achieved primarily through the activities of local chapters and, secondarily, through efforts of the staff, officers, and committees of the headquarters.

Campus-based chapters in the United States and other countries serve as links within their respective communities to promote interaction among counselor educators, students, alumni, and local professionals. The chapters provide a forum for interaction, sharing of concerns, discussion of issues, and support for common interests. Chapters schedule meetings and solicit speakers on a variety of topics relevant to counselors, thereby serving as a resource for continuing education. Chapters conduct service activities and organize social gatherings to facilitate interactions among members.

International headquarters activities include the functions of the CSI International Office, which is responsible for maintaining the database and records of the organization, ordering and distributing certificates and pins, corresponding with and supporting chapters and members, and distributing information about CSI. The international headquarters is responsible for the dissemination of the *Exemplar,* the quarterly publication of the Society, as well as continuously updating the CSI Web page. Members use the CSI Web site to apply for or renew membership; transfer chapters; register for conferences; and access many sources of information essential to leaders and members about awards, grants, fellowships, and more.

Regarding the quality of articles published in the *Exemplar,* there have been several instances when articles on topics associated with both practitioner and researcher interests have been cited in refereed journals. Many young authors have a chance to begin publishing through service to the membership of CSI by publishing in the *Exemplar*. Likewise, many of the profession's scholars (e.g., Edwin Herr, Courtland Lee, Don C. Locke, Jane Myers) contribute to the *Exemplar* through special issues and invited summaries of their research and clinical practice.

The headquarters also serves as a database networking source to link CSI chapters and members throughout the world. This has been an especially valuable resource for members who have moved to new locations after graduation and seek to affiliate with the nearest CSI chapter.

Annual meetings of CSI are held during the annual convention of the American Counseling Association (ACA) in the spring of each year. The conference includes time for an executive council meeting, leadership training seminar, annual assembly of chapters business meeting, an awards ceremony, and an informal gathering of members for the exchange of information and socialization.

Since the time of its chartering, CSI as an organization and many of its individual members have assumed leadership roles at the state, regional, national, and international levels in promoting the counseling needs of persons of all ages as well as the concerns of counselors themselves. In a world where diversity and cultural richness are an asset, CSI has flourished through its leadership, for example by including scholars, leaders, and specialists who articulate the important role counselors perform in advancing social equality for all persons.

Collaboration

At the grassroots level, CSI provides recognition ceremonies, awards, fellowships, professional development grants, professional development programs, conferences, social functions, and assistance to the counselor education programs of which CSI is a part. In addition, CSI awards fellowships and internships to individuals nominated by their chapters to attend CSI Day leadership development activities and to participate in year-round activities of the Society.

In addition, the annual awards program recognizes outstanding entry-level and doctoral students, practitioners, supervisors, scholars, leaders, chapter faculty advisers, and chapters for their outstanding programs and activities. Included are grants to chapters for professional development and service projects, research grants designed to enhance the scientific and practice basis for professional counseling, and advocacy funds for projects that contribute to equity for counselors and their clients wherever they are needed.

Over the years, the Council for Accreditation of Counseling and Related Educational Programs (CACREP) and CSI have collaborated in recognizing chapters located in CACREP-accredited programs. In addition, CSI uses the CACREP (2009) Standards as one measure of whether a counselor education program is suitable for supporting a new chapter. CSI's goal is to encourage every counselor education program to strive for and ultimately attain national accreditation by CACREP (see Council for Accreditation of Counseling and Related Educational Programs). To that end, all new and reactivating chapters must have administrative support to become nationally accredited by CACREP within 5 years of application to become a chapter.

In its earliest years, CSI collaborated with the then new National Board for Certified Counselors (NBCC) by publishing the professional pamphlet Client Rights and Responsibilities that was suitable for framing in counseling offices. Thousands were distributed by NBCC and CSI to clients, syndicated columnists, and others. In addition, professionals who request new membership in the Society must hold a counselor credential, and the National Certified Counselor is one of the appropriate credentials accepted.

CSI also supports activities of the Association for Counselor Education and Supervision (ACES) and continues to encourage members to attend its meetings both nationally and regionally. Both ACA and ACES have provided conference space and ancillary time for CSI to have meetings and programs.

Advocating for the Profession and Those Whom We Serve

Perhaps the most notable of CSI collaborative efforts was its invitation to all the divisions and credentialing and accrediting bodies of the profession to participate in two national conferences on leadership on counselor advocacy. The outcomes of these meetings are available on the CSI Web site and have guided the activities of the Society and its advocacy committee. Through the efforts of countless volunteers, CSI has been at the forefront of efforts to promote excellence in the profession and to advocate for its place among service providers. Plans are underway to initiate this kind of professional involvement on a regular basis. The goal is to help CSI remain relevant and complementary in its efforts on behalf of the profession as it continues to grow in membership and scope.

Contributed by Thomas J. Sweeney,
Executive Director, Chi Sigma Iota,
Greensboro, NC

Reference

Council for Accreditation of Counseling and Related Educational Programs. (2009). *CACREP accreditation manual: 2009 standards.* Alexandria, VA: Author.

Additional Resource

Chi Sigma Iota Web site: http://www.csi-net.org

■ Child Abuse

Child abuse is a broad term often referring to physical abuse, sexual abuse and exploitation, emotional abuse, and neglect of a person under the age of 18 years. Although each state in the United States, each U.S. territory, and the District of Columbia have their own legal definitions of child abuse, the Child Abuse Prevention and Treatment Act (CAPTA) provides a minimum definition of child abuse (U.S. Department of Health and Human Services, 2003). CAPTA's definition extends the basic components of child abuse to include lack of action on the part of a parent or caretaker to prevent potential or actual serious harm, injury, or death of a child. In addition, the World Health Organization (2004) defined child abuse as

> all forms of physical and/or emotional ill-treatment, sexual abuse, neglect or negligent treatment or commercial or other exploitation, resulting in actual or potential harm to child's health, survival, development or dignity in the context of relationship of responsibility, trust or power. (p. 6)

Prevalence of Child Abuse

Each state is required to report yearly child abuse statistics to the Administration of Children and Families in the U.S. Department of Health and Human Services. Although some states report abuse statistics under an umbrella heading, many states report types of abuse in specific categories (i.e., physical, sexual, emotional, neglect). Many children experience multiple forms of abuse, making accurate statistics difficult.

In 2005, there were 3.5 million investigations of child abuse in the United States and Puerto Rico, resulting in 899,000 children being identified as victims of child abuse and 1,460 deaths (U.S. Department of Health and Human Services, 2007). Of the reported child abuse victims, 50.7% were female. One half of the children were Caucasian, 23% were African American, 17% were Hispanic, 2.3% were multiple races, 1.2% were American Indian and Alaskan Native, 0.8% were Asian, 0.2% were Pacific Islander, and 5.5% were classified as "other" (i.e., did not respond or could not be classified for some reason). Thirty percent of children abused were 0 to 3 years of age, 24.1% were ages 4 to 7 years, 19.8% were ages 8–11 years, 19.8% were ages 12–15 years, and 5.9% were ages 16–17 years. Three fourths of these children had no recorded history of victimization. Abusers included parents (79.4%), strangers (6%), family members (6.8%), partners of parents (3.8%), caregivers

(0.8%), family friends (0.6%), foster parents (0.4%), and legal guardians (0.3%). Child abuse occurs at all socioeconomic levels in all areas of the United States.

The reporting of suspected child abuse and neglect is mandated by all states and territories. **Mandatory reporters** are defined by each state and often include school and daycare personnel, medical personnel, professional counselors, social workers, and other professionals working with children. Some states have a universal mandate, meaning that every citizen of the state must report suspected child abuse or neglect.

Children who are documented victims of child abuse and are in immediate danger are removed from their homes and placed in foster care or in the homes of other family members. In some cases, parental rights are terminated by the state, and children are placed in an adoptive home, permanent foster care, or a group home.

Consequences of Child Abuse

The victims of child abuse often suffer long-term effects, depending on the type of abuse, frequency, duration, severity, child's age and developmental level, and the relationship between the victim and abuser. Survivors of child abuse often have a variety of problems, including shaken baby syndrome, impaired brain development, poor physical health, depression, anxiety, eating disorders, suicide attempts, dissociative disorders, panic disorders, personality disorders, attention-deficit/hyperactive disorder, posttraumatic stress disorder, reactive attachment disorder, cognitive difficulties, social difficulties, delinquency, alcohol and drug abuse, and criminal behavior.

Emotional/Psychological Abuse

Nearly all states include emotional abuse/injury/maltreatment as part of their child abuse definitions, and about 7.1% of confirmed cases of child abuse are considered emotional abuse (U.S. Department of Health and Human Services, 2007). **Emotional abuse** is anything that impairs the child's emotional or social development, including such behaviors as belittling, ignoring, threatening, withholding love, criticizing, or being verbally or physically rejecting. Emotional abuse is often difficult to prove, and child protective services may not be able to intervene without physical proof, resulting in a low percentage of confirmed cases. In addition, emotional abuse is often paired with other forms of abuse.

Neglect

Neglected children are the largest group of victims of abuse in the United States. **Neglect** is defined as failure to provide for a child's basic needs and can be physical (e.g., not providing food, shelter, or supervision), medical (e.g., not providing medical or mental health treatments), educational (e.g., not educating a child or providing special educational opportunities), and emotional (e.g., exposure of a child to adult abuse, lack of nurturing or affection, permitting alcohol or drug use, not providing psychological care). Parents who are unable to provide for a child's needs, such as consistent shelter or food, are differentiated from parents who are financially able to but choose not to provide for their child's needs.

Physical Abuse

Physical abuse is anything that causes physical injury to a child and can be manifested as bruises, broken bones, sprained muscles, cuts, burns, or bites and may result from being shaken, thrown, kicked, hit with the hand or an object, or choked. Genital mutilation is also considered a form of physical abuse. Regardless of intent, all injuries inflicted by an adult on a child are considered physical abuse. Physical abuse is one of the easiest types of abuse to prove, due to the obvious evidence.

Sexual Abuse and Sexual Exploitation

All states include **sexual abuse** and sexual exploitation in their child abuse definitions; however, some states specify types of sexual abuse whereas other states have a general definition. When a child is in a sexual situation with an older person, regardless of touch, the child is being sexually abused; thus, indecent exposure, forcing a child to watch pornography, touching a child's genitals, penetration, a child touching an adult's genitals, rape, and sodomy are all forms of child sexual abuse. **Sexual exploitation** occurs in cases of child prostitution or when a child participates in the production of pornographic material. Sexual abuse is often difficult to prove because of a lack of evidence and because the child, fearing retribution or shame, remains silent.

Contributed by Edina L. Renfro-Michel,
Montclair State University,
Montclair, NJ

References

U.S. Department of Health and Human Services, Administration on Children, Youth and Families. (2003). *The Child Abuse and Prevention Treatment Act: Including Adoption Opportunities and Abandoned Infants Assistance Act as amended by the Keeping Children and Families Safe Act of 2003.* Washington, DC: Author.

U.S. Department of Health and Human Services, Administration on Children, Youth and Families. (2007). *Child maltreatment 2005.* Washington, DC: Author.

World Health Organization. (2004). *Managing child abuse: A handbook for medical officers.* New Delhi, India: Author. Retrieved April 12, 2007, from http://www.searo.who.int/LinkFiles/Publications_Combine_Child_Abuse_WHO_dt15sept.pdf

Additional Resources

Administration for Children and Families Web site: http://acf.hhs.gov

Child Welfare Information Gateway Web site: http://www.childwelfare.gov

Crosson-Tower, C. (2007). *Understanding child abuse and neglect* (7th ed.). Boston: Allyn & Bacon.

■ Circumscription, Compromise and Self-Creation, Gottfredson's Theory of

Linda Gottfredson created a **theory of circumscription, compromise, and self-creation** that specifically articulates the stages of career development of children and adolescents and defines key concepts influencing their view of themselves and the world-of-work. Her theory incorporates elements of developmental and cognitive psychology and considers both hereditary and environmental factors that influence career choice. In Gottfredson's (2002, 2005) model, concepts of gender role and social class are important factors in understanding how individuals circumscribe or narrow their view of acceptable career options. Once young people create a circumscribed view of acceptable career options, they compromise or adjust their aspirations within this narrowed "cognitive map" to accommodate an external reality. Thus, circumscription refers to a process in which individuals reject alternatives viewed as unacceptable, and compromise is a process by which they abandon their most preferred alternatives for more accessible ones.

Key Concepts of Gottfredson's Theory

Circumscription is the process of vocational choice in which an individual eliminates occupational alternatives that conflict with self-concept. In this model, self-concept is an important factor that refers to both an individual's public and private view of self and incorporates many elements such as appearance, abilities, gender, values, and place in society. As children begin to recognize distinctions among jobs, they rule out entire sets of occupations as socially unacceptable for themselves.

Stages of Circumscription
Stages of circumscription are the four developmental phases that all children experience, but at different rates depending on their cognitive ability. The stages may overlap and the ages associated with the stages are only approximate.

1. **Orientation to size and power** (ages 3 to 5 years): Children begin to classify people in the simplest ways, such as big and powerful versus little and weak, and recognize there is an adult world. They recognize occupations as adult roles and no longer report that they would like to be animals (e.g., horses), fantasy characters (e.g., princesses), or inanimate objects (e.g., trees) when they grow up, but rather they see themselves in adult work roles such as teacher or truck driver.

2. **Orientation to sex roles** (ages 6 to 8 years): Children think in concrete terms and make simple distinctions. They understand the concept of sex roles and believe their own sex is superior. Their vocational aspirations reflect what they believe to be appropriate for their own sex and mirror the cultural sex-typed occupations in the world around them, such as nurse or teacher for girls and athlete or police officer for boys.

3. **Orientation to social valuation** (ages 9 to 13 years). Children become sensitive to social evaluation;

recognize distinctions among social classes; rank occupations in prestige the same way adults do; and understand the link between income, education, and occupation. By the end of this stage, children have ruled out large sections of the occupational world as being inappropriate for their gender, social class, or intellectual ability and have a narrowed range of acceptable classes of occupations.

4. **Orientation to internal, unique self** (ages 14 years and older). Adolescents become increasingly aware of their own personality, interests, values, and life-style needs and have occupational preferences that reflect their understanding of themselves and what is most accessible in their world.

Compromise

Compromise is the process by which adolescents abandon their most preferred alternatives for less compatible but more accessible ones. External barriers such as the unavailability of certain educational or employment opportunities, unfair hiring practices, and family obligations restrict the range of realistic alternatives, and people begin to modify their aspirations to reflect external reality. The theory proposes four principles that govern the compromise process:

1. **Developing conditional priorities.** When individuals are faced with small discrepancies between their most preferred occupational choice and what is most realistic, they will give highest priority to satisfying their interests and then their need to match prestige and sex type. When there are moderate tradeoffs, individuals will most avoid a compromise to prestige level. When faced with a major compromise, individuals will sacrifice interests before prestige and sex type.
2. **Opting for the "good enough."** Individuals usually settle for a good occupational choice, not necessarily the best choice, because they are either unable or unwilling to go thorough the demanding process of balancing their view of themselves with what is realistically attainable in order to obtain their most ideal choice.
3. **Staving off the "not good enough."** Individuals who are not satisfied with the available choices in their social space will avoid making commitments to any choice. Avoidance might include searching for more alternatives, reconsidering options, and delaying decisions or commitments.
4. **Accommodating to compromise.** Individuals can adjust psychologically to even major compromises to field of work, less to compromises in prestige that are counter with their view of their social standing, and least to compromises to their acceptable range of sex-type occupations.

Self-Creation

Self-creation refers to the belief that all individuals are capable of improving their options and implementing their self-concept through their career choices. However, due to

hereditary and environmental influences, individuals vary greatly in personal traits such as optimism and perseverance that affect their ability to navigate the compromise process Although the principles of compromise apply to individuals who are beginning their adult lives, once adults have satisfied many of their family responsibilities they are less concerned with implementing a desired social self and more likely to pursue dreams that reflect their private view of themselves.

Counseling Implications

Gottfredson suggested that professional counselors attend to ways in which clients have unnecessarily narrowed their career options at earlier ages and focus on the career options young people reject as well as on the ones they say they prefer. Counseling with the circumscription and compromise model also focuses on how to encourage "constructive realism," which is based not only on choice constraints but also on ways to expand choice. Gottfredson recommended that professional counselors help clients develop a wide range of experiences in order to be better able to discover their unique interests, values, and abilities. Professional counselors can also help clients learn not only ways to shape themselves but also ways to modify their environments to bring out their best qualities and traits.

Contributed by Marion L. Cavallaro,
The College of New Jersey, Ewing, NJ

References

Gottfredson, L. S. (2002). Gottfredson's theory of circumscription, compromise, and self-creation. In D. Brown & Associates (Eds.), *Career choice and development* (4th ed., pp. 85–148). San Francisco: Jossey-Bass.

Gottfredson, L. S. (2005). Applying Gottfredson's theory of circumscription and compromise in career guidance and counseling. In S. Brown & R. Lent (Eds.), *Career development and counseling: Putting theory and research to work* (pp. 71–100). Hoboken, NJ: Wiley.

Classical Conditioning

Classical conditioning, also known as **respondent conditioning,** is a historically important learning model that serves as a foundational piece for the work of professional counselors. The components and process of classical conditioning are fundamental knowledge counselors must have when using the learning model in the counseling process.

Ivan Petrovich-Pavlov (1849–1936) was a 1904 Nobel-Prize-winning Russian scientist trained in biology and medicine. In the study of digestion, he used dogs to experiment with components of salivation in the presence of food. In the process of these studies, he noticed that the dogs that had salivated as expected at the presence of food began to salivate at the presence of white lab coats. Pavlov determined that the dogs had learned that the lab coats signified food, thus producing the response a dog would normally have to food. From this discovery, Pavlov (1927/1960) developed a model known today as classical conditioning.

Important terms in this model include the **unconditioned stimulus (UCS),** which is something that elicits a response that is not learned (unconditioned) but that occurs reflexively; the **unconditioned response (UCR),** which is the reflexive response given to a UCS; the **conditioned stimulus (CS),** which is something that usually does not elicit the desired response but is paired with a UCS in order to condition a subject to provide a desired response; and a **conditioned response (CR),** which is the desired response that a subject gives that is not normally elicited by a stimuli. The response has been learned (conditioned) to be given due to the pairing of the CS with the UCS. In sum, in classical conditioning there is an association or pairing that occurs between an old stimulus and a new stimulus in order to get the new stimulus to produce the same response as the old stimulus.

Using Pavlov's experimentation with digestion and dogs, classical conditioning is demonstrated in the following model:

1. UCS (dog food) leads to UCR (salivation).
2. CS (bell ringing) is paired with UCS (dog food) many times.
3. CS (bell ringing) leads to CR (salivation) without presence of food.

Extinction, Spontaneous Recovery, and Generalization

Although an unconditioned stimulus has been paired with a conditioned stimulus to produce a conditioned response, this condition is not permanent. If the pairing is not reinforced, the conditioned response will soon fade. That is, after a few trials with the conditioned stimulus followed by no food, the conditioned response of salivation will disappear. The term Pavlov used to describe this phenomenon was **extinction.** It is interesting that in these experiments, there was a reappearance (weaker, but still present) of the conditioned response (salivation) in response to the bell alone after the dogs were given a rest from exposure to the conditioned stimulus. This phenomenon was called **spontaneous recovery.**

Further investigation revealed yet another process. A third, different stimulus that closely resembled the first conditioned stimulus could elicit the learned, or conditioned response, just as the conditioned stimulus did. When a different bell was introduced to the dogs, they would salivate to that bell just as they had to the conditioned stimulus bell. No pairing was needed at all. This process was labeled **generalization.**

Applications to Counseling Practice

Classical conditioning paradigms serve counselors as they attempt to understand a client's issues and as they assist in the growth and development of clients in the counseling process. Lights, tones, shades, temperature changes, and words are examples of stimuli that produce natural responses. These natural stimuli can be paired with an infinite number of alternative stimuli. Such pairings lead to the alternative stimuli producing the same response as the natural stimuli. Hence, responses such as changes in heart rate, rate of breathing, pupil dilation, and primary emotional responses such as fear may be elicited from a variety of stimuli that would typically not produce such responses. Attribution of meaning to words, attitudes toward others or to events, and behavioral and emotional responses can all be classically conditioned, which can confuse the presentation of a client in the counseling session. A counselor who understands classical conditioning can use such findings as counseling content.

Classical conditioning theory has served as the foundation for several behavioral techniques, such as counter conditioning and systematic desensitization. Joseph Wolpe (1959) developed a technique called **counter-conditioning.** This involves a new learning experience in which a previously negative stimulus is paired with a new and favorable experience. In his classic example, Wolpe worked with cats that had been made to be fearful of certain situations by the pairing of shocks and harsh sounds with those situations. He later began pairing the same situations with food, and the cats' fear diminished.

Systematic desensitization works under the same principles. A once-feared situation is paired, in steps, with relaxation in order to pair a relaxed state with the once-feared situation methodically. Thus, the client who fears snakes is relieved of those fears by pairing a relaxed condition with orderly steps leading to closeness to snakes until the client can think about, see, and even touch snakes while remaining relaxed.

Conditioning has also been used in the counseling process in an attempt to curb smoking and alcohol drinking habits. Again, the pairing of an experience with a negative stimuli produces a negative state for the client so that a shock following the swallowing of a drink of alcohol will eventually lead to uneasy feelings about alcohol consumption entirely. These kinds of **aversion therapy** approaches that attempt to produce extinction have had mixed results.

In sum, classical conditioning has provided a foundation for counselors in understanding client issues and providing treatment to help resolve such concerns. Many behavioral techniques are a direct application of this paradigm and should be a staple in a counselor's arsenal of techniques.

Contributed by Paul B. Hastings and
Elisabeth D. Bennett,
Gonzaga University, Spokane, WA

References

Pavlov, I. P. (1960). *Conditioned reflexes: An investigation of the physiological activity of the cerebral cortex* (G. V. Anrep, Ed. and Trans.). New York: Dover Publication. (Original work published 1927)

Wolpe, J. (1958). *Psychotherapy by reciprocal inhibition.* Stanford, CA: Stanford University Press.

Additional Resources

Films for the Humanities. (1975). *Classical conditioning, Ivan Petrovich Pavlov* [Video cassette recording]. Princeton NJ: Author.

Smith, W. I., & Moore, J. W. (1966). *Conditioning and instrumental learning.* New York: McGraw Hill.

■Client-Centered Counseling

Carl Rogers, the founder of **client-centered counseling,** was born January 8, 1902, outside of Chicago. One of the most influential psychologists of the 20th century, Rogers grew up in a home that he described as caring, affectionate, controlling, and religious. Rogers was a bright, somewhat withdrawn, and sensitive child who had a close relationship with his mother. As a result of his strict religious upbringing, he decided to major in religion at the University of Wisconsin, and at the age of 22, he went off to attend Union Theological Seminary in New York City. It was at this time that he married Hellen Elliot against his parents' wishes. Increasingly being encouraged to question his career path at Union Theological Seminary, Rogers eventually left the seminary to pursue a master's degree in psychology at Columbia University. After obtaining his degree, he worked as a child psychologist at the Rochester Society for the Prevention of Cruelty to Children. In 1931, he pursued his doctorate in clinical psychology from Columbia University.

Although Rogers began treating individuals from a psychodynamic approach, he eventually questioned the aloof nature of the therapeutic relationship as well as the deterministic nature of this approach. Influenced by **Otto Rank** (a psychoanalyst who split from Freud), existential philosophers, and humanistic thinkers, Rogers increasingly began to take on an existential-humanistic framework and to emphasize the importance of focusing on the present, free will, and an egalitarian relationship with clients. This eventually led to his belief that facilitating client growth in a **nondirective** fashion by offering a therapeutic relationship that embodied humanistic qualities was the most effective way of helping clients. Rogers was given a professorship at The Ohio State University in 1940 and in 1942 published *Counseling and Psychotherapy,* his first book that emphasized his philosophical approach to working with clients.

In 1945, Rogers went to the University of Chicago to establish a counseling center. In 1946, he became the president of the American Psychological Association (APA). During the 1940s, Rogers began applying his humanistic philosophy to group settings. After bringing together counselors to discuss problems they might encounter when working with soldiers returning from World War II, Rogers found that his client-centered approach was eliciting strong emotions from these counselors and noticed that they were sharing deeper parts of themselves in this group setting. These group discussions are often seen as the beginning of the **encounter group movement,** which was to become particularly popular in the 1960s and 1970s and had a major influence on the counseling and therapy groups seen today.

In 1951, Rogers published a major work on his theory, *Client-Centered Therapy.* As his approach grew in popularity, many of his humanistic ideas were adopted by counselors and therapists. In 1957, Rogers wrote an article that described the **necessary and sufficient conditions** for counseling, which highlighted the following underlying tenets to his counseling approach:

1. Two persons are in psychological contact.
2. The first, whom we shall term the client, is in a state of incongruence, being vulnerable or anxious.
3. The second person, whom we shall term the therapist, is congruent or integrated in the relationship.
4. The therapist experiences unconditional positive regard for the client.
5. The therapist experiences an empathic understanding of the client's internal frame of reference and endeavors to communicate this experience to the client.
6. The communication to the client of the therapist's empathic understanding and unconditional positive regard is to a minimal degree achieved. (Rogers, 1957, p. 96).

As a result of this article and the books he had written, his nondirective, client-centered approach was soon to be seen by some as the most important contribution to psychotherapy in the 20th century. As he continued to become increasingly popular, in 1957 Rogers won the APA's first Distinguished Contribution Award. Although Rogers returned to the University of Wisconsin around this time, he found that he disliked the politics of higher education and eventually took a research position in 1964 at the Western Behavioral Studies Institute (WBSI) in La Jolla, California. He left WBSI in 1968 and started the Center for the Studies of the Person, which focused on his humanistic approach to education and counseling.

As Rogers reached his later years, he became increasingly interested in social justice issues. It was during this time that Rogers could be found facilitating workshops and discussion groups between Catholics and Protestants in Northern Ireland, Blacks and Whites in South Africa, and concerned individuals in the former Soviet Union. As Rogers increasingly began to view the qualities inherent in his therapeutic approach as a philosophy of living, he began to use the name "person-centered counseling" instead of client-centered counseling. In 1980, he published his last book, *A Way of Being,* which stressed this viewpoint.

Rogers's philosophy had at its core a number of humanistic tenets. For instance, he believed that people were born with an **actualizing tendency;** that is, if placed in a nurturing environment, the individual has a natural tendency to reach his or her full potential and to be genuine and real, or congruent, in relationships. He also believed that individuals had a need for positive regard, which could, at times, take precedence over the actualizing tendency if significant others were to place **conditions of worth** on the individual. Such conditions occur when significant others place an expectation on an individual to respond in a certain manner, even if the desired response is not how the person wants to respond. This, said Rogers, would create a false self, or as Rogers put it, a person who is incongruent, not genuine, or not real. Rogers believed that a therapeutic environment could counteract the conditions of worth if the counselor could embody three core conditions: congruence, unconditional positive regard, and empathy.

Congruence or Genuineness

Congruence, sometimes called **genuineness,** is the ability of the professional counselor to be real in the relationship. Rogers believed that counselors should not hide their true selves from clients and should risk being themselves. Although advising against moment-to-moment sharing of feelings by the counselor, he did stress the importance of the counselor expressing ongoing feelings he or she might have toward the client, whether they were positive or negative. He also warned counselors that the purpose of counseling was for client self-revelation and not for counselor self-disclosure and that any counselor disclosure of feelings should be done with this in mind.

Unconditional Positive Regard

Unconditional positive regard (UPR), sometimes called acceptance, was the second quality that Rogers believed was critical to an effective helping relationship. UPR means that a counselor accepts the client regardless of the feelings and thoughts expressed. It allows the client to feel safe and trusting in the therapeutic environment and to know that the deepest feelings and most unusual thoughts could be shared without fear of recrimination, rejection, or criticism. Such deep respect for the client's hidden feelings and thoughts allows clients to share their deepest parts of self and enables clients to see how they have been incongruent or false in their life.

Empathic Understanding

Empathic understanding was the last quality Rogers highlighted. Rogers believed that the professional counselor must show the client that she or he is being heard at the deepest levels. Stressing that this is more than "reflecting feelings," Rogers pointed out that empathy can be shown in many ways, including the counselor's use of metaphors, analogies, nonverbals, sensitive touching, careful listening and responding, and reflection. Rogers often said that a helper can come to understand the world of the client "as if" it were his own world, keeping in mind that no one can actually be inside the world of another. Such deep understanding, said Rogers, allows the client to hear deep, often hidden, parts of self.

Rogers believed that if a counselor could embody the characteristics of congruence, unconditional positive regard, and empathic understanding, she or he would create a therapeutic environment that would facilitate the development of certain client characteristics. For instance, clients would tend to be more in touch with their feelings and thoughts, more real or genuine in relationships, more accepting of others, have increased self-regard, have more of an internal locus of control, have a greater sense of free will, and be able to see their choices more clearly.

In January 1987, Carl Rogers was nominated for the Nobel Peace Prize, and in February of the same year, he died of heart failure following surgery for a broken hip. Over his lifetime, Rogers wrote dozens of books, chapters in books, and articles expanding on this theory, with his most well-known books being *Client-Centered Therapy* (1951), *On Becoming a Person* (1961), *Carl Rogers on Encounter Groups* (1970), *Becoming Partners: Marriage and Its Alternatives* (1972), *Carl Rogers on Personal Power* (1977), *Freedom to Learn* (1969), and *A Way of Being* (1980).

Contributed by Ed Neukrug,
Old Dominion University, Norfolk, VA

References

Rogers, C. R. (1942). *Counseling and psychotherapy: Newer concepts in practice.* Boston: Houghton Mifflin.

Rogers, C. R. (1951). *Client-centered therapy: Its current practice, implications, and theory.* Boston: Houghton Mifflin.

Rogers, C. R. (1957). The necessary and sufficient conditions of therapeutic personality change. *Journal of Consulting Psychology, 21,* 95–103.

Rogers, C. R. (1961). *On becoming a person: A therapist's view of psychotherapy.* Boston: Houghton Mifflin.

Rogers, C. R. (1969). *Freedom to learn: A view of what education might become.* Columbus, OH: Merrill.

Rogers, C. R. (1970). *Carl Rogers on encounter groups.* New York: Harper & Row.

Rogers, C. R. (1972). *Becoming partners: Marriage and its alternatives.* New York: Delacorte Press.

Rogers, C. R. (1977*). Carl Rogers on personal power.* New York: Delacorte Press.

Rogers, C. R. (1980). *A way of being.* Boston: Houghton Mifflin.

Additional Resources

Kirschenbaum, H. (1979). *On becoming Carl Rogers.* New York: Delacorte Press.

Kirschenbaum, H. (2009). *The life and work of Carl Rogers.* Alexandria, VA: American Counseling Association.

Kirschenbaum, H., & Henderson, V. (Eds.). (1989). *The Carl Rogers reader.* Boston: Houghton Mifflin.

■ Clinical Mental Health Counseling

Mental health counseling is a specialty area within the counseling profession. According to the **American Mental Health Counselors Association (AMHCA),** mental health counseling is defined as the provision of professional counseling services, including the application of principles of psychotherapy, human development, learning theory, group dynamics, and the etiology of mental illness and dysfunctional behavior, to individuals, couples, families, and groups for the purposes of promoting optimal mental health, dealing with normal problems of living, and treating psychopathology. Unlike counselors in other specialties (e.g., school, college, marriage, and family), mental health counselors focus more on the clinical skills of diagnosing psychopathology and treatment planning. In addition, mental health counselors are more likely to be familiar with the process of third-party reimbursement. Today, mental health counselors find employment in a number of settings, including private practice, community mental health centers, agency settings, substance abuse rehabilitation facilities, hospitals, prisons, and other government agencies.

Origins of Mental Health Counseling

Mental health counseling traces its roots to the 1940s and 1950s when a shift in thinking resulted in radical changes to both the scope and delivery of treatment for the mentally ill. A 1959 study under the aegis of the Joint Commission on Mental Illness and Health suggested that an increase in the number of mental health workers was needed to address the problems related to the current care of mental patients adequately. In response to this call for additional resources, President John F. Kennedy signed into law the **Community Mental Health Centers Act** in 1963. This act allocated federal funding for the establishment of community mental health centers designed to make mental health treatment more accessible. To meet the needs of the community in the best way, these centers provided the following services: short-term inpatient care, outpatient care, partial hospitalization, crisis intervention, and community education and outreach.

Theoretical Foundations of Mental Health Counseling

As a profession, mental health counseling is differentiated from other helping professions (e.g., psychiatry, psychology, social work) by the theoretical foundations on which it is based. Central to the professional identity of mental health counseling is the emphasis on human development across the life span (Palmo, 1996). Mental health counselors use developmental approaches to help identify baseline behaviors of their clients and to explain specific events in the context of the client's lived experiences. Similarly, mental health counselors also assume an ecological perspective when working with their clients. Recognizing that events do not occur in a vacuum, mental health counselors attempt to understand their clients through their own unique developmental context. Finally, mental health counselors focus on holistic wellness as a way to prevent mental illness. To meet the requirements of many third-party reimbursement companies, mental health counselors address wellness by designing interventions that both enhance wellness and remediate mental illness.

Academic Requirements and Credentialing Standards of Mental Health Counselors

Although the terms *mental health counseling* and *community counseling* are often used interchangeably and practitioners in both specialties work in similar settings, there are distinct differences in the academic requirements for each specialization. In 1988, the **Council for Accreditation of Counseling and Related Educational Programs (CACREP)** adopted separate standards for mental health counselors. The revised CACREP standards, effective July

1, 2009, call for clinical mental health counseling degree programs to require 54 semester hours of graduate study, with a planned increase to a 60-semester-hour program scheduled for July 1, 2013. In addition to specific course work that focuses on diagnosis, treatment planning, third-party reimbursement, and psychopathology, mental health counseling trainees also must complete 600 hours of supervised internship.

The credentials most mental health counselors seek are **National Certified Counselor (NCC), Certified Clinical Mental Health Counselor (CCMHC),** and **Licensed Professional Counselor (LPC)** or **Licensed Mental Health Counselor (LMHC;** titles vary across states). The NCC is a voluntary certification that has been offered by the **National Board for Certified Counselors (NBCC)** since 1983. According to NBCC, as of 2007 approximately 42,000 counselors held this professional credential. The CCMHC also is a voluntary certification offered by NBCC. It is designed to recognize those who have advanced specialty training in clinical mental health settings. Several insurance carriers require the CCMHC credential for counselors to become authorized mental health providers in their network. More than 1,100 counselors hold the CCMHC credential. The LPC and LMHC are state-issued licenses that protect the practice and use of the title **professional counselor.** In order to become licensed, individuals must satisfy their respective state's licensing requirements. Although these requirements vary by state, they all include some combination of educational background, supervised counseling experience, and successfully passing a comprehensive counseling practice examination. Since the first licensure law was enacted in Virginia in 1976, 49 states (as of 2007, California is the only exception) as well as the District of Columbia and Puerto Rico have established similar laws.

Professional Organizations for Mental Health Counselors

In addition to joining the **American Counseling Association (ACA),** many mental health counselors also choose to join the **AMHCA.** Established in 1976, AMHCA was created to represent the interests of professional counselors who had the following characteristics in common: (a) academic preparation at the graduate level; (b) positions in community mental health, private practice, or agency settings; (c) belief in the delivery of a wide range of mental health services; and (d) no professional home due to the uniqueness of their position (Smith & Robinson, 1995). Although a division of ACA, AMHCA is run as an autonomous organization with its own operating budget (see American Mental Health Counselors Association).

Clinical mental health counseling is one of several specialty areas in which professional counselors choose to practice. Professional counselors working in mental health positions are often required to become licensed and credentialed so that they can work with managed-care companies to see clients. To help mental health counselors remain current in their training and professional knowledge, several organizations exist to provide professional development and networking opportunities.

Contributed by Morgan Litchfield and Joshua C. Watson, Mississippi State University–Meridian, Meridian, MS

References

Palmo, A. J. (1996). Professional identity of the mental health counselor. In W. J. Weikel & A. J. Palmo (Eds.), *Foundations of mental health counseling* (2nd ed.). Springfield, IL: Thomas.

Smith, H. B., & Robinson, G. (1995). Mental health counseling: Past, present, and future. *Journal of Counseling & Development, 74,* 158–162.

Additional Resources

Gerig, M. (2007). *Foundations for mental health and community counseling: An introduction to the profession.* Upper Saddle River, NJ: Pearson Education.

Gladding, S. T., & Newsome, D. W. (2004). *Community and agency counseling* (2nd ed.). Upper Saddle River, NJ: Prentice Hall.

Lewis, J. A., Lewis, M. D., Daniels, J. A., & D'Andrea, M. J. (2003). *Community counseling: Empowering strategies for a diverse society* (3rd ed.). Pacific Grove, CA: Brooks/Cole.

Cognitive Behavior Modification, Donald Meichenbaum's Theory of

Cognitive behavior modification is a multifaceted, psychoeducational approach to counseling developed by **Donald Meichenbaum.** It focuses on helping clients learn new ways of thinking and behaving to cope with problematic situations. Through the use of empirically supported cognitive and behavioral change strategies, clients modify their internal dialogue, or **self-statements,** and develop and practice new behavioral skills. **Cognitive restructuring** is the process of helping clients recognize and modify this inner dialogue and develop coping self-statements to guide new ways of behaving. Meichenbaum also developed **stress inoculation training (SIT),** a semistructured, graded method of helping clients cope specifically with stressful situations that combines elements of both cognitive restructuring and behavioral change processes.

Cognitive Restructuring

Cognitive restructuring is an essential component that helps clients to recognize problematic self-statements that interfere with their life situations and to develop new coping self-statements to use in all aspects of their changed behavior. Through a collaborative approach with their counselor, clients discover their underlying self-talk and generate facilitative inner dialogue that is first modeled by their counselor and then practiced in therapy and subsequently in real-life situations. During the first stage of cognitive restructuring, clients learn through a process of Socratic questioning that

self-talk is a normal process that influences behavior and emotions and that self-defeating, negative self-statements can directly influence and cause distressing emotions and problematic behavior. Next, clients are taught to recognize their self-defeating thoughts before, during, and after a specific problem situation. For example, a client who experiences fear of speaking in public might identify negative self-statements before giving a speech, such as "I know I am going to forget my lines" or "They will think I don't know what I am talking about." Negative self-statements during the speech might include "Everyone can tell I am nervous" or "I wish this were over," and after the speech such thoughts might include "I really blew that one" or "I sounded terrible." At this stage, clients also learn how these self-defeating thoughts interfere with their performance.

Once clients have identified negative self-statements, they are taught the difference between negative, self-defeating thoughts and positive, self-enhancing thoughts and then generate specific coping thoughts to use during each stage of their challenging situation. For the client fearful of public speaking, coping self-statements before the speech might be "I've practiced and know what I want to say" and "I've done well before." During the speech, facilitative self-statements could include "I'll focus on what I know" or "Just take a deep breath." After the speech, the client could use rewarding self-statements such as "I handled that well" and "People looked interested." In order to stop the negative self-statements and switch to coping self-statements, clients are taught to recognize certain cues during the situation, such as rapid breathing, sweaty palms, or certain recurring negative thoughts, as a sign to stop the negative inner dialogue and start the facilitative self-talk.

During the final stage of cognitive restructuring, clients practice their new internal dialogue. First, the counselor models the use of coping self-statements through recreating the problematic situation with the use of imagery and verbalizing the facilitative self-talk throughout all phases of the behavior. Clients then practice their new coping self-statements by imagining the distressing situation while verbalizing their self-enhancing self-statements. Through practice and counselor feedback, clients learn how to stop their negative self-statements and switch to coping self-statements. Once clients are comfortable practicing their new internal dialogue in the counseling environment, homework assignments are given to practice the coping self-statements in real-life situations.

SIT

Meichenbaum designed SIT to help clients learn how to cope specifically with stressful situations by using a variety of cognitive and behavioral strategies in a semistructured graded approach. Similar to a vaccine that inoculates patients by first exposing them to a very mild form of the disease so that their body can form antibodies to protect them during an actual exposure, SIT prepares clients for real-life stressors by first teaching them cognitive and behavioral coping skills that they practice in a graded manner, first in the counseling environment and then in actual life situations. SIT is a collaborative process that is flexible and designed for each client's unique situation and includes aspects of each of three phases.

Conceptual Phase

During the conceptual phase, it is essential for professional counselors to establish warm, collaborative relationships with their clients and convey genuine acceptance and optimism for client change. Clients learn to observe their behaviors and recognize their thoughts, feelings, physiological reactions, and interpersonal behaviors during stressful situations. A central goal of this stage is for clients to understand how their negative inner speech is causing emotional distress and interfering with their performance and to redefine their problems in ways that will give them a sense of self-control and hopefulness.

Skills Acquisition and Rehearsal Phase

In the skills acquisition and rehearsal phase, clients learn and practice a variety of cognitive and behavioral coping skills to use in the stressful situation. Cognitive strategies include problem solving and cognitive restructuring so that clients can develop new coping self-statements that will enhance their performance. Behavioral strategies include relaxation and/or social skills training that the clients rehearse in the counseling environment where they can practice and receive counselor feedback. The cognitive and behavioral coping skills are integrated so that clients can develop a self-enhancing, coping dialogue to accompany their newly learned stress-reduction behaviors.

Application and Follow-Through Phase

The focus of this final stage, the application and follow-through phase, is to help clients gradually implement their coping strategies in real-life situations and generalize their learning to a range of stressful situations. Initially, clients practice their new coping skills in the counseling setting through imagery rehearsal and behavioral practice. Similar to the process of systematic desensitization, clients imagine coping with progressively more stressful scenes while relaxed. Unique to SIT, however, is the combination of using cognitive coping self-statements and skills while engaged in the graduated imagery. Clients imagine themselves in the stressful situation, experiencing stressful thoughts and feelings, and then use certain stress sensations as cues to use their newly formulated coping strategies. Throughout this process, clients are engaged in coping self-statements to guide and monitor their behavior. Once clients can successfully imagine coping with stressful situations in the counseling setting, they are then given graduated homework assignments to practice their coping strategies in day-to-day stressful situations. During follow-up sessions, clients and counselors evaluate and modify the coping strategies, and booster sessions at 3, 6, and 12 months are used to phase out counseling while providing reinforcement and relapse prevention.

Counseling Applications

Cognitive behavior modification has been used to help clients cope with a wide variety of concerns, such as anger management, impulse control, shyness, anxiety, phobias,

and depression. SIT has been applied specifically to assist clients struggling with performance and/or stressful life situations. In medical settings, SIT has been used to help clients prepare for medical and dental procedures, manage pain, and help medical staff cope with stress. Clients suffering from test anxiety, public speaking anxiety, social phobias, posttraumatic stress, and athletes working to improve their performance have found the coping skills training of SIT effective in managing their stress.

Contributed by Marion L. Cavallaro,
The College of New Jersey, Ewing, NJ

Additional Resources

Meichenbaum, D. (1977). *Cognitive behavior modification: An integrative approach.* New York: Plenum.

Meichenbaum, D. (1985). *Stress inoculation training.* New York: Pergamon Press.

■ Cognitive Developmental Theory

Cognitive developmental theory describes the ways in which individuals make meaning of experience based on different thought processes. Its primary assumption is that reasoning and behavior are strongly related to cognitive complexity. The theory stresses the importance of helping individuals enhance their meaning-making systems in order to achieve a better person–environment match.

Individuals have an innate drive to develop, and growth occurs throughout the lifetime. There appear to be no sex differences in development, and stage growth has been found to occur in all cultures. Progression through stages is affected by interactions between the person and the environment, and change involves both physiological as well as psychological transformations. Progression through the stages is linear, stages cannot be skipped, and the cognitive developmental sequence is essentially invariant and irreversible; however, cognitive development is domain specific. **Domains** are major aspects of human functioning that include thinking, judging, feeling, relating, conceptualizing, and understanding. It is possible to develop in one domain and not another, therefore stage growth is not generalizable across all domains.

Applying the basic tenets of the theory, various stage theories across several domains of development have been specified, including Piaget's (1963) cognitive and intellectual development, Kohlberg's (1958) moral development, Perry's (1970) intellectual and ethical development, Hunt's (1971) conceptual development, Loevinger's (1976) ego development, Fowler's (1981) faith development, Gilligan's (1982) morality of care and women's development, and Kegan's (1982) subject–object theory of development.

Piaget's Theory of Cognitive Development

Jean Piaget is commonly known as a founding cognitive developmental theorist. It was his constructs that became the premise for other developmental stage theories. Piaget identified the developmental process and described a model of hierarchical stages differentiating the meaning-making processes of children and adolescents. In four sequential stages,

Piaget characterized the progressively complex manner in which children understand the world. Ages corresponding with each stage were assigned; however, follow-up research indicated age variability in children's development. Therefore, the assigned ages should not be considered rigid norms but rather typical ranges. Table 1 describes the primary characteristics of each stage.

Forming the foundation for cognitive developmental theory, Piaget identified a unifying set of principles about meaning-making that can be applied across different functional domains. Specifically, stages within each domain signify qualitatively different ways in which to make meaning of experience. The stage in which an individual is currently functioning represents the prevalent style of comprehending the environment. Individuals are defined by the stage they use most frequently, but they do not function solely in one stage at any given time. Depending on the domain and situation, individuals may function at one stage higher or one stage lower than their preferred, modal stage.

Although not rigidly fixed in any one stage at a given time, stage development is nonetheless sequential and hierarchical, thus an individual's behavior positively correlates with his or her level of psychological complexity. Individuals with higher levels of stage development are better able to adapt to their environment.

Cognitive developmental stage theories that address various domains of functioning focus on the process of growth and development. The process of development, as defined by Piaget, includes organization of information for adaptation to the environment. The mechanisms for achieving this include both **assimilation** and **accommodation** to modify existing schema. **Schemata** are mental constructs for organizing information. When individuals encounter new information, they attempt to assimilate it by fitting the information into already existing schemata. If this is not possible, it causes the individual to experience disequilibrium, or an unbalancing of cognitive structures. It is then necessary to accommodate the information by altering existing schema or creating new schema, thus resolving the cognitive dissonance and reestablishing equilibration, or cognitive balance. As the brain grows, it has more capacity for assimilating and accommodating new information, but physical growth alone is not enough to stimulate psychological growth; experience is also needed. When individuals experience difficulty equilibrating, pathology may ensue.

Cognitive developmental theory's view of pathology is that individuals become maladaptive when their current level of development is insufficient at enabling them to function effectively in the environment. Pathology also results from **decalage,** in which individuals become stuck in their current stage when experiencing high levels of stress or overwhelming situations. The theory's therapeutic objective is to determine at which level of development an individual is currently functioning, constructively mismatch by applying interventions that are one stage more advanced, and promote growth toward more adaptive functioning. The role of the therapist varies based on the client's level of development. For individuals functioning at lower stages, the therapist is structured and direct, whereas the therapist is predominantly nondirective and unstructured with those at higher stages.

Deliberate Psychological Education

Clinical and educational interventions have been designed with the aim of providing the conditions necessary for promoting cognitive development. One such model is deliberate psychological education (DPE), in which individuals participate in a significant role-taking experience followed by guided reflection. This model emphasizes the need for providing balance between the experience and reflection, balance between support and challenge, and continuity. DPEs have been used successfully in a variety of contexts.

Professional counselors functioning at higher levels of cognitive development have been found to be more empathic and autonomous, exhibit greater flexibility in counseling techniques, and have greater self-awareness. Specifically related to multicultural counseling, cognitive complexity is correlated with counselors' ability to adopt the perspectives of others, refrain from judgment, and engage in critical thinking,

Table 1. Piaget's Stages of Development

Stage of Development	Age Range (in Years)	Characteristic
Sensorimotor	0–2	Use senses and manipulate the body as well as other objects to learn about themselves and the environment. Move from reflexive actions (e.g., sucking, grasping) to differentiated and intentional actions. Develop object permanence and basic intuition.
Preoperational	2–7	Find meaning in symbolic representations predominantly through the use of language. Move from sensorimotor to conceptual reasoning. Only able to attend to one characteristic of a condition (**centration**), therefore egocentric (i.e., unable to take the perspective of others). Move from **animism** (i.e., ascribing life to inanimate objects and thus believing one can control the environment) to a greater awareness of reality. Prelogical thought as evidenced in belief in **immanent justice** (i.e., the belief that people get what they deserve).
Concrete operational	7–11	Can engage in logical thought but pertaining only to concrete physical situations. Develop ability for **conservation** (i.e., the quantity of objects remains the same no matter how they are arranged). Engage in **reversibility** (i.e., the ability to mentally reverse an action taken on an object). Able to take the perspective of another (reduced **egocentrism**).
Formal operational	11–adulthood	Begin to develop the ability to think abstractly and apply logic to abstractions. Begin to recognize multiple perspectives and consider multiple approaches to solving problems through hypothetical-deductive reasoning.

all of which have been related to knowledge and awareness of diversity issues and culturally sensitive practices.

Contributed by Tammi F. Milliken,
Old Dominion University, Norfolk, VA

References

Fowler, J. W. (1981). *Stages of faith.* San Francisco: Harper & Row.

Gilligan, C. (1982). *In a different voice: Psychological theory and women's development.* Cambridge, MA: Harvard University Press.

Hunt, D. E. (1971). *Matching models in education: The coordinating of teaching models with student characteristics.* Toronto, Ontario, Canada: The Ontario Institute for Studies in Education.

Kegan, R. (1982). *The evolving self: Problem and process in human development.* Cambridge, MA: Harvard University Press.

Kohlberg, L. (1958). *The development of modes of moral thinking and choice in the years 10 to 16.* Unpublished doctoral dissertation, University of Chicago, Chicago.

Loevinger, J. (1976). *Ego development.* San Francisco: Jossey-Bass.

Perry, W. G., Jr. (1970). *Forms of ethical and intellectual development in the college years: A scheme.* New York: Holt, Rinehart, & Winston.

Piaget, J. (1963). *The origins of intelligence in children.* New York: Norton.

■ Cognitive Dissonance

Leon Festinger (1957) developed the theory of dissonance and asserted personal cognitive processes involve voluntary and involuntary exposure to contradictory information. **Cognitive dissonance** is a psychological concept used to explain the discomfort a person feels when a discrepancy exists between what he or she already knows or believes and new information or interpretation that is contrary to his or her original beliefs or behavior. This phenomenon occurs when there is a need to accommodate new ideas or behaviors and a potential need to incorporate the new cognitions or beliefs. According to this theory, there is a tendency for individuals to seek consistency with previously held beliefs or behaviors; therefore, confirmatory thoughts and beliefs are more readily accepted and incorporated into people's cognitions.

The theory of dissonance has two principles. First, dissonance occurs most often when an individual must choose between two incompatible beliefs or actions, with the greatest dissonance occurring when the two alternatives are equally attractive (Atherton, 2005). The strength of the cognitive dissonance is affected by the amount of evidence present to challenge previously held beliefs, the importance attached to the beliefs, and an individual's inability to rationalize or explain away the conflict. For example, this process can be seen within a counseling setting when an individual has learned that his or her partner has been intimate with someone else. This situation confronts previously held beliefs that the relationship was an exclusive one between the two partners. The consequence of this new knowledge often leaves a couple struggling to incorporate this new information into their preexisting knowledge of the relationship. In this example, because of the challenge to previously held beliefs about the relationship, the importance of the relationship, and the difficulty of just explaining away the problem, couples must often struggle to create new beliefs about the relationship that are compatible with the new information.

The second principle explores several ways in which an individual can reduce dissonance. An individual may choose to reduce the importance of the beliefs, add beliefs that are more compatible to the originally held ideas, and/or change the dissonant beliefs so that they are no longer inconsistent (Atherton, 2005). This principle can be seen when an individual is confronted by difficulties in establishing a career direction, for example. A student who is doing poorly in college when majoring in prelaw may respond to this new information in several ways: He or she did not want to be a lawyer (reducing the importance of the beliefs), he or she did poorly in school because of outside factors and just needs to focus and try harder (which holds onto the original beliefs and moves forward), or the student may assess that he or she lacks the necessary talent to succeed in prelaw and switches majors (a complete change in direction). These strategies were originally observed by Leon Festinger's (1957) investigation of a doomsday cult after the prophecy of the end of the world was proven false. The fringe members of the cult chose to leave after being confronted with the contradictory facts, whereas the more resolute members, those who held the strongest beliefs, persisted in their beliefs and readjusted their beliefs to incorporate the idea that they had misinterpreted the signs and, thus, continued their involvement in the cult.

Cognitive dissonance is an important concept in the field of counseling and can be a motivator for behavioral or attitudinal change. The tension or emotion felt during periods of cognitive dissonance may impel an individual to seek counseling. This tension can be sudden, with a new awareness or insight into a situation, or can build slowly over time. When there is an inconsistency between attitudes and beliefs, change may occur; therefore, cognitive dissonance applies to situations involving attitude formation and change. It is especially pivotal for problem solving and decision making. Dissonance appears to be natural in the process of change. What is most interesting is how people choose to resolve the uncomfortable level of tension (Levine, 2003).

Contributed by Carol Klose Smith,
Winona State University, Winona, MN

References

Atherton, J. S. (2005). *Learning and teaching: Cognitive dissonance and learning.* Retrieved October 7, 2007, from http://www.learningandteaching.info/learning/dissonance.htm

Festinger, L. (1957). *A theory of cognitive dissonance.* Stanford, CA: Stanford University Press.

Levine, R. (2003). *The power of persuasion—How we're bought and sold.* New York: Wiley.

Cognitive Therapy

Cognitive therapy (CT) is a system of psychotherapy that was developed by **Aaron T. Beck** in the 1960s. It is also referred to as **cognitive–behavior therapy (CBT).** CT focuses on cognitions, or the way humans tend to think. It is based on the premise that the way an individual perceives or thinks about situations will determine how he or she feels about them. For example, a client who fails a test and thinks "I lack intelligence and I am a failure" is likely to feel more emotionally upset than the client who thinks, "I didn't do too well this time but I know that I am capable of doing better." The goal of the professional counselor is to help clients uncover their underlying thoughts and understand relationships between thinking, feeling, and behaving. Clients being treated with CT learn that their thoughts affect the way they feel. They also learn to identify distortions in thinking patterns.

CT proposes that perceptions are biased and individuals tend to distort events using cognitive errors or errors in information processing. Some of these cognitive errors are given in the following list, along with an example for each type of error:

- *Arbitrary inference.* A student who has had a very busy day thinking at the end of it, "I am really incompetent."
- *Overgeneralization.* After an argument with her father, a teenage girl thinking, "All older men are impossible to talk to—I will therefore avoid talking with them."
- *Selective abstraction.* A woman finding the number of a female colleague of her husband on his desk and thinking, "I know he is having an affair."
- *Magnification.* A person giving a presentation thinking, "If I have to look at my notes even once, my audience will think I'm a useless presenter."
- *Minimization.* A person who wins an award and is thinking, "This was just luck—I didn't deserve to win."
- *Personalization.* A student who obtains a grade of B on a paper thinking, "My teacher hates me—I must have done something to offend him."
- *Absolutist dichotomous thinking.* A housewife thinking, "Unless my children and my house look perfect at all times, I am a worthless wife and mother."

When people are in psychological or physical distress, they tend to think unclearly and are prone to errors in information processing. Cognitive therapy helps people to identify their distressing thoughts and to evaluate how realistic the thoughts are. They then learn to change their erroneous or distorted thinking. Clients who are thinking more realistically tend to feel better.

Beck is professor emeritus of psychiatry at the University of Pennsylvania, School of Medicine, and is president of the Beck Institute for Cognitive Therapy and Research. His daughter, Judith Beck, is director of this institute and is expanding on the work of her father. Extensive empirical research on CT supports its effectiveness in reducing symptoms and relapse rates for a variety of mental disorders. It is effective in treatment in conjunction with medication or on its own. There are currently more than 400 published outcome studies on CT and CBT. Beck first established empirical support for CT in the treatment of depression. He then applied CT to disorders in the following sequence: suicidal behaviors, anxiety disorders, phobias, panic disorder, personality disorders, and substance abuse. Beck also researched the efficacy of CT to treat interpersonal problems, anger, hostility, and violence. Most recently, he turned his attention to applying CT to schizophrenia. Other researchers have supplemented Beck's empirical analyses of CT, making it one of the most widely researched counseling approaches. CT is currently used with adults of all ages, as well as with children and adolescents, in individual, group, couples, and family counseling.

Beck was first trained in psychoanalysis and practiced this form of psychotherapy; however, he was not able to establish empirical support for psychoanalysis in his work with clients experiencing depression. This led to his development of CT, which Beck noted was influenced in the 1950s and 1960s by the work of George Kelly and Albert Ellis. Beck focused his research investigations on identifying idiosyncratic ways of thinking that were shared by people diagnosed with a particular mental disorder. He proposed that all people operate from individual **core schemas,** which are a network of systems of beliefs that have been learned from past experiences. For example, in clients with depression, clients' core schemas incorporate a negative view of themselves, their experiences, and their future. In clients diagnosed with anxiety, there is a sense of physical or psychological danger. Suicidal clients demonstrate patterns of thinking reflecting hopelessness and problem-solving deficits. Beck used the term **automatic thoughts** to explain the large volume of thoughts that go through people's minds so rapidly that they are often unaware of them and unable to stop them. Clients in CT learn how to identify negative, harmful, and repetitive automatic thoughts; stop them; and replace them with more positive and beneficial thoughts. Positive thoughts in turn influence core schemas that guide an individual's behaviors.

CT is a structured and short-term form of therapy, lasting approximately 6 to 25 sessions. It is focused on the present, and emphasis is placed on solving problems and initiating behavioral change. The counselor and client collaboratively engage in setting goals and defining what the client is working toward in counseling. The counselor identifies biased information processing through Socratic dialogue focused on responses to questions such as, "What is the evidence for that belief?" "How else might you interpret that situation?" and "If it is true, what are the implications?" Counselors use a variety of techniques to help clients think about themselves and their experiences differently. These include challenging absolutes, reattribution, labeling of distortions, decatastrophizing, challenging all-or-nothing thinking, and listing advantages and disadvantages. Clients learn skills in counseling that they can use throughout their lives.

Counselors using CT have access to a variety of structured instruments to assess and assist clients. Beck developed questionnaires and surveys to help measure constructs such as depression (Beck Depression Inventory), anxiety (Beck Anxiety Inventory), hopelessness (Beck Hopelessness Scale), and suicidal behaviors (Scale for Suicidal Ideation, Suicide Intent Scale). These scales are widely used by practitioners in mental health settings. Clients are required to work between sessions with tools such as the Dysfunctional Thought Record) in which clients record situations and their accompanying emotions and automatic thoughts, thought sampling, and a variety of scales and questionnaires.

Contributed by Christine Suniti Bhat,
Ohio University, Athens, OH

Additional Resources

Beck, A. T. (2005). The current state of cognitive therapy: A 40-year retrospective. *Archives of General Psychiatry, 62,* 953–959.

Beck Institute for Cognitive Therapy and Research: http://beckinstitute.org

Beck, J. S. (1995). *Cognitive therapy: Basics and beyond.* New York: Guilford Press.

College Admissions Counseling

College admissions counseling is the practice in which a highly qualified counseling professional assists students through the college selection process. College counseling professionals can be professional high school counselors, specific college placement counselors in a high school, or independent college counselors who are paid by the students and their families. Most of the college counseling process takes place during a student's 11th- and 12th-grade years, but effective college counseling can begin as early as middle school.

There are several key components to the college counseling process, including academic advising, student self-reflection, college exploration, and informational and technical support through the process. **Academic advising** begins during middle childhood and continues through the college years, but the most important academic years in terms of college counseling are the student's high school years. It is the role of the college counselor to guide the student in taking the most appropriate academic course load. The professional counselor should advise the student to take a well-balanced, rigorous course load that will allow the student to excel because many colleges are looking to see that a student has been challenged each year. The junior and senior years are the most critical years in terms of college admissions. Professional counselors can help students through this stressful time by meeting with them regularly, keeping students well informed, validating their feelings, and showing ongoing support.

Self-reflection is one of the most important components of the college admission process. In order for students to begin their college exploration journey, they need to take a look at who they are and assess their interests, desires, and

life goals. Professional counselors can help the self-reflection process by offering interest inventories, career exploration inventories, and college search assessments. Professional counselors should also meet with students individually and in groups to facilitate this process.

After spending time in the self-reflection stage, the student **explores different colleges** with a professional counselor. It is the counselor's role to be informed about different colleges and to stay abreast of new information and new programs at colleges. College counselors often visit colleges, meet admissions representatives, attend conferences, and use online tools to keep up with this information. During this period, usually in the spring of a student's junior year and fall of a student's senior year, professional counselors help students build an appropriate list of colleges to which they might apply. Typically, counselors recommend students apply to six to eight colleges. Students should have at least two "likely" schools, two "target" schools, and two "dream" schools on this list. It is also important for students to visit the colleges they are interested in as part of the exploration process.

College counselors should provide **informational and technical support** to the student throughout the college application process. Information on preparation and registration for standardized college admissions tests, such as the SAT and ACT, and assistance with college application procedures, such as submitting applications, requesting transcripts, sending standardized test score reports, requesting teacher and counselor recommendations, writing college admission essays, and scheduling college admission interviews, are especially important. It is important to understand that counselors are not responsible for financial counseling. Counselors should, however, be able to refer parents and students to appropriate financial counselors and resources.

Like all counseling processes, college counseling is a cyclical progression. In the spring of the senior year, a student will have to make a choice about where to attend college. At this point, professional counselors should revisit the process of self-reflection to help the student in making this choice.

Contributed by Lauren M. Klein,
Ridgewood High School, Ridgewood, NJ

Additional Resources

American College Testing Web site: http://www.act.org

College Board Web site: http://www.collegeboard.com

National Association for College Admission Counseling Web site: http://www.nacanet.org

Peterson's Guide to Colleges Web site: http://www.petersons.com

College Counseling

College counseling is a broad concept that has two distinct descriptions. In higher education, *college counseling* is a general term used to describe a campuswide service available to students, faculty, and staff. The emergence of the vocational guidance movement was instrumental in bringing counseling into the mainstream of higher education; therefore, people often confuse the terms *career counseling* or *educational planning* with *college counseling*. The two terms cannot be used interchangeably because the two types of service are distinct.

College counseling arose after World War II, when counseling centers on campus became responsible for addressing the educational and vocational needs of returning veterans. During the 19th century, faculty advisers were supplemented by and replaced with professional counselors. Diagnosis and psychological testing originated and were implemented at this time. Today, there are more than 700 institutions of higher learning in the United States that provide college counseling. The primary purpose of college counseling is to provide direct interventions to students whose personal, social, emotional, psychological, or behavioral problems interfere with their ability to function in the academic environment.

As college campuses have increased in size and became more diverse, the college counseling services have changed to meet the needs of the students. Many college counseling centers have moved away from the traditional approach of addressing transitions from home to college and academic issues to a more clinical approach, such as diagnosis and treatment (e.g., depression, eating disorders) and diversity issues (e.g., multiethnic issues, religion and spirituality issues). College counselors recognize the great need for counseling and mental health services to address the adjustment and developmental concerns, health and social problems, environmental issues, and serious mental illnesses experienced on college campuses (Schwitzer & Choate, 2007). College counseling centers ordinarily provide the following array of services: crisis intervention and counseling, individual counseling and psychotherapy, group counseling and psychotherapy, couple and relationship counseling, career assessment and testing, identification of cases involving domestic abuse and sexual assault, appropriate referrals to outside agencies and therapists, administration of psychoeducational evaluations (e.g., testing for learning disabilities, attention-deficit/hyperactivity disorder), and furnishing self-help materials and resources to further students' development and ability to cope with dilemmas. In addition, college counselors frequently provide consultation and outreach programming to faculty and staff, supervise counselor trainees, research topics related to student development, and respond to changes and challenges in higher education. College counselors assist students wanting to learn more about themselves, crises, relationship or marital problems, difficulties with studying and academic challenges, roommate issues that cannot be resolved by resident assistants, homesickness, emotional concerns, and bothersome moods. College counselors spend 60% of their work hours providing direct services to students, with an average of 24.1 hours spent providing individual and group counseling. In addition, college counselors spend more than 10 hours per week performing administrative duties (Smith et al., 2007).

College counseling services are generally administered through a student service department or division. The clinical service director usually reports to the main director of counselor services, who, in turn, reports to the vice-president of student affairs. Occasionally, the vice president of student affairs may report to the president of the college. Most college counseling takes place at a central location on campus, and students are usually self-referred. Generally, services are provided at no charge, except for a few selected assessments. The majority of the services are provided in the college counseling center; however, there are times when students are referred to other agencies and private counselors for more extensive counseling over a period of time.

The internal organization of the professional staff that provides college counseling varies, but the professional staff ordinarily includes psychologists, professional counselors, and interns or counselors-in-training. On most campuses, all professional staff members possess desired qualifications for college counseling, including a doctorate in counseling or clinical psychology, counseling, or social work; at least 1 year of clinical experience; and licensure or eligibility for licensure in the state of the position. Some college counseling is provided by professional counselors who have a master's degree in counseling or a related field, are licensed or license-eligible for the state of the position, and have a few years of work experience as a counselor in a college environment. In addition, many college counseling centers have interns who are in the process of becoming psychologists and professional counselors and who are supervised by the professional staff. The interns provide some services alone and provide other advanced services with a professional staff member present.

A low percentage of students use college counseling. Students may recognize their need for guidance and support, but their perception of counseling may be colored by stigma, fears, and uncertainty. Other students are not aware of the college counseling services available on their campuses. Usually, women, athletes, students involved in fraternities and sororities, dormitory residents, and off-campus residents are most aware of the college counseling on their campuses. The **American College Counseling Association,** a division of the America Counseling Association, strives to promote awareness among the general public, students, parents, and administrators of the value of counseling services on college campuses (see American College Counseling Association). Today, college counselors are seeing an increase in the number of students receiving college counseling; however, it is their aim to continue to increase students' awareness of college counseling's benefits in enhancing their collegiate lives.

Alternatively, professional school counselors provide a different perspective of college counseling. School counselors' description of college counseling is endorsed by the National Association for College Admission Counseling. They generally provide college counseling by assisting students with postsecondary transitions and reinforcing the students' academic potential to succeed in college. School counselors are professionals who are certified or licensed in school counseling with the training and experience to address the academic, personal/social, and career development needs of students. The college admission counseling used in this specialty may include college exploration, scholarship searches, assistance with the college admission process, advising on selection of majors, and career planning.

Contributed by Nykeisha Moore,
University of Iowa, Iowa City, IA

References

Schwitzer, A., & Choate, L. (2007). College students' needs and counseling responses. *Journal of College Counseling, 10,* 3–5.

Smith, T., Dean, B., Floyd, S., Silva, C., Yamashita, M., Durtschi, J., et al. (2007). Pressing issues in college counseling: A survey of American College Counseling Association members. *Journal of College Counseling, 10,* 64–78.

Additional Resource

Lippincott, J. A., & Lippincott, R. B. (Eds.). (2007). *Special populations in college counseling: A handbook for mental health professionals.* Alexandria, VA: American Counseling Association.

■ Commission on Rehabilitation Counselor Certification

The **Commission on Rehabilitation Counselor Certification (CRCC)** is an independent, not-for-profit organization that sets and oversees the criteria and standards for rehabilitation counseling services in the United States and Canada. The Commission was established in 1974 and has certified more than 35,000 rehabilitation counselors since its inception.

As a certifying body, the CRCC initiates projects and continues to examine the knowledge base, skills, competencies, and job functions empirically that are essential to the successful performance of practicing rehabilitation counselors. The CRCC exam is the final step in the certification process of rehabilitation counselors (CRCC, 2007), leading to the granting of the credential **Certified Rehabilitation Counselor (CRC)** or **Canadian Certified Rehabilitation Counselor (CCRC).**

In addition to setting and overseeing the criteria and standards for the CRC and CCRC credentials, the CRCC has also developed and administered certification credentials for the following:

- CRC-Master Addictions Counselor
- CRC-Clinical Supervisor
- CRC-Master Addictions Counselor-Clinical Supervisor

The CRCC requires that rehabilitation counselors adhere to its *Code of Professional Ethics* (CRCC, 2008) and specifically delineates the scope and practice for rehabilitation counselors through the inclusion of the following techniques and modalities:

- Assessment and appraisal
- Diagnosis and treatment planning
- Career/vocational counseling

- Individual and group counseling interventions (including medical and psychosocial adjustment to chronic illness and disability)
- Case management, referral, and service coordination
- Research and program evaluation
- Interventions to remove environmental, employment, and attitudinal barriers
- Consultation services among various parties and systems
- Consultation about and access to rehabilitation technologies
- Job evaluation, job analysis, and job placement services (CRCC, 2006, pp. 1–2)

The CRCC requires that rehabilitation counselors renew their certification every 5 years. Renewal of the certification can be achieved by (a) documentation of minimally accrued 100 clock hours of relevant continuing education activities or (b) successfully passing the CRC exam. The CRCC holds full accreditation by the National Commission for Certifying Agencies.

Contributed by Hanoch Livneh,
Portland State University, Portland, OR

References

Commission on Rehabilitation Counselor Certification. (2006). *CRCC certification guide.* Schaumburg, IL: Author.

Commission on Rehabilitation Counselor Certification. (2007). *Scope of practice for rehabilitation counseling.* Retrieved June 18, 2007, from www.crccertification.com/downloads/35scope/scope_of_practice_%200307I.pdf

Commission on Rehabilitation Counselor Certification. (2008). *Code of professional ethics.* Retrieved August 25, 2008, from http://www.crccertification.com/pages/30code.html

Additional Resource

Commission on Rehabilitation Counselor Certification Web site: http://www.crccertification.com

■ Computer-Assisted Career Guidance Systems

Computer technology and a rapidly changing job market have affected how career guidance is delivered. Sophisticated **computer-assisted career guidance systems (CACGS)** provide career development tools used by millions of people in various educational sites throughout the country. Different program versions are available for personal computers and online access.

CACGS development began in the late 1960s when the International Business Machines Corporation created interactive computer technology that allowed users to carry on dialogues with their computers. Intrigued by this invention, early career theorists such as Donald Super, JoAnne Harris, David Tiedeman, and Martin Katz developed systems to provide easily accessible applications of career theories. Later, in the 1970s, career practitioners such as Joseph

Impelleteri designed the Computer Occupational Information System, which students could use to explore vocational-technical educational programs and occupations to make career decisions.

CACGS are interactive tools that aid in organizing and processing career information. Four common components of CACGS are assessment, occupational information, educational information, and job search information. Many of these systems have large comprehensive databases that allow users to engage in sophisticated searches of occupations, college majors, educational institutions, scholarships, apprenticeships, and available jobs. Specific occupational information, such as working conditions and work settings, job duties and responsibilities, training requirements, salary, and labor market projections, is available. CACGS may also include assessment instruments that measure vocational interests, personal and work values, abilities, skills, and personality characteristics. On some systems, users are able to complete résumés and practice their job interview knowledge and skills.

In 1976, the **National Occupational Information Coordinating Committee (NOICC)** was formed and provided funding for the development of state **career information delivery systems (CIDS).** NOICC distributed free software to schools and community agencies that allowed users to go online to use these state-developed systems. CIDS provided state-specific information on educational programs, job listings, internship opportunities, and scholarships. CIDS provided an inexpensive alternative for CACGS, whose private leasing fees, at that time, were too costly for many schools and agencies. The development and use of CIDS resulted in reducing the costs of CACGS and encouraged private CACGS publishers to develop online versions. Costs for 1 year leasing of commercially available CACGS can range from $150 to $1,850. Currently, many of these systems have online capabilities that provide links to many career exploration and planning resources, including access to educational institutions and financial aid.

Purpose of CACGS

CACGS help users gain a greater understanding of self, make vocational choices, and receive vocational guidance with the use of computers. When used in conjunction with career counseling, CACGS help individuals with career planning and decision making by providing the most up-to-date information available. Comprehensive systems include activities and strategies that incorporate the common steps in the career planning process. Examples of these activities and strategies are (a) assessing abilities, interests, and values; (b) occupational searching based on self-assessments; (c) selecting an educational or training site; (d) conducting a job search; (e) writing a résumé; and (f) interviewing for employment. The most recent feature of CACGS has been CD-ROM technology that adds video and sound to the systems. Users can watch demonstrations of employment interviews, view workers performing specific job functions, or tour an educational institution.

The Center for the Study of Technology in Counseling and Career Development at Florida State University has conducted research on the effectiveness of these systems with the center's clients. These studies have found the systems to be effective tools for career exploration and making career decisions. Users have expressed satisfaction with the systems, rating them as being user-friendly, enjoyable to use, and needing minimal counselor assistance when navigating through the different components. The interactive nature of these systems allows users to be actively engaged in the career decision-making process. The online systems can be accessed at any time and are cost effective, and the large databases are frequently updated. Several of the most popular and often used CACGS are SIGI, SIGIPLUS, and SIGI[3]; DISCOVER; Guidance Information System (GIS); Computerized Heuristic Occupational Information and Career Exploration (CHOICES); and O*NET.

SIGI, SIGIPLUS, and SIGI[3]

SIGI, developed by Martin Katz (1975) in the 1960s, with revisions in 1975 and 1983, was intended for use by students about to enter high school or attending 2-year colleges. Values clarification and its importance in career decision making provided the underlying theoretical framework for SIGI's development, which initially included five subsystems: values, locate, compare, planning, and strategy. SIGIPLUS, produced in 1996 by the Educational Testing Service (ETS), broadened the subsystem components to introduction, self-assessment, search, information, skills, preparing, coping, deciding, and next steps. The use of both SIGI and SIGIPLUS was expanded for use in colleges and universities and by adults making life and career transitions. In 2000, the program became available in a Web-based version that contained more than 500 links to online resources. Valpar International Corporation acquired SIGI Plus from ETS in May 2004 and discontinued the CD-based version to make the system entirely Web-based. All the SIGI Plus content and components remained the same, and a new and more modern user interface was added. SIGI[3] was last updated in 2006, and more than 100 new occupations added. The 2007 update includes a new personality type component based on Holland's Realistic, Investigative, Artistic, Social, Enterprising, and Conventional codes. The values, interests, and skills surveys have been expanded, and the user interface has been revised to be more guidance oriented.

DISCOVER

DISCOVER, published by American College Testing Program (1984), provides research-based assessments and a comprehensive career guidance process for use by middle school, high school, and college students as well as adult learners. The program is divided into four modules with icons in the main menu titled "halls." Students enter the halls, or modules, as they navigate through the program. When students click on Hall 1, they learn about self and careers by engaging in abilities, interests, and values assessments and evaluating their life roles and career transitions.

Hall 2 contains occupational information and occupational characteristics from the World-of-Work Map. Students can match their vocational interests to the specific demands of the job and job market to make career choices. Hall 3 is designed to help students choose educational majors and institutions and to access financial aid information; Hall 4 provides information on employability skills (e.g., résumé preparation, employment interviewing) and the job search. Students can also access internship and military job information. Career counselors can determine which module(s) or hall(s) students can explore on the basis of individual student needs. For example, if self-assessments have been completed, the counselor may begin the student in Hall 2 to explore occupations that match vocational interests, abilities, and values. DISCOVER has a multimedia version and is available online. Program licenses are held by all types of educational institutions, government agencies, private counseling practices, businesses, military bases, and libraries. The system is updated annually to keep up with changes in the job market and educational sites.

GIS

GIS is published by Riverside and is an electronic data system that provides access to 10 files: occupational information, military information, 2-year and 4-year colleges, graduate and professional schools, state vocational schools, financial aid, majors, and careers. The user can enter scores from off-line inventories such as the Career Decision-Making Inventory (Harrington & O'Shea, 1992), the Career Assessment Inventory (Johannson, 1986), the Strong Interest Inventory (Strong, 1994), and the Self-Directed Search (Holland, Fritzsche, & Powell, 1994). An optional online interest inventory, the Harrington-O'Shea's Career Decision-Making System (Harrington & O'Shea, 1992), is also available.

CHOICES

CHOICES was originally developed as a CIDS, but it also contains the elements of a CACGS because of its comprehensiveness and access to large databases. CHOICES has been adopted by approximately 30 states. It is used for obtaining career information and making career decisions. Users identify personal preferences to access information on educational institutions (e.g., majors, geographic location, student population, tuition, athletics, housing), programs of study, and financial aid. Students can compare occupational characteristics on 17 topics (e.g., job demands, training or education required, salary, aptitudes, interests, work sites, temperaments) of two occupations simultaneously. States can customize the database to provide information on local jobs, apprenticeships, coops, and assistantships. CHOICES is used primarily in educational settings, and in some states the program is Web-based.

O*NET

O*NET is the Web-based version that has replaced the traditional hardbound copy of the *Dictionary of Occupational Titles* (4th ed.) published by the U.S. Department of Labor. This database, updated regularly, contains descriptions of 812 occupations by 277 descriptors. The content model provides the theoretical and empirical foundation for O*NET and reflects occupations by job-oriented and worker-oriented descriptors that are organized into six domains: (a) worker characteristics (e.g., abilities, occupational interests, work values, work styles), (b) worker requirements (e.g., basic skills, cross-functional skills, knowledge, education), (c) experience requirements linked to previously performed work activities (e.g., work experience and training, basic skills and cross-functional entry skill requirements, licenses or credentials that demonstrate acquired knowledge and skills), (d) occupation-specific information (e.g., specific work tasks, tools, technology needed to perform the job), (e) labor market characteristics (e.g., employment projections and trends), and (f) occupational requirements (e.g., job behaviors, organizational characteristics that influence work performance, work context or the physical and social aspects of work). O*NET provides links to all 50 states, which post local job listings and information (e.g., salary, location), educational (e.g., educational training institutions), and labor market services (e.g., wage data, employment trends and projections). Users are able to complete online and download the O*Net Interest Profiler, O*Net Ability Profiler, and O*Net Work Importance Profiler. These inventories assess users' vocational interests using Holland's six occupational types, perceptions regarding abilities and skills (i.e., verbal, arithmetic reasoning, computation, spatial, form perception, clerical perception, motor coordination, finger dexterity, and manual dexterity), and six work values (i.e., achievement, independence, recognition, relationships, support, and working conditions). O*NET is free to online users.

Ethical Considerations When Using CACGS

CACGS provide greater accessibility to career information to more individuals, especially those who can often access online resources easier than traditional face-to-face counseling (e.g., individuals with physical disabilities). There are limitations and concerns, however, associated with the use of these systems. Security and confidentiality of the information are major concerns and a potential disadvantage for their use. Passwords and identification codes are needed to maintain confidentiality. The same ethical guidelines apply when using CACGS for career counseling that would apply in conventional career counseling approaches. The **National Career Development Association** in 1997 approved guidelines for delivery of career-related services using the Internet. These guidelines should be carefully reviewed. The **American Counseling Association's** (2005) *ACA Code of Ethics* has also identified ethical standards for the use of online counseling, and the **National Board for Certified Counselors** (2007) has also developed standards, The Practice of Internet Counseling, which can be accessed on the organization's Web site. Other limitations that counselors should consider prior to using CACGS with clients are the appropriateness of the instruments for the user (e.g., cross-cultural value differences), the reliability and validity of scores generated from online inventories, system failure, downtime and slow data transmission rate, the computer proficiency of the user, and client readiness. The purpose and limitations of the program should be carefully explained to clients, and they should be advised that it is only one of many other tools that can be used in the career decision-making process. Counselors should closely monitor clients' progress, with assistance provided throughout the process. For optimal counseling effectiveness, CACGS should be used with the assistance of career counselors who can individualize the program for clients as well as interpret the information in the context of clients' abilities, interests, personalities, and values.

The following Web sites can be used to access CACGSs online:

- American's Career Kit (America's Job Bank and America's Talent Bank): http://www.ajb.dni.us
- Career InfoNet: http://www.acinet.org
- COIN JR: http://www.coinedu.com/products/docs/CoinJr.pdf
- CHOICES: http://www.careerware.com
- DISCOVER: http://www.act.org/discover/index.html
- O*NET: http://www.onetcenter.org
- SIGI³: http://valparint.com/sigi3.htm

Contributed by Adriana G. McEachern, Florida International University, Miami, FL

References

American Counseling Association. (2005). *ACA code of ethics*. Alexandria, VA: Author.

American College Testing Program. (1984). *DISCOVER. A computer-based career development and counselor support system*. Iowa City, IA: Author.

Harrington, T., & O'Shea, A. (1992). *Harrington-O'Shea Career Decision-Making System*. Circle Pines, MN: American Guidance Service.

Holland, J. L., Fritzsche, B. A., & Powell, A. B. (1994). *Technical manual for the Self-Directed Search*. Lutz, FL: Psychological Assessment Resources.

Johannson, C. B. (1986). *Career Assessment Inventory*. Upper Saddle River, NJ: Pearson Education.

Katz, M. R. (1975). *SIGI: A computer-based system of interactive guidance and information*. Princeton, NJ: Educational Testing Service.

National Board for Certified Counselors. (2007). *The practice of Internet counseling*. Retrieved June 26, 2008, from http://www.nbcc.org/webethics2

National Career Development Association. (1997). *NCDA guidelines for the use of the Internet for provision of career information and planning services*. Retrieved June 26, 2008, from http://ncda.org/about/poles.html

Strong, E. K. (1994). *The Strong Interest Inventory*. Palo Alto, CA: Consulting Psychologists Press.

Additional Resources

Harris-Bowlsbey, J., Dikel, M. R., & Sampson, J. P. (Eds.). (2004). *The Internet: A tool for career planning* (2nd ed.). Tulsa, OK: National Career Development Association.

Niles, S. G., & Harris-Bowlsbey, J. (Eds.). (2005). *Career development interventions in the 21st century* (2nd ed.). Upper Saddle River, NJ: Pearson Merrill Prentice Hall.

Zunker, V. G. (Ed.). (2006). *Career counseling: A holistic approach* (7th ed.). Belmont, CA: Thomson Brooks/Cole.

■ Computer-Based Testing

Computer-based testing involves the use of computer technology, software programs, or Internet sites for the administration, analysis, and interpretation of testing instruments used in the assessment and evaluation process. The rapid advancement of computer and related technology has resulted in an increased ability for professional counselors to take advantage of existing testing resources when assessing clients in educational and clinical settings. Computer-based tests are available to assess a wide variety of domains, including but not limited to diagnosis of psychopathology, personality, behavior, intelligence, ability, career development (or exploration), and relationships. There are a vast number of computer-based assessment tools available to counseling professionals. Examples of instruments that offer the option of using computer technology are the Beck Depression Inventory–II, Strong Interest Inventory, Personality Assessment Inventory, Myers–Briggs Type Indicator, and Marital Satisfaction Inventory. There are also testing instruments that fall under a parallel use of assessment instruments, known as computer-adaptive testing. The Graduate Record Examination is a good example of **computer-adaptive testing,** a technology that enables the computer program to assess a client's ability level rapidly and then structure test items in a manner that best determines the test taker's aptitude, usually more quickly and accurately than a paper-and-pencil version of the test.

Once primarily the province of the psychology field, assessment has become increasingly easier to access by those working as mental health counselors, marriage and family counselors, and school counselors. Computer technology has enabled professional counselors to make wider use of assessments, although counselors need to consult their state statutes to determine whether their credential limits the type of testing they may conduct. Also, test publishers may require specific graduate training and academic degrees in order to purchase software and other materials necessary to use certain instruments.

The accessibility of assessment tests through advanced technology has benefited the profession. Counselors, however, must not lose sight of the guidelines laid out in the American Counseling Association's (2005) *ACA Code of Ethics* in Section E: Evaluation, Assessment, and Interpretation. Although access to computer-based testing may be far-reaching, counselors are ethically bound to receive supervised instruction and training in the specific instruments they may choose to use. In addition, many tests can be scored and interpreted with narrative reports generated through computer software. In such cases, counselors are called on to understand the construct of what the test is measuring.

Drummond and Jones (2006) identified a number of benefits and drawbacks of using computer-based testing. Advantages include (a) rapid and cost-effective collection of data; (b) potential for greater scoring accuracy; (c) computer-generated analysis and written narrative reports; (d) faster, and sometimes immediate, feedback for both client and counselor; (e) ability with some tests to adapt the structure and order of test items to best fit a client's response to previous items; and (f) reduction in time spent on routine counselor tasks because of information generated by testing software. Several disadvantages associated with computer-based testing are (a) interpretations can be confounded because the client's emotional state at the time of testing is not accounted for; (b) the normative data used for computer-based instruments may be insufficient; (c) although information collection may be economical, the start-up costs for equipment and supplies can be expensive; (d) some traditional and widely used instruments may not easily convert to computer formats; (e) there is a lack of the human involvement that is so important to a therapeutic relationship; (f) standards for obtaining computer-based tests are not highly monitored; and (g) becoming properly trained in testing and procedures for specific tests can be expensive and time-consuming.

If professional counselors choose to make use of the advantages of computer-based testing, they should not consider these tools as the sole determinant of a client's presentation during the evaluation and case conceptualization process. Testing results must be used in conjunction with a client interview and information gathered from other resources whenever possible. Doing otherwise would not serve the client's best interests.

Contributed by David F. March,
Stetson University, DeLand, FL

References

American Counseling Association. (2005). *ACA code of ethics*. Alexandria, VA: Author.

Drummond, R. J., & Jones, K. D. (2006). *Assessment procedures for counselors and other helping professionals* (6th ed.). Upper Saddle River, NJ: Pearson Merrill Prentice Hall.

Additional Resources

American Psychological Association Testing and Assessment Web page: http://www.apa.org/science/faq-findtests.html

Association for Assessment in Counseling and Education Web site: http://www.theaaceonline.com/resources.htm

Association of Test Publishers. (2005). *Guidelines for computer-based testing*. Washington, DC: Author.

Bartram, D., & Hambleton, R. (2006). *Computer-based testing and the Internet: Issues and advances*. West Sussex, England: Wiley.

■ Confidentiality

Confidentiality is the client's right to privacy in the counseling relationship. Confidentiality is an ethical concept that appears in most ethical codes established among professional counseling organizations. The American Counseling Association's (2005) *ACA Code of Ethics* outlines confidentiality for practicing counselors. Professional counselors are to communicate the parameters of confidentiality in a culturally competent manner. Counselors are to respect the client's right to privacy and do not share client information without clients' consent or sound legal or ethical justification. Other professions, licensing organizations, or credentialing agencies may address confidentiality. Confidentiality is one of the first topics counselors address with clients when informing them about the counseling experience. Confidentiality is a concept taught in counseling programs and is the foundation for the trust element between counselor and client. It is especially important to inform clients of the limits of confidentiality.

Although confidentiality is meant to protect the client, confidentiality has limits. It protects the client from having information disclosed without the consent of the client. Universal exceptions to confidentiality include (a) client consent, (b) child abuse, and (c) harm to self or others. In addition, confidentiality may be breached on a judge's order. Another exception may be consultation among counseling professionals while protecting the client's privacy, including discussions with supervisors according to protocol within an agency. It is also important for counselors to be sensitive to cultural implications regarding confidentiality.

Professional counselors hold ongoing discussions with clients about how, when, and with whom information is to be shared as well about the limits of confidentiality. Counselors respect clients' rights to privacy and do not share confidential information without clients' consent. Counselors transmit client information in a way to ensure confidentiality and keep client records in a secure location. When a client is a minor or unable to give consent, professional counselors seek out a third party who can give consent for the client. In a consultant role, counselors disclose information necessary to achieve the purposes of the service provided. It is the counselor's responsibility to provide clients with the information regarding confidentiality, its limits, and the client's right to privacy.

Contributed by Annette P. Bohannon,
Sylacauga, AL

Reference

American Counseling Association. (2005). *ACA code of ethics*. Alexandria, VA: Author.

Additional Resources

Gladding, S. (2006). *Counseling: A comprehensive profession* (5th ed.). Upper Saddle River, NJ: Pearson Merrill Prentice Hall.

Health Insurance Portability and Accountability Act of 1996. Retrieved June 5, 2007, from http://www.cms.hhs.gov/HIPAAGenInfo/Downloads/HIPAALaw.pdf

Conflict Resolution

Conflict resolution is the process by which individuals or groups resolve differences surrounding beliefs or opinions about a set of circumstances. The process of conflict resolution involves negotiation, mediation, facilitation, and arbitration in an attempt to avoid violence or other consequences (Cheldelin & Lucas, 2004). When using conflict resolution strategies, individuals should look for **win-win opportunities** rather than looking for opportunities that provide advantage to one of the parties involved. Professional counselors in all fields of expertise use conflict resolution strategies. School counselors are often involved in structured conflict resolution programs in their school districts. These programs are used as alternatives to traditional disciplinary programs. Regardless of setting or age of individuals, the focus of conflict resolution begins with the relationship between the conflict and the problem. In order to begin the conflict resolution process, it is important to help differentiate the perceptions of the presenting problem from the reality of the problem. The primary components of the conflict resolution process include negotiation, mediation, facilitation, and arbitration.

Negotiation

Negotiation relates to two parties being willing to give up something each wants in exchange for something else (Cheldelin & Lucas, 2004). Negotiation, which can also be referred to as compromising or contracting, can come in several forms (Barsky, 2000). Parties involved in **power negotiation** compete for the strongest influence in order to win the conflict. Power negotiations are known for degrading acts of lying, cheating, and stealing in order to gain advantage over the opposing party (Cheldelin & Lucas, 2004). **Rights negotiation** often revolves around the legal system's view of what is right. It also incorporates the rules, regulations, norms, and traditions of the parties involved (Barsky, 2000). Rights negotiation can quickly become power negotiation if parties argue over whose rights take precedence.

Interest-based negotiations (another type of negotiation) are used to determine some common ground or interest between opposing parties (Barsky, 2000). Professional counselors can then help the parties to communicate effectively what it is they really want. Opening the lines of communication allows the parties involved to build a collaborative relationship. Interest-based negotiations work toward the improvement of common interest rather than winning an argument (Cheldelin & Lucas, 2004).

The purpose of **transformation-based negotiations** is to focus on the empowerment and recognition of individuals involved in the conflict (Barsky, 2000; Cheldelin & Lucas, 2004). **Empowerment** allows individuals to be more aware of their own strengths and personal value (Barsky, 2000). **Recognition** involves the process of active listening and being able to relate emotionally to the individuals' situation (Cheldelin & Lucas, 2004). Transformation-based negotiations require commitment from all parties in order to gain a different perspective, which in turn changes behavior. Regardless of the type of negotiation used, professional counselors can use negotiation strategies to help clients with a variety of issues (e.g., resolving marital discord, solving classmate disagreements, managing group home relationships).

Mediation

Professional counselors can be involved in a variety of mediation activities (e.g., school-based peer mediation programs, divorce mediation, and custody negotiations). **Mediation** involves use of a third party, presumably an impartial person, to assist in resolving a dispute between two or more people. Although mediation is considered a voluntary process, which means that parties involved can stop the mediation at any time (Cheldelin & Lucas, 2004), there are some cases of mediation that are mandated by the judicial system (Barsky, 2000). Many legal jurisdictions encourage mediation before going to court. A mediator plays an independent role and usually has no decision-making power. Mediators work toward clarifying the needs and wants of each party, use problem-solving skills to come to an agreement, advise parties on effective solutions, and develop a contract outlining the commitment of each party (Cheldelin & Lucas, 2004). Although professional counselors may use mediation strategies in a variety of settings, one clear example would be helping a divorcing couple to reach agreement about child custody arrangements. The professional counselor could help the couple clarify their needs and desires with regard to child visitation and develop a contract suitable to both parties.

Facilitation

Facilitation is a process of analysis by a third party, the facilitator (Cheldelin & Lucas, 2004). Because facilitation works best for large groups, the facilitator must be adept at using group-related skills. Active listening, reflection of feeling, paraphrasing, clarifying the needs and wants of each group, and keeping the conversation focused on the issue are just a few skills needed in order to facilitate properly.

The process of analysis begins with the facilitator conducting separate meetings with each group. This initial meeting builds trust and allows the facilitator to clarify the issue. After ground rules are established, the facilitator and the parties start to problem solve and create new avenues for a working relationship. An action plan and contractual commitment of both parties conclude the facilitation. The facilitator then summarizes the process of analysis (Cheldelin & Lucas, 2004). Professional counselors may use the process of facilitation to conduct group interviews with conflicting groups of students in a school setting, for example, meeting with each of the groups to develop ground rules and strategies for resolving the problem.

Arbitration

Different than other forms of conflict resolution, **arbitration** involves decision-making power on the part of the arbiter. Arbitration involves a third neutral party, the arbitrator, to hear both parties and make an executive decision based on the information given. Even though parties use written or oral arguments that include evidence justifying their dispute, arbitration is still considered less formal than traditional court hearings. If the arbitration is binding, there can be no follow-up litigation to continue arguments. If the arbitration is nonbinding, parties must go back into the legal system in order to continue arguments (Barsky, 2000).

Some individuals choose to use a combination of conflict resolution processes. One hybrid, **"med-arb,"** is a combination of mediation and arbitration. It allows a third party to hear the statements of each disputing party and to use problem-solving skills to incorporate mediation, but med-arb gives the decision-making power back to the parties involved (Cheldelin & Lucas, 2004). This type of med-arb is often used in divorce or custody procedures. In this type of process, professional counselors might make decisions about the best interest of the children in a custody evaluation. The professional counselor would present his or her evaluation and recommendations to the parties for their approval. If the parties do not agree on the recommendations, then they could pursue other relief through the court system.

Because conflict is inevitable, the process of conflict resolution is an essential skill for professional counselors. If conflict is handled properly, the individuals and groups involved will learn to grow and to build successful relationships. Professional counselors should always conduct some form of assessment related to the conflict in order to determine the best tactic for developing resolution. It should be noted that not every tactic is suitable for every individual or group. Professional counselors should take an objective approach in helping individuals or groups arrive at the best possible solution.

Contributed by Angel Cole Golson
and Carl J. Sheperis,
Mississippi State University,
Starkville, MS

References

Barsky, A. E. (2000). *Conflict resolution for the helping professions*. Belmont, CA: Wadsworth/Thomson Learning.

Cheldelin, S. I., & Lucas, A. F. (2004). *Academic administrator's guide to conflict resolution*. San Francisco: Jossey-Bass.

■ Conjoint Family Therapy

Virginia Satir (1916–1988) was among the pioneers in family therapy and developed **conjoint family therapy.** She was known for her commanding presence, her deep respect for and abiding confidence in human beings, her novel interventions, her inspiring meditations, and her contributions to the professional literature. She has been described as a "master therapist," the "mother of family therapy," the "Carl Rogers of family therapy," and the "Columbus of family therapy."

Upon obtaining a master's degree in social work at the University of Chicago in 1942, she launched a private practice and began work with families in 1951. Subsequently she, Don Jackson, and Jules Riskin founded the Mental Research Institute in Menlo Park, California, where formal training in family therapy was introduced. Her first book, *Conjoint Family Therapy* (Satir, 1964), has been a classic

mainstay in teaching and practice settings. In 1977, Satir founded the Avanta Network, an organization where her teachings and materials are archived and the Satir Growth Model continues to be promoted.

Essential Philosophical Underpinnings

Satir contended that people have the resources as well as the capacity to make changes in their lives that contribute to health, overall functioning, and success. She grounded her work on the premise that people are essentially good with a propensity for growth and change. She communicated her abiding faith in people and the essence of her philosophy by saying,

> Human beings are a marvel, also a treasure, and indeed a miracle. My approach, the Human Process Validation Model, is based on the premise that all we manifest at any point in time represents what we have learned, consciously, implicitly, cellularly. Our behavior reflects what we have learned. Learning is the basis of behavior. To change behavior, we need to have a new learning. To accomplish new learning, we need a motive, a purpose, a nurturing context, and a trust in something from the outside to help us. (Avanta, 2004, p. 1)

Satir viewed families systemically and rarely viewed interactions as causally related. Her focus was on process and patterns rather than on content. She also considered family dynamics and interactions vertically (i.e., intergenerationally) and horizontally (i.e., peers within a subsystem).

Satir believed that functional communication occurs when words, nonverbal responses, and feelings are congruent with the message. On the basis of her work with families, Satir identified unhealthy communication patterns in which families often engage: placater, blamer, intellectualizer (being super reasonable), and distracter (being irrelevant). **Placaters** are often apologetic, self-blaming, and self-deprecating. People who placate are particularly vulnerable when paired with someone who relies heavily on blaming (i.e., **blamers**), which is characterized by criticism, intimidation, threats, outbursts, and commands. Other individuals self-protect with extreme logic and objectivity. To this end, **intellectualizers** maintain control and avoid affective experiences. In contrast, **distracters** avoid internal discomfort or gain attention by distracting or changing the subject with irrelevant comments.

Satir explained that children may adopt these communication strategies to maintain a sense of self-worth and connection within their families. Although these strategies are functional and appropriate in childhood, they often become obsolete in adulthood. They often result in feelings of being unloved, unwanted, rejected, alone, and powerless. In an effort to promote healthy communication among family members, Satir encouraged people to adopt a fifth posture, **congruence.** Congruent responses flow from accurate self-awareness, internal harmony, and confidence. Internal experiences, facial expressions, words, and posture are consistent, integrated, and believable.

Approach to Intervention

Because change often involves vulnerability, Satir emphasized that ethical therapists must ensure clients' psychological safety in the counseling relationship. In addition, she maintained that they must demonstrate congruence with clients. As Satir connected with clients, she fully accepted their circumstances, their fears, and oftentimes their desperation. She endeavored to communicate her belief that change was possible and that clients had resources to change.

She described a six-phase process of change, beginning with the existing, predictable status quo (Phase 1). Change is invited or provoked by a disturbance or disruption in Phase 2, which may include external crises or even the introduction of a therapist into the system. The disruption evokes chaos and demands rearrangement. As behaviors that maintained balance in the initial status quo are abandoned, individuals and families experiment with new interactions that do not have predictable outcomes in Phase 3. Therapists' active and consistent presence in this phase of therapy provides grounding, support, and assurance. In Phase 4, families recognize options and possibilities and experience increasingly congruent patterns of communication. Solidification of new behaviors and interactions is predicated on practice (Phase 5), which ultimately leads to a new status quo, increased balance, comfort, and equality in the final phase (Phase 6).

Although Satir's interventions have been documented and replicated, she eschewed a technique-oriented therapy. To reduce the work of Virginia Satir to a series of steps or a collection of techniques would be a disservice to her viewpoint and her vigor. She emphasized the personhood of the therapist and his or her engagement with clients as the primary change agent. Her work with clients was characterized by experiential engagement, touch, connection, intensity, and intimacy. Although Satir's approach to family therapy focuses more on personhood than intervention, her most famous interventions involve movement (e.g., **family sculpting;** see Family Sculpting) and fantasy (e.g., **family reconstruction, parts parties**).

Contributed by Sandy Magnuson,
University of Northern Colorado,
Greeley, CO; S. Allen Wilcoxon,
University of Alabama, Tuscaloosa, AL;
and Ken Norem, Couples and Family
Counseling Associates, Greeley, CO

References

Avanta. (2004). *Virginia's philosophy.* Retrieved March 19, 2007, from http://avanta.net/writings/biography/bio-philosophy.html

Satir, V. (1964). *Conjoint family therapy.* Palo Alto, CA: Science and Behavior Books.

Additional Resources

AVANTA—The Virginia Satir Network Web site: http://www.avanta.net

Satir, V. (1976). *Making contact.* Berkeley, CA: Celestial Arts.

Satir, V. (1998). *The new peoplemaking.* Mountain View, CA: Science and Behavior Books.

Satir, V., & Baldwin, M. (1983). *Satir step by step: A guide to creating change in families.* Palo Alto, CA: Science and Behavioral Books.

■ Conjoint Sexual Therapy

William Masters and **Virginia Johnson** developed a unique method of treating sexual problems—working with couples instead of individuals. This approach was based on the assumption that the partner and the relationship as a whole were affected by the sexual distress. Masters and Johnson found that working with couples provided a more effective means of identifying the full dimension of sexual problems because input was from both partners. Masters and Johnson's approach, **conjoint sexual therapy,** involved two therapists—a man and a woman working together as a cotherapy team. It was believed that the team approach provided greater objectivity and balance to treatment because male and female viewpoints were represented. The conjoint treatment of sexual problems was designed to reduce performance anxiety, increase nonverbal communication between partners, remove blame from the sexual problem, and locate sexuality as just one aspect of the relationship.

Conjoint sexual therapy made use of physiological and psychological information and involved a rapid, intensive approach to treating sexual dysfunctions. Typically, couples were seen daily for approximately 12 to 14 days. The benefit of such an approach was that it reduced anxiety and freed the couple from the distractions of daily activities in order to devote undivided attention to their own relationship. Treatment was designed to meet specific needs of each couple. Because sexual functioning was viewed as a function of autonomic arousal, Masters and Johnson identified obstacles that blocked effective sexual functioning. Anxieties regarding sexual activity were initially removed by prescribing no sexual contact. Couples were introduced to **sensate focus** (Masters, Johnson, & Kolodny, 1986), a pleasuring exercise designed to help couples rediscover areas of their bodies that were sensually pleasurable. This exercise made use of a "hand-riding" technique that provided a more direct, nonverbal means of communicating what each partner found pleasurable and avoided guessing what a partner liked or disliked. Sexual intercourse was gradually reintroduced over the course of treatment.

The purpose of gradually reintroducing genital contact was to desensitize couples to the fear/spectator/failure cycle that was often deeply ingrained in many sexual problems. Conjoint sexual therapy moved the focus of sexual functioning toward an individual taking responsibility for what he or she found arousing and learning how to arouse his or her partner.

General features of the Masters and Johnson treatment model were supplemented by additional methods designed to treat specific sexual disorders. **Erectile disorder** was treated using cognitive restructuring and reframing that addressed the performance fears associated with sexual intercourse. For example, the Masters and Johnson model would help the man understand that he cannot make himself achieve an erection. Rather, the man was instructed on how to set the stage for his own reflexes to take over. Once an erection was achieved, the man was restrained from attempting sexual intercourse too quickly. This minimized performance fears and the likelihood of rapid erection loss.

Treatment of **Premature ejaculation** made use of the "squeeze technique" (Masters, Johnson, & Kolodny, 1988) that helped recondition the ejaculatory reflex. Just prior to ejaculation, the woman was instructed to place her thumb just below the head of the penis on the bottom side while placing the first and second fingers on the corresponding top side of the penis. A moderately firm pressure was then applied for about 4 seconds. The squeeze technique reduced the urge to ejaculate and was applied as many times as necessary to achieve ejaculatory control.

Vaginismus involved the use of a set of plastic dilators. After a pelvic exam, the physician instructed the woman on how to insert the dilators. The smallest dilator (about the size of a finger) was inserted and held in place for about 10 to 15 minutes. Over a period of several days, this process continued until the female partner could hold the largest dilator (about the size of a penis). In this way, the involuntary spasms were reduced, and sexual intercourse was slowly reintroduced.

The Masters and Johnson treatment model was developed for heterosexual couples, and there is a lack of research on this model with same-sex couples. Because homosexuality was declared a mental disorder during the initial development of this treatment model, Masters and Johnson focused on sex therapy among heterosexual couples. In fact, Masters and Johnson (1979) discussed reparative therapy research between 1968 and 1977 on same-sex couples. Thus, while there is some room to adapt this treatment model to same-sex couples, this was never done by Masters and Johnson, per se.

Contributed by Stephen W. Johnson,
University of Texas at El Paso,
El Paso, TX

References

Masters, W. H., & Johnson, V. E. (1979). *Homosexuality in perspective*. Toronto, Ontario, Canada: Bantam Books.

Masters, W. H., Johnson, V. E., & Kolodny, R. C. (1986). *Masters and Johnson on sex and human loving*. Boston: Little, Brown.

Masters, W. H., Johnson, V. E., & Kolodny, R. C. (1988). *Human sexuality* (3rd ed.). Glenview, IL: Scott, Foresman.

■Consultation and Collaborative Consultation

Consultation and collaboration are transactive processes that necessarily engage people with a diversity of expertise as team members in the creation of solutions to mutually defined problems. Whatever the particular orientation (e.g., behavioral, psychodynamic, organizational), most contemporary models of **consultation** accept the basic triadic nature characterized by interactions among the **consultant** and the **consultee** on behalf of the **client system,** which may be a person, family, organization, group, or other social unit (Brown, Pryzwansky, & Schulte, 2006; Dougherty, 2005).

As a problem-solving process, consultation typically proceeds through a series of stages characterized by their relatively greater emphasis on **entry** into the client system, problem **identification, planning** a course of action for problem resolution, **implementation** and **evaluation** of promising plans, and **disengagement** from the client system (see Dougherty, 2005). Consultation begins with a focus on establishing an effective working relationship between the consultant and the consultee and engaging the client system. Once an initial contract outlining the work to be accomplished and the roles of the participants has been established, the emphasis shifts to a fuller exploration of the problem situation and a deeper understanding of what makes this situation problematic for the participants. Goals are established, and possible avenues for meeting these goals are explored. This stage gives way to the development of an action plan as the relative merits of each course of action are evaluated in terms of likely outcome, ease of implementation, and relative value in resolving the problem situation. During implementation, plans are tested against intended outcomes, necessary revisions enacted, and plans modified or substantially revised as actual outcomes are measured against those intended. Implementation, therefore, is an iterative process that moves between planning, action, and evaluation. Because consultation is essentially an empowering process intended to enhance the functioning of the client system, consultants must necessarily reduce their involvement over time. As the client system gains the capacity to address its own problems successfully, the consultant becomes progressively disengaged from the system.

Although some authors use collaboration and consultation interchangeably or in combination (Schulte & Osborne, 1993), others have argued that collaboration and consultation can be distinguished by their relative focus on the nature of the interaction as either direct or indirect (Brown et al., 2006). **Collaborative consultation** is not unlike other forms of consultation in that it accepts the client as a voluntary partner in a process of empowerment intended to resolve a problematic work situation and designed to improve the capacity of the client to cope with similar problems in the future. Collaborative consultation, however, recognizes that the consultant and consultee must necessarily work together along a problem-solving continuum from mutual definition of the problem, to development of an agreed-on plan, to collaborative implementation and evaluation of any interventions. Collaborative consultation, therefore, is characterized as a special form of consultation in which each participant to the consultation is seen as an "expert" in contributing to the resolution of a problem situation (Lusky & Hayes, 2001).

Because collaborative consultation also includes members of the client system, it most commonly engages them as part of a team (Hayes, 2000). In such a collaborative relationship, the focus is on there being multiple "experts," and the consultant, consultee, and other members of the client system (e.g., family members, teachers, students, administrators, agency personnel, and coworkers) come together as equal participants in solving a specific issue (Dettmer, Dyck, & Thurston, 2005; Idol, Nevin, & Paolucci-Whitcomb, 1994). The collaborative consultant attempts to understand the consultee's intended purposes for consultation and to engage the consultee as well as other members of the client system in elaborating categories of evidence for intervention. In the data-gathering phase of consultation, the collaborative consultant seeks input from members of the client system in order to create a shared vision of the process for intervention, with the primary goal to help participants find workable approaches to problems that will enable the participants to develop a more responsive plan for future action. Rather than using a detached objective evaluation, problems are framed, analyzed, and solved within the context of issues pertinent to members of the client system (Dettmer et al., 2005; Idol et al., 1994). Once the issues are identified, they can be used to guide the development of an intervention that is grounded in the practices and language of the client system.

Because team members must share a common goal and work toward its realization, teams more than groups are challenged to become collaborative rather than merely cooperative. In particular, this distinction means that members will not only have to learn to work together but that the ends toward which they are working must be the same. Developing effective working relationships with people in the client system and trying to understand difficulties they encounter during the process also help the consultant establish credibility. In addition, it is important that the consultant help members of the client system to understand how the process works and help build the capacity of the system to carry out agreed-on interventions. It is critical that team members be willing to support the consultant's work, and the consultant needs to seek input from all stakeholders in the client system. Whatever the outcome, the process has the potential to be a growth experience for all participants, because each participant informs the other participants' practice of working in a collaborative manner and ability to do so.

Contributed by Richard L. Hayes,
University of South Alabama, Mobile, AL

References

Brown, D., Pryzwansky, W., & Schulte, A. (2006). *Psychological consultation and collaboration: Introduction to theory and practice* (6th ed.). Boston: Allyn & Bacon.

Dettmer, P. A., Dyck, N. T., & Thurston, L. P. (2005). *Consultation, collaboration, and teamwork for students with special needs* (5th ed.). Boston: Allyn & Bacon.

Dougherty, A. M. (2005). *Psychological consultation and collaboration in school and community settings* (4th ed.). Pacific Grove, CA: Brooks/Cole.

Hayes, R. L. (2000). Making meaning in groups: A constructivist developmental approach. In K. Fall & J. Levitov (Eds.), *Modern applications to group work* (pp. 263–280). Huntington, NY: Nova Science.

Idol, L., Nevin, A., & Paolucci-Whitcomb, P. (1994). *Collaborative consultation.* Austin, TX: PRO-ED.

Lusky, M., & Hayes, R. L. (2001). Collaborative consultation and program evaluation. *Journal of Counseling & Development, 79,* 26–38.

Schulte, A. C., & Osborne, S. S. (1993, April). What is collaborative consultation? The eye of the beholder. In D. Fuchs (Chair), *Questioning popular beliefs about collaborative consultation.* Symposium presented at the annual meeting of the Council for Exceptional Children, San Antonio, TX.

■ Continuous Development and Discontinuous Development

The nature of change is one of the fundamental issues facing practice, research, and theory in the fields of counseling and human development. The debate on how change is best captured and described is not new; however, modern theorists and researchers agree that, much as in the debate over the comparative importance of nature versus nurture, change involves both continuous and discontinuous aspects.

Continuous development is change that results from small shifts in behavior, cognition, or emotional states. This view of change is also referred to as quantitative growth or development. Continuous development is stable and predictable; occurs consistently; and, for the most part, is slower. In terms of theory, behaviorists, social learning theorists, and information processing cognitive theorists assert that developmental change is primarily continuous in nature. Different counseling theories and techniques may be thought to bring about continuous change in clients. Existential techniques that assist clients in the constant process of discovering meaning in their lives may be considered quantitative. A person's search for meaning and purpose may be a gradual process that occurs throughout a lifetime. Similarly, person-centered therapy techniques assist clients in gradually moving to a higher level of personal functioning. A person-centered counselor uses empathy, genuineness, and acceptance to work as a catalyst for a client to change into the person he or she would like to be.

Discontinuous development is change that results from a major reorganization in behavior, cognition, or emotional states. This is also referred to as qualitative growth and development. Discontinuous development is unstable and unpredictable; occurs inconsistently; and, in general, occurs more quickly. In terms of theory, the grand stage theories of Erickson, Freud, and Piaget assert that developmental change is primarily discontinuous in nature. Different counseling theories and techniques may be thought to bring about discontinuous change in clients. For example, cognitive-behavior therapy is based on the idea that restructuring self-talk will result in transformation of clients' moods and behaviors. Rational emotive behavior therapy techniques assist clients in replacing irrational beliefs with positive rational thoughts, and this in turn changes the way they respond to situations. Once clients undergo cognitive restructuring, they are likely seeing the world through a different lens and react to situations that arise in daily living differently.

Counseling involves both the larger changes associated with discontinuous development and the smaller changes observed through continuous development. A particular counseling theory or technique may reflect more of one than the other. In addition, particular clients may be able to make striking changes in their lives and outlook over a comparatively short period of time, whereas others may need more time to make even the slightest shifts. When professional counselors and clients join to form a therapeutic relationship, they can expect to see both small continuous changes and large discontinuous changes occur.

Contributed by Richard P. Lanthier and Correta J. Mallery, George Washington University, Washington, DC

Additional Resources

Emde, R. N., & Harmon, R. J. (Eds.). (1984). *Continuities and discontinuities in development.* New York: Plenum Press.
Miller, P. H. (2002). *Theories of developmental psychology* (4th ed.). New York: Worth.

■ Control Group

A **control group** is used in an experimental design to provide support for the contention that any change occurring in the participants is due to the treatment, or independent variable, and not to extraneous factors. The participants are divided randomly into two equivalent groups (i.e., control group and experimental group) so that any differences that may exist before the treatment are evenly distributed and are reflected in the posttest scores of both groups. The **experimental group** would then receive the treatment, and the control group would receive no treatment, receive the treatment after the experimental group completed the treatment, or receive a placebo treatment. Any extraneous differences in the experiences of the two groups during the experimental process that the researcher cannot control are also reflected in the posttest scores of both the control group and the experimental group. There is no way to ensure that both groups will have identical experiences for the duration of the research because some participants may seek other forms of treatment or some unforeseeable form of local history might affect members of one group and not the other. The control group design, however, increases the probability that the resulting difference between the posttest scores of the two groups will reflect only the difference that is attributable to the independent variable.

In order to examine the effect of a meditation intervention on feelings of well-being, the researcher would randomly assign participants to an experimental group and a control group. In a **no-treatment control group,** the experimental group would receive the meditation treatment, and the control group would receive no treatment at all. Data would then be collected on both groups to measure feelings of well-being. In a **waiting-list control group,** the experimental group would receive the meditation treatment, whereas the control group would not receive any treatment, data would be collected on both groups to measure feelings of well-being, and then the control group would receive the meditation treatment. Further data might then be collected to measure feelings of well-being in the waiting-list control group. In a **placebo control group,** the experimental group would receive the meditation treatment, and the control group would receive a treatment that is not expected to be effective in bringing about change in well-being in the participants. The placebo is used to provide support that any change that is due to nonspecific factors, such as the participants' expectation that they will improve because of the intervention and the attention that the participants receive from the researchers, is reflected in the posttest scores of both groups.

Contributed by Kathryn A. Oden, Texas A & M University–Commerce, Commerce, TX

Additional Resources

Gall, M., Gall, J., & Borg, W. (2007). *Educational research: An introduction* (8th ed.). Boston: Allyn & Bacon.
Heppner, P., Kivlighan, D., & Wampold, B. (2007). *Research design in counseling* (3rd ed.). New York: Brooks/Cole.

■ Core Conditions

The **core conditions,** also known as **facilitative conditions,** were integral components of **Carl Rogers's client-centered** or **person-centered therapy.** Rogers (1957) originally identified and described three core conditions that he believed should be provided and communicated by the counselor: genuineness, respect, and empathy. He asserted that providing these conditions was both necessary and sufficient for facilitating the development of an effective counseling relationship and promoting client growth. In order for the core conditions to be effective, Rogers emphasized that the professional counselor must effectively communicate them and they must be perceived by the client.

The core condition known as **genuineness** refers to the degree to which the professional counselor is authentic. More specifically, a genuine counselor possesses thoughts, feelings, and behaviors that are consistent, or congruent. Genuineness on the part of the professional counselor facilitates the client's trust and provides the client with a model for authentic living.

A second core condition essential for counselor effectiveness is an attitude of **respect** for the client. Rogers described respect as an unconditional positive regard for, or prizing of, the client as a person. Although the professional counselor may disapprove of particular behaviors performed by the client, the counselor should always maintain a positive regard or respect for the client. This attitude of respect fosters a healthy client–counselor relationship and engenders self-respect on the part of the client.

Third, in order to facilitate a client's growth, a professional counselor should possess and effectively communicate **empathy** for the client. More specifically, an empathic counselor strives both to understand accurately and describe verbally the subjective aspects of the client's experience, including beliefs, views, meanings, and emotions. When a client perceives a professional counselor as empathic, she or he is also likely to feel supported and respected by the counselor (see Client-Centered Counseling).

More recently, a number of theorists have developed and described specific counselor skills that support the counselor's efforts to provide and communicate the core conditions. These skills include immediacy, concreteness, self-disclosure, and confrontation. The use of **immediacy** involves the professional counselor's communication of his or her here-and-now experience and may take one of three forms. First, the counselor may share here-and-now subjective experiences with the client, such as "I'm wondering whether it would be more productive for us to focus on a specific goal or to spend additional time exploring the range of your personal concerns." Second, the counselor may share subjective impressions of the client in the moment, for example, "I get the feeling that there is something deeply personal that you would like to discuss, but you're not sure that you're ready to talk about it." Third, the counselor may share impressions regarding the nature of the client–counselor relationship: "Right now I feel like our interaction is highly collaborative and that we're both optimally engaged in the problem-solving process." The preceding examples also illustrate how a professional counselor may use immediacy to communicate genuineness, empathy, or respect, respectively.

Another counseling skill that is useful for providing the core conditions is **concreteness**, or the ability to help a client turn something that is vaguely understood and intangible into something that is clear and concrete. Feelings, problem situations, and counseling goals are some examples of aspects of an individual's life that professional counselors help make more concrete. The counselor uses questions or leading statements to elicit concrete details from the client. After the client has provided the counselor with a fuller, more detailed description of what was previously vague, the counselor summarizes the description to provide the client with a more concrete understanding. In addition to facilitating the client's self-understanding, concreteness also facilitates the counselor's empathy for the client.

A counselor skill particularly relevant to the core condition of genuineness is the use of **self-disclosure.** The content of counselor self-disclosure may include sharing details of his or her personal life and/or sharing his or her here-and-now responses to the client. With regard to the latter, it is important for the professional counselor to recognize that her or his opinions and feelings are subjective and, as such, do not represent objective truths. Furthermore, in addition to communicating openness, a counselor also has a professional obligation to self-disclose in a manner that contributes to the growth and welfare of the client. By judiciously self-disclosing in a manner that is sensitive to the client's feelings and needs and contributes to the counseling process, the effective counselor is able to model genuineness while also communicating respect for the client.

Another counseling skill that supports the core conditions and should be used judiciously is confrontation. A **confron-tation** response is one in which the professional counselor describes client inconsistencies that usually fall into one of three primary categories: (a) inconsistencies among the client's thoughts, feelings, and actions; (b) inconsistencies between the client's behaviors and goals; or (c) inconsistencies between the client's self-perceptions and how the client is perceived by others. Effective confrontation requires considerable social skill on the part of the counselor. Considerable care should be taken to communicate respect for the client and to ensure that the confrontation contributes to the client's growth and welfare. When used effectively, a confrontation response can promote a client's awareness of the relationship between behaviors and specific consequences. In addition, confrontation can facilitate increased client congruence and the attainment of desired counseling goals.

Contributed by Mark B. Scholl,
Long Island University,
C.W. Post Campus, Long Island, NY

Reference

Rogers, C. R. (1957). The necessary and sufficient conditions of therapeutic personality change. *Journal of Consulting Psychology, 21,* 95–103.

Additional Resources

Cain, D. J. (2001). Defining characteristics, history, and evolution of humanistic psychotherapies. In D. J. Cain & J. Seeman (Eds.), *Humanistic psychotherapies: Handbook of research and practice* (pp. 3–54). Washington, DC: American Psychological Association.

Cormier, L. S., & Cormier, W. H. (1998). *Interviewing strategies for helpers: Fundamental skills and cognitive behavioral interventions* (4th ed.). Pacific Grove, CA: Brooks/Cole.

■ Correlation and Regression

The constructs of correlation and regression are relational and predictive research procedures. These functions provide information about the relationship between variables of interest. Contained within these constructs are various operations that are explored in detail in the following sections.

Correlation

A **correlation** represents a relationship shared by two variables. These variables may share two types of relationships, referred to as either positive or negative. The polarity of the relationship illustrates the direction between the two variables and may range from either +1.00 to −1.00. The range of the relationship between the variables indicates the strength shared by both variables. Positive correlations indicate that as one variable increases in its value, the other variable will increase as well. Conversely, negative correlations signify that as one variable increases in its value, the other variable decreases (see Correlation Coefficient).

The relationships between variables may be depicted using a scatterplot or scattergram. A **scatterplot** or **scattergram** is a visual depiction the relationship between two variables. The scatterplot or scattergram is a two-dimensional figure that contains an x axis (abscissa) and a y axis (ordinate). The independent variable being measured is placed on the x axis, and the dependent variable in the study is found on the y axis. Each participant in the study or data point is entered into the scatterplot or scattergram in order to illustrate the relationship between the variables.

For example, a counselor may wish to explore the relationship between a student's grade point average (GPA) and his or her SAT scores. The researcher may use a scatterplot to view the relationship between the two variables in order to determine the relationship (see Figure 1).

Canonical Correlations

Canonical correlations measure the relationship between two sets of data as well as shared underlying factors. Similar to factor analysis, canonical correlations provide insight into shared, underlying structures of components. As a result, canonical correlations illustrate common factors found between two sources of data, whereas correlations in general provide information about the strength of a relationship between two random variables.

For example, a counselor may want to use canonical correlations to examine the relationship between subscales of the Minnesota Multiphasic Personality Inventory–2 and the Million Clinical Multiaxial Inventory–III in order to determine common factors shared between instruments.

Regression

Regression is a relationship between variables in a manner similar to a correlation; however, a regression explores the relationship between an independent variable (i.e., predictor variable) and dependent variable (i.e., criterion variable). The examination of such a relationship provides the opportunity to determine the value of the dependent variable based on the value of the independent variable.

A **regression line** is based on an equation that attempts to provide an optimal prediction for variables. The regression line equation provides the opportunity for researchers to determine a best-fitting line for the variables of interest. The

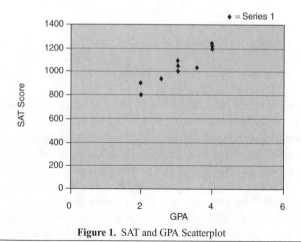

Figure 1. SAT and GPA Scatterplot

Note. GPA = grade point average.

best-fitting line is the line of prediction that is closest to all points in the scatterplot. This line depiction allows for the opportunity to examine the relationship between the independent variable and dependent variable.

The **regression equation** used in order to determine the regression line is expressed as $Y = \mathbf{b}X + \mathbf{a}$. The Y value in the equation represents the predicted value of the independent variable. The b component of the equation depicts the slope of the regression, which is produced by the amount of change in the dependent variable due to the independent variable. The X value in the regression equation is the score value of the independent variable. Last, the a component of the equation represents the Y intercept. The Y intercept of the equation provides information for the value of the dependent variable when the independent variable (X) is 0. The equation may encompass the values of additional predictor variables, such as in the case of multiple regression. The Y value of the equation in this manner is the function of the combination of all the values of the independent variables and their standardized variance.

The **coefficient of multiple determination (R)** illustrates the relationship shared between two variables. The proportion of the dependent variable's variability may be encompassed by the value of the independent variable (Mertler & Vannatta, 2005). In other words, the coefficient of multiple determination provides researchers with the opportunity to know how much of the difference observed in the dependent variable can be expected, due to knowing the value of the independent variable.

For example, if a counselor wanted to study the outcome of treatment (i.e., dependent variable) based on the treatment modality (i.e., independent variable), he or she would examine the coefficient of multiple determination value in order to view the proportion of treatment outcome explained by the treatment modality.

Types of Regression

There are two primary types of regression: simple regression and multiple regression. **Simple regression** is a statistical procedure that allows for the prediction of a dependent variable through the measurement of an independent variable. The independent variable in simple regression refers to the variable being used in order to determine the value of the dependent variable; therefore, simple regression provides the opportunity to make a prediction regarding some variable of interest based on the knowledge obtained by a predictor variable.

If a school counselor wanted to predict the success of students in early college programs, he or she might use regression. For example, the counselor might wish to predict the success of students in the early college program (i.e., criterion variable) based on the students' GPA (i.e., predictor variable).

Multiple regression is an extension of a simple regression; however, instead of using one predictor variable (i.e., independent variable), multiple regression uses several predictor variables. The combination of predictor variables in multiple regression is used to examine the influence on a criterion variable (i.e., dependent variable). Therefore, the information obtained through the use of predictor variables provides information about the value of the dependent variable (i.e., $Y' = b_1 X_1 + b_2 X_2 + b_3 X_3 + \ldots b_i X_i + a$.)

For example, if a vocational counselor wanted to predict employment success (i.e., criterion variable), he or she might collect information pertaining to income, education, and location (i.e., predictor variables). These predictor variables may influence employment success and subsequently lead to predictions regarding future employment success.

There are four concepts that relate specifically to multiple regression: beta weights, homoscedasticity, colinearity and multicolinearity, and multiple regression coefficient. **Beta weights** represent the unique contribution of each independent variable in the multiple regression equation (Mertler & Vannatta, 2005). Beta weights are the standardized coefficients of the independent variable and may affect the value of the dependent variable independently of the other predictor variables. For example, if a community counselor wanted to determine the amount of influence program adherence had on treatment success without the influence of other predictor variables, he or she might examine the beta weight of adherence in order to determine its independent contribution to the multiple regression equation.

Homoscedasticity is a statistical assumption that is used to examine the variance (i.e., difference) between variables. The assumption of homoscedasticity posits that the variance in values for one continuous variable is approximately the same as the variance in all the scores of another continuous variable (Mertler & Vannatta, 2005). In this sense, homoscedasticity is similar to the homogeneity of variance. In other words, homoscedasticity assumes that the distribution of scores in one variable used in multiple regression is the same distribution in the other variables as well. Violation of the homoscedasticity assumption will result in a decreased correlation coefficient. Homoscedastic analysis, which may be performed through statistical software packages, will illustrate homoscedastic assumption violations.

For example, if a counseling researcher wanted to explore the difference between scores on the SAT and ACT and how these scores might negatively influence the prediction of college success, she or he might examine the variance value between these variables. The examination of value difference may provide the researcher with the opportunity either to adjust or remove variables that are reducing the predictive power of the multiple regression equation.

Colinearity and multicolinearity represent the degree of relationship shared between independent variables. The stronger the relationship between the multiple predictor variables, the more unstable the predictive equations and the more limited the value of the multiple correlation coefficient (Mertler & Vannatta, 2005). Thus, if the independent variables are highly correlated (i.e., measuring the same construct), they may not contribute uniqueness to the prediction of the dependent variable. Analysis of data sets, specifically correlation matrices, will illustrate strong relationships shared between independent variables. Removal or replacement of highly correlated independent variables will reduce both colinearity and multicolinearity.

For example, if a counseling researcher is concerned that the independent variables in his or her regression equation (e.g., Beck Depression Inventory and Beck Anxiety Inventory) may be measuring similar constructs, he or she may examine the degree of colinearity or multicolinearity. The examination of these values will provide information about the amount of overlap shared between independent variables.

Multiple correlation coefficient represents the value of the relationship between a dependent variable and the multiple independent variables. The coefficient is similar to the value of the correlation coefficient; however, the multiple correlation coefficient represents the amalgamation of the independent variables. The multiple correlation coefficient is expressed as R^2, which is the proportion of the dependent variable's variance explained by the combination of the independent variables.

For example, a counseling researcher finds that the multiple correlation coefficient is equal to 36% when examining graduate student success (i.e., criterion variable) predicted by scores on the Graduate Record Examination, letters of recommendation, and GPA (i.e., predictor variables). He or she may then suggest that 36% of graduate student success is predicted by independent variables.

Contributed by James M. Devlin,
Texas A&M University–
Corpus Christi, Corpus Christi, TX

Reference

Mertler, C. A., & Vannatta, R. A. (2005). *Advanced and multivariate statistical methods* (3rd ed.). Glendale, CA: Pyrczak.

Additional Resource

Tinsley, H. E., & Brown, S. D. (Eds.). (2000). *Handbook of applied multivariate statistics and mathematical modeling.* San Diego, CA: Academic Press.

■ Correlation Coefficient

The **Pearson product–moment correlation coefficient**, typically denoted by r, is the statistic used to describe the linear relationship between two or more variables or sets of scores. In particular, a correlation coefficient provides information on the direction and magnitude of the relationship between variables. The **direction** of the relationship between variables is determined by the valence sign preceding the correlation coefficient value. A **positive correlation** (+) indicates that both variables appear to trend in the same direction. The variables can either both increase or both decrease in value. Alternatively, when the variables appear to trend in opposite directions a **negative correlation** (−) is noted. In a negative correlation, the value of one variable increases as the value of the other decreases, creating what is known as an inverse relationship between the variables.

The **magnitude,** or strength, is determined by the numeric value of the correlation coefficient. Correlation coefficient values have a range from 0 to 1 in both the positive and negative direction. A value of −1.00 represents a perfect negative correlation, whereas a value of +1.00 represents a perfect positive correlation. A zero correlation ($r = .00$) indicates that no correlation exists between the variables. Typically, the closer the correlation coefficient value is to either pole (−1.00 or +1.00), the stronger the relationship between the variables.

Because most correlations will not be perfect correlations or zero correlations, further analysis is often needed to fully understand what a calculated correlation coefficient truly means. When further analysis is warranted, researchers often compute the **coefficient of determination** to evaluate the strength of the relationship between variables. The coefficient of determination is obtained by squaring the correlation coefficient value and is denoted as r^2. This new statistic allows researchers to determine the proportion of variance in one variable that can be predicted from the other variable. For example, assume that two variables (X and Y) are found to have a correlation of .80. The coefficient of determination for these variables would be .64 (the square of .80). This means that 64% of the variance in variable Y can be predicted based on the information that is known about the relationship between variables X and Y.

In addition to interpreting the direction and magnitude of the correlation coefficient, researchers should also attend to the **significance level** of the correlation coefficient. Significance levels are computed for each correlation coefficient produced and are a good measure of the consistency or reliability of the observed relationship between the two variables. When interpreting significance levels, it is important to consider the size of the sample from which the data were collected.

An important caution is that the correlation coefficient value may not necessarily be a good indicator of the relationship between variables, even when the coefficient of determination demonstrates a large amount of variance predicted and a significant alpha level indicates an appropriate level of risk acceptable as Type I error. A **spurious correlation** may occur because correlations may be overestimated or underestimated in several ways. These include when either the sample size is very large or small, reliability estimates of assessment tools used to measure the variables are small, the variables being correlated are not distinct enough, or there is a third variable that is (or several variables that are) responsible for the correlation. Counselors should examine psychometric data of assessment tools, the sample for which the correlation is calculated, and additional variables that may influence the relationship between the two variables.

Types of Correlation Coefficients

Researchers using correlation designs quickly discover that there are several types of correlation coefficients that can be used. Selecting the appropriate coefficient depends on the type of data collected for each variable. In particular, researchers should pay attention to whether or not the data are quantitative (interval or ratio) or categorical (nominal or ordinal).

The most widely used of all the correlation coefficients is the **Pearson product–moment correlation coefficient (r)**. The Pearson product–moment correlation is used when

quantitative data are collected for both variables and a linear relationship exists. Conceptually, the Pearson produce–moment correlation is a ratio of the covariability of two variables together and their individual variability measured separately. All of the correlation coefficients are easily computed when using the SPSS statistical package. Although the Pearson product–moment correlation is the most commonly reported correlation coefficient, there are variations of the Pearson product–moment correlation that are more appropriate under certain circumstances. One such variation is the **Spearman rank correlation coefficient (r^s)**. The Spearman rho is a special case of the Pearson r that is used when assessing the relationship between two sets of ordinal (ranked) data. Another variant of the Pearson r is the **point-biserial correlation coefficient (r^{pb})**. It is used when the data for one variable are quantitative in nature and the data for the other variable are nominal and dichotomous. Similar to the point-biserial correlation coefficient is the **phi coefficient (Φ)**. The phi coefficient is used when both variables produce nominal and dichotomous data.

Although they are not considered special cases of the Pearson product–moment correlation, there are other measures of association that are used in correlation research. One of these measures is the **coefficient of contingency (C)**. It is similar to the phi coefficient in that both variables produce nominal data; however, the requirement for the data to be dichotomous is not present. Another measure of association commonly used is the **biserial correlation coefficient (r^b)**. The biserial correlation coefficient measures the relationship between a quantitative and dichotomous variable with the dichotomous variable representing ordinal data. Finally, the **tetrachoric correlation coefficient (r^{tet})** can be used to assess the relationship between two ordinal and dichotomous sets of data. It is differentiated from the Spearman rank correlation previously discussed in this entry by the fact that its data are ranked into discrete rather than continuous categories.

All of the measures described in this entry are used when the data are linear in nature; however, there are times when nonlinear relationships are found. In these cases, a separate measure is needed to assess the level of association between the two variables. When nonlinear (i.e., curvilinear) relationships are noted, the **eta coefficient (η)** is used. It is interpreted in much the same way as the Pearson product–moment correlation except that negative coefficient values cannot occur.

Contribution by Joshua C. Watson,
Mississippi State University–
Meridian, Meridian, MS

Additional Resources

Chen, P. Y., & Popovich, P. M. (2002). *Correlation: Parametric and nonparametric measures.* Thousand Oaks, CA: Sage.

Gravetter, F. J., & Wallnau F. B. (2006). *Statistics for the behavioral sciences* (7th ed.). Belmont, CA: Wadsworth.

Howell, D. C. (2007). *Statistical methods for psychology* (5th ed.). Pacific Grove, CA: Duxbury.

Council for Accreditation of Counseling and Related Educational Programs

Established in 1981 as the premier accrediting organization for graduate counselor preparation programs in the United States, the **Council for Accreditation of Counseling and Related Educational Programs (CACREP)** promotes the professional competence of counseling practitioners and counselor educators by setting educational training standards used by colleges and universities wishing to achieve accredited status. CACREP's primary purpose is to advance the educational preparation of future counselors by implementing a high-quality accreditation review process that continually fosters program development and improvement in an effort to prepare counseling professionals who can serve the needs of a diverse and complex society.

In its 25 years of existence, CACREP's reputation for offering a high-quality educational review process has grown exponentially. Currently, more than 200 institutions across the United States offer CACREP-accredited counseling programs. Furthermore, most state licensing boards for professional counseling model their educational requirements on CACREP's required curriculum. In addition, many countries around the world are using the CACREP (2009) Standards as a model for the development of their own counselor preparation programs, and several international programs have expressed an interest in seeking some form of recognition and/or accreditation from CACREP.

Legitimate accrediting agencies, like CACREP, are recognized and maintained on a registry by either the Council for Higher Education Accreditation (CHEA) or the U.S. Department of Education. CACREP has been recognized by CHEA and its organizational predecessors since 1987 to review counseling master's-degree programs in the following areas: career counseling; college counseling; community counseling; marital, couple, and family counseling/therapy; mental health counseling; school counseling; and student affairs. In addition, CACREP's recognized scope of accreditation includes doctoral-degree programs in counselor education and supervision. CACREP is also a founding member of the Association of Specialized and Professional Accreditors (ASPA) and subscribes to the ASPA Code of Good Practice.

CACREP's accreditation review process takes approximately 1 year to complete and includes the following steps:

1. *Self-study and application.* Programs conduct a self-study to determine how well they meet the CACREP Standards.
2. *Initial review.* CACREP conducts an initial review of the application documents to determine the readiness of the program to proceed in the review process.
3. *On-site visit.* When the initial review reveals a program's readiness to proceed, CACREP schedules a team of trained counselor educators and/or counseling practitioners to visit the institution for a 3-day, on-site review.
4. *Team report.* In a written report, the team designates each standard as either being "met" or "not met" by the program and includes requirements for bringing the program into compliance with any unmet standards. CACREP sends this report to the institution's chief executive officer, dean, and program faculty for review and response.
5. *Institutional response.* Institutions are given 30 days to address the relative accuracy of the report and to provide any additional supporting evidence of how the program meets the Standards.
6. *Accreditation decisions.* The CACREP board meets twice yearly to render accreditation decisions on programs that have completed the process. On the basis of the information obtained through the process, the board renders one of the following decisions: (a) Accredited—awarded for an 8-year period to programs judged as meeting all of the CACREP Standards, (b) Accredited for a 2-year period—given to programs that substantially meet the CACREP Standards but that may have minor deficiencies to be address in a follow-up report; or (c) Denial—rendered when programs cannot demonstrate substantial compliance with the CACREP Standards.

Lending credibility to this accreditation review process and to the continued relevancy of the accreditation standards is CACREP's built-in requirement for a comprehensive review and revision of the Standards every 7 years. Over the years, the revision process has been instrumental in ensuring the inclusion of standards that provide counselors with an understanding of working in a culturally diverse society. Graduates of CACREP programs are well equipped to serve in many types of settings, including schools, hospitals, colleges and universities, and private practice and with many types of clientele.

The heart and soul of CACREP's expertise and service, however, is derived from its well-trained cadre of volunteers. The accreditation process is a peer review process, in which programs voluntarily submit themselves to an in-depth review against a set of standards. CACREP maintains a database of more than 300 trained volunteers who sit on the Board of Directors, serve as initial reviewers, and/or conduct the on-site team visits. CACREP maintains a small staff to coordinate the volunteer services for the programs.

Contributed by Carol L. Bobby,
CACREP, Alexandria, VA

Reference

Council for Accreditation of Counseling and Related Educational Programs. (2009). *CACREP accreditation manual: 2009 standards* (3rd ed.). Alexandria, VA: Author.

Additional Resources

Council for Accreditation of Counseling and Related Educational Programs Web site: http://www.cacrep.org

Council for Higher Education Accreditation Web site: http://www.chea.org

U.S. Department of Education Web site: http://www.ed.gov/admins/finaid/accred/index.html

The Council on Rehabilitation Education

The **Council on Rehabilitation Education (CORE)** is the accrediting institution for rehabilitation counselor education (RCE) programs. CORE was established in June of 1971 and was incorporated as a not-for-profit organization in 1972. The CORE Standards for Rehabilitation Counselor Education Programs (CORE, 2007) include mission and objectives, program evaluation, general curriculum requirements, knowledge domains and education outcomes, clinical experience, administration and faculty, and program support and resources.

Individuals from the National Rehabilitation Counseling Association (NRCA), the National Council of State Agencies for the Blind, the National Council of Rehabilitation Education (NCRE), the American Rehabilitation Counseling Association (ARCA), and the Council of State Administrators of Vocational Rehabilitation are appointed to CORE as board members for a 4-year term. Two people from the public are also appointed to the board.

The **Commission on Standards and Accreditation** is responsible for evaluating an RCE program and reporting to CORE the decision of granting or denying accreditation. The commission consists of 15 to 20 people who serve a term of 3 years. The individuals are nominated from NRCA, NCRE, ARCA, Commission on Rehabilitation Counselor Certification, the National Association of Non-White Rehabilitation Workers, the Department of Veterans Affairs, the National Association of Multi-Cultural Rehabilitation Concerns, the Vocational Evaluation and Work Adjustment Association, and the International Association of Rehabilitation Professionals.

Contributed by Cindy M. Trevino,
St. Mary's University, San Antonio, TX

Reference

Council on Rehabilitation Education. (2007). *Standards for rehabilitation counselor education programs.* Retrieved August 25, 2008, from http://www.core-rehab.org/Standards.html

Additional Resources

American Rehabilitation Counseling Association Web site: http://www.arcaweb.org

National Council on Rehabilitation Education Web site: http://www.rehabeducators.org

National Rehabilitation Counseling Association Web site: http://nrca-net.org

Counseling, Stages of

Counseling is a formal process whereby a professional counselor and a client engage in a relationship designed to address or manage any or all of the following: the way a person thinks (cognition); the way a person feels (emotion); and the way a person acts (behavior). The helping process evolves through a number of stages, allowing theoretical orientation and client need to determine variation and duration of each stage. The counseling process is similar across theories and can be viewed as consisting of three major divisions or stages: relationship building, action, and termination.

Initial Stage: Relationship Building

The **relationship-building** stage of counseling establishes a working bond between client and professional counselor, thus providing the therapeutic foundation for client self-exploration and change. Although the specificities of the relationship may vary according to theoretical orientation, counselors' attributes in the helping relationship include interest, empathy, understanding, insight, and acceptance. In addition, it is the responsibility of the counselor to encourage rapport with the client, keep appointments, monitor the duration of the session, put the client's welfare first, provide a safe environment for the client, educate the client about the counseling process, obtain informed consent, and operate within the ethical guidelines of the counseling profession. The primary goal in the first stage of counseling is to create and maintain a relationship that ensures the safety of the client while affording opportunities for self-exploration, self-awareness, and resolution of the problem.

Middle Stage: Action

The middle stage of counseling, **action,** includes identifying problems, creating goals, exploring alternatives, and taking action. Identifying and clarifying clients' problems include activities directed toward the gathering and synthesizing of client information. It is in this stage that the professional counselor participates in active listening skills, such as using direct eye contact, nodding, providing encouraging remarks, and paying close attention to the body language and posture of the client in order to identify discrepancies in verbal and nonverbal forms of communication. Techniques used may be direct (conducting an assessment), whereas others may be indirect (understanding social, cultural, and familial influences). Frequently included are therapeutic interactions designed to encourage focus, reflection, and definition of the problem.

Helping clients create goals requires that the counselor and client work collaboratively to identify desired changes and to design action plans that lead to goal attainment. This shared effort reduces the struggle for power in the relationship between the professional counselor and client, thus promoting movement toward the empowerment of the client. At this point in the counseling process, the client assumes an active role by increasing personal responsibility and making choices designed to promote growth. It is the counselor's responsibility to ensure that goals identified during this stage are observable, realistic, attainable within a reasonable period of time, and selected (owned) by the client.

The next step is for the counselor to encourage the client to explore and evaluate options, examine possible action strategies, identify a reasonable plan of action, and implement the selected plan. The exploration process may require confrontation and self-disclosure in an attempt to promote clarity and action on the part of the client. A variety of techniques may be implemented, depending on the willingness of the client to be an active participant. Written plans and contracts are often used to encourage active participation, goal clarification, and effective outcome evaluation. This may evoke client anxiety and fear as a result of unexpected repercussions resulting from changed behavior patterns and unanticipated obstacles. It is, therefore, important that the client, in collaboration with the counselor, identify and explore potential obstacles, contingency plans, and effective ways to deal with frustration and setbacks.

Final Stage: Termination

The final stage of the counseling process, **termination,** provides closure to the counseling relationship. Ideally occurring after accomplishment of the counseling goals, this stage affords the opportunity to evaluate progress, summarize accomplishments, and examine lessons learned from participation in the counseling process. Major themes, learning, and insights occurring during the counseling process are reviewed and reinforced. During this final stage, the counselor assists the client in dealing with emotions and thoughts resulting from the ending of the client–counselor relationship. Termination resulting in referral is indicated if the client is failing to make progress, the counseling relationship is not productive, or working with the client is beyond the counselor's level of competency.

Contributed by Suzanne D. Mudge, Our Lady of the Lake University, San Antonio, TX, and Ashlea R. Worrell, St. Mary's University, San Antonio, TX

Additional Resources

Bramer, L. M. & MacDonald, G. (1996). *The helping relationship: Process and skills* (6th ed.). Needham Heights, MA: Allyn & Bacon.

Corey, M. S., & Corey, G. (2007). *Becoming a helper* (5th ed.). Belmont, CA: Thomson Brooks/Cole.

Egan, E. (1998). *The skilled helper: A problem–management approach to helping* (6th ed.). Pacific Grove, CA: Brooks/Cole.

■ Counseling Association for Humanistic Education and Development

The **Counseling Association for Humanistic Education and Development (C-AHEAD)** is one of the founding divisions of the American Counseling Association (ACA). Focusing on humanistic issues (see Humanistic Theories) in counseling and education, C-AHEAD is dedicated to (a) promoting meaningful, ethical, and holistic lives for professional counselors and clients; (b) exploring the factors of the counselor–client interaction that foster personal growth and development; (c) celebrating and nurturing all forms of human diversity; and (d) working to promote resilience in counselors and mitigate the negative effects of personal, societal, or professional events.

C-AHEAD has a long history as an association, evolving along with the counseling profession itself. Originally founded in 1931 under the name of the Teachers College Personnel Association, the organization was dedicated to "personnel workers" (i.e., counselors) involved in training of teachers (Allen, 1962). In 1946, the name was changed to Personnel Section of the American Association of Teachers Colleges, evolving again in 1951 to the Student Personnel Association for Teacher Education, or SPATE. It was then in 1952 that SPATE joined with three other organizations to form the American Personnel and Guidance Association (APGA), later ACA (Kaplan, 2002). With its emphasis on humanistic education and counseling, C-AHEAD has directly contributed to the counseling profession through its focus on getting to know the client as a person rather than a diagnosis and has continued championing the ethical regard for the dignity of all persons. In this way, C-AHEAD has been instrumental in defining the counseling profession as unique and separate from other helping professions, such as social work or psychology.

Today, C-AHEAD continues its work fostering the wellness and mental health of clients and counselors. "Giving back" as an organizational philosophy has resulted in the Empty Plate project, in which funds are collected from ACA members to benefit a local food pantry in the community hosting the annual convention. The annual Wellness Center at the convention is a series of events that enhance counselor wellness. In addition, benefits for members include a twice-yearly, peer-reviewed journal, the *Journal of Humanistic Counseling, Education and Development,* and a twice yearly newsletter, the *Infochange.* As the "division with vision," C-AHEAD works to identify issues or topics of interest to the counseling profession and provide a venue for exploration of those issues or topics. In the past, these have included hot-topic debates at the annual ACA convention, special issues and special sections of the *Journal,* and hosting activities at the association's booth in the convention exhibit hall. In the future, these initiatives and others are a reminder that counseling as a profession will remain the core of the association's identity.

Contributed by Colette T. Dollarhide, The Ohio State University, Columbus, OH

References

Allen, C. H. (1962). The history of SPATE: 1931–1962. *Journal of Student Personnel Association for Teacher Education, 2*(1), 1–5.

Kaplan, D. M. (2002). Celebrating 50 years of excellence. *Journal of Counseling & Development, 80,* 261–263.

■ Counseling Skills, Basic

Learning to be a professional counselor takes a lifetime of practice and courage: practice in the art of helping others to reach their desired state of being and courage for the professional counselor to face his or her own self-doubt, personal prejudices, and frustration. To begin the journey, a person must learn basic **counseling skills.** The skills of attending, responding, reflecting, paraphrasing, summarizing, confronting, and interpreting are basic skills that aid in building the counseling relationship (Carkhuff, 1987; Egan, 2007; Ivey & Ivey, 2007).

Attending skills are used to convey to the client that the professional counselor is listening, interested, and focused on the client. Attending behaviors encourage clients to talk, convey empathy, and assure clients they are being heard. Attending behaviors can also help clients reduce their anxiety by relaxing and feeling more comfortable in the counseling setting. These behaviors may include, but are not limited to, head nodding, facing the client, leaning toward the client in an open posture, verbal following (listening), and maintaining eye contact (when appropriate). Egan (2007) encouraged counselors to display attending skills by maintaining SOLER: Squared up, Open stance, Leaning toward client, making Eye contact, and Relaxed body position.

Responding refers to the use of open- and closed-ended questions to acknowledge a client. Open-ended questions are those that clients cannot easily answer with a "yes" or "no." Open-ended questions are often used to begin a counseling session, encourage a client to elaborate, increase client communication, and ask for specific examples. Closed-ended questions are those that can easily be answered with a "yes" or a "no" or a one- or two-word response. Closed-ended questions are used to obtain specific information, narrow the topic of discussion, interrupt a talkative client, and identify specific problems or issues. Examples are "Are you living with your spouse?" (closed) and "What do you argue about?" (open).

Reflecting is a response to a client's verbal content or emotion. Reflecting content demonstrates that the counselor is clearly hearing the client's verbal statements, whereas reflection of feeling ensures accurate identification of the client's emotions. Reflection helps clients to feel understood, express more feelings, discriminate among various feelings, and manage the feelings being experienced. Paraphrasing and summarizing are often used in reflecting content. Reflection also involves the counselor observing the client's nonverbal behaviors, listening closely to what the client is saying, and verbally reflecting feelings back to the client. The counselor should try to match the feeling and intensity of what the client is saying and provide feedback to the client. Often, counselors may use the feedback from "You feel _____ because _____." Counselors should check with the client for accuracy of the reflection. A client's cultural affiliation may determine the response to reflection of feeling. In some cultures, the restraint of feelings is valued. In general, men seem to have more difficulty than women exploring emotions.

Paraphrasing reflects the content of what the client has communicated. Paraphrasing conveys understanding on the part of the counselor, helps the client simplify and focus on what he or she has said, encourages the client to elaborate, and provides the counselor a means to check the accuracy of perceptions. Paraphrasing is often used if the counselor has a hypothesis about what is going on with the client or if the client has presented the counselor with a great deal of information and the counselor is confused. Accuracy of understanding on the part of the counselor should be confirmed by the client. Translating what the client is saying into the counselor's own words in a paraphrase might include, "It sounds like you are having a hard time telling your spouse you want a divorce because of his reaction. Is that right?"

Summarizing is a reflection of two or more paraphrases or reflections that condense the client's messages of the session, covering more information over a longer period of time. Summaries are used to collapse multiple elements of a client's statements, identify a common theme that has emerged over a number of sessions, interrupt excessive rambling, and review progress that has occurred over a number of sessions. Summarizing may also be used to open a session, end a session, pace a session, and serve as a transition when changing topics. Introductory stems that may be used in summarizing include "It seems that," "Let's see if I understand you correctly. . . . Last week you stated that," "Earlier today you indicated that," "I am sensing that you are now feeling."

Confronting involves bringing to the client's attention discrepancies or inconsistencies in the client's thoughts, feelings, or behavior. Without making judgment, the professional counselor helps the client to see these discrepancies and work to resolve them. Confrontation should be done in a respectful, gentle, and encouraging manner that allows the client to explore these discrepancies further. One example of confronting would be,

> Help me understand . . . you say that you want to improve your academic performance in your college classes, yet you continue to stay out late drinking with friends and skip class the next day. How might that be standing in the way of your stated goals?

Finally, **interpreting** assists the client in identifying the underlying meaning of his or her narrative from an alternate perspective. The counselor helps the client focus not just on the explicit but also implicit messages being communicated. Theoretical orientation and multicultural considerations are important when using interpretation skills. Beyond simply interpreting the response, the counselor also works with the client to develop alternative responses and actions to facilitate the counseling goals.

The art of counseling others is complex and takes both time and practice to develop fully. Although theory and experience guide counselors in working with clients, the use of basic counseling skills is a foundation for effective counseling

Contributed by Julia S. Chibbaro and
Kerry E. Sebera, University of West
Georgia, Carrollton, GA

References

Carkhuff, R. R. (1987). *The art of helping* (6th ed.). Amherst, MA: Human Resource Development Press.

Egan, G. (2007). *The skilled helper: A problem-management and opportunity development approach to helping* (8th ed.). Belmont, CA: Wadsworth.

Ivey, A. E., & Ivey, M. B. (2007). *Intentional interviewing and counseling: Facilitating client development in a multicultural society* (6th ed.). Belmont, CA: Brooks/Cole.

Additional Resources

Evans, D. R., Hearn, M. T., Uhlemann, M. R., & Ivey, A. E. (2008). *Essential interviewing* (7th ed.). Belmont, CA: Brooks/Cole.

Young, M. E. (2005). *Learning the art of helping: Building blocks and techniques.* Upper Saddle River, NJ: Pearson Education.

■ Counselors for Social Justice

Counselors for Social Justice (CSJ) became an officially recognized division of the American Counseling Association (ACA) in September 2002. The formation of CSJ was predicated on the belief that counseling professionals needed to make a more concerted effort to address oppressive sociopolitical structures that are often manifested in client problems. The prevailing thought was that CSJ would help make social justice a clearer presence in the counseling field, meet the growing need for professional counselors to be change agents, and expand the counselor's role to include social justice advocacy (Ratts, D'Andrea, & Arredondo, 2004).

History of CSJ

The inception of CSJ began as a grassroots effort in the early 1990s by counselor educators and professional counselors who gathered to examine ways counseling professionals could more adequately address the social, political, and economic forces that negatively affect clients' lives (J. Lewis, personal communication, September 7, 2006). These informal gatherings, which took place at national conferences across the United States, grew out of dissatisfaction with the counseling profession's insufficient intervention in issues of oppression affecting individuals and their families. These informal meetings, initially led by Michael D'Andrea and Don C. Locke, were instrumental in the development of CSJ, because they started the conversation regarding how professional counselors can address oppressive sociopolitical structures. The ideas that took shape at these meetings led Stuart Chen-Hayes, Mark Pope, Anita Jackson, Mary Arnold, Jo Hayslip, and Judy Lewis to conceive the idea of becoming an officially recognized division.

On October 14, 1998, key individuals, including Mary Smith Arnold, Patricia Arredondo, Bob Barrett, Mary Patrick Burke, Ann Chapman, Stuart Chen-Hayes, Ann Coles, Michael D'Andrea, Judy Daniels, Robert Davison-Aviles, Faith Deveaux, Julie Dinsmore, Ned Farley, Michael Hutchins, Kelly Kenny, Mark Kenny, Mark Kiselica, Judy Lewis, Rod Merta, Vivian McCollum, Beverly O'Bryant, Mark Pope, Portia Rothschild, Azara Santiago-Rivera, Rebecca Toporek, Janet Windwalker-Jones, and Richard Yep, met at ACA headquarters in Alexandria, Virginia (J. Lewis, personal communication, September 7, 2006). At this meeting, concrete steps were taken to make CSJ a division. In April 1999, the ACA Governing Council granted CSJ

organizational affiliate status; CSJ's membership grew to the requisite level for divisional status, which was granted on September 27, 2002.

Structure of CSJ

CSJ members include students, mental health counselors, school counselors, psychologists, and counselor educators. A number of branches across the country offer a CSJ division, including Illinois, New Mexico; Washington; Washington, DC; and Florida (CSJ, 2007, para. 1).

CSJ sponsors a variety of activities, events, and awards that promote social justice and social advocacy. A "Day of Action" is held at the annual ACA national convention and provides counselors and counselor educators with opportunities to take action on a social justice issue. CSJ has also created awards to recognize the accomplishments of individuals who advocate for social justice and social change. The first award was named in honor of the late Mary Smith Arnold (1946–2003). The Mary Smith Arnold Anti-Oppression award honors "counselors and counselor educators who have an exemplary record of challenging multiple oppressions in the counseling professions as well as in their local schools and communities" (CSJ, 2006, para. 2).

The second award is titled the CSJ 'Ohana Award. This award was created by Michael D'Andrea and Judy Daniels of the University of Hawaii, Manoa. This award honors individuals in counseling who affirm diversity and advocate for social justice in the spirit of nine elements of the indigenous Hawaiian concept of 'Ohana, or extended family. These include (a) alama: caring, (b) ha'aha'a: humility, (c) na'auuo: intelligence, (d) lokomaika'i: generosity, (e) kupono: integrity/honesty, (f) aloha: unconditional love, (g) mana: spiritual power, (h) 'olu'olu: courtesy, and (i) koa: courage" (Counselors for Social Justice, 2006). This award is given annually at the ACA national conference.

A newsletter and e-journal are also available on the CSJ Web site. The newsletter, titled *CSJ Activist,* is published quarterly. Michael D'Andrea served as the newsletter's first editor, helping to establish and provide structure to the *CSJ Activist*. Articles published in the newsletter cover diverse topics and focus on promoting social justice issues within the counseling profession.

In collaboration with Psychologists for Social Responsibility, CSJ is developing an e-journal titled *Journal of Social Action (JSA)*. Debuting in spring 2007, *JSA* is published twice a year under the editorship of Rebecca Toporek and Tod Sloan. Issues focus on social justice work and peace building carried out by helping professionals.

ACA Advocacy Competencies

The ACA advocacy competencies, which were endorsed by the ACA Governing Council in 2003, are heavily promoted by CSJ. The competencies were developed in 2001 by a task force appointed by Jane Goodman, then past-president of ACA (J. Goodman, personal communication, October 18, 2006). This taskforce included the following CSJ members: Judy Lewis, Mary Smith Arnold, Reese House, and Rebecca

Toporek. The ACA advocacy competencies were developed in an effort to provide a conceptual framework to address issues of oppression at the micro- and macrolevel (Rubel & Ratts, 2007). Specifically, the competencies encourage counselors to provide services at the client/student level, school/community level, and public arena level. A description of the ACA advocacy competencies is available on the CSJ Web site.

The establishment of CSJ as a division of ACA has been an important development in the history and evolution of the counseling profession. CSJ provides professional counselors with a venue to address social justice issues, and it has the potential to transform counselor education, research, and training practices. Moreover, the development of CSJ has been key in making counselors aware of how oppression affects people's lives and encouraging the use of the ACA advocacy competencies when working with individuals and organizations. This is particularly important given the increasing body of research demonstrating the negative impact oppression has on people's lives and the need to use both microlevel and macrolevel interventions and strategies.

Contributed by Manivong Ratts,
Seattle University, Seattle, WA

References

American Counseling Association. (2003). *Governing Council minutes.* Alexandria, VA: Author.

Counselors for Social Justice. (2006). *Mary Smith Arnold Anti-Oppression and 'Ohana honors awards.* Retrieved December 1, 2006, from http://www.counselorsforsocial justice.com/ohana.html

Counselors for Social Justice. (2007). *CSJ branches.* Retrieved February 5, 2007, from http://www.counselors forsocialjustice.com/branches.html

Ratts, M., D'Andrea, M., & Arredondo, P. (2004). Social justice counseling: A "fifth force" in the field. *Counseling Today, 47*(1), 28–30.

Rubel, D., & Ratts, M. (2007). Diversity and social justice issues in counseling and psychotherapy. In D. Capuzzi & D. R. Gross (Eds.), *Counseling and psychotherapy: Theories and interventions* (4th ed., pp. 47–67). Upper Saddle River, NJ: Pearson Education.

Additional Resource

Counselors for Social Justice Web site: http://www.counsel orsforsocialjustice.com

■ Creative Arts in Counseling

While celebrating his 70th birthday, Freud gathered with acquaintances and suggested that he (and indeed all mental health practitioners) owed creative artists an enormous intellectual debt. He proposed that they, not he, had first unearthed the unconscious.

One could argue that each counseling theorist and every related technique always involve creativity and the arts in some fashion. Many would agree that counseling certainly can be classified among the professional fields more as an art than as a science, and to be an effective counselor, he or she must be creative. However, therapies that are considered traditional or more like "talk therapies" differ in theory from those that involve the creative arts. Yet, although differences between the two groupings of therapies can be made in theory, the differences are often less distinct in practice. Many professional counselors now combine both in their practices, and even among theorists considered to be founders of traditional therapies, creative arts played some part in their practices. For example, talk therapies are often attributed to theorists such as Freud; Jung; Rogers; Adler; and, more recently, White and Epston (1990); however, such theorists either included the creative arts in their practices or their theories and practices have been adapted to approaches that include the creative arts. Freud focused on dreams and humor. Jung emphasized archetypes unveiled in art, particularly mandalas, and he hypothesized that play and dramatization could release blocked psychic energy. Axline, who is considered the founder of play therapy, adapted Rogers's theory and practices. Espenak related her dance therapeutic approach to Adler's theory (Gladding, 2005). White and Epston, in their work with narrative therapy, espoused a basic premise in the importance of story and how individuals can re-story their lives. Indeed, early on, Freud (1956) supported the power of story in the therapeutic process and found storytellers to be valuable allies.

Although they are often used in combination, some features of the two therapeutic foci can be distinguished. Traditional therapies for the most part are focused on cognitive, emotional, and behavioral components that are communicated by verbal exchange, whereas therapies that involve the creative arts (a) make use of an object that is available to the senses, (b) create an experience that may be unusual for the client, (c) engage the client and professional counselor in a relationship about a shared experience of an object, (d) often involve multiple modalities, and (e) stimulate a variety of neurological processes.

First, creative arts therapies always include a **sensual object,** one that is available to the senses but substantially different from speech. A sensual object includes, but is not limited to, dance/movement, drawing, literature, imagery/visualizing, cinema, psychodrama, games, music, and play. Although a case can be made that talk is a distinctive feature, the distinction does not include language. Song, poetry, and stories are creative arts used in therapies, and they all involve language.

Second, by focusing on an unusual sensual object rather than on a more usual verbal exchange, a client will likely experience a familiar issue in a new and unusual way and, thus, exchange a well-rehearsed verbal response as a defense mechanism for a new way of expressing memories. Such memories, including feelings about them, can be reorganized and understood from a new perspective. By including a sensual object, the counselor provides the client with an opportunity for an emotional and/or behavioral response that differs from usual responses, often called the client's "tape."

Third, as a counselor and client interact by focusing attention on a shared sensual object, their relationship can become more than interactive; it becomes transactive. Their experiences are no longer dyadic but move to a unity, a togetherness joined and unified by the triadic relationship. Client and counselor are united almost within a single intentional experience because of the "thirdness" (i.e., the unifying sensual object). In such a transactive relationship, the professional counselor is naturally nondirective and accepting and can begin to view the object as a symbol. Through such symbols, a counselor can enter the client's world and gain the client's perspective. This process develops the counselor's and client's empathy for one another, and defenses are lowered for both client and counselor. A shared attention about a sensual object presents an opportunity for a special "aboutness," that is, a thirdness that can establish an unusual relationship and a new way for a client to express concerns and even to gain a different perspective about prior experiences and present situations.

Fourth, counseling approaches that include the creative arts are active rather than passive and naturally involve multiple modalities, both expressive and receptive. When more than listening and speaking are involved, activities enhance learning, especially when sensory and motor activities are combined. Movement such as dance and drawing and even writing are motor activities, and when they are combined with music, viewing art and drawings, and listening to a poem or story read, they are receptive but also active.

Finally, counseling approaches that include creative arts emphasize modalities and, therefore, neurological functions other than, or usually in addition to, speaking and listening. For the most part, language functions are processed in specific areas of the left hemisphere, whereas most creative arts approaches involve additional parts of the neurological system, such as the right hemisphere and even directly the limbic system and amygdala, two areas of the brain known to be involved with emotions. Learning is usually enhanced when a brain is more active.

A **metaphor** of a commonly known workplace may help to clarify the differences between traditional and creative arts therapies. Because everyone would likely agree that counseling is about doing work, theories and approaches to counseling can be compared metaphorically with a place of work, wherein the unconscious is what counselors' work is about. A workplace has several entrances, most obvious of which is the front door. Traditional counseling approaches attempt to enter through the verbal processes, the front door in this metaphor. To carry forward the workplace metaphor, other therapies make use of creative arts as ways to enter the backdoor or windows, and some creative arts seem to open a cellar door stealthily.

Including creative arts in a counseling practice can be advantageous (Junge, 1994). According to Gladding (2005), one major advantage for the counselor in using the creative arts in counseling is playfulness, which he saw as a balance against the more serious concerns. He also proposed other reasons for incorporating creative arts into a counseling practice. The use of the creative arts (a) promotes connectedness, (b) involves participatory actions, (c) provides a focus on things visual, (d) uncovers new dimensions while expanding experiences, (e) establishes a new sense of self,

(f) involves concreteness for multisensory reflections, (g) develops insight into a variety of new situations under safe conditions, and (h) builds rapport and socialization through cooperation. The creative arts apply to all developmental stages as well as to clients with special needs. In addition, connecting through creative arts is universal because they apply in one way or another to all cultures; creative arts are multicultural.

Although increasing use by professional counselors and anecdotal testimony can be seen as support for the inclusion of creative arts in counseling, actual research on effectiveness is lacking or at best sparse. Empirical studies using statistical designs may not be appropriate for examining counseling approaches; it is very difficult to isolate one approach when dealing with the complexities required in treating clients. However, qualitative studies such as single or multiple case designs and/or an observational method such as structural analysis of movement sessions, as suggested by Gladding (2005), can be useful for understanding how individuals within groups influence one another.

Contributed by Dale-Elizabeth Pehrsson, University of Nevada Las Vegas, Las Vegas, NV

References

Freud, S. (1956). *Delusion and dream and other essays* (P. Rieff, Ed.). Boston: Beacon Press.

Gladding, S. T. (2005). *Counseling as an art: The creative arts in counseling* (3rd ed.). Alexandria: VA: American Counseling Association.

Junge, M. B. (1994). *A history of art therapy in the United States*. Mundelein, IL: American Art Therapy Association.

Shrodes, C. (1950). *Bibliotherapy: A theoretical and clinical-experimental study*. Unpublished doctoral dissertation, University of California, Berkeley.

White, M., & Epston, D. (1990). *Narrative means to therapeutic ends*. New York: Norton.

Additional Resources

Association for Creativity in Counseling, a division of the American Counseling Association, Web site: http://www.aca-acc.org/

National Coalition of Creative Arts Therapies Associations Web site: http://www.nccata.org/

■ Crisis Intervention

A **crisis** is a time-limited period of upset and disequilibrium triggered by a precipitating event during which individuals' typical methods of coping and problem solving fail them. During times of crisis, people are vulnerable to both opportunities for growth and potential for negative mental health outcomes.

Erich Lindemann was one of the first people to document crisis responses and to lay the groundwork for modern crisis intervention. In 1942, he treated the survivors of a fire that ravaged the Coconut Grove Nightclub in Boston, killing 493 people. He documented the responses that patients had to the grief and trauma they experienced and reported that caretakers might be able to help prevent crises by teaching people how to mourn appropriately and adequately. Lindemann's colleague, Gerald Caplan, expanded Lindemann's work by applying preventative psychiatry and public health principles.

Types of Crisis

There are five different types of crisis that fit this definition: developmental, environmental, existential, situational, and psychiatric. **Developmental crises** are caused by events that are considered normal aspects of human growth and development (e.g., marriage, having a child, graduating from college, changing careers, aging). **Environmental crises** are caused by either natural or human events that affect the majority of people in a specific environment (e.g., hurricanes, famine, flood, oil spill, pandemic flu, economic depression, war). **Existential crises** are triggered by personal realizations around purpose, meaning, or other existential themes that create cognitive dissonance, anxiety, or inner conflict (e.g., realization that a person's life is less significant than he or she had hoped). **Situational crises** are triggered by a precipitating event, often perceived as unexpected, shocking, random, or beyond the control of the individual (e.g., rape, car accident, death, being laid off). **Psychiatric crises** are situations that are affected by mental health or substance abuse concerns (e.g., psychotic break, manic episode, drug or alcohol relapse or overdose).

Six-Step Model of Crisis Intervention

Since Lindemann's and Caplan's work, researchers have studied the unique skill set that helping professionals need to possess in order to intervene appropriately with clients in crisis. In particular, James and Gilliland (2005) developed a six-step model that outlines how counselors can assess the needs of their clients in crisis. A summary of this model follows.

Step 1: Defining the problem. Because one client's challenge is another client's crisis, it is important for a professional counselor to understand the client's perception of the problem and of the precipitating event. Using attentive listening skills to empathize with a client in crisis and fully understand the situation and that client's reaction is important. Also paramount in this first step are basic assessment skills, including examining the severity of the crisis, the client's level of emotional distress, the client's behavioral and cognitive functioning, and the client's potential level of lethality (i.e., how likely is this client to harm him- or herself or someone else).

Step 2: Ensuring client safety. Although this is listed as the second step, ensuring client safety is something that should be present throughout this model. Safety is defined as both physical and psychological safety and includes the client's safety as well as the safety of those around the client. If the initial step of defining the problem indicates that there is physical or psychological risk to the client or those the client might have contact with, it is the responsibility of the professional counselor to take steps to ensure their safety. Although the steps to ensure safety are not prescriptive (i.e., they need to be tailored specifically to meet the client's needs), some typical examples of steps to promote safety include notifying medical, police, or support personnel; involving child protective services; and developing a safety plan with the client.

Step 3: Providing support. During a crisis, professional counselors need to demonstrate that they care about and fully accept their clients, no matter what the nature of the crisis is or the counselors' own value systems. Professional counselors can provide that support and help their clients feel less alone, less worthless, and more accepted by using skills like accurate empathy, unconditional positive regard, and direct communication.

Step 4: Examining alternatives. Often clients in crisis are paralyzed in respect to their decision making and may not see a range of opportunities and supports available to them. Once a client is safe and feels supported and the problem has been defined, professional counselors can think through an array of possibilities and then narrow those down to a few to discuss with their client. In this case, the ability of professional counselors to whittle down the list to a few that are appropriate and realistic, so as not to overwhelm their clients further, is important. Finding the balance between being directive enough to help the client make decisions and not making decisions for the client is important.

Step 5: Making plans. Once the alternatives have been examined and discussed with the client, a plan should be developed that identifies supports (e.g., friends, family, groups, organizations, resources) that will be immediately available to the client and coping mechanisms that will provide the client with something positive and constructive that can be done immediately (e.g., writing, a spiritual group, a physical activity). In this step, it is important for the client to be as involved as possible in coconstructing the plan in order to begin to reestablish control over his or her actions and autonomy from the professional counselor.

Step 6: Obtaining commitment. The natural outgrowth of a well-designed and coconstructed plan is obtaining commitment. This involves getting clients in crisis to commit to taking at least one step toward restoring the equilibrium in their lives that had been disrupted by the crisis state. This step might involve the client stating what step(s) will be taken and how and when they will be accomplished. It is important for counselors to ensure that clients are being realistic and honest in their commitment prior to termination of the crisis intervention session. Professional counselors can then follow up with their clients to check the progress made on the coconstructed plans.

Contributed by Carrie A. Wachter,
Purdue University, West Lafayette, IN

Reference

James, R. K., & Gilliland, B. E. (2005). *Crisis intervention strategies* (5th ed.). Belmont, CA: Wadsworth/Thomson Learning.

Additional Resources

Caplan, G. (1964). *Principles of preventative psychiatry.* New York: Basic Books.

Greenstone, J. L., & Leviton, S. C. (2002). *Elements of crisis intervention: Crises and how to respond to them* (2nd ed.). Pacific Grove, CA: Brooks/Cole.

James, R. K. (2007). *Crisis intervention strategies* (6th ed.). Belmont, CA: Thomson Brooks/Cole.

■ Criterion-Referenced Assessment

In general, a **criterion-referenced assessment** is used to determine what individuals can do and what they know, not how they compare with others. The assessment is typically designed to measure how well an individual has learned or mastered a particular body of knowledge or set of skills without regard to how well other individuals at the same age or grade level have learned or mastered the knowledge or skill. There are two major types of criterion-referenced assessments used today: minimum competency-based assessments and standards-based assessments.

The **minimum competency-based assessment** has historically been used for the purpose of determining whether or not an individual graduating from a given educational program or course has reached minimum proficiency as deemed by a specific set of a predetermined foundation or basic skills considered necessary for all individuals to acquire in order to graduate from the given program or course. For example, beginning in the 1970s and 1980s, many states have mandated the use of minimum competency assessments, including, but not limited to, high school graduation qualifying examinations.

On the other hand, in response to the No Child Left Behind Act of 2001 (Public Law 107-110) and the standards-based educational reform movement, many states, school districts, and schools now administer **standards-based assessments,** the other major type of criterion-referenced assessment. Unlike the minimum competency-based assessment, the standards-based assessment is typically designed to measure an individual's mastery of a more rigorous set of learning targets as defined by a set of state-specific or school-district-specific, subject-area, grade-level, curriculum-content standards or expectations. This criterion-referenced assessment is typically designed to align with the principles of the standards-based educational reform movement as called for in the 1993 National Education Goals Panel publication, *Promises to Keep: Creating High Standards for American Students.*

Regardless of whether or not the criterion-referenced assessment is a minimum competency assessment or a standards-based assessment, a score on the criterion-referenced assessment will report how well each individual is doing relative to the predetermined performance level on a specified set of knowledge or skills (basic skills or rigorous learning targets). Each individual's criterion-referenced score is typically presented as a performance standard (e.g., below basic, basic, proficient, advanced) that serves to indicate the degree to which the individual has attained mastery of the defined knowledge or set of skills. The performance-level score or standard, therefore, serves to describe how good is good enough.

For each criterion-referenced assessment, the performance-level score or standard can be defined in a number of ways. For example, in a physical education class, a performance standard might be defined by whether or not an individual is able to perform a set of physical activities to perfection. These activities might include running in place for several minutes, walking on a balance beam without falling, and jumping rope for a specified number of minutes. If the individual is able to perform all of these physical activities to perfection, he or she would be deemed as having mastery of the performance standard. Not every individual may successfully complete each activity; however, the performance standard is clearly described.

In summary, in today's educational setting, the use of criterion-referenced assessments, especially standards-based assessments, is a rapidly growing movement in which a heavy focus is placed on the use of the assessment in order to determine what individuals should know and be able to do. The scores on the criterion-referenced assessments are now tied to accountability systems where the results have an impact on teaching and learning.

Contributed by Patricia J. McDivitt,
Data Recognition Corporation,
Maple Grove, MN

Reference

National Education Goals Panel. (1993). *Promises to keep: Creating high standards for American students.* Washington, DC: Author.

Additional Resources

McDivitt, P. J. (2004). Training educators to develop good educational tests. In J. E. Wall & G. R. Walz (Eds.), *Measuring up: Assessment issues for teachers, counselors, and administrators* (pp. 422–442). Austin, TX: PRO-ED.

McMillan, J. H. (1997). *Classroom assessment: Principles and practice for effective instruction.* Needham Heights, MA: Allyn & Bacon.

Popham, W. J. (2002). *Classroom assessment: What teachers need to know.* Boston: Allyn & Bacon.

■ Cross-Cultural Communication

Cross-cultural communication refers to the ways in which individuals from differing cultures communicate with each other. As an interdisciplinary area of study, cross-cultural communication has its origin in anthropology, communication studies, cultural studies, and psychology and is often referred to as **intercultural communications.** In the field of counseling, cross-cultural communications are typically considered as exchanges between counselors and clients; however, they also occur between the counselor and professional colleagues or between clients and others.

Cross-cultural communications can be both verbal and nonverbal. **Verbal communication** involves the medium (e.g., formal languages, dialects), delivery (e.g., intonation, cadence), and content of human speech. **Nonverbal communication** denotes those cues not involving spoken language, such as eye contact, kinesics (e.g., facial expressions and body language), gesturing, and proxemics (i.e., personal and interpersonal space and territoriality). Individuals from differing cultures often have different patterns of both verbal and nonverbal communication; such differences may be observable not only across specific cultures (e.g., national origin) but also across broader constructs, such as race and ethnicity, as well as subcultures like regional origin or religious affiliation.

It is important to note that cultural differences in communication go beyond matters of "style," because they are often based on underlying systems of meaning-making and may be indicative of a culture's core values (Geertz, 1973). For example, an individual's rigid use of formal titles in addressing perceived authorities (e.g., counselors, teachers) may stem from a cultural emphasis on respect for authority figures or elders. Cross-cultural competence, therefore, entails both becoming knowledgeable about specific differences in communication patterns and seeking to understand how these patterns may provide insight into an individual's cultural worldview.

The need to acknowledge and understand differences in communication patterns is true for all participants in cross-cultural communications, because professional counselors should be as aware of their own cultural backgrounds and their impact on the process as they are of their clients'. Part of this self-awareness involves understanding reactions when confronted with difference, which Bennett (1998) suggested can be characterized as ranging from **ethnocentric,** or exclusively using one's own set of standards and customs to judge others, to **ethnorelative,** in which judgments and behaviors are adapted to a range of cultural differences. Bennett's developmental model of intercultural sensitivity describes the transition from the first stance to the latter through a series of six stages: (a) denial of the existence of cultural differences, (b) defense against difference and negative perception of difference, (c) minimization of the importance of differences, (d) acceptance of differences in both self and others, (e) adaptation to difference through shifting frames of reference and modifying behavior in culturally appropriate ways, and (f) integration of these skills across many different cultural contexts. Through continuous, productive experiences with cross-cultural communications—as well as self-reflection on those experiences—professional counselors and clients may move toward a more ethnorelative stance in their communication.

In recent years, cross-cultural communications have received growing attention in the field of counseling. This has occurred through an expansion of cross-cultural training in counselor education, as well as professional organizations' recognition of cross-cultural competency as an ethical mandate (American Counseling Association, 2005). With the increasing globalization of society, expanded access to counseling through technology, and de-stigmatization of counseling for many cultural groups, developing competence in cross-cultural communications remains of foremost concern for counselors.

Contributed by Lynn E. Swaner,
Long Island University,
C.W. Post Campus, Long Island, NY

References

American Counseling Association. (2005). *ACA code of ethics.* Alexandria, VA: Author.

Bennett, M. J. (Ed.). (1998). *Basic concepts of intercultural communication: Selected readings.* Yarmouth, ME: Intercultural Press.

Geertz, C. (1973). *The interpretation of cultures.* New York: Basic Books.

Additional Resources

Gudykunst, W. B. (Ed). *Cross-cultural and intercultural communication.* Thousand Oaks, CA: Sage.

Sue, D. W., Carter, R. T., Casas, J. M., Fouad, N. A., Ivey, A. E., Jensen, M., et al. (1998). *Multicultural counseling competences: Individual and organizational development.* Thousand Oaks, CA: Sage.

■ Cross-Cultural (Multicultural) Supervision

Cross-cultural supervision or **multicultural supervision** is a complex triadic relationship of a supervisor, supervisee, and client that involves the intersection of diverse cultural backgrounds in the relationship. Multicultural supervision involves discussions of relevant cultural issues in a combined effort to provide effective counseling and supervisory processes for the triad. A debate exists regarding how broadly to define the word *culture* in the context of this relationship. Proponents of the narrow definition of culture argue that cross-cultural supervisory relationships involve individuals from different racial and ethnic backgrounds, whereas proponents of a broad or inclusive definition of culture argue that the term *multicultural supervision* more accurately describes the complex cultural identities encountered in the triadic relationship of the supervisor, supervisee, and client. The inclusive definition of culture includes race, ethnicity, language, class or socioeconomic status, sexual identity, gender, religious or spiritual identity, ability status, and age. Defining the supervisory relationship as a multicultural encounter acknowledges that all people have numerous cultural identities that interact with each other and may become more or less salient across time and situation. The broad definition of culture also helps to avoid stereotyping by acknowledging within-group differences and allows supervisors and supervisees to examine how various aspects of their cultural identities may influence the supervisory and counseling relationships. As the general population becomes more diverse, the number of supervisor–supervisee–client triads composed of individuals with complex cultural characteristics will continue to increase.

The goals of multicultural supervision include addressing cultural issues in the supervisee–client and the supervisor–supervisee relationships and fostering cultural competence in the supervisee to facilitate culturally competent counseling on behalf of the client. It is the responsibility of the supervisor to initiate the discussion of cultural issues in the supervisory relationship. As such, the supervisor should address the inherent power differential present between the supervisor and supervisee as well as how various aspects of the supervisor's and supervisee's cultural identities may influence the working alliance in supervision. Supervisors are also responsible for promoting the supervisee's awareness of cultural issues and ensuring that supervisees develop culturally competent attitudes, knowledge, and skills. Supervisors may challenge supervisees to explore their cultural heritage and biases or assumptions about various cultural groups. Supervisors may also ensure that supervisees are approaching case conceptualization from a multicultural perspective and using culturally appropriate interventions with clients.

Despite recognition of the U.S. population's growing diversity and the increased recognition of the importance of addressing multicultural issues in supervision, cross-racial and cross-cultural issues have not been widely addressed in the counseling literature. The literature on multicultural supervision has predominately been conceptual in nature, with limited but increasing numbers of empirical studies. Empirical studies have primarily examined the relationship between racial and ethnic background and supervision satisfaction and/or the working alliance in supervision. Findings indicate that African American supervisees expect supervisors to be less empathic and respectful than do White supervisees (Vander Kolk, 1974), racial and ethnic minority supervisees identify supervisor liking as the factor most significantly related to satisfaction with supervision (Cook & Helms, 1988), supervisor race and racial matching in the supervisory relationship does not influence supervisees' level of satisfaction with supervision (Hilton, Russell, & Salmi, 1995), and racial and ethnic minority supervisors spend more time discussing multicultural issues in supervision than do White supervisors (Hird, Tao, & Gloria, 2005). In addition, supervisors may increase the likelihood of positive outcomes in multicultural supervision through facilitating open discussion of multicultural issues, creating a supportive environment, demonstrating knowledge of a supervisees' culture, providing guidance on culture-specific issues, and demonstrating an awareness of power and privilege in the supervisory triad.

Racial identity development models have been applied to multicultural supervision as another means of predicting supervisory outcomes (Cook, 1994; Chang, Hays, & Shoffner, 2003). Supervisor and supervisee dyads can be described as parallel (similar levels of racial development), progressive (supervisor at a more advanced level of development than supervisee), or regressive (supervisee at a more advanced level than supervisor; Chang et al., 2003; Cook, 1994). Research indicates that progressive dyads and paral-lel dyads at advanced levels of identity development are most effective in fostering strong working alliances in supervision and in promoting multicultural competence in supervisees (Constantine, Warren, & Miville, 2005; Ladany, Brittan-Powell, & Pannu, 1997).

The multicultural supervision literature clearly states that the supervisor must ensure that the topic of multiculturalism is an integral facet of the supervision dialogue. This dialogue must include cultural awareness in general, the counselor–client relationship, and the supervisory relationship. Given that supervisees are more likely to have enrolled in a multicultural counseling course, it is the responsibility of the supervisor to seek continuing education opportunities, consultation, and supervision of multicultural supervision issues.

Contributed by Amy L. McLeod and Catherine Y. Chang, Georgia State University, Atlanta, GA

References

Chang, C. Y., Hays, D. G., & Shoffner, M. F. (2003). Cross-racial supervision: A developmental approach for White supervisors working with supervisees of color. *The Clinical Supervisor, 22,* 121–138.

Constantine, M. G., Warren, A. K., & Miville, M. L. (2005). White racial identity dyadic interactions in supervision: Implications for supervisee's multicultural counseling competence. *Journal of Counseling Psychology, 54,* 490–496.

Cook, D. (1994). Racial identity in supervision. *Counselor Education and Supervision, 34,* 132–141.

Cook, D. A., & Helms, J. E. (1988). Visible racial/ethnic group supervisee's satisfaction with cross-cultural supervision as predicted by relationship characteristics. *Journal of Counseling Psychology, 35,* 268–274.

Hilton, D. B., Russell, R. K., & Salmi, S. W. (1995). The effects of supervisor's race and level of support on perceptions of supervision. *Journal of Counseling & Development, 73,* 559–563.

Hird, J. S., Tao, K. W., & Gloria, A. M. (2005). Examining supervisor's multicultural competence in racially similar and different supervision dyads. *The Clinical Supervisor, 23,* 107–122.

Ladany, N., Brittan-Powell, C., & Pannu, R. (1997). The influence of supervisory racial identity interaction and racial matching on the supervisory working alliance and supervisee multicultural competence. *Counselor Education & Supervision, 36,* 284–304.

Vander Kolk, C. J. (1974). The relationship of personality, values, and race to anticipation of the supervisory relationship. *Rehabilitation Counseling Bulletin, 18*(1), 41–46.

Additional Resources

Ancis, J. R., & Ladany, N. (2001). A multicultural framework for counselor supervision. In L. J. Bradley &

N. Ladany (Eds.), *Counselor supervision: Principles, process, and practice* (pp. 63–89). Philadelphia: Taylor & Francis.

Pope-Davis, D. B., & Coleman, H. L. K. (Eds.). (1997). *Multicultural counseling competencies: Assessment, education and training, and supervision.* Thousand Oaks, CA: Sage.

■ Cultural Competence

Cultural competence (or **multicultural competence**) is generally defined as the development of a counselor's awareness of his or her cultural identity and belief systems and the knowledge and skills to work with diverse populations (Sue, Arredondo, & McDavis, 1992). More specifically, Sue et al. (1992) proposed 31 standards for three areas of multicultural competence. Arredondo et al. (1996) operationalized multicultural competencies that allowed for the adoption and inclusion of cultural competence into counselor training programs. In addition, Arredondo et al. extended the scope of multicultural competencies to include other diverse identities (e.g., religion, sexual orientation, ability or disability, gender, or age) and promote systemic change and social advocacy. To gain cultural competence, a counselor is responsible for obtaining training in skill sets to work with culturally different individuals by incorporating the following areas:

- *Attitudes and beliefs.* Counselor's awareness of self as a cultural being, exploring his or her own bias, values, assumptions;
- *Knowledge.* Information about the racial, cultural, and ethnic groups with whom the counselor plans to work and understanding the worldview of the client;
- *Skills.* Tools that enable the counselor to be ready to work with clients of various backgrounds by using culturally appropriate intervention strategies.

Multiculturalism is considered the "fourth force" in counseling (Pedersen, 1990); thus, the need for cultural competence counselor training is imperative. Sue et al. (1992) listed five reasons a multicultural perspective was needed in counselor education: (a) The United States is becoming more diverse; (b) traditional, monocultural, counseling approaches and techniques have been found ineffective with minority populations; (c) counselors are part of the larger society, which has been oppressive to minorities; (d) research in counseling has reflected White, middle-class values and has pathologized minorities based on the assumption that they do not have "the right culture"; and (e) counselors who are not trained in cultural competency are potentially harmful to their minority clients. Furthermore, service providers who do not gain knowledge in these three areas of competencies are seen as **culturally incompetent,** that is, practicing from a culturally encapsulated vantage point; not considering the client's worldview; and, overall, acting unethically.

Multicultural Competence in Research and Assessment

The value of multicultural competence is also reflected in the increased number of publications discussing multicultural competence. Over the past 20 years, there has been a consistent increase in empirical research on multicultural counseling competencies. Experimental and quasi-experimental studies consistently indicate that multicultural competence training tends to improve counseling process and outcome. Manese, Wu, and Nepomuceno (2001) suggested that using an integrative multicultural approach, in which an organizational commitment to multiculturalism and contact with minority groups are present, leads to increased multicultural competence. Counselors with multicultural counselor training and who use culturally consistent verbalizations consistently receive higher ratings of client counseling satisfaction. Studies also show underserved minority populations have lower attrition rates when they are paired with a counselor who has had culturally sensitive training.

Most multicultural competence research falls into two categories: (a) investigating counselor multicultural competence response and behavior and (b) scale-specific research. The majority of empirical multicultural counseling research has focused on intrapersonal characteristics of counselors, such as their demographics, identity, and multicultural counseling training. Other variables explored in empirical research on multicultural counseling competencies include clients' perception of counselor training, scale development, and objective ratings of counselors' multicultural counseling competencies.

Although there has been an increase in multicultural competency research, particularly within the last 20 years, it is not without its limitations. An overwhelming majority of research publications on multicultural competency are based on self-report measures that examine variables such as demographics, personality, and attitude that are not reflective of actual counseling behaviors. Much of the literature on multicultural competence is not empirical in nature. Dunn, Smith, and Montoya (2006) found that out of more than 800 multicultural competence articles, only 137 were quantitative in nature. Many of the instruments used in multicultural competence research tend to have poor correlation with one another, indicating that multicultural competency is a multifaceted construct that is still being defined. Of the 137 studies examined by Dunn et al., 29 multicultural instruments were used, yet only 6 of the instruments were used in more than 1 study. Participants in research on multicultural competency tend to be female, European American, approximately 36 years old, and middle to upper-middle class. In addition, only a small number of authors have published empirical studies in this area. As traditional methods of empirical research are often historically based on European American norms and standards, the movement in multicultural competency research may involve nontraditional means such as multimethod studies and qualitative research.

It is important for clinicians to evaluate their level of multicultural competency, making multicultural competence assessment a major area of research in counseling. The most widely used assessments are included in Table 1.

Table 1. Commonly Used Multicultural Counseling Assessments

Assessment	Type	Target Population	Description
Cross-Cultural Counseling Inventory (LaFromboise, Coleman, & Hernandez, 1991)	Observer-rated	Counselors and counselor trainees	Measures cross-cultural competence; used in determination of counselor effectiveness with culturally diverse clients
Multicultural Counseling Inventory (Sodowsky, Taffe, Gutkin, & Wise, 1994)	Self-report	Practitioners providing direct services, therapy/counseling	Measures cultural competency as assessed through four subscales: Multicultural Counseling Skills, Multicultural Awareness, Multicultural Counseling Knowledge, and Multicultural Counseling Relationship. Higher scores indicate a greater degree of mulicultural competency.
Multicultural Awareness-Knowledge-and-Skills Survey (D'Andrea, Daniels, & Heck, 1991)	Self-report	Counseling trainees	Assesses multicultural awareness, knowledge, and skills based on Sue et al.'s (1982) model of cross-cultural counseling
Multicultural Counseling Knowledge and Awareness Scale (Ponterotto, Gretchen, Utsey, Rieger, & Austin, 2002)	Self-report	Counselors and counseling trainees	Assesses multicultural competency through two subscales, Knowledge and Awareness. Higher scores indicate greater self-perceived multicultural competencies
Multicultural Counseling Competence and Training Survey (Holcomb-McCoy & Myers, 1999)	Self-report	Professional counselors	Assesses self-perceived multicultural competence, based on Association for Multicultural Counseling and Development's Multicultural Competencies and Explanatory Statements; behaviorally stated items and demographic items (gender, age, race, year of graduation)

Models of Competency Training for Students

The value of integrating a multicultural perspective and multicultural training competence has been noted by the increased number of counselor training programs offering multicultural-related courses. In 1982, the American Psychological Association (Ponterotto, 1996) found that only 4.3% of psychology departments incorporated a diversity or multicultural course in its program, whereas a more recent study by Ponterotto in 1996 found that 89% of counseling psychology and counselor educator programs incorporated at least one multicultural or diversity course in their training. Today, most counseling programs now require a preliminary course in multicultural competency, where students gain awareness, knowledge, and skills necessary to begin working with culturally diverse clients. The American Counseling Association (2005) and the Council for Accreditation of Counseling and Related Educational Programs (2009) have incorporated multicultural competencies into their standards.

There are currently four major models of multicultural competency training: (a) the separate course/"cookbook" approach, which consists of a one-semester course that gives a brief overview of general cross-cultural issues; (b) the area of concentration model, in which core courses are combined with skill-building and experiential activities; (c) the interdisciplinary model, in which students are encouraged to take courses outside of their department; and (d) the integrated approach, in which there is program development and implementation of multicultural competencies. The integrated approach has become more widely used by counselor education programs.

Originally developed to address the potential harm traditional counseling methods can have on diverse clients and to keep pace with the U.S.'s changing demographics, multicultural competence has been and will continue to be a hot topic in the counseling field. As more research is performed and more clinicians adopt a multiculturally competent perspective, the standards for cultural competency may become better defined, and the delivery of services to diverse populations may look different to future clinicians

Contributed by Sharon Blackwell Jones,
Allison Smith, and Kimber Shelton,
The University of Georgia,
Athens, GA

References

American Counseling Association. (2005). *ACA code of ethics.* Alexandria, VA: Author.

Arredondo, P., Toporek, R., Brown, S. P., Jones, J., Locke, D. C., Sanchez, J., et al. (1996). Operationalization of the multicultural counseling competencies. *Journal of Multicultural Counseling and Development, 21,* 42–78.

Council for Accreditation of Counseling and Related Educational Programs. (2009). *CACREP accreditation manual: 2009 standards.* Alexandria, VA: Author.

D'Andrea, M., Daniels, J., & Heck, R. (1991). Evaluating the impact of multicultural counseling training. *Journal of Counseling & Development, 70,* 143–150.

Dunn, T., Smith, T., & Montoya, J. (2006). Multicultural competency instrumentation: A review and analysis of reliability generalization. *Journal of Counseling & Development, 84,* 471–482.

Holcomb-McCoy, C., & Myers, J. (1999). Multicultural competence and counselor training: A national survey. *Journal of Counseling & Development, 77,* 294–302.

LaFromboise, T., Coleman, H., & Hernandez, A. (1991). Development and factor structure of the Cross-Cultural Counseling Inventory–Revised. *Professional Psychology: Research and Practice, 22,* 380–388.

Manese, J. E., Wu, J. T., & Nepomuceno, C. A. (2001). The effect of training on multicultural counseling competencies: An exploratory study over a 10-year period. *Journal of Multicultural Counseling & Development, 29,* 31–40.

Pedersen, P. (1990). The multicultural perspective as a fourth force in counseling. *Journal of Mental Health Counseling, 12,* 93–95.

Ponterotto, J. (1996). Multicultural counseling in the twenty-first century. *The Counseling Psychologist, 24,* 259–268.

Ponterotto, J. G., Gretchen, D., Utsey, S., Rieger, B., & Austin, R. (2002). A revision of the Multicultural Counseling Awareness Scale. *Journal of Multicultural Counseling and Development, 30,* 153–180.

Sodowsky, G. R., Taffe, R. C, Gutkin, T. B., & Wise, S. L. (1994). Development of the Multicultural Counseling Inventory: A self-report measure of multicultural competencies. *Journal of Counseling Psychology, 41,* 137–148.

Sue, D. W, Arredondo, P., & McDavis, R. J. (1992). Multicultural counseling competencies and standards: A call to the profession. *Journal of Counseling & Development, 70,* 477–486.

Sue, D. W., Bernier, J., Durran, M., Feinberg, L., Pedersen, P., Smith, E., et al. (1982). Position paper: Multicultural counseling competencies. *The Counseling Psychologist, 10,* 45–52.

Cultural Identity

Cultural identity is the extent to which individuals perceive themselves included and aligned with a cultural group (i.e., a group that has a shared system of meaning and symbols and norms and rules for conduct). By way of contrast, the term *racial identity* concerns race (social categorizations based on phenotypic features and geographic ancestry, such as American Indian or Asian American), and the term *ethnic identity* concerns ethnicity (a sociolinguistic group typically associated with the nation of ancestry, such as Lakota Sioux or Vietnamese American). Cultural identity is therefore more circumscribed than racial identity but less narrow than ethnic identity.

Research indicates that socialization in childhood profoundly shapes cultural identity, with the family of origin playing the most salient role but with peer models and local contextual norms also contributing substantially. Cultural identity, however, can be augmented or diminished over time; for example, adults who did not identify with a cultural group during their childhood can come to identify strongly with that group by engaging in relationships and activities that transmit cultural traditions and values. In contrast, individuals who as children strongly identified with one cultural group may come to identify more strongly with a different cultural group if they continuously invest themselves in that culture's mores and systems (e.g., through acculturation following immigration). An individual may have multiple cultural identities; however, a particular cultural identity may be more salient at a given time and place.

Although cultural identity is commonly described in terms of a continuum (i.e., weak to strong identification), cultural identity is necessarily multifaceted. For example, individuals may strongly identify with several aspects of their native culture (e.g., communication styles) but may not internalize or may outright reject other aspects (e.g., traditional gender roles). Hence, counselors optimally should ascertain how individuals perceive and experience their cultural heritage rather than assume that an ostensibly strong cultural identity equates with conformity to all cultural norms. For example, rather than acting on an assumption that an Asian American client will respond better to directive interventions than to person-centered therapy, the counselor should first test such assumptions based on typical cultural values by inquiring about previous instances when the client found interventions that were helpful, by evaluating the acculturation of the client to Western values of individualism, and so on. Knowledge of a client's cultural identity should guide hypotheses, but it should not automatically determine a counselor's response to a client (i.e., stereotype confirmation bias). Counseling is a one-on-one relationship between therapist and client that is informed by many contextual factors influencing the client's cultural identity and its associated psychological functions.

Cultural identity serves several psychological functions. First and foremost, cultural identity provides an interpretive framework (worldview) based on cultural values and beliefs through which events are evaluated. For example, individuals from different cultures may interpret the same physical proximity between two people in a conversation as either friendly or aggressive, depending on their worldview. Second, cultural identity contributes to the maintenance of a sense of belonging (collective identification) with a group. Strength of cultural identity can therefore be a distal indicator of self-confidence and the degree to which an individual successfully relates to culturally similar others. Third, cultural identity contributes to the regulation of behavior in terms of cultural norms. Individuals who identify with a particular culture but do not conform to cultural norms may experience cognitive dissonance or social pressure to conform. Fourth, cultural identity implicitly differentiates an individual from others who do not share the same cultural characteristics. In particular, cultural identity is associated with "dis-identification" with and/or opposition to groups seen as undesirable or oppressive.

To the extent that cultural identity provides access to support networks and a sense of inclusion, cultural identity is positively associated with mental health and well-being. In situations in which a cultural group is isolated or disempowered by another group, cultural identity may buffer against negative outcomes or contribute to the personalization of collective group trauma. In general, cultural identity tends to be stronger in cultures characterized by collectivistic values and/or by a history of systematic oppression.

Contributed by Timothy B. Smith,
Brigham Young University, Provo, UT

Additional Resources

Hays, P. A. (2001). *Addressing cultural complexities in practice: A framework for clinicians and counselors.* Washington, DC: American Psychological Association.

Mokros, H. B. (Ed.). (1996). *Interaction & identity.* New Brunswick, NJ: Transaction.

■ Culture

Culture is defined as the values, norms, worldviews, and typical ways of life adopted by any group and then passed on from one generation to the next. It characterizes how individuals develop meaning and relate with others. Culture is commonly viewed within four contexts or types: universal, ecological, national, regional, and racio-ethnic.

Universal culture is the commonality that is shared by all cultures and humankind. For example, people's bodily functions transcend cultural boundaries—when they are hungry their bodies need nourishment, when they are frightened their instincts tell them to run, when they are tired their bodies need to rest. Other cultural universals are found in gender roles, marriage, entertainment, and government.

Ecological culture refers to four overlapping levels of environmental factors that have an impact on culture and human development. First, individuals are viewed within **microsystems,** or their most direct and immediate environmental interactions such as family, church, or school contexts. The second level is the **mesosystem,** which is the infusion of two microenvironments, such as the connection between work and family. The third level includes the external aspects in environments that have direct impact on individuals, such as their neighborhood or workplace, which is referred to as the **exosystem.** Last, the **macrosystem** consists of the overall larger cultural context, values, traditions, and mores (Bronfenbrenner, 1979).

Culture is a very fluid and uniquely personal concept. It consists of a multitude of layers and dimensions. It is possible for individuals of seemingly identical cultures to maintain differences within their group. Two dimensions of culture are national and regional. **National culture** relates to the nation as a whole. **Regional culture** specifies the ethnic, linguistic, or religious differences that exist within a nation. Often, natives of a particular group are oblivious to the influences of their nationality or regional culture until they interact with someone of a different culture. For instance, national culture is evident when people from the United States travel to other countries; in and around Europe, it is often stated that they can be spotted on the streets before they even utter a word. Likewise, two individuals who are both from America, one from Itta Bena, Mississippi, and the other from Los Angeles, California, are similar in nationality but maintain vastly different meanings and values from their regional cultures.

Another dimension or type of culture is racio-ethnic. **Racio-ethnic** culture relates directly to an individual's race or attitudes that are derived based on his or her race. This term is often used to describe, isolate, or separate racio-ethnic minority groups, such as African Americans, Asian Americans, and Hispanic Americans, from mainstream behaviors, values, and mores.

Important Culture Terminology

In moving from the various types of culture into terms that define this phenomenon, it is important to understand that every group develops a distinct set of rules, behaviors, and standards by which the members of the group perceive and interact within their world. These traditions are taught and passed on from one generation to the next. This process is called socialization.

Socialization molds and shapes how individuals think, what they think about, and how they form their opinions and make decisions or determine outcomes (Sue & Sue, 2003). Throughout the socialization process, individuals gain an understanding of their culture's uniqueness through repeated social interactions with other cultures. This process is called **enculturation.** As the process of enculturation provides an understanding of the uniqueness of an individual's culture, cultural pluralism is a concept that provides an appreciation and acceptance of the differences, specific needs, and strengths that exist among and between groups. **Cultural pluralism** embraces unity and diversity. This term is commonly interchanged with the term *multiculturalism.* It is often stated that **cultural relativism** is the opposite of cultural pluralism because cultural relativism views all cultures equally from a neutral perspective, and the characteristics of a culture are understood on their own merit as opposed to being understood through the filter of a different culture.

Unlike cultural relativism, in which differences are viewed from a neutral perspective, **stereotype** is a negative behavior whereby differences are noticed about a particular group, then the differences are negatively labeled. From that point, every person affiliated with that group is generalized, oversimplified, or judged within this negative category. Stereotypes are typically derived from history and social interactions between cultural groups.

Another concept that impedes cultural competence is defined with the term **cultural encapsulation.** The encapsulated view is narrow and rigid, limited to the dominant culture's perspectives with disregard of any cultural variation (Wrenn, 1962). This type of cultural view is a hindrance to counselors' effectiveness because it overlays universal concepts of "healthy" and "normal" without the benefit of intentionally conceptualizing clients as individuals within their unique cultural contexts (Sue & Sue, 2003).

Segregation is a term that refers to the process of social or legal separation of people, typically on the basis of their race and ethnicity. Segregation can also occur along lines of class, gender, orientation, and disability. **Ethnicity** describes a social group with shared history, sense of identity, and affiliation that is tied to common geographical and cultural roots. The term **diversity** refers to the differences among people or groups of people reflected in a variety of forms, including but not limited to race, culture, gender, age, sexual orientation, perspective, socioeconomic status, class, language, religion, ethnicity, and disability.

To provide a broader understanding of culture, the terms *subculture, microculture,* and *minority group* describe social cultural groups that are smaller than the mainstream or society at large, thus providing a broader understanding of components of the larger culture within society. **Subculture** refers to a social group that has adopted a shared perspective and life-style that are different from the cultural mainstream, such as the biker culture or the hip hop culture. Some subcultures derive from demographic differences from the mainstream, such as the baby boomer culture and the culture of affluence. Subcultures can have geographical influences but are primarily influenced by trends, music, and media. The term *subculture* is used interchangeably with the term *microculture;* however, the two terms are different. **Microculture** refers to a select group of individuals who identify themselves as different. They share a set of norms, attitudes, and values that give them distinctiveness. Microcultures imply a greater connection with the mainstream or dominant culture. Interactions within microcultures interpret and convey ideas and values to the larger culture, or macroculture. For instance, the social interactions that take place in the family, the classroom, and the school convey the overall values of the neighborhood. Finally, the term **minority group** historically referred to the group that was smaller in number compared with other groups in a particular society; however, that is not the current cultural usage of the term. From a cultural perspective, the term *minority group* is used to designate groups that are perceived as having less power or status than the majority or dominant group. The term is widely used to refer to racial, ethnic, and cultural groups that are protected by law.

Implications for Counselors

Cultural factors have significant implications for counseling research, training, and practice. Historically, the models for mental health professionals have been based primarily on White, European, middle-class, heterosexual, and able-bodied populations with exclusion and embedded bias to variations among race, ethnicity, class, sexual orientation, and disability; however, cultural norms, ideologies, and traditions influence multiple dimensions of the therapeutic process and provide a framework for a deeper understanding of affect, behavior, and personality (Kirmayer, 1989). It is important for competent counselors to challenge their own assumptions and biases. Clients are not culturally homogenous. In efforts to diagnose clients accurately and treat clients from diverse backgrounds, it is imperative to understand that culture shapes the experiences and expressions of emotional distress and social problems. Consequently, in counselor training and practice, the behavior of individuals should not be conceptualized without taking into account individuals' social-cultural contexts.

Contributed by Lea R. Flowers,
Georgia State University, Atlanta, GA

References

Bronfenbrenner, U. (1979). *The ecology of human development: Experiments by nature and design.* Cambridge, MA: Harvard University Press.

Kirmayer, L. J. (1989). Cultural variations in the response to psychiatric disorders and emotional distress. *Social Science Medicine, 29,* 327–339.

Sue, D. W., & Sue, D. (2003). *Counseling the culturally different: Theory and practice* (4th ed.). New York: Wiley.

Wrenn, C. G. (1962). The culturally encapsulated counselor. *Harvard Educational Review, 32,* 444–449.

Additional Resources

Helms, J. E., & Cook, D. A. (1999). *Using race and culture in counseling and psychotherapy: Theory and process.* Needham, MA: Allyn & Bacon.

Vontress, C. E. (2002). Culture and counseling. In W. J. Lonner, D. L. Dinnel, S. A. Hayes, & D. N. Sattler (Eds.), *Online readings in psychology and culture* (Unit 10, chap. 1). Available on Western Washington University, Department of Psychology, Center for Cross-Cultural Research Web site: http://www.wwu.edu/~culture

◼Culture-Fair and Culture-Free Assessments

Culture-fair and **culture-free assessments** are typically associated with intelligence tests and refer to assessments that are constructed to eliminate or minimize irrelevant influences of cultural and societal factors (i.e., cultural bias) on the results of the assessments, thereby producing test results that better separate a person's natural ability from cultural and societal influences. The goal of culture-free assessments is to generate assessment results that accurately reflect the ability or achievement of individuals from culturally diverse backgrounds through the use of content that does not favor one cultural group over another. This is accomplished by including items that are equally familiar to all the cultural groups being assessed. Despite attempts to eliminate cultural bias from assessments, the best that test developers can accomplish is to reduce the effects of cultural bias, thus leading to culture-fair assessments. Culture-fair assessments, therefore, are assessments that attempt to be equitable to individuals from different cultural groups and that have been normed on various cultural groups. Originally, the term used to describe these assessments was *culture free;* however, the preferred term is *culture-fair* assessments.

Cultural bias in assessments can be related to **content bias** (i.e., content of the assessment items favor one group over another, either by using items that are stereotypical to one group or experiences that are more relevant for one group over another), **inappropriate standardization sample** (i.e., norm group does not include or includes only a small sample of individuals from the same cultural background as the individual being assessed), **slope bias** (i.e., minority group test scores have lower validity coefficients than majority group scores), and **intercept bias** (i.e., minority group test scores systematically underpredict performances on a criterion; Zurcher, 1998).

Some have argued that because cultures differ in their perspectives on problem solving and concrete and abstract thinking and that intelligence represents cultural knowledge, the notion of culture-free and culture-fair assessments is nonsensical and impossible to achieve (Scarr, 1994). Given that the construct of testing and intelligence varies from culture to culture, culture-fair assessments are an idealized abstraction that is never achieved in the real world. Although some assessment inventories may be more culturally fair than others, it is impossible for any assessment instrument to be equally fair to all cultural groups.

Contributed by Catherine Y. Chang and
Amy L. McLeod, Georgia State
University, Atlanta, GA

References

Scarr, S. (1994). Culture-fair and culture-free tests. In R. J. Sternberg (Ed.), *Encyclopedia of human intelligence* (pp. 322–328). New York: McMillan.

Zurcher, R. (1998). Issues and trends in culture-fair assessment. *Intervention in School and Clinic, 34,* 103–106.

■ Curative Factors

Curative factors are elements of the group experience that facilitate change. First identified and researched by Irvin Yalom (Yalom & Leszcz, 2005), these interdependent curative factors, also known as **therapeutic factors,** can be found in all types of groups, with varying degrees of importance depending of the purpose of the group. Following are the 11 identified factors:

- **Instillation of hope.** This factor involves personal expectations that the group can help facilitate change. Structural changes such as better attendance as well as dynamic changes such as deeper levels of sharing can be outcomes of faith in the group modality. When a group member reports, "I took what I learned from group and applied it to my marriage and it really helped," the other group members' belief in the group process as an agent of change is enhanced.

- **Universality.** Through mutual sharing of personal issues, members realize they are not alone in their struggles. For example, as one member discusses a difficulty with trusting people, other group members are relating to those feelings. This often prompts others to express similar issues. The overlapping concerns reduce feelings of isolation and facilitate feelings of relief and belonging.

- **Imparting information.** Common to psychoeducational groups, imparting information is often facilitated by didactic instruction by the group leader or through advice or suggestions about how to cope with issues offered by the group members or group leader. Examples are information on parenting techniques, communication skills, and sleep hygiene.

- **Altruism.** Altruism is the concept that helping fellow group members is growth enhancing. Altruism is unique to group and provides members of the group other ways to change in addition to talking about their own issues. Group members most often help each other through encouragement, reassurance, and advice.

- **The corrective recapitulation of the primary family group.** Given the assumption that most people have had less than satisfactory experiences in their family of origin, the group provides a safe place to work through unresolved family issues and maladaptive roles and patterns. For example, a member who has adopted a dependent role in the family of origin may enact that role in group by idolizing the group leader. The group can help the member identify this pattern and experiment with adapting and changing the role.

- **Development of socializing techniques.** Occurring in all types of groups, the acquisition of social skills can be explicit (e.g., training or role plays) or implicit (e.g., insight regarding nonverbal behavior among group members). When a group member says to another member, "It's hard to trust what you say because you never look me in the eye when you are talking to me," opportunities surface for a person to learn about his or her public persona and make changes when there is a discrepancy between how he or she is perceived and how he or she wants to be perceived.

- **Imitative behavior.** Group members may experiment with new behaviors and attitudes by adopting personality characteristics of other group members. For example, a shy member may learn from a more outgoing member by first observing the new behavior and then gradually practicing elements of the behavior in group.

- **Interpersonal learning.** Group acts as a social microcosm, allowing group members, through self-observation, to gain awareness of their social selves. The group provides feedback to help each member gain insight into productive and maladaptive social patterns and also provides the social laboratory for possible change. For example, when the group provides feedback to a member that he or she is coming across as arrogant and aggressive when speaking to other members, the group member is given the opportunity to reflect on that feedback, compare it with his or her own self-assessment, and experiment with change. The group can continue to give feedback to the member as he or she attempts different ways of relating.

- **Group cohesiveness.** Akin to a magnetic force, this dynamic bonds the group together. This factor is synonymous with feelings of group loyalty, unity, and togetherness. Just as the counselor–client relationship is vital to change in individual counseling, group cohesiveness is the therapeutic relationship among the members of the group. Group members forge the alliance through warmth, acceptance, and genuineness.

- **Catharsis.** Catharsis is the expression of intense, usually repressed, emotions. The ventilation of the emotion, coupled with acceptance of the emotion by the group, produces the curative aspect. For example, when a group member sobs deeply over the loss of a loved one, the expression of the core emotion can be helpful to the group member; however, in group, how the group responds to the outpouring of emotion is also key. For the ventilation to be curative, the group must serve as a safe container for the emotion by listening and not distracting, and then allow for processing of the residual feelings.

- **Existential factors.** Consistent with Yalom's theoretical orientation, these factors illuminate the givens of existence that confront every human being. Due to their universal nature, they are present in group. How each member deals with the givens of freedom, death, meaninglessness, and isolation provides insight into the member's intra- and interpersonal life.

Contributed by Kevin A. Fall, Loyola University New Orleans, New Orleans, LA

Reference

Yalom, I. D., & Leszcz, M. (2005). *The theory and practice of group psychotherapy* (5th ed.). New York: Basic Books.

D

Decision Accuracy

Professional counselors make a wide range of decisions in their work. **Screening decisions** assess whether an observed phenomenon is significantly discrepant from the norm. **Diagnostic decisions** determine the specific nature of the discrepancy. **Prognostic or treatment decisions** determine the nature or efficacy of intervention. **Placement decisions** determine the educational or vocational fit between persons and their schooling or work assignment. Although a wide range of tests support human decision making, it is important to recall that psychological tests do not make decisions. Humans make decisions. The accuracy of human decisions should be enhanced by the use of a test.

A simple way to assess the accuracy of tests in supporting decisions is to compare the results of testing with known outcomes. The ability of a test to identify the presence of a phenomenon (such as pedophilia) accurately is called **sensitivity** or **true positive rate**. The ability of a test to identify the absence of a phenomenon accurately is called **specificity** or **true negative rate**. Inaccurately identifying the presence of a phenomenon when it is absent is called **false positive error**. Inaccurately identifying the absence of a phenomenon when it is present is called **false negative error**. The ratio of total correct decisions divided by the total number of decisions is called **efficiency**. Decision rules can be adjusted to enhance sensitivity, specificity, and error rates. Enhancing sensitivity often comes at the cost of increased false positive error. Similarly, enhancing specificity often comes at the cost of increased false negative error. People make a value judgment in deciding which errors are more damaging and which decision rules should be used. As an example, a sample efficiency matrix for a screening test for pedophilia is provided in Figure 1. With a sample of 50 known pedophiles and 50 known nonpedophiles, the test correctly identified 30 pedophiles and 48 nonpedo-

philes. It incorrectly labeled 2 known nonpedophiles as pedophiles and 20 known pedophiles as nonpedophiles. Overall, the test made 78 correct decisions out of 100.

It is an oversimplification to evaluate the test merely according to its overall efficiency. Seventy-eight percent efficiency might seem to be very good until the risks of the errors involved are considered. To be inaccurately labeled a pedophile can be devastating. The social and emotional costs associated with such an error are significant in someone's life. To misidentify a pedophile as a nonpedophile can also be devastating. The pedophile needs treatment, and children need to be protected. The particular risks of each kind of error must be evaluated, and decisions must be made regarding which errors to protect against and which errors are easier to tolerate.

Another approach to assessing whether a test enhances decision making is to compare the results of a decision that was made using one test with the results of a decision that was made using a different test, a different version of the same test, or no test at all. This approach relies on estimating incremental validity. **Incremental validity** assesses whether a test enhances the prediction of some criterion. The criterion to be predicted may be job performance, clinical diagnosis, treatment outcome, or any other relevant criterion. Because the criteria may vary, estimates of incremental validity are highly sensitive to the context of the decision and the nature of the test data. A test may provide significant incremental validity in one context but not in another. For example, the Minnesota Multiphasic Personality Inventory–2 (MMPI-2) was designed to describe psychopathology and may help with decisions about treatment. In a different context, such as admission to graduate school, the MMPI-2 may add no incremental validity to the decisions, which may be based on other more germane assessments or admissions data. Counselors should carefully consider the context of the decision and the nature of the test data when evaluating the benefit of using a test.

Estimates of incremental validity are also very dependent on the measurement of the criterion. If the measure of the criterion is unreliable or invalid, then the estimate of incremental validity may be spurious. Professional counselors should carefully consider the measurement of the criterion to evaluate whether the test is of value in their decision-making process.

Typically, more predictors of a phenomenon result in greater total variance accounted for in the criterion. So it is with psychological tests. Although each additional test administered to a client may provide some degree of improved accuracy, the costs of time and energy for the client to complete the test and the counselor to score and interpret the test may not justify the small value added to the decision-making

	50 Known Pedophiles	50 Known Nonpedophiles	
Test-Identified Pedophiles	30 (True Positives) 30/50 = .60 (Sensitivity)	2 (False Positive Error)	30 + 2 = 32 (Test-Identified Pedophiles)
Test-Identified Non-pedophiles	20 (False Negative Error)	48 (True Negatives) 40/50 = .96 (Specificity)	20 + 48 = 68 (Test-Identified Nonpedophiles)
	30 + 20 = 50 Known Pedophiles	2 + 48 = 50 Known Nonpedophiles	30 + 48 = 78 Correct Decisions 78/100 = .78 (Efficiency)

Figure 1. A Sample Efficiency Matrix for a Screening Test for Pedophilia

process. Although more variance may be accounted for, it is important to assess whether the added predictive ability is worth the effort expended to obtain the data.

Contributed by Lane Fischer, Brigham Young University, Provo, UT

Additional Resource

Hunsley, J., & Haynes, S. N. (Eds.). (2003). Incremental validity and utility in clinical assessment (Special section). *Psychological Assessment, 15*(4).

Defense Mechanisms

According to early psychoanalytic theory, the basic premise of symptom formation held that anxiety or tension arises in an individual due to intrapsychic conflict. To cope with the resulting discomfort, the individual develops a symptom that functions to alleviate the original anxiety. This behavior was later defined more clearly as a **defense mechanism,** an unconscious intrapsychic process that serves to provide relief from emotional conflict and anxiety.

Sigmund Freud was the first to introduce this concept, which is probably the most robust, enduring, and least controversial component of psychodynamic theory. Freud's later work expounded on the concepts of resistance in treatment, repetition compulsion, transference, countertransference, and mastery of developmental functions, all of which are explained within the context of defense mechanisms and their function in psychotherapy. Defense mechanisms are widely accepted as a crucial aspect of clinical assessment among many schools of psychotherapy. This is largely because defense mechanisms are easily observed in clinical situations and in everyday life.

Anna Freud also described and explained defense mechanisms and delineated new mechanisms on the basis of her clinical experience with children. She pointed out that although defenses may become symptoms and form psychopathology, they also fulfill vital functions in personality development. Neo-Freudians such as Klein and Kernberg built theoretically on these ideas and added additional defenses, such as splitting, primitive idealization, and omnipotence. Recent attempts to define behavior and defense mechanisms have led to the recognition of behaviors more commonly reported or observed in today's short-term therapy settings. These include self-assertion, substitution, physical incorporation and expulsion, and dissociation.

Defense mechanisms have been classified as four types: (a) those that are almost always pathological, such as when they allow individuals to obscure their ability to perceive reality; (b) those that are immature and typically used in childhood and adolescence and mostly abandoned by adulthood because they lead to socially unacceptable behavior; (c) those that are neurotic and common to everyone but not optimal for coping with reality because they lead to problems in relationships and work; (d) and those that are mature defense mechanisms that optimize an individual's ability to love, work, and experience pleasure.

Table 1 lists and defines defense mechanisms and provides an example of each. The first 10 listed (indicated by[a]) were the original 10 defense mechanisms written about by Sigmund Freud. Other defenses defined in the literature include distortion, withdrawal, acting out, blocking, externalization, inhibition, intellectualization, rationalization, sexualization, asceticism, humor, and suppression.

Contributed by Leslie Flint Armeniox, Center for Creative Counseling, Greensboro, NC

Additional Resources

Buckley, P. (1995). Ego defenses: A psychoanalytic perspective. In H. R. Conte & R. Plutchik (Eds.), *The Einstein series: Vol. 10. Ego defenses: Theory and measurement* (pp. 38–52). New York: Wiley.

Freud, A. (1966). *The writings of Anna Freud.* New York: International Universities Press.

Trimboli, F., & Farr, K. L. (2000). A psychodynamic guide for essential treatment planning. *Psychoanalytic Psychology, 17,* 336–359.

Table 1. Defense Mechanisms

Defense Mechanism	Definition	Example
Repression[a]	Expelling and withholding an idea from conscious awareness, often accompanied by highly symbolic behavior.	She repressed her memories of early physical abuse for nearly 20 years and believed she had a normal childhood.
Sublimation[a]	Channeling instincts or impulses by changing their aim or object from a socially inappropriate one to one that is socially valued	Aggressive instincts are frequently channeled or sublimated through competitive sports.
Reaction formation[a]	Managing unacceptable impulses by permitting expression of the impulse in antithetical form	Although he secretly loathed his sister and wanted to kill her, to all outward appearances he expressed love and devotion to her and even took her into his home to care for her when she was injured in an accident.
Undoing[a]	Making efforts to extricate oneself from uncomfortable thoughts, actions, events, or consequences through ritualistic, placative, or magical means and/or efforts to undo the behaviors and suspected motives, actions, and thoughts of others through ritualistic, placative, or magical means	When she became anxious, she would eat large quantities of food and then ritualistically purge, even after she became aware that the behavior was unhealthy. Binging and purging was an almost magical solution to her discomfort.
Isolation[a]	Separating of affect from content, resulting in repression or displacement	When surgeons operate, they isolate their affect so that it does not affect their performance.
Projection[a]	Having frank delusions about external reality, usually persecutory, which include both perception of one's feelings toward another and subsequent action on that perception; can include attributing one's own unacknowledged feelings to others, severe prejudice, hypervigilance to external danger, and injustice collecting	Members of White supremacist hate groups believe that they are protecting themselves and others from the hate, violence, and wrong-doings of target minority groups. One might say they have projected their own feelings onto members of minority groups in order to justify their behavior.

(Continued on next page)

Table 1. Defense Mechanisms *(Continued)*

Defense Mechanism	Definition	Example
Introjection (or identification)[a]	Internalizing the characteristics of a loved object in order to feel closer to that object, thus reducing anxiety; also internalizing the aggressive characteristics of a feared object, thereby putting the aggression under one's own control	When the boy's parents separated and his father moved to an apartment, the boy began to carry his books in a briefcase and wear a tie to school in an effort to feel closer to his father and reduce his anxiety.
Regression[a]	Returning to a previous stage of development or functioning to avoid anxieties or hostilities involved in later stages, often the result of disequilibrium at a later phase of development	When the 5-year-old girl's mother became pregnant with her second child, the girl regressed and began sucking her thumb, refused to eat unless fed from a bottle, and asked to sleep with her parents in their bed.
Turning against the self[a]	Directing negative feelings of judgments toward the self rather than others	The girl's cutting behavior was a manifestation of her depression and negative thoughts toward herself.
Reversal[a]	Reversing an instinct into its opposite	The young man became celibate and pursued the priesthood rather than address his unconscious feelings of sexual attraction toward children.
Denial	Lacking acknowledgment of external reality (what one sees or hears); related more to perception of external reality than internal reality	The woman was in denial about her brother's sexual abuse of her daughters, even though her oldest daughter reported the abuse.
Identification with the aggressor	Incorporating within the self the mental image of a source of frustration from the outside world; a combination of identification and introjection	The boys joined the local gang rather than continue to be bullied by the gang members.
Altruism	Vicarious but constructive and instinctually gratifying service to others; distinguished from altruistic surrender	The woman created a life that revolved around her volunteer work with refugees and said she was never happier than when she was actively helping others.
Projective identification	Splitting off and projecting parts of the self and internal objects onto an external object, which then becomes possessed by, controlled, and identified with the projected parts differs from projection in that the individual feels some identification with the projection	The client put her therapist on a pedestal and described her as a wise and loving Earth mother who would always put others before herself. The client aspired to be like this and believed that by participating in counseling, she would become more like her counselor.
Devaluation (external)	Having the tendency to depreciate, tarnish, and discount the importance of one's outer and inner objects (minor image-distorting) to regulate self-esteem and mood	The man frequently criticized the behaviors of others behind their backs and felt better about himself in comparison.
Devaluation (internal)	Reducing in worth some aspect of the self; overly critical of self; may include devaluation of groups to which the person belongs	She was constantly thinking self-critical and demeaning thoughts related to her weight, academic performance, and social skills. She was overheard saying, "It can't be a cool group if they allow me to be a member."
Splitting	Involving a division of internal and external into (a) parts, as distinct from wholes, and (b) good and bad part or objects; may occur regarding the self or object	The young man reported that the healthy part of him wanted to quit using cocaine, but the wild "bad" part of him needed the drug to have fun.
Omnipotence	Attributing greater or excessive importance to one's self to regulate self-esteem and mood	The man described himself as "the father of his profession" and gave no credit to others' contributions.
Primitive denial	Rejecting an aspect of external reality or the blocking of awareness of an internal reality	The alcoholic repeatedly denied that he struggled with alcoholism and declared that he had always been in control of his drinking, even though he had liver damage from his alcohol use and had been arrested three times for driving under the influence of alcohol.
Primitive idealization	Consciously or unconsciously overestimating an aspect of another person	She believed her father was the perfect man and thus was shocked when she discovered he had had multiple extramarital affairs.
Self-assertion	Having the ability to express feelings and set boundaries in a socially appropriate manner for the purposes of self-protection, advancement, or intimacy	After leaving her abusive marriage, the client's goal was to learn how to assert herself so that she could have healthy relationships and not become a victim again.
Self-observation (also called observing ego)	Having the ability to be self-aware, acknowledge behavior, and act upon this awareness in a socially appropriate way, preferably for the benefit of self and others	By participating in a support group, the client was able to become more observant of his behavior with others, reflect upon it, and try new behaviors that were effective and helpful.
Substitution	Attempting to rechannel positive affect when the original object of the affect is unavailable, unobtainable, or inappropriate or to rechannel negative affect when the individual has imposed sufficient organization on the situation to discharge the affect in a substitute, socially appropriate, releasing, or gratifying manner	While the couple had many reasons to feel angry, they intentionally rechanneled their anger through martial arts.
Incorporation (physical)	Assimilating something from the environment in order to reduce discomfort through nurturance	A half gallon of Rocky Road ice cream was her usual antidote for a broken heart.
Incorporation (indirect)	Drawing comfort or relief from the words, actions, or presence of others	When he became anxious, he would visit his family because they were always ready with words of support to boost his self-esteem and mood.
Expulsion (physical)	Involving simple, unplanned expressions of emotion or tension, physical outbursts or destruction of an object, or implied threat to attack an object	When employees openly disagreed, the company president had temper tantrums that consisted of throwing objects and yelling at others.
Expulsion (verbal)	Verbally expressing/releasing an affect or a verbal attack on an object; largely impulsive behavior that does not reflect conscious planning or logical argumentation	His verbal expulsion became so severe when he was driving that others diagnosed his "road rage" and refused to ride with him.
Dissociation	Temporary and drastic modifying of character or sense of personal identity to avoid distress or trauma in order to distance from reality and make it appear unreal	When the counselor asked about history of sexual abuse, the client dissociated to the extent that she lost time and was unable to focus on the session or participate in a conversation.

(Continued on next page)

Table 1. Defense Mechanisms *(Continued)*

Defense Mechanism	Definition	Example
Displacement	A subconscious redirecting of affect from an object perceived to be dangerous or unacceptable to an object felt to be acceptable; can refer to displacement of aggressive and sexual impulses	The man was upset about being fired from his job and displaced his anger by slapping his wife.
Fixation	Having an intense psychological association with a past event or series of events that trigger certain feelings or behaviors in a person when confronted with similar events or series of events	Due to her early dependency and attachment issues, she hoarded food and ate secretly whenever she was placed in a new foster home.
Compensation	Involving a person consciously or unconsciously covering up weaknesses, feelings of inadequacy, frustrations, desires, or incompetence in one life area by gratification or drive toward excellence in another area	As mid-life approached, he realized he had not accomplished his career goals and compensated by driving a Porsche and spending money on lavish meals for his friends.

[a]Indicates 1 of original 10 defense mechanisms described by Sigmund Freud.

Deficit Model

The **deficit model,** often referred to as the **cultural deficit model,** is based on the belief that environmental factors rather than biological factors influence behavior. These environmental factors ordinarily refer to cultural attributes related to race, ethnicity, and social class; accordingly, it was assumed that a deprived cultural background had an impact on ability and performance. The deficit model was used to explain behavior and often to segregate people into groups. In recent decades, the deficit model has been used to segregate children in school by ability and to explain the reasons some groups of children do not perform as well as their peers.

In education, the deficit model focuses on the child having deficits that prevent him or her from performing well in school. These deficits might include a lack of cognitive and linguistic abilities or a lack of intrinsic motivation to learn, often attributed to the child's race, ethnicity, or economic status. Students who are members of minority groups or whose background is considered low income are often viewed as having more learning deficits than do other children.

Even though the deficit model is not considered an appropriate educational model and alternatives such as the cultural difference model and the bicultural model were proposed, many federal programs, including project Head Start, Reading Recovery, and No Child Left Behind, are based on the deficit model. These programs are based on the assumption that there are children who are so deprived that the only way to mediate their deficits is through educational intervention.

In addition to educational practice, the deficit model is used in other areas, such as counseling. It is used to label as defiant behaviors that are not consistent with those of the dominant culture. The deficit model is not an appropriate response to differences that exist among groups of people. A more appropriate response is to recognize that all cultural groups have beliefs, attitudes, and behaviors that are appropriate for the group. These cultural norms are a product of each group's socialization process. For professional counselors working with children and adults who are culturally different, the deficit model is not an appropriate tool; rather, professional counselors should work to understand the culture of each client and develop a protocol based on an understanding of the cultural group. An alternative to the cultural deficit model for counselors is a multicultural approach. There are several variations to the multicultural approach. In practice, some counselors may consider a **strength-based model** (Smith, 2006), a **cultural-specific model** (Sue, 1990), or other approaches that focus on an understanding of the needs of culturally diverse populations.

Contributed by Margaret King,
Ohio University, Athens, OH

References

Smith, E. (2006). The strength-based counseling model. *The Counseling Psychologist, 34,* 13–79.

Sue, D. W. (1990). Cultural-specific strategies in counseling: A conceptual framework. *Professional Psychology: Research and Practice, 21,* 424–433.

Additional Resources

Goodman, Y. (1969). Culturally deprived child: A study in stereotyping. *Equity and Excellence in Education, 7*(4), 58–63.

Persell, C. H. (1981). Genetic and cultural deficit theories: Two sides of the same racist coin. *Journal of Black Studies, 12,* 19–37.

Riessman, F. (1962). *The culturally deprived child.* New York: HarperCollins.

Valencia, R. (Ed.). (1997). *The evolution of deficit thinking: Educational thought and practice.* Washington, DC: Falmer Press.

Degrees of Freedom

The term **degrees of freedom (symbol *df*)** refers to the estimation of the independence of a set of scores or the number of scores that may vary in a statistical calculation. Degrees of freedom are governed by the number of observations (*n*) in a data set and cannot exceed that number of observations. For instance, when the mean of a set of numbers is calculated, 1 degree of freedom is lost for that group of scores. In the group of scores, 4, 6, 8, 10, 12, the mean of the distribution is 8. For the mean to remain the same, only four of the scores can vary, so the degrees of freedom are 4 for this set of scores. Calculating the mean limits the number of scores that can vary within the distribution of scores, such that $n - 1$, or 4 degrees of freedom, results after estimation of the mean. Degrees of freedom are lost for each estimate of the parameters of the distribution.

Developing a variance estimate using the analysis of variance or F ratio results in the loss of 1 degree of freedom for each computation of the variance. The degrees of freedom for both numerator and denominator are written $df = n - 1$. Computation of the analysis of variance requires variance estimates of the between-groups variance and the within-groups estimate of variance. For instance, if the researcher was attempting to determine differences between three groups with 5 participants assigned to each group, the degrees of freedom for the between-groups estimate would be 2 ($df = 3 - 1$), whereas the within-groups estimate would be 12 ($df = 15 - 3$), or the total number of participants minus the total number of groups. Correctly calculating the degrees of freedom in statistical analysis is critical to appropriate estimates of the statistic.

Contributed by Katherine Dooley,
Mississippi State University,
Starkville, MS

Additional Resources

Hinkle, D. E., Wiersma, W., & Jurs, S. G. (1998). *Applied statistics for the behavioral sciences* (5th ed.). Boston: Houghton Mifflin.

Howell, D. C. (2007). *Statistical methods for psychology* (5th ed.). Pacific Grove, CA: Duxbury/Thompson Learning.

Pagano, R. R. (2007). *Understanding statistics in the behavioral sciences* (8th ed.). Belmont, CA: Wadsworth/Thomson Learning.

Delirium

Delirium is an acute disturbance of a person's global cognitive functioning. This state of mental confusion is usually characterized by distractibility, disorientation, disordered thinking, memory deficits, defective perception, agitation, emotional lability, and changes in the sleep–wake cycle. To determine the presence of the disorder, both the *Diagnostic and Statistical Manual of Mental Disorders* (4th ed., text rev.; American Psychiatric Association [APA], 2000) and the *International Statistical Classification of Diseases and Related Health Problems* (10th ed.; World Health Organization, 2007) require the following two elements: determination of the presence of delirium and identification of its underlying cause, if possible. The following should be present to diagnose delirium: (a) a disturbance of consciousness such as a cloudy awareness, accompanied with deficits of attention; (b) a change in cognition such as a memory or language problem not caused by dementia; and (c) acute onset with daily fluctuations. Delirium usually develops abruptly

or within hours or days; presents a fluctuating course, with symptoms changing in intensity over any 24-hour period and worsening at night; and exhibits a transient nature, with most cases resolving within days or weeks. In addition, the degree of severity ranges from mild to very severe.

Delirium can be classified on the basis of the level of movement or muscular activity associated with mental processes (psychomotor activity). **Hyperactive delirium,** which accounts for approximately 25% of the cases, is characterized by increased psychomotor activity, strong agitation, and delusions. **Hypoactive delirium** (approximately 25% of cases) is characterized by decreased psychomotor activity and lethargy. **Mixed delirium** (approximately 35% of cases) presents features of both. Psychomotor activity is normal in approximately 15% of the cases (APA, 2000).

The prevalence of delirium in the general population is about 0.4%, but, overall, delirium is more frequent in older populations and in populations of people with preexisting cognitive impairment and certain medical or surgical problems. Rates vary according to the population assessed, setting of the study, and method of identification used. Older adults (65 years or older) present prevalence rates of 10% to 40% during the course of a hospitalization, whereas patients with AIDS and cancer present prevalence rates of 17% to 40% and 25% to 85%, respectively (APA, 2000).

Delirium can have various causes, such as fever, exhaustion, lack of essential metabolic nutrients, brain trauma, neurological disorder, drug intoxication or withdrawal, or combinations of these. Treatment of delirium includes treating the underlying disorder, removing contributing factors, applying behavioral techniques, managing possible complications, and supporting the patient and family. The disorder is frequently misdiagnosed, and failure to provide appropriate treatment may lead to life-threatening and costly complications and long-term loss of function. For this reason, early recognition of delirium and implementation of treatment for its underlying cause(s) are essential.

Treatment outcome varies. Delirium may be reversible with treatment of the underlying cause(s). In most cases, the disorder only lasts about 1 week, but it may take several weeks for cognitive function to return to normal levels. Full recovery is common, although in some cases the complications can be very negative, with the person losing ability to function or engage in self-care; exhibiting diminished capacity to interact with others; having strong side effects of the medication used to treat the disorder; and, infrequently, progressing into stupor or coma. For this reason, it is essential to contact a health care provider when a rapid change of mental status is observed in a person.

Related disorders include dementia (i.e., a progressive decline in cognitive and intellectual functions that involves deficits in memory, behavior, learning, and communication; see Dementia) and delirium tremens (i.e., a severe form of alcohol withdrawal that involves sudden and severe neurological, cognitive, and emotional changes).

Contributed by Carlos P. Zalaquett,
University of South Florida, Tampa, FL

References

American Psychiatric Association. (2000). *Diagnostic and statistical manual of mental disorders* (4th ed., text rev.). Washington, DC: Author.

World Health Organization. (2007). *International statistical classification of diseases and related health problems* (10th rev.). Retrieved September 18, 2007, from http://www.who.int/classifications/apps/icd/icd10online/

Additional Resource

American Psychiatric Association. (1999). *Practice guidelines for the treatment of patients with delirium*. Washington, DC: Author.

Dementia

Dementia is a cognitive mental disorder that has multiple symptoms, the most common of which is memory impairment. Other symptoms may include language deficiencies, difficulty planning/organizing, inability to recognize familiar objects, and reduced ability to carry out physical activities in spite of intact physical functioning. These symptoms interfere with an individual's everyday performance and represent a significant decline in the level of normal functioning.

There are several types of dementia, including dementia of the Alzheimer's type, vascular dementia, and dementia due to other causes. The causes of dementia include general medical conditions (e.g., head trauma, Parkinson's disease), the effects of substances (e.g., drugs), or multiple factors (e.g., chronic drug abuse and head trauma or HIV disease). Some types of dementia progress slowly (e.g., Alzheimer's), whereas the onset of others is more sudden (e.g., head trauma). The incidence of dementia varies depending on age, region of the country, and type of cognitive impairment. Research indicates that the incidence of dementia, especially dementia of the Alzheimer's type and vascular dementia, generally increases with age. It has been estimated that more than 5 million people in the United States have Alzheimer's disease and that it is the seventh leading cause of death in the United States (American Psychiatric Association, 2000). The specific criteria that mental health professionals normally evaluate include cognitive changes (e.g., recent memory, understanding written and oral communication, reasoning ability), personality changes (e.g., withdrawal, inappropriate friendliness, depression, anxiety, suspiciousness, insomnia), problem behaviors (e.g., wandering off, agitation, restlessness), and changes in daily functioning (e.g., getting lost, difficulty handling money, trouble shopping, difficulty driving).

The assessment and diagnosis of dementia may involve a team of mental health and medical professionals. For example, counselors may provide a general functioning screening through intake interviews, client history taking, and administering various questionnaires. Psychologists and psychiatrists may provide an assessment of psychological functioning, whereas medical personnel (e.g., psychiatrists, neurologists) usually arrive at a formal diagnosis. Assessment of cognitive and behavioral functioning may include such techniques as the standardized mini-mental status examination, Clock Drawing Assessment, Time and Change Test, Functional Activities Questionnaire, Blessed Information Memory Concentration Test, Blessed Orientation Memory Concentration Test, and the Wechsler Adult Intelligence Scale.

Treatment for dementia is related to the type involved. For example, treatment for dementia of the Alzheimer's type might include medication, counseling, and psychoeducation, as well as family counseling. Support for caretakers is especially important and is usually addressed as part of a comprehensive family counseling program.

Contributed by Thomas H. Hohenshil,
Virginia Tech, Blacksburg, VA

Reference

American Psychiatric Association. (2000). *Diagnostic and statistical manual of mental disorders* (4th ed., text rev.). Washington, DC: Author.

Additional Resource

Alzheimer's Association Web site: http://www. alz.org/

Descriptive Research

Descriptive research is a commonly used research method in the counseling profession. Descriptive methods allow the researcher to describe the phenomenon of interest, such as trends, opinions, preferences, and relationships between variables. It can also provide information about group differences. Descriptive studies are appropriate when the goal of the research is to describe inherent characteristics (e.g., ethnicity, socioeconomic status, disability), characteristics that should not be manipulated because of ethical reasons (e.g., drug abuse, dangerous behavior), or characteristics that cannot be manipulated for practical reasons (e.g., participation in counseling, school placement). Descriptive methods include such methods as survey research, causal comparative research, correlational research, historical research, case study research, field study research, and exploratory research.

Survey research is widely used in the counseling profession and can yield valuable information about participants' thoughts, characteristics, perceptions, and attitudes regarding various phenomena. It is classified as both a method of descriptive research as well as a data collection method that can be used in other research designs (see Survey Research in Counseling). In addition, survey research allows the researcher to collect data from a larger sample than would be possible using experimental research designs, potentially increasing generalizability of the research findings. For example, professional school counselors could administer an electronic survey nationally to high school students to investigate the prevalence and effects of cyberbullying. The researchers could ask the following questions: How widespread is cyberbullying? Who is doing it and to whom? What forms does it take? How are students affected by it? Researchers have multiple data collection options with this type of research; surveys can be mailed and conducted via telephone or e-mail or in person. The researcher can also opt to use a combination of a few data collection strategies to enhance response rates and gain deeper understanding. Survey research can be conducted longitudinally, studying one set of participants over time, or by a cross-sectional approach, in which data are collected from different groups at the same time. Although survey research is relatively inexpensive and easy to conduct, it does have limitations. The primary limitation associated with survey research is that the accuracy of the results is limited largely by the honesty of the respondents. Low response rates can also be a concern; for instance, if a survey has a response rate of 60% (which is considered acceptable), the results only represent the views of the respondents and not necessarily the remaining 40% of the potential sample. There are circumstances when researchers seek not only to describe the status quo of the phenomena under investigation but to also make comparisons between groups.

Causal comparative studies allow the researcher to make group comparisons on one or more variables of interest. For example, a researcher may be interested in examining the willingness to participate in psychotherapy groups among African American students and Asian American students. These types of studies can aid in understanding group differences but do not afford the researcher the ability to make inferences about causation. Because causal comparative research compares characteristics of preexisting groups, the researcher is faced with limited control. The researcher cannot control the independent variable or extraneous or confounding variables, which significantly limits the internal research validity of the study. Making group comparisons is essential to comprehending many of the issues counselors seek to understand, as is the examination of relationships through the use of correlational studies. Caution, however, should be used when interpreting group differences research; counseling researchers are encouraged to use proxy variables (i.e., a variable that theoretically represents another variable).

Although both causal comparative and correlational methods are used to study inherent characteristics of participants, there is a key difference between the two. Causal comparative studies focus on examining group comparisons, and although correlational studies can be used to make comparisons, their main focus is to study the magnitude of the relationship between two variables. **Correlational studies** can be used to describe the relationship between two variables, such as the relationship between grade point average and number of hours spent studying for exams or the relationship between feelings of self-efficacy and participation in group counseling. A wide range of correlational coefficients is reported in the professional counseling literature, and the consumer should be knowledgeable about the guidelines for interpreting the strength of the relationship. A correlation of 1.0 describes a perfect relationship, whereas a correlation of 0 indicates that there is no relationship between the variables of interest. Other coefficients are heavily tied to sample size, significance level, and so on, and, therefore, the strength of the correlation cannot easily be determined by looking only at the coefficient. Correlations can be positive or negative,

which allows the researcher to describe the direction of the relationship. A correlation is positive when both factors are going in the same direction; they both go up, or they both go down, such as increased age in school children and increased competence in mathematical computation. A correlation is negative when the variables are inversely related; when one factor goes up, the other goes down, such as increased participation in conflict resolution programs among middle school students and decrease in the number of discipline referrals. It is important for the consumer to keep in mind that a strong relationship between two variables (participation in pre–job placement career counseling and high level of job satisfaction) does not mean that one factor causes the change in the other. The aforementioned research methods are all means to describe the current state of affairs by using a systematic approach to data collection and interpretation. These methods are concerned with collecting data related to present events in order to describe trends, opinions, preferences, and relationships between variables and group differences. There are times when circumstances dictate that the researcher examine past events in order to understand the variables under investigation.

Historical research involves the observation and interpretation of past events. Historical research can be either qualitative or quantitative or a combination of both methods. This type of research can be used to understand a past event, a person, an institution, or a profession (e.g., counseling) more completely. The aim of historical research is to understand the past in relation to the present or the present in relation to the past. Although this type of inquiry can enhance understanding, it is limited in large degree because researchers are not able to generalize present findings on the basis of past events. The observation that occurs in historical research happens after the fact; therefore, many of the events were unplanned and result in many uncontrolled factors. Because of this lack of control, the researcher must make inferences about what occurred as well as the reasons why it occurred. Frequently, historical researchers must draw their conclusions on the basis of sources such as documents and reported observations from others. When researchers are able to gain access to their sources and are primarily concerned with direct observations of and conversations with their participants, they frequently engage in case study and field study research.

Case study research falls under the qualitative paradigm, and consumers of research in the counseling profession are familiar with it. Case studies are frequently conducted to understand a single participant, group, program, event, or setting more fully. Data are collected through interviews, observations, and document analysis. Case studies provide the reader with rich narratives and thick descriptions of the participants' experiences. The credibility of these studies is enhanced by prolonged engagement with the participants and verbatim accounts of their experiences. Case studies are conducted in the natural setting and are largely concerned with capturing the context that surrounds the entity of interest. The perspectives of the participants define what is real in case study research and interpretations are made inductively;

that is, conclusions are drawn on the basis of specific events and participant descriptions.

Field study research is another type of descriptive research that is qualitative in nature. Field study research also relies heavily on interviews, observations, and document analysis. This research method allows the researcher to be immersed in the natural setting where the phenomena under investigation are occurring. This unique approach allows the researcher to capture idiosyncrasies and unique elements that may be missed if the study was conducted under more controlled conditions. Field study requires the researcher to take detailed field notes and account for all elements of their experiences. Consumers of field research can experience phenomena through all five senses as a result of the extensive description provided by the researcher. Field study research can yield valuable information to consumers about various counseling milieus, programs, settings, and associated systems.

Exploratory research combines both qualitative and quantitative research methods to explore phenomena when existing measures are not applicable or there is no extant theory related to the phenomena. Exploratory designs typically begin with the gathering of qualitative data, such as interviews and observations. The results from the qualitative analysis are used to help determine the nature of data collection for the quantitative phase. For example, a researcher, studying the effects of conjugal loss on participants, would meet with and interview a few participants from the initial sample in order to identify themes, ideas, and salient beliefs. The researcher would then construct a quantitative survey based on the responses of these participants, and the survey would be administered to the larger sample. This type of survey construction helps to ensure that the items on the survey are grounded in the experiences of the participants and not in the researchers' theoretical assumptions about the phenomena.

Contributed by Laurae Wartinger,
Sage Graduate School, Troy, NY

Additional Resources

Best, J. W., & Kahn, J. V. (2003). *Research in education* (10th ed.). Boston: Allyn & Bacon.

McMillan, J. H. (2004). *Educational research: Fundamentals for the consumer* (4th ed.). Boston: Pearson.

■ Descriptive Statistics

Descriptive statistics is a branch of inductive logic and mathematics used by counseling researchers to organize and summarize data sets in numerical and graphical form. Descriptive statistics is usually contrasted with inferential statistics. As mathematical tools, **inferential statistics** help researchers make generalizations and decisions regarding populations, whereas descriptive statistics illustrate the various properties of data samples in terms of centralizing tendencies and measures of variability.

In order to answer empirical questions, counseling researchers collect samples of data, usually for statistical analysis. In their natural state, data sets are unorganized and amorphous. As a means to understand and display coded observations, researchers use graphs and tables. One of the best ways to organize a data set is to tabulate the scores in a frequency distribution.

A **frequency distribution** simply counts the number of observations for any variable under consideration and reports the number of times that the observation occurred in the data set. Frequency distributions can reveal representative scores and show the typical data values. In addition, frequency distributions can give some indication of the dispersion of scores. For example, Table 1 displays a frequency distribution for the variable of age. Each column expresses something about the variable. The column Participant's Age contains all the ages and the frequency (f) column displays how many times a particular age occurred in the sample. According to Table 1, the most frequently occurring age for the data set was 21, which occurred 13 times. The last three columns reveal frequency percentages for each age. As an example, 21-year-olds accounted for 22% of all of the ages in the data set.

Another use of frequency distributions has to do with dispersion of scores. Inspection of Table 1 reveals that the most frequently reported ages are the younger ages (ages 20, 21, and 22 years). There are 19 different ages reported in the table. Looking at the cumulative percentage column, it can be seen that by 22 years of age, 61% of the ages, or over half, have been tabulated. Over half of the ages reported are below age 24 years, suggesting positive skew (see Skewness).

In addition to the tabulations of scores, data sets can be described using graphical forms. One such graphical form is the frequency polygon (see Figure 1). A **frequency polygon** displays data along two axes. The horizontal axis usually lists the values of the variable under consideration, and the vertical axis displays the frequency count for that value. Taller peaks indicate greater frequency, whereas shorter peaks indicate lesser frequency. The frequency polygon in Figure 1 is based on the frequency distribution for age. As seen in the frequency distribution, the majority of age values occur at the younger end of the age range (19–22 years old).

Table 1. Frequency Distribution for the Variable Age

Participant's Age (in Years)	f	%	Valid %	Cumulative %
19	2	3.4	3.4	3.4
20	10	16.9	16.9	20.3
21	13	22.0	22.0	42.4
22	11	18.6	18.6	61.0
24	1	1.7	1.7	62.7
25	1	1.7	1.7	64.4
29	3	5.1	5.1	69.5
31	3	5.1	5.1	74.6
33	1	1.7	1.7	76.3
34	1	1.7	1.7	78.0
38	2	3.4	3.4	81.4
40	1	1.7	1.7	83.1
41	1	1.7	1.7	84.7
42	4	6.8	6.8	91.5
43	1	1.7	1.7	93.2
45	1	1.7	1.7	94.9
47	1	1.7	1.7	96.6
50	1	1.7	1.7	98.3
59	1	1.7	1.7	100.0

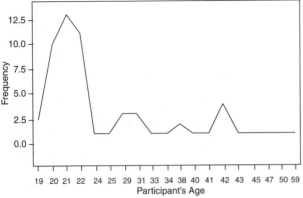

Figure 1. Frequency Polygon for the Variable Age

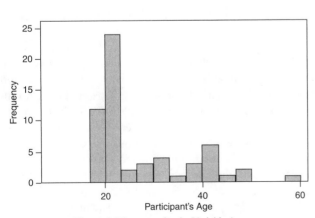

Figure 2. Histogram for the Variable Age

Another method for depicting data is to use graphical representations of data sets. One such graph is called a **histogram**. Used with quantitative and continuous variables, histograms illustrate the grouping tendencies and spread of scores for a data set. Histograms are made up of connecting bars that show the frequency of scores on some measured variable. The taller the bars, the more frequent the score in a data set. Figure 2 shows a histogram for the variable age used previously in the frequency distribution example. On the horizontal axis, ages are listed, and on the vertical axis, the frequency count is listed.

Comparable to a histogram is the more commonly known bar graph. **Bar graphs** are similar to histograms, but in a bar graph there are spaces between the columns or bars. The spaces separating the bars denote a qualitative difference between the levels of the variable. Qualitative variables differ in kind, whereas quantitative variables differ in amount. Again, the taller the bar, the more frequent that element is present in the data set. The bar graph in Figure 3 shows the frequency between women and men in a data set.

As stated earlier, descriptive statistics include numerical and graphical depictions of data sets. Numerically, there are several indices used in describing data sets. The most well-known of these are the measures of central tendency and the measures of variability. **Measures of central tendency** help describe the ways in which data sets cluster around the mid-point. Measures of central tendency include mean, median, and mode (see Central Tendency). The **mode** is the most frequently occurring or typical score in a data set, whereas the median is the geographic center of a data set. The **median** represents the location in a data set, where half the scores are above and half the scores are below. The **mean** is the arithmetic average and represents the balance point of a data set.

Measures of variability give counseling researchers a way of describing the dispersion of scores (see Variability). If the amount of dispersion around the mean is known, then it is possible to compare individual scores with the average. These indices describe data sets as being homogenous or heterogeneous. Measures of variability include range, variance, and standard deviation. The **range** is a gross estimate of variability and represents the arithmetic difference between the maximum and minimum score. The **variance** is the average squared distance from the mean in a data set and provides the counseling researcher an estimate of the spread of scores around the mean. The **standard deviation** is the square root of the variance and estimates the average distance from the mean.

In Table 2, it is possible to see the descriptive statistics for the variable of age. The most frequently reported age (mode) was 21. The median was slightly higher at 22. That means that half of the ages were below 22 and half the ages were above 22. The average age was a little over 27 years old. Because the mean is greater than the median, this suggests skewness or a nonnormal distribution. The range was 40 years, which suggests a large spread of ages. The variance was 95.66 "squared" years. Because it is not usual to talk about age in squared units, the standard deviation is more informative here. The standard deviation was almost 10 years (9.781 years), so the average distance from the mean in

Figure 3. Bar Graph for the Variable Sex

Table 2. Descriptive Statistics for Age

Variable Age	Value
N	59
M	27.42
Median	22.00
Mode	21
SD	9.78
Variance	95.66
Range	40

this data set was almost a decade, which suggests a heterogeneous group when it comes to the variable age.

Contributed by David M. Carscaddon,
Gardner-Webb University,
Boiling Springs, NC

Additional Resources

Cohen, B. H. (2001). *Explaining psychological statistics* (2nd ed.). New York: Wiley.

SPSS Inc. *SPSS interactive graphics 16.0.*

■ Developmental Counseling

Developmental counseling, a wellness approach to counseling, is based on stages that individuals go through during normal human growth. Counseling from the developmental perspective is predicated on the belief that the problems individuals have are directly related to a developmental task in life. Developmental counseling studies the progressive psychological changes that occur in individuals as they age. Developmental counseling has as its focus the goal of facilitating the development of clients by helping them to be aware of the issues that drive their lives and learning how to control those issues.

Developmental counseling differs from other therapeutic approaches because its basic concepts are developmental and psychosocial rather than pathogenic and intrapsychic. Developmental counselors recognize that their clients are affected by physical, environmental, and cultural patterns that can move clients to a higher level or can confront clients with issues and personal crises that stall or limit their development.

As early as the 1950s, the developmental approach was central to the identity of counselors. Figures such as Erikson (see Ego Psychology: Erikson's Psychosocial Stage Theory), Kohlberg (see Moral Development), and Piaget (see Cognitive Developmental Theory) provided stage theories for conceptualizing development over the life span. The 1960s highlighted development over the life span as a central focus in counseling. Life-span development comprises chronological stages that individuals pass through as they age. Each stage brings with it a set of tasks or crises that must be accomplished or overcome in order for progression to occur. **Blocher** (1966), in his book *Developmental Counseling,* introduced a comprehensive developmental approach to counseling based on the principles of Erik Erikson's life stage theory. Erikson believed that human development is determined by interactions between the mind, body, and culture.

The developmental approach posits that the counseling process is influenced by successful navigation through life's crises and is organized around a set of ideas and principles regarding the relationship between human beings and their physical and social environments. Developmental counseling often includes components involving giving and receiving information and is closely tied to learning behaviors. Its impact is evident in school counseling, which is concerned with helping children to attain their age-appropriate goals related to education, career, and society.

Contextual developmental theories, popularized in the early 1980s by J. W. Fowler (see Spirituality in Counseling) and Carol Gilligan (see Moral Development), are complementary to stage theories because they emphasize the role of social and cultural influences in the lives of individuals over the life span. Contextual development points out that human beings are vulnerable to cultural factors that can lead to frustration and failure, ultimately limiting their development.

Developmental counseling is viewed as an eclectic approach in that it involves systems that deal with a wide range of human needs. It is comprehensive, goal oriented, growth producing, dynamic, and technique driven. Developmental counseling attempts to help the client achieve optimal psychological development by enhancing higher levels of functioning and overcoming crises in order to further growth.

The overarching objective of this type of counseling is to enhance personal and psychological development, with emphasis on prevention and education. Carl Rogers endorsed the developmental approach when he indicated that the purpose of most of the helping professions was to enhance the personal development and psychological growth of the client.

Contributed by Vivian J. McCollum,
Albany State University, Albany, GA

Reference

Blocher, D. H. (1966). *Developmental counseling.* New York: Ronald Press.

Additional Resource

Blocher, D. H. (2000). *Counseling: A developmental approach* (4th ed.). New York: Wiley.

■ Developmental Milestones

Developmental milestones are specific tasks or events that are used as markers to indicate movement in an individual's growth process. Development is measured by comparing the individual's skills to the established milestones of "normal" or expected growth in specific domains. Development milestones are indicated in several domains; these domains include physical, psychosocial, and cognitive development.

Physical Milestones

Measuring development in the **physical domain** focuses on physical ability and agility. A child can turn his or her head to a noise and ball a hand into a fist from the moment of birth. By 3 months of age, that same child can wring his or her own hands in frustration and repeat a series of body motions with enjoyment. Between 3 to 6 months of age, a child can roll over, grasp desired objects, and handle objects with curiosity. Crawling often occurs between the 6th and 12th months and walking between the 9th and 18th months. Complex motor skills that include writing, climbing stairs, and repeating sequences of body movements to complete a goal are developed by the age of 5 years. Middle childhood (6–12 years old) is marked by gains in complex physical movements such as skillful running, throwing, and riding a bicycle. Physical skill and prowess peak in early adulthood (20–40 years old) before development begins to slow, and by 40 years of age, clear physical skill degeneration is present. Decline in fertility and physical stamina is evident in middle adulthood (40–60 years old), proceeded by a clear decline in physical strength in late adulthood (over 60 years old). Milestones of physical development were created by **T. Berry Brazelton** and are updated periodically by the American Medical Association and the American Academy of Pediatricians.

Psychosocial Milestones

Development in the **psychosocial domain** focuses on relationships with others, emotional maturity, and ability to interact successfully with the environment. Seeking to feel soothed and calm when upset or hurt is instinctive, and infants universally seek to be soothed when they cry. The simple act of being soothed leads to the first attachment bonds. Between birth and 2 years of age, the primary attachment bond is with a caregiver or caregivers. Children ages 2 to 5 years increase their sphere of connection through preschool, play groups, or siblings. Around this same time, children show gender role awareness, preferred playmates, and racial awareness. Friendship and gender segregation occur between the ages of 6 to 12 years and facilitate gender identity. Interest in a sexual partner(s) and dating occurs in adolescence (12–18 years old). Working toward initiation into adulthood predominates in adolescence as individuals begin to assume adult responsibilities. Life choices, such as finding a mate, earning a living, and making a home, are the focus of early adulthood (20–40 years). Middle adulthood (40–60 years) may involve coping with the death of parents and the changing family. A shift in identity, social power, and psychological resilience comes with retirement and the potential loss of a partner and friends in late adulthood (over 60 years). Seminal theorists in this domain of development include Erik Erikson, Mary Ainsworth, Carol Gilligan, and John Bowlby.

Cognitive Milestones

Language development, problem solving, and creativity are the hallmarks of this domain of development. From birth to 2 years of age, a child begins to gain rudimentary language skills, including cooing, following a voice, smiling when the speaker sounds happy, and visually tracking the face of a speaking person. Spoken language appears around 2 years of age with simple one-word utterances; however, vocabulary rapidly grows to hundreds of words by the age of 5 years. Problem solving, along with reading and writing skills, accelerates between 6 to 12 years of age as language skills become more refined. Abstract thinking and the development of adult similar interests, including politics, philosophy, world and local events, and money issues, begin to take shape as the child moves into adolescence (12–18 years). The development of postformal operational thought occurs between 20 to 40 years of age and marks the movement toward the achievement of wisdom attained typically after 60 years of age. Seminal theorists in this area of cognitive

development include Noam Chomsky, Jean Piaget, William Perry, Arthur Chickering, and Lawrence Kohlberg.

This is not an exhaustive list of developmental milestones but rather a representation of the types of demonstrated behaviors or skills that define each domain across the life span. These milestones are indicators of the various stages of development and, barring any medical illness, trauma, or environmental factors that may accelerate or change the process, represent typical development. Individuals develop at different rates in different domains. A child may excel in verbal skills but lag behind in problem-solving ability. Typically, these children catch up to their cohort and show no long-term deficits. Areas of development overlap; cognitive growth is closely tied to psychosocial development, which is inextricably linked to physical growth. An enriched environment can accelerate skill development and allow milestones to appear earlier in the developmental process.

Delays in development may indicate that an individual simply has a slower growth process. Significant delays in achieving specific developmental milestones may indicate more serious underlying conditions. Physical development slows and eventually stops as the body begins degeneration; however, psychosocial and cognitive development do not degenerate or terminate as an individual ages unless a medical condition occurs (e.g., Alzheimer's).

Contributed by Mary-Jeanne Raleigh,
New England College, Henniker, NH

Additional Resources

Berk, L. (2006). *Child development* (7th ed.). Needham Heights, MA: Allyn & Bacon.

Seifert, K. L., Hoffnung, R. J., & Hoffnung, M. (2000). *Lifespan development* (2nd ed.). Boston: Houghton Mifflin.

■ Developmental Scores: Age-Equivalents and Grade-Equivalents

An understanding of **developmental scores** depends on an understanding of norms. **Norms** help in the transformation of assessment data, typically raw scores, into information that is meaningful to people who will use the results. When developmental scores are used, the result is a transformation of the assessment result by placing the score along a developmental continuum (i.e., ordinal scale) representing the test takers by age or by school grade. An **age-equivalent score** is reported in chronological years and months, and a **grade-equivalent score** is reported as grade and month in the grade. Thus, an age-equivalent score of 6-2 would indicate the raw score was the median (midpoint) score for members of the norm group who had a chronological age of 6 years and 2 months (74 months), whereas a grade-equivalent score of 6.2 would mean the raw score was the median for members of a norm group who had completed 2 months (i.e., .2) of the sixth grade. A grade-equivalent score is different from a grade norm score that would yield the percentile rank a given score would have in a distribution of scores from a norm group of students in the same grade. Developmental norms are only appropriate for assessment of characteristics that have a progression over time. Typically, they are used for assessment of children who are in early adolescence or younger, that is, students who are not yet in secondary school. Most often, educators and parents are the recipients of assessment results that have developmentally normed, age-, or grade-equivalent scores, and counselors should consider the limitations of such scores when presenting them.

Grade-equivalent scores are based on the instruction received by the members of the norm group and are subject to variation due to instructional scheduling, including summer vacation. A student may receive little or no formal instruction between Grade 4.9 and Grade 5.1, but without an understanding of the norming process, parents, teachers, or counselors might assume that a grade equivalent of 5-1 was 3 months more advanced than 4-9. More important, a grade-equivalent score does not indicate that students are ready for a higher grade if the score is above grade or that they are not qualified for their current placement if the score is below grade level. A student could achieve a grade-equivalent score that is above grade and not have mastered essential skills for the higher grade, and, likewise, a student could have a score below grade due to attitude and personality-based attention errors but could have actually mastered the essential skills. Finally, grade-equivalent scores are a placement of the score in the norm group and not an analysis of the skills. In other words, the grade-equivalent score simply tells the professional counselor where the child's score fell on the distribution of scores for children at the grade level. A fourth grader who has a grade-equivalent score of seventh grade in math is not necessarily ready for seventh-grade math. Furthermore, the norm group should be appropriate for the examinee. For example, if subject-matter grade norms are based on a different curriculum than the curriculum used in the counselee's school, the grade equivalence would not be meaningful. Similarly, age-equivalent scores for the mastery of subject matter could be distorted by the student's age when starting school.

Professional counselors typically deal with developmental norm scores that are age and grade equivalents of academic assessments. Assessment of change over time or development is an appealing and useful concept; however, if age- and grade-equivalent scores are used to assess change, the limitations of change scores of any type should be considered. Elementary school counselors might encounter age-equivalent scores based on physical development. Some cautions about age-equivalent scores are the wide range of physical attributes that present no cause for concern, the uneven rate of development of many physical characteristics, and the correlation between physical attributes. For example, a student's weight could result in an age-equivalent score above or below his or her chronological age but one that was considered normal (average range) for the student's height. Professional counselors would be most likely to encounter age-equivalent scores for physical characteristics if they were members of child study teams.

Developmental scores present challenges for people who are interested in dealing with assessment data using statistics based on an assumption of normal distributions and equal intervals represented by score units. Age- and grade-equivalent scores are considered ordinal (relative rank) scores and cannot properly be added, subtracted, or used to produce descriptive statistics such as mean. Even during the school year, each month does not represent equal units of instruction or educational development. For example, December is usually less that a full month of instruction due to holiday breaks. Likewise, children develop more in essential skills such as reading between Grade 2 and Grade 3 than between Grade 8 and Grade 9. Physical growth is notorious for occurring in "spurts," and some children reach their maximum physical growth at an earlier age than others. Thus, the knowledge and skills of the counselor are critical for the accurate and successful interpretation of age- and grade-equivalent scores.

Contributed by Robert H. Pate Jr.,
University of Virginia, Charlottesville, VA

Additional Resources

American Educational Research Association, American Psychological Association, & National Council on Measurement in Education. (1999). *Standards for educational and psychological testing.* Washington, DC: American Psychological Association.

Pearson Assessments. (2007). *Interpretation problems of age and grade equivalents.* Retrieved June 27, 2007, from http://ags.pearsonassessments.com/assessments/age_grade.asp

University of Minnesota, Office of Measurement Services. (2006). *Glossary of measurement terms.* Retrieved June 27, 2007, from http://oms.umn.edu/oms/index.php?select=mstp&mstp=testsandservices&testsandservices=glossary

■ *Diagnostic and Statistical Manual of Mental Disorders*

As its name implies, the ***Diagnostic and Statistical Manual of Mental Disorders*** (4th ed., text rev.; *DSM-IV-TR;* American Psychiatric Association [APA], 2000) is a reference manual that is used to classify and describe mental disorders. The first edition of the manual was published in 1952. Different categories of mental disorders are described in the *DSM-IV-TR,* and the specific **criteria** that must be present before a person is diagnosed with various disorders are addressed. The following considerations are addressed for each disorder: diagnostic features; recording procedures; associated features and disorders; specific culture, age, and gender features; prevalence, course, familial patterns; and differential diagnosis. The major groups of mental disorder diagnoses include disorders first diagnosed in infancy, childhood, or adolescence; delirium, dementia, and amnestic and other cognitive disorders; mental disorders due to a general medical condition; substance-related disorders; schizophrenia and other psychotic disorders; mood disorders; anxiety disorders; somatoform disorders; factitious disorders; dissociative disorders; sexual and gender identity disorders; eating disorders; sleep disorders; impulse-control disorders not elsewhere classified; adjustment disorders; personality disorders; and other conditions that may be a focus of clinical attention (i.e., V-codes). Health and mental health professionals use the *DSM,* and a *DSM*-based diagnosis is almost always required by third-party payers (e.g., insurance companies, Medicaid) to provide reimbursement of services to mental health care providers. The *DSM-IV-TR* is 943 pages and identifies approximately 300 mental disorders. In the *DSM-IV-TR,* the causes and treatment of mental disorders are not addressed.

The *DSM* uses a **multiaxial assessment system** that includes five axes, each of which relates to a unique domain that is intended to help mental health providers in conceptualizing clients, applying interventions and treatments, and predicting client outcomes. Following are the five axes:

- **Axis I—Clinical Disorders and Other Conditions.** All of the mental disorders or conditions are listed on this axis except personality disorders and mental retardation.
- **Axis II—Personality Disorders and Mental Retardation.** Personality disorders and mental retardation are listed on this axis; prominent, maladaptive personality features and defensive mechanisms may also be listed on Axis II.
- **Axis III—General Medical Conditions.** Current medical conditions that are potentially relevant in understanding or managing the client's mental disorder are listed on Axis III.
- **Axis IV—Psychosocial and Environmental Problems.** Psychosocial and environmental problems that may affect the diagnosis, treatment, and prognosis of the mental disorders (e.g., environmental events or deficiencies, life stresses, inadequate social supports and relations, economic, educational, or occupational problems) are listed on this axis.
- **Axis V—Global Assessment of Functioning.** This axis includes the provider's judgment of the individual's overall level of functioning; on the basis of the Global Assessment of Functioning Scale, the person is ascribed a number from 1 to 100.

The *DSM-IV-TR* addresses **culture-bound syndromes,** or syndromes that are only found in people in certain areas of the world. Most of the behaviors and experiences of the person are considered by others in the cultural context to be illnesses, and most have local names. An example of a culture-bound syndrome is *taijin kyofusho,* a culturally distinctive phobia seen in the Japanese culture. Symptoms of this syndrome include a fear that one's body and its functions displease, embarrass, or offend others in their odor, appearance, movements, or expressions.

Contributed by Victoria Kress,
Youngstown State University,
Youngstown, OH

Reference

American Psychiatric Association. (2000). *Diagnostic and statistical manual of mental disorders* (4th ed., text rev.). Washington, DC: Author.

Additional Resources

Morrison, J. (2006). *Diagnosis made easier: Principles and techniques for mental health clinicians.* New York: Guilford Press.

Zimmerman, M. (1994). *Interview guide for evaluating DSM-IV psychiatric disorders and the mental status examination.* East Greenwich, RI: Psych Products Press.

■ *Dictionary of Occupational Titles/O*NET*

The ***Dictionary of Occupational Titles (DOT)*** was created in 1939 by the U.S. Department of Labor to meet the need for a standardized list of occupational descriptions for use in job placement organizations. The first edition presented more than 17,000 job titles using a special coding system that designated jobs as skilled, semiskilled, or unskilled. Shortly after its creation, the public employment service system primarily used the *DOT* to match World War II veterans with their job skills.

The *DOT*'s second revision was published in 1949, its third in 1965, and its fourth in 1977. Since then, the only revisions have been in the form of supplements to the fourth edition. The *DOT* has been updated with new job categories that were added based on the changes in technology, skills, and workforce needs. The *DOT* was last updated in 1991 and has now been replaced by **O*NET (Occupational Information Network),** an online occupational information Web site. The O*NET Web site system serves as the principal source of occupational data in the United States, and the online database provides extensive information on characteristics of both workers and occupations. In the O*NET's online system are the *U.S. Dictionary of Occupational Titles,* the *Dictionary of Occupational Titles,* the *Directory of Occupational Titles,* and the *Occupational Job Outlook.*

The most recent edition of the *DOT* provides information on nearly 13,000 occupations (fewer than the number in the original 1939 version) and is meant to supply labor market information to employers and workers concerning the occupations for which the American workforce must be prepared and the competencies and job requirements needed to perform those jobs successfully. The *DOT* details the duties of each job and the training needed to successfully perform the role. Employers, job counselors, workforce development professionals, placement agencies, and training organizations use the *DOT* to structure jobs, create job descriptions, monitor labor market information, and develop training programs and compensation systems. The *DOT*'s content helps workers design their résumés to take into account certain competencies, skills, and educational requirements and can offer information that allows workers to determine what jobs are most suitable for them.

The *DOT* has now been replaced by O*NET, and because the *DOT* has undergone several major changes in content organization, the job categories and codes are quite different than they once were. These are now referred to as the O*NET Content Model. Currently, a person can search O*NET in a number of ways, with several features from which to choose. O*NET Descriptors allow a person to search in the categories of knowledge, skills, abilities, work activities, interests, and work values. Searching under the job families category, a person finds a list of occupational umbrellas, such as community and social services, management, and production. Searching under high growth industries, a person finds occupations such as aerospace, biotechnology, and homeland security. Finally, there is a search category for science, technology, engineering, and mathematics disciplines.

Once an occupation is selected from the list, the reader will find a very detailed description about that job. The following information is provided for each occupation: the tasks performed in the job; the tools and technologies needed or used in the job; the knowledge, skills, and abilities required; the work activities performed; the work context (e.g., hours worked, physical environment, contact with others); the job "zone" (describing how much preparation and training is needed to perform the job); interests (using John Holland's realistic, investigative, artistic, social, enterprising, and conventional model); work styles (such as analytical thinking and attention to detail); a list of related occupations; and national wages and employment trends.

Another search option is a skills search. A worker can complete an online checklist of personal skills, and O*NET will provide a list of the occupations best suited for the worker's skill set, along with links to each occupation.

The *DOT,* now O*NET, is a useful tool for professionals in the employment and counseling areas. Although the *DOT* was replaced by O*NET, copies of the 1991 *DOT* are still available for purchase from the U.S. Government Printing Office. A complete electronic copy of the 1991 *DOT* is available on the Internet. O*NET updates its database twice each year with the latest workforce information. For more information about *DOT,* visit O*NET online or the U.S. Department of Labor's *DOT* site.

Contributed by Shelly Prochaska Trent,
Society for Human Resource
Management, Louisville, KY

Other Resources

DOT (electronic version):http://www.occupationalinfo.org
O*NET Web site: http://www.onetcenter.org
U.S. Department of Labor *DOT* Web site: http://www.oalj.dol.gov/libdot.htm

▊ Disability

Disability is defined as a physical or mental impairment that substantially limits at least one of life's major activities (i.e., walking, seeing, hearing, speaking, breathing, learning, working, and taking care of oneself). According to the U.S. Census Bureau (2000), approximately 12.6% of working-age individuals (over 21 million people in the United States) reported having a disability. The highest prevalence was for physical disabilities (7.9%), followed by mental (4.4%), sensory (3.0%), and self-care (2.2%).

Society's attitudes and behaviors toward individuals with disabilities are often negative and discriminatory, and this attitude is often referred to as **ableism.** People with disabili-

ties often acknowledge that the most difficult barriers are the limiting attitudes of people who are uninformed about disability. It is not uncommon for others to underestimate a person's ability because of the disability. For example, a person with a physical disability may also be assumed to have cognitive limitations, an assumption that is not necessarily accurate. Attitudinal barriers are particularly troublesome for people with hidden or **invisible disabilities** that are not readily observable, such as learning or psychiatric disabilities. For instance, these individuals may even need to justify the existence of their disability because others may not recognize the disability or believe it is credible or real.

In the field of disability, language and terminology have evolved over the years. A recent shift from using the term *disabled person* to *person with a disability,* called **people-first language,** acknowledges the individuality of people while avoiding objectification. The term *handicapped* has fallen into disuse and, in fact, is no longer used in federal legislation.

The U.S. Rehabilitation Act of 1973, the 1990 Americans With Disabilities Act, and the Individuals With Disabilities Educational ActIDEA, and related case law, provide legal guidance regarding the treatment of persons with disabilities. These laws center on preventing discrimination and providing equitable access to education, employment, and public facilities. For example, a person with a disability who wants to attend college cannot be discriminated against during the admission process and must be provided with reasonable accommodations such as extended time or assistance with note taking in order to provide equal access. Public facilities need to be accessible to individuals with disabilities, and accommodations such as providing sign language interpreters must be made.

A person with a disability must meet specific criteria in order to receive the protection of disability law. Generally, the guidelines include having a documented physical or mental disability that substantially limits one or more of the major life activities, a history of disability, and/or the perception that a person has a disability. There are an estimated 54 million people of all ages in the United States who meet these criteria, with learning disabilities being the most prevalent. There are also many people who have conditions and issues that do not rise to the level of a disability under the law. For example, not all individuals who have a psychiatric diagnosis (e.g., major depressive disorder, bipolar disorder) are considered to be disabled. A person diagnosed with bipolar disorder or attention-deficit/hyperactivity disorder who is being effectively treated with medication may not have active symptoms that substantially limit one or more of life's major activities. In this situation, the person still has a disorder, but the treatment with medication serves as a mitigating factor. A person with a vision loss that is corrected with glasses would also not qualify as having a disability. The disability must have a significant functional impact with considerable limitations to be regarded as a disability under the law.

Counseling interventions will clearly vary depending on the nature and duration of the disability. Acceptance of the disability can also vary greatly, which will affect the counseling process. If the person was born with a disability, such as blindness, the person may have come to terms with the disability by adulthood, whereas someone who becomes blind later in life may significantly struggle with acceptance. Generally speaking, counseling interventions are best guided by a framework that includes an understanding of disabilities, a familiarity with U.S. legal and ethical obligations, and a foundation of respect for and appreciation of strengths and challenges. It is equally important to assess the personal impact of the disability for the client. Many in the disability community advocate a shift from the medical model to the social interaction model, in which the focus is on inclusion and looking at the person from a holistic, strength-based perspective. In other words, rather than focusing only on the disability and treating it, the counselor would also attend to abilities and strengths for the person. Although the movement has been influenced by legislative efforts, it has also been greatly affected by many famous individuals who have contributed to people's perspective on and expectations of those with disabilities. The influence of Franklin Roosevelt, Helen Keller, Ray Charles, Stephen Hawking, and Christopher Reeve have all helped shaped the culture's view of what is possible despite a disability. Technology, too, has allowed many to participate in society who otherwise would have been unable. Voice activation, screen readers, and many other types of **assistive technology** have allowed individuals with disabilities to use computers and compete with their peers who are not disabled in academic and employment settings.

Counseling theories, many based on a strengths perspective, easily lend themselves to working effectively with a person who has a disability, including providing professional counselors with a healthy and realistic lens through which to view the client and guiding interventions. A holistic approach, viewing the disability as only one part of the person, allows the professional counselor to focus on the person's strengths also. Counseling interventions based on this mind-set and approach lead to productive outcomes.

Contributed by Elaine Weir Daidone
and Christine Harrington,
Middlesex County College, Edison, NJ

Reference

U.S. Census Bureau. (2000). *United States census 2000.* Retrieved August 25, 2008, from http://www.census.gov/main/www/cen2000.html

Additional Resources

Americans With Disabilities Act Web site: http://www.ada.gov

Individuals With Disabilities Educational Improvement Act Web site: http://www.idea.ed.gov

National Organization on Disability Web site: http://www.nod.org

■Dissociative Disorders

Dissociative disorders are a category of mental disorders that are often characterized by an interruption in consciousness, memory, identity, or perception. This interruption can result in a significant disruption of a person's social, familial, and occupational functioning. Dissociation, described as a symptom, occurs along a continuum of severity and is a process that allows the mind to separate or compartmentalize specific thoughts and memories from consciousness. These thoughts and memories are not necessarily forgotten. They are considered to be repressed and may return spontaneously when triggered by objects, events, or sensory information in a person's environment.

Dissociative disorders develop as a means to cope with a traumatic event, a series of traumatic events, or intensive distressing events in the recent or distant past. Individuals exposed to traumatic events (e.g., chronic sexual, physical, and/or emotional abuse; violence; natural disasters) use dissociation as a coping mechanism, which literally allows the person to detach from a situation or event too traumatic to integrate into consciousness. Children who experience chronic abuse or live in highly unpredictable households are at greater risk of developing dissociative disorders. In addition, symptoms of dissociative disorders, or even of one or more of these disorders, are also seen in other mental illnesses, including posttraumatic stress disorder, panic disorder, and obsessive-compulsive disorder.

Dissociative disorders are characterized by a variety of symptoms, including memory loss (amnesia) of specific times, events, or people; mental health problems, including depression, anxiety, or other mental illnesses; a sense of being detached from oneself (depersonalization); a distorted or unreal perception of the people and things in the immediate surroundings (derealization); and a blurred sense of identity.

Types of Dissociative Disorders

There are four major types of dissociative disorders: depersonalization disorder, dissociative amnesia, dissociative fugue, and dissociative identity disorder. Each of these dissociative disorders is characterized by a distinct method of dissociation.

Depersonalization disorder is characterized by a feeling of distance or detachment from one's own experience, body, or self. Individuals with depersonalization disorder often describe their experience in terms of a dream-like state or feeling spaced out, resulting in a sense of limited control over their actions and movements. They often believe the world is unreal or distorted. The combination of these experiences can severely affect a person's level of functioning.

Dissociative amnesia, formerly known as psychogenic amnesia, is more extensive than normal forgetfulness and is characterized by memory loss typically associated with extreme distress or a traumatic event. As a result, individuals usually block out critical personal information. It is important to differentiate dissociative amnesia from other types of amnesia, including amnesia of a physical (e.g., head injury) or physiological (e.g., dementia) type or amnesia associated with substance use (e.g., blackout.). Dissociative amnesia has four subtypes: localized amnesia, selective amnesia, generalized amnesia, and systematized amnesia.

Dissociative fugue is a disconnection from one's identity, resulting in an individual suddenly and unexpectedly taking physical leave of the environment and setting off on a journey of some kind. Although people experiencing a dissociative fugue are often unaware and confused about their identity, they typically are able to function, with their faculties intact, in their new environment. In rare instances, a person in a dissociative fugue may take on a new identity. A fugue episode can last anywhere from a few hours to days or even months and then ends as abruptly as it began. A person "coming out" of a fugue state may feel disoriented, depressed, and angry and have no recollection of what occurred during the fugue episode or how he or she arrived in such unfamiliar circumstances.

Dissociative identity disorder (DID), formerly known as multiple personality disorder, is probably the most controversial of the dissociative disorders and the most misunderstood. DID is characterized by a disturbance of identity that results in two or more distinct and separate personality states or identities controlling an individual's behavior. People with DID describe hearing voices inside their heads. They also report encounters with unfamiliar people who claim to know them, find themselves somewhere without knowing how they got there, or find items they do not remember purchasing among their possessions.

The commonly used term *switching* is actually a change in the presence of a personality state or states, usually occurring in times of stress. Each personality state may exhibit differences in speech, mannerisms, attitudes, thoughts, gender orientation, and memories. Personality states exist to serve a purpose in the person's life (i.e., to fill a role), whether that is sheltering other personality states from traumatic memories, expressing certain emotions, or performing specific responsibilities in the person's life. Often, these personality states develop in response to severe and chronic abuse and are often misdiagnosed.

Treatment of Dissociative Disorders

Treatment of dissociative disorders can entail individual, group, and family counseling coupled with prescribed psychiatric medications to treat symptoms and other co-occurring disorders. Specific types of treatment differ, depending on the professional's theoretical orientation and training. Some professionals use hypnosis or eye movement desensitization and reprocessing to recover traumatic memories, whereas others use more traditional counseling techniques, such as cognitive-behavioral therapy. Regardless of theoretical approach to treatment, the most essential facet is the trust and a sense of safety in the therapeutic alliance. Although treatment may be extensive and emotionally painful, people with dissociative disorders learn new coping skills and are able to lead healthy and productive lives.

Contributed by Melissa Deroche-Philpot, Arkansas State Hospital, Little Rock, AR

Additional Resources

Haddock, D. B. (2001). *Dissociative identity disorder*. New York: McGraw-Hill.

International Society for the Study of Trauma and Dissociation Web site: http://issd.org

Schwartz, H. L. (2000). *Dialogues with forgotten voices: Relational perspectives on child abuse trauma and the treatment of severe dissociative disorders*. New York: Basic Books.

■ Divorce and Separation

Divorce, a legal term, is defined as the dissolution of marriage prior to the death of either spouse and is often preceded by **separation.** Separation may also occur when a marriage was never legally formed. In contrast to divorce, **annulment** means that a marriage is considered to have been invalid in the first place. When expectations are vastly different within a couple or family and the differences are unresolved or marital quality is diminished, the outcome may be a decision to separate or divorce.

There are many reasons cited for divorces, including infidelity, abuse, addictions, differences in values, and a person's perspective on marriage or work outside the home. Historically, the primary reason given for divorce was financial discord between husband and wife. Intrapersonal issues, including a spouse's depression, anxiety, or self-dislike, may be as common as interpersonal problems, including arguments, problems with money, or child-rearing issues. Emotional (e.g., complex personality differences or inability to communicate about emotions or issues) and sexual compatibility (e.g., expectations placed on sexual behaviors in and outside the marriage) have risen as primary reasons for divorce in more recent studies. Individuals in a marriage may see their roles as husband or wife in a different way. For example, one person in the marriage may adopt a more traditional view than the does the other spouse. According to Munson and Sutton (2006), the 2005 divorce rate in the U.S. population was slightly less than 50%.

Individuals, couples and families may seek counseling at different stages of divorce or separation. Depending on the stage of divorce or separation and the presenting issue, a variety of counseling strategies and approaches may be used. Individuals or couples who enter therapy before a physical separation or divorce occurs may be helped through counseling to reunify the marriage. Some individuals or couples, however, may enter counseling wanting solutions for coping as they go through a divorce. Many families seek counseling to assess or treat children whose parents are seeking a divorce. Reactions to divorce may be different between and within families, thus requiring a variety of skills and knowledge from counselors.

Rich (2002) identified four stages of divorce: shock and disbelief, initial adjustment, active reorganization, and life reformation. Counselors can work through these stages with their clients. **Shock and disbelief** that is related to experiencing divorce can be worked through using reality testing and learning to tell about the process. The **initial adjustment stage** usually includes beginning to deal with immediate changes. Clients may be helped in dealing with relocation, legal matters, and changes in the new family structure. The conclusion of legal matters can be a beginning of the **active**

reorganization stage. This stage may also open the door for the formation of new friendships and possibly romantic relationships. Finally, the **life reformation stage** is similar to the acceptance stage in grief counseling. Clients begin to solidify their values and accept their new life. The integration of old and new values and old and new lives is important in this stage.

Couples in crisis may enter counseling prior to the decision to separate or divorce. One issue that counselors may face is the difference in values between two individuals regarding the need to divorce or the steps that can be taken in order to continue the marriage. Issues that may be brought into counseling before separation include infidelity, finances, and parenting differences. Cognitive-behavioral methods are often used to help couples make changes and address predictable problems. Professional counselors often work with communication issues in counseling through a variety of techniques, including experiential methods that allow the couple to communicate in the counseling session. Many marriage counselors believe that quality of communication is the best predictor of successful marriage.

Families involved in divorce often seek counseling to gain strategies in coping with the changes divorce may cause. All members of the family may be going through different stages of grief. Counseling may include education about grief and loss and working through stages of grief. Counselors may choose to work with the entire family or individual members of the family at this time. Counselors should be aware of any significant reactions that family members may be having as a result of what might be a traumatic event.

If the family entering counseling is a stepfamily or newly blended family, education about the different needs of individuals may be necessary. Some issues that may arise include children's relationships with the stepparent and stepsibling(s). Change for most children is difficult, and children may need counseling to handle the feelings associated with change. Stepfamilies can work in counseling to establish routines, traditions, and a new "normal" within the context of a different family setting. One-on-one time between the biological children and their parent without the stepparent is often important in adjustment. Stepparents may view the time spent alone between the biological parents and child as a threat to the new family dynamics. The professional counselor can often help the individuals in the family unit learn to listen to each other and respect the needs of each other in the new family.

Children and Divorce

Children may experience many short-term and long-term consequences of divorce. In a longitudinal study, Wallerstein, Lewis, and Blakeslee (2000) found that the long-term effects of divorce on children were cumulative and that the effects might be most significant when children of divorce reach their 20s and 30s. The implications of this study indicate that parents should work toward giving children more control when they are younger, and counselors may need to revisit the work with children as they enter adulthood.

Children of divorce can show a variety of reactions, and the reactions can range in severity. Children usually experience a reaction to loss of one parent or change in their current situation. Many children believe that if their parents can fall out of love, they may also stop loving them. Self-blame is a common reaction to divorce, as is the belief that the child can fix the parents' marriage. Children may also begin to try to please both parents or fix the problems. Parents should be careful not to change the role of children. For example, the son should not be made "man of the house," and the children should not have to take care of their parents. Most children will have some reactions to their parents' divorce or separation. In some cases, there is an immediate reaction, and in some families, the reaction is delayed. Most children want their parents to be married regardless of the type of marriage that existed (e.g., violent, intense, unhappy). Many children believe that the divorce is their fault or that they can do something to reunite their parents.

Professional counselors can help parents who are divorcing by teaching them ways to explain the divorce to the children appropriately. Counselors can encourage the parents to meet with the child, together if possible. The parents should explain how the child's life will be both different and similar. Both parents should explain that the child will be able to continue to see the parents and that the parents continue to love the child the same. It is important that the parents explain that the divorce is not a result of anything the child did and that the child does not have the ability to reunite the parents. Parents should be encouraged to answer all the child's questions truthfully, yet developmentally appropriately. For example, if a child asks which parent wanted the divorce or if infidelity was involved, the parents should say that those are grown-up topics that only the grown-ups will discuss. Parents should be encouraged not to lie to children because it causes some children to disregard their instincts.

Many children exhibit behavior problems as a reaction to divorce or a way to try to save the marriage. Children should not be involved in marital conflict. Counselors can give parents the tools to communicate without involving the child so that he or she does not feel the need to resolve parental conflict, communicate for parents, or choose sides. Children may show adjustment issues by being sad, having more anxiety, needing order and structure, or becoming angry or having new fears. Counselors and parents can look for signs of a more severe reaction that needs more intense mental health care. These reactions may include severe changes in eating or sleeping habits, talk of suicide or suicidal ideations, extreme violence or aggression, or dissociative reactions. Children's ability to cope with divorce may depend on several factors. These factors include level of conflict between the parents, the child's personality, the child's resiliency, and the child's age or developmental level. Parents who are divorced or separated may need help in coparenting, a process by which the parents communicate effectively, make decisions together, and allow the child to stay out of the middle of decisions. Parents often also need help in setting limits and boundaries with their children after divorce.

Professional counselors who are involved in divorce cases may be called into the legal realm to testify in court proceedings or provide information. Counselors may protect themselves or the family by using contracts that discourage parents from using the counselor in the courtroom. Some judges may order that a psychological evaluation of the parents and family be completed. A psychological evaluation usually uses tests and interviews. Counseling during divorce is not the same as a psychological evaluation. The counselor working with the family should also not be in the role of independent evaluator, because the counselor would be working in a dual relationship in this case. Counselors may want to seek the advice of an attorney if subpoenaed in a divorce case. Although many people may believe that their life may be better after divorce or that their unhappiness may be alleviated, Wallerstein and Blakeslee (1989) found that at least one member of the divorced couple missed the life that he or she had left behind or did not have relief from unhappiness after the divorce.

Contributed by Jennifer Savitz-Smith,
Columbia, SC

References

Munson, M., & Sutton, P. (2006). *Births, marriages, divorces, and deaths: Provisional data for 2005. National vital statistics reports* (Vol. 54, No. 20). Hyattsville, MD: National Center for Health Statistics.

Rich, P. (2002). *Divorce counseling homework planner.* New York: Wiley.

Wallerstein, J., & Blakeslee, S. (1989). *Second chances: Men, women and children a decade after divorce.* New York: Houghton Mifflin.

Wallerstein, J., Lewis, J., & Blakeslee, S. (2000). *The unexpected legacy of divorce: The 25 year landmark study.* New York: Hyperion.

Additional Resources

Gladding, S. T. (2007). *Family therapy: History, theory, and practice* (4th ed.). Upper Saddle River, NJ: Merrill Prentice Hall.

Levy, D. (1993). *The best parent is both parents: A guide to shared parenting in the 21st century.* Norfolk, VA: Hampton Roads.

Nichols, M. P., & Schwartz, R. C. (2005). *Family therapy: Concepts and methods* (7th ed.). Boston: Pearson Education.

■ Domestic Violence

According to the National Domestic Violence Hotline (NDVH; 2007), **domestic violence** is defined as "a pattern of abusive behavior in any relationship that is used by one partner to gain or maintain power and control over another intimate partner" (para. 1). Other definitions have delineated the difference between the nature of violent acts versus the types of relationships in which the violence occurs. **Violence** can be described as physical, sexual, emotional, economic, or psychological abuse that is designed to exert power and control. Although the general public may consider extreme physical violence that causes significant injury to be more typical of domestic violence, the reality is that victims of domestic violence are more commonly subjected to other types of abuses, such as slapping, pushing, and grabbing that produce no visible signs. Although these acts may not constitute **battering** (i.e., repeated forceful blows), the effects of these acts are still severe and can have long-term effects (Dutton, 2006). In addition to physical violence, a partner can inflict abuse in a variety of forms. According to the NDVH (2007), **abuse** can be defined as "physical, sexual, emotional, economic or psychological actions or threats of actions that influence another person," which can include "any behaviors that frighten, intimidate, terrorize, manipulate, hurt, humiliate, blame, injure or wound someone" (para. 2).

When considering the types of relationships in which domestic violence can occur, the term *domestic* denotes a relationship that exists related to a person's family unit. These relationships can include marital relationships, intimate partnerships (e.g., same-sex couples, cohabitating couples), and/or dating relationships. Domestic violence can occur as male-on-female violence, female-on-male violence, and same-sex-partner violence. In addition, domestic violence can affect people of any age, gender, race, sexual orientation, religion, socioeconomic status, or education level. Because society's definition of what constitutes a relationship has changed, **intimate partner abuse** and **intimate partner violence** are other terms used to describe domestic violence that occurs between two people who are in an intimate relationship.

Prevalence

According to the Bureau of Justice Statistics (BJS; 2008), intimate partner violence has been on the decline for the past 15 years. In a report developed using statistics from the National Crime Victimization Survey, the BJS reported that women are subjected to nonfatal intimate partner violence more than are men. More specifically, the statistics related to nonfatal intimate partner victimizations between 2001 and 2005 indicated that women were more than 5 times more likely the victim of nonfatal violence than were men. The National Institute of Justice reported that women are twice as likely to be victims of intimate partner violence as are men (Tjaden & Thoennes, 2000).

A major factor contributing to a person becoming a victim of intimate partner violence as an adult is if he or she experienced physical violence as a child at the hands of a parent or caregiver. According to Campbell et al. (2003), it is likely that half of all women who are murdered are victims of intimate partner violence. Of these homicides, physical violence occurred in 70% to 80% of the relationships, typically perpetrated by the male partner regardless of who was in the end murdered. According to the BJS (2008) report, homicides committed by intimate partners accounted for 30% of women killed and 5% of men killed.

Regarding racial groups, the NIJ study (Tjaden & Thoennes, 2000) reported little difference in the incidence of physical violence against women between White and non-White groups; however, when non-White groups were examined more closely, the research showed differences among various racial groups. For example, American Indians and Alaska Natives reported experiencing more violent victimization, such as physical assaults, rapes, and/or stalking, than did other racial groups. Hispanic women reported fewer rapes than did non-Hispanic women. Asian/Pacific Islander women and Asian/Pacific Islander men in heterosexual relationships reported significantly lower rates of violence than did other non-White racial groups.

History of Domestic Violence

The history of domestic violence is really a social history of beliefs about domestic violence through the ages rather than the fact that domestic violence has occurred throughout history. Domestic violence has been chronicled as dating to the Middle Ages, when violence was justified as a way to rid women of the influences of the devil (Dutton, 2006). Women were routinely murdered in order to suppress witchcraft, which at the time was believed to be linked to male impotence. Scholars have written about the tolerance of domestic violence in English common law and the early American colonies (Davidson, 1977; Martin, 1976). One example of this tolerance is embedded in the adage "rule of thumb." According to English common law, the origins of rule of thumb date to the practice of allowing a husband to correct his wife or children by beating them with a stick as long as the stick was no thicker than his thumb. Many other scholars, however, have given accounts in which family violence was considered illegal and immoral. In 1869, John Stuart Mill wrote *The Subjection of Women,* which is hailed as the first document to draw attention to the predicament of battered women (Dutton, 2006). In addition, Pleck (1987) described the views of the Puritan colonies toward wife beating, considering it sinful and punishable with severe consequences. Later, tort law was used to afford women some rights against husbands who were physically abusive. Later in the mid-1800s, scholars such as Elizabeth Stanton and Susan B. Anthony advocated for a closer look at violence in marriages. In a message to Congress in 1904, President Theodore Roosevelt condemned wife battery, calling such acts brutal and cruel (Dutton, 2006).

Although some attention was focused on domestic violence during the earlier part of the 20th century, the focus began to wane, with a shift toward domestic violence as a "family secret." Police began to consider situations of family violence as "domestic disturbances," in which interference was typically avoided if possible. There was renewed focus on family violence in the 1970s and 1980s. In 1971, Erin Pizzey developed the first domestic violence shelter for women who were leaving abusive relationships (Dutton, 2006). In 1976, the National Organization for Women formed a task force to research the prevalence of domestic violence (WomenSpace, 2007). In 1978, the National Coalition Against Domestic Violence (NCADV) was developed from a grassroots effort to provide a voice to survivors of domestic violence. In the late 1970s and early 1980s, several federal government initiatives continued the focus on domestic violence: (a) The Office of Domestic Violence in the U.S.

Department of Health and Human Services was established (closed in 1981), (b) Congress held the first hearings on domestic violence, (c) the U.S. attorney general established the Task Force on Family Violence, (d) the U.S. surgeon general identified domestic violence as a major health problem, and (e) the first legislation was passed by Congress to designate the month of October as Domestic Violence Awareness Month (WomenSpace, 2007). In 1995, the U.S. Congress passed the Violence Against Women Act (VAWA), acknowledging domestic violence as a gender-related crime and providing funding for programs for communities to address domestic violence. VAWA has consistently been reauthorized and funded, with the last reauthorization occurring in 2005 (U.S. Department of Justice, 2007).

Risk Factors

Physical abuse in childhood can be a predictor of adults who are more likely to experience domestic violence than are other people. In addition, other risk factors that increase the likelihood a person will become a victim of domestic violence include (a) low self-esteem, (b) low academic achievement, (c) lack of social networks, and (d) social isolation. In addition, there are many reasons why victims of domestic violence may delay leaving an abusive partner. Many victims lack the resources to leave an abusive situation because they have children; have employment issues; or do not have property, bank accounts, or credit cards. Victims may fear losing custody of their children or not being able to care for their children because of a decline in the family's standard of living in single-parent homes. Societal messages that focus on the importance of making a marriage work can override the desire to leave an abusive relationship. Victims may rationalize that the abuser's violence is due to substance abuse, stress, or past childhood abuse. Relationship patterns that can affect domestic violence are (a) marital conflict and/or instability, (b) male dominance in the family, (c) poor family functioning, (d) emotional dependence and insecurity, (e) belief in strict gender roles, and (f) desire for power and control in relationships. Signs and symptoms of domestic violence can vary from verbal messages to physical injury. Victims of domestic violence often deal with a range of consequences, from conveyed messages of embarrassment, shame, or guilt from an intimate partner to physical violence such as bruising, broken bones, or sexual assault. Typically, physical injuries occur most frequently to the head, face, neck, chest, breasts, and abdomen. Repeated exposure to domestic violence can lead to medical conditions such as traumatic brain injury, posttraumatic stress disorder, sexually transmitted diseases, and ulcers, as well as many other physical and emotional health conditions.

Prevention

Although victims of domestic violence often seek counseling for trauma that can occur due to their experiences, professional counselors can also make a vital contribution by focusing on prevention and advocacy. Given the historical perspective discussed earlier, it is clear that domestic violence is a societal issue that must be addressed on a broader scale. Society as a whole must examine beliefs about the tolerance of this type of violence. Stemming from issues related to violence in the media, the objectification of women, and the **machismo** of men, society must begin to rethink how it accepts or does not accept violence perpetrated by intimate partners.

One of the crucial issues regarding a change in societal norms is prevention. The key to prevention related to domestic violence is to change the environment systematically, reducing the likelihood that domestic violence will occur. There are three levels of prevention to consider: primary, secondary, and tertiary. At the center of primary prevention is addressing the societal norms that may still support violence (e.g., objectification of women, male dominated power). Primary prevention is more than simply raising awareness, providing education, and intervening early. It is more about changes in culture and society as a whole. Many of the organizations that address domestic violence work on a **primary prevention** level. The National Coalition Against Domestic Violence (NCADV) is an organization that works at the state, regional, and national level to provide community resources, legislative agendas, and educational programming. NCADV's (2007) mission is "to organize collective power by advancing transformative work, thinking and leadership of communities and individuals working to end the violence in our lives" (para. 1). In **secondary prevention,** the focus is on the response after the violence occurs. The majority of communities have developed programs to help victims of domestic violence once it has occurred, such as women's shelters that provide safety, housing, and counseling, as well as many other resources designed to help victims of domestic violence. NDVH is an organization that provides a 24-hour hotline for victims of domestic violence, providing crisis services and safety planning. **Tertiary prevention** focuses more on rehabilitation issues and is designed to address issues that are more long term related to domestic violence. Intervention programs for perpetrators of domestic violence are good examples of tertiary prevention efforts. To be successful, all levels of prevention must be addressed in a systematic, consistent way.

Because professional counselors and other helping professionals often see firsthand the consequences and effects of domestic violence, they are in a unique position to advocate for the total eradication of this problem. Through advocacy, professional counselors can provide a voice to victims who often do not have the ability to speak for themselves. Professional counselors and helping professionals should consider advocating at the local, state, and national levels to ensure that the issue of domestic violence and its victims receive the proper amount of attention and funding to end this crisis.

Contributed by Robin Wilbourn Lee,
Middle Tennessee State University,
Murfreesboro, TN

References

Bureau of Justice Statistics. (2008). *Intimate partner violence in the U.S.* Retrieved January 8, 2008, from http://www.ojp.usdoj.gov/bjs/intimate/ipv.htm

Campbell, J. C., Webster, D., Koziol-McLain, J., Block, C., Campbell, D., Curry, M. A., et al. (2003). *Risk factors for femicide in abusive relationships: Results from a multisite case control study.* Retrieved October 15, 2007, from http://www.ajph.org/cgi/reprint/93/7/1089

Davidson, T. (1977). *Wifebeating: A recurring phenomenon throughout history.* In M. Roy (Ed.), *Battered women* (pp. 1–23). New York: Van Nostrand Reinhold.

Dutton, D. G. (2006). *Rethinking domestic violence.* Vancouver, British Columbia, Canada: University of British Columbia Press.

Martin, D. (1976). *Battered wives.* New York: Pocket Books.

National Coalition Against Domestic Violence. (2007). *About us.* Retrieved October 15, 2007, from http://www.ncadv.org/

National Domestic Violence Hotline (2007). *Get educated.* Retrieved October 15, 2007, from http://www.ndvh.org/educate/what_is_dv.html

Pleck, E. H. (1987). *Domestic tyranny: The making of social policy against family violence from colonial times to the present.* New York: Oxford University Press.

Tjaden, P. & Thoennes, N. (2000). *Extent, nature, and consequences of intimate partner violence.* Retrieved October 15, 2007, from http://www.ncjrs.gov/pdffiles1/nij/181867.pdf

U.S. Department of Justice. (2007). *Office on violence against women.* Retrieved October 15, 2007, from http://www.usdoj.gov/ovw/index.html

WomenSpace (2007). *WomenSpace herstory.* Retrieved October 15, 2007, from http://www.enddomesticviolence.com/aboutus/WomenspaceHerstory.asp

Other Resources

National Coalition Against Domestic Violence Web site: http://www.ncadv.org

National Domestic Violence Hotline: http://www.ndvh.org

■ Double Blind

An experiment in which participants do not know to which group they are assigned is referred to as a "blind" or **single-blind** study. In a **double-blind** study, neither the study participants nor the researchers know which group is being exposed to a particular treatment (i.e., independent variable) until after data are collected or the study is complete. This procedure is used to control the impact of various types of bias more rigorously or to control extraneous variables that may unduly influence the relationship between the experimental variables. These variables include the placebo effect, observer bias, and the possible conscious or unconscious bias of the experimenter. The **placebo effect** occurs when specific outcomes of a treatment are due to participants' expectations or beliefs that a treatment will work rather than their having actually been given a viable treatment. Although using a blinding procedure does not eliminate the possibility of the placebo effect, it does allow the researcher to compare whether the effects of the treatment under study are greater for the experimental group than for the group receiving the inactive treatment. Participants in a study may also change their behavior when they are aware of being observed or when they guess the hypothesis of the study and attempt to please the researcher, a phenomenon known as **observer bias** or the **Hawthorne effect.**

Experimenter bias occurs when the outcome of a study is influenced by the expectations of the researcher, rather than being influenced by input from the participants, often by overemphasis on expected behaviors and failure to notice unexpected behaviors. A double-blind procedure controls for both observer bias and experimenter bias by concealing which group is receiving the treatment under study from both the participants and the researchers carrying out the experiment. Thus, double-blind studies are considered to meet a more stringent scientific standard than studies that do not use blinding procedures or use only a single-blind procedure. For example, in testing the efficacy of a cognitive-behavioral treatment on depression using a double-blind procedure, the control group might instead receive treatment focused on dream analysis with neither the participants nor the counselors knowing which treatment is being tested.

Ethical considerations when using this procedure include informed consent specifically indicating that participants may be placed in a group that will not receive an active treatment during the course of the study, a debriefing that informs participants of any information that was withheld from them at the onset of the study, and making the experimental treatment available to those who were in the control group.

Contributed by Laura T. Easter,
University of Virginia, Charlottesville, VA

Additional Resource

Lafountain, R. M., & Bartos, R. B. (2002). *Research and statistics made meaningful in counseling and student affairs.* Pacific Grove, CA: Thomson Learning.

◼ Duty to Warn and Protect

Professional counselors, spurred by the courts, have a dual ethical and legal responsibility to protect others from potentially dangerous clients, to protect clients from being harmed by others, and to protect clients from themselves. The delicate balance between confidentiality and the duty to warn and protect others must be handled on a case-by-case basis. The majority of individual state laws require counselors to breach confidentiality in order to warn and protect someone who is in danger. All states and U.S. jurisdictions now have mandatory reporting statutes for suspected physical, sexual, or emotional child abuse or neglect. There are also several states with mandatory reporting statutes for elder abuse or abuse of other persons presumed to have limited ability to care for themselves. Remley and Herlihy (2001) explained,

A duty to protect from harm arises when someone is especially dependent on others or is some way vulnerable to the choices and actions of others. Persons in a vulnerable position are unable to avoid risk of harm

on their own and are dependent on others to intervene on their behalf. When counselors, through their confidential relation with clients, learn that a vulnerable person is at risk of harm, they have a duty to act to prevent the harm. This is a higher duty than the duty to maintain confidentiality. (p. 95)

It is important to disclose only information pertinent to the current problem (e.g., to help prevent a suicide attempt). Duty to protect includes not only others who are reasonably identifiable victims but also the clients themselves, such as those who are suicidal. In its revised *ACA Code of Ethics*, the American Counseling Association (ACA; 2005) addresses a sensitive and controversial topic with the inclusion of a new standard to give counselors guidance when trying to best meet the needs of the terminally ill and palliative end-of-life care for terminally ill clients. Standard A.9.c. states,

Counselors who provide services to terminally ill clients who are considering hastening their own deaths have the option of breaking or not breaking confidentiality, depending on applicable laws and the specific circumstances of the situation and after seeking consultation or supervision from appropriate professional and legal parties. (p. 6)

The duty to warn did not have a sudden onset brought on by a specific court case, but rather for years, mental health professionals were involved in giving expert testimony about the likelihood that a potential patient was mentally ill and a threat to the physical safety and well-being of self or others. Although the decision in 1976 in the *Tarasoff v. Regents of the University of California* case is the landmark court case in which the duty to warn (and breach confidentiality) was decided, there were other court cases that preceded it. Under what conditions a counselor has a duty to warn (or protect) a potential victim, law enforcement officials, or another person of a client's dangerousness has been the focus of ever-increasing lawsuits (Austin, Moline, & Williams, 1990).

In the *Tarasoff* case, a young man named Prosenjit Poddar admitted to his psychologist, Lawrence Moore, that he wanted to kill an unnamed girlfriend (who was easily identifiable as Tatiana Tarasoff) when she returned from a trip to Brazil. Dr. Moore proceeded to notify campus authorities and his superiors of the threat that Poddar had made. The campus police picked Poddar up and detained him for questioning but found that he was "rational." Once he agreed to stay away from Tarasoff, they released him. Dr. Moore's superiors ordered all records of this situation with Poddar destroyed. Shortly after Tarasoff returned from her trip, Poddar killed her. Tarasoff's parents sued the officers, mental health practitioners, the head of the medical center (i.e., Cowell Hospital at the University of California, Berkeley) where Poddar was treated as an outpatient, and the Board of Regents of the University of California for negligence in failure to warn Miss Tarasoff or her family of Poddar's threats.

The responsibility to protect the public from dangerous actions of violent clients entails liability for civil damages when counselors neglect this duty by (a) failing to diagnose or predict dangerousness, (b) failing to warn potential victims of violent behavior, (c) failing to commit dangerous clients, and (d) prematurely discharging dangerous clients from a hospital (Austin et al., 1990). Although a lower court dismissed the *Tarasoff* suit in 1974, the parents appealed, and the California Supreme Court ruled in favor of the parents in 1976, holding that a failure to warn an intended victim was professionally irresponsible. The court's ruling requires that psychotherapists breach confidentiality when the general welfare and safety of others is involved. Because this was a California case, courts in other states are not bound to decide a similar case in the same way. In fact, the court decisions over the years appear to be both conflicting and confusing to mental health professionals. Also, there is no consensus among the states about the particular circumstances in which a counselor has a duty to warn. Not only is it difficult at times for counselors to determine an exception to confidentiality, it is especially challenging to predict dangerousness because human behavior is not always predictable (Remley & Herlihy, 2001).

Under the *Tarasoff* decision regarding the duty to warn "where the patient has communicated to the psychotherapist a serious threat of physical violence against a reasonable identifiable victim or victims" (Moline, Williams, & Austin, 1998, p. 89), the psychotherapist must first accurately diagnose the client's tendency to behave in dangerous ways toward others. Deciding whether a particular client is dangerous is a challenge for every counselor. This first duty is judged by the standards of professional negligence. Whereas with the first *Tarasoff* ruling in 1974, the lower court cited a "duty to warn," this duty was expanded by the California Supreme Court into a "duty to protect" third parties from dangerous clients. Professional counselors can protect others through traditional clinical interventions, such as reassessment, recommending medication changes, referral, or hospitalization, as well as warning potential victims, contacting the police, or informing the state child or elder protection agency (Corey, Corey, & Callanan, 2007). Additional caution must be demonstrated in taking steps that convey respect while treating clients in the least restrictive environment or in ways that are the least disruptive or intrusive for the client. Choices of action for the counselor on a continuum may range from the least intrusive action (e.g., obtaining a promise from the client not to harm anyone else) to the most intrusive action (e.g., involuntary hospitalization; Remley & Herlihy, 2001).

Since the 1976 California court ruling in the *Tarasoff* appeal, professional counselors have been seriously concerned about the ethical and legal ramifications of the duty to warn and protect. Whereas for many years the *ACA Code of Ethics* stated that confidentiality was to be broken if there was "clear and imminent danger," the current 2005 *ACA Code of Ethics* states in Section B.2.a. that confidentiality is broken when there is "serious and foreseeable harm." Of equal concern to counselors is the potential liability in court actions in dealing with clients who are dangerous to others.

Following is a list of suggestions that are related to duty to warn and protect issues associated with counseling suicidal clients who are minors and that are applicable to protecting both clients and counselors:

- Professional counselors should know the privileged communication or confidentiality laws in the state where they are employed (Sheeley & Herlihy, 1989).
- Counselors should have available and circulate descriptions and explanations of confidentiality and its limits. It has become a "standard of care" practice to address the limits of confidentiality before any therapeutic process begins (Moline et al., 1998).
- Counselors should keep apprised of related court decisions and also be well versed in their respective state licensure board stipulations, because the *Tarasoff* decision does not apply in every state (Sheeley & Herlihy, 1989).
- Counselors should be familiar with mental health professional organization's representative codes of ethics. The courts usually look to professional standards of ethics to examine the standard of care and how the ordinary and prudent practitioner might act under similar circumstances and determine whether a legal duty by a counselor has been breached. This standard of behavior is usually established by the testimony of experts (Moline et al., 1998).
- When employed by a school district, counselors should communicate the need for related school board policies (Sheeley & Herlihy, 1989).
- When counseling minors, counselors should develop policy handbooks and document confirmation that they received the materials (Sheeley & Herlihy, 1989).
- Counselors should keep accurate notes and records. Federal and/or state law may require adequate record keeping (Moline et al., 1998). The courts may view a failure to keep records as a failure to give service. Clear and concise record keeping is mandatory for a successful review by the legal system, insurance companies, and supervisors. Record keeping protects both the client and counselor by demonstrating that treatment occurred and that the evaluation and counseling plan were consistent with the standards of the profession.
- Counselors should consult with professional peers concerning doubts about client assessments and treatment interventions and only reveal information germane to the consultation (Sheeley & Herlihy, 1989).
- Counselors should know an attorney to contact for legal assistance, especially if their records are subpoenaed or they are required to testify, or both (Moline et al., 1998).
- Counselors should be certain to have professional liability insurance and understand the coverage included in their policy. Although places of employment usually have a professional liability insurance plan, ACA, the American School Counselor Association, and other mental health professional organizations make this coverage available to their members.

Other instances when counselors may have a duty to protect clients who are harming self include eating disorders, substance abuse, reckless and/or promiscuous sexual behavior, cult membership, and criminal activity. There are also circumstances (e.g., a client is known to have a disease that is both communicable and life threatening) according to the 2005 *ACA Code of Ethics* (Standard B.2.b. Contagious, Life-Threatening Diseases) where counselors may be justified in disclosing information to an endangered third party but are not necessarily obligated to take this course of action. Counselors are especially challenged when working with minors and dealing with balancing confidentiality and duty-to-protect dilemmas about such things as youth sexuality, counseling minors about birth control or abortion, and whether or not to notify parents. Counselors need to be aware of their own values, competence, and scope of practice and refer clients who could be better helped by another mental health professional.

Contributed by George T. Williams,
The Citadel, Charleston, SC, and
Lori Ellison, Texas A&M–Commerce,
Commerce, TX

References

American Counseling Association. (2005). *ACA code of ethics*. Alexandria, VA: Author.

Austin, K. M., Moline, M. E., & Williams, G. T. (1990). *Confronting malpractice: Legal and ethical dilemmas in psychotherapy*. Newbury Park, CA: Sage.

Corey, G., Corey, M. S., & Callanan, P. (2007). *Issues and ethics in the helping professions* (7th ed.). Pacific Grove, CA: Thomson Brooks/Cole.

Moline, M. E., Williams, G. T., & Austin, K. M. (1998). *Documenting psychotherapy: Essentials for mental health practitioners*. Thousand Oaks, CA: Sage.

Remley, T. P., Jr., & Herlihy, B. (2001). *Ethical, legal, and professional issues in counseling*. Upper Saddle River, NJ: Prentice Hall.

Sheeley, V. L., & Herlihy, B. (1989). Counseling suicidal teens: A duty to warn and protect. *School Counselor, 37,* 89–97.

Tarasoff v. Regents of the University of California, 17 Cal.3d 425, 551 P.2d 334, 131 Cal. Rptr. 14 (1976).

Eating Disorders

Eating disorders involve chronic and continuous disruptive eating habits. Disruptive eating habits include severe oscillations or extremes that occur in eating patterns such as under-eating (i.e., restriction), overeating (i.e., binging), body perception distortions (i.e., perceiving oneself as "fat" when not overweight), and a host of compensatory behaviors (e.g., fasting, dieting, exercising, laxative and diuretic use, purging) that attempt to self-correct excess imbalances in food intake (i.e., binge eating). The two primary eating disorders are anorexia nervosa and bulimia nervosa. The lifetime prevalence of anorexia nervosa for female adolescents and women (0.9% of population) is 3 times higher than for male adolescents and men (0.3% of population; Hudson, Hiripi, Pope, & Kessler, 2007). The cultural factors associated with the prevalence of anorexia nervosa include industrialized cultures where food is plentiful (i.e., anorexia nervosa is less common in cultures where food is scarcer), age (i.e., anorexia nervosa typically begins in midadolescence, and earlier onset is associated with better outcomes), and gender (i.e., more than 90% of anorexia nervosa cases are female; American Psychiatric Association [APA], 2000). The lifetime prevalence of bulimia nervosa for female adolescents and women (1.5% of population) is 3 times higher than for male adolescents and men (Hudson et al., 2007). The cultural factors associated with the prevalence of bulimia nervosa include industrialized cultures (i.e., bulimia nervosa occurs in the population similarly across industrialized countries), race (i.e., clinical studies indicate that the majority of bulimia nervosa clients are White), gender (i.e., more than 90% of bulimia nervosa clients are female), and age (i.e., bulimia nervosa typically occurs in late adolescence or early adulthood; APA, 2000).

Anorexia Nervosa

Anorexia nervosa is an eating disorder in which an individual's intense fear of gaining weight and distorted body image converge to influence the individual's refusal to maintain a minimally normal body weight (at least 85% of weight normal for a person's age and height).

There are four diagnostic criteria in the *Diagnostic and Statistical Manual of Mental Disorders* (4th ed., text rev.; *DSM-IV-TR;* APA, 2000) for anorexia nervosa: (a) refusal to maintain a minimally normal body weight for age and height; (b) intense fear of gaining weight or becoming fat even though underweight; (c) disturbance in the way in which one's body or shape is experienced, undue influence of body

weight or shape on self-evaluation, or denial of the seriousness of the current low body weight; and (d) amenorrhea (in girls and women). It is important to clarify that "minimally normal body weight" is 85% of weight expected for age, height, and build or the inability to gain weight during periods of growth (adolescence) whereby the individual falls below the 85% threshold. It is important to note that being underweight or failing to gain weight during periods of growth (adolescence) does not by itself indicate an eating disorder, but it does warrant further examination. Thus, professional counselors need to take into account a person's weight history because some people have long histories of being underweight despite healthy eating patterns. Counselors should consult physicians or dieticians to assess the first criterion for anorexia nervosa. The second and third criteria of anorexia nervosa are fundamentally related because a person's intense fear of gaining weight (second criterion) and body image distortion (third criterion) conspire to continue a pattern of eating restriction despite significant associated weight loss and unhealthy weight levels. There are two subtypes of anorexia nervosa: the restricting type (i.e., person chooses restricting food intake rather than binging and purging) and the binge-eating/purging type (i.e., person engages in binging and purging; includes vomiting or misuse of laxatives, diuretics, or enemas). The distinction between a person with bulimia nervosa and anorexia nervosa binge-eating/purging type is that only the former is able to maintain a normal range of body weight. In order for the anorexia nervosa binge-eating/purging type to maintain a significant underweight level, the person would also need to have engaged in restriction of food intake (restricting type), making the distinction rather fine. The fourth criterion (i.e., amenorrhea) can be assessed through client self-report, although the counselor should encourage the client to see her physician to rule out other medical reasons (e.g., hormonal imbalances, thyroid disorders) for amenorrhea other than anorexia nervosa.

The treatment efficacy research for anorexia nervosa is considerably weaker than that for bulimia nervosa. The literature on the efficacy of treatment for anorexia nervosa is sorted according to the stage of anorexia nervosa (i.e., acute anorexia nervosa and weight-restored anorexia nervosa) as well as client age (adolescent or adult). In **acute anorexia nervosa** (i.e., the client is below the 85% threshold of appropriate weight), family therapy with adult clients has some preliminary supporting evidence of treatment efficacy compared with medication management or routine treatment (e.g., nonspecific supportive psychotherapy), but the weight gain outcomes have been modest, and the majority of clients were still significantly underweight. Family therapy, however, does have treatment efficacy for acute anorexia nervosa with adolescent clients when the focus includes putting the parents in charge of refeeding the adolescent (Berkman et al., 2006). In **weight-restored anorexia nervosa** (i.e., focus is maintaining the client's weight in the acceptable range and relapse prevention), cognitive-behavioral therapy has some preliminary evidence of treatment efficacy for adult clients but not for adolescents. Thus, there is currently a gap in treatment efficacy for acute anorexia nervosa for adults and weight-restored anorexia nervosa for adolescents, and there is a need for further efficacy studies on the adult client population. Other treatment approaches for anorexia nervosa that have potential treatment efficacy include motivational enhancement therapy (i.e., focuses building client motivation to change) and expressive therapies (i.e., example, guided imagery), although both of these approaches need randomized clinical trials (Kaplan, 2002). For a systematic review of the literature on the efficacy of treatment for anorexia nervosa that includes medical interventions only, psychological treatments only, or combinations of medical and psychological treatments, see Berkman et al. (2007).

Bulimia Nervosa

Bulimia nervosa is an eating disorder in which an individual's eating habits tend to follow a complementary pattern of binge eating followed by various compensatory behaviors (e.g., vomiting; misusing laxatives, diuretics, or other medications; fasting, dieting; excessive exercising).

There are five diagnostic criteria in the *DSM-IV-TR* for bulimia nervosa: (a) recurrent episodes of binge eating; (b) recurrent inappropriate compensatory behavior in order to prevent weight gain (e.g., self-induced vomiting; misuse of laxatives, diuretics, enemas, or other medications; fasting; excessive exercising); (c) binge eating and inappropriate compensatory behaviors occur, on average, at least twice a week for 3 months; (d) self-evaluation is unduly influenced by body shape and weight; and (e) disturbance does not occur exclusively during episodes of anorexia nervosa (APA, 2000). **Binge eating** (first criterion) is defined as eating an excessive amount of food (e.g., type of food consumed varies, but high-calorie sweets are common) over a discrete period of time (within any 2-hour period) as well as lacking self-control over volume of food consumed or ability to stop eating. Binge eating, however, requires both overconsumption of food and a lack of self-control over eating behavior, which means that choosing to overeat periodically although retaining the ability to regulate what is consumed and being able to stop when satiated would not constitute a binge-eating episode. In contrast to persons with anorexia nervosa who are significantly underweight, persons with bulimia nervosa often maintain a body weight within the normal range for their age, height, and build. The primary method that persons with bulimia nervosa use to maintain their normal range body weight despite their frequent binge eating episodes is compensatory behaviors (second criterion). The two subtypes of bulimia

nervosa (i.e., purging type and nonpurging type) are categorized on the basis of which compensatory behaviors individuals use (third criterion). Persons with bulimia nervosa engage in binge eating, although the purging subtype uses vomiting or misuse of laxatives, diuretics, or enemas to compensate, whereas the nonpurging subtype chooses other compensatory behaviors such as fasting or excessive exercise. The binging and compensatory behavioral pattern is strongly influenced by the fourth criterion of self-evaluation tied heavily to body shape and weight. For example, the full pattern may include (a) individuals feel dissatisfied with their current body shape and/or weight, (b) they feel bad (low self-esteem), (c) they deal with their low self-evaluation through binge eating, (d) they compensate for binge eating with one or more compensatory behaviors (e.g., excessive exercise), and (e) the pattern repeats when they begin feeling dissatisfied with their body image and/or weight again.

The research on treatment efficacy for bulimia nervosa is significantly stronger than for anorexia nervosa. Cognitive-behavioral therapy, in either individual or group therapy modalities, is the dominant treatment approach for bulimia nervosa with the strongest treatment efficacy (Shapiro et al., 2007). Cognitive-behavioral therapy has been found in randomized clinical trials to reduce the core behavioral symptoms of binge eating and purging (e.g., decreases in days binging and vomiting) and psychological symptoms (e.g., decreasing the drive for thinness and body dissatisfaction) of bulimia nervosa in both short-term and long-term periods. Cognitive-behavioral therapy has been found to be superior in treatment efficacy for bulimia nervosa compared with interpersonal psychotherapy, supportive expressive therapy, and behavior therapy. Another treatment that has some preliminary evidence of treatment efficacy for bulimia nervosa is guided imagery therapy (Berkman et al., 2006). The clinical trials on treatment efficacy have been conducted with mostly White clients (more than 80%) with bulimia nervosa in the age range of 17 to 64 years, therefore the treatment efficacy for clients diagnosed with bulimia nervosa who are non-White and/or younger than 17 years has not yet been established. For a systematic review of the literature on the treatment efficacy of bulima nervosa that includes medical interventions only, psychological treatments only, or combinations of medical and psychological treatments, see Berkman et al. (2006)

Other Eating Disorders

Other eating disorders include **eating disorder not otherwise specified (NOS)** and the proposed **binge-eating disorder.** The eating disorder NOS diagnosis includes disorders of eating that do not meet the criteria for any specific eating disorder (APA, 2000). Previously, the newly proposed binge-eating disorder was included as an example of the eating disorder NOS diagnosis. Examples of eating disorder NOS are (a) girls and women who meet all the anorexia nervosa criteria except amenorrhea (i.e., have regular menses); (b) persons who meet all the anorexia nervosa criteria except that their weight loss, although significant, is still within the normal range for their height, weight, and build; (c) persons who meet all of the bulimia nervosa criteria except that their binge eating and inappropriate compensatory behaviors occur less frequently than twice per week and/or have a duration of less than 3 months; (d) persons of normal body weight who repeatedly use inappropriate compensatory behaviors after consumption of small amounts of food (e.g., the purging behavior may occur in the absence of a binge-eating episode); and (e) persons regularly chewing and spitting out, but not swallowing, large amounts of food (APA, 2000).

The proposed criteria for binge-eating disorder include recurrent episodes of binge eating (definition for binge eating is same as for bulimia nervosa) and binge-eating episodes associated with three or more of the following eating patterns: (a) eating much more rapidly than normal; (b) eating until feeling uncomfortably full; (c) eating large amounts of food when not feeling physically hungry; (d) eating alone because of being embarrassed by how much one is eating; (e) feeling disgusted with oneself, depressed, or guilty after overeating; (f) feeling marked distress regarding binge eating; (g) binge eating occurring at least 2 days a week for 6 months; and (h) binge eating not associated with the regular use of inappropriate compensatory behaviors (e.g., purging, fasting, and excessive exercising) and not occurring exclusively during the course of anorexia nervosa or bulimia nervosa (APA, 2000).

Regarding the research on treatment efficacy for binge-eating disorder, cognitive-behavioral therapy has been studied most often although there is still a need for additional treatment research. Berkman et al. (2006) indicated that cognitive-behavioral therapy is helpful with clients with binge-eating disorder in reducing the number of binge days or binge episodes. Cognitive-behavioral therapy, offered in group format, does have treatment efficacy with binge-eating disorder because it is associated with significantly more abstinence from binge eating than wait list controls; however, there is a need for treatment research on cognitive-behavioral therapy that is administered individually to establish efficacy. For a systematic review of the literature on the treatment efficacy for binge-eating disorder that includes medical interventions only, psychological treatments only, or combinations of medical and psychological treatments, see Berkman et al. (2006).

Professional counselors will regularly encounter clients with major disruptions in eating patterns. It is essential that counselors properly differentiate between subtypes of anorexia nervosa and bulimia nervosa to facilitate both accurate diagnosis and the use of the most efficacious counseling treatments with clients.

Contributed by Darren A. Wozny,
Mississippi State University–
Meridian Campus, Meridian, MS

References

American Psychiatric Association. (2000). *Diagnostic and statistical manual of mental disorders* (4th ed., text rev.). Washington, DC: Author.

Berkman, N. D., Bulik, C. M., Brownley, K. A., Lohr, K. N., Sedway, J. A., Rooks, A., et al. (2006). *Management of eating disorders* (Evidence report/technology assessment No. 135. AHRQ Publication No. 06-E010). Rockville, MD: Agency for Healthcare Research and Quality.

Hudson, J. I., Hiripi, E., Pope, H. G., & Kessler, R. C. (2007). The prevalence and correlates of eating disorders in the National Comorbidity Survey Replication. *Biological Psychiatry, 61,* 348–358.

Kaplan, A. S. (2002). Psychological treatments for anorexia nervosa: A review of published studies and promising new directions. *Canadian Journal of Psychiatry, 47,* 235–242.

Shapiro, J. R., Berkman, N. D., Brownley, K. A., Sedway, J. A., Lohr, K. N., & Bulik, C. M. (2007). Bulimia nervosa treatment: A systematic review of randomized controlled trials. *International Journal of Eating Disorders, 40,* 312–336.

■ Eclecticism to Integration in Counseling

After playing a vital role in the development of Freud's psychoanalysis, Adler and Jung became the first of a long line of individuals who broke with Freud or the psychoanalytic model and developed their own theories (Seligman, 2001). As the field of psychotherapy grew, the tradition was that the typical clinician learned the values, principles, and techniques of a theoretical model, often an offshoot theory from psychoanalysis. Almost all clinicians acknowledge, however, that no one theory explains all personality development and the psychological disturbances that individuals experience. Some people now estimate that there are more than 300 counseling and psychotherapeutic approaches, and increasing numbers of mental health practitioners are using an integration of these approaches.

From the early 1900s into the 1950s, little was said about **eclecticism** as a distinctive viewpoint of psychotherapy. In fact, the term *eclecticism* was practically unknown in the mid-1940s. In the 1950s and 1960s, **Frederick Thorne** and Roy Grinker Sr. were almost its only advocates. In his early training in the Columbia University psychology department, Thorne's (1973) disillusionment with behaviorism's sterility helped to instill in him the motivation to dedicate almost 15 years to rigorous evaluation and testing of various counseling theories and their techniques. He believed no counseling theory and its appropriate techniques had all of the answers for treating each individual's unique needs. It then followed that wisdom and competence depended on clinicians mastering all that was known in psychology so that they would know enough to treat these unique needs. Thorne set forth a complete system of practice based on an eclectic theory of psychotherapy. He systematically selected and combined compatible elements from various schools/systems into a unified eclectic whole; however, his theory or rigorous method never garnered a following, and presently few clinicians even know of Thorne.

In contrast to theories or schools centering on a prominent authority, early eclecticism never became a school or system with a leader and a dedicated following. This even follows Thorne's (1973) intention that eclecticism should not become a special approach in competition with other approaches. For Thorne, the clinician must tailor the scientific application of specific parts of theories and techniques to each individual's need. That there are no real authorities guiding clinicians who describe themselves as eclectic is fascinating because studies from 1981 through 2001 reported from 30% to 75% of clinicians described themselves this way (Murdock, 2004; Walborn, 1996).

Proponents of individual theoretical models continuously criticized the lack of leading authorities because many clinicians were initially trained to model their therapy after a primary theorist (e.g., Freud, Jung, Adler, Rogers, Ellis, Perls, Wolpe, Glasser). A related common criticism directed at eclectic clinicians was that they haphazardly selected methods or techniques with no unified rationale. When novice or undereducated counselors used this approach, it was mockingly referred to as "electric" because they might randomly try methods or techniques that "turn them on" (Gladding, 2002, p. 38). In addition, Eysenck (1970) used "lazy eclecticism" (p. 140) to refer to clinicians who put together a random bag of interventions without any prevailing logic. A more customary term for describing clinicians who carelessly, uncritically, and unsystematically combine various therapeutic approaches is *syncretism.*

Since most clinicians and theorists acknowledge that there are limitations to each theoretical model, it is curious how more current clinicians and theorists have creatively described their theoretical approach, many using an adaptation of the *eclecticism* term. The following list briefly describes the work of some current clinicians and theorists.

- Marianne and Gerald Corey (2006) used the term **integrative approach** to encompass the dimensions of thinking, feeling, and behaving when describing human experiences. They advocated examining all of the current theories to decide what concepts and strategies clinicians want to incorporate into their style.
- Linda Seligman (2001, 2004) organized her presentation of psychotherapy theories and her technical and conceptual skills around four broad categories: "background, emotions, thoughts, actions" (p. 5), called by the acronym **BETA.** She indicated that therapeutic use of her BETA categories is enhanced because integrated and eclectic approaches are increasingly becoming the norm.
- In the first edition of his book, Cavanagh (1982) proposed healthy eclecticism as the model of choice. In his second edition, Cavanagh and Levitov (2002) favored technical eclecticism as the process of combining a variety of techniques into a workable unit but opposed unsystematic eclecticism and theoretical eclecticism.
- In the eighth edition of their classic textbook, Corsini and Wedding (2008) included, for the first time, a chapter titled "Integrative Psychotherapies" (pp. 481–511). In this chapter, Norcross and Beutler (2008) mentioned the four most popular paths to integrative psychotherapy: **technical eclecticism** (i.e., taking techniques from various therapeutic systems without adopting their originating theories), **theoretical inte-**

gration (i.e., integrating the theories and techniques from two or more therapies), **common factors** (i.e., determining core ingredients that therapies share and creating new treatments based on these commonalities, such as therapeutic alliance), and **assimilative integration** (i.e., selectively combining various techniques from other theories into a single, coherent theory such as rational emotive behavioral therapy), plus their own approach, "systematic eclectic or systematic treatment selection" (pp. 482–483; i.e., blending several of the paths to integrative psychotherapy).
- Lazarus (2008) described multimodal therapy as systematic, comprehensive, personalized, individualized, and technically eclectic.
- Ivey and Ivey (2003) described their orientation as developmental/integrative. They believed that there were several roads toward the best outcome of effective interviewing.
- Ellis (2008) stressed the importance of "thinking/feeling/wanting" and "of behavior" (p. 187) and used a wide variety of techniques that drew from different theoretical orientations.
- Young (as cited in Seligman, 2001) developed REPLAN ("relationship, efficacy, practicing, lowering, activating, new"; p. 526) as an acronym to represent six common factors that serve as the foundation for the specific techniques that adapt his model to the individual client.

These illustrations provide samples of the varied terminologies presently used in describing the evolution of eclecticism. Norcross and Beutler (2008) suggested that eclecticism, or the more popular term **integration,** is the most frequently used theoretical approach of English-speaking therapists. As the 21st century begins, some have proposed that clinicians are entering the fourth force of psychotherapy—the first being the psychodynamic approaches; second, the cognitive and behavioral approaches; and third, the existential-humanistic approaches (Seligman, 2001). This fourth force is an integration of these first three therapeutic systems to form a comprehensive and holistic system in order to understand clients as fully as possible.

The goal of the integration of therapies is to improve the desired effect of psychotherapy and its application to individuals, groups, and systems. With the maturing of the field of psychotherapy, integration (or eclecticism) has evolved as a primary viewpoint/approach, with many well-known advocates. Integration encourages the clinician to examine various theories and techniques and to incorporate those parts that are the best fit and the most effective for this particular person in need.

Contributed by Ernie Cowger,
Louisiana Tech University,
Barksdale Air Force Base, LA

References

Cavanagh, M. E. (1982). *The counseling experience.* Monterey, CA: Brooks/Cole.

Cavanagh, M. E., & Levitov, J. E. (2002). *The counseling experience: A theoretical and practical approach* (2nd ed.). Prospect Heights, IL: Waveland Press.

Corey, M. S., & Corey, G. (2006). *Groups: Process and practice* (7th ed.). Belmont, CA: Thomson Brooks/Cole.

Corsini, R. J., & Wedding, D. (2008). *Current psychotherapies* (8th ed.). Belmont, CA: ThomsonBrooks/Cole.

Ellis, A. (2008). Rational emotive behavior therapy. In R. J. Corsini & D. Wedding (Eds.), *Current psychotherapies* (pp. 187–222). Belmont, CA: Thomson Brooks/Cole.

Eysenck, H. J. (1970). A mish-mash of theories. *International Journal of Psychiatry, 9,* 140–146.

Gladding, S. T. (2002). *Counseling: A comprehensive profession* (2nd ed.). New York: Macmillan.

Ivey, A. E., & Ivey, M. B. (2003). *Intentional interviewing and counseling: Facilitating client development in a multicultural society.* Pacific Grove, CA: Thomson Brooks/Cole.

Lazarus, A. A. (2008). Multimodal therapy. In R. J. Corsini & D. Wedding (Eds.), *Current psychotherapies* (pp. 368–401). Belmont, CA: Thomson Brooks/Cole.

Murdock, N. L. (2004). *Theories of counseling and psychotherapy: A case approach.* Upper Saddle River, NJ: Pearson Education.

Norcross, J. C., & Beutler, L. E. (2008). Integrative psychotherapies. In R. J. Corsini & D. Wedding (Eds.), *Current psychotherapies* (8th ed., pp. 481–511). Belmont, CA: Thomson Brooks/Cole.

Seligman, L. (2001). *Systems, strategies, and skills of counseling and psychotherapy.* Upper Saddle River, NJ: Prentice Hall.

Seligman, L. (2004). *Technical and conceptual skills for mental health professionals.* Upper Saddle River, NJ: Pearson Education.

Thorne, F. C. (1973). Eclectic psychotherapy. In R. J. Corsini (Ed.), *Current psychotherapies* (pp. 445–486). Itasca, IL: Peacock.

Walborn, F. S. (1996). *Process variables.* Pacific Grove, CA: Brooks/Cole.

Additional Resources

Corey, G. (2001). *The art of integrative counseling.* Belmont, CA: Thomson Brooks/Cole.

Thorne, F. C. (1967). *Integrative psychology.* Brandon, VT: Clinical Psychology.

Ecological Counseling

Ecological counseling is an approach to counseling developed in the early 2000s that looks at health, helping, and change through the perspective of person–environment interaction. Its most important principle is that what people do and how they make meaning of their lives are the result of each person's interaction with his or her social and physical environment at any given point in time. As the pioneering social psychologist Kurt Lewin succinctly put it, behavior is a function of both person and environment. Through examining person–environment interaction in detail, ecological

counseling is able to open up additional levels of conceptualization and intervention that can be applied across diverse counseling theories, making it an important **metatheory** of counseling.

Although ecological counseling has engaged a wide range of disciplines, including community counseling, sociology, and social work, in attempting to relate person and environment, it has been shaped by three primary influences. From **Kurt Lewin's field theory,** it took the conviction that behavior is best understood as the outcome of a person's evaluation and interaction with the social/physical environment. From **Urie Bronfenbrenner's developmental theory,** it drew a framework for describing how each person is embedded in a multilayered, complex web of environmental relationships that promote development through recurring interactions. From **constructivism,** it took the view that truth and meaning are not simply objectively "out there," external to thought and language, but constructed by individuals and cultures.

These influences lead to key assumptions made by the ecological approach. First, ecological counseling focuses on examining persons within contexts. Persons and environments are not separate; they are always related, and their interaction is where professional counselors should look to understand their clients and work for change. Second, ecological counseling holds that human beings are neither entirely determined by nor radically independent of their environments. The two are interwoven: Using the resources and opportunities provided by their environments, clients seek to live meaningful lives, and in doing so, they change their environments. Thus, change in either person or environment will affect the other. Finally, ecological counseling takes a pragmatic and eclectic view of counseling theory, borrowing tools from different theories to effect change.

To conceptualize cases, ecological counseling makes use of a framework derived from Bronfenbrenner's concept of the **ecosystem,** a person's set of interactions with different levels of the social/physical environment. The ecological approach considers the interactions at each level as contributing both positively and negatively to clients' situations and as possible places to intervene for change. The levels of the ecosystem range from **proximal** (close) to **distal** (far).

The **microsystem** is the most proximal level of the ecosystem and consists of contexts in which there is face-to-face contact with the client (e.g., family, coworkers, small groups). The **mesosystem** consists of relationships among microsystems (e.g., home and school, work and family, church and civic organizations). The **exosystem** consists of those larger systems in which a person does not participate but whose decisions influence a person (e.g., religious bodies, governments, corporations, health care systems, the media, zoning boards). Finally, the **macrosystem** is the most distal influence on the client, consisting of the structures and cultural apparatus of a society (e.g., laws, language, economies, stereotypes, roles, ideals, climate).

Clients regularly inhabit a particular portion of their ecosystem, called their **ecological niche.** This portion of the ecosystem regularly influences a client's life. Assessment focuses on the ecological niche and the enduring patterns of meaning or **life patterns** with which clients approach their environments. The interaction between these two constitutes a **life space,** characterized by a better or worse fit.

Problems are the result of a poor fit, or **discordance,** between a client's life patterns and ecological niche. The goal of ecological counseling is to work for increased **concordance** between person and environment, leading to a mutually beneficial interaction. This optimal fit balances support with challenge, helping clients cope better with their problems while also encouraging their development. In reality, there is never any perfect match between person and environment; the goal of the ecological approach is to provide a good-enough match to promote development.

Just as in case conceptualization, the ecological approach considers the different levels of the ecosystem as potential places to intervene. As a metatheory, ecological counseling does not seek to create new interventions but seeks to use a wider variety of interventions from traditional person- or system-focused counseling linked together through the ecological framework. Thus, an ecological counselor might work with a client diagnosed with chemical dependency through individual motivational interviewing, family therapy, changing peer groups through Narcotics Anonymous, community advocacy to obtain just and affordable housing for the client's family and others in that position, and engaging the content of the client's faith tradition to help her or him make spiritual sense of her or his struggles. Moreover, ecological counseling can consider any level of the ecosystem to be a client: a person, a family, an organization, a government, even a society.

With increased scope, however, comes increased unintended consequences. Thus, the ecological approach stresses that interventions should be parsimonious, attempting the smallest changes that have a likelihood of success. Parsimonious changes often come from within the ecosystem and use local resources and ideas. Moreover, clients' autonomy must be honored through goal setting that is collaborative, getting the client to consider the entire spectrum of possible outcomes.

Ecological counseling brings an important perspective to many areas of counseling. For instance, while providing a framework for advocacy, the ecological perspective also asks when advocacy at different levels of the ecosystem is most parsimonious for different problems. The ecological perspective also moves beyond a simple contrast between spirituality and religion at the microsystemic level to a more nuanced picture of the influence of religious traditions and organizations on individuals at more distal levels of the ecosystem, even if these individuals are not formally affiliated with any religious organization. As these examples show, the ecological approach not only provides an important framework for counseling practice, it also provides an important perspective for advancing counseling theory and research.

Contributed by Joseph A. Stewart-Sicking, Loyola University Maryland, Baltimore, MD

Additional Resources

Bronfenbrenner, U. (1979). *The ecology of human development: Experiments by nature and design.* Cambridge, MA: Harvard University Press.

Conyne, R. K., & Cook, E. P. (Eds.). (2004). *Ecological counseling: An innovative approach to conceptualizing person–environment interaction.* Alexandria, VA: American Counseling Association.

Moen, P., Elder, G. H., & Luscher, K. (Eds.). (1995). *Examining lives in context: Perspectives on the ecology of human development.* Washington, DC: American Psychological Association.

Eco-Map

An **eco-map** is a graphical representation of the various social systems that constitute an individual's or family's life, such as friends, family, neighborhood, employment, professional affiliations, school, places of worship, community services, and other social systems (see Figure 1 for a sample eco-map). The purpose of the eco-map is to identify the various relationships and the scope of the relationships (i.e., strength, quality, impact) that an individual or family has with various social systems for use in prioritizing treatment needs and designing treatment interventions. The eco-map is typically completed by the client and professional counselor with paper and pencil and can be drawn spontaneously, or

Use each circle to represent the various social systems that exist around you, identifying the benefits that you receive from each and any distress or challenges that you encounter from each. Additionally, identify any special relationships that may exist in each and any social systems you do not feel connected with or supported by and any other important information. Examples of social systems may include neighborhood, school/employment, place of worship, friends, family, and other social systems that have significance to you.

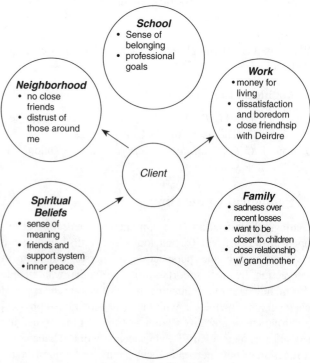

Figure 1. Sample Eco-Map

counselors may choose to use a previously developed outline. There is also software available for use in developing eco-maps (e.g., SmartDraw). The development of an eco-map typically requires approximately 10 to 15 minutes to complete, allowing for varying degrees of dialogue throughout the process. The eco-map can be used as an assessment tool, often at the onset of individual or family counseling. Eco-maps provide information to the client and the professional counselor regarding the various social systems with which the individuals or families are engaged as well as the degree of engagement with each system, thus providing a holistic or ecological view of the client.

Eco-Maps depict social systems as resources and strengths as well as sources of conflict and stress, thereby providing essential information to the client and counselor for use in treatment planning. Various symbols are used to illustrate the complexities of the relationships that the individual has with the various social systems. For instance, a dotted line connecting the individual to the social system indicates a tenuous relationship, whereas no line indicates that no connection exists between the individual and the social system. In addition, arrows are used to indicate the direction of the relationship and, as such, the impact of the relationship on the individual. For instance, an arrow directed from the individual to a particular social system indicates that energy is being taken from the individual and given to the social system, thereby depleting some of the individual's energy, whereas an arrow directed toward the individual from a social system indicates that energy is being provided to the individual from the social system.

Eco-maps were developed by family system practitioners to promote a sociocontextual view of the client. As such, eco-maps allow the individual to be viewed in conjunction with various social systems that make up the social environment, thereby taking a broader view of the individual into account and incorporating this view into the treatment process. This approach is contrary to adopting an intrapsychic view of the client that examines only the client in isolation from other individuals and social systems. As a result of the eco-map's origins in family counseling, they are often used in conjunction with **genograms,** another graphical mapping tool designed to provide a transgenerational view of an individual's family and the various relationships existing among family members.

In addition to providing essential information about a client's social connections (or lack thereof) in a quick and easy manner, as an assessment tool, the eco-map provides a significant intervention for the client by promoting exploration of social connections in the therapeutic context. Furthermore, the professional counselor may adapt eco-maps for a variety of uses in the counseling process. They can be used to direct treatment strategies by identifying specific client assets or strengths (e.g., neighborhood support, spiritual and/or religious connections) that should be incorporated into the therapeutic process, promoting conceptualization of the client from an alternative dimension, and assisting the client and counselor in identifying specific gaps or needs to be addressed in counseling. Through the identification of specific social system needs and the subsequent development of counseling strategies to address such needs, the use of an eco-map at various stages of counseling can provide continuous feedback to the client and counselor regarding treatment outcomes. Eco-maps have been found to be effective tools for collecting significant data related to the client's environment and, as such, have proven effective in assessment and treatment planning (Ferguson, 1999; Ray & Street, 2005).

As with all assessment practices in counseling, the assessment process offers an opportunity for the counselor and client to explore a particular area jointly and collaboratively. The counselor, therefore, facilitates the development of the eco-map, guiding the client through a series of exploratory questions to gain information related to each social system. Guiding questions that may be used by the counselor to assess the relationship that a client has with his or her neighborhood might include the following: "How well do you know your neighbors?" "In what ways do you socialize with your neighbors?" "What does your neighborhood mean to you?" and "Who is significant to you in your neighborhood and why?" The eco-map can empower the client as he or she goes through the process of developing it and subsequently uses it to develop therapeutic goals and to evaluate personal progress toward goal attainment. Because eco-maps can so easily be used by individuals and families and can promote client control in the assessment process, their use can often increase the engagement of clients in counseling and provide a deeper level of meaning to the counseling process.

Finally, eco-maps allow objective evaluation of the client's progress because the outcomes are both visible and tangible. Although the benefits of using an eco-map can be significant, as with all assessment tools, it should only be used in conjunction with other assessment tools to ensure comprehensive assessment practices. Care should be taken to ensure that the use of the eco-map as a clinical tool does not interfere with the development and maintenance of the therapeutic relationship but rather that it enhances the relationship. This is of particular importance when the counselor uses a computer program to develop the eco-map.

Contributed by Nancy G. Calley,
University of Detroit Mercy, Detroit, MI

References

Ferguson, D. (1999). Eco-maps: Facilitating insight in learning-disabled sex offenders. *British Journal of Nursing, 8,* 1224–1230.

Ray, R., & Street, A. F. (2005). Ecomapping: An innovative research tool for nurses. *Journal of Advanced Nursing, 50,* 545–552.

Additional Resources

Hodge, D. (2000). Spiritual ecomaps: A new diagrammatic tool. *Journal of Marital and Family Therapy, 26,* 217–228.

Vodde, R., & Giddings, M. M. (2001). The field system ecomap: A tool for conceptualizing practicum experiences. *Journal of Teaching in Social Work, 20,* 41–61.

Education Resources Information Center

The **Education Resources Information Center (ERIC)** is an Internet-based digital library with education research and information sponsored by the Institute of Education Sciences of the U.S. Department of Education. ERIC was developed in 1966 to provide free access to more than 1.2 million bibliographic records of journal articles, nonjournal materials, and other education-related bibliographic materials. In addition to digital material, ERIC also offers more than 115,000 full-text, PDF-formatted documents from more than 600 education-related journals. Most materials published in 2004 and beyond include links to other sources, including publishers' Web sites.

Specific bibliographic information offered by ERIC includes journal articles, books, conference papers, policy papers, research syntheses, and other education-related materials. Users of ERIC are instructors, students, parents, education researchers, librarians, administrators, media, and businesses. ERIC can be used to search for material with methods such as search, find, manage, and link. Search refers to using basic or advanced search options. Find allows users to locate relevant materials. Manage involves scanning through search criteria and search results. Link allows users to access available full-text materials in PDF or on the publishers' Web sites.

Computer Sciences Corporation, which is under contract to the U.S. Department of Education, operates ERIC. ERIC's contract supports the development and management of the digital collection, Web site, and associated technologies. Two expert advisory panels have been authorized to foster the ongoing development and transformation of ERIC to meet the changing needs of consumers.

Contributed by Teresa M. Christensen,
Old Dominion University, Norfolk, VA

Additional Resource

Education Resources Information Center Web site http://www.eric.ed.gov

Effectance Motivation

Effectance motivation is defined as a feeling of efficacy in transactions whereby behavior has an exploratory, varying, experimental character and produces changes in the stimulus field. Effectance motivation deals primarily with the concept of competence, which reflects an effective interaction with the environment. **Robert White** (1959), one of the original theorists in this area, believed that theories of motivation based on primary drives (e.g., psychoanalysis) are inadequate in explaining exploratory behavior, manipulation, and general activity. In essence, the theory of basic instincts falls short in its account of the effective ego, and there is no compelling reason to identify either pleasure or reinforcement with drive reduction or to conceptualize motivation as a source of energy external to the nervous system. Rather, it is better to consider animal and human behavior in the context of stimulation and contact with the environment being sought

and welcomed, elevated tension and mild excitation being cherished, and novelty and variety seemingly being enjoyed for their own sake.

Competence, in a broad biological sense, refers to an organism's capacity to interact effectively with its environment. Competence can be considered an innate attribute of organisms that are capable of basic or little learning; however, in mammals such as human beings, with their highly adaptable nervous system, interaction with their environment is slowly attained through prolonged feats of learning. It may be necessary, then, to treat competence as having a motivational aspect because its persistence and directedness lead to feats of learning. As such, motivation needed to attain competence cannot be derived solely from sources of energy conceptualized as drives and instincts. Humankind and animals capable of higher order learning develop a competence that is not found at birth and certainly does not arrive simply through maturation. This competence or behavior includes visual exploration; grasping, crawling, and walking; attention and perception; language and thinking; exploring novel objects and places; manipulating surroundings; and producing effective changes in the environment. This competence is derived from activities that are playful and exploratory in character but show direction, selectivity, and persistence in interacting with the environment. This motivation can be designated by the term *effectance,* and the feeling produced can be characterized as a feeling of efficacy.

Effectance motivation is neurogenic; its "energies" are simply those of living cells that make up the nervous system. External stimuli also play an important part, but this part is secondary to the "energy" providing clarity with environmental stimulation. The effectance urge represents what the neuromuscular system wants to do when it is otherwise unoccupied or is gently stimulated by the environment. Satisfaction lies in the arousal and maintaining of activity rather than in the slow decline toward bored passivity. The motive or arousal does not need to be as intense and powerful as hunger, pain, or fear can be when aroused. Strongly aroused drives such as pain and anxiety can be conceived as overriding the effectance urge and capturing the energies of the neuromuscular system. Effectance motivation, however, regularly occupies the spare waking time between episodes of homeostatic crisis. Independent of primary drives, it can have high adaptive value when, for human beings, so little is innate and so much has to be learned. Young animals and children learn at a slow rate during infancy; therefore, without an effective level of interaction with their surroundings, they simply would not learn enough unless they worked steadily at the task between homeostatic crisis. Therefore, strong motivation reinforces learning in a narrow sphere whereas moderate motivation engages exploration and experimentation, which leads to competent interactions without reference to an immediate pressing need.

Because there is no consummatory climax in effectance motivation, satisfaction, or the feeling of efficacy, must be considered in the series of transactions and trends of behavior rather than a goal that is achieved. Effectance motivation is aroused by stimulus conditions that offer difference-in-sameness. The response is novel and variable. The organism is then led to find out how the environment can be changed and what consequences are derived from these changes. Interest is best sustained when the resulting action affects the stimulus to produce further difference-in-sameness. When action begins to have less effect, interest wanes. Effectance motivation decreases when exploration no longer presents new possibilities.

Both the cognitive and active aspects of behavior can be attributed to the arousal of playful and exploratory behavior. Change in the stimulus field may happen during passive times or times of random movement without the intent of exploration. The neural basis of effectance motivation, however, does not refer to any and every kind of neural action. It refers to a particular type of behavior or activity. It does not include reflexes and other kinds of automatic response or well-learned habitual patterns, even those that are complex and highly organized. In addition, it does not include behaviors caused by deep arousal or behavior that is highly random and discontinuous. White (1959) stated that the urge toward competence is inferred specifically from behavior that shows a lasting focalization, with characteristics of exploration and experimentation. When this type of activity is aroused in the nervous system, effectance motivation is being aroused. It is characteristically selective, directed, and persistent, and instrumental acts will be learned for the sole reward of engaging in them.

Effectance motivation aims for the feeling of efficacy, not for the vitally important learning that comes as its consequence. It may lead to continuing exploratory interests or active adventures when in fact there is no longer any gain in actual competence or any need for it in terms of survival. The motive here is capable of yielding surplus satisfaction well beyond what is necessary to get the biological work done. Effectance motivation can be conceived as undifferentiated in young children, yet distinguishes motives such as cognizance, construction, mastery, and achievement in later life. They are differentiated through life experiences that emphasize some aspect of the cycle of transaction with the environment. It may be that the satisfaction of effectance contributes significantly to feelings of interest, which sustain day-to-day actions with continuing elements of novelty.

Contributed by Megan Scharett and Michael T. Garrett, University of Florida, Gainesville, FL

Reference

White, R. W. (1959).Motivation reconsidered: The concept of competence. *Psychological Review, 66,* 5.

Additional Resources

Fortune, A. E., Lee, M., & Cavazos, A. (2005). Achievement motivation and outcome in social work field education. *Journal of Social Work Education, 41,* 115–129.

Margolis, H., & McCabe, P. P. (2006). Improving self-efficacy and motivation: What to do, what to say. *Intervention in School and Clinic, 41,* 218–227.

■ Ego Development, Loevinger's Theory of

Ego development is a construct pioneered by **Jane Loevinger** and more recently refined by Susanne Cook-Greuter (1994). Although Loevinger (1979) preferred the term *self-development,* she chose the term *ego development* to encompass moral judgment, interpersonal relations, and the framework within which a person perceives himself or herself and others. Ego in this sense is what philosopher Ken Wilber called the **proximate self** (i.e., that which one considers self in contrast to the rest of the world). Cook-Greuter more colloquially stated that ego development is the template for the story that people tell about themselves and their world—and their story changes as they evolve. Loevinger (1973) emphasized that ego development happens in the real world, so it is necessary to look there to understand ego development rather than to arbitrary definitions. Toward this end, she concluded that a projective test was the best way to ascertain how a person made sense of the world.

Loevinger's stages were crafted and continually revised by data. Loevinger's ego development stages evolved from four levels adapted from Harry Stack Sullivan (i.e., impulsive, conformist, conscientious, and autonomous) and grew to include 10 stages. The first 2 are really prior to any sense of ego or self (presocial and symbiotic), whereas the final 8 (impulsive, self-protective, conformist, self-conscious, conscientious, individualistic, autonomous, and integrated) refer to an increasingly complex sense of self that, with each stage, requires a greater ability to take the perspective of others and make self an object awareness. The impulsive and self-protective stages are considered preconventional in that the person is very impulsive and self-centered and lacks an ability to take the perspective of others. The conformist, self-conscious, and conscientious stages are conventional, characterized by an increasingly complex balance between valuing one's own perspective and the perspectives of others. In the individualist stage, the person not only can hold multiple perspectives but reflects critically on his or her own role in cocreating reality. Loevinger had little to say about her two later stages, noting that there was not enough data at the time she was working to refine them further.

Cook-Greuter refined Loevinger's later stages of development through the same intense data analysis that Loevinger used to confirm the existence of the earlier stages. Cook-Greuter (1994) described ego development as "a sequence of consecutive stages of how human beings make sense of themselves and their experience. It explains both the strengths and the limits of a given meaning-making system and shows the next 'logic' of experience that a developing person will enter into" (p. 120). Cook-Greuter concluded that there were postconventional stages (i.e., individualist, construct aware, ego aware, and unitive) that, although rare, could be discerned in the types of responses given to the sentence stems in the Sentence Completion Test. She estimated that about 10% of adults function at preconventional levels of ego identity, 80% at conventional levels, and 10% at postconventional levels.

The quantitative scale to measure ego development is the Washington University Sentence Completion Test (WUSCT). A more recent version by Cook-Greuter is the Sentence Completion Test Integral (SCTi). These are projective tests that present 36 sentence stems (e.g., "When I am criticized…") that the respondent then completes. Each response is rated by at least one, and preferably two, trained raters using scoring manuals. (There are three manuals currently: Loevinger, Wessler, & Redmore, 1970; Hy & Loevinger, 1996; and a third being compiled by Cook-Greuter that adds responses from postconventional ego stages.) Both the WUSCT and the SCTi have excellent score reliability (.85 to .94; Loevinger & Wessler, 1970) and construct validity (Manners & Durkin, 2001). Their only drawback is the time it takes to score a protocol; a trained rater can usually score a protocol in 30 to 60 minutes.

Loevinger's construct is generally respected in the field of personality. Critics of Loevinger's construct note that her work does not provide a theory of change process. In other words, the theory still does not account for the factors that are correlated with growth in ego level. The research on experiences that correlate with change or growth in ego identity indicates the experiences are interpersonal in nature, disequilibrating to the individual, personally salient, and emotionally engaging (Manners & Durkin, 2000). **Disequilibrating** means that the experiences introduce dissonance into the person's current worldview. The idea behind this factor is that when people cannot resolve the dissonance at their current level of ego development, they are motivated to seek a new way of experiencing the world, which can be found in the next level of ego development. Again, if the issue around which a client is experiencing dissonance is interpersonal in nature, personally salient, and emotionally engaging, there is a higher likelihood that the person will grow into the next level of ego development to resolve the dissonance. Because a person can be healthy or unhealthy at any given level, growth is not a necessity, but it does give a person more tools to use in navigating life.

Counseling Implications

Although only a few counselor educators have used ego development as a research construct, its increased use in coaching and counseling for wellness points to a growing relevance for the construct in the field of counseling. Understanding a client's level of ego development provides important information about how that client views the world, the types of things likely to be threatening to the client, and the things the client values. This added knowledge increases the probability that the counselor will meet the client where the client is developmentally and use more appropriate language interventions with the client.

Contributed by Elliott Ingersoll,
Cleveland State University, Cleveland, OH

References

Cook-Greuter, S. (1994). Rare forms of self-understanding in mature adults. In M. E. Miller & S. R. Cook-Greuter (Eds.), *Transcendence and mature thought in adulthood: The further reaches of adult development* (pp. 119–147). Lanham, MD: Rowan & Littlefield.

Hy, L. X., & Loevinger, J. (1996). *Measuring ego development* (2nd ed.). Mahwah, NJ: Erlbaum.

Loevinger, J. (1973). Ego development: Syllabus for a course. *Psychoanalysis and Contemporary Science, 2,* 77–98.

Loevinger, J. (1979). The idea of the ego. *The Counseling Psychologist, 8,* 3–5.

Loevinger, J., & Wessler, R. (1970). *Measuring ego development: Volume 1.* San Francisco: Jossey Bass.

Loevinger, J., Wessler, R., & Redmore, C. (1970). *Measuring ego development 2: Scoring manual for women and girls.* San Francisco: Jossey Bass.

Manners, J., & Durkin, K. (2000). Processes involved in adult ego development: A conceptual framework. *Developmental Review, 20,* 475–513.

Manners, J. & Durkin, K. (2001). A critical review of the validity of ego development and its measurement. *Journal of Personality Assessment, 77,* 541–567.

Additional Resources

Loevinger, J. (1976). *Ego development.* San Francisco: Jossey Bass.

Westenberg, M. P., Blasi, A., & Cohn, L. D. (Eds.). (1998). *Personality development: Theoretical, empirical, and clinical investigations of Loevinger's conception of ego development.* Mahwah, NJ: Erlbaum.

Wilber, K. (2006). *Integral spirituality: A startling new role for religion in the modern and postmodern world.* Boston: Shambhala.

Ego Psychology: Erikson's Psychosocial Stage Theory

In 1950, **Erik Erikson** first published *Childhood and Society,* in which he described eight stages of **ego identity.** His **psychosocial theory,** sometimes termed **ego psychology,** was an alternative to previous psychoanalytic theories that he believed neglected the positive social contributions to ego development. Erikson was originally a child analyst who developed his theory of ego development from his work with children in Vienna, Austria, supplemented by his and others' research and historical/literary accounts of American Indians and American, German, and Russian cultures.

Erikson's eight stages of development span the entire life cycle. Each stage is described by two ego qualities, one that demonstrates that the individual has successfully met the challenges of this particular critical period and one that demonstrates a general lack of success. This should not be interpreted to mean that stage development has an all-or-nothing outcome. Although Erikson gave no specific guidelines for measuring successful development, he believed an individual's relative success at each stage could be evaluated by examining the individual's behavior, unconscious inner states, and subjective sense of health or disease. In addition, although each new stage presented a new challenge or crisis, each stage was also affected by the individual's success in negotiating previous stages.

Stage 1: Basic Trust Versus Basic Mistrust

According to psychosocial theory, the primary task of the infant is to develop a general sense that the world is a predictable place, where, in general, his or her basic needs are met and where, at a very rudimentary level, he or she has a sense of self that is all right. When an infant experiences a world with little predictability; where needs are often ignored, unmet, or interfered with; or where there appears to be little meaning in the caregivers' actions, then a basic sense of **mistrust** develops. The infant may have a fractured sense of self, or a general sense that either he or she is not all right or that the world is not nurturing, dependable, or meaningful. Individuals who develop more mistrust than **trust** may appear relatively normal, although pessimistic, or in more severe cases the individual may be habitually depressed, incapable of close relationships, or psychotic.

Stage 2: Autonomy Versus Shame and Doubt

The developing child with a relative sense of basic trust engages in simple decision making. She or he learns to stand on her or his own two feet both literally and figuratively. Children test their willfulness, their ability to control themselves, and their environment. The successful outcome of this sensitive period facilitates the development of an individual who can make decisions to benefit self or others, an individual who can be both cooperative and **autonomous,** and an individual who can generally regulate thoughts and emotions with pride instead of a loss in self-esteem. On the other hand, poor negotiation of this stage may result in overcontrolling behavior, either of self or others. Individuals lacking autonomy may have difficulty making decisions. They may seem incapable of purposeful testing of their environment. **Shame,** which some believe is rage turned inward, may result, leaving the individual feeling small, self-conscious, angry, and evil or sneaky. **Doubt,** frequently coupled with shame, may lead to an individual's nagging suspicion that he or she is a puppet subject to the will of the puppeteer or that his or her decisions or sense of control is always suspect and subject to revocation at any time.

Stage 3: Initiative Versus Guilt

Initiative, as opposed to autonomy, involves planning or attacking and is not so much about testing control as it is about directing an individual's energies toward a goal, fantasy, or accomplishment. Developing initiative allows people to act on their dreams; to construct, experiment and plan; to create things for both good and evil. The danger for the child at this stage is that the child's superego evaluates the child's motives, motives that may be greedy, jealous, spiteful, manipulative, outlandish, or self-serving. If the child is particularly punitive or controlling, he or she may then become **guilt-ridden** or inhibited, constricted and self-righteous or develop psychosomatic complaints. Adult manifestations of thwarted initiative are hysteria, inhibition, impotence, or the opposite behavior—being a show-off. It may also be displayed as moralistic hypervigilance.

Stage 4: Industry Versus Inferiority

In Stage 4, which coincides with Freud's latency period, children learn the skills and tasks required to become productive members of society eventually. In industrialized societies, these skills may be those taught in school. In other cultures, the skills may be those necessary to meet the needs for food, clothing, and shelter. Common to all cultures is a training period during which the child is taught to work in collaboration with others, not just to play at what interests the child but to work at a task deemed important by society. Those who do not develop a sense of competence in this stage are left with a sense of **inferiority.** Erikson noted another serious danger at this age: Individuals who equate their value with the work to which they have been assigned may become thoughtless conformists, tools of people who will exploit them.

Stage 5: Identity Versus Role Confusion

Stage 5 coincides with the advent of puberty and is a period of integration, during which adolescents must integrate their new sense of sexuality with the aptitudes and competencies recognized by themselves and others and fit these personal qualities into a future career. This task is more difficult because of adolescents' concern about appearances and their tendency toward idealism. Adolescents who are unable to define their sexual **identity,** their aptitudes or competencies, or a suitable future career are likely to experience an intolerable confusion that leads to adopting the identity of someone else (e.g., a hero or a group identity). Similarly, adolescents who are unable to integrate their self-assessments with those of others to find a suitable niche in society may find their identity in the eyes of a lover. In either case, the individual has failed to develop a unique identity, and the resulting condition, which Erikson called **role confusion,** leaves the individual subject to the beliefs and values of others, in a sense without a personal rudder.

Stage 6: Intimacy Versus Isolation

The security of a personal identity enables the individual to enter into close relationships with others without feeling engulfed, negated, or diminished. The task at this age is to commit to other people or affiliations and learn to negotiate one's own needs and expectations with the needs and expectations of others. This allows a person to feel enhanced by sexual relationships, intimate relationships, close friendships, and other close affiliations, as opposed to struggling in these relationships to preserve a sense of self or abandoning his or her self in the service of others. Individuals who are unable to maintain a sense of identity while in a close relationship are prone to distance themselves from **intimacy** and become **isolated.** Those who feel threatened by the demands of others may also feel forced to defend themselves, to become hostile or antagonistic, and others may view them as self-absorbed and/or unethical.

Stage 7: Generativity Versus Stagnation

As people accept the inevitability of death and nonexistence on earth, they must confront the enduring value of their lives.

The mark that a person leaves behind can be described as **generativity,** and it may be manifested in a person's children, either biological or those children whom he or she has mentored. It can also be manifested in the works people leave behind (e.g., creative endeavors, their products, or an example for others to follow). Those who are unable to extend their interests beyond themselves, who remain focused on personal need satisfaction, are likely to feel impoverished or let down by others. Erikson describes this as a pervading sense of **stagnation.**

Stage 8: Integrity Versus Despair

The individual who arrives at this stage with a sense of **integrity** has accepted the natural order of things, including death. This individual may recognize past mistakes but accept his or her life for what it was, imperfect but nonetheless deserving of dignity, often because it had to be the way it was. Those who are not reconciled to their own death or the choices they made in life often fear death and **despair** that life will end before they can make it right. Erikson believed that disgust was at the base of this despair, disgust for the way people had lived their lives, the lost opportunities, or the inability to create a life to their liking.

A Critique of Erikson's Psychosocial Theory

Erikson's theory has been criticized for being ethnocentric, because it was based primarily on Western cultures. It has also been criticized for its gender bias, in that there is a greater focus on autonomy and achievement than on community and inclusion. Because Erikson's psychosocial theory does not account for the variation often seen in the development of identity and intimacy, some have suggested that Erikson missed a stage or ordered the stages incorrectly, particularly around the periods of adolescence and young adulthood. Young women, for example, may orient toward the development of intimacy before focusing on identity development. Furthermore, today many theorists believe that identity development continues well into adulthood and is not, as Erikson theorized, solidified by the time of young adulthood.

Nevertheless, Erikson's psychosocial theory has made a significant contribution to the field of human development. His theory is relatively consistent with other theories of development (e.g., theories of cognitive development, moral development, spiritual development, Freud's theory of psychosexual development, and other theories of ego development). In addition, Erikson's psychosocial theory of development spans the entire life span from infancy to old age, and it is the only major life-span theory specifically focused on social–emotional development. It was one of the first developmental theories to account for the interaction between nature, nurture, and individual human motivation.

Contributed by Barbara L. Carlozzi,
Oklahoma State University,
Stillwater, OK

Reference

Erikson, E. (1950). *Childhood and society.* New York: Norton.

Additional Resources

Crain, W. (1992). *Theories of development: Concepts and applications* (3rd ed.). Englewood Cliffs, NJ: Prentice Hall.
Kroger, J. (2007). *Identity development: Adolescence through adulthood* (2nd ed.). Thousand Oaks, CA: Sage.
McAdams, D. P. (2006). *The redemptive self: Stories Americans live by.* New York: Oxford University Press.
Miller, P. H. (1993). *Theories of developmental psychology* (3rd ed.). New York: Freeman.

■ Ethical Principles

Counseling professionals define ethics differently, depending on theory, morality, and practicality. Some emphasize theory rather than practice in examining "good" or "right" helping behaviors. Others embrace rules, principles, and standards governing appropriate conduct and acceptable practice. Regardless of the perspective, counseling professionals agree that ethics guide thinking and behavior. Culture and social values, worldviews, and life experiences influence how people think and behave when defining and resolving problems and how they conduct themselves and define acceptable practice.

Principles recognized in the counseling profession as foundational guidelines for ethical standards include nonmaleficence, beneficence, justice, and fidelity. Counselors are challenged to recognize and understand the relevance of cultural and social influences on these principles in today's diverse world. The following offers a discussion of the four principles, poses questions for consideration, and offers ideas to help counselors function at a higher ethical level by infusing cultural and social justice perspectives into the principles.

Nonmaleficence

The principle of **nonmaleficence** mandates that counselors purposefully engage in counseling behaviors that avoid harm. Ethical practice in a diverse world mandates that counselors consider cultural values and worldviews as determinants of what may or may not be harmful. The implementation of nonmaleficence spans from using appropriate helping techniques to avoiding practicing outside a counselor's scope of competence with diverse clients. Counselors striving to do no harm have an ethical responsibility to question the cultural dictates underlying a client's behavior and to examine the influences of these dictates on their interpretations of the behaviors, particularly when assessing, diagnosing, and designing treatment plans. The following scenario and queries illustrate this principle.

A school counselor interacts with an African American child and notices the child does not make eye contact. The counselor interprets the lack of eye contact as shy behavior. *(What cultural values are motivating the thinking and behavior of the client?)* The counselor decides to increase the child's self-esteem by teaching the child to make eye contact when talking. *(How might this helping technique be harmful to the client?)*

One way to implement nonmaleficence in a culturally appropriate context in this scenario is to identify cultural dictates by becoming knowledgeable of thematic African American values, particularly those related to communication styles and children's roles with adults. The counselor can then use the cultural knowledge as a foundation for determining how to respond to questions of cultural values motivating thought and behavior and for selecting helping techniques that address the needs and issues of clients.

Beneficence

The principle of **beneficence** mandates that counselors engage psychologically and intellectually in good behavior as they provide services and promote client outcome. Ethically, counselors operate within the client's cultural and social contexts rather their own. Section A of the American Counseling Association's (ACA; 2005) *ACA Code of Ethics* illustrates beneficence in developing a counseling relationship and states,

> Counselors encourage client growth and development in ways that foster the interest and welfare of clients and promote formation of healthy relationships. Counselors actively attempt to understand the diverse cultural backgrounds of the clients they serve. Counselors also explore their own cultural identities and how these affect their values and beliefs about the counseling process. (p. 4)

Counselors striving toward positive outcomes are aware, knowledgeable, and skillful in discerning the impact of the differences between them and their clients. They balance decisions about helping with the cultural beliefs, values, and assumptions of clients and commit to actions that increase growth. Good behavior depends on the counselor's ability to weigh the beliefs and values that the counselor and client bring to the table and how both influence outcome. Questions and ideas to help counselors carry out the principle of beneficence follow.

- A counselor should ask what his or her cultural and social beliefs, values, and assumptions about abilities, class, ethnicity, gender, race, sexual orientation, and religion are and should complete assessments (e.g., Ibrahim's Worldview Assessment) and surveys (e.g., reading Pedersen's culturally biased assumptions) to identify and monitor personal and culturally biased assumptions and beliefs.
- What are the client's cultural and social beliefs, values, and assumptions about abilities, class, ethnicity, gender, race, sexual orientation, and religion? Counselors can identify and use creative helping tools, such as collages, that provide information about cultural and social worldviews and quality of life.

Justice

The principle of **justice** mandates that counselors should act fairly toward clients. Counselors should recognize unique situations, backgrounds, and cultures of clients and operate with reasonable and impartial helping behaviors. They should relate to clients (regardless of ability, age, ethnicity gender, race, religion, sexual orientation, and socioeconomic status) as equal beings entitled to the same economic, political, and social privileges and opportunities as others. Counselors do not discriminate against clients due to a monolithic view of the world; rather, they recognize cultural and social implications for how life is experienced in a just and unjust society. They possess multicultural and advocacy competencies to help clients live more fully by being creative in identifying interventions consistent with clients' cultural and social values. For example, counselors working with clients who self-identify as female and value a relationally oriented life approach may choose to use a collectivistic intervention, such as group work, to display helping that is more respectful of cultural and gender values and beliefs. As counselors begin the process of justice, they may ask questions such as, How does their theory of counseling influence them to act fairly toward all clients? What are they doing to ensure that they interweave equal treatment into their counseling?

Fidelity

The principle of **fidelity** mandates that counselors generate thoughts and actions that promote the development of trusting and therapeutic relationships. Counselors displaying this principle are honest, trustworthy, and loyal when offering promises and commitments. They are informed about their clients' cultures, practice within a culturally appropriate context, and are able to anticipate situations that may discount the importance of the client's culture and subsequent effects on the quality of the relationship and effectiveness of trust. Counselors can adhere to the principle of fidelity by being cautious with language that may trivialize client problems. For example, to tell a client, without respect for the client's cultural and social contexts, that "everything will be okay" may provide an inaccurate assessment of the world in which the client lives and provide a false sense of security that may have an impact on the client's psychological or emotional health. Counselors have ethical mandates such as informed consent and confidentiality designed to help guide their practice of fidelity. It is significant that to meet these mandates, counselors must infuse culturally appropriate values, assumptions, and worldviews into their thoughts and actions to ensure that the mandate is interpreted and enacted within a culturally appropriate framework (Corey, Corey, & Callanan, 2007; Pack-Brown & Williams, 2003). Counselors may also position themselves to meet the ethical principle of fidelity by posing and responding to critical questions such as, How do they professionally and culturally define faithfulness? How is trust defined, developed, and displayed in the client's cultural and individual worldviews?

The four principles discussed here contribute to the formation of a culturally intentional and ethical helping foundation. Each reflects rules defining and modifying human behavior in a cultural and social context. Regardless of the theoretical or practice orientation of the counselor, only through practicing competently will the counselor be able to avoid doing harm (nonmaleficence)

> within an environment that meets the expectations for the relationship that is agreed upon by the counselor and client (fidelity), in a way that recognizes the client's unique situation, background, and culture (fairness), and helps bring about a positive outcome for the client (beneficence). (Pack-Brown & Williams, 2003, p. 78)

Contributed by Sherlon P. Pack-Brown,
Bowling Green State University,
Bowling Green, OH

References

American Counseling Association. (2005). *ACA code of ethics*. Alexandria, VA: Author.

Corey G., Corey, M. S., & Callanan, P. (2007). *Issues and ethics in the helping professions*. Belmont, CA: Thomson Brooks/Cole.

Pack-Brown, S. P., & Williams, C. B. (2003). *Ethics in a multicultural context*. Thousand Oaks, CA: Sage.

Additional Resource

Pedersen, P. (1987). Ten frequent assumptions of cultural bias in counseling. *Journal of Multicultural Counseling and Development, 4,* 16–24.

■ Ethnicity

Many nations have become more pluralistic as people from ethnic and cultural groups have moved throughout the world. These demographic shifts have increased the pluralities and complexities of ethnic and cultural identities that exist among and within groups of people and, in the process, have influenced the language used in conversations about ethnicity.

Although a broad definition of the word *ethnicity* sometimes includes cultural and physical characteristics and is used interchangeably in the literature with the concept of **race,** the concepts are different. To use the terms synonymously is to ignore the rather complex relationship that exists between race and ethnicity. The construct of race is based on a biological foundation (i.e., heredity and physical traits) whereas **ethnicity** refers to a person's affiliation with a particular ethnic group of people who share a social or cultural history (e.g., Irish, Italian, Jewish, American Indian, Cambodian, Chinese, African American). Within each ethnic group is a multiplicity of cultural patterns based on a common language; religion; physical characteristics; customs; geographical location; family; ancestry; or a subculture of a larger cultural, religious, racial, or gender group. For some people, ethnicity involves a loose group identity with little or no cultural traditions in common. Family may have moved away from cultural roots and assimilated into the more dominant culture. Therefore, a person's ethnicity is fluid, often appearing seamless, shifting as a person becomes more aware and accepts the multitude of cultural patterns that weave together to create his or her unique ethnic self.

Another concept associated with ethnicity is **ethnocentrism,** which is derived from the Greek word *ethnos,* meaning "nation" or "people," and implies a strong allegiance to a group. Ethnocentrism is a belief that an individual's own ethnicity is superior to all others. Inherent in this belief of superiority about a person's own beliefs, values, and attitudes is an allegiance to a given standard against which all other groups are measured. Ethnocentric views may lead to intolerance, segregation, and oppression.

There has been a growing awareness in the mental health field of the need to eliminate ethnic and racial disparities in counseling and to understand better the role that ethnicity plays in seeking services, diagnosis, and treatment. Ethnicity as a social construct can be used to divide people into subgroups to influence the perceptions of others negatively or positively. Narrowly defined concepts of ethnicity and ethnic identity often fail to capture and communicate the complexity of individuals and groups of people. Negative and positive messages about ethnicity influence the development of self-esteem and an ethnic identity as people learn to accept, deny, and disown parts of themselves within a cultural context.

Contributed by Ann Shanks Glauser,
The University of Georgia, Athens, GA

Additional Resources

Adams, M., Bell, L. A., & Griffin, P. (Eds.). (1997). *Teaching for diversity and social justice*. London: Routledge.

Williams, C. B. (1999). Claiming a biracial identity. Resisting social constructions of race and culture. *Journal of Counseling & Development, 77,* 32–37.

■ European Americans, Counseling

Although **European Americans** are considered to belong to the dominant culture in the United States, the umbrella term *European American* actually comprises many diverse ethnic cultures that professional counselors need to learn about in order to develop their cultural competency. The term *European American* is more narrowly defined than either of the terms *Caucasian* or *White*. The term *Caucasian* originated from anthropology as a crude definition of race based on the evaluation of skull features. Contemporary use of the term *Caucasian* is synonymous with the term *White*. The term *White* refers to persons living in the United States whose origins were European, North African, and Middle Eastern regions. The U.S. Bureau of the Census began to use the term *European American* in the late 1970s to replace the term *White,* although since that time, the U.S. Census Bureau has returned to the latter term. European American refers to a person living in the United States who either has previous generations of family from Europe or is a first-generation immigrant from Europe. European Americans immigrated to the United States in two major waves, 1800–1850 and 1880–1920. The first wave, 1800–1850, included Northern and Western Europeans (e.g., Germans, Irish, Scots, English, and French), whereas the second wave, 1880–1920, included Southern and Eastern Europeans (e.g., Italians, Greeks, Poles, and Ukrainians).

Demographically, the 2000 U.S. census indicated that Northern Europeans make up the largest percentage of the U.S. population (30.9%), followed by Western Europeans (18.6%), Southern Europeans (7.1%), and Eastern Europeans (4.9%). In comparison with the 1990 U.S. census, the percentage of the U.S. population that was made up of Northern, Western, and Eastern Europeans significantly decreased while only Southern Europeans increased in numbers. Collectively, in 1990, European Americans accounted for 84.2% of the U.S. population, whereas in 2000, European Americans had dropped to 60.4% of the U.S. population. The four European American subgroups highlighted in this entry (i.e., German Americans, Greek Americans, Italian Americans, and Irish Americans) were chosen in part because of the large numbers who immigrated to the United States (Germans, Italians, and Irish), representation of northern (Irish and Germans) and southern European regions (Italians and Greek), and both the similarities the subgroups share and the differences between them in the cultural dimensions that are discussed. The generalizations made are broad, and readers are reminded that within-group differences are ordinarily as substantial or more substantial than between-group differences. To help orient professional counselors to the different examples of European American culture, several cultural dimensions were selected, including individualism versus collectivism, family structure (i.e., patriarchal, matriarchal, or egalitarian), cultural values, communication style, and counseling attitudes.

Individualistic Versus Collectivistic

Individualistic cultures tend to promote autonomy, independence, and achievement of their members, whereas **collectivist cultures** tend to put the needs of the group ahead of the needs of the individual members, thus valuing cooperation, relationships, and a sense of community. On the continuum of individualistic to collectivistic, the Irish Americans are the most individualistic, followed by German Americans (mostly individualistic), whereas both Italian and Greek Americans tend to reflect more collectivistic cultures. Irish Americans tend to emphasize independence because they do not see extended family as a source of support and tend to keep problems from them out of fear of embarrassment (individualistic). Irish Americans do have collectivistic cultural elements as well, including a strong emphasis on the Irish American mother–son bond as the most significant relationship in Irish American families, which is actually considered more important than Irish marriages. The involved Irish American mother role continues throughout the Irish American son's adult life. Protestant German Americans emphasize individual responsibility and rigid boundaries to protect privacy and prefer to live separately from their extended family (individualistic) while at the same time maintaining a strong emotional attachment to their extended family. Both Irish American daughters and German American children reflect some collectivistic ele-

ments, such as reciprocity of care, in their relationships where they are expected to take care of their elderly parents. Greek Americans tend to be more collectivistic because they are both family and community oriented, and Greek American women are socialized to attend to the family's needs because the culture assigns a strong value to motherhood, and mothers encourage daughters to help care for younger siblings as well as elderly family members. Greek American men, however, tend to be more individualistic than are their wives, as demonstrated by their active social life outside of the family that at times may result in extramarital affairs. The Greek American male practice of "kefi" is the present-oriented, spontaneous, nature-oriented (explained away as satisfying natural urges) practice of extracurricular sexual activity that is permitted as long as men do not divorce their wives or abandon their children. Similar to Greek Americans, family is primary for Italian Americans. Family members are to remain physically, emotionally, and psychologically close to meet family needs and care for elderly members. Italians place a strong value on neighborhood relationships, and they prefer their extended family to live in the same neighborhood.

Patriarchal, Matriarchal, and Egalitarian Family Structures

Family structure is concerned with how families are organized in terms of power and decision-making authority and include **patriarchal structure** (male-dominated authority), **matriarchal structure** (female-dominated authority), or **egalitarian structure** (shared authority among men and women). German, Greek, and Italian American families tend to be patriarchal, whereas Irish American families are typically matriarchal. In German, Greek, and Italian American families, the father is head of the household, an authoritarian disciplinarian who is less available emotionally to children (more so for German and Greek American fathers), provider to family, and major decision maker. Traditionally, the father's authority is not challenged, and a woman is expected to support her husband's decisions and not to challenge her husband publicly. German, Greek, and Italian American mothers typically assume a complementary traditional role in taking care of household tasks, being the emotional heart of the family, and managing child-rearing responsibilities whereby mothers are usually more involved with children than are fathers. Alternatively, the role of the Irish American mother is primary in Irish families. They manage all family members, including the father, who tends to be a peripheral family figure, and children and handle family responsibilities and burdens with little emotional expression. Similar to German, Greek, and Italian American fathers, Irish American mothers closely supervise their children to protect the family name in the community.

Cultural Values

Cultural values articulate what a cultural group defines as vitally important in life. German, Greek, and Italian American cultures all place family as a key cultural value, whereas Irish American Catholics traditionally have viewed the church as being more important than family. In German, Greek, and Italian American cultures, there is an expectation that first loyalty is to the family. All four ethnicities are concerned with how the family is perceived in the community (**family honor** or reputation) although for Irish Americans, it is primarily related to the importance of family members' compliance with the Catholic Church's authority. The cultural value placed on family relates to the family as being the source of support during difficult times rather than outsiders providing support (for German, Greek, and Italian Americans) and duty to family in terms of caring for family members across the life span (for German, Greek, Italian, and Irish Americans). Other cultural values include the importance of **work ethic** (for German and Italian Americans), education (for German, Greek, Irish Americans for both genders, and Italian Americans only to the extent that education meets family needs), ethnic identity (German and Irish Americans tend to be more guarded due to their histories, whereas Greek and Italian Americans emphasize their cultural traditions), adaptability and resilience (for German, Greek, Irish, and Italian Americans), efficiency (for German Americans), respectability (for German, Greek, Irish, and Italian Americans), warmth (for Italian Americans), spontaneity (for Italian Americans), and fate (for Irish and Italian Americans).

Communication Style

European American cultures vary considerably in terms of their communication style, which includes levels of emotional expressiveness, use of colloquial language, expressing/demonstrating affection, conflict management strategies, and nonverbal behavior. In terms of emotional expressiveness, German, Irish, and Greek Americans (particularly Greek American men) tend to be more emotionally reserved, whereas Italian Americans are the most emotionally expressive. Italian Americans are also known for their facial and kinesthetic expressions. The Irish Americans are most known for their use of colloquial language that includes slang, colorful expressions, and phrases, in part because colloquial language could be used by Irish Americans to remain evasive, masking their true feelings and beliefs on controversial topics. There is wide variance in expression or demonstration of affection even within families because German Americans tend not to express affection verbally (e.g., "I love you") and prefer to demonstrate love through deeds. Similarly, Irish and Greek Americans tend not to demonstrate affection in front of children although Italian Americans prefer to show affection regularly among family members as a sign of warmth and connection. In terms of expressing appreciation for the achievements of children, both Irish American mothers and Italian Americans prefer to withhold praise from their children, but for different reasons. Irish American mothers are concerned that their children will become conceited, whereas Italian Americans worry that encouraging too much individual success can result in children separating from family when they become adults.

The European American ethnic cultures differ in terms of how they prefer to handle conflict. German Americans tend to be rigid and less expressive and may choose emotional cutoff rather than change rules to be more developmentally appropriate. Greek and Irish Americans (mostly Irish American men) often avoid conflict, although Irish American mothers do communicate discipline to children through use of ridicule, belittling, criticism, and sarcasm. Although Italian Americans will avoid difficult issues, they are the cultural group that seems most comfortable with overtly arguing within the family. As expected, Italian Americans are the most emotionally expressive ethnicity discussed here and therefore also are the most nonverbally expressive in terms of demonstrative gestures in conversation.

Counseling Attitudes

German Americans tend to be highly independent, thus attending counseling sessions goes against this value and is often a last resort to address a family-related crisis. Seeking help is seen as weakness, failure, lack of work ethic, or the result of irresponsible choices. Greek Americans are concerned about family reputation in the community and, therefore, prefer to seek counseling from non-Greek Americans about somatic complaints rather than psychological issues because the latter are thought to be influenced by previous generations (i.e., genetics) and so Greek American families tend to hide these issues from the community. Irish Americans may view counseling as similar to confession (disclose sins and seek forgiveness) and see problems as private matters between an individual and God, which makes it harder for them to seek counseling or any outside help from extended family or community when issues occur. Irish American clients often need third-party referrals to begin counseling. Italian Americans tend to mistrust outsiders and, therefore, rely heavily on family. Family members protect the family's honor and avoid any behavior that would disgrace the family, which includes talking about the family to outsiders, including counselors. Italian Americans believe problems should be handled within the family and tend to underutilize counseling, but when they do go, they are concerned that they will be seen as failures. As a result, going to therapy needs to be reframed as "caring for family" rather than "family failure."

European Americans are a significant proportion of many professional counselors' practice, and, therefore, it is important for professional counselors to continue to develop their cultural competency. Professional counselors need to learn about the cultural nuances of European American subgroups in order to retain those subgroups that currently use counseling services as well as better serve the European American subgroups that underutilize counseling services.

Contributed by Darren A. Wozny,
Mississippi State University–
Meridian, Meridian, MS

Reference

U.S. Bureau of the Census. (2000). *2000 U.S. census of population and housing.* Washington, DC: Author.

Additional Resources

Baruth, L. G., & Manning, M. L. (2007). *Multicultural counseling and psychotherapy: A lifespan perspective* (4th ed.). Upper Saddle River, NJ: Merrill Prentice Hall.

McGoldrick, M., Giordano, J., & Garcia-Preto, N. (2005). *Ethnicity and family therapy* (3rd ed.). New York: Guilford Press.

Exchange Theory

Social psychologists and sociologists constructed the **exchange theory,** or **social exchange theory,** in the 1950s. John Thibaut, Harold Kelley, George C. Homans, and Peter M. Blau were the principal theorists who initially defined and expanded exchange theory as the negotiated exchanges occurring between people. Individuals in relationships negotiate exchanges through a subjective cost–benefit analysis, wherein each seeks to maximize personal benefits and minimize personal costs. Given that the initial theorists drew from economic theory, a simple formula for exchange theory is total reward minus total cost in any relationship (Rewards – Costs = Exchange). Relationships are satisfying to the degree that each person evaluates the behaviors received as having more positive benefits than negative costs. When a person in a rocky marriage determines that the costs outweigh the benefits, the person would be inclined to leave. Homans asserted that both parties in an interaction were subjectively aware of the potential and respective profits and payoffs available to each party. Such a linear view of relationships and interactions may be criticized for being overly rational and lacking cultural sensitivity. Choice generally involves more than a simple rational assessment of costs and rewards; emotional and cultural values influence choice. Even though Thibaut and Kelly saw mutual exchange and social interaction as influenced by the interdependence of participants, the rational and linear structure gives exchange theory an individualistic cultural bias and may not be appropriate for collectivist cultures.

Exchange theory has been applied to counseling. Clients seek professional counselors for help with their problems, whereas counselors need clients for their livelihoods and to maintain their professional identities. Professional counselors must be mindful of the power and ethical implications of their professional role in the exchange. There are two major tenets of exchange theory. First, individuals negotiate exchanges based on subjective cost–benefit analysis. For example, the counselor might help a client weigh the costs and rewards of staying in a relationship. Second, social life is characterized by scarcity, and people must choose and make decisions. The counselor might help clients who have multiple marriage prospects to recognize that in the United States, they can marry only one person and that they must choose one partner over another based on what they consider the costs and rewards of each relationship.

Contributed by Rolla E. Lewis,
California State University,
East Bay, CA

Additional Resources

Blau, P. M. (1964). *Exchange and power in social life.* New York: Wiley.

Homans, G. C. (1958). Social behavior as exchange. *American Journal of Sociology, 63,* 597–606.

Thibaut, J. W., & Kelley, H. H. (1959). *The social psychology of groups.* New York: Wiley.

Existential Counseling

Unlike other theoretical orientations, **existential theory** is grounded in a philosophical context, extending its reach to include an individual's view of self, life, and the world. At the heart of the existential journey is humanity's search for meaning. For human beings, to experience a sense of their own mortality and to construct meaning in the shadow of their eventual death reframe their perception of reality, drawing them from the past or future to focus more fully on their present experience.

The word **existentialism** is rooted in the Latin, *exsistere,* meaning to exist; to be; or perhaps more appropriately, to emerge or to become (Traupman, 1966). Philosophically, existentialism arose in reaction to earlier concepts of rationalism and empiricism. Rejecting Descartes's hypothesis that conscious thought is the ultimate reality, existentialists such as Kierkegaard (1813–1855), Nietzsche (1844–1900), Heidegger (1889–1976), Sartre (1905–1980), and Buber (1878–1965) maintained that humanity's reality is inextricably linked to people being in, and part of, their world. Thus, consciousness is not an end unto itself.

Søren Kierkegaard (1844/1957) first used the word *existentialism* in this context. He focused on angst as well as on humanity's confrontation of meaninglessness through the experience of existence. Human beings are thrown into existence, and they are free to create their meaning, leading to responsibility and the defining of their personal reality. **Friedrich Nietzsche**'s term for the absence of meaning, purpose, or order in life is **nihilism,** or nothingness. This could be seen as the rejection of extrinsic morality that represents a universal source of right and wrong. The result of nihilism is a state of individual angst, anxiety, or spiritual dread. Thus, Nietzsche places the responsibility for moral living in the hands of the individual and the freedom of choice.

Influenced in part by Kierkegaard and Nietzsche, **Martin Heidegger** (1927/1996) contributed the temporal concept of **dasein,** meaning being there or being in the world, an undeniable essence that is neither a part of the world nor a part of the individual, but simply the result of existing. Being in the world means that a person's focus is turned toward other individuals and worldly purposes and not toward the experience of the moment. Heidegger also saw time as a matter of possibilities instead of in a linear sense. He believed that human fulfillment comes not from the world but through experiencing the moment.

Jean-Paul Sartre (1943/1966), a French existentialist and companion of Simone de Beauvoir, was influenced by

Kant, Hegel, and Heidegger. During World War II, he was held as a prisoner of war for 9 months by German troops. He continued his work after the war in Paris and sought to disprove the philosophical concept of **determinism,** the idea that all actions, events, thoughts, and decisions are the result of previous occurrences. Denying determinism means that humans have a free will and the ability to make choices based on the moment rather than on the past. Humans are on a journey of becoming.

Martin Buber (1946/1970) in his book *I & Thou* enhanced this premise with his concept of existence as encounter with, or experience of, other. There can be no I without another. Through the experience of other, each individual is changed. Buber believed that people can experience the other on a number of levels, with nature, humans, or spiritually with a higher power. They can also see other as an object, an it. Through **depersonification,** experience of other as object is in fact an encounter with self, whether positive or negative. Buber saw death as something that invigorated and created urgency in people's lives. It draws them into the present, and, in turn, allows them to be more fully present when experiencing the other. Individuals such as Paul Tillich and Gabriel Marcel applied these concepts to human spirituality as well. This rich history of existential philosophy provides a solid foundation for existential psychology and counseling theory.

Existential Counselors

Existential counselors assist clients in finding meaning, making choices based on their own unique value system, and accepting responsibility for the outcomes of their choices, whether positive or negative. Therapy facilitates client awareness, leading to meaning, where there was once an **existential vacuum,** or meaninglessness. Three counseling theorists are most well known for their work in the evolution of existential counseling. Over the past 60 years, Victor Frankl, Rollo May, and Irvin Yalom have contributed to the theory and practice of existential counseling that remains the foundation upon which tens of thousands of counselors base their practice today.

Victor Frankl was born in Vienna, Austria, and was largely influenced by his experiences as a concentration camp survivor during the Holocaust in World War II. A keen observer of human behavior, he noted that during the deprivations of captivity, some men died while others not only survived but grew emotionally, morally, and spiritually. He posited that humans could survive the most deplorable of conditions, learn, and grow if they believed that there was meaning to their existence. Frankl believed that all human acts, even suffering, had meaning. His (1946) book, *Man's Search for Meaning,* described his experiences in the concentration camps and outlined the counseling process that he named **logotherapy.** *Logos* is of Greek origin, referring to meaning; word; or, perhaps spiritually, the Word.

The basic principles of logotherapy, and in essence existentialism, are (a) people's main motivation for living is to find meaning in their life journey, which is possible even in the most challenging conditions; (b) they have the freedom to

make personal choices in what they do, what they think, and how they react to experience, even if the experience is one of suffering; and (c) with the freedom to choose comes personal responsibility. Frankl wrote that the imperative of logotherapy, which emphasizes personal responsibility, is "Live as if you were living already for the second time and as if you had acted the first time as wrongly as you are about to act now!" (Frankl, 1946/1984, pp. 131–132). With this mind-set, it is as if the past can still be changed in the present.

In a world devoid of predetermined meaning, Frankl challenged people to seek out meaning in their lives, to follow the innate drive to pursue meaning in their life journey, their will to meaning. In doing this, each moment becomes more salient, creating an appreciation of the present. So the measure of a meaningful life lies in the quality of the journey rather than in the length or other quantitative measures.

Rollo May was an American who is best known for his works, *Love and Will* (1969), *The Art of Counseling* (1965), and *The Courage to Create* (1975). Like Frankl, he asserted the worth and dignity of all people, including their freedom to make decisions. He believed that humans possess rational thought and can use it morally to determine what is right and wrong. May viewed human evolution in stages that have nothing to do with age but everything to do with the development of a genuine perception of people's place in the world and their acceptance thereof. May applied the concepts of existentialism to both counseling and to society as a whole, becoming a critic of cultural narcissism and capitalistic manifestations in the world.

Irvin Yalom is well-known for his many publications, which include *Existential Psychotherapy* (1980), *The Theory and Practice of Group Psychotherapy* (1970), and *When Nietzsche Wept* (1992). His style of therapy focuses on the here and now of the counseling process. In both group and individual therapy, he used his own thoughts, feelings, and intuitions to experience the client's subjective reality fully. The relationship he shared with his clients was essential in facilitating a genuine awareness and acceptance of themselves. In doing so, Yalom believed that the process of psychotherapy was as important to understand as the content that fueled the process.

In the (1980) book *Existential Psychotherapy,* Yalom sought to consolidate the ideas of many existential philosophers and practitioners. He organized the book into four themes that frequent the lives of both clients and counselors. Often referred to as **Yalom's ultimate concerns,** they are death, freedom/responsibility, isolation, and meaninglessness. The definitions of the concerns are given in the following list:

- **Death.** Each life is finite.
- **Freedom/Responsibility.** People have the freedom to choose their own paths in life, but they must assume responsibility for the choices they make.
- **Isolation.** People are ultimately alone in the world.
- **Meaninglessness.** Life is devoid of predetermined meaning. People are responsible to create and recreate their own meaning.

Yalom has taken foundational concepts in existential theory and made them tangible for the general practitioner through personal illustrations and examples. This has expanded the reach and acceptance of existential counseling in contemporary American psychotherapy.

Other theorists, such as Carl Rogers and Fritz Perls, included aspects of existentialism in their theoretical premises. Because of its constant link to the human condition and universal questions, existential theory can be incorporated into most therapeutic applications today.

Contributed by Grafton T. Eliason and
Jeff L. Samide, California University of
Pennsylvania, California, PA

References

Buber, M. (1970). *I and thou* (W. Kaufmann, Trans.). New York: Charles Scribner's Sons. (Original work published 1946)

Frankl, V. E. (1984). *Man's search for meaning.* New York: Washington Square Press. (Original work published 1984)

Heidegger, M. (1996). *Being and time* (J. Stammbaugh, Trans.). Albany: State University of New York Press. (Original work published 1927)

Kierkegaard, S. (1957). *The concept of dread* (W. Lowrie, Trans.). Princeton, NJ: Princeton University Press. (Original work published 1844)

May, R. (1969). *Love and will.* New York: Dell.

May, R. (1975). *The courage to create.* New York: Norton.

May, R. (1989). *The art of counseling.* Gardner Press. (Original work published 1965)

Sartre, J. P. (1966). *Being and nothingness: An essay on phenomenological ontology* (H. Barnes, Trans.). New York: Citadel Press. (Original work published 1943)

Traupman, J. C. (1966). *The new college Latin & English dictionary.* New York: Bantam Books.

Yalom, I. D. (1985). *The theory and practice of group psychotherapy* (3rd ed.). New York: Basic Books.

Yalom, I. D. (1980). *Existential psychotherapy.* New York: Basic Books.

Yalom, I. D. (1992). *When Nietzsche wept.* New York: Basic Books.

Additional Resource

Tomer, A., Eliason, G., & Wong, P. (Eds.). (2007). *Existential and spiritual issues in death attitudes.* Boca Raton, FL: Taylor & Francis–Erlbaum.

■ Ex Post Facto Research Design

Ex post facto research design examines the relationships or differences between independent and dependent variables "after the fact," or after data are collected for a dependent variable. Thus, the researcher examines how one or more preexisting conditions (i.e., independent variables) may have caused significant differences on the dependent variable, typically scores on a measure. Ex post facto research is a quantitative design, but it differs from experimental and quasi-experimental research because the researcher does not manipulate any of the variables under study. Common statistical methods in ex post facto research include correlation, t test, and analysis of variance.

In ex post facto research, the researcher can randomly sample from a preexisting group but cannot randomly assign participants to groups. Therefore, the level of internal validity is low, although the researcher can infer some cause and effect based on the findings. In addition, the lack of randomization creates low external validity, and, therefore, the study lacks generalizability beyond the participants of the study. Because the researcher does not randomly assign and select participants, there may be compounding variables that affect the outcome. Ways in which to control for extraneous variables in ex post facto design are through comparing homogenous groups and analysis of covariance, a statistical method that controls for differences in scores.

Following are examples that illustrate ex post facto research design. Tang et al. (2004) conducted an ex post facto study examining self-efficacy in counseling students. The researchers examined the relationship between self-efficacy and the following factors: age, work experience, courses taken, and number of internship hours. All of these factors were preexisting, thereby making it an ex post facto research study. Another example of ex post facto research was a study conducted by Utsey, McCarthy, Eubanks, and Adrian (2002) that investigated the relationship between anxiety, racism, and self-esteem in White graduate and undergraduate students. Similar to the first example, the researchers did not manipulate any of the variables (i.e., the anxiety, racism, or self-esteem), thereby making this an ex post facto study. In both examples, the factors were not manipulated, but rather the relationship is examined between factors.

Contributed by Travis W. Schermer,
Kent State University, Kent, OH

References

Tang, M., Addison, K. D., LaSure-Bryant, D., Norman, R., O'Connell, W., & Stewart-Sicking, J. A. (2004). Factors that influence self-efficacy of counseling students: An exploratory study. *Counselor Education and Supervision, 44,* 70–80.

Utsey, S. O., McCarthy, E., Eubanks, R., & Adrian, G. (2002). White racism and suboptimal psychological functioning among White Americans: Implications for counseling and prejudice prevention. *Journal of Multicultural Counseling and Development, 30,* 81–95.

Additional Resource

Wiersma, W., & Jurs, S. (2004). *Research methods in education: An introduction* (8th ed.). Boston: Allyn & Bacon.

■ Experiential Family Counseling

Experiential family counseling is a therapeutic approach based on a way of being in the world that emphasizes immediate, in the moment, here-and-now experience because of the belief that such experience helps to bring forth increased self-expression and freedom of the human spirit. The approach is based on the proposition that given the proper conditions or environment, every life form is oriented toward growth (Satir & Baldwin, 1983) and that a person's experiences are the essential phenomena of existence (Kempler, 1981). According to Kempler, intimate experiences that include interaction with others help a person to develop self-awareness and skills that can be used to cope with future experiences. To help family members experience increased authenticity in their interactions, experiential family counseling uses the intimate involvement of the counselor's personhood as a therapeutic tool. Thus, becoming capable of authentic, immediate emotional expression is a pathway toward meaningful shared experience and the means to personal and family fulfillment.

Psychopathology occurs when a person has a restricted capacity for experience and growth and for living authentically in the world (Felder & Weiss, 1991). Growth is inhibited by a person's living of experiences solely in the cognitive realm and bypassing emotions that accompany deep intimate experiencing (Whitaker & Bumberry, 1988). The result is repressed creative freedom and intuition, which thwarts the full expression of self. The individual experiences a lack of integration, a separation between the intuitive and the analytic (Felder & Weiss, 1991). The person's capacity to tolerate the positive anxiety of risk taking that accompanies change is diminished (Whitaker, 1989). In contrast, deeper experiencing leads to acceleration in personal growth. **Family dysfunction** is seen as being the result of family members suppressing feelings and denying impulses necessary for relating authentically with one another, thereby preventing a deepening of their intimate experience. These blocks to authentic relationships may appear in a family as rules against having and expressing feelings, rules against seeing life as what it is, or rules against asking for what a person wants (Loeschen, 1991).

After World War II, Carl Whitaker, Dick Felder, John Warkentin, and Thomas Malone began developing experiential counseling at the Atlanta Psychiatric Clinic. According to Felder and Weiss (1991), although **Carl Whitaker** named this counseling process, he considered that theory might be useful for beginners but that counselors should give up theory as soon as possible in favor of just being themselves. **Virginia Satir,** one of the first women to play a major role in the development of experiential approaches to individual and family counseling, strongly believed that a healthy family life involved an open and reciprocal sharing of affection, feelings, and love. On the basis of the conviction that people were capable of new understanding, continued growth, and change, her goal was to improve relationships through the deepening of shared experiences within the family unit. Other notable experiential theorists include Walter Kempler, Alvin Mahrer, and Avrum Weiss.

The Counseling Process

Experiential counselors attempt to resonate with their clients' inner thoughts and feelings in an effort to see the world in which their clients exist while identifying inner resources that can be tapped in order to enhance well-being. These innate resources may have become blocked by family and societal rules, resulting in deviation from the authentic self (Satir, 1983). The therapeutic session itself is used as a laboratory where the client is able to experiment with and entertain new experiences and, therefore, learn new skills (Kempler, 1981). Symptomatic behaviors extinguish themselves naturally when client strengths and inner resources are nurtured (Loeschen, 1991), and clients develop their capacity to be all of who they are in the here and now. The objectives are to help clients learn to develop their personhood by allowing themselves to just be (Whitaker, 1989) as well as to enhance clients' potential for becoming more fully and completely human (Satir & Baldwin, 1983).

The therapeutic relationship should elicit a recurrence of the dynamics that have been problematic for clients in the past. The counselor uses authentic emotional intensity to initiate client self-discovery that results in an intense and intimate corrective experience. This corrective experience helps clients to modify the symbolic representations responsible for the faulty meanings upon which they are defining their external reality. This process is negotiated by attention to, and manipulation of, current encountering through insistence that the client stay in the moment (Kempler, 1981). The objective is to create symbolically the relational experiences that have been absent in the client's life and to provide corrective experiences in response that help clients to increase their capacity to experience; to grow; and to become increasingly authentic, increasingly healthy, and more whole (Felder & Weiss, 1991).

The counselor accesses deeply personal and unconscious aspects of the personhood of the authentic self, bringing those aspects into counseling as an intervention and as acknowledgement of the coauthorship of the therapeutic relationship. The counselor honors the authentic self, thereby modeling good spiritual, emotional, and psychological health for clients. In general, what the counselor shares with the client is the counselor's experience of the client's experience. The professional counselor must experience the same feelings, not necessarily the same content, of the client's experience (Felder & Weiss, 1991). The counselor's willingness to expose himself or herself provides a model for the client that feelings and emotions are not destructive and that being open to feelings and emotions is a necessary step for growth to take place (Satir & Baldwin, 1983).

Having all family members present is not a necessary condition for conducting experiential family counseling, although it is preferred for this modality. The solution is to think systemically about the counseling process, regardless of who is actually in the session. In other words, no matter which family members decide to come for counseling, the entire family is considered to be the client (Felder & Weiss, 1991). The family is understood to be a system in which everyone and everything is affected by, and in turn affects, everyone and everything else. Any problematic situation is a result of these multiple effects (Satir & Baldwin, 1983); thus, experiential family counseling is interactional in its conceptual framework, with change in any part of the family system changing the whole system.

Experiential Counseling Techniques

From an experiential perspective, to adhere to any specific set of techniques without an examination of the context of the "in-the-moment relationship" with the client would limit the possibilities of coexperience and, therefore, limit the potential authenticity of the therapeutic encounter (Felder & Weiss, 1991). Although specific techniques may be useful, what is most important is the way clients feel about themselves and about the possibilities for change (Satir & Baldwin, 1983). The basic goal of any technique is to help to release the client from unresolved and repressed emotions around relationships so that the client is better able to live in the present.

When doing experiential family counseling, interventions are devised in keeping with clients' willingness and ability to explore images, body movements, eye contact, and verbalizations (Korb, Gorrell, & Van De Riet, 1989). The use of music, art, drama, body movement exercises, and games to provide the client with new and deeper experiences in touching, seeing, hearing, feeling, and expressing may be of value (Satir, 1983). Specific techniques include family sculpting (see Family Sculpting) and choreography that stimulate affective intensity; touching/sensitivity exercises; family art therapy that helps free families to express themselves; and psychodrama, visualization, and role-playing that are based on the idea that for experience to be real it must be felt and exposed in the present (Nichols & Schwartz, 2001). Additional therapeutic tools that may be useful are humor, metaphor, and reframing of a situation to place the problem in a different context (Satir & Baldwin, 1983).

To be meaningful, techniques need to be tailor-made for the situation and used with flexibility (Satir & Baldwin, 1983). The most powerful interventions are in the present, awareness oriented, and based on the premise that clients learn through the discovery process. In the development and administration of any intervention, the counselor is authentic, whole, and genuine, just as the client is encouraged to be (Korb et al., 1989). The process of therapy and use of intervention should result in several positive outcomes for clients. Family members should learn to identify and then capitalize on unused and untapped innate inner strengths as they realize their inherent potential, learn to honor and cherish their authentic self, and begin to embrace the wonderment of their humanity.

Contributed by Laura R. Ritchie,
University of North Carolina at
Charlotte, Charlotte, NC

References

Felder, R. E., & Weiss A. G. (1991). *Experiential psychotherapy: A symphony of selves.* Lantham, MD: University Press of America.

Kempler, W. (1981). *Experiential psychotherapy within families.* New York: Brunner/Mazel.

Korb, M. P., Gorrell, J., & Van De Riet, V. (1989). *Gestalt therapy: Practice and theory* (2nd ed.). New York: Pergamon Press.

Loeschen, S. (1991). *The magic of Satir: Practical skills for therapists.* Desert Hot Springs, CA: Event Horizon Press.

Nichols, M. P., & Schwartz, R. C. (2001). *Family therapy: Concepts and methods* (5th ed.). Boston: Allyn & Bacon.

Satir, V. (1983). *Conjoint family therapy* (3rd ed.). Palo Alto, CA: Science and Behavior Books.

Satir, V., & Baldwin, M. (1983). *Satir step by step: A guide to creating change in families.* Palo Alto, CA: Science and Behavior Books.

Whitaker, C. (1989). *Midnight musings of a family therapist* (M. O. Ryan, Ed.). New York: Norton.

Whitaker, C. A., & Bumberry, W. M. (1988). *Dancing with the family: A symbolic-experiential approach.* New York: Brunner/Mazel.

Additional Resources

Bumberry, W. B. (Producer), & Tenenbaum, S. (Producer). (1986). *A different kind of caring: Family therapy with Carl Whitaker* [Videorecording]. United States: Brunner/Mazel.

Elliot, R., Greenberg, L. S., & Lietaer, G. (2004). Research on experiential psychotherapies. In M. Lambert, A. Bergin, & S. Garfield (Eds.), *Handbook of psychotherapy and behavior change* (pp. 493–539). New York: Wiley.

Satir, V., Banmen, J., Gerber, J., & Gomori, M. (1991). *The Satir model.* Palo Alto, CA: Science and Behavior Books.

▌Experimental Research Designs

Experimental research designs serve as blueprints for how a quantitative study will be conducted. The design of the study includes elements of random assignment, manipulation or categorization of the independent variable, measurement of a dependent variable, and control of extraneous variables.

The primary purpose of research designs is to facilitate causal inference (internal validity) and increase the generalizability of the study (external validity) by controlling for factors that may influence the results, known as extraneous variables. **Random assignment** refers to the equal likelihood that a participant will be placed in a **treatment group,** thereby receiving a treatment or intervention, or **control/ comparison group,** in which a participant receives no treatment or an alternative treatment/intervention. Random assignment controls for the presence of extraneous variables by equally distributing such variables across both groups.

When a treatment is either provided or withheld from a group, it is referred to as a **manipulated independent variable.** For example, a school counselor wants to know whether participation in a study skills program may increase standardized test scores. Participants are randomly assigned to either the experimental condition, in which they attend a study skills group and a treatment is provided, or a control group, in which participants do not attend any group and the treatment condition is withheld. Not all variables can be manipulated, such as comparisons between sex and ethnicity.

These types of independent variables are referred to as factors or organismic variables because they are not manipulated.

Extraneous variables are variables outside the scope of the study that may influence the results. Using the example given, participants who receive tutoring after school may have an unintended effect on the results of the study, because the presence of tutoring was not defined as a variable in the study. Random assignment controls for the presence of extraneous variables by equally distributing such variables across both treatment and control groups. When an extraneous variable is known to have an effect on the results of a study because it is related to the independent and dependent variables, it is known as a **confounding variable.** For example, if it is known that tutoring has an effect on improving study skills and increasing test scores and is not identified as a variable in the study, then tutoring is a confounding variable. The researcher would need to make sure, then, that students who receive tutoring were either (a) eliminated from the study (in both the treatment and control groups), (b) equally dispersed in both treatment and control groups, or (c) addressed as another independent variable in the study.

The purpose of the experimental research design is to test whether change in the dependent variable occurs as a result of the administration of a treatment or intervention. The **dependent variable** is a measure of a construct. Differences may be assessed between experimental and control group/comparison groups through the use of an instrument or measure to determine change in the dependent variable. In the example given, the construct being measured by the standardized test may be achievement; thus, the test score serves as the dependent variable, and the presence or absence of the treatment condition (the study skills group) is the independent variable.

The researcher needs to be cautious not to imply cause and effect from the results of the study. Simply because there is a change in the dependent variable does not mean that the change is due to the treatment or intervention. The researcher needs to explore the potential effect of any extraneous variables or threats to experimental validity. Gall, Gall, and Borg (2007) outlined three essential characteristics for causation: (a) a relationship is evident between the independent and dependent variables, (b) a time-ordered sequence is apparent, and (c) the influence of any confounding variables has been eliminated.

There are two general types of experimental designs: between-groups design and within-subject design. In a **between-groups design,** the researcher is interested in comparing two or more groups in order to test the effect of an intervention or treatment for a group that receives a treatment or intervention (see Between-Groups Design). Statistical tests may be conducted to determine whether there are differences between the treatment and control groups. From the results of the tests, inferences may be made about the effectiveness of the treatment or intervention. In a **within-subject design,** the researcher is interested in identifying changes over time in one or more groups (see Within-Subject Design). In this type of study, a group of individuals completes a pretest in order to establish a baseline for a particular topic of interest, (e.g., depression, wellness). The pretest is typically followed by a treatment or intervention. A posttest is administered in order to see if there is any change in the baseline after the treatment or intervention. Statistical tests may be conducted to determine whether there are differences between the pretest and posttest scores. From the results of the tests, inferences may be made as to the effectiveness of the treatment or intervention. In a within-subject design, participants may be exposed to multiple treatments, such receiving both individual and group therapy. A researcher could obtain a baseline measure, by using a wellness inventory for example, and then administer the instrument again after clients participated in a series of individual sessions and then again after they participated in a series of group sessions. The researcher may need to conduct the study with participants receiving each intervention (individual or group counseling) in a different sequence in order to address the extraneous variable of ordering (which intervention was administered first).

Experimental design can be further divided into four models: (a) true experimental, (b) quasi-experimental, (c) preexperimental, and (d) single-subject research designs. A **true experimental design** contains elements of random assignment and the presence of a control or comparison group (see True Experimental Design). Thus, in a true experimental design, the independent variable is manipulated. In a **quasi-experimental design,** there is no random assignment, so there may not be manipulation of an independent variable (see Quasi-Experimental Research Designs). Quasi-experimental designs are often used to examine differences across demographic characteristics. **Preexperimental designs** do not use random assignment or a control or comparison group (see Preexperimental Research Design). Such studies may not produce results that are generalizable. In a **single-subject research design,** a single participant (or group or unit) receives some type of initial measure, known as a baseline, followed by periodic measures after implementation of some treatment or intervention that may be compared with the baseline to indicate the potential effect of the intervention. The goal of this study is to examine a specific phenomenon of a single participant (see Single-Subject Research Design).

For example, a counselor is interested in whether participation in group counseling in addition to individual counseling would benefit adolescent clients diagnosed with disruptive behavior disorders. An outcome instrument is used to assess changes in behavior. If the counselor opted to compare the progress of clients who received both individual and group counseling (perhaps through a within-subject design) but did not compare results to any comparison group (e.g., participants who only received individual counseling), then this is known as a preexperimental design. Although the counselor may be able to show that clients improved, the results are limited in that the counselor does not know if the changes were above and beyond the improvement in clients who received individual counseling only. If the counselor compared the scores between clients who received individual and group counseling and clients who received individual counseling only, then the study is termed quasi-experimental. A comparison group is present, but there is no control for extraneous variables. The control for extraneous variables is achieved by a true experimental design, in which clients are randomly assigned to either individual counseling only or individual and group counseling. Each of these types of designs is explained in greater detail elsewhere in this encyclopedia.

While a true experimental design may control for many extraneous variables, studies with a rigid design still have some limitations. For example, results in an experimental setting may not be generalizable to nonexperimental settings if the experiment is too tightly controlled and simply unrealistic to implement in a nonexperimental setting.

Contributed by Richard S. Balkin,
Texas A&M University–Commerce,
Commerce, TX

Reference

Gall, M. D., Gall, J. P., & Borg, W. R. (2007). *Educational research: An introduction* (8th ed.). Boston: Allyn & Bacon.

Additional Resources

Heppner, P. P., Wampold, B. E., & Kivilighan, D. M. (2007). *Research design in counseling* (3rd ed.). Boston: Thomson Higher Education.

Vogt, W. P. (2007). *Quantitative research methods for professionals*. Boston: Allyn & Bacon.

External Validity, Threats to

External validity refers to the extent to which a given set of research results can be applied outside of the confines of a particular study. In other words, research has external validity if it is generalizable to a variety of populations (population validity) and settings (ecological validity). To increase the external validity of a study, careful **participant selection** is essential to maximize **population validity** (i.e., the degree to which sample characteristics are generalizable to the population of interest). The following is a quintessential example of research that lacks external validity. In the 1948 presidential election, telephone polling indicated that Republican Thomas Dewey would easily defeat Democrat Harry Truman. At that time, however, Republicans were more affluent, more likely to have telephone service, and therefore more likely to be reached by telephone. The researchers were embarrassed when Truman then won the election. In this case, the researchers erroneously generalized results from their sample to the U.S. population at large. In the field of counseling, it is also important to consider participant selection when assessing the generalizability of research. For instance, an intervention for the treatment of depression that is developed and tested solely with college students would not necessarily be effective if used with senior citizens.

Ecological validity refers to how closely research conditions mimic "real life," or the degree to which the research context extrapolates to real settings. Increasing ecological validity may improve external validity. An example is a researcher studying counselor trainees and their effectiveness at communicating with clients. The researcher does not have permission to view trainee sessions with clients but is allowed to observe trainee role plays with classmates. Can the researcher generalize observations from role plays to actual client sessions? The answer may depend on how true-to-life the role plays feel to the participants. The trainee and the classmate may feel that the simulation is real and behave as they might in an actual counseling session. If the situation feels artificial, however, their behavior might not reflect reality. For instance, if both parties read from a script, this would likely feel less realistic than it might if they were improvising the session. In this research scenario, improving the authenticity of the situation would likely boost external validity. Threats to ecological validity can take many forms, including reactivity, interaction of testing and treatment, interaction of selection and treatment, multiple treatment interaction, novelty/disruption effects, history effects, and issues relating to the measurement of the dependent variable, as well as the timing of measurement.

Reactivity

When assessing the ecological validity of a given study, an important component to consider is reactivity. **Reactivity** refers to the fact that if people believe others are watching, they may behave differently than they might otherwise. In research, reactivity poses a threat to external validity because participants, knowing they are being studied, may display behavior that is not typical for them. Therefore, study findings may not generalize to "the real world." It is important to note that these reactivity effects are also cited as threats to internal validity.

The following are variations and extensions of reactivity. Named for a 1920's study of worker productivity in the Hawthorne factory, the **Hawthorne effect** refers to the phenomenon in which individuals react to increased attention by changing their behavior. In the Hawthorne study, researchers found a significant increase in productivity but discovered that this was not caused by any intervention. Rather, the workers were aware that they were being watched and worked harder. Similarly, in counseling research, if participants (e.g., clients, supervisors, students) know that they are being observed, they may react to this increased attention by changing their behavior.

Demand characteristics emerge when research participants adjust responses to conform to their beliefs about the researcher's purpose. As an example, a professional counselor may know that a researcher is observing her or his counseling session. The counselor may believe (correctly or incorrectly) that this researcher is a well-known Adlerian therapist, so she or he may unconsciously use more Adlerian interventions during the session than normally.

In contrast, **experimenter expectancy** takes place when a researcher unconsciously guides participants toward the desired response. For instance, subtle changes in experimenter tone may cue participants to react in a certain manner. An example is a scenario in which a researcher interviews clients from a community mental health clinic regarding their satisfaction with obtained services. The researcher may more clearly enunciate the answer choices that indicate satisfaction than the choices that convey dissatisfaction, especially if the researcher has a vested interest in demonstrating client satisfaction. A potential solution to this problem would be to assign a neutral party to conduct the interviews.

Evaluation apprehension occurs when the knowledge that one is being studied results in increased arousal, leading to better or worse performance than would be seen otherwise. For instance, student counselors who know they are being watched during a session may be so nervous that their performance suffers. Conversely, the extra stress may produce better performance in some individuals.

Often used in an educational context, the term **Pygmalion effect** refers to a self-fulfilling prophecy in which students perform better than they might otherwise if teachers expect high achievement. Similarly, in a mental health setting, clients may detect counselor expectancies. If the counselor believes that a particular group of clients will improve, they may—due to the therapist's belief, not the intervention.

Finally, the **placebo effect** means that a given intervention will work simply because someone believes it will. For instance, some clients may believe that counseling will improve their symptoms, so their symptoms do indeed improve after treatment. The counseling may not be effective by itself, but the client's belief in its efficacy may lead to positive change.

Interaction of Testing and Treatment

In certain situations, it may be difficult to differentiate between the effects of measuring the success of a given treatment from the treatment itself. For example, a researcher may interview a participant to evaluate the participant's reaction to a particular counseling intervention. The participant may, however, find the interview process itself to be therapeutic and give answers that do not reflect her or his true feelings about the intervention in question.

Interaction of Selection and Treatment

Researchers need to be aware that participants may self-select into treatment groups; therefore, subsequent changes may result from preexisting differences and not from the treatment itself. For instance, in a particular study, clients may be given a choice between traditional counseling and an innovative new intervention. Any outcome differences noted may not be due to the counseling approaches themselves but rather to personality differences between participants who self-selected into the two groups.

Multiple Treatment Interaction

In many cases, it is difficult to isolate the effects of a single intervention. If a client has had multiple interventions, including individual counseling, group counseling, and medication management, it becomes more challenging to argue that one treatment in particular led to change.

Novelty/Disruption Effects

In some cases, a given intervention may result in change simply because it is new and/or unanticipated, known as **novelty or disruption effects.** An example is middle school students who are working on improving their peer relations and have become accustomed to traditional school-based group counseling. A researcher may then introduce these students to an outdoor ropes course in which they engage in physical activities together, performing "trust falls" and the like. The intervention may not be effective in and of itself, but the fact that it is new and exciting may yield positive change in the students' peer relations.

History Effects

History effects take place when data are collected during a time in which unusual contextual factors exist. These factors may be due to events within or outside the study. **Local history effects** refer to when a particular group or subgroup in a study is affected by an event or certain dynamics. Consequently, results cannot easily be generalized to different times and settings.

An example of a history effect is a researcher interested in gauging college students' attitudes toward on-campus violence; however, the researcher collected data during the 2-week period following the horrific shootings at Virginia Tech in Blacksburg, Virginia. Data collected during the aftermath of that tragedy may not be representative of college student attitudes during a more typical time period.

Measurement of the Dependent Variable

The way in which the dependent variable is measured can affect obtained results. An example is a longitudinal study in which counselor trainees are given surveys regarding their preferred learning environments at the beginning and the end of a semester. In this scenario, the survey given at the beginning of the semester is long and arduous, tiring the students and producing rather simplistic answers. The survey at the end of the semester is much shorter, and the students are able to complete it more easily. Any differences found may not reflect true change over the course of the semester but rather differences in the instrumentation itself.

Timing of Measurement Effects

Sometimes, the timing of the measurement of the dependent variable may influence results. For instance, in the preceding example, counseling students were asked to complete surveys at the beginning and the end of the semester. If the students were scheduled to take their final exam immediately after completing the second survey, they might be distracted, worried, and motivated to finish the survey as quickly as possible; therefore, results may not reflect reality and may not generalize to other settings. The researcher may obtain very different results if the survey is administered the next day.

In summary, it is crucial to gauge external validity carefully when planning research. If a study has little or no application to the real-world settings in which counselors function, valuable resources, including time, money, and effort, may be wasted. To maximize external validity of a given study, the researcher must consider both population and ecological validity.

Contributed by Jennifer Douglas Vidas,
George Washington University,
Washington, DC

Additional Resources

Campbell, D. T., & Stanley, J. C. (1963). *Experimental and quasi-experimental designs for research.* Chicago: Rand-McNally.

Pettigrew, T. F. (1996). *How to think like a social scientist.* New York: HarperCollins.

■ Eye Movement Desensitization and Reprocessing

Eye movement desensitization and reprocessing (EMDR) is an eight-phase integrated treatment model developed by **Francine Shapiro.** It is a time-efficient, comprehensive methodology that allows individuals to process disturbing thoughts and experiences through eye movements or other left–right stimulation, such as hand tapping and auditory stimulation. EMDR lends itself to a variety of theoretical orientations because it incorporates psychodynamic, experiential, behavioral, cognitive, body-based, and systems perspectives.

EMDR assists an individual's neurological system to process information that seems to be "locked" in the nervous system as a result of a particular experience. This locked information is often in the form of images, sounds, thoughts, and emotions related to the experience. It becomes triggered throughout the individual's life whenever reminders are encountered. The individual frequently experiences emotional or physical discomfort, such as feelings of fear or helplessness when traumatic experiences are triggered. EMDR allows the nervous system to unlock and process the original experience through specific patterns of eye movements. It is believed that the eye movements are similar to those that occur during REM sleep, during which the rapid eye movements may be helping the individual process unconscious material in the brain.

As previously mentioned, EMDR is an eight-phase treatment protocol. The first phase includes history taking and the development of a treatment plan. The second phase assesses the individual's coping skills and strengthens them, if necessary. Phases 3 through 6 involve identifying a target for EMDR; the individual chooses the most vivid image related to the distressing event, as well as the negative beliefs, emotions, and body sensations that are related to the event. The individual also identifies a preferred positive belief about the self, and both the positive belief and the intensity of the negative emotions are rated for validity. The individual is then instructed to focus on the image, negative thoughts, feelings, and body sensations as the clinician implements one

of the various bilateral stimulation methods for approximately 20 to 30 seconds. The individual is then asked what he or she notices, and this process is repeated until the client no longer reports distress associated with the disturbing event. The individual is then instructed to think about the positive belief while focusing on the event, and the clinician again uses bilateral stimulation. The individual generally reports greater confidence in the positive belief, as well as desirable emotions and body sensations, after repeating this part of the process several times. During Phase 7, the individual is instructed to keep a journal noting any related material that arises throughout the week. The individual is also reminded of ways to self-soothe in the case that distressing material surfaces between appointments. The final phase of EMDR is completed in the following appointment when the clinician and individual reevaluate the previous work done and any progress made in the previous week. EMDR continues until all of the related past, current, and future scenarios that elicit distress are processed.

EMDR is one of the most widely researched treatments for posttraumatic stress disorder. Several studies indicate that EMDR is not only empirically supported but that it is also the treatment of choice for trauma survivors. Outcome research consistently demonstrates that EMDR is an effective approach that results in decreased clinical symptoms, trauma resolution, and strengthened coping skills. Moreover, some studies reveal that EMDR is more efficient than behavior therapy and pharmaceuticals.

The body of knowledge for the application of this approach to diverse clinical populations is growing rapidly. EMDR has been the subject of more research and case reports than any other method for the treatment of trauma. It has also been used in the treatment of anxiety disorders, sleep disorders, dissociative disorders, personality disorders, eating disorders, grief, attachment difficulties, and stress. Furthermore, it is useful for both children and adults.

EMDR is increasingly used in international relief efforts. Humanitarian Assistance Programs (EMDR-HAP) have been established to help trauma victims of natural disasters or human violence around the world. In EMDR-HAP, volunteers provide free EMDR treatment and train local mental health professionals in the model. Training in EMDR can be obtained through the EMDR Institute or by a licensed, EMDR-trained clinician.

Contributed by Amy Wickstrom,
San Diego Center for Play Therapy,
San Diego, CA

Additional Resources

Shapiro, F. (1995). *Eye movement desensitization and reprocessing: Basic principles, protocols, and procedures.* New York: Guilford Press.

Shapiro, F., & Forrest, M. (1997). *EMDR.* New York: Basic Books.

Factitious Disorder

Factitious disorder refers to deliberately exaggerating, inducing, or feigning symptoms of physical or mental illness for the sole purpose of fulfilling the patient role. Three subtypes of factitious disorder have been identified: (a) predominantly psychological signs and symptoms, (b) predominantly physical signs and symptoms, and (c) combined psychological and physical symptoms (American Psychiatric Association [APA], 2000).

Factitious disorder is distinct from malingering and somatoform disorders. Both factitious disorder and **malingering** involve faking or inducing symptoms of physical or mental illness; however, the malingerer derives some external reward over and above filling the patient role. For example, the malingerer may avoid criminal charges by mimicking psychosis, gain financially by defrauding an insurance company, or cope adaptively by faking illness to secure release from a hostage situation. In contrast, the person diagnosed with factitious disorder has no extrinsic motive for the feigning behavior. Although both feature symptoms that have no legitimate medical origin, factitious disorder also differs from somatoform disorders. A person with a **somatoform disorder** believes that she or he is ill, which is in a sharp contrast to the person with factitious disorder, who deliberately misleads health care professionals.

Cases documenting factitious disorder include a wide range of physical and mental disorders. The more commonly fabricated physical symptoms and illnesses include seizures, gastrointestinal bleeding, and breast cancer. Individuals with factitious disorder use a vast array of methods to simulate or induce physical symptoms. These methods include simply exaggerating pain and discomfort, dramatically enacting tics or seizures, deliberately tampering with test samples, and introducing bacteria into the bloodstream. The more severe and chronic form of factitious disorder is commonly referred to as **Munchausen syndrome** (Feldman, Hamilton, & Deemer, 2001).

Persons with factitious disorder may undergo multiple unwarranted surgeries, exposure to unnecessary medications, and painful medical procedures (Feldman, 2004). One risk of factitious disorder is that genuine iatrogenic illness or symptoms, those that result from medical procedures or medication, may result from treatments of the fabricated illnesses. The diagnosis of factitious disorder does not preclude the existence of another authentic mental disorder.

Cases documenting feigned mental illness also include a broad range of disorders, including bipolar disorder, amnesia, dissociative identity disorder, and substance abuse. Gregory and Jindal (2006) reviewed the admission records of a university psychiatric hospital in upstate New York. Six patients of the 100 admissions reviewed were given a diagnosis of factitious disorder at discharge. Among these 6 patients, depression, suicidal ideation, and hallucinations were the most prevalent of the fabricated symptoms.

More common in women than in men, factitious disorder generally has its onset in early adulthood, often following a hospitalization for a valid medical condition. Patients presenting with factitious disorder frequently describe elaborate and sometimes bizarre medical histories. Factitious episodes tend to be intermittent; however, those with more chronic forms of factitious disorder may experience a string of hospitalizations over the course of many years.

A potential fourth subtype of factitious disorder, factitious disorder by proxy, is under investigation and is included in Appendix B of the *Diagnostic and Statistical Manual of Mental Disorders* (4th ed., text rev.; *DSM-IV-TR;* APA, 2000) as a proposed diagnosis. Using the proposed criteria, **factitious disorder by proxy** would be reserved for those who (a) intentionally produce or fabricate symptoms, either physical or psychological, in another person under their care; (b) are motivated by a desire for the vicarious experience of the patient role; and (c) evidence no external incentives (Lasher & Sheridan, 2004).

Factitious disorder by proxy, also known as **Munchausen by proxy,** has been the focus of contention within the field. Appendix B of the *DSM-IV-TR* suggests that the perpetrator of the behavior would receive a factitious disorder by proxy diagnosis while the victim would receive a diagnosis of either physical abuse of a child or physical abuse of an adult; however, a number of professionals argue that these harmful behaviors are not the product of mental disorder and should be recognized instead as child abuse (Lasher & Sheridan, 2004).

Contributed by Cheree Hammond,
University of Virginia,
Charlottesville, VA, and Lennis G.
Echterling, James Madison University,
Harrisonburg, VA

References

American Psychiatric Association. (2000). *Diagnostic and statistical manual of mental disorders* (4th ed., text rev.). Washington, DC: Author.

Feldman, M. D. (2004). *Playing sick? Untangling the web of Munchausen syndrome, Munchausen by proxy, malingering, and factitious disorder.* New York: Brunner-Routledge.

Feldman, M. D., Hamilton, J. C., & Deemer, H. N. (2001). Factitious disorder. In J. M. Oldham & M. B. Riba (Eds.), *Somatoform and factitious disorders* (Vol. 20, pp. 129–160). Washington, DC: American Psychiatric.

Gregory, R. J., & Jindal, S. (2006). Factitious disorder on an inpatient psychiatry ward. *American Journal of Psychiatry, 76,* 31–36.

Lasher, L. J., & Sheridan, M. S. (2004). *Munchausen by proxy: Identification, intervention and case management.* Binghamton, NY: Hawthorne Press.

Factor Analysis

Factor analysis is a statistical procedure based on the work of Charles Spearman (1927), who noted that multiple correlations could be accounted for via a simple model of derived data (Manly, 1986). Specifically, Spearman noticed that any two rows of a correlation matrix are almost proportional if the diagonals are removed or ignored. On the basis of this observation, Spearman derived a model expressed as $X_i = a_i F + e_i$, where F represents a variable described as the "factor" value and X_i is a standardized score with a mean of 0 and a standard deviation of 1. In addition, e_i represents the portion of X_i that is specific to the described element within the matrix under study, and a_i represents the specific correlations derived within the matrix under study.

The primary purpose of factor analysis is to reduce a set of variables to a smaller number of factors using this model. Quite often this technique is used as a preliminary measure of how a large set of variables might group according to the intercorrelational structure of the data. For example, a researcher is likely to use a factor analytic design in the construction of an instrument where subscales are likely to emerge. In this case, a researcher may apply a factor analysis to sample data of the instrument items to determine whether specific items "load" together in the form of a broader factor. Solving for F allows a researcher to identify factor loadings within a correlation matrix and to determine the strength of the relationships existing within each identified factor. Ultimately, this provides a basis for comparison among the variables under study such that a researcher can determine how influential a particular factor is in accounting for the relationships under study.

More specifically, **factor loading** is the term used to describe the percent of the variance of a specific variable explained by a derived factor. In any application of factor analysis, the individual variables under study will vary in terms of the strength of their influence on the factor where the variables have loaded. For example, a researcher may wish to develop an instrument to assess career satisfaction. Items might include references to quality of life, satisfaction with the culture of a particular work environment, the positive challenge existent in a specific career, and so on. In this example, if indeed these did represent the derived factors, the strength of the individual items' (i.e., the variables) mathematical relationship to the factor where they have loaded will vary. *Factor loading* is the term used in evaluating the strength of these relationships.

Types of Factor Analysis

There are two distinctly defined types of factor analysis: exploratory and confirmatory. In **exploratory factor analysis,** the primary focus is on the exploration of a possible underlying factor structure among a set of identified variables where there is no predetermined hypothesis regarding the structure. This represents the most common application of factor analysis. Exploratory factor analysis is often used in the beginning stages of the research process when no prior studies have revealed existing relationships among the variables under study.

Confirmatory factor analysis, on the other hand, is a statistical procedure applied for the purpose of confirming a hypothesized factor structure. In other words, confirmatory factor analysis is used when a relationship among the variables under study has been previously established, and the factor loadings are predicted prior to the application of data analysis procedures. In this case, there is an implicit hypothesis that suggests the outcome of the factor analysis. Thus, it is not uncommon for a researcher to use confirmatory factor analysis following a study in which exploratory factor analysis has been applied to establish initial relationships among variables.

Procedure for a Factor Analysis

The application of a factor analysis to a set of data involves a three-step process. The first step is the identification of initial factor loadings. These factor loadings are often derived via a **principal components analysis,** in which uncorrelated factors are identified. Because the solutions inherent in this type of analysis are infinite and difficult to interpret, the second step in a factor analysis is to rotate the identified factors. Factor rotation involves a procedure whereby these initial factors are transformed in order to identify new factors. Factor rotation is generally necessary to facilitate the interpretation of the initially derived factors.

There are two broad categories for defining a factor rotation, orthogonal and oblique. In an **orthogonal factor rotation,** the new factors are uncorrelated. This type of rotation is not frequently used, because the results are generally more difficult to interpret. The primary reason for this difficulty is that, in general, factors derived in a study of human behavior are not uncorrelated.

In an **oblique factor rotation,** the new factors are correlated. The most common oblique factor rotation is the **varimax rotation,** which generally has the highest value in terms of identifying individual variables with a single factor (Manly, 1986). In the case of an oblique factor rotation, the factor axes are allowed to form acute or obtuse angles, indicating a relationship among the factors under study.

An oblique factor rotation is likely to be used in the development of an instrument as a way to assess potential groupings of items. In this case, it is highly unlikely that the derived items are completely uncorrelated; therefore, the use of an orthogonal rotation is not justified.

The final stage of the application of a factor analysis involves calculating and interpreting the factor scores. The final interpretation of a factor analysis is somewhat subjective for two primary reasons. First, the researcher generally chooses the type of factor rotation used. Although the researcher makes this choice on the basis of the intended study and the relationships known to exist among the variables, it is not based on results of a specific empirical procedure. In addition, the number of factors identified and reported is generally up to the researcher, although the number, too, is usually suggested by the data. It is within this phase of a factor analysis that the researcher will determine how many factors to report and how these might be named according to the specific variables that have loaded on the derived factors. There are several customary methods that involve eigenvalues and scree tests used to determine how many factors to report on the completion of a factor analysis.

Eigenvalues

The **eigenvalue** associated with a specific factor represents a measure of the variance in all of the variables under study accounted for by that factor. It is the specific statistic most frequently used to assess the level of variance explained by a particular factor and is often the measure used to determine whether a particular factor will be reported and defined by a researcher. Essentially, the eigenvalue represents the numerical strength of the identified factors. In any factor analysis, all of the variables under study will be associated with an identified factor; however, one of the primary functions of a factor analysis is to assess the utility of the derived factors, and this is often decided on the basis of the eigenvalues associated with each identified factor. Lower associated eigenvalues indicate a smaller contribution to the explanation of variances in the variables. Often, factors with low associated eigenvalues are ignored as being redundant with more significant factors. Mathematically, an eigenvalue is the sum of squared values in the column of a factor matrix or the variance in a set of variables explained by a factor or component. Practically, the eigenvalue is used to assess the usefulness or the applicability of a derived factor. According to the Kaiser criterion (Dunteman, 1989), researchers use an eigenvalue of 1 or more as the determinant of including a particular factor. The final results of a factor analysis rely on the researcher deciding how many of the derived factors are useful in describing and accounting for the variance among the variables under study.

Scree Test

The **scree test** is a visual mechanism for determining the number of factors that should be identified and used as the result of a factor analysis. The scree test dates to Cattell (1966) and is based on a visual analysis of data that might resemble scree, that is, an accumulation of loose stones or rocky debris. In a pile of gravel or small stones, there is a point at which the scree begins to level off, usually after dropping off sharply. The application of a scree test includes graphing the data and visually deciding where this occurs on the derived graph. In using this method, a researcher will include all of the factors identified prior to where the scree seems to level off. Cattell

reported that the process, which led to the development of the scree test, was one that had him extracting the principal components of correlation matrices and then looking for various signs in the resultant eigenvalues.

The utility of factor analysis as a method for analyzing data is dependent on the research question posed. Factor analysis is, however, widely used and is typically applied in studies where the reduction of data is desired. As previously noted, this is often the case when a researcher wishes to develop an empirically derived assessment tool. In addition, factor analysis is frequently used in studies where a primary hypothesis relates to the categorizing of the variables under study.

Contributed by Virginia A. Kelly,
Fairfield University, Fairfield, CT

References

Cattell, R. B. (1966). *The scientific analysis of personality.* Chicago: Aldine.

Dunteman, G. H. (1989). *Principal components analysis* (Publication No. 69). Thousand Oaks, CA: Sage.

Manly, B. F. J. (1986). *Multivariate statistical methods: A primer.* New York: Chapman & Hall.

Spearman, C. (1927). *The abilities of man: Their nature and measurement.* New York: Macmillan.

■ Family Counseling

Couples counseling and **family counseling** (or therapy) arose as a response to the traditional individualistic, and particularly psychoanalytic, understanding of mental illness. Its beginnings are rooted in clinical observation and experimentation in psychiatric hospitals. In the 1940s and 1950s, clinicians working closely with patients with schizophrenia noticed that when patients improved, often someone else in the family became worse. These observations led researchers to consider the relationship between family organization and mental health. In 1954, a team of clinicians led by Gregory Bateson found that certain communication patterns within families were related to severe mental illness. Independent scientist-practitioners around the globe began including family members in psychiatric treatment with favorable results. The defining tenet of couples and family counseling is that systems rather than individual clients are the unit of analysis.

Systems Theory

Traditionally, science has used experimental control to explore cause-and-effect relationships. These isolated fragments of information were the best attempt to understand the bigger picture of human relationships (Laszlo, 1996). Relationships are, however, complex entities, in that the whole is greater than the sum of individuals. A growing sensitivity toward complexity and holism by the natural and social science fields required a new paradigm for understanding relationships. **Systems theory** privileges patterns and interactions among various phenomena under study and has given rise to a number of disciplines and subtheories, such as cybernetics (i.e., the science of control and communication processes in biological and artificial systems), factor analysis (i.e., a statistical technique used to detect structure in the relationship between variables; see Factor Analysis), and information theory (i.e., a branch of mathematics that studies the definition, measurement, and transmission of communication; Laszlo, 1996).

Key to systems theory is the belief in **homeostasis,** or that systems regulate stability through reciprocal feedback mechanisms. Therefore, instead of conceptualizing dilemmas as isolated intrapsychic processes, a systemic lens allows problems to be viewed as situated within a client's interconnected, multilevel context. Systems theory suggests that the organization of societal, familial, interactional, and intrapersonal levels involve repetitive and problem-maintaining patterns. These patterns work to maintain stability and may be difficult to change even when considered dysfunctional for the overall system. Professional counselors intervene at various contextual levels, or layers, that serve to define a person's experience of mental health to create change in a system.

These layers are used at every stage of the therapeutic process, from initial assessment through termination. Societal factors that professional counselors pay particular attention to are patterns of discourse, gender socialization, and cultural privileges and injustices. Key familial factors include organization, reciprocal behavioral sequences, triangles, and intergenerational cutoffs and attachments. On the individual level, professional counselors are interested in identifying characteristic ways of relating, temperament, and attachment styles. It is essential to understand the relationship of a client's experiences at each systemic level and the combination of those experiences to understand a client's dilemmas and ascertain avenues for change and healing. Thus, whether professional counselors are treating clients presenting with anxiety, marital problems, or individual psychological problems such as schizophrenia or bipolar disorder, interventions are aimed at interactional patterns between the client and others. Several guiding assumptions and evidence-based research serve to support the efficacy of marital and family therapy as an effective approach to treating mental illness.

Assumptions Guiding Systems Theory and Family Counseling

The emphasis professional counselors place on using relationships in the treatment of mental disorders is based on several guiding assumptions. First, professional counselors are generally limited to a 1-hour-per-week role in client lives, with the client's natural support system as ancillary to the therapeutic relationship. Subjugating the family system in this way may hinder counseling process and outcome. Second, the assumption that change in the interaction between counselor and client generalizes to others in the client's life is a hypothetical endeavor. Systems theory promotes seeing change happen between client and significant others in the therapy room. Third, dependency and attachment are not merely seen as childhood traits, but innate needs (Bowlby, 1988). Dependency and attachment shape a person's sense of self and oth-

ers. Because the self is deeply embedded in relationships, a client's dilemmas are frequently healed through relationships. This also implies that change in the client's life affects others with whom the client comes in contact. Moreover, failure to consider how others may be affected by client change may undermine the change process and runs the risk of posing damage to intimate relationships.

Research Supporting Couple and Family Counseling

Law and Crane's (2000) seminal research demonstrated that individual treatment that included at least one significant other reduced health care utilization. Treatment of specific presenting problems, including conduct disorder; adolescent substance abuse; childhood behavioral and emotional disorders; alcohol abuse; marital problems; domestic violence; and severe mental disorders, namely schizophrenia and mood disorders, has been supported by rigorous research on couple and family counseling approaches (American Association for Marriage and Family Therapy, 2002; Sprenkle, 2002). The efficacy of couple and family counseling in the aforementioned areas suggests that systemically oriented therapy may also be an effective approach for a multiplicity of mental health issues.

Contributed by Stephanie I. Falke,
Loma Linda University,
Loma Linda, CA

References

American Association for Marriage and Family Therapy. (2002). *FAQ's on MFT's: Frequently asked questions on marriage and family therapist.* Retrieved April 15, 2007, http://www.aamft.org/faqs/index_nm.asp

Bowlby, J. (1988). *A secure base.* New York: Basic.

Laszlo, E. (1996). *The systems view of the world: A holistic vision for our time.* Cresskill, NJ: Hampton Press.

Law, D. D., & Crane, D. R. (2000). The influence of marital and family therapy on health care utilization in a health-maintenance organization. *Journal of Marital and Family Therapy, 26,* 281–291.

Sprenkle, D. H. (Ed.). (2002). *Effectiveness research in marriage and family therapy.* Alexandria, VA: American Association for Marriage and Family Therapy.

Additional Resources

Gurman, A. S., & Jacobson, N. S. (Eds.). (2002). *Clinical handbook of couple therapy* (3rd ed.). New York: Guilford Press.

Hoffman, L. (2002). *Family therapy: An intimate history.* New York: Norton.

Nichols, M. P., & Schwartz, R. C. (2006). *Family therapy concepts and methods* (7th ed.). Boston: Pearson.

■ Family Life Cycle

The concept of what constitutes a **family life cycle** has changed over the years, but what has remained constant is the notion that time is linear. Historically, in the 1930s, the family life cycle approach rested on the assumption that most families passed through an orderly progression of stages, each with its own characteristics affecting the roles and status of family members. Significant disagreement about the stages emerged as research was conducted in the 1960s and 1970s, leading to the position that no single set of classifications was realistic or valuable. Traditionally, a family life cycle model outlined movement in a family from being single and unattached to being married or partnering to parenting and childrearing. Next would follow the stages of child development to the movement of children out of the home and the transition of older adults facing later life issues.

Life cycle models presume that as family members face significant transitions, family life cycle events come into play. Life in families is complex and interactive and proceeds in a linear time frame. Intergenerational phases of development affect and influence one generation and another generation reciprocally, so that dynamics within a family may reflect curvilinear relationships. The family life cycle revolves around the entering, exiting, and possible reentering of members through marriage and partnering and the addition of one or more children, first incorporating infants, then young children, then adolescents. As children mature into young adults, at some point they move toward independence. The manifestation of this independence differs markedly, depending on cultural background and beliefs, so inquiring about what constitutes an appropriate reason for leaving home must be explored. The impact of culture is critical, and life cycle events and transitions must be contextualized within the culture of the family, the extended family, and the community at large.

Life cycle stages must be regarded with the full appreciation and acknowledgement that variations occur among ethnic groups and families of different social and economic makeup, so no one progression should be stereotyped. A recent model includes six stages, based primarily on family expansion and contraction: (a) the single young adult, (b) joining and forming a new dyad, (c) family with young children, (d) family with adolescents (this stage can also simultaneously include the care giving of aging parents), (e) family launching children and moving on, and (f) the family in later life (Carter & McGoldrick, 1999).

The family life cycle has also been conceptualized as predictable, linear, and time-bound and focusing on generally anticipated real-life events. These would include (a) the infant family, (b) the preschool family, (c) the grade school family, (d) the adolescent family, (e) launching family, (f) mentoring family, (g) retired family, and (h) elderly family.

The criticisms of the stage models of life cycle development have focused on their limitations as linear approaches that are incompatible with a systemic family framework. From a systems perspective, life events involve interactive and ongoing dynamic processes among family members. Stage models tend to describe what were considered traditional nuclear families, reflective of too small a proportion of society and not inclusive of the vast diversity found in family structures today. Because there is no single explanation of transitions, developmental tasks, or life events, a fixed stage model does not fully capture the complexity of

family development in all its constellations, and too much information may be overlooked by a strict adherence to a stage model. Nevertheless, the utility of the model continues to be recognized.

Viewing the family life cycle means attending to and exploring significant transition points— times of disruption, change, and adaptation. Life cycle models generally include not only the transition points but also the emotional issues faced by the family unit as well as the developmental tasks that need to be completed. These are times to assess the functionality of family members in terms of stability and change, flexibility and rigidity. The life cycle transitions represent situations of potential stress and also opportunities to identify the resiliency and resources within and outside of the family context. Exploring how family members negotiate significant life cycle events helps to determine intervention strategies and assists in helping family members locate their strengths as well as identify patterns that have become dysfunctional and require change.

While many life cycle events are predictable, the complexity of the life cycle picture across diverse family structures is not commonly attended to in the literature, as the following examples demonstrate. **Blended families** have issues involved in reorganizing and adapting to a new family structure. The number of **single-parent-headed households** has been rising steadily in the United States, and frequently these families must negotiate with extended family members during key life cycle events. **Gay and lesbian families** have faced societal stressors that may become reduced as acceptance of this family composition grows on a national level. Families facing infertility and adoptive families confront particular challenges and will benefit from supportive counseling throughout their compelling family life cycle events. Families without children also have life cycle issues although they do not involve raising children. Finally, multiethnic, immigrant, and intergenerational families navigate transition points not necessarily identified in the more traditional life cycle map (McBride, 2003).

It is expected that there will be more revisions in the conceptualization of the family cycle, given that family life itself periodically reorganizes as individual development progresses and aligns with changes in the larger society. The conceptual and empirical status of this area continues to evolve and be a fruitful one for investigation.

Professional counselors can be most productive and helpful in working with individuals and family members by understanding people's life experiences and how people have negotiated life cycle events. Major life events affect all human beings across gender, class, language, culture, geographical location, and so on; therefore, counselors can use their knowledge of family life cycle events as points of entry into their work with families. Counselors gather assessment data and develop intervention strategies through tracking the patterns of communication, dysfunction, successful coping strategies, handling of crises, resiliency, and patterns of relationship among family members, and the most valuable information is commonly revealed during moments of significance in the life cycle of the family. It is important for counselors to appreciate how individuals and family members define and view family as well as understand the impact of family history, and the family life cycle lens is often the one that provides a clear view.

Contributed by Faith Deveaux, Lehman College of the City University of New York, Bronx, NY

References

Carter, B., & McGoldrick, M. (Eds.). (1999). *The expanded family life cycle: Individual, family, and social perspectives* (3rd ed.). Boston: Allyn & Bacon.

McBride, J. L. (2003). *Family behavioral issues in health and illness.* New York: Haworth Press.

Additional Resource

Walsh, F. (Ed.). (2003). *Normal family processes: Growing diversity and complexity* (3rd ed.). New York: Guilford Press.

■ Family of Origin

Family of origin is conceptualized as an organism or living unit in which an individual initially develops physically, mentally, and emotionally (Hovestadt, Anderson, Piercy, Cochran, & Fine, 1985). It is within the framework of people's experiences in their family of origin that their self-image, values, behaviors, attitudes, and relationship-building skills develop. Throughout individuals' lives, these early family-of-origin experiences continue to affect their growth and development.

Kerr and Bowen (1988) stated that relationships from individuals' family of origin are "templates" from which they interact with others in later life, particularly in relationships that demand intimacy (e.g., with significant others, children, close friends). Bowen (1978) maintained that unless individuals explore and resolve learned patterns of behaviors from past generations, they are likely to repeat them in current relationships. This influence of the family of origin persists whether an individual retains old family (of origin) connections or not.

Gladding (2007) defined family of origin as the "family in which a person grew up" (p. 6; i.e., all human beings begin life by being part of a family or family system). Each individual family member's experiences are also other family members' experiences, because family system processes affect all members of the family or family system; therefore, each family member plays a role in the family system that maintains a balance, or **homeostasis.** In other words, in the crucial years of development in the family of origin, individuals build relationships unconsciously patterned on the interactions with other members in the family, striving hard at all costs to maintain homeostasis. Unconsciously, each member of the family slips into a particular role. These roles may be overt or covert. For example, a child may unwittingly take on a role as a troublemaker in order to divert family attention from the marital discord of his or her parents.

The principle of homeostasis explains why as one member in a dysfunctional family system (e.g., alcoholic family)

changes a role, other members will unconsciously try to change that person back to recreate dysfunctional patterns of behavior. In addition to overt and covert roles, an individual also lives with overt and covert rules, family secrets, multiple myths, multiple and sometimes conflicting loyalties, diverse boundaries, patterns of intimate interaction, economic and political influences, and experience of loss. For example, a family may have an unspoken rule that it is not appropriate to discuss topics such as sex or religion. Although there has been no formalization of the rule within the family, the rule is conveyed through interactions and nonverbal behavior.

Individuals carry with them family-of-origin dynamics (e.g., people are never far from home, no matter how many miles they physically distance themselves). In the growing-up years, falling in love is quite often a search for someone with whom an individual can "work out" family-of-origin issues, which means that individuals unconsciously choose someone who is like or totally unlike their family of origin to recreate roles played in the family of origin. In order to build mature and meaningful relationships, it is imperative that individuals address their family-of-origin issues.

Family-of-Origin Work

Family-of-origin work typically looks at the family into which a client is born and the families of origin of the client's parents. Counseling involves examining old family messages, values, communication styles, traditions, and ways of dealing with feelings. Family-of-origin work can help individuals in (a) understanding their origins and learning from the past, so that old unhealthy patterns will not be perpetuated, either in themselves or in their intimate relationships; (b) understanding the consequences of injustice that was directed at them; (c) breaking free of the past; (d) detecting generational issues and dealing with them; (e) detecting and dealing with the roots of any bitterness or resentment; (f) addressing any unresolved guilt; and (g) improving current and extended family relationships.

Lawson and Gaushell (1988) developed the **family autobiography intervention** to help individuals focus on family-of-origin dynamics, providing the opportunity to revisit and explore relationships with parents, siblings, and any other close members in the family, as well as to scrutinize the presence and pressure of these patterns in current relationships. The goal is to unravel old patterns or characteristics of interpersonal behavior habituated in an individual's family of origin. The family autobiography consists of a genogram, a timeline of important family events, a description of interactions in a person's family of origin, and an explanation of how these events affect the individual's current life situation. Some family counselors believe that if individuals can go back in time and deal directly with past as well as present issues with their families of origin, there is an opportunity for reconstructive change in their current family life and other meaningful relationships (Holcomb-McCoy, 2004).

Contributed by Phyllis Benjamin and Carl J. Sheperis, Mississippi State University, Starkville, MS

References

Bowen, M. (1978). *Family therapy in clinical practice.* Northvale, NJ: Aronson.

Gladding, S. T. (2007). *Family therapy: History, theory, and practice* (4th ed.). Upper Saddle River, NJ: Simon & Schuster.

Holcomb-McCoy, C. (2004). Using the family autobiography in school counselor preparation: An introduction to a systemic perspective. *The Family Journal: Counseling and Therapy for Couples and Families, 12,* 21–25.

Hovestadt, A. J., Anderson, W. T., Piercy, F. P., Cochran, A. W., & Fine, M. (1985). A Family-of-Origin Scale. *Journal of Marital and Family Therapy, 11,* 287–297.

Kerr, M. E., & Bowen, M. (1988). *Family evaluation: An approach based on Bowen theory.* New York: Norton.

Lawson, D. M., & Gaushell, H. (1988). Family autobiography: A useful method for enhancing counselors' personal development. *Counselor Education and Supervision, 28,* 162–167.

Family Sculpting

Family sculpting, an arts-based intervention with roots in psychodrama, is a visible metaphor for a person's perceptions of family. First used in 1951 by **Virginia Satir,** the technique was further developed by Satir and other experiential family therapists, including Bunny Duhl, Fred Duhl, John Banman, and David Kantor. Its premise is the illustration of family patterns of interrelationships, communication, and behavior by creating static scenes or "sculptures" with family members. Its nonverbal nature offers the potential for creating intensity and circumventing verbal defenses. Family sculpting provides information about patterns of relationships, boundaries, and alliances and highlights perceptions of family members. By sculpting desired or ideal portrayals of family interactions, family members can portray hopes and identify changes to work on between sessions. The technique may be used on a voluntary basis in the training of counselors. It also has applications for use as a catalyst for change in organizational training and development sessions.

Family sculpting sessions require three roles: (a) the **sculptor** (client) who sculpts players chosen by the sculptor to portray members of the family (in a classroom or group setting) or the actual family member themselves; (b) the **facilitator,** or professional counselor, who supports, protects, and guides the sculptor; and (c) the family members or **role players.** In a classroom or training session, remaining audience or class members observe and comment in the feedback stage.

The basic protocol involves the professional counselor asking a member of the family to arrange or pose the others in a meaningful scene of family life, which may include the sculptor. Distance, touch, facial expressions, closeness, and positioning of arms and legs are all expressive indicators. The scene is processed carefully with the leadership of the professional counselor.

Contributed by Katherine Ziff, Ohio University, Athens, OH

Additional Resources

Costa, L. (1991). Family sculpting in the training of marriage and family counselors. *Counselor Education and Supervision, 31,* 121–132.

Gladding, S. T. (2005). *Counseling as an art: The creative arts in counseling* (3rd ed.). Alexandria, VA: American Counseling Association.

Satir, V., Banmen, J., Gerber, J., & Gomori, M. (1991). *The Satir model: Family therapy and beyond.* Palo Alto, CA: Science and Behavior Books.

Feminist Identity Development Model

In 1985, **Downing and Roush** established the first feminist identity development stage model of several currently present in the literature (see Reid & Purcell, 2004; Whipple, 1996). Downing and Roush's model was based on several factors, including Cross's (1971) racial identity development model, general identity development models, and research on sex role transcendence and consciousness (Hansen, 2002). According to the **feminist identity development model,** the development of a feminist identity is a process whereby women and girls make sense of their position in the world, integrating their awareness of sexism, issues of power, and concerns of male privilege through alliance with other women and pride in their femininity.

It was the intention of Downing and Roush to provide a model that could inform clinical practice with women. The model alerts professional counselors to the complex and potentially painful process women undertake when developing a feminist identity. With an increased awareness of this process, professional counselors can more effectively and efficaciously serve these women.

Stages of the Model

Downing and Roush's feminist identity development model consists of five discrete stages. The authors acknowledged that the model is not entirely linear; women may recycle through the stages at different points in their lives. In addition, the model is intended for conceptualizing only women's feminist identity.

The first stage of the model, **passive acceptance,** embodies an immersion in the predominant societal views of women and traditional female gender roles. Women in this stage are resistant to notions of a power differential between the sexes and gender discrimination. They are also often reluctant to engage in social interactions or experiences with individuals they perceive as embracing a feminist identity. At the end of Stage 1, women begin to experience more openness to ideas challenging traditional views of women's status in society. In addition, an event or series of events, either positive or negative, occur that propel women into the second stage.

Stage 2, **revelation,** is a time marked by personal crisis in which a woman experiences a shift in her cognitive schema. That which she has always known to be true has been shown to be false, and she is faced with the daunting task of reforming her understanding of her world. As she works to put together these pieces, she does so by rejecting the patriarchal values that inform traditional male and female gender roles rather than by embracing a pro-woman stance.

Stage 3, **embeddedness–emanation,** is a two-part stage. The initial half of this stage, embeddedness, is distinguished by a woman's immersion into the company of other women to the exclusion, or near exclusion, of men. This stage is also characterized by a unilateral acceptance of feminist values. The lack of questioning of feminist values is reminiscent of the unquestioning acceptance of patriarchal values seen in Stage 1. For many women, embeddedness is often very difficult to achieve and maintain, because they often have multiple significant relationships with men, such as fathers, husbands, and sons. Through the value they place on these relationships, women begin to conceptualize the world as less polarized; all men need not be avoided. They also gain awareness that rage is not their most effective tool and develop more advantageous coping skills. By the end of this stage, women remain guarded in their interactions with men as they further their establishment of a more flexible worldview. This developing worldview accepts that there are men who are content with traditional gender roles and deny their position of privilege; however, there are others who revile this inequity and are actively working toward creating a world in which power is more freely shared.

Stage 4 is **synthesis.** At this point, women integrate their own personal and cultural values with the feminist principles they had unquestioningly accepted previously. This integration results in the establishment of a unique feminist identity and the opportunity for that identity to be embraced by a woman. This identity also facilitates identifying men to include in the women's lives.

In the fifth and final stage, **active commitment,** the feminist identity developed in the synthesis stage is used to advance social change for women. This may involve voicing opposition to issues of gender inequality as they present themselves in the woman's world, supporting social or political campaigns that strive for gender equity, or working to promote peace throughout the world. It is noteworthy that women rarely achieve this stage, and many women advocates are actually working within the revelation or embeddedness–emanation stages.

Validity of the Model

Since its presentation in 1985, Downing and Roush's model has received considerable empirical attention. Studies investigating this model have predominantly used three instruments specifically developed in hopes of quantitatively assessing the stages of this model. According to Hansen (2002) and Hyde (2002), however, studies based on these three instruments (the Feminist Identity Scale [Rickard, 1989], the Feminist Identity Development Scale [Bargad & Hyde, 1991], and the Feminist Identity Composite [Fischer, Tokar, Good, Hill, & Blum, 2000]) have resulted in mixed support for the five-stage model. Moradi, Subich, and Philips (2002) provided an overview of research studies based on this model of feminist identity development. The studies they reviewed explored various attitudes, beliefs, and behaviors related to feminist identity, including perception of women's sociocultural roles, body

image, disordered eating, and dating behaviors. Ultimately, it is unclear from the current research whether this inconsistent support is due to deficits in the model or limitations in the construction of the instruments.

Although this model has been highly influential and has served as a framework for considerable clinical and empirical work, repeated critiques of the model exist. Foremost, the model does not appear to address diversity issues such as class, race, ethnicity, age, sexual orientation, gender identity, or ability status. It also assumes universality among all women. For example, the model assumes that all women will initially experience anger at the revelation of their relative powerlessness. This would be especially questionable for women of color, who may possess a heightened and early awareness of their oppressed status. It also presupposes ways in which women move beyond the anger into a pro-woman stance. This would also very likely be a highly individualized and culturally informed process.

The model has also been critiqued as highly value laden. Foremost, it bestows an inferior status on women functioning in earlier stages of the model, and it indicates a need for women to obtain the final stage of active commitment. The model also assumes that women will typically first reject men and then learn to incorporate them into their new worldview. This assumption devalues the experience of women who choose to maintain close relationships exclusively with other women.

Finally, critics have questioned whether Downing and Roush's stages are in fact true stages. It was suggested by Hyde (2002) that the stages of this model were more representative of dimensions. This critique was based in part on the inability of current measures of feminist identity development to capture the five stages adequately. It was suggested by Downing (Hansen, 2002) that perhaps the model would be more adequately assessed with qualitative measures.

Despite these critiques, the Downing and Roush model has served as a valuable means to undertake empirical consideration of feminist identity development. Given the numerous unanswered questions remaining in this line of research, further exploration of this construct is warranted to advance the conceptualization of feminist identity; its development; and its effects on the thoughts, feelings, and actions of women.

Ultimately, Downing and Roush's model serves as a seminal work in the field of counseling. Through its empirical and clinical influence, this feminist identity development model has been critical in advancing the way in which the counseling profession conceptualizes feminist identity development.

Contributed by Claudia Brasfield
and L. Shane Blasko,
Georgia State University, Atlanta, GA

References

Bargad, A., & Hyde, J. S. (1991). A study of feminist identity development in women. *Psychology of Women Quarterly, 15,* 181–201.

Cross, W. E. (1971). The Negro-to-Black conversion experience: Toward a psychology of Black liberation. *Black World, 20,* 13–27.

Downing, N. E., & Roush, K. L. (1985). From passive acceptance to active commitment: A model of feminist identity development for women. *The Counseling Psychologist, 13,* 695–709.

Fischer, A. R., Tokar, D. M., Good, G. E., Hill, M. S., & Blum, S. A. (2000). Assessing women's feminist identity development. *Psychology of Women Quarterly, 24,* 15–29.

Hansen, N. D. (2002). Reflections on feminist identity development: Implications for theory, measurement, and research. *The Counseling Psychologist, 30,* 87–95.

Hyde, J. S. (2002). Feminist identity development: The current state of theory, research, and practice. *The Counseling Psychologist, 30,* 105–110.

Moradi, B., Subich, L. M., & Phillips, J. C. (2002). Revisiting feminist identity development theory, research, and practice. *The Counseling Psychologist, 30,* 6–43.

Reid, A., & Purcell, P. (2004). Pathways to feminist development. *Sex Roles, 50,* 759–769.

Rickard, K. M. (1989). The relationship of self-monitored dating behaviors to level of feminist identity on the Feminist Identity Scale. *Sex Roles, 20,* 213–226.

Whipple, V. (1996). Developing an identity as a feminist family therapist: Implications for training. *Journal of Marital & Family Therapy, 22,* 381–396.

▮ Feminist Theory

Feminist theory is best viewed as a kaleidoscope. There are many facets, which take on different forms and colors depending on who is doing the twisting of the instrument's wheel. Feminist theory is an overarching perspective of how women are considered in the context of counseling. Effective feminist counseling first calls for the therapist to self-examine her or his value systems. Next, the professional counselor views the client as competent, establishes an egalitarian counseling relationship, and has a goal of empowering the client. Feminist theory is not a specific set of techniques but a set of values that include paying attention to women's issues connected specifically to gender and the context of the client's world. It is informed by feminist political philosophy, multiculturalism, and social change. It is not prescriptive, nor does it endorse a particular established theory. The client's experience of oppression in political and environmental situations is a topic for examination. The client is not necessarily seen as having pathology but as surviving by coping with life issues. Feminist theory started as a grassroots political theory that morphed into the counseling sphere. Feminist theory falls into several basic types: liberal feminism, radical feminism, cultural feminism, and women of color feminism, to name a few.

Liberal feminism was a reaction to women's oppression by men and is rooted in the 18th and 19th centuries, when philosophical discussions of natural rights and enlightenment pointed the way to looking at both men and women as rational human beings, who should be treated as such. Women's right to vote and the inclusion of contemporary women in psychological and medical studies are from these roots. This is the first wave of feminism.

The second wave of feminism, known as **radical feminism,** occurred between 1960 and 1980. Gender oppression in capitalism and the resulting repressive political and social systems are the themes of this movement, building a foundation for feminist therapy. The book *Feminine Mystique* by Betty Friedan (1963) was a catalyst in this movement worldwide.

The third wave of feminism began in the mid 1980s with a new emphasis on political activity, including women's issues in the workplace, especially sexual harassment. Although the second wave was focused on the White middle-class woman, the third wave sought to expand to an idiosyncratic narrative of gender and sexual identity. **Cultural feminism** examines how a woman's life is unique because she is female. A contemporary offshoot of this approach is how feminist managerial styles are beginning to be seen as more productive—that is, collaborative rather than patriarchal top-down.

Global feminism has several divisions, depending on location. **Women of color feminism** is about creating inclusiveness for all women, regardless of skin color. **Black feminism** maintains that Black women experience the effects of both sexism and racism. Postcolonial and third-world feminism do not favor Western theories of feminism. The thrust is to fight oppression of women within the cultural context of each individual country, especially those once ruled by colonialism.

Although not within the typology of most references to feminism, two other classifications are often mentioned that overlap with the basic types already mentioned: social feminism and ecofeminism. Social (or socialist) feminism includes race, ethnicity, economics, social class, women's roles, women's work, and the patriarchal/capitalistic context. A central focus is large-scale society as a whole. **Ecofeminism** comes from the belief that male domination hurts women and the environment. The concept of the harmony of people and nature is viewed as being better understood by women than by men.

The types of feminist theory already discussed in this entry are the main ones, but the list of the various intellectual traditions is much longer. Other types of feminist theories include (a) separation, (b) "French" feminism, (c) psychoanalytic, (d) materialist, (e) anti-pornography movement, (f) pro-porn artists, (g) queer theory, (h) reformist, and (i) lesbian. All of these have some overlapping ideology and are fluid and dynamic. As the political and economic scene changes and evolves, so will all of these types of feminism.

Major Tenets of Feminist Theory

The grassroots of feminist theory are from a pluralistic base of a reaction to the isms in society, such as racism, ageism, and chauvinism, as well as an assumption that all types of oppression can eventually be eliminated. There are some major tenets that are found in all forms and aspects of feminist theory: (a) Men and women are equal in political, social, and economic spheres; (b) patriarchy is a dominant idea that oppresses all women; (c) the personal is political; (d) problems and psychological symptoms are a result of coping in a hostile environment; (e) it is impossible to practice value-free counseling; and (f) the counselor's role is to create an egalitarian relationship.

Application of Feminist Theory

Feminist counseling is informed by feminist theory. All feminist theories subscribe to the position that women have been unable to be full participants in all social spheres and institutions. Some professional counselors may have been practicing from a feminist theoretical perspective without labeling themselves as such. They have done this by establishing the egalitarian relationship that is the core of some theoretical orientations.

Applying a feminist perspective in the counseling setting is a matter of exploring the client's perception of where she sees her place in her particular community. It is also a matter of the professional counselor being attuned to how contextual variables may affect the presenting problem of the client. The professional counselor may have to be the one to bring the client into awareness of the issues of feminism that are relevant. The professional counselor must, however, also proceed with caution in order not to impose her or his own values on the client.

The woman is viewed in the greater context of socioeconomic status, education, culture, ethnicity, and gender identity. She is not a problem to be cured but a person who has to learn about the oppression she is experiencing in relation to her personal and social location, and through that discovery process, she becomes empowered to create a better life for herself. Consciousness-raising and awareness are crucial components in the counseling process, as are analysis of social and gender roles, resocialization, and social activism.

Consciousness-raising in the second half of the 20th century was introduced in the second wave of the feminist movement. Actual implementation covers a wide spectrum of activities, including fiction and nonfiction feminist books; political activism; women's groups that are either educational, psychoeducational, or therapeutic; or individual therapy. The issue usually centered around violence and abuse, imbalance of power, autonomy, sexuality, and body image. The direct or indirect result of raising consciousness of issues may or may not be actual change of behavior or attitude.

Many would argue, however, that consciousness-raising has led to analysis of social and gender roles, not just in the individual but in the collective society. Issues include male privileges, gender inequalities, and stereotyping gender-based behavior. The advent of the birth control pill in the 1960s allowed women to define their roles as wife and mother, allowing planning and spacing of children or not having children at all. There was, and in some circles still is, a confusion of what exactly is a primary role for women in U.S. society. Women have more choices than ever before regarding marital status, care giving, education, and career. As a result, women today carry more roles than women did prior to 1960. More choices may mean more difficulties for the client, and women's career issues and the roles that others expect her to fill can often be a topic of counseling.

Resocialization is tied to this analysis of social and gender roles, and in some ways to consciousness-raising. The term *resocialization* is not found in most of the current literature in women's studies, having been absorbed into role analysis.

Social activism arose before feminist theory in the 100-year-long battle for women to obtain the right to vote in the United States and in the Women's Christian Temperance Union movement. Jane Addams of Hull House and Margaret Sanger, who brought the need for birth control into the open, were also social activists. Today, social activism continues to focus on those who are marginalized in society, with an ever-expanding definition of who comes under that heading.

Advocacy takes on many issues; the "pink" campaign against breast cancer and the "red dress" movement to raise awareness of heart disease in women are two significant health issues highlighted by the media in the 21st century. Because feminist theory incorporates a holistic, environmental approach, health issues are also part of the counseling realm. More directly connected to counseling, national screening days for depression and anxiety are a part of this advocacy movement, and the benefits are not exclusive to women.

Feminist theory sees gender as a social construction and argues against set roles in life for women based on their biology. Feminist counselors help women to discover other roles that they can take on because they are based on clients' desires and not on exterior, imposed expectations.

A feminist practitioner seeks to balance the power equation in the counseling relationship by aiming to use strategies that convey the counseling process as a journey on which client and counselor are together, rather than as a forum where a client is diagnosed and then encouraged to achieve a preset level of wellness. Feminist counselors may use techniques such as appropriate self-disclosure, thorough informed consent, building a safe environment for the client, explaining his or her theoretical orientation, striving for an egalitarian relationship of client and counselor, helping clients in articulating their own values, and joint development of goals.

Feminist practitioners must stay attuned to the community in which they counsel. The feminist practitioner should seek out experiences in the community to enhance self-understanding of potential clients. Application of that knowledge, however, must always respect the client's developmental acculturation level and help the client process her comfort in her primary community and other communities in which the client may function. Although it is rare in the literature, a feminist counselor may use the same techniques when counseling both men and women. Men can also suffer from oppression and so may benefit from the feminist perspective.

Spirituality can also be essential in feminist theory. Spiritual and religious ties can be a vital part of the client's support system and foundational sense of life meaning. Some congregations or denominations may or may not support the counselor's value systems, but if the values are meaningful to the client, the counselor is respectful of those values. In the processing of a spiritual or religious component, the feminist counselor should consider this context as all other contexts of the client's life and not automatically make the assumption that it is oppressive. The counselor would be wise, however, to help the client process this life factor, as she or he does all other life factors, for awareness and empowerment in the situation.

Feminist practitioners are holistic in their approach and consider the medical issues in their clients' lives. It is almost impossible to separate what is happening to the female body from what happens to her emotions and functioning. Mood disorders and anxiety are often accompanied by, or may be precipitated by, medical factors. Menstrual or menopausal symptoms can affect a client's view of life, depending upon their severity. A woman may have a more difficult time obtaining medical treatment when needed, either because of no access to health care or restrictions on health insurance. For example, women are often labeled as "enablers" when the husband is an alcoholic. The reality may be that she is a survivor in a difficult situation, struggling to keep the family together, particularly if there are children.

Women's issues are both idiosyncratic and common, no matter where the woman resides. The difference is in degree. Physical, sexual, and emotional abuse; sex trafficking; economic difficulty; lack of education and opportunity; childbearing; a voice in government; a voice in business; leadership in community; business, and church—all of these are issues for women that intertwine with the tenets of feminist therapy, and they can be addressed when working from a feminist perspective.

Contributed by Rosemarie Scotti Hughes, Regent University, Virginia Beach, VA

Reference

Friedan, B. (1963). *The feminine mystique.* New York: Norton.

Additional Resources

Borysenko, J. (1996). *A woman's book of life: The biology, psychology, and spirituality of the feminine life cycle.* New York: Riverhead Books.

Boston Women's Health Book Collective. (2005). *Our bodies, ourselves.* New York: Simon & Schuster.

Enns, C. Z. (2004). *Feminist theories and feminist psychotherapies: Origins, themes, and diversity* (2nd ed.). New York: Haworth Press.

Lips, H. M. (2006). *A new psychology of women: Gender, culture, and ethnicity* (3rd ed.). New York: McGraw Hill.

■ Five-Factor Model

The **five-factor model** is arguably the most influential and widely endorsed taxonomy of personality to emerge in the past 25 years. Sometimes referred to as the **Big Five**, the model classifies personality traits along five bipolar dimensions that capture the array of personality descriptors found in many languages. Because the factors are dimensions rather than types, most people fall between the two poles, resulting in a bell-curve distribution for each of the five domains.

Represented by the acronym **OCEAN,** the domains include (a) **openness,** which describes the degree to which a person is imaginative or curious; (b) **conscientiousness,** which assesses a person's ambitiousness; (c) **extraversion,** which addresses sociability; (d) **agreeableness,** which describes the desire to avoid conflict; and (e) **neuroticism,** which encompasses persistent negative emotional states such as depression and anxiety. Combinations of the five personality dispositions have been linked with a number of behavioral outcomes. Academic achievement, for example, has been correlated with high conscientiousness and low neuroticism. Alcohol consumption, on the other hand, has been associated with high extraversion and low conscientiousness. The possibility that interactive combinations of traits may have an impact on health behaviors or serve as buffers from disease has spurred research in the area of behavioral medicine.

To assess the five domains identified in the model, a number of instruments have been developed. The **NEO Personality Inventory–Revised (NEO-PI-R;** McCrae & Costa, 1991) seems to be the most comprehensive and widely used measure. Research using the NEO-PI-R has identified six facets in each of the five trait domains that further differentiate the dimensions. In the domain of agreeableness, for example, are facets labeled "trust," "straightforwardness," "altruism," "compliance," "modesty," and "tendermindedness." Numerous studies have replicated the five factors across age groups, genders, and cultures. The factors appear stable throughout adulthood, especially after 30 years of age, and are considered to be biologically based.

The five-factor model is relevant to professional counselors because it addresses variations in normal personality and can assist in selecting targeted interventions. In addition, personality disorders as well as psychological conditions classified on Axis I of the *Diagnostic and Statistical Manual of Mental Disorders* (4th ed., text rev.; American Psychiatric Association, 2000) have been associated with varying profiles of the five factors. As the primary means of measuring personality domains, the NEO-PI-R assesses both strengths and weaknesses and complements a brief model of treatment. Because personality is especially salient to career planning, counselors may find the five-factor model a useful adjunct in vocational counseling. For clients, knowing their placement on the five factors enhances self-understanding and provides a means of evaluating the match between their disposition and the demands of their environment.

Although the five-factor model has been embraced by most researchers, critics have argued that reducing the vast array of traits to merely five results in a loss of specificity and that the model ignores some important aspects of personality. Alternative models consisting of 6, 7, and 10 factors have emerged. Other critics have noted that the domain identified as openness lacks the replicability of the other dimensions. In cross-cultural studies, this factor has been alternately conceptualized as intelligence and conventionality. Future research will likely clarify whether the factor has greater applicability to some cultures more than to others. Despite these criticisms, the five-factor model has spurred a tremendous volume of research and generated support from the majority of personality researchers who concur that it captures the central components of personality.

Contributed by Sarah L. Hastings,
Radford University, Radford, VA

References

American Psychiatric Association. (2000). *Diagnostic and statistical manual of mental disorders* (4th ed., text rev.) Washington, DC: Author.

McCrae, R. R., & Costa, P. T. (1991). *Professional manual for the Revised NEO Personality Inventory (NEO PI –R) and Neo Five-Factor Inventory (Neo-FFI)*. Lutz, FL: Psychological Assessment Resources.

Additional Resources

Costa, P. T., & McCrae, R. R. (1992). The NEO Personality Inventory: Using the five-factor model in counseling. *Journal of Counseling & Development, 69,* 367–372.

Malouff, J. M., Thorsteinsson, E. B., & Schutte, N. S. (2005). The relationship between the five-factor model of personality and symptoms of clinical disorders: A meta-analysis. *Journal of Psychopathology and Behavioral Assessment, 27,* 101–114.

McCrae, R. R., & Costa, P. T. (2003). *Personality in adulthood: A five-factor theory perspective* (2nd ed.). New York: Guilford Press.

Gender Identity Development

Everyone has a **gender identity,** an image of her- or himself as possessing primarily feminine or masculine characteristics. Gender characteristics can be different, depending on the culture in which a person is raised, and they are reinforced by social structures such as religion and school. Many cultures, however, have similar gender expectations. Williams and Best (1994) found that people in 30 countries largely agreed on what constituted masculine and feminine gender characteristics. Some characteristics of gender expression seem to have some basis in genetics, such as aggression and rough physical play found in most human males across cultures and many other animal species as well.

Gender identity is different from sex, although people often use the term *gender* when they are referring to a person's sex. Gender identity most often, but not always, matches the biological sexual characteristics with which a person is born and, thus, is a social expression of sex, so females act and look like females and males act and look like males. **Sex** is the biological sex a person is born with, as identified by genitalia. Gender is the social expression of this sex. **Sexual orientation** refers to the sex of the person to whom a person is sexually attracted, and sexual identity refers to the sexual orientation with which a person identifies.

Gender identity can be considered as being a continuum rather than a dichotomy. A feminine gender identity would ordinarily endorse behaviors and attitudes such as affectionate, soft-spoken, cheerful, and relational and would endorse characteristics such as self-sufficient, ambitious, and aggressive less so. A person with a masculine gender identity would endorse the opposite. People who score in the middle range of the continuum, androgynous, score high on both feminine and masculine characteristics; people who score low on both characteristics are considered undifferentiated. Most people fall somewhere along the continuum, with some feminine characteristics and some masculine characteristics.

Some argue that socialization plays a role in gender role identification, because parents and others in society expect, and at times force, children to conform to gender stereotypes. According to Kolhberg (1966), children begin to label their own and others' sex when they are around age 2 years, soon after they begin to sort out what it means in terms of activity and behavior. This is **gender labeling,** or gender typing. At this point, children understand that they are boys or girls and can label themselves accurately. **Gender stability** occurs during the preschool years as children begin to understand that sex is stable and that little girls will grow up to be women and little boys will grow up to be men. At this age, however, children can believe that boys who wear ponytails or a dress will grow up to be a girl and that girls who dress like a boy and play with boys' toys will grow up to be a man; that is, sex can be changed by displaying differing gender characteristics. **Gender constancy** is achieved around age 6 to 8 years when children understand that sex is unaffected by the clothes a person wears or the activity in which a person engages. Children understand stereotypical gender roles in play as early as preschool and punish peers who engage in cross-gender play. Boys are more harshly judged than girls in cross-gender play by both peers and parents. Some children (and adults) experience incongruence between their biological sex and their gender identity, or gender dysphoria (Money, 1994). If this incongruence causes significant difficulties in social, occupational, or other areas of functioning, a diagnosis of gender identity disorder may be given (see Sexual and Gender Identity Disorders). Many people who experience gender dysphoria seek hormone treatment and sex reassignment surgery to help create the appearance of the external genitals typical of the other sex to match their internal lived experience.

There has been much discussion concerning whether socialization or biology produces gender differences. One study done by Imperato-McGinley et al. (as cited in Rathus, Nevid, & Fichner-Rathus, 2008) following 18 boys born with damaged genitalia until adulthood provides some interesting insight. The boys' testes and internal male organs were formed, but their external organs resembled those of girls; therefore, they were raised as girls. Once they reached puberty, the internal organs released male hormones, and they developed male secondary sex characteristics. Of the 18 children raised as girls, 16 chose to switch and live life as male; 1 identified as male but continued to live as female, including wearing dresses; and the final child continued to see herself as female and sought sex reassignment surgery. This study supports the idea that gender identity is related to biology. On the other hand, the first question often asked when a child is born is, "Is it a boy or girl?" and the child is treated differently based on the answer. The answer to the nature versus nurture question is likely to be much like other areas of human development: It is a combination between these two factors (see Nature Versus Nurture). The environment helps express or stunts the genetic potential.

Nearly all research regarding gender identity has been done with children assumed to be heterosexual. The models of **gender identity development** in children reflect the heterocentric views of culture at this time. Examples given of how girls are more likely to play with dolls and boys to play with trucks are examples of this heterocentric focus. Boys are also said to be more active, physical, and noisy in their play, whereas girls are more quiet and calm. Children who are homosexual or transgender may not fit these molds. A lack of recognition of these gender differences can create anxiety and confusion for a child who is not drawn to express gender in the same way as other children of the same sex. In a unique study on the gender identity development of lesbians, Levitt and Horne (2002) found that lesbians later identifying as butch stated knowing at a very young age, as young as 4 or 5 years, that they were attracted to women. Butch children tried to dress as boys, preferred boy activities, and rejected typical gender expressions of little girls. These **butch lesbians** reported that they experienced difficulties and harassment in childhood because of their gender but reported little confusion about their homosexual identity. **Femme lesbians,** on the other hand, often did not recognize their homosexuality until adulthood and often not until after having sexual encounters with men. These femme lesbians reported that they matched the gender expectations of little girls and were accepted into society as girls. They stated they had much more difficulty with confusion and acceptance as lesbians. Butch and femme are common gender expressions in lesbian communities and influence social expectations and dating within these communities.

To date, research on gender has focused on the sex of the participants and looked for expected gender expressions of this sex. It was not considered that the participants (children) whom the researchers were examining did not identify with the expected gender expression of their sex. If this aspect of individuality was considered, there would be a much better picture of how young gay and lesbians develop their gender identity throughout the life span instead of starting in adolescence. At this point, young gays or lesbians are behaving abnormally if they express the opposite gender than the sex with which they were born, such as a young male child who wants to paint his nails and play with Barbie dolls. If it were considered that this individual was perhaps transsexual or transgender, then his gender identity development would be seen as normal, and it would be possible to learn more about how this complex and critical aspect of identity develops in a much broader perspective. Gender identity development is complex and has not been fully explored. Until homosexuality and transsexuality are included in research, information will be incomplete.

Contributed by Darlene Daneker,
Marshall University,
South Charleston, WV

References

Kohlberg, L. (1966). A cognitive developmental analysis of children's sex role concepts and attitudes. In E. E. Maccoby (Ed.), *The development of sex differences* (pp. 82–174). Stanford, CA: Stanford University Press.

Levitt, H. M., & Horne, S. G. (2002). Explorations of lesbian-queer genders: Butch, femme, androgynous, or "other." *Journal of Lesbian Studies, 6*(2), 25–39.

Money, J. (1994). The concept of gender identity disorder in childhood and adolescence after 39 years. *Journal of Sex and Marital Therapy, 20,* 163–177.

Rathus, S. A., Nevid, J. S., & Fichner-Rathus, L. (2008). *Human sexuality in a world of diversity*. Boston: Allyn & Bacon.

Williams, J. E., & Best, D. L. (1994). Cross-cultural views of women and men. In W. J. Lonner & R. Walpass (Eds.), *Psychology and culture* (pp. 191–196). Boston: Allyn & Bacon.

■ Gender Roles

Sex type refers to biologically linked features that are determined by chromosomal information, whereas **gender** focuses on the cognitive, social, and emotional schemas associated with being male or female. One of the most important aspects regarding gender is that it is socially constructed. **Gender role socialization** refers to how individuals (e.g., parents, peers) and institutions (e.g., schools, media, religion, cultures) define and control the ways boys, girls, men, and women think, act, and view themselves and others. As a result, **gender roles** are defined as functions, positions, and sometimes duties of a man or woman in a society based on assumptions of how males and females behave when they work, play, express feelings, and interact with the world around them. Socialization is different (and often unequal) for males and females.

Immediately after a person's birth, many people quickly begin to socialize a boy and girl differently. These expectations continue in school, where a teacher might say, "Boys do better in math" and "Girls do better in English." Unfortunately, these statements may contain hidden stereotypes. Some gender roles may also infer that boys need to participate in sports and that dance is exclusively for girls, but when parents, peers, or society dictate such standards, these boys and girls may grow to be adults with significant limitations and pressures if their interests do not match these gender prescriptions.

The transition from gender roles in children to gender roles in adults is not accidental but is, in fact, learned through direct messages from people around the child (see Gender Identity Development). Although understanding gender is important for healthy development in children, gender roles may contain hidden stereotypes.

Culture also has a tremendous effect on the ways gender roles are shaped. There are a few interesting examples of how culture celebrates the gender role passages from girl to womanhood and boy to manhood. For girls, in many Latino families, the *quinceañera*, a lavish celebration, signals transition from young girl to woman. In the Jewish culture, the bar mitzvah (i.e., the announcement of a boy becoming a man) and bat mitzvah (i.e., the celebration of a girl becoming a woman) signal new roles and responsibilities for the new man or new woman. Gender roles in these examples are designed to welcome the individual into the culture and support and encourage that person's future as a man or woman.

Some look at theories of evolution to defend the need to maintain separate functions or roles for men and women. For example, some argue that to survive as a human race, men needed to be the hunters and, therefore, the leaders and protectors, whereas women were destined to be gatherers who were meant to nourish and maintain the home. The implication is that these gender roles should still play a big part in how society assigns men's and women's "duties" today, and, therefore, one might conclude that a man's role is to venture out into the world to find a job and provide for his family, whereas a woman's primary concern is to be a mother and take care of the home. The problem with this prescription is that it may limit the participants and not allow for the couple to change the rules to the roles.

There has been an increasing amount of research on **gender role conflict,** which has been defined as the feeling of fear, anxiety, anger, dissonance, and limited emotionality when people are faced with changing gender roles that contradict their previously learned gender expectations (Blumenfeld, Zuniga, Hackerman, & Casteneda, 2000). This limitation in expression has been directly linked to a host of physical ailments.

There seems to be a relationship between gender role conflict and homophobia, reflecting the often overlapping nature of gender and sexual orientation. Some restrictions in gender roles may come from the fear that one gender might act more like the other gender because of "homosexual tendencies." This means that a man should be warned not to figure skate for fear of being labeled gay, and a woman should not enjoy playing basketball because of the possibility of being labeled a lesbian.

Both men and women now have a wider choice of careers, mostly because the perception of gender roles has gradually changed over time. The growing number of women who have become lawyers, judges, politicians, and police officers, for example, has helped to support the contention that girls and women are very successful in nontraditional fields when given the opportunity. Men who are now staying at home to help raise children, teaching at the elementary level, and taking singing or acting classes have also found themselves to be happy in careers and activities once thought to be only for women. This might have been difficult to consider 20 years ago, but their successes today still depend heavily on support from families, employers, media, and government. For example, more men might seek paternity leave from work if employers and politicians made it financially possible to do so.

The roles of power and sexism also have an impact on career development for women. Women have historically been paid, and continue to be paid, less than men, sometimes for the same amount of work or type of work. Women's traditional duties, such as caretaker, teacher, or nurse, are not as respected as the traditional roles of their male counterparts, and women continue to find more resistance than do men when seeking positions of leadership and power. As a result, when a woman's role is devalued or confined, it damages that woman's self-worth. She is not only "different" in the society, but also "unequal." Feminists have long argued that this will not improve unless people first recognize that sexism exists on both an overt and covert level.

This examination of gender roles, up to this point, has primarily focused on the existence of two genders. It is important to remember that in numerous cultures room has been made for additional genders to survive. In some areas in Indonesia, those born as intersex (i.e., with male and female genitalia) are looked upon as a third gender with high legal and social status in that tribe. It is interesting that the Native North Americans have been known to have third and fourth genders. Male *berdache* is their term used to represent a third gender (i.e., men who assume many of the female traditional roles), whereas their fourth gender, called female *berdache,* occurs when women assume gender roles traditionally reserved for men. They are not only well-accepted gender types but also highly regarded and thought to possess spiritual power (Jacobs, Thomas, & Lang, 1997).

In conclusion, gender roles function best when there is allowance for fluidity in their definitions and their application does not become restrictive or oppressive. Research in marriage and family therapy indicates that most debates on gender roles do not involve women wanting to be the same as men or men wanting to be the same as women. The responses from most of these studies reveal that women primarily want to know how they can obtain what they want in life using all of their abilities and that most men want the same thing; therefore, the goal would be for both women and men to embrace and use both commonalities and differences between the genders.

Contributed by Michael G. Laurent,
California State University,
Northridge, CA

References

Blumenfeld, W. J., Zuniga, X., Hackerman, H., & Casteneda, C. (Eds.). (2000). *Readings for diversity and social justice.* New York: Routledge.

Jacobs, S., Thomas, W., & Lang, S. (Eds.). (1997). *Two-spirit people: Native American gender identity, sexuality, and spirituality.* Chicago, IL: Illiani Books.

Additional Resources

Newman, B., & Newman P. (2006). *Development through life: A psychosocial approach* (9th ed.). Belmont, CA: Thomson Wadsworth.

Wade, C., & Tavris, C. (2007). *Psychology* (8th ed.). Upper Saddle River, NJ: Pearson.

■ Generational Characteristics

According to Strauss and Howe (1991), a **generation** is a group of individuals distinguished by birth year or "age location" in history who may share similar characteristics. People within generations often share peer personalities that tend to be sequential in nature, often repeating throughout time. These peer personalities have similar attributes and collective mindsets that people may either embrace or find objectionable. Generations typically span an average of 22 years and can be divided into four life cycles. These life cycles are (a) youth (0 to 21 years), (b) rising adults (22 to 43 years), (c) midlife

(44 to 65 years), and (d) elderhood (66 to 87 years). In these life cycles, generational types emerge (e.g., idealistic, reactive, civic, and adaptive) that usually occur in some type of fixed order. Most generations can be distinguished based on social movements defined as eras or events that have a significant impact on the social environment. Typically, people recognize a social movement by noting that during a specific time period or thereafter, the world became significantly altered and an unfamiliar and/or new world emerged. These social movements have the most impact on peer personalities (i.e., attitudes, moods, and/or values and beliefs) and can significantly affect or change these personalities.

As many as 18 U.S. generations have been outlined, spanning four centuries, beginning with the Puritans (1588–1617) and ending with the most recent generation born in the 2000s. Of these generations, those that have living members include (a) the GI generation (born 1901–1924); (b) the Silent generation (born 1925–1942); (c) the Baby Boomers (born 1943–1960); (d) Generation X, also known as the Xers (born 1961–1981); (e) the Millennials, also called Generation Y (born 1982–2000); and (f) those born after 2000, which have been described as Generation Z, the Homelanders, or the New Silent Generation (Strauss & Howe, 1991).

The **GI generation** (GI stands for either "general issue" or "government issue") is best described as good citizens and team players. They see themselves as "general" or "regular" people. The growth of government played a significant part in the lives of members of the GI generation by providing education and employment opportunities, which in turn made them protective of government. Members of the GI generation may be civic minded and are characterized by military triumph because of the significant impact of the attack on Pearl Harbor and World War II. Their energy is characterized by the most prominent comic strip figure of that era: Superman. Superman typifies the GI generation members' attitude of strength and commitment to "good." This generation was heavily influenced by male dominance. Members of the GI generation were the United States' first Boy and Girl Scouts and later the first "senior citizens." Their children are members of the Silent and Baby Boomer generations, and their grandchildren typically fall within Generation X. Members of the GI generation include Walt Disney, Charles Lindbergh, John Wayne, Ann Landers, Katharine Hepburn, Sidney Poitier, and Jimmy Stewart. Presidents from the GI generation include Lyndon B. Johnson, Richard Nixon, Ronald Reagan, Gerald Ford, John F. Kennedy, Jimmy Carter, and George H. W. Bush.

The **Silent generation** is characterized as not having a distinct identity but as being considerably influenced by their role models (the virtuous members of the GI generation) or their juniors (the fiery Baby Boomers). The Silent generation dislikes the name "Silent" but recognizes the meaning of the label. This generation experienced few casualties in war and experienced low rates of social pathologies such as crime, suicide, and illegitimate births. They have experienced tremendous prosperity but seem to lack the passion and exuberance of the members of the GI generation and the Baby Boomers; however, this apathy has developed into a

sense of humanity, fairness, and social conscience, giving this generation the ability to listen and mediate. A focus on the helping professions grew out of the Silent generation. Some of the greatest humanitarians, performers, comedians, and songwriters, including Martin Luther King Jr., Sandra Day O'Connor, Marilyn Monroe, Elvis Presley, Clint Eastwood, Jack Nicholson, and Barbara Streisand, also grew out of this generation. Notably, there are no presidents from the Silent generation, but presidential candidates include Walter Mondale, Michael Dukakis, Gary Hart, and Jesse Jackson.

The **Baby Boomers** are viewed as a generation in which "self" is all-important. The expectations of their GI parents were that Baby Boomers would be cherished and revered. The optimism that was lacking in the Silent generation existed threefold in the Baby Boomers. The social movement most prevalent to the Baby Boomers was the consciousness revolution, which occurred in the 1960s. This revolution was rebellion against many of the characteristics of the GI generation and a rejection of the "fatherly" attributes such as the value of the sciences, conformity, patriotism, community, and patience. Baby Boomers were negative, rebellious against authority, fractious, and introspective. They found career success in more creative occupations such as art, religion, philosophy, and media rather than in science and math. Their focus on self and spirituality later developed into a focus on church, leading to the most prominent movement in religion of this generation in the United States: evangelicalism. The Boomer generation may be the most difficult to describe, given that half were born to the optimistic members of the GI generation and the second half were born to the members of the more pessimistic Silent generation. Because of these parental differences, these groups vary from liberal to conservative, modernists to evangelicals. One of the reasons the Baby Boomer era is considered such an extraordinary time is the sheer number of momentous events that occurred during this era, such as the civil rights movement; the women's movement; the Vietnam War; Sputnik; the sexual revolution; free speech movement; Dr. Spock; advent of the television age; discovery of the polio vaccination; *Brown v. Board of Education;* Watergate; the resignation of Richard Nixon; Woodstock; the Kent State massacre; the Apollo moon landing; and the assassinations of John F. Kennedy, Robert Kennedy, and Martin Luther King Jr. Members of the Baby Boomer generation are Oprah Winfrey, Bill Gates, Steven Jobs, Oliver North, Janis Joplin, Donald Trump, and Jane Pauley. Presidents include William J. Clinton and George W. Bush. Political leaders include Newt Gingrich, Dan Quayle, and Al Gore Jr.

Generation X (Xers) can be characterized as being a dichotomy between how their elders (the Boomers) viewed them versus how they viewed themselves. According to the Baby Boomers, Xers are soulless, ambivalent, indecisive, ruined, and often stupid. They are referred to as the "lost" generation because of their focus on personal gratification and a lack of focus on issues the Boomers found important, such as ideals, spirituality, and the value of freedom. In contrast, Xers view themselves as sharp, practical, and realistic and believe these characteristics are due to how they were raised (by Baby Boomers). Notably, the term *X* is more of a pejorative term, coined to describe the angst Xers felt because of their lack of connection with much of the Baby Boomer culture and their feelings that they were overshadowed by the Boomer generation. The Generation X childhood was plagued by cynicism and economic woes (e.g., dramatically increasing poverty rates, gas shortage, inflation, recession, rise of college tuitions, and decline of salaries). Xers felt it was necessary to grow up fast, with a forced focus on self-reliance and independence. They consider themselves survivors of the excess they witnessed with the Boomer generation. If the Boomers were focused on "self," what was left for the Xers was a "nightmare of self-immersed parents, disintegrating homes, schools with conflicting missions, confused leaders, a culture shifting from G to R ratings, new public-health dangers" (Strauss & Howe, 1991, p. 321). Xers were criticized for their lack of intellectual abilities, a judgment based on their declining test scores, and their questionable moral status, a judgment based on high crime rates, premarital sex, and rampant substance abuse. They later reversed those trends (e.g., higher test scores, declining crime rates, declining teen pregnancy rates). During the Generation X era, the majority of women worked outside the home, divorce rates began to rise, and latchkey children were the norm. Generation X witnessed the fall of the Berlin Wall and the disintegration of the Cold War, the AIDS-HIV crisis, *Roe v. Wade,* the introduction of MTV, increase of gang violence, Iran hostage crises, Challenger shuttle explosion, and the first Gulf War. Members of Generation X include Tom Cruise, Michael Jordan, Whitney Houston, Brad Pitt, Tiger Woods, and Julia Roberts.

The **Millennials,** also known as **Generation Y,** are the last generation that has been defined. Members of the Millennial generation actually coined the term *Millennial* to distinguish themselves from the apathetic Generation Xers (Howe & Strauss, 2000). Although contraceptives and abortion were commonplace in the Generation X era, fertility clinics are more the norm in the Millennial era. Because their parents had challenges with fertility or made very deliberate choices to have children, Millennials are special and highly valued. As opposed to their Xer counterparts, Millennials are optimistic, positive, upbeat, and team players. They are more conservative and trusting of authority, electing to follow rules rather than question (as did Baby Boomers) or resent (as did Xers) the rules. Crime, violent deaths, teen pregnancy, divorce and abortion rates are declining. The Millennials are a very protected and supervised generation, growing up in a very child-focused environment, unlike the independent, latchkey environment of the Xers. Society made a significant shift to focus on child and adolescent issues, such as education (e.g., mandatory kindergarten), positive TV programming (e.g., Barney), safety (e.g., prenatal care, child car seats), and products (e.g., clothes, toys, electronics). At this point, Millennials outnumber Boomers and Xers. They are a diverse group, and they value this diversity. It is interesting that the first surge of Millennials was more likely to have parents who were members of the Baby Boomer generation, and the second surge was more

likely to have parents from Generation X. Historically, it is the elders (in the case of Millennials, the Boomers) who set the tone for the culture. For the Boomers, this was an opportunity to address their weaknesses and focus on institutions, standards, and teamwork. For the Xers, their focus on family was a reaction to the lack of focus they felt they received as children. Members of the Millennial generation include Kirsten Dunst, LeAnn Rimes, Mary-Kate and Ashley Olsen, LeBron James, and Serena Williams. Events that shaped the Millennials are September 11, 2001; Columbine; the Oklahoma City bombing; Princess Diana's death; the Bill Clinton/Monica Lewinsky scandal; and the O.J. Simpson trial.

The newest generation (i.e., those born after 2000) has been described by various names, including the **Homelanders, Generation Z,** and the **New Silent Generation.** Although the characteristics of this generation are being developed, it is possible to look to previous generations to understand the possible peer personalities that may develop. It is clear that current events (e.g., the Iraq War, the digital age, globalization, instant communication, a growing focus on environmental concerns, the ever-present threat of terrorism) will have a major impact on this generation similar to the impact social movements have had on all generations.

Contributed by Robin Wilbourn Lee,
Middle Tennessee State University,
Murfreesboro, TN

References

Howe, N., & Strauss, W. (2000). *Millennials rising.* New York: Vintage Books.

Strauss, W., & Howe, N. (1991). *Generations: The history of America's future, 1584 to 2069.* New York: Morrow.

Additional Resource

Hicks, R., & Hicks, K. (1999). *Boomers, Xers, and other strangers.* Wheaton, IL: Tyndale House.

◼ Genogram

Genograms are also commonly referred to as family diagrams. They are visual mappings of three or four generations of a family and are widely used by physicians and mental health practitioners to record family data. Genograms aid counselors in exploring family structure, major life events, relationship patterns, illnesses, migration history, and multigenerational legacies for effective assessment and intervention with diverse clients in the counseling process. Genograms can also aid counselors in generating clinical hypotheses, which can guide therapeutic interventions in clinical work.

Symbols represent the essential elements of the genogram. Members of the family are represented by squares for males and circles for females (see Figure 1). Relationships among members in the family are represented by lines: Solid lines connect the marital unit as well as the children to the marital unit or marital units. Children are placed in chronological order, with the oldest sibling to the left. Demographics (e.g., age, place of birth, date of birth, education), medical

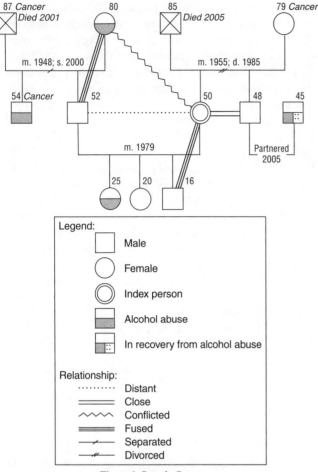

Figure 1. Sample Genogram

ailments (e.g., depression, cancer), abuse of any nature (e.g., domestic violence, child abuse, incest), legal complications (e.g., jail and/or prison sentences), emotional or mental challenges (e.g., hospitalization for suicide), and family dynamics (e.g., triangles, collusions, emotional cutoffs) are noted by symbolic representation in the genogram.

Genograms are usually used in the beginning of the counseling relationship. The professional counselor informs the client that some information about the client and client's family is needed to aid in better understanding the presenting problem. As the professional counselor interviews the client, the counselor takes note of critical events and tracks relationship dynamics and intergenerational patterns in the client's multigenerational family history. The counselor also inquires about recent life cycle changes and transitions such as births, marriages, divorce, or deaths. How a family deals with changes gives important information about the family's adaptive style. The professional counselor also notes if there are any unresolved losses in the client's life and family history. If so, intervention may consist of transforming the losses by developing appropriate rituals to grieve and resolve the loss. If information on the genogram reveals a history of cancer or alcohol abuse in the family (see Figure 1), the professional counselor assesses how these patterns relate to the presenting problem. Interventions in such situations depend on the counselor's therapeu-

tic judgment that is based on hypotheses generated about the functioning, relationship, roles, and the individual functioning of the client.

Used in cross-cultural counseling situations, genograms not only provide a platform for therapeutic inquiry about family structure and roles, family functioning, resilience, and family relational patterns but also a roadmap for the exploration of meaning systems in relation to the sociocultural context of the family. Much has been written about the genogram, its variants, and its uses. Genograms, for example, have been adapted and developed for specific uses in career counseling and in clinical work with clients to explore issues of spirituality; intimacy, sexuality, and related problems; and cultural factors, including immigration.

Contributed by Soh-Leong Lim, San Diego State University, San Diego, CA

Additional Resources

Beck, R. L. (1987). The genogram as process. *American Journal of Family Therapy, 15,* 343–351.

Magnuson, S., & Shaw, E. S. (2003). Adaptations of the multifaceted genogram in counseling, training, and supervision. *The Family Journal, 11,* 45–54.

McGoldrick, M., Gerson, R., & Shellenberger, S. (1999). *Genograms: Assessment and intervention* (2nd ed.). New York: Norton.

■ Gerontological Counseling

Demographic trends in population growth show that the United States will experience significant increases in the number of older individuals because of substantial decreases in mortality and related increases in life expectancy and because the members of the large Baby Boomer generation are beginning to reach retirement age. Government statistics show that although the 1900 census showed 3 million Americans over age 65 years, the number had increased to 35 million in 2000 and is estimated to grow to 90 million by 2060. In addition, people over 85 years of age will account for 23% of the total population by that date (Wilmoth & Ferraro, 2007). **Gerontological counseling** is a specialty area that requires professional counselors who work with adults over the age of 65 years to acquire specific skills as defined by the Gerontological Competencies of the Association for Adult Development and Aging (AADA; 1990).

Gerontology is a multidisciplinary field that includes sociology, biology, medicine, nursing, psychology, and social work, and there is a large body of knowledge that informs professional counselors about the different aspects of aging. Research has shown that therapeutic outcomes in mental health counseling are effective with the individuals who are older and that these outcomes are equal to those achieved when working with younger adults. However, few multicultural training programs include specific preparation for working with the aging. There is much diversity in the aging population because its members span 25 to 30 years. These differences are apparent in health status, cognitive functioning, social engagement, and cultural diversity.

There are specific challenges in working with those over 65 years of age. Although the following presenting issues may occur anytime during the life span, they are more common in the older population. Chronic illness, disability, the loss of loved ones to death, and prolonged care giving for family members who have severe cognitive or physical impairments (e.g., spouses and grown children) may prompt older individuals to seek counseling.

Depression is a major presenting problem for older adults, but it is sometimes difficult to diagnose because of other health issues and somatic complaints. It is, therefore, important for professional counselors to become knowledgeable about age-related changes and how the depression spectrum can manifest in individuals over 65 years. Suicide assessment is critical because suicide rates are relatively high, particularly for older men and even more so for older White men.

Individuals who are older than 65 years generally have less exposure to and less formal education about counseling and outpatient services; therefore, the effective professional counselor should be sensitive to these concerns, particularly during the first sessions. Older clients may be accompanied by family members, such as adult children, and wish them to be involved in counseling and treatment decisions. The Gerontological Competencies, as approved by AADA for use by professional counselors and human development workers, provide specific guidelines that ensure effective counseling practice with older adults and should be used as an essential resource for those who choose to work with this population.

Other adaptations may become necessary during counseling. Although crystallized intelligence is normally stable in individuals who are older, some cognitive changes do develop. There can be a general slowing, with some decrease in the attention span and working memory. Hearing and vision changes are common. A professional counselor who adopts a slower speech pattern gives evidence of empathy; one who shouts does not. When preparing disclosure statements and other client forms, it is helpful to use larger print on nonglossy paper. Handicapped parking and wheelchair access should be available, and accommodations for walkers should be made.

Individuals who are elderly are often better at regulating emotions, so there may be less obvious emotionality (Knight, 2004). Research has shown that there is personality stability across the life span (Haan, Millsap, & Harta, 1987); therefore, professional counselors should be aware that they are observing lifelong patterns of personality functioning. The various ways that society makes it difficult for the older population can create problems that bring them to counseling. Ageism can cause older adults to appear suspicious and operate from a negative worldview. The social context in which they live (e.g., alone, with children, in institutional settings) may have radically changed their lifestyle and not be in their locus of control. Their customary coping skills may no longer be adequate. Older adults may give evidence of an identity crisis as they deal with a new developmental stage.

The creation of a sound therapeutic relationship with the older client is as important as with younger adults. Respect for the client is imperative; the effective professional counselor is aware of his or her own prejudices, biases, and susceptibility toward ageism. Effective gerontological counselors should also have expertise in aging issues (e.g., chronic illness, dementia, disability, prolonged care giving, grief, and loss) and be informed about community resources that are available. Finally, professional counselors should be aware that the accumulated knowledge of people and relationships that older adults have amassed can be an asset. Gerontological counselors who are open to learning from their clients have a rich and readily available resource.

Contributed by Lydia B. Smith,
University of North Carolina at
Charlotte, Charlotte, NC

References

Association for Adult Development and Aging. (1990). *Gerontological competencies for counselors and human development specialists.* Retrieved August 20, 2008, from http://www.uncg.edu/~jemyers/jem_info/docs/competencies.htm

Haan, N., Millsap, R., & Harta, E. (1987). As time goes by: Change and stability in personality over fifty years. *Psychology and Aging, 1,* 220–232.

Knight, B. G. (2004). *Psychotherapy with older adults* (3rd ed.). Thousand Oaks, CA: Sage.

Wilmoth, J. M., & Ferraro, K. F. (2007). *Gerontology: Perspectives and issues.* (3rd ed.). New York: Springer.

Additional Resources

Association for Adult Development and Aging Web site: http://www.aadaweb.org/

Scogin, F. (2000). *The first session with seniors: A step-by-step guide.* San Francisco: Jossey-Bass.

Sheik, J. I. (Ed.). (1996). *Treating the elderly.* San Francisco: Jossey-Bass.

■ Gestalt Therapy

Gestalt therapy is a phenomenological, existential, and behavioral-based therapy that emphasizes wholes, the therapist–client relationship, and being in the present moment. It was initially formulated by Frederick (Fritz) Perls (1893–1970) in the 1940s, with the notable help later from Laura Perls and Paul Goodman. **Fritz Perls** studied psychiatry and worked briefly with Karen Horney and Wilhelm Reich. He was influenced strongly by the Freudian psychoanalytic tradition in which he was trained.

Gestalt therapy takes a Reichian perspective on mind–body unity and attends to the importance of bodily tension and nonverbal behavior. Central to Gestalt therapy is a focus on direct experience, a humanistic belief in the innate movement of organisms toward equilibrium, and existential contact, characterized by the mutuality and inclusion of Buber's "I–thou" relationship. In "I–it" relationship moments, a therapist might hypothesize, summarize, or otherwise *think about* the client; in **"I-thou"** moments, client and therapist harmoniously encounter one another, present and energized with their whole beings and ready for spontaneous therapeutic "work" to emerge.

Consequently, great emphasis is placed on the development of the counselor as a whole person, who having worked on her or his own "unfinished business," is less reactive, more present, and has more available energy in facilitating the client's work.

The term *gestalt* derives from the focus it places on wholes, patterns, configurations, or gestalts, as opposed to various forms of reductionism. It also applies principles investigated by Gestalt psychologists (e.g., Max Wertheimer, Wolfgang Köhler), such as understanding that organisms will tend to complete incomplete figures, the importance of figure–ground (i.e., foreground–background) shifts, and the role of attention and personal/social construction of meaning involved in perception as a creative act.

Gestalt therapy is deeply aligned with an Eastern non-Aristotelian philosophical approach as well, especially in its embracing of multivalent logic (i.e., both–and as opposed to either–or), field theory (i.e., people and their environments are a related system in constant change), process (e.g., being genuine, present in the ongoing now), and a "paradoxical theory" of change (fostering the natural Taoist "flow" of being who one is, rather than pushing toward an ideal). Implicit in the Gestalt field-theory model is a **homeopathic treatment** methodology, or treating the person and person-in-environment (including family and culture) as a whole system, which is generally at odds with the **allopathic treatment** of isolated parts and independent symptoms common in medical models.

Change is seen as a natural state; therefore, Gestalt counselors often look at the obstacles to creative response. Such neurotic disturbances arise when there is an imbalance between the individual and the environment. Six characteristic channels of resistance are most prevalent. Although described here independently, a single individual may use several together. **Introjection** is the indiscriminate acceptance of a foreign body. The individual who introjects never fully develops a personality. The "topdog–underdog" conflict is a helpful metaphor for understanding the typical polarized internal struggle between an introject and the resistance to it. **Projection** is the reverse of introjection. In projection, the tendency is to make the environment responsible for what begins in the self. When a projector uses the word *it* or even *you, he, or she,* the individual often means *I.* Encouraging the projector to experiment with *I* language can often be helpful in reowning disowned projections. **Confluence** occurs when the individual feels no boundary between self and other. Confluence often leads to what are commonly called "psychosomatic problems," and those clients stuck in confluence often demand likeness and are intolerant of differences. **Retroflection,** meaning "turning back against," involves doing to oneself what one would like to do to the environment and others. This involves a boundary drawn sharply inside, in which the individual and "self" are made distinct. **Deflection** occurs when individuals distance themselves from opportunities for healthy contact. Examples may include avoiding eye contact, overly polite phony behaviors, or talk about things other than the present self, all of which lead to weakened or absent con-

tact. **Egotism** is an excessive concern for internal processes so prominent that the individual does not recognize possibilities for contact.

Gestalt therapy aims to help the individual move to maturation with clear, flexible boundaries and to make a transition from neurotic manipulation of the environment to quality contact and satisfaction of needs. Through various experiments, the individual may have experiences during session that offer opportunities to complete unfinished business that has previously prevented healthy contact. Because such impasses are certain to interfere with the individual's ability to maintain contact and stay in the now, a patient history will only elaborate what is already present in the moment, and because the important gestalts will emerge first, attention to the obvious in the present is the pathway to completion. To facilitate this awareness, the Gestalt therapist attempts to create a "safe-emergency," directing the individual's ongoing awareness to the present, providing support through the therapeutic relationship, attending to breathing as needed to stay with anxiety, and frustrating attempts to escape the present.

A Gestalt therapist may use a number of techniques in helping a client. Each of these is approached with an experimental attitude and a radical respect for the client. Techniques may include silence, active listening, attending, clarification, confrontation, self-disclosure, feedback, open and closed questions, reframing, and drawing attention to body awareness. Although many techniques are shared with other theoretical orientations, a number have grown out of the theory itself, such as dialogue (the **empty chair technique** being the classic model, in which a client moves from one chair to another, with each chair holding a place for different perspectives, allowing them to be externalized and discussed); bringing unfinished business into the present (similar to regression in hypnosis); focusing on and giving voice to bodily sensations (e.g. asking "what are you aware of in your chest right now" or "what would your tears say if they could talk?"); exaggeration (which helps awareness of the obvious); and, in groups, the **hotseat** (where individuals take turns doing work with a facilitator in front of, and sometimes interacting with, the group).

Contributed by Brian J. Mistler,
University of Florida, Gainesville, FL

Additional Resources

Feder, B. (2000). *Beyond the hot seat: Gestalt approaches to group.* Montclair, NJ: BeeFeeder Press.

Gestalt Therapy Resources Online Web site: http://gestalt.onlinepsy.com

Kempler, W. (1974). *Principles of Gestalt family therapy.* Costa Mesa, CA: Kempler Institute.

Korb, M., Gorrell, J., & Van De Riet, V. (2002). *Gestalt therapy practice and theory.* Gouldsboro, ME: Gestalt Journal Press.

Perls, F., Hefferline, R., & Goodman, P. (1951) *Gestalt therapy: Excitement and growth in the human personality.* New York: Julian Press.

Gifted Students, Counseling

What is considered **"gifted"** varies from culture to culture. In terms of high intellectual ability, which is usually the focus of special programs for students identified as gifted, specific criteria vary; however, a score on a standardized achievement or ability assessment is commonly used, often with a cutoff determined by a particular program. An error range is often not acknowledged. Because profound giftedness may be at a level several standard deviations above the mean, a large group of individuals of any age labeled "gifted" may represent a range of ability. Extreme difference may mean extreme personal challenges. Any of these factors may contribute to counseling concerns during the school years and beyond.

Counseling concerns are sometimes related to identification itself (e.g., discomfort with the label, poor fit in a one-size-fits-all program) or nonidentification (e.g., gifted underachievers not believed to deserve participation in a program, gifted students with acting-out behavior, abilities not recognized or nurtured). Programs offering challenge or other experiences beyond the regular classroom may be narrow in focus (e.g., simply a more rapid curriculum) or broad (e.g., an array of options geared to one or more of several kinds of intelligence, such as verbal, musical, and spatial). Counseling concerns may be related to a poor fit in a narrow-focus program, with consequent doubts about ability, to interests not matching a special curriculum, or to students being selected because of high grades but not adapting well to a gifted program curriculum that requires higher level thinking and independent learning. Common presenting issues related to gifted students and these concerns may involve underachievement and incongruent interests or personality conflicts within familial, social, and occupational settings. These issues may present in adulthood or persist into adulthood.

A growing clinical and research-based literature has argued for differential counseling responses for individuals with high ability, and both proactive and reactive approaches have been described. Professional counselors in any setting should be aware of characteristics that have been associated with giftedness, such as multifaceted sensitivity, intensity, desire to succeed, and overexcitability (e.g., psychomotor, sensual, intellectual, imaginational, emotional). These characteristics may be inappropriately pathologized by educators and counselors, may exacerbate difficulties during normal developmental transitions or after unexpected or traumatic life events, and may contribute to difficulties with relationships. **Asynchrony,** a mismatch between cognitive and social/emotional development, is a common phenomenon among gifted youth. This concept also applies to those with extreme talent, who may not handle great attention and power emotionally. Young gifted children may also be precociously concerned and distressed about future career planning, social justice issues, wars, and natural disasters. High expectations from self and others, overcommitment during secondary-level school years, perfectionism, anxiety, and high stress have been discussed as representing the dark side of giftedness. Sensitivities and intensities may also be factors in substance abuse, self-harm, and interpersonal conflict throughout the life span.

It should be noted that empirical literature about pertinent social and emotional needs, concerns, and development is often based on samples that fit high-achieving, high-motivation, mainstream-culture stereotypes, because those are the students who are typically identified for programs and easily accessed. Some of those studies have found that giftedness is an asset; others have seen it as burdensome. There is no consistent empirical evidence that gifted individuals are more or less likely than the rest of the population to have mental health concerns—except in regard to creatively gifted adolescents, who have been linked with psychological vulnerability more than have academically or intellectually gifted teens. Regardless, characteristics coupled with giftedness in the literature may not represent a broad spectrum of individuals with exceptional talent or keen intellect, including, for example, individuals from nonmainstream cultures, unsupportive families, or difficult circumstances; those not proficient in the dominant language of the country where they reside; those with learning or other disabilities; those experiencing challenging developmental transitions, recovering from trauma, or experiencing depression; those who are uncomfortable in the inherently competitive school environment; underachievers; and delinquents. Characteristics commonly associated with giftedness, however, may indeed characterize gifted individuals who are not identified for programs.

Counseling Implications

Professional counselors can be helpful to gifted individuals, whether young children, adolescents, young adults, or older adults. With clients of any age, counselors can normalize sensitivities and developmental challenges for individuals who do not discuss these aspects of their lives elsewhere. Counselors can affirm personal strengths beyond those related to performance, with which significant others may be preoccupied. Counselors' unconditional regard and empathy can provide an oasis for those who are anxious about evaluation. They can recognize and address serious concerns in gifted children and adolescents, who, according to researchers, are not likely to ask for help even when highly distressed. Gifted individuals at any age may not have developed an expressive vocabulary, and some, accustomed to controlling situations intellectually, may restrict their emotions because they feel uneasy when control is threatened. Some may protect a public image of success and invulnerability. They also may not want to disappoint those who are heavily invested in them and may not believe anyone can understand their thoughts and feelings.

Like other significant persons in highly capable individuals' lives, counselors, including those with high ability themselves, may have biases and attitudes about giftedness that can interfere with establishing a trusting and effective relationship. Counselors may lack knowledge about gifted persons' experiences of development, characteristics connected with giftedness, and appropriate counseling approaches. They may be unwittingly competitive with gifted clients regarding humor, vocabulary level, and sophistication of thought. They may be in awe of giftedness, unable to recognize or empathize with clients' distress. Counselors may also forget that young gifted children are not simply "little adults." In addition, gifted clients may remind counselors of their own school experiences with peers, with the latter not taking presenting issues seriously or identifying too thoroughly to be objective. It is important for counselors to self-reflect about attitudes related to giftedness.

Gifted individuals of any age are part of a continuum from being "ideal" clients to being extremely difficult to work with. Their cognitive ability can help them make sense of complex phenomena and experiences and do the hard work of counseling, but it can also be reflected in manipulation and tight self-protection. Thinking may be disordered. The growing amount of literature related to the social and emotional development of gifted persons offers guidance to counselors in any venue. Professional counselors can help to identify giftedness, normalize characteristics associated with it, affirm the complexity of it, use a developmental framework when pondering it, and offer a rare opportunity for clients to be unconditionally received. Professional school counselors can successfully and proactively use small-group work with gifted students, with the focus on development, normalizing feelings and sensitivities, and validating struggle. Gifted youth typically develop trust more easily when groups are homogeneous according to ability. In any venue and with any approach, professional counselors who enter the world of gifted clients knowledgeably, respectfully, and sensitively will have taken an important first step in establishing trust and working toward positive outcomes.

Contributed by Jean Sunde Peterson,
Purdue University, West Lafayette, IN

Additional Resources

Mendaglio, S., & Peterson, J. S. (Eds.). (2007). *Models of counseling gifted children, adolescents, and young adults.* Waco, TX: Prufrock Press.

Peterson, J. S. (2008). *The essential guide to talking with gifted teens: Ready-to-use group discussions about identity, stress, relationships, and more.* Minneapolis, MN: Free Spirit.

Webb, J. R., Amend, E. R., Webb, N. E., Goerss, J., Beljan, P., & Olenchak, F. R. (2005). *Misdiagnosis and dual diagnosis of gifted children and adults: ADHD, bipolar, OCD, Asperger's, depression, and other disorders.* Scottsdale, AZ: Great Potential Press.

■ Ginzberg's Theory of Career Development

Eli Ginzberg was an economist who significantly affected society in a variety of ways. Career development for individuals became a focus for his research, leading to the 1951 work with associates, *Occupational Choice: An Approach to a General Theory.* In a collaborative effort with Sol W. Ginsburg, a psychiatrist-psychoanalyst; Sidney Axelrad, a sociologist; and John L. Herma, a psychologist, Ginzberg worked

for three decades developing his theory. Believing the economy of a developing society is based on an effective workforce, Ginzberg became interested in career decision making. His theory brought new direction to career development that began with Frank Parsons's (1909) trait and factor approach. Ginzberg's approach was psychologically based and focused on ego functions that adolescents use. He was more interested in the process than the content of occupational choice. Ginzberg and associates identified three periods in the choice process (i.e., fantasy, tentative, and realistic) to describe the qualities of occupational choices appearing at different ages. During the **fantasy period,** individuals identify occupations at young ages based on what they have observed or been introduced to through experiences. Throughout the **tentative phase,** interests are the basis for choice. Abilities begin to emerge and are compared with interests. Values emerge in later adolescence as the basis for choosing an occupation. Maturation is critical through the tentative period because development is occurring at a rapid rate. There is a move in the **realistic period** toward realistic choices as the individual matures and gains greater ability, particularly through educational opportunities.

This developmental approach elaborates on four ego functions. First, as individuals mature, they are better able to make significant occupational choices through their ability to project a psychological future, sometimes called "time perspective." Second, "delay function" is the ability to wait for valued goals and postpone gratification, which produces a more realistic career decision than one based on immediate gratification. The third ego function is identifying a person's abilities and resources. What is the reality associated with entering a particular occupation? Is this realistic based on the individual's abilities and educational opportunities? What are the educational requirements and how will they be carried out? The fourth ego function is about attitude: How motivated is a person to meet necessary academic and experiential requirements to obtain a career goal?

The developmental approach states career choice in adolescence is a process that occurs over time between ages 10 to 21 years. Decisions the adolescent makes provide direction for his or her career that are irreversible. Ginzberg believed career decisions were a compromise between an individual's need and the reality of his or her ability to succeed at that choice. The key elements to the theory of occupational choice are (a) it is a process, (b) the process is irreversible, and (c) compromise is essential in every choice. In later work, Ginzberg (1972) reformulated the theory and no longer confined occupation choice to young adulthood but stated that occupation choice coexisted with a person's working life. His reformulated theory describes occupational choice as a lifelong process of making decisions based on new experiences and realities of the world-of-work. Individuals continue to seek an optimum fit between their career goals and opportunities within the working world.

Critics of Ginzberg's research found the theory was less applicable with women because research had been carried out solely with young men. Ginzberg's career theory has historical significance but has been replaced by modern theories, including Holland's (1973) and Tiedeman and O'Hara's (1963) that look at career development throughout the life span, including opportunities to change and move past careers chosen in adolescence. The belief that career choice is irreversible is no longer subscribed to by counselors and other career professionals. Ginzberg's (1972) further research led to additional modifications that influenced his stance. His quest to broaden and revise his theory continued throughout his life, but his initial work created a foundation for the field of career development.

Contributed by Carolyn W. Kern,
University of North Texas, Denton, TX

References

Ginzberg, E. (1972). Toward a theory of occupational choice: A restatement. *Vocational Guidance Quarterly, 20,* 169–176.

Ginzberg, E., Ginsburg, S. W., Axelrad, S., & Herma, J. L. (1951). *Occupational choice: An approach to a general theory.* New York: Columbia University Press.

Holland, J. L. (1973). *Making vocational choices: A theory of careers.* Englewood Cliffs, NJ: Prentice Hall.

Parsons, F. (1909). *Choosing a vocation.* Boston: Houghton Mifflin.

Tiedeman, D. V., & O'Hara, R. P. (1963). *Career development: Choice and adjustment.* New York: College Entrance Examination Board.

Additional Resource

Ginzberg, E. (1989). Career development. In D. Brown, L. Brooks, & Associates (Eds.), *Career choice & development* (pp. 169–191). San Francisco, CA: Jossey Bass.

■ Grief

Appalled by the treatment of dying patients, **Elizabeth Kübler-Ross** developed a series of lectures for medical students to help assist patients with death and dying. Over time, Kübler-Ross (1969) developed five stages of grief that she first featured in the book, *On Death and Dying.* These **five stages of grief** encompass thoughts, feelings, and behaviors through which most people progress when they are confronted by their own death or other circumstances of grief and loss. Although most people tend to move through these five stages sequentially, Kübler-Ross proposed that a person might revisit or skip stages as necessary until the final stage of acceptance is achieved. Kübler-Ross's five stages are denial, anger, bargaining, depression, and acceptance. They are described as rational coping strategies for accepting the loss that death represents for the patient and/or family members who are close to the patient.

In the first stage of **denial,** Kübler-Ross described the patient and family as rejecting the facts and the reality of death as the ultimate outcome. Searching for any other explanation or treatment that might prove the physician wrong, the patient and family will go to great lengths to avoid confrontation of death and mortality. Although most people move beyond this stage when they are ready, Kübler-

Ross has identified several people who were able to maintain a perspective of denial until the very end. This ability to keep the finality of death at bay through denial is a rarity. Because death is too difficult to confront on a constant basis, it is common for dying patients to move in and out of denial to address their thoughts associated with death as they are able. It is important for others to remember that the patient and family will raise the subject when they are ready to discuss it, and pushing the conversation is never advisable.

In the **anger** stage, the patient and family adopt a "Why me?" indignant attitude. Kübler-Ross stated that it is important for caregivers and medical workers to understand that individuals with terminal illness have the right to be angry due to the injustice that death represents. Caregivers need to be sensitive to the patient's need to experience anger as a healthy and appropriate response. Outbursts and negativity that a patient and family may direct toward caregivers is not a personal attack but a way for these people to process the anger that is a natural and normal response when confronted by death and dying. Often in the anger stage, the patient may experience an overwhelming need for control and become difficult about little things. In an effort to control what remains of their environment and to avoid the pain of their recent and impending losses, patients may lash out in anger to reject anyone who might be available to help. Tolerance for rational and irrational expressions of anger may be difficult for caregivers struggling with their own fears about death and dying and can create defensiveness.

In the third stage of **bargaining,** the patient and family might make promises to themselves, or more often to their God, in exchange for a reversal of the diagnosis or a miracle cure. Like children who are denied a request by their parents, patients and family members often resort to bargaining when angry outbursts have not produced desired results. Kübler-Ross cautioned caregivers about brushing comments aside that might be associated with bargaining because they often related to issues of guilt. Secret agreements with God that promise good or new behavior to counterbalance old transgressions may be important for the patient or family members to process. Deep, unconscious, or hostile wishes can precipitate guilt that is unhealthy for the individual and prevent the client from moving toward the optimal stage of acceptance. Active listening skills in a warm and accepting therapeutic environment are most helpful for patients who are dealing with guilt related to the bargaining stage.

The fourth stage is **depression.** Kübler-Ross described this depression as different from the type of depression that is related to the desire for changes in daily living. Individuals in the depression stage do not long for the alleviation of suffering or understanding from others because they recognize the futility in desiring immortality. This depression reflects the letting go of material things and all attachment to things associated with living. In this preparatory type of grieving, the patient does not respond to the attempts of others to cheer them up. The patient in the depression stage desires connection with others that is based on tangible things that are still within their scope of reality and not on false hope for recovery. Awareness and acknowledgement of loss in separating from what they have loved in life are what these patients and family members seek most. Caregivers need to be sensitive to their patient's need to grieve for a future that has been lost and to provide an environment that will facilitate the patient's progression through this stage.

The fifth and final stage is **acceptance.** This stage is one of peace in which the patient usually adopts a quiet state where nonverbal communication becomes more important than verbal communication. Acceptance is not a happy stage but rather a state that is almost devoid of feelings. The patient or family member has had the opportunity to express previous feelings of anger, envy, depression, and loss and has been given time and space to mourn the ending of relationships and the attachment to places, people, and things. Caregivers need to be aware of the importance of silence in being with a person who is in the final stage of acceptance and how nonverbal communication can be instrumental in assisting this individual to prepare for death. This stage is not giving up or the lack of fight in a person but rather the peaceful state of being that comes after wrestling with issues relating to the impending loss that death represents. It is important to note that a person who has reached the stage of acceptance is not necessarily close to death and that everyone moves through the stages at his or her unique pace.

Throughout this process, hope is emphasized as the mediating factor that is necessary for every person to cope effectively with the traumatic reality of death and dying. If the patient and family are not permitted to move through these five stages at their own pace, anxiety and hopelessness can interfere with their ability to progress toward acceptance and peace. Kübler-Ross stated that the need for hope does not imply the need for a cure or an unrealistic idea about eluding death. For the person dealing with terminal illness, hope provides an opportunity to look forward without despair and hopelessness. Hope emphasizes each person's ability to live in a meaningful way that can transcend even death.

Until her death in 2004, Kübler-Ross studied and wrote about death and dying to sensitize caregivers and families to the uniqueness of terminally ill patients and their needs. Using her own experience of death and dying, she was able to provide the means for appropriate communication that is instrumental in working with patients and their families. In many of her writings, Kübler-Ross cautioned caregivers about their need to understand their own fears about death and dying that can interfere with the progress of the patient and bring about unconscious concerns that can be troublesome for the caregiver on a personal level. Her writings emphasize the importance of timing as critical to working with people who are experiencing terminal illness and of the need for caregivers to remain mindful that the pace should be set by the patient and not by the caregiver's own goals in therapy.

Caregivers may find Kübler-Ross's (1981) later work, *Living with Death and Dying: How to Communicate With the Terminally Ill,* particularly helpful in working with children and families. This book offers case examples that illustrate the importance of communication and strategies for eliciting what the patient might be experiencing in safe and compassionate ways. Illustrations in the text include draw-

ings made by children who were close to death and unable to articulate their thoughts and feelings about death. As the groundbreaking researcher in the sensitive field of death and dying, Kübler-Ross has left a body of work that is widely considered the definitive work for counseling patients and family members dealing with terminal illness.

Contributed by Carol Z. A. Salisbury,
Loyola University Maryland,
Baltimore, MD

References

Kübler-Ross, E. (1969). *On death and dying.* New York: Simon & Schuster.

Kübler-Ross, E. (1981). *Living with death and dying: How to communicate with the terminally ill.* New York: Simon & Schuster.

■ Group Co-Leadership

Group co-leadership is a treatment delivery structure in which two group leaders simultaneously and collaboratively work with the same set of group members. Designed to facilitate development within and between group members, this mutual work can be classified in three main models of co-leadership: junior–junior (i.e., two inexperienced group workers are paired, and they alternate responsibilities for a portion of a session or across sessions), senior–junior (i.e., a more experienced group worker is paired with one with less experience to model and supervise effective group work), and senior–senior (i.e., experienced group workers with a well-developed relationship are paired, fluidly dividing leadership responsibilities as the needs arise in the group).

Co-leadership can be used across a range of counseling theoretical orientations and treatment-delivery settings or contexts, as well as with an assortment of types, foci, and populations of groups. In fact, a perusal of articles in the *Journal for Specialists in Group Work* reveals that many articles related to group interventions present strategies, techniques, and applications of group counseling delivered with a co-leadership structure. Although the efficacy of co-leadership is acknowledged as being dependent on a variety of factors, co-leadership is, in particular, widely used as a training vehicle in counselor preparation programs.

The merits of co-leadership consist of three general categories of advantages: pragmatic or organizational benefits, benefits for co-leaders, and benefits for group members. Pragmatic benefits of co-leadership include the ability to accommodate more clients in a single group and a greater assurance for coverage and continuity of leadership during emergencies, vacations, or staff transitions. Benefits for co-leaders include shared planning; combined input on case conceptualization; exploration of leader biases and reactions; and learning from one another's differing styles, use of techniques, or specialized training. Benefits for group members are arguably the most important and involve the increased diversity of modeling and feedback that results from two leaders. Co-leadership offers an opportunity for group members to be exposed to complementary individuals, who may differ in style or perspective and even disagree but who can effectively communicate and cooperatively work together. Co-leadership dyads composed of leaders of opposite genders can be especially useful in eliciting family-of-origin dynamics and then assisting in fostering a corrective emotional experience for group members. Despite potential benefits, it is advised that co-leadership be used judiciously.

Although there has been considerable anecdotal and theoretical writing related to co-leadership over the last 50 years, there has comparably been little empirical research. Current conceptual and empirical writings related to co-leadership attribute this primary limitation to relational difficulties between co-leaders (e.g., Dugo & Beck, 1997; Fall & Wejnert, 2005; Okech & Kline, 2005, 2006). Drawbacks involve interpersonal issues between the co-leaders that negatively affect the group. Complications can result from ineffective or incomplete communication, a lack of trust or respect, unexpressed or unresolved interpersonal conflict, and competition or jealousy between co-leaders. In addition, uncoordinated co-leadership efforts (e.g., a dominating or exceedingly passive co-leader, collusion with a group member) can easily become destructive forces in the group. Prevention and amelioration of these potential difficulties may be possible through intentional preparation of co-leaders and ongoing attention focusing on the development of their relationship. Such efforts can be subsumed within the context of clinical supervision, where there can be a focus on increasing the level of disclosure, acceptance, and trust between co-leaders.

Contributed by Melissa Luke,
Syracuse University, Syracuse, NY

References

Dugo, J. M., & Beck, A. P. (1997). Significance and complexity in the early phases in the development of the co-therapy relationship. *Group Dynamics: Theory, Research, and Practice, 1,* 294–305.

Fall, K. A., & Wejnert, T. J. (2005). Co-leader stages of development: The application of Tuckman and Jensen (1977). *Journal for Specialists in Group Work, 30,* 309–327.

Okech, J. E. A., & Kline, W. B. (2005). A qualitative exploration of group co-leader relationships. *Journal for Specialists in Group Work, 30,* 173–190.

Okech, J. E. A., & Kline, W. B. (2006). Competency concerns in group co-leader relationships. *Journal for Specialists in Group Work, 31,* 165–180.

Additional Resource

Luke, M., & Hackney, H. (2007). Group co-leadership: A critical review. *Counselor Education and Supervision, 40,* 280–293.

■ Group Leader Personal Qualities

No formula exists for the exact combination of qualities a person must possess to be an effective group leader. Instead, the appropriateness of an individual leader for a particular group depends on a complex interaction of factors: the leader's personal qualities and preferred leadership style, the type and purpose of the group, the stage of the group, and the needs of group members. The most effective group leaders modify their leadership patterns to coincide with the purposes of the group and its members.

Despite the difficulty in identifying a particular personality type or a list that encompasses all traits associated with effective leadership, specialists in group work have compiled lists of desirable personal qualities for group leaders. Few leaders possess all these qualities; however, three qualities rise to the top, suggesting their importance for any group leader's success.

The first quality is **self-awareness.** Self-aware group leaders are willing to know and be themselves and to work on their own psychological well-being. They know their personal and interpersonal sensitivities and insensitivities, patterns of confusion and misperceptions, and personal reactivity. Self-aware group leaders understand how their own cultural identities, personal histories, and history of their own cultural groups affect the ways they perceive and respond to group members. They exhibit clear-headedness in their efforts to be fair, honest, equitable, nondefensive, and as free as possible of biases and prejudices. Without self-awareness and interpersonal competency, it is difficult or impossible for group leaders to apply knowledge, skills, and experiences effectively.

Second is **flexibility** (or tolerance for ambiguity). Group leaders must be creative problem solvers who are able to think intuitively and respond instantly to subtle nuances in group members' behavior and group process. Flexibility requires self-awareness. Effective leaders are able to identify their behavioral and emotional impact on group members and modify their leadership style to meet the needs of the group.

Third is **caring.** Effective group leaders care about others and communicate their caring in ways others can understand. The quality of caring is thematic in the group literature, beginning with Lieberman, Yalom, and Miles's (1973) intensive study of encounter groups, in which caring was prominently featured in all three of the most successful leadership styles these researchers identified.

In addition to the three qualities already discussed, the following list represents a synthesis of the most frequently cited qualities associated with effective group leadership. **Self-confidence** encompasses self-assurance, a sense of personal power, comfort with oneself and others, courage to show oneself, comfort in a position of authority, and confidence in ability to lead. The next qualities are closely related and frequently overlap: **responsibility** to the group and to oneself as a professional, which includes dependability and reliability; **honesty; trustworthiness; genuineness,** which includes openness and the courage to show and to share oneself sensitively and thoughtfully; and **courage,** which includes strength, willingness to be honest and to confront in caring and respectful ways. **Self-acceptance** is defined as the courage to accept one's own imperfection, which allows room for group members to see themselves as imperfect and forgive themselves for mistakes. Group leaders, like individual counselors, need to feel and communicate **empathy; respect; compassion; presence,** the ability to be fully present and attentive, yet maintain clear boundaries; and **objectivity,** the ability to maintain the "as if" quality while feeling empathy, to monitor feelings and responses, and to recognize transference and countertransference.

Additional qualities include **creativity** and **spontaneity; inventiveness; humor,** which encompasses playfulness and the ability to find humor in life's challenges; **enthusiasm;** and **charisma.** Although this final quality appears on some lists but not others, it merits attention. Charismatic leaders believe in themselves, are persuasive, radiate power to the extent that others are inclined to listen, inspire and stimulate others, and have a vision or sense of mission. Depending on personality and interpersonal style, charisma may manifest forcefully and dramatically, or it may be quiet and understated. Along with group composition and member needs, this complex interaction moderates the effects of a charismatic leader on positive outcome. For example, early research in encounter group outcomes indicated that when group members with low ego strength and high expectations were paired with leaders who were high in charisma, aggressive stimulation, individual focus, support, and confrontation, the result was a high number of dropouts and "casualties" harmed by the group experience.

Group Leadership Style

The literature on group leadership and group dynamics strongly supports the relationship between **group leader personal qualities** and **leadership style.** Group leaders bring to group their preferred ways of perceiving the world and experiences in relating to self and others. Leadership style typically evolves from basic personality and ways of interacting. In reviews of group research spanning more than 50 years, Richard Bednar and colleagues (e.g., Bednar & Kaul, 1999) recognized that the personal qualities of group leaders and leadership style affect group members' behavior, perceptions and evaluations, group dynamics, and outcomes and that leaders and members reciprocally affect one another. Bednar and others who reviewed individual counseling and group research commented on the commonalities in counselor function and effects found in individual counseling and group work. They recognized the difficulty in attempting to identify the personal qualities of counselors and the leadership styles that accounted for systematic variations in positive and negative outcomes.

The categories of leadership style most frequently described in current group literature were first identified in Kurt Lewin's early studies of group dynamics in the 1940s: authoritarian, democratic, and laissez-faire. **Authoritarian** (sometimes called **autocratic**) group leaders view themselves as experts, tend to be somewhat rigid and conventional, give advice, demand obedience, and expect conformity and are often charismatic and manipulative. Group structure is often leader centered, with information filtered through the leader. The leader's personality is strongly emphasized; therefore, the leader is given a high level of power and trust. The power vested in authoritarian leaders usually protects them from exposure of their personal vulnerabilities. These leaders may be friendly and persuasive as they direct the group, but they engage in little self-disclosure. Leader-centered groups are sometimes referred to as "guru oriented"; however, not all authoritarian leaders may view themselves as "gurus." Rather, effective leaders using this style may lead in a manner that recognizes and meets the needs of the group. An authoritarian leader can achieve a great deal during periods of crisis. This style of leader may also meet the needs of culturally diverse group members who expect the leader to assume the expert role.

Democratic group leaders tend to be less directive and more group centered, trusting group members to develop their own potential. They function as facilitators of group process through cooperation, collaboration, and shared power and responsibility. Democratic leaders facilitate conditions to promote self-awareness, self-exploration, expression, and calculated risk taking without fear of rejection for group members.

Laissez-faire leaders take little responsibility for leading the group and instead leave this responsibility to the group itself. These leaders may be very accepting of group members, but they provide little structure or direction. Some leaders may believe the group must take care of itself from the beginning. In groups with high-functioning members, this style could result in productive outcomes; however, in other groups, this style could result in members feeling frustrated, confused, and possibly hostile. Novice group leaders may adopt a laissez-faire style due to lack of skill or knowledge or in an attempt to appear nonthreatening. Others adopt this style to defend against making difficult decisions and thereby increase their popularity or to avoid what they perceive to be authoritarianism.

Aspects of Lewin's typology are evident in the six categories of leadership style Lieberman et al. (1973) identified in their groundbreaking research into encounter group processes and outcomes. These styles and their associated personal qualities were (a) **energizers** (caring, charismatic, risk takers, exhibiting a high level of emotional expressiveness, supportive, encouraging, warm, and genuine), (b) **providers** (caring, personal in style, ability to conceptualize and communicate meaning to group members), (c) **social engineers** (group focused, moderate in caring, providing support and affection, low on charisma and high in peer orientation), (d) **impersonals** (distant, combining a somewhat high level of emotional stimulation with low levels of caring, structure, and support), (e) **laissez-faires** (moderate-to-high ability to conceptualize and communicate meaning but low in caring, emotional expressiveness, and stimulation, providing little structure and direction for the group), and (f) **managers** (high use of control in structuring and directing the group). Lieberman et al. identified energizers, providers, and social engineers as the most successful styles. Most group leaders operate primarily from one style; however, effective leaders are able to draw on their knowledge, skills, experience, and personal qualities and modify their style as needed.

Contributed by Carmen F. Salazar,
Texas A&M University–Commerce,
Commerce, TX

References

Bednar, R. L., & Kaul, T. J. (1999). Experiential group research: Can the cannon fire? In A. E. Bergin & S. L. Garfield (Eds.), *Handbook of psychotherapy and behavior change* (4th ed., pp. 631–663). New York: Wiley.

Lieberman, M. A., Yalom, I. D., & Miles, M. B. (1973). *Encounter groups: First facts.* New York: Basic Books.

Additional Resources

Corey, M. S., & Corey, G. (2006). *Groups: Process and practice* (7th ed.). Belmont, CA: Brooks/Cole.

Posthuma, B. W. (1999). *Small groups in counseling and therapy: Process and leadership* (3rd ed.). Boston: Allyn & Bacon.

■ Group Leadership

The facilitator or leader of a counseling or therapy group is vital to the success of the group. The group leader role is instrumental in the type of dynamics that occur within the group and the outcomes of its members. Although there is much that remains unknown about effective group facilitation, several characteristics and behaviors of leaders are related to group effectiveness.

Screening and Selection of Members

The American Counseling Association's (ACA; 2005) *ACA Code of Ethics* states in Section A.8.a. that

> counselors screen prospective group counseling/therapy participants. To the extent possible, counselors select members whose needs and goals are compatible with the goals of the group, who will not impede the group process, and whose well-being will not be jeopardized by the group experience. (p. 5)

For example, one important variable to consider in the screening and selection process is the motivation level of the potential group member.

Preparation of Members for Group

A strong case can be made for preparing group members to enter a therapeutic group. It has been shown that **pregroup preparation,** also called **pregroup training,** is related to the development of group cohesion, or how much the group members feel connected to the group. Leaders can help members understand how behavior change occurs in a group and how the group will function. There is no standard method of preparation, yet Couch (1995) suggested a four-step model that includes (a) identifying the clients' needs, expectations, and commitment; (b) challenging myths and misconceptions; (c) providing information; and (d) screening individuals for group fit. Preparation prior to the beginning of group requires that a leader have an understanding of group dynamics and an ability to convey hope, trust, and safety to group members while also reducing the anxiety about what group counseling is about, a typical concern for new members.

Positive Leader–Member Relationship

Research strongly underscores that for group members, a supportive relationship with the leader is necessary for client change (Dies, 1994). It is also helpful for group members to have a positive view of the leader. It is not surprising that group leaders who are warm, supportive, and genuinely interested in individual members, as well as the group as a whole, have more members who make more progress toward their goals. Five common leader behaviors have been described as core mechanisms of group process and change (Lieberman, Yalom, & Miles, 1973; Polcin, 1991; Yalom & Leszcz, 2005):

- **Caring.** Group leaders must be able to demonstrate caring, openness, honesty, and genuine concern for all group members.
- **Meaning attribution.** Group leaders are able to define cognitively or describe what is occurring in the group and to attribute meaning to specific events in group. Dies (1994) stated that meaning attribution provides structure for the group in that it helps group members understand and make sense out of their actions and the actions of others.
- **Executive function.** Executive function provides the limits, rules, and norms so that the group can operate.
- **Emotional stimulation.** Leaders must encourage sharing on an affective as well as on a cognitive level.
- **Feedback.** Group leaders need to provide effective positive and corrective feedback to group members and encourage group members to provide feedback to each other.

Use of Structure by the Leader

Structure is a broad term that includes a variety of different techniques and interventions that are directly geared toward the development and maintenance of a healthy group. For example, structure is conveyed when the group leader discusses the group's norms. Typical **norms** include rules around attendance, confidentiality, and how communication occurs (e.g., taking turns, using *I*-statements, being an active participant). Too little structure is problematic for the group, particularly in the early sessions, yet too much structure may also result in passivity and lack of spontaneity in the group. Some of the core mechanisms of group leaders described earlier are also important structuring methods (i.e., executive function and meaning attribution). The following group leader strategies help provide structure and safety in the group (Morran, Stockton, & Whittingham, 2004):

- **Linking** connects members' similarities and themes that occur in the group. This helps members see their commonalities with others.
- **Blocking** is an effective leadership method geared toward protecting group members from potentially damaging interactions. Group leaders need to stop non-beneficial and harmful interactions.

- **Processing** is used by the group leader to help members look at a significant happening in a deeper way and understand their feelings, thoughts, and behaviors.
- **Interpreting** provides a potential hypothesis for why a particular behavior or event occurred.
- **Self-disclosing** occurs when "group leaders reveal their personal feelings, experiences, or here-and-now reactions to group members" (Morran et al., 2004, p. 98).
- **Modeling** involves the group leader or a group member demonstrating a specific skill or behavior that will be helpful for group members to demonstrate also.
- **Tracking** allows the group leader to monitor and keep track of what is occurring in the group. This helps the group leader be clear as to what is happening in group and which topic or interaction needs additional focus.

Group Cohesion

An essential leader behavior is to foster a group climate that is safe, positive, supportive, and yet strong enough to withstand at times intense emotions, challenges, and interactions between members. Yalom and Leszcz (2005) described **cohesion** as the "glue of the group," the "*we*-ness," of the group or how strongly the members feel about their group. Although often studied at one time period, cohesion seems to be a dynamic process that changes over the life of the group and needs continual attention from the leader.

Effective group leadership is paramount to the group's success. Despite the limited amount of research on the essential components of group leadership, the Association for Specialists in Group Work (ASGW) has outlined training standards to provide guidelines for group leader training. These standards have established two levels of training: core training and specialist training (Conyne, 1996). Core training includes both cognitive and experiential components that are the foundation for learning basic knowledge and skills. The distinction made between core training and specialized training highlights the fact that therapeutic groups are complex and diverse. This increased diversity means that different types of groups (i.e., task/work, guidance, psychoeducational, counseling, and psychotherapy groups) with different goals, emphases, populations, and problem areas will require different leader skills.

Contributed by Maria T. Riva,
University of Denver, Denver, CO

References

American Counseling Association. (2005). *ACA code of ethics*. Alexandria, VA: Author.

Conyne, R. K. (1996). The Association for Specialists in Group Work training standards: Some considerations and suggestions for training. *Journal for Specialists in Group Work, 21,* 155–162.

Couch, R. D. (1995). Four steps for conducting a pregroup screening interview. *Journal for Specialists in Group Work, 20,* 18–25.

Dies, R. R. (1994). Therapist variables in group psychology research. In A. Fuhriman & G. M. Burlingame (Eds.), *Handbook of group psychotherapy: An empirical and clinical synthesis* (pp. 114–154). New York: Wiley.

Lieberman, M. A., Yalom, I. D., & Miles, M. B. (1973). *Encounter groups: First facts.* New York: Basic Books.

Morran, D. K., Stockton, R., & Whittingham, M. (2004). Effective leader interventions for counseling and psychotherapy. In J. L. DeLucia-Waack, D. A. Gerrity, C. R. Kalodner, & M. T. Riva (Eds.), *Handbook of group counseling and psychotherapy* (pp. 37–48). Thousand Oaks, CA: Sage.

Polcin, D. L. (1991). Prescriptive group leadership. *Journal for Specialists in Group Work, 16,* 8–15.

Yalom, I. D., & Leszcz, M. (2005). *The theory and practice of group psychotherapy* (5th ed.). New York: Basic Books.

Additional Resources

Association for Specialists in Group Work Web site: http://www.asgw.org for documents on ASGW best practice guidelines for group workers, training standards, and diversity competent group workers

DeLucia-Waack, J. L., Gerrity, D. A., Kalodner, C. R., & Riva, M. T. (Eds.). (2004). *Handbook of group counseling and psychotherapy*. Thousand Oaks, CA: Sage.

Fuhriman, A., & Burlingame, G. M. (2001). Group psychotherapy training and effectiveness. *International Journal of Group Psychotherapy, 51,* 399–416.

Gladding, S. T. (2003). *Group work: A counseling specialty* (4th ed.). Upper Saddle River, NJ: Merrill Prentice Hall.

■ Group Leadership Style

Leadership style refers to the general approach the counselor takes to group leadership. There are as many styles of therapeutic group leadership as there are group leaders. Styles are influenced by the personality and theoretical background of the group leader; the purpose of the group; the type of group; and its stage of development, setting, and membership. A useful way to categorize leadership styles is based on the classic work of Lewin (Lewin, Lippitt, & White, 1939), who divided group leadership styles into authoritarian, democratic, and laissez-faire, which have also come to be known as Theory X, Theory Y, and Theory Z leadership styles, respectively.

Authoritarian, or **Theory X group leadership,** is shown by group leaders who take total responsibility for and control of the group. All decision making is assumed by the leader, who sets the agenda, rules, and goals for the group and who also determines and directs group interventions. Often, interaction among members is actively discouraged; members are either engaging directly with the leader or observing and learning from others' interactions with the leader. This style is also typical of groups in which the leader uses a confrontational approach, such as certain ex-offender or substance abuse groups, traditional Gestalt groups, and traditional rational-emotive behavior therapy groups.

In **democratic,** or **Theory Y group leadership,** the leader is a facilitator rather than a director. Those who practice democratic leadership see the potential in group members to make decisions, set agendas and goals, and interact therapeutically with each other. The leader provides information, comments on and leads discussion into group process, and works to set norms encouraging group member interaction and self-revelation and seeking feedback from other group members. For the democratic leader, the therapeutic value of the group derives from both the actions of the counselor and the interactions of its members. This approach is exemplified by Rogers, Yalom, and similar writers.

The third type of leadership style, **laissez-faire** or **Theory Z group leadership,** is essentially a group in which the leader exhibits little or no leadership. In contrast to democratic style and in opposition to authoritarian leadership, in the laissez-faire approach, the leader abdicates responsibility for decision making and assumes that the group members themselves have the potential, ability, and responsibility to determine the course of the group, with the leader assuming little responsibility for group goals and outcomes.

Group Leadership Effectiveness

Lieberman, Yalom, and Miles (1973), after failing to find differences in the effectiveness of encounter group leaders based on their theoretical orientation, used factor analysis to distill four leadership functions operating across theoretical backgrounds: emotional stimulation, caring, meaning attribution, and executive function (see Group Leadership). Analysis of these leadership functions discovered significant differences in outcomes based on leadership function use. The most effective leaders, with the fewest dropouts and highest member satisfaction, were those leaders who scored high in **caring** (e.g., supportiveness, warmth, acceptance) and **meaning attribution** (e.g., explaining, interpreting) with moderate levels of **emotional stimulation** (e.g., challenging, confronting, stimulating catharsis and self-disclosure) and **executive function** (e.g., setting limits and rules, managing time, interceding). Yet those leaders who were more authoritarian, with high emotional stimulation and executive function, tended to produce high dropout rates and more severe casualties. Similarly, those with low caring, executive function, and emotional stimulation (i.e., laissez-faire) also produced negative results. These results support the use of a more democratic leadership style, a style in which the leader enables members and sets boundaries but does not aggressively dominate the group, keep members from interacting, or insist on self-disclosure and catharsis before members are ready.

This recommendation, however, can oversimplify the question of the ideal leadership style. To be effective, the leader not only should adopt a style that is congruent with his or her own skills, theoretical background, and personality but one that is also appropriate for the group's level of development, its purpose, and the makeup of its members.

Group Development

Several group development models are recognized, but they generally follow the basic linear pattern of a formation period, a working period, and a closing stage. Different leadership styles are generally required for different stages of group development. For example, the early stages of a group typically would require more executive function activity from the leader (e.g., setting boundaries, establishing the group goals, establishing group procedures). Executive function activity at the formation stage may involve the use of more structured activities. As the group develops, the leader can become increasingly democratic as members become more cohesive, take leadership roles themselves, learn to recognize group processes, attend to each other's needs, and actively work together on achieving group goals.

Other Factors in Choosing a Leadership Style

In choosing a style of leadership, the counselor must also pay attention to other ecological factors, such as the culture of the group members, the setting in which the group is placed, and the purpose of the group. The culturally proficient counselor recognizes that individuals' expectations of leaders vary with cultural background. For example, Asian cultures often value respect for authority, and, thus, group members with Asian backgrounds may be less likely to challenge the group leader, be more likely to expect the counselor to take the role of expert, and be less self-revealing of emotions. To be successful, the counselor's choice of leadership style must be guided by the cultural realities of the group members. The type and purpose of the group are also factors in leadership style; for example, a task-oriented or educational group may require a more authoritarian style to keep the group directed toward its institutionally sanctioned task. Settings, as well as the expectation of payers and clients and the counselor's own theoretical background, may also affect the choice of leadership style.

Contributed by Christopher Engle,
University of Cincinnati,
Cincinnati, OH

References

Lewin, K., Lippitt, R., & White, R. K. (1939). Patterns of aggressive behavior in experimentally created social climates. *Journal of Social Psychology, 110,* 271–301.

Lieberman, M. A., Yalom, I. D., & Miles, M. B. (1973). *Encounter groups: First facts.* New York: Basic Books.

Additional Resources

Corey, M. S., & Corey, G. (2002). *Groups: Process and practice* (6th ed.). Pacific Grove, CA: Brooks/Cole.

Gladding, S. T. (2003). *Group work: A counseling specialty* (4th ed.). Upper Saddle River, NJ: Merrill Prentice Hall.

Yalom, I. D. (1975). *The theory and practice of group psychotherapy* (2nd ed.). New York: Basic Books.

■ Group Member Roles

A **role** is an expected pattern of behavior that recurs as the characteristic social functioning of a person, comprising the actions and activities assigned to, or required or expected of, a person in a particular setting, organization, society, or relationship. A **formal role** is a specific role assigned to a group member, such as secretary or timekeeper. An **informal role** is one that is not specified but is chosen or developed by the interactive behaviors of a group member, such as an opinion seeker or opinion giver. Group members' roles should not be equated with the members' individual personalities; group members manifest roles based on their interactions in the group.

Group members' roles evolve as the group forms, and the role assumed by a group member defines the relationship to the rest of the group members. Roles are fluid, however, and can change over time. Member roles are influenced by internal and external factors. Four broad influences have been identified: (a) the expectations of self and others, (b) personality factors, (c) the characteristics of the leader, and (d) the characteristics of the group. For instance, the group's composition is a variable of influence, as noted in (d), because mixed gender or mixed ethnic groups affect members' interactions, often based on cultural norms or social status.

Group members, like group leaders, bring varying levels of experience to a group. Past experiences in groups produce certain member reactions that may be carried over to future group experiences. Group leaders can enhance the therapeutic experience for their members when they understand the dynamics of the various roles group members bring to the setting. Group members may become stuck in a role, or roles may be flexible to the degree that group members are able to accommodate changes in the group's process. Such changes may fluctuate, depending on the developmental phase of the group's life cycle and changing conditions in the group itself.

Classification systems of group member roles vary in description within the field of group study. Rugel (1991) described MacKenzie's system from the Tavistock perspective, which names four functional roles: structural, social, divergent, and cautionary roles. Trotzer (2006) discussed the functional dynamics previously named within the context of the roles named "the client, the helper, the model and the reality check" (p. 207). Simply, the **client** is a group member who receives the group's attention. The **helper** is a group member who offers assistance to others through support, encouragement, listening, understanding, or even confrontation. The **model** is a group member who demonstrates behavior that may be emulated by others due to the socially adaptive nature of the behavior and its value for others who have the opportunity to identify with the effective patterns. Finally, the **reality check** is a group member who offers the function of assisting other members to select options based on realistic and constructive criteria. A **cautionary role,** according to MacKenzie's terminology, is a role played by a group member who demonstrates avoidance to participation and overdependence on other group members to assume the client role.

In most of the literature on groups, member roles are divided into three groups: roles that function as facilitative or building roles; maintenance or task roles; and self-serving, individual roles (see Table 1). Although certain group member roles are facilitative and promote growth in a group, others impede group process and progress. Some roles include those that relate to the socioemotional behaviors of the group members. For instance, a facilitator or encourager acts to

Table 1. Group Member Roles

Role	Actions
Facilitative and building roles	
Facilitator	Assists the group leader, often speaks on behalf of the group
Encourager	Makes others feel comfortable, praises others' ideas
Harmonizer	Mediates to keep emotions controlled within the group, helps to resolve disagreements
Neutralizer	Offers cognitive solutions, often avoids emotions
Compromiser	Detaches ego from ideas by admitting error and fallibility or compromises own ideas for the sake of the group
Gatekeeper	Keeps group operating within agreed-upon norms
Task and maintenance roles	
Initiator	Moves the group to take action, makes suggestions
Information seeker/giver	Deals with information about the group's tasks
Opinion seeker/giver	Deals with the group's values in relation to its tasks
Coordinator	Focuses other members on the group's activities
Evaluator	Judges how well the group is doing what it is supposed to do
Observer	Provides feedback to the group
Individual-centered roles	
Aggressor	Disagrees with other members' ideas, imposes own ideas
Blocker	Impedes group progress by resisting wishes of others, brings up old business
Recognition seeker	Calls attention to self at the expense of others
Informer	Talks about other members outside of the group
Nonparticipator	Avoids group participation, often silent, or can be intimidating
Know-it-all	Wants to improve self-image by offering information as factual

keep a friendly feeling within the group, whereas a gatekeeper or expediter often acts similar to a referee to keep the group behavior within its set norms. Other roles relate to the instrumental or task actions of the group, such as opinion seekers, timekeepers, or recorders. Participants who pursue individual roles often actively work against the group's functioning, such as those group members who tend to dominate conversations, demand a disproportionate amount of the group's attention, or speak in judgmental terms.

Group leaders must be in tune with the group's dynamics in order to help the group members gain awareness of their particular modes of behavior and of whether their interactions within the group are constructive or counterproductive to the work and purpose of the group. Ideally, maintenance and task roles should be balanced, with sufficient attention given to both socioemotional and task functioning.

Some member role problems can negatively affect the group's development. For example, **role collision** occurs when a group member functions outside of the group in a particular role and then finds that role is incompatible with what the group expects the member to perform within the group. **Role incompatibility** occurs when an individual's needs and the group's desires do not match well, and the individual feels pressured into an undesired role within the group, making the individual's needs and the group's desires not match. Perhaps more troubling is **role confusion,** when a member is unsure of the role he or she is expected to play in the group. A group member may also experience **role** transition anxiety when changing from one role in the group to another role. Any of these problems can be significant if group members find themselves giving more attention to clarifying or adjusting to their roles than to the actual ongoing group process.

Contributed by Jeri L. Crowell, Fort Valley State University, Fort Valley, GA

References

Rugel, R. P. (1991). Closed and open systems: The Tavistock group from a general system perspective. *Journal for Specialists in Group Work, 16,* 74–84.

Trotzer, J. P. (2006). *The counselor and the group: Integrating theory, training and practice* (4th ed.). Philadelphia: Taylor & Francis.

Additional Resource

Gladding, S. T. (2003). *Group work: A counseling specialty* (4th ed.). Upper Saddle River, NJ: Prentice Hall.

Group Member Roles: Problems and Types

A role is defined as a "dynamic structure within a person" (Munich, 1993, p. 26), based on an individual's needs, cognitions, and values. Roles are activated by interactional, group, or situational stimuli or by defined positions. Each person has an available "repertoire of goals" (Munich, 1993, p. 27) that they may access. Roles require action on the part of the individual fulfilling the roles.

The mid-1930s to the 1950s were particularly influential in the practice of modern group work. Lewin's (Lewin, Lippitt, & White, 1939) pioneering analysis of group dynamics, Benne and Sheats's (1948) classification of member roles, and Bales's (1950) contributions on interaction process are some of the seminal works that have enriched the practice of group counseling and the current understanding of group roles.

Members of a group tend to assume or play a particular role within the group. Group leaders who have an awareness of group member roles are better positioned to understand the dynamics at work within their groups. Roles are often subconsciously assumed, and they manifest in particular behaviors or ways of interaction within the group. Often, roles are an unconscious coping mechanism or a form of avoidance or resistance.

Individuals may assume different roles in different groups or may assume different roles based on the particular mix of personalities in the group. For example, although an individual may be the quiet onlooker in a group of assertive or talkative people, that member may assume the role of information or opinion giver in a group made up of less assertive or talkative people.

Roles are usually different from the overall identity of an individual (Gladding, 2008); however, roles can sometimes be consistent across different settings and different groups. Some individuals are unable to differentiate themselves from the role they have assumed from a young age, and this role becomes intertwined with their overall identity (Gladding,

2008). In the case of adult children of alcoholics, maladaptive behavior patterns adopted during childhood to cope with a chaotic environment may continue to be used in relationships as adults. Four such maladaptive roles of adult children of alcoholics have been identified: hero, scapegoat, lost child, and mascot (Harris & MacQuiddy, 1991).

Problems Associated With Roles

Four major problems are associated with the fulfillment of group roles (Hare, 1962): role collision, role incompatibility, role confusion, and role transition. **Role collision** is experienced when two or more persons in the same group hold roles that overlap, leading to tensions focused on actions to be carried out and lines of responsibility (Hare, 1962). For example, role collision could occur in a group where more than one person assumes the role of leader. Role collision may also take place when there is a conflict between the role an individual is expected to play in two settings (Gladding, 2008). For example, an individual who plays the role of initiator or energizer in the work setting might experience role conflict when playing the role of follower in a counseling group.

Role incompatibility occurs when an individual is forced to meet expectations for different roles that are incompatible (Hare, 1962). For example, the roles of friend and disciplinarian are incompatible. According to Gladding (2008), role incompatibility takes place when a member is assigned an unwanted role or a role the member does not feel comfortable carrying out. For instance, a member may be elected to lead a group despite a lack of interest or confidence in assuming a leadership role.

Role confusion takes place when there is a lack of agreement in the group regarding the functions of a particular role (Hare, 1962). When a group member is unsure of what role to play in the group, role confusion or role ambiguity is experienced (Gladding, 2008). Group members who experience role confusion and are not proactive about seeking clarification regarding roles are likely to experience heightened stress, and they may feel a sense of hostility toward the leader for not providing clear direction (Corey, 2008).

Finally, **role transition** occurs in groups when a member gives up one role to take on another role (Hare, 1962). When members are expected to take on a new or enhanced role as the group progresses, but they do not feel comfortable doing so, the transition could be a source of stress (Gladding, 2008). For example a member who is relatively quiet in the early phases of the group may be expected or challenged to participate more as the group progresses. This challenge might come from the leader, or from other participants, or even from within the member.

Types of Roles

One way of categorizing the types of roles in a group is to assess their function. Benne and Sheets (1948) classified group roles into three broad areas: (a) group task roles, (b) group building and maintenance roles, and (c) individual roles. This classification (with minor modifications in some cases) has been used by group theorists over the years.

Group task roles are focused on the task of the group and serve to facilitate or coordinate group efforts. Such roles allow the group to progress and achieve goals, maximizing participation and cooperation while minimizing unnecessary conflict or unproductive work. Examples of group task roles include initiating, contributing, information or opinion seeking, information or opinion giving, elaborating, coordinating, orienting, evaluating or critiquing, energizing, recording, or serving as a procedural technician (Benne & Sheets, 1948).

Group building and maintenance roles (or vitalizing roles) focus on the functioning of the group as a group. They contribute to the group's well-being and enhance the likelihood of group members bonding on social and emotional levels. Group members who fulfill building and maintenance roles tend to foster a sense of cohesiveness and connectedness within the group. Examples of maintenance roles include encouraging, harmonizing, compromising, gate keeping, expediting, standard setting, observing and commenting on group process, and following (Benne & Sheets, 1948).

Individual roles tend to impede the progress of the group because they are focused on the satisfaction of individual needs or goals that may be irrelevant to group tasks or the effective functioning of the group. Members of a group with individual goals usually have a hidden agenda (which they may or may not be aware of), and that agenda is not aligned with the group goals. These types of goals are sometimes referred to as blocking roles. Group leaders must be astute at identifying such individual roles and intervening appropriately to ensure that the entire group does not become unproductive. Examples of individual goals are aggressing, displaying hostility, blocking, seeking recognition, self-confessing, seducing others and acting the playboy/playgirl, dominating, excessive help seeking, and special interest pleading (Benne & Sheats, 1948). Specific interventions or techniques that may be used by group leaders to address individual or blocking roles in groups may be found in the additional resources listed at the end of this entry.

Contribution by Christine Suniti Bhat,
Ohio University, Athens, OH

References

Bales, R. F. (1950). *Interaction process analysis*. Cambridge, MA: Addison-Wesley.

Benne, K. D., & Sheats, P. (1948). Functional roles of group members. *Journal of Social Issues, 4*, 2.

Corey, G. (2008). *Theory and practice of group counseling* (7th ed.). Belmont, CA: Thomson Brooks/Cole.

Gladding, S. (2008). *Group work: A counseling specialty* (5th ed.). Upper Saddle River, NJ: Merrill Prentice Hall.

Hare, A. P. (1962). *Handbook of small group research*. New York: The Free Press of Glencoe.

Harris, S. A., & MacQuiddy, S. (1991). Childhood roles in group therapy: The lost child and the mascot. *Journal for Specialists in Group Work, 16,* 223–229.

Lewin, K., Lippitt, R., & White, R. K. (1939). Patterns of aggressive behavior in experimentally created social climates. *Journal of Social Psychology, 10,* 271–301.

Munich, R. L. (1993). Group dynamics. In H. I. Kaplan & B. J. Sadock (Eds.), *Comprehensive group psychotherapy* (3rd ed., pp. 21–32). Baltimore: Williams & Wilkins.

Additional Resources

Corey, M. S., & Corey, G. (2006). *Groups: Process and practice* (7th ed.). Belmont, CA: Thomson Brooks/Cole.

Yalom, I. D., & Leszcz, M. (2005). *The theory and practice of group psychotherapy* (5th ed.). New York: Basic Books.

■ Group Norms

Group norms are those practices, rules, or guidelines established by the group in its formative stages that influence its operation and functioning. Norms usually play a significant role in whether or not the group is effective in helping members attain desired goals. By definition, group norms affect the direction and flow of group process toward goal attainment. Norms can be classified as either constructive or destructive. Constructive norms are usually overt and explicit, whereas destructive norms are primarily covert and implicit.

Constructive norms are those standards of behavior that assist in establishing a group atmosphere conducive to members achieving their goals. Constructive norms are usually openly identified and endorsed by the group as the standards of conduct necessary for success in a group. Examples of this type of norm are (a) the importance of confidentiality, (b) regular and punctual attendance, (c) giving constructive feedback, (d) sharing meaningful aspects of oneself that identify personal problems and concerns, (e) focusing on the here and now, and (f) providing support to members yet also challenging them to look at problematic behaviors. Constructive norms are usually viewed as an important ingredient in the development of the high levels of trust and cohesion necessary for members to engage in productive work in group.

Destructive norms, occasionally referred to as limiting norms, are detrimental and may significantly inhibit progress toward members' goals. They are typically hidden, unidentified, and/or unconsciously held rules of behavior that often block the growth of trust, cohesion, intimacy, and risk taking necessary for member growth. In essence, destructive norms may secretly replace previously established constructive norms and may be diametrically opposed to them. The following two examples demonstrate how a constructive norm initially established to set a desired level of open expression of emotion in a group is found to be in direct conflict with a more destructive norm actually condoned and practiced in the group.

Example 1: Many groups establish an explicit norm that members are free to choose their level of participation and that no one will be unduly pressured to disclose; however, an unspoken, yet practiced norm may exist that in order to be fully accepted as a valued and respected member of the group, a participant must disclose deeply intense and personal emotions. Such a norm may be viewed as intimidating and threatening by more reserved members who agreed to join the group based on the explicit, openly identified norm that disclosures were voluntary. Enforcement of this unspoken, implicit norm may cause some members undue anxiety, which can be detrimental to their continued participation and progress in the group.

Example 2: Although a group may have established an explicit norm that catharsis is highly encouraged, a more pervasive, implicit norm not to engage in an intense expression of emotions may actually exist. Significant emotionality may be regularly ignored or ridiculed by the group members experiencing this type of response after a catharsis, and members could easily feel minimized or ostracized by the group.

In both cases, the group facilitator is charged with the responsibility of recognizing and openly confronting and challenging the continued existence of the destructive norm actually being practiced in the group. Table 1 identifies several constructive norms, each of which is followed by its corresponding destructive norm. Obviously, the constructive norms are easily identified as significantly more effective than the destructive norms in helping members grow and change in an effort to reach their established goals.

Contributed by Don C. Combs,
University of Texas at El Paso,
El Paso, TX

Table 1. Constructive Norms and Corresponding Destructive Norms

Constructive Norms	Destructive Norms
Confidentiality considered important and necessary	Confidentiality regularly breached without consequence
Regular and punctual attendance required	Absences and lateness tolerated and not confronted
Constructive feedback sanctioned	Destructive, hurtful feedback permitted without consequence
Closeness and intimacy highly valued	Closeness and intimacy deemphasized, even ridiculed
Open expression of emotion accepted, even encouraged	Open expression of emotion downplayed and/or ignored

Additional Resources

Corey, M. S., & Corey, G. (2006). *Groups: Process and practice* (7th ed.). Belmont, CA: Thomson Brooks/Cole.

Gladding, S. T. (2004). *Group work: A counseling specialty* (4th ed.). Upper Saddle River, NJ: Merrill Prentice Hall.

■ Group Work Assessment

Having generally demonstrated that groups are effective in producing cognitive, behavioral, and emotional change, group work scholars have now shifted to examining what makes groups effective (DeLucia-Waack & Bridbord, 2004). Research on group work is now examining how such variables as group climate, group dynamics, therapeutic factors, and leader and member characteristics affect group member outcomes. **Assessment measures** exist for measuring a variety of different aspects of group work. **Screening and selection instruments** are being used to help select members who are most likely to be most successful in a group. **Leadership instruments** are commonly used to assess the behavior skills of group leaders and behaviors for training, supervision, and research purposes. **Measures of group climate** are used to understand therapeutic factors and perceptions of group environment. Understanding the common elements and active ingredients that contribute to positive group outcomes depends on having appropriate assessment tools. This entry briefly reviews measures related to screening and selection, leader behavior and skills, group climate, therapeutic factors, and in-session group member behavior.

Screening and Selection Instruments

Four measures are typically used to select group members, assess attitudes toward groups, and assess interpersonal behavior that may affect group members' ability to function successfully in groups. Elements (Schutz, 1992), the Group Psychotherapy Evaluation Scale (Van Dyck, 1980), and the Hill Interaction Matrix–A & B (Hill, 1965) focus on the behaviors and skills of group members that are necessary to participate successfully in groups. The Group Therapy Survey (Slocum, 1987) assesses misperceptions toward group interventions that may interfere with clients seeking or participating in such treatment.

Assessment of Group Leadership Behavior and Skills

Several measures have been developed to assess and rate group leadership behaviors to give feedback to leaders as part of training experiences and to understand the relationship between group leadership behaviors and effective groups. The Skilled Group Counseling Scale (Smaby, Maddux, Torres-Rivera, & Zimmick, 1999), Trainer Behavior Scale (Bolman, 1971), Group Counselor Behavior Rating Form (Corey & Corey, 1987), and Leadership Characteristics Inventory (Makuch, 1997) assess specific leadership skills and can be rated by group leader, coleader, supervisor, or group member. In contrast to these behavior scales, the Corrective Feedback Self-Efficacy Instrument (Page & Hulse-Killacky, 1999) focuses specifically on self-efficacy for giving corrective feedback, whereas the Group Leadership Self-Efficacy Instrument (Page, Pietrzak, & Lewis, 2001) is a more general measure of the self-efficacy of group leadership skills. The Core Group Work Skills Inventory (Wilson, Newmeyer, Rapin, & Conyne, 2007), based on the (2000) Association for Specialists in Group Work: Professional Standards for the Training of Group Workers, assesses perceived importance and personal confidence in implementing specific group leadership behaviors. These skills have been used as pre- and postmeasures to assess change in practicum experiences for beginning group leaders as well as to examine relationships between perceptions of group leadership, group climate, and behavior change.

Assessment of Group Climate

Two measures of group climate and environment have been used extensively with a range of groups from task/work to counseling and therapy groups: the Group Climate Questionnaire–Short (MacKenzie, 1983, 1990) and Group Environment Scale (Moos, 1986). Such measures have been used to assess group stage and levels of cohesion as well as to provide feedback to group leaders of the members' perceptions of the group climate.

Assessment of Group Therapeutic Factors

Yalom and Leszcz (2005) suggested that 12 therapeutic factors form the basis for what makes groups effective. The 12 factors are altruism, catharsis, cohesiveness, existentiality, family reenactment, guidance, hope, identification, interpersonal learning input (feedback), interpersonal learning output (new behavior), self-understanding, and universality (see Curative Factors). Several instruments have been designed to assess therapeutic factors in groups, including the Therapeutic Factors Scale (Yalom, 1975), Curative Factors Scale–Revised (Stone, Lewis, & Beck, 1994), and Therapeutic Factors Inventory (Lese & McNair-Semands, 2000). The Critical Incidents Questionnaire (Kivlighan & Goldfine, 1991) asks group members to describe the most important event in a given session and explain why it was important; the responses are then rated in terms of therapeutic factors. Practitioners use the assessment of key therapeutic factors to understand how groups affect group members and create change. Most recently, Kivlighan and Holmes (2004) used a cluster analysis of studies of therapeutic factors to differentiate groups into four types: affective insight groups, affective support groups, cognitive support groups, and cognitive insight groups, each with differently valued therapeutic factors.

Ratings of In-Session Group Behavior

Some of the oldest group assessment instruments are those that were designed to rate in-session group leader and member behavior based on videotapes, audiotapes, or transcripts of actual group sessions. These instruments are similar to coding schemes that are intended to recognize overall patterns of interactions within sessions or entire groups

The Groups Sessions Rating Scale (Cooney, Kadden, Litt, & Getter, 1991; Getter, Litt, Kadden, & Cooney, 1992) focuses on the differential use of therapeutic interventions in coping skills training and short-term interactional group therapy. The Hill Interaction Matrix (Hill, 1965, 1973) categorizes statements into four quadrants that focus on interpersonal interaction and discussion skills. The Interaction Process Analysis (Bales, 1950) measures task and social-emotional interpersonal behavior using 12 categories that emphasize problem-solving behavior. Systems for Multiple Level Observation of Groups (Bales, Cohen, & Williams, 1979) codes on three dimensions: dominant–submissive, unfriendly–friendly, and instrumentally controlled–emotionally expressive. The Group Observer Form (Romano & Sullivan, 2000) examines group cohesiveness, here-and-now focus, and group conflict. The Group Cohesiveness Scale (Budman & Gurman, 1988) rates aspects of group connectedness. The Individual Group Member Interpersonal Process Scale (Soldz, Budman, Davis, & Demby, 1993) is multidimensional (i.e., presence/absence of a behavior, locational and object designations, and intensity or significance of the behavior). These scales are used to map interactions behaviorally to further the understanding of group process and dynamics and the interplay between group leader and member behavior.

Ongoing Issues in Group Assessment

There are several important ongoing issues in the assessment of group phenomena that will help the field to advance. There is a need for continuity and uniformity among measures that would allow comparing results across studies. Measures of group dynamics and outcome that yield reliable and valid scores need to continue to be developed and used systematically in studies. Reliability must be established in terms of test–retest reliability and how reactive measures are to interventions and over time. Validity must be established in terms of what constructs are actually being measured and the consistency across instruments and raters. The use of measures that yield reliable and valid scores will then lead to the development of clearly established norms that can be used to compare specific samples and act as a baseline for future studies.

Contributed by Janice L. DeLucia-Waack,
University at Buffalo, SUNY, Buffalo, NY,
and Amy Nitza,
Indiana University–Purdue University,
Fort Wayne, IN

References

Association for Specialists in Group Work. (2000). Association for Specialists in Group Work: Professional standards for the training of group workers. *Journal for Specialists in Group Work, 25,* 327–354.

Bales, R. F. (1950). *Interaction process analysis: A method for the study of small groups.* Cambridge, MA: Addison-Wesley.

Bales, R. F., Cohen, S. P., & Williams, S. A. (1979). *SYMLOG: A system for the multiple level observation of groups.* New York: Free Press.

Bolman, L. (1971). Some effects of trainers on their T-groups. *Journal of Applied Behavioral Science, 7,* 309-325.

Budman, S. H., & Gurman, A. S. (1988). *The theory and practice of brief therapy.* New York: Guilford Press.

Cooney, N. L., Kadden, R. M., Litt, M. D., & Getter, H. (1991). Matching alcoholics to coping skills or interactional therapies: Two-year follow-up results. *Journal of Consulting & Clinical Psychology, 59,* 598–601.

Corey, M. S., & Corey, G. (1987) *Group counseling: Process and practice* (3rd ed.). Monterey, CA: Brooks/Cole.

DeLucia-Waack, J. L., & Bridbord, K. (2004). Measures of group process, dynamics, climate, leadership behaviors, and therapeutic factors: A review. In J. L. DeLucia-Waack, D. Gerrity, C. R. Kalodner, & M. Riva (Eds.), *Handbook of group counseling and psychotherapy* (pp. 120–135). Thousand Oaks, CA: Sage.

Getter, H., Litt, M. D., Kadden, R. M., & Cooney, N. L. (1992). Measuring treatment process in coping skills and interactional group therapies for alcoholism. *International Journal of Group Psychotherapy, 42,* 419–430.

Hill, W. F. (1965). *Hill Interaction Matrix.* Los Angeles: University of Southern California.

Hill, W. F. (1973). Hill Interaction Matrix (HIM) conceptual framework for understanding groups. In J. W. Pfeiffer &

J. E. Jones (Eds.), *The 1973 annual handbook for group facilitators* (pp. 159–176). San Diego, CA: University Associates.

Kivlighan, D. M., Jr., & Goldfine, D. C. (1991). Endorsement of therapeutic factors as a function of stage of group development and participant interpersonal attitudes. *Journal of Counseling Psychology, 38,* 150–158.

Kivlighan, D. M., Jr., & Holmes, S. E. (2004). The importance of therapeutic factors: A typology of therapeutic factor studies. In J. L. DeLucia-Waack, D. Gerrity, C. R. Kalodner, & M. Riva (Eds.), *Handbook of group counseling and psychotherapy* (pp. 23–36). Thousand Oaks, CA: Sage.

Lese, K. L., & McNair-Semands, R. R. (2000). The Therapeutic Factors Inventory: Development of the scale. *Group, 24,* 303–317.

MacKenzie, K. R. (1983). The clinical application of a group climate measure. In R. R. Dies & K. R. MacKenzie (Eds.), *Advances in group psychotherapy: Integrating research and practice* (pp. 159–170). New York: International Universities Press.

MacKenzie, K. R. (1990). *Introduction to time-limited group therapy.* Washington, DC: American Psychiatric Press.

Makuch, L. (1997). *Measuring dimensions of counseling and therapeutic group leadership style: Development of a leadership characteristics inventory.* Unpublished doctoral dissertation, Indiana University, Bloomington.

Moos, R. H. (1986). *Group Environment Scale manual.* Palo Alto, CA: Consulting Psychologists Press.

Page, B. J., & Hulse-Killacky, D. (1999). Development and validation of the corrective feedback self-efficacy instrument. *Journal for Specialists in Group Work, 24,* 37–54.

Page, B. J., Pietrzak, D. R., & Lewis, T. F. (2001). Development of the group leader self-efficacy instrument. *Journal for Specialists in Group Work, 26,* 168–184.

Romano, J. L., & Sullivan, B. A. (2000). Simulated group counseling for group work training: A four-year research study of group development. *Journal for Specialists in Group Work, 25,* 366–375.

Schutz, W. C. (1992). Beyond FIRO-B—Three new theory driven measures–Element B: Behavior, Element F: Feelings, Element S: Self. *Psychological Reports, 70,* 915–937.

Slocum, Y. S. (1987). A survey of expectations about group therapy among clinical and non-clinical populations. *International Journal of Group Psychotherapy, 37,* 39–54.

Smaby, M. H., Maddux, C. D., Torres-Rivera, E., & Zimmick, R. (1999). A study of the effects of a skills-based versus a conventional group counseling training program. *Journal for Specialists in Group Work, 24,* 152–163.

Soldz, S., Budman, S., Davis, M., & Demby, A. (1993). Beyond the interpersonal circumplex in group psychotherapy: The structure and relationship to outcome of the individual group member interpersonal process scale. *Journal of Clinical Psychology, 49,* 551–563.

Stone, M. H., Lewis, C. M., & Beck, A. P. (1994). The structure of Yalom's Curative Factors Scale. *International Journal of Group Psychotherapy, 44,* 239–245.

Van Dyck, B. J. (1980). An analysis of selection criteria for short-term group counseling clients. *Personnel and Guidance Journal, 59,* 226–230.

Wilson, F. R., Newmeyer, M., Rapin, L. S., & Conyne, R. K. (2007). *Core Group Work Skills Inventory.* Retrieved September 12, 2007, from http://www. asgw.org/instrumentation.asp

Yalom, I. D. (1975). *The theory and practice of group psychotherapy.* New York: Basic Books.

Yalom, I. D., & Leszcz, M. (2005). *The theory and practice of group psychotherapy* (5th ed.). New York: Basic Books.

Additional Resources

Beck, A. P., & Lewis, C. M. (Eds.). (2000). *The process of group psychotherapy: Systems for analyzing change.* Washington, DC: American Psychological Association.

Wheelan, S. A. (2005). *Handbook of group research and process.* Thousand Oaks, CA: Sage.

Group Work, Developmental Stages of

Human groups are capable of developing through an orderly sequence of stages toward a more organized, mature level of interdependent, cooperative functioning in a manner similar to that described by psychology theories of individual human development. Bales and Schutz were early proponents of group stage models. Although many group experts (e.g., Cohen, Smith, Gazda, Lacoursiere, Rogers, Yalom) by the late 1970s had described their own versions of group development, recent authors of prominent group work textbooks (e.g., Corey, Gladding, Trotzer, Yalom) have identified group developmental stage theory as a foundational group dynamic factor essential to understanding and working with groups.

Tuckman (1965) and Tuckman and Jensen (1977) identified five stages as the best fit for the various developmental sequences described in the existing literature at those times. Most models that propose a different number of stages vary only in the way the models partition the same overt behavioral and underlying theoretical sequences and can therefore be logically transformed into the five-stage model. Tuckman's simplified list of the key issues of each of the five stages includes **forming, storming, norming, performing,** and **adjourning/mourning.**

Salient, underlying psychological and interpersonal issues that are most important to and motivate most individual and group activity at various periods of group existence are often called **themes.** Although specific themes may have recurring relevance in the development of the group, key themes are most cogent at certain times during the group's development, and, if these themes are not sufficiently addressed and resolved or normed, the group will not progress into a well-formed, highly productive group or team. Conversely, adequately addressing and norming these critical dimensions of personal functioning and interpersonal interaction as they manifest in subsequent group interaction facilitate cohesive and collaborative group functioning, thereby enhancing group process and outcome.

Stage 1

During the first stages of group development, **forming,** members are interested in establishing safety and security with other members and the leaders, how the group will operate to achieve its goals, and what behavioral rules and contributions are expected of them. How well group participation can meet the individual member's needs and help the member achieve personal goals and what kinds of relationships with and interactive patterns are possible and expected by other members are also important. Finally, determining whether further effort expended will prove to be beneficial to members' personal goals is typical of Stage 1 behavior.

It is crucial to understand that leaders, who are sometimes assisted by members, must perform both task and social-emotional functions at each stage of group development. Although many basic orientation, norm clarification, and goal identification tasks must often be accomplished during the first, or forming, stage of group development, the primary underlying psychological themes of Stage 1 are emphasizing similarities; committing to the group process; and, most salient, **avoiding rejection.** If successful, initial efforts to avoid rejection will allow members to accomplish the important early goals of orientation and exploration of group expectations, norms, and meaning before deciding to commit energy to the complex tasks of developing deeper personal cooperative working relationships with other members and with the group as a unit. A second major theme of the first stage of group development is **emphasizing similarities** or searching for commonality among members. Developing common ground allows members to establish basic behavioral ground rules and expectations or norms quickly so that further exploration and group involvement may be undertaken. Members are less likely to be rejected if they are perceived to have things in common with other members. Through emphasizing similarities, members manage to avoid rejection and gain initial levels of acceptance into the group. Members make a **commitment** to remain in the group and to work toward goal accomplishment. Ironically, it is only after safety is established through orientation activity and members are able to convince themselves that they will not be rejected that they can afford the luxury of increasing their personal commitment to the group and move ahead as if basic structure and acceptance are unimportant.

Stage 2

The second stage in group development, characterized as the **storming** stage by Tuckman, involves searching for uniqueness and testing to what extent other members, the group leaders, and the group as a unit can accept the individual members with all their unique abilities and limitations, attractiveness and unattractiveness, and so on. The issue becomes, then, "Can I be accepted and belong in this group as the 'real, whole me?'" or "Can the group only accept the restricted identity I presented in order to gain admission in Stage 1?" Major themes of Stage 2 are **emphasizing differences** in order to **establish unique individual identities** and to **norm the disagreement–differentiation process.** For complex group tasks requiring considerable commitment from members, this differentiation of identity is central to the process. Establishing norms for the safe delivery and processing of disconfirmatory feedback and disagreement is essential. Disagreement and emphasis on individual differences lead to the adoption and differentiation of member roles and an individualization of identity. As the power and dominance hierarchy is established and members learn that the expression of negative feelings and disagreement will not result in personal rejection, a feeling of closeness begins to develop in the group. Groups can now disagree and tolerate the tension necessary for maximum self-exploration, change, and growth while still retaining their members and group identity.

Stage 3

As the limits of relationships have been tested and the amount of member-influencing power has been established, members learn that they can disagree and express negative feelings without fear of rejection. During this **norming** stage, closeness begins to develop, and the group increases in **cohesiveness,** a dominant theme of Stage 3 and a criterion for the development of full cooperative teamwork. Intimacy and closeness are important issues. Warm feelings are often expressed, and belonging becomes compatible with individual differences. The degree of intimacy needed for norming depends on the group purpose and setting. Once this sense of commitment to "groupness" has been established and strengthened in Stage 3, the cooperative potential of the group is used to strengthen **collaboration** toward task accomplishment and productivity. Stage 3 involves reinforcing and increasing members' bonding with, attraction to, and identification with other members and the group (cohesiveness) in order to increase the efficiency of **cooperative interactive work** toward individual and group goals (collaboration).

Some experts do not distinguish between Stages 3 and 4, because working toward goal achievement is important in both. Stage 3 work, however, is more important for developing cooperative teamwork than for actual individual or group goals achieved. It is therefore justifiable to consider Stage 3 distinct from Stage 4 and important in its own right.

Stage 4

In Stage 4, the original primary goals of the group become both the overt and underlying focus of the group's activity. Cooperative efforts toward task accomplishment are the major focus of Stage 4; therefore, **performing** is given major emphasis. The type of work depends on the purpose, goals, and mission of the group or organization. **Helping others and contributing to group goals** and **working as a cooperative team** to create high levels of **task accomplishment, goal achievement,** and **collaborative productivity** are the major themes of Stage 4. In counseling and therapy groups, personal exploration; risk taking; catharsis; insight; restructuring of cognitive and affective processes; resolution of problems; learning new psychological, interpersonal, and group skills and behavior; and psychological growth, change, and remediation are all themes appropriate to Stage 4.

Stage 5

Because Stage 4 represents such a high level of group productivity and takes considerable planning, selection, and group effort to achieve, a major goal of some groups is to reach and then maintain high levels of cooperative group productivity; however, other groups, including most counseling and therapy groups, have a finite purpose and should reach conclusion. In the earlier conceptual models reviewed by Tuckman (1965), this concluding aspect of groups was not mentioned or not emphasized by most theorists; however, by the time of the subsequent review by Tuckman and Jensen (1977), the inclusion of a termination stage had gained considerable support. They, therefore, added **adjourning** or **mourning** as a fifth stage in their comprehensive model to complete forming, storming, norming, and performing. Grieving, leaving, and maximizing transfer of learning and accomplishments may be viewed as the major themes of Stage 5. If Stage 5 is addressed and resolved, the group will disband appropriately, and the members will feel good about living productively and independently without the assistance of the group. Of course, these guidelines apply more directly to time-limited, closed groups in which all members begin and end together.

Contributed by Donald E. Ward,
Pittsburg State University,
Pittsburg, KS

References

Tuckman, B. W. (1965). Developmental sequence in small groups. *Psychological Bulletin, 63,* 384–389.

Tuckman, B. W., & Jensen, M. A. C. (1977). Stages of small group development revisited. *Group and Organizational Studies, 2,* 419–427.

Additional Resource

Cohen, A. M., & Smith. (1976). *The critical incident in growth groups: Theory and technique.* La Jolla, CA: University Associates.

■ Group Work Dynamics: Content and Process

Kurt Lewin (1951) defined **group dynamics** as the powerful processes that take place in group. These include the continuous movement and progression of the group and the interacting forces that have an impact on the group and its functioning. Lewin is generally thought to be the prime initiator of group dynamics and emphasized conceptual systems to understand group dynamics. He developed **field theory** and force field analysis to identify the dynamics taking place in the group at any particular time. Field theory is a conceptual system that explains the dynamics observed in groups, and it proposes that there are numerous influences, both attracting and repelling, that continually affect group members and their behavior in the group. Force field analysis identifies the helping and restraining forces acting on the group.

Furthermore, Bion (1961) applied psychoanalytic theory to groups and was particularly instrumental in increasing the attention given to the collectivistic dynamics and away from a more individualistic focus of group member dynamics. He proposed that the group needed to be perceived as a unit that shows mental activity to further the task of the group, mobilize its resources, relate to external realities, and make decisions. The inclusion of the group as a whole is perceived in its totality, in which each of the individual members contributes from a personal perspective, but there is also a collective functioning. Bion proposed three basic assumptions for groups: **dependency,** in which members feel helpless and look to the leader for support; **fight or flight response,** in which the group feels in danger and uses one of these actions as a response; and **pairing,** in which members have hopeful fantasies of being saved and of the group being constructive.

Aspects of group dynamics that have been studied include leadership patterns (Lewin, Lippitt, & White, 1939), group decision-making processes (Marrow, 1957), response patterns and roles (Bales, 1950), sequential stage theory (Moreland & Levine, 1988), basic themes (Bion, 1961), primary issues (Schultz, 1962), norms (Sherif, 1936), interaction of personal and environmental factors (Lewin, 1951), communication and cohesion (Thibaut & Kelly, 1959), power (French, 1956), motives and goals (Zander, 1996), conflict (Deutsch, 1949), interpersonal attraction (Newcomb, 1963), and communication networks (Shaw, 1964). Group dynamics involve both content (structural components) and process (interaction components). These aspects relate to group content and process components discussed in the remainder of this entry.

Group Content

Structural components (i.e., **group content**) refer to norms, developmental stages, roles, leadership factors, and information. **Norms** are the conscious and unconscious standards and expectations for how group members will behave and relate. The norms form the group's culture, and members are included or excluded according to these norms. **Developmental stages** are the phases of growth (i.e., beginning, conflict/transition, cohesion, termination) that groups encounter, and considerable evidence is available that confirms the existence of stages (Brown, 2003b). **Roles** define the expectations for appropriate behavior and ways of relating to others. Roles are used to differentiate one position from another and can be assigned or assumed. **Leadership factors** refer to the attitudes and behaviors that define effective leadership. **Information** relates to topics, issues, tasks, and concerns of group members. Information can be expressed about past, current, and/or future events and situations; can focus on outside-the-group concerns; and is used to provide structure and directions for group discussions.

Group Process

Process components refer to the here and now experiencing in the group that reflects how the group is functioning, the quality of relationships among group members and with the group leader(s), and the expressed and hidden issues and concerns that are of major importance for group members. (Brown, 2003a; Yalom & Leszcz, 2005). Observation and understanding of the group's dynamics reveal the current process for the group, and the identification and understanding of these dynamics allow the group leader to intervene more effectively and to help the group accomplish its tasks. Helpful process components include level of participation, communication patterns, feelings expressed, resistance and defenses, and conflict management by the group.

Level of participation refers to the characteristic extent of the interaction, input, and response for individual members and for the group as a whole. **Communication patterns** include both verbal and nonverbal communication. Verbal communication patterns can demonstrate inclusion or exclusion, deference, location of the perceived power and influence, group norms for expected emotional expression, and comfort or discomfort with what is taking place in the group at a given time. Nonverbal communication is the major and most important part of communication and can be valuable information about what the group and its members are experiencing at a deep level. Behaviors such as voice tone, body positioning, facial expression, body movements or lack of movement, and clusters of gestures all convey deep and important messages about current emotional states. There are characteristic individual member verbal and non-verbal communication patterns, and characteristic group-as-a-whole communication patterns that, observed over time, indicate how members are relating.

Feelings expressed can be an important indicator of overt or hidden issues in the group, as well as indicators for individual members' emotional states, sensitivities, and resistance. Hidden, disguised, and suppressed feelings are important and significant for group members and for the group as a whole. **Resistance** is an indicator of sensitive material that is threatening and, thus, must be defended against, suppressed, or repressed. **Defenses** include denial, deflection, intellectualization, and displacement. **Conflict** can be revealing of the group's fear, need, or wishes, and the most important signal is how the group manages conflict. Common group strategies for conflict management are denial, suppression, ignoring, and working to resolve the conflicts.

Group process is understood through group members' reactions, responses, and feelings, all of which explain the meaning of the behavior of both the groups and the individuals in the group. Also provided through process are clues about the group's underlying concerns, of which they may not be consciously aware. **Process commentary** is a means by which the group leader brings concerns to the group's attention and makes visible how the group is acting to suppress, avoid, ignore, and resist significant issues in the group and how this behavior is affecting the group and its functioning; process commentary also reveals members' shared fears, hopes, wishes, and fantasies. Process commentary is the responsibility of the group leader and is an important intervention when the group becomes mired, the discussion is circular, members appear confused, and some-

thing important for the group and its members is being suppressed or ignored.

Contributed by Nina W. Brown,
Old Dominion University,
Norfolk, VA

References

Bales, R. (1950). *Interaction process analysis*. Reading, MA: Addison-Wesley.

Bion, W. (1961). *Experiences in groups*. New York: Basic Books.

Brown, N. (2003a). Conceptualizing process. *International Journal of Group Psychotherapy, 53,* 225–244.

Brown, N. (2003b). *Psychoeducational groups: Process and practice*. New York: Routledge.

Deutsch, M. (1949). Trust and suspicion. *Journal of Conflict Resolution, 2,* 265–279.

French, J. R. P., Jr. (1956). A formal theory of social power. *Psychological Review, 63,* 181–194.

Lewin, K. (1951). *Field theory in social science*. New York: Harper.

Lewin, K., Lippitt, R., & White, R. (1939). Patterns of aggressive behavior in experimentally created "social climates." *Journal of Social Psychology, 10,* 271–299.

Marrow, A. (1957). *Making management human*. New York: McGraw-Hill.

Moreland, R., & Levine, J. (1988). Group dynamics over time: Development and socialization in small groups. In J. McGrath (Ed.), *The social psychology of time* (pp. 151–181). Newbury Park, CA: Sage.

Newcomb, T. M. (1963). Stabilities underlying changes in interpersonal attraction. *Journal of Abnormal and Social Psychology, 66,* 376–386.

Schultz, W. (1962). *Investment in human beings*. Chicago: University of Chicago Press.

Shaw, M. (1964). Communication networks. *Advances in Experimental Social Psychology, 1,* 111–147.

Sherif, M. (1936). *The psychology of group norms*. New York: Harper.

Thibaut, J., & Kelly, H. (1959). *The social psychology of groups*. New York: Wiley.

Yalom, I., & Leszcz, M. (2005). *The theory and practice of group psychotherapy* (5th ed.). New York: Basic Books.

Zander, A. (1996). *Motives and goals in groups*. New Brunswick, NJ: Transaction.

■ Group Work Evaluation

Effective group work is grounded in its plan for evaluation. The Association for Specialists in Group Work (ASGW; see Association for Specialists in Group Work) offers important best practices guidelines for conducting ethical professional group work (ASGW, 2007). These group work standards are provided for the reader to underscore the link between ethical principles and evaluation practices in group work.

There are three main methods for evaluating the effectiveness of group work: process evaluation, outcome evaluation, and member satisfaction. Each method of evaluation may be conducted through informal or formal means and may be conducted before, during, and after completion of the group. Group work evaluation methods are applicable for each of the four types of groups: task, psychoeducation, counseling, and therapy (ASGW, 2007, Sections A.4, B.7).

Process Evaluation

Group work is multidimensional, having both elements of content (what is said/not said) and process (how the content evolves and who is a part of the evolution). **Process evaluation** focuses on the elements that shape the how and who of group work. Bales (1970) defined group process observation as "who does what to whom in the process of their interaction" (p. 72). The group process elements may include (a) progress of group and member goals, (b) leader behaviors and techniques, (c) group dynamics and interventions, (d) development and evolution of group norms, and (e) emergence of therapeutic factors. Group facilitators may also address fidelity to the group plan or group treatment model through observation of when and how the movement of the group varies from the plan. Using process evaluation in conjunction with fidelity evaluation provides an important link between the actual practice of the group plan and the original model or empirical support for the group plan. As an example, during the process evaluation of a psychoeducational group, it is noted that one of the facilitators frequently uses probes that entail deep interpersonal information and focuses on interventions that are consistent with group therapy process. Addressing the discrepancy may lead to a greater understanding of the differences in the two types of groups, the role of the facilitators, and potential gaps in the psychoeducational model for the population attending the group (ASGW, 2007, Section B.3).

Processing should happen during sessions, before and after each session, at the time of termination, and at post-termination follow-up (ASGW, 2007, Sections C.1, C.2). Process evaluation may be done through self-reflective journaling by the leader(s) and members, active interaction during the group itself, and formal assessment methods (e.g., group process scales and questionnaires).

Outcome Evaluation

Accountability in group work requires assessing whether the member accomplished goals while participating in the group. Typically, group leaders establish a baseline measurement of the group members' behavior and then monitor the degree of change that occurs at various points in the group (e.g., mid-group, every 3 months, at termination/completion of the group, at a prearranged follow-up point). Effective outcome evaluation begins with understanding the purpose or goals of the group (ASGW, 2007, Section C.3).

Goals are related to the needs of members and the core purpose of the type of group. Goals of task groups are often solution based or work-product oriented. Goals of psycho-educational groups include developing skill sets, gaining information, and promoting new competencies. Goals of counseling groups include promoting interpersonal growth,

developing interpersonal communication skills, and enhancing coping. Goals of therapy groups include remediation of existing difficulties (see Bauman & Waldo, 1998, for an in-depth discussion).

Outcome evaluation in group work may be conducted with standardized self-report scales, member interviews, group leader observations, or any combination of these methods. When group leaders plan for objective, group-themed measures taken during pregroup member screenings and at regular intervals during the existence of the group, they are addressing the ethical standard of assessing the benefits that occur from group participation (ASGW, 2007, Sections B.7, C.3). There are numerous multifactorial clinical instruments that may be used for pre- and postgroup evaluation (see Corcoran & Fischer, 2000). One example for use with adults is the Symptom Checklist–90–Revised (Derogatis, 2004). The Child and Adolescent Functional Assessment Scale (Hodges, 1994) is worth consideration for measuring outcomes with children and adolescents, given the focus on functioning. An outcome measure that targets a specific outcome could also be chosen. For example, in a group for survivors of a natural disaster, a life-functioning scale might be chosen as the outcome measure.

Member Satisfaction

The third important construct in evaluating group work entails assessing the general satisfaction of group members. **Member satisfaction** with the group may vary greatly, given the stage of group development; for example, early excitement may give way to natural conflict as the group grows. Satisfaction may also vary, given the status of attendance for the group members. If attending a court-ordered or mandatory treatment group, the member satisfaction rating may be influenced by the circumstances of attendance. Member satisfaction may be assessed during in-group processing, at various points during the group, or at termination of the group. The Session Evaluation Questionnaire (Stiles, Gordon, & Lani, 2002) is one type of instrument for assessing session satisfaction.

Ultimately, comprehensive group work evaluation involves creating a plan that includes all three methods of evaluation. Each method gives group facilitators a part of the picture; yet the adage that the group (whole) is greater that the sum of its members (parts) is also true for evaluation. Creating such an evaluation plan will advance group work practice through understanding of what (process evaluation) works for whom (outcome evaluation and member satisfaction).

Contributed by Debra A. Pender,
Northern Illinois University,
DeKalb, IL

References

Association for Specialists in Group Work. (2007). *Association for Specialists in Group Work best practice guidelines*. Retrieved August 9, 2007, from http://www.asgw.org/PDF/Best_Practices.pdf

Bales, R. (1970). *Personality and interpersonal behavior*. New York: Holt, Rinehart & Winston.

Bauman, S., & Waldo, M. (1998). Improving the goals and process (GAP) matrix for groups: Incorporating feedback from the field. *Journal for Specialists in Group Work, 23,* 215–224.

Corcoran, K., & Fischer, J. (2000). *Measures for clinical practice: A sourcebook.* New York: Free Press.

Derogatis, L. R. (2004). *Symptom Checklist–90–R.* Minneapolis, MN: Pearson Assessments.

Hodges, K. (1994). *Child and Adolescent Functional Assessment Scale.* Ypsilanti: Eastern Michigan University, Department of Psychology.

Stiles, W. B., Gordon, L. E., & Lani, J. A. (2002). Session evaluation and the Session Evaluation Questionnaire. In G. S. Tryon (Ed.), *Counseling based on process research: Applying what we know* (pp. 325–343). Boston: Allyn & Bacon.

Additional Resources

Burlingame, G. M., Fuhriman, A., & Johnson, J. (2004). Process & outcome in group counseling and psychotherapy: A perspective. In J. DeLucia-Waack, D. A. Gerrity, C. R. Kalodner, & M. T. Riva (Eds.), *Handbook of group counseling and psychotherapy* (pp. 49–62). Thousand Oaks, CA: Sage.

Conyne, R. K. (1999). *Failures in group work: How we can learn from our mistakes.* Thousand Oaks, CA: Sage.

DeLucia-Waack, J. L. (1997). Measuring the effectiveness of group work: A review and analysis of process and outcome measures. *Journal for Specialists in Group Work, 22,* 277–293.

DeLucia-Waack, J. L., & Bridbord, K. H. (2004). Measures of group process, dynamics, climate, leadership behaviors, and therapeutic factors: A review. In J. L. DeLucia-Waack, D. A. Gerrity, C. R. Kalodner, & M. T. Riva (Eds.), *Handbook of group counseling and psychotherapy* (pp. 120–135). Thousand Oaks, CA: Sage.

Ogles, B. M., Lambert, M. J., & Fields, S. A. (2002). *Essentials of outcome assessment: Essentials of mental health practice.* New York: Wiley.

▪ Group Work, Key Ethical Issues in

Group work is a powerful and multifaceted counseling specialty and, therefore, requires constant monitoring of ethical decision making. Group workers face ethical situations that are, in some ways, different from problems faced by practitioners of individual psychoeducation, counseling, and therapy. Multiple clients with individual and shared group goals working with one or more skilled leaders produce countless choice points for interaction. Whether the group is a task, psychoeducational, counseling, or therapy group, it is desired that it be led by a professional who has core training in group work and specialty training for the specific type of group gained through formal course work, continuing education, or mentoring.

Many counseling programs provide only core training in group work, whereas employment settings often require the provision of a wide range of groups. Professionals in counseling and related professions must work within their **scope of practice** and adhere to professional codes of conduct such as the 2005 American Counseling Association (ACA) *ACA Code of Ethics,* the 1998 National Board for Certified Counselors *Code of Ethics*, the 2004 American School Counselor Association *Ethical Standards for School Counselors,* and the 2000 American Mental Health Association *Code of Ethics.*

Group practitioners have guidance from three Association for Specialists in Group Work (ASGW) documents: Best Practice Guidelines (revised in 2007); Professional Standards for the Training of Group Workers (2000), and Principles for Diversity-Competent Group Workers (1999). In addition, the American Group Psychotherapy Association's 2007 Practice Guidelines for Group Psychotherapy can be applied to many group practice settings. Active use of these documents can greatly assist the group work professional to identify common potential ethical dilemmas and prepare appropriate responses to them. Because group work is contextual, it is impossible to define thoroughly all ethical decision-making opportunities and challenges; however, excellent moral decision-making models are available in the counseling literature to assist in identifying the moral considerations and sequential steps a counselor can use in practice (Forester-Miller & Davis, 1996; Hansen & Goldberg, 1999)

One of the most significant ethical issues in group work is that **confidentiality** cannot be protected as it can be in individual work. Although group facilitators are required to abide by rules of confidentiality in the same way that counselors working with individuals are required to do so, the presence of a group greatly changes the confidentiality dynamic. Because each of the individual members of a group owns the confidence, out-of-group communication cannot be controlled. Group members must reasonably understand the limits of protection for anything shared in a group setting. Furthermore, cultural norms may influence the understanding of confidentiality. One of the most common examples of this situation is that group members may share their own group experience with others, thereby disclosing information about the contents of the group (e.g., a depression group) and perhaps about other members of the group and their personal information. Members may encounter each other in social situations and introduce each other with reference to participation in a counseling group. Each of these examples demonstrates the unintended consequences of members breaking confidentiality.

Informed consent is also critical in group work. Treatment settings (e.g., employment settings) often require individuals to participate in a group, and treatment progress may be documented on levels of participation. Group facilitators must balance codes of ethics and employment-setting or treatment-setting requirements in making assignments to groups in such settings. When group leaders provide members with information about participation requirements and consequences, information in advance about the general group plan, and information about how they will plan for each group session, the potential for ethical lapses can be reduced.

Group member screening is intended to help both the group facilitator and potential group member determine whether the group is an appropriate match for the client. Providing advance organization through member preparation increases the potential for productive participation by the group member. Discussion of the role of the member in an anxiety group, for example, may assist in preparing the member to talk about the fears.

As communities continue to become more multicultural and complex, increased attention to **diversity** has become central to the practice of counseling and is a key ethical consideration in the practice of group work. In group work, multiple levels of diversity are always in play, not only cultural, sexual, lifestyle, gender, age, and religious as might naturally be expected, but also more subtle forms of diversity, for example, style of language, cultural or geographical idioms, multiple perceptions of shared events in the group, and perceptions of homogeneous or heterogeneous formation of groups. Respect of diversity has become more concrete in recent years and is reflected in the latest revisions of the *ACA Code of Ethics* (ACA, 2005) and the ASGW Best Practice Guidelines (ASGW, 2007).

Moral principles that guide all mental health work are particularly important when applied to group work (see Ethical Principles). Each of the professional association documents mentioned earlier includes the assumption of moral action in several areas, including beneficence (doing good for others), nonmaleficence (doing no harm), and autonomy. In the practice of group work, the contexts for ethical decision making greatly influence ethical choice points. For example, in consideration of nonmaleficence, the group leader has to protect group members from intentional harm by activities of the group or responses of other group members. Furthermore, the group facilitator must consider refraining from actions that would risk harm. For example, group pressure may influence members to disclose at an uncomfortable level (group pressure) or push people to actions that may not be appropriate (group think). The skilled facilitator will acknowledge the autonomy of individual members to elect their levels of participation while educating about a range of participation styles.

Contributed by Lynn S. Rapin,
Cincinnati, OH

References

American Counseling Association. (2005). *ACA code of ethics*. Alexandria, VA: Author.

American Group Psychotherapy Association. (2007). *Practice guidelines for group psychotherapy*. New York: Author.

American Mental Health Counselors Association. (2000). *Code of ethics*. Alexandria, VA: Author.

American School Counselor Association. (2004). *Ethical standards for school counselors*. Alexandria, VA: Author.

Association for Specialists in Group Work. (1999). *Principles for diversity-competent group workers*. Alexandria, VA: Author.

Association for Specialists in Group Work. (2000). *Professional standards for the training of group workers*. Alexandria, VA: Author.

Association for Specialists in Group Work. (2007). *Best practice guidelines*. Alexandria, VA: Author.

Forester-Miller, H., & Davis, T. (1996). *A practitioner's guide to ethical decision making*. Alexandria, VA: American Counseling Association.

Hansen, N. D., & Goldberg, S. G. (1999). Navigating the nuances: A matrix of considerations for ethical-legal dilemmas. *Professional Psychology: Research and Practice, 30,* 495–503.

National Board for Certified Counselors. (1998). *Code of ethics*. Greensboro, NC: Author.

Additional Resources

Association for Specialists in Group Work Web site: http://www.asgw.org

Rapin, L. S. (2004). Guidelines for ethical and legal practice in counseling and psychotherapy groups. In J. DeLucia-Waack, D. Gerrity, C. Kalodner, & M. Riva (Eds.), *Handbook of group counseling and psychotherapy* (pp. 151–165). Thousand Oaks, CA: Sage.

Group Work, Key Historical Events in

Corsini (1957) divided the history of group work into three eras: (a) origins (before 1899), (b) pioneer (1900–1930), and (c) modern (after 1930). The true origins of group work can be traced back to antiquity, that is, whenever three or more people met for a common conscious purpose. Plato's Academy, where students of Socrates gathered to improve their enlightenment, is one such example.

Group work also took root when famous people, whose practice was not primarily in the area of group, drew attention to group work or lauded the idea. Sigmund Freud and Alfred Adler each praised the concept of working with groups of clients, but they never practiced group therapy. **Jacob Moreno,** creator of **psychodrama,** proclaimed group work as the third most important revolution in the history of psychiatry; the first two were viewing the mentally ill as sick rather than as possessed by demons and Freud's extending help to neurotics as well as psychotics.

Early pioneers of group work included Joseph Pratt, Jane Addams, and Jesse Davis. **Joseph Pratt** worked with patients recovering from tuberculosis (TB) in Boston at a time when TB sanitariums isolated patients with this infectious disease. Patients quarantined in sanitariums for 6 months to a year became discouraged and depressed. Pratt was among the first to write about his experiences working in groups, noting that not only was the method time effective but patients also provided emotional support to each other. **Jane Addams** organized immigrants at Hull House in Chicago. Those groups engaged in reading, crafts, and social activities for the purpose of learning more about social skills, hygiene, and nutrition. Addams's groups emphasized common needs and goals of members and rallied the support system to help members identify with a larger social community. **Jesse**

Davis, who was principal of Grand Rapids High School in Michigan, directed that every student experience one class each week on vocational guidance, using groups to teach career exploration, social skills, and values.

The formation of professional societies helped establish group work as a legitimate specialty. In 1941, Moreno named his organization the **American Society of Group Psychotherapy and Psychodrama.** Then, in 1943, **Samuel Slavson** founded the **American Group Psychotherapy Association.** Both organizations published journals, thereby providing group work with a research base.

Corsini (1957) tracked all journal articles published in the United States containing the word *group* in the title and noticed a tremendous growth after World War II. He attributed this growth to the high number of veterans suffering from posttraumatic stress (then called "battle fatigue") and a shortage of professionals trained to help them. Leaders not only found group methods time effective, but they also noticed the positive effects of peers who had experienced the reality of combat.

In 1946, **Kurt Lewin,** a social and Gestalt psychologist at the Massachusetts Institute of Technology, conducted experiments to investigate human communication and interaction. To escape the summer heat of Boston, he moved his operation to Bethel, Maine, where he was able to rent space in a school closed for the summer. He met with his graduate student assistants each evening to discuss the day's experiments on communication. It soon became apparent that distinct communication patterns existed both in the experiments and in the roundtable evening discussions. Lewin founded the **National Training Laboratory** (now the **NTL Institute**) dedicated to understanding and investigating group dynamics, interpersonal behavior, and intergroup conflict. Group leadership training for both sensitivity training and organizational task group leadership continues at the NTL Institute in 2008.

At about the same time, the **Tavistock Institute of Human Relations** was founded in London, England, with a grant from the Rockefeller Foundation. Originally called the Tavistock Group because the founders had met at London's Tavistock Clinic, this talented assortment of psychiatrists, psychologists, and anthropologists worked with groups of British Army veterans. Primarily influenced by Sigmund Freud and his followers, many other well-known therapists (e.g., Wilfred Bion, John Bowlby, Melanie Klein, Carl Jung, R. D. Laing) have participated at Tavistock over the years. After World War II, the Tavistock Clinic was incorporated into the newly established British National Health Service, and the Tavistock Institute became a charitable foundation offering training in organizational consultation. Founding members of Tavistock influenced world affairs; for example, Ronald Hargreaves became deputy director of the World Health Organization and Brigadier General John Rawlings Rees became the first president of the World Federation for Mental Health.

Another postwar influence on group work was the contributions of **W. Edwards Deming,** who pioneered **total quality management** in Japanese industrial settings. These organizational task groups focused on quality control in manufacturing, on customer satisfaction, and on participatory management. Some suggested these methods contributed to Toyota overtaking General Motors as the largest producer of automobiles.

In the 1960s, group practice became so popular that *The New York Times* designated 1968 as "the year of the group" (Gladding, 2003). That decade's **human potential movement** proposed that the well-being of individuals took precedence over the desires of institutions and attempted to increase public awareness and foster social change. Examples of social activism in the 1960s included mounting protest over racial inequality, growth of the women's movement, demonstrations against U.S. involvement in Vietnam, and the hippie movement.

Carl Rogers found himself using his person-centered counseling more and more often in group rather than in individual settings. By the mid-1960s, Rogers decided to work exclusively in groups. He called these "basic encounter groups" (Rogers, 1970) and later shortened the title to **encounter groups.** He established a training center near his home in La Jolla, California. Encounter groups quickly grew in popularity.

Fritz Perls conducted numerous Gestalt therapy leadership training workshops at the **Esalen Institute** in Big Sur, California. **William Shutz** also offered encounter group training workshops at Esalen. Shutz introduced a theory of interpersonal relations in which a group member's needs for inclusion, control, and affection explained his or her interactions. The Fundamental Interpersonal Relations Orientation-Behavior was the instrument he created to measure those dimensions, and the test was frequently used during group work.

The 1970s were marked by the growth of group research and the realization among practitioners that improvement of practice was an ethical responsibility. **Irvin Yalom** (1975) described **curative factors** found in group methods (e.g., cohesion, catharsis, self-understanding, interpersonal learning, installation of hope). **Lieberman, Yalom, and Miles** (1973) conducted research to identify helpful **leader characteristics.** This work provided conceptual entry points for research on groups by using systematic and insightful observations of real clients.

George Gazda was the first president of two new professional organizations devoted to group work. In 1973, the **Association for Specialists in Group Work (ASGW)** was founded as a division of the American Counseling Association. In 1991 the American Psychological Association (APA) added **Division 49—Group Psychology and Group Psychotherapy**—to its fold. APA Division 49 began publishing its journal, **Group Dynamics,** in 1997. The **Journal for Specialists in Group Work** has been in continuous publication since 1975.

Professional associations help to guide and shape the field. For example, in 1990, the ASGW published **professional training standards** that distinguished between core group competencies and the four group specialty areas of group counseling, group therapy, group guidance, and organizational groups. ASGW also guided practitioners through ethical dilemmas with their *Professional Standards for Group Counseling* (1983), now called *ASGW Best Practices Guidelines*. One example of how the *ASGW Best Practice Guidelines* (1998) address group-specific ethical dilemmas are guidelines for addressing confidentiality among group members. ASGW (1999) was the first organization to establish **diversity competencies for group leaders.** Professional associations such as ASGW, American Group Psychotherapy Association, and Division 49 provide common ground for both practitioners and researchers to improve the field of group work.

Contributed by George R. Leddick,
Association for Specialists in Group
Work, Commerce, TX

References

Association for Specialists in Group Work. (1983). *ASGW professional standards for group counseling*. Alexandria, VA: Author.

Association for Specialists in Group Work. (1990). *Professional standards for the training of group workers*. Alexandria, VA: Author.

Association for Specialists in Group Work. (1998). Guidelines for best practice. *Journal for Specialists in Group Work, 23,* 237–244.

Association for Specialists in Group Work. (1999). ASGW principles for diversity-competent group workers. *Journal for Specialists in Group Work, 24,* 7–14.

Corsini, R. J. (1957). *Methods of group psychotherapy*. New York: McGraw-Hill.

Gladding, S. T. (2003). *Group work: A counseling specialty* (4th ed.). Upper Saddle River, NJ: Pearson Education.

Lieberman, M. A., Yalom, I. D., & Miles, M. B. (1973). *Encounter groups: First facts*. New York: Basic Books.

Rogers, C. R. (1970). *Carl Rogers on encounter groups*. New York: Harper & Row.

Yalom, I. D. (1975). *The theory and practice of group psychotherapy* (2nd ed.). New York: Basic Books.

Additional Resources

Bednar, R. L., & Kaul, T. J. (1994). Experiential group research: Can the cannon fire? In A. E. Bergin & S. L. Garfield (Eds.), *Handbook of psychotherapy and behavior change* (4th ed., pp. 631–663). New York: Wiley.

Gladding, S. T. (2007). *Groups: A counseling specialty* (5th ed.). Upper Saddle River, NJ: Pearson Education.

Group Work, Key Legal Issues in

Specific laws and statutory rules that influence or regulate the practice of group work vary across jurisdictions. It is incumbent on professional counselors to investigate the local, state, and federal statutes that regulate their licenses and practice accordingly. Most states include group work in the definitions common to all forms of counseling practice. In addition, the legal practice of group work may be defined by the ethical standards of professional associations. For example, the licensure boards of 19 states as of 2007 have adopted the American Counseling Association's (ACA; 2005) *ACA Code of Ethics* in some form to define legislated practice. The Commonwealth of Massachusetts's Board of Allied Mental Health and Human Services Professions identifies the *ACA Code of Ethics* as its official guide to determine standards of conduct, except where they contradict specific codes or laws. The State of Ohio's administrative code describing ethical practice and professional conduct for counselors cites the *ACA Code of Ethics* "as an aid in resolving ambiguities which may arise in the interpretation of the rules of professional ethics and conduct" (Cluse-Tolar et al., 2008, p. 24); therefore, specific ethical guidelines that apply to group work may be considered equivalent to legal mandate in some states. For professional counselors leading groups, these include (but would not be limited to) ACA code A.8.a. on ethical screening of group work members; A.8.b. protecting clients in a group work setting, and B.4.a. addressing the limits of confidentiality (ACA, 2005). Counselors should scrutinize the laws and regulations for the state(s) in which they are licensed to identify any legal guidelines specifically defining the practice of group work as well as associated professional standards, such as ethics, used to guide or define legal expectations for group practice. As already mentioned, all legal standards for counseling practice that are addressed by law extend to the activities conducted in groups; however, there are several specific legal concerns that are particularly relevant to the practice of group work.

Limits of Confidentiality and Informed Consent

Individual state statutes and/or rules usually govern the extent and limits of **confidentiality** on the part of the counselor and the client's right to **privileged communications** in the context of a judicial or administrative setting. Although the privilege belongs to the client, it is the counselor's responsibility to uphold the privilege by maintaining confidentiality (Wheeler & Bertram, 2008). To meet legal and ethical guidelines, counselors must explain the extent and limits of the group members' privilege as well as the legal limitations counselors have for maintaining confidentiality in a group setting prior to consenting to group membership in psychoeducational, counseling, or therapeutic groups. Corey (2008) suggested that, depending on the laws of the particular state, the legal privilege of confidentiality may not even apply to clients receiving treatment in a group setting. It is critical for group leaders to alert group members that even though they will be disclosing information to a professional ethically and legally bound to maintain confidentiality, other group members will be hearing the same information and may have no such responsibility or mandate and for which there is no legally defined expectation of privilege. An exception to the expectations for group members can be found in the District of Columbia's Official Code (2001), which requires that mental health professionals provide group members with a written statement that prohibits unauthorized disclosure of information obtained in a group setting and the consequential civil liability of any person who violates that code. Most individuals in a group, however, have no legal or ethical duty to keep confidential information that is shared in a group. Group members need to be made aware that group counselors are not able to guarantee confidentiality on the part of others.

The limits of confidentiality and client privilege in group work are especially important when working in groups with children, adolescents, or impaired adults who are not capable of understanding the concepts of confidentiality and whose privilege may be restricted or assigned by law. This latter limitation as it applies to children is addressed by the Ethical Standards for School Counselors (American School Counselor Association, 2004) in which the professional school counselor is advised in Standard A.6.c. to clearly state "that confidentiality in group counseling cannot be guaranteed. Given the developmental and chronological ages of minors in schools, the counselor recognizes the tenuous nature of confidentiality for minors renders some topics inappropriate for group work in a school setting" (p. 3).

Potential group members also need to know that if a court orders the release of records for group sessions, such as group progress notes, the documentation might reveal information that could be damaging to the other group members who may have no connection to the litigation. Again, the limits of an individual's privilege will vary from state to state, and group members should be informed in advance of the limitations of the protection afforded by their state's statutes or administrative codes. Group workers should obtain signed informed consent from potential group members as part of the pregroup screening process. Counselors should also remind group members of the limits of protection throughout the course of the group and especially when a member appears about to disclose information that might be potentially damaging if revealed outside the group.

Practicing Beyond the Scope of Training as a Group Worker

There are legal consequences for counselors performing any treatment that, by the prevailing standards of the mental health professions in the community, would constitute failure to meet the minimum criterion of performance when measured against generally prevailing peer performance. "Should the counselor fail to bring to that relationship the skill and care of a qualified group counselor practicing within the expert discipline of the profession, the counselor may be liable for breach of professional duty to clients" (Wheeler & Bertram, 2008, p. 44). The scope of practice for group workers is restricted to the specific methods, techniques, or modalities for which the counselor has received appropriate training and can justify competence. Most state statutes specifically name the practice of group work as one of several modalities regulated by scope of practice regulations. The Association for Specialists in Group Work (ASGW) has published *Best Practice Guidelines* (1998) and *Professional Standards for the Training of Group Workers* (2000) that define the scope of practice for the profession of group work. In the event of criminal or civil action against a group leader for practice concerns, it is likely that the plaintiff or the judicial

body will consider published ethics codes (such as the *ACA Code of Ethics*) or practice standards (such as the ASGW documents mentioned) in the case of group work practice.

Protecting Group Members From Harm

Group dynamics can be very powerful and helpful forces; however, group processes such as scapegoating, coercion, excessive hostility, or misdirected personal attacks on the part of the leader or by group members who are permitted to participate in such behaviors unsanctioned by the leader can be emotionally damaging to a vulnerable group member. Most governance bodies, such as state licensure or certification boards, have laws or rules that mandate counselors take appropriate action to protect their clients from harm. Corey (2008) stated,

> Group leaders are expected to practice within the code of ethics for the particular profession and abide by legal standards. . . . If group members can prove that personal injury or psychological harm was caused by a leader's failure to render proper service, either through negligence or ignorance, the leader is open to a malpractice suit. (p. 64)

Group counselors are responsible for facilitating groups in a manner that does not harm group members. Section A.8. of the *ACA Code of Ethics* (ACA, 2005) specifies that

> Screening: Counselors screen prospective group counseling/therapy participants. To the extent possible, counselors select members whose needs and goals are compatible with goals of the group, who will not impede the group process, and whose well-being will not be jeopardized by the group experience; [and] b. Protecting Clients: In a group setting, counselors take reasonable precautions to protect clients from physical, emotional, or psychological trauma. (p. 5)

Again, because some states have adopted the *Code of Ethics* to define or clarify their standards for practice, counselors should be knowledgeable of professional ethics as well as specific laws. Professional counselors who fail to fulfill their legal duty of protecting clients against harm may be found guilty of wrongful injury in the event of a civil suit for negligence or malpractice if a group member can establish that the procedures used in the group were not within the realm of acceptable practice standards or scope of training and/or experience of the group practitioner.

Other Legal Mandates Relevant to Group Workers

The practice of group work obligates counselors to all other obligations established by statutes and/or rules governing their license.

> The counselor's duty to each member of a group is the same as in individual counseling sessions: Professional services must be rendered according to the rec-

ognized standard of care expected of a competent counselor. Should the counselor fail to bring to that relationship the skill and care of a qualified group worker practicing within the expert discipline of the profession, the counselor may be liable for breach of professional duty to clients. (Wheeler & Bertram, 2008, p. 44)

Infractions such as contributing to the delinquency of a minor, failing to inform parents of information to which they are legally entitled, being an accessory to a crime, filing a false report or record, withholding records, committing an act of sexual misconduct, fraudulently billing for services, or practicing while impaired are justification for legal action against group leaders. Group practitioners are responsible for professional performance as mandated by the licensure laws of their state. Group counselors who fail to fulfill these requirements may be found guilty of criminal behavior, misdemeanors, or felonies; may have their licenses sanctioned or revoked; and may be civilly liable for monetary damages or fines.

Generally accepted best practice standards, ethical codes, and the intention of legislative statute and rules written by licensing boards may all be considered during court proceedings or hearings before administrative bodies when judging the actions of a group counselor and in determining client harm in the case of any of the situations described. For this reason, group counselors should know the legal guidelines that govern their license and practice accordingly in the context of group work.

Contributed by Alicia M. Homrich,
Rollins College, Winter Park, FL

References

American Counseling Association. (2005). *ACA code of ethics*. Alexandria, VA: Author.

American School Counselor Association. (2004). *Ethical standards for school counselors*. Alexandria, VA: Author.

Association for Specialists in Group Work. (1998). Best practice guidelines. *Journal for Specialists in Group Work, 23,* 237–244.

Association for Specialists in Group Work. (2000). Professional standards for the training of group workers. *Journal for Specialists in Group Work, 25,* 327–342.

Cluse-Tolar, T., Barson, L, Camerino., J., Cohen, R., Holubec, O., Kress, V. W., et al. (2008). *Ohio Counselor, Social Worker, & Marriage and Family Therapist Board laws & rules.* Retrieved August 20, 2008, from http://cswmft.ohio.gov/pdfs/4757.pdf

Corey, G. (2008). *Theory and practice of group counseling.* Belmont, CA: Thomson Brooks/Cole.

District of Columbia Official Code, Division 1, Title 7, Subtitle C. Chapter 12, Subchapter VI. § 7-1206.03. Notice requirement—Clients in group sessions. (2001).

Wheeler, A. M., & Bertram, B. (2008). *The counselor and the law.* Alexandria, VA: American Counseling Association.

Additional Resources

American Psychological Association publishes a series of individual books titled *The Law and Mental Health Professionals* for 29 states as a resource for both mental health professionals and attorneys addressing areas pertinent to mental health law. See http://books.apa.org/subpages/mental.cfm

Fischer, L., & Sorenson, G. P. (1995). *School law for counselors, psychologists, and social workers* (3rd ed.). White Plains, NY: Longman.

Gazda, G. M., Ginter, E. J., & Horne, A. M. (2001). *Group counseling and group psychotherapy: Theory and application.* Boston: Allyn & Bacon.

National Board for Certified Counselors (http://www.nbcc.org/stateboardmap) offers links to all state licensing board Web sites where the major laws and rules governing the practice of counseling can be found for individual states.

Stone, C. B. (2005). *School counseling principles: Ethics and law.* Alexandria, VA: American School Counseling Association.

■ Group Work, Key Organizations in

The field of group work is supported by several professional organizations that promote the training, development, and practice of group work. Specific organizations include the Association for Specialists in Group Work, American Group Psychotherapy Association, American Society of Group Psychotherapy and Psychodrama, National Training Laboratory, Tavistock Institute of Human Relations, and Esalen Institute. Membership in these organizations provides a network of individuals who are dedicated to the organization's mission, professional growth via leadership and mentorship opportunities, and representation ranging from the local to national/international levels.

Association for the Specialists in Group Work

The **Association for the Specialists in Group Work (ASGW),** a division of the American Counseling Association (ACA), was established to promote quality group work training, group practice, and research in order to elevate the foundation of basic counseling skills to a level of sophistication in the interpretation of group process phenomena, effective facilitation within various types of groups, and the intricate interaction between group members. ASGW has established guidelines for best practices in group work, principles for diversity competence in group work, and training standards for core group work skills and group work specializations. Group counselors and students are welcome to join ASGW. The benefits of membership in ASGW include networking at the state, regional, and national levels with other professionals involved in group counseling; opportunities to attend annual conferences and workshops; and a subscription to the *Journal for Specialists in Group Work* and the ASGW *Together* newsletter (see Association for Specialists in Group Work).

American Group Psychotherapy Association

The **American Group Psychotherapy Association (AGPA)** is an interdisciplinary association dedicated to standards of enhancing practice, theory, and research of group psychotherapy for mental health care professionals in the fields of psychiatry, psychology, counseling, social work, psychiatric nursing, marriage and family therapy, pastoral counseling, creative arts therapy, and substance abuse counseling. Group psychotherapy provides a form of therapy that helps individuals with mental or emotional disorders to learn about themselves and their disorders and to make significant changes to improve the quality of their lives.

The leadership of group practice and the growth of both AGPA and ASGW have been furthered through the collaboration of elected officers and members. In addition to the emphasis on training and promotion of group practice, both AGPS and ASGW provide counselors and students opportunities for certification as a group practitioner. Certification conveys that the group practitioner has met the national standards of practice, has professional accountability, and continues excellence in professionalism through continuing education.

American Society of Group Psychotherapy and Psychodrama

The **American Society of Group Psychotherapy and Psychodrama (ASGPP)** was founded by J. L. Moreno, a pioneer of role theory. ASGPP is an organization dedicated to professional standards of training, practice, research, and ongoing developments in group psychotherapy, psychodrama, and sociometry at national and international levels. ASGPP is an approved continuing education provider for the National Association of Alcohol and Drug Abuse Counselors, National Board for Certified Counselors, and the National Registry of Group Psychotherapists. Available to professionals and students, membership in ASGPP includes the benefits of receiving the *Journal of Group Psychotherapy, Psychodrama, and Sociometry* as well as The Psychodrama Network News and opportunities to attend an annual conference, regional meetings, and training programs.

National Training Laboratory

Based on the work of Kurt Lewin in social psychology, the **National Training Laboratory (NTL)** promotes organizational leadership and proactive change via team building, learning labs, and consulting services using principles of applied behavioral sciences to resolve complex business problems in the workplace. These principles strengthen the relationships of individuals working together as a group through open group dialogue and acceptance of the diversity and self-efficacy of all members. In addition, NTL offers certificate programs in Appreciated Inquiry, Diversity Leadership, and Organization Development that are targeted to the mid-senior-level professional. Last, through a partnership with the American University School of Public Affairs, NTL offers a 2-year master's-degree program in organizational development. This weekend program is designed for individuals who are interested in organizational consulting and training.

Tavistock Institute of Human Relations

The mission of the **Tavistock Institute of Human Relations** is to promote human well-being and development by advancing the theory, methodology, and evaluation of change within group, communities, and organizations. From multidisciplinary and social/organizational perspectives, the Tavistock Institute provides services for consultation, research, and organizational development based on an applied evaluation orientation. The Tavistock Institute promotes the training of group dynamics through workshops, such as leadership coaching for business and management practices and innovative delivery of public services while supporting the emotional well-being of personnel. In addition, Tavistock also provides collaborative evaluations of an agency's procedures, including recommendations for achieving a more desired outcome.

Tavistock is a registered charity and a not-for-profit organization funded through research grants and contracts for research projects, consultancy, training, and publishing. The Tavistock Institute has an interdisciplinary staff with expertise in applied research and evaluation, consultation, group relations training, organization and change, and coaching certification. Tavistock produces the international social sciences journal, *Human Relations,* and is involved in the editorial works of *Evaluation—The International Journal of Theory, Research and Practice.*

Esalen Institute

Founded by Michael Murphy and Richard Price, the **Esalen Institute** is a center for humanistic alternative multidisciplinary education that fosters personal and social transformation aimed at the exploration and enrichment of the human potential through experiential/didactic workshops, think-tank forums, and restorative retreats. On the Big Sur coastline in California, Esalen welcomes Western and Eastern philosophers, artists, writers, philanthropists, and those who seek healing for themselves as individuals and as agents for society. Esalen offers intensive monthly work study programs of growth groups, including Gestalt, meditation, creative arts, massage, relationships, and somatics work. These growth groups focus on awareness, reverence, balance, and healing while simultaneously facilitating harmonious individual and community development. Esalen is approved by the California Board of Behavioral Science to be a provider of continuing education credit to marriage and family therapists and licensed clinical social workers.

Contributed by Sandra K. Terneus,
Tennessee Tech University,
Cookeville, TN

Additional Resources

Association for Specialists in Group Work Web site: http://www.asgw.org

American Group Psychotherapy Association Web site: http://www.agpa.org

Society of Group and Psychotherapy and Psychodrama Web site: http://www.asgpp.org
National Training Laboratory Web site: http://www.ntl.org
Tavistock Institute Web site: http://www.tavinstitute.org
Esalen Institute Web site: http://www.esalen.org

■ Group Work, Key People in

Group work has advanced through the contributions of countless individuals. The individuals recognized in this entry represent a partial and alphabetized listing of people who laid the foundation and devoted their careers to the advancement of group work. Numerous other practitioners and scholars have made important contributions to research and best practices in group work but are not acknowledged due to space limitations.

- **Alfred Adler** (1870–1937) wrote extensively on the social nature of people and began conducting "collective counseling" in 1922, when he counseled in a group format (Gladding, 2003). Specific attention was given to the relationship between children's presenting problems and their family history. Adler's belief in the social needs of individuals made group work an especially appropriate format (Horne & Rosenthal, 1997).
- **Richard D. Allen** was the first to use the term *group counseling* (about 1931), a term he applied to what we now refer to as group guidance (Gazda, Horne & Ginter, 2001; Gladding, 2003).
- **Dwight Arnold** formed and led the American Personnel and Guidance Association (now the American Counseling Association) interest group for group counseling in 1966, which later became the Association for Specialists in Group Work (ASGW).
- **Wilfred Bion** (1897–1979) was a member of the Tavistock Institute. Bion focused on group dynamics and believed that processes within groups differed from those of families (Gladding, 2003). Specifically, he focused on the individual and his or her relation/attraction to the group culture.
- **Gary Burlingame,** a professor at Brigham Young University, has focused on the outcomes of groups, group treatment models for various client populations, and group interventions following disasters and how change occurs during group.
- **Robert Conyne** is professor emeritus of counseling, University of Cincinnati, and an ASGW Fellow, past editor of *Journal for Specialists in Group Work* (1979–1985), past ASGW president (1995–1996), and recipient of the ASGW Eminent Career Award. A strong proponent of expanding the concept of group work, he chaired the ASGW Professional Training Standards Committee when the concept of group work types was created. Writings include more than 250 works on group work, prevention, and ecological approaches to group work.
- **Gerald Corey** is professor of human services and counseling at California State University at Fullerton. Corey has written extensively on group work and emphasized the need for group leaders to both attend

therapeutic groups as a participant and be trained in groups for leaders. He is an ASGW Fellow.
- **Donald Dinkmeyer** applied Adlerian concepts to group interventions with specific populations and developed the Systematic Training for Effective Parenting group intervention. He is a recipient of the ASGW Eminent Career Award.
- **Helen Driver** wrote *Counseling and Learning Through Small-Group Discussion* (1958), a significant text in the field of group work.
- **Jack A. Duncan,** of Virginia Commonwealth University, cofounded ASGW in 1973 (with G. Gazda and K. Geoffroy) and was an ASGW president (1975–1976) and ASGW Fellow. Duncan coauthored a group counseling for children textbook and chaired one of the early national group counseling conferences at the College of William and Mary.
- **Addie Fuhriman**, professor emeritus of Brigham Young University, is an influential researcher in the areas of process and outcome variables in groups, comparisons of individual and group counseling, and characteristics of group treatment.
- **George M. Gazda,** research professor emeritus at The University of Georgia, cofounded ASGW in 1973 (with J. Duncan and K. Geoffroy) and was its first president (1973–1975) and first Fellow. He has authored, coauthored, edited, and coedited 16 books and 10 revisions, most of which are on group counseling and psychotherapy, and more than 100 journal articles and monographs. He has made over 500 professional presentations at local, national, and international meetings.
- **Kevin Geoffroy** cofounded ASGW in 1973 (with J. Duncan and G. Gazda).
- **Samuel Gladding** is a professor at Wake Forest University and author of *Group Work: A Counseling Specialty* (2003), now in its fourth edition. He is a past president of ASGW (1993–1994), an ASGW Fellow, and recipient of the ASGW Eminent Career Award.
- **Arthur M. Horne** is a distinguished research professor emeritus at The University of Georgia. He is an ASGW Fellow, past editor of *Journal for Specialists in Group Work* (1992–1995), ASGW past president (1999–2000), and recipient of the ASGW Eminent Career Award. His research and emphasis within group counseling include training, systematic models of group counseling and applications, and group effectiveness.
- **Diana Hulse-Killacky** is a professor at Fairfield University who has advocated for models emphasizing group work competencies across the counselor education curriculum. She developed the Corrective Feedback Instrument–Revised, which is used in establishing group norms. She is past president of ASGW (1988–1989), an ASGW Fellow, and recipient of the ASGW Eminent Career Award.
- **Dennis Kivlighan** is a professor at the University of Maryland, College Park. His research includes process and outcomes in group, counselor factors in relation to group, and group climate.

- **Walter Lifton** suggested 14 therapeutic forces in relation to group counseling (Capuzzi, Gross, & Stauffer, 2006). Lifton is past president of ASGW (1980–1981), an ASGW Fellow, and recipient of the ASGW Eminent Career Award.
- **Clarence Mahler** made extensive contributions to group dynamics and group counseling in school settings (Gazda et al., 2001).
- **Merle Ohlsen** is professor emeritus at the University of Illinois and Holmstedt Distinguished Professor at Indiana State University. One of the original group work specialists who was instrumental in helping to initiate ASGW (Horne, 1987), Ohlsen was president of ASGW (1997–1978) and is an ASGW Fellow.
- **Zipora Schechtman** of the University of Haifa, in Haifa, Israel, was a major contributor to research procedures for group work with children.
- **Rex Stockton,** Chancellor's Professor at Indiana University, is a past president of ASGW (1982–1983), an ASGW Fellow, and recipient of the ASGW Eminent Career Award. Stockton's group work and research focuses on group leadership, clients' experiences of group, interpersonal feedback exchange, and therapeutic factors within group.
- **James Trotzer** is one of the leaders in the formation of institutes for training in group counseling. He developed a problem-solving group model and was president of ASGW (2004–2005) and is an ASGW Fellow.
- **John Vriend** examined group counseling process interventions and effective group leadership skills. He was president of ASGW (1978–1979) and is an ASGW Fellow and recipient of the ASGW Eminent Career Award.
- **Irvin Yalom** formulated the 11 curative factors in group therapy and wrote one of the most widely used texts on group therapy, *The Theory and Practice of Group Counseling and Psychotherapy* (2005), now in its fifth edition.
- **David G. Zimpfer** explored trends in the status and history of group counseling, group counseling outcome evaluation, life-skills focus in groups, and solution-focused theory in groups (Capuzzi et al., 2006). He is an ASGW Fellow and recipient of the ASGW Eminent Career Award.

Contributed by Jeanmarie Keim and
Daniel L. Stroud, University of
New Mexico, Albuquerque, NM

References

Capuzzi, D., Gross, D., & Stauffer, M. D. (2006). *Introduction to group work*. Denver, CO: Love.

Driver, H. (1958). *Counseling and learning through small-group discussion*. Madison, WI: Monona.

Gazda, G. M., Horne, A., & Ginter, E. (2001). *Group counseling and group psychotherapy: Theory and application*. Needham Heights, MA: Allyn & Bacon.

Gladding, S. T. (2003). *Group work: A counseling specialty* (4th ed.). Upper Saddle River, NJ: Prentice Hall.

Horne, A. M. (1987). The leadership of Merle Ohlsen. *Journal of Counseling & Development, 65,* 525–531.

Horne, A., & Rosenthal, R. (1997). Research in group work: How did we get where we are? *Journal for Specialists in Group Work, 22,* 228–240.

Yalom, I. (2005). *The theory and practice of group counseling and psychotherapy.* New York: Basic Books.

Group Work, Multicultural and Diversity Competence in

Cultural competency guidelines geared specifically for group workers are provided in the *Principles for Diversity-Competent Group Workers* endorsed by the **Association for Specialists in Group Work (ASGW;** 1999). This document, which is based on the seminal work of Sue, Arredondo, and McDavis (1992) and the subsequent operationalizing of the multicultural competencies by the **Association for Multicultural Counseling and Development (AMCD;** 1996; see Association for Multicultural Counseling and Development), takes a broader focus on diversity and includes race, ethnic and cultural heritage, gender, socioeconomic status, sexual orientation, abilities, religious and spiritual beliefs, and all other apparent or unapparent differences within a group setting.

The competencies address three characteristics: (a) group worker's awareness of self, (b) group worker's awareness of group members' worldviews, and (c) diversity-appropriate intervention strategies. Each of these characteristics is further discussed in relationship to three domains: (a) attitudes and beliefs, (b) knowledge, and (c) skills.

Group Worker's Awareness of Self

Diversity-competent group workers need to understand their own attitudes and beliefs and increase awareness of their own cultural identity with respect to various social statuses. Examination of diverse cultural identities necessitates the parallel examination and knowledge of oppression in society and the impact of racism, sexism, ableism, classism, and homophobia. Group workers are encouraged to develop skills related to seeking consultation and training in enhancing their understanding and effectiveness in working with various cultural groups.

Group Leader's Awareness of Group Members' Worldviews

In addition to knowing themselves in a cultural context, group workers need to examine their attitudes and beliefs about other cultural groups. This requires a personal examination of stereotypes, biases, and prejudices toward other racial, ethnic, and religious groups; sexual minorities; people with disabilities; people who are poor; and people who are elderly. Group workers need to increase their knowledge about the cultural heritage, history, traditions, and impact of sociopolitical forces (e.g., immigration, prejudice, discrimination, oppression) on people who belong to these groups. Furthermore, group workers need to develop skills to familiarize themselves with relevant research and educational experiences and actively involve themselves with various culturally diverse groups and individuals outside of the group setting.

Diversity-Appropriate Intervention Strategies

Examination of attitudes and beliefs about the religious/spiritual beliefs, indigenous helping practices, and other intrinsic helping practices is critical in the type of interventions provided. Group leaders need to increase their knowledge base about culturally responsive intervention strategies by understanding institutional barriers that may prevent group members from participating in the groups, recognizing potential bias in assessment instruments, and considering how specific linguistic and other cultural factors may negatively affect group evaluation results. A diversity-competent group leader would, therefore, have the skills to engage in a variety of verbal and nonverbal facilitative functions, exercise institutional interventions on behalf of group members when appropriate, and address the different linguistic and spiritual needs of group members in a culturally responsive manner. Diversity-competent group leadership skills can be further enhanced by conforming to *ASGW Best Practice Guidelines* (ASGW, 1998), which involve three broad group worker functions (i.e., planning, performing, and processing).

Planning for Diversity-Competent Group Work

Diversity-competent group leaders can take a number of steps toward planning for effective group work with diverse clientele. The group leader should partner with representatives of the target population whenever possible in order to meet the population's unique needs (Conyne & Bemak, 2004). For example, transportation and child care needs may have to be considered for better outreach to low-income populations.

Merchant (2006) described three types of diversity-related groups: (a) culture-specific groups geared toward addressing the needs of a particular cultural group (e.g., support group for lesbian mothers), (b) intercultural learning groups designed to promote better relations and reduce bias and discrimination between groups (e.g., diversity training group, race-relations group), and (c) other content-focused groups where the purpose of the group is to focus on other content goals (e.g., substance abuse) but addressing diversity is an important consideration in the group. (For a more complete discussion, see Merchant, 2006.) Planning for groups will vary depending on the type of diversity-related group offered.

Diversity issues can be identified early in the screening process, both as a way to address specific needs of members and to set the tone and norm of acceptance of diversity in the group. The group leader, for instance, can work collaboratively with a gay member in determining conditions that would create a safe group environment.

Performing Diversity-Competent Group Work

Several leadership skills need to be considered in the performance of diversity-competent group work. A brief discussion on each of the skills, as delineated by Merchant (2006), follows:

- **Preparing group members for multicultural group work.** Providing an informed consent that describes the nature and expectations of the group and emphasizes acceptance and respect for cultural differences can facilitate better preparation for group members.
- **Structuring.** Group leaders need to modify group content, process, and activities to accommodate or respond to cultural differences.
- **Norming.** Group leaders need to intentionally create a norm of valuing cultural differences through the use of verbal and nonverbal cues.
- **Modeling cultural respect and sensitivity.** Group leaders play an important role in demonstrating that all cultures are valued and all members are treated equally.
- **Demonstrating neutral but active leadership.** The group leader needs to use discretion in sharing personal values in order to avoid cultural similarity and alignment with some members and alienation with others. A neutral but active approach communicates impartiality and valuing of all members in the group.
- **Working through cultural conflict.** The pressure to be politically correct can cause both group members and group leader to be less than genuine. Group leaders need to be attentive to cultural conflict when it emerges in the group process.
- **Attending to interplay of multiple cultural identities and differences in communication styles.** Communication needs to be understood in relation to differences in communication styles and level of consciousness regarding an individual's cultural identity. For instance, miscommunication can quickly develop between an African American man who is very aware of racism but not sexism and a European American woman who is very aware of sexism but not racism.
- **Being sensitive to language needs.** Language interpretation can create unique challenges in a group context due to simultaneous conversations and noise interference. The use of interpreters should be carefully managed to ensure the best outcome for both the group member requesting the service and the rest of the group members.
- **Advocating and exercising institutional intervention skills.** Group leaders may find it necessary to intervene at an institutional level, such as connecting members to community resources or advocating on behalf of the group member.
- **Incorporating spiritual healing or seeking consultation when appropriate.** As appropriate, group leaders can invite spiritual healers or incorporate practices that would allow for healing in a cultural context.

Processing Group Work

Formative and summative evaluations of the group need to be implemented and understood within a cultural context. Assessment tools should be culturally relevant and used with sensitivity. In summary, diversity-competent group work involves a thorough examination of the counselor's own worldview and others' worldview and using best practice methods that are culturally relevant.

Contributed by Niloufer M. Merchant,
St. Cloud State University,
St. Cloud, MN

References

Association for Multicultural Counseling and Development. (1996). *Operationalization of the multicultural counseling competencies.* Alexandria, VA: Author.

Association for Specialists in Group Work. (1998). ASGW best practice guidelines. *Journal for Specialists in Group Work, 23,* 237–244.

Association for Specialists in Group Work. (1999). ASGW principles for diversity-competent group workers. *Journal for Specialists in Group Work, 24,* 7–14.

Conyne, R. K., & Bemak, F. (2004). Teaching group work from an ecological perspective. *Journal for Specialists in Group Work, 29,* 7–18.

Merchant, N. M. (2006). Multicultural and diversity-competent group work. In J. P. Trotzer (Ed.), *The counselor and the group: Integrating theory, training, and practice* (4th ed., pp. 319–349). New York: Routledge, Taylor & Francis.

Sue, D. W., Arredondo, P., & McDavis, R. J. (1992). Multicultural counseling competencies and standards: A call to the profession. *Journal of Counseling & Development, 70,* 477–486.

Additional Resources

DeLucia-Waack, J. L., & Donigian, J. (2004). *The practice of multicultural group work: Visions and perspectives from the field.* Belmont, CA: Brooks/Cole.

DeLucia-Waack, J. L., Gerrity, D. A., Kalodner, C. R., & Riva, M. T. (Eds.). (2004). *The handbook of group counseling and therapy.* Thousand Oaks, CA: Sage.

■ Group Work, Planning for

Understanding the components of planning a group is an essential part of facilitating effective group work. The planning of a group is usually done by the group's facilitator or facilitators and requires careful attention to a number of pre-group details. Before starting, not only is it important for group leaders to have appropriate training in actually leading groups, they must also have adequate knowledge and expertise regarding their group's intended subject matter and theme. Planning for group work is important because it allows for thoughtfulness, focus, clarity, and intentionality regarding the intended group's purpose, target population, rationale, objectives, and evaluation procedures. When a group is well planned, it increases the chances for potential members to make informed decisions about whether or not the intended group is appropriate for them and it increases its likelihood for success. Group workers should have a clear framework for planning and should consider the differences between planned-theme groups versus spontaneous-content groups, homogenous versus heterogeneous groups, open groups versus closed groups, and large versus small groups.

Purpose

The first step in planning is identifying the purposes for the group. Most groups, whether they are task groups, psychoeducational groups, counseling groups, or psychotherapy groups, develop around a specific purpose or theme. In most cases, group purposes are developed to help individuals increase their knowledge of a particular topic, learn new ways of coping, or learn more about themselves and how they relate to others. Examples of topical group purposes include helping children of alcoholic parents cope, helping victims of sexual abuse move toward survivorship, or helping individuals with substance abuse recovery. Although many individuals join specific groups because of their topical purpose, many also join because of the group's therapeutic potential (e.g., an opportunity to reduce social isolation, a safe environment to connect with others who share the same concern).

Planned Theme Versus Spontaneous Content

The degree of focus on content is an important factor in planning a group. Many groups tend to be **theme-oriented** groups and focus on helping specific populations cope with a variety of life issues (e.g., women dealing with domestic violence, children coping with divorce, men managing the stressors of fatherhood, individuals overcoming addictions). Theme groups have a very specific focus and only admit group members who are dealing with the group's intended focus. On the other hand, groups can also be planned as **spontaneous-content groups.** This means they do not have a set theme but provide a venue for individuals to talk freely about a variety of topics and concerns. Although spontaneous-content groups have some criterion for group participation (e.g., members share common characteristics such as age, personal challenge), these groups are designed to provide general support and personal growth. An example of a spontaneous-content group would be a women's general personal growth group. Participants meet regularly to discuss openly whatever concerns or challenges are most significant for them at the time of the group's meeting. Group members support each other, give feedback, and provide a venue for collective empowerment and personal development. These groups often meet weekly or bimonthly, may have fluctuating membership, and can last for several months or years.

Homogeneity Versus Heterogeneity

Planning for group work requires attention to determining whether the group will be **homogeneous** (i.e., all group members share the same concern or life challenge) or **heterogeneous** (i.e., group members have different issues, but work to resolve their concerns together). It is important to consider cultural diversity issues relative to group composition in both homogeneous and heterogeneous groups. This includes a consideration of group members' participation based not only on their presenting concern but also taking into consideration their race, sexual orientation, religion, gender, age, and physical ability as variables for potential membership selection. Having a culturally diverse group can increase the therapeutic value and real-life experiences for members because it replicates the diversity that exists in the world.

Open Group Versus Closed Group

Group planners will also need to determine whether their group will it be an **open group** (i.e., one in which members enter and leave the group at different times, but the group continues its focus) or **closed group** (i.e., one in which only a set number of members are allowed to participate from beginning to end). Allowing continuous new membership into a group can fuel its energy and excitement, but it can also inhibit the development of group cohesion due to constantly changing member dynamics. Closed group membership provides clear benefits; however in some circumstances, permitting open group membership may be the only practical way to meet the needs of the population to be served by the group.

Large Group Versus Small Group

It is important to remember that there is no set membership size for task, psychoeducational, counseling, or psychotherapy groups. Rather, the appropriate size of any group is ultimately determined by the nature of the group, its purpose, the age of its participants, and environmental or economic conditions. For example, in determining the most desirable size for a task group whose goal is to plan a regional community conference on the needs of Hispanic families, it is important to focus on having experienced and knowledgeable representatives from each local agency that serves Hispanic populations and families, rather than just concentrate on a set number of participants with little expertise in the area. Furthermore, when planning a psychoeducational group to increase workers' knowledge of job-related stress and anxiety prevention, it may be advantageous to present the information to a large group of people at one time (e.g., as many as 50 or more workers in a large room or auditorium). Such service delivery not only gets information out to a large group of people at one time, but it can serve to curtail financial costs during times of economic scarcity. Next, in planning for counseling and psychotherapy groups where intermember interaction is essential to success, a desirable size is typically thought to be 5 to 12 participants. Some counseling groups actually work better with fewer members. If the group is dealing with a very sensitive topic (e.g., sexual abuse, sexual identity issues), members may feel less vulnerable and safer in disclosing their experiences in a smaller rather than larger group. Also, if a counseling or psychotherapy group is too large, members who may want to speak may not have adequate opportunities to share their feelings because too many individuals are participating, resulting in a fight for "air time." The maturity level of members also affects optimal size. In planning a psychotherapy group for 10- to 12-year-old boys dealing with attention-deficit/hyperactivity disorder and anger management issues, a smaller rather than larger group may be most desirable.

Strategies for Effective Planning in Group Work

Planning for group work is labor intensive in the beginning, but paying attention to the previously discussed details in this entry can increase the chances of a successful group experience. The following are some suggested strategies for group work planning:

1. Conduct an initial needs assessment of the community/population. Facilitators should explore what salient issues need to be addressed.
2. Facilitators should include evaluation methods during and after the group. This can be done by asking participants to identify which aspects of the group are working or have worked and which ones are not working or did not work for them. They should ask what improvements can be made in the future.
3. Facilitators should stay current and up-to-date in the field of group facilitation through continued professional development. This can be done by taking additional group courses, attending professional conferences, and/or participation in the Association for Specialists in Group Work (ASGW).
4. Facilitators should read and reread the *ACA Code of Ethics* (American Counseling Association, 2005), the ASGW (2000) *Professional Standards for the Training of Group Workers*, and the ASGW (1998) *Principles for Diversity-Competent Group Workers*.
5. Facilitators should seek supervision and always engage in self-evaluation to make sure they have the professional and personal competencies needed to be effective in group work planning and facilitation.

Contributed by Angela D. Coker,
The University of Missouri–St. Louis,
St. Louis, MO

References

American Counseling Association. (2005). *ACA code of ethics.* Alexandria, VA: Author.

Association for Specialists in Group Work. (1998). *Principles for diversity-competent group workers.* Retrieved August 21, 2008, from http://www.asgw.org

Association for Specialists in Group Work. (2000). *Professional standards for the training of group workers.* Retrieved August 21, 2008, from http://www.asgw.org

Additional Resources

Association for Specialists in Group Work. (1998). Best practice guidelines. *Journal for Specialists in Group Work, 23,* 237–244.

Corey, M. S., & Corey, G. (2004). *Process and practice groups* (7th ed.). Belmont, CA: Brooks/Cole.

Gladding, S. (2003). *Group work: A counseling specialty* (4th ed.). Upper Saddle River, NJ: Prentice Hall.

◼ Group Work Techniques

Group work techniques generally are activities and/or experiments designed to engage group members and group leaders in an interactive process whereby themes and topics can be revealed, shared, and processed. The general purpose of these techniques is to create a dialogue between participants and generate observational data that can be used to challenge and/or encourage people to learn and apply lessons revealed within the context of the group to their within-group interactions and, by extension, to their everyday lives.

It is important to note that the use of group work techniques is not without controversy. Many proponents of group counseling considered the use of particular techniques an act that de-emphasized the Rogerian, client-centered aspects of therapy. Person-centered theorists argued that a focus on technique detracted from the therapist's empathy, genuineness, and unconditional positive regard and that the core conditions they valued might be reduced to artificial gestures that might create dialogue but that would no longer tap into deeper levels of emotion and personal value. Other scholars, however, disagreed with this notion and produced other models by which group work techniques became more central to the effectiveness of group dynamics.

Ivey's microskills movement, for example, emphasized the importance of mastering particular interviewing strategies and statements that maximize the effectiveness of individual and group counseling. Gestalt therapists have introduced numerous techniques that have become major staples of group counseling, such as the empty chair and making the rounds. Solution-focused therapists have adapted techniques based on the miracle question and various scaling exercises that allow group members to engage more deeply in the group process. There are also empirically validated approaches that provide particular structures and approaches to certain groups, such as outpatient groups for the clinically depressed. This is not to say that the techniques are the only elements that matter when it comes to conducting an effective group, but it is clear that the shift toward attending to group techniques has become a dominant message in the fields of counseling and psychology. Understanding some of these techniques will aid the counselor when conducting group work.

Examples of commonly used group techniques include setting tone, drawing out, cutting off, linking, focusing, modeling, role playing, pairing, and making the rounds. Setting tone provides a backdrop for the way in which all groups are formed and can significantly affect the effectiveness and delivery of the subsequently presented techniques on the aforementioned list. Each technique listed, from drawing out to making the rounds, symbolizes a greater step toward the macrolevel characteristics of a particular group. Drawing out and cutting off, for example, tend to involve brief statements and fairly simple actions on the part of the group leader, whereas pairing and making the rounds involve more involved and complex approaches by the group leader. A brief discussion of each technique can better illustrate its properties.

Setting Tone

Setting tone, also known as **structuring,** is a way of overtly setting a style and putting a climate in place for a group to follow. It provides the foundation for most group activities and dynamics because the members of the group can set this norm, which defines the general approaches that all the participants should adopt when participating in the group. The tone of a group significantly affects the amount of cohesiveness that members have. A group with a serious tone may engage in activities that bring about deep discussion of intense subject matter, whereas a group with a humorous tone may otherwise keep issues at a surface level. In either case, the group has a set of expectations that creates an environment within which members feel able to discuss and process issues because of how they will be received. The tone of a group is important to set early on, while the group is at an initial stage, in order to allow the group's leader and members to orient themselves to one another.

Drawing Out

Drawing out is a relatively basic technique whereby a group facilitator directly engages group members to contribute to a topic being discussed during the course of a group session. It is used to obtain specific information from members and to encourage people to speak. Numerous methods can be used to draw members out, such as directly asking them to respond ("What do you think about this?"), using minimal encouragers ("Tell me more"), or reflecting and/or paraphrasing responses ("So, we all appear to be saying that this issue has no easy answers"). This technique is designed to help members overcome certain forms of resistance that may develop at certain stages of group. It is important to note that this is not meant to be a form of interrogation, but rather it is a way of encouraging members to elaborate and produce greater dialogue during session.

Cutting Off

Cutting off is a technique that is the direct opposite of drawing out. The group facilitator may use this technique to discontinue dialogue about material that does not appear to be related to the main topic of the group, discourage a particular member from speaking too much about a topic that will take needed emphasis away from other members, or steer the group into a relevant discussion about the here-and-now moments of the session as opposed to the there-and-then matters. It is important to note that this is not simply interrupting conversation, nor "shutting someone up." The facilitator uses this technique to focus the group's attention on material that he or she judges to be more relevant and is directly aligned with specific group goals.

Linking

Linking is a technique whereby a group facilitator specifically points out to group participants the connections they share for the purpose of connecting members to each other in a literal (content-based) and figurative (interpersonally based) manner. As an example, a member who states during the course of group that he is "uncomfortable with talking about feelings" could be linked to another member who states later in the same group that she is "someone who is afraid of letting certain feelings out." The group facilitator can point out to these members that they both "seem to feel uncertain about how to express certain feelings." By linking these two statements together, the leader may encourage dialogue between these two (and perhaps others as well) whereby they may feel connected to each other in a deeper way, possibly because they are harboring similar feelings about similar life situations and/or experiences that may not have otherwise been shared during the normal course of the group.

Focusing

Focusing is an interpretive technique whereby a group facilitator specifically points out to group members underlying themes that appear to exist underneath the surface-level communications that are occurring between them during the group process. Instead of merely pointing out literal connections that exist between the content of expressed statements (which is mentioned in the linking section), the group facilitator makes an interpretation of the meaning behind the content. As an example, a member who states during the course of group that she is "uncomfortable with expressing herself around her parents" can be linked to another member who states later in the same group that he is "unable to be honest with his spouse about certain issues." It is also possible to focus the members on the similarity of their feelings of anxiety by having the facilitator ask these members to "explore with each other what commonalities they might have regarding the antecedents to their anxiety, how they experience it, and how their anxiety interferes with them getting what they need from life."

Modeling

Modeling is the specific learning of a skill or behavior through the use of observation and imitation. The effectiveness of modeling is largely determined by the rewards and consequences that are given to the learner for appropriately demonstrating the specific skill or behavior that is being modeled. It is for this reason that a learner (i.e., the person attempting to learn the behavior or skill) first chooses a model (i.e., the person demonstrating the behavior or skill) who is typically rewarded when the skill or behavior is performed. The learner assumes that if the model's behavior is followed properly, the same rewards will come the learner's way.

Group members, however, may choose an inappropriate model and imitate behaviors that are counterproductive to the development of the group. An example is a learner who models the behavior of another group member who puts down other members of the group because of the perceived amount of power and attention that will be granted in return. The learner may be able to model the behavior, but the behavior can be counterproductive to the group dynamics as well as to the identity of the learner who has adopted this pattern of behavior. Although working with bullying behavior is often slow and complex work, setting tone and using the leadership skill of cutting off may be important first steps to open the way for exploring the members' feelings about being in a group where members put each other down and helping members who bully to find more social ways to have their needs met. When the modeling process is structured

into the group session, such as is the case when social skills training groups are conducted, the leader can often have more control of the process. In this instance, the specific skill or behavior to be learned is typically operationally defined in either a single concrete step or a series of steps. The learner typically watches the model demonstrate the specific skill or behavior and then performs what has been observed. An example of this technique in action would be teaching people to make *I*-statements during the course of a group by having them start each sentence they utter with the phrase "I feel." The group facilitator begins the exercise by demonstrating the skill in front of the entire group and asking other members to follow this behavior as they subsequently join in the discourse. The group facilitator has modeled the *I*-statement skill successfully if the other members choose to imitate this behavior during their participation. Furthermore, the members help to reinforce the performance of this skill by serving as models for subsequent speakers.

Role Playing

Role playing is a form of modeling in which members enact hypothetical situations designed to simulate real-world scenarios that they may encounter outside of the group. Specific attention is given to the role player's use of particular skills or those behaviors the group facilitator and any other designated participants observe. The group facilitator can direct the exercise from the observational position or participate in this exercise as well. Feedback is shared between role player(s) and observers after the exercise has been completed in order to aid everyone's understanding of the skill or behavior that has been played out during the session. An example of this skill in action would involve a member who would like to communicate feelings more directly to a significant other. The significant other, who is not a member of the group, can be simulated (or role-played) by another member of the group who poses as this particular individual. The member would be asked to simulate a typical conversation that the member would have with this significant other while other members of the group (including the role player who is acting as the significant other) observe the member's use of feeling words during this simulation exercise. Feedback is given to the member after the exercise is over in order to have this individual learn how to use feeling words better. This process can be repeated after the feedback is shared in order to see if the member can readily apply the newly learned skill by having the member redo the role play.

Pairing

Pairing (or subgrouping) is a technique that involves forming a small contingency of members within a larger group. This act may not need to be done in a directed fashion, because group members who find things in common with each other may spontaneously pair off or form a subgroup at any time during the course of a group. It is often advantageous for a group facilitator to pair members who match or complement each other in some way in order to encourage deeper levels of disclosure between members. As an example of the complementary function of pairing, a group facilitator may chose to pair group members who are particularly good at using feeling words with members who are not particularly good at using this skill. As a result of working in pairs, it may be possible for members who are not particularly strong when it comes to using these words to become better at the skill because of the modeling their paired member is able to demonstrate. Caution must be used with this technique, however, in order not to divide the larger group of members from one another further by having them only communicate through subgroups. The group facilitator should encourage all members to share their experience of working within their pairs (or subgroups) in order not to reinforce the notion of subgrouping as a norm or weaken whole-group cohesion.

Making the Rounds

Making the rounds, a technique taken from the Gestalt school of group therapy, forces a group member to "go around" the group and address each individual member, one at a time, by saying something that this member may not normally speak about during the normal discourse of the group session. For example, a group member who has difficulty expressing feelings to people may be asked by the group facilitator to address each group member one at a time by going around the group and stating "I feel _____ about you because _____." The purpose of this technique is to allow the member in question to fully experience on an interpersonal and intrapersonal level what it is like to say these statements and process how the other members react to hearing these statements. Leaders may modify their use of this technique to serve multiple purposes.

Making the rounds can help other group members gain a sense of how the rounds-making member characteristically interacts while doing this activity: a phenomenon sometimes referred to as contact style. For example, if a group member tends to tense up when making feeling statements toward a particular subset of group members (e.g., the opposite sex, persons of a different race, younger group members), the group can call attention to this observation. It is anticipated that the rounds-making member upon hearing this data may be able to make adjustments to the contact style.

Making the rounds can also draw out a form of resistance that may be blocking the rounds-making member from effective contact and communication. Perhaps the group member in the previous example has an awkward contact style with female group members because of unfinished business with a maternal caregiver. To explore a member's resistance to expressing feelings, the member may be asked to speak to each member in turn, saying, "I cannot talk to you about my feelings because _____." By making the rounds, this group member may become more aware of the historical antecedents to his or her contact style and become freer to change the contact approach

One other purpose of making the rounds is to allow a group member to confirm or refute hypotheses about the self. Perhaps the member in the previous example has a belief that "real adults don't wallow in feelings" or that "having feelings is dangerous"; by having the member go around the group and state to each member, "I don't have any feelings, right?" an opportunity is created for each member to challenge that belief by calling attention to verbal and nonverbal behaviors the rounds-making individual exhibits while performing the activity. The result of this task may allow the rounds maker to experience a variety of perspectives and opinions that provide rich data on the basis of which changes to self-acceptance and contact style can be made.

Contributed by Adam P. Zagelbaum,
Sonoma State University,
Rohnert Park, CA

Additional Resources

Corey, G. (2004). *Theory and practice of group counseling.* Belmont, CA: Brooks/Cole.

Day, S. (2007). *Groups in practice.* Boston: Lahaska Press.

■ Group Work Terminology

Effective group work begins with an understanding of the language of group workers. Essential terms include, but are not limited to, *contagion, group content, group process, group rules, group cohesion, groupthink, nominal group technique, scapegoating, polarizing, power, processing,* and *resistance.*

Contagion is the tendency of group members to behave in similar ways. This includes the process by which emotions and behaviors can be transmitted from one person to another (Forsyth, 1999). For example, one person crying in a group can stimulate crying or feelings of sadness in other members.

Group content refers to the actual words, ideas, and information shared within a group. This includes the purpose of the group and all of the facts that are exchanged by the members. For example, in a group designed to deal with depression, the content would include information about depression (such as diagnostic criteria or medications), details from group members about how symptoms are affecting their lives, and other facts that are shared.

Group process refers to the naturally occurring dynamics or interactions in a group that tell facilitators about the relationships of group members with one other. This includes the energy exchange between members and/or facilitators as well as the reactions of members/facilitators during the course of the group (Jacobs, Masson, & Harvill, 2006). Process variables include, but are not limited to, body language; eye contact; tone of voice and rate and inflection; language that is used; and who talks, when, to whom, and how. Group process and its interpretation are affected by multicultural factors and necessitate an understanding of the cultural context in which behaviors are learned and displayed.

Group rules are the guidelines by which groups are run. These guidelines are established to specify acceptable limits of member conduct and may be discussed before and during the group sessions. These rules often include confidentiality, attendance, promptness, eating/drinking during the session, and cooperation. Sometimes these rules or guidelines are explicit. For example, guidelines about the limits of confidentiality might be presented in an informed consent document, or the order of issues to be addressed in a meeting may be published in an agenda. Sometimes they are implicit, informally held operating procedures that are learned through group participation. For example, in some groups, members act as though there were a rule that prohibited open discussion of conflict even though no such explicit rule exists. In other groups, member self-disclosure is encouraged and supported, even without explicit discussion about how self-disclosure is to be treated. Implicit norms are often affected by culture and members' past experiences and, thus, may not be understood by all group members. Whether explicit or implicit, norms affect how members communicate and behave in a group.

Group cohesion is one of the important factors of change in group work and involves a felt bond, togetherness, or solidarity that members share with one another or the group as a whole (Yalom & Leszcz, 2005). It refers to the condition of members' perceiving a sense of warmth, belonging, value, acceptance, and support within the group. Cohesion has particular importance for group counseling, as distinct from individual counseling, because of its emphasis on intragroup relationships. Yalom believed that group cohesion was one of 11 therapeutic factors (i.e., instillation of hope, universality, imparting information, altruism, corrective recapitulation of the primary family group, development of socializing techniques, imitative behavior, interpersonal learning, group cohesiveness, catharsis, and existential factors; see Curative Factors) that form a basis for the therapeutic process and successful outcomes in groups.

Groupthink refers to the harmful power to conform that a group may exert over the members. Groupthink occurs when the members in a highly cohesive group are selective in gathering information and desire unanimity at the expense of quality decisions. This mentality in a group can be detrimental to the growth of members and can impede the problem-solving ability of the group by decreasing motivation to generate alternative ideas and choices (Janis, 1982). Some examples of the negative consequences of groupthink include the decision process that led to the disastrous Bay of Pigs invasion and the mass suicide of the members of the closed, Jonestown, Guyana, religious community.

Nominal group technique is a structured small-group technique, often associated with task or work groups, that can help members think about a problem situation and emphasizes individual input into group planning or decision making (Asmus & James, 2005). Delbecq, Van de Ven, and Gustafson (as cited in Gladding, 2003) offered a systematic six-step process in which the group leader first introduces the problem for which members silently generate possible solutions. Each individual in turn then shares one idea until all potential solutions have been recorded. In Step 3, members discuss the list of ideas to clarify any questions. Then they individually rank their top choices, which are tallied and presented to the group. This vote is then discussed in Step 5 and a revote is the final step, particularly if new information has been shared that prompts members to reconsider their previous decision.

Scapegoating occurs when individuals in a group direct their hostility toward one of the members, blaming that member for the group's difficulties. This action may result from their anxiety or dissatisfaction with the member, the group, or the leader. For example, some less active members of a group may scapegoat a more talkative member, blaming the member for dominating the group and for the group's lack of progress, which may in fact be a result of those members' own difficulty opening up and trusting others. It is important for a facilitator to recognize this phenomenon, protect the scapegoat, and reveal the dynamic to the group members, particularly when it occurs in the early stages of group development.

Polarization "occurs when a group becomes divided into different and opposing subgroups or camps" (Gladding, 2003, p. 290). Polarization may occur naturally and unintentionally, such as when group members intensify their position in relation to other members as a result of discussing a salient or emotionally charged issue or have chance encounters outside of the group time. If the polarization is due to intentional acts by group members or threatens to become normative in the group, then specific attention by the leader may be warranted.

Power is "the capacity to bring about certain intended consequences in the behavior of others" (Gardner, 1990, p. 55) and "affect another person's goal accomplishment" (Johnson & Johnson, 2000, p. 249). Members' struggle for power within a group affects the dynamics, is related to how members deal with conflict, and is reflective of member relationships outside of the group that are played out in the interactions within the group.

Processing is

> capitalizing on significant happenings in the here-and-now interactions of the group to help members reflect on the meaning of their experience; better understand their own thoughts, feelings, and actions; and generalize what is learned to their life outside the group" (Stockton, Morran, & Nitza, 2000, p. 345).

Member growth often takes place when the process is brought to the awareness of the group by the facilitator and discussed. For example, a leader who is aware of a lengthy period of silence in the group might bring that to the group's attention with a statement, "It has gotten very quiet in the group," or by asking a process question such as "What are you all aware of in this moment?"

Resistance in therapy is, at its core, intrapsychic in nature and reflective of an individual's feelings of pain, anxiety, fear, and shame associated with the competing demands of problem resolution and protection of oneself. As Cullari (1996) described it, resistance involves "conflicts arising from simultaneous attempts at self-preservation and self-transformation both within the client and between the client, the therapist, and society" (p. 9). Resistance may be a sign of a person feeling unsafe, having something to hide, or harboring a fear of the unknown (about what he or she might reveal), or it may be related to a fear of change and the disturbance that change might have on an individual's life. It is a protective mechanism that attempts to reduce anxiety and may be viewed as a natural reaction to a person's circumstances rather than an inappropriate or problem behavior on the part of a group member. Resistance may also be interpersonal in nature, such as an individual's reaction to an external force of power or authority, real or perceived, that is pressuring or coercing him or her to behave in a particular way (Egan, 2007). Early psychoanalytic work stressed resistance as integral to the therapeutic process, not a difficulty to be avoided, eliminated, or quickly conquered. It is a phenomenon worthy of careful analysis, by client and counselor, of its function in order to help the individual recognize the resistance and understand its source and purpose. Group facilitators are encouraged to interpret a group member's resistant behavior in light of the member's context and the reason for the behavior; the resistant behavior may make sense and have a distinct purpose. Moreover, leaders are directed to examine their own reactions to resistant group members and to use those thoughts and feelings as an important resource to respond effectively and provide critical learning opportunities for group members (Corey, 2004).

Contributed by Lorraine J. Guth,
Indiana University of Pennsylvania,
Indiana, PA, and Kelly A. McDonnell,
Western Michigan University,
Kalamazoo, MI

References

Asmus, C. L., & James, K. (2005). Nominal group technique, social loafing, and group creative project quality. *Creativity Research Journal, 17,* 349–354.

Corey, G. (2004). *Theory and practice of group counseling* (6th ed.). Belmont, CA: Thomson Brooks/Cole.

Cullari, S. (1996). *Treatment resistance: A guide for practitioners.* Needham Heights, MA: Allyn & Bacon.

Egan, G. (2007). *The skilled helper: A problem-management and opportunity-development approach to helping* (8th ed.). Belmont, CA: Thomson Brooks/Cole.

Forsyth, D. R. (1999). *Group dynamics* (3rd ed.). Belmont, CA: Wadsworth.

Gardner, J. W. (1990). *On leadership.* New York: Free Press.

Gladding, S. T. (2003). *Group work: A counseling specialty* (4th ed.). Upper Saddle River, NJ: Merrill Prentice Hall.

Jacobs, E. E., Masson, R. L., & Harvill, R. L. (2006). *Group counseling strategies & skills* (5th ed.). Belmont, CA: Thomson Higher Education.

Janis, I. (1982). *Groupthink: Psychological studies of policy decisions and fiascos* (2nd ed.). Boston: Houghton Mifflin.

Johnson, D. W., & Johnson, F. P. (2000). *Joining together: Group theory and group skills* (7th ed.). Needham Heights, MA: Allyn & Bacon.

Stockton, R., Morran, D. K., & Nitza, A. G. (2000). Processing group events: A conceptual map for leaders. *Journal for Specialists in Group Work, 25,* 343–355.

Yalom, I. D., & Leszcz, M. (2005). *The theory and practice of group psychotherapy* (5th ed.). New York: Basic Books.

■ Group Work Theory

Group work theory is a set of interrelated concepts that explain the function, process, and dynamics of group behavior. Multiple broad-based theories such as field theory and systems theory explain group dynamics in a general context. More specific theories, such as focal conflict theory, relate particularly to group counseling and therapy. Traditional theories of psychology, such as psychodynamic and rational emotive behavioral theory, have also been applied to explain group dynamics.

Group Theory (Field Theory, General Systems Theory, Focal Conflict Theory)

Lewin's field theory highlighted the interaction between all of the parts of a person's environment. A **field** is defined as the totality of coexisting facts that are conceived as mutually interdependent (Lewin, 1951). Previously, an individual's psychological and biological characteristics were paramount in explaining behaviors. Lewin proposed that the context or environment of the action must be considered along with the individual's internal needs. A person's internal state was influenced by his or her social milieu.

Field theory has been applied extensively to explaining group change. In particular, the model helps explain how factors of a group mutually influence each other and how this process molds change in the group. Leadership style and group dynamics, for example, have been studied in-depth. These topics reflect examples of interdependent parts that affect the group as a whole. One particular study that is often cited demonstrated how a democratic leadership style leads to more positive group change when compared with authoritarian or permissive styles.

Ludwig von Bertalanffy also stressed how the whole of a system is greater than a sum of its parts with **general system theory (GST).** The interaction between parts was of greater concern than a reductionistic analysis of individual elements. GST formulated integral group concepts such as dynamic systems and open versus closed systems. When applied to group work, GST encourages leaders to focus on interactions of members and features of the group as a whole more than on the analysis of individuals. Although GST is similar to field theory, GST focuses more on external factors whereas field theory explores interactions between internal factors, such as personality and environmental variables.

Group theories have also been developed specifically for use in group counseling practice. Whitaker's **focal conflict theory (FCT)** explains how groups can foster healthy integration of core issues experienced by group members. According to Whitaker, long-term issues, called **nuclear conflicts,** such as a rejection from parents as a child, are reexperienced throughout life. When nuclear conflicts, in this case a theme of rejection, are reexperienced in groups, they are termed **focal conflicts.** Groups act as a catalyst for core issues to emerge. These conflicts are reexperienced in a more adaptive manner, and the core conflicts are ameliorated.

Group Counseling Theories

Psychodynamic Approaches

Psychoanalytic group counseling theory is based on Sigmund Freud's psychodynamic/psychoanalytic theory. This theory focuses on the group leader—the expert—analyzing unconscious needs and motivations of group members by observing their interactions. The underpinnings of this theory are realizing an individual's unconscious thoughts by the group leader using specific techniques such as free association, interpretation, and analysis of the transference relationship. This type of group would also focus on group members' psychosexual stage progression (i.e., oral, anal, phallic, latency, and genital; see Psychosexual Stages of Development). The goal of this long-term group therapy is change in personality.

Object relations therapy is based on the idea that an individual, early in life, has drives that are satisfied through attachment to specific objects/people, primarily parents. These early life interactions set a foundation for an individual's relationship patterns later in life. Through therapy, an individual works through self-destructive relational patterns. The therapist is a very active participant in the group session, paying close attention to projection from the group member as well as transference. The main goals are to create a corrective emotional experience and change self-defeating relationship patterns (see Object Relations).

According to **self-psychology,** supportive experiences, such as positive interactions with parents early in life, help create a healthy self and self-esteem. Dissonance can develop early in life if problematic experiences occur. This conflict can be internalized and developed into unwanted narcissistic or other problematic personality characteristics. The group experience helps members fulfill a need to be involved with others, the need to feel attached, and the need to feel appreciated. Empathy and insight are the primary tools of the group experience.

Cognitive and Behavioral Approaches

Rational emotive behavioral group counseling theory is based on Albert Ellis's rational emotive behavioral theory (REBT). Overall, REBT groups vary in length of time in group (several months to a weekend) and whether the group will be open or closed. The group leader is often direct and can assume a teaching role, but the members may also give feedback and suggestions during group sessions. The basis of this theory is that an individual's thoughts, not the surrounding circumstances, produce feelings and behaviors. It makes use of identifying self-defeating thoughts and developing more realistic patterns of thought (see Rational Emotive Behavior Therapy).

Beck's cognitive therapy has been widely applied in groups in addressing depression and anxiety. Maladaptive mental structures for organizing life experiences, called schemes, cause depression and anxiety. The purpose of the group is to help members develop more adaptive patterns of thinking. Three primary areas addressed are members' negative views of self, the world, and the future. Group leaders and members use Socratic dialogue to develop logical conclusions that challenge members' maladaptive thinking.

William Glasser originated **reality therapy,** and Robert Wubbolding expanded on it. This therapy is based on choice theory, which emphasizes how individuals make healthy or unhealthy choices to fulfill basic needs, including belonging, power, freedom, and fun. Group leaders and members analyze their perceived wants and needs, identify how they attempt to meet these needs, evaluate the effectiveness of these actions, and create new plans to make healthier choices to meet those needs. Group leaders are active, didactic, and structured in their leadership style (see Reality Therapy).

Interpersonal psychotherapy highlights how dysfunctional relationship skills are developed early in life and perpetuated by interpersonal conflict and loss throughout life. The group itself represents the interpersonal worlds for the members and provides a safe setting for improving communication and relationship skills. Throughout the group experience, members provide positive feedback that reinforces healthy relationship skills and enhances self-esteem. Gaining insight, providing feedback, and communicating support are three essential components of this group experience.

Humanistic Approaches

Person-centered group theory is based on the work of Carl Rogers. This theory takes a humanistic perspective; a qualified group leader uses an unstructured format in which trust in the group members' inner resources leads to change and allows the members to help guide others in the group. The group leader and members use active listening skills and confrontation in a positive way when needed. The main goal of the group is development of self-awareness and awareness of others, leading to self-actualization.

Existential therapy is based on several premises: People have freedom to make choices, healthy individuals seek meaning in their lives, and people can choose to live their lives to the fullest. Through action and reflection, the leader helps members realize their full potential and how to live up to choices made in life. This leads to more personal responsibility. The overall desired outcomes of group revolve around having group members become more self-aware, become more aware of their choices, find new meaning in their lives, be authentic with themselves, and become more interpersonally responsible.

Contributed by Jennifer L. Marshall,
University of Cincinnati–Raymond
Walters College, and Trey Fitch,
University of Cincinnati–Clermont
College, Cincinnati, OH

Reference

Lewin, K. (1951). *Field theory in social science: Selected theoretical papers.* New York: Harper.

Additional Resources

Gottman, J., Swanson, C., & Swanson, K. (2002). A general systems theory of marriage: Nonlinear differences equation modeling of marital interaction. *Personality & Social Psychology Review, 6,* 326–340.

von Bertalanffy, L. (1951). Theoretical models in biology and psychology. *Journal of Personality, 20,* 24–38.

Whitaker, D. S. (2000). Theory-building, theory-use and practice in group psychotherapy. *Group Analysis, 33,* 559–573.

■ Group Work Training

The framework of the Association for Specialists in Group Work (ASGW) professional training standards cannot be fully appreciated apart from understanding the contributions of Mullan and Rosenbaum's 1962 model for the training of group psychotherapists (Conyne, Wilson, & Ward, 1997). According to this model, effective training of group psychotherapists required (a) didactic instruction (e.g., history of group psychotherapy, leader skills), (b) clinical workshops (e.g., training groups with suggested number of hours), (c) personal work (i.e., participating in a group as a client), and (d) supervised experience (e.g., provision of support and promotion of personal introspection). Since then, other group leader training models have demonstrated remarkable similarities (e.g., Fenster & Colah, 1991; Gallagher, 1994; Yalom, 1985), thus reaffirming key aspects of Mullan and Rosenbaum's seminal work.

Accordingly, in 1983 ASGW instituted *Professional Standards for Group Counseling.* With the establishment of knowledge competencies, skill competencies, and supervised clock hours, graduate-level counseling programs now had guidelines for instruction and preparation in group counseling. In 1990, revisions to this seminal document reflected a broader understanding of ways in which counselors interact with groups. Adopting the term **group work** in the revised title, the *Association for Specialists in Group Work Professional Standards for the Training of Group Workers* (ASGW, 1992) identified core training standards that were essential to all counselors as well as additional specialized training required for those integrating group work into their professional practice. Specialized training was delineated by distinguishing among four major types of groups: task groups, counseling groups, psychoeducation groups, and psychotherapy groups (ASGW, 1992).

By 2000, the training standards were again revised, reflecting the influence of a decade of scholarly debate and discussion. Retaining the distinction between core training standards and specialization training standards, specific content instruction (e.g., course work and knowledge objectives) and clinical instruction (e.g., group skills and group experience) were specified. Revisions also sought to clarify the distinction between task group facilitation, psychoeducational group leadership, group counseling, and group psychotherapy. In part, these changes provided increased specificity by distinguishing what group leaders do from why they do it:

- *Specialization in task and work group facilitation.* The application of principles of normal human development and functioning through group-based cognitive, affective, behavioral, or systemic intervention strategies applied in the context of here-and-now interaction that promote efficient and effective accomplishment of group tasks among people who are gathered to accomplish group task goals

- *Specialization in psychoeducation group leadership.* The application of principles of normal human development and functioning through group-based educational and developmental strategies applied in the context of here-and-now interaction that promote personal and interpersonal growth and development and the prevention of future difficulties among people who may be at risk for the development of personal or interpersonal problems or who seek enhancement of personal qualities and abilities

- *Specialization in group counseling.* The application of principles of normal human development and functioning through group-based cognitive, affective, behavioral, or systemic intervention strategies applied in the context of here-and-now interaction that address personal and interpersonal problems of living and promote personal and interpersonal growth and development among people who may be experiencing transitory maladjustment, who are at risk for the development of personal or interpersonal problems, or who seek enhancement of personal qualities and abilities

- *Specialization in group psychotherapy.* The application of principles of normal and abnormal human development and functioning through group-based cognitive, affective, behavioral, or systemic intervention strategies applied in the context of negative emotional arousal that address personal and interpersonal problems of living, remediate perceptual and cognitive distortions or repetitive patterns of dysfunctional behavior, and promote personal and interpersonal growth and development (ASGW, 2000)

In addition, the modifications of the training standards brought them into alignment with the Council for Accreditation of Counseling and Related Educational Programs accreditation standards (ASGW, 2000).

Core Training Standards

Core training standards for all counselors require both a cognitive understanding (i.e., knowledge proficiencies) of group work and experiential application (i.e., skill proficiencies). To accomplish this goal, a minimum of one graduate course in group work, with at least 10 supervised clock hours in observation and participation as a group member and/or leader, is required to satisfy the current Association for Specialists in Group Work Professional Standards for the Training of Group Workers (ASGW, 2000). More specifically, the core training standards require that knowledge and skills objectives be met in seven areas: nature and scope of practice; assessment of group members and social systems in which they live and work; planning of group interventions; implementation of group interventions; leadership and coleadership; evaluation; and ethical practice, best practice, and diversity-competent practice. Representative examples of these seven areas across both knowledge and skill objectives are provided in Table 1.

Table 1. Core Training Standards: Knowledge and Skills Objectives

Standard	Examples	
	Knowledge Objective	Skill Objective
Nature and scope of practice	Identify and describe the nature of group work and the four specializations	Prepare a professional disclosure statement for practice in a chosen area of specialization
Assessment of group members and the social systems in which they live and work	Identify principles of group dynamics	Observe and identify group process events
Planning group interventions	Identify the impact of group member diversity on group member behavior and group process	Collaboratively consult with targeted populations to enhance ecological validity of planned group intervention
Implementation of group interventions	Identify therapeutic factors within group work; identify group work approaches that are indicated and contraindicated	Attend to and acknowledge group member behavior
Leadership and coleadership	Identify group leadership styles and approaches	Engage in reflective evaluation of one's personal leadership style
Evaluation	Identify methods of evaluating group process in group work	Contribute to evaluation activities during group participation
Ethical practice, best practice, diversity-competent practice	Identify best practices in group work	Implement best practices in group work

Specialization Guidelines

Programs that train group work specialists must provide a philosophy of training to cover the types of ASGW-recognized group work (i.e., task, psychoeducation, counseling, or psychotherapy) supported by the program for which training is provided (ASGW, 2000). Commensurate course work is also required. For example, for specialization in group psychotherapy, courses might be taken in abnormal human development and/or treatment of psychopathology, in addition to particular course work in group psychotherapy (ASGW, 2000). Like the core training standards, experiential minimum clock hours are specified for specialization training. For both task and psychoeducation group specializations, the Standards specify a minimum of 30 supervised clock hours in which the trainee facilitates or conducts a group. For specializations in group counseling or group psychotherapy, the trainee is required to put in a minimum of 45 supervised clock hours conducting the appropriate group (ASGW, 2000).

Programs wishing to grant specialization training must also implement a clear and coherent curriculum plan that demonstrates the resources to help trainees substantially advance their understanding and skills relative to the seven core training areas previously discussed (ASGW, 2000).

Contributed by Mark D. Newmeyer,
University of Cincinnati,
Cincinnati, OH

References

Association for Specialists in Group Work. (1983). *ASGW professional standards for group counseling*. Alexandria VA: Author.

Association for Specialists in Group Work. (1992). Association for Specialists in Group Work professional standards for the training of group workers. *Journal for Specialists in Group Work, 17,* 12–19.

Association for Specialists in Group Work. (2000). Association for Specialists in Group Work professional standards for the training of group workers. *Journal for Specialists in Group Work, 25,* 327–342.

Conyne, R. K., Wilson, F. R., & Ward, D. (1997). *Comprehensive group work: What it means and how to teach it*. Alexandria, VA: American Counseling Association.

Fenster, A., & Colah, J. (1991). The making of a group psychotherapist: Needs and goals for graduate and postgraduate training. *Group, 15,* 155–162.

Gallagher, R. E. (1994). Stages of group psychotherapy supervision: A model for supervising beginning trainees of dynamic group therapy. *International Journal of Group Psychotherapy, 44,* 169–183.

Yalom, I. D. (1985). *The theory and practice of group psychotherapy* (3rd ed.). New York: Basic Books.

Additional Resources

Association for Specialists in Group Work Web site: http://www.asgw.org/training_standards.htm

Conyne, R. K., & Bemak, F. (Eds.). (2004). Teaching group work [Special issue], *Journal for Specialists in Group Work, 29*(1).

■ Group Work, Types of

Group work focuses on harnessing the curative forces that can emerge from people gathering in groups to achieve a common purpose. To organize the myriad of group interventions that have emerged, the **Association for Specialists in Group Work (ASGW)** proposed a four-fold typology (ASGW, 2000), which included task group consultation, group psychoeducation, group counseling, and group psychotherapy. In addition, leaderless or peer-led support groups are discussed in this entry.

Task Groups and Work Consultation

Task group consultation focuses on facilitating an existing work group to establish and accomplish defined goals. Skillful work group consultants typically have studied organizational development, management and consultation, and other practices that assist groups in accomplishing identified work goals and have mastered such skills as obtaining goal clarity, facilitating group decision making, managing conflict, and blending interpersonal factors with the predominant task focus. These groups function in the context of a larger organizational structure and include such groups as task forces, committees, community organizations, discussion groups, volunteer groups, and learning groups whose purpose is to achieve work goals.

Rather than focus on individual growth, task groups focus on accomplishing a common goal. Although the group itself determines the content, the group leader manages the group dynamics as a means of enhancing group performance. Once the goal is accomplished, the group is disbanded. For example, a task force may be formed in a school to determine ways to improve school attendance. Group members may gather data, generate ideas, and set goals to be implemented by the staff. Once the program has been implemented, the task force may be terminated.

One of the earliest forms of task group consultation was **training-groups** (or **T-groups**), originally formed in 1947 and based on Kurt Lewin's field theory, which studied group process and experimented with group behaviors. T-groups help managers gain a greater understanding of the group processes and dynamics among their employees, increase leadership efficacy, and improve management of group conflict. T-groups were the precursor to what is now known as **sensitivity groups or team-building.** Techniques used to facilitate greater awareness and change include self-observation and self-disclosure, vicarious learning, feedback, catharsis, and universality.

Encounter groups, an outgrowth of T-groups, are a form of interpersonal process group that was popular in the 1960s and 1970s and involved small to moderately large groups meeting for several hours a week or, in the case of **marathon groups,** even 24 hours in a row. The goal was to increase members' awareness of themselves and their impact on others using verbal and experiential methods to get participants to experience and express intense emotions and process them in the here and now. Although encounter groups were typically led by professionals, often arising from the Gestalt school, they were at times also led by people not trained as mental health professionals, which resulted in concern when the groups' intense emotional impact resulted in a negative effect on individuals with mental health problems who were involved in the groups.

A form of task group supporting physical, mental, and spiritual health goals is the **social advocacy group.** Although these groups may be professionally led, they are often leaderless groups that involve a small group of members (8–10) and are generally oriented around a common purpose (e.g., reducing pollution by an area corporation, providing peer supervision for counselors, faith-based support).

Social advocacy was also an important component in **consciousness-raising groups,** which were initially formed in the 1960s and 1970s by radical feminists to give women a place to talk to each other and to gain greater awareness of their commonality of experience, which historically they did not discuss because of societal role expectations. Subjects covered by these groups included spousal conflicts, abortion, surviving rape, and so on. These groups were often thought of as a form of political action, encouraging women to view their problematic experiences less as neuroses and more as social issues. The focus was on changing social issues, as determined by the members, rather than on changing the woman's mental or emotional state or behavior.

Both school and community counselors lead or participate in task groups to address individual and systemic issues. When-

ever a school counselor assembles a group of school personnel to develop a plan to assist an individual student, the counselor has created a task group. Group members are selected based on the nature of the problem and may include administrators, teachers, special education specialists, counselors, and school psychologists. The team works together to determine what services may best assist the student and identifies how these services can collaborate to maximize the benefits of the interventions. In the area of mental health counseling, the current best practice models encourage a team-based approach in which counselors, social workers, and community-based services work together to implement services.

Group Psychoeducation

Group psychoeducation refers to providing educational experiences in a group format, typically to promote the goals of primary and secondary prevention. Leaders of psychoeducational groups must understand principles of instruction and theories of human development, be skillful in the integration of information and the use of structured exercises, and have knowledge on the topic addressed by the group that they are able to translate into an educational plan for the group members. Members are presented with information relevant to the group topic, engaged in activities that illustrate and reinforce the topic, and provided the opportunity to integrate the information and activities through group processing. At times, clients are placed in psychoeducational groups in order to learn more about a common issue (e.g., anger management) and learn more about group processes while they wait to enter a counseling or psychotherapy group.

Psychoeducational groups are often used in school counseling or community mental health settings as prevention or supportive intervention for commonly shared problems. School counselors, mental health professionals, or paraprofessionals may conduct groups to enhance parent–child relationships, called **parent education groups.** These groups teach parenting skills to help parents learn new and more effective ways to address discipline and communication issues with their children in order to improve these relationships. Another type of group school formed by counselors is **guidance groups** of 6 to 10 students that are generally focused on a specific issue or skill deficit shared by the students. Some examples of guidance groups are new student groups, study skills groups, friendship groups, and anger management groups.

Some school counseling groups can also be defined as life skills groups, although they may be led by professionals or paraprofessionals in mental health settings as well. **Life skills groups** offer psychoeducational and behavioral interventions to assist a small number of group members (8–10) who demonstrate deficits in skills, such as resolving conflict, communicating with others, cooperation, problem solving, or other skills necessary for healthy functioning. Life skills groups are also popular in group homes and mental health agencies to improve the functioning of the patients once they move into noninstitutionalized environments.

Community mental health agencies or hospitals often use psychoeducational groups to help clients with chronic mental illness (e.g., schizophrenia, bipolar disorder) and their families learn more about their mental health issues. The groups provide information about the illness experienced, common caregiver issues, available supports for clients and their families, and advocacy issues, and they offer social support to group members dealing with a common experience.

Group Counseling

Group counseling uses the group's interpersonal dynamics to address common career, personal, social, and developmental concerns. Using skills that facilitate interpersonal problem solving as well as interactive feedback and support, the leader works within a here-and-now framework that maximizes the use of major group counseling strategies, techniques, and procedures. Leader skills include using pacing appropriate to stages of group development, intervening effectively with critical incidents, and responding appropriately to disruptive members. Group counseling addresses the personal and interpersonal problems of living and generally is aimed at people who are experiencing difficulty with life transitions or who are seeking to enhance personal abilities and qualities.

Group counseling is used in both schools and community mental health settings. In schools, counselors may identify a common area of concern, such as grief and loss issues. A group may then be formed around this general topic, thus providing students with an opportunity to examine issues that may be affecting their social and academic progress. The school counselor may identify certain predictable life issues for which group counseling would be appropriate. Examples of these issues include transitioning to a new school, adjusting to parental divorce, and coping with the end of a relationship. Group counseling may also address more specific topics such as incarceration of a parent or dealing with the deployment of family members by the military.

In a similar manner, group counseling that occurs in mental health settings can provide an avenue for general exploration of personal issues within the group context. Groups may focus on addressing topics to enhance growth as well as topics around coping with loss. **Relationship groups** are one example of a counseling group that focuses on enhancing relationship skills. They are highly effective in helping people learn about their interpersonal styles and to make changes in the way they relate with others. The changes are usually based on shared group feedback, thus helping people see that their interpersonal style may be problematic and, therefore, leads to difficulties in communicating and relating with others. These counseling groups are led by trained mental health professionals who work with a small number of participants (5–8) to establish an atmosphere of trust where members feel they can be honest about who they are and honest in their communication with each other. One type of relationship group is the **couples group,** which is a professionally led counseling group with four to six couples who meet to work on enhancing their relationships.

In the 1950s, **remotivation groups** were developed to help regressed mental health patients who had been institutionalized to improve socialization and self-esteem. Currently, they are used primarily with severely depressed patients and individuals who are older living in long-term

care facilities. Similarly, **reminiscing groups** of five to seven participants are therapeutic in increasing the sense of self-worth and coping abilities of older individuals. The other group members listen and ask questions to help the speaker expand on his or her memories. The groups may be ongoing or time limited, providing members a chance to tell the stories of their lives.

Group Psychotherapy

Group psychotherapy addresses core issues presented by group members who have experienced significant psychological or emotional dysfunction. Such groups may examine antecedents to the current behavior as well as focus on remediation of perceptual and cognitive distortions that maintain dysfunctional thinking, repetitive patterns of behavior, and acute or chronic psychological distress. Group leaders need to be knowledgeable about normal and abnormal human development, assessment and diagnosis of psychological disorders, and treatment of psychopathology in addition to their knowledge of the theory and practice of group psychotherapy. Additional training in family therapy and family pathology is beneficial, given the need to explore the connection between past events and present functioning and to be able to address family-systemic issues that may arise in these groups. Although clients with serious mental health disorders may benefit from other group formats such as psychoeducational groups, the goal of group psychotherapy is to assist members in examining the emotional origins of their current functioning and engaging in personality reconstruction. For example, groups for individuals who have been sexually molested as children will help members examine the dynamics that underlie the abuse from an individual, family, and community perspective.

An intense form of group psychotherapy requiring specialized training is **psychodrama groups,** developed by J. L. Moreno to use storytelling and enactment as a therapeutic medium. During psychodrama groups, a member of the group tells stories about significant incidents in his or her life while other group members act out those memories. The experiential nature of the group increases the understanding of both the storyteller and the other group members of the events and the resulting emotional impact. Psychodrama groups can be very intense, and leaders require supervision from a therapist trained in psychodrama who has worked to prepare the group members for the intense nature of the group work and who has developed a safe place for the work to occur. Following the reenactment, the member processes the experience and works to integrate the affective, cognitive, and behavioral experiences. The group may also enact a healing scene as directed by the storyteller, demonstrating how the members of the group would ideally like things to be in the situation or relationship previously acted out.

Leaderless or Peer-Led Support Groups

The **leaderless group** or **peer-led support group** is a special form of group that does not fit neatly into the ASGW typology of groups but that makes a critical contribution to the physical and mental health of people with a wide variety of problems. These groups provide support for people who share a common problem such as alcoholism (Alcoholics Anonymous, Al-Anon, Al-a-teen), weight management (Take Off Pounds Sensibly), or drug addiction (Narcotics Anonymous), among others. Generally, there is no limit to the number of people in the group. These groups facilitate the increased well-being of people who are dealing in isolation with issues such as divorce or other social adjustment situations (e.g., grief groups) or mental (e.g., bipolar disorder) or physical (e.g., arthritis) illness. In the last two decades, there has also been an increase in the emergence of job support groups that provide opportunities for networking and development of job search skills for people who have recently become unemployed. With recent advances in electronic communication, support groups are increasingly being held as virtual or online groups. Another example of a peer-led group is the consciousness raising groups popular during the early and middle stages of the women's movement and the men's groups that emerged shortly thereafter. These groups were formed to raise consciousness about gender issues.

Contributed by Leigh Falls, Sam Houston State University, Huntsville, TX, and Susan Furr, University of North Carolina at Charlotte, Charlotte, NC

References

Association for Specialists in Group Work. (2000). Association for Specialists in Group Work professional standards for the training of group workers. *Journal for Specialists in Group Work, 25,* 327–342.

Additional Resources

Andrews, H. B. (1995). *Group design and leadership: Strategies for creating successful common-theme groups.* Boston: Allyn & Bacon.

Conyne, R. K., & Wilson, F. R. (1998). Toward a standards-based classification of group work offerings. *Journal for Specialists in Group Work, 23,* 177–184.

Grotjahn, M., Kline, F. M., & Friedmann, C. T. H. (1983). *Handbook of group therapy.* New York: Van Nostrand Reinhold.

Moreno, J. L. (1988). *The essential Moreno: Writings on psychodrama, group method and spontaneity.* New York: Springer.

Pinney, E. L., & Slipp, S. (1982). *Glossary of group and family therapy.* New York: Brunner Mazel.

Waldo, M., & Bauman, S. (1998). Regrouping the categorization of group work: A goals and process (GAP) matrix for groups. *Journal for Specialists in Group Work, 23,* 164–176.

Halo Effect

The **halo effect** is the subjective, usually positive, perception of an individual's traits or abilities that is generalized to the individual's other traits and abilities. Usually, first impressions are generalized to subsequent additional traits and abilities of the considered individual, group, thing, or service. The halo effect was originally described by Thorndike (1920) after he discovered that estimates of employees' various traits (e.g., intelligence, industry, technical skill, reliability) were highly and evenly correlated. Evaluators' "ratings were apparently affected by a marked tendency to think of the person in general as rather good or rather inferior and to color the judgments of the qualities by this general feeling" (Thorndike, 1920, p. 25).

The halo effect may also apply to consideration of groups, things, and corporate entities. For example, a well-groomed and attractive person is more likely to be considered intelligent and competent in a job interview. New product lines introduced under a well-regarded brand name are more likely to be perceived favorably in the market. Prestigious universities are more likely to be granted research funding regardless of a particular application's merit. The opposite, or "devil effect," may also apply. For instance, a significantly obese individual may be considered less successful or less self-disciplined when being socially evaluated.

A counselor might choose to appropriate the strength of a given client trait or skill and apply it as a "halo effect" to other traits and skills in the client's life. For example, use of the halo effect could foster self-esteem and self-management, for example, "It sounds like your determination to set a personal record in track and field might also play a strong role in improving your grades." The professional counselor is, however, also cautioned to be aware of the negative side of the halo effect when assessing clients' situations. For example, a wise counselor knows to look beyond the halo effect of a well-dressed, successful client when probing for addictive processes or substance abuse. Finally, counselors can educate clients about the influences of the halo effect when drawing conclusions about others. For example, a client working to overcome codependent habits may benefit from understanding that individuals who excel in one area of life (e.g., business, politics, personal charisma) may not excel in others (e.g., personal commitments or intimate relationships).

Contributed by Carol M. Smith, Liberty
University, Lynchburg, VA

Reference

Thorndike, E. L. (1920). A constant error in psychological ratings. *Journal of Applied Psychology, 4*, 25–29.

Additional Resource

Lachman, S., & Bass, A. (1985). A direct study of halo effect. *Journal of Psychology, 119*, 535.

Havighurst's Developmental Tasks

According to **Robert Havighurst,** human development is a lifelong process that is characterized by six stages: (a) infancy and early childhood, (b) middle childhood, (c) adolescence, (d) early adulthood, (e) middle age, and (f) late maturity. During each stage, the individual accomplishes different tasks, either in sequence or simultaneously, according to his or her biological, social, and cognitive development. Havighurst suggested that the individual's ability to master the developmental tasks in each stage can have a profound impact on later stages of development because some developmental tasks acquired at later stages are building on previously established skills. In addition, Havighurst postulated that the developmental sequence of different tasks also varies across social classes and cultures. Although an individual's biological predisposition may determine his or her readiness for further development in some developmental tasks, most tasks are acquired through socialization and social learning, such as close supervision and guidance from teachers, parents, and/or peers. Hence, a developmental sequence in one culture or social class might not necessarily be the same sequence in another culture or social class. The six developmental stages and corresponding developmental tasks are presented in the following list (Havighurst, 1962):

I. Developmental tasks of infancy and early childhood
   1. Learning to walk
   2. Learning to take solid foods (>2 years old)
   3. Learning to talk
   4. Learning to control the elimination of body wastes
   5. Learning sex differences and sexual modesty
   6. Forming concepts and learning language to describe social and physical reality
   7. Getting ready to read
   8. Learning to distinguish right and wrong and beginning to develop a conscience

II. Developmental tasks of middle childhood
   1. Learning physical skills necessary for ordinary games

2. Building wholesome attitudes toward oneself as a growing organism
3. Learning to get along with age-mates
4. Learning an appropriate masculine or feminine social role
5. Developing fundamental skills in reading, writing, and calculating
6. Developing concepts necessary for everyday living
7. Developing conscience, morality, and a scale of values
8. Achieving personal independence
9. Developing attitudes toward social groups and institutions

III. Developmental tasks of adolescence
1. Achieving new and more mature relations with age-mates of both sexes
2. Achieving a masculine or feminine social role
3. Accepting one's physique and using the body effectively
4. Achieving emotional independence of parents and other adults
5. Preparing for marriage and family life
6. Preparing for an economic career
7. Acquiring a set of values and an ethical system as a guide to behavior—developing and ideology
8. Desiring and achieving socially responsible behavior

IV. Developmental tasks of early adulthood
1. Selecting a mate
2. Learning to live with a marriage partner
3. Starting a family
4. Rearing children
5. Managing a home
6. Getting started in an occupation
7. Taking on civic responsibility
8. Finding a congenial social group

V. Developmental tasks of middle age
1. Assisting teenage children to become responsible and happy adults
2. Achieving adult social and civic responsibility
3. Reaching and maintaining satisfactory performance in one's occupational career
4. Developing adult leisure time activities
5. Relating oneself to one's spouse as a person
6. Accepting and adjusting to the physiological changes of middle age

VI. Development tasks of late maturity
1. Adjusting to decreasing physical strength and health
2. Adjustment to retirement and reduced income
3. Adjusting to the death of a spouse
4. Establishing an explicit affiliation with one's age group
5. Adopting and adapting social roles in a flexible way
6. Establishing satisfactory physical living arrangements

In the stage of infancy and early childhood, children not only learn to control and use their bodies but also learn to

form different perceptions of their surroundings. These perceptions may include different conceptualizations of physical entities, human beings, and abstract concepts. Once these skills are developed, the child enters the second stage, middle childhood. During the middle-childhood stage, the child further refines previously established skills to a more advanced level of integration. In other words, the child combines and embraces both physical and cognitive abilities into one entity. The child refines and develops new concepts and skills. The child then accumulates these newly acquired abilities into an imaginary pool of reference, which can be drawn on in the future. Once the child masters these relatively self-centered developmental tasks, the focus will be directed toward the interpersonal level as the child approaches the end of the middle-childhood stage and enters adolescence.

In short, childhood development links the initial establishment and internal awareness of oneself, both physically and cognitively, to the emergence of social awareness. Failing to do so (e.g., lack of self-awareness, lack of other-awareness, lack of effective communication, and lack of coping skills) can result in the exhibition of externalizing behaviors (e.g., noncompliant behaviors, disrespectful behaviors, aggression toward others) as presented by many clinically disturbed children in counseling. Counseling for this particular stage of development thus should emphasize the development of a child's sense of and perception of self and progress into the awareness of others and the fundamental skills for social interaction that prepare a child for future development.

Desire for social interactions and the development of social relationships are the major characteristics of adolescents. Through these social and emotional exchanges, the adolescent verifies the inner concept and solidifies the virtue that will guide behaviors. These attitudes and beliefs may also play a large role in producing emotions in different situations. Subsequently, the young adult develops emotional independence and claims to have individual thoughts; however, the desire for interpersonal relationships and intimacy continues throughout adulthood. The adult becomes a responsible citizen, partner, and parent while simultaneously achieving career aspirations. Next, the older adult prepares the next generation of children to achieve their own developmental tasks. Finally, when all of these different developmental tasks (e.g., emotional independence, development of intimacy, career development, nurturance of the next generation) are accomplished, the mature adult eventually adjusts to physical limitations, loss of loved ones, and a new form of social roles and relationships.

Hence, the development from late adolescence to late adulthood is characterized by separation from caregivers to individuation of self and progresses into attachment through other meaningful relationships (e.g., partners, friends, work, children). Failure to do so may lead to emotional disturbances (e.g., depression, anxiety) if environmental triggers are presented. Counseling individuals in these stages of development should focus on exploring and understanding the individual's constructed meaning of relationships, the development of meaningful relationships, and the restoration of and bereavement over past meaningful relationships. These relationships can be an individual's relationships with a partner or colleagues, relationships between self and work, relationships between parent and child, and so on.

By identifying the sequence of these developmental tasks and emphasizing the fact that the sequence is not identical for all cultures and social classes, Havighurst's discernment of human development has conveyed an important message to practitioners: Careful consideration is especially important when working with children and adolescents because rapid and frequent developmental changes characterize these stages. In order to have a better assessment of a client's development, professional counselors need to consider at least three levels: individual, societal, and cultural. Professional counselors should also tailor their interventions uniquely to each client within a developmental context.

Contributed by Sin-Wan Bianca Ho,
University of Southern Mississippi,
Hattiesburg, MS

Reference

Havighurst, R. J. (1972). *Developmental tasks and education.* Philadelphia: McKay.

Health Management Organization

A **health management organization (HMO),** often referred to as a **health maintenance organization** or **managed care system,** consists of a mixture of organizations, including providers, financial and management companies, and payees, designed to manage accessibility and quality in the delivery of health care services, outcomes, and costs. HMOs administer somatic and mental health care services under the auspices of a party other than the practitioner or the client. This system, which became widely used during the 1980s, differs from the traditional fee-for-service system that is controlled primarily by practitioners and service demand.

HMOs were developed as a response to the rapidly escalating costs for patient and client care fostered by the fee-for-service system. Third-party payers developed the HMO system to help provide more effective cost control of services and better quality services. The HMO system stresses time-limited interventions, cost-effective methods, evidence-based clinical approaches, and an increased focus on preventative rather than curative strategies. Typically, members receive their care from in-network providers. Unless referred by their provider to an outside specialist, the network will not cover the costs of services by other health care providers or services not covered by their plan.

Contributed by Shawn L. Spurgeon,
The University of Tennessee at
Knoxville, Knoxville, TN

Additional Resource

Starr, P. (1984). *The social transformation of American medicine.* New York: Basic Books.

Helping Relationships, Key Ethical Issues in

The **2005 American Counseling Association's (ACA)** *ACA Code of Ethics* provides ethical principles to guide the actions of its members. It contains eight subsections, the first of which is Section A: The Counseling Relationship. Section A addresses a number of critical ethical concerns, including client welfare, professional counselor roles and relationships, working with multiple clients, working with terminally ill clients, fees and bartering concerns, termination and abandonment issues, and technology applications. Although not a distinct plan of action for every ethical dilemma, the *ACA Code of Ethics* provides guidance for professional counselors to interpret and determine correct actions through the lens of their own unique situations with clients.

A brief introduction that provides users with the general context prefaces each section of the *Code.* Section A: The Counseling Relationship is introduced with the concept of **autonomy;** that is, professional counselors foster healthy client development in ways that promote client welfare through the cultural worldview of the client. It encourages professional counselors to explore their own cultural values in light of how these values affect the counseling relationship. This section is also introduced with an understanding that counselors should provide some services at a reduced rate or pro bono as a service to the public.

The primary responsibility of professional counselors is to promote the best interests of clients and to value their right to autonomy. Professional counselors do this by involving clients in the counseling process and adequately and accurately documenting the work of counseling. A significant addition to the 2005 *ACA Code of Ethics* is the change in language related to family. Previously, professional counselors were advised to solicit involvement from the client's family when possible to maximize the opportunities for success. That language has changed to "support network involvement," reflecting the culturally relevant concept that not all support systems are made up of family members.

While acknowledging current practices, the *Code* recognizes that counseling has roots in vocational guidance. In Section A, the *Code* directs professional counselors to facilitate successful career matches with clients by ensuring that the employment considerations are commensurate with the clients' skills, abilities, talents, and interests.

Section A addresses, at least to an extent, the role of **informed consent** in the client–counselor relationship. Informed consent, put simply, allows the client to have the right to enter or not enter into the counseling relationship. Consent is provided within the relevant cultural context and in language understandable by the client and includes information about the type of services the client can expect from the professional counselor. Other portions of the *Code* address informed consent in further detail, and other entries in this encyclopedia provide more in-depth information on this topic.

Another important consideration in this section is the attention paid to nonmaleficence and counselor values. **Nonmaleficence,** or the directive to do no harm, is a guiding principle of the counseling profession. The *ACA Code of Ethics* addresses this underlying moral principle specifically and reminds practitioners to avoid harm where possible and to mend any unintentional or unavoidable harm suffered by clients, students, and research participants. In addition, professional counselors are reminded that their own values play a role in the counseling process and are cautioned against imposing their personal belief systems on clients.

Section A receives a great deal of attention in the profession because it defines roles and relationships with current and former clients. There has long been debate over what have been called dual relationships in the profession. Essentially, a **dual relationship** is an additional relationship outside of the client–counselor relationship. The 2005 *Code* recognizes that these multiple roles are not always damaging and may even be potentially beneficial. An example might be attending the graduation of a client who had struggled academically during the counselor's and client's work together. The *Code* outlines clear directions to the professional counselor that require such an occurrence be initiated by the client and evaluated for potential consequences. Consultation plays a key role in evaluating the potential for harm, and professional counselors are encouraged to engage in consultation as a routine part of ethical decision making.

There is continued controversy about romantic or sexual relationships with current or former clients or their family members. Such relationships with current clients or their family members are expressly prohibited in the *Code*. A question is, however, what constitutes a family member in the *Code?* It is easy to see how difficult it could be to assess the amount of damage done to clients' extended family members who have relationships with professional counselors. It is clearer that these types of relationships with clients are viewed as universally damaging and are thus forbidden; however, the *Code* may permit professional counselors to enter sexual or romantic relationships with former clients 5 or more years after the conclusion of the counseling relationship. The professional counselor is required to assess the role of the prior counseling relationship as well as whether entering into this new relationship has the potential to damage the former client in any way and document that assessment in writing. If harm is possible, the professional counselor is instructed not to enter into the relationship.

Professional counselors routinely find themselves in multiple roles. They may be counselors, teachers, supervisors, evaluators, or researchers. The *ACA Code of Ethics* addresses role changes during the client–counselor relationship and directs professional counselors to obtain an additional informed consent with each change to allow the client the opportunity to understand the implications of the role change and refuse to enter into those services if needed. This is related to other portions of Section A that provide guidance for working with multiple clients and clients in group settings where both individual and group counseling may be offered.

Working with more than one client at a time often results in issues related to appropriate treatment methods and confidentiality. Professional counselors must screen and protect clients who are invited to participate in counseling that involves multiple clients. In addition to ensuring this is the best treatment option for the client, counselors have added confidentiality concerns in that confidentiality cannot be guaranteed, given there are several participants. Confidentiality is regularly the basis for a large portion of the ethical inquiries made to ACA.

Section A of the 2005 *Code* includes an addition to the previous *Code* related to working with **terminally ill clients** who elect to hasten their own deaths. Previously considered a duty to warn issue, the *Code* now allows counselors who work with such clients the option to break or not break the client's confidentiality when making such personal determinations related to end of life care. The *Code* is culturally respectful in its recognition that rational suicide may be an option for some mentally healthy and competent adults who are terminally ill. It also allows the professional counselor the option to refer clients whose choices conflict with the counselor's personal values.

An additional consideration is related to **fees, bartering, and gifts.** Previously considered to have negative consequences, bartering is now viewed as ethical when culturally appropriate and beneficial to the client. Again, this must be initiated by the client, evaluated for negative consequences, and entered into with written consent. Similarly, receiving gifts from clients may be ethical practice if the purpose and value of the gift are taken into consideration. Although these remuneration directives allow professional counselors to make choices based on individual circumstances, the *Code* clearly prohibits accepting private fees or other additional compensation from clients who are eligible for services provided by the counselor's employer.

The part of Section A that addresses **termination and referral** suggests that professional counselors should consider the end of the counseling relationship when they begin such relationships. Although clients have the right to leave the counseling process as they choose, counselors have a professional and ethical obligation to terminate formally. Professional counselors are prohibited from abandoning clients without referral. Professional counselors may end relationships when the services have reached a natural conclusion, when benefit is no longer occurring, or the counselor can no longer assist, as well as in rare instances when clients experience harm as the result of services. Upon recognition that termination is needed, counselors appropriately transfer or refer clients to other practitioners. Transfer or referral must also occur when services are interrupted due to illness, vacation, or extended leave. Essentially, if the counselor is no longer available to the client for some reason, the counselor is obligated to make provisions for the client to receive alternative care.

Finally, Section A addresses the burgeoning use of **technology** in the provision of counseling services. The *Code* acknowledges both the benefits and limitations of technology and provides for the ethical use of electronic communication, distance counseling using technology applications, and the World Wide Web and mandates fair access to such services. Although technological, cultural, and other changes related to current practice are clearly evident in the 2005

ACA Code of Ethics, it is the best interests of clients that ultimately drive consideration in Section A.

Contributed by Donna S. Starkey, Delta
State University, Delta, MS

Reference

American Counseling Association. (2005). *ACA code of ethics.* Alexandria, VA: Author.

Additional Resources

American Counseling Association Web site: http://www.counseling.org

Kocet, M. (2006). Ethical challenges in a complex world: Highlights of the 2005 *ACA Code of Ethics. Journal of Counseling & Development, 84,* 228–234.

■ Helping Relationships, Key Legal Issues in

Legal issues in the helping relationships begin in the training phase and extend throughout the career of the professional counselor. Students in counselor education programs, also known as counselors-in-training, must be familiar with the American Counseling Association's (ACA; 2005) *ACA Code of Ethics* and must obey the laws and policies of their placements and internship settings (Section F.8.a.). Counselor educators and agency and school personnel who are supervising counselors-in-training are obligated to ensure that clients understand that they are being counseled by a trainee/intern and must ultimately assume legal responsibility for the work of the trainee/intern.

Most states require professional counselors to be licensed or certified beyond having a master's degree in the field. **Licensure statutes,** part of statutory law, serve to regulate practice and to define the scope of practice in the profession. The specific requirements for licensure or certification vary widely across the states. Professional counselors are also affected by **case law** (when court decisions set legal precedents that must be followed by the profession) and by **administrative law** (which develops regulations [e.g., state boards] to govern practice). Professional counselors may be prosecuted under civil and/or criminal law for various violations, some of which are discussed in this entry.

Informed Consent

The legal obligation to the client begins with informed consent and may even continue after the termination phase of counseling has occurred. **Informed consent** is a legal standard of care adopted first by the medical profession and more recently by the field of psychology. The essence of informed consent is that the counselor is responsible for ensuring that the client enters counseling with an awareness of both the practical issues (e.g., fees, cancellation policies, charges for missed sessions, duration of sessions, interactions with managed care, limits of confidentiality) and the clinical issues (e.g., process of diagnosis, potential benefits and risks of participation, theoretical orientation, areas of specialization).

The client (or the client's parent/guardian in the case of minors, as discussed later in this entry) must have the capacity for consent, understand what the counselor has explained, and enter counseling voluntarily. These are the legal aspects of informed consent, a practice that should take place during the initial meeting and continue throughout counseling. Section A.2. of the 2005 *ACA Code of Ethics* discusses the legal and ethical obligations of the professional counselor regarding informed consent.

Professional disclosure forms are sometimes used by counselors to cover the practical and clinical issues previously listed that may arise in counseling, to introduce the counselor's background and training, and to outline counselor and client rights and responsibilities. These forms must contain accurate information regarding the counselor's credentials and qualifications to provide services, as specified in Section C.4. of the 2005 *ACA Code of Ethics.*

With regard to counseling minors or dependent adults, the legal decision-making power and right to claim privilege (discussed later in this entry) generally rests with the parent, guardian, or legally appointed representative; however, the professional counselor should include the minor or dependent adult as much as possible in the informed consent process and should, whenever possible, honor confidentiality in the counseling relationship (see 2005 *ACA Code of Ethics,* Sections A.2.d., B.5.a., B.5.b., and B.5.c.). Many states have enacted laws granting unemancipated minors limited rights to confidentiality in specific situations and/or emergencies, although age of consent and the types of legal rights vary widely across the states. These laws are called **minor consent laws.**

Termination Procedures

There are also several legal issues related to termination of clients. According to the 2005 *ACA Code of Ethics* (see Section A.11.), termination must occur when the client no longer needs, is not benefiting from, or is being harmed by the services of the professional counselor or when the professional counselor is in danger of being harmed by the client. Counselors may also terminate a client for refusal to pay agreed-on fees (see Section A.11.c.) or in the event that the client sues the counselor. The professional counselor must not, however, abandon the client through termination of the relationship and should provide appropriate support in the form of referrals to other services. In addition, the professional counselor must arrange for the appropriate and confidential transfer of clients and their files in the event of counselor's death, incapacitation, or decision to leave the practice of counseling (see Sections B.6.h. and C.2.h.).

Competence and Misconduct

One primary legal issue that arises in the counseling relationship is **competence** (i.e., counselors should not treat or counsel clients outside their realm of competence or their scope of practice). In cases where counselors are unfamiliar with clients' problems or issues, they should either gain competence through consultation (see Sections B.8.c. and

C.2.e. of the 2005 *ACA Code of Ethics*) and/or professional development, or they should refer the client to another counselor. An incompetent counselor is in breach of ethical duties, which can easily result in harm to a client through negligence or willful violation of ethics. **Professional negligence** is also known as **malpractice,** which leaves the counselor and institution where the counselor is practicing vulnerable to a malpractice suit. The 2005 *ACA Code of Ethics* can be used by clients as the basis for registering a complaint or filing a lawsuit against a professional counselor.

A commonly reported violation of the law in the counseling profession is **sexual misconduct,** which is also the most damaging form of a dual relationship. Sexual relationships with current clients are strictly prohibited (*ACA Code of Ethics,* Section A.5.a.), and sexual relationships with former clients and their family members are discouraged in general and prohibited for 5 years after the termination of the professional relationship (Section A.5.b.). A client could also sue a counselor for neglecting to obtain informed consent, for misdiagnosis, for improper treatment, for abandonment, or for spurious reasons. Due to the threat of malpractice, counselors in private practice are advised to purchase **malpractice insurance.**

Because many states legally require counselors to take notes as part of the counseling relationship and counselors can be prosecuted for incomplete, inaccurate, altered, or missing notes, record keeping represents another key legal issue for counselors. Section B.6. of the 2005 *ACA Code of Ethics* discusses the issue of records in depth. The professional counselor is legally obligated to secure client records, to maintain confidentiality with regard to records, to store and dispose of records appropriately, and to protect confidentiality of client records even after the client is deceased (see Section B.3.f.). The specific process for and time limit on storing client records varies from state to state. In addition, clients have a right to access their records (see 2005 *ACA Code of Ethics*, Sections A.2.b. and B.6.d.).

Privacy and Confidentiality

The **Health Information Portability and Accountability (HIPAA)** privacy rule, initially signed into law in 1996, expands the protection of psychotherapy notes by requiring a patient's authorization for release of information to insurance companies and by prohibiting insurance companies from denying services when the patient refuses to authorize such release. In addition, HIPAA allows patients to access their records, although it also allows therapists to decide whether or not to allow clients to see psychotherapy notes. Although HIPAA guarantees minimum standards for privacy, some state laws grant more extensive rights to clients and patients.

Confidentiality, the ethical duty of counselors not to disclose client-related information without permission or unless mandated to do so, is an even more complex legal issue in the helping profession. In most states, the professional counselor is legally obligated to maintain confidentiality regarding the content of counseling sessions, unless an exception to confidentiality applies. Sections B.1. and B.2. of the 2005

ACA Code of Ethics address this issue. The *Code* states, "Counselors do not share confidential information without client consent or without sound legal or ethical justification" (Section B.1.c.). Clients should be told their rights to confidentiality and the limits of confidentiality as part of the informed consent process, and they should be involved as much as possible in decisions to disclose confidential information (Sections B.1.d. and B.2.d.). Common exceptions to confidentiality include child and elder/dependent adult abuse, suicide and involuntary hospitalization, and duty to warn.

Child and Elder Abuse

In general, counselors should follow an assessment process to determine if the specific details of the case warrant a breach of confidentiality. There are cases in which the counselor is legally mandated to breach confidentiality and other cases in which the counselor can decide whether or not to breach. For example, if the counselor determines that child abuse has or even may have occurred, the counselor is required to notify officials (i.e., the police and/or a child welfare agency). Mandates regarding reporting child and elder/dependent adult abuse are examples of statutory law. The **Child Abuse Prevention and Treatment Act (CAPTA)** was enacted in 1974 and has been updated several times since, most recently in 2003. CAPTA provides funding for preventing and investigating child abuse, and state laws vary with regard to the specific requirements and procedures for reporting abuse. Similar laws apply with respect to elder and dependent adult abuse.

Duty to Warn

Regarding suicide, most states allow counseling professionals to assess the degree of danger and decide whether or not to breach confidentiality and/or hospitalize the client involuntarily. A professional counselor is not generally held responsible for a client's attempted or completed suicide, provided that the counselor was competent in the assessment and treatment of the client and maintained adequate documentation of the situation. However, clients have sued therapists for malpractice after an attempted suicide, and clients' families have also sued in cases of completed suicide. Such lawsuits have increased in recent years, although they still remain low in comparison with other types of malpractice suits. As previously mentioned, there has not yet been a significant legal ruling that holds therapists responsible for a client's death by suicide when they are following the principle of reasonable standard of care.

In *Bellah v. Greenson* (1978), the California Court of Appeals ruled that the therapist's duty to warn does not extend to suicide, although the therapist is required to take reasonable steps to assess clients accurately and to prevent suicide whenever possible. On the other hand, the Maryland Court of Appeals ruled in *Eisel v. Board of Education of Montgomery County* **(1991)** that school counselors have a duty to notify parents when a student is suicidal; this decision expands the responsibility of the school counselor regarding the prevention of suicide. The recent case of *Shin v. M.I.T.,* which was settled in 2004, called into question the responsibility of the mental health community to notify parents when college-age students are in danger of committing suicide.

State laws vary in terms of the counselor's duty to warn intended victims when clients are potentially violent. The most well-known case in the field of counseling and psychotherapy is ***Tarasoff v. Regents of the University of California*** (1976), which was heard on appeal by the Supreme Court of California. This seminal case became the precedent for the "duty to warn" law, in which counselors and other professionals are required to notify law enforcement and the intended victim in cases when threats of violence to an identifiable third party are made by the client. Three well-known variations on the ruling are *Bradley Center v. Wessner* (1982), *Jablonski v. United States* (1983), and *Hedlund v. Superior Court* (1983). Two recent cases, one from Ohio and one from California, have expanded duty to warn responsibilities of professional counselors. In *Morgan v. Fairfield Family Counseling Center* (1997), the Ohio Supreme Court ruled that a therapist is only legally protected if he or she hospitalizes a potentially violent client, a finding that contradicts the immunity typically granted to therapists acting under *Tarasoff*. In *Ewing v. Goldstein* (2004), the Superior Court of Los Angeles ruled that the communication of intent to harm an identifiable third party could come from either the patient (i.e., the essence of *Tarasoff*) or a family member (see Duty to Warn and Protect).

The issue of breaching confidentiality with regard to contagious, life-threatening diseases (see 2005 *ACA Code of Ethics*, Section B.2.b.) such as HIV is fraught with conflict. Although the *Code* states that the professional counselor "may be justified in disclosing information to identifiable third parties" (p. 7), some states have passed HIV confidentiality statutes that expressly forbid such disclosure. In these cases, the professional counselor may feel caught between the obligation of duty to warn others versus the obligation to maintain confidentiality with clients. Two possible remedies in these cases include helping the client to become willing to disclose the information to others and informing clients of HIV transmission laws in states that enforce criminal penalties against individuals who knowingly expose others to the virus.

Another difficult issue with regard to breaching confidentiality relates to end-of-life decisions. The 2005 *ACA Code of Ethics* states that professional counselors may or may not choose to work with clients who are considering end-of-life options, as in the case of a terminal illness (Section A.9.b.) The *Code* also states that counselors may decide to breach confidentiality in such cases, unless the law requires them to do otherwise (Section A.9.c.). Currently, only one state, Oregon, legally permits terminally ill individuals to end their lives through the voluntary ingestion of prescribed, lethal medications through the Death With Dignity Act.

A related issue is **privilege,** which is a client's confidential communications that are protected by law within the context of the individual counseling relationship. Counselors can refuse to testify or share a client's records in a court of law unless the client requests their participation (i.e., waives

privilege) or privilege is overruled by a court-ordered breach. When ordered by a court to release confidential information, the professional counselor should attempt to secure the client's written authorization and to limit the disclosure as much as possible (see Section B.2.c. of the 2005 *ACA Code of Ethics*). ***Jaffee v. Redmond* (1996)** was a landmark decision by the United States Supreme Court that effectively established the right to privileged communication between psychotherapists and patients in federal courts. The earliest case regarding privilege in psychotherapy was in 1952 with *Binder v. Ruvell,* in which a circuit court in Illinois ruled that confidential communications between a psychiatrist and patient should be considered privileged.

Technology

The professional counselor has several legal obligations with regard to the use of technology. HIPAA requires certain patient-related communications to be securely delivered when using electronic sources such as the Internet or faxes (see also 2005 *ACA Code of Ethics*, Section B.3.e.). When counselors make use of technology, they must ensure that they are not violating the law, as specified in Section A.12.e. of the 2005 *ACA Code of Ethics*. The informed consent process must be carried out when counselors intend to use technology in their communications with clients (e.g., disclosing to clients the difficulty of ensuring confidentiality with regard to e-mail and other electronically transmitted communication) or if they decide to engage in online counseling. In such cases, the professional counselor must give clients alternative sources for obtaining help, such as crisis hotline numbers (see Section A.12.g.), or alternative ways to reach the counselor (see Section A.12.h.).

At times, legal and ethical realms may be in conflict with one another, as when the ethical guidelines of the profession call on the counselor to take a certain action but the law may require another action. In these cases, the 2005 *ACA Code of Ethics* advises counselors to be familiar with the ethical guidelines and to attempt to resolve the dilemma by adhering to both the guidelines and the law whenever possible (Section H.1.b.).

Contributed by Suzy R. Thomas,
Saint Mary's College of California,
Moraga, CA

Reference

American Counseling Association. (2005). *ACA code of ethics.* Alexandria, VA: Author.

Additional Resources

Corey, G., Corey, M. S., & Callanan, P. (2007). *Issues and ethics in the helping professions* (7th ed.). Belmont, CA: Thomson Brooks/Cole.

Remley, T. P., Jr., Hermann, M. A., & Huey, W. C. (Eds.). (2003). *Ethical & legal issues in school counseling.* Alexandria, VA: American School Counselor Association.

Sperry, L. (2007). *Dictionary of ethical and legal terms and issues: The essential guide for mental health professionals.* New York: Routledge.

Helping Relationships, Key People in

The helping relationship is therapeutic and serves as a medium for implementing strategies and techniques. Originally, however, helping relationships consisted of the expert counselor providing directives by way of actions or communication to a client. There are several key figures who facilitated the understanding of the helping relationship and led to the belief that clients are the experts of their own lives and the counselor serves to empower clients through the therapeutic relationship.

Carl Rogers, considered to be one of counseling's most influential therapists, was the first to use the term *helping relationship*. Some of his most significant books include *Client-Centered Therapy* (1951), *On Becoming a Person: A Therapist's View of Psychotherapy* (1961), and *A Way of Being* (1980). Rogers's beliefs about the helping relationship were influenced by phenomenological concepts. His theory purports that people's need for positive regard from others drives the development of their self-concept and that self-regard is learned through internalization of experiences. As a result, a person's developed/emerged self-concept regulates personality and behavior. According to Rogers (1971), a helping relationship promotes "growth, development, maturity, improved functioning, [and] improved coping with life" (pp. 2–3). Various studies led Rogers to conclude that clients considered the helping relationship successful when they trusted their counselor, felt understood by him or her, and felt independent in making choices about their own dilemma/issue; thus, a therapist's empathy, unconditional positive regard, and congruence or genuineness were more important to the efficacy of counseling than the counselor's theoretical approach.

Robert R. Carkhuff's work validated the efficacy of Rogers's core conditions (i.e., empathy, unconditional positive regard, and congruence/genuineness) in the therapeutic alliance. Carkhuff, Rogers's former student, took Rogers's core conditions and operationalized these concepts into measurable skills. Some of Carkhuff's significant work was completed alongside **Charles Truax.** Both of these men solidified the importance of the core conditions in the counseling relationship; however, Carkhuff eventually parted ways with Rogers and, much like Gerard Egan, came to the conclusion that insight was insufficient in the success or progress of the client. Carkhuff began to value the merits of behavioral therapy and attempted to integrate the two approaches to counseling. Although Carkhuff's theoretical approach is aligned with Rogers's approach, Carkhuff took it a step further by addressing more of the "initiative" dimensions in therapy. According to Carkhuff, the responsive dimension of counseling consists of empathy, respect, and specificity, whereas the initiative dimension consisted of genuineness, self-disclosure, confrontation, immediacy, and concreteness. Carkhuff's model proposed that there were three phases to counseling: exploring, understanding, and acting. He also indicated that the following skills would facilitate this process: attending, responding, exploring, personalizing, understanding, initiating, and acting. In essence,

Carkhuff believed that the counselor should help clients integrate the core conditions into their own personal lives and help clients translate insight into action. In other words, the role of the counselor is to help clients help themselves.

Jerome D. Frank established that there were commonalities among the various theoretical orientations. In essence, the therapeutic relationship was central to all theoretical approaches. In addition, the therapy goals of the various theories of counseling included (a) increasing client's motivation, (b) enhancing self-efficacy, (c) providing new learning experiences, (d) raising/lowering emotional arousal, and (e) providing opportunities for implementation of new behaviors (Young, 2001). Frank's work led to the recognition of common methods and techniques that could be used to promote Rogers's core conditions. These methods and techniques, integral to the therapeutic relationship, are known as basic helping skills, microskills, or therapeutic building blocks. The therapeutic building blocks or skills known to facilitate the relationship between counselor and client include invitational, reflecting, advanced reflecting, challenging, goal-setting, and solution skills. The most important skills in building the helping relationship are invitational, reflecting, and advanced reflecting skills. **Invitational skills** consist of nonverbal skills and opening skills. Examples of nonverbal skills are eye contact, body position, and physical distance. Open-ended questions, closed-ended questions, and minimal encouragers are examples of opening skills. Examples of **reflecting skills** are paraphrasing clients' statements and reflecting the clients' underlying feelings. Reflection of underlying meaning and summarizing clients' stories are examples of advanced reflecting skills.

Gordon Allport believed that psychoanalytic psychology often overanalyzed, whereas, behavioral psychology did not analyze sufficiently; thus, he created his own theory on personality that focused on conscious motivations and current context. Allport believed that the self developed via seven functions: (a) sense of body, (b) self-identity, (c) self-esteem, (d) self-extension, (e) self-image, (f) rational coping, and (g) propriate striving. He also believed that as the self developed, personal traits/dispositions were being developed. He categorized these traits into three domains: cardinal, central, and secondary. Allport's contributions to helping relationships include the books *Becoming* (1955), *Pattern and Growth in Personality* (1961), *The Individual and His Religion* (1950), and *The Nature of Prejudice* (1954).

Gerard Egan is a professor emeritus at Loyola University of Chicago. His most influential work in the field of counseling is *The Skilled Helper: A Problem-Management and Opportunity-Development Approach to Helping* (Egan, 2002). His main contribution is organizing the approach to the helping relationship into a problem-management model. He has also strongly emphasized the methods and communication skills involved in the helping relationship. Egan believed his model of helping was a practical framework that included methods and skills that could be used by the counselor to facilitate the helping relationship. His work was influenced by Carl Rogers and can be classified as person focused. It includes the core conditions of Rogers; however,

Egan does not subscribe to the belief that Rogerian therapy is sufficient. In other words, although Egan values the core conditions in his therapy, his experience has been that not all clients who have insight act upon their revelations. Egan's model of counseling goes one step further in emphasizing client action. According to Egan (2002), two principal goals of the client are "managing specific problems in living more effectively or developing missed opportunities and unused resources, and the other relating to their general ability to manage problems and develop opportunities in everyday life" (p. 7). Egan's model can be categorized into four stages: (a) Stage 1—helping clients clarify key issues, (b) Stage 2—helping clients determine outcomes, (c) Stage 3—helping clients develop strategies for accomplishing goals, and (d) Stage 4—helping clients implement their plans/goals. Throughout the model, ongoing evaluation of counseling and client action is essential. Egan believed that what the client did between the first and second session was a strong indicator of the success of counseling.

Allen E. Ivey and **Mary Bradford Ivey** have also been key contributors to the helping relationship. Allen E. Ivey is a distinguished university professor (emeritus) at the University of Massachusetts, Amherst, and president of Microtraining Associates. Mary Bradford Ivey is vice-president of Microtraining Associates; served as a visiting professor at various universities; and was a school counselor in Amherst, Massachusetts, public schools. Although both of these therapists value and have been influenced by the person-centered Rogerian methods, they experienced that these methods alone were not sufficient in helping clients. Their main contribution to the helping relationship is the identification of microskills, or units of communication, that facilitate the interviewing process/interaction with the client. Microskills is a foundational approach that facilitates other theories aimed at promoting client growth and development. In other words, the goal of this theory is to understand the world through the eyes of the client. The Iveys have organized their microskills into a hierarchy and emphasized that counselors must master ethics, multicultural competence, and wellness prior to continuing their training as counselors.

Contributed by Veronica Castro,
The University of Texas–Pan American,
Edinburg, TX

References

Allport, G. (1950). *The individual and his religion: A psychological interpretation.* New York: Macmillan.

Allport, G. (1954). *The nature of prejudice.* Cambridge, MA: Addison-Wesley.

Allport, G. (1955). *Becoming: Basic considerations for a psychology of personality.* New Haven, CT: Yale University Press.

Allport, G. (1961). *Pattern and growth in personality.* New York: Holt, Rinehart & Winston.

Egan, G. (2002). *The skilled helper: A problem-management and opportunity-development approach to helping.* Pacific Grove, CA: Brooks/Cole.

Rogers, C. R. (1951). *Client-centered therapy, its current practice, implications, and theory.* Boston: Houghton Mifflin.

Rogers, C. R. (1961). *On becoming a person: A therapist's view of psychotherapy.* Boston: Houghton Mifflin.

Rogers, C. R. (1971). The characteristics of a helping relationship. In D. L. Avila, A. W. Combs, & W. W. Purkey (Eds.), *The helping relationship sourcebook* (pp. 2–18). Boston: Allyn & Bacon.

Rogers, C. R. (1980). *A way of being.* Boston: Houghton Mifflin.

Young, M. E. (2001). *Learning the art of helping: Building blocks and techniques* (3rd ed.). Upper Saddle River, NJ: Merrill Prentice Hall.

Additional Resources

Carkhuff, R. R. (1969). *Helping and human relations: A primer for lay and professional helpers: Vol.1. Selection and Training.* New York: Holt, Rinehart & Winston.

Ivey, A. E., & Ivey, M. B. (2007). *Intentional interviewing and counseling: Facilitating client development in a multicultural society.* Belmont, CA: Thomson Brooks/Cole.

■ High-Stakes Testing

High-stakes testing uses standardized test scores to make important educational decisions with serious consequences for students and schools. State proficiency and graduation tests, Advanced Placement examinations, the SAT, and ACT are examples of high-stakes tests used for various purposes, such as determining promotion and retention, educational placement, and entrance into special programs and college. High-scoring students may be rewarded with scholarships and admission to highly selective colleges. Students who do not achieve passing scores can be retained, placed in remedial programs, or have diplomas withheld, severely limiting their educational and career options.

Since the early 1980s, the educational reform movement has used high-stakes test results to increase school accountability. Federal and state high-stakes testing programs provide rewards and sanctions such as program funding, financial incentives, supplemental instruction and tutoring, and school reconstitution to improve test performance. The No Child Left Behind Act (NCLB; U.S. Department of Education, 2002) dramatically shifted federal education policy from individual students to school accountability by holding school districts responsible for the academic achievement of all students. States are required to administer standardized tests in mathematics and reading in Grades 3–8 and 10–12 and publish school report cards listing annual yearly progress toward academic achievement, disaggregating scores by ethnicity and other groups.

Although the NCLB goal of closing the achievement gap between higher performing and lower performing groups is generally accepted, the choice of high-stakes methodology is controversial. Proponents suggest that using high-stakes test scores provides an objective measure and uniform standards in making educational decisions, including promotion and graduation. High-stakes tests increase expectations, raise the quality of instruction, and motivate students and teachers.

School sanctions require tutoring for students with failing scores, and parents can transfer their children to schools with higher scores.

Critics cite research indicating that high-stakes testing programs do not increase academic performance or raise scores on other test measures (Center for Public Education, 2006). The use of a single criterion-referenced test negatively affects minority students who traditionally score poorly on standardized tests and fails to address the complex socioeconomic factors affecting minority student performance. Retention sanctions increase dropout rates and have an impact on students with disabilities, English language learners, and students of racial or ethnic minorities.

High-stakes testing position statements of the American Counseling Association (2005), American School Counselor Association (2002), American Educational Research Association (2000), and numerous educational associations agree that high-stakes decisions should be based on multiple criteria, not on a single test score. Students who do not achieve benchmark scores should be provided multiple opportunities to take the test or alternative tests and to engage in meaningful remediation programs to improve their performance.

Standardized tests used for high-stakes decisions must produce valid and reliable scores for the purposes intended. Content should be limited to curriculum that students have the opportunity to learn at their developmental level with adequate instruction and resources. Multiple assessment measures and authentic assessment can reduce high-stakes test failures and keep educational and career pathways open for disadvantaged students.

Contributed by Jane Webber, Seton Hall University, South Orange, NJ

References

American Counseling Association. (2005). *Position on high-stakes testing.* Alexandria, VA: Author.

American Educational Research Association. (2000). *AERA position concerning high-stakes testing in preK–12 education.* Washington, DC: National Academy of Education.

American School Counselor Association. (2002). *Position statement: High-stakes testing.* Alexandria, VA: Author.

Center for Public Education. (2006). *Research review: Effects of high-stakes testing on instruction.* Retrieved October 12, 2007, from http://www.centerforpubliceducation.org/site.

U. S. Department of Education. (2002). PL 107-110. *No Child Left Behind* (NCLB) Act. Retrieved October 10, 2007, from http://www.ed.gov/policy/landing.jhtml?src=rt

Additional Resources

Amrein, A. L., & Berliner, D. C. (2002). High-stakes testing, uncertainty, and student learning. *Education Policy Analysis Archives, 10*(18), 1–65.

Brown, D., Galassi, J. P., & Akos, P. (2004). School counselors' perceptions of the impact of high-stakes testing. *Professional School Counseling, 8,* 31–39.

Johnson, D. D., & Johnson, J. B. (2006). *High stakes: Poverty, testing, and failure in American schools* (2nd ed.). Lanham, MD: Rowan & Littlefield.

■ HIV/AIDS, Counseling Clients With

The **human immunodeficiency virus (HIV)** came to public awareness in 1981 and has created a pandemic, leading to the deaths of 25 million people worldwide representing every sector of society. Worldwide, 40 million people are currently infected with HIV, and up to 25% may be unaware that they are infected (Centers for Disease Control and Prevention [CDC], 2005). It is an insidious infection, invading and slowly disabling the immune system, leaving the person vulnerable to opportunistic infections that others without HIV successfully fight off. It is transmitted by contact with the blood, semen, or vaginal fluids of an infected person; through unprotected sex or shared needles; and from an HIV positive mother to her baby during birth or breastfeeding. Fortunately, the virus does not survive long outside the body and cannot be spread by casual touching, by coming into contact with surfaces in the environment, by coughing, by swimming, or by kissing or sharing food with an infected person, despite widely held mistaken beliefs to the contrary. HIV is the virus that in time causes **acquired immunodeficiency syndrome (AIDS).** There is no known cure.

In 2005, approximately 1 million Americans were living with the virus; an additional 40,000 Americans receive an HIV diagnosis each year (CDC, 2005). Men make up 77% of this population; among men, 59% are exposed to the virus by means of sexual contact with a male partner, 20% by intravenous drug use alone, and 8% had both exposures; only 11% of men acquired the infection from heterosexual contact. Among women, however, heterosexual contact accounts for 65% of HIV infections, and 33% are from sharing needles used to inject intravenous drugs. The African American population has been disproportionately affected by the virus, and 44% of Americans living with HIV are African American. The fastest growing population of new AIDS diagnoses in America in 2008 is African American women in stable heterosexual relationships who had carefully followed established practices to avoid exposure and, thus discover, along with the presence of the virus, that their partners must at some point have engaged in risky behavior that accounts for the exposure.

Circumstances leading the client to be tested for HIV are varied. An infected person may be symptom free for years, and testing is often prompted by disclosure by an infected partner or former partner. HIV testing is also routinely done during unrelated hospital stays, including childbirth, and during prenatal care. Free, rapid testing is also increasingly available at health fairs and sexually transmitted disease clinics and on university campuses.

HIV Diagnosis and Mental Health Assessment

Counseling is often recommended for clients diagnosed with HIV. They are often overwhelmed emotionally and inundated with medical information; thus, the initial mental health assessment requires exceptional sensitivity, and the professional counselor must allow ample time to develop rapport. Clients are often shaken and feel the situation is hopeless; therefore, professional counselors will want to include a suicide assessment. Clients with HIV/AIDS are likely to have counseling issues related to the source of exposure (i.e., risky behavior and sexual infidelities); therefore, it is important to assess for addictions, impulsive behavior, and mania. Because HIV/AIDS is a highly stigmatizing condition, clients may experience rejection from family, friends, and society; therefore, clients should be assessed for mood disorders.

Mental Health and the Progression of HIV/AIDS

Once they receive their initial diagnosis, people living with HIV often begin their journey with the virus burdened with obsolete and terrifying information. Some expect imminent death after receiving a diagnosis of HIV. The reality is much more complex and ambiguous. In the current era of highly active antiretroviral therapy medications, clients' postexposure life span has been greatly extended, and many clients live with the diagnosis for more than 20 years in reasonably good health. Improvements also make it possible for clients to take fewer pills than were required a decade ago. Challenging gastrointestinal side effects are reduced but still present, at least initially. In addition to nausea and diarrhea, side effects can include fatigue, anemia, lipodystrophy (i.e., redistribution of fat deposits in a way that changes body shape), and peripheral neuropathy (i.e., nerve pain in the extremities). The medicines work well if taken faithfully and correctly. Nonetheless, there is no known cure for HIV at this time, and although medications slow its progression, so far they do not stop it. As a result, many clients come to counseling with an acute awareness of their mortality that may be unusual for their age, and for a young client, this may strain even supportive relationships with peers.

Life planning may be particularly confusing as clients disentangle the lethargy of depression from realistic prognosis for their health, which may be ambiguous. Counseling may be helpful to clients with HIV as they consider long-term commitments, such as the possibility of pursuing careers, relationships, academic goals, and parenting of children while managing their HIV disease, that have become increasingly realistic. With proper adherence to medical treatment, the rate of perinatal transmission of the virus from HIV positive mother to baby has diminished to under 2% (CDC, 2005). Access to HIV services and medications is available in the public sector for low-income clients funded by federal grants under the Ryan White CARE Act.

The point at which an HIV-infected person's diagnosis changes to **AIDS** is another major landmark in the course of the disease, and this change may trigger acute depression and anxiety. The lived experience of the client may be unchanged after receiving this new label, but once the client has AIDS, clients may become deeply discouraged, and self-blaming, and stigma may increase. One criterion for AIDS diagnosis is related to the lab value for CD4 (T-cells), a type of infection-fighting white blood cell. The CD4 count is in the range of about 1,000 in a healthy adult and declines gradually over the life span of the HIV-positive client, indicating

reduced capacity to fight infection. When it dips, even briefly, below 200, the person's diagnosis becomes AIDS. The diagnosis is also changed to AIDS the first time that the client has an opportunistic infection such as Pneumocystis pneumonia, which is rare in the general population but common in persons with a compromised immune system. Once a person receives an AIDS diagnosis, that diagnosis remains with the client for the duration of life, with all its emotional challenges, even if the person's health improves dramatically and remains good.

Counseling and the Social Dimension of HIV/AIDS

Development of trust in the counseling relationship depends critically on the sensitive issue of confidentiality regarding HIV status. The requirement for counselor confidentiality regarding a client's HIV status is quite clear, except when the client may, by failing to disclose his or her status when engaging in risky behaviors, put the life of another person at risk without that person's knowledge. The *ACA Code of Ethics* (American Counseling Association, 2005), like the ethics codes of other mental health professions, recognizes the tension between legitimate confidentiality concerns and duty to warn an unprotected sexual partner of an HIV positive client. Counselors are encouraged by the *Code* to use professional judgment in negotiating with a client who has not disclosed this information to make a plan to do so. The Centers for Disease Control and Prevention (2005) has responded to the public health dimension of HIV transmission by recommending supportive educational programming oriented toward HIV-positive individuals, termed "prevention for positives." The counseling response will simultaneously address client fears of rejection and stigma upon disclosure, fears that may be realistic. Participation in support groups can help to mitigate these fears of isolation.

Support groups and therapy groups are extremely helpful to persons living with HIV/AIDS, although their focus has shifted from the early years of the epidemic, when end-of-life issues dominated, to wellness (e.g., living with the virus, sharing stories, coping with relatives, coping with social stigma, dealing with comorbid mental health concerns, self-valuation despite the uncertain future). Groups provide community to clients whose social and spiritual supports are unavailable, cultivating mutual empathy and instilling hope. Support groups can be effective places to explore the spiritual dimension; quite apart from religious belief, clients typically share a deep desire to find meaning in their HIV experience. Some may find artistic expression, become involved in client advocacy, or work in community outreach for HIV prevention. Confidentiality concerns, although always important in groups, are heightened in the HIV-positive population. Fear of being recognized by others whose discretion is unknown is a frequent barrier to participation in support groups, just as it is to visiting the HIV doctor.

Clients living with HIV/AIDS are often especially mindful of their family relationships and protective of close friends and family members. Paradoxically, they often avoid disclosure of their status to those whom they trust the most in order to spare them the distress of knowing their loved one has a life-threatening condition. Intimate relationships are often adversely affected by withholding information about the client's HIV diagnosis, including relationships with children and adolescents. Issues about disclosure and risk of rejection in existing and new relationships are prevalent in counseling settings and in support groups.

Counseling Support for Grief and Hope in the Presence of HIV

Even with the best care, clients living with HIV do experience fatigue and, at some point, diminished functioning; counseling must address both emotional and existential dimensions of many forms of loss. For example, the prospect of loss of independence, especially while young, may become a source of intense anxiety and shame. Clients may lose or fear they will lose valued relationships to rejection when their HIV status becomes known. They may lose HIV-positive friends to illness and death, and they may lose social identities associated with work they can no longer do. Grief work will be of ongoing value in individual and group counseling as clients come to terms with loss and reconstruct their lives. Some forms of loss are unavoidable; however, discrimination by an employer, school, daycare center, or landlord on the basis of HIV status, is illegal under the Americans With Disabilities Act.

For a client with HIV, the role of medical patient itself may generate counseling concerns. Clinical settings, straining to meet community needs, may seem impersonal, and clients have heightened sensitivity to interactions with care providers. Multidisciplinary HIV/AIDS clinics sometimes incorporate mental health services. This has some advantages, including efficiency, some degree of support for interdisciplinary collaboration, and easier access to psychotropic medications; however, some clients prefer to receive counseling outside of the medical environment, hoping that their changed self-image, depression, anger, and disorientation will be addressed more holistically elsewhere, and with less pathologizing. Clients with HIV, as they regain strength and adjust to changes in their relationships and routines, become increasingly concerned with integrating the HIV/AIDS experience into their larger lives. It becomes important to revise their sense of self and community in a meaningful way and to be recognized as a person living with HIV, both humbled and emboldened, and not merely as a patient with HIV/AIDS. Medical progress related to HIV/AIDS continues at a rapid rate, and treatments are improving significantly.

Contributed by Lynn Schlossberger,
Family Service of Greater Baton Rouge,
Baton Rouge, LA

References

American Counseling Association. (2005). *ACA code of ethics*. Alexandria, VA: Author.

Centers for Disease Control and Prevention. (2005). *HIV/AIDS surveillance report, HIV/AIDS infection in the United States and dependent areas*. Retrieved May 1, 2007, from http://www.cdc.gov/hiv/topics/surveillance/basic.htm#aidsrace

Additional Resources

Mental Health AIDS Web site: http://www.mentalhealthaids.samhsa.gov/index.asp

National Institute for Mental Health Web site: http://www.nimh.nih.gov/dahbr/dahbr.cfm

Holland's Personality Types

John Holland (1966, 1985) developed a typology of six **vocational personalities** and six corresponding work environments to use in classifying particular persons or jobs. Holland postulated that an individual with a particular personality type would be happiest and most fulfilled working in a similar work environment. ("Types" like to be with similar "types.") Thus, work environments matching an individual's vocational personality type reinforce and satisfy the individual, leading to success and satisfaction in the job. In contrast, work environments not matching the individual's personality type are of less interest to the individual and will lead to dissatisfaction in the job.

The six vocational personalities and work environments Holland delineated are Realistic, Investigative, Artistic, Social, Enterprising, and Conventional. The following descriptions of Holland's personalities refer to "pure" types that are represented on a **hexagonal model** (see Figure 1), although in reality most people share some characteristics with most of these types, if not all of them. On the hexagon, those personality types that are closest to each other tend to have the most characteristics in common, whereas those furthest apart have the least in common. Holland indicated that people tend to have a dominant vocational personality type, with one to two other personality types of lesser importance. These combinations of vocational personality types result in career options that span a huge variety of work environments. Descriptions of the vocational personality types in their purest forms are described in this entry.

Realistic personality types are "doers" who favor activities where they can manipulate objects, tools, machines, and animals. They enjoy learning by doing in task-oriented settings and value practicality, tradition, and common sense.

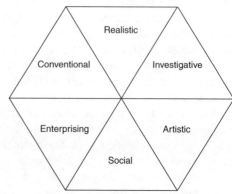

Figure 1. Holland's Hexagonal Model

Note. From *Holland's Hexagon* (ACT Research Report No. 29), by J. L. Holland, D. R. Whitney, N. S. Cole, and J. M. Richards Jr., 1969, Iowa City: The American College Testing Program. Copyright 1969 by The American College Testing Program. Reprinted with permission.

These types like the outdoors and physical activity, including athletics. They prefer to work with things rather than with people, ideas, or data and tend to communicate frankly and directly. Realistic types often see themselves as skilled in mechanical activities, but they may be uncomfortable or less skilled with human relations.

Investigative personality types are intellectual and observant and enjoy research, math, and science activities. They are "analyzers" who favor activities where they can explore or develop knowledge of the world. Investigative types tend to be precise by nature and value independence, curiosity, and learning. People in this category use logic and enjoy solving highly complex, abstract problems. They are introspective and focused on creative problem solving, often work autonomously, and prefer solving problems through experimentation and science.

Artistic personality types are "creators" who prefer activities by which they can create art forms or products. Beauty, originality, independence, and imagination are important to them. These personality types tend to be intuitive and imaginative and enjoy creative activities such as composing or playing music, writing, drawing or painting, and acting in or directing stage productions. People in this category typically need flexibility and ambiguity and have an aversion to convention and conformity. Artistic types tend to be impulsive and emotional, and communicate in an expressive and open manner.

Social personality types are "discussers" who are drawn to activities involving information, training, developing, or interacting and talking with other people. They value cooperation, generosity, and service to others, preferring interpersonal and educational activities. They generally focus on human relationships and enjoy social activities and solving interpersonal problems. Social types seek opportunities to work as part of a team and solve problems through discussions. They usually communicate in a warm and tactful manner.

Enterprising personality types are "persuaders" who prefer activities where they can manipulate people to attain organizational, personal, and economic gains. This type of person values risk taking, status, and competition. They are energetic, ambitious, adventurous, sociable, and self-confident and enjoy leadership roles. Enterprising types are often successful public speakers, but they may be viewed as domineering. They see themselves as assertive and skilled in leadership and speaking, but lacking in scientific abilities.

Conventional personality types are "sustainers" who prefer to follow traditions, rules, and customs. They tend to be careful, conforming, organized, and reliable. These types are comfortable working within an established chain of command, rarely seek leadership roles, and need detailed instructions for any task they are assigned. They have an aversion to ambiguity, dislike being in the spotlight, and are thorough and persistent in carrying out assignments. Conventional types value accuracy, stability, dependability, and efficiency.

According to Holland, an individual's vocational personality type will solidify, or stabilize, between the ages of 18 to 30 years, and it will be hard to change after that. The more stable or consistent a person's personality type, the more likely the person will find a suitable job environment. Holland's theory is the basis for career assessments such as the Self-Directed Search and the Strong Interest Inventory.

Contributed by Rita A. Baker,
Davidson College, Davidson, NC

References

Holland, J. L. (1966). *The psychology of vocational choice: A theory of personality types and model environments.* Waltham, MA: Blaisdell.

Holland, J. L. (1985). *Making vocational choices: A theory of vocational personalities and work environments* (2nd ed.). Englewood Cliffs, NJ: Prentice Hall.

Holland, J. L., Whitney, D. R., Cole, N. S., & Richards, J. M., Jr. (1969). *Holland's hexagon* (ACT Research Report No. 29). Iowa City, IA: The American College Testing Program.

Homophobia and Heterosexism

Homophobia describes an array of negative attitudes, beliefs, and actions toward gay, lesbian, bisexual, transgender, or questioning (GLBTQ) individuals and their culture. Weinberg (1972) defined homophobia as "the dread of being in close quarters with homosexuals" (p. 4). Use of the word was intended to characterize an individual's antihomosexual attitudes and reactions as forms of prejudice stemming from a fear of GLBTQ individuals. Use of the term *homophobia* challenged the ideology of homosexuality as pathology and identified the "problem" with homosexuality as those who were intolerant of persons with a GLBTQ orientation. The term *homophobia* has been used to label the antihomosexual thoughts and reactions of individuals as well as the oppressive and discriminatory policies and practices of political, corporate, and religious organizations. The term *heterosexism* has also been used to describe antihomosexual responses and is discussed later in this entry.

Despite the widespread use of the term *homophobia,* appropriate use of the term in literature and research has become an area of concern. Literary use of homophobia to describe many forms of bias and discrimination toward GLBTQ individuals has contributed to ambiguity regarding the meaning and understanding of antihomosexual responses. Not all discriminatory policies and actions toward homosexuals are based on a phobia or fear; hence, the use of the term *homophobia* may inaccurately describe the source of certain types of antigay responses (e.g., those stemming from membership in political or religious organizations).

Research on antihomosexual responses has been difficult because of the lack of a clear operational definition of the term *antihomosexual responses.* The nature and etiology of various forms of antihomosexual responses have not been accurately represented with current terminology. Research findings suggest that antihomosexual responses are more characteristic of a prejudice than a phobia. These findings support the use of the term **homoprejudice** in place of homophobia. Research identifying interventions that are effective in reducing homoprejudice is necessary.

Internalized homophobia describes an acceptance and internalization of negative attitudes, feelings, and beliefs toward homosexual features in oneself and others. Internalized homophobia can complicate the healthy development of GLBTQ individuals. For instance, GLBTQ individuals may experience severe emotional discomfort and a devalued self-esteem as a result of internalizing negative attitudes and beliefs about their own sexual orientation; hence, internalized homophobia makes it difficult for GLBTQ individuals to find acceptance and pride in their sexual orientation.

The term **heterosexism** has often been used synonymously with homophobia to describe antihomosexual acts and attitudes. However, heterosexism can be distinguished as a cultural ideology that purports heterosexuality to be the societal norm and distinctively superior to homosexuality, whereas homophobia refers to individual attitudes and responses that stem from a heterosexist ideology. Heterosexism and homophobia are intrinsically related in that individuals acquire homophobia through cultural socialization that is based on heterosexist values. Heterosexism creates a hierarchical structure that provides for societal and political privileges for heterosexual individuals and establishes a rationale for prejudicial, discriminatory, oppressive, and even hostile acts toward homosexual individuals. Because homophobia and heterosexism are acquired through learning, they can also be deconstructed through learning. Counselors can help GLBTQ and heterosexual clients who are dealing with homophobia by providing them with accurate information to dispel many of the myths and stereotypes regarding homosexuality. Through education and exploration, counselors can help clients examine the basis of their antihomosexual responses and work toward developing more accepting and affirming attitudes toward homosexuality.

Unfortunately, counselors can perpetuate homophobia and heterosexist ideals in their work with GLBTQ clients. For instance, counselors who are not aware of the influence that homophobia and heterosexism have had on their views of GLBTQ individuals risk misunderstanding and erroneously assessing the presenting problems of these clients. Moreover, counselors who harbor homophobic beliefs (i.e., homosexuality is wrong, immoral, and deviant) are likely to be judgmental and pejorative in their communications with GLBTQ clients. For instance, a counselor's inquiry as to whether or not a female client has a husband or boyfriend conveys a judgment that heterosexuality is understood and that homosexuality will not be comfortably approached. The **Association for Lesbian, Gay, Bisexual, and Transgender Issues in Counseling (ALGBTIC)** has established a set of counseling competencies (ALGBTIC, 2008) to ensure that counselors are adequately prepared to work sensitively and effectively with GLBTQ clients. Counselors should work toward acquiring these competencies prior to working with clients from the GLBTQ communities (see Association for Lesbian, Gay, Bisexual and Transgender Issues in Counseling).

Although many GLBTQ individuals seek counseling for problems that are similar to the problems that heterosexual individuals have, GLBTQ clients may face unique problems that are related to their experiences with homophobia and heterosexism. For instance, a homosexual victim of physical violence may blame herself or himself for the violence as a result of internalizing antihomosexual beliefs. Counselors must be able to help GLBTQ clients explore the role that homophobia and heterosexism may play in their presenting problems. Counselors can help GLBTQ clients recognize the negative impact that societal prejudices have had on their perceptions of homosexuality and how their socialization may be hindering their development of a healthy identity. Identifying what issues are external to GLBTQ clients helps counselors and clients to focus on issues that are within the client's control and develop effective strategies to resolve them.

Contributed by Ginger L. Dickson,
University of Texas at El Paso,
El Paso, TX

References

Association for Lesbian, Gay, Bisexual, and Transgender Issues in Counseling. (2008). *Competencies for counseling gay, lesbian, bisexual, and transgendered (GBT) clients.* Retrieved August 25, 2008, from http://www.algbtic.org/resources/competencies.html

Weinberg, G. (1972). *Society and the healthy homosexual.* New York: St. Martin's Press.

Additional Resource

Herdt, G. (Ed.), & Stein, T. S. (Managing Ed.). (2004). Homophobia and sexual prejudice [Special issue]. *Sexuality Research & Social Policy, 1*(2).

▪ Human Growth and Development, Key Ethical Issues in

The preamble of the American Counseling Association's (ACA; 2005) *ACA Code of Ethics* states, "ACA members are dedicated to the enhancement of human development throughout the life span." Human development can be defined as the changes an individual experiences throughout the life span. These changes occur in cognitive, physical, social, and emotional domains at rates unique to each individual. In the Introduction to Section A: The Counseling Relationship, promoting human growth and development of clients, particularly their values, beliefs, and cultural backgrounds, is the primary goal of counselors in their work with clients. Salient ethical issues related to human development found in other sections of the *Code* fall into three general areas: the ability to give consent, professional competence, and evaluation and assessment.

Section B.5.: Clients Lacking Capacity to Give Informed Consent addresses the ability to give consent for counseling services, handling of records, or assessment. When explaining **informed consent** to clients, professional counselors should communicate with clients in developmentally appropriate ways. If clients are unable to give consent because of their minor status or cognitive developmental level, assent should be sought from the client and consent from a parent or legal guardian.

Section C: Professional Responsibility addresses a counselor's preparation for counseling all clients, particularly clients of diverse backgrounds. Professional counselors should gain the appropriate knowledge, credentials, self-awareness, sensitivity, skills, and supervision prior to counseling children, adolescents, or others who may have developmental delays. Counselors who are learning to work with new populations (e.g., young children) should work under supervision and take further steps to ensure client progress and prevent client harm.

Section E: Evaluation, Assessment, and Interpretation addresses the use and interpretation of different forms of client **evaluations.** Professional counselors use varying methods to evaluate and assess clients in order to choose appropriate treatment methods. Most assessment and evaluation tools are designed for use with clientele of specific developmental levels, and counselors should take this into account. Those tools should only be used with clientele for which they are designed. For example, tools designed for adults should not be used with children. When any method of assessment or evaluation is used, its nature and purpose should be explained to the client at the appropriate developmental level. Furthermore, the results of any assessment or evaluation should be presented to the client in a way that is understandable to the client.

Contributed by Steve Rainey, Kent State University, Kent, OH

Reference

American Counseling Association. (2005). *ACA code of ethics.* Alexandria, VA: Author.

Additional Resources

Cottone, R. R., & Tarvydas, V. M. (2003). *Ethical and professional issues in counseling* (2nd ed.). Upper Saddle River, NJ: Pearson Education.

Remley, T. P., Jr., & Herlihy, B. (2005). *Ethical, legal, and professional issues in counseling* (2nd ed.). Upper Saddle River, NJ: Pearson Education.

■ Human Growth and Development, Key Historical Events in

For much of history, children were not the focus of developmental study. For example, until the 17th century, the average life span was only 30 to 40 years. Childhood ended around 6 to 7 years of age, which was when most children were expected to enter the workplace. By age 12 years, most girls were married. Because there was very little distinction between the child's world and the adult's world, there was little need for an understanding of child development. The dominant view was that children were miniature adults, with miniature personalities and qualities; however, some early philosophers did address child development. **Plato** wrote about the development of the mind of the child, which included the development of a spirit and soul. **Aristotle** was

the first to introduce the concept of "development" and proposed three levels of human development, each of which was 7 years long, ending at age 21 years.

It was not until the 17th century that a strong interest in child development began. During this time, the world saw a great increase in industry, commerce, and city living. With the rise of the middle class came the realization that children could benefit from attending schools and becoming educated rather than being sent to work at an early age, which had been the common practice.

During this time, a Puritan view of child development began. During the Puritan era in the 1700s in the United States, Christian religious leaders believed that children were born in sin, a long-held tenet of Catholicism, and that it was the duty of parents and adults to guide children from their natural evil ways, by physical punishment if necessary. Although harsh, this was the first time that the world of children and the world of adults were separated. The belief that children were born in sin began to change when **John Locke** (1634–1704) asserted that a child's mind was **tabula rasa,** a blank slate, and that children's development is shaped by their life experiences. These life experiences are strongest during the early years of life, and adults are influential in providing positive experiences to help their children develop appropriately. Another philosopher-theorist, **Jean-Jacques Rousseau** (1712–1778), did not believe that children were born tabula rasa but instead believed that children develop according to nature's plan. Rousseau, unlike Locke, had no faith in the environment, especially the social environment, to help children develop in a positive manner. He believed that human nature is good until corrupted by society.

By the 19th century, the field of human development had a major problem. At this time, there were many seemingly brilliant theories about how children develop, but there was little to no empirical evidence to support most of the bold theories of the time. It was during this time that many researchers began to favor empirical findings over broad, comprehensive theory. This movement toward empiricism and away from theory was called the "child study movement" and it was led by **G. Stanley Hall** (1844–1924), one of the most influential developmentalists. Hall was a diligent researcher and for many years collected and published questionnaire data on the thinking of school children. It was his empirical approach, rather than his effort at grand theory, that set the direction of human development for the next century.

By the 1920s, the field of human development was largely a research-oriented and atheoretical field. During this time, human development was focused on the observation of children and not experimentation. From the 1920s to 1950s, many researchers were measuring development empirically without explaining how development was occurring. Influential researchers were measuring intelligence and cognitive growth without a theory as to how or why the mind grew. There was a focus on determining normative behavior of infants and children (i.e., how children should behave and think at certain ages). There was a large increase in longitudinal studies in which infants would be tested and retested throughout their lives. Now, the field of human development was able to predict later characteristics and growth from earlier characteristics, although this growth was not explained because of the lack of theory. In essence, the field of human development became focused on measuring development but could not explain how or why development occurred.

During the 1950s, a revolutionary figure, **Jean Piaget** (1896–1980), emerged in the field of human development. Piaget's contribution to child development was highly influential, partially because of the explanatory power of his theory. Piaget's theory was made up of concepts of cognitive processes as well as other concepts from biology and philosophy. Piaget's theory, simplistic yet comprehensive, stated that the mind changed through interaction with the environment; it did not just collect experiences but changed from them in order to develop more complex ways of thinking about the world. Piaget was one of the first developmentalists to create a bold, comprehensive theory of child development that was supported empirically. Despite some minor modifications in research methodology, Piaget's theory has held up to rigorous empirical inquiry for the past 50 years. Thus, with Piaget, modern developmental psychology was born.

It was also during the 1950s that a new view of human development, the life-span perspective, started. **Erik Erikson** (1902–1994) was the first to offer a detailed theory of how people develop throughout the life span. Erikson, much like Piaget, created a comprehensive theory of development that has been well supported through empirical investigation. The shift toward a life-span perspective gained popularity in the 1960s and then became a strong movement in the 1970s. In addition to Erikson's contributions, the popularity of the life-span perspective was also due, in part, to the numerous longitudinal studies that had been started many decades earlier. The life-span perspective is quintessential in today's understanding of human development; however, it is just a perspective and not a theory. The life-span perspective only offers a way to look at a particular individual's human development.

Today, professional counselors integrate theory and research into an understanding of human development and look upon views of the past, such as children being miniature adults, as antiquated; however, the field of human development is far from mature. Although there are many theories and a vast amount of empirical research supporting them, there is not one theory that fully explains the development of people throughout the life span. There is little integration of theories and much disagreement among theorists and researchers. The field of human development, however, may be so immense that no single theory will ever adequately explain it. It may be best to accept that the field will remain a collection of discrete theories and research.

Contributed by Jason J. Barr,
Monmouth University,
West Long Branch, NJ

Additional Resources

Ariès, P. (1960). *Centuries of childhood: A social history of family life* (R. Baldick, Trans.). New York: Knopf.

Hunt, M. (1993). *The story of psychology.* New York: Anchor Books.

■ Human Growth and Development, Key People in

Theories of human growth and development are fundamental to understanding individuals and families in the counseling process. Many scholars have made substantial contributions to the understanding of how people grow and change. Urie Bronfenbrenner and Robert Kegan represent key contributors to the understanding of human development, the former from a bioecological perspective and the latter from a constructivist developmental perspective. These two perspectives share the notion that development refers to stability and change in the individual and in environmental processes throughout the life span.

Urie Bronfenbrenner, born in 1917 in Moscow, Russia, was a distinguished and widely published developmental psychologist, an authority on childrearing, and a human ecologist. His life was devoted to scholarly work in developing theory and designing research in human development; in applying theory and research to public policy and practice; and in sharing his findings in developmental research through articles, lectures, and discussions. He played an active role in the design and implementation of developmental programs in the United States and abroad and was a founder of Head Start in the United States. He was the Jacob Gould Schurman professor emeritus of human development and psychology at Cornell University when he died in 2005 at the age of 88 years.

Bronfenbrenner was best known for the creation of **bioecological systems theory** that stressed the interrelatedness of ecological levels on child development. In his theory, originally known as the ecological systems theory, he suggested that all settings must be considered when explaining child development. Bioecological systems theory proposed that the biological disposition, resources, and demand characteristics of the child, in combination with the system of relationships in the environment, came together to shape the child's development. Prior to the development of this groundbreaking theory, researchers, each in his or her own discipline, studied the child, family, society, economic frameworks, and political structures as separate entities.

Urie Bronfenbrenner's bioecological systems theory focuses on both the quality and context of the child's environment. Bronfenbrenner described the child as developing within a nested structure, situated at the center and surrounded by concentric layers made up of individuals and groups that directly or indirectly affected the individual's development. These include the microsystem, mesosystem, exosystem, macrosystem, and chronosystem layers or levels. The first level (**microsystem**) includes all those in direct, close relationship with the child over a significant amount of time. Parents, teachers, caregivers, extended family, peers, and church groups are examples of those who have the most immediate effect on the child. The **mesosystem** is the layer that provides the connection between the structures, such as the child's microsystems. Examples include the connection between teachers and parents, between the church and the neighborhood, and/or between parents and extended family. The **exosystem** is the layer that defines the larger social system, and although it does not directly affect the child, it does influence the child's development because of its interaction with structures in the microsystem. Examples include parental workplace schedules, community-based family resources, school systems, and government. The **macrosystem** is the outermost layer of the child's environment and includes cultural values, customs, norms, laws, and media. These larger principles influence the interactions among all other layers. The **chronosystem** relates to both internal changes and external events over time that affect the child's development. Examples are growth and development within the child and change in the family structure.

The increasingly complex interactions between the layers of a child's environment in contemporary society provide a clear view of the problems seen in youth and in families; these interactions also offer direction to stop the breakdown of ecological systems. Bronfenbrenner's cross-cultural research on families and their support systems and on human development and the status of children and his bioecological approach have united the social sciences across disciplines, allowing findings to emerge that identify key elements in social structure across societies that are vital to the development of human potential. During his life, he authored more than 300 articles and chapters and 14 books, including *Two Worlds of Childhood: U.S. and U.S.S.R.* (1970), *The State of Americans: This Generation and the Next* (1996), and *The Ecology of Human Development: Experiments by Nature and Design* (1979).

Robert Kegan was born in 1946 in St. Paul, Minnesota. He earned his doctorate in developmental psychology from Harvard University; joined the human development faculty of the Harvard Graduate School of Education in 1977; and in 2008 serves as the William and Miriam Meehan professor in adult learning and professional development, the educational chair of the Institute for Management and Leadership in Education, and the codirector of the Change Leadership Group. He has devoted his scholarly career to teaching, research, writing, and consulting about adult development, adult learning, and professional development. His **constructive developmental theory,** based on the work of Jean Piaget, describes how individuals make meaning throughout the life span as a result of the interaction between self and the other.

Kegan's theory represents a lifelong process of evolution through which a person knows the world and becomes that type of person because of a series of subjective meanings made in a relational context and grounded in an objective framework. He conceptualized stages of evolutionary balances, or orders of consciousness, visualized as a helix, with both vertical and horizontal movement. The bottom-to–top motion represents individual movement from an egocentric, simple, undifferentiated, unintegrated system, heavily influenced by the environment, to a more allocentric, complex, differentiated, and integrated system more in control of the environment. The right-to-left motion goes from a stance of favoring inclusion to favoring independence, thus recogniz-

ing that successful adaptation requires differentiation, separation, and autonomy as well as integration, attachment, and inclusion. Each balance or stage is supported by a culture of embeddedness (environment) that must perform three functions in order for the individual to be allowed to remain in the stage and then move on from it. These functions are holding the person by providing support and establishing trust, letting go in a timely fashion so the person can move on, and remaining intact so that the person can look back and reflect on the past in relation to the present. The absence of any one of these functions can inhibit a person's developmental movement.

Each stage Kegan described represents the construction and organization of thought, feeling, and social relating within the meaning-making system of the individual. Movement to a higher stage occurs when an individual faces a conflict or crisis that cannot be resolved within the current order of consciousness. The stages are summarized in the following list:

0. *Incorporative balance.* This stage occurs during the first 18 months of life and is characterized by the "me" stage in which an infant's reflexes (moving and sensing) are the fundamental groundwork of personality development. The infant is his or her reflexes, and there is no differentiation between subject and object. The culture of embeddedness is the primary caretaker.
1. *Impulsive balance.* This stage occurs roughly between the ages of 2 to 7 years and is characterized by a new sense of self where reflexes become object to the child. At this stage, the child is subject to impulses and perception (i.e., when the child perceives that an object has changed, the object itself has changed in the child's experience). In the same way, the child is subject to impulses and lacks impulse control. The culture of embeddedness is the family.
2. *Imperial balance.* This stage occurs during preadolescence and is characterized by the emergence of a self-concept and the ability to take on the role of another. The child also recognizes a private world that others cannot easily enter. Children are subject to needs, wishes, and interests, while their impulses and perceptions are now object (i.e., they are now able to regulate their impulses and become more self-sufficient). The culture of embeddedness consists of institutions that recognize roles, such as school, family, peers, and so forth.
3. *Interpersonal balance.* This stage reflects the stage that most people reach during their lifetime. This stage is characterized by the person who is able to make needs, wishes, and interests object, while roles and relationships are now subject. Consequently, individuals tend to hold on to the ideals and beliefs that were instilled in them as children, to internalize the values of society, and to experience difficulty dealing with others whose values and beliefs differ from their own. An individual at this stage only knows self in relation to others and is defined in terms of traditional roles
4. *Institutional balance.* This stage is characterized by people who now make their relationships, roles, and

values object and become subject to larger institutions, such as family and work. The individual at this level can separate his or her own thoughts and feelings from those of others and demonstrate increased autonomy and a sense of self that is distinct from others.

5. *Interindividual balance.* This stage is rarely achieved before age 40 years and is characterized by people who now reflect on (make object) institutions and are able to coordinate, direct, or create these systems. The individual at this stage has an increased capacity for intimacy, for seeking out new information, and for engaging in the active process of transformation.

Robert Kegan authored or coauthored several books, including *The Evolving Self* (1982), *In Over Our Heads: The Mental Demands of Modern Life* (1994), *How the Way We Talk Can Change the Way We Work: Seven Languages for Transformation* (Kegan & Lahey, 2001), and *Change Leadership: A Practical Guide for Transforming Our Schools* (Wagner & Kegan, 2006).

Contributed by Leila F. Roach, Stetson University, DeLand, FL

References

Bronfenbrenner, U. (1970). *Two worlds of childhood: U.S. and U.S.S.R* (with the assistance of J. C. Condry). New York: Russell Sage Foundation.

Bronfenbrenner, U. (1979). *The ecology of human development: Experiments by nature and design.* Cambridge, MA: Harvard University Press.

Bronfenbrenner, U. (1996). *The state of Americans: This generation and the next.* New York: Free Press.

Kegan, R. (1982). *The evolving self: Problems and process in human development.* Cambridge, MA: Harvard University Press.

Kegan, R. (1994). *In over our heads: The mental demands of modern life.* Cambridge, MA: Harvard University Press.

Kegan, R., & Lahey, L. L. (2001). *How the way we talk can change the way we work: Seven languages for transformation.* San Francisco: Jossey-Bass.

Wagner, T., & Kegan, R. (2006). *Change leadership: A practical guide for transforming our schools.* San Francisco: Jossey-Bass.

Additional Resources

Bronfenbrenner, U., & Morris, P. A. (1998). The ecology of developmental processes. In W. Damon (Series Ed.) & R. M. Lerner (Vol. Ed.), *Handbook of child psychology: Vol. 1. Theoretical models of human development* (5th ed., pp. 993–1028). New York: Wiley.

■ Humanistic Theories

Humanism first evolved from philosophical perspectives that questioned humankind's place in the universe, asking "What does it mean to be fully experientially human?" and "How does that understanding illuminate the fulfilled or vital life?" (Schneider, Bugental, & Pierson, 2001, p. xx). Humanistic theories attempt to describe the phenomenologically constructed world of the client by exploring the potential of humanity through the nature and experience of values, spirituality, meaning, emotions, transcendence, intentionality, healthy relationships, the self, self-actualization, creativity, mortality, holism, intuition, and responsibility (among other topics).

Humanistic theories arose as a reaction to an increasingly industrialized world, Freudian psychoanalysis, and behaviorism. Humanistic theories first emerged in the writings of Alfred Adler, Carl Jung, Karen Horney, and Victor Frankl and came into full expression in the works of Abraham Maslow, Rollo May, Gordon Allport, Carl Rogers, Charlotte Buhler, Virginia Satir, Albert Ellis, and Fritz Perls, among others (Association for Humanistic Psychology, n.d.). Each of these theorists made unique contributions to the field of professional counseling. The foundation of humanistic theories is the strong belief in the innate power of the client to move, with understanding and self-awareness, in the direction of growth and better functioning in all life endeavors. This common thread reveals a humanistic foundation.

It is within the humanistic counseling tradition that the **core conditions** of counseling emerged: unconditional positive regard, empathy, congruence, authenticity, caring for the client, phenomenological assessment strategies, self-discovery, and insight. These core conditions permit therapeutic intervention in life areas that were previously inaccessible, such as love, hope, meaning of life, loss, relationships, creativity, holism, spirituality, freedom, transcendence, personal growth, social justice, multicultural and gender issues, responsibility, and interdependence.

Critics of humanistic theories suggest that humanism has contributed to individualism/autonomy over cooperation/collectivism, the drive for self-actualization over the building of community, and the minimizing of the influence of social oppression in the lives of women and persons of color. In contrast, humanistic counselors posit that **human agency** (i.e., the ability of individuals to chose their direction through intentionality) and **self in relationship** (i.e., the awareness that individuals are only known in relationship with others) allow both sociocentric and idiocentric societies to thrive as individuals dedicate themselves to live to their fullest potential within their constructed social reality.

Current practitioners of humanistic theories are found in various theoretical schools, including person-centered counseling, existential counseling, and Gestalt counseling, as well as in more contemporary approaches that include family therapy, transpersonal psychology, ecopsychology, and constructivism (Association for Humanistic Psychology, n.d.). The professional counseling association addressing humanistic theories is the Counseling Association for Humanistic Education and Development, a division of the American Counseling Association.

Contributed by Colette T. Dollarhide, The Ohio State University, Columbus, OH

References

Association for Humanistic Psychology. (n.d). *Humanistic psychology overview*. Retrieved March 19, 2007, from http://ahpweb.org/aboutahp/whatis.html

Schneider, K. J., Bugental, J. F. T., & Pierson, J. F. (Eds.). (2001). *The handbook of humanistic psychology: Leading edges in theory, research, and practice*. Thousand Oaks, CA: Sage.

Additional Resource

Bankart, C. P. (1997). *Talking cures: A history of Western and Eastern psychotherapies*. Pacific Grove, CA: Brooks/Cole.

Hypothesis Testing

Hypothesis testing is an approach to decision making involving the systematic evaluation of speculative suppositions about the relationship between variables in a study. In using a logic-based process, decisions are based on evaluation of the plausibility of specific suppositions (null hypotheses) in the context of evidence.

Specifying a Null Hypothesis

Hypothesis testing begins with the specification of a null hypothesis. **Null hypotheses (H_o)** test that there is no effect or relationship between variables of interest. In a bit of paradoxical logic, null hypotheses are statements that express the opposite of the decision maker's true belief about a given relationship between study variables. When evidence suggests that null hypotheses are implausible in the context of evidence, they are rejected in favor of other alternative hypotheses or suppositions that are consistent with the decision maker's true beliefs.

Forms of Alternative Hypotheses

There are a number of different types of hypotheses, which vary depending on the question of interest and the specific research design. Three examples are relational hypotheses, difference hypotheses, and evaluative hypotheses.

Relational hypotheses describe the extent to which two variables are associated with each other. For example, a relational hypothesis might posit a relationship between body weight and depression. This type of hypothesis might be tested with a correlational methodology.

Difference hypotheses focus on the extent to which the value of one variable is greater or less than the value of another variable. In the previous example about body weights and depression, a difference hypothesis might posit a difference in the depression rates of groups of people who vary in their discrepancy from ideal weight. This hypothesis might be evaluated by comparing the depression levels of people from three different weight groups (e.g., underweight, average weight, overweight). This type of hypothesis would be used in an experimental design using analysis of variance statistical methods to explore the difference among the means of the three groups.

Evaluative hypotheses focus on the impact or effect of one variable (e.g., independent variable) on one or more other variables. For example, an evaluative hypothesis might explore the impact of one or more weight-loss regimens over a period of time. This might take the form of comparing, for example, Weight Watchers® participants with those not on any program and monitoring their weight loss. This type of hypothesis would likely be used in a causal comparative or treatment/control experimental methodology.

Establishing Criteria for Making Decisions

Hypothesis testing involves the use of specific techniques that guide the decision maker toward accurate decisions. The procedure is rooted in the scientific method and is designed to produce conclusions that are valid and reliable. Two related concepts, significance levels and statistical significance, are important to planning for a decision process that is valid and reliable.

Significance levels are predetermined criteria for evaluating the extent to which the data evidence is inconsistent with the null hypothesis. The decision maker should determine the cutoff criterion (significance level) before looking at the evidence that will be used to make the decision. This decision is usually based on considerations of statistical power and confidence (i.e., risk level) of the final decision (e.g., values of α and β).

Statistical significance is a term used to describe threshold criteria for evaluating empirically based decisions after the application of appropriate statistical tests of significance (e.g., *t, z, F*). In simple terms, if the evidence exceeds the critical threshold (i.e., cutoff point), the result is deemed statistically significant (i.e., null hypothesis is rejected). If the data do not sufficiently meet the threshold, then the conclusion of nonsignificance is reached (i.e., alternative hypotheses not supported).

Significance levels and statistical significance usually go hand in hand and correspond to a planning phase and a result evaluation phase of the hypothesis-testing process. Collectively, significance levels and statistical significance are often thought of as risk levels in that they specify the level of accepted risk for making decisional errors. A conventional level of significance is .05, suggesting that the result must be reliable 95% of the time before deciding to reject the null hypothesis.

Type I and II Errors

Two types of errors are associated with hypothesis testing. The first type of error (**Type I error**), or false alarm, occurs when a decision is made to reject a null hypothesis when the null hypothesis is, in fact, true. The likelihood of a Type I error occurring is described as alpha (α). A **Type II error** occurs when a decision is made to retain the null hypothesis that should have been rejected because the null hypothesis was indeed false. The likelihood of a Type II error is described by (β). There is a need to balance the likelihood of making Type I and Type II errors, because efforts to decrease Type I errors directly increase the probability of Type II errors and

	Truth Value of Hypothesis	
	Hypothesis is false	Hypothesis is true
Decide to reject the null hypothesis. Decide that the null hypothesis is false.	Hit (power) True positive Null hypothesis is rejected accurately based on evidence (1-β).	Type I error False positive Null hypothesis is rejected accurately based on faulty evidence (α).
Decide to retain the null hypothesis. Decide that the null hypothesis is true.	Type II error False negative Null hypothesis is not rejected and therefore deemed plausible based on lack of sufficient evidence (β).	Hit True negative Null hypothesis is not rejected and therefore deemed plausible based on accurate information (1-α).

Figure 1. The Hypothesis Testing Model

visa-versa. Figure 1 illustrates how these errors are associated with hypothesis testing.

Not withstanding unreliable and/or unsystematic decisions, thoughtful clinicians and other decision makers do, in fact, make erroneous decisions from time to time. The likelihood of making errors as well as good decisions is variable and is based on several parameters of the situation. **Statistical power** is a concept that concerns the potential for any decision maker to discover an effect that actually exists. In terms of the confusion matrix, power is simply the probability of the correct rejection of the null hypothesis. Although an extended discussion of power is beyond the scope of this entry, power is influenced by several aspects of the situation, including most practically the sensitivity of the assessment instrument, the threshold criteria for a particular diagnostic decision, and perceived or real consequences of making an error.

In summary, the goal of hypothesis testing is to reject null hypotheses that are inconsistent with the decision maker's true belief. In doing so, the decision maker can accumulate evidence that is consistent with alternative hypotheses that are more consistent with his or her true beliefs. The overall accuracy (validity and reliability) of conclusions based on a hypothesis-testing procedure is evaluated by applying statistical tools.

Contributed by Richard J. Ricard,
Texas A&M University–Corpus Christi,
Corpus Christi, TX

Additional Resources

Cherry, A. L. (2000). *A research primer for helping professionals.* Belmont, CA: Brooks/Cole

Heppner, P. P., Kivlighan, D. M., & Wampold, B. E. (1999). *Research design in counseling* (2nd ed.). Belmont, CA: Wadsworth Brooks/Cole.

Huck, S. W. (2004). *Reading statistics and research* (4th ed.). Boston: Allyn & Bacon.

Identity Formation

Erikson (1968) described identity development as a normative crisis during which adolescents struggle with critical issues such as vocation and ideology. Identity achievement and identity diffusion are concepts developed by Erikson to describe the ways individuals are or are not successful in working through the task of resolving their process of "identity versus role confusion" (see Ego Psychology: Erikson's Psychosocial Stage Theory). A sense of confidence comes from identity achievement, and this confidence, in turn, can be a strong foundation from which to resolve other significant adult development issues; however, those adolescents who experience identity diffusion can experience confusion about a variety of issues over the course of their lives.

Marcia (1966) expanded on Erikson's theory and developed the concept of "status" by examining the level of commitment in combination with the existence of a crisis and how these elements affected an individual's process of identity development. Marcia's identity status model proposes levels of commitment and crisis as they relate to ideology, vocation, and sexual orientation. Marcia developed four types of status: **identity achievement** (i.e., being in crisis and developing a commitment to one's preferences), **moratorium** (i.e., being in crisis and not being committed to one's preferences), **foreclosure** (i.e., not being in crisis and accepting parents' or others' ideas about ideology/vocational choice/sexual orientation), and **diffusion** (i.e., not being in crisis and not actively exploring ideas about ideology, vocational choice, sexual orientation). Examples of each status as it relates to career selection are provided in Figure 1.

Marcia (1980) determined that understanding the identity development process required flexibility, according to an individual's culture, career, and family relationships. Regardless of the level of success in resolving an identity crisis during adolescence, confusion can emerge at various times throughout adulthood; therefore, flexibility can be of great value in dealing with life's challenges.

According to Marcia's model, the identity formation process for men and women is very similar (Kroger, 1997); however, research involving college students found that women attribute more significance to their identity development in areas related to sexuality, relationships, and maintaining work and family responsibilities than did the male participants. Finally, there are several models of identity formation or development related to cultural identity development (see Feminist Identity Development Model; Racial Identity Development Models, Minority; Sexual Identity

	No Commitment Made	Commitment Made
No Crisis Experienced	**Diffusion Status** This individual lacks clear direction. *Example:* "I really haven't thought about what to do after high school. I guess I'll wait and see what happens."	**Foreclosure Status** This individual has developed a premature identity without exploration. *Example:* "My folks always encouraged me to attend college and become a doctor and this sounds like a good idea to me."
Crisis Experienced	**Moratorium Status** This individual has explored values and is in the process of "becoming." *Example:* "I've been going to the career counseling center at school and we've begun to narrow my options, but I want to spend more time exploring my preferences and career options before I make a decision about a major."	**Identity Achievement Status** This individual has explored a number of options and feels self-aware and self-knowledgeable. There is a sense of confidence and commitment. *Example:* "I have visited professionals in this field and researched my options and feel confident about going to dental school."

Figure 1. Examples of the Four Identity Statuses as They Apply to Career Development

Development; Spiritual Identity; White Racial Identity Models).

Contributed by Mary Fawcett,
Winona State University, Winona, MN

References

Erikson, E. H. (1968). *Identity: Youth and crisis.* New York: Norton.

Kroger, J. (1997). Gender and identity: The intersection of structure, content, and context. *Sex Roles, 36,* 747–770.

Marcia, J. E. (1966). Development and validation of ego identity status. *Journal of Psychology and Social Psychology, 3,* 551–558.

Marcia, J. E. (1980) Identity in adolescence. In J. Adelson (Ed.), *Handbook of adolescent psychology* (pp. 159–187). New York: Wiley.

Additional Resource

Marcia, J. E. (1993). The relational roots of identity. In J. Kroger (Ed.), *Discussions on ego identity* (pp. 101–120). Hillsdale, NJ: Erlbaum.

Immigrants and Refugees

Immigrants are people who have made a permanent move voluntarily to a country like the United States, whereas

refugees are immigrants who move to another country involuntarily, often to escape war or economic or political conditions in their home country. By contrast, some reasons immigrants may choose to move to a new country include educational, employment, or other economic advancement opportunities and personal familial reasons such as marriage, adoption, or reuniting with other members of their family. In the last census, 26 million, or roughly 1 in 10 people in the United States, had been born in another country (U.S. Census Bureau, 2000). The foreign-born population that originally came from Europe to the United States has been decreasing as a percentage of the U.S. population, whereas the percentage of foreign-born people who came from Asia and Latin America has been increasing.

Cultural Adjustment

For both immigrants and refugees, the cultural adjustment process in the new country may take a toll. Many reactions are possible at various times, ranging from excitement or curiosity to dissatisfaction, anxiety, anger, depression, grief, or alienation. Psychosomatic symptoms and identity confusion are also possible. **Culture shock** describes the reaction to cultural differences around language and communication difficulties, legal barriers to employment, and difficulties in dealing with differences in ways of conducting business and obtaining basic services. Individual reactions, however, vary widely and may not necessarily require counseling.

The degree of **acculturative stress** that an individual may experience is related to the level of tolerance for ethnic diversity that is present in the new culture, the degree of difference between the two cultures, and the existence of bilingual educational and mental health services. Individual predictors of adjustment include gender, self-confidence, interpersonal interest, lack of ethnocentrism, a positive attitude toward acculturation, prior knowledge of the new language and culture, previous intercultural experience, voluntary movement to the new culture, educational level, and employment status. In the host culture, positive attitudes toward newcomers and the presence of a home culture community are factors. There have been several models describing various stages of cultural adjustment. Many of them include an initial positive period of excitement, followed by dissatisfaction, grief, depression, or anger when cultural differences become problematic, and then eventual acceptance and appreciation of the new culture. The most positive adaptation approach for immigrants and refugees is **bicultural** (i.e., to have ties to both cultures). Developing involvement in two communities can provide two cultural support systems. Interpersonal support is helpful during the cultural adjustment process, and a professional counselor can be one source of support. A professional counselor can also aid in the development of networking skills for making new friends.

Job loss or shrinkage is a major change immigrants and refugees experience that may result in economic, social, or psychological stress. It is difficult to maintain socioeconomic status in a new culture if a person is not fluent in the language, the person's previous occupation does not exist in the new culture, or there are licensing or educational barriers to continuing an occupation. Loss of a job has multiple effects: The original career may be mourned, a sense of personal identity may be lost, and a new job may not pay as well, contributing to economic stress. Experiencing job exploitation, racism, and other forms of discrimination may also add stress for some immigrants and refugees.

People without official immigration documentation face additional stress and may be reluctant to seek counseling or other services and reluctant to disclose much information about their personal history, employment, or psychological concerns out of fear that their undocumented status may be revealed. The term **undocumented workers** is preferable to **illegal aliens** because it acknowledges the productive status of these people as well as their need for official documentation. Undocumented workers are ineligible for many social assistance programs, but they may be eligible for some children's programs and emergency medical care. Their American-born children are fully eligible for all educational and economic benefits of citizenship. Beginning May 1, 2006, more than 1 million people in several cities demonstrated for humane treatment and legal residence for undocumented Americans on "A Day Without Immigrants." Boycotts and store closures highlighted the economic contributions of immigrants.

Refugees who may have left their homes involuntarily; experienced the effects of war; or were traumatized because of their ethnicity, religion, or political beliefs are more at risk than other immigrants for psychological problems. Each year, from 70,000 to 125,000 refugees (U.S. Census Bureau, 2000) enter the United States and make up a substantial part of annual entry to this country. These refugees may have experienced traumas, including physical torture, sexual abuse, refugee camp internment, or family deaths. Refugees, in many respects, are like disaster victims and might be helped in similar ways. Depression and posttraumatic stress disorder may be frequent diagnoses.

Impact of Immigration

The impact of acculturation on immigrant and refugee families may last for many generations. Although economic and adjustment issues may be paramount for first-generation immigrants, second-generation children may be placed in the awkward role of family translator if their language proficiency is superior to that of their parents, upending traditional family structure. Intergenerational conflict can be another source of stress for immigrants and refugees whose children and grandchildren may acquire different values from growing up in the new culture. The mental health of recent immigrants has sometimes been associated with a healthier mental outlook than that of second- and third-generation immigrants. Maintenance of language and culture has been associated with well-being for recent immigrants, whereas increased Americanization may be associated with increased likelihood of a psychiatric disorder. For many ethnic groups, high school grades and time spent on homework decreased for second and third generations. There is some indication that cultural parenting styles, ways of speaking, and reluctance to acknowledge psychological problems may continue for three generations and beyond. Third and later generations may continue to face discrimination based on ethnicity, even though their identity and cultural experience are primarily mainstream American. The **Hansen effect** refers to third-generation immigrants who wish to recapture their lost culture, perhaps by taking what has become a foreign language, enrolling in ethnic studies classes, or in other ways becoming acquainted with their ancestral history and cultural roots.

United States Immigration Policies

Throughout the history of the United States, there have been policies related to immigration that have often reflected prejudicial negative societal attitudes toward immigrants from many ethnic backgrounds. These issues continue to affect immigrant clients today, and professional counselors are advised to keep this context in mind when working with them. A brief outline of some of these events and policies is included in the following list:

- 1790: U.S. Naturalization Law limits citizenship to "free White persons."
- 1858: California passes a law to bar entry of Chinese and "Mongolians."
- 1862: California "Anti-Coolie" Act inhibits Chinese immigration and taxes employers who hire Chinese workers.
- 1870: Naturalization Act is revised to allow African American citizenship, but Asians are still excluded.
- 1878: In *In re Ah Yup,* the court ruled that Chinese were not eligible for naturalized citizenship.
- 1882: Chinese Exclusion Act suspends immigration of laborers for 10 years. The law was renewed in 1892 and in 1902, with no ending date. It was also made applicable to U.S. possessions in 1904.
- 1894: U.S. circuit court in Massachusetts declares in *In re Saito* that Japanese are ineligible for naturalization.
- 1898: *Wong Kim v. U.S.* decided that Chinese born in the United States cannot be stripped of their citizenship.
- 1902: The Expatriation Act declares that any American female citizen who marries a foreign national would lose her citizenship.
- 1913: California passes Alien Land Law prohibiting "aliens ineligible to citizenship" from buying land or leasing it for longer than 3 years. Over the next 10 years, Arizona, Washington, Louisiana, New Mexico, Idaho, Montana, and Oregon follow.
- 1922: Cable Act declares that any American female citizen who marries "an alien ineligible to citizenship" would lose her citizenship.
- 1923: *U.S. v. Bhagat Singh Thind* declares Asian Indians not eligible for naturalized citizenship. *Frick v. Webb* forbids aliens "ineligible to citizenship" from owning stocks in corporations formed for farming.
- 1924: Oriental Exclusion Act denies entry to virtually all Asians.

- 1944: The draft was reinstated for Nisei. The 442nd Regimental Combat Team gains fame. Exclusion orders are revoked.
- 1956: California repeals its alien land laws.
- 1965: Immigration Law abolishes "national origins" as the basis for allocating immigration quotas to various countries. All countries are now equal.
- 1986: Immigration Reform and Control Act imposes civil and criminal penalties on employers who knowingly hire undocumented aliens and allows amnesty and access to citizenship for many undocumented workers.
- 1996: Antiterrorism and Effective Death Penalty Act expedites the deportation of criminal aliens and limits asylum. Illegal Immigration Reform and Immigrant Responsibility Act bars permanent residence to anyone falsely claiming citizenship and allows potential deportees to be incarcerated for up to 2 years before being brought before an immigration board.
- 2006: More than a million people demonstrate, demanding that U.S. immigration laws be reformed.

Counseling Implications

Professional counselors of immigrant and refugee clients need to assess many areas relevant to the immigrant experience, including languages spoken, birthplace and immigration status, immigrant generation, geographic location of other relatives (e.g., continuing immigration, proximity of the home country), socioeconomic status, religious background and current spirituality, political identification, level of acculturation, and experiences with prejudice or discrimination.

For example, the language or languages spoken may be suggestive of cultural traditionalism, because non-English-speaking clients tend to be more traditional; however, immigrant parents often strongly encourage their children to speak both their native tongue and English. Bilingual second-generation immigrants may prefer to speak English, which they may have learned in school and through the media. After exploring when and where English was learned, the professional counselor should give the client the choice of language to use in the session if possible. Bilingual professional counselors may be able to use "language switching" to help moderate the emotional involvement of clients because using a nonnative language may allow the client to distance from intense emotions

The professional counselor can help the client distinguish between individual problems and the broader social problems that may affect the client, such as poverty, substandard housing, stress from creditors, possible deportation, possible exposure to environmental toxins, difficulties associated with communicating in another language, and the complexities of dealing with government agencies. After considering these external influences, the professional counselor can then assist the client in exploring his or her individual and cultural strengths and identifying community resources.

Professional counselors who work with immigrants and refugees may consider simultaneously educating the client about the counseling process; applying individual, group, and family counseling techniques as appropriate; empowering the client by serving as a cultural resource guide, culture broker, and advocate; and working with indigenous healers from the client's culture.

It is essential to note that immigrants and refugees are an extremely diverse group. They come from many countries and various cultures within a country, and they will have different experiences depending on the timing of their coming to the United States or waves of immigration from the same country. Emphasis needs to be placed on exploring the individual client's own experiences and not erroneously generalizing from information about his or her immigrant group.

Contributed by Wanda M. L. Lee,
San Francisco State University,
San Francisco, CA

Reference

U.S. Census Bureau. (2000). *United States census 2000.* Retrieved August 25, 2008, from http://www.census.gov/main/www/cen2000.html

Additional Resources

Chung, R. C. (2001). Psychosocial adjustment of Cambodian refugee women: Implications for mental health counseling. *Journal of Mental Health Counseling, 23,* 115–126.

Lee, W. M., Blando, J., Mizelle, N., & Orozco, G. (2007). *Introduction to multicultural counseling for helping professionals* (2nd ed.). New York: Routledge.

Yeung, A. S., & Change, D. F. (2002). Adjustment disorder: Intergenerational conflict in a Chinese immigrant family. *Culture, Medicine and Psychiatry, 26,* 509–525.

Yost, A. D., & Lucas, M. S. (2002). Adjustment issues affecting employment for immigrants from the former Soviet Union. *Journal of Employment Counseling, 39,* 153–170.

Implosive Therapy

Each counseling theory has a unique perspective on the psychological factors contributing to phobias and other anxiety-related disorders (e.g., obsessive-compulsive disorder). From these theoretical perspectives, a variety of techniques have been developed to reduce the debilitating symptoms associated with phobic anxiety. In 1957, Thomas G. Stampfl blended principles of the psychodynamic and behavioral orientations and produced **implosive therapy,** which aims to eliminate the internal triggers (e.g., self-criticisms or faulty cognitions) of anxiety (Stampfl & Levis, 1967). With implosive therapy, the professional counselor uses imagery related to a conditioned trigger to provoke maximum anxiety levels in the client within a safe environment. When this anxiety response can no longer be sustained, the conditioned trigger is eliminated as well as the symptomatic behavior associated with it (Troester, 2006). The professional counselor continues this procedure until the symptoms are diminished to the level desired.

Stampfl and Levis (1968) specifically matched the learning theory elements of behaviorism with the sources of anxiety proposed in psychodynamism. They viewed phobias as resulting from an original traumatic event in the client's life that he or she blocked from consciousness using neurotic cognition and behavior. The client also used these mechanisms (i.e., neurotic cognition and behavior) to avoid stimuli linked to the original event or conditioned stimuli. Stampfl proposed that the original event occurred during the client's developmental years via relationships (i.e., parental and social) or pain-eliciting experiences. Consequently, he developed implosive therapy as an attempt to present verbally and systematically "as good an approximation as possible the sights, sounds, and tactual experiences originally present in the primary conditioning event" (Stampfl & Levis, 1968, p. 33), allowing the client to reprocess these stimuli.

Similar to other behavioral techniques, the stimuli are organized on a continuum according to their ability to provoke an anxiety response. For example, if a client becomes extremely anxious about the presence of germs and becoming contaminated, the counselor would work to identify a hierarchy of germ-related scenarios that would produce increasing levels of anxiety. The avoidance serial cue hierarchy (ASCH) organizes the stimuli presented as imagery in implosive therapy according to the stimuli's relationship to the original negative experience and their location in the client's consciousness. Located on the lowest tiers of this system, **symptom-contingent cues** are those anxiety prompts of which the client is conscious and are directly associated with symptomatic behavior. In the previous example, the client may already be aware that he or she is uncomfortable when shaking hands with people because of a fear of germs. Composing the remainder of the ASCH, **hypothesized sequential cues** are the anxiety prompts the client suppresses to prevent an anxiety response and are, therefore, subconscious (Stampfl & Levis, 1967).

The counselor suggests the symptom-contingent cues on the basis of the client's report of the circumstances surrounding episodes of symptomatic behavior. The counselor also suggests the hypothesized sequential cues, deriving them from the symptom-contingent cues and psychodynamic theory. In other words, the counselor must begin to hypothesize the root of the developed anxiety and create a system of cues to elicit anxiety responses in the client. Stampfl and Levis (1967) reported the following areas as common in ordering the hypothesized sequential cues: aggression, punishment, psychosexual stages (e.g., oral), sexuality, rejection, pain, loss of control, morality, and reactivity of the autonomic nervous system and the central nervous system. Counselors can rate the suggested cues by measuring the client's anxiety response. Imagery eliciting higher levels of anxiety indicates a stimuli network that demands further exploration (Stampfl & Levis, 1967).

In implosive therapy, the counselor presents imagery associated with symptom-contingent cues first because the client is conscious of them and finds them less disturbing. The elimination of these lower level anxiety cues grants the client access to those cues that have been repressed because of the potential anxiety they provoke (Stampfl & Levis, 1967). In this respect, the counselor guides the client to more intensive imagery according to the client's ability to process the imagery; however, the counselor does not plan each session in this way and instead seeks to promote high levels of anxiety for the duration of the session, relying mainly on the speed and amount of material presented. A graduated system dictates the overall course of implosive therapy, but not for any specific session. In addition, self-directed imagery sessions promote similar conditions, and implementation in the client's home augments the efficacy of the therapeutic process (Goldberg & Green, 1986).

Stampfl and Levis (1967) suggested that the implosive therapy process can be initiated after two or three sessions that explore the problematic symptoms, the anxiety prompts perpetuating them, and their connection to the client's life. Typically, the client's symptoms can be noticeably reduced in 15 sessions lasting 1 hour and reduced enough to cease therapy by 30 sessions of the same duration. In some cases though, sessions consist of approximately 100 minutes of intense anxiety elicitation as a consequence of the case severity of the case or the session limitations (Goldberg & Green, 1986). Stampfl and Levis (1967) suggested that implosive therapy is effective in the treatment of anxiety-driven reactivity in anxiety disorders, depression, affective disorders, paranoia, alcoholism, speech disorders, and schizophrenia.

*Contributed by Daniel R. Russell and
Carl J. Sheperis, Mississippi State
University, Starkville, MS*

References

Goldberg, R., & Green, S. (1986). A learning-theory perspective of brief psychodynamic psychotherapy. *American Journal of Psychotherapy, 40,* 70–82.

Stampfl, T. G., & Levis, D. J. (1967). Essentials of implosive therapy: A learning-theory-based psychodynamic behavioral therapy. *Journal of Abnormal Psychology, 72,* 496–503.

Stampfl, T. G., & Levis, D. J. (1968). Implosive therapy—A behavioral therapy? *Behavior Research & Therapy, 6,* 31–36.

Troester, J. D. (2006). Experiences with implosive therapy. *Clinical Social Work Journal, 34,* 349–360.

■ Impulse Control Disorders

Impulse control disorders are characterized by an overpowering and persistent inability to refrain from a maladaptive behavior. The primary indicator of these disorders is impulsivity, in which an individual experiences loss of control in specific situations or circumstances. The impulsive behavior is preceded by an upsurge of tension that diminishes or remits following the action. Many disorders in the *Diagnostic and Statistical Manual of Mental Disorders* (4th ed., text rev.*; DSM-IV-TR;* American Psychiatric Association, 2000) entail overwhelming urges (e.g., substance abuse disorders, sexual disorders), but they have other defining symptoms as well. The category, **impulse control disorders not elsewhere classified,** is distinct from other impulse control diagnoses in that these disorders are specifically defined by loss of control. Intermittent explosive disorder, kleptomania, pyromania, pathological gambling, trichotillomania, and impulse control disorders not otherwise specified (NOS) are in this category.

Intermittent explosive disorder is a loss of control involving aggressive outbursts that result in destruction of property or assault of others. The intensity of the violent behavior exceeds what would be considered a typical reaction to a stressor or event. Discrete episodes of violent behavior may include intentionally damaging property, harming another person physically, or threatening to harm someone. Individuals who have this disorder may experience physical symptoms preceding the aggressive acts such as tingling, palpitations, or chest tightness. After the act, they may become fatigued and/or depressed.

Aggressive behavior is a symptom of several mental disorders, including delirium, dementia, substance intoxication, substance withdrawal, conduct disorder, oppositional defiant disorder, and panic disorder. Other disorders should be ruled out before assigning a diagnosis of intermittent explosive disorder. In addition, purposeful angry or aggressive acts may occur in the absence of a mental disorder in someone who is malingering or who is reacting to a life event.

Individuals with **kleptomania** compulsively steal items that they may not need or that have little monetary value. The theft is preceded by feelings of anxiety and followed by a sense of relief or pleasure. Other disorders, such as conduct disorder, antisocial personality disorder, or bipolar disorder, may include stealing as a behavior; however, kleptomania is distinguished from other mental disorders because the stealing is not done to express anger and the individual feels guilt and remorse as a result of the theft. Kleptomania occurs more often in women than in men. It is a rare condition; only about 5% of identified shoplifters are thought to have kleptomania.

Pyromania (literally, obsession with fire) is the deliberate setting of multiple fires in order to decrease tension and experience pleasure. Individuals with this disorder are fascinated by fires and may engage in behaviors such as setting off false alarms, befriending firefighters, or collecting fire paraphernalia. Like kleptomania, this behavior is not done for profit or revenge. The act of fire starting is not a result of other mental disorder symptoms such as cognitive impairment, delusions, or mania. Persons who have pyromania are usually not disturbed by the destruction resulting from their actions, even though the fires may cause serious injury or loss of life. Pyromania is rare; it is most often found in males, particularly those with poor social skills and learning difficulties.

Pathological gambling is classified as an impulse control disorder because the essential feature is an inability to resist persistent, overwhelming urges to gamble. Individuals with this disorder typically start gambling for the thrill rather than for the money; however, they tend to wager larger and larger amounts to mitigate their losses, leading to personal, social, and occupational problems. Symptoms of pathological gambling include a preoccupation with gambling, an inability to cut back on gambling, feeling remorseful after gambling, borrowing money or stealing to gamble, lying to others about gambling, and gambling to escape problems or relieve anxiety.

Substance abuse, anxiety, attention-deficit/hyperactivity disorder, and depression (including suicide attempts) may be present in individuals with pathological gambling. There is also evidence that certain personality disorders, such as antisocial personality disorder, narcissistic personality disorder, and borderline personality disorder, may be related to pathological gambling.

Individuals with **trichotillomania** compulsively pull out their hair, leaving noticeable bare patches. There is an increase of tension or anxiety before pulling the hair and a sense of pleasure or relief after the pulling. Hair may be pulled from any part of the body, and some may even pull hair from pets, stuffed animals, or even other people. The individual with trichotillomania experiences distress and tries to conceal the hair loss. If the person also eats the pulled hair, the condition is trichophagia, which can cause serious complications such as intestinal obstruction or malnutrition. Other conditions, such as scalp infections, male-pattern baldness, certain autoimmune diseases, and other mental disorders (e.g., obsessive-compulsive disorder), should be considered before giving a diagnosis of trichotillomania. Children may develop a benign form of hair pulling that does not persist more than a few weeks that should not be considered trichotillomania.

The impulse control disorder NOS category is reserved for those conditions in which impulse control is the main feature, but the criteria for a specific impulse control disorder are not met. Skin picking, an individual damaging his or her own skin by repetitively and compulsively scratching or picking, is an example.

Contributed by Hunter D. Alessi,
Southeastern Louisiana University,
Hammond, LA

Reference

American Psychiatric Association. (2000). *Diagnostic and statistical manual of mental disorders* (4th ed., text rev.). Washington, DC: Author.

Indigenous Healing Approaches

The terms **indigenous healing** and **traditional healing** refer to the helping approaches and strategies that originated in various countries and were used by ethnic populations for thousands of years before the arrival of modern medicine. **Indigenous** societies have access to a unique cultural and environmental knowledge base. These practices emerged from the confluence of culture, history, philosophy, and natural resources in various world regions. The World Health Organization (2007) estimated that traditional healing approaches were used by 65% to 85% of the world's population as their primary form of health care. An **indigenous per-**

spective considers people to be an integral part of the natural world, wherein humans convey spirituality, balancing energies, interconnectedness, embedded social networks, and harmony with nature. For example, Sue and Sue (1999) described the interconnected nature of the belief systems, with harmony and balance being an optimal condition, and they emphasized the importance of interdependence. Healing must involve the entire group rather than just an individual.

The indigenous perspective of **wellness/health** is based on the premise that humankind is an integral part of nature and that a major indication of health is balance; therefore, the individual and the world thrive when this complex system of interrelationships is honored and maintained in harmony. Illness, disharmony, and disease are perceived within a larger, holistic context inclusive of mind, body, spirit, emotions, and interrelationships. Imbalance on every level of life, from the most personal inner life to the most overt behavior, is construed to be a condition for disharmony and, potentially, illness or disease. Optimal health encompasses humankind's connection with the natural world, and, conversely, illness, disease, and spiritual unrest are associated with the dislocation and removal of people from native lands, the introduction of colonization, and the decimation of the indigenous culture.

Every society and culture have designated individuals as healers who may cure not only physical problems but also difficulties related to psychological issues and abnormal behaviors. These **indigenous healers,** who have an understanding of the historical and cultural worldview of their people, are believed to have particular skills and wisdom that assist individuals in problem solving and decision making. Indigenous healers include shamans, priests, chiefs, or ministers, depending on the cultural system and region.

Treatment Approaches

Effective treatment requires the convergence of a skilled, compassionate practitioner and a committed client. The unique quality of each healer's approach is not simply accepted, it is prized. Another equally important facet of the treatment process is the client's choice to heal. Clients' preferences are always honored. If a healer were to disregard the client's preferences, or to exert even subtle force, the establishment of harmony would be subverted.

The goal of indigenous healing is to return the individual to a state of harmonious balance, both within him- or herself and in relationship to the outer world. Intervention strategies include a knowledge of and access to indigenous helping resources and networks within a particular community. Professional counselors may use an integrative approach, drawing from both Western and traditional models. In some instances, a traditional healer and professional counselor might collaborate to deliver services to indigenous and/or ethnic minority populations. Professional counselors should encourage clients to share their worldview and cultural belief systems. Within this context, the professional counselor may make a determination regarding the potential use of indigenous helping methods to assess whether this would be a match for the client. Sue and Sue (1999) have suggested that professional counselors take a more active role in their work with indigenous clients. For example, in some instances, a professional counselor might intervene in an institutional setting to remove institutional barriers inhibiting clients' success.

Despite empirical findings that suggest that the use of indigenous methods is efficacious, modern Western mental health services can be in conflict with indigenous healing practices. Some of the potential areas of conflict are rooted in the values inherent in the worldviews of each paradigm. For instance, a Western perspective of counseling and healing values independence and individuality, whereas indigenous societies and many ethnic minority cultures value collectivist perspectives. Professional counselors are encouraged to examine the philosophical underpinnings that inform their practice and take into consideration how the differences between independent and interdependent perspectives play a part in their own practice. Yeh, Hunter, Madan-Bahel, Chiang, and Kwong (2004) discussed the efficacy of indigenous methods such as cuento therapy for anxiety reduction and mindfulness-based (informed by a Buddhist perspective) cognitive therapy in the treatment of depression.

Cuento therapy uses folktales in the treatment of children and adolescents to convey cultural values and customs. Cuento therapy encompasses a method of enhancing clients' adaptive emotional and behavioral functioning by "(a) improving their attentional processes; (b) modeling salient cultural values, beliefs and behaviors; and (c) modeling appropriate relationships with parental figures" (Costantino & Malgady, 1986, p. 640). Multicultural counseling theorists suggest that practitioners may need to acknowledge a fully holistic approach in working with clients who come from indigenous cultures. For example, the worldview and tradition of shamanic healers encompass mind, body, and spirit within the context of the larger cosmos. This is considered to be a universal perspective among indigenous healers.

In conclusion, professional counselors must demonstrate multicultural competence as an important facet of overall professional competence. The professional counselor's knowledge base must, therefore, include an awareness of and openness to indigenous resources and methods of treatment. With access to Western and indigenous perspectives and approaches, professional counselors will be prepared to provide effective service to an increasingly diverse client population.

Contributed by Debra Behrens,
University of California, Berkeley,
Berkeley, CA

References

Costantino, G., & Malgady, R. G. (1986). Cuento therapy: A culturally sensitive modality for Puerto Rican children. *Journal of Consulting and Clinical Psychology, 54,* 639–645.

Sue, D. W., & Sue, D. (1999). *Counseling the culturally different: Theory and practice* (3rd ed.). New York: Wiley.

World Health Organization. (2007). *The world health report 20007: A safer future.* Geneva, Switzerland: Author.

Yeh, C. J., Hunter, C. C., Madan-Bahel, A., Chiang, L., & Kwong, A. (2004). Indigenous and interdependent perspectives of healing: Implications for counseling and research. *Journal of Counseling & Development, 82,* 410–419.

Additional Resources

Cunningham, C., & Stanley, F. (2003). Indigenous by definition, experience or world view. *British Medical Journal, 327,* 403–404.

Jackson, Y. (Ed.). (2006). *Encyclopedia of multicultural psychology.* Thousand Oaks, CA: Sage.

Ponterotto, J. G., Casas, M. J., Suzuki, L. A., & Alexander, C. M. (Eds.). (2001). *Handbook of multicultural counseling.* Thousand Oaks, CA: Sage.

Whitbeck, L. B., Adams, G. W., Hoyt, D. R., & Chen, X. (2004). Conceptualizing and measuring historical trauma among American Indian people. *American Journal of Community Psychology, 33,* 3–4.

▪ Individual Psychology

Alfred Adler developed a theory of personality and maladjustment and an approach to counseling and psychotherapy that he called **individual psychology.** Adler (1870–1937) was born in a suburb of Vienna, Austria. He attended public school in Vienna and then trained as a physician at the University of Vienna. Adler entered private practice as an ophthalmologist. A short time later, he switched to general practice and then to neurology. In 1902, he was invited by Sigmund Freud to join the Vienna Psychoanalytic Society. Due to significant theoretical disagreement with Freud, Adler resigned from the Society in 1911. He spent the remainder of his life developing a personality theory and approach to counseling and psychotherapy so far ahead of his time that Albert Ellis (1970) declared, "Alfred Adler, more than even Freud, is probably the true father of modern psychotherapy" (p. 11). Corey (2005) stated that Adler's most important contribution was his influence on other theoretical perspectives. Adler's influence has been acknowledged by, or his vision traced to, neo-Freudian approaches, existential therapy, person-centered therapy, cognitive-behavioral therapies, reality therapy, family systems approaches, and constructivist and social constructionist (e.g., solution-focused and narrative) therapies.

Basic Concepts

Individual psychology, or **Adlerian psychology,** is often misunderstood as primarily focusing on individuals; however, Adler chose the name individual psychology (from the Latin, *individuum,* meaning indivisible) for his theoretical approach because he eschewed reductionism. He emphasized that persons cannot be properly understood as a collection of parts but rather should be viewed as a whole. Adlerian theory is a holistic, phenomenological, socially oriented, and teleological (i.e., goal-directed) approach to understanding and working with people. It emphasizes the proactive, form-giving, and fictional nature of human cognition and its role in constructing the "realities" that persons know and to which they respond. Adlerian theory asserts that humans construct, manufacture, or "narratize" ways of viewing and experiencing the world and then take these **fictions** for truth. It is an optimistic theory affirming that humans are not determined by heredity or environment. Rather, they are creative, proactive, meaning-making beings, having the ability to choose and to be responsible for their choices.

Personality Theory

Adler affirmed that humans are characterized by unity across the broad spectrum of personality: cognitions, affect, and behavior. **Life style** or **style of life,** the Adlerian nomenclature for personality, is a cognitive blueprint containing the person's unique and individually created convictions, goals, and personal beliefs for coping with the tasks and challenges of life. This life plan is uniquely created by each person, begins as a prototype in early childhood, and is progressively refined throughout life. The social context of children includes both the values of their culture of origin and their experiences within their **family constellation,** which is Adler's phrase for the operative influences of the family's structure (including a person's position in the family or **psychological birth order**), values, and dynamics. Children perceive others and the world as paralleling their first social environment, their family, and eventually frame or filter the larger experience of life—and interpersonal relationships—on the basis of these initial relationships and perceptions.

According to Adlerian theory, humans are proactive in regard to the development of the style of life. This idea is inherent in the Adlerian construct known as the creative power of the self, or the creative self. Because of this creative power, people function like actors authoring their own scripts, directing their own actions, and constructing their own personalities within a socially embedded context. Humans coconstruct the realities to which they respond.

The central human directionality is toward competence or self-mastery, what Adler called **striving for superiority.** This is the individual's creative and compensatory answer to the normal and universal feelings of insignificance and disempowerment and the accompanying beliefs that one is less than what one should be (i.e., **feelings of inferiority**). Striving for superiority is the natural human desire to move from a perceived negative position to a perceived positive one.

Individual psychology is a relational theory. It asserts that humans are socially embedded and that knowledge is relationally distributed. Adler stressed that persons cannot be properly understood apart from their social context. Consequently, the Adlerian perspective on the tasks of life—love, society, work, spirituality, and self—is a relational one. These tasks of life address intimate love relationships, relationships with friends and fellow beings in society, relationships at work, the relationship with self, and the relationship with God or the universe.

The cardinal tenet of Adler's theory, *Gemeinschaftsgefühl* (translated as community feeling or social interest), is a social-contextual one. Community feeling and social interest are the two most common translations. Both are needed for a holistic understanding of *Gemeinschaftsgefühl*. Community feeling is the affective and motivational aspects, and social interest is the cognitive and behavioral aspects. Thus, true community feeling (i.e., sense of belonging, empathy, caring, compassion, and acceptance of others) results in social interest (thoughts and behaviors that contribute to the common good, the good of the whole at both micro- and macrosystemic levels). True social interest is motivated by community feeling.

The aforementioned striving for superiority occurs in a relational context as well, and this striving may occur in either a socially useful or a socially useless manner. The manner a person chooses constitutes the Adlerian criterion for mental health: Healthy development follows the goal of community feeling and social interest; maladjustment is the consequence of pursuing narcissistic self-interest.

The Counseling Process

Adlerian counseling embraces a nonpathological perspective. Clients are viewed as discouraged. All persons struggle with feelings of inferiority. When persons creatively respond with courage and community feeling/social interest to the challenges of life and the concomitant feelings of inferiority, they are considered to be functioning well. When they do not, or if they respond without community feeling/social interest, they are discouraged and may have what Adler called an **inferiority complex.** Persons with an inferiority complex are more concerned with how others perceive them than they are with finding solutions to problems. They tend to be passive and withdrawn. Persons compensating for inferiority feelings by a **superiority complex** tend to be arrogant and boastful. In both cases, they are discouraged but responding to overwhelming feelings of inferiority in different ways.

Adlerian counseling is commonly viewed as consisting of four phases. The first and most important phase is titled relationship. The client–counselor relationship in Adlerian counseling is variously described as cooperative, collaborative, egalitarian, optimistic, and respectful. Success in the other phases of the Adlerian approach (i.e., analysis, insight, reorientation) is predicated on the development and continuation of a strong counselor–client relationship.

Adlerians take a process view of individuals and consequently do not see assessment as an event that categorizes clients with static diagnostic labels. Assessment is ongoing, a continual process. Most Adlerians do some form of **style of life (life style) analysis** as a part of their assessment, either formally or informally. This assessment usually includes eliciting information about the client's childhood family constellation and asking the client for **early recollections,** a projective assessment whereby clients share memories of specific childhood events. According to individual psychology, early memories are seen as invented, selected, and altered by the individual to reflect current attitudes and perspectives.

The fundamental goal of Adlerian counseling is to help clients experience and assimilate new information that is discrepant from existing cognitive structures (style of life). Clients have an opportunity to create perceptual alternatives and modify or replace growth-inhibiting beliefs or personal narratives with growth-enhancing ones. The ultimate goal for Adlerians is the development or expansion of clients' social interest. Congruent with Adlerian personality theory, the goals of Adlerian counseling are relationally focused.

Adlerians use a variety of cognitive, behavioral, and experiential techniques for achieving the goals of counseling. Adlerian counseling is immensely flexible, and, consequently, Adlerians select techniques based on the unique needs and problems of each client.

Applications

Some Adlerians view individual counseling as the preferred method. Many Adlerians practice couples and family counseling. The majority of the parent education curricula currently available are based on Adlerian principles. In addition, many professional school counselors find Adlerian counseling a useful approach for their work. Adlerian group therapy has also remained an important counseling modality. Given that Adlerians believe that humans are socially embedded and knowledge is relationally distributed, the application of individual psychology principles in groups and on a systemic level is also popular.

Contributed by Richard E. Watts and Daniel Eckstein, Sam Houston State University, Huntsville, TX

References

Corey, G. (2005). *Theory and practice of counseling and psychotherapy* (7th ed.). Belmont, CA: Brooks/Cole.

Ellis, A. (1970). Humanism, values, rationality. *Journal of Individual Psychology, 26,* 11.

Additional Resources

Carlson, J., Watts, R. E., & Maniacci, M. (2006). *Adlerian therapy: Theory and practice.* Washington, DC: American Psychological Association.

Watts, R. E. (Ed.). (2003). *Adlerian, cognitive, and constructivist psychotherapies: An integrative dialogue.* New York: Springer.

■ Individual Psychology Counseling Techniques

Individual psychology (or Adlerian counseling and psychotherapy) is a theoretically consistent and technically eclectic approach. Adlerians are **multimodal** in the sense that they regularly use techniques from a broad range of theoretical perspectives based on the client's presenting problem(s) and specific needs. Adlerians have however created techniques of their own. Although not an exhaustive listing, this entry discusses several of the most prominent.

Encouragement

For Adlerians, **encouragement** is both an attitude and a way of being with clients. Clients present for counseling because they are discouraged and lack the confidence and "courage" to engage successfully in the tasks or problems of living. The

process of encouragement helps build hope and the expectancy of success in clients. Adlerians use encouragement throughout the counseling process to help clients create new patterns of behavior, develop more encouraging perceptions, and access resources and strengths. These skills of encouragement include, but are not limited to, communicating confidence in clients' strengths, assets, and abilities, such as identifying and drawing on past successes; helping clients distinguish between what they do and who they are (deed vs. doer); assisting clients in generating perceptual alternatives for discouraging fictional beliefs; focusing on clients' efforts and progress; and communicating affirmation and appreciation to clients.

Style of Life (or Life Style) Analysis

There are several different ways for professional counselors to conduct a **style of life analysis.** Some conduct the interview in the first session, whereas others take two to three sessions to complete it. Some interviewers use a standard format for the assessment, whereas others may collect the information informally. Regardless of the specific way that Adlerian counselors conduct the interview, they do typically include an interview that leads to a formulation or summary of the client's style of life. These interviews, based on clients' memories of their family of origin, have common subject areas that are explored. Interviewers first ask about siblings and how similar or different clients were relative to their siblings. Next, clients are asked about the influence of their parents. This gives the professional counselor information about the client's perceived ordinal position (or psychological birth order), the family constellation (how each person related to the other), and the family atmosphere (the overarching "mood" of the family). Next, Adlerian counselors ask about the client's childhood physical development, sexual development, social development, and school experience. Professional counselors also ask about clients' local community and socioeconomic status to help determine clients' views of themselves and the family's position in the larger world.

The final phase of the interview is the collection of early childhood recollections. Early memories are not coincidences; they are often projections. What clients selectively attend to from the past is reflective of what they believe and how they behave in the present and what they anticipate for the future. Each early recollection elicited by the professional counselor should be a single, specific incident, preferably occurring before the age of 10 years. Interviewers collect anywhere from three to eight early memories.

Having gathered all the aforementioned data, the clinician has the information necessary to create tentative hypotheses about a client's style of life regarding patterns of behavior and ways of viewing himself or herself and his or her world. Next, the professional counselor presents these hypotheses to the client.

The Question

In using **the question,** professional counselors ask a variation of the question, "How would your life be different if, all of a sudden, you didn't have this problem anymore?" There are variations for dramatic or explanatory purposes (e.g., "Suppose I gave you a pill?" "What if you had a magic wand?" "What if you woke up in the morning and no longer had this problem?"). There are three possible responses to the question. One reflects a clearly **psychogenic symptom,** meaning that the cause and relief from the symptom are purely psychological in nature (e.g., malingering, avoiding responsibility). The second type reflects a **somatogenic symptom,** meaning that the cause and relief from the symptom are purely physical in nature (e.g., chronic pain or illness). The third type of response is a combination of the psychogenic and somatogenic responses. The question forces clients to think in terms of a new reality where they are no longer burdened by their presenting problem. As a result, clients will either be unable to hide what their symptom is doing *for* them (i.e., the usefulness, or "purpose" of the behavior), or they will feel a sense of encouragement because they begin to understand that they have the resources and abilities to overcome the problem.

Hypothesis Interpretation

The purpose of using **hypothesis interpretation** is to convey to the client that more than one explanation for behavior exists and that the counselor wants to check out his or her own hunches to see if they are on the mark. When using this technique, phrasing is important. For example, after reviewing the style of life assessment, a professional counselor may start the interpretation process with "Could it be that?" or "Is it possible that?" Interpretations phrased in this way provide the client an opportunity to let the professional counselor know if he or she is on the right track. Observing an "ah-ha" moment in the client's expression (recognition reflex) or a quick glance of disapproval in response to the interpretation would be enough for the professional counselor to continue or to move in a different direction. Phrasing interpretations as hypotheses is an effective way to diminish resistance in the counseling relationship.

Acting As If

In the traditional approach to using the **acting as if** technique, professional counselors ask clients to begin acting as if they were already the person they would like to be, for example, a confident individual. Using this procedure, counselors ask clients to pretend, and counselors emphasize that the clients are only acting. The purpose of the procedure is to bypass potential resistance to change by neutralizing some of the perceived risk. The professional counselor suggests a limited task, such as acting as if an individual had the courage to speak up for himself or herself. The expectation is that the client will successfully complete the task. If the task is not completed successfully, then the counselor explores with the client what prevented a successful experience.

An approach to acting as if that is more reflective asks clients to take a reflective step back prior to stepping forward to act as if. This process encourages clients to reflect on how they would be different if they were acting as if they were the person they desire to be. By using reflective questions, professional counselors can help clients construct perceptual

alternatives and consider alternative behaviors prior to engaging in acting as-if tasks.

Catching Oneself

This technique involves encouraging a client to **catch oneself** in the act of performing the presenting problem. Clients may initially catch themselves too late and fall into old patterns of behavior; however, with practice, clients can learn to anticipate situations, recognize when their thoughts and perceptions are becoming self-defeating, and take steps to modify their thinking and behavior. Catching oneself involves helping clients identify the signals or triggers associated with their problematic behavior or emotions. When triggers are identified, clients can then make decisions that stop their symptoms from overwhelming them.

The Pushbutton Technique

The purpose of the **pushbutton technique** is to help clients become aware of their role in maintaining, or even creating, their unpleasant feelings. The pushbutton technique has three phases. In Phase 1, clients are asked to close their eyes and recall a pleasant memory (e.g., a time when they felt happy, loved, successful). Clients are to re-create the image in their minds in as specific detail as possible and focus on the positive feelings generated by the pleasant memory. In Phase 2, clients are asked to close their eyes and recall an unpleasant memory (e.g., a time when they felt sad, unloved, unsuccessful). As in Phase 1, clients are to recall the memory in all its clarity and, this time, strongly focus on the unpleasant feelings created by the memory. In Phase 3, clients are asked to retrieve another pleasant memory or return to the one used in Phase 1. They are to recall the memory in specific detail and strongly focus on the positive feelings. After they have relived the pleasant memory and positive feelings, clients are instructed to open their eyes. They are then asked to share what they learned from the exercise. Clients usually make the connection between beliefs and feelings. If clients fail to do so, professional counselors should help them understand that certain thoughts or images usually generate certain types of feelings. After making sure the connection is made, counselors then give clients two make-believe pushbuttons to take for a homework assignment. These pushbuttons control the images clients create. When they push the negative pushbutton, they create unpleasant images that negatively affect how they feel. When they push the positive pushbutton, they create pleasant images that positively affect how they feel. These pushbuttons affirm that feelings or behaviors are typically a choice. When they return for the next counseling session, the discussion with the professional counselor can focus on which button clients have been pushing and the purpose of the choice.

Contributed by Richard E. Watts, Sam Houston State University, Huntsville, TX; Todd F. Lewis, The University of North Carolina at Greensboro, Greensboro, NC; and Paul R. Peluso, Florida Atlantic University, Boca Raton, FL

Additional Resources

Clark, A. J. (2000). *Early recollections: Theory and practice in counseling and psychotherapy.* New York: Brunner/Routledge.

Eckstein, D., & Kern, R. (2002). *Psychological fingerprints: Lifestyle assessments and interventions* (5th ed.). Dubuque, IA: Kendall/Hunt.

Powers, R. L., & Griffith, J. (1987). *Understanding life-style: The psycho-clarity process.* Chicago: The Americas Institute of Adlerian Studies.

Shulman, B. H., & Mosak, H. H. (1988). *Manual for life style assessment.* Bristol, PA: Accelerated Development/Taylor & Francis.

■ Inferential Statistics

Quantitative research uses **inferential statistics** to describe research findings. Inferential statistics are used to identify or to infer whether or not results obtained from a sample can be carried over to a population and with how much confidence the results can be generalized. Inferential statistics differ from descriptive statistics (i.e., measures of central tendency, variability, relative position, and relationship) in that inferential statistics assume something rather than summarize it. Often, research studies begin by using descriptive statistics (a summarization of data) and then shift to more advanced statistics. Ordinarily, the larger the sample size used, the better the data may be described and summarized and the greater the chance of being able to generalize to an entire population (Mertler & Vannatta, 2005).

An example is a researcher who is inquiring whether two or more groups are different from each other on a specific variable, particularly about whether or not a particular specialty area in a counseling program predicts higher scores on the National Counselor Examination (NCE). The researcher obtains a sample from the entire population of counseling student specialties and performs inferential statistical analyses on the obtained data to determine whether or not there is statistical significance between the specialty areas (e.g., independent variables/groups) and earned NCE scores (e.g., dependent variable).

Key Concepts in Inferential Statistics

Significance level and effect size are two key concepts in inferential statistics. **Statistical significance level** is a numerical value that is set by the researcher and, in the counseling profession, is known as **probability** (*p*) or the **alpha level** (α). It is most often set at .01 ($p < .01$) or .05 ($p < .05$). For example, for an alpha level of .05, 95% of the time there is no chance of a Type I error occurring. Another way to say this is that there is an allowance for a 5% chance of a Type I error (i.e., stating significant differences between groups when there are none). It can be said that the lower the probability (alpha level, significance level), the lower the chance for a Type I error. For instance, if the researchers found statistical significance ($p < .01$) in counseling students specializing in mental health counseling and implications for higher scores on the NCE, this would mean that the chance of this being incorrect is less than 1 out of 100, which is a higher level of significance than $p < .05$. Inferential statistics can be used to test hypotheses made about a specific sample drawn from a population and then produce a probability. Subsequently, researchers can be more confident when they reject the null hypothesis (i.e., find statistical significance) and accept the alternate when discussing their research results.

The strength of the relationship between variables is determined by computing the **effect size** (LaFountain & Bartos, 2002). Effect size is represented as ES or partial η^2. Effect size indicates functional importance and tells the magnitude of a finding. Typically, the effect size is determined by the researcher, similar to the alpha level, and reflects what result the researcher hopes to find. To calculate effect size in an experimental study, the following formula is generally used:

$$ES = \frac{M_{\text{experimental}} - M_{\text{control}}}{SD_{\text{control}}}$$

The effect size is an important dimension of statistical analysis because it contextualizes how researchers interpret a statistically significant result. The effect size is a way to quantify the strength of the relationship between the variables of interest. Knowing the effect helps researchers make meaningful interpretations because it highlights the size of the difference as opposed to just the statistical significance. It is an important dimension to add because a statistically significant result can emerge from a very large sample size and not be a true representation of the strength of the relationship between the variables (see Power).

Parametric Tests

Several types of inferential statistics can be produced using parametric tests. A **parametric test** can be described as a statistical procedure for interval and ratio scales of measurement because the scales yield parameters (e.g., mean, standard deviation). Types of parametric tests include, but are not limited to, *t* test, analysis of variance (ANOVA), multivariate analysis of variance (MANOVA), and analysis of covariance (ANCOVA). Parametric tests are said to be more powerful than nonparametric tests, although certain criteria must be met in order to use them. One criterion that must be met involves independent observations of data established through randomization when drawing observations from the population. Another criterion of a parametric test is that, within the population, the variable must be normally distributed. Finally, in a population, there must be equal variances when more than one sample is used in the study (see Parametric Statistics).

Nonparametric Tests

Other types of inferential statistics can be elicited through nonparametric tests. **Nonparametric tests** are used to analyze data that use nominal and ordinal scales of measurement. Nominal scales are used for naming, and ordinal scales are used for ranking. With nonparametric tests, it is not necessary to meet the previously stated criteria required for parametric analysis. This makes nonparametric tests more flexible, but less powerful, than parametric statistics; that is, the criteria must be met for parametric analysis, whereas nonparametric statistics are more distribution free (e.g., not restricted by parametric requirements). Some examples of nonparametric tests are the chi-square test, Mann–Whitney *U* test, Wilcoxon matched-pairs signed-ranks test, and the Kruskal–Wallis test (see Nonparametric Statistics).

Benefits and Limitations of Inferential Statistics

Inferential statistics can be useful to determine whether or not there is statistical significance and, consequently, whether to accept or reject specific hypotheses. Moreover, inferential statistics provide a common language among counselors for quantitative research findings. Inferential statistics allow counselors to draw from a specific sample and consequently generalize or infer something about a larger population.

Although inferential statistics can be helpful in testing hypotheses and identifying statistical significance, there are limitations to be noted. For instance, just because statistical significance is found, this does not mean that a large difference exists. Although small differences can be important at times, it is helpful to use larger samples to conduct inferential statistical analyses and find larger differences among means, although this can be difficult and costly.

Contributed by Carrie Alexander-Albritton and Nicole R. Hill, Idaho State University, Pocatello, ID

References

LaFountain, M. R., & Bartos, B. R. (2002). *Research and statistics made meaningful in counseling and student affairs*. Pacific Grove, CA: Brooks/Cole.

Mertler, C. A., & Vannatta, A. R. (2005). *Advanced and multivariate statistical methods* (3rd ed.). Glendale, CA: Pyrczak.

Additional Resource

Pyrczak, F. (2006). *Making sense of statistics* (4th ed.). Glendale, CA: Pyrczak.

■ Information-Processing Model

The **information-processing model** describes a widely used approach in the study of memory, defined as the ability to store and retrieve information that is experienced, imagined, and learned. As exemplified by the classic work of Atkinson and Shiffrin (1968), the information-processing model describes the process humans use to register, encode, store, and retrieve information. This representation shows how humans process information through entry points of the sensory registers, where the information either fades away or is determined to be meaningful. Selected information is passed on for further mental and symbolic processing in short-term, or working, memory, where it is either forgotten or transferred into long-term memory. If transferred into long-term memory, the information can be stored and retrieved as necessary. Thus, the interplay and manipulation of information

provide an explanation of the processes of receiving, analyzing, and acting on information received. How the information is eventually expressed is based on the reception, understanding, and meaning derived from the received information.

Sensory Memory

The initial process of stimulus perception is associated with the flow of information from the senses into the sensory register for a brief time. Although the sensory register has the capacity to hold enormous amounts of temporal information without attending to or selecting the information for further processing, the duration is extremely brief, meaning the information in **sensory memory** begins to fade away within 1 to 3 seconds. The process of selective attention to stimuli further influences the integration and transfer of information through various filters related to the stimulus, such as personal meaningfulness and previously learned stimuli. During this attention process, selected information flows into short-term memory, or working memory, while factors involved in forgetting (e.g., passage of time, masking) discard extraneous stimuli.

Short-Term Memory

Short-term memory, or **working memory,** is the process whereby selected information from the sensory registers is stored and actively processed. Organizing and grouping stimuli in short-term memory occur in a manner that separates the information into meaningful units, called **chunking**. Chunking allows an individual to process more information by grouping data into larger informational units, such as numbers, phonetics, strings of digits, and visual encoding (e.g., data, maps, diagrams). **Encoding** in short-term memory occurs phonologically or visually or in terms of meaning. Maintenance (rote rehearsal) and elaborative rehearsal mechanisms provide processes to link new short-term information to long-term memory. **Rote rehearsal** is the repeating of information without intention to enhance memory. On the other hand, **elaborative rehearsal** is a method of processing new meaningful data by associating or connecting the information to familiar material in long-term memory. Without rehearsal of information, retention and retrieval time for short-term memory is limited to 7 ± 2 stimuli for 15 to 20 seconds through decay (passage of time) or interference from other information.

Long-Term Memory

Information in **long-term memory** is dynamic, highly organized, catalogued, and cross-referenced. The human mind stores memory units in three types of long-term memory. **Semantic memory** represents the most structured categorization and is where general facts, hierarchies, and categorical and abstract information are stored. **Episodic memory** centers on personal experience and specific events, including both personally experienced and meaningful events; a person can have a memory of a meaningful event even if he or she was not physically present to witness it. Semantic memory and episodic memory describe information that is intentionally committed to memory until needed again, known as **explicit memory. Implicit memory,** in contrast, defines information that either was unintentionally stored or unintentionally retrieved from long-term memory. Personal meaning appears to determine the encoding processes in long-term memory. Storage and retrieval capacity for long-term memory is immense and limited only to retrieval failure or interference theory, known as proactive, retroactive, and output interference. The interference effect describes the difficulty or failure to learn when there are existing conflicting associations in memory. In essence, **proactive interference** occurs when current new information is lost or challenged by old learning that continues to intrude in memory. Conversely, **retroactive memory** subscribes to the perspective that new learning interferes with previously learned information or old information. Interference that occurs during the activity of information retrieval is known as **output interference.**

By focusing on the process of how humans receive, store, integrate, retrieve, and respond to information, the complexity of understanding human learning is strengthened. The information-processing model provides useful insight for thinking about the executive control processes through which individuals use their senses and mind to acquire, store, integrate, respond, and retrieve information in the process of learning.

Contributed by Wanda P. Briggs,
Winthrop University, Rock Hill, SC

Reference

Atkinson, R., & Shiffrin, R. (1968). Human memory: A proposed system and its control processes. In K. Spence & J. Spence (Eds.), *The psychology of learning and motivation: Advances in research and theory* (Vol. 2, pp. 742–775). New York: Academic Press.

Additional Resource

Massaro, D. W., & Cowan, N. (1993). Information processing models: Microscopes of the mind. *Annual Review of Psychology, 44,* 383–425.

■ Informed Consent

Informed consent is an important ethical and legal concept developed by the medical field and defined as the process of providing sufficient information to a person so that he or she can make a well-informed decision before undertaking an action, procedure, or relationship. In the mental health field, informed consent sets the stage and boundaries in counseling and supervisory relationships, allowing involved persons to establish a mutual understanding about the experience they are about to share, including the potential risks and benefits of the services to be rendered. Informed consent begins with the first session and continues throughout the professional relationship. Important issues to be addressed in informed consent include limits of confidentiality, maintenance of records, the education and training of the service provider, emergency contact information, fees, and billing

arrangements. A professional disclosure statement is a helpful and recommended way to share necessary information.

In a counseling relationship, informed consent may specifically focus on the need for clients to understand their rights, practical and legal boundaries in the counseling relationship, and the theoretical approach of their counselor, including possible techniques that may be used. In a supervisory relationship, the clear and forthright discussion of informed consent issues by supervisors and supervisees can help to ensure that the learning potential of supervision is realized to the fullest extent possible by supervisees. Specific issues that may be addressed include the evaluative and gate-keeping role of the supervisor, dual relationships, workplace policies and procedures, and responsibilities of both the supervisee and supervisor. Informed consent is also the initial means by which supervisors not only model effective communication but also work to assuage any presenting concerns of supervisees. Supervisory contracts may be used to formalize agreed-on goals and logistical matters.

Informed consent is also a central component of any research study and must be received before any data are gathered from a participant. Issues to be addressed include what participation in the research entails; the purpose for collecting information from the participant; how the information will be used; how data will be handled, including issues of confidentiality; and potential risks and/or benefits involved for the participant. With all informed consent processes, consent must be received from a parent or guardian regarding the involvement of a minor or any legal adult who is not able to comprehend the informed consent issues fully.

Informed consent is a vital legal and ethical process that offers clients and supervisees practical and professional information about if and how their counselor or supervisor can provide desired services. Most important, informed consent protects all persons by clarifying the boundaries and processes of the relationship while facilitating the effective use of the services.

Contributed by Timothy D. Rambo,
University of Virginia, Charlottesville, VA

Additional Resources

American Counseling Association. (2005). *ACA code of ethics.* Alexandria, VA: Author.
Borders, L. D., & Brown, L. (2005). *The new handbook of counseling supervision.* Mahwah, NJ: Erlbaum.

■ Institutional Review Board for the Protection of Human Subjects

In 1966, Henry Beecher published an article in the *New England Journal of Medicine* titled "Ethics and Clinical Research." Beecher articulated disturbing examples of unethical treatment of human subjects in American medical research and categorized them into several types. He also speculated on the causes of such ethical failures in American medicine. He identified researchers' needs to obtain funding, competition for publication, and the desire for career advancement as factors that seemed to lead to ethical lapses.

Although Beecher had previously cited numerous examples of unethical research, in 1973 the Tuskegee Syphilis Study conducted by the U.S. Public Health Service came to the attention of the general public and motivated congressional hearings. The Tuskegee researchers had withheld available treatment for syphilis from 399 African American sharecroppers. The participants believed that the medical procedures they endured were treatments, when in fact, they were assessments of the course of an untreated disease. The congressional hearings eventually resulted in the National Research Act, the National Commission for Protection of Human Subjects of Biomedical and Behavioral Research, and the Belmont Report.

The **Belmont Report** articulated three basic ethical principles and three major applications of those principles. The basic principles were **respect for persons, beneficence,** and **justice.** The applications were **informed consent, assessment of risk and benefits,** and **selection of subjects.** The Belmont Report was the guiding document that laid the foundation for Title 45: Code of Federal Regulations: Part 46: Protection of Human Subjects, which is commonly called 45 CFR 46.

The statutory adoption of 45 CFR 46 resulted in the creation of **institutional review boards (IRBs).** Under 45 CFR 46, any entity that applies to the federal government for a grant, contract, or cooperative agreement that involves human subjects in research must establish an IRB. The IRB is to review research procedures to protect the rights and safety of human subjects. Any researcher at an institution that receives federal funding must submit a research application to the IRB for permission to use human participants.

Although some research is conducted without federal funds, it is best practice to have all research proposals reviewed to ensure protection of human participants. A common interpretation of the law is that if any research at an institution is conducted with federal funds, then all research at the institution is subject to IRB approval. This has placed increased demands on each institution's IRB and researchers. In recent history, concerns about ethical oversight and research practices have resulted in the federal government temporarily placing a stop on all funding and ongoing research at several institutions. For example, federally funded studies at the University of Alabama at Birmingham were halted in 1999, and research trials were halted in the same year at Virginia Commonwealth University. Research at Rush–Presbyterian–St. Luke's Medical Center was halted when a study of medication to treat strokes enrolled patients that were ineligible because of the undue risks placed on them in the study. The same factors (funding, publication, and advancement) that Beecher identified in 1966 are still viable and can cloud the ethical judgment of otherwise caring professionals.

When researchers intend to use human subjects or data resulting from assessments of human participants they submit a proposal to the appropriate IRB associated with their institution. Each IRB will have its own format, but IRBs are reasonably similar across settings. The applications will typically identify the researcher, the participants, the recruitment process, the procedures, the risks and protections against risks, and the informed consent procedure and documentation.

The full IRB consists of at least five members with varying backgrounds who are typically experienced researchers at the institution. The IRB must also include a nonscientist and a community representative. Inclusion of the nonscientist and community representative is particularly important because they may see research risks from the perspective of potential participants. An initial review of the proposal may determine that the apparent risks require review by the full board, or an initial review of the minimal risks in a proposal may result in it being reviewed on an expedited basis by a subcommittee of the full board. Initial review may also result in the decision that the proposal meets the criteria to be exempt from federal oversight under 45 CFR 46. Although some research is eligible for exemption, it is the purview of the IRB to determine the exemption and not the researcher's prerogative.

Best counseling practice is for researchers to submit all proposals to the IRB and receive guidance from it. The IRB serves as an objective body that is not influenced by the demands of funding, publication, or career advancement. Typically, when there are inadequate protections in place for the identifiable risks, the IRB will recommend revision of the procedures to ensure that human participants are less likely to be harmed. Sometimes the risks of conducting a study will outweigh any possible benefits and may not be mitigated by any possible protections. In those cases, the IRB can reject a proposal and deny permission to use human subjects altogether.

Contributed by Lane Fischer,
Brigham Young University, Provo, UT

Reference

Beecher, H. K. (1966). Ethics and clinical research. *New England Journal of Medicine, 274,* 1354–1360.

Additional Resources

Belmont Report: http://ohsr.od.nih.gov/guidelines/belmont.html

Dunn, C., & Chadwick, G. (1999). *Protecting study volunteers in research: A manual for investigative sites.* Boston: Center Watch.

Nuremberg Code: http://ohsr.od.nih.gov/guidelines/nuremberg.html

Sieber, J. E. (1992). *Planning ethically responsible research: A guide for students and internal review boards. Applied Social Research Methods Series* (Vol. 31). Newbury Park, CA: Sage.

Title 45: Code of Federal Regulations: Part 46: Protection of Human Subjects Web site: http://www.hhs.gov/ohrp/humansubjects/guidance/45cfr46.htm

Vanderpool, H. Y. (1996). *The ethics of research involving human subjects.* Frederick, MD: University Publishing Group.

Intelligence

In counseling, the term **intelligence** refers to a general collection of mental abilities involved with problem solving. Because intellectual mental abilities are not directly observable, most theories of intelligence are based on the measurement of hypothetical constructs or domains. **Francis Galton** is often credited as the first theorist of intelligence who attempted to verify hypotheses about intelligence through empirical investigation. Galton postulated that perceptual abilities were highly influential in the development of higher faculties of intelligence. Although Galton's theories of intelligence have not withstood the test of time, his greatest legacy is perhaps the statistical methods he invented, or improved on, to study intelligence (e.g., correlation and regression methodologies) that continue to be used in contemporary science.

Widely influenced by Galton were French physicians **Alfred Binet** and **Theodore Simon,** who in 1904 created the first formal measures of intelligence. These tests measured several abilities and identified children performing below the average. Soon after the successful use of the Binet intelligence test in France, **Lewis Terman** revised the intelligence test with the help of his colleagues at Stanford University in 1916. The **Stanford–Binet** became the standard for all intelligence tests to follow. During this revision, Terman adopted **William Stern's** concept of mental quotient, which was calculated by dividing an individual's mental age, based on test performance, by his or her chronological age to derive what was called a **ratio IQ** (intelligence quotient). Future revisions of the test discontinued the use of a quotient in favor of a point-scale format. Modern measures of intelligence, including the Stanford–Binet Intelligence Scale, Fifth Edition; Wechsler Intelligence Scale for Children–Fourth Edition; and the Woodcock–Johnson Tests of Cognitive Abilities–Third Edition, use a mathematical transformation of a raw score in a point-scale format based on deviance from normality, which technically makes IQ an inaccurate description.

Also influenced by Galton was **Charles Spearman,** who in 1912 developed factor analysis, a tool used to determine statistically the factors that cause scores to be more or less similar. Because factor analysis can provide a numerical value for the number of factors in a data set, it provided the empirical foundation for testing different theories of intelligence and determining whether intelligence was one or many abilities. Most of Spearman's research led him to believe intelligence was a single entity that contributes generally across problem-solving areas, which he named *g* for the general factor. Spearman metaphorically referred to *g* as "mental energy." Spearman also noted the existence of *s*, or specific factors to represent skills in a specific area often as a result of training (e.g., spelling).

Louis Thurstone, in 1938, was the first to include a more diverse set of intelligence tests that measured an array of abilities. After analyzing the correlations using factor analysis, Thurstone determined that there was no single *g* factor, but rather seven distinctly separate primary mental abilities (i.e., verbal comprehension, word fluency, number, spatial ability, associative memory, perceptual speed, and reasoning or induction). Many psychologists after Thurstone have agreed with his theory of multiple intelligences, including **Howard Gardner.** Gardner presented eight primary intelligences (i.e., linguistic, logical-mathematical, musical, spatial, bodily-kinesthetic, intrapersonal, interpersonal, and naturalistic) and held that brain damage could reduce ability in single areas without affecting others.

Building on Thurstone's work with factor analysis, **Raymond Cattell,** along with **John Horn,** presented the idea of two distinct intelligences that repeatedly emerged in factor analytic studies. Cattell and Horn referred to these two intelligences as fluid and crystallized. **Fluid** describes an individual's reasoning ability without reliance on learned knowledge, whereas **crystallized** is strongly reliant on learned knowledge. In subsequent research studies, additional factors also began to emerge. In 1993, **John Carroll** analyzed the data from hundreds of factor analysis studies and concluded that a three-stratum model, which described intelligence using a hierarchy, provided the best fit to the data. According to Carroll's three-tier hierarchy, *g* was placed at the top, followed by eight cognitive abilities, which were then followed by specific factors that influenced the eight broader abilities. The ideas of these three psychologists came to form the **Cattell–Horn–Carroll theory of cognitive abilities**.

Contemporary theories of intelligence have been most influenced by understanding neurobiology and functional brain networks. Eysenck's (1982) discovery that simple reaction-time measures were positively correlated with psychometric *g* led **Jensen** (1993) and others to believe that *g* is based on, and results from, individual differences in the speed of information processing in nerve pathways. Other biological markers have also been found to be correlated with intelligence. The number of synapses in the brain has positively correlated with higher levels of education; individuals with more gray matter in the brain tended to score higher on intelligence tests; and brain size, when adjusted for an individual's height, has a positive correlation with intelligence. Functional brain studies have revealed developmental differences in apotosis between individuals who scored high on intelligence measures from individuals who scored low on intelligence measures. Other researchers have focused more on constructs, such as **working memory** and **executive functions,** that are most dependent on frontal lobe functions and are highly correlated with *g*. Future revisions of intelligence theories will most likely be from discoveries in neuropsychology and brain sciences rather than in psychometrics.

The vast accumulation of research on the topic of intelligence suggests the term *intelligence,* and what it is meant to confer, is much too broad to be covered in a single definition. Intelligence is best understood at differing levels, including genetics, neurology, cognitive, psychological, and social levels. Regardless of the breadth of the subject and despite the numerous applications of intelligence measures as well as the controversial eugenic applications, theories of intelligence and the applications of such measures continue to be one of the most fruitful areas of psychology and will continue to be so.

Contributed by Scott L. Decker,
Kimberly B. Oliver, and Jessica A.
Carboni, Georgia State University,
Atlanta, GA

References

Eysenck, H. J. (Ed.). (1982). *A model for intelligence.* Berlin, Germany: Springer-Verlag.

Jensen, A.R. (1993). Spearmans hypothesis tested with chronometric information processing tasks. *Intelligence, 17,* 47–77.

Additional Resources

Flanagan, D. P., & Ortiz, S. O. (2002). Best practices in intellectual assessment: Future directions. In A. Thomas & J. Grimes (Eds.), *Best practices in school psychology* (Vol. 4, pp. 1351–1372). Bethesda, MD: National Association of School Psychologists.

Kosslyn, S. M., & Rosenberg, R. (2006). *Psychology in context* (3rd ed.). Boston: Allyn & Bacon.

Sattler, J. M. (2001). *Assessment of children: Cognitive applications* (4th ed.). La Mesa, CA: Sattler.

■ Intelligence Testing

The first successful effort to measure intelligence is generally credited to **Alfred Binet** and his colleague, **Theodore Simon,** in the early 1900s (Wood & Wood, 2002). The Ministry of Instruction in Paris, France, was in search of an objective means of identifying children whose intelligence was too low for them to benefit from regular classroom instruction. A wide variety of tests were used by the two men in order to include items that discriminated between older and younger children. Binet and Simon first published their intelligence scale in 1905 and later revised it in 1908 and 1911. Binet proposed that a person who scored 2 years below his or her chronological age was viewed as retarded and should be placed in special education classes. Of course, a flaw existed in his thinking because a 4-year-old with a mental age of a 2-year-old is substantially more intellectually deficient than a 12-year-old with the mental age of a 10-year-old. This flaw was addressed in Germany during 1914 by the work of William Stern, who used a simple formula for calculating an index of intelligence by dividing the mental age by the chronological age, which provided an intelligence quotient or IQ (Hockenbury & Hockenbury, 2006; Wood & Wood, 2002).

Lewis Terman of Stanford University translated and adapted Binet's test, and the revision was referred to as the Stanford–Binet Intelligence Scale. Originally published in 1916, it was the first test to use Stern's formula for IQ and was for many years the standard used for intelligence testing in the United States (Hockenbury & Hockenbury, 2006).

World War I was a significant event leading to widespread use of intelligence testing in the testing programs carried out by the U.S. Army (Boake, 2002). Implemented by a Committee on the Psychological Examination of Recruits, chaired by Robert Yerkes, the Army intelligence tests were group-administered examinations. Tests of intelligence before the war were individually administered and, therefore, time-consuming. Yerkes and colleagues modified these tests into a group-administration format by using multiple-choice questions. The **Army Alpha** test was used to assess literate English-speaking individuals, and the **Army Beta** test was used to assess a minority of recruits who were either illiterate or non-English speaking. More than 1,726,966 recruits were administered either the Alpha or Beta exams (Yerkes, 1921). The Alpha and Beta examinations consisted of a series of subtests that could be administered in less than an hour.

David Wechsler was trained as a psychological examiner by the U.S. Army. Wechsler scored the Alpha test and later administered individual psychological tests (Stanford–Binet or the Yerkes Point Scale) to soldiers who had failed both the Alpha and Beta tests. After the war, Wechsler provided oversight of the testing of adults of widely varying cultural and socioeconomic backgrounds and ages at a large hospital in New York City. Wechsler developed a new intelligence test, the Wechsler Adult Intelligence Scale (WAIS), which was first published in 1955. The WAIS has been revised and restandardized several times, most recently in 1997 as the WAIS-III, and continues to be one of the most widely used psychological tests. A contribution of the WAIS was the inclusion of Verbal and Performance (nonverbal) subtests yielding separate IQ scores for each area as well as an overall IQ score. Wechsler also published the Wechsler Intelligence Scale for Children (WISC). Since the 1960s, the Wechsler intelligence tests have remained the most commonly administered intelligence tests.

Process of Testing Intelligence

Wechsler developed the deviation IQ, a means of calculating an IQ score based on a statistical representation that is commonly used in other tests today: the normal curve or the bell-shaped curve. A comparison of an individual's IQ as a standard score with the scores of others in the same general age group is used. An average score for a particular age group was fixed at a standard score of 100, and a standard deviation for each group was set at 15. This standard score is commonly referred to as a **deviation IQ score.** The distribution of IQ scores among the general population follows the normal bell-shaped curve, with 68% of the scores falling between 85 to 115, which is viewed as being in the "normal" range, and 95% of the general population's scores falling between 70 to 130. Only 0.1% of examinees scored lower than 55 or higher than 145 (see Figure 1).

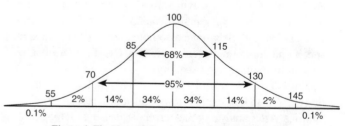

Figure 1. The Normal Curve of Distribution of IQ Scores

Note. IQ score of 100 ± 15 (85–115) represents a normal range.

The Wechsler scales are based on the early subtests that were used in the Stanford–Binet and in the U.S. Army Alpha and Army Beta tests. The Wechsler scales takes approximately 1 to 2 hours to administer and score, and the examiner requires extensive training. The test is individually administered and requires the examinee to answer questions, construct block designs, use pictures to solve problems, and recall information. Wechsler provided a classification table with commonly used diagnostic labels (see Table 1).

More recently, **Howard Gardner** presented the **theory of multiple intelligences,** which views intelligence as a number of different mental abilities with different skills and products valued in various cultures. He noted that in individuals with brain damage, some mental abilities are spared when others are lost. Gardner suggested that mental abilities are independent and cannot be accurately reflected with IQ scores, and he presented eight distinct and independent intelligences: linguistic, logical-mathematical, musical, spatial, bodily-kinesthetic, interpersonal, intrapersonal, and naturalistic. Robert Sternberg agreed with Gardner that intelligence was much more than what could be reflected in a conventional IQ score, and he has proposed a theory of three distinct forms of intelligence: analytic, creative, and practical. Sternberg disagreed with Gardner's notion of multiple intelligences and contended that an individual would be able to manage just fine if tone deaf and lacking musical intelligence in most societies (Hockenbury & Hockenbury, 2005); however, Sternberg pointed out that if an individual was unable to reason and plan ahead, he or she would be unable to function in any culture. Although Gardner's theory appreciates the strengths that a person may have that are not necessarily represented on traditional intelligence tests, the mental health profession continues to rely on earlier works in the field of intelligence testing. David Lohman has written extensively about the topic of intelligence and has noted that "some of the most important changes in the format of intelligence tests that were administered were dictated more by the demands for efficiency and reliability than by psychological theory" (Lohman, 1997, p. 2). A number of instruments have emerged as standard measures of intelligence that are used by counselors who have obtained specialized training and skills.

Contemporary Instruments

Intelligence tests are generally classified two ways: by the length of administration time and by the number of individuals who can be tested in a single administration (Erford, 2007). Instruments designed to offer a quick IQ score are considered brief and generally take from 20 to 60 minutes to administer. Instruments designed to offer a more comprehensive picture of cognitive functioning typically take between 60 to 180 minutes to administer. Clearly, the more comprehensive instruments offer richer data to assist the counselor in diagnosis and treatment. In addition, the brief instruments have limitations such as testing only a few domains of intelligence while overlooking others. Still, both brief and comprehensive intelligence testing can offer the clinician useful information for treatment planning. Counselors must be mindful that states set standards regarding who is qualified to administer and interpret intelligence tests. Professional associations, including the American Counseling Association (ACA), also offer professional and ethical guidelines for professionals trained in test administration and interpretation. The *ACA Code of Ethics* (ACA, 2005) reminds counselors to use only instruments "for which they have been trained and are competent" (p. 12).

As previously mentioned, the Wechsler scales are the most common instruments used to measure intelligence in individuals. The WAIS-III is designed for administration to individuals ages 16 to 89 years. Other scales are the WISC-IV for children ages 6 to 16 years and the Wechsler Preschool and Primary Scale of Intelligence–Third Edition for children ages 2 years and 6 months to 7 years and 3 months. A Spanish version of the WISC-IV is also available.

Other highly regarded contemporary measures of comprehensive intelligence are also available. The Stanford–Binet Intelligence Scales is currently in its fifth edition. Also available are the Woodcock–Johnson: Tests of Cognitive Abilities–Third Edition and the Kaufman Assessment Battery for Children–Second Edition (KABC-II). The KABC-II is designed to be a culturally fair measure of intelligence for children ages 3 to 18 years.

Depending on the purpose of testing, counselors may prefer the use of a brief instrument to assess intelligence. The Kaufman Brief Intelligence Test–Second Edition is one of the most common brief tests of intelligence in contemporary use. Other brief instruments commonly used today are the Wechsler Abbreviated Scale of Intelligence (WASI) and the Slosson Intelligence Test–Revised (SIT-R). The WASI is appropriate for use with individuals ages 6 years and above, whereas the SIT-R is appropriate for individuals ages 4 years and above. Professional counselors may be attracted to such measures due to their lower relative cost and ease of use. Counselors should be cautioned that brief intelligence tests offer a limited sampling of the client's full range of cognitive functioning and may be considered screening or provisional data.

A final category is intelligence tests designed for group administration. Group administration has received scrutiny for many, some quite obvious, reasons. For example, group administration does not facilitate close monitoring of the test taker, there is less opportunity to establish examiner–client rapport, and there is some evidence to show that children with emotional disturbances perform better on individually administered intelligence tests. Still, group intelligence testing is essential and practical in situations that require the collection of data from a large number of individuals. Thus, professional counselors working in schools frequently administer group intelligence tests. A common instrument in

Table 1. Wechsler Classification Categories

IQ	Classification
130 and above	Very superior
120–129	Superior
110–119	High average
90–109	Average
80–89	Low average
70–79	Borderline
69 and below	Mentally retarded

contemporary use is the Cognitive Abilities Test, Form 6 (CogAT). The CogAT is designed to test abilities using verbal, quantitative, and nonverbal subtests in students from grades kindergarten through 12. Another popular instrument for group administration is the Multidimensional Aptitude Battery–Second Edition (MAB-II). The MAB-II can be administered in about 100 minutes and is appropriate for both individual and group use (Erford, 2007).

Applications for Professional Counselors

Intelligence testing is an area that has both school and clinical applications. School counselors are often charged with the responsibility of test administration. Often, school counselors use both group-administered and individually administered intelligence tests to assist in assessing qualifications of students for gifted and talented programs, initial screenings for special education, and qualification for other school-based programs.

Professional counselors who work in clinical settings, including rehabilitation counseling, generally use results from intelligence testing in development of treatment plans. Treatment planning should be driven by assessment, which may include a measure of cognitive functioning. Many counseling theories focus treatment on the development of insight in the client, leading to improvement in the client's life. Counseling students are often trained to identify core issues and facilitate change with their clients. Such an approach may be appropriate when working with clients who have average or higher intelligence; however, many clients have lower than average cognitive functioning. This is especially true for counselors working with court-ordered clients and clients in rehabilitation systems. Progress in counseling might be seen as a direct function of the client's ability to process what is discussed both in and between sessions (Heppner & Fitzgerald, 1987); thus, a measure of intelligence is essential for counselors to understand which counseling approaches may best fit the needs of clients.

Professional counselors who work with clients whose intelligence is shown to be below the norm might embrace alternative methods when working with these clients. For example, counselors may set aside their preferred orientation to take on a more psychoeducational approach. At least one source (Glickman & Gulati, 2003) recommends skills training with individuals who require counseling but have delayed cognitive functioning.

Contributed by Gabriel I. Lomas,
University of Houston–Clear Lake,
Houston, TX, and Robert Sindylek,
Texas A&M University at Galveston,
Galveston, TX

References

American Counseling Association. (2005). *ACA code of ethics.* Alexandria, VA: Author.

Boake, C. (2002). From the Binet-Simon to the Wechsler-Bellevue: Tracing the history of intelligence testing. *Journal of Clinical and Experimental Neuropsychology, 24,* 383–405.

Erford, B. T. (Ed.). (2007). *Assessment for counselors.* Boston: Houghton Mifflin/Lahaska Press.

Glickman, N. S., & Gulati, S. (2003). *Mental health care of deaf people: A culturally affirmative approach.* Mahwah, NJ: Erlbaum.

Heppner, P. P., & Fitzgerald, K. M. (1987). Human intelligence: Implications for counseling. *Journal of Counseling & Development, 65,* 266–267.

Hockenbury, D., & Hockenbury, S. (2005). *Psychology* (4th ed.). New York: Worth.

Lohman, D. F. (1997). Lessons from the history of intelligence testing. *International Journal of Educational Research, 27,* 1–20.

Wood, S. A., & Wood, G. W. (2002). *The world of psychology.* Boston: Allyn & Bacon.

Yerkes, R. M. (1921) Psychological examining in the United States Army. *Memoirs of the National Academy of Sciences, 15,* 1-890.

Additional Resource

Essentials of Psychological Assessment Series, published by Wiley.

■ Internal Validity

Internal validity is an important construct that is useful in research design and psychological testing and is considered the "basic minimum without which any experiment is uninterpretable" (Campbell & Stanley, 1963, p. 5). There are a variety of factors related to the researcher (test administrator), research participant (test taker), and the environment in which the research (test) is conducted that may affect internal validity. These threats to internal validity basically decrease the likelihood that the results of the experiment are due to relationships among or between the independent and dependent variables. Simply put, the primary focus of internal validity is on the relationships between variables. (Note: The terms *intervention, treatment, test,* and *manipulation* are used to represent what is "changed" in the experiment, but only one term is not sufficient because of the diversity of the examples given in this entry.)

Participant Threats

Participant reaction biases include participant expectancies, participant reactance, and evaluation apprehension. All of these factors threaten internal validity because participants may act differently when they know that they are being observed. **Participant expectancies** occur when the participant consciously or unconsciously tries to behave in the way the experimenter expects; that is, the participant is overly cooperative. Participants may often base their behavior on the demand characteristics, which can be eliminated with good research design (see Research Setting Threats section in this entry), of the experimenter or the setting. **Participant reactance** is when the participant intentionally tries to act counter to the experimenter's hypothesis; that is, the participant is uncooperative. This could be the result of a desire for autonomy or independence (see Brehm, 1966). **Evalua-**

tion apprehension is when participants' responses are affected by a desire to appear consistent with social or group beliefs. This response style can polarize responses and lead to inappropriate conclusions. These biases can be reduced or eliminated by guaranteeing a participant anonymity, use of cover stories, use of unobtrusive observations, and use of indirect measures.

Other participant-based threats to internal validity include history, maturation, participant mortality, compensatory rivalry, resentful demoralization, and diffusion of treatment. All of these effects appear to be treatment effects in repeated-measures studies that do not include a randomly assigned control group. One of the ways to control these effects is to add a randomly assigned control group.

History effects are changes in the attitudes, beliefs, or the behavior of a large group's members (e.g., members of a city, country, or culture) that occur over time, usually as the result of an abnormal event or experience (e.g., a hurricane). These changes can occur over a short period of time (e.g., a week or a few minutes) or a long period of time (e.g., Great Depression).

Maturation effects are related to history effects but are different because these changes are specific to a person or small group of people rather than to a large group. Maturation effects are usually due to normal developmental events (e.g., puberty) or life experiences (e.g., graduation from high school) whereas history effects are abnormal events. Also, changes can occur over a short period of time (e.g., such as fatigue) or a long period of time (e.g., puberty).

Participant mortality (also known as **attrition**) occurs when some research participants fail to complete an investigation. Participants may withdraw equally from all conditions in the investigation (known as homogeneous attrition), which is not usually a risk to internal validity because individual differences associated with attrition should remain constant across all conditions. That is, the participants are withdrawing for reasons that are not systematically related to the condition to which they are assigned. However, if people are withdrawing from one or a few conditions more than others (known as heterogeneous attrition), it is a threat to internal validity because their withdrawal could be systematically related to the condition to which they were assigned. Thus, heterogeneous attrition is a threat to internal validity. For example, participants may be selectively withdrawing from one condition because in that condition they are asked more personal questions than they are willing to answer; meanwhile, participants remain in the control condition because they are not asked those questions. This creates a sampling (selection) bias between the groups.

Corrections for this problem include personal and stimulating participant recruitment techniques such as personal invitations to each participant and/or explaining the importance of the participant's role (hopefully to increase participant commitment to the study and avoid attrition altogether), frequent rest breaks, and noncoercive reinforcement to complete the study. Another possibility is to have the control participants complete the experimental task after data collection is complete, assuming that some of these participants will withdraw, which could then equalize the conditions.

Compensatory rivalry by participants receiving less desirable treatments occurs when individuals in the control group make efforts to perform so well that they try to outperform those in the treatment group in order to look "as if" they do not need the treatment. For example, students in a control group for an intervention to improve reading may work very hard to show they do not need the intervention. This behavior, if systematic, may influence outcomes, which may then indicate little or no difference between groups. In the worst case scenario, the outcomes could falsely suggest that no treatment is better than the treatment.

Resentful demoralization of participants in less desirable treatment conditions may be observed in participants who perceive that their treatment or lack thereof is somehow undesirable. They then may feel demoralized or even that they have little sense of control over their current environment. These feelings may be reflected in low posttest scores. The differences between the groups may be due to the differences between the individual participants rather than to the treatment.

Diffusion or imitation of treatment may occur when the control group (i.e., group with no intervention) accidentally or inadvertently is exposed to part or all of the treatment or intervention. This may influence the outcomes so that they indicate no difference between the treatment and control group when, indeed, there is a difference.

The previous threats to validity can be controlled by random selection and assignment, double-blind methodology, careful standardization of procedures and protocol, and regular retraining of experimental staff.

Researcher Threats

Researcher threats occur when the experimenter intentionally or unintentionally influences research outcomes. This may manifest itself as experimenter bias, experimenter drift, or compensatory equalization of treatments.

Experimenter bias occurs when the researcher manipulates the participant data collection, the methods, or setting to influence the outcome either to confirm or disconfirm hypotheses. A common way to control for this is use of double-blind methodology, which prevents the experimenter from recognizing the treatment group or hypotheses.

Experimenter drift occurs when the experimenter begins to deviate from the original research protocol, possibly due to boredom, familiarity, or fatigue. To solve this problem, it may be helpful to have periodic protocol review and retraining, as well as frequent task shifts between conditions or experimenters.

Compensatory equalization of treatments is likely when researchers or support staff involved provide some type of service, treatment, or extra benefit to those who are in the control group (i.e., not receiving intervention), perhaps in an effort to compensate for their not receiving the treatment, intervention, or manipulation of the variable. The extra experiences may compensate for the lack of treatment and affect the outcome scores so that they are similar to the treatment group, thus showing no difference between the treatment group and the control group when there is really a difference. Efforts to control this would include double-blind methods, randomization of selection and assignment, careful training, and standardization of the research protocol.

Research Setting Threats

Research setting threats occur when something in the research design or setting systematically influences the participants and outcomes. These include such problems as regression to the mean, testing effects, selection bias, interactions with selection, and instrumentation.

Regression to the mean, which is related to maturation, is the tendency for people who receive extreme scores on a particular measure to score closer to the mean when retested later. Regression to the mean occurs because of the differences between measured scores and a participant's true ability. Measured scores will vary due to transitive states (e.g., wakefulness, "good" guessing), whereas true ability is stable; therefore, when the transitive states change, the measured scores will change, most often to reflect a person's true ability (i.e., the mean).

Testing effects are related to regression to the mean. A testing effect is the tendency for most people to perform better on a task after having experienced the same or a similar task in the past. Some potential explanations for testing effects include learning (e.g., test takers could develop strategies for some questions), practice (i.e., familiarity with the test format), social desirability (i.e., participants' answers may change because they learn what was socially expected after the first testing), and attitude polarization (i.e., attitudes become more extreme after people have been asked to think about them). These effects can co-occur with regression to the mean, which serves to increase error in the measurement of the dependent variable. Large samples and random selection and assignment help to obviate this problem.

Selection bias occurs when treatment conditions begin with nonequivalent groups. This may be due to inappropriate sampling procedures, participant self-selection biases (e.g., participants select paid vs. nonpaid studies), and participant mortality/attrition. This can be rectified by matching or random selection and assignment to groups.

Interactions with selection may occur when some aspect of participant selection interacts with other threats to validity and exacerbates the validity problems. One example would be maturation interaction with selection, such as in a longitudinal study when participants mature and no longer wish to participate. The chances of selection problems can be reduced by using large samples random selection and random assignment.

Instrumentation could be due to either human or equipment error. For example, the equipment for the experiment may wear over time or be difficult to set up, causing variations in calibration for each administration. Furthermore, it is possible that the device may not be sensitive enough to detect differences or may even have floor and ceiling effects. These problems could cause random or systematic errors that could make it difficult to interpret the outcomes of the study. This can be controlled by using a control group, retraining, frequent checks, and evaluation of equipment used.

Demand characteristics include a participant's reactivity to the experimenter or setting characteristics that may influence the participant's behavior. For example, often setting characteristics such as two-way mirrors can increase anxiety and change participants' behavior. Another possibility is that the experimenter's actions could provide information about the expected treatment that could affect a participant's behavior. This can be controlled by random assignment, double-blind methodology, standardization of setting, and experimenter training.

Contributed by Gayle Morse and
Donald F. Graves,
The Sage Colleges in Troy and Albany, NY

References

Brehm, J. W. (1966). *A theory of psychological reactance.* New York: Academic Press.

Campbell, D. T., & Stanley, J. C. (1963). *Experimental and quasi-experimental designs for research.* Chicago: Rand McNally.

Additional Resources

Heppner, P. P., Wampold, B. E., & Kivlighan, D. M., Jr. (2008). *Research design in counseling* (3rd ed.). Belmont, CA: Wadsworth.

Pelham, B. W., & Blanton, H. (2007). *Conducting research in psychology: Measuring the weight of smoke* (3rd ed.). Belmont, CA: Thomson/Wadsworth.

■ International Association of Addiction and Offender Counselors

The **International Association of Addictions and Offender Counselors (IAAOC)** is a division of the American Counseling Association (ACA). IAAOC members include professional addictions counselors, corrections counselors, students, and counselor educators who share the goal of assisting clients who struggle with addictive and/or criminal behaviors. The mission of IAAOC is to provide leadership in, and advancement of, the professions of addiction and offender counseling. What follows is a review of IAAOC's history, a synopsis of IAAOC's mission and goals, a presentation of the services afforded members, and IAAOC's future goals as they pertain to the counseling profession.

History

Chartered in 1972, IAAOC was originally the Public Offender Counselor Association (POCA). POCA focused on the promotion of quality rehabilitation services to public offenders as well as the representation of the interests and concerns of professional counselors who provided those services. On November 25, 1974, POCA became incorporated, and in December of that year, it gained status as a division of the American Personnel and Guidance Association (APGA), which later became the American Association of Counseling and Development (AACD), now known as ACA. On July 16, 1990, in order to (a) more accurately reflect its membership orientation and scope (which included a large contingency of addictions counselors), (b) recognize the pervasive relationship between addiction and issues pertinent to offending clients (e.g., rehabilitation, education, recidivism), and (c) clarify public perception of the work accomplished by its membership, POCA changed its name to IAAOC, a motion that was officially accepted by AACD on November 19, 1990.

Mission and Goals

IAAOC focuses on the recognition of the professional counselor as a qualified practitioner in the fields of addictions and forensic treatment services. IAAOC's leadership supports local, state, national, and international efforts through (a) the promotion of quality educational and professional presentations at all levels, (b) legislative and advocacy activities aimed at meeting the needs of both the professional counselors and the clients they serve, (c) collaborative efforts across divisions of ACA, (d) the provision of specialized training and cutting-edge techniques for counselors and counselors-in-training, (e) the development of graduate students and professional members through research and various other grant opportunities, and (f) the maintenance and enhancement of communication among leaders and members. Finally, IAAOC was an active stakeholder in the development and promotion of the **Master Addictions Counselor** credential through the National Board of Certified Counselors, which recognizes appropriate graduate education and specialized training as a foundation for addictions counselors.

Member Services

IAAOC offers members several benefits, particularly means of communication between its members and other interested parties. These include the *Journal of Addictions & Offender Counseling (JAOC)*, the *IAAOC News*, and the IAAOC Web site. Each has a rich history of its own.

Similar to the developmental history of IAAOC, *JAOC* has its own "coming of age" story. At its inception, POCA collaborated with the National Employment Counselors Association (NECA) and shared in the sponsoring of the *Journal of Employment Counseling (JEC)*. Given similar organizational missions and the collegial relationship between POCA and NECA, as well as the economics of publishing a professional journal, the two organizations shared *JEC* between 1979 and 1981. Each organization had its own section of the journal that was maintained by a different editor and editorial board. In 1981, POCA established the *Journal of Offender Counseling (JOC)*, which in 1990 was renamed *JAOC*.

JAOC is published biannually by ACA in April and October. Publishing trends have changed slightly over time and have reflected the shift in organizational membership. Whereas the journal between 1979 and 1998 originally published articles that had a heavier emphasis on offender counseling (with a focus on career, education, and training issues; Charkow & Juhnke, 2001), between 1999 and 2004 the emphasis shifted more to addiction counseling with a clinical focus (e.g., treatment issues, diverse client groups, and comorbid complications; Juhnke, Charkow-Bordeau, & Evanoff, 2005).

Current and future directions for the journal include (a) an online submission and review format, (b) a manuscript classification system to encourage a variety of research submissions (i.e., quantitative, qualitative, innovative approaches,

and position papers), and (c) a call for manuscripts that target specific topics (e.g., forensic counseling; the impact of multiculturalism; the importance of spirituality; families and addictions/violence; process addictions; age-specific interventions for children, adolescents, and people who are elderly).

The original *POCA Report,* the association's first newsletter, was published by the Inmate Students of the Graphic Arts Program at the Hampden County House of Correction in Springfield, Massachusetts. The name changed in September of 1990 and today *IAAOC News* is published four times a year and is housed at the editor's university setting. The newsletter is the primary communication tool that IAAOC leaders use to connect with the membership. Typical features include a president's message, an editor's message, book and movie reviews (that are pertinent to addiction and offender counseling), the publication of meeting minutes, calls for award nominations, and special feature articles.

In response to the advent and popularity of the Internet as a means of information and communication, the **IAAOC Web site** was established in 2003. The Web site, which connects members and distributes divisional information, offers numerous resources, including a review of IAAOC's history, mission, and bylaws; IAAOC's current officers and committee chairs; calls for proposals and award nominations; and access to electronic versions of both current and archival issues of the newsletter. Also included are calls-for-action, where current divisional advocacy efforts are posted; updates and messages from IAAOC's president; and a members-only section. The ACA division page has a link to the IAAOC Web site.

IAAOC's Future

In 2008, the Council for Accreditation of Counseling and Related Educational Programs (CACREP) has recognized the efforts that IAAOC has made in the area of addiction counseling educational standards. Two important developments with long-reaching impacts are imminent. First, a specialty area of Addictions Counseling will likely be added to the 2009 CACREP Standards. This will provide an opportunity for the standardization of addictions counseling education at the master's and doctoral levels. Second, IAAOC emphasized the need for addiction-related knowledge and practice across the counseling curriculum, a recommendation that was accepted by CACREP and will likely be implemented in the new Standards.

IAAOC stands on the brink of a potential wave of increased exposure in the profession of counseling. More important, IAAOC's leadership is excited about the pending increase in competent counselors who will be able to recognize the impact of addictive disorders across client populations. Regardless of where the future of IAAOC lies, the organizational mission will remain, namely that IAAOC will continue to be a high-quality resource organization that supports prevention, treatment, research, training, and advocacy for the addicted and forensic/criminal justice populations.

Contributed by W. Bryce Hagedorn,
University of Central Florida,
Orlando, FL

References

Charkow, W. B., & Juhnke, G. A. (2001). *Journal of Addictions and Offender Counseling* submission patterns, topic areas, and authors: 1979–1998. *Journal of Addictions & Offender Counseling, 22,* 12–20.

Juhnke, G. A., Charkow-Bordeau, W. B., & Evanoff, J. C. (2005). *Journal of Addictions and Offender Counseling* submission patterns, topic areas, and authors: 1999–2004. *Journal of Addictions & Offender Counseling, 26,* 52–58.

Additional Resource

International Association of Addiction and Offender Counselors Web site: http://www.iaaoc.org/index.asp

◼ International Association of Marriage and Family Counselors

The **International Association of Marriage and Family Counselors (IAMFC)** is a division of the American Counseling Association (ACA) that promotes excellence in the practice of couples and family counseling by creating and disseminating publications and media products, providing a forum for exploration of family-related issues, involving a diverse group of dedicated professionals, and emphasizing collaborative efforts. IAMFC encourages professional counselors to think systemically and to advocate for the worth and dignity of all families.

IAMFC was cofounded by Thomas Sweeney and Martin Ritchie at Ohio University in 1986 because there was no ACA division that specifically served the interests and needs of marriage and family counselors. IAMFC was incorporated in 1987, with Thomas Sweeney as president. In April 1989, ACA (then the American Association of Counseling and Development) Governing Council approved IAMFC as an organizational affiliate when Robert Smith was president. IAMFC recruited sufficient members to attain full ACA divisional status in 1990. Robert Smith became executive director, and Jon Carlson became the editor of *The Family Journal.* David Kaplan chaired the ethics committee and helped establish the IAMFC Code of Ethics. Others who were instrumental in the early development and growth of IAMFC include Patricia Love, Lynn Miller, Don W. Locke, Judith Lewis, and Scott Hinkle. In 1994, the National Academy for Certified Family Therapists was established as a collaborative effort with IAMFC. IAMFC continues to grow and is one of the largest divisions of ACA.

Contributed by Martin H. Ritchie,
University of Toledo, Toledo, OH

◼ International Students, Counseling

International students pursue academic goals in countries other than their own. Through this transition, international students leave the familiarity of their country, family, and friends to embark on their academic journey. According to the Institute of International Education's Open Doors Report 2007, international students account for more than a half million students enrolled in U.S. colleges and universities for the 2006–2007 academic year, with an 810% increase in new enrollment. As indicated by these statistics, professional counselors providing services to international students must be aware of and knowledgeable about several pertinent areas, including culture shock, acculturation, transitional issues faced by students, factors that impede counseling, and counseling considerations.

In working with international students, it is important to remember that although some characteristics may be shared because of their common experiences as international students in a foreign country, they are a heterogeneous group, and there are differences based on individual cultural groups that may affect their adjustment. International students may face several challenges in the form of sociocultural, environmental, and physiological adjustments, including language barriers, academic differences, racial discrimination and prejudice, financial difficulties, inadequate social support, and postgraduation issues that increase their acculturative stress. On the other hand, factors that may decrease international students' acculturative stress are relationships with host nationals, emotional support from family, support for academic programs (Mallinckrodt & Leong, 1992), willingness to learn new cultures, and opportunities to study English (Hayes & Lin, 1994). In addition, international students face several psychological challenges related to these concerns, including depression, alienation, anxiety, sense of loss, and helplessness. Acculturative stress often accompanies emotional pain, such as feelings of powerlessness, marginality, inferiority, loneliness, and perceived alienation and discrimination (Sandhu & Asrabadi, 1998). Culture shock and acculturation are important concepts that are associated with many of these challenges.

Culture Shock and Acculturation

Culture shock is a sequential and cyclical process of adapting to a new environment and culture that results from external changes and differences in the physical environment (e.g., climate, food, transportation) and internal changes such as role differentiation and status loss (Pedersen, 1991, 1995; Ward, Bochner, & Furnam, 2001). As the following list shows, culture shock has four phases (Pedersen, 1995; Winkelman, 1994):

1. *Honeymoon phase.* This phase is marked by fascination with cultural differences, optimism, and excitement.
2. *Crisis or disintegration phase.* In this phase, aspects of cultural difference that were fascinating initially are later perceived as sources of irritation and disappointment.
3. *Reorientation and reintegration phase.* International students become reoriented in the host culture and are now able to view the positive and negative aspects of the host culture.
4. *Adaptation or resolution phase.* There is a sense of belonging to several cultures at the same time and a greater sense of stability. Students can navigate through the new culture and resolve problems.

As culture shock encapsulates the various stages of adjustment for international students during their transition to a foreign country, issues related to acculturation broaden the perspective of cross-cultural transition that can challenge their personal and cultural identity and worldview (Arthur, 2004). **Acculturation** refers to changes in cultural attitudes, values, and behaviors that result from contact between two distinct cultures. **Acculturative stress** can be a manifestation of acculturation in which there is a marked deterioration of the general health status of an individual; it encompasses physical, psychological, and social aspects that are explicitly linked to the acculturation process (Poyrazli, Kavanaugh, Baker, & Al-Timimi, 2004).

Berry's (1990) acculturation model is a primary model for understanding the acculturation process. It is based on four styles that encompass the extent to which individuals maintain their original identity and engage in participation with other cultural groups. The model may be applied to international students' experiences in the following manner. In the first style, **integration,** international students maintain positive attitudes toward both culture of origin and host culture. For example, international students may welcome the various customs and festivals of their host country, while at the same time having deep admiration for their own festivals. In the second style, **assimilation,** international students accept the host culture and reject major cultural features of the culture of origin. For example, international students may find themselves preparing and enjoying the various cuisines from their host country, with a decreased interest in dishes from their home country. In the third style, **separation,** international students hold on strongly to the culture of origin while avoiding contact with host culture. For example, international students may find themselves within an "ethnic enclave," where they only associate with people and customs from their home country and are not open to learning or experiencing anything about their host country. In **marginalization,** the fourth style, international students harbor negative attitudes toward both cultures and societies. For example, international students may isolate and alienate themselves from their culture of origin as well as the host culture.

Challenges for International Students

Language difficulties can be a challenging issue for international students, because a lack of English skills is likely to affect international students' academic performance and, in turn, affect their psychological adjustment. Research of English language fluency in relation to acculturative stress demonstrated that higher frequency of use, fluency level, and the degree to which participants felt comfortable speaking English predicted lower levels of acculturative distress (Yeh & Inose, 2003). The decrease in acculturative distress results in smoother interactions for international students with people in the new cultural setting, leading to greater feelings of adjustment. Academic differences are an area that can also be a concern for international students because they are navigating different academic systems, especially regarding their interaction with professors and classmates.

Some of the educational stressors include performance expectations, system adjustment, and test-taking anxiety. Racial discrimination and prejudice are concerns that may have been unanticipated because many international students have been in the majority racial group in their home countries. Particular prejudices that members of the host culture may hold for various international students can serve as a barrier and may lead to low self-esteem and self-confidence. Some international students also face anxieties because of fear of immigration authorities. In the post–September 11, 2001, era of higher education, the discussion regarding international students on U.S. campuses has taken on greater urgency. Because immigration rules and regulations restrict opportunities for employment outside of the college or university and restrict federal financial aid, financial problems are more difficult to resolve than for American students. Any unexpected shift in financial resources can threaten an international student's educational pursuit as well as other aspects of living, which may result in stress. Social support may be an issue for international students who socialize primarily with other international students. They may feel discouraged and dissatisfied with their support system, which in their home country may be relied on as a way to validate their self-concept and provide emotional support. Finally, it can be stressful for students to decide whether to stay in the host country or return to their countries at the conclusion of their studies. They must examine the advantages, disadvantages, and the implications involved with all the options considered. One of the issues they face if they decide to return home is reverse culture shock because they must readjust to their culture, family, and friends as their self-concept and worldview have been altered to include their experiences in the United States.

Factors That Impede Counseling

Although international students face the aforementioned challenges, there are factors that may prevent them from seeking counseling services. International students who are funded by their government may be fearful that their counseling appointment will be reported to their government officials, and, consequently, they will be asked to return home, which will result in shame to the students' families. In addition, there may be the somatization of psychological problems expressed through physiological disorders; therefore, international students' stress-related symptoms may be identified first by medical providers because the students would seek services from student health. Finally, as a result of cultural differences in beliefs about mental health issues, international students may be unfamiliar with the basic concept of counseling and may hold negative or inappropriate expectations due to misconceptions.

Counseling Considerations

Many international students are reluctant to use campus counseling services. They may delay seeking services because of the uneasiness in seeking help from counselors and the stigma attached to such services. Even when they seek services, they are more likely than American students to terminate the therapeutic relationship prematurely (Pedersen, 1991). Several suggestions for enhancing cultural sensitivity within the counseling process for international students are listed here:

- Counselors who work with international students can provide group and workshop services in locations outside of the counseling center to decrease stigma (e.g., English-as-second-language departments, international program offices) and address such topics as stress management techniques, assertive communication skills, academic transitions, and effective study skills. Through these services, international students build social relations with American students and other international students. In addition, these services can be used as a way to make a referral for individual counseling, if needed based on the severity of symptoms.

- Student expectations are often for the counselor to act an authoritarian role of teacher and expert; thus, counselors should provide concrete, tangible help (e.g., campus and community resources) at the beginning of the counseling relationship. Counselors who are active and directive will build trust in the counseling relationship.

- Proactive approaches are needed to increase the visibility and accessibility of counseling through cooperative efforts with international student offices and organizations and advisory boards run by international students. For example, counselors can provide short presentations for international students on topics such as the stages of culture shock at orientation programs to lessen the stigma related to counseling.

- It is important to be aware of cultural biases in standardized assessments tools. Counseling centers can use an acculturative stress scale with international students to determine particular areas in which they may be having difficulty. For example, the Acculturative Stress Scale for International Students (Sandhu & Asrabadi, 1994) examines acculturative stress and can be implemented in treatment planning.

- International student mentors, both of American and international students, can be paired with incoming international students and trained by counseling center staff in areas of communication, detecting signs of distress, and referral of cases to mental health professionals. Training can also be conducted with international students' advisers about signs of psychological distress.

- Cultural diversity in a counseling center staff can help convince international students that their unique issues will be understood. Other ways to make international students feel more comfortable with counseling are to have diverse facilitators and to conduct groups and workshops with one male and one female facilitator because expectations of gender roles may vary from culture to culture.

- Issues related to culture shock and acculturation can be addressed in the therapeutic relationship as counselors build their awareness and understanding of issues related to cross-cultural transitions. Counselors can normalize international students' experiences by exploring the cultural differences and similarities and help students reconcile cultural conflicts that they experience (Arthur, 2004).

- Incorporating stress management techniques that address international students' acculturative stress can be beneficial in the reduction of anxiety and frustration. Techniques can address cognitive self-care that enhances students' sense of power, and relaxation methods such as breathing, imagery, and meditation can be used. In addition, physical self-care can be promoted through massage, exercise, and healthy eating habits (Mori, 2000).

Contributed by Shari-ann H. James,
University of Central Florida,
Orlando, FL

References

Arthur, N. (2004). *Counseling international students: Clients from around the world.* New York: Kluwer Academic/Plenum.

Berry, J. W. (1990). Psychology of acculturation: Understanding individuals moving between cultures. In R. W. Brislin (Ed.), *Applied cross-cultural psychology* (pp. 232–253). Newbury Park, CA: Sage.

Hayes, R. L., & Lin, H. R. (1994). Coming to America: Developing social support systems for international students. *Journal of Multicultural Counseling and Development, 22,* 7–16.

Institute of International Education. (2007). *Open doors report 2007.* Retrieved July 11, 2008, from http://open doors.iienetwork.org/?p=113743

Mallinckrodt, B., & Leong, F. T. (1992). International graduate students, stress, and social support. *Journal of College and Student Development, 33,* 71–78.

Mori, S. (2000). Addressing the mental health concerns of international students. *Journal of Counseling & Development, 78,* 137–145.

Pedersen, P. B. (1991). Counseling international students. *The Counseling Psychologist, 19,* 10–58.

Pedersen, P. B. (1995). *The five stages of culture shock.* Westport, CT: Greenwood Press.

Poyrazli, S., Kavanaugh, P. R., Baker, A., & Al-Timimi, N. (2004). Social support and demographic correlates of acculturative stress in international students. *Journal of College Counseling, 7,* 73–82.

Sandhu, D. S., & Asrabadi, B. R. (1994). Development of an acculturative stress scale for international students: Primary findings. *Psychological Reports, 75,* 435–448.

Sandhu, D. S., & Asrabadi, B. R. (1998). An acculturative stress scale for international students: A practical approach to stress management. In C. P. Zalaquett & R. J. Wood (Eds.), *Evaluating stress: A book of resources* (Vol. 2, pp. 1–33). Lanham, MD: Scarecrow Press.

Ward, C., Bochner, S., & Furnam, A. (2001). *The psychology of culture shock* (2nd ed.). East Sussex, England: Routledge.

Winkelman, M. (1994). Culture shock ad adaptation. *Journal of Counseling & Development, 73*, 121–126.

Yeh, C. J., & Inose, M. (2003). International students' reported English fluency, social support satisfaction, and social connectedness as predictors of acculturative stress, *Counselling Psychology Quarterly, 16*, 15–28.

Additional Resources

Arthur, N., & Pedersen, P. (Eds.). (2008). *Case incidents in counseling for international transitions.* Alexandria, VA: American Counseling Association.

Institute of International Education Open Doors Web site: http://opendoors.iienetwork.org/

Singaravelu, H., & Pope, M. (2007). *A handbook for counseling international students in the United States.* Alexandria, VA: American Counseling Association.

Interpretation of Assessment

The **interpretation** of an assessment is the explanation or communication of test results to an individual, such as a client or third party. Professional counselors who administer assessments are required to assist clients in interpreting relevant data. Counselors must have the ability to interpret test scores competently and present test results to clients accurately. There are three components to the process of interpreting assessment results: counselor interpretation of the assessment, counselor presentation of the assessment results, and client interpretation of the assessment results. The first component relates to the counselor's process of attributing meaning to the client's test scores. The second component is the process of communicating the meaning of the test results to clients. The third component is the client's perspective of the implications of the test results.

Counselor Interpretation of Assessment

When preparing to interpret the results of an assessment, professional counselors must first have a clear understanding of the test scores. Generally, the meaning of test results is enhanced by similarities among the assessment data. At times, there may be inconsistencies in test results for a particular client, which may pose a challenge for counselors to ascertain the meaning of the data. Counselors integrate the results of the assessment with other information about the client to develop hypotheses that are explored with clients in the feedback session. Counselors must give careful consideration to the delivery of assessment results to clients. For example, some clients become defensive when presented with undesirable test scores. Counselors should, therefore, never solely present test scores to clients during the feedback session.

When preparing to interpret assessment results, professional counselors ask the following questions: What is the meaning of the test scores? What are the cultural considerations in interpreting assessment results? How do test scores compare with other data gathered about the client? How do I expect the client to respond to the results?

Counselor Presentation of Assessment Results

When presenting the results of assessments to clients, counselors review the purpose of testing, report the test scores, discuss the meaning of the test scores, and explain the implications of the assessment results. It is often helpful if counselors remind clients of the primary reasons for the assessment. This aids the client with conceptualizing the results of the assessment. In addition, explaining the kind of information that is generated from the tests that the client took helps the client to understand the rationale for testing. For example, "The test where you indicated whether the two designs were the same or different was designed to measure spatial ability." Any limitations of a particular test should be explained to the client.

When communicating test results to clients, counselors attempt to avoid overwhelming clients with a vast amount of qualitative data. Test scores or technical information is not essential when communicating test results to clients. Assessment results must be communicated in a manner that is understandable to clients. Likewise, counselors should avoid the use of jargon, because technical language may interfere with clients' ability to understand the assessment's results. The use of visual aids, such as profiles, helps to organize and simplify the information that is presented to clients.

Counselors aim to provide information that has meaningful implications for the types of decisions that clients must make. Counselors must be cautious not to present the results of the assessment in absolute terms; rather, counselors should present the results in terms of probabilities. The purposes of the assessment, as well as any limitations about interpretation of the assessment results, should be discussed with clients. Counselors can elicit valuable information by posing the following questions to themselves: What was the purpose of the client taking the assessment? What are the client's strengths and weaknesses as revealed by the test results? Is the counselor prepared to discuss test results in relation to the client's past, present, and future behavior? Are the interpretations explained at a level that the client can understand?

Client Interpretation of Assessment

After professional counselors explain the meaning of test scores to clients, they should encourage clients to participate in the interpretation of assessment results. Providing clients with an opportunity to discuss their performance on the assessment assists them with understanding the assessment data. Counselors can obtain feedback from clients with statements such as "Do you recall this test?" and "What were your thoughts about this test?" Counselors should be aware of clients' feelings toward the information and acknowledge clients' perceptions of the assessment results. Other examples of statements that can be used to elicit feedback include "How do these assessment results compare with what you expected?" and "How do you feel about what has been discussed?" This cooperative engagement helps to avoid passivity on the client's part or defensiveness about the assessment results. It also increases the probability that clients will be more accepting of the assessment results and use the data when making decisions.

Contributed by Kacie M. Blalock,
North Carolina A&T State University,
Greensboro, NC

Additional Resources

Hood, A. B., & Johnson, R. W. (2007). *Assessment in counseling: A guide to the use of psychological assessment procedures* (4th ed.). Alexandria, VA: American Counseling Association.

Lichtenberg, J. W., & Goodyear, R. K. (Eds.). (1999). *Scientist-practitioner perspectives on test interpretation*. Needham Heights, MA: Allyn & Bacon.

Interviewing

Clinical interviewing is a process wherein the professional counselor uses counseling skills to help the client report data and information that will facilitate the counseling process. Interviews, the most common method of assessment in counseling, have the potential to elicit data and information regarding a broad range of clients' experiences, strengths, and needs. Interviews are often used to gather information regarding a client's demographic characteristics; presenting concern; current life situation (e.g., relationships, living arrangements); and family, occupational, educational, developmental, physical health, and mental health history. Professional counselors can use information gathered from interviews to diagnose clients' problems and determine optimal methods for helping clients to improve functioning. Professional counselors use a wide variety of essential skills (e.g., open-ended questions, closed-ended questions, prompts, clarifications, reflection of content, and reflection of feeling) to facilitate clinical interviews. Some clinical interviews also involve use of stimuli such as pictures and sentence completion tasks. Counselors use different interviewing skills and stimuli, depending on the purpose and structure of the interview. Although hundreds of published interview protocols are available for counselors to use, all interviews can be classified as structured, semistructured, or unstructured.

Structured interviews consist of a series of scripted questions or prompts that the interviewer presents in the same order and manner during each interview. Because many elements of structured interviews are controlled, this type of interview provides consistency of content across different counselors, clients, and time periods. Structured interviews are well suited for research, gathering identification data, suicide risk assessment, or in large mental health settings where the intake counselor may be different than the assigned counselor, and they are likely to produce more reliable results compared with other types of interviews. Often, these types of interviews are based on the American Psychiatric Association's (2000) *Diagnostic and Statistical Manual of Mental Disorders* (4th ed., text rev.) and are used to help counselors determine the best diagnosis for a client. Structured interviews tend to be detailed and exhaustive. In some settings,

this amount and type of information is necessary. The need for information is counterbalanced by the concern that the process may alienate or distance clients who are experiencing pain and have a need to share information on their own terms. Similarly, counselors may feel limited by the lack of flexibility to ask follow-up questions or to otherwise explore clients' concerns in the interview. Limitations of structured interviews may be most apparent when (a) the counselor's theoretical approach is nondirective, (b) the client is unable to focus on an interview due to the degree of distress or impairment, (c) the client desires more flexibility or a greater degree of relational contact, or (d) the client is willing and able to provide the information needed via less formal means. Professional counselors who use structured interviews must take care to build rapport prior to the interview, evaluate whether a particular interview is developmentally and culturally appropriate for a client, note clients' responses to the interview process, and provide an opportunity for clients to voice their questions and concerns regarding the interview process upon the conclusion of the interview.

Like structured interviews, **semistructured interviews** provide specific question formats and topics to be addressed; however, the professional counselor has the power to customize the interview by modifying questions, altering question sequence, or constructing follow-up questions. The semistructured interview has the advantage of providing a degree of structure while allowing for a degree of flexibility. A variety of diagnosis-focused semistructured interview formats are available, and professional counselors may find themselves using semistructured interviews to facilitate the client-intake process. For example, an organization may require that counselors discuss certain elements of a client's presenting problem, mental health history, family of origin, current relationships, and occupational or educational status during the first session. The professional counselor, however, will decide how to order these topics and follow up on each; thus, the counselor can devote more time and energy to some areas of concern than to others. Semistructured interviews are more susceptible to counselor error and bias than are structured interviews; therefore, semistructured interviews are not considered as reliable as structured interviews. Professional counselors who use semistructured interviews must have well-developed essential counseling skills that will help them to facilitate exploration while still keeping sight of the larger purpose of the interview.

Unstructured interviews involve an assessment process wherein there are no scripted or standardized questions. Professional counselors who use unstructured interviews tend to follow the client's lead when establishing the focus area of the interview. In this way, counselors use highly developed, open-ended questioning and reflecting skills to assist the client to explore an area of focus. Some professional counselors prefer the unstructured interview format because it allows greater opportunity to develop rapport and to elicit client concerns from the client's own perspective. Although unstructured interviews provide for the greatest amount of flexibility and adaptability, these interviews are the least reliable and most subject to counselor error compared with structured and semistructured interviews. Professional counselors who use unstructured interviews must focus on the initial purpose of the interview, use essential skills to facilitate the interview, and constantly self-monitor reasons for pursuing and emphasizing topics or details during the unstructured interview process.

Contributed by Casey A. Barrio Minton,
University of North Texas,
Denton, TX

Reference

American Psychiatric Association. (2000). *Diagnostic and statistical manual of mental disorders* (4th ed., text rev.). Washington, DC: Author.

Additional Resources

Erford, B. T. (Ed.). (2006). *Counselor's guide to clinical, personality, and behavioral assessment.* Boston: Houghton Mifflin/Lahaska Press.

Hersen, M., & Turner, S. M. (Eds.). (2003). *Diagnostic interviewing* (3rd ed.). New York: Kluwer.

Rogers, R. (2001). *Handbook of diagnostic and structured interviewing.* New York: Guilford.

■ Item Analysis

In classical test theory, **item analysis** traditionally depends on the two concepts of item difficulty and item discrimination. **Item difficulty** is the percentage (expressed in decimal point format) of test takers who correctly respond to a test item either by getting the answer correct or by endorsing the trait or characteristic under examination. It is reported as a p value (ranging from 0 to 1.00) and is calculated by dividing the number of persons who correctly answered the item by the number of test takers. Higher numbers mean the question is easier. Item difficulty levels are known as **p values**, but this should not be confused with the same name used in connection to levels of statistical significance.

The "correct" answer for psychological assessment instruments measuring constructs would simply be an answer that endorses the construct. For example, on an instrument measuring depression, a reply that positively signifies a depressive symptom would be a correct answer. An item that queried, "Do you find yourself often discouraged?" would have a higher item difficulty level (more would "pass" it) than the question, "Do you frequently have thoughts about suicide?"

Authors of tests calculate item difficulty in order to improve the instrument. Teachers frequently compute item difficulty in consideration of grade changes. Sometimes an item will appear to be easy or hard to the test maker, but when item difficulty is actually calculated after the test is scored and reviewed, the test creator is sometimes surprised. Sometimes an "easy" question will confuse high-performing students because of poor wording, or a "hard" question will prove too easy, and even those without true knowledge can guess at the answer. In the later case, **distractors** (also known as **foils**) of poor quality may be to blame.

An item with a p value of .9 is considered very easy, because 90% of test takers correctly answered or endorsed the item. Likewise, an item with a p value of .15 is very difficult because only 15% chose the "keyed" answer or positively endorsed the trait, attitude, or characteristic addressed.

In general, items with difficulty levels or p values of .5 will yield the most variation in test score distributions. In choosing the level of item difficulty or trying to set a range of p values for an item set, the purpose of the test and the population being tested are among considerations. To provide maximum differentiation, all items should cluster around .5. This would make the test mean around 50%, which is too low for many practical purposes such as licensing, certification, or university classroom tests. When a test is too difficult for the group, the test has an inadequate floor, and when the test is too easy, it has an insufficient ceiling.

Persons who possess a high degree of the trait will score higher on each item than those who do not possess the trait or only possess it at a low level. If this is the case, then there is positive **item discrimination.** To use the previous example, professional counselors may want to differentiate or discriminate people into two groups: those who are depressed from those who are not depressed. One way to measure how well items discriminate is to calculate the **discrimination index.** Each item will have a discrimination index.

A discrimination index can be calculated for each item using the **extreme groups method.** In this method, the proportion (0 to 1.00) of correct answers from those persons with a total score in the lower range of the entire group would be subtracted from the proportion of correct answers from those persons scoring in the upper range. The proportion from the group of persons with a total score in the top 27% should be compared with the proportion from those scoring in the bottom 27%. Simply put, for each item, each group (i.e., the highest 27% and the lowest 27%) has its own item difficulty, and an index of discrimination involves subtracting the item difficulty of the low-scoring group from the item difficulty of the high-scoring group. The resultant calculation for each item will yield the **index of discrimination (D)** that ranges from -1.00 to $+1.00$. Note D is only one type of index of discrimination. This method of determining whether an item differentiates between those who truly have more or less of the trait is an internal method. External methods involve using an external criterion to inspect for differentiation or discrimination.

The correlation of an item with the total test score (internal method) or with an external criterion (external method) is yet another way to investigate the degree of item discrimination. There are a variety of correlational indexes that can be used, depending on the nature of the variables. The most common correlation is the **point biserial (r_{pb}) correlation,** which is used when the criterion measure (e.g., total score) is continuous and the item scores are dichotomous (e.g., correct–incorrect). The point biserial correlation coefficient ranges from -1.00 to $+1.00$.

With both the index of discrimination and correlational indexes, a positive value indicates positive item discrimination, a negative value indicates negative discrimination, and low values indicate low or no discrimination. Items demonstrating high positive discrimination (e.g., over .50) would probably be retained, whereas items with negative or low absolute values should be rejected, unless the item is checking for mastery and all or nearly all examinees are expected to mark the item *correct*. Items with a discrimination index of between .20 and .50 should probably be modified. Of course, overall item difficulty serves as a mediator of the index of discrimination; that is, easier items ordinarily have lower discrimination indexes because item difficulty truncates or suppresses the range of scores on one of the variables, thus lowering the resulting correlation or index.

Item discrimination indexes are sometimes used as **indexes of item validity.** For nearly all tests, the most essential quality for items to have is the power of discrimination. Very easy items do not discriminate well, but a teacher may want to include them in classroom tests for motivational reasons, especially at the beginning of a test. Should nobody correctly answer an item, then the index of discrimination would be equal to zero. Items that are extremely difficult may be desired if a critical objective is being measured, even if the discrimination happens to be low. In most cases, a test maker wants items to be of moderate difficulty, because these show the most positive discrimination.

In classroom tests, it is important to check that the false answers (distracters) are positively discriminating as well. Occasionally, only the correct or keyed answers are examined in item analysis, but this should definitely not be the case. All answers should be checked to be sure they are contributing to the discrimination ability of the item.

The statistics and discussion thus far in this entry are based on classical test theory, but **item response theory (IRT)** uses many similar concepts. The **item characteristic curve (ICC),** sometimes called the item trace curve, is used in IRT to analyze items. In the item characteristic curve, the strength of the attribute is represented on the horizontal axis, and the likelihood of passing the item is scaled along the vertical axis. Typically, the ICC will take on the shape of an "S." If the examiner extends a line from .50 of the vertical axis (representing a 50% chance of passing or endorsing an item) to the ICC, the ICC is intersected at a point representing a certain strength of the attribute. This 50% point of each item will be matched with a strength point. The further out on the horizontal axis (i.e., the greater the strength of the attribute), the more difficult the item is. Thus, the ICC provides a wonderful visual of item difficulty for each item (see Figure 1).

At this same pivotal point on the graph, the ICC will have a certain slope. The steeper the slope, the more item dis-

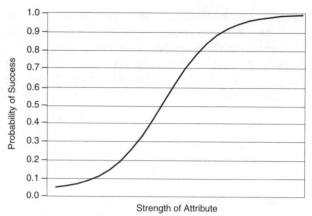

Figure 1. Item Characteristic Curve

crimination is demonstrated. An ICC that looks like an elongated S leaning to the right will provide less item discrimination than an ICC with a straighter and steeper S shape. If the ICC is very flat, this indicates almost no item discrimination, and if the ICC is the shape of a backward S, then negative item discrimination would be evidenced.

If many items were graphed on the same graph, the items shifted to the right would be the more difficult items. Where the ICC intersects the vertical axis, the strength of the attribute is either zero or is at least at a minimum. The likelihood of passing the item at this point is equivalent to a false positive, meaning that someone with very little or none of the characteristic in question would have the likelihood of passing or endorsing the item. Ideally, this likelihood for an item would be zero, although if there are five possible answers, the false positive likelihood might be .20 because of chance (if the question is a measure of knowledge).

The item analysis concepts discussed in this entry are basic and commonly used in test development, but there are other more advanced item analysis concepts not discussed. A few of the topics not discussed include item bias, qualitative item analysis, factor analysis, computerized adaptive testing, differential item functioning, considerations of speed, and various software programs used in item analysis.

Contributed by V. Van Wiesner III, Sam Houston State University, Huntsville, TX

Additional Resources

Anastasi, A., & Urbina, S. (1997). *Psychological testing* (7th ed.). Upper Saddle River, NJ: Prentice Hall.

DeVellis, R. F. (2003). *Scale development: Theory and applications* (2nd ed.). Thousand Oaks, CA: Sage.

Jews, Counseling

American Jews are a diverse group of people linked through a common history; ethnic and cultural heritage; and, often, religious practices. The general U.S. population is estimated at nearly 300 million, and American Jews constitute between 5 to 6 million of this estimate (U.S. Census Bureau, 2000). There is significant variability among Jews with regard to their self-identification (i.e., cultural, ethnic, and religious) and their observances of Jewish holidays and customs. For example, there are three main lineages for American Jews (i.e., Ashkenazim, Sephardim, and Mizrachim). The Ashkenazim are Jews who trace their family history to Eastern Europe. The Sephardim are Jews who trace their family history to the Iberian Peninsula (i.e., Spain and Portugal). The Mizrachim are Jews who trace their family history to Northern Africa and/or Western Asia. In addition, there are also several active denominations among American Jews, including Hasidic, Orthodox, Conservative, Reform, and Reconstructionist. These groups are differentiated from one another by the degree of their adherence to Jewish orthodoxy. Finally, some Jews self-identify as secular or cultural Jews and divorce themselves from many, if not all, of the religious traditions associated with Judaism.

Despite within-group differences, there are several important considerations. First, all Jews are subject to marginalization in one form or another. For example, anti-Semitic activity continues to be a major problem. **Anti-Semitism** includes the oppression and denigration of Jews and the systematic discrimination against Jews. Internalized anti-Semitism is equally troublesome; this occurs when a Jew takes on the dominant group's (i.e., other religions' or nationalities') views of Jews, downplays any negative experiences of Jews, and accepts the views of the dominant group. Anti-Semitism has also created fear and healthy paranoia in American Jews, so much so that passing (i.e., concealing one's Jewish identity) is common. This paranoia and subsequent desire to blend into the dominant culture were likely results of the long history of anti-Semitism that culminated in the Shoah. The Shoah (Hebrew for "catastrophe") refers to the Nazi genocide of 6 million Jews; hence, it is critical for counseling professionals to understand the stress that results from historical and contemporary experiences with anti-Semitism.

Another important consideration is that some Jews may not openly self-identity as Jews until they determine that the environment is safe for such a disclosure. As noted previously, the long history of anti-Semitism has contributed to Jews now being hesitant or unwilling to disclose their identity. Hence, counselors need to tread cautiously when inquiring about religious and ethnic background. Counselors can work to create an environment that is affirming of diversity and follow the client's lead with regard to the depth of disclosure about the client's Jewishness. Once a client's Jewish identity has been described by the client, counselors could inquire about the client's adherence to the practice of Judaism.

Counseling professionals should engage in a self-assessment regarding their attitudes, behaviors, thoughts, and feelings about Jews, Judaism, and Jewish culture. This is important so that any anti-Semitic stereotypes or beliefs can be addressed through education, supervision, consultation, and personal counseling. Failure to do so would constitute a breach of counselor ethics. In addition, Jewish and non-Jewish counselors must consider particular issues when working with Jewish clients. For example, Jewish counseling professionals must not assume that their beliefs and practices regarding Judaism are shared by their clients. In this case, counselors should encourage clients to explore and discuss their own feelings and thoughts about their own Jewish identity. Furthermore, Jewish counselors must consider the potential problems associated with internalized anti-Semitism in themselves and their clients. Non-Jewish counseling professionals have different issues to consider when working with Jewish clients. The primary concern for non-Jewish counselors is to be knowledgeable about Judaism. Being able to communicate this understanding (e.g., recognizing Judaism as more than a religion) to Jewish clients should facilitate the development of a more positive working alliance; this, in turn, should lead to more positive counseling outcomes.

Like with any good treatment, a good rapport and a positive working alliance are key goals for counselors beginning to work with Jewish clients. Some suggestions for successfully accomplishing these goals include knowing about the history and present experiences of Jews, including anti-Semitism and stereotypes, as well as not letting assumptions guide treatment plans. In addition, counselors can appropriately distinguish clinical (i.e., actual) paranoia from healthy paranoia or cultural mistrust. Finally, counselors need to understand the complex nature of Jewish identity.

Scholars have theorized a number of typical presenting problems that could emerge when counseling Jews, including (a) Jewish identity issues, (b) body image and gender identity, (c) child-rearing practices, (d) interfaith or interdenominational couples, (e) issues surrounding conversion to/from Judaism, (f) sexual orientation and religion, and

(g) experiences related to anti-Semitism. Of course, American Jews may also seek counseling for personal growth or to receive treatment for any mental health disorder.

Contributed by Lewis Z. Schlosser,
Seton Hall University, South Orange, NJ

Reference

U.S. Census Bureau. (2000). *United States census 2000.* Retrieved August 25, 2008, from http://www.census.gov/main/www/cen2000.html

Additional Resources

Langman, P. F. (1999). *Jewish issues in multiculturalism: A handbook for educators and clinicians.* Northvale, NJ: Aronson.

Levitt, D. H., & Balkin, R. S. (2003). Religious diversity from a Jewish perspective. *Counseling and Values, 48,* 57–66.

Schlosser, L. Z. (2006). Affirmative psychotherapy for American Jews. *Psychotherapy: Theory, Research, Practice, Training, 43,* 424–435.

Job Satisfaction/Dissatisfaction

One of the most widely studied constructs in the vocational field is job satisfaction. Generally, **job satisfaction** is an individual's overall attitude of liking (job satisfaction) or not liking (job dissatisfaction) a job. This global perspective is expanded through a facet approach to identifying specific factors or variables that significantly affect job satisfaction. These factors include overall attitude toward work, coworkers, job conditions, pay, job mobility, nature of the work, supervision, and job benefits. Additional elements that exist beyond the job itself that are purported to have an effect on job satisfaction include global life and relationship satisfaction, work–family balance, organizational citizenship, and perceptions of performance and success (Iaffaldano & Muchinsky, 1985; Williams, 2004).

Job satisfaction is perceived to be the outcome of a developmental match between work situations and an individual's self-definition. **Vocational adjustment** is the relationship of job satisfaction to an individual's occupational self-concept. Individuals who report lower levels of job satisfaction experience an increase in physical and psychological symptoms, including anxiety, depression, burnout, and poorer health. Such outcomes support efforts both within professional settings and through counseling interventions to enhance job satisfaction for identifiable individuals and groups. Frequently used assessments of job satisfaction include the Job Descriptive Index, the Job Satisfaction Survey, the Job Diagnostic Survey, the Minnesota Satisfaction Questionnaire, and Hoppock's Job Satisfaction Measure.

Contributed by David J. Bergen,
High Point University, High Point, NC

References

Iaffaldano, M. T., & Muchinsky, P. M. (1985). Job satisfaction and job performance: A meta-analysis. *Psychological Bulletin, 97,* 251–273.

Williams, J. (2004). *Job satisfaction and organizational commitment.* Boston: Boston College, Sloan Work and Family Research Network.

Additional Resource

Spector, P. E. (1997). *Job satisfaction: Application, assessment, causes, and consequences.* Thousand Oaks, CA: Sage.

Johari Window

The **Johari Window** is a model of communication developed in the 1950s by Joseph Luft and Harry Ingham that is used to understand how interpersonal interaction may increase self-awareness. This model has been used to conceptualize individual and group counseling processes. The Johari Window divides personal awareness into four quadrants, and each quadrant represents different forms of the "self." Quadrant I, the public or open self, represents information that is known to self and others. Quadrant II, the blind self, is where others can see things about an individual of which he or she is unaware. Quadrant III, the private or hidden self, represents things that an individual knows about him- or herself but does not reveal to others, possibly because of shame, guilt, self-protectiveness, or other reasons. Quadrant IV, the unknown or potential self, represents that information of which neither an individual himself or herself or others are aware. Figure 1 depicts the Johari Window.

A dynamic relationship exists between the four quadrants; a change in one quadrant affects all other quadrants. The Johari Window is particularly useful in group work. As clients move through group stages, changes in quadrants are likely to occur. In a new relationship, such as in the initial stage of group development, Quadrant I is small. As the relationship develops and passes through growth stages from impersonal to interpersonal, Quadrant I expands. Safety and trust must exist for Quadrant II to shrink, resulting in acceptance of negative or positive feedback from others. Quadrant III shrinks as Quadrant I grows; it becomes safer as a relationship grows to reveal things people know or feel about themselves and others.

An example is a client who enters group counseling for an eating disorder. The client may initially present little information about the severity of her eating disorder and other related clinical symptoms to others in the group. This may be due to the client or others genuinely not having enough information (Quadrant I) and/or the client choosing not to reveal information about her symptoms (Quadrant III). As the group

	Known to Self	Unknown to Self
Known to Others	**Quadrant I** Public Self Open Arena	**Quadrant II** Blind Self Shadow
Unknown to Others	**Quadrant III** Private Self Hidden Façade	**Quadrant IV** Unknown Self Potential

Figure 1. The Johari Window

progresses, additional information may be presented to the group (Quadrant I increases and Quadrant III decreases) and the group may have insight into the client's eating disorder unknown to the client (Quadrant II). Quadrant II will decrease as group members interact with the client; this will in turn lead to an increase in Quadrant I. Quadrant IV represents aspects of awareness about the client's eating disorder that is not known to anyone in the group due to group dynamics (e.g., duration, size, content, process).

Contributed by Danyell Facteau and
Danica G. Hays, Old Dominion
University, Norfolk, VA

Additional Resources

Lowry, M. (2005). Self-awareness: Is it crucial to clinical practice?: Confessions of a self-aware-aholic. *American Journal of Nursing, 105*(11), 72CCC–72DDD.

Luft, J., & Ingham, H. (1955). The Johari window, a graphic model of interpersonal awareness. *Proceedings of the Western Training Laboratory in Group Development.* Los Angeles: University of California Los Angeles.

South, B. (2007). Combining mandala and the Johari window: An exercise in self-awareness. *Teaching and Learning in Nursing, 2,* 8–12.

Jungian Psychology

Carl Gustav Jung was born July 26, 1875, in Kesswil, Switzerland. His father was a Protestant minister, and at an early age, Jung saw faults in his father because Jung thought that his father was unable to convey his faith effectively. Jung's disenchantment with his father's spirituality was the genesis of Jung's lifelong search for his religion, eventually culminating in the theory known as **Jungian psychology** or Jungian analytical psychology.

To Jung, a relationship to the symbolic life is how individuals relate to the symbols inside themselves. It is the crux of his theory of individuation, a lifelong inner journey of self-discovery. Jung postulated that growth happens when an individual works with symbols in dreams and follows the symbols wherever they lead. Jungian psychology centers around the contrast of descent into the underworld and the natural ascent back to the outer world.

Jung was one of Freud's disciples at the turn of the 20th century, defending Freud's radical psychoanalytic theory with its heavy emphasis on the psychosexual and irrational nature of the psyche. In 1913, Jung resigned as president of Freud's International Psychoanalytic Association because he eventually came to disagree with Freud's sexual trauma theory. He saw delusions as archetypes, not repressed memories as Freud postulated, and published his disagreements in *Symbols of Transformation* (Jung, 1916/1956). After a public and humiliating break with Freud, Jung experienced a period of isolation when he wrote volumes about the collective unconscious and the **process of individuation.** Jung's last book, *Man and His Symbols* (Jung, Henderson, von Franz, Jaffé, & Jacobi, 1964), which he wrote before his death but was published after he died, illustrated his focus in the last

part of his life on the intersections among culture, spirituality, and archetypes. The International Association for Analytical Psychology was founded in Zurich in 1966 as a training institute for individuals interested in Jung's theory. It offers accreditation in becoming a Jungian analyst. Jung's ideas serve as the foundation for the Myers–Briggs Type Indicator, a commonly used personality inventory. Jung's ideas have influenced play therapy with children, art therapy, and the integration of the symbolic life in psychotherapy.

Archetypes

Jung's construct of **libido** is life force, in opposition to Freud's view of libido as sexual energy (Schwartz, 2003). The **self** is the soul within people trying to change, grow, and relate within this libidinal life force; therefore, Jung's theory is considered the psychology of the soul. Jung indicated that all people have **ego,** the function of which is to relate to the outer world and maintain a connection with the inner world. Jung believed that an archetypal world was represented in the human psyche's evolution over 2 to 3 million years, just as the structure of the human body evolved. In the human **psyche** are **archetypal patterns** or complexes. A **complex** is a centrally organized constellation of feelings that have an autonomous quality and are typically outside of consciousness, therefore uncontrollable by the psyche. For example, if an individual lost his mother to a sudden, unexpected automobile accident when he was a child, this individual might develop a complex about death. His complex might compromise all of the emotions accumulated during the course of his childhood and adult life about his mother's death and the impact it might have had on him or any other psychosocial deficit related to losing his nurturing mother figure at an early age. An **archetype,** then, is a symbol of a particular image that has an emotional component that predisposes individuals to perceive the world in similar patterns based upon repeated human experiences that are inherited psychically. Some of the most prominent archetypes are the divine child, the hero, the trickster, the Self, Christ (Savior), and mother Earth.

Structure of Psyche

At birth, Jung believed there was no ego consciousness. Jung said the ego is embedded in the Self. At birth, ego deintegrates, exemplified by eye moving, the calming of a distressed infant, sucking, being comforted, and crying, all of which form ego. Deintegration of the ego is followed by reintegration. At 4 years of age, humans have a substantial ego. The archetype of the Self is about symbol and image. Infants interpret their world symbolically and conceptualize their world in images (Green, 2007). The first language is the language of self-image and metaphor, then comes *daddy, momma* words and then "I exist, I like, I am a child, I hate, I love." At night, the Self rises up in dreams as symbols, and Jung stated that the Self cleanses repressed ego anxieties from the day via dream work.

Although the conscious mind comprises the ego, the unconscious mind consists of the collective unconscious and the personal unconscious (Jung, 1963). The **collective unconscious** is a suprapersonal structure, a virtual storehouse of archetypes, where images, symbols, and myths are passed down from primordial man to modern humans. The **personal unconscious** is a repository of repressed memories, fantasies, wishes, traumas, and desires that accumulate over the course of a life span. In the personal unconscious exists the shadow, which carries both the benevolent and malevolent portions of the personality. Jung believed that by integrating the shadowy aspects of the personality through analysis, psychic healing and wholeness could occur.

Jung stated that the infant was not an empty slate; the psyche carries contrasexual images. Men carry the **anima** (female traits) and women carry **animus** (male traits). Together, the anima and animus form a *heiros gamos,* a union representing the union of polarities within the personality, exemplified by the yin and yang in Eastern religions, or Adam and Eve from the Christian biblical story of creation.

Personality Typology

Four functions of a person's psychology process how internal and external stimuli are perceived:

1. **Sensation.** Perceiving through physical stimuli and categorized by people who are concrete
2. **Thinking.** Involving cognitive processing and using intellect to analyze and interpret
3. **Intuition.** Basing perceptions on "gut" feelings in contrast to sensate functioning
4. **Feeling.** Emphasizing emotions and values, opposite of thinking

In addition to the four functions, there are two attitudes for perceiving the world. **Introverts** reflect from within their inner world and recharge their batteries in solitude. **Extraverts** first examine the external stimuli, then relate this stimuli to their interior life, gaining energy from being around crowds of people.

Jungian Psychotherapy

Numinas is the experience of spirituality, which, Jung theorized, ultimately heals the fractured and tormented psyche. In psychotherapy, Jung believed that numinosity was evidenced by the ritualistic entrance into the inner world, which followed the following stages:

1. **Entrance.** Inner world
2. **Chaos.** Client moves everywhere, reflection of chaos of broken attachment in inner self, therapist is anchor of chaos
3. **Struggle.** Between good and evil, light, and darkness (pain wish to hurt, jealousy, intense negative affects); therapists provide symbolic outlets
4. **Resolution.** Therapy is managing tension between opposites simultaneously; internal transformation of hope comes up, hope when tension between opposites is managed; feeling of resolution of struggles creates positive feelings

5. **Exit.** Back into outer world; therapeutic space is safe and protected, which allows transformation of pain; archetypal patterns of creation and destruction (enter and exit); clients' Self knows where to go, which strengthens ego, then clients fall back into darkness.

In Jungian psychotherapy, clients must first strengthen themselves. Therapists stay at the feeling level of the client. Before moving into the working phase, Jung stated that the therapist must build trust with the client. Once trust is formed, the client is free to enter into the symbolic realm, and to deintegrate into affect. For example, if a client presents with depression, the analyst will see what image comes up in depression by assisting the client in switching off the energies of the ego and symbolically painting the image of depression. By entering the feeling, the client changes the affect. The Jungian approach to psychotherapy depends on clients trusting and allowing the symbols to lead them into healing by containing the images. The successful nature of Jungian psychotherapy depends on the cultivation of the **transference,** or as Jungians describe it, "working in the transference." Transference, according to Jung, was the crux of psychotherapy—the emotional chemistry between the analyst and client where unconscious, archetypal material was projected onto the therapist, not so much determined from the client's personal past or childhood relationships, but projections from a suprapersonal or archetypal past. Psychotherapy is only as effective as the extent to which both the analyst and client are changed within the transferential and countertransferential projections, out of which numinous healing and growth can occur.

In summary, Jungians (a) make sense of symbols through an extensive process of personal analysis with a Jungian analyst, (b) make sense of rage and how the client symbolizes rage, (c) maintain an analytical attitude that is both involved and detached at the same time, and (d) use techniques such as sand trays and dream analysis.

Contributed by Eric J. Green, Johns Hopkins University, Baltimore, MD

References

Green, E. (2007). The crisis of family separation following traumatic mass destruction: Jungian analytical play therapy in the aftermath of Hurricane Katrina. In N. B. Webb (Ed.), *Play therapy with children in crisis: Individual, group, and family treatment* (3rd ed., pp. 368–388). New York: Guilford Press.

Jung, C. G. (1956). *Symbols of transformation: An analysis of a prelude to a case of schizophrenia* (R. F. C. Hull, Trans.). New York: Pantheon Books. (Original work published 1916)

Jung, C. G. (1963). *Memories, dreams, and reflection.* New York: Pantheon.

Jung, C. G., Henderson, J. L., von Franz, M.-L., Jaffé, A., & Jacobi, J. (1964). *Man and his symbols.* New York: Dell.

Schwartz, S. E. (2003). Jungian analytical theory. In D. Capuzzi & D. R. Gross (Eds.), *Counseling and psycho-*

therapy: Theories and interventions (3rd ed., pp. 68–90). Upper Saddle River, NJ: Pearson.

Additional Resources

C. G. Jung Institute Zurich Web site: http:// www.junginstitut.ch/
Jung Institute of Chicago Web site: http://www.jungchicago.org
Jungian Conferences Web site: http://www.jungconference.org

◼ Juvenile Offenders

A **juvenile offender** is anyone, typically under the age of 18 years, who has been charged and tried in a court of law. The maximum age of a juvenile offender may vary from state to state. Law enforcement agencies arrest an estimated 2.2 million persons under the age of 18 years each year (Office of Juvenile Justice and Delinquency Prevention, 2007). Most chronic juvenile offenders begin their delinquency behaviors before age 12 years and some as early as age 10 years. The four most frequent juvenile offenses are simple assault, misdemeanor larceny, injury to personal property, and disorderly conduct.

The two main types of juvenile offenders are status offenders and delinquent offenders. **Status offenders** are individuals who are typically under the age of 18 years and who have been accused of behavior that would not be a crime if committed by an adult. These offenses include truancy, undisciplined behaviors, curfew violations, and underage alcohol or tobacco usage. **Delinquent offenses** would be a crime regardless of the age of the offender. All of these juveniles are seen in juvenile courts, where much of the focus is on rehabilitation, instead of in adult courts, where the focus is more on punishment.

Contrary to previous beliefs that treatment away from home is more effective than treatment near an individual's community, juvenile court systems are now examining alternative ways to deal with juvenile offenders. Instead of being placed in detention centers or training schools (now termed *Youth Development Facilities*), the current trend involves allowing the juveniles to live in their home community, which has reduced costs and increased treatment success and parental involvement. Consistent with this trend, more than half of all the individuals in juvenile cases receive pro-

bation, restitution, community service, or referrals to community programs instead of commitment to a training school. Treatment options consist of a wide range of interventions, including outpatient, inpatient, and community-based services (e.g., therapeutic group homes, foster care, in-home preservation services). The juvenile justice system, families, and mental health agencies continue to seek the most effective treatment for juvenile offenders in their communities.

There is no one single cause that leads to juvenile criminal activity. Professionals who work with juvenile offenders need to be aware of both causal and behavioral components that may increase the chances of a juvenile engaging in criminal behaviors. Examples of causal factors are mental health issues, family problems, lack of resources (e.g., financial issues), friends who may exhibit at-risk behaviors, and violence. Some examples of behavioral factors are defiant behaviors, failing in school, drug and alcohol abuse, and low self-esteem. Care should be exercised when evaluating juvenile offenders because many of these factors, which may have contributed to the negative behaviors, vary from individual to individual and are not predispositions to criminal behavior in all youth.

Contributed by David A. Scott,
Clemson University, Clemson, SC

Reference

Office of Juvenile Justice and Delinquency Prevention. (2007, March). *OJJDP statistical briefing book*. Retrieved March 30, 2007, from http://ojjdp.ncjrs.gov/ojstatbb/crime/qa05101.asp?qaDate=2005

Additional Resources

Capuzzi, D., & Gross, D. R. (2008). *Youth at risk: A prevention resource for counselors, teachers, and parents* (5th ed.). Alexandria, VA: American Counseling Association.

Grisso, T., & Schwartz, R. G. (2000). *Youth on trial: A developmental perspective on juvenile justice*. Chicago: University of Chicago Press.

MacKenzie, D. L. (2006). *What works in corrections: Reducing the criminal activities of offenders and delinquents*. New York: Cambridge University Press.

Kurtosis

The shape of a frequency distribution is dictated by a number of measures, including those of central tendency (i.e., mean, median, mode) and dispersion (e.g. range, standard deviation, skew, kurtosis). Kurtosis is but one of a number of helpful statistics that allow researchers to quickly make sense of a large amount of data. **Kurtosis** is derived from the Greek language and refers to the "peakedness" of a distribution. The peakedness of a distribution is affected by the position of individual scores around the mean. The closer the scores are gathered around the mean, the more peaked the distribution and the greater the kurtosis. The more dispersed the scores are from the mean, the flatter the distribution and the lower the kurtosis. According to their kurtic properties, distributions are described in three general shapes: **mesokurtic** (normal distribution), **leptokurtic** (tall and thin), and **platykurtic** (flat or plateau-like). Figures 1–3 demonstrate these three general shapes superimposed with a normal curve for data sets created in SPSS.

Kurtosis is represented by numeric values, which can be easily derived from SPSS. A mesokurtic, or normal distribution, has a kurtosis value of 0 (technically from –1.00 to +1.00). A leptokurtic distribution, demonstrating more peakedness, has a positive kurtosis value (i.e., >1.00), and a platykurtic distribution, being flatter than the normal distribution, has a negative kurtosis value (i.e., <–1.00).

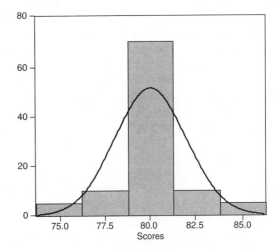

Figure 2. Leptokurtic Distribution

Note. $N = 100$. Minimum to maximum statistic range = 75–85; $M = 80$; $SD = 1.95$; Kurtosis = 2.166; $SE = 0.478$.

The following examples show how to envision the different shapes and how the shapes might occur. In order to gain a better understanding of how eighth graders are performing in math, the fictional ABC school district has decided to test the students. There are five middle schools in the district and a total of 500 eighth-grade students. On a particular assessment, students have the possibility of scoring between 0 and 100. The district will view scores as < 65 *very poor,* 66–75 *poor,* 76–85 *average,* 86–95 *very good,* and > 95 *excellent.* If

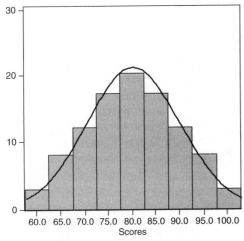

Figure 1. Mesokurtic Distribution

Note. $N = 100$. Minimum to maximum statistic range = 60–100; $M = 80$; $SD = 9.67$; Kurtosis = –0.596; $SE = 0.478$.

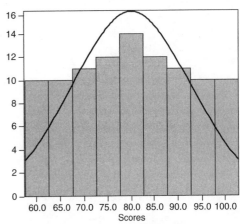

Figure 3. Platykurtic Distribution

Note. $N = 100$. Minimum to maximum statistic range = 60–100; $M = 80$; $SD = 12.43$; Kurtosis = –1.095; $SE = 0.478$.

the scores from the math test are represented by a mesokurtic distribution, the scores approximate a normal distribution. This means all levels of math knowledge and skills were present. A few students scored *very poor* (< 65), and a few scored *excellent* (> 95), but, by far, most of the students scored around the mean and fell within the average range of performance. This also is reflected in a substantial difference between the highest and the lowest score, or a large range.

If the math scores are represented by a leptokurtic distribution, it is understood that on this test, nearly all students possessed generally the same or a very similar level of math knowledge and skills. The scores were tightly clustered around the mean with few extreme scores, resulting in significantly fewer points separating the highest and lowest scores. Math scores in this pattern are more likely to be found if students are ability grouped and receive the same math curriculum and instruction.

Finally, if the scores are represented in a platykurtic distribution, all levels of math knowledge and skills were present, and the test scores were equally distributed across the scoring intervals, from *very poor* to *excellent*. A platykurtic distribution in this case might suggest to the school district that math instruction on the five individual campuses is very different, with each campus yielding uniform results of different math skills and abilities.

Contributed by Cullen T. Grinnan,
Our Lady of the Lake University,
San Antonio, TX

Additional Resources

Coolidge, F. L. (2000). *Statistics: A gentle introduction.* London: Sage.

Jaegar, R. M. (1993). *Statistics: A spectator sport* (2nd ed.). Newbury Park, CA: Sage.

Language Acquisition Theories

Counseling is fundamentally communication; it involves words accompanied by tones of voice, rapidity of speech, gestures, facial expressions, and so forth. Communication includes cognition and emotion and points of view and values, and it occurs in cultural contexts tied to language. It is important that professional counselors understand how individuals initially develop language as well as how they acquire other languages, particularly in the case of immigrants whose first language may not be English, because language acquisition influences communication in the counseling relationship. There are several language acquisition theories with which counselors should be familiar, including those of Chomsky, Lambert, Krashen, and Baugh.

Noam Chomsky: Language Acquisition Device

Noam Chomsky was an early pioneer who contributed to understanding language acquisition. His theory includes the idea that individuals have innate capability, which he called the **language acquisition device (LAD),** and this innate ability allows the individual to develop language and grammar. Chomsky stated that there are mental mechanisms in place that were solely related to linguistics. Salient content includes acquisition, learning, situational factors, and linguistic input. Every individual goes through the invariant sequence of language development, moving from the most basic to the most complex. The journey is from vocabulary to syntax to structure to sentence formation to paragraph to complex sentences. Attitudes and motivation are pivotal to the speed with which people learn language.

Language acquisition is informal (e.g., home, movies, social circles, radio, TV). It is not studied but acquired without pressure or expectation. Language acquisition is defined as communication at its basic level. The **survival language** of everyday use (e.g. directions, going to the restroom, reading a menu) is considered acquired language. In contrast, **language learning** can be defined as what takes place in a formal environment (e.g., lab, school, language class, night school for immigrants). All elements of a new language are studied and learned. The goal is competence in academic language.

Professional counselors can be misled when clients have **acquisition language.** Counselors can think that **English language learner (ELL)** clients have sufficient language to carry on a counseling session, but they might not. It is imper-ative that counselors be aware of where ELL clients are relative to the language-learning process. Clients who have mastered language learning can baffle counselors because they may have excellent formal skills in a second language but only have access to their native language for expressing emotions. Professional counselors, when encouraging clients to access their feelings, can design strategies to help them.

Situational factors and linguistic input are factors in the development of language. **Situational factors** include who talks to whom and the environment in which the communication takes place (e.g., loving, stressful, familiar, strange). This environmental setting, according to Chomsky, can be formal or informal, familiar or unusual. **Linguistic input** includes what is understandable and comprehensible. It must be adjusted to clients' competence in a second language for comprehension to occur. Professional counselors do not have control over every aspect of their clients' language, but counselors can activate LAD by encouraging clients to express themselves using their most basic forms of language to communicate, even if it is their native language. Counselors may be able to tap feelings that clients do not have the skills to express in their formal language. Counselors who communicate a profound respect for the most basic forms of clients' language will have a greater probability of successfully accessing clients' feelings.

Wallace Lambert: Model of Second Language Acquisition

Wallace Lambert's model of second language acquisition distinguishes between language being additive or subtractive. For example, when professional counselors communicate **additive perspectives,** they value, welcome, and affirm the identity of clients, especially those aspects of identity that are inherent in the first language of ELL clients. Consequently, clients feel valued and affirmed for who they are. Additive perspectives may motivate clients to commit to the struggle intrinsic to expressing feelings in a language that is not their feeling language. If counselors communicate **subtractive perspectives,** clients feel devalued because they cannot express themselves in formal English to the counselors' liking. As a result, clients may feel alienated, frustrated, and angry. Language, the most basic aspect of culture used as a means to express self, is diminished; therefore, it is very likely that clients will not be motivated to try to communicate with counselors, and in all probability they will not continue in counseling.

Stephen Krashen: Language Acquisition

Steven Krashen had two distinct concepts of language development. He called one language acquisition and the other language learning. Krashen believed that a client's first language is acquired, not learned; **language acquisition** is a subconscious process that results from informal, natural communication. Language is a means of communication, not an end in itself. It develops as a result of the desire to enter into authentic relationships with others. Krashen's **monitor hypothesis** considers second-language learning as a conscious process of study, practice, and analysis in formal settings. It includes the editing of language before it is spoken. Given time and practice, individuals will begin to apply the rules of grammar, syntax, and other rules of language in an effective way.

When clients come to counseling, it may be that they have never used English in a counseling setting. Although it may be evident that they enjoy communicating in English in safe environments with family members and friends, in the classroom, or on the playground, it cannot be assumed that confidence in familiar settings translates to confidence in new settings. Professional counselors who are sensitive to these realities will have conversations with clients about their caution, timidity, and tentativeness when making an effort to speak to the counselor in English. Counselors can use these conversations to build rapport and encourage clients to persevere in counseling.

Krashen observed that if people feel pressured, inadequate, or disrespected, they would not produce language or want to participate. In response to this observation, Krashen developed the **affective filter hypothesis,** which maintains that if persons feel safe, supported, and valued, learning will occur. It behooves counselors to learn all that they can about language acquisition so that they increase their competency in providing a relaxed, respectful, and confidence-building environment for effective rapport with English-language learners.

Krashen provided evidence to support another hypothesis, the **natural order hypothesis** that holds that people will learn second languages naturally if they already know grammar, syntax, and other language rules in their first language. What these second-language learners need is support, time, and encouragement, and counselors need patience while clients are struggling to communicate in a second language.

On the other hand, if clients do not have sufficient language development in their first language (e.g., Spanish), it might be imperative for them to have counselors who speak their first language. Such ELL clients need to be able to make themselves understood, and this is almost impossible if their command of their first language is severely limited. Making an effort to speak in a second language may be too stressful, intimidating, and demanding for effective counseling.

When input is understandable, language acquisition will become natural and understandable over time. This **input hypothesis** encourages professional counselors to speak in familiar rhythms with words simple enough for clients to comprehend. Conversations about communication can benefit both clients and counselors.

John Baugh: Linguistic Profiling

Baugh's most significant contributions are his contributions to professional understanding of spoken vernacular. His research on **linguistic profiling,** what he labeled the auditory equivalent of racial profiling, can help counselors become aware of clients' emotional reactions when they listen to clients either on the telephone or in person. Baugh concentrated on African American vernacular and led the professional dialogue regarding the intersection of the economic, educational, and legal implications of vernacular. Many times, clients speak in a vernacular that may or may not be familiar to counselors or even respected by them. If clients feel comfortable expressing their feelings in their vernacular, professional counselors will be better able to appreciate and understand the subtle meaning behind the words chosen by clients.

The discussion in this entry regarding ELL and language development can be applied to people who speak a vernacular of English. It is essential for counselors to be aware of this when counseling individuals who speak an English vernacular at home and in their communities. Counselors can use the research that Baugh and his colleagues have provided to be effective with such populations who are considered ELL because they are not proficient in academic English, or academic English is not their emotional language.

Contributed by Emiliano Gonzalez and Marie Faubert, University of Saint Thomas, Houston, TX

Additional Resources

Baker, C., & Jones, S. P. (1998). *Encyclopedia of bilingualism and bilingual education*. Philadelphia: Multilingual Matters.

Baugh, J. (2000). *Beyond Ebonics: Linguistic pride and racial prejudice*. New York: Oxford University Press.

Baugh, J., & Sherzer, J. (Eds.). (1984). *Language in use: Readings in sociolinguistics*. Englewood Cliffs, NJ: Prentice Hall.

■ Language Development and Communication Disorders

Language development includes expressive and receptive language and involves motor and cognitive functions. Language development is generally conceptualized in either of two ways. In the evolutionary interpretation, based on **Jean Piaget's** theory, symbols precede signs, and children begin to understand words at the end of the 2nd year. The acquisition of logically based concepts begins at school age, when children start to link language and culture to concepts. Before then, language is diffuse and egocentric. Children make words that have personal meanings to them. According to Piaget's theory, humans have concepts they want to communicate and they invent words to symbolize those concepts.

Another approach to language development is based on the notion that communication is social from the beginning, an approach espoused by **Lev Vygotsky.** Children have concepts and put words with them, but the words may have different meanings than the meanings adults attach to the words. This is because children's concepts are different from the concepts of adults, and they must go through a series of steps to gain adult conceptual structure.

Because of the close association of language to learning and information processing, language development affects success in school, the workplace, and society. How language development is affected in these areas forms the basis for diagnosing a language disorder in the *Diagnostic and Statistical Manual of Mental Disorders* (4th ed., text rev.; *DSM-IV-TR;* American Psychiatric Association [APA], 2000). It is estimated that 2% to 5% of otherwise nonimpaired children have difficulties in acquiring receptive and expressive language.

There are three major categories of **communication disorders:** linguistic deficits, nonlinguistic deficits, and extralinguistic deficits. Language requires the interaction of physical structures of hearing and sound production, linguistic structures, communication skills, domains of language, and knowledge of language. **Linguistic structure** includes substructures that are often associated with language disorders. Language pathologists view these substructures as (a) **phonological systems** (i.e., rules for putting sounds together to form words of the language, for example, phones, phonemes); (b) **semantic systems** (i.e., meaning attached to words, also called lexicon or vocabulary bank); (c) **morphological, syntactical, or grammatical systems** (i.e., how words are put together to make meaning and formulate sentences); and (d) **pragmatic systems** (i.e., how language is used in society; Moore & Pearson, 2003).

Communication disorders are discussed in the Disorders Usually First Diagnosed in Infancy, Childhood, or Adolescence section of the *DSM–IV–TR* (APA, 2000). Five communication disorders are identified: expressive language disorder, mixed receptive-expressive language disorder, phonological disorder, stuttering, and communication disorder not otherwise specified. If another deficit is present, such as mental retardation or environmental deprivation, the language difficulty must be in excess of that problem to be classified as a language disorder. If a speech-motor or sensory deficit or neurological condition is present with any language disorder, it should be coded on Axis III.

A person has an **expressive language disorder** if expressive language skills are substantially below receptive language development and nonverbal intelligence. A diagnosis is made using standardized testing and observation of limitations to vocabulary, errors in tense, difficulty recalling words, and difficulty forming sentences. An expressive language disorder can be distinguished from a mixed receptive-expressive language disorder because the latter disorder includes significantly more difficulty in **receptive language** (e.g., hearing, discerning, and understanding word sounds). If another developmental disorder, such as autism, is present, the language disorder is not diagnosed even though language differences will be present.

Developmental communication disorders of articulation or linguistic and grammatical processing have been linked to the FOXP2 gene, which is involved in procedural learning and sequencing of movement of the face and may be associated with other areas of speech. Autism and dyslexia have, however, not been conclusively linked to this gene.

Phonological disorders are the most common communication disorders in younger children because children often cannot distinguish sounds or categorize them to give the sounds meaning; however, with effective therapy, the probability for eventual normal speech is high for children with phonological disorder. Some indications of this disorder are lack of fluency, abnormal rapid or erratic rhythm, substitution of one sound for another, omission of sounds, errors in use of sounds, and disorganization of speech (e.g., cluttering). Severity ranges from sound distortions to sound substitutions to, the most severe, sound omissions. Common phonological disorders include lisping, delayed onset of speech, and errors often called **developmental dyspraxia.** Sometimes this disorder is caused by physical impairments of hearing, cleft palate, cerebral palsy, mental retardation, or psychosocial problems.

When working with possible disorders of language development, particularly phonological disorders, culture must be considered. The syntax of words in different languages may not be the same; for example, the subject of a sentence may come before or after the verb, and modifiers may be arranged differently. Studies have found that normal language development varies based on cultural behaviors and the physical structures used to make sounds that make up different languages; therefore, comparing language development across cultures may lead to misdiagnosis of a disorder when none exists. When working with bilingual individuals, the counselor should be mindful of the first language of the individual and differences in first- and second-language cultures.

Stuttering is a problem with the fluency of speech. It may take the form of repetitions of sounds, prolonged sounds, interjections, pauses within words, pauses in speech that are called blocking, word substitutions, excess physical tension when producing words, or monosyllabic whole-word repetitions. Although stuttering has not been associated with a specific gene, first-generation offspring are more likely to experience stuttering. Ten percent of female and 20% of male offspring from fathers with a speech disorder stutter. About 3 times more boys than girls stutter. The onset of stuttering ordinarily occurs between ages 2 and 7 years.

Language disorders that have their onset in adulthood are generally caused by traumatic brain injury, stroke, dementia, or psychosocial contexts of older persons. The highest risk groups for head injury are the 15- to 29-year-old and the 75-year-old and older age groups. Strokes are also caused by trauma to the brain and cause **aphasia** (difficulty naming) and **anomia** (difficulty finding words). Early treatment results in the greatest improvement.

Later onset disorders may also be caused by degenerative disorders such as Parkinson's disorder, progressive supranuclear palsy, HIV-associated dementia, dementia of Alzheimer type, dementia associated with multiinfarct dementia, and other dementia. As people age, the structural aspects of language change and the complexity of grammar decreases.

The effects of aging on morphology may be small because the underlying skills to process information at the word level do not require large units of information in the working memory. Thus, older people may change their speech habits because of their situation or attitude.

Although many communication disorders are successfully treated and most children achieve normal speech by their late teenage years, some disorders continue through adulthood. Speech difficulties may also be associated with other disorders such as developmental coordination disorder, attention-deficit/hyperactivity disorder, mood disorders, autistic disorder, Tourette's disorder, hearing impairment and other sensory deficits.

Contributed by Glenda P. Reynolds,
Auburn University–Montgomery,
Montgomery, AL

References

American Psychiatric Association. (2000). *Diagnostic and statistical manual of mental disorders* (4th ed., text rev.). Washington, DC: Author.

Moore, S., & Pearson, L. (2003). *Competencies and strategies for speech-language pathology assistants.* Clifton Park, NY: Delmar Learning.

Additional Resources

Battle, D. E. (1998). *Communication disorders in multicultural populations* (2nd ed.). Newton, MA: Butterworth-Heinemann.

Homer, B. D., & Tamis-LeMonda, C. S. (2005). *The development of social cognition and communication.* New York: Erlbaum.

Murray, L. L., & Clark, H. M. (2006). *Neurogenic disorders of language: Theory driven clinical practice.* Clifton Park, NY: Delmar Learning.

■ Latin American Clients: Culture and Counseling Implications

Although the Latin American population shares the commonality of a Spanish language and cultural heritage, it is equally defined by its diversity. This within-group diversity emanates largely from the distinct lands of its peoples' origin. The term **Latino/a** refers to individuals of diverse Hispanic-based national origins, including Mexico, the countries of Central America, the Spanish-speaking countries of South America, the Spanish-speaking countries of the Caribbean, and the U.S. territorial island of Puerto Rico.

During the 1980s, the Latino/a population in the United States increased five times as fast as the rest of the nation, reaching 22.3 million by 1988. This minority group constituted about 33.7 million (approximately 11%) of the total U.S. population (U.S. Census Bureau, 2006). It is projected that by 2050, the Latino population will increase to 102.6 million, which will make up approximately 25% of the U.S. population (Bernal & Sáez-Santiago, 2006). The challenge for professional counselors who encounter clients from this fast-growing population is to develop "evidence-based, culturally sensitive

interventions" (Bernal & Sáez-Santiago, 2006, p. 121). Culturally sensitive interventions should include awareness of culture; knowledge of norms, language, lifestyle, and customs; an ability to distinguish between culture and pathology; and the capacity to integrate all of these dimensions when counseling. Consequentially, it is appropriate that counselors be able to identify specific needs and preferences of the various subgroups of the Latino population correctly.

Values

Specific needs and preferences of the various Latino subgroups are based on characteristics of language, socioeconomic status, country of origin, and level of acculturation. Some basic values that seem to be common among Latino subgroups are *dignidad* (worthiness) and *respeto* (personal respect). Also related to the areas of dignity and respect are *simpatía,* or the promotion of smooth social relationships; power distance, or the promotion of respect toward powerful individuals; and lineality, which stresses the role of authority in the solution of problems.

The values of **confianza** (mutual generosity) and **personalismo** (relating to and trusting people rather than institutions) are also very important to Latin Americans. Both the professional counselor and client must recognize a mutual duty to honor their relationship; if *confianza* is not felt mutually, the client might shut down emotionally, thus causing the counseling relationship to suffer dramatically. All of these defining characteristics demonstrate the manner in which Latin Americans favor collaboration and interdependence over confrontation and competition. These cultural values regulate many social interactions among Latin Americans.

Familismo, a very important value for the Latin American culture, emphasizes loyalty, reciprocity, strong bonds, and interdependent functioning (Andrés-Hyman, Ortiz, Añez, Paris, & Davidson, 2006). A strong emphasis is placed on family relationships and childbearing as an integral part of family life and the feminine gender role. Women often define themselves through their family and children instead of independently or as part of a couple. Group goals are highlighted rather than individual ones; family support that reaches beyond the extended family to include cousins, godparents, and close friends, or *compadres/comadres,* is encouraged; and elders and parents are at the pinnacle of the hierarchy of respect. There is significant resistance against placing grandparents in a nursing home, because they are considered to be an integral part of the family. Many believe that cooperation, mutual assistance, and problem solving should involve the family as a whole; therefore, it is extremely important that family members be provided the opportunity to participate in the counseling treatment and healing process. Because Latina women are usually extremely dedicated to their families and the good of their children, they are more likely to attend counseling sessions to promote emotional growth and appropriately manage sex role conflicts. In addition, the emphasis on a wife's quiet submission and the husband's dominance and independence may make it more difficult for Hispanic women to communicate directly and assertively with their husbands in therapy.

Marianismo and *machismo* are terms that describe the conceptualization of gender roles in Latin American culture. ***Marianismo*** stresses the self-sacrifice of women and their wish to aspire to humility and kindness, to transmit religious and cultural traditions and norms, and to remain chaste before marriage (Andrés-Hyman et al., 2006). Latin American parents are often reluctant to give their daughters information about sexuality and have established rules regarding dating and contact with boys and men. Dating may be prohibited until after the age of 15 years, which is also the time when the *quinceañera* is held, which is the traditional coming-of-age ceremony for Latina girls. After maintaining her virginity until marriage, motherhood grants Latin American women a higher status of spiritual superiority to men and, consequently, a greater amount of power.

Machismo in Latin American culture emphasizes the virtues of responsibility to family and community, honor, humility, and hard work. Some positive components of this value include that men are to be family oriented, hardworking, brave, proud, and interested in the welfare and honor of their loved ones, including providing for, protecting, and defending their families and less fortunate members of society. Other descriptions include forcefulness of personality, strength of will, honor, autonomy, dignity, commitment, responsibility, self-assertiveness, and self-confidence.

Religion plays a key role in Latino beliefs and cultural traditions. Forms of prayer and spiritual guidance can be used to help the Latino client find possible solutions to the problem. The concept of ***espiritismo*,** or spiritism, has been found to be effective when working with Latino/a clients in counseling and psychotherapy sessions. The use of *espiritismo* is an important part of religious faith that might provide an important source of emotional support for the Latino client. When using this technique, professional counselors must be active in pointing out the client's ailment, demonstrating their ability to diagnose and to be an "expert." Essentially, professional counselors are expected to be familiar with the *espiritismo* rituals and traditions.

Catholicism also has a major influence in Latin American groups and can be viewed as a source of comfort in times of stress. Strong beliefs exist about the importance of prayer, and most Latinos participate in Mass. Consequences of these beliefs are that many Latin Americans have difficulty behaving assertively. Life's misfortunes are seen as inevitable, and Latinos often feel resigned to their fate *(fatalismo)*.

Mental Health Concerns

Depression and other mood disorders cross all national, cultural, ethnic, and gender boundaries. Approximately 1 in 3 Latinos has a lifetime history of mental disorder, and 19% experienced an episode of mental disorder in the past 12 months (Vega, Sribney, Aguilar-Gaxiola, & Kolody, 2004). Collective evidence suggests that the prevalence of mental disorders among recent immigrants is similar to the prevalence in their homeland but that the prevalence increases with additional time in the United States. Latinos are unlikely to use mental health services, but rather they seek care from general practitioners and the public health clinic system.

These mental health issues are increased with the current levels of socioeconomic status for Latinos. According to the U.S. Census Bureau (2006), almost 60% of the school-age Latino population either drop out or never finish their high school education, which can determine earning potential and directly influence socioeconomic status. Poverty, income level, and lack of education can contribute to a higher prevalence of mental health and societal problems.

Traditional gender roles in the Latino community may further contribute to an unwillingness to talk about feelings of depression. Latinos tend not to recognize depression as an illness, partly because of a strong cultural stigma against mental illness. Latinos are more likely to attribute their decreased energy level, stress, and other symptoms to external factors, such as lack of money or other problems over which they have no control. If Latinos do recognize that they are depressed, they are less likely to know where to seek treatment and frequently visit a general health care provider rather than a mental health professional. Often, the health care programs lack the resources to provide treatment for depression, especially the psychotherapy options that Latinos tend to prefer instead of medications. Given the growing presence of Latinos throughout the United States, it is imperative that systems of care in all states and locales systematically examine the use of services and quality of care by race or ethnicity.

Counseling Implications

Counseling Latin Americans requires specialized training and the practice of culturally sensitive interventions. One main aspect of counseling Latin American clients is establishing trust and an effective therapeutic alliance based on the values of *personalismo.*

The use of language is another important factor in the counselor–client relationship. Language barriers can interfere with the therapeutic process and delay the establishment of rapport and trust. Communication between people of different cultural backgrounds involves much more than overcoming the language barrier. Hidden cultural differences can often cause a great deal of misunderstanding and friction. These differences are a serious problem because they are mostly invisible and inaudible, but they affect the true meaning of the messages. Knowledge of language often works in collaboration with the expression of emotional experiences, such as emotional expressions, mannerisms, and verbal style. If these are misinterpreted, the course of treatment could be affected (Bernal & Sáez-Santiago, 2006). One of the major obstacles is the limited availability of bilingual counselors and other workers in the mental health field. Moreover, U.S. residents who are limited in English-language proficiency are less likely to seek and receive needed mental health services (Alegría et al., 2007). Spanish-speaking clients with counselors of similar ethnicity and language experienced lower dropout rates, more treatment sessions, and improved therapeutic outcome. This further supports the importance of having professional counselors who are able to offer culturally sensitive skills in a counseling relationship.

Other types of cultural conflicts may exist in addition to a language barrier. Conflicts that involve being caught between two cultures with opposing, or at least different, values and beliefs might hinder counseling outcomes. Participating in counseling itself may pose a conflict for Latinos whose cultural values promote seeking help and comfort from within the family rather than from strangers or outsiders. It is often almost impossible to avoid the presence of these cultural conflicts in therapy. Moreover, if professional counselors are not aware of the conflicts, it is very likely that the conflicts will be reenacted in therapy. Rather than viewing cultural conflicts as a contamination of or hindrance to the therapeutic process, these conflicts offer a unique opportunity to enhance patients' and counselors' awareness of their cultural environment.

Clinicians must familiarize themselves with the many ways in which Latinos construe and organize their lives and contexts. Being attuned to these cultural meanings is crucial to developing a therapeutic alliance. Because of the diversity of cultural features specific to each nationality, socioeconomic status level, or acculturation level, in addition to individual variations, it is impossible to have an exhaustive knowledge of Latinos' cultural characteristics. The professional counselor must withhold assumptions and presumptions about the meanings of culturally different patients' narratives until these meanings are either researched outside of the session or explored further with the Latino patient. If these cultural meanings are misread as distortions, treatment disruptions will occur. In contrast, if understood correctly, clients will often stay in counseling and narrate their stories.

Contributed by José M. Maldonado,
Jennifer Ascolese, and Lauren Aponte,
Monmouth University,
West Long Branch, NJ

References

Alegría, M., Mulvaney-Day, N., Woo, M., Torres, M., Gao, S., & Oddo, V. (2007). Correlates of past-year mental health service use among Latinos: Results from the National Latino and Asian American Study. *American Journal of Public Health, 97,* 76–83.

Andrés-Hyman, R. C., Ortiz, J., Añez, L. M., Paris, M., & Davidson, L. (2006). Culture and clinical practice: Recommendations for working with Puerto Ricans and other Latina(os) in the United States. *Professional Psychology: Research and Practice, 37,* 694–701.

Bernal, G., & Saéz-Santiago, E. (2006). Culturally centered psychosocial interventions. *Journal of Community Psychology, 34,* 121–132.

U.S. Census Bureau. (2006). *Hispanic Americans by the numbers.* Retrieved September 4, 2007, from http://www .infoplease.com/spot/hhmcensus1.html

Vega, W. A., Sribney, W. M., Aguilar-Gaxiola, S., & Kolody, B. (2004). 12-month prevalence of *DSM-III-R* psychiatric disorders among Mexican Americans: Nativity, social assimilation, and age determinants. *Journal of Nervous and Mental Disease, 192,* 532–541.

■ Law of Effect

The **law of effect** is one of two general principles of learning formulated by Edward L. Thorndike. Based on Thorndike's experiments with animals at Columbia University at the beginning of the 20th century, the law of effect describes the conditions for acquiring new behaviors. For Thorndike, learning was a trial-and-error process in which an animal or a person interacts with and adapts to the environment in a stimulus–response fashion. For example, when a counselor presents nonverbal or verbal praise to a client for sharing information, the client tends to make more personal disclosures as a way of adapting to the counseling situation. Thorndike's law of effect is generally understood as a precursor to Skinner's operant conditioning theory (see Operant Conditioning).

At its center, the law of effect is a statement about reward and punishment and their relative effect on behavior. Originally, the law of effect states that if several behaviors were generated to a common situation, only those behaviors that produced "satisfaction" or that fulfilled some need would tend to be repeated. Likewise, behaviors that produced discomfort would not likely be repeated. Thorndike believed behaviors are mostly tied to the environment. The more a behavior brings about satisfaction, the more the behavior would be connected to a specific situation. Greater dissatisfaction leads to weaker connections. Later, Thorndike revised the law of effect to reflect his modified belief that, when it comes to learning, reward is more powerful than punishment.

Contributed by David M. Carscaddon,
Gardner-Webb University,
Boling Springs, NC

Additional Resources

Hearst, E. (1999). After the puzzle boxes: Thorndike in the 20th century. *Journal of Experimental Analysis of Behavior, 72,* 441–446.

Thorndike, E. L. (1911). *Animal intelligence.* New York: Macmillan.

■ Learning Theory

Learning theories attempt to explain the cognitive processes involved in the acquisition of knowledge or skills. Four major perspectives defining how human learning occurs are behaviorism, cognitivism, constructivism, and postconstructivism.

Behaviorism

Ivan Pavlov's research on the digestive system of dogs led to the development of the earliest behaviorist model of learning. Based on stimulus–response theory, the model known as **classical conditioning** focused on the acquisition of involuntary responses rather than on the development of new behaviors. In classical conditioning, an **unconditioned stimulus** or event that produces a natural, involuntary **unconditioned response** is paired with a formerly neutral **conditioned stimulus** until the neutral stimulus comes to elicit the **conditioned response.**

John Watson, credited as the founder of **behaviorism,** used the principles of classical conditioning to create a coherent theory of learning in the early part of the 20th century. Thorndike, Tolman, Guthrie, Hull, and Skinner provided additional behaviorist models over the next 4 decades. Three principles are common to all behaviorist models of learning: (a) **Learning** is defined as any change in overt behavior with no attempt made to describe or explain cognitive activity or processes, (b) environmental factors determine and shape behavior and learning, and (c) the concepts of **contiguity** (i.e., associations created when two events overlap or occur simultaneously) and reinforcement are basic to defining the learning process. **Thorndike's law of effect** defined the role of **reinforcement** in learning and described responses occurring prior to a satisfying outcome as more likely to be repeated than those occurring prior to an aversive outcome (see Law of Effect).

B. F. Skinner's theory of operant or respondent conditioning became one of the most popular behaviorist models for instructional design and educational practice. Operant conditioning used a simple feedback system incorporating independent and dependent variables and a variety of reinforcers and reinforcement schedules. Independent variables are variables manipulated by the experimenter; dependent variables are affected by independent variables but not manipulated by the experimenter. Operant conditioning differed from classical conditioning in that responses were voluntary and repeated or repressed according to anticipated consequences. **Generalization** was said to occur when reinforcement produced the desired response to new but similar stimuli.

Cognitivism

Cognitivism, or **cognitive information processing (CIP),** replaced behaviorism in the late 20th century as the dominant paradigm for understanding human learning and mental functioning. CIP expanded the findings of behaviorism to include the existence of internal mental states and explained learning in terms of a systems approach in which the learner actively processes new experiences. Processing information and learning were thought to occur as a result of these efforts. Processing functions include input, organization, storage, retrieval, and categorization. Schemas, mental maps, and scripts were used to organize and relate new information with previous knowledge.

Gestalt theorists Wertheimer, Kohler, Koffka, and Lewin emphasized the role of perception, insight, and purpose as critical elements of learning. They described the individual as a functioning organism constantly evaluating conscious experiences and making sense of those events based on personal perspective. In Gestalt models of CIP, the individual learned by thinking about events and responding to them.

Jean Piaget used principles from behaviorism and Gestalt models of CIP to propose a theory of child development and learning influenced by neurological development and environmental exposure to a variety of experiences. Piaget contended children developed mental maps, or **schema,** to understand and respond to forces in the environment. Piaget also contended that mental processing and resulting schema became more sophisticated over time and could be identified in four basic developmental stages: the **sensorimotor stage** (birth to 2 years), **preoperational stage** (ages 2–7 years), **concrete operations stage** (ages 7–11 years), and **formal operations stage** (age 11 years and upward). Individuals make sense of novel experiences by a process of **assimilation** or **accommodation.** Information similar to previously learned information is easily assimilated into an existing schema; dissimilar experiences require the child to accommodate new schema to restore mental equilibrium. By encountering new conditions, the child uses the two processes to acquire and use extended cognitive structures.

Theories of CIP from the 1960s and 1970s focused on memory structure and function, metacognition, transfer of learning, artificial intelligence, and mathematical learning models. These theories were united by their emphasis on the learner's internal mental processes with little emphasis on a developmental perspective.

Information processing theory, first described by George Miller, produced two constructs fundamental to an understanding of human cognition. One was the concept of chunking as a way to describe how short-term memory operates. The other was the **test-operate-test-exit (TOTE)** construct as a way to describe instinctive processing and learning structure. **Chunking** refers to the ability to hold only 5 to 9 "chunks" of meaningful information at one time in short-term memory. New information is combined by the learner into meaningful chunks in order to be more easily remembered and retrieved. Miller's concept of the short-term memory having a limited capacity remains a basic element of subsequent theories of memory. The TOTE paradigm replaced stimulus–response as the defining model of learned behavior. Individually preselected goal attainment was identified as the motivation for learning and behavior. In the TOTE model, a stated goal is tested to determine whether it has been met. If not, additional operations are performed until the goal is either attained or abandoned. The iterative process has become the basis for subsequent theories of learning and problem solving. Miller's information processing theory provided a linear-sequential view of learning and memory, established **planning** as a fundamental cognitive process, and defined human behavior as hierarchically organized.

David Ausubel focused primarily on verbal learning and emphasized the hierarchical nature of knowledge and the role of preparation to facilitate learning. Ausubel's **subsumption theory** described learning as the process of "subsuming" new information into existing cognitive structures. Ausubel proposed the concept **advanced organizer,** a learning device designed to activate existing schema or mental patterns so that new information could be more easily understood and related to an individual's understanding.

Robert Gagne analyzed the processes of learning and instruction and identified nine instructional "events" as essential conditions for learning. These events, to be presented sequentially, are reception, expectancy, retrieval, selective perception, semantic encoding, responding, reinforcement, retrieval, and generalization. In Gagne's model, when new information is properly presented and reinforced, learning will occur; thus, the responsibility for learning rests with the instructor.

Constructivism

Constructivist theories describe learning as a process created or constructed by the learner using individual knowledge based on individual experience to make sense of new information. Cognitive development is viewed as an individual, internal process created within a social setting. Others from the social setting or culture provide the means for the learner to discover new concepts and understanding on his or her own. Social interaction is thought to extend knowledge construction by providing the learner with opportunities to clarify ideas, identify inconsistencies, and solve problems in realistic settings by sharing them with others. The term *constructivism* has been applied to the theories of Bruner, Vygotsky, and Bandura. Similar theories include generative learning and knowledge building. Basic to all of these is the focus on the learner's exploration within a given framework or structure provided or supported by others.

Jerome Bruner's discovery learning identifies learning as an active process based on developmental readiness and occurring when individuals question, explore, or experiment using inductive reasoning to "discover" interrelationships between novel and familiar experiences. Basic to Bruner's model are the principles of readiness, spiral organization, and extrapolation. The learner selects and organizes information, constructs hypotheses, and makes decisions by relying on mental models that provide meaning and allow the learner to extrapolate or apply the information given in similar situations.

Social factors and language acquisition are the basis of cognitive development according to **Lev Vygotsky's social development theory. Vygotsky** claimed cognitive development was complex and lifelong, not an achievement measured in developmental stages. He used the phrase **zone of proximal development** to describe the distance between what the learner knew and what could be known using "scaffolding" or help from others. **Scaffolding** leads the learner to higher levels of problem solving and understanding than could be achieved independently. Vygotsky emphasized the role of culture and language as tools used to deal with the environment. By internalizing these tools, individuals could achieve higher levels of thinking and extend cognitive development. Vygotsky's principles of guided participation, continuous change, and the role of social community shaped current understanding of cognitive development.

Albert Bandura's social learning theory defines human behavior as ongoing reciprocal interactions between the individual and cognitive, behavioral, and environmental experiences. Although not denying the role of individual discovery, social learning theory stresses the impact of observation and modeling on learning. The effectiveness of modeling is mediated by four processes: attention, retention, reproduction, and motivation. Bandura found that learning and performance were separate phenomena and that observational learning could be self-reinforcing rather than dependent on external reinforcement.

Postconstructivism

Recent work in cognitive processing includes theories of componential analysis, multiple intelligences, and Sternberg's triarchic theory of intelligence. **Componential analysis** attempts to define cognitive functioning by isolating and testing separate cognitive processes. The model identifies four components of information processing: encoding; problem-solving strategy formation; implementation; and generalization. **Howard Gardner's theory of multiple intelligences** suggests cognition and learning are not a unitary construct but a modular mental process with different types of skills or knowledge being learned and developed in diverse ways. Gardner speculated that future understanding of learning would require isolating the areas of the brain responsible for different types of intelligence. Gardner identified eight human intelligences: linguistic, logical-mathematical, spatial, bodily-kinesthetic, musical, interpersonal, intrapersonal, and naturalistic.

Sternberg's triarchic theory of intelligence includes three subtheories: the componential, the experiential, and the contextual. The **componential subtheory** defines how behavior is generated, the **contextual subtheory** relates cognition to the external world, and the **experiential subtheory** addresses the relationship between using a given behavior in a specific situation and the amount of experience the individual has with that behavior or situation. Cognitive processing involves the interaction of these three subtheories. The componential subtheory identifies five principles of instruction that contribute to learning and performance: relevance, real-world applications, explicit directions for dealing with variations of the concept taught, attention to multiple intelligences, and acknowledgement of individual learning style.

Contributed by Rosalie R. Hydock,
Scottsdale, AZ

Additional Resources

Domjan, M. P. (2006). *The principles of learning and behavior* (5th ed.). Belmont, CA: Wadsworth.

Hergenhahn, B. R., & Olson, M. H. (2004). *An introduction to theories of learning* (7th ed.). Upper Saddle River, NJ: Prentice Hall.

◼ Legal Issues in Counseling

Ethical guidelines are not the only standards governing the practices of professional counselors. There are numerous legal obligations that professional counselors must be aware of and with which they must comply. Often, ethical standards and legal statutes may appear synonymous because many licensure laws integrate ethical standards when developing statutes and regulations; however, ethical and legal standards are not the same, and professional counselors should not assume that if they are in compliance with their professional ethical standards, they are also in compliance with the laws of the state governing their professional licenses or certifications. State laws may permit ethical standards to govern professional behaviors, but the law is able to supersede ethical guidelines when the public is considered to be at risk.

Professional ethical standards are often national in scope and govern all members of the profession, independent of the residence and location of practice of the professional counselor. Laws differ from state to state, and although the legal terminology may be similar, there may be subtle interpretations and definitions of the laws according to the state. For this reason, professional counselors must be aware of the laws in their state to determine the legal implications for their counseling practices. The following legal issues are explored to aid counselors in understanding several legal terms that directly affect counseling practices and to assist in avoiding legal complaints.

Negligence and malpractice are often connected in legal complaints. **Negligence** refers to professional behaviors that fall below and interfere with an acceptable standard of care (Granello & Witmer, 1998). A professional counselor may not intentionally try to cause harm to a client; however, when negligent behavior causes harm, malpractice may have occurred. **Malpractice** is the failure in behavior and skill to provide a standard of care in similar circumstances by similar professionals in good standing.

When a client believes that she or he has been harmed due to the negligence of a counselor, the client can file a grievance, or tort. A **tort** is a legal complaint filed when a client believes she or he has encountered harm due to negligence of the counselor. Compensation for negligence is sought by filing a tort, which is categorized as a civil liability. The burden of proof rests on the plaintiff, who must prove the following four components of negligence: (a) A client–counselor relationship existed resulting in a duty to the client (legal duty of care), (b) a standard of care was breached and fell below the standard of care (breach of duty), (c) the client was harmed as a result of the negligence (real loss), and (d) a causal relationship existed between the harm encountered and professional conduct (proximate cause; Granello & Witmer, 1998). Misdiagnosis and inappropriate delivery of treatment have been the cause of numerous negligent malpractice suits. In malpractice cases, plaintiffs must prove their case by a preponderance of the evidence. This means the plaintiff's complaint and evidence of negligence, using these four elements, must be more convincing than the counselor's defense against the malpractice complaint.

Due to the nature of the counselor–client relationship, the professional counselor assumes direct liability for the client. **Liability** is a legal obligation of the counselor to provide a standard of care to the client. There are several types of torts likely to affect professional counselors: defamation, right of privacy, and emotional distress (Krauskopf & Krauskopf, 1965). **Defamation,** which includes both libel and slander, alleges the professional counselor has committed harm through some form of communication. **Libel** is a falsely written statement about a living individual that caused direct harm and was performed with intentional malice disregarding the rights of the client. **Slander** is intentional defamatory spoken statements that caused harm and was performed with intentional malice disregarding the rights of the client.

If written documents such as counseling notes, assessments, reports, and diagnoses or verbal communications with others about the client are (a) proven to be false, (b) shown to have caused harm to the client, and (c) performed with the intent to cause malice and disregard the client's rights, then a civil liability malpractice libel or slander complaint may be filed by a client.

Laws regarding minor consent often differ across states more than other legal statutes. **Informed consent** is the formal permission granted by a client that initiates the legal agreement to begin treatment. In most legal circumstances when a minor enters into treatment through parental consent, it is imperative for professional counselors to obtain consent from the custodial parent. If proper consent is not obtained, counselors can be sued for malpractice. Legally, parents have a right to know about their child's treatment although ethically it is helpful if the parents agree to confidentiality for the child client, except when there is potential harm or abuse. A minor child is able to consent to treatment in most circumstances but is unable to refuse treatment (Lawrence & Kurpius, 2000).

In some circumstances, children can consent to treatment without parental consent, referred to as minor consent. **Minor consent** occurs in one of four ways: (a) with parental consent, (b) involuntary treatment by the parent's initiation, (c) by order of a court (Lawrence & Kurpius, 2000), or (d) minor consent laws passed by individual states. There are other situations when a minor does not require parental consent for treatment. The most common situation involves a minor being **court ordered** for treatment. In many states, a **mature minor** is defined as a child over the age of 16 years who is able to comprehend the reasons and consequences for counseling. Finally, an **emancipated minor** is defined in most states as an individual under the age of 18 years who lives separately from parents and is able to manage daily affairs independently. In addition, in many states a minor may also enter into treatment through minor consent when the minor is (a) waiting to gain parental consent, (b) in need of drug treatment, (c) assessed to be a risk to self or others, and/or (d) the alleged victim of abuse or sexual assault.

Some professional counselors mistakenly believe that by acting in accordance with their professional ethical standards they are also in compliance with the laws in their practicing state. The reality, however, is that ethical codes do not encompass all the legal statutes that are required for professional practices of a licensed counselor. It is the obligation of the professional counselor to become aware of the laws governing the licensee in order to provide clients with the appropriate legal standard of care and to practice professional counseling lawfully to prevent malpractice suits.

Contributed by Lisa R. Jackson-Cherry,
Marymount University, Arlington, VA

References

Granello, P., & Witmer, M. (1998). Standards of care: Potential implications for the counseling profession. *Journal of Counseling & Development, 76,* 371–380.

Krauskopf, J., & Krauskopf, C. (1965). Torts and psychologists. *Journal of Counseling Psychology, 12,* 227–237.

Lawrence, G., & Kurpius, S. (2000). Legal and ethical issues involved when counseling minors in nonschool settings. *Journal of Counseling & Development, 78,* 130–136.

Additional Resources

Braun, S., & Cox, J. (2005). Managed mental health care: Intentional diagnosis of mental disorders. *Journal of Counseling & Development, 83,* 425–433.

Rowley, W., & MacDonald, D. (2001). Counseling and the law: A cross-cultural perspective. *Journal of Counseling & Development, 79,* 422–429.

Wheeler, A. M., & Bertram, B. (2008). *The counselor and the law: A guide to legal and ethical practice* (5th ed.). Alexandria, VA: American Counseling Association.

■ Liability Insurance

Licensed professional counselors, student counselors, and counselor education instructors are aware that there is an assumed risk of lawsuits in their profession. Counselors assume risk every day when they meet with a client for assessment, treatment planning, and counseling. With any form of risk, there may be a need for liability insurance. **Liability insurance** is a means to limit the financial liability of counselors because of errors and omissions (i.e., negligence) in their professional practice. Counselors are exposed to a certain amount of professional liability because they are expected to have extensive knowledge and training in their area of expertise and are expected to perform counseling-related services according to the standards of the profession. Although there is no ethical standard in the counseling profession encouraging liability insurance, it is a good practice to protect professional integrity, personal assets, and possible loss of licensure and finances when a complaint is brought against a professional counselor. The primary way to avoid litigation is to follow the professional code of conduct for counselors.

The American Counseling Association's (ACA; 2005) *ACA Code of Ethics* is designed as a guidebook for counseling professionals. Counselors are expected to adhere to a best practice standard, refer to the *Code*, and consult with other professional colleagues to decrease risk of potential harm to clients. If an ethical decision-making model is adhered to, there is less likelihood of having a validated liability claim. Because incidents may occur, it is imperative that licensed professional counselors maintain liability insurance as a safeguard.

The concept of insurance is traced back to Babylonia, when traders were encouraged to insure that their goods would reach the destination without being stolen or lost. The need for insurance carried over into the societies of the Phoenicians, Greeks, Romans, and Europeans. It covered seaborne commerce, life insurance, protection from fire or shipwreck, and captivity by pirates and provided assistance during sickness and poverty. Since the 1900s, there has been a growing trend in the insurance industry to cover all areas where there is a high risk of harm. If clients believe they have been harmed in some way, whether this claim is baseless or founded, they can seek relief through the court system. The cost of legal defense can be enormous; thus, as society becomes more litigious, insurance policy sales will continue to grow ("The History of Insurance," 2007).

Liability insurance was originally designed to protect individuals or companies when an unexpected event required compensation to an individual who had incurred a loss of some kind. In its basic form, liability insurance is a type of insurance directly designed to protect individuals at risk for being sued by a third party because of negligence. As a result, when a claim is made, the insurance carrier has the right to defend the insured. Particular fields of practice are encouraged to obtain liability insurance because the very nature of their profession means that members of the profession may engage in activities that may put others at risk for injury or loss (Matthews, 1992).

Many companies offer professional liability insurance for professional counselors, counseling students, and counseling educators. Some important aspects to consider when deciding on an insurance carrier is the reputation of the agency, the requirements to obtain the insurance, the cost of coverage, the amount of coverage offered by the agency, and the reputation for protection of the insured. Some carriers that are designed to meet the needs of the counseling and psychology fields are the organizations that practitioners are involved with as members. Liability insurance can be obtained from ACA, American Mental Health Counselors Association, National Association of Alcoholism and Drug Abuse Counselors, American Psychological Association, and Healthcare Providers Service Organization. Most of these carriers have a 1 million dollar per occurrence maximum, and a 3 million dollar annual aggregate.

Contributed by Rosanne Nunnery and
Carl J. Sheperis, Mississippi State
University, Starkville, MS

References

American Counseling Association. (2005). *ACA code of ethics.* Alexandria, VA: Author.

The history of insurance. (2007). Retrieved October 2, 2007, from the *Columbia Electronic Encyclopedia* (6th ed.) at http://www.infoplease.com/ce6/bus/A0858849.html

Matthews, J. L. (1992). *How to win your personal injury claim.* Berkeley, CA: Nolo Press Self-Help Law.

■ Licensure

Prior to the 1970s, there were basically only two credentials that affected counselors: state certification in school counseling (administered by a state department of education or similar body) and licensure as a psychologist (administered by a state psychology licensure board). State certification in school counseling controlled who could be a school counselor in a public school. State psychology licensing boards controlled who could practice "psychology," which included counseling and psychotherapy, independently or in private practice. **Licensure,** in this sense, is the process through which a governmental agency gives permission to qualified citizens to use a title and practice a specific profession (e.g., counseling) after certain criteria have been met. **Certification,** similar to licensure, is the recognition by an agency or association of those professionals who have met certain standards. If, in the past, a counselor was not interested in working in a school or in private practice, **credentials** (e.g., licensure, certification) were not an issue. State and private agencies and other employers of counselors simply developed their own requirements for hiring counselors. At that time, counselors with doctoral degrees were routinely licensed as psychologists, but that began to change in the mid 1970s when state psychology boards became more restrictive when reviewing qualifications.

With licensure as a psychologist becoming more restrictive (a movement led by the American Psychological Association), professional counselors, led by the Association for Counselor Education and Supervision and the American Personnel and Guidance Association (now the American Counseling Association) began to advocate for separate licensing laws governing private, independent counseling practice. In 1976, Virginia became the first state to enact a separate licensure law for counselors holding a master's degree, and today 49 states license counselors separately as "professional counselors." During this same time, other specialties represented by professional associations, such as the American Association for Marriage and Family Therapy, began to push for separate licensure as well. Today, most states separately license psychologists, counselors, marriage and family therapists, and social workers, thus adding somewhat to the confusion surrounding licensure relative to independent practice in the helping professions. Generally speaking, licensure in counseling requires a minimum of a master's degree in counseling or a closely related field, numerous hours of supervised clinical experience after obtaining the master's degree, and passage of a licensure examination. Similar requirements exist for licensure in marriage and family therapy and social work, whereas licensure in psychology requires a doctoral degree.

One aspect of licensing that has generated recent interest and concern is reciprocity. Many professionals who are licensed as professional counselors move from one state to another state over the course of their professional lives. In doing so, some will have difficulty meeting the counselor licensure requirements of the state where they are relocating. This occurs because states have various counselor licensure laws, which, while similar, have different provisions. One of the ways some states have attempted to deal with this problem is through reciprocity. In its purest sense, **reciprocity** between state licensure boards involves the mutual or cooperative interchange of rights and privileges through the acceptance of licenses granted by each other automatically without further review. In reality, there are very few states, if any, that have the kind of reciprocity agreements that automatically give recognition to counselors licensed by another state. Those states with reciprocity often have some caveat stating that the applicant must hold a license from a state that

is substantially equivalent to or more stringent than the license being sought.

Reciprocity is one method considered when discussing portability. **Portability** is the ability to carry, move, or transfer an individual license between states. One method is licensure by **endorsement** (i.e., acknowledging and validating a license from another state), which is an abbreviated application for those holding a license in another jurisdiction. Generally, this means the license must be substantially equivalent (including previous examination scores) and often means meeting other specific requirements. Another method to help with the problem of portability has been developed by the American Association of State Counseling Boards (AASCB). This alliance has created a service to facilitate professional mobility for licensed professional counselors who can deposit (store) their credentials (e.g., education, supervised experience, examination scores, work history) in a central location, allowing the information to be forwarded to a counselor licensure board in another state. There are specific requirements to become eligible as a registrant with AASCB, including a fee for service.

Contributed by Brent M. Snow,
University of West Georgia,
Carrollton, GA

Additional Resources

American Association of State Counseling Boards Web site: http://www.aascb.org
American Counseling Association Office of Professional Affairs (2008). *Licensure requirements for professional counselors.* Alexandria, VA: Author.

Life Events

Life events refer to the events that occur in the daily lives of individuals (e.g., births, deaths, marriages, life's transitions). Life events generally are short lived as opposed to enduring conditions, such as poverty, although life events may have enduring consequences for the individual. Both positive and negative life events, including stress, wellness, illness, depression, and coping strategies, have been associated with various constructs.

Life events were first studied by **Thomas Holmes** and his student, **Richard Rahe,** when they sought to examine the relationship between stress and wellness. They surveyed 5,000 individuals and requested that they assign numerical ratings to different life events, both positive and negative (e.g., death of a spouse, marriage, retirement). Each rating reflected the participants' opinion of how much "social readjustment" was required following an event. Holmes and Rahe found a positive correlation between the life events and illness. From their research, Holmes and Rahe (1967) developed the **Social Readjustment Rating Scale (SRRS),** an instrument that assigned points to a variety of life events. The original instrument identified 43 life events (e.g., death of spouse, divorce, trouble with boss, vacation) and ranked the event according to their potential negative impact on an individual's health.

The SRRS is also known as the Schedule of Recent Events (SRE) or simply the Life Events Scale. When using the SRE, individuals review the list of events and mark those that occurred in the past 12 months. The more life events experienced over the past year, the higher the score on the SRE and the greater the risk of developing health problems. The possible criterion-referenced interpretive scores are low (a score of less than 149), mild (a score between 150 and 200), moderate (a score between 200 and 299), and major (a score of 300 or more). The SRE was revised and is now known as the Holmes–Rahe Scale. Additional research (Holmes & Masuda, 1974) has adapted the scale by asking participants to rate the degree of adjustment (to change) necessary for each life event experienced. The researchers assigned a value of 50 to the marriage event and instructed the participants to think of each event experienced as relative to getting married (i.e., was the experienced event more or less stressful than the event of getting married).

The Holmes–Rahe Scale or some variation of the instrument has been a popular device used both by mental health practitioners and researchers for understanding and managing stress. Much of its appeal can be attributed to its ease of use and intuitive feel, which are also responsible for its migration from the domain of psychological journals to the mainstream media. It continues to be a well-known and frequently used instrument for assessing the impact of various life events on individuals' stress levels and identifying the levels at which stress might increase the susceptibility to illness and mental health problems.

Life Events in Counseling

Professional counselors can educate their clients about the impact, both positive and negative, that life events can have on clients' physical and mental health. In addition, professional counselors can use assessment of life events to facilitate discussions related to life events and the impact of these events on clients. Clients can be encouraged to examine the role that life events have on their life currently as well as learn to recognize when life events happen. They can also be encouraged to examine the impact that the life event will have on the individual and his or her family as well as begin to explore ways to adjust to those life events.

Research Related to Life Events

In spite of its widespread use, there is an ongoing debate about whether or not there is a direct link between life events and stress and if additional factors should be considered. For example, individuals may experience the same life event but not experience the same level of stress. Thus, one argument suggests the importance of examining not only the event but also examining how stressful the individual perceives the event to be as well as his or her coping strategies. For example, individuals who lack social support or who have a pessimistic outlook on life may experience more stress in coping with life changes (events) than those who have a more optimistic outlook on life.

Rahe, as well as a number of supporters of Holmes and Rahe's research, has acknowledged the validity of arguments

such as these and has made improvements to the original SRE. Rahe's Stress and Coping Inventory (SCI) added measurements of coping skills and access to health and wellness resources. There are two versions of this revised instrument: the SCI, which can take up to an hour to complete, and the Brief Stress and Coping Inventory, which takes approximately 15 minutes to complete.

Further research has expanded the work of Holmes, Rahe, and others and resulted in second-generation tools, such as the PERI: Psychiatric Epidemiology Research Interview Life Events Scale (Dohrenwend, Askenasy, Krasnoff, & Dohrenwend, 1978) and the Life Events and Coping Inventory (Dise-Lewis, 1988), which was designed to measure how normal children react to changing life events. The High School Readjustment Scale was developed by Tolor, Murphy, Wilson, and Clayton (1983) to study the relationship of stress and life events in high school students. Windle (1987) studied older adolescent girls to determine the relationships between stressful life events and general mental health and temperament.

Other studies have used a modified version of the Holmes–Rahe Scale, separating controllable from noncontrollable events, to determine whether there were differences. One such study of 197 university students by Stern, McCants, and Pettine (1982) found that uncontrollable events caused more stress than controllable events, suggesting the need for subsequent research on which instruments, such as the Holmes–Rahe Scale, distinguish between controllable and noncontrollable events.

These studies are samples of the research that continues to examine the link between life events and stress. Although this exploration continues, many individuals continue to turn to the Holmes and Rahe SRE as a practical barometer of levels of stress and a warning of possible health issues.

Contributed by Gibson Scheid,
Gibsonworks, Oakland, CA

References

Dise-Lewis, J. E. (1988). The Life Events and Coping Inventory: An assessment of stress in children. *Psychosomatic Medicine, 50,* 484–499.

Dohrenwend, B. S., Askenasy, A. R., Krasnoff, L., & Dohrenwend, B. P. (1978). Exemplification of a method for scaling life events: The PERI Life Events Scale. *Journal of Health and Social Behavior, 19,* 205–229.

Holmes, T. H., & Masuda, M. (1974). Life changes and illness susceptibility. In B. S. Dohrenwend & B. P. Dohrenwend (Eds.), *Stressful life events: Their nature and effects* (pp. 45–72). New York: Wiley.

Holmes, T. H., & Rahe, R. (1967). Holmes–Rahe Social Readjustment Rating Scale. *Journal of Psychosomatic Research, 11,* 213–218.

Stern, G. S., McCants, T. R., & Pettine, P. W. (1982). Stress and illness: Controllable and uncontrollable life events' relative contributions. *Personality and Social Psychology Bulletin, 8,* 140.

Tolor, A., Murphy, V. M., Wilson, L. T., & Clayton, J. (1983). The High School Social Readjustment Scale: An attempt to quantify stressful events in young people. *Research Communications in Psychology, Psychiatry and Behavior, 8,* 85–111.

Windle, M. (1987). Stressful life events, General mental health, and temperament among late-adolescent females. *Journal of Adolescent Research, 2,* 13.

Additional Resource

Chiriboga, D. A. (1989). The measurement of stress exposure in later life.In K. S. Markides, C. L. Cooper, & U. K. Chichester (Eds.), *Aging, stress, and health* (pp. 13–41). London: Wiley.

■ Life-Span, Life-Space Career Theory

Donald Edwin Super (1910–1994) emerged as a leader of career development in the 1940s, and he proposed the initial elements of his theory of vocational development in 1953 (Super, 1953). In contrast to career development theorists who focused on the matching of individual and career traits as an event, Super viewed career as a process that continually unfolded throughout an individual's lifetime. Over the next 40 years, Super engaged in continual revision of this theory to include greater attention to developmental tasks, life roles, and contextual influences. In 1990, at the age of 80 years, Super published a final major revision of his **life-span, life-space career theory.** Perhaps one of the most complex and well-studied career development theories to date, life-span, life-space theory includes attention to three main constructs: self-concept, life span, and life space.

Self-Concept

Super originally described **self-concept** as a person's self-perceptions of personality traits, qualities, competencies, and preferences. Super believed that self-concept develops throughout the lifetime as individuals identify similarities and differences between themselves and others. According to Super, self-concept influences a person's ideas about the occupations that will be best for that individual; in other words, a person's career choice is a reflection of his or her self-concept. Just as he proposed that career development is a lifelong process, Super envisioned self-concept as an ever-evolving influence on an individual's career choice. In turn, he proposed that career decisions and life experiences affect the continued development of the self-concept.

Life Span

Super's life-span, life-space theory is founded on the assumption that individuals engage in a lifelong process of career development that involves a series of developmental stages and tasks. Although Super initially presented career development as a relatively linear process, he later revised his theory to reflect the observation that individuals cycle and recycle through the various stages throughout their lives. As individuals move through the life stages and encounter developmental and adaptation tasks, their ability and readiness to cope with the challenges of each stage, known as **career adaptability,** is crucial (Super, Osborne, Walsh,

Brown, & Niles, 1992). Various cognitive and affective characteristics are associated with career maturity, including decision-making skills, self-appraisal skills, and occupational exploration skills. Professional counselors can work to assess and develop an individual's career adaptability to improve the individual's ability to meet the demands of each developmental task successfully.

Super proposed the following five major life stages: growth, exploration, establishment, maintenance, and disengagement. Although he believed progression through the stages and developmental tasks to be flexible, he proposed approximate age ranges for each stage. The **growth** stage typically occurs from birth until age 14 years; substages or developmental tasks include curiosity, fantasy, interest, and capacity. Although children may not be intentional about career development, the early years are an important time for development of a self-concept that will later guide an individual's career process. During the growth stage, children begin to gain an awareness of self and a basic understanding of the world-of-work. Younger children engage in **curiosity** and **fantasy** as they use their natural curiosity and role-play to express and explore the concept of work. Soon children develop likes and dislikes and begin to develop and express **interest** in various careers. Finally, young adolescents gain a better understanding of their talents and abilities and how these relate to work as they engage in a substage Super called **capacity.**

Super suggested that the **exploration** stage takes place from ages 15 to 24 years as individuals make tentative choices related to careers. Substages or developmental tasks include crystallization, specification, and implementation. During **crystallization,** individuals begin to clarify the types of work that may be of interest to them. Later, individuals move from a tentative plan to a specific occupational choice in a process Super termed **specification.** Individuals prepare to exit the exploration stage when they engage in **implementation,** a process wherein individuals actively pursue a career choice through entry-level work or further training and education.

Individuals generally engage in Super's third stage, **establishment,** between the ages of 25 and 45 years. During this time, individuals establish themselves in a chosen career field. Important substages or developmental tasks include stabilizing, consolidating, and advancing. **Stabilizing** occurs as individuals use actual work experience to assess the degree to which their career choices are appropriate for them. As individuals move through the **consolidating** substage, they work to become productive employees and gain favorable reputations. The final substage, **advancing,** occurs as individuals gain higher pay, status, and responsibility based on their recognized reputations.

Super proposed that workers between 45 and 65 years of age experience a fourth stage, **maintenance,** as they adjust to changes and innovations in their chosen fields. Substages within maintenance include holding, updating, and innovating. During the **holding** substage, workers seek to maintain their place and status in light of new competition, family concerns, and other demands. Workers may choose to maintain their level of success through **updating** their skills and **innovating,** creating new ideas or applying knowledge in new ways, in their chosen fields.

Super proposed a final stage, **disengagement,** in his model. Disengagement includes deceleration, retirement planning, and retirement living. **Deceleration** occurs at approximately age 65 years when workers begin to experience decreased interest in work. During the substage of **retirement planning,** individuals begin to formulate plans for retirement. Individuals implement these plans during the final substage of **retirement living.**

Life Space

Super recognized that occupational choice and job advancement are not always central areas of focus for everyone, and he suggested that various life roles affect career choice and development. Super used the term **life-space** to describe the interplay of nine roles (i.e., child, student, leisurite, citizen, worker, spouse or partner, homemaker, parent, and pensioner) over the course of a person's life. Super suggested that individuals enact these roles in the home, community, school, and workplace. Super emphasized that each individual assigns unique meanings to the life roles and chooses the level of importance ascribed to the specific life roles; therefore, individuals often reflect varying priorities across their career based on their balancing of life roles.

Super's life-career rainbow, a vital concept in his theory, provides a pictorial representation of the interconnections of the various life roles throughout the life span. In one of his last revisions of life-span, life-space theory, Super (1990) transformed the life-career rainbow into the **archway of career determinants.** In addition to accounting for the various life roles, Super turned attention to the various societal and contextual influences on an individual's career development. Super envisioned the self, one's self-concepts, and the developmental stages at the top of the archway. These three were supported, however, by columns depicting individual characteristics (e.g., needs, values, interests, intelligence, aptitudes, special aptitudes) and societal influences (e.g., economy, society, labor market, community, school, family, peer groups).

Donald Super's numerous contributions to the field of career counseling were significant in shaping and redefining the concept of career development in the 20th century. Even after his death, scholars continue to expand his theory through research and development.

Contributed by Cheyenne Pease-Carter
and Casey A. Barrio Minton,
University of North Texas, Denton, TX

References

Super, D. E. (1953). A theory of vocational development. *American Psychologist, 8,* 185–190.

Super, D. E. (1990). A life-span, life-space approach to career development. In D. Brown, L. Brown, & Associates (Eds.), *Career choice and development: Applying contemporary theories to practice* (2nd ed., pp. 197–261). San Francisco: Jossey-Bass.

Super, D. E., Osborne, W. L., Walsh, D. J., Brown, S. D., & Niles, S. G. (1992). Developmental career assessment and counseling: The C-DAC model. *Journal of Counseling & Development, 71,* 74–80.

Additional Resource

Niles, S. G., & Harris-Bowlsbey, J. (2005). *Career development interventions in the 21st century* (2nd ed.). Upper Saddle River, NJ: Pearson Education.

■Locus of Control

Locus of control is a concept developed to explain the attribution of life event outcomes. People with an **internal locus of control** believe that their own actions, abilities, and efforts produce the outcome. For example, a person with an internal locus of control may believe that getting good grades in school depends on studying hard for tests, paying attention in class, and working hard on assignments. People with an **external locus of control** believe that forces outside themselves determine the outcome of their behavior. For example, a person with an external locus of control may believe that getting good grades in school depends on luck, ease of the class, and the teacher's grading policy.

Because people with an internal locus of control attribute success to their own abilities and efforts, they tend to be more achievement oriented, and, as a general rule, they obtain more education and better paying jobs. People with an external locus of control may not be motivated to put forth the effort needed to be successful because they believe success is not related to anything they themselves do.

People can have both an internal and external locus of control for success and failure, and these differences can be healthy or harmful. For example, if they are consistently rejected when applying and interviewing for jobs, they may attribute this rejection to lack of qualifications, inability to do the job well, or poor interviewing skills, all beliefs stemming from an internal locus of control. When these same individuals obtain a job, however, they may believe it was because they were the only applicant, there is something wrong with the place of employment because no one else wanted the job, or the place of employment was desperate, all beliefs stemming from an external locus of control. This shift in locus of control is not healthy and may be related to low self-esteem.

On the other hand, after being rejected repeatedly when applying and interviewing for jobs, individuals with an external locus of control may believe that these rejections were due to the unrealistic early hour of the interview, lack of sleep, or lack of ability of the interviewer to appreciate what the applicant had to offer. When these same people obtain a job, they may believe it is due to performing well during interview, doing a good job, and being well prepared, all stemming from an internal locus of control. A balance of internal and external locus of control is best.

As a person grows older and experiences more in life, the locus of control ordinarily shifts. In general, it shifts more toward the internal end of the continuum and, paradoxically, more to the external at the same time. For example, as individuals gain experience in life and integrate these experiences, they learn that effort or lack of effort affects the outcomes. They also learn that there are many things a person has no control over and no matter how hard he or she works, the efforts may have no effect over the outcome, such as is the case with the death of loved ones. This lack of control can create challenges for people who have a strong internal locus of control and can result in their trying harder to gain control, or they can learn from people with an external locus of control that sometimes things happen that a person cannot control, and such a result is acceptable.

Contributed by Darlene Daneker,
Marshall University, Charleston, WV

Additional Resources

Butcher, E., & Hebert, D. J. (1985). Locus of control similarity and counselor effectiveness: A matched case study. *Journal of Counseling & Development, 64,* 103–109.

Locus of Control Survey Web site: http://www.dushkin.com/connectext/psy/ch11/survey11.mhtml for a short test on locus of control

Longitudinal and Cross-Sectional Designs

Longitudinal and cross-sectional designs are two types of descriptive research designs. Researchers use **cross-sectional designs** to look at relationships between variables at one point in time. **Longitudinal designs,** by contrast, involve measurements taken from samples of the same population at two or more times. Although cross-sectional designs allow researchers to identify associations between or among variables, longitudinal designs are needed to measure legitimate change over time. As descriptive designs, neither cross-sectional nor longitudinal designs involves experimentation, and neither can demonstrate causal effects.

Longitudinal studies may be prospective or retrospective. In **prospective designs,** data are collected on at least two occasions, with the data being current at the time collected. In **retrospective designs,** the researcher obtains data relating to a previous time, typically by asking participants to recall that time or by pulling data from existing records. For example, a prospective study may conduct two surveys about attitudes toward psychotherapy, with one done before and one after a televised documentary on the topic. A retrospective study may survey participants after the documentary, asking them about their attitudes before and after they watched the program.

In longitudinal studies, the same cases may or may not be followed over time. A **panel design** involves collecting information from the same people at different points in time. In a **trend study** (sometimes called a **repeated cross-sectional study**), different samples from the same population are used. An example is researchers who are interested in how attitudes toward gay marriage change in a state because of the passage of civil union legislation. With a panel design, researchers could survey a group of people shortly before the legislation took effect and then survey them again a year later. They could then look for changes in the attitudes of these individuals. With a trend study, researchers could survey two separate groups of individuals. They would then look at any differences between the two samples in attitudes toward gay marriage. Assuming that both were sufficiently large random samples of the population of interest, any observed differences were likely due to changes in the overall population rather than due to differences between the participants in the two samples.

Cross-sectional studies have a number of advantages over longitudinal ones. Because there is no need to make measurements over time, they are quicker to complete and, thus, typically less expensive as well. There is also no need to worry about **attrition,** the loss of participants during the course of the research.

By contrast, a longitudinal study takes longer than a cross-sectional study to complete because the data are typically collected at more than one point in time. Retrospective designs, as previously described in this entry, would be an exception. When the same participants are followed over time, attrition becomes a concern because some participants decline to continue participation or cannot be located for follow-up. Attrition can be a significant threat to the validity of the research because the remaining participants may no longer be representative of the population of interest. Financial cost of a study typically increases with its duration and with efforts to reduce attrition, so longitudinal studies tend to be more expensive than cross-sectional studies.

Another disadvantage of cross-sectional designs is that they are subject to cohort effects. **Cohort effects** occur when observed differences between age groups or cohorts are due to differences in generation and experiences rather than age. An example is a researcher who is interested in whether typing speed decreases with age. A cross-sectional study might find that young adults typed more quickly than did adults who were over 65 years; however, this might have nothing to do with age-related declines. It may simply be because the younger age group grew up using computers and, thus, obtained much more experience typing.

A primary disadvantage of cross-sectional designs is that it is impossible to determine the nature of any association found. Social science researchers often point out that correlation does not mean causation. When variables A and B correlate, it may be that A causes B, or that B causes A, or that both A and B are caused by another variable. An example would be a cross-sectional study that found a correlation between parental marital conflict and adolescent substance abuse. It is possible that parents' marital conflict makes a teenager more likely to abuse substances, but it is also possible that the child's substance abuse leads to the marital conflict. A longitudinal study allows the researcher to determine which of these came first. Although this is not sufficient to demonstrate causation, establishing the sequence of events is an important step toward explaining causation.

This still leaves the possibility that some other factor(s) may have caused both the conflict and the substance abuse. Longitudinal studies can lead to better explanations by matching on one or more relevant variables. This allows the researcher to eliminate those matched variables as possible causes of any observed changes. In the previous example, researchers might match subjects on parental substance abuse. This matching would eliminate the possibility that the observed association between teen substance abuse and marital conflict is spurious, due only to the association of these variables with parental substance abuse.

Longitudinal studies, thus, have the potential to lead to better understanding of the relationships among variables. In situations not amenable to experimentation, longitudinal designs may be the best designs available. It is common for researchers to reap the advantages of each design by beginning with a cross-sectional study and using its findings to design an appropriate longitudinal study to elaborate on those findings.

Contributed by Deb Cohen,
University of Delaware, Dover, DE

Additional Resource

Erford, B. T. (Ed.). (2008). *Research and evaluation in counseling.* Boston: Houghton Mifflin/Lahaska Press.

Male Development

Daniel Levinson (1978) wrote *The Season's of a Man's Life,* which is still considered a seminal work on male development. Levinson's research is still one of the most influential works in adult **male development.** Levinson and his research team found that a man's **life structure** evolves through a relatively orderly sequence for all men. **Life structure** refers to the alternating times of stability and change in which critical life choices are being made. Eras in the life structure consist of periods of stability followed by more transitional, structure-changing periods that are often less stable and sometimes chaotic. **Transitional periods,** lasting 4 to 5 years, form a bridge between stable periods. Each change can be completed on a continuum of well to poorly relative to each man's own perceived life satisfaction at that point in his life. **Marker events,** such as being fired or divorced, are events in a man's life requiring some sort of adaptation.

Levinson's theory reveals four overlapping eras, each lasting about 25 years. Each **era** is distinguished by biological, psychological, and social aspects that form the "skeletal structural" of the life cycle. Within these four major eras, a series of developmental periods, including cross-era transitions between early, midlife, and late adulthood, provide the sources of renewal or stagnation that shape the character of an individual man's developmental sequence.

The following six characteristics (Levinson, 1978) define the eras of a man's life cycle:

1. For every period. there is a typical age of onset. There is a range of 2 or 3 years on either side of the average.
2. All of the periods occur in a fixed sequence. That means a man must progress from Phase 1 to 2 and not skip to Phase 4, for example. Being stuck in one phase begins the decline of each man's successful sequential progression from one period to another.
3. In contrast with hierarchical stages in which an individual "progresses" from a lower level to a higher one, this sequence is more a circular progression.
4. Each era features some type of successful–unsuccessful evaluation both by the man himself and by the external world.
5. Rather than being separate and distinct stages, all periods are overlapping and connected.
6. There is a cultural universality of the eras and periods. Levinson stressed that such sequences are universal within all societies throughout the entire spectrum of the human race. Although a particular man goes through the periods in a unique way, the sequence is universal.

Levinson's Stage Theory

The major task of **early adult transition** (ages 17–22 years) is characterized by such tasks as questioning the nature of the world and a man's place in it. One of the major findings from this age period was that all the men of Levinson's (1978) sample formed a life in early adulthood that was quite different from their parents' lives. **Discontinuity** was the term used to characterize a marked shift in the direction of such young men's lives relative to either their own adolescence or the core values of their parents. Culturally, it should be noted that such a trend is more characteristic of Western than Eastern men, who do still tend to retain values similar to their parents' values into adulthood.

Early adulthood begins around age 22 years (plus or minus 2 years) and lasts about 6 to 8 years. It is during this time that the "novice adult" is forging beginning links between the valued self and the adult society. Coupled with a sense of adventure and wonder, there is also a compelling "I must make something of my life" driving existential motivation.

In the **age 30 transition** (28–33 years), the provisional quality of earlier times is replaced with a more authentic sense of oneself as an adult. For most men, there is an age 30 "crisis" in which the man feels that although his present life is in many ways intolerable, he is nonetheless unable to form a better one.

Transition to the **settling down phase** involves a transitional shift, in which men make new choices or reaffirm old decisions if they are still consistent with their current dream. "Moving up the ladder" is a metaphor Levinson used frequently in describing male development. Success at each stage moves a man higher up the ladder, whereas stagnation or failure keeps him stuck or even descending. A man starts on the bottom rung of the ladder. If successful, he pursues a personal enterprise or project and ascends the ladder; if he is discouraged or feels like a failure, upward mobility is halted. Men step onto the ladder as junior members in the hopes of later ascending to being senior members of the adult world.

One of Levinson's most famous developmental phrases for men is that of **becoming one's own man (BOOM).** Speaking in his own voice with a greater sense of authority carries the equal burden of greater stress and responsibility and more letting go of the little boy inside him. During this

BOOM period, the man individuates himself and develops his own unique identity.

Levinson called the period of early adulthood (age 22–40 years) a **novice phase** that consisted of formulating a life dream and giving it a place in the man's life structure; forming a mentor relationship, usually with an older man; being both happy and prosperous in an occupation; and establishing a significant loving relationship, often involving marriage with a partner.

The **entering middle adulthood transitional phase** (ages 40–45 years) is characterized by such existential questions as, What have I done with my life? What is it that I truly want to give and receive for myself and the significant others in my life? How can I best actualize my desires, talents, and aspirations? The following four specific polarities can be successfully resolved and/or result in a feeling of failure, depending on both the man's own personal opinion as well as the messages he receives from significant others relative to their judgments of his effectiveness in moving up the ladder by becoming more successful: (a) the young–old polarity, (b) the destruction–creation polarity, (c) the masculine–feminine polarity, and (d) the attachment–separateness polarity. **Leaving a legacy** is yet another task of this era, a term frequently used in contemporary times to indicate the importance of a man leaving something behind to prove the worth of his existence.

The **entering middle adulthood** phase (45–50 years) is characterized by a series of changes in major defining marker events. The variability of men's level of satisfaction with this season of life begins to forge a major gap between happy and unhappy overall life judgments. The men being judged and judging themselves as being stagnant and/or stepping downward on the ladder often feel they lack both internal and external resources for creating a minimally adequate structure to their life.

The **age 50 transition** (50–55 years) has a series of transitions that are similar to the age 30 transition into middle adulthood. Although the age 50 transition can involve further refining and defining of a man's own personal dream, it can also be a time of great discouragement and despair, depending on where a man is on his existential ladder. An important consideration for men in counseling at this point in their lives is that, according to Levinson, there will be at least a moderate crisis in either the midlife or age 50 transition.

Ages 55 to 60 years involve **building a second middle adult structure,** which provides a vehicle for completing middle adulthood. This is often a time of great rejuvenation characterized by a sense of fulfillment. From about ages 60 to 65 years, the **late transition** terminates middle adulthood and creates the initial formation of a major turning point in the life cycle, marking the final era of a man's life.

Additional Issues in Male Development

Levinson noted that his work focused mostly on middle-age development rather than on late adulthood. Hillier and Barrow (2005) cited important statistics relative to men in later life. Specifically, the population of men age 65 years and older has greatly exceeded the percentage growth of the U.S. population of men as a whole. Furthermore, men 85 years and older are the most rapidly growing age group of those men over 65 years of age. A similar trend is evident worldwide.

Increased life expectancy is a significant factor in male development. Although men still do not live as long as women (75 years for men vs. 81 years for women, on average) decreases in death due to diseases such as heart disease, cerebrovascular disease, and pneumonia have increased men's longevity significantly over the past several decades. With the exception of diabetes, men have higher death rates than women for the following rank-ordered leading causes for death: heart disease, tumors, strokes, pulmonary disease, pneumonia and flu, chronic liver disease, accidents, diabetes, and suicide. White men over age 85 years are at highest risk of suicide (U.S. Census Bureau, 2008). As men live longer, retirement and leisure life will be increasingly important in their lives.

Shepard (2007) explored the importance of adult men of all ages confronting and changing attitudes, stressing that men need to change the trend of being disconnected from vulnerable feelings such as sadness and fear as well as from their nurturing and soothing capacities. Adult men need to develop an emotional vocabulary, connect with their children, and develop the capacity for intimacy.

O'Neil (2001) stressed that a psychology of men is one of the least studied or developed models in psychology. Questions that need to be investigated and answered in future research include such topics as multiculturalism and masculinity, at what age and how should men be educated about the psychology of men, and how feminist ideas relate to the psychology of men.

Contributed by Daniel Eckstein and Andrew Benesh, Sam Houston State University, Houston, TX

References

Hillier, S., & Barrow, G. (2005). *Aging, the individual, and society.* Belmont, CA: Thomson Brooks/Cole.

Levinson, D. (1978). *The seasons of a man's life.* New York: Random House.

O'Neil, J. M. (2001). Promoting men's growth and development: Teaching the new psychology of men using psychoeducational philosophy and interventions. In G. R. Brooks & G. E. Good (Eds.), *The new handbook of psychotherapy and counseling with men: A comprehensive guide to settings, problems, and treatment approaches* (Vol. 2, pp. 639–663). San Francisco: Jossey–Bass.

Shepard, D. (2007) Male development and the journey toward disconnection. In D. Comstock (Ed.), *Diversity and development* (pp. 133–160). Belmont, CA: Thomson Brooks/Cole.

U.S. Census Bureau. (2008). *American factfinder.* Retrieved July 13, 2008, from http://www.factfinder.census.gov

■ Mattering to Others in Counseling

All human beings have the innate desire and need to matter to others, to feel significant to others, and to be needed and wanted by others. Desiring that others take interest in their thoughts, ideas, and feelings is fundamental to humans and paramount to human development across the life span. The feeling of being needed, of being significant to others, of mattering, puts meaning in individuals' lives. **Morris Rosenberg** (Rosenberg & McCullough, 1981) first conceptualized the construct of mattering to others as an integral component of individuals' self-concepts. He hypothesized that all individuals experience varying perceptions of **general mattering** (i.e., mattering in a broad sense to society, workplaces, and communities) and of **interpersonal mattering** (i.e., mattering to specific other individuals). Mattering to others is essential to individuals' sense of self (i.e., all people want to matter to others) and to society (i.e., as an element of social bonding and connection) and plays a crucial role in helping relationships.

Mattering to others is also understood through individuals' self-perceptions of their importance and significance to the world around them and to others in their lives. If individuals do not intrapersonally recognize and believe that they matter, they will not actually experience mattering to others; therefore, the mattering process begins with external, interpersonal dynamics but ultimately takes place on an internal level and affects an individual's internal sense of self and self-concept. The antithesis of mattering is the perception of not mattering, or believing one is insignificant and unimportant to others. The experience of not mattering to others can be detrimental to individuals. Without the perception that they matter, it is easy for individuals to feel "lost" or that they do not "belong."

Mattering to others may vary in degree and form. **Attention mattering** is a cognitive experience and perception of mattering to others; individuals matter if others simply recognize them and acknowledge that they exist. People perceive that they matter when others pay attention to them, and if they do not receive others' attention, they may feel ignored. **Relationship mattering** implies a deeper relationship between an individual and important persons. Relationship mattering can also be bidirectional in these specific relationships, involving two forms of mattering: importance and reliance. The importance form of mattering involves the idea that we, as human beings, matter to others if they reciprocate the interest and concern. Because caring relationships are bidirectional, the "flow" of mattering in the relationship goes both ways. Others are able to show individuals that they care and are interested in individuals' lives. The second form of relationship mattering involves people relying on others in their lives. People matter to others if they depend on them for their needs or wants. As people rely on each other, they are ensured that they matter to each other and can offer each other something that others cannot.

Mattering in the Counseling Relationship

Because individuals need others to pay attention to them, take an interest in them, and consider them important, matter-ing may play a crucial role in counseling relationships. Both professional counselors and clients in counseling relationships want to experience mattering. Through the helping and counseling interventions they perform and the relationships they form, counselors want to matter to their clients. Professional counselors matter to clients if the clients are accountable to them and committed to growth, change, and the counseling relationship. When counselors perceive that they matter to the individuals they are helping, their sense of mattering to their clients will bring greater meaning to their professional lives, and their desire to help others will increase.

Just as professional counselors want to experience a sense of mattering to their clients, most clients need and want to matter to their counselors as well as to others. Through mattering to others, individuals meet their basic needs for relationships; for those who experience not mattering to others, the thought of no longer being needed is shocking. Clients may enter counseling with feelings of hopelessness and helplessness. They can feel as if they are invisible in their lives and matter to no one. Overall, individuals may have greater well-being and feel successful in their lives if they perceive that people value them.

Similarly, clients who perceive that their counselors care for them, that they are important, and that they matter may have greater investment in the counseling process. Clients who believe they matter to their counselors are likely to be more productive in counseling, have a greater sense of trust in their counselors, and increase counseling outcomes. Professional counselors are in appropriate positions to attend to clients, demonstrate how important clients are to the counselor and counseling process, and illustrate to clients that counselors rely on clients for successful counseling goals and outcomes. Thus, professional counselors and clients can experience the positive consequences of the flow of mattering between them. This flow of mattering can be optimized by the professional counselor in a number of ways in order to strengthen the counseling relationship. Mattering in the counseling relationship provides professional counselors another method for helping clients to find and make meaning in their lives.

Contributed by Andrea Dixon,
University of Florida, Gainesville, FL

Reference

Rosenberg, M., & McCullough, B. (1981). Mattering: Inferred significance and mental health among adolescents. *Research in Community and Mental Health, 2,* 163–182.

Additional Resources

Elliott, G. C., Kao, S., & Grant, A. M. (2004). Mattering: Empirical validation of a social psychological construct. *Self and Identity, 3,* 339–354.

Rayle, A. D. (2006). Mattering to others: Implications for the counseling relationship. *Journal of Counseling & Development, 84,* 483–487.

Mental Health Practitioners

Mental health practitioners are professionals trained to assist clients with developmental and psychological issues, from coping with difficulties in life to serious mental and emotional disorders. Although there is a significant amount of overlap among the services provided by mental health practitioners, the mental health professions may be distinguished by their emphasis and training. The mental health practitioners described in this entry include professional counselors, psychologists, psychiatrists, psychoanalysts, social workers, psychiatric nurses, marriage and family counselors or therapists, and psychotherapists.

Professional Counselors

Professional counselors work with clients across a wide spectrum of concerns, such as prevention, career concerns, and coping strategies as well as more serious psychological disorders. Professional counselors are distinguished from other mental health professionals by their emphasis on wellness, prevention of psychological difficulties, and focus on optimizing human development across the life span. In many states, counselors can also administer psychological tests.

Professional counselors work in a variety of settings, such as community mental health centers, health maintenance organizations, employee assistance programs, schools, substance abuse programs, hospitals, family agencies, and private practice. Counselors are required to have a master's degree in counseling or a related program, and many universities offer doctoral degrees in counselor education. Professional counselors are licensed in 49 states and the District of Columbia and are eligible to be reimbursed by many insurance providers.

Psychologists

Psychologists provide a range of services to clients, from the diagnosis and treatment of psychological disorders to administering psychological tests, and may specialize in many areas, such as clinical, counseling, and school psychology. Psychologists practice in a wide variety of settings, including inpatient settings, community mental health centers, schools, and private practice. A doctoral degree is required for licensure, although bachelor's and master's degrees in psychology are available. Psychologists are licensed in all 50 states and are eligible to be reimbursed by insurance providers.

Psychiatrists

Psychiatrists are physicians who focus on working with clients with serious psychological disorders. Many psychiatrists work from a biomedical approach, focusing on the biological aspects of the treatment of psychological disorders, such as prescribing medication. Some psychiatrists also use psychotherapeutic approaches. The educational requirements for psychiatrists include a medical degree and a residency program in psychiatry. Psychiatrists are licensed in all 50 states.

Psychoanalysts

Psychoanalysts are mental health professionals who conduct psychoanalysis with clients. They engage in long-term, in-depth psychotherapy, which is designed to resolve a client's unconscious conflicts. In addition to a graduate degree in a related field, training involves undergoing psychoanalysis and several years of study at a psychoanalysis institute. Psychoanalysts may practice in a variety of settings, but they often are in private practice. Some states offer licensure for psychoanalysts.

Social Workers

Social workers provide a broad range of services, such as administering social programs; implementing public policy; advocating for social change; and conducting therapy with individuals, families, and groups. Social workers focus on working with clients within their social context, such as families and communities. Social workers are distinguished from other mental health professionals by their emphasis on the client's social context, public policy, and advocacy for change in social systems.

Social workers practice in a variety of settings, including community agencies, health maintenance organizations, inpatient settings, nursing homes, and private practice. Independent licensure requires a master's degree, and many universities offer bachelor's and doctoral degrees. Social workers are licensed in all 50 states and are eligible to be reimbursed by insurance providers.

Psychiatric Nurses

Psychiatric nurses are registered nurses who have received specialized training in the care of clients with serious mental and emotional disorders. Most psychiatric nurses work in inpatient settings and can conduct individual and group therapy. Registered nurses may choose to pursue master's or doctoral degrees in psychiatric nursing. With such advanced training, in some states it is possible for psychiatric nurses to practice independently. Furthermore, in some states, they may prescribe medications. Psychiatric nurses are licensed or regulated in all 50 states. It is possible for psychiatric nurses to receive insurance reimbursement.

Marriage and Family Counselors or Therapists

Marriage and family counselors or therapists focus on relationship issues in their work with individuals, couples, and families. They use a systemic approach and focus on making changes in the family system. Marriage and family counselors or therapists practice in a variety of settings, such as community mental health centers, private practice, and hospitals. Marriage and family counselors or therapists must have at least a master's degree. Many states license or certify marriage and family counselors or therapists. In addition, in some states, working with couples and families is within the scope of other licensed mental health professionals. Marriage and family counselors or therapists are often reimbursed by insurance providers.

Psychotherapists

Psychotherapist is a commonly used term that does not have a clearly defined professional identity; that is, counselors, psychologists, psychoanalysts, social workers, or psychiatrists may refer to themselves as psychotherapists, usually as a generic way to describe what they do while counseling clients. In many states, counseling and psychotherapy are defined synonymously. Some professionals specify that psychotherapy focuses on the remediation of serious psychological problems, which often involves long-term therapeutic relationships.

Contributed by Jacqueline A. Walsh,
California University of Pennsylvania,
California, PA

Additional Resources

Corey, M. S., & Corey, G. (2007). *Becoming a helper* (5th ed.). Belmont, CA: Thomson.

Gladding, S. T. (2004). *Counseling: A comprehensive profession* (5th ed.). Upper Saddle River, NJ: Merrill Prentice Hall.

MacCluskie, K. C., & Ingersoll, R. E. (2001). *Becoming a 21st century agency counselor.* Pacific Grove, CA: Brooks/Cole.

◼ *Mental Measurements Yearbook* and the Buros Institute

Since 1938, the ***Mental Measurements Yearbook (MMY)*** has offered critiques of major, commercially available testing and assessment instruments in the English language. The first volume was published in 1938 by **Oscar K. Buros,** who founded the **Buros Institute of Mental Measurements (BIMM)** a year later in 1939 (BIMM, 2004). Experts in the field of testing and assessment have contributed to subsequent volumes of the *MMY* and are now recognized as "distinguished reviewers" by the BIMM when they make six or more contributions to this comprehensive resource (Spies & Plake, 2005). The *MMY* offers relevant and timely information, including the test name, acronym, author, publisher, copyright date, purpose, cost, form, scales/scores derived, test population, typical administration time, and objective reviews by testing professionals. *MMY* is currently in its 16th volume (Spies & Plake, 2005) and is published every 2 to 8 years, with each volume offering new or recently revised/updated versions of major tests in the field of testing and assessment.

MMY test summaries are designed to inform professionals about tests and their various uses. Specifically, the *MMY* was "developed to stimulate critical thinking and assist in the selection of the best available test for a given purpose, not to promote the passive acceptance of reviewer judgment" (Spies & Plake, 2005, p. xi). These independent reviews add to the credibility of assessment instruments because there is no inherent motive to market the examinations to the professional public. In addition to *MMY*, BIMM publishes a companion publication called *Tests in Print (TIP)*, which presents all the major, commercially available tests in the English language but in a briefer format than *MMY* because it lacks the independent test reviews *MMY* provides. One of the main differences between these two resources is that *TIP* has a listing of all major, commercially available tests that have been listed in all the *MMY*s from 1938 if they are not obsolete or out of print. The first *TIP* volume was published in 1961, some 33 years after the first *MMY*. *TIP* is currently in its seventh volume (published 2006) and is published every 3 to 13 years.

Both *MMY* and *TIP* have bibliographies and references that identify additional test reviews, analysis, and research studies using each of the identified test instruments. For any test, cross-referenced codings are provided in the *MMY* and *TIP* so that a person can find further information about a test or its revisions. Some indexes common to both resources are test titles, acronyms, subject categories, publisher directory, names (e.g., tests, authors, reviews, references), and scores/scales indexes for not only overall test scales but also their subscales for all the major test instruments in the field of assessment. *TIP*, unlike *MMY*, has an additional index identifying tests that have recently gone out of print. *MMY* and *TIP* have critical assessment information for people in the fields of education, psychology, and business to help assist test examiners make better decisions regarding appropriate test selection and test usage (BIMM, 2004).

The online version of *MMY* allows instant access to a comprehensive index of tests from 1985 to the present. This is particularly convenient for students or professionals who need to access important information about potential assessment instruments. There is a per title fee for each test review, although students may be able to receive these reviews free of charge through subscriptions purchased by many university libraries. BIMM provides one of the best testing resources for anyone interested in researching a particular assessment or interested in determining what instruments may be available to evaluate a certain personality characteristic or personal domain.

Professional counselors can use these important resources best by becoming familiar with the content of the reviews as they investigate tests that are potentially beneficial to those they serve. Reading test reviews helps determine how widely and in what contexts tests are used and the preparation, experience, and cost necessary for their use. Testing becomes a tool to serve clients better by assisting counselors in diagnosis and treatment of psychiatric disorders. For professionals experienced in test use, these resources offer current information regarding tests and their implementation. The *MMY* and *TIP* are essential resources for counselors who use testing in their professional practice.

Contributed by Scott Rasmus, Lifespan,
Inc., Hamilton, OH, and Matthew
Buckley, Delta State University,
Cleveland, MS

References

Buros Institute of Mental Measurements. (2004). *Publications catalog.* Retrieved May 31, 2007, from http://www.unl.edu/buros/bimm/html/catalog.html

Spies, R. A., & Plake, B. S. (Eds.). (2005). *The sixteenth mental measurements yearbook*. Lincoln: University of Nebraska Press.

Additional Resource

Buros Institute of Mental Measurements Web site: http://www.unl.edu/buros

Mental Retardation

Mental retardation can be defined as significantly below average intellectual and adaptive functioning. **Intellectual functioning** is measured by an individual's IQ score obtained from a standardized intelligence test. **Adaptive functioning** refers to an individual's ability to meet the standards of independent living as appropriate for an individual of that particular age. In order to meet the criteria for diagnosis of mental retardation, an individual ordinarily has an IQ score below 70 (i.e., more than 2 standard deviations below the mean on an individualized test of intelligence) and demonstrates significant delays in at least two of the following areas of adaptive functioning: communication, self-care, home living, social skills, use of community resources, self-direction, functional academic skills, work, leisure, health, and safety. The onset of the characteristics of mental retardation occurs before the age of 18 years. The overall prevalence for this disorder ranges between 1% to 3% of the U.S. population, depending on how mental retardation is defined and measured (American Psychiatric Association [APA], 2000). Boys are more frequently diagnosed with mental retardation than are girls.

There are four degrees of severity of mental retardation: mild, moderate, severe, and profound; each reflects a specific level of intellectual impairment. **Mild mental retardation** includes IQ scores between 50–55 and 70; approximately 85% of individuals with mental retardation can be classified in this category. The intellectual functioning of most individuals diagnosed with mild mental retardation will reach approximately the sixth-grade level. **Moderate mental retardation** includes IQ scores between 35–40 and 50–55 and includes approximately 10% of those individuals diagnosed with mental retardation. Intellectual functioning of most individuals with moderate mental retardation reaches approximately the second-grade level. **Severe mental retardation** includes IQ scores between 20–25 and 35–40; approximately 3% to 4% of individuals diagnosed with mental retardation can be classified in this category. **Profound mental retardation** includes IQ scores below 20–25; only 1% to 2% of individuals with mental retardation are classified in this category (APA, 2000).

Although the specific causes of mental retardation are sometimes unknown, there are some factors related to the onset of the disorder. Some of these factors include genetic conditions, such as fragile X syndrome and Down syndrome; prenatal or early environmental issues, such as fetal alcohol syndrome and premature birth; and other health disorders, such as infections. In approximately 30% of all individuals with mental retardation, no etiology can be determined.

Mental retardation is coded on Axis II of the multiaxial system of the *Diagnostic and Statistical Manual of Mental Disorders* (4th ed., text rev.; APA, 2000).

There is no "cure" for mental retardation; however, many individuals with this diagnosis can receive behavioral, psychopharmacological, and educational interventions to help them reach their fullest potential. Behavioral interventions are often used to increase adaptive skills and decrease maladaptive behaviors. Psychopharmacological interventions are used to alleviate some of the cognitive, behavioral, or psychiatric difficulties that may occur along with mental retardation. Finally, special education interventions are implemented in the least restrictive environment to educate children diagnosed with mental retardation. In addition to the aforementioned interventions, opportunities exist in the community to help individuals with mental retardation live as independently as possible. For example, employment opportunities for individuals with mental retardation have increased. Supervised residential settings also exist where several individuals with mental retardation live together. Overall, many individuals with mental retardation live productive and independent lives, whereas others require a greater degree of structure to be successful.

Contributed by Kristi Bracchitta,
College of Mount Saint Vincent,
Riverdale, NY

Reference

American Psychiatric Association. (2000). *Diagnostic and statistical manual of mental disorders* (4th ed., text rev.). Washington, DC: Author.

Additional Resources:

American Association on Intellectual and Developmental Disabilities. (2002). *Mental retardation: Definition, classification, and systems of supports* (10th ed.). Washington, DC: Author.

Handen, B. L. (1997). Mental retardation. In E. J. Mash & L. G. Terdal (Eds.), *Assessment of childhood disorders* (3rd ed., pp. 369–407). New York: Guilford Press.

Murphy, C. C., Boyle, C., Schendel, D., Decoufle, P., & Yeargin-Allsopp, M. (1998). Epidemiology of mental retardation in children. *Mental Retardation and Developmental Disabilities Research Reviews, 4*, 6–13.

Mental Status Examination

The **mental status examination (MSE)** is used by medical and psychological practitioners. The psychological community uses the MSE to obtain a clinical snapshot of a client's signs and symptoms for level-of-care admission screenings (e.g., inpatient, partial hospitalization, day treatment) and as part of standardized intake documents to obtain a baseline for future treatment. The medical community primarily uses specialized applications of the MSE, called the **mini-mental state examination (MMSE;** Folstein, Folstein, & McHugh, 1975) and the **standardized mini-mental state examination (SMMSE;** Molloy, Alemaychu, & Robert, 1991) to determine the cognitive state of geriatric medical patients with dementia and to assess stroke and head trauma victims.

The MSE assists the clinician in organizing the signs and symptoms needed to develop a differential diagnosis. Conducting a proper and complete MSE is essential to ensure quality diagnostic formulations and to apply the appropriate treatment in outpatient and inpatient settings. Observations should focus on factual examples because these will serve as the cornerstone of the diagnostic picture according to the criteria in the *Diagnostic and Statistical Manual of Mental Disorders* (4th ed., text rev.; American Psychiatric Association, 2000). These observations may be obtained through the use of checklists (e.g., whether a patient's speech is normal, soft, loud, pressured, incoherent, rapid), standardized questions, or circular Socratic questioning. Regardless of the method of questioning, a complete MSE must address several key areas. These include appearance, movement and behavior, mood and affect, thought and content, perceptions, thought process, judgment and insight, and intellectual functioning and memory.

Appearance includes the patient's age, race, hygiene, grooming, posture, and clothing choice. Clinicians note aspects of the client's appearance that would stand out to an observant viewer. Clients may be disheveled and have body odor/halitosis, or they may appear excessively well groomed, bizarrely dressed, or dressed in militaristic manner. Clients may be overweight, average weight, underweight, or emaciated. They may have a noticeable hairstyle or an unnatural hair color. They may have scars, tattoos, jewelry, glasses, or braces. These initial observations may match larger themes that become evident as the interview continues.

Movement and behavior are descriptive terms used to describe clients' walk (e.g., limp, shuffle, assisted), eye contact, facial expressions, and general manner of conducting themselves. The professional counselor should describe the client's gestures, any presence of tics, overactivity, and mimicry and whether or not he or she is combative or aggressive. The professional counselor should mention the client's attitude toward the examiner. Is the client's manner seductive, friendly and cooperative, playful, defensive, hostile, attentive, or interested? Is the client alert and coherent in his or her responses?

Mood and affect describe the qualities that relate to the client's emotions. A client's **affect** is the current external expression of his or her mood; it is subject to frequent change. A client's **mood** is the pervasive way he or she feels most of the time. A client's affect may appear blunted, expansive/euphoric, constricted, flat, silly, guarded, or labile. A client's mood may be depressed, euphoric, irritable, angry, pleasant, fearful, apathetic, or neutral. The professional counselor should note the quality and intensity of the client's observable affect and whether it is congruent with his or her reported underlying mood. Incongruence between affect and mood may indicate a possible psychotic disorder or guarded presentation. The counselor should also note if the client is able to express a full range of appropriate emotions (i.e., emotions congruent with context). A restricted range of emotions may indicate a depressive or manic episode;

response to internal stimuli; or a guarded, obsessed, or distracted state. The client may also be experiencing symptoms, such as insomnia, hypersomnia, disordered eating, and diminished libido, that may have an impact on his or her affect and mood. It is also important to note any substance use and the use (or lack of use) of psychotropic medications that may affect the patient's underlying mood and observable affect. Mood and affect should be assessed with respect to the environmental stressors at hand. For example, extreme or odd affect and mood may occur following traumatic events such as the death of a spouse or a serious accident.

Thought content pertains to the details of the client's cognitions. These include suicidal or homicidal ideation, depressive thoughts, symptoms of dissociations, delusions, obsessions, phobias, and feelings of paranoia. The client may exhibit thought broadcasting (i.e., in which the client believes other people can hear his or her thoughts) or thought insertion (i.e., in which the client believes another person is inserting thoughts into the client's head). The professional counselor should explore positive endorsements of any abnormal thought content areas. For example, if clients report they are suicidal, the clinician should ascertain if there is a plan, the lethality risk, if there have been past attempts, if they have access to means, and whether or not a note has been written or personal items given away (see Suicide Assessment).

Perceptions refer to a client's illusions (e.g., seeing an unidentified flying object when others see correctly that is a weather balloon or a plane), derealizations (e.g., out-of-body experiences or feeling that one's body is changing its shape or size), and hallucinations (i.e., visual, auditory, tactile, olfactory, gustatory). When assessing hallucinations, the professional counselor should determine whether they are command (i.e., ordering the client to do things) or persecutory in nature, the number of voices, and their age and gender. Obtaining detailed information on hallucinations may be useful in ruling out malingering. Perceptions may also include déjà vu, feelings as if the client has been somewhere or done something before, or *jamais vu,* a familiar place or feeling that the patient should remember but cannot.

Thought process refers to the connections between thoughts and their relationship to the conversations at hand. A client's thought process may be logical or illogical, coherent or incoherent, or it may be circumstantial, tangential, loose, flight of ideas, or rambling. The patient may express neologisms (i.e., nonsense words or real words used out of place) or may include irrelevant details or repeated words or phrases. Odd or uncommon thought processes may include clang associations (i.e., associations resulting from sounds), word salad (i.e., a total incoherence of speech found in severely regressed psychotic patients), or a flight of ideas (i.e., a disturbance in the flow of thought manifested through rapid speech with abrupt changes of topics).

Judgment and **insight** questions assess the client's ability to make commonsense decisions in everyday situations (e.g., Why is it better to build a house out of brick than of wood? What should you do if you see a train approaching a broken track?). Judgment can be poor, adequate, impaired, critical, automatic, or impulsive. Insight refers to clients' ability to appreciate their surroundings and how well they understand the environment. Clients may have impaired insight, including, but not limited to, denying their disorder.

Intellectual functioning and **memory** questions assess the level of intellect (e.g., superior, average, retardation, dementia), fund of knowledge (e.g., identifying the last four presidents), ability to perform calculations (e.g., counting backward by 7 from 100—also called serial 7s), and ability to think abstractly (e.g., What does "There is no use crying over spilt milk" or "The mouse that has but one hole is soon caught" mean? "How are a mountain and a lake similar?" "What do the numbers 49 and 121 have in common?" "How are scissors and a copper pan alike?"). Memory questions are designed to assess immediate memory ability (e.g., asking the client to repeat a series of numbers backward and forward), recalling common objects after 5 minutes (e.g., ball, man, pencil, and cat), and remote memory (e.g., recalling events that are days or years old). The professional counselor should also note clients' orientation to the environment in terms of who they are (e.g., name, type of work), when it is (e.g., year, season, month, day), and where they are (e.g., country, state, city, building, floor).

The professional counselor often applies shorthand notations for several common terms and conditions. The notation, OX3, indicates orientation in the three spheres; person (who he or she is), place (where he or she is), and time (when it is). Suicidal ideations are represented by SI, and HI indicates suicidal ideations and homicidal ideations, respectively. The + or − sign indicates the presence or absence of signs or symptoms. SA refers to substance abuse, and H/V or H/A often refers to either visual or auditory hallucinations, respectively. For example "HI−, SI+ w/plan to hang self; H/V−, H/A−, SA+ 3–4 beers, 2 X week" would indicate a client who denies homicidal ideation and visual or audio hallucinations, indicates suicidal ideation with a plan to kill himself by hanging, and drinks 3–4 beers twice a week.

The MMSE and SMMSE are specialized applications of the MSE used to screen cognitive problems in older adults along with assessing differential dementia and stage of the disease. Folstein et al. (1975) developed the MMSE for use in hospitals to assess patients who were elderly for dementia. The SMMSE was created by Molloy et al. in 1991. This instrument drastically improved the interrater and intrarater reliability and shortened administration time.

The SMMSE consists of 20 items and is scored on a 30-point scale, with scores lower than 23 indicating significant cognitive impairment. The SMMSE is broken down into several categories, including clients' orientation (e.g., naming their location, the year, month, day of the week), memory and registration (i.e., recalling three common words like *ball, car,* and *man*), attention and calculation (i.e., counting backward from 100 by 7s or 3s, spelling *w-o-r-l-d* backward), and language and fine motor ability (e.g., naming common objects such as a watch and pencil; following simple commands like "take a paper in your hand, fold it in half and place it on the floor"; and copying a simple diagram).

Contributed by Brian Van Brunt, New England College, Henniker, NH

References

American Psychiatric Association. *Diagnostic and statistical manual of mental disorders* (4th ed., text rev.). Washington, DC: Author.

Folstein, M., Folstein, S. E., & McHugh, P. R. (1975). "Mini-mental state" a practical method for grading the cognitive state of patients for the clinician. *Journal of Psychiatric Research, 12,* 189–198.

Molloy, D. W., Alemaychu, E., & Robert, R. (1991). A Standardized Mini-Mental State Examination: Its reliability compared to the traditional mini-mental state examination. *American Journal of Psychiatry, 48,* 102–105.

Additional Resources

Robinson, D. J. (2002). *The mental status exam explained.* Port Huron, MI: Rapid Psychler Press.

Trzepac, P. T., & Baker, R. W. (1993). *The psychiatric mental status examination.* Oxford, United Kingdom: Oxford University Press.

■ Meta-Analysis

Research within counseling subspecialties has increased considerably over the past 2 decades. As a result, counseling professionals and counselor educators have the daunting task of synthesizing and interpreting findings from individual studies that may yield equivocal or even contradictory recommendations and conclusions. From this accumulation of information, counseling researchers, as they devise future studies, must impose some order on and coherency to the mass of statistical findings. Similarly, counseling practitioners must have an efficient way of filtering the research as they plan their interventions. Although there are multiple ways to integrate results across studies, **meta-analysis** has assumed a significant role in quantitatively summarizing and reviewing the counseling and psychotherapy research literature (Chan & Rosenthal, 2006).

First proposed in the 1970s (Glass, 1976), meta-analysis has several key advantages. It attempts to minimize the subjectivity inherent in more conventional research synthesis procedures such as narrative literature reviews or vote counting methods (i.e., counting up the number of findings pro or con for a particular research conclusion; Gall, Gall, & Borg, 2007; Hunter & Schmidt, 2004). Through meta-analysis, researchers have a more standardized way to reexamine statistically the quantitative outcomes of previous studies, with the aim of locating general trends in the findings and expressing them as an overall "average" result. In other words, the results from a meta-analysis provide an aggregate picture of the phenomenon under investigation.

Basic Procedures and Outcome Measure

Instead of collecting raw data, a meta-analysis uses quantitative information already gathered and reported in published empirical studies and technical reports. It is conducted in a relatively straightforward manner. Researchers (a) identify pertinent studies based on clearly predetermined criteria for inclusion in the meta-analysis sample, including, for example, those investigations with the same or similar dependent and independent variables; (b) obtain copies of the publications; (c) code the studies to meet the purpose of the meta-analysis; (d) cull the key statistical results from each selected study; (e) synthesize the findings using certain statistical indexes; and (f) generate overall conclusions based on the strength of these indices (Gall et al., 2007; Glass, McGaw, & Smith; 1981; Hunter & Schmidt, 2004). Because the outcomes from various studies are measured on different scales, their statistical results are transformed into a common metric called an **effect size (ES)**. This effect size then becomes the outcome measure or the dependent variable in a meta-analysis.

The **ES index** estimates the magnitude of an independent variable's effect on the dependent variable, usually expressed as a proportion (ratio) of explained variance. Typically, an effect size ranges between 0 and 1, with higher values reflecting a larger effect and a greater amount of explained variance in the dependent variable. However, because effect sizes are scaled in standard deviation (*SD*) units, it is entirely possible for them to be substantially higher than 1, indicating a "very effective" treatment, and less than 0, suggesting a possible "harmful" treatment effect.

An effect size comparing the means from two groups is easily calculated by subtracting the mean (*M*) of the intervention (experimental) group at postintervention from the mean of the control (comparison) group at postintervention divided by the pooled or weighted standard deviation of the two groups. This index is comparable to a Cohen's *d* and is interpreted similarly to a *z* score. This ratio can also be represented as a mathematical formula,

$$\frac{M_{\text{intervention}} - M_{\text{control}}}{SD_{\text{pooled}}},$$

where SD_{pooled} is the square root of the average of the squared standard deviations taken from each group's distribution. The formula for the denominator is:

$$SD_{pooled} = \sqrt{\frac{SD_c^2 + SD_i^2}{2}}.$$

Confidence intervals are often placed around effect sizes. A *d* index can be computed from a variety of statistics such as a correlation (*r*), *t* value, and Hedges's *g* (see Kline, 2004; Sink & Stroh, 2006; Thompson, 2002, 2006). Effect sizes can also be calculated using pre- and posttest scores of a single group in studies without a control or comparison group. Such effects are often of a higher magnitude than those attained when control or comparison groups are used.

To reiterate, in a meta-analysis the dependent variable is the effect size calculated from each investigation's quantitative results. Because the effect size is based on standard deviation units, this index is used to convert the numerical outcomes from each reviewed study into a common measure. Effect sizes reflect the relative magnitude of an effect in a metric common across studies. Once the statistical findings from each study included in the meta-analysis have been transformed into an effect size, researchers can then compare effect sizes over studies using any one of the commonly used statistical procedures. For example, effect sizes from all meta-analyzed studies can be averaged, correlated, and tested using appropriate statistical procedures (Glass et al., 1981). In addition, effect sizes can be interpreted in terms of percentile ranks and confidence intervals (Thompson, 2006).

A positive effect size index value reflects that the intervention group outperformed the control group, and a negative score has the reverse meaning. Furthermore, although there are no definitive criteria to determine practical significance of research results, Cohen (1992) suggested threshold numbers (cutoffs) for categorizing the magnitude of a *d* effect size: Small, medium, and large are the absolute values, 0.2, 0.5, and 0.8, respectively. As a rule, the stronger (or higher) the effect sizes, the more convincing the evidence is that the statistically significant results are useful for counseling practice. Finally, effect sizes of the same magnitude are equivalent across studies because they have been standardized; that is, a 0.50 effect size from one investigation is equivalent to a 0.50 effect size from another study, indicating that the intervention examined in both studies was equally effective.

In counseling studies that compare the impact of an independent variable on participants' scores in the experimental and control groups, an effect size of +1.00 indicates that the experimental group changed 1 standard deviation more than did the control group. If the effect size was –1.00, the control would have outperformed the experimental group by one standard deviation. Put differently, if a counseling researcher using a meta-analysis procedure found a mean effect size of 1.00 (a large effect size) across a variety of similar studies, this value would signify that the average counseling client in one sample scored in the 84th percentile of the other (control) group's score distribution (i.e., 1 standard deviation above the mean is the 84th percentile rank). A small effect size of 0.33 indicates that the average client scored at the 63rd percentile of the total score distribution (i.e., .33 standard deviation above the mean is the 63rd percentile rank).

Effect size magnitudes are affected by the psychometric properties (e.g., reliability coefficients) of the measures used, the absolute difference among group means, the shape of the score distribution, and the sample size (Sink & Stroh, 2006; Thompson, 2002). As such, relatively small effects (i.e., ES < 0.30) may still possess some practical value, and the reverse can be true for large effects. Therefore, if the results of a meta-analysis indicate an average effect size of 0.20 across multiple studies examining the efficacy of a particular counseling intervention, the researcher should not immediately assume this intervention has minimal clinical value. Counselors and researchers need to view the derived effect sizes within their research context (Thompson, 2006). For example, practitioners wondering if they should use a new counseling procedure or not must look at, for instance, the quality of studies used in the meta-analysis, the characteristics of the outcome measure on which the effect size is based (e.g., is it number of days of hospitalization, intervention cost, long-term recidivism rates following treatment, or subjective self-reports of psychological pain or discomfort?), how the dependent variables were measured, and so on.

Thus, the interpretation of the practical or clinical significance of every effect size eventually rests with the counseling researcher (Thompson, 2002; Vacha-Hasse & Thompson, 2004). Any effect size should always be situated within the context of previous related counseling literature, the studies' research designs and procedures, and clinical impact of the findings. An effect size is only an aid to interpretation of the results, not the final word on the utility of the research findings. Next, an example of a meta-analytic study from the counseling literature is summarized.

Example of Meta-Analysis in Counseling Research

A meta-analytic study was conducted to investigate the efficacy of multicultural educational interventions (Smith, Constantine, Dunn, Dinehart, & Montoya, 2006). The researchers noted that studies on multicultural competence have resulted in contradictory findings on the effects of multicultural educational interventions. Some studies have indicated significant ethnic and gender effects on multicultural counseling competence. Others have indicated no statistical difference in multicultural competence based on ethnicity or gender.

To investigate the effect of multicultural educational intervention on multicultural competence, Smith et al. (2006) conducted two meta-analyses. The first examined survey studies. Typically, data in these studies were gathered via questionnaires sent to existing groups. Analysis was conducted by comparing those who reported having been trained in multicultural education to those without training. The second meta-analysis was a review of outcome-based studies. In these studies, data were gathered before and after the multicultural educational intervention. Most of these studies used an experimental or quasi-experimental research design.

Smith et al. (2006) determined the studies to be included in the meta-analysis based on set criteria that included (a) time frame during which the study was conducted, (b) English as the language in which the article was written, (c) the dependent variable measured quantitatively, and (d) a comparison of different formats of multicultural educational interventions in the study. On the basis of these criteria, 45 studies were included in the first meta-analysis, and 37 were included in the second.

For the first meta-analysis, the overall, or omnibus effect size, as measured by Cohen's d ($d = .49$; 95% confidence interval .41– .56) indicated a moderate effect. This demonstrates that, on average, those who reported previous participation in multicultural educational interventions had multicultural counseling competence that was about .5 standard deviation above their nontrained counterparts.

For the second meta-analysis, the omnibus effect size (Cohen's $d = .98$; 95% confidence interval .77 – 1.19) indicated a strong effect. This finding suggests that, on average, those who participated in multicultural educational training grew in their multicultural counseling competence by about 1 standard deviation. In these analyses, neither ethnicity nor

gender had a significant effect on multicultural counseling competence. Thus, the researchers were able to show in both meta-analyses that although there are contradictions in the studies on multicultural competence, there is an overall positive effect of multicultural educational interventions.

Comments and Criticisms of Meta-Analysis

Although meta-analysis has many advantages, it is not without its critics (see Bushman & Wells, 2001, or Hunter & Schmidt, 2004, for thorough discussions). A criticism of meta-analysis is that poorly designed studies are given equal weight as studies that are more carefully designed and executed; thus, a good meta-analysis of poorly designed studies will produce questionable results. On the other hand, merely excluding these "poor" studies brings subjectivity to the process. Another criticism of meta-analysis is that it relies heavily on published studies. This makes the procedure susceptible to **publication bias** because studies that show nonsignificant results are generally harder to publish (i.e., the **file drawer effect**). In interpreting the results of a meta-analysis, it is important to note that studies with nonsignificant results are not well represented in the public domain.

Even though these disadvantages are noteworthy, meta-analysis is a research tool that provides practitioners and researchers with a reliable way of comparing results across a group of related counseling studies. The derived effect sizes are versatile quantitative indices. As with all research methods, there are caveats to meta-analysis. Interpretation of effect sizes must always be contextualized to the research and clinical settings from which the research findings were drawn.

Contributed by Christopher A. Sink and Nyaradzo Mvududu, Seattle Pacific University, Seattle, WA

References

Bushman, B. J., & Wells, G. L. (2001). Narrative impressions of literature: The availability bias and the corrective properties of meta-analytic approaches. *Personality and Social Psychology Bulletin, 27,* 1123–1130.

Chan, F., & Rosenthal, D. A. (2006). Advanced research methodology in rehabilitation. *Rehabilitation Counseling Bulletin, 49,* 219–222.

Cohen, J. (1992). A power primer. *Psychological Bulletin, 112,* 155–159.

Gall, M. D., Gall, M. D., & Borg, W. R. (2007). *Educational research: An introduction* (8th ed.). New York: Longman.

Glass, G. V. (1976). Primary, secondary, and meta-analysis of research. *Educational Researcher, 5,* 3–8.

Glass, G. V., McGaw, B., & Smith, M. L. (1981). *Meta-analysis in social research.* Beverly Hills, CA: Sage.

Hunter, J. E., & Schmidt, F. L. (2004). *Methods of meta-analysis: Correcting error and bias in research findings* (2nd ed.). Thousand Oaks, CA: Sage.

Kline, R. B. (2004). *Beyond significance testing.* Washington, DC: American Psychological Association.

Sink, C. A., & Stroh, H. (2006). Practical significance: Use of effect sizes in school counseling research. *Professional School Counseling, 9,* 401–411.

Smith, T. B., Constantine, M. G., Dunn, T. W., Dinehart, J. M., & Montoya, J. A. (2006). Multicultural education in the mental health professions: A meta-analytic review. *Journal of Counseling Psychology, 53,* 132–145.

Thompson, B. (2002). "Statistical," "practical," and "clinical": How many kinds of significance do counselors need to consider? *Journal of Counseling & Development, 80,* 64–71.

Thompson, B. (2006). Role of effect sizes in contemporary research in counseling. *Counseling and Values, 50,* 176–186.

Vacha-Haase, T., & Thompson, B. (2004). How to estimate and interpret various effect sizes. *Journal of Counseling and Psychology, 51,* 473–481.

■ Microskills Counseling

Microskills are a hierarchy of specific skills that professional counselors use when interviewing clients. The microskills model is frequently used to teach counselors-in-training the basics of individual and group counseling. The microskills approach, developed by Allen E. Ivey and Mary Bradford Ivey, sees client growth and development as the aim of counseling.

The 18 skills covered in this approach are common to most theories (see Table 1). The technical skills are taught first and then practiced. The aim is for the counselor to learn to identify and classify each skill, then develop competence using the skill at a basic, intentional, and finally, teaching level. A beginning counselor is expected to have basic competence with all the skills and, hopefully, intentional competence with several. Even novice counselors should begin to develop teaching competence so that they can teach clients how to listen and express feelings. Microskills are organized into a hierarchy representing the successive steps of intentional interviewing. The base of the hierarchy is ethics, multicultural competence, and wellness. These foundational principles are emphasized throughout the model.

To begin an interview, a professional counselor uses attending behavior and the basic listening sequence. Attending behavior is used to encourage the client to tell his or her story. **Attending behavior** includes eye contact, vocal quality, verbal tracking, and body language. Questions allow the counselor to direct the interview. There are two basic styles: closed and open questions. **Closed questions** can be answered in a few words and are used to focus the interview or obtain information that is more specific (e.g., Does your dad live with you?). **Open questions** encourage the client to talk more freely (e.g., "Tell me more about that"). Professional counselors are urged to ask essential open questions like "What else?" or "How did that affect you?" **Observation**

Table 1. Microskills Summary

Skill	Definition	Example
Attending behavior	Use visuals (eye contact), vocal qualities, verbal tracking, and body language.	Open posture of counselor is one example.
Open and closed questions	Closed generally start with *is, are, do;* open require more than two–three word responses.	*Closed:* "Is the teacher yelling at you a lot?" *Open:* "What was your old school like?"
Observational skills	Notice nonverbal behavior, verbal behavior, discrepancies, and conflict.	Note when client looks away, pauses, or changes the topic.
Encouraging	Use verbal and nonverbal prompts to continue talking.	Counselor nods head or says "Uh-huh."
Paraphrasing	Feedback the essence of what has just been said in the counselor's own words plus important main words of client.	"So you are a good student and a good athlete."
Summarizing	Clarify what has been said over a longer time span; used to begin an interview, before moving to a new topic or stage, and to end an interview.	"Today we've talked about your organizational issues around balancing school and a job."
Reflection of feeling	Acknowledge and make explicit the emotions a client is experiencing.	"It looks like you feel sad about quitting your job but maybe a little excited about going back to school, is that right?"
Five-stage structure	Use checklist to ensure a complete interview.	*Stage 2:* "What concern brought you here today?"
Confrontation	Use supportive challenge, in which discrepancies are noted and fed back to the client.	"On the one hand you want to go to college next year, but on the other hand you feel burnt out and would like to wait a year."
Focusing	Direct conversation around the client, main theme, others, family, or culture.	"What help have you gotten from your friends?"
Reflection of meaning	Stress the deeper thoughts relating to understanding values and attitudes.	"What does it mean that your parents are getting a divorce?"
Interpretation/reframe	Provide a new way of thinking about a concern or problem.	"You seem to react very strongly to any criticism from your husband."
Logical consequences	Help client anticipate the consequences of actions, thoughts, feelings, and behaviors.	"If you do this . . . , then . . ."
Self-disclosure	Share self through personal life experience.	"I was raised in a military family."
Feedback	Provide accurate data on how the counselor or others view the client.	"I think your teachers and I would agree that you have all the tools to be successful."
Information/advice	Share specific information with the client.	"This online site will give you information about college majors."
Directives	Give client specific actions to take and what results to expect.	"If you stop and close your eyes and breathe slowly for a minute, you will begin to relax."
Skill integration	Integrate the microskills into a well-formed interview and generalize the skills to situations beyond the session.	Counselor will integrate skills and add them to own natural helping style.

skills are used to track nonverbal behavior, verbal behavior, and discrepancies or inconsistencies between counselor and client that are vital to be aware of in establishing a helping relationship. Videotaping sessions is suggested to help the novice develop observation skills. **Encouraging, paraphrasing,** and **summarizing** communicate to the client that the professional counselor hears the story, sees the client's point of view, and empathizes with an experience or perspective. Feelings are observed, reflected, and explored.

A framework or decision-making wheel (see Figure 1) for each counseling session integrates skills and maps out five stages. Stage 1, initiating the session, includes rapport and structuring. Stage 2, gathering data, focuses on drawing out client stories or concerns. Stage 3, mutual goal setting, establishes what the client hopes to get out of the session. Stage 4, working, requires exploration of alternatives, confrontation, and restoring. Stage 5, terminating, makes generalization and acting on new stories more likely to occur. At the center of the wheel and present in each stage is the positive asset of search and wellness. **Positive assets** are identified so that strengths can be used in problem resolution. The positive assets are the hub of the wheel of the five stages. The wheel symbolizes that the professional counselor and client work together on issues.

In the step-by-step model, active listening is followed by confrontation, focusing, reflection of meaning, and influencing skills. **Confrontation** allows clients to identify conflicts and work toward resolution of a problem. **Focusing** attention in the interview on various aspects of client issues helps examine multiple perspectives and explore potential solutions. **Reflection** of meaning moves the client toward a deeper understanding of life experiences. Finally, the counselor uses **influencing skills,** such as interpretation, logical consequences, self-disclosure, feedback, and information, to help the client move toward growth and change.

The microskills approach provides a framework that uses a single skills-introduction format to developing counseling competence. Counselors-in-training practice the individual skills in groups by rotating through the counselor, client, and observer roles. Microskills incorporate a wellness approach that encourages identification and use of positive assets in helping clients solve problems. After the individual skills are

mastered, the professional counselor is advised to reflect on these skills in order to refine a natural, personal, and authentic style and begin integrating theories into practice. Microskills are designed to be used intentionally so that the counselor can predict the expected consequence or response for most clients. Microskills are the tools all professional counselors need to conduct counseling sessions.

Contributed by Mary E. McCormac,
Marymount University, Arlington, VA

Additional Resources

Ivey, A. E., & Ivey, M. B. (2007). *Intentional interviewing and counseling* (6th ed.). Monterey, CA: Thomson Brooks/Cole.

Ivey, A. E., Pedersen, P. B., & Ivey, M. B. (2008). *Group microskills: Culture-centered group process and strategies.* Hanover, MA: Microtraining Associates.

MicroTraining Institute Web site: http://www.emicrotraining.com

◼ Milan Systemic Family Therapy

The original **Milan group** was formed in Milan, Italy, in 1967 by psychoanalytically trained psychiatrist **Mara Selvini Palazzoli** with the intent of including families in the treatment of children. Other original team members included Luigi Boscola, Gianfranco Cecchin, and Guiliana Prata. When the psychoanalytic approach proved inadequate for family work, the Milan group incorporated the systemic concepts of Gregory Bateson and Paul Watzlawick. Although **Milan systemic family therapy** shared roots with the **Mental Research Institute (MRI)** of Palo Alto, California, and strategic family therapy, the Milan model focused on how families perceive interactions and how power struggles within a family lead to communication sequences that either alienate or make a villain of an individual within the family system.

The Milan group originated the use of **positive connotation,** whereby the therapist reframes family behaviors as positive attempts to solve problems and maintain equilibrium within the system. The Milan group developed intervention techniques such as hypothesizing, circular questioning, neutrality, and rituals to bring about change in the family system. Their viewpoint was that systems formed around problems, and by altering rules and patterns, family members could choose another way to relate to one another, thereby changing the old rules and patterns. Ideally, Milan systemic family therapy was conducted with two therapists who were observed by a team behind a one-way mirror. Sessions were scheduled once a month for 10 to 12 months. This allowed interventions time to work between appointments.

Hypothesizing provided a therapeutic framework for inquiry through circular questioning, and the therapeutic team would meet before the first session to generate tentative hypotheses. **Circular questioning** was developed not only to explore family concerns but also to enlighten families and help them move away from linear thinking and shift toward a circular causality perspective. The therapist asked each family member questions about perceptions of events and

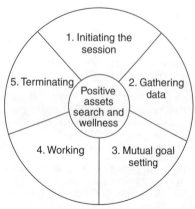

Figure 1. Decision-Making Wheel

relationships. The process allowed the family to see problems in a relational context and develop new understandings of the interconnectedness of family interactions and concerns. New information gained through circular questioning could be used to rethink previous hypotheses if necessary.

The Milan group espoused therapeutic **neutrality** in their work. By maintaining neutrality, therapists could avoid appearing biased or judgmental, but neutrality proved to be problematic. The neutral stance was often perceived by families as cold and distant; therefore, it sometimes interfered with rapport. Also, neutrality in the face of abuse and domestic violence ignored real safety issues. Theoretically, neutrality is based on the need for maintaining a nonjudgmental stance and fully comprehending the context of family interactions. The intention of neutrality was never to overlook ill treatment or danger.

Paradoxical in nature, **rituals** served to elucidate systemic maintenance of problem behaviors, making it impossible for such behaviors to continue covertly; thus, the behaviors lost power and the rigid recursive patterns and rules were broken, which allowed healthier patterns to emerge. Rituals were prescribed to address problem behaviors or to establish boundaries. They were also prescribed to highlight that systematic rules and patterns can have positive connotations.

In 1980, the original Milan group split. Selvini Palazzoli and Prata continued their systemic work and research focusing on work with clients with schizophrenia and anorexia nervosa. Boscolo and Cecchin concentrated on training and have refined many of the original ideas while integrating second-order cybernetics and social constructivism into the Milan approach. Today, Milan systemic family therapy concepts are an essential aspect of integrated approaches that use language and family strengths to facilitate change when working with families.

Contributed by Charlotte Daughhetee,
University of Montevallo, Montevallo, AL

Additional Resources

Boscolo, L., Cecchin, G., Hoffman, L., & Penn, P. (1987). *Milan systemic family therapy.* New York: Basic Books.

Campbell, D. (1999). Family therapy and beyond: Where is the Milan approach today? *Child and Adolescent Mental Health, 2,* 76–84.

Gladding, S. T. (2007). *Family therapy history, theory and practice.* Upper Saddle River, NJ: Merrill Prentice Hall

Nichols, M. P., & Schwartz, R. C. (2004). *Family therapy concepts and methods* (6th ed.). Needham Heights, MA: Allyn & Bacon.

Selvini Palazzoli, M., Boscola, L., Cecchin, G., & Prata, G. (1980). Hypothesizing-circularity-neutrality: Three guidelines for the conductor of the session. *Family Process, 6,* 3–12.

■ Mixed Method Designs

Mixed method designs refer to research designs that use a combination of quantitative and qualitative methods to collect, analyze, interpret, and report data. Mixed method designs, which are based on the philosophy of pragmatism, emerged in response to the call for increased methodological diversity in the last 2 decades. Viewed as a major methodological improvement in recent research, mixed method designs allow researchers to combine strengths and offset the weaknesses of both quantitative and qualitative methods.

Dimensions of Mixed Method Designs

There are two major dimensions to consider in formulating mixed method designs. One dimension pertains to the decision of whether to give an equal status to both quantitative and qualitative methods or whether to allow one method to predominate (i.e., **paradigm emphasis dimension**). Figure 1 illustrates three basic options to prioritize the data: (a) Quantitative and qualitative data are of equal weight, (b) quantitative data are of greater weight than qualitative data, or (c) qualitative data are of greater weight than quantitative data. The other dimension, the **time order dimension,** assesses whether to carry out quantitative and qualitative research methods simultaneously or in sequence. Figure 1 shows that three basic options are available for the time order of data collection: (a) quantitative data and qualitative data are collected concurrently; (b) quantitative data are collected first, followed by collection of qualitative data; or (c) qualitative data are collected first, followed by collection of quantitative data. The time order dimension delineates two major designs of the mixed method research: concurrent and sequential designs.

In **concurrent designs,** quantitative and qualitative data are collected and analyzed at the same time to answer a single type of research question. Status for both forms of data can be equal or unequal. Data analysis for each research strand is usually separate. Results of the data analysis for each method are usually integrated to form overall inferences at the end of the study. Interpretation typically involves discussing the extent to which the data triangulate or converge. These designs are useful for attempting to confirm, cross-validate, and corroborate study findings.

| | | Time Order Dimension | |
		Concurrent	Sequential
Paradigm Emphasis Dimension	Equal Status	QUAL + QUAN	QUAL → QUAN QUAN → QUAL
	Unequal Status	QUAL + quan qual + QUAN quan + QUAL QUAN + qual	QUAL → quan qual → QUAN QUAN → QUAL quan → qual

Figure 1. Matrix of Mixed Method Research Designs Dimensions

Note. QUAL = qualitative; QUAN = quantitative; + = concurrent; → = sequential. Capital letters denote higher priority or weight, and lowercase letters denote lower priority or weight. From "Mixed Methods Research: A Research Paradigm Whose Time Has Come," by R. B. Johnson, and A. J. Onwuegbuzie, 2004, *Educational Researcher, 33,* p. 14–26. Copyright 2004 by Sage. Adapted with permission.

Luzzo's (1995) study of gender differences in college students' career maturity and perceived barriers in career development provides an example of concurrent design. In the study, quantitative data, in the form of scores on the measure of career mature attitudes, career decision-making skills, and vocational congruence, and qualitative data, in the form of tape-recorded verbal responses to open-ended interview questions, were collected simultaneously. Of the 401 participants, 128 participated in the qualitative part in addition to responding to the quantitative measures. The order in which the participants completed the quantitative questionnaires and participated in the interview was counterbalanced. After analyzing the quantitative and qualitative data separately, the results were integrated to examine the career-related gender differences.

In **sequential designs,** one type of data (e.g., quantitative) is first collected and analyzed to provide a basis for the collection of another type of data (e.g., qualitative). Both forms of data can have an equal or unequal status. When the two forms of data have an unequal status, the dominant method usually is the focus of the study, and the less dominant method is used to augment the study. Inferences from one research method lead to questions to be researched using the other method. Data from both methods are connected, and integration usually occurs at the data interpretation stage and in the discussion of findings. Also called **two-phase designs,** sequential designs are particularly useful for explaining relationships and expected findings.

McCaughey and Strohmer (2005) used a two-phase sequential design to identify prototypes as an indirect measure of attitudes toward disability groups. In the first phase, 51 participants listed five examples of a mental disability and five examples of a physical disability that were familiar to the general pubic. The responses were summed into six basic-level disability categories: schizophrenia, mental retardation, attention-deficit/hyperactivity disorder, spinal cord injury, visual impairment, and hearing impairment. Then, in the second phase, 71 participants listed at least 10 phrases that describe a person in each of the six disability groups. The order of disability groups was alternated to ensure each disability was presented to an equal number of participants and to control possible extraneous variables (e.g., task fatigue) in the data-collection process. Analysis of participants' attributes produced insight into the richness and distinctiveness of prototype images of each disability group.

More complex **nested designs** can be advanced by mixing quantitative and qualitative methods in formulating research questions and selecting methods of data collection, and they can also be advanced during data analysis and interpretation. For instance, open-ended questions can be embedded in a Likert-scale survey questionnaire to collect quantitative and qualitative data concurrently on the same phenomenon. Alternatively, embedded data may be collected sequentially before or after the other data set. In nested designs, different components of the mixed method studies are connected in a network or web rather than in a linear or cyclic sequence. Data analysis usually involves transforming the data, and integration usually occurs during the data-analysis stage.

Frequently, the less prioritized form of data is included to help answer an altogether different question. Nested designs are useful for gaining a broader perspective on the topic at hand and for studying different groups or levels in a single study.

Guernina (1998) used a nested design to study adolescents with eating disorders. Twenty-three participants between ages 14 to 16 years were randomly selected and divided into two groups. The experimental group participants used a diary to describe their thoughts and feelings over 2 days about the amount of food and drink and the type of action undertaken at a certain time. The diary also included questions on decision making and how to develop strategies to have a balanced diet. After the diary was distributed to the experimental group, both groups completed a standardized self-administered Eating Attitudes Test (EAT) as the pretest. On completion of the diary keeping, the experimental group participants returned the diary and joined the control group to complete the posttest questionnaire (i.e., EAT). Results showed that the control group participants reported more problems at the posttest. In the diary, the experimental group reported more problems at the pretest. Qualitative data in the form of diary entries were nested and collected to identify the meanings participants gave to eating experiences and to examine changes between the pre-and posttests of eating disorders.

Purposes of Mixed Method Designs

Mixed method designs enable researchers to gather information in a way that uses the best features of both quantitative and qualitative data collection and analysis. They allow researchers to create more user-specific and complex designs than either the quantitative or qualitative paradigm allows. At the same time, the mixed method designs are inherently more complex and demand expertise across the quantitative and qualitative methodologies. They often require translation of one form of data into the other form to integrate and compare data sets, and they make it necessary to collect additional data to reconcile inconsistent results between different research strands. With emerging procedures, a notation system, and specific designs, mixed method designs have emerged as a separate and distinct design and a useful alternative to experiments, surveys, grounded theory, case study, ethnography, and others. Mixed method designs represent a genuine effort to be reflexive and critical of the research practice and will become more useful and accountable to broader audiences.

Mixed method designs are usually used for the following five purposes (Greene, Caracelli, & Graham, 1989). The most common purpose is **triangulation.** Also known as convergence or corroboration, triangulation often requires concurrent designs and uses different data sources, data collection and analysis procedures, and research methods to assess the same conceptual phenomenon in order to increase validity and credibility of the research results. A second purpose for mixed method designs is to achieve **complementarity,** which aims at clarifying and illustrating results from one method with the use of another method. The complementarity designs focus on the overlapping, as well as different, aspects of a phenomenon in order to enrich the understanding of what is being studied. Quantitative and qualitative results are often used to address different issues and provide different but nonconflicting conclusions or interpretations.

A third purpose of the mixed method designs is **development.** Mixing methods for development involves the sequential use of quantitative and qualitative methods where results from the first method are used to shape the second method. The goal of development is to increase the strength and sensitivity of additional research methods with the assistance of data generated by a previously implemented research method. A fourth purpose of the mixed method designs is **initiation.** Initiation designs focus on the discovery of paradox and contradiction. The intent is to challenge results obtained through one method in order to generate new interpretations, suggest new areas for further explorations, or recast the entire research question with questions or results from the other method.

A fifth purpose of the mixed method designs is **expansion.** The intent of expansion is to extend the breadth and range of inquiry by using different methods for different inquiry components. Expansion has two goals. The first is similar to complementarity and focuses on applying research methods that are particularly strong in analyzing specific situations. Results from different methods shed light on different components of the study. For instance, in evaluation contexts, a mixed method expansion study may use qualitative methods to assess program processes while using quantitative methods to examine program outcomes. The second goal of expansion is similar to development in that expansion involves capitalizing on the strengths of research tools to investigate situations that these tools are particularly strong at analyzing. The results generated by one method are then used to help analyze the results generated by different research methods. Expansion designs provide richness and detail to the study by exploring specific features of each method.

Contributed by Li Cao, University of
West Georgia, Carrollton, GA

References

Greene, J. C., Caracelli, V. J., & Graham, W. F. (1989). Toward a conceptual framework for mixed-method evaluation designs. *Educational Evaluation and Policy Analysis, 11,* 225–274.

Guernina, Z. (1998). Adolescents with eating disorders: A pilot study. *Counseling Psychology Quarterly, 11,* 117–124.

Johnson, R. B., & Onwuegbuzie, A. J. (2004). Mixed methods research: A research paradigm whose time has come. *Educational Researcher, 33*(7), 14–26.

Luzzo, D. A. (1995). Gender differences in college students' career maturity and perceived barriers in career development. *Journal of Counseling & Development, 73,* 319–322.

McCaughey, T. J., & Strohmer, D. C. (2005). Prototypes as an indirect measure of attitudes toward disability groups. *Rehabilitation Counseling Bulletin, 48,* 89–99.

Additional Resources

Creswell, J. W., & Plano Clark, V. L. (2007). *Designing and conducting mixed methods research.* Thousand Oaks, CA: Sage.

Tashakkori, A., & Teddlie, C. (Eds.). (2003). *Handbook of mixed methods in social & behavioral research.* Thousand Oaks, CA: Sage.

Teddlie, C., & Tashakkori, A. (2006). A general typology of research designs featuring mixed methods. *Research in the Schools, 13*(1), 12–28.

■ Mood Disorders

The predominant feature shared by all of the diagnosable **mood disorders** appearing in the *Diagnostic and Statistical Manual of Mental Disorders* (4th ed., text rev.; *DSM-IV-TR;* American Psychiatric Association [APA], 2000) is a disturbance in mood that causes clinically significant distress or impairment in a person's social or occupational functioning or in his or her ability to fulfill other important life roles. Normal life experiences, culturally expected reactions, and developmental or age-appropriate changes that affect mood but do not result in clinically significant distress or impairment typically do not warrant a mood disorder diagnosis. For example, bereavement or normally expected grief reactions often share similarities with diagnosable depressive disorders; however, normal grief reactions typically do not warrant a mental disorder diagnosis. Furthermore, competent diagnosis of mood disorders requires an understanding of variations in symptom presentation that can result from individual differences due to such common demographics as age, gender, ethnocultural background, religious affiliation, socioeconomic status, or nation of origin.

Mood disorders are divided into three categories: depressive disorders, bipolar disorders, and two disorders defined by their etiology. Depressive disorders include major depressive disorder, dysthymic disorder, and depressive disorder not otherwise specified (NOS). Bipolar disorders include Bipolor I disorder, Bipolar II disorder, cyclothymic disorder, and bipolar disorder not otherwise specified (NOS). Mood disorder due to a medical condition and substance-induced mood disorder are both etiologically defined.

The primary characteristic of **major depressive disorder** is the occurrence of one or more major depressive episodes. The features of a **major depressive episode** include a period of 2 weeks or more during which the person experiences depressed mood or loss of interest or pleasure in all or almost all activities; characteristic physiological symptoms such as change in weight, change in sleep, or fatigue; characteristic psychological symptoms such as feelings of worthlessness, undue guilt, or diminished concentration or ability to think; or recurrent thoughts of death or suicidal ideation without or with a clear plan for committing suicide (APA, 2000). Major depressive disorder may reflect a single major depressive episode or recurrent episodes. Severity of the disorder ranges from mild to severe with psychotic features. The clinical course can vary according to whether the individual partially or fully recovers between episodes, whether onset is postpartum, or whether episodes return predictably during specific seasons of the year. Children and adolescents may experience irritable, rather than depressed, mood. Additional variations in symptoms and features are described in the *DSM-IV-TR* (APA, 2000). If schizophrenia or another psychotic disorder is present or if a bipolar disorder is present, a diagnosis of major depressive disorder normally is not made.

The primary characteristic of **dysthymic disorder** is the presence of chronically depressed mood, occurring most of the time, for at least 2 years. During this period, the person also experiences such features as change in appetite, change in sleep, fatigue, low self-esteem, hopelessness, and difficulties with concentration or decision making (APA, 2000). In children and adolescents, mood may be irritable, and the minimum duration to make the diagnosis is 1 year. A diagnosis of dysthymic disorder is not made if the person has ever experienced a bipolar disorder, experiences a major depressive disorder during the 2-year period, or the symptoms occur during schizophrenia or another psychotic disorder. Occasions in which major depressive disorder and dysthymic disorder may co-occur are outlined in the *DSM-IV-TR*.

The diagnosis of **depressive disorder NOS** includes situations in which the person's experience is characterized by a clinically significant change in mood, but the full criteria are not met for dysthymic disorder or for any of the variations or subtypes of major depressive disorder.

The primary characteristic of **Bipolar I disorder** is the occurrence of one or more **manic episodes.** The features of a manic episode include a period of 1 week or more during which the person experiences elevated, expansive, or irritable mood that is persistent and distinctly abnormal; a grandiose or inflated self-esteem; decreased need for sleep; racing thoughts or rapidly occurring flight of ideas; distractibility or being easily drawn to unimportant stimuli; significantly increased focus on goal-directed activity in the social, occupational, sexual, or other realm; or clinically significant overinvolvement in activities that are pleasurable but have high potential for pain or negative consequences (e.g., gambling binges, extravagant buying sprees, or hypersexuality; APA, 2000). Over the course of the disorder, Bipolar I disorder may reflect the occurrence of only a single manic episode or recurrent manic episodes, one or more manic episodes along with one or more major depressive episodes, or one or more manic episodes along with one or more hypomanic episodes or mixed episodes. It is notable that the diagnosis is made when an individual experiences one or more manic episodes, whether or not he or she has ever experienced a major depressive episode. The nature and severity of the most recent episode usually are described; severity can range from mild to severe with psychotic features. Furthermore, when a person's symptoms require hospitalization, there is no minimum duration (i.e., a 1-week duration is not necessary to make the diagnosis). As with major depressive disorder, the clinical course can vary according to whether the individual partially or fully recovers between episodes, whether onset is postpartum, or whether episodes return predictably during specific seasons of the year. It also is noted

when the episodes of a bipolar disorder repeat, or cycle, in rapid succession. Additional variations in symptoms and features are described in the *DSM-IV-TR* (APA, 2000).

Bipolar II disorder is diagnosed when, over the course of time, an individual experiences recurring major depressive episodes, as previously described in this entry, along with hypomanic episodes. The features of a **hypomanic episode** include a period of at least 4 days during which the person experiences noticeably and persistently elevated, expansive, or irritable mood and characteristic hypomanic symptoms such as inflated self-esteem, decreased sleep, becoming hypertalkative, having racing thoughts, increased goal-directed activity, and overpursuit of pleasurable activities with potentially negative consequences (APA, 2000). In comparison with the manic episode characteristic of Bipolar I disorder, there is a clear disturbance in usual mood and functioning that is observable by others and different from the person's typical adjustment, but the change is not severe enough to impair functioning markedly or require hospitalization, and no psychotic features are present. Unlike Bipolar I disorder, which just requires the presence of manic episodes, a diagnosis of Bipolar II disorder is made only when the person has had experiences of both hypomanic episodes and major depressive episodes.

Cyclothymic disorder shares some similarities with dysthymic disorder. The primary characteristic of **cyclothymic disorder** is the presence of numerous periods in which hypomanic symptoms are present as well as numerous periods during which depressive symptoms that do not meet the full criteria for a major depressive episode are present over a course of at least 2 years. In children and adolescents, the minimum duration to make the diagnosis is 1 year. As with dysthymic disorder, a diagnosis of cyclothymic disorder is not made if the person experiences a major depressive episode, manic episode, or mixed episode during the 2-year time period. Occasions in which cyclothymic disorder may co-occur with Bipolar I disorder or Bipolar II disorder are outlined in the *DSM-IV-TR* (APA, 2000).

The diagnosis of **bipolar disorder NOS** includes situations in which the person's experience is characterized by clinically significant change in mood, but the full criteria are not met for cyclothymic disorder or any of the variations or subtypes of Bipolar I or Bipolar II disorders or the symptoms occur during schizophrenia or another psychotic disorder.

The remaining mood disorders indicate mood symptoms that are due to the direct physiological effects of a physical medical condition (i.e., **mood disorder due to general medical condition**) or are due to intoxication, withdrawal, or the consequences of problematic substance use (i.e., **substance-induced mood disorder**). Examples are depressed mood due to hypothyroidism (general medical condition) and mood disturbance due to cocaine withdrawal (substance induced). These disorders may occur with depressive, manic, or a mixture of features. The final diagnosis among the mood disorders, **mood disorder NOS,** describes situations in which an individual experiences clinically significant mood difficulties that do not meet the criteria for any other mood disorder and are not better captured by depressive disorder NOS or bipolar disorder NOS.

Contributed by Alan M. "Woody" Schwitzer,
Old Dominion University,
Norfolk, VA

Reference

American Psychiatric Association. (2000). *Diagnostic and statistical manual of mental disorders* (4th ed., text rev.). Washington, DC: Author.

Additional Resources

Neukrug, E., & Schwitzer, A. (2006). *Skills and tools for today's counselors and psychotherapists: From natural helping to professional counseling.* Belmont, CA: Thomson Brooks/Cole.

Seligman, L. (2004). *Diagnosis and treatment planning* (3rd ed.).New York: Plenum Press.

Moral Development

The modern understanding of **moral development** has been developed primarily by Lawrence Kohlberg and Carol Gilligan. Both Kohlberg and Gilligan developed models of moral development as ways to explain how individuals develop identity and view the world. Kohlberg saw this process as a series of stages that individuals moved through as they became more aware of their place in society. Gilligan, in response to Kohlberg's stages appearing to apply primarily to men, developed a perspective of development for women that described women connecting with others in finding individual identity. **Lawrence Kohlberg's** (1981) model illustrates a progressive sequence that an individual moves through when making a moral decision. The primary concern at each stage is the principle of justice. Kohlberg believed that individuals were guided along the stages by a set of principles, which he described as a guide for choosing among behaviors, rather than simply abiding by social rules. The progression from Stage 1 to Stage 6 is a fluid movement, as demonstrated in the following list. There are three levels with two stages in each. Kohlberg's model has been criticized for its assumption that advanced moral development is reflected by autonomy. In addition, he developed the model using only male participants. Kohlberg's model follows:

Level I.   Preconventional Level

Stage 1—Obedience and punishment: In this stage, there is literal obedience to rules in order to avoid punishment. Individuals are focused only on themselves and the physical consequences of their choices.

Stage 2—Individualism and moral reciprocity: An individual separates his or her own needs and points of view from those in authority. There is awareness that others have individual interests that may conflict. Individuals may begin to make self-serving deals: "You scratch my back, I'll scratch yours."

Level II.   Conventional Level

Stage 3—Mutual interpersonal expectations: The individual is aware of relationships to other immediately connected individuals. A sense of shared feelings, agreements, and expectations begin to emerge and take precedence over individual interests. The desire to be seen as "good" takes over.

Stage 4—Social system and conscience maintenance: In this stage, the individual considers the viewpoint of the larger system when making decisions. There is also a transitional phase here where the individual begins to consider himself or herself outside of a societal context.

Level III.   Postconventional Level

Stage 5—Social contract: The individual considers moral and legal points of view, recognizes any conflicts, and finds it difficult to integrate the conflicts. There is a sense that the individual would like to uphold the basic legal rights, values, and contracts of society even if these conflict with the concrete rules of a group.

Stage 6—Universal ethical principles: There is identification with the moral point of view in which social arrangements are grounded. The basic moral premise of respect for other individuals is used as an end, not a means.

Carol Gilligan (1982) argued that there is the lack of consideration for girls and women's development in Kohlberg's model, because female moral development involves a relationship orientation. Gilligan described women as understanding the world through connections, relationships, and an ethic of caring. She described the **ethic of caring** as being what drives morality for women, a concept that may conflict with a male-dominated society. Gilligan suggested that the central moral dilemma for women was an ongoing conflict between the self and others. Women have a distinct moral language, a language of selfishness and responsibility, a language that defines the moral problem as one of obligation to exercise care and avoid hurt. This is the basis for the three stages outlined in the following list with which women resolve moral conflicts: orientation to individual survival, goodness as self-sacrifice, and morality of nonviolence.

- Stage 1—Orientation to individual survival: This stage focuses on the self. The goal here is one of individual survival. The transition between this stage and the second stage occurs when the individual is able to move from a level of selfishness to having a sense of responsibility to others.
- Stage 2—Goodness as self-sacrifice: This stage occurs when good is equated with doing for others. Self-sacrifice is seen as goodness. The transition to the final stage occurs when the individual fully realizes that she is a person too.
- Stage 3—Morality of nonviolence: This final stage is the resolution of the conflict between selfishness and responsibility, when equilibrium is found between the

expectations of conformity and caring in the social ideals of womanhood and individual needs. At its core is the realization that an individual will not harm others or herself in the choices she makes.

Contributed by Jennifer L. Pepperell,
Minnesota State University, Mankato, MN

References

Gilligan, C. (1982). *In a different voice: Psychological theory and women's development.* Cambridge, MA: Harvard University Press.

Kohlberg, L. (1981). *The philosophy of moral development: Moral stages and the idea of justice.* San Francisco: Harper and Row.

Motivation

Motivation involves the instinct and drive to accomplish a task or goal and is an important factor in determination of behavior. Such tasks or goals range from satisfying hunger to obtaining a certain job or degree. Whatever the accomplishment pursued, certain aspects exist behind how and why individuals accomplish the task or goal. Motivating factors differ for each individual; however, motivation can be divided into two categories: intrinsic and extrinsic motivation.

Intrinsic motivation consists of internal factors within a person, which are defined as biological drives or instincts. Intrinsic motivation is characterized as an internal desire to complete the task or obtain the goal. The completion of such tasks or goals evokes a sense of satisfaction and accomplishment. For example, when a client wants to quit smoking, intrinsic motivation for doing so would be an internal desire to make a healthier life-style choice. In addition, quitting smoking would bring a certain sense of accomplishment, which represents an internal or intrinsic motivating factor.

Extrinsic motivation represents the rewards or pressures found from external factors, such as the recognition received for completing a task or goal or the desire to avoid the disappointment that may surface from important individuals in a person's life should the task not be completed. Extrinsic motivators are thought to be more powerful than intrinsic motivating factors. Continuing with the example of helping a client quit smoking, better health insurance rates, pleasing one's family, or simply not smelling like cigarette smoke would all represent extrinsic or external motivating factors.

Whether the motivation comes from intrinsic or extrinsic factors, a significant component behind the progression of motivation is the expectations of the individual: expectations of what will or will not occur should a task be completed or a goal reached. For example, in taking a standardized test, an individual's expectations for how he or she wants to score will motivate the level of studying and preparation as well as the amount of anxiety experienced going into the exam. Motivation is only one factor, but an important one, in determining behavior both for counselors and clients.

Contributed by Tonya R. Hammer and
Dana L. Comstock, St. Mary's
University, San Antonio, TX

Additional Resources

Maslow, A. H. (1970). *Motivation and personality.* New York:Harper & Row.

McClelland, D. C. (1987). *Human motivation.* New York: Cambridge University Press.

Motivational Interviewing

Motivational interviewing (MI) is a client-centered, directive counseling approach cofounded by **William R. Miller** and **Stephen Rollnick.** Since its introduction in 1983, MI has been applied to a wide range of issues in medicine, corrections, counseling, and education. The research evidence supporting MI's effectiveness is both broad and deep. Miller and Rollnick's Web site lists randomized clinical trials that demonstrate that MI has been effective in helping people who have had problems in the following areas: eating, exercise, trauma, hypertension, diabetes, substance use disorders, smoking, gambling, pregnancy, stroke, psychosis, anxiety, and HIV. MI has also been shown to be effective with diverse populations, including adolescents, gay men, Native Americans, African Americans, and Latinos.

MI was designed as an alternative to the traditional American counseling approach to alcohol addiction. This traditional approach, known as the **Minnesota model (MM),** holds that clients with alcohol addiction possess a personality that habitually uses the defense of denial. Accordingly, it is thought that such clients are inherently resistant to examining the costs of their drinking. As such, MM counselors use strong confrontational techniques to "break" a client's inborn denial and resistance. Although MM is popular and influential in the United States, there is scant evidence supporting its effectiveness.

Why does MM lack effectiveness? Miller and Rollnick's (2002) answer is based on their novel blend of two psychological theories. These theories are self-perception, in which people do what they hear themselves saying they should do, and psychological reactance, in which people experience unsolicited advice as a diminution of their personal freedom and hence act contrary to the advice in order to preserve this freedom. They theorized that MM's confrontational style leads to client psychological reactance in the form of "no-change" verbalizations. In turn, they noted that such verbalizations reinforce a client's self-perception as a "non-changer."

MI contrasts with MM in two key ways. First, in MI, a client's ambivalence about change is not viewed as a pathological trait personality feature to be conquered; rather, this ambivalence is understood as a normal part of the change process. Second, client motivation is not seen as an immutable personality trait but rather as a state function of the counselor–client relationship. Given their interpersonal (vs. trait) conception of client ambivalence and motivation, Miller and Rollnick (2002) based MI on Carl Rogers's necessary conditions for therapeutic change (i.e., empathy, congruence, unconditional positive regard).

Essential Elements of Motivational Interviewing

MI's essential elements can be captured in the mnemonics: FRAMES and OARES (Poirier et al., 2004). FRAMES stands for **F**eedback, **R**esponsibility, **A**dvice, **M**enu, **E**mpathy, and **S**elf-Efficacy. The contents of this mnemonic are fully supported by research on the active ingredients of effective brief interventions (Bien, Miller, & Tonigan, 1993). OARES lists techniques that embody the MI approach: **O**pen-ended questions, **A**ffirm, **R**eflective listening, **E**licit self-motivational statements, and **S**ummarize. A counselor practicing MI weaves these elements through the various phases of this approach.

Phases of Motivational Interviewing

MI proceeds in distinct, essential phases. MI opens with intense use by the counselor of open-ended questions (OARES's O), listening reflectively (OARES's R & FRAMES's E), and summarizing client statements (OARES's S). The rationale for this opening is that it produces a safe, supportive interpersonal environment where clients can explore both the positives and negatives of their maladaptive behavior. Such an exploration will naturally yield some client statements supporting change. These statements are reinforced by the counselor through the use of reflection. The selective reinforcement of the client's own pro-change statements by counselor reflection will then produce more client change statements (OARES's E). The counselor also seeks to promote client-driven change by providing both affirmation (OARES's A) and objective feedback (FRAMES's F) about the consequences of the target behavior to the client. Thus, in MI, it is the client's (vs. counselor's) responsibility (FRAMES's R) to see change enacted.

One core skill for the MI counselor is the ability to recognize when the client's change/no-change "decisional balance" has tipped toward change. Negotiating a change plan before this tip can lead to psychological reactance and the client arguing the no-change side. Waiting too long to negotiate a change plan can lead to frustration for the client. Miller and Rollnick (2002) noted clients who have just moved through the tip point do the following: demonstrate a quiet resolve, ask questions about change, envision change, and begin small experiments with change.

At this point in the counseling process, MI counselors diverge from the traditional nondirective stance of Rogerians in that they offer clients advice or options. Once a client's decisional balance tips toward change, counselors are often asked by clients for advice on what to do next. Miller and Rollnick (2002) cautioned that a counselor should not give unsolicited advice or one-option advice because both can provoke psychological reactance. Instead, they hinted that advice (FRAMES's A) should be presented as a "menu of options" (FRAMES's M) from which the client can choose.

MI's final phase involves negotiating a change plan. This planning involves both setting goals and considering options. Miller and Rollnick reminded counselors to monitor for client ambivalence because it can resurface at any point. They recommended that if such ambivalence reemerged, counsel-

ors should return to the skills they used before the decisional balance tip (i.e., the skills of asking open-ended questions, listening reflectively, summarizing client statements, and selectively reinforcing client pro-change statements through reflection). At times, clients may perceive that they lack the skills (i.e., self-efficacy) to enact the change goals. If so, the MI counselor can provide (or refer for) the necessary skills training (FRAMES's S).

MI Adaptations

There have been two major adaptations of MI. These are motivational enhancement therapy and brief motivational interviewing. Motivational enhancement therapy is a manualized adaptation of MI designed for research use. Brief motivational interviewing is an adaptation designed for health care workers with severely limited time to intervene with patients. MI should not be equated with the global term *brief intervention*, which encompasses multiple approaches including some antithetical to MI and its adaptations. Barry (1999) provided detailed online descriptions of approaches used in the Brief Intervention.

In both their training materials and books, Miller and Rollnick (2002) strongly encouraged counselors not to lose sight of the "spirit" of MI when learning or using the techniques of this approach, cautioning that no matter how appropriate or skillfully applied, any technique delivered in a coercive counselor–client interpersonal ecology is doomed to fail.

Contributed by Cass Dykeman, Oregon State University, Corvallis, OR

References

Barry, K. L. (1999). *Brief interventions and brief therapies for substance abuse.* Retrieved August 1, 2007, from http://www.ncbi.nlm.nih.gov/books/bv.fcgi?rid=hstat5.chapter.59192

Bien, T. H., Miller, W. R., & Tonigan, J. S. (1993) Brief interventions for alcohol problems: A review. *Addiction, 88,* 315–336.

Miller, W. R., & Rollnick, S. (2002). *Motivational interviewing: Preparing people for change* (2nd ed.). New York: Guilford Press.

Poirier, M. K., Clark, M. M., Cerhan, J. H. Pruthi, S., Geda, Y. E., & Dale, L. C. (2004). Teaching motivational interviewing to first-year medical students to improve counseling skills in health behavior change. *Mayo Clinic Proceedings, 79,* 327–331.

Additional Resource

Miller and Rollnick's Web site: http://www.motivationalinterview.org

■ Multicultural Assessment Standards

In the counseling profession, the term **multicultural** is used to describe an inclusive way of being that includes appreciation and valuing of cultural and linguistic differences.

Identifying as a counselor practicing from a multicultural perspective assumes an understanding of how differences in race, gender, class, ethnicity, age, religion/spiritual beliefs, sexual identity, socioeconomic status, and level of ability influence the individual cultural experience. A multicultural perspective also assumes that a person has acquired knowledge of how the experiences and worldview of the counselor and client affect the counseling relationship and process

To encourage the development of multicultural awareness, knowledge, skill, and overall competency for counselors, counselor trainees, and counselor educators, the Council for Accreditation of Counseling and Related Educational Programs (CACREP; 2001) developed a set of standards that guide counselor education training, and the American Counseling Association (ACA; 2005) published the *ACA Code of Ethics* as a guide for ethical practice. These standards serve to guide the training and practice of counselors and set forth guidelines for counselors to follow when conducting ethical research. Specifically, the Assessment core area of the CACREP training standards and Section G of the *ACA Code of Ethics* address fair and ethical assessment practices. The counseling profession has further developed and implemented a set of standards for multicultural assessment. A leader in the development of the **Standards for Multicultural Assessment** is the Association for Assessment in Counseling and Education (AACE; 2003b). AACE developed the standards for multicultural assessment from five critical source documents. They are the Code of Fair Testing Practices in Education (Joint Committee on Testing Practices, 2002), *Responsibilities of Users of Standardized Tests* (3rd ed., AACE, 2003a), the *Standards for Educational and Psychological Testing* (American Educational Research Association, American Psychological Association, & National Council on Measurement in Education, 1999), the Multicultural Counseling Competencies and Standards (Association for Multicultural Counseling and Development, 1992), and the *Code of Ethics and Standards of Practice* (ACA, 1995). The Standards for Multicultural Assessment (AACE, 2003b) serves as a guide for the selection of appropriate testing and assessment instruments, the administering and scoring of these instruments, the interpretation of scoring, and the application of results. In addition, these standards help guide practice, training, and research related to assessment and evaluation in the counseling field. Assessment standards are a critical component of counselor training, practice, and research.

Need for Multicultural Assessment Standards

Multicultural assessment standards (AACE, 2003b) aid the counseling process because they help to provide an understanding of the various approaches to assessment and evaluation. Without assessment standards, professional counselors operate at a disadvantage in their ability to conceptualize the client's mental and emotional status from a cultural perspective. The counselor who is not aware of multicultural assessment standards risks harming the client or, at the very least, counseling from a deficit perspective. Regarding research, a lack of multicultural assessment standards would contribute to the production and dissemination of faulty and inaccurate professional literature. Such practices will inevitably cause more harm and misunderstanding than help. If there were no assessment standards that took into account the obvious cultural differences that exist, the counseling profession would operate from a model that would endorse a "good for all" methodology. Such an approach would not follow a developmental model or value each person's uniqueness of culture.

Multicultural assessment standards (AACE, 2003b) are used to evaluate and determine the minimal level of skill needed to test or assess an individual client's need for counseling interventions appropriately, to guide ethical counseling practices, and to understand the most useful way of engaging in test and assessment research. In short, the multicultural assessment standards are the guidelines that drive ethical and appropriate training, practice, and research.

Counselor Training

The multicultural assessment standards (AACE, 2003b) guide counselor training by requiring the study of and practice using assessment and testing instruments. This guideline helps the counselor develop the ability to select and administer tests and assessment tools that are appropriate to the cultural needs of the client. For example, prior to administering a test or assessment tool, a culturally competent counselor would evaluate the usefulness of a test on the basis of the norm-reference group on which the test was standardized and the cultural context of the client. This evaluation aids in selecting the most appropriate test or assessment tool for the client. Another example of what a culturally competent counselor would do is to select a test or assessment instrument in which all the test forms had been appropriately modified to meet the needs of the client. Counselor preparation training should reinforce the idea that a given test should suit the ability of the client, thus meeting the individual needs of the client. An example of this would be for a professional counselor to avoid administering the Beck Depression Inventory (Beck, Steer, & Brown, 1996) without language modification to a client who speaks English as a second language.

When interpreting the results of a test or assessment tool, the counselor should understand that the race, gender, age, ethnicity, affectional orientation, partner status, and socioeconomic status of the client can influence test results. Counselor training in the use of various tests and assessment tools should include detailed instruction in the use of fair and equitable test-taking procedures for clients. An example of this would be to ensure that a client with a documented learning disability be given an appropriate amount of time to take and complete an assessment instrument. A lack of attendance to this detail would serve to invalidate the results of an assessment instrument and would have the potential to cause harm to the client through misdiagnosis and labeling.

Counseling Practice

The multicultural assessment standards (AACE, 2003b), as they relate to the practice of counseling, serve to guide fair treatment and equity for the client and ensure best practices that benefit client growth and development. As an example, the professional counselor, prior to administering any assessment, should fully explain the nature, purpose, and implications of all intended methods of assessment in a manner and language that the client can understand. If the need arises, the counselor should provide an interpreter who has the ability to fully understand and speak the language of both the counselor and the client to ensure accurate dissemination of information. At the conclusion of any assessment, the counselor should put forth the same effort to ensure that the client fully understands the results of the assessment.

Prior to the administration of any assessment or test for a person with a documented disability, the culturally competent counselor evaluates the need for either multiple or alternative testing to meet the needs of the client best. As a further example, the professional counselor should appraise the need for using multiple sources of information about a client. In addition, the culturally competent counselor recognizes the potential for bias in any test or assessment tool. In the documentation of the results of testing and assessment, the counselor should account for and acknowledge bias when it exists.

Counseling Research

The purpose of multicultural assessment standards (AACE, 2003b) in research is to guide the student, counselor, and counselor educator in ethical research practices that contribute to the body of literature in the area of testing and assessment in a pluralistic society. To this end, the standards of research suggest a number of guidelines for the research investigator to follow that will ensure ethical practice. An example of the guidelines is for a researcher to ensure, when possible, that participants for a research study be representative of the population to be studied. By contrast, if participants of a study differ from the population that was used to norm reference an assessment tool, the researcher should be diligent in clearly articulating such differences in the presentation of results. Another example of an assessment standard guideline is that reports of participant or group differences in test scores should include contextual information that will aid in the accurate interpretation of a report or results. A final example is that when reporting assessment results, researchers should clearly articulate concerns that exist regarding the validity or reliability of an assessment tool or test in relation to the appropriateness of the testing instrument for persons who are from diverse or underrepresented populations. To this end, it is important that in the near future multicultural assessment standards guide the development and practice of research into the reliability and validity of testing instruments and their use with diverse populations. For example, multicultural assessment standards can serve to guide the development of new testing instruments as well as the investigation of existing tests and measures of assessment. Specifically, increased attention could be directed to the norm reference group when exploring the validity and reliability of scores derived from a testing instrument. To do so would serve to minimize the potential for culture-bound test items. In this case, such standards will help to ensure an equality of testing practices in a diverse and pluralistic society.

AACE has served as the leader in the development of multicultural assessment standards. Without these standards of practice, students, counselors, and educators would be operating from a deficit perspective with respect to their ability to conceptualize and understand the client as a whole person. In addition, without these standards, there would be increased chance of causing harm to the client or examinee and producing faulty assessment data.

Contributed by Linwood G. Vereen,
Idaho State University, Pocatello, ID

References

American Counseling Association. (1995). *Code of ethics and standards of practice*. Alexandria, VA: Author.

American Counseling Association. (2005). *ACA code of ethics*. Alexandria, VA: Author

American Educational Research Association, American Psychological Association, & National Council on Measurement in Education. (1999). *Standards for educational and psychological testing* (3rd ed.). Washington, DC: American Psychological Association.

Association for Assessment in Counseling and Education. (2003a). *Responsibilities of users of standardized tests* (3rd ed.). Alexandria, VA: Author.

Association for Assessment in Counseling and Education. (2003b). Standards for multicultural assessment. Retrieved September 7, 2007, from http://aac.ncat.edu/Resources/documents/STANDARDS%20FOR%20MULTICULTURAL%20ASSESSMENT%20FINAL.pdf

Association for Multicultural Counseling and Development. (1992). *Multicultural counseling competencies and standards*. Alexandria, VA: Author.

Beck, A. T., Steer, R. A., & Brown, G. K. (1996). *Beck Depression Inventory* (2nd ed.). San Antonio, TX: PsychCorp.

Council for Accreditation of Counseling and Related Educational Programs. (2001). *CACREP accreditation standards and procedures manual*. Alexandria, VA: Author.

Joint Committee on Testing Practices. (2002). *Code of fair testing practices in education* (2nd ed.). Washington, DC: Author.

▌Multicultural Counseling

Multicultural counseling denotes the provision of counseling services where relevant cultural traits are incorporated in the context of the counseling process. **Cultural traits** include ethnicity, race, gender, sexual identity, socioeconomic status, disabilities, age, and spirituality. Educators recognized the need for culturally competent counseling as early as the 1950s; however, certain developments over the past 30 years have elevated the status of multiculturalism to that of a general theory, or **fourth force,** in the field of counseling. These developments include (a) an increasingly diverse and global society; (b) a shift from a monocultural perspective to the valuing of a pluralistic society, including respect for the culturally unique attributes of individuals; and (c) empirical evidence that traditional counseling services have failed to meet the needs of a diverse clientele. Multiculturalism is now a recognized philosophical framework, complementary with the humanistic, behavioral, and psychodynamic theories (Pedersen, 1991).

This shift has served as a catalyst for the development of essential multicultural models that delineate instructions or tenets for mental health professionals in the practice of effective multicultural counseling. For a comprehensive description of the models, readers should refer to Mollen, Ridley, and Hill (2003). The tripartite model of multicultural counseling competencies and the multidimensional model for developing cultural competence are two such influential models in the multicultural literature. The **tripartite model of multicultural counseling competencies** (Ponterotto, 1997) defines the skills, knowledge, and awareness necessary for effective work with clientele of various cultures. The **multidimensional model for developing culture competence** (Sue, 2001) adds to these three components an awareness of social justice, focus (e.g., cultural competence that includes the individual, professional, organizational, and societal levels of intervention), and understanding of specific attributes of five ethnic groups.

Models, in turn, have informed the development of **multicultural counseling competencies** for counseling professionals (e.g., Sue et al., 1998). Although still evolving, these competencies have been adopted as guidelines in the formation of multicultural training in counselor education programs. Training topics that are aligned with these competencies include multicultural concepts and issues, understanding the worldviews and sociopolitical history of specific populations, communication and intervention skills specific to a diverse clientele, and ethical multicultural knowledge and practice. Multicultural training increases students' awareness and understanding of the importance of personal culture, biases, and ethnic and racial identity statuses in the counseling process by making use of these competencies. In addition, effective training develops students' roles as change agents, advocates, and facilitators of indigenous healing (see Cultural Competence).

Also emerging as a tenet of effective multicultural counseling and training is an emphasis of an emic, versus etic, approach with clientele. Initially, work with clients in the field of counseling assumed an etic approach. **Etic** refers to a universal perspective, or viewing a client's culture through a lens that is external to and potentially incongruent with the client's culture. This approach posits that general forms of helping would be universally beneficial to all persons, regardless of individual cultural differences. With the growing recognition of the impediments of this approach with diverse clientele, many professional counselors have shifted to an emic approach. **Emic** refers to a culture-specific perspective of the world, with focus on the intrinsic cultural differences that are meaningful to an individual client. An example of services provided from an emic perspective would be the use of indigenous healing practices, theories, or techniques specific to the client's culture.

Multicultural counseling will continue to evolve through continued dialogue, thereby establishing a more universal understanding of its characteristics and features and allowing a systematic application of multicultural competencies. Furthermore, empirical studies related to multicultural counseling should reflect a more balanced approach to qualitative and quantitative research methods. Future studies might identify effective counseling services for specific populations and examine alternative healing practices and outcomes on the basis of the use of these practices with specific populations. In addition, investigations should continue to expand the understanding of the strengths and coping skills inherent in each population.

Future directions of multicultural counseling related to counselor training include (a) the development of more accurate and reliable measures of student multicultural counseling competence; (b) the application of empirical studies verifying effective multicultural training practices for counseling students; (c) the implementation of field-based or longitudinal empirical studies to verify the lasting effects of multicultural training; (d) intensified recruitment practices of culturally diverse students and counselor educators; (e) eventual infusion of multicultural counseling across all training courses and internships; and (f) increased student orientation toward a more proactive, social justice stance.

Contributed by Krista M. Malott,
Villanova University, Villanova, PA,
and Tina R. Paone, Monmouth
University, West Long Branch, NJ

References

Mollen, D., Ridley, C. R., & Hill, C. L. (2003). Models of multicultural counseling competence: A critical evaluation. In D. B. Pope-Davis, H. L. K. Coleman, W. M. Liu, & R. L. Toporek (Eds.), *Handbook of multicultural competencies in counseling and psychology* (pp. 21–37). Thousand Oaks, CA: Sage.

Pedersen, P. B. (1991). Multiculturalism as a generic approach to counseling. *Journal of Counseling & Development, 70,* 6–12.

Ponterotto, J. G. (1997). Multicultural counseling training: A competency model and national survey. In D. B. Pope-Davis & H. L. K. Coleman (Eds.), *Multicultural counseling competencies: Assessment, education and training, and supervision* (pp. 111–130). Thousand Oaks, CA: Sage.

Sue, D. W. (2001). Multidimensional facets of cultural competence. *The Counseling Psychologist, 29,* 790–821.

Sue, D. W., Carter, R. T., Casas, J. M., Fouad, N. A., Ivey, A. E., Jensen, M., LaFromboise, T., et al. (1998). *Multicultural counseling competencies: Individual and organizational development.* Thousand Oaks, CA: Sage.

Additional Resources

Lee, C. C. (Ed.). (2006). *Multicultural issues in counseling: New approaches to diversity* (3rd. ed.). Alexandria, VA: American Counseling Association.

McGoldrick, M., Giordano, J., & Garcia-Preto, N. (Eds.). (2005). *Ethnicity & family therapy* (3rd ed.). New York: Guilford Press.

Pope-Davis, D. B., Coleman, H. L. K., Liu, W. M., & Toporek, R. L. (Eds.). (2003). *Handbook of multicultural competencies in counseling and psychology*. Thousand Oaks, CA: Sage.

Sue, D. W., & Sue, D. (Eds.). (2003). *Counseling the culturally diverse: Theory and practice* (4th ed.). Hoboken, NJ: Wiley.

■ Multiculturalism as a Fourth Force

The descriptor of "fourth force" indicates that a theoretical concept has had a substantial and distinguishable impact on the field of counseling equivalent to the three preexisting forces of psychodynamic, behaviorism, and humanism–existentialism. The concept of **multiculturalism as a fourth force** characterizes multiculturalism as a general theory of human behavior essential to the understanding and practice of counseling. Proponents assert that the field of counseling will be and is being revolutionized by multiculturalism, affecting the manner in which clients and their concerns are conceptualized and influencing the way counseling professionals understand themselves and their role in the counseling relationship. Multiculturalism holds that culture is so central to the act of counseling that human behavior should not be evaluated, assessed, or interpreted apart from its cultural context.

Multiculturalism has been defined in various ways in the behavioral sciences literature. Competing explanations are based on philosophical assumptions about the meaning and influence of difference as it relates to human behavior. Some authors emphasize the social and political significance of race and ethnicity. Others advocate a broader definition of multiculturalism that includes demographic, ethnographic, and status variables such as gender, language, and social class, respectively. Although each approach and its assumptions about culture have different implications for training and practice, unifying factors of multicultural counseling approaches include modifying traditional theories and techniques to account for culture and expanding the repertoire of effective counseling interventions for use with culturally diverse clients. In addition, multicultural counseling approaches regard culture as a significant influence on multiple dimensions of the therapeutic process, such as symptomatology, modes of coping, and response to treatment.

Multiculturalism is a relatively recent term; however, the practice of questioning the applicability of traditional counseling theories and techniques to culturally diverse populations and amending traditional theories and techniques to attend to culture has an established history. The 1950s witnessed the birth of the multicultural counseling movement, and the 1960s witnessed the movement in its infancy with African American clinicians leading the charge for the counseling profession to be responsive to all Americans. During the 1970s, research demonstrated clinicians' bias and stereotyping in the areas of assessment, diagnosis, and intervention with racial and ethnic minority clients. Many authors discussed the need for culturally sensitive and relevant practice as a means to alleviate oppression, racism, and social injustice within and outside the counselor's office.

The multicultural perspective has since evolved from the work of individual counselors to become an influential force within the professional counseling community. The influence of multiculturalism is evidenced by the endorsement of guidelines for the training and practice of multiculturally competent helping professionals by the American Counseling Association and the American Psychological Association. Guidelines for psychological practice with girls and women; guidelines on multicultural education, training, research, practice, and organizational change; and guidelines for counseling lesbian, gay, bisexual, and transgender clients have also been developed. Through such scholarship, multiculturalism has begun to influence accreditation criteria, curriculum reform, and training guidelines in the counseling field.

Critiques of considering multiculturalism as a fourth force include (a) there are no accepted standards for describing multiculturalism as a theory, (b) measurable competencies for application or adequate standards of practice are limited, and (c) it is unreasonable to think counselors can attend to such a large range of factors simultaneously. Moreover, multiculturalism is closely associated with highly emotional terms like *reverse discrimination, affirmative action,* and *racism*. Some authorities suggest that defining multiculturalism broadly enough to include everyone is no different than viewing cultural difference as individual difference, rendering the concept meaningless.

Most recently, feminist scholars have further broadened the concept of multiculturalism to include a focus on the intersection of multiple cultural identities (e.g., race, class, gender, religion, sexual orientation, and socioeconomic status) and the resulting clinical implications. In addition, current research has promoted an increase in the development and validation of inventories that assess counselors' multicultural awareness, knowledge, and skills. Future directions include continued empirical validation of such instruments, an emphasis on social justice and advocacy for diverse clients, and a movement toward international initiatives.

Conceptualizing multiculturalism as a fourth force acknowledges the centrality of culture to the practice of counseling. Proponents assert that the accuracy and effectiveness of counseling interventions may be enhanced by interpreting client behavior in a cultural context. In a related way, client conceptualization and treatment may be protected from the clinician's own culturally encapsulated self-reference criteria and assumptions. Particular to the counselor–client relationship, proponents of multiculturalism as a fourth force assert that a culture-centered perspective allows for the best chance of improving helping behaviors with diverse clientele.

Contributed by Telsie A. Davis and Julie R. Ancis, Georgia State University, Atlanta, GA

Ancis, J. R. (Ed.). (2004). *Culturally responsive interventions: Innovative approaches to working with diverse populations*. New York: Brunner-Routledge.

Jackson, M. (1995). *Multicultural counseling: Historical perspectives.* In J. Ponterotto, J. Casas, L. Suzuki, & C. Alexander (Eds.), *Handbook of multicultural counseling* (pp. 3–15). Thousand Oaks, CA: Sage.

Pedersen, P. B. (Ed.). (1999). *Multiculturalism as a fourth force.* Philadelphia: Taylor & Francis.

Ponterotto, J., Casas, J., Suzuki, L., & Alexander, C. (Ed.). (1995). *Handbook of multicultural counseling.* Thousand Oaks, CA: Sage.

■ Multimodal Therapy

Multimodal therapy is a comprehensive, holistic approach to assessment and treatment developed by **Arnold Lazarus** (2005). The model is built on seven broad, interrelated modalities of human functioning: behavior, affect, sensation, imagery, cognition, interpersonal relationships, and drugs/biological processes. The final modality addresses broad lifestyle and health questions, including nutrition, medication, exercise, sleep, and self-care. The first letter of each modality forms the acronym **BASIC ID**, a framework that describes the client in great detail and is the central assessment and treatment system of multimodal therapy.

Grounded in social-cognitive theory, the multimodal therapy model is broader than traditional affect-behavior-cognition systems and uses imagery and sensory training techniques extensively. Lazarus characterized multimodal therapy as technical eclecticism, that is, selecting the most effective techniques for the client from various theories without the need to accept a technique's theoretical assumptions.

The core of multimodal therapy is a unique comprehensive assessment model used to identify problems and goals quickly and match empirically supported techniques to each goal. Assessment is conducted through session interviews, detailed elaboration of problems, modality profiles constructed by the client, and formal instruments.

At the end of the first session, the client is assigned the 15-page Multimodal Life History Inventory as homework to complete gradually over several days and to bring to the next session. The detailed written questionnaire provides a thorough picture of the client's problems and style and is divided into six parts: general information, personal and social history, description of the presenting problem, expectations regarding therapy, the modality analysis of current problems, and the Structural Profile. Each modality is rated on a 1–7 scale in the Structural Profile Inventory (SPI), a 35-item survey that provides a rank order of the client's preferred areas of functioning. Similar counselor and client SPI profiles predict therapy outcomes that are more positive.

The professional counselor reviews the inventory thoroughly before discussing it with the client during the third session, although treatment can begin in the first session. After the client identifies salient problems on the Modality Profile, the counselor matches the most effective treatments

to client priorities in each area. The counselor systematically develops an individualized action plan for the client with the goal of reducing ineffective behaviors by learning new skills. When the counselor uses techniques in the client's primary modalities, successful treatment outcomes are likely. The more modalities addressed in treatment, the more durable the outcomes and the less likely the client is to relapse.

The multimodal counselor is humanistic and positive, flexibly varies direct and indirect styles, and adapts techniques depending on the client's immediate needs. Nearly half of the 39 techniques listed in *The Practice of Multimodal Therapy* (Lazarus, 1989) are behavioral, and one fourth are cognitive strategies. Lazarus frequently used didactic and psychoeducational approaches, such as coaching, advice giving, skills training, and homework. Because the client cannot directly change emotions, goals and techniques for the affective modality are addressed through the other six modalities. As examples, in the **deserted island fantasy,** the client shares what the professional counselor would learn if the client and counselor were on a deserted island together. In **time tripping,** the client moves forward or backward in time to experience an event or resolve a problem.

Several unique techniques characterize multimodal therapy. **Bridging** is used when the professional counselor responds in the client's preferred modality to develop connections and rapport before branching out to address other modalities and ways of responding. The counselor uses tracking to help the client identify the **firing order** of modalities used to respond to stressors and to use the same sequence of modalities in treatment. Thus, SICSA would indicate sensation first, then imagery, cognition, sensation, and affect. The counselor might conduct a second-order BASIC ID assessment when a problem impasse requires a more specific approach after typical treatments are not successful. Second-order BASIC ID analyzes a problem from one modality in greater detail.

Keat's HELPING Approach

Donald Keat (1990) applied the framework of the BASIC ID to his work with children and adolescents. In order to address school and environmental problems that were not part of the BASIC ID, Keat expanded the system to the BASIC IDEAL. Three additional letters represented education (E), adults in the child's life (A), and learn the client's culture (L). Keat later adapted the BASIC ID to **HELPING,** an easy-to-understand multimodal model for parents, teachers, and children representing health (H); emotions (E); learning, school (L); people/personal relationships (P); imagination/interests (I); need to know/thinking (N); and guidance of actions, behaviors, and consequences (G).

The multimodal counselor selects from a broad range of creative and developmentally appropriate treatments for children and adolescents. Techniques may include physical exercise, diet (H); relaxation training, anger management (E); tutoring, biofeedback (L); family council meetings, peer helpers, friendship training (P); hero imagery, *I am Loveable and Capable* (I); bibliotherapy, cue words (N); and behavioral contracts, games (G). The HELPING model has been applied extensively to multilevel school counseling concerns. Successful group counseling applications of the HELPING model in school settings have addressed social skills and interpersonal relationships, friendship skills, academic achievement, problem solving, motivation, and test-anxiety reduction.

Use of Multimodal Therapy

Lazarus emphasized the effectiveness of "broad spectrum" multimodal therapy for multifaceted problems in a managed care environment that requires accountability and effective time-limited treatment. In *Brief but Comprehensive Psychotherapy: The Multimodal Way,* Lazarus (1997) described how multimodal therapy can be an effective brief therapy model using empirically supported treatments that are best for the client.

The model has been used successfully with clients with a broad range of problems, such as anxiety, obsessive-compulsive disorder, phobias, chronic pain, divorce, and learning disabilities, and the model has been applied to counseling couples; families; and clients in groups, schools, and hospitals. Brunell and Young (1982) applied multimodal therapy to inpatient problems in their *Multimodal Handbook for a Mental Hospital.* Controlled studies in Europe have indicated durable positive results in children with learning disabilities, obsessive-compulsive patients, and phobic clients. The complexity, multiple interactions, and individualized nature of multimodal therapy treatment present challenges to researchers, and case studies make up the majority of the literature on effectiveness.

Contributed by Jane Webber, Seton Hall University, South Orange, NJ, and J. Barry Mascari, Kean University, Union, NJ

References

Brunell, L., & Young, W. (1982). *Multimodal handbook for a mental hospital.* New York: Springer.

Keat, D. B. (1990). *Multimodal therapy with children.* Norwood, NJ: Ablex.

Lazarus, A. A. (1989). *The practice of multimodal therapy.* Baltimore: Johns Hopkins University Press.

Lazarus, A. A. (1997). *Brief but comprehensive psychotherapy: The multimodal way.* New York: Springer.

Lazarus, A. A. (2005). Multimodal therapy. In J. C. Norcross & M. R. Goldfried (Eds.), *Handbook of psychotherapy integration* (2nd ed., pp. 231–263). New York: Oxford University Press.

Narrative Therapy

The leading figures in **narrative therapy** are **Michael White** and **David Epston.** Their theory was first announced in their book *Narrative Means to Therapeutic Ends* (White & Epston, 1990). Narrative therapy has several distinct therapeutic views, including personal narratives, social narratives, narrative letters, externalizing the problem, the use of therapeutic questions, and unique instances/outcomes. Narrative therapy shares commonalities with the following philosophies/ theories: humanistic, existential, solution-oriented, feminist, linguistic, Foucaultian, brief, phenomenological, and social constructivism.

Narrative therapists believe people construct meaning from their experiences. These constructions are then used to create personal narratives that connect the perceived experiences in life. Such personal narratives, therefore, define both the way people understand themselves and the way they view their personal problems; for example, "People don't like me.... There must be something wrong with me because no one likes me.... I should keep my distance from people."

Intertwined with these personal narratives are social (also known as cultural) narratives that are primarily made up of rules and guidelines described and prescribed by the dominant culture. These social narratives have their origins in the work of **Michael Foucault** (Foucaultian philosophy) who suggested societies maintain power over individuals by creating and supporting agreed-on object truths (e.g., acceptable body size for women); therefore, narrative therapists attend to issues of oppression and power exerted by the dominant culture.

Clinical Approach

The narrative therapist approaches working with a client as a collaborative effort designed to assist the client to reauthor his or her own story. Rather than interpreting life events reported by the client, the narrative therapist is far more interested in helping the client discern new meaning within such events. The therapist accomplishes this through implementation of several therapeutic vehicles.

The primary approach used by narrative therapists is to investigate the story of the client by having the client tell and retell the story from various angles. This method enables the client to move from a thin description (i.e., one story line with only one probable outcome) to a thicker description (i.e., multiple story lines providing multiple outcomes). As a result, the narrative therapist helps the client discover alternatives and explore expanded cognitive and/or behavioral possibilities.

Another goal in narrative therapy is to help clients understand that they are not the problem; the problem itself is the problem. The therapist accomplishes this through helping the client externalize the problem. Questions that are used include queries designed to help the client envision the problem as a separate entity (e.g., What color is it? What is its shape? What name do you have for it?). Once the problem is "seen" by the client, the narrative therapist moves on to assisting the client to recognize the power the problem has been allowed to assume over the client's life (e.g., What does it do to get you to do things against your better judgment? What does it say when you try to ignore it? What does it whisper in your ear to get you to do that?). Following the client's recognition of this dynamic, the narrative therapist then helps clients recognize the power and control they actually have and can exert over the problem, a method known as **unique instances/outcomes** (e.g., How were you able to make it grow smaller? What did you do to make it be quiet for those 5 minutes? How did you get it to agree with you in that case?).

Because a narrative therapist believes change occurs when the client has reauthored the story, **narrative letters** are often used as a means of reminding the client of progress, encouraging continued change, and chronicling the highlights from the previous session. These letters are typically brief and to the point and are often sent to be received by the client between sessions.

Example of a Narrative Letter

Dear Jane,

I am writing to congratulate you on your decision to directly address the "foolish liar." As we talked about last session, it has been in your life for over 5 years, and it is time for it to go.

One of the things that stood out last session was your insistence that you can get it to stop simply by going for a walk. You said that each time you have done this, it has gone away. I agree with you that this is a good plan of attack.

Experience tells us that the "foolish liar" will try other means to get you to see your body in a negative way. So, you need to be prepared for anything it throws your way.

Before next week, I want you to take note of the ways in which the "foolish liar" tries to get you to do what it wants, and how you were able to defeat it.

Once again, congratulations.

Sincerely,

Bill

Narrative therapy suggests that people's stories about their problems assume a life of their own. Through effective therapy, however, these stories can be reauthored through various techniques, equipping and enabling clients to experience both the problem and themselves differently.

Contributed by Bill McHenry,
Shippensburg University,
Shippensburg, PA,
and Jim McHenry, Edinboro
University, Edinboro, PA

Reference

White, M., & Epston, D. (1990). *Narrative means to therapeutic ends.* New York: Norton.

Additional Resources

Dulwich Center Web site: http://dulwichcentre.com.au/
Freedman, J., & Combs, G. (1996). *Narrative therapy: The social construction of preferred realities.* New York: Norton.

■ National Board for Certified Counselors, Inc.

Created in 1982, the **National Board for Certified Counselors, Inc., and Affiliates (NBCC)** provides the world's largest certification system for professional counselors. This certification system promotes quality counseling by identifying counselors who have voluntarily met specific, preset standards. NBCC's national certifications allow counselors who are certified to increase professional visibility and enhance their careers by providing an important and professionally relevant method to promote skills and education. Regardless of location, all counselors who are certified by NBCC must follow established procedures in order to be able to identify themselves as National Certified Counselors (NCCs).

NBCC's principal credential, the **NCC,** provides national recognition for professional counselors and functions as a "general practice" certification. Requirements include educational course work, professional endorsements, documented experience, and satisfactory performance on a standardized national counselor examination (see National Counselor Examination for Licensure and Certification). After obtaining NCC certification, professional counselors who want to demonstrate areas of expertise may pursue one of NBCC's specialty certifications: the National Certified School Counselor (NCSC) for school counseling, the Certified Clinical Mental Health Counselor (CCMHC) for clinical mental health counseling, and the Master Addictions Counselor (MAC) for addictions counseling. Holding a specialty certification through NBCC offers counselors extra recognition. Some NCSCs receive monetary stipends, whereas CCMHCs have been recognized by insurance carriers such as TRICARE/CHAMPUS. MACs are also eligible to seek substance abuse professional status. The NCC certification is a pre- or corequisite of all specialty certifications offered by NBCC. Specialty certifications entail additional educational, experience, and examination requirements.

NBCC's national certifications allow counselors who are certified to distinguish themselves professionally by providing a uniform definition of counselor certification. This common language promotes the referral process, given the differences in state laws regarding counselor licensure. State licensure, or state certification, refers to state laws that govern the practice of counseling and determine who can identify themselves as counselors. Currently, 49 states, the District of Columbia, and Puerto Rico regulate the practice of counseling. It is important to note that national certification is not in competition with state licensure, and, in fact, NBCC has actively supported efforts to achieve counselor licensure in a number of states since its formation in 1982; rather, state licensure authorities and NBCC use common elements to recognize counseling professionals. The national certification process recognizes those who voluntarily continue to meet standards set by counseling experts; state licensure defines who may legally self-identify as professional counselors practicing in that particular state (see Licensure). Common to both processes are NBCC examinations, which are used by each state in the licensure process.

In addition to the state licensure efforts, NBCC continues to advocate for professional counselors by communicating with decision makers about the importance of recognizing professional counselors who have demonstrated a range of skills. NBCC is a founding member of the **Fair Access Coalition on Testing,** a nonprofit organization dedicated to the appropriate access of tests to competent testing professionals. Other NBCC partnerships are focused on achieving much-needed changes to federally funded programs such as Medicare and TRICARE to incorporate qualified professional counselors as recognized service providers. NBCC has also worked in collaboration with organizations in times of national crisis; hundreds of NCCs responded to the terrorist attacks on September 11, 2001, and the 2005 hurricane disasters. With more than 42,000 certified counselors in 2007, NBCC continues to work with and for professional counselors to strengthen the counseling profession and to offer a registry of qualified counselors to the public.

Contributed by Kristi McCaskill,
National Board for Certified
Counselors, Greensboro, NC

Additional Resources

Clawson, T. W., Henderson, D. A., Schweiger, W. K., & Collins, D. R. (2004). *Counselor preparation* (11th ed.). New York: Brunner-Routledge.
National Board for Certified Counselors Web site: http://www.nbcc.org

National Board for Certified Counselors Code of Ethics

The **National Board for Certified Counselors (NBCC)** is the world's largest credentialing board for professional counselors and applicants for credentials in general and specialty counseling areas. Applicants must do more than meet the identified standards for a credential; they must also agree to conduct themselves in accordance with and in adherence to the NBCC (2005) *Code of Ethics*. The **NBCC *Code of Ethics*** provides a minimal ethical standard for the professional behavior for all counselors who are certified by NBCC and assures those served of some resource in the case of a perceived ethical violation by a counselor who is certified by NBCC.

The NBCC *Code of Ethics* applies to all those credentialed by NBCC, regardless of other affiliation or professional identification. Those certified by NBCC who agree to conduct themselves in accordance with the NBCC *Code of Ethics* are investigated in accordance with policies as described in the NBCC *Ethics Case Procedures* if there is a complaint lodged against the counselor or his or her counseling practice. The **NBCC *Ethics Case Procedures*** are the sole process used in examining and determining whether a counselor who is certified by NBCC has committed a violation of the NBCC *Code of Ethics*.

The NBCC *Code of Ethics* was originally approved in July 1982 and has been amended several times, most recently in October 2005. The current NBCC *Code of Ethics* comprises seven sections, and each section is named for and pertains to a particular aspect of professional counseling. The sections are A: General Expectations, B: Counseling Relationship, C: Counselor Supervision, D: Measurement and Evaluation, E: Research and Publication, F: Consulting, and G: Private Practice. In each section are statements describing how counselors who are certified by NBCC are expected to behave. For example, one statement in the section on Private Practice reads, "In advertising services as a private practitioner, certified counselors must advertise in a manner that accurately informs the public of the professional services, expertise, and techniques of counseling available." The current NBCC (2005) *Code of Ethics* is currently available on the NBCC Web site.

Contributed by Joseph P. Jordan,
National Board for Certified
Counselors, Greensboro, NC

Reference

National Board for Certified Counselors. *Code of ethics*. Greensboro, NC: Author.

Additional Resources

American Counseling Association. (2005). *ACA code of ethics*. Alexandria, VA: Author.

Herlihy, B., & Corey, G. (2006). *ACA ethical standards casebook* (6th ed.). Alexandria, VA: American Counseling Association.

National Board for Certified Counselors Web site: http://www.nbcc.org

Remley, T. P., & Herlihy, B. (2005). *Ethical, legal, and professional issues in counseling* (2nd ed.). Upper Saddle River, NJ: Merrill Prentice Hall.

National Board of Certified Counselors Standards for the Ethical Practice of Internet Counseling

The **National Board for Certified Counselors (NBCC)** requires persons credentialed by NBCC to comply with the **NBCC (2005) *Code of Ethics.*** In addition to the standards of behavior contained in the NBCC *Code of Ethics*, NBCC has promulgated **Standards for the Ethical Practice of Internet Counseling,** which is part of a larger document titled *Practice of Internet Counseling* (NBCC, 2007). These Standards are an attempt to provide guidelines for a rapidly evolving and constantly changing method of counseling service delivery (i.e., Internet or other electronically assisted methods of providing counseling to clients).

In January of 1998, a Forum on Internet Mental Health Practice convened in Bethesda, Maryland, at the invitation and sponsorship of NBCC. Twenty-one representatives from various mental health professional membership organizations and representatives from key federal agencies attended, with the stated purpose of discussing and identifying ethical issues in the provision of behavioral health care services using Internet technologies. What emerged from this discussion was a set of core principles that attempted to address these concerns (DuMez, 2000).

NBCC developed a document titled *Practice of Internet Counseling* from these core principles. The first part of this document provides a taxonomy for face-to-face and technology-assisted counseling and is followed by a section with an extensive explanation for various types of counseling. The next section lists definitions related to technology-assisted counseling (e.g., telecounseling, e-mail-based counseling). The final section contains the *Standards for the Ethical Practice of Internet Counseling.*

These *Standards* are divided into the following three sections: Internet Counseling Relationship; Confidentiality in Internet Counseling; and Legal Considerations, Licensure, and Certification. The first section, Internet Counseling Relationship, provides guidelines and parameters for online counseling relationships. For the sake of brevity, the term *online* in this document refers to Internet, telephone, or other electronically assisted methods. For example, the first standard in this section discusses taking steps to verify the identity of an Internet client in order to address possible imposter concerns. This standard thereby seeks to negate one of the inherent difficulties in online counseling: not seeing someone face-to-face and thereby being unable to confirm his or her identity. Subsequent standards in this section deal with similar concerns specific to online counseling relationships (e.g., discussing alternative means of communication should there be a technological problem, obtaining parental consent for service in the case of minor clients).

The second section, Confidentiality in Internet Counseling, provides recommendations pertaining specifically to confidentiality issues in online counseling. This includes using encryption methods to ensure security of client–counselor communications, informing clients how long electronic communications are maintained, security measures used by the online counselor, and following appropriate release of information procedures.

The third section, Legal Considerations, Licensure, and Certification, addresses issues specific to online counseling. One standard states that professionals who provide online counseling services should review and familiarize themselves with all pertinent ethical codes regarding the provision of online counseling services as well as all local, state, provincial, or national statutes related to online counseling services. Another standard calls for online counselors to provide links on their Web site to all appropriate certification or licensure boards to which the counselor is accountable to facilitate client protection.

It should be noted, however, that these standards are to be used in conjunction with and supplemental to the most recent version of the NBCC (2005) *Code of Ethics* and are based on the principles of ethical practice embodied in that code (see National Board for Certified Counselors Code of Ethics). Counselors who provide Internet or other electronically assisted counseling services would benefit from frequently reviewing these standards, as well as applicable ethical codes, in order to ensure compliance with these standards for the provision of services.

Contributed by Joseph P. Jordan,
National Board for Certified
Counselors Inc. and Affiliates,
Greensboro, NC

References

DuMez, E. (2000). Cyberpaths to ethical competence. In J. W. Bloom & G. R. Walz (Eds.), *Cybercounseling and cyberlearning: Strategies and resources for the millennium* (pp. 379–404). Alexandria, VA: American Counseling Association and CAPS.

National Board for Certified Counselors. (2005). *Code of ethics.* Greensboro, NC: Author.

National Council for Certified Counselors. (2007). *Practice of Internet counseling.* Retrieved July 23, 2008, from http://www.nbcc.org/webethics2

Additional Resources

American Counseling Association. (2005). *ACA code of ethics.* Alexandria, VA: Author.

Bloom, J. W., & Walz, G. R. (2000). *Cybercounseling and cyberlearning: Strategies and resources for the millennium.* Alexandria, VA: American Counseling Association and CAPS.

■ National Career Development Association

The **National Career Development Association (NCDA)** is the premier organization for career development, career counseling, and career education. It is a valuable resource for career counselors across specialty areas and for anyone seeking assistance with career development in his or her life. NCDA is a division of the American Counseling Association (ACA) and has a long history of promoting career development across the life span through activities, publications, and the sharing of public information related to careers. NCDA serves diverse groups and fosters the interests of specific groups such as college and university counselors, counselor educators and researchers, K–12 counselors and educators, graduate students, and private practitioners. Furthermore, NCDA provides information and guidance for consumers of career counseling who are seeking education and assistance in career exploration.

NCDA was founded in 1913 and was originally called the National Vocational Guidance Association. In 1985, the group changed its name to the National Career Development Association to broaden services to span career information, career education, and career counseling across many settings. The purpose of NCDA is to provide and promote professional opportunities in career development, to publish and provide public information regarding career standards and activities, and to advocate for and support career development initiatives.

NCDA is at the forefront of establishing and implementing professional standards, guidelines, and competencies in the area of career development. The most recent professional publication is the *NCDA Code of Ethics* (NCDA, 2007) that is based on and adapted from the *ACA Code of Ethics* (ACA, 2005). The ethical standards provide direction for career counselors and consumers and assist in ensuring competence and consistency in career counseling practices. Relevant information, such as a section on career counseling and the Internet, is provided to career counselors and consumers so that information and practices are up-to-date.

One of NCDA's most comprehensive documents is the **Career Counseling Competencies** (NCDA, 1997), which focuses on career knowledge and skills in the following areas: career development theory; individual and group counseling skills; individual/group assessment; information resources; program promotion, management, and implementation; coaching, consultation, and performance improvement; diverse populations; supervision; ethical/legal issues; research/evaluation; and technology. The competencies are tailored to professionals at or above the master's level of education and indicate the minimum competencies needed to provide effective career counseling. Although the competencies are general, they can be specifically applied to special settings so that career counseling professionals can adapt them in order to maximize skills and services.

NCDA sponsors a variety of activities, events, and resources for professionals in career development. Major advocacy events include National Career Development Week and National Career Development Day, which are typically held in November. Poster and poetry contests, K–12 activities, media kits, and specialty products are offered to allow members and nonmembers to celebrate career development. In addition, a summer conference is held annually where many professional development opportunities and resources in career counseling are available.

Membership in ACA is recommended but not required for membership in NCDA. Basic information and resources are accessible through the organization's Web site. Benefits of NCDA membership include updates on the latest information regarding career development and professional opportunities, networking opportunities with other career development professionals, and mentoring programs for beginning career counselors. Another membership benefit is receiving *The Career Development Quarterly,* the official journal of NCDA. Articles in this publication provide the latest information in career development research and practice. Other NCDA publications include *Career Developments* (the NCDA newsletter published quarterly) and a Career Resource Store (available on the Web site) where materials and publications are available for purchase at a discounted member rate. The Web site also provides an area called "Career Center" where jobs for career development professionals are posted. In addition, guidelines for consumers who are selecting a career counselor are offered.

Contributed by Tamara E. Davis,
Marymount University, Arlington, VA

References

American Counseling Association. (2005). *ACA code of ethics.* Alexandria, VA: Author.

National Career Development Association. (1997). *Career counseling competencies.* Retrieved July 2, 2007, from http://www.ncda.org/pdf/counselingcompetencies.pdf

National Career Development Association. (2007). *Code of ethics.* Retrieved July 2, 2007, from http://www.ncda.org/pdf/code_of_ethicsmay-2007.pdf

Additional Resource

National Career Development Association Web site: http://www.ncda.org

■National Counselor Examination for Licensure and Certification

The National Board for Certified Counselors (NBCC) develops, owns, and administers the **National Counselor Examination for Licensure and Certification (NCE).** A 200-item, nonsectioned test that measures knowledge, skills, and abilities essential for providing quality counseling services, the NCE is used not only for national certification purposes but is also an important element of most state counselor licensure processes. The exam's theoretical basis stems from the areas identified by the Council for Accreditation of Counseling and Related Educational Programs (CACREP), the accreditation organization for counselor education programs. NBCC also incorporates research of counseling work behaviors and services as a part of the NCE's fundamental design. All questions are classified by both the CACREP core area and the work behaviors, as outlined in Table 1.

NCE test items contain a "stem" and four possible response choices. Candidates have 4 hours to complete the 200 questions. NBCC creates a new version of the NCE for each administration. Every item underscores an extensive

Table 1. Council for Accreditation of Counseling and Related Educational Programs Core Areas and Work Behaviors Underlying Questions on the National Counselor Examination

Content Area	Work Behavior
Human growth and development	Fundamentals of counseling
Social and cultural foundations	Assessment and career counseling
Helping relationships	Group counseling
Group work	Programmatic and clinical intervention
Career and lifestyle development	Professional practice issues
Appraisal	
Research and program evaluation	
Professional orientation and ethics	

review and field testing process before official use as a scored question on the NCE. The maximum score achievable on the NCE is 160. A modified Angoff procedure is used to establish the minimum passing score for each version. Candidates receive a detailed score report that provides a score from each subarea (i.e., the eight CACREP areas and five work behavior analysis areas) and a total score. Each version of the NCE contains 40 field-tested items. Candidates are not scored on their answers to these questions; however, NBCC gathers statistical data to determine the suitability of the items for use in the future. If the statistical data substantiate the soundness of an item, the question can be used in future versions.

NBCC convenes various committees to conduct the necessary steps to construct an examination that will produce valid and reliable scores. The committees do the following tasks:

1. Classify items according to the Detailed Content Outline derived from the national job analysis of professional counselors.

2. Refine the item pool by rejecting items that are too specialized, that is, considered to be "out of the domain" in terms of the content knowledge considered to be necessary for a minimally competent professional counselor.

3. Create new items that are linked to the current examination framework in order to expand the examination item pool and to keep the content of the examination items current.

4. Review each item every time it is scheduled to be used on an examination. The committee checks for psychometric properties of each item and ensures content accuracy, content distribution and overlap, and verification of quality items. The items are also rechecked for potential gender, race/ethnicity, geographical/cultural, or other types of bias.

5. Review each form of the NCE to ensure the examination contains the specified number of items, with representative sampling of tasks within each major category. The committee is guided by the test specifications, which were empirically derived from the job analysis study.

6. Review after each administration of the NCE and in conjunction with the committee and staff psychometricians the properties of each of the items and of the examination as a whole.

All questions, each form of the NCE, and the answer sheet are copyrighted; therefore, any unauthorized use of examination content or materials is prohibited. Disclosure of the examination content is a violation of the NBCC *Code of Ethics*.

Contributed by Kristi McCaskill,
National Board for Certified
Counselors, Greensboro, NC

Additional Resources

National Board for Certified Counselors, Inc. and Affiliates. (2001). *Official preparation guide for the National Counselor Examination for Licensure and Certification.* Greensboro, NC: Author.

National Counselor Examination for Licensure and Certification Web site: http://www.nbcc.org/nce

◼ National Employment Counseling Association

The **National Employment Counseling Association (NECA;** 2007) is one of two divisions of the American Counseling Association (ACA) that provide leadership for counselors specializing in employment services and career development. The other division is the National Career Development Association (NCDA; see National Career Development Association). Herr (2000) drew a distinction between these two professional organizations by stating that NCDA's focus is more concerned with theory, emerging issues, and career development throughout the life span, whereas NECA's focus is on labor exchange, labor market trends, counseling models useful for job seekers, and the impact of government policies on employment and unemployment.

NECA was originally chartered in 1966. The organization emerged during the decade when occupational opportunities and vocational education programs expanded under the 1963 Vocational Education Act and 1968 Amendments (Herr & Shahnasarian, 2001). NECA attracts members working in diverse settings, such as private practice; business and industry; community agencies; schools, colleges, and universities; and federal, state, and local government. NECA's mission is to assist members with their charge of preparing individuals to understand and navigate the work world. The organization supports its mission through a focus on (a) developing standards and guidelines, (b) highlighting best practices, (c) promoting legislative advocacy, and (d) offering network and continuing education opportunities (NECA, 2007).

In 2000, NECA and NCDA combined their two respective journals to produce a one-time joint special issue highlighting the benefits of more collaboration and partnership between the two organizations. The special issue was preceded by previous discussions between editors of the journals over a 2-year period. The editors hoped to spark further collaboration and connection between members of both organizations (Amundson & Niles, 2000). Previously, NECA also contributed to the development and support of the Career Development Facilitators (CDF), a certification process outlining competencies, education, and experiences of career service providers. This certification was a collaborative response to issues of career and job transitions, unemployment, and entering the changing world-of-work (Splete & Hoppin, 2000). This initial CDF certification has since taken a more international face and has evolved into the Global Career Development Facilitator (GCDF) credential. NECA also began its sponsorship of the Working Ahead curriculum, leading to a graduate-level GCDF certification (Brawley, 2002).

NECA offers two types of annual membership: professional/regular and student/retired. Members have access to employment counseling standards, which offer guidance for competencies in employment counseling programs such as Workforce Development, Welfare Reform, School-to-Work, and One-Stop Career Centers. NECA members also receive the quarterly *NECA Newsletter* and the quarterly *Journal of Employment Counseling*. NECA is an approved provider of continuing education for the National Board for Certified Counselors and offers an annual 2-day professional development workshop (NECA, 2007).

Contributed by Kathleen Kellum and
Tarrell Awe Agahe Portman,
University of Iowa, Iowa City, IA

References

Amundson, N. E., & Niles, S. G. (2000). Editors' introduction to the joint special issue on collaboration, partnership, policy, and practice in career development. *Journal of Employment Counseling, 37,* 51–52.

Brawley, K. (2002). Working Ahead: The national one-stop workforce system and career development facilitator curriculum training for instructors. In G. R. Walz, S. Lambert, & R. Kirkman (Eds.), *Careers across America 2002: Best ideas in career development conference proceedings* (pp. 27–32). Greensboro, NC: ERIC Counseling and Student Services Clearinghouse. (ERIC Document Reproduction Service No. ED 465906)

Herr, E. L., (2000). Collaboration, partnership, policy, and practice in career development. *Journal of Employment Counseling, 37,* 53–61.

Herr, E. L., & Shahnasarian, M. (2001). Selected milestones in the evolution of career development practices in the twentieth century. *The Career Development Quarterly, 49,* 225–232.

National Employment Counseling Association. (2007). *National Employment Counseling Association.* Retrieved July 13, 2007, from http://geocities.com/employment-counseling/neca.html

Splete, H. H., & Hoppin, J. M. (2000). Emergence of career development facilitators. *Journal of Employment Counseling, 37,* 107–116.

Additional Resource

National Employment Counseling Association Web site: http://geocities.com/employmentcounseling/

National Rehabilitation Counseling Association

The **National Rehabilitation Counseling Association (NRCA)** was the first professional organization to form as a division of the **National Rehabilitation Association.** By forming a distinct professional organization in 1958, members of NRCA emphasized the importance of the counseling relationship in the provision of rehabilitation services. More recently, in 2005, NRCA became a separate and independent organization representing rehabilitation counselors. Rehabilitation counselors work in a variety of employment settings, including vocational rehabilitation agencies, nonprofit and for-profit institutions, and private practice. NRCA defines **rehabilitation counseling** as "a profession, rather than a particular skill area within the context of general counseling or guidance, that transcends the variety of employment settings, for example, state-federal, mental health, drug, and hospital programs" (Kirk & La Forge, 1995, p. 47). **Rehabilitation counselors** are dedicated to developing self-sufficiency in persons with disabilities. NRCA advances the profession of rehabilitation counselors through its influence on licensure and certification, ethical standards and best practice guidelines, training and professional development, and advocacy.

NRCA has taken an active role in promoting the licensure and certification of rehabilitation counselors. The establishment of the **Commission on Rehabilitation Counselor Certification (CRCC)** provided for certification that ensured the profession and public that **Certified Rehabilitation Counselors** meet minimum standards of education and training. Rehabilitation counselors must possess a master's degree in rehabilitation counseling or a related counseling area (e.g., a master's degree in mental health counseling) and have specific work experience in rehabilitation counseling to be considered for certification or licensure.

An additional focus of NRCA was to join with CRCC and the American Rehabilitation Counseling Association to establish ethical standards for the profession. The **Code of Professional Ethics for Rehabilitation Counselors** (NRCA, 2001) and **Scope of Practice Statement for Rehabilitation Counseling** set minimum ethical standards and guidelines for the practice of rehabilitation counseling. Furthermore, these standards delineate the knowledge and skills required to provide effective rehabilitation counseling services and set parameters for training of rehabilitation counselors. NRCA is also dedicated to fostering ongoing professional development of rehabilitation counselors through research. The *Journal of Applied Rehabilitation Counseling* is published quarterly to keep NRCA members and others abreast of current issues in rehabilitation counseling, innovations, and best practice approaches as well as legislation affecting rehabilitation counseling.

In addition to promoting credentialing, another primary concern of NRCA is advocacy. NRCA strives to ensure quality, equity, and parity in the delivery of rehabilitation counseling services. Rehabilitation counselors recognize that their services are of value to individuals of diverse multicultural backgrounds who have disabilities. Rehabilitation counselors also work to serve the larger community in which individuals with disabilities live and work. NRCA advocates for legislation and training standards that allow for the best-practice provision of services that allow recipients to become self-reliant, self-sufficient, contributing members of the community.

The American Counseling Association (ACA) recognizes that much of the early background of counseling was vocational counseling. In 2003, the Governing Council of ACA passed a motion reaffirming a previous position that rehabilitation counselors are, first and foremost, counselors. ACA indicated in its position statement that rehabilitation counselors with degrees from Council on Rehabilitation Education programs and those trained in programs accredited by the Council for Accreditation of Counseling and Related Educational Programs are considered to have equivalent training when considered for state licensure.

NRCA offers multiple opportunities for membership in a range of categories from professional to affiliate members, depending on qualifications. Membership is open to rehabilitation counselors, rehabilitation counselor educators, researchers in rehabilitation, graduate students, and related affiliates. Professional members not certified by CRC must hold a minimum of a master's degree from an accredited rehabilitation counseling program and have a minimum of 1 year of experience working in a rehabilitation setting. Professional members who do not hold degrees from accredited rehabilitation programs may qualify for membership if their degree is from a related accredited program and they have completed a minimum of 2 years of experience working in a rehabilitation setting. Students currently enrolled in accredited 4-year institutions in a curriculum leading to a degree in rehabilitation services may also qualify for membership. Individuals holding bachelor's degrees in rehabilitation services or those employed in rehabilitation practice at an ancillary level may also qualify for membership.

Contributed by Donna S. Starkey, Delta State University, Cleveland, MS, and Veronica Renee Harrison, Mississippi State University, Starkville, MS

References

American Counseling Association. (2003). *Governing Council motion form.* Retrieved July 23, 2008, from http://www.rehabeducators.org/docs/pdf/american_counseling_association_motion.pdf

Kirk, F., & La Forge, J. (1995). The National Rehabilitation Counseling Association: Where we've been, where we're going. *Journal of Rehabilitation, 61*(3), 47–50.

National Rehabilitation Counseling Association. (2001). *Code of professional ethics for rehabilitation counselors.* Retrieved July 23, 2008, from nrca-net.org/prof_devl.html

Additional Resource

National Rehabilitation Counseling Association Web site: http://nrca-net.org

Native Americans, Counseling

Native Americans are a highly racially and ethnically diverse group whose ancestors inhabited the Americas before European contact and settlement. Native Americans are variously known as American Indians, indigenous people, aboriginal people, and original Americans, although there is little agreement among non-Natives or among Native American people themselves about the most suitable designation. There are approximately 4.5 million Native Americans in the United States representing over 500 federally and state recognized tribes, with 37% living in urban areas and 63% living in small town, rural and reservation areas (U.S. Census Bureau, 2000).

Native American Values

Among Native American tribes, there are many differences in histories, cultural practices, religious beliefs, attitudes, and living conditions. There are also many similarities that are based on common worldviews and common core value systems, including (a) harmony (i.e., a nonaggressive and noncompetitive approach to life, especially if the goal of aggression and competition is individual gain); (b) reciprocity and generosity (i.e., in the form of gift giving and receiving and sharing personal resources, even when people cannot afford to do so); (c) a belief in immanent justice, personal choice, and noninterference with others' choices or decisions; (d) a belief in not speaking ill of others so that a person's ill speaking does not return to harm the speaker; (e) a present time orientation and a belief in the good of living fully in each moment given; (f) a respect for elders; and finally (g) the importance of the good of the community over the good of the individual. In contrast, the mainstream American value orientation consists of a preference for (a) competition in the promotion of self-interests, (b) saving and dominating rather than giving and sharing, (c) a belief that the justice a person receives is based on his or her mastery over all, (d) a belief that criticism of others is a good thing and will result in their improvement as well as increase the speaker's dominance over the criticized, (e) a future time orientation (i.e., living for what will happen tomorrow), (f) a regard for youth, and (g) the importance of the individual over the importance of the community. Native American worldviews resemble a circle, with power, resources, and support shared among equals. Mainstream American worldviews resemble a pyramid, with one person on top who has gotten there through competitive actions and with power, resources, and support distributed according to the importance of the person on each descending row, until there is little left for people at the bottom of the pyramid. These highly divergent value systems can cause Native American people to suffer acculturation stress as they attempt to meet the demands of the society around them while still remaining true to their own beliefs and value systems.

Historical and Current Experiences of Native American People

There are also similarities that stem from colonization, oppression, and less access to full participation in the American economy. Examples of these practices are treaties to which Native Americans were forced to acquiesce and were then broken by the U.S. government, leading to loss of lands and opportunities to choose one's own path; being called by pejorative names (e.g., savage); being told that Native Americans have low intelligence and need to have decisions made for them as wards of the government; being forced to give up Native American languages and religions; having children taken and placed in boarding schools, with parents often not seeing their children again for years; being placed on reservations only to be removed again at the discretion and pleasure of the U.S. government; having fewer educational opportunities; being subject to discriminatory hiring, promotion, and wage increase practices; and being victimized by interracial violence at twice the rate of all other U.S. residents (U.S. Department of Justice [USDOJ], Office of Justice Programs, Bureau of Justice Statistics, 2001). These practices, which have been perpetrated on Native American people over the last 500 years, have led to intergenerational trauma, anxiety, depression, loss of will, loss of hope, and loss of life.

Key Concerns and Challenges of Native American People

There are vibrant Native American communities that celebrate their own cultures and traditional life ways. Native Americans as a group also experience tremendous social and mental health challenges related to poverty, low educational attainment, substance abuse/dependence, diabetes and other chronic debilitating diseases, interpersonal violence, incarceration, and depression/suicide. Although Native American people have developed coping strategies to deal with these social, health, and mental health issues, such as using humor, telling "Indian" stories, and participating in spiritual rituals, Native American people have greater vulnerabilities and protective factors (e.g., resources to deal with mental health issues, healthy families and communities, and societal support for their values and beliefs) than any other American ethnic group. These problems have spanned generations and appear to be intractable, with seemingly little progress over the last 100 years in solving the problems or diminishing their consequences. More recent research, however, is beginning to address these concerns in greater depth by investigating intertribal similarities and differences in order to understand etiology, construct culturally sensitive counseling models, develop targeted counseling strategies, and confront social injustices.

Poverty

The 2000 census data (U.S. Census Bureau, 2000) show that the rate of poverty among Native Americans nationwide is approximately 25.9%, almost 3 times that of Caucasian Americans. In some areas of the country, Native incomes on average are approximately half those of Caucasian Americans, with Native Americans about a third less likely to have jobs.

Unemployment rates among Native Americans range from 25% to 50% among the 25 largest tribes in the nation, 50% or more across all reservations, and upwards of 80% on the large northern reservations. In addition, approximately 90,000 Native families are homeless, 15% of the homes that Native Americans live in are overcrowded, 12% of Native Americans do not have access to indoor plumbing, and 17% of Native American households do not have phone service (U.S. Census Bureau, 2000). Although the reasons for this poverty are very complex and not well understood, the rates of poverty may be associated with lower educational attainment, the lack of employment opportunities both on reservations and in urban areas for Native American people, and discrimination in employment practices.

Substance Abuse and Comorbid Mental Health Concerns

The most serious mental health challenge among Native Americans is alcohol/drug abuse and dependency. Although exact rates are difficult to determine, research has shown that alcohol and drug abuse accounts for 72% of outpatient visits to the Indian Health Service for persons less than 40 years of age (Silmere & Stiffman, 2006). There is, however, significant tribal variation in rates of alcohol use, drug abuse, and co-occurring psychological diagnoses. For example, some tribes have reported total abstinence from alcohol among their members, some have reported heavy episodic drinking, and some have reported that tribal members engaged in continuous binge drinking.

Regarding drug abuse, studies report high lifetime prevalence rates (i.e., using illicit substances or the abuse of prescription drugs at least once) in the range of 45% to 55% among Native American adolescents and adults. Across studies, the most commonly abused drugs are marijuana, cocaine, methamphetamines, and inhalants (Silmere & Stiffman, 2006; USDOJ, Office of Justice Programs, Bureau of Justice Statistics, 2001). In these studies, ceremonial substances such as peyote, are not typically considered illicit drugs.

Concomitant with chemical abuse are other serious problems. For example, alcohol-related mortality rates from motor vehicle crashes are 184% higher among Native Americans than among other ethnic groups. Native Americans tend to experience more incidents of alcohol-related cirrhosis of the liver, suicide, and homicide. Domestic abuse is 3.5 times greater among Native Americans than among other groups. Fetal alcohol syndrome is 3 times greater among Native Americans than among the rest of the U.S. population, and at least 50% of all court referrals and criminal acts are related to alcohol abuse among Native American youth (USDOJ, Office of Justice Programs, Bureau of Justice Statistics, 2001).

Studies have reported comorbid mood, behavioral, and other diagnoses as high as 82% (Alcántara & Gone, 2007; USDOJ, Office of Justice Programs, Bureau of Justice Statistics, 2001). Especially distressing is the rate of co-occurring depression and suicide among Native American youth, with some studies reporting that 1 out of every 200 Native youth attempt suicide and that 4 times as many complete suicide as youth from all other population groups combined.

Diabetes

Diabetes is a serious public health challenge among Native American people. The prevalence of Type II diabetes among Native Americans has reached epidemic proportions, with rates of diabetes ranging from twice as high (12.2% compared to the 6.5% overall national rates) to 4 times as high as the general U.S. population (Silmere & Stiffman, 2006). In one tribe, diagnosed diabetes has been reported at 50%, which is the highest prevalence rate across all other racial/ethnic groups worldwide. Moreover, studies show that Native Americans are significantly less likely to adhere to treatment protocols than the general population. This is compounded by the cycle of poverty that creates an inability to afford medication. Indeed, complications from diabetes are one of the major causes of death among Native Americans, with Native people 3 times more likely to die from diabetic complications than Caucasian Americans.

Incarceration

Native Americans are also overrepresented at all levels of incarceration at 1.6 times higher in the federal system to 4 times higher in local and county jails than Caucasian Americans. Researchers have estimated that 1 out of 3 Native Americans will be jailed during their lifetime and that 1 in 2 American Indian families will have a relative die in jail (USDOJ, Office of Justice Programs, Bureau of Justice Statistics, 2001).

School Dropout Rates

Native Americans are also estimated to drop out of high school at 2 to 3 times the rate of Caucasian Americans; however, newer programs that allow Native American youth to complete high school courses in nonstandard sequences and at nontraditional times may be helping more Native students obtain their diplomas and continue on into personally satisfying post–high school opportunities. The success of these programs is still being evaluated, but it is likely that high school completion will increase as alternative programs continue to be developed. Nevertheless, addressing the wage and employment gap between Native Americans and members of the American ethnic majority may demand a broader solution than educational progress and achievement.

Counseling Strategies

Emerging counseling research and practical professional experience suggest ways to ameliorate the effects of centuries of social injustice among Native Americans. Studies examining the use of traditional healing ceremonies have had mixed effects; however, treatment strategies that include Native American counselors, elders, spiritual leaders, families, and even the employers of Native American people are showing promising results in managing chemical abuse and other mental health issues. Moreover, family involvement has been shown to be related to overall successful functioning of Native American young people, including increasing educational achievement; health and safety behavior; self-sufficiency; and emotional, social, behavioral, and cognitive competence. The provision of diabetes education and counseling on tribal grounds has been met with satisfaction among Native American adults. The inclusion of sexual health education could also be included in these psychoeducational opportunities, as could the provision of career counseling for employment seekers as ways to increase successful career development. Finally, professional counselors need to become highly involved in social justice issues. Examining discriminatory practices in education and employment and supporting initiatives that promote equity can diminish the root causes of mental health challenges and promote successful life opportunities among Native American people.

Contributed by Sherri Lou Turner,
University of Minnesota, Minneapolis, MN

References

Alcántara, A., & Gone, J. P. (2007). Reviewing suicide in Native American communities: Situating risk and protective factors within a transactional-ecological framework. *Death Studies, 31,* 457–477.

Silmere, H., & Stiffman, A. R. (2006). Factors associated with successful functioning in American Indian youths. *American Indian and Alaska Native Mental Health Research, 13,* 23–47.

U.S. Census Bureau. (2000). *American Indian and Alaska Native (AIAN) data and links.* Retrieved July 23, 2008, from http://factfinder.census.gov/home/aian/index.html

U.S. Department of Justice, Office of Justice Programs, Bureau of Justice Statistics. (2001). *American Indians and crime.* Retrieved August 3, 2007, from http://www.ojp.usdoj.gov/bjs /pub/pdf/aic.pdf

Additional Resource

Lapidus, J. A., Bertolli, J., McGowan, K., & Sullivan, P. (2006). HIV-related risk behaviors, perceptions of risk, HIV testing, and exposure to prevention messages and methods among urban American Indians and Alaska natives. *AIDS Education and Prevention, 18,* 546–559.

■Nature Versus Nurture

Nature versus nurture is the phrase used to describe the debate between the influences of heredity and environment in physical, behavioral, and psychological traits. Philosophers and scientists as early as Aristotle have attempted to sort the impact of **nature** (heredity) and **nurture** (environment) on individual developmental processes. If the primary influences on development were found to be in nature, genetics counseling would become preeminent. If the primary responsibility were found to be in nurture, studies of factors that would enhance development would take preeminence. Height and hair color are traits that have a large genetic component; however, intelligence, personality traits, and even the development of certain psychiatric disorders can be traced to both genetic and environmental influences.

Researchers investigating the nature versus nurture debate often use twins as a research sample. Studies with twins help to differentiate between those traits or characteristics believed to be based in genetics and those that occur as the result of environmental influences. One example of the classic twin study is fraternal or identical twins separated at birth. Such an approach affords researchers the opportunity to study genetically similar individuals who have been exposed to different environments. Simply put, if twins raised separately share common characteristics, these can be assumed to be based in nature (i.e., genetics). Fundamental differences in characteristics may then be attributed to the environments in which the twins were raised (i.e., nurture). Researchers also investigate the interaction between genetic and environmental influences as well as the correlation between the two in order to strengthen the evidence for the influence of genetic factors.

The counseling field is ripe with examples of genetic and environmental influences. The *Diagnostic and Statistical Manual of Mental Disorders* (4th ed., text rev.; *DSM-IV-TR;* American Psychiatric Association [APA], 2000) specifies all recognized diagnostic categories of mental disorders. Within each category, the *DSM-IV-TR* provides information on familial patterns and genetic predispositions for mental disorders. For example, individuals who have a first-degree biological relative with a history of depression are more vulnerable to developing posttraumatic stress disorder than do individuals without this family history. Individuals with schizophrenia have distinctly different brain imaging patterns than those who do not. Having a first-degree biological relative with this disorder places a client at 10 times the risk for developing schizophrenia. This risk is clearly based in nature rather than nurture because a similar predisposition is not found in individuals whose adoptive parent has schizophrenia.

In addition, adoption studies have provided evidence that there are both genetic and environmental influences in the development of antisocial personality disorder, somatization disorder, and substance use and abuse disorders. In fact, having a biological or adoptive parent with either of these disorders increases a child's risk for the development of the disorders (APA, 2000). There is not a neat separation of the effects of influences from genetics (i.e., nature) versus those from environmental forces (i.e., nurture). Although the debate continues, contemporary theorists recognize the interaction (i.e., the epigenetic approach) between these two powerful factors to determine traits. Concern is less over whether nature or nurture is more powerful than over how these factors interact to influence development.

Contributed by Sondra R. Dowdle,
Mississippi State University, Starkville, MS,
and Donna S. Starkey, Delta State
University, Cleveland, MS

Reference

American Psychiatric Association. (2000). *Diagnostic and statistical manual of mental disorders* (4th ed., text rev.). Washington, DC: Author.

Additional Resources

Moore, D. S. (2001). *The dependent gene.* New York: Holt.

Rutter, M. (2003). Commentary: Nature–nurture interplay in emotional disorders. *Journal of Child Psychology and Psychiatry, 44,* 934–944.

Needs Assessment

Needs assessment is an essential component of planning, implementing, and continually evaluating programs. Counseling programs use needs assessment to monitor their programs continually and to improve them. For example, the Council for Accreditation of Counseling and Related Educational Programs requires counseling programs to perform a complete program evaluation every 3 years. Through an analysis of these evaluations, it is possible to determine which areas of the program are satisfactory, which areas of the program may have improved since the last evaluation, and which areas of the program may need improvement. In this way, needs assessment is continually involved in locating areas of programs and interventions that need to be improved or deleted. In addition, the needs assessment process is essential for deciding what new programs or services are necessary in an area and what current programs are providing.

The needs assessment process involves three components. The first component is to decide what needs are currently being met. The second component is to decide what needs are not being met. Basically, needs assessment can be defined as the process of determining what is and what should be. Once this is determined, a third component is to design interventions and programs to meet the identified needs.

There are some basic steps to most needs assessments. First, it is critical to define the exact purpose of the needs assessment. When working toward defining the purpose, it is important to operationalize the purpose so that it may be assessed. Once this is clear, the stakeholders associated with the purpose must be identified. **Stakeholders** are any individuals who have an association with the purpose. For example, if the purpose is to define the extent of bullying in a middle school, stakeholders may include students, parents, teachers, administrators, custodians, school resource officers, cafeteria workers, secretaries, school counselors, and bus drivers. It is essential to define all of the possible stakeholders to gain the most information, but it is also important that everyone involved feels they have input into the outcomes. There are several methods used in the actual needs assessment, such as key informants, community forums, field surveys, focus groups, social indicators, and rates under treatment. In addition, there are differing methods to gather the information, such as interviews, surveys, focus groups, records review, data analyses, and reports studies.

Once the assessment has been completed, the data must be analyzed. Professional counselors are in an excellent position to facilitate the understanding of the results of the needs assessment. It is important the data be disseminated to each interested group on a level that is appropriate for that particular group. For example, when making a presentation to students, the content and medium chosen may be different than the information and medium chosen to present the information to a consortium of community agencies. In developing and revising interventions and programs based on needs assessments, goals and objectives need to be outlined concretely. It is ideal to involve all stakeholders in this process, attending to potentially conflicting goals and objectives and outlining clearly specific criteria for outcomes.

In conclusion, there are three basic components to needs assessment. Needs assessment allows individuals to determine what is, what should be, and what method should be devised to close the gap between the first two. Needs assessments may vary greatly in terms of level of comprehensiveness, complexity, cost, length of time to be conducted, information received, and effectiveness.

Contributed by Valerie L. Schwiebert,
Western Carolina University,
Cullowhee, NC

Additional Resources

Gupta, K., Sleezer, C., & Russ-Eft, D. (2007). *A practical guide to needs assessment.* London: Pfeiffer.
Reviere, R. (1996). *Needs assessment: A creative and practical guide for social scientists.* New York: Taylor & Francis.

Neo-Freudian Approaches

Orthodox classical psychoanalysis has traditionally been associated with the work of **Sigmund Freud.** During the early decades of the psychoanalytic movement, major figures such as Jung, Adler, Ferenezi, and Rank diverged significantly from Freud's theory of sexuality, based on the notion of instinctual drive, as well as his theory of development. This divergence from Freud's established psychosexual approach became known as the **neo-Freudian approach.** Neo-Freudians have challenged Freud's original concepts of the instinctual drive, the Oedipus complex, and the motivational primacy of sex and aggression (Fine, 1990; Mitchell & Black, 1995).

Departures from orthodox classical analysis can be seen in successive generations through the developments of ego psychology, interpersonal psychoanalysis, Kleinian psychoanalysis, object relations, and self-psychology. Ego psychologists differed from Freud in that they were interested in preoedipal disturbances prior to language development as well as the Oedipal conflict. Ego psychologists broadened Freud's concept of transference to include a greater understanding of psychic disturbances. Major contributors to **ego psychology** were **Anna Freud** (1895–1982), **Heinz Hartmann** (1894–1970), **Margaret Mahler** (1897–1985), and **Edith Jacobson** (1897–1978; Fine, 1990; Mitchell & Black, 1995). Anna Freud's study of the ego and its characterological defenses was the basis for her defense theory. Mahler's developmental ego psychology has provided an understanding of the psychological symbiotic embeddedness of the child–mother psychological relationship. Hartmann became known as the father of ego psychology. Jacobson posited that biology and experience continuously interacted and mutually influenced each other.

In his work with people with schizophrenia, **Harry Stack Sullivan** (1892–1949) made two psychoanalytic contributions: interpersonal field theory and the methodology of participant observation. Sullivan did not view individual psychology as an object to study; instead, he suggested in his interpersonal field theory that personality manifests itself only in relation to others, much like Martin Buber's I–thou concept, in which there is no *I* without a *thou*. Sullivan, therefore, was most interested in the dynamics of interpersonal relationships. **Clara Thompson** (1893–1958) integrated Sullivan's interpersonal theory with **Erich Fromm's** (1900–1980) theory about what is currently referred to as interpersonal psychoanalysis (Mitchell & Black, 1995). The central concept in contemporary **interpersonal psychoanalysis** is the idea of the self as organized horizontally versus Freud's notion of the self as being organized vertically.

Melanie Klein (1882–1960) and her contemporary **Wilford Bion** (1897–1979) had a significant impact on contemporary psychoanalysis (Mitchell & Black, 1995). Klein was responsible for the concept of an infantile fantasy life and the use of projective identification—an extension of Freud's concept of projection—as a defense mechanism. Bion is noted for his description of **attacks on linking,** or how the mind can attack its own processes.

During the 1940s, the British Psychoanalytic Society split into three groups: Kleinian disciples, classical Freudians, and a new group of object relations theorists. Major **object relations** figures included **W. R. D. Fairbairn, D. W. Winnicott, Michael Balint, John Bowlby,** and **Harry Guntrip.** These theorists maintained Klein's idea that an infant was wired for human interaction, but they disagreed with her idea of constitutional aggression deriving from the death instinct. Fairbairn's concepts of the splitting of the ego and internal objects can be best understood in terms of how relationships are shaped according to an individual's internalized patterns of his or her earliest significant relationship. Winnicott's concepts of the **transitional object** and **holding environment** are often used by current clinicians. In Balint's view, a rupture in the early relationship creates what he termed the *basic fault* (Balint, 1968). Bowlby's concept of instinctual attachment has contributed to the relationship between psychoanalysis and other disciplines (e.g., information processing, biology, anthropology, ethnology). Guntrip was an analysand of Winnicott and Fairbairn. His concept of the regressed ego has contributed to the approach by poplar psychology of the inner child.

Although **Erik Erikson** (1902–1994) and **Heinz Kohut** (1923–1981) were heavily influenced by Freudian ego psychology, each created a different psychoanalytic vision of ego psychology (Mitchell & Black, 1995). Erickson is remembered for his theoretical contribution of ego development, in which an individual's identity develops as the ego unfolds across psychosocial stages or crises. Each stage corresponds with a libidinal phase of drive maturation. The most widely known concept was Erickson's concept of **ego identity,** which is associated with adolescence. Kohut's elaborations of ego psychology provided the basis for explorations of the phenomenology of selfhood through his theory

of self-psychology. Kohut is remembered for his initial contributions of his reformulation of Freud's concept of narcissism as well as his methodological innovation of sustained empathic immersion and the theoretical concepts of selfobjects and selfobject transferences.

Contemporary Freudian revisionists include **Otto Kernberg, Roy Schafer, Hans Loewald** (1906–1993), and **Jacques Lacan** (1901–1981; Mitchell & Black, 1995). These clinicians sought to assimilate many of Freud's concepts and observations into their own theoretical concepts and have revised the basic principles of analytic neutrality, frustration, and regression. Kernberg integrated features of Freud's traditional instinct theory and Freud's structural model, Klein and Fairbairn's object relation theories, and Jacobson's developmental theory. Kernberg's ideas have remained relative to some of the basic features of Freudian thought, but he added the ideas of borderline and narcissistic phenomena along with the concept of primitive object relations. Schafer's idea of **narratives** can be seen in current psychodynamic techniques (Schafer, 1992). Loewald redefined Freud's ideas into a theory of object relations; Lacan redefined Freud's ideas in his discovery of the linguistic nature of the unconscious.

Contemporary neo-Freudian approaches have come about because of the changing times. Orthodox psychoanalysis has been replaced by other forms of psychotherapy and psychiatric medications. The insurance industry's and government's control over payments has increased the use of brief and solution-focused symptomatic treatments; however, most psychotherapies have been influenced both by classical and contemporary psychoanalytic concepts.

Contributed by Luellyn Switzer and
Carl J. Sheperis, Mississippi State
University, Starkville, MS

References

Balint, M. (1968*). The basic fault*. London: Tavistock.

Fine, R. (1990). *The history of psychoanalysis*. Northvale, NJ: Aronson.

Mitchell, S. A., & Black, M. J. (1995). *Freud and beyond: A history of modern psychoanalytic thought*. New York: Basic Books.

Schafer, R. (1992). *Retelling a life*. New York: Basic Books.

■ Nonexperimental Research

Nonexperimental research includes the detailed observation, description, and documentation of variables as they naturally occur. Nonexperimental research describes variables without implementation of an intervention. Unlike experimental research, nonexperimental research does not involve the direct manipulation of the independent variable by the researcher and does not include random assignment of participants, thereby eliminating the ability to draw cause-and-effect connections between independent and dependent variables. Although nonexperimental research is deemed weaker than experimental research in terms of causal assessment (i.e., internal validity), it is frequently used in social science research because many variables (e.g., depression, anxiety, marital satisfaction) cannot be ethically manipulated.

Nonexperimental designs can be either quantitative or qualitative, depending on the goals of the researcher, but they are typically associated with quantitative research. The four major types of nonexperimental quantitative research include descriptive, correlational, causal–comparative, and survey.

Descriptive research is the broadest category of nonexperimental research and includes detailed descriptions of the variables being studied. This form of nonexperimental research is typically conducted when very little information is known about a construct or phenomenon and is frequently seen as the starting point for the development of theories or the generation of hypotheses. Data for descriptive research are most often collected through the use of questionnaires or interviews and can be used to assess basic descriptive statistics, such as frequencies, percentages, and averages (see Descriptive Research). For example, a researcher might be interested in knowing how many panic attacks a claustrophobic person experienced following systematic desensitization therapy. This would be an example of descriptive research because it assesses the frequency of an observed event.

Correlational research is a form of nonexperimental research that is used to describe the relationship between two or more variables being investigated. With correlational research, the researcher is interested in understanding the extent to which the variables being investigated covary. Correlations are used to quantify the strength and direction of a relationship between variables and are statistically demonstrated with a numerical value known as the **correlation coefficient** that ranges from −1.0 to +1.0. The direction of a correlation is determined by whether or not the correlation coefficient is positive or negative. If positive, then an increase (or decrease) in one variable will result in an increase (or decrease) in the other variable. Either way, both variables are moving in the same direction. The strength of the correlation is determined by the actual numerical value of the correlation coefficient. The closer the correlation coefficient comes to 1.0 (positive or negative), the stronger the correlation. A correlation coefficient of zero indicates no correlation, and, therefore, there is no relationship between the variables (see Correlation Coefficient). An example of correlational research would involve exploring the relationship between level of depression and grade point average in freshman college students.

Causal–comparative research, also known as **ex post facto research,** is a form of nonexperimental research that explores the relationship between the independent and dependent variable when it is impossible or unethical to manipulate the independent variable. The term *ex post facto* actually means "after the fact," indicating that the evaluation of the dependent variable took place after the independent variable had occurred. Unlike quasi-experimental research, which involves the direct manipulation of the independent variable by the researcher, the researcher does not influence the independent variable in causal–comparative research.

Instead, the researcher evaluates the impact of the independent variable on the dependent variable after the independent variable is present or has already occurred (see Ex Post Facto Research). An example of causal–comparative research would be evaluating the level of parental marital satisfaction after the birth of a child. Given that a researcher could not assign (manipulate) participants to have children, a causal–comparative study would be appropriate for assessing post-childbirth marital satisfaction.

The final form of nonexperimental quantitative research is known as **survey research.** When conducting survey research, most researchers are interested in gaining information about prevalence, distribution, and interrelations of variables within a population. Survey research uses self-report information and direct questioning in order to elicit information about how, what, and to what extent some variable is occurring within the selected population. This type of nonexperimental research is used frequently because it can generate large amounts of information in a relatively short amount of time. The primary means of conducting survey research are personal interviews, telephone interviews, self-administered questionnaires, or a combination of these three (see Survey Research in Counseling). One example of survey research would be attending an autism support group meeting and having attending parents fill out a survey on levels of nonfinite grief. In this instance, the researcher would be able to assess quickly the grief level of the parents in attendance.

Contributed by Kristi B. Cannon,
St. Mary's University, San Antonio, TX

Additional Resources

Heppner, P. P., Wampold, B. E., & Kivlighan, D. M. (2008). *Research design in counseling* (3rd ed.). Belmont, CA: Wadsworth.

McMillan, J. (2003). *Educational research: Fundamentals for the consumer* (4th ed.). Boston: Pearson.

■ Nonparametric Statistics

Also known as distribution-free tests, **nonparametric tests** are a class of statistical procedures that make few assumptions about the distribution of scores in the underlying population that is represented by the research. In particular, nonparametric tests do not require the dependent variable to be normally distributed, and there is no assumption that scores in the underlying population of interest will fall along a symmetrical bell curve. Nonparametric tests are used with nominal or ordinal data or when interval or ratio data are not distributed normally.

These procedures are commonly used when data fail to meet one or more of the assumptions of parametricity, thus precluding the use of parametric tests such as *t* tests, analysis of variance (ANOVA), or Pearson product–moment correlations; however, there is debate in the literature about the value of using nonparametric tests, even in these situations. Proponents of nonparametric procedures raise several arguments for their use in counseling research. First, they point out that nonparametric tests, unlike their parametric counterparts, remain valid no matter how scores are distributed. Second, because these tests are based on ranks rather than raw scores, the risk of having conclusions distorted by the presence of a few extreme scores in the data set is eliminated. Finally, proponents note that counseling researchers often use parametric tests with ordinal data, such as scores based on Likert-type scales. Opponents of the use of nonparametric tests counter that, in most situations, parametric tests are robust enough to yield valid conclusions even when there are some violations of the assumptions of parametricity. In addition, when violations of parametricity are minor or absent, they argue that nonparametric tests require more participants to achieve the same level of statistical power as equivalent parametric procedures.

The **chi-square test** is a procedure designed for studies in which all the variables in a study are categorical (i.e., nominal), such as ethnicity, choice of occupation, or type of therapy. It can be used with two or more categorical variables, where each variable contains two or more separate categories. All scores, however, need to be independent; that is, the same person cannot be in multiple categories of the same variable. Chi-square is a flexible test that can be used in a number of different ways. It can be used in a similar manner as t tests and ANOVAs to examine the possibility that there are differences in the proportion of participants who fall into each category of one variable on the basis of which group they are a part of on another variable. For example, a chi-square test could examine whether there is a significant difference in the percentage of people who remain married 6 months after completion of therapy, based on whether they received individual, group, or couples counseling. Chi-square can also be used to test the possibility that there is a significant relationship between two variables and to answer research questions such as whether there is a relationship between mental health counselors' gender and their preferred choice of employment setting (private practice or agency/hospital). Unlike the Pearson product–moment correlation, chi-square does not provide information on the strength of the relationship between variables. To obtain that information, researchers need to follow up the chi-square with other procedures, such as the phi coefficient or Cramér's V test.

Another nonparametric test is the **Mann–Whitney U test.** This procedure compares the sum of ranks of scores taken from two different groups of individuals. Although based on a different set of calculations, the **Kolmogorov–Smirnov Z procedure** also tests whether two groups have been drawn from the same population. It is equivalent to the Mann–Whitney U except that it has more power when samples are smaller than approximately 25 participants; consequently, it is the preferred procedure when sample sizes are small. Both of these tests are analogous to an independent samples t test and yield information about whether there is a significant difference between two different groups. For example, if researchers examining differences in the educational aspiration levels of Grade 9 versus Grade 11 students defined the dependent variable in an ordinal way (e.g., high

school, 2-year degree, 4-year degree, graduate degree), a t test would be unsuitable for the analysis. In such a situation, either the Mann–Whitney U or Kolmogorov–Smirnov Z procedure would be needed to determine whether there is a significant difference between aspirations by grade level.

The **Kruskal–Wallis test** extends the Mann–Whitney U test to situations in which there are three or more groups of different participants for the independent variable. As such, it is a nonparametric test that is analogous to the one-way ANOVA procedure. It is used to determine whether there is a significant difference in the sum of ranks somewhere among the comparison groups. Post-hoc tests, such as a series of Bonferroni-corrected Mann–Whitney U tests, are required to determine precisely which groups are different from each other. If the previously mentioned example was expanded to include students in every grade from 9 to 12, a Kruskal–Wallis test would provide information about whether there is an overall effect of grade on educational aspirations, and, if there was a significant effect, Mann–Whitney U tests could then be used to identify which specific pairs of grades were different from each other.

The **Wilcoxon's signed-ranks test** is the nonparametric equivalent to the related samples t test. It is used to compare two groups of data that are not independent from each other, such as when the same individuals are measured twice or when each participant in the first group is matched with a specific participant in the second group. The test involves ranking the amount and direction of change for each pair of scores to determine whether the two groups differ significantly. For example, a professional school counselor who is examining the effectiveness of a self-esteem program for prevention of bullying could ask students to rank how confident they were about responding to bullies before and after the program. A Wilcoxon's signed-ranks test would reveal whether there was a significant difference, on average, in students' rankings of their confidence.

Friedman's rank test is similar to Wilcoxon's signed-ranks test in that it is designed for use with repeated measures or matched scores; however, it can be used when there are more than two comparison groups. To continue the previous example, the professional school counselor may decide to explore the long-term effectiveness of the self-esteem program by measuring students' confidence rankings 6 months later. In this case, the Friedman's rank test could be used to determine whether there is a significant change somewhere over the three time periods, and post hoc tests could be used to determine which specific times were significantly different than other ones.

Contributed by José F. Domene,
Trinity Western University, Langley,
British Columbia, Canada

Additional Resources

Howell, D. C. (2008). *Fundamental statistics for the behavioral sciences* (6th ed.). Belmont, CA: Thomson.

Huck, S. W. (2008). *Reading statistics and research* (5th ed.). Boston: Pearson.

Nonverbal Communications

Nonverbal communications are messages expressed through nonlinguistic means. The varying types of nonverbal communications, or nonverbals, include high- and low-context communication (i.e., ways that members of various cultures deliver messages), paralanguage (i.e., voice qualities and independent utterances), kinesics (i.e., face and body behaviors), chronemics (i.e., using and structuring time), and proxemics (i.e., personal and interpersonal space and territoriality). All behavior has communicative value. When verbal and nonverbal messages are incongruent, individuals are more likely to believe the nonverbal communicative signals they experience because nonverbals tend to reveal hidden truths and are more difficult to conceal than verbal messages. An individual's use of nonverbals is conditioned by multiple factors, including his or her biology (e.g., sex, age), physiology (e.g., disorders), psychology (e.g., personality), and sociocultural background (e.g., where raised as a child).

Persons of diverse cultures deliver messages in specifically distinct manners. Members of cultures in which **high-context communication** is used rely heavily on subtle, nonverbal cues to maintain social harmony. The group is valued over the individual, and there is the general belief that members of the same culture have had similar experiences from which inferences may be drawn. Many things go unsaid, because members assume that the common background of the culture is sufficient to explain what is happening. In other words, there is an internalized understanding of communication based on culture and less explicit communiqués, with actual verbal comments to others tending to be indirect and ambiguous. High-context communication cultures include various Asian and African countries, specifically Japan and Kenya, in which members demand reliance on close-knit groups and often are distrustful of outsiders. People in **low-context communication** cultures, including Spanish and Italian individuals, use language primarily to express thoughts, feelings, and ideas as clearly as possible; the meaning of a statement lies in the words spoken and self-expression is highly valued. Verbal comments are usually calculated and germane. Similarity of experiences or background is used to a lesser extent than in high-context cultures because there is usually greater variation within low-context cultures. Rather, knowledge is considered to be public, transferable, and accessible. Relationships occur on a more widespread basis, and there is more trust for those not already a part of in-groups. High-context cultural communication is often used for impression management, or saving face; whereas, low-context cultural communication is used for corroborating specifics and details. With close friends, individuals are more likely to engage in low-context communication.

Paralanguage nonverbals include personal voice features and the vocal characteristics that differentiate people. They comprise timbre, resonance, volume, tempo, pitch, rhythm, and disfluencies. Timbre is an individual's organically determined voice register, whereas resonance indicates prolongation of sound. Voice volume encompasses the loudness or intensity with which an individual speaks, and voice tempo is known as the rate or speed of an individual's sequential delivery of words. Pitch is the highness or lowness of an individual's voice, and rhythm is a combination of the patterns created by pitch, volume, syllabic duration, and tempo. Disfluencies occur when a speaker stammers, emitting such sounds as *uh, er,* and *um.* The qualities of an individual's voice can influence others' perceptions, because people who are viewed to have attractive voices are perceived as better communicators. Paralanguage is more powerful than verbal language because listeners are often more aware of it than they are of actual verbal content. Laughter is a form of paralanguage through which persons from varying cultures exhibit very specific behaviors. For example, when Japanese women giggle, they tend to do so in a high, feminine pitch and cover their mouths and noses with one hand, typically held vertically. Also, when confronted with rudeness, Japanese people may laugh, smile, or giggle nervously in reaction. Voice volume is important when considering cultural paralanguage. For example, Kenyans typically consider shouting in the street or talking too loudly indoors unacceptable behavior, and Spaniards and Italians may accept loudness as a standard cultural characteristic.

Another component of nonverbal communications is **kinesics,** or how individuals communicate through facial and body movements. Kinesics includes facial expressions, eye gazes (e.g., contact, movement, direction), gesticulations, touch, posture, and stride. An individual's mood is often displayed on his or her face, and the face and eyes tend to be the most noticeable parts of a person's body. Signs that individuals are lying include averting gaze and touching their face. Ambiguous gestures, such as fidgeting, often reveal signs of discomfort. Touch can influence liking and compliance, leading to disclosure, acceptance, and strong relationships. An individual's posture and orientation to others are indicative of attitude and authority. In cultures, various facial and body movements can have multiple meanings, thus lending to misinterpretation and confusion. What is easy to understand in one culture is not comprehensible in another. In North America, individuals consider regular eye contact while speaking to one another to be respectful, but in certain African tribes, eye contact is rude and violates social customs. A commonly used gesticulation for one cultural group of people can have a very different meaning for another. For example, sticking up one's middle and pointer fingers can be interpreted as meaning the number 2, as is the case in North America, or it can stand for victory, which holds true in Great Britain. The extent to which an individual shows emotion on the face is also determined by cultural upbringing. North Americans are encouraged to be open with emotional expression, whereas the Japanese are taught to mask negative emotions and replace them with either smiles or no facial emotion at all.

Chronemics refers to how people perceive, manage, and react to time as well as the messages inferred from how time is used. A person's concept of time can be central to how he or she views the world, affecting individual perspective on punctuality, daily agendas, and sense of urgency. The ways in which an individual uses time can illustrate values regarding time, and it can even demonstrate a person's status. For example, important people may be seen by appointment only, and it is acceptable for a person of higher status to keep one of lower status waiting, but the opposite is not true. An individual's time usage is often greatly affected by culture and the time system that is in place. There are two types of systems, the first being **monochromic time,** which refers to linear time that is scheduled by the clock and is usually planned in advance. Time is segmented into precise units and viewed as a commodity. There is rigorous adherence to planning, and time commitments are taken very seriously. North Americans live in a monochromic system. The other type of system, **polychromic time,** is less stringent and related to intuitive decisions made as situations play out. Relationships are considered far more important than schedules. Plans may be changed easily, and time commitments are looser and more like possibilities than obligations. Spain and many Central and South American cultures adhere to polychromic time.

Proxemics, the study of how people use the space around them, is the last major component of nonverbal communications. Personal territories are the areas that serve as extensions of individuals' physical beings or the geographical spaces that they feel belong to them. These can include an individual's home, bed, or desk at work/school. An individual's cultural background directly affects how much room is needed to feel comfortable physically. North Americans prove to be uncomfortable when interacting with people of Middle Eastern cultures, who interact with others at a distance at which they can feel another person's breath. When an individual's personal space is invaded, he or she will often use barrier behaviors in order to regain comfort. These barrier behaviors include breaking eye contact; backing away from the other communicator; and placing an object, like a purse or book, between him- or herself and the too-close communicator. North Americans have four spatial zones in which they choose to communicate with others; how far away they stand while communicating is dependent on their feelings for the other communicator. The first zone is **intimate distance,** and it occurs from an individual's skin to 18 inches from himself or herself. This zone is most often used with people who are trusted and emotionally very close. The second spatial zone occurs from 18 inches to 4 feet. This is known as **personal distance** and is used with others who are considered somewhat close. The third zone is known as social distance and occurs from 4 to 12 feet. **Social distance** usually indicates business communication, such as when salespersons talk to customers. The farthest zone, which occurs from 12 feet outward, is the public distance zone. The **public distance** zone is used in teaching and public speaking and is not considered appropriate for two-way communication because it does not lend itself to reciprocating interactional communications.

Nonverbals aid communicators by serving as complements to verbal communications. They lend themselves to identity management, defining relationships, and conveyance of emotions. Nonverbal behaviors can present an image designed to impress others, such as sitting up straight and smiling during an interview. They can also betray secrets, such as when an individual claims that things are well but simultaneously wrings his or her hands, which reveals that there may be more to his or her personal story. In many cultures, deception is more likely to be revealed through nonverbals, such as fidgeting, blinking, shifting posture, and hesitation, because they are not as conscious as verbal messages. Nonverbals elucidate feelings that people are unaware of and unwilling to express, and they can have multiple meanings. For example, a smile can be innocent or not, and a yawn can indicate boredom or lack of sleep. In today's culturally diverse world, it is crucial that all individuals exercise caution when interpreting or responding to others' nonverbal behaviors because nonverbal messages contain great variability from one culture to the next and, more specifically, from one person to the next.

Contributed by Rebecca M. Goldberg
and Andrea Dixon,
University of Florida, Gainesville, FL

Additional Resources

Adler, R. B., Rosenfeld, L. B., & Proctor, R. F., II. (2004). *Interplay: The process of interpersonal communication* (9th ed.). New York: Oxford University Press.

Poyatos, F. (2002). *Nonverbal communication across disciplines: Volume II. Paralanguage, kinesics, silence, personal and environmental interaction.* Philadelphia: Benjamins.

■Norm-Referenced Assessment

Norm-referenced assessment uses comparisons of an individual to a sample of other people to facilitate counseling decisions. Although the terms *assessment* and *testing* are highly related and frequently used interchangeably, assessment is different from testing. Assessment is the utilization of data in the decision-making process. Testing is the process by which data are generated for assessment. In addition, norm-referenced assessment is different from both ipsative and criterion-referenced assessment. **Ipsative assessment** relies on intraindividual variation only and is extremely limited in the inferences and decisions that it can support. It can help the professional counselor understand variations in the individual across time or across attributes, but it cannot support any inference of normalcy or deviance. **Criterion-referenced assessment** relies on the comparison of an individual's performance relative to a measurable standard and is a very powerful alternative or supplement to norm-referenced assessment.

Norm-referenced assessment facilitates several types of decisions that professional counselors make in their work. These include screening decisions, diagnostic decisions, prognostic decisions, and treatment/intervention decisions. Screening decisions generally respond to the question: Is this observation notably different from what is typical? Diagnostic decisions usually follow screening decisions and respond to the question: Given that this observation is notably different from the typical response, what is the specific nature of the difference? Prognostic and intervention decisions usually follow diagnostic decisions and respond to the question: Given the nature of the notable difference, what is the typical course of this attribute over time and what is the best way to nurture or diminish its development?

Norm-referenced assessment typically uses data generated by norm-referenced measures. Measurement is the assignment of numbers to observations according to rules. In the case of norm-referenced measures, the number assigned to an observation indicates the individual's attribute or performance relative to the measured attribute or performance of a reference group. Aggregated data from the reference group create the **norm.**

The measured attributes or performance of a reference group can be characterized by the central tendency and the variability of the scores within the group. An individual observation can then be characterized as deviation from the central tendency relative to the variability of the group. In whatever scores or units the original measurement may be, they are converted to units called z scores. These z scores are the fundamental standard scores used in norm-referenced assessment.

A z score is computed by subtracting the arithmetic mean of the scores from the observed score and dividing the result by the standard deviation of the scores as follows:

$$z = (X - M) \div SD.$$

In the z score is found all three components of a norm-referenced measurement: individual (X) deviation from the average (M) relative to the standard variation (SD) within the group.

Because the computation of z scores results in units that include negative numbers and decimals that can be lost in transcription, they often undergo linear transformation into other scales that mean the same thing. A common linear transformation results in T scores. T scores are created by multiplying the z score by 10 and adding 50. Linear transformations effectively remove the decimals and negative values in the scores while preserving their original meaning.

Another common form of norm-referenced scores is the percentile rank. Rather than referring to the mean, percentile ranks reference an individual's performance to the number of people scoring below that score in the norm group. Hence, the 50th percentile rank represents the score below which 50% of the people in the norm group scored. The 90th percentile rank represents the score below which 90% of the norm group scored. Whether the reference point is the mean or the number of scores below the observed score, norm-referenced measures always compare an individual to the performance of the group.

It is essential to evaluate the adequacy of the reference group for the decision to be made. For example, if a counselor is making a screening decision about the behavior of an 8-year-old child, it is best if the child is compared with other 8-year-olds rather than children much younger or much older. Norm groups may be evaluated along any number of factors, including age, gender, ethnicity, education, and

locale. Any norm-referenced decision should be couched in terms of the reference group. For example, a screening decision might be stated as, "Sarah's measured reading performance was significantly higher than that of other girls of her age in this school district." A good rule of thumb is to ask whether the individual to be tested is reasonably represented by similar people in the reference group.

Examples of common norm-referenced tests include the Wechsler Intelligence Scale for Children–Fourth Edition and the Minnesota Multiphasic Personality Inventory–2. Each of these measures generates scores that are linear transformations of z scores that represent an individual's deviation from the mean relative to the typical variation in the standardization group. The publishers of each of these measures have been careful to obtain observations across a wide range of ages, ethnicities, education levels, and geographic locations so that the norm-group reasonably represents most people in the United States.

Because individuals are ultimately unique, and no reference group is entirely adequate to represent all people, there are controversies around the use of norm-referenced data in decision making. A norm-referenced score may be a misrepresentation of true skills or an oversimplification of the rich diversity of an individual's gifts.

Contributed by Lane Fischer,
Brigham Young University, Provo, UT

Additional Resources

Drummond, R. J., & Jones, K. D. (2006). *Assessment procedures for counselors and helping professionals* (6th ed.). Upper Saddle River, NJ: Pearson Merrill Prentice Hall.

Murphy, K. R., & Davidshofer, C. O. (2005). *Psychological testing: Principles and applications* (6th ed.). Upper Saddle River, NJ: Pearson Prentice Hall.

Salvia, J., Ysseldyke, J. E., & Bolt, S. (2007). *Assessment in special and inclusive education* (10th ed.). Boston: Houghton Mifflin.

■ Normal Curve, Normal Distribution

A **normal curve,** also known as the **bell curve** because the graph resembles the shape of a bell, is a symmetrical probability distribution, being highest in the middle and lowest on either side (see Figure 1). The graph shows the distribution, or spread, of scores obtained from a given test, assuming enough data are collected. The graph also shows the probability of finding a certain value (score) by calculating the area under the normal curve. Most psychological and physical measurements are normally distributed within a population, called a **normal distribution,** and, therefore, most research hypotheses assume that the study variables are distributed normally within the population. That is, most scores are close to the average, and relatively few tend to fall toward either extreme; therefore, as the figure shows, 68% of the scores fall within 1 standard deviation, with an equal number of scores above and below the mean; 95% of the scores fall within 2 standard deviations of the mean; and almost all (99.7%) fall within 3 standard deviations of the

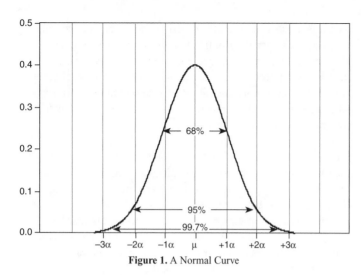

Figure 1. A Normal Curve

mean. This 68–95–99.7 principle is commonly known as the empirical rule.

In the class of normal curves, the standard normal distribution is the most widely observed distribution. This allows for probabilities to be calculated on the basis of a single curve whose mean (μ) is 0 and standard deviation (*sd*) is 1. This is also called the *z* distribution. The figure shows that the *x* axis (horizontal) represents the variable in question (e.g., height), whereas the *y* axis (vertical) is the number of scores (e.g., number of people who have a particular height). Although it is assumed that the normal distribution is symmetrical, the actual shape of the curve may vary from being relatively steep (leptokurtic) to fairly flat (platykurtic; see Kurtosis). Steep curves result from low standard deviations, whereas flat curves result from high standard deviations.

In a normal distribution of scores, the mean is equal to the median, which is equal to the mode (see Central Tendency). For example, if enough women in a given population are sampled for their height, it may be found that the mean height of women is 5 feet 5 inches with a standard deviation of 3 inches. When all the obtained scores (i.e., height measurements) are plotted, the distribution of scores would show that 68% of measurements are located within 1 standard deviation above and below the mean (i.e., between 5' 2" and 5' 8"). The mean height would represent the peak of the curve, which would also represent the median (middle value) and the mode (most frequent value).

Contributed by Alia Sheikh, Newcastle University, Newcastle, United Kingdom

Additional Resources

Anastasi, A., & Urbina, S. (1997). *Psychological testing* (7th ed.). Upper Saddle River, NJ: Prentice Hall.

Aron, E. N., & Coups, E. J. (2006). *Statistics for psychology* (4th ed.). Upper Saddle River, NJ: Pearson Merrill Prentice Hall.

Howitt, D., & Cramer, D. (2005). *Introduction to statistics in psychology* (3rd ed.). Upper Saddle River, NJ: Pearson Merrill Prentice Hall.

Norms

Norm is the standard by which something is compared. In the case of standardized assessment, a norm represents typical performance on whatever variable is being examined. Norms are one of the main features that differentiate norm-referenced from criterion-referenced tests. **Criterion-referenced tests** are typically used in the context of evaluating whether a person has mastered a set of information. For example, in a counseling theories class, the instructor may administer a final exam to the students and identify a specific number of items that must be answered correctly for a student to pass the course. The required number of correct answers that a student must minimally attain is the **criterion.**

On the other hand, many tests used by professionals in the fields of mental health and education are norm-referenced. A standardized achievement test, for example, has norms that tell a test user what number of correct answers constitutes typical or average test performance for individuals who are at a particular grade level or chronological age. Thus a **norm-referenced test** score tells the test user about the test taker's relative standing in comparison to the test taker's peers (see Norm-Referenced Assessment).

Purposes of Norms

There are many different ways that characteristics of human beings are operationally defined. In addition, comparing one person to a norm group can serve several purposes. Following are some of the purposes for doing a normative comparison.

Assessing a Person's Global Level of Functioning
Norms are used to evaluate aspects of an individual's daily functioning across multiple domains within a broad category, such as overall intellectual ability or general activities of daily living. Norms from these instruments that cover broad domains allow a test user to compare one person's functioning level to the level of many other individuals of a similar chronological age or with a similar diagnosis to obtain a sense of the relative competence (or severity) of symptoms.

Evaluating Facets of an Individual's Personality, Temperament, or Degree of Psychopathology
Norms can be used to gauge the degree of prominence of a particular personality or interpersonal characteristic. For example, instruments such as the NEO Personality Inventory–Revised, the Myers–Briggs Type Indicator, and the Minnesota Multiphasic Personality Inventory–2 (MMPI-2) offer test users norms to compare an individual's preferences or symptom complaints to a large number of other individuals in the standardization sample. If a person has a high score on a particular scale, such as the Depression scale on the MMPI-2, it means that in comparison with all the individuals who took the test during norming, the number of items related to depressive symptoms were endorsed more frequently by this person than they were by the participants from the norming sample.

Assessing a Person's Rate of Development in a Particular Domain

Human development occurs across many realms, including motor skills, social skills, cognitive ability, speech and language, and academic progress; tests and other instruments exist that assess a person's rate of development in each of those areas. Some individuals experience symptoms, problems, or delays in one specific domain of development. The norms for standardized instruments enable a test user to compare one individual's rate of development with the "typical" rate of development for most people. For example, the entire category of developmental disorders given in the *Diagnostic and Statistical Manual of Mental Disorders* (4th ed., text rev.; American Psychiatric Association, 2000) has in common the diagnostic criteria of a child's behavior developing at a markedly slower rate than what is typical for a given chronological age.

The Norming Process

The process of test development and norming can best be explained in the context of a specific example. Test development begins with a test author defining the variable to be assessed. For example, a test author might decide to create an instrument that measures students' reading achievement in elementary school. The author would first clearly articulate what is meant by the term *reading achievement* and then create a set of items intended to measure what was articulated and defined as reading achievement. Test questions in the item pool would range in difficulty from very easy to extremely challenging.

After determining that scores on the test items are valid and reliable, the next step in the norming process is to generate a standardization sample. A perfect way to ensure that a norm group is truly representative would be to sample the entire population of elementary students; however, it is not practically possible to obtain test scores from that entire group of students. Instead, the test developer will attempt to create a standardization sample whose composition parallels, or mirrors in proportion, the general population of elementary students. Students will be recruited in such a way that there are equal numbers of children to represent different chronological ages and grade levels. In addition, in norm development, an effort is often made to generate a student sample that represents the general population in ethnicity, geographic location, socioeconomic status, and gender. The more similar the sample is to the general population, the more likely it is that the norm-referenced score will be a valid and reliable indication of that student's relative standing.

It is important to note that the particular characteristics a test author controls within the participant pool depend on what the test is measuring. For example, if the test was an instrument measuring severity of eating disorder symptoms, instead of controlling for grade level, the author creating the standardization sample might attempt to control for the vari-able of treatment modality. Controlling for this variable could be done by obtaining representative participants who were receiving inpatient treatment, others who were receiving intensive outpatient treatment, and others who were receiving moderate-to-minimal outpatient treatment. Among this group, the test author might also attempt to develop norms for different intervals of chronological age.

Returning to the example of reading achievement, the test author would obtain a large number of first graders, second graders, and so on. Ordinarily, test authors will attain a minimum sample of 100 participants at each age or grade level when developing a screening test or 200 participants for diagnostic tests. Each grade level group in the sample would be administered the same pool of test items. Then the author would calculate the average raw score and standard deviation for each group of students. Raw score means and standard deviations for each grade level would then be plotted on a bell curve, with the raw scores being transformed to some type of standardized scale and then smoothed or calibrated.

There are a variety of standardized scores that examiners and test developers use to interpret client performance. Examples include standard scores ($M = 100$; $SD = 15$, a T score ($M = 50$; $SD = 10$), or a z score ($M = 0$; $SD = 1$). Any one of these standardized scores is intended to convey similar information about a test taker, that is to convey how the test taker's responses to the test items compare with the responses of all of the test taker's peers in the standardization sample.

The test manual for any standardized instrument provides technical information about the characteristics of the standardization sample and also provides tables to use to convert an individual's raw score to a standardized score, thereby allowing comparison of that individual's performance with the performance of other individuals who took the same test, even though those individuals may be older or younger than the target client.

Contributed by Kathryn C. MacCluskie, Cleveland State University, Cleveland, OH

Reference

American Psychiatric Association. (2000). *Diagnostic and statistical manual of mental disorders* (4th ed., text rev.). Washington, DC: Author.

Additional Resources

Dorfman, W. I., & Hersen, M. (Eds.). (2001). *Understanding psychological assessment*. New York: Springer.

Groth-Marnat, G. (2003). *Handbook of psychological assessment* (4th ed.). New York: Wiley.

Sattler, J. M., & Hoge, R. D. (2006). *Assessment of children: Behavioral, social, and clinical foundations* (5th ed.). La Mesa, CA: Sattler.

Object Relations

Object relations theory is a theory posited by a diverse group of psychoanalytic theorists who, in extending Freud's insights regarding the objects of libidinal energy, modified or in some cases replaced Freud's drive theory with a theory of personality development based on the quality of an individual's early relationships. Object relations theory proposes that out of interactions with its primary caregiver(s), the infant develops its capacity and patterns for relating to self, others, and the world. Furthermore, it is the quality of an individual's relationships, rather than the management of instinctual conflicts, that becomes the measure for health and pathology. In contrast to Freud, who argued that humans are primarily motivated by "pleasure seeking" (i.e., they seek to reduce anxiety caused by instinctually driven conflicts), object relations theorists propose that humans are motivated primarily to seek connections or relationships with others (i.e., object seeking). Key figures include W. R. D. Fairbairn, Otto Kernberg, Melanie Klein, Margaret Mahler, and D. W. Winnicott.

W. R. D. Fairbairn developed the "purest" object relational approach, arguing that humans are "object-seeking" rather than "pleasuring seeking," as Freud had proposed. Relationships, rather than instincts, were the primary human motivation. He saw "internal objects" as compensation for failed actual relationships, arguing that a pattern of dysfunctional relationships had its roots in the compulsive repetition of these internalized relational patterns.

Otto Kernberg reconceptualized psychopathology in terms of the quality of an individual's object relations. For instance, borderline and narcissistic personality disorders lie along a continuum of object relatedness between inability to relate to others as separate from a person's own needs and wishes (e.g., psychosis) and healthy, mature interactions that exhibit a stable sense of self and boundaries.

Melanie Klein, primarily known as a child analyst, contributed to understanding the richness of the child's inner world (e.g., "internal objects") and its impact on relationships. She saw play as the child's equivalent to free association. She understood development as oscillating between a more self-protective, narcissistic stance (the "paranoid-schizoid position") and a more mature stance in which an individual could express concern for others (the "depressive position").

Margaret Mahler is known best for her contributions to understanding the "psychological birth" of the individual, as traced through a series of stages and substages from "normal autism" (the infant does not distinguish itself from its pri-

mary caregiver) to "individuation" (the child understands both himself or herself as having individual characteristics and others as separate individuals).

D. W. Winnicott is most known for his concept of "transitional objects," which are objects that belong to a special "space" between the inner and outer worlds and that help the child maintain a sense of continuity when interruptions in care occur (e.g., the teddy bear to help the child go to sleep by himself or herself). He argued that "good enough" mother–infant interactions provide a holding environment that facilitates the infant's development of a sense of self and other.

The term **object** is derived from Freud's early writings, in which he designated anything that could serve as a focal point for discharge of instinctual energy as an object. Common objects were the mother, the mother's breast, and other significant persons. Less common objects might include animals or other things that were "overvalued" (e.g., fetish objects). In contrast to Freud's focus on the infant's use of the object for need satisfaction and pleasure, however, it was the infant's internal experience of the object that preoccupied the object relations theorists. More specifically, object relations theory focuses on how a sense of self develops as separate from its objects, how these social relationships are subjectively experienced, and the consequences of those experiences for personality development and for psychopathology. The following abbreviated account of these concerns can provide only the broad contours of a complex and richly nuanced process.

According to object relations theory, infants come into the world with an inability to distinguish themselves clearly from objects in their environment. They may perceive they create the objects that satisfy their needs for hunger and comfort by simply wishing the objects to be present. Only gradually, through their interactions with caregivers (especially the mother) are infants able to build up the structures that enable them to perceive themselves and their environment as related but separate. This occurs through complex processes that include perception, representation, fantasy, and memory. From these processes, along with early encounters with caregivers, infants construct and hold in memory representations not only of these objects from their environment but of themselves in relation to these objects (hence, the term *object relations*). What is important to note is that the objects to which the infant relates are not simply the external objects in the environment but the infant's intrapsychic representation of these objects. The quality and patterns of an individual's interactions with these "internal objects" are pivotal to the development of personality and also provide a template for all subsequent relations.

The development of the person via his or her interaction with and representation of primary caregivers can be a perilous journey, with successes or failures along the way contributing to health or various psychopathologies. According to Winnicott (1972), parents' contributions to this process include their bringing a certain level of "wantedness" and expectations for the infant that influence their interactions with the child and convey an initial sense of meaning and identity. This is especially true for the mother, whose ability to anticipate and meet the infant's needs for food and comfort allows the infant to experience a necessary but temporary sense of omnipotence and creativeness that the infant will later use to construct a separate sense of self; however, the mother's inevitable failure to meet the infant's needs perfectly has the salutatory effect of helping the infant form a sense of external reality by creating (a not yet understood) frustration and anxiety with which the infant must cope. How the infant copes with these feelings highlights the infant's role in the journey to becoming a separate but interrelated self.

The infant's longings to regain the lost ideal eventuate in a **splitting** of its experience so that the times of failed need satisfaction are separated from the more pleasant times when needs were satisfied. This splitting occurs on both a self and object level so that infants come to experience themselves and their objects as alternately "all good" or "all bad" (often manifest in an idealization of the parents). If the environment sufficiently satisfies needs (i.e., good enough) and if infants do not feel overwhelmed by their own internal processes, then gradually they build up tolerance to delay in having their needs met and are able to move toward a position of distinguishing self and other (inner and outer reality). They recognize that good and bad, comfort and discomfort, belong to the same object or self, and they are more able to integrate their experiences. Too much frustration of needs or inability to move beyond infantile wishes and splitting become the basis of various pathological ways of relating, which are replicated in all subsequent relationships. For instance, an individual might idealize others, demanding they serve as perfect objects, vilifying them when they fail and repeating the search for another ideal object. By contrast, healthy maturation involves both a capacity for object relatedness, in which self and object are distinct but related, and the ability to integrate experiences of good and bad without defensive splitting.

During the transition from the inability to distinguish one's objects and oneself to a state of clear differentiation, certain objects in the infant's world (e.g., teddy bear, blanket, musical tune, mannerism) take on a special significance because of their ability to form a bridge between the infant's fantasy world, in which needs are perfectly met, and the external world of reality, where needs are sometimes frustrated. These transitional objects assist infants in their movement from being "merged" with the mother to being a separate other through the objects' ability to allay anxiety by enabling infants to recall an image of the mother's care during her absence. Thus, these special objects allow a certain continuity to the experience of infants that helps them develop a capacity to recognize and accept reality and to develop eventually into a healthy, mature adult able to interact realistically with others.

This brief outline of the development of the self highlights only the broad contours of agreement among object relations theorists on the importance of the quality of an individual's early relationships and the role of his or her internal mental life for the formation of personality. This overview glosses over important distinctions among those included under the object relations banner (e.g., the "British" school vs. the interpersonal or relational school in America, the role of fantasized vs. real objects, the importance of the original drive model).

Contributed by Stephen Parker,
Regent University, Virginia Beach, VA

Reference

Winnicott, D. (1972). *Playing and reality*. New York: Routledge.

Additional Resources

Greenberg, J., & Mitchell, S. (1983). *Object relations in psychoanalytic theory*. Cambridge, MA: Harvard University Press.

Kernberg, O. (1976). *Object-relations theory and clinical psychoanalysis*. New York: Aronson.

■ Observer Bias

Observer bias occurs when observers' expectations lead to systematic errors in identifying and/or recording behavior. Observer bias is similar to expectancy effects, which may be more likely when observers are aware of a hypothesis or previous research.

Observer bias may occur in either quantitative and qualitative research. Quantitative observer bias occurs when any action by observers has a negative effect on the validity or reliability of the data they collect. An example of this type of bias is observer omission. This is the failure to record the occurrence of a behavior that fits one of the categories on the observational schedule. Observer omission can occur as a result of personal bias (e.g., having some stake in the type of data collected) or when behaviors being observed occur rarely or too frequently. Researchers can avoid observer omission by simplifying the observation schedule or assigning multiple observers to a setting. Providing cues and reminders may also help maintain the observer's vigilance. In quantitative studies, in order to improve validity and reliability, the researcher can prevent contaminating information from the observers by simplifying the observation schedule or assigning multiple observers to a setting. Observer bias can also be affected by reliability decay. Reliability decay is the tendency for observational data recorded during the later phases of data collection to be less reliable than those collected earlier. Researchers can avoid reliability decay by frequently checking on observers during the course of study to keep them performing at a satisfactory level. Calculating rates of interobserver agreement can minimize the effects discussed here.

Observer bias in qualitative research refers to the cultural assumptions (i.e., preconceived ideas that the observer may have about his or her own culture versus other cultures), which all researchers bring to their work, that help determine their method of research and their observations. The more involved the researcher is, the greater the degree of subjectivity likely to be reflected in the observations. Researchers try to reduce the effect of their personal biases on their findings by conscientiously recording their thoughts, feelings, and reactions about what they observe as well as what they observe. Observer bias is countered by self-reflection, concomitant coding and interpretation (i.e., peer review), triangulation (i.e., use of multiple data sources, data collection methods, researchers or theoretical perspectives), structural corroboration, member checks, and use of low inference indicators (e.g., quotation).

Contributed by E. Claire Brown and
Carl J. Sheperis,
Mississippi State University, Starkville, MS

Occupation

The term **occupation,** for most people, refers to their employment. In a broad sense, a person's work or job can be synonymous with occupation; however, an occupation can contain multiple jobs and multiple tasks within each job. For example, Reggie works as a registered nurse (occupation). Monday through Friday, Reggie provides children wellness visits and administers vaccinations at a governmental health agency (one job with multiple tasks). Every other weekend, Reggie works two 12-hour shifts on the neonatal unit at a local hospital (different job with different tasks, but same occupation). Individuals considered to be in the same occupation can have different jobs. They may also hold different positions. For example, as time goes by, Reggie is given some administrative responsibilities and a different title at the health center (a different position, but same occupation).

Occupation differs from **career** in that it does not typically support the importance of other life roles, leisure activities, or growth throughout the life span. Career is considered more a person's long-term pursuit of work and leisure in a given area of interest (his or her work history or life history). In a career, an individual may hold several occupations, and a series of jobs held by one person is that person's career. For example, after 20 years of working for the health center and the hospital, Reggie is offered a position at a local university teaching nursing students. Reggie's occupation is no longer registered nurse. It is now instructor/professor; however, Reggie's career is still primarily defined as a nurse or helping professional.

The United States Department of Labor (DOL) Bureau of Labor Statistics collects, analyzes, and disseminates data regarding occupations through the use of the Standard Occupational Classification (SOC) system. There are more than 820 occupations defined in the 2000 SOC system. Definitions may include typical job duties, skills, education, or experience. DOL also publishes the *Occupational Outlook*

Handbook (OOH), which is a more practical publication for professional counselors. It is used as a reference to assist clients with career exploration (i.e., to discover the training and education needed for any occupation, earnings, expected job prospects, what workers do on the job, and potential working conditions). In addition, the *OOH* provides job search tips and how to find out information about the job market in each state.

Another publication, the Occupational Information Network (O*NET), is also a source of occupational information. It replaced the *Dictionary of Occupational Titles,* which was last updated in 1991. The O*NET provides comprehensive information on key attributes and characteristics of workers and occupations, and it is often used by employees of state employment service offices to classify applicants and job openings and to file occupational information. The codes used by the O*NET are provided by the SOC.

Contributed by Chadwick Royal,
North Carolina Central University,
Durham, NC

Additional Resources

Bolles, R. N. (2007). *What color is your parachute?* Berkeley, CA: Ten Speed Press.

Occupational Information Network Web site: http://online.onetcenter.org/

Occupational Outlook Handbook Web site: http://www.bls.gov/oco/

Sharf, R. (2005). *Applying career development theory to counseling* (4th ed.). Pacific Grove, CA: Brooks/Cole.

Standard Occupational Classification system Web site: http://www.bls.gov/soc/

Zunker, V. (2005). *Career counseling: A holistic approach* (7th ed.). Pacific Grove, CA: Brooks/Cole.

Occupational Information

Occupational information is defined as data or facts about a job, position, task, field, or employment to use in making decisions about future work. Gathering and interpreting occupational information and selecting the appropriate resources are essential components of **career planning.** Career counselors need to master a variety of types and sources of occupational information to be informed and effective; they also need to know the limitations of occupational information. For example, the Internet is a valuable source of large volumes of up-to-date information that is immediately accessible; however, some clients may not have access to the Internet or may question the validity of the source.

Occupational information may include, but not be limited to, duties and nature of the work, work settings and conditions, training, methods of entry, earnings and benefits, advancement, and employment outlook. The sources of occupational information include, but are not limited to, literature, computer-based systems, direct observation, parents and advisers, courses, the Internet, professional associations, career centers, audio/video tapes, CD-ROMs, and Webinars.

Formal sources, such as the nationally recognized *Occupational Outlook Handbook,* are public and easily replicable, whereas informal sources, such as interviews with employees currently working in the field, may offer unique insights into specific personal aspects of a career.

Career counselors need to be aware of a client's comfort level with various sources, such as when a lack of technological skills causes a client to reject Internet sources or a strong family connection causes a client to rely on personal sources (such as family, ministers, elders). Career counselors need to make a professional judgment regarding the client's use of occupational information: Is the information being incorporated into career planning thoughts or is it being ignored. Also, too much information can be as detrimental to the career planning process as too little, because the client may feel overwhelmed or immobilized by all the facts. Similarly, the timing of when the information is provided affects the client's use of that information, because if the general facts about the occupation (such as the nature of the work) are processed before the client has chosen that particular career path, then more details may be sought (such as opportunities for advancement) after the choice is made. Obtaining client feedback helps the counselor with diagnosing the effects of comfort level, too much information, and timing, as well as the client's awareness of these issues. Although the nature of occupational information has changed over the years in terms of content, the need for such information during career/life planning has remained constant. Exploration of occupational information by the client and professional counselor is viewed as one of the critical ingredients for effective career intervention.

Data become occupational information at the point where data "inform" an individual's decision-making process. The counselor and the client pursue occupational information for either the purpose of education (to inform, expand, correct) or motivation (to stimulate, challenge, confirm). The client's experience with the occupational information presents the greatest challenge for the counselor (e.g., the difference between reading facts about a career and learning about what was read). The practice of gathering, sorting, evaluating, and using information may depend on the client's ethnicity, race, gender, cultural or socioeconomic background, and a multitude of other variables and can have an effect on vocational maturation and future work lives.

Contributed by Melanie Reinersman,
National Career Development Association

Additional Resources

Gysbers, N. C., Heppner, M. J., & Johnston, J. A. (2009). *Career counseling: Contexts, processes, and techniques.* Alexandria, VA: American Counseling Association.

Hoppock, R. (1976). *Occupational information.* New York: McGraw-Hill.

National Career Development Association. (1992). *Guidelines for the preparation and evaluation of career and occupational information literature.* Retrieved May 16, 2007, from http://www.ncda.org

◼ *Occupational Outlook Handbook*

The *Occupational Outlook Handbook (OOH)* is published every other year by the Bureau of Labor Statistics, a division of the U.S. Department of Labor. The **Bureau of Labor Statistics** compiles and analyzes economic and job market data to understand changes and trends for occupations in America.

Prior to the Industrial Revolution, occupational choice was limited. As Americans gained greater access to education, this changed. In 1936, Franklin D. Roosevelt's Advisory Committee on Education recommended that vocational education should reflect actual employment options. As a result, the Bureau of Labor Statistics was commissioned in 1940 to provide the educational community with accurate employment information, including the difficult task of predicting future trends. The first *OOH* was given to returning World War II veterans in a collection of pamphlets bound with a shoestring.

The *OOH* is currently published in both print and online formats and provides 10-year projections of national employment conditions for approximately 270 occupations. Because conditions may vary by location, state and regional employment data should be consulted along with information from the *OOH*. The OOH provides information on the nature of each occupation, including job qualifications, necessary training or education, earnings, work conditions, advancement, employment outlook, related occupations, and sources of additional information. The *OOH* is an important resource for individuals who are exploring potential careers or who are considering career changes. Career counselors and professional school counselors make frequent use of the *OOH* in helping clients and students.

Contributed by John Hawkins,
Mississippi State University, Starkville, MS

Additional Resource

Occupational Outlook Handbook Web site: http://www.bls.gov/oco/

◼ Occupational Stress

Occupational stress has become a prominent health issue as a result of scientific research that brought to light linkages between occupational stress and serious health problems. More specifically, occupational stress has been associated with mental health concerns such as depression and anxiety, physical health problems including hypertension and cardiovascular disease, and unhealthy coping behaviors (e.g., cigarette smoking). The salience of occupational stress as a health issue is underscored by the chronicity of stressful experiences associated with work as well as the large portion of a person's life spent at work.

Occupational stress most commonly has been defined as chronic psychological and physiological strain elicited by ongoing work-related stressors (i.e., events, conditions, demands associated with a person's work). The experience of strain can result in fatigue, tension, poor concentration, tearfulness, indecisiveness, irritability, and anger suppression and outbursts; it can also be involved in decreases in immune system functioning and increases in blood pressure, respiration, and heart rate. Work stressors that relate to strain include working in unpleasant (e.g., noisy settings) or unsafe conditions (e.g., working with dangerous machinery), perceiving oneself as unable to perform a particularly difficult task competently, having unclear responsibilities, sensing that one has more tasks than can be competently completed in an expected amount of time, and experiencing conflict between one's home and work life.

Although the immediate physiological response to a stressor has the adaptive function of preparing an individual to act in terms of "fight or flight," the continuous arousal of the physiological stress response clearly is detrimental to a person's physical health (see Stress). For example, the neurochemicals cortisol and epinephrine, which are released during the experience of stress, have been found to weaken immune system functioning. Moreover, hypertension (i.e., chronically elevated blood pressure), which is often associated with work strain, is a risk factor for heart disease, strokes, and kidney disease. Furthermore, occupational stress can indirectly undermine physical health by causing an increase in unhealthy coping behaviors such as excessive use of alcohol or caffeine, cigarette smoking, illicit drug use, overeating, and unhealthy eating (e.g., frequently eating fast-food or junk food) or by eliciting risky behaviors (e.g., driving without wearing a safety belt).

From a psychological perspective, ongoing occupational strain is generally considered to cause a phenomenon known as **burnout.** Burnout can be characterized as a state of emotional exhaustion (i.e., feeling a depletion of emotional resources), cynicism (i.e., negative attitudes toward others), and reduced personal accomplishment (i.e., reduction in feelings of competence); burnout can also be described as a syndrome characterized by emotional, physical, and cognitive fatigue. In addition to engendering burnout, severe forms of chronic strain have been linked to depression, general anxiety, and posttraumatic stress disorder. Negative psychological consequences (e.g., anxiety) resulting from severe forms of chronic stress have been found to last for years (in extreme cases as long as 50 years). Furthermore, even seemingly benign experiences of strain may have subtle effects on behavior, such as a decrease in the likelihood that help will be offered to someone in need.

Researchers have found that the development of negative consequences of strain, such as burnout, can be affected by certain psychological factors. For example, **Type A personality** characteristics (e.g., tendency to be time conscious, competitive, restless) are predictive of chronic strain. In contrast, other personality characteristics that reflect personal agency (i.e., viewing self as having resources such as high self-efficacy, internal locus of control, and self-esteem to cope with situations) and positive emotionality (e.g., tendency to be optimistic and hopeful) may protect against the impact of stressors. A prominent psychosocial factor affecting the experience of strain is social support. A perceived lack of social support by coworkers or superiors has been

found to be one of the strongest predictors of strain. Social support at work or from relationships outside of work has been found to be a strong buffer against strain.

Although the literature on occupational stress has remained focused on the notion of strain, work-related stress is indeed a complex concept that can be conceptualized in a number of ways. For example, the relationship between stress and performance suggests that individuals tend to perform better under moderate levels of stress and less well under either very low or very high levels of stress. Thus, the effect of a particular stressor could be viewed as either positive or negative, depending on the level of stress. Furthermore, individuals differ widely in how they experience certain stressors; that is, some individuals may experience a severe reaction to a given stressor, whereas others may experience a minimal reaction or even a positive reaction, commonly referred to as **eustress.**

Models of Occupational Stress

A number of theoretical frameworks have been offered to explain this complexity. According to the **cognitive appraisal model,** strain is produced by an individual's active evaluation of the level of threat imposed by a stressor. This model suggests that the experience of strain depends in large part on how individuals perceive events rather than on the nature of the events themselves. The cognitive appraisal model further hypothesizes that individuals first evaluate events by assessing the potential harm of a threat and, then, determining their ability to overcome the threat or cope with the harm effectively. Thus, high levels of strain are experienced when the harm is assessed to be great and a person's ability to avoid or cope with the harm to be inadequate. In **demand/control theory,** on the other hand, strain is engendered by high levels of responsibility along with low decision-making authority. In other words, in this view, strain is determined by demands placed on workers and the authority afforded them. Alternatively, the **person–environment model** suggests that occupational stress is related to the extent to which a person's abilities (e.g., aptitudes, skills, knowledge) and needs (psychological and physical) correspond with the requirements and rewards supplied by the work (e.g., tasks, conditions, expectations, rewards). A good fit, then, between the person and work is hypothesized to engender positive experiences, such as eustress or career satisfaction, whereas a poor match is predicted to lead to strain and decreased levels of satisfaction.

In addition to being detrimental to an individual's psychological and physical health, occupational strain is a substantial cost to organizations. Specifically, occupational stress has been found to be associated with increases in sick days and employee turnover. Many work-related injuries are considered to be the result of strain. The costs of injuries, sick days, and turnover to the bottom line of businesses have led some organizations to take steps to promote and safeguard the health of employees from a holistic standpoint by implementing interventions that can be classified in terms of three levels. Primary interventions are designed to change the prevalence and severity of strain by removing or reducing stressors and to promote an organizational concern for health and safety. Secondary interventions are aimed at enhancing employees' awareness of stress and stress-management skills. Tertiary interventions involve the rehabilitation of employees who are experiencing negative effects of stress and can include personal counseling.

The interdisciplinary field of occupational health psychology emerged to address specifically the need for research to clarify the etiology and ramifications of occupational stress and, ultimately, to inform the development of effective interventions. Furthermore, the National Institute for Occupational Safety and Health and the Department of Labor Occupational Safety and Health Administration in the United States (created as a result of the Occupational Safety and Health Act of 1970) continue to champion the creation and maintenance of healthy work environments. Toward the same ends, the European Union established the European Agency for Safety and Health at Work in 1996. As research continues to shed light on the complex nature of occupational stress, individuals, organizations, and governments alike can take greater steps toward preventing and mitigating the harmful effects. Given the swift and wide-sweeping economic changes of globalization, such efforts will certainly continue to be of great value in the years to come.

Contributed by Shawn T. Bubany and
Jo-Ida C. Hansen,
University of Minnesota,
Minneapolis, MN

Additional Resources

Clarke, S., & Cooper, C. L. (2004). *Managing the risk of workplace stress*. London: Rutledge.

Cooper, C. L. (1998). *Theories of organizational stress*. New York: Oxford University Press.

Quick, J. C., & Tetrick, L. E. (2004). *Handbook of occupational health psychology*. Washington, DC: American Psychological Association.

■ Offenders, Adult

One area of great importance in the counseling profession is practice in corrections settings with adult offenders. As the number of adults under correctional supervision approaches 6 million (Beck, 2000), more professional counselors will find themselves working with offenders and their families.

The criminal justice system comprises three major parts: law enforcement, the courts, and corrections. These parts form a continuum, and corrections is the end result for individuals convicted of a criminal offense. Individuals arrested and tried as adults are known as **adult offenders.** Although the age at which an individual can be tried as an adult varies from state to state, in general, crimes committed by a person who is older than 17 years tend to be considered adult crimes; however, the severity of the offenses, for example homicide or sexual assault, may result in the age limits being decreased.

Professional Counselors as Part of the Process

Professional counselors are needed throughout the criminal process. Although prisons and jails are the most visible cor-

rectional facilities for adults, probation, parole, and alternatives to incarceration such as diversion programs also fall under the umbrella of corrections and count for more than two thirds of the adult correctional population (Young & LoMonaco, 2001).

The number of individuals under some form of correctional control continues to increase. Between 1990 and 1998, the increase in the number of state and federal prisoners averaged almost 7% annually (Beck & Mumola, 1999). At the end of 2001, there were an estimated 5.6 million adults who had at some point served time in state or federal prisons, including 4.3 million former prisoners and 1.3 million adults in prison at that time. Nearly a third of former prisoners were still under correctional supervision, including 731,000 on parole, 437,000 on probation, and 166,000 in local jails (U.S. Department of Justice, n.d.). These individuals and their family members often need the services provided by professional counselors in a wide variety of settings. Of jail inmates, 31% grew up with a parent or guardian who abused alcohol or drugs, about 12% had lived in a foster home or institution, and 46% had a family member who had been incarcerated (U.S. Department of Justice, n.d.). In addition, the large number of individuals who cycle in and out of jails and prisons could benefit from counseling intervention. It is important to note that nearly two thirds of the 3.8 million adults incarcerated between 1974 and 2001 occurred as a result of an increase in first incarceration rates, whereas one third occurred as a result of an increase in the U.S. population, that is, the increased proportion over this period of time of individuals age 18 years and older. Thus, increases in incarceration were due less to population increases in the United States than to changes in laws and sentencing guidelines.

A relationship exists between offender populations and the individuals and families with whom professional counselors come into contact in other settings. For example, about 16% of male and 23% of female jail inmates have been identified as mentally ill (Young & Smith, 2000). Almost 60% of female state prisoners report experiencing physical or sexual abuse (Greenfield & Snell, 1999). In addition, over 75% of incarcerated individuals have substance-abuse-related disorders (Mumola, 1999).

Racial and ethnic minorities are disproportionately represented behind bars and make up over 65% of the prison populations (U.S. Department of Justice, n.d.). The lifetime likelihood of going to prison is 29% for African American men, 16% for Hispanic men, and 4% for White men (Bonczar & Beck, 1997). As professional counselors strive to promote cultural competence, they should be aware of practices and policies that adversely affect certain groups in correctional populations.

The population of incarcerated women has nearly doubled since 1990 (Alleyne, 2006; Beck, 2000). Much of this increase is due to changes in drug laws and harsher sentencing for drug-related offenses. Indeed, the proportion of women convicted of violent crimes or property crimes has decreased whereas the proportion of drug offenders has grown (Greenfield & Snell, 1999). Many of these women would benefit from appropriate treatment for substance abuse that takes into consideration their life histories and circumstances. Professional counselors employed in treatment settings, as well as in correctional settings, are well positioned to address these needs.

When women go to prison, more than 70% of them leave behind children under the age of 18 years. These children and their caregivers often need support and counseling. It is important to assist these families at the earliest opportunity because there is a strong correlation between maternal incarceration and future criminal behavior and imprisonment among affected children (Alleyne, 2006; Bloom & Steinhart, 1993).

Treatment Considerations

Treatment of adult offenders includes addressing the needs of incarcerated individuals when they are in the prison setting, when they have finished their mandated sentence, and when they are out of prison, as well as addressing the needs of offenders' families throughout the process. Turnbo and Murray (1997) discussed an array of mental health needs for inmates, including services to address mental illness (including sex offenses), substance abuse, suicide prevention, transitional care, hospice, development of prosocial values, HIV/AIDS, and self-help groups and services to address the needs of women and special needs populations. The authors also emphasized the importance of the mental health needs of prison staff, including employee assistance programs, family and employee assistance teams, and employee development/human resources management.

Dvoskin and Spiers (2004) aptly noted that a prison comprises a community of individuals who mutually depend on one another; inmates depend on prison officials and staff for order and safety, and prison officials depend on inmates for compliance with rules and as a labor force. Ironically, most aspects of the prison environment are not conducive to building a safe and productive community. Loss of freedom and control; anger at the legal system; humiliation and negative social stigma (e.g., "Convicts are supposed to suffer for their crimes"); fear for one's life, of being raped, or of never again being free; and concern about their families with no ability to address their needs foster in inmates a negative self-concept and vulnerability to antisocial attitudes and behavior. Mental illness and co-occurring disorders exacerbate unproductive intrapersonal dynamics (Edens, Peters, & Hills, 1997). Coupled with these inherent factors is the prison environment, with slamming cell doors, cramped quarters, loud noises, horrible smells and sanitation problems, violence, drug abuse, and continual verbal commands ranging from turning out the lights to when to shower. These elements create a chaotic, stressful, and often violent living situation that is counter to facilitating a therapeutic environment. Mental health treatment within a prison system is largely focused on enhancing the maintenance of security in the prison by decreasing incidences of unpredictable violent behavior of mentally ill inmates (Dvoskin & Spiers, 2004; Lewis, 2000). Shenson, Dubler, and Michaels (1990) argued that although prisoners in the United States have a constitutional right to appropriate health care, mental health needs are not a priority, and care for mental health needs is often woefully lacking.

Interventions that are focused on helping inmates understand and accept their interdependence and work cooperatively within a prison community not only help develop more productive and less stressful living conditions but also help reinforce appropriate socialization for the inmates' eventual return to life outside of prison. These interventions include psychoeducational group work (e.g., interpersonal communication, assertiveness, sensitivity training) and cognitive and behavioral strategies focused on impulse control. Bayse, Allgood, and Van Wyk (1991) found that inmates exposed to family life education had decreased negative attitudes, which assisted in reintegrating inmates with their families. Dvoskin and Spiers (2004) advocated for a model of mental health treatment in a prison setting that includes working with direct line staff (e.g., correctional officers, nurses) to engage inmates in talking about their challenges while maintaining the order essential to a safe prison environment. In this way, professional counselors act in a consultative role to develop in prison staff a therapeutic orientation to their work.

Transition counseling and **recidivism prevention** are central concerns when inmates are freed from prison after fulfilling their sentences or on parole. Professional counselors should take a supportive stance and seek interventions designed to strengthen family relationships and develop and maintain a positive social support system. Bahr, Armstrong, and Gibbs (2005) identified that decreased recidivism for released prisoners was linked to the number of close relationships within a family network, the quality of parent–child relationships, employment, and reliable housing. Factors identified as increasing recidivism included socializing with friends (away from family) more than four times a week, drug abuse, conflicted relationships within the family network, and other family members on probation or in jail. Treatment should be focused on helping ex-inmates maintain parole conditions, including maintaining contact with parole officers and being in compliance with the conditions of parole. Family counseling is essential in helping strengthen family relationships and addressing transitional concerns. In this way, effective rehabilitation decreases recidivism and, thus, helps prevent crime.

Families of incarcerated inmates are significantly affected socially, emotionally, and economically by having parents or siblings in a prison system. Confusion often emerges in children and is manifested in acting-out behavior, longing for the incarcerated family member, and being socially ostracized by peers, all of which can complicate family functioning. How parents respond to questions about the incarcerated family member affects relationships and children's sense of safety and of self. Parents with an incarcerated spouse face raising children and supporting their families by themselves, which increases stress and tests their coping strategies. Counseling interventions should focus on helping identify and strengthen support systems (both extended family and community) for families and helping to strengthen the parental roles within the family. Supportive and corrective interventions for disruptive behavior in children are also important in strengthening family functioning. Professional counselors are encouraged to remain sensitive to the numerous stressors (e.g., economic decline, social stigma, lack of resources) these families face and focus on maintaining collaborative relationships with the family.

Contributed by Laura R. Simpson and
Matthew Buckley,
Delta State University, Cleveland, MS

References

Alleyne, V. (2006). Locked up means locked out: Women, addiction and incarceration. *Women & Therapy, 29,* 181–194.

Bahr, S. J., Armstrong, A. H., & Gibbs, B. G. (2005). The reentry process: How parolees adjust to release from prison. *Fathering, 3,* 243–265.

Bayse, D. J., Allgood, S. M., & Van Wyk, P. H. (1991). Family life education: An effective tool for prisoner rehabilitation. *Family Relations, 43,* 254–257.

Beck, A. J. (2000). *Prison and jail inmates at midyear 1999* (U.S. Department of Justice Publication No. NJC 181643). Washington, DC: U.S. Government Printing Office.

Beck, A. J., & Mumola, C. J. (1999). *Prisoners in 1998* (U.S. Department of Justice Publication No. NJC 175687). Washington, DC: U.S. Government Printing Office.

Bloom, B., & Steinhart, D. (1993). *Why punish the children? A reappraisal of the children of incarcerated mothers in America.* San Francisco: National Council on Crime and Delinquency.

Bonczar, T. P., & Beck, A. J. (1997). *Lifetime likelihood of going to state or federal prison* (U.S. Department of Justice Publication No. NCJ 160092). Washington, DC: U.S. Government Printing Office.

Dvoskin, J. A., & Spiers, E. M. (2004). On the role of correctional officers in prison. *Psychiatric Quarterly, 75,* 41–59.

Edens, J. F., Peters, R. H., & Hills, H. A. (1997). Treating prison inmates with co-occurring disorders: An integrative review of existing programs. *Behavioral Sciences & the Law, 15,* 439–457.

Greenfield, L. A., & Snell T. L. (1999). *Women offenders* (U.S. Department of Justice Publication No. NJC 175688). Washington, DC: U.S. Government Printing Office.

Lewis, C. F. (2000). Successfully treating aggression in mentally ill prison inmates. *Psychiatric Quarterly, 71,* 331–343.

Mumola, C. J. (1999). *Substance abuse and treatment, state and federal prisoners, 1997* (U.S. Department of Justice Publication No. NJC 172871). Washington, DC: U.S. Government Printing Office.

Shenson, D., Dubler, N., & Michaels, D. (1990). Jails and prisons: The new asylums? *American Journal of Public Health, 80,* 655–656.

Turnbo, C., & Murray, D. W. (1997). The state of mental health services to criminal offenders. In T. R. Watkins & J. W. Callicutt (Eds.), *Mental health policy and practice today* (pp. 298–311). Thousand Oaks, CA: Sage.

Young, D. S., & LoMonaco, S. W. (2001). Incorporating content on offenders and corrections into social work curricula. *Journal of Social Work Education, 37,* 475–491.

Young, D. S., & Smith, C. J. (2000). When moms are incarcerated: The needs of children, mothers, and caregivers. *Families in Society: The Journal of Contemporary Human Services, 81,* 120–141.

U. S. Department of Justice, Bureau of Justice Statistics. (n.d). *Criminal offenders statistics.* Retrieved January 25, 2008, from http://www.ojp.usdoj.gov/bjs/crimoff.htm#prevalence

Additional Resources

Bureau of Justice Statistics Web site: http://www.ojp.usdoj.gov/bjs

Correctional Services Corporation Web site: http://www.correctionalservices.com

Criminal Offenders Statistics Web site: http:www.ojp.usdoj.gov/bjs/crimoff.htm

Sentencing Project Web site: http:www.sentencingproject.org

■Operant Conditioning

Operant conditioning was the term used by **B. F. Skinner** to describe the use of consequences to modify the incidence rate and structure of a behavior. Skinner, an experimental psychologist, stressed the methods of behavior and looked for principles to illustrate and foretell behavioral patterns as well as ways to transform behavior (Kalodner, 2007). In addition to B. F. Skinner, Edward Thorndike and John Watson are major theorists in the development of operant conditioning. **Edward Thorndike** was the first to theorize that satisfying consequences to a response would reinforce the experience, thus causing the behavior to occur more frequently. Likewise, annoying consequences would lessen the occurrence of the behavior. **John Watson** was also interested in experimenting with changes in human behavior. He paired an unconditioned stimulus (a bell) with a conditioned stimulus (a white rat). He then demonstrated that this pairing could lead a child to experience a fearful reaction not only to the white rat but also to white cotton or Watson's white hair. Playing a major role in the development of psychology, these behavioral approaches proposed that learning is composed of connecting certain responses with certain stimuli. Learning occurs as the connection causes a change in response to events (stimuli) in the environment.

There are four major types of operant conditioning: positive reinforcement, negative reinforcement, punishment, and extinction. In the process of **positive reinforcement,** a behavior is strengthened if it is followed by a positive reinforcer. For instance, when a rat presses a bar in his cage and receives food, the food becomes a positive condition for the rat and will strengthen the behavior of pressing the bar. Likewise, **negative reinforcement** also involves strengthening a behavior, but the reinforcer comes in the form of stopping or avoiding a negative condition. One such scenario would involve the rat receiving a slight electrical shock. When the rat presses the bar, the shock subsides. Subsequently, each time the rat receives a shock and presses the bar, the shock subsides. This reoccurring reinforcer causes the behavior to be "stamped in."

In addition to positive and negative reinforcement, punishment and extinction are widely used in operant conditioning. The purpose of **punishment** in operant conditioning is to weaken a behavior; thus, the behavior is less likely to happen again (Archer & McCarthy, 2007). Positive punishment and negative punishment are both used to weaken a behavior. **Negative punishment** reduces a behavior by removing a satisfying stimulus when the behavior occurs. For example, if the rat had previously received food by pressing a bar but now receives food for not pressing the bar, the rat will eventually stop pressing the bar. With **positive punishment,** a disagreeable stimulus follows the behavior. In order to avoid the punishment, the organism will also avoid the behavior. If the rat had been receiving food when the bar was pressed and now receives a shock, the rat will learn to stop pressing the bar. On the other hand, **extinction** is a very simple concept. It is accomplished by simply removing the reinforcement to the behavior, thus stopping the behavior.

Generalization, chaining, and shaping are also aspects of operant conditioning. **Generalization** is simply applying the behavior in more than one similar situation. Chaining and shaping, however, are more complex processes in operant conditioning. In everyday human affairs, behaviors occur in intricate sequences. **Chaining** refers to the sequencing of events leading to behaviors. For example, an individual might drive to work, get out of the car, go into the building, unlock the office, turn on the computer, and read the mail. Providing reinforcement to the final behavior of reading the mail would reinforce the entire chain. **Shaping** involves reinforcing a less complex form of the desired behavior. Once the less challenging behavior has been established, behaviors are initiated that gradually move a little closer to the desired activity. At each level of advancement, the organism receives reinforcement for the appropriate behavior. Actually, shaping occurs every day as individuals move through life experiences and establish careers.

In summary, operant conditioning came to the forefront of behavioral science in the 1930s and since that time has been an important aspect of a behavioral approach to psychology. The most important contribution of this feature of behaviorism is the identification, measurement, and modification of learning. In operant conditioning, the learner always plays an active role in absorbing and applying knowledge from the surrounding environment.

Contributed by Jan C. Lemon and
Carl J. Sheperis,
Mississippi State University,
Starkville, MS

References

Archer, J., & McCarthy, C. J. (2007). *Theories of counseling and psychotherapy: Contemporary application.* Upper Saddle River, NJ: Pearson Education.

Kalodner, C. (2007). Theories of counseling and psychotherapy. In D. Capuzzi & D. Gross (Eds.), *Counseling and psychotherapy theories and interventions* (pp. 243–261). Columbus, OH: Merrill Prentice Hall.

Additional Resources

Skinner, B. F. (1953). *Science and human behavior.* New York: Macmillan.
Journal for the Experimental Analysis of Behavior
Journal of Applied Behavior Analysis

■ Oppression: Historical Contexts

Oppression has been defined by scholars and educators in various fields as a system that demeans and disadvantages people by denying them equal access to services, advantages, and rewards because of their membership in a particular cultural group (e.g., ethnic minorities, religious minorities, sexual minorities, women, individuals with disabilities). Oppression involves the abuse of power whereby a dominant group engages in unjust, harsh, or cruel activities that perpetuate an attitude or belief reinforced by society and maintained by a power imbalance. It involves beliefs and actions that impose undesirable labels, experiences, and conditions on individuals, making prejudice and discrimination in areas such as race, ethnicity, religion, gender, class, and sexual orientation a persistent social reality.

In the counseling and psychology literature, the term *oppression* is often discussed in relation to privilege. These concepts can be viewed as existing on opposite ends of the same continuum. Thus, in contrast to oppression, **privilege** refers to the benefit of having access to services, advantages, and rewards in society based on an individual's membership in a particular group, irrespective of merit. Ideas, attitudes, and behavior that reinforce the notion that one group's beliefs and standards are superior to those of other groups perpetuate systems of privilege and oppression. These systems may operate in the workplace, education, housing, media, and the legal system, and they result in inequities for some and unearned advantages and opportunities for others. Social inequities, cultural imposition of a dominant group on minority groups, and cultural disintegration and re-creation of the oppressed groups characterize systems of oppression.

Hanna, Talley, and Guindon (2000) described two mutually inclusive modalities of oppression: oppression by force and oppression by deprivation. They contended that oppression can be manifested in three ways, yielding three types of oppression: primary, secondary, and tertiary. **Primary oppression** refers to overt acts of oppression, including oppression by force and oppression by deprivation. **Secondary oppression** involves individuals benefiting from overt oppressive acts. Individuals involved in secondary oppression do not actively engage in oppressive acts but also do not object to others who do engage in overt oppressive acts and benefit from the aggression. **Tertiary oppression,** also known as internalized oppression, refers to minority group members identifying with the dominant message in an effort to seek acceptance by the dominant group. Like secondary oppression, tertiary oppression can be passive in nature.

Internalized oppression is a central theme in ethnic minority psychotherapy. The internalization of a dominant group's message that an individual is inferior to those in power and that an individual's identity is consistent with an oppressor's stereotyped perceptions leads to a devalued self-worth among the oppressed. Internalized oppression has been linked to a range of psychiatric problems, including depression, anxiety, posttraumatic reactions, identity confusion, substance abuse, domestic violence, and eating disorders, as well as to physical ailments such as high blood pressure.

Feminist scholars have broadened the discussion of oppression to include the complexity of multiple intersecting identities and the resulting clinical implications. The terms **double jeopardy** or **triple jeopardy** are used to refer to individuals who often experience compounded oppression or multiple oppressions due to having multiple marginalized identities associated with characteristics such as race, class, gender, religion, or disability. Such individuals may also suffer from marginalization due to factors associated with language, immigration and migration status, and generation of residence in the United States. Possessing multiple marginalized identities often requires effective coping strategies and resilience in order to survive and thrive in an oppressive environment.

Paulo Freire's writings on oppression have significantly influenced the fields of education and counseling. In his most well-known work, *Pedagogy of the Oppressed,* Freire (1970) discussed the banking concept of education, in which learners are passive recipients of information that is deposited by expert teachers who consider the learners to know nothing. Such education attempts to control thinking, promote passivity, and stifle creativity, alienating human beings from their own decision making and process of inquiry. In contrast, the revolutionary educator uses problem posing or liberating education, in which students become critical co-investigators who are in dialogue with the teacher. Freire's concept of *conscientizacào,* or the process of developing a critical consciousness, has been applied to the counseling literature. Clients and professional counselors are encouraged to develop an awareness of self within their social context as a way of fostering insight and effective action. Critical consciousness is the process whereby individuals develop an awareness of oppressive systems in which they live and develop strategies to empower themselves. An example may be an abused woman who develops an awareness of related power and control issues, moves beyond self-blame, and takes action to terminate such a relationship.

Application to Counseling

All counseling may be viewed as cross-cultural because every individual is a cultural being with multiple cultural identities; however, the counseling field has been traditionally monocultural and ineffective regarding persons of color, women, persons with disabilities, older persons, sexual minorities, and non-Christians. The counseling relationship has been viewed as mirroring the state of cultural and racial relations in the larger society. Professional counselors frequently reflect the attitudes, beliefs, and practices of the dominant society. Oppressive attitudes and behaviors on the part of the counselor often result in clinician bias and reinforcement of stereotyping, culturally insensitive assessment and intervention practices, misdiagnosis of individuals from oppressed groups based on majority norms, and the characterization of reactions as intrapsychic pathology as opposed to culturally and contextually influenced expressions of distress in response to oppressive circumstances. Thus, many people who identify with marginalized cultural groups may be at an increased risk of experiencing oppressive conditions in the counseling relationship.

Given the pervasiveness of oppression, professional counselors must acknowledge and understand how prejudice and discrimination negatively affect counseling. They must also be able to identify and understand the intersection of multiple cultural identities, recognize that clients may be managing multiple oppressions at any given time, and understand the potential impact this has on the counseling relationship. To address oppression appropriately in the counseling process and enhance the counseling relationship for all clients, the Association for Multicultural Counseling and Development approved the *Multicultural Counseling Competencies* (MCC; Arredondo et al., 1996). These competencies, endorsed by both the American Counseling Association and the American Psychological Association, propose specific guidelines for the training of multiculturally competent helping professionals (see Cultural Competence).

In addition to the MCC, there has been an increased focus on social justice and social action related to multicultural counseling. In this context, professional counselors should be not only aware and knowledgeable about oppression but should take action against the causes and conditions of oppression. Guidelines for psychotherapy with girls and women; guidelines on multicultural education, training, research, practice, and organizational change; and guidelines for counseling lesbian, gay, bisexual, and transgendered clients have also been developed.

The counseling and educational literature suggests several strategies for addressing oppression and privilege issues at both training and practice levels. These strategies include developing an awareness of self, fostering empathy, increasing critical consciousness, and building coalitions. Specifically, educators and counselors should encourage students and clients to explore their cultural identities, become knowledgeable about the sociocultural and historical backgrounds of their students and clients, and apply this awareness and knowledge to inform culturally relevant practice.

Future Directions

The fields of counseling and psychology have moved from a focus on intrapsychic factors to an analysis of the interplay between intrapsychic and contextual forces, such as oppression and its impact on psychological functioning. More recent perspectives have moved from a dualistic approach and pointed to the complex interplay of oppression and privilege that varies across context. This position considers the significant impact of multiple cultural identities on the human experience and the counseling relationship, and, in this view, culture is regarded as central to accurate clinical assessment, interpretation, and treatment. Recent research has focused on the development of inventories that assess awareness of and attitudes toward oppression and privilege, the effects of multiple oppressions on individuals' mental health, and counseling interventions designed to decrease the deleterious effects of oppression on mental health.

Contributed by Julie R. Ancis and
Telsie A. Davis,
Georgia State University, Atlanta, GA

References

Arredondo, P., Toporek, R., Brown, S. P., Jones, J., Locke, D. C., Sanchez, J., et al. (1996). Operationalization of the Multicultural Counseling Competencies. *Journal of Multicultural Counseling and Development, 24,* 42–78.

Freire, P. (1970). *Pedagogy of the oppressed.* New York: Herder & Herder.

Hanna, F. J., Talley, W. B., & Guindon, M. H. (2000). The power of perception: Toward a model of cultural oppression and liberation. *Journal of Counseling & Development, 78,* 430–441.

Additional Resources

Arredondo, P. (1999). Multicultural counseling competencies as tools to address oppression and racism. *Journal of Counseling & Development, 77,* 102–108.

Comas-Díaz, L., & Greene, B. (Eds.). (1994). *Women of color: Integrating ethnic and gender identities in psychotherapy.* New York: Guilford.

Sue, D. W., & Sue, D. (2003). *Counseling the culturally different: Theory and practice* (4th ed.). New York: Wiley.

U.S. Department of Health and Human Services. (2001). *Mental health: Culture, race, and ethnicity—A supplement to mental health: A report of the surgeon general.* Rockville, MD: U.S. Department of Health and Human Services, Substance Abuse and Mental Health Services Administration, Center for Mental Health Services.

■ Oppression, Types of

Oppression has been defined in the counseling literature as an equation: oppression = prejudice × power. **Prejudice** is the maintenance of incorrect conscious or unconscious attitudes, feelings, and beliefs that members of a cultural group are inferior or that a group's cultural differences are unacceptable. All people have prejudice. **Power** is the ability to control access to resources, including control of the images of what is culturally appropriate. Power and power over others are maintained and used on individual, cultural, and systemic levels. All people do not have the same access to power and power over others. Although oppression is common between groups, in that the dominant group demonstrates power over nondominant groups, oppression may be seen within groups, depending on the combination of cultural statuses of individuals of a particular group. Regardless of the type of oppression, the result is always the limitation of access to appropriate or equitable individual, cultural, and systemic resources.

There are multiple oppressions addressed by varied levels of theory and research in the counseling and social justice education literature. **Ableism** is oppression by persons with no disabilities against persons with disabilities (e.g., developmental, emotional, physical, learning disabilities). **Ageism** is oppression by persons ages 18 to 49 years against children, adolescents, and persons 50 years and older. **Beautyism** is oppression by persons with dominant standards of beauty against overweight persons or persons with other nondominant appearances. **Classism** is oppression by wealthy and upper-middle-class persons against poor, working-class, or lower-middle-class persons. **Familyism** is oppression by persons of traditional family configurations against single persons, single parents, same-gender parents, same-gender couples, divorced persons, cohabiting couples, adoptive/foster families, and other nontraditional family configurations.

Genderism is oppression by traditionally gendered persons against transgendered (e.g., transsexuals, cross-dressers, gender benders, drag kings and queens), and gender-variant (e.g., intersex persons, masculine women and girls, feminine men and boys) persons. **Heterosexism** is oppression by heterosexuals against lesbian, bisexual, gay, two-spirit, queer, and questioning persons. **Immigrationism** occurs when citizens attempt to exclude others from citizenship or legitimate immigration status; this oppression limits the ability of potential immigrants and, often, the most recent immigrants to access individual, cultural, and systemic resources. **Linguicism** is oppression by dominant-language speakers against nonspeakers of the dominant language or persons who speak with an accent or with little fluency in the dominant language.

Racism is oppression, typically by Whites of various ethnicities, against people of color and multiracial people in countries where White/European colonization and racial/ethnic influence dominate. In countries lacking White/European colonization and influence, racism is a dominant racial/ethnic group limiting access to individual, cultural, and systemic resources by members of other racial/ethnic groups. **Religionism** is oppression by members of a dominant religious group (in the United States, Christians) against nondominant religious, spiritual, and/or nonreligious persons and groups (e.g., Jews, Muslims, Hindus, Jains, Buddhists, Earth-Centered, Pagans, atheists, agnostics). **Sexism** is oppression used by men or boys against women or girls.

The definitions, theory, and research regarding the oppressions listed in this entry continue to evolve in counseling, social justice education, and other disciplines (Lewis, Arnold, House, & Toporek, 2002). Professional counselors need awareness, knowledge, and skills in advocacy, including the ability to name, address, and challenge oppressions in clients, systems, and society at large. Evidence-based research and practice interventions related to anti-oppression in counseling and counselor education are an important focus for the counseling profession.

Contributed by Stuart F. Chen-Hayes, Lehman College of the City University of New York (CUNY), NY

Reference

Lewis, J., Arnold, M. S., House, R., & Toporek, R. (2002). *ACA advocacy competencies.* Retrieved March 29, 2007, from http://counselorsforsocialjustice.com/advocacy competencies.html

Additional Resources

Adams, M., Bell, L. A., & Griffin, P. (2007). *Teaching for diversity and social justice* (2nd ed.). New York: Routledge.

Lewis, J. A., & Arnold, M. S. (1998). From multiculturalism to social action. In C. C. Lee & G. R. Walz (Eds.), *Social action: A mandate for counselors* (pp. 51–66). Alexandria, VA: American Counseling Association and ERIC Counseling and Student Services Clearinghouse.

Pope, R., & Reynolds, A. (1991). The complexities of diversity: Exploring multiple oppressions. *Journal of Counseling & Development, 70,* 174–180.

◼ Outcome Research

Outcome research in counseling attempts to describe, interpret, and predict the impact of counseling interventions for "final" endpoints. **Final endpoints** are those outcomes or end results that make a difference, such as improved functioning, increased capacity for decision making, or less anxiety. Outcome research is comparative. In essence, outcome research seeks to find out whether a counseling intervention is better than or worse than no intervention at all, if one intervention is better than another intervention, and to what degree an intervention is better or worse than no intervention or another intervention. "Better than" can be defined in terms of measurable outcomes for the people experiencing the intervention, whether the measurable outcome is self-perceived or observed.

Heppner, Wampold, and Kivlighan (2008) divided outcome research strategies into seven categories: treatment package, dismantling, constructive, parametric, comparative outcome, common factors control group design, and moderation design. The **treatment package strategy** asks the question of whether a treatment package or intervention has an impact on a variable. For example, does assertiveness training help increase the ability of introverted middle school students to self-advocate appropriately when compared with another group of introverted middle school students who did not receive the assertiveness training?

The **dismantling strategy** asks the question of which elements in an effective treatment package or multifaceted intervention are necessary and which are nonessential. Perhaps the best way to conceptualize this strategy is to think of

the treatment package as an exam and each treatment element in the package as a question on the exam. The goal is to see if the exam will have the same validity and reliability if the number of test items is reduced, or in the counseling situation, will the intervention still have the same effect, with greater parsimony, if treatment elements are removed.

The **constructive strategy** seeks to determine whether or not the addition of a new component to an already-supported treatment adds to the overall effectiveness. One example of the constructive strategy is a study completed by Smith, Compton, and West (1995). The investigators provided two groups the Personal Happiness Enhancement Program (PHEP), which had already been shown to be effective in increasing a sense of well-being and reducing symptoms of depression and anxiety, and provided one of the two groups with additional instruction in meditation. The PHEP-plus-meditation group showed significantly greater improvement on all dependent measures over the PHEP-only group.

The **parametric strategy** involves assessing how an optimal quantity of counseling components may add to the outcome. For example, if reviewing goals once a session is shown to lead to positive outcomes, does reviewing goals two or three times per session increase the positive outcome?

The **common factors control group strategy** tries to ascertain whether a specific therapeutic intervention or specific ingredient accounts for an outcome or if therapeutic change results from common factors in counseling, such as the therapeutic alliance. For example, is the assignment of homework responsible for a positive outcome (e.g., decreased depression) or is the decrease in symptoms primarily a result of the counselor–client relationship?

The **comparative outcome strategy** poses the question of which of two or more effective treatments is most effective or most efficient (i.e., less costly or less time-consuming). L. Miller, Barrett, Hampe, and Noble (1972) demonstrated that both reciprocal inhibition and traditional psychotherapy were effective in treating phobic children, and both treatments were shown to be more effective than no treatment in a group of children in a control group. The **moderation design strategy** seeks to address the notion that certain types of clients might respond better to certain types of treatments. For instance, individuals with a high need for structure may respond better to highly structured treatment regimens, whereas individuals with a low need for structure may respond better to low-structure treatments. In such cases, counselors look to see the interaction of need for structure and structure level of the counseling intervention with the hope of finding the most effective intervention for a particular client type.

Comparisons can also be made regarding cost effectiveness. Self-perceived or observed outcomes are frequently used to help inform best practice, whereas outcomes research focused on cost effectiveness is frequently used to inform public policy. Project Match is a prime example of outcomes research in which the results were used to look at cost effectiveness for treatment of alcohol abuse and dependence and subsequently has led to policy decisions regarding such issues as effective duration of treatment programs (Cisler, Holder, Longabaugh, Stout, & Zweben, 1998; Holder et al., 2000; W. Miller, Zweben, DiClemente, & Rychtarik, 1995).

Contributed by E. H. Mike Robinson III,
University of Central Florida,
Orlando, FL

References

Cisler, R., Holder, H. D., Longabaugh, R., Stout, R., & Zweben, A. (1998). Actual and estimated replication costs for alcohol treatment modalities: Case study from Project MATCH. *Journal of Studies on Alcohol, 59,* 503–512.

Heppner, P., Wampold, B., & Kivlighan, D. (2008). *Research design in counseling* (3rd ed.). Belmont, CA: Thomson.

Holder, H. D., Cisler, R. A., Longabaugh, R., Stout, R. L., Treno, A. J., & Zweben, A. (2000). Alcoholism treatment and medical care costs from Project MATCH. *Addiction, 95,* 999–1013.

Miller, L., Barrett, C., Hampe, E., & Noble, H. (1972). Comparison of reciprocal inhibition, psychotherapy and waiting list control for phobic children. *Journal of Abnormal Psychology, 79,* 269–279.

Miller, W., Zweben, A., DiClemente, C., & Rychtarik, R. (1995). *Motivational enhancement therapy manual.* Rockville, MD: National Institute on Alcohol Abuse and Alcoholism.

Smith W., Compton, W., & West, W. (1995). Meditation as an adjunct to a happiness enhancement program. *Journal of Clinical Psychology, 51,* 269–273.

Additional Resources

Dimmitt, C., Carey, J., & Hatch, P. (2007). *Evidence-based school counseling: Making a difference with data-driven practices.* Thousand Oaks, CA: Corwin.

Erford, B. (2008). *Research and evaluation in counseling.* Boston: Houghton Mifflin.

Paradoxical Intention

Paradoxical intention, an approach used in counseling and psychotherapy, was first used by Viktor Frankl in the 1920s when treating patients with high levels of anxiety. Frankl defined paradoxical intention as a process in which "the patient is encouraged to do or wish to happen, the very thing he fears" (Frankl, 1969, pp. 102–103). For example, someone who has significant anxiety of leaving his or her house for fear of having a heart attack would actually be encouraged by the professional counselor to plan a trip far away from home in order to increase his or her heart rate and "promote" a heart attack. The client would work to embrace the target of his or her particular apprehension by directly addressing the "anticipatory anxiety" (leaving the house), which Frankl believed was the key to stopping the endless cycle of anxiety. Logically, an individual cannot both fear and wish for the same thing. Thus, as Frankl suggested, a person who experiences a great deal of anticipatory anxiety cannot maintain that anxiety when performing the behavior. If a person can be encouraged to wish for the thing that he or she fears, the cycle of anxiety can be broken.

Paradoxical intention is most effectively used not as a simple technique for reducing anxiety in the client but rather as an overall change in attitude toward the object of angst. The professional counselor works with the client to embrace the attitude that the anxiety will not be harmful and that it is the avoidance of the anxiety that reduces the client's overall efficacy. A further component of the paradoxical approach is the presence of humor in the counseling relationship, which is used to encourage a healthy distance between the client and the anxiety.

Contributed by James D. Raper,
Syracuse University, Syracuse, NY

Reference

Frankl, V. E. (1969). *The will to meaning: Foundations and applications of logotherapy.* New York: New American Library.

Additional Resources

Ascher, L. M. (1989). *Therapeutic paradox.* New York: Guilford Press.

Frankl, V. (2004). *On the theory and therapy of mental disorders: An introduction to logotherapy and existential analysis* (J. M. DuBois, Trans.). New York: Brunner-Routledge.

Omer, H. (1981). Paradoxical treatments: A unified concept. *Psychotherapy: Theory, Research, Practice, Training, 18,* 320–324.

Seltzer, L. F. (1986). *Paradoxical strategies in psychotherapy: A comprehensive overview and guidebook.* New York: Wiley.

Parametric Statistics

Parametric statistics involve estimating the specific value of an unknown population parameter (estimation) or making a decision about a hypothesized value of an unknown population parameter (hypothesis testing). To use a parametric statistic, certain assumptions must be met: The distribution of the population(s) on some variable must be normal and the variances equal. In statistical hypothesis testing, data from a randomly drawn sample are used to make inferences about the normally distributed population from which the sample was drawn. Statistical tests are performed on the sample data to make a conclusion about the null hypothesis; that is, is the null hypothesis likely or unlikely to be true. The statistical tests presented in this section are the t test, one-way analysis of variance (ANOVA), factorial ANOVA, multivariate analysis of variance (MANOVA), analysis of covariance (ANCOVA), multivariate analysis of covariance (MANCOVA), and post hoc comparisons.

t test

The t test, also known as the **Student's distribution** or **Student's distribution of t,** is used to test statistical hypotheses about sample means. It may be used to test one mean, differences between two independent means, and differences between two **dependent means.** The null hypothesis for a single mean involves testing whether the mean differs significantly from a numerical value ($H_o: \mu_x = K$). For example, a professional school counselor wants to know if the mean IQ score of students in the school district differs significantly from the IQ score for the norm group of the IQ test. If the mean IQ score for the norm group is 100, the null hypothesis would be $H_o: \mu_x = 100$. The null hypothesis test between two **independent means** involves testing whether the two means differ significantly ($H_o: \mu_1 - \mu_2 = 0$). The two means represent different measures of the same variable (e.g., two types of behavior therapy). When testing the hypothesis, it is assumed that Sample 1 is drawn randomly from a normally distributed Population 1 and that an independent Sample 2 is drawn randomly from a normally distributed population.

The samples may be drawn from the same or different normally distributed populations. It is also assumed that their variances are equal (i.e., homogeneity of variance).

Differences between two dependent means may be determined for repeated measures of the same sample or repeated samples of the same measure, where the null hypothesis is $H_o: \mu_1 - \mu_2 = 0$. **Repeated measures** of the same sample may be illustrated by comparing the mean pretest and posttest reading comprehension scores for a randomly selected group of third graders from a particular school. The same measure is used for the pretest and the posttest. To illustrate repeated samples of the same measure, the effects of a specific behavior therapy on two randomly selected samples taken from the same population can be compared. When testing the hypothesis of dependent means, it is assumed that Samples 1 and 2 are drawn randomly from normally distributed populations with the same variance.

The distribution representing t shares similar characteristics with the normal distribution z. Like the normal distribution, the t distribution is symmetrical and unimodal and has a mean of zero. The shape of the t distribution is, however, more leptokurtic than the normal distribution, which means that the curve representing t is narrower at the peak and wider at the tails. The standard deviation for t is larger than that of the normal distribution, where ($\sigma = 1$). The t distribution also depends on the number of degrees of freedom (df). For t tests involving a single mean, $df = n - 1$, where n is the total number of participants in the sample. The t tests involving independent means has $df = (n_1 - 1) + (n_2 - 1)$, where n_1 is the total number in Sample 1 and n_2 is the total number in Sample 2. The degrees of freedom for tests of dependent means is similar to that of the single mean, $df = n - 1$. In this case, n represents the number of pairs of scores.

ANOVA

The t test is limited to the test of a single mean or the difference between two means. It is not an adequate test if the researcher is interested in comparing differences among three or more means. Multiple t tests would need to be conducted to examine each possible combination of two means. For example, the hypothesis test $H_o: \mu_A = \mu_B = \mu_C$ has three combinations of mean comparisons (i.e., $H_o: \mu_A = \mu_B$, $H_o: \mu_A = \mu_C$, and $H_o: \mu_B = \mu_C$). A t ratio is computed for each combination, increasing the likelihood of committing at least one Type I error—that is, of obtaining a "significant difference" when no true difference exists. If the three tests are independent with a significance level of .05 for each test, the probability of a false positive is .14 $[p = 1 - (.95)^3]$. To address this issue, **Sir Ronald Fisher** developed the **ANOVA**. ANOVA permits the simultaneous comparison of two or more means using an F ratio with a single specified level of significance. For $H_o: \mu_A = \mu_B = \mu_C$ and a significance level of .05, the probability of a Type I error is .05 ($p = 1 - .95$). In the case of two means, it leads to the same conclusions as the t test. In fact, the t test may be considered a special case of ANOVA when the number of means is two.

In a one-way ANOVA, the means refer to treatment conditions or different levels of the independent variable. If k is used to represent the number of treatment conditions, and the letters A, B, and C are used to represent the k treatments, then the population means may be expressed as μ_A, μ_B, and μ_C. The null hypothesis involves testing whether any of the means differ ($H_o: \mu_A = \mu_B = \mu_C = \ldots = \mu_k$). Like the t test, an ANOVA may be used to compare means of independently drawn samples or repeated measures of dependent samples.

The ANOVA for independent measures examines variations within each sample (within-groups variation) and between the different samples (between-groups variation). These variations are called **sum of squares** *(SS)*. For the total sample, the total sum of squares is a measure of the total variation present in the data without regard to group ($SS_{total} = SS_{within} + SS_{between}$). The estimate of variance for within groups is SS_{within}/df_{within}, where $df_{within} = n_{total} - k$ (n_{total} is the total number of cases and k is the number of groups). It is referred to as the **mean square within** or **mean square error**. The estimate of variance for between groups is $SS_{between}/df_{between}$, where $df_{between} = k - 1$ (k is the number of groups). The statistic used to test the hypothesis is based on the ratio of the two variance estimates, $F = s^2_{between}/s^2_{within}$, with df_{within} and $df_{between}$.

The variation examined in the ANOVA for repeated (dependent) measures is the same as for independent measures ($SS_{total} = SS_{within} + SS_{between}$). However, in ANOVA for repeated measures, the SS_{within} is partitioned into two parts: (a) $SS_{subjects}$, a measure of the variability due to individual differences and (b) $SS_{residual}$, a measure of variability due to random error or chance. For $SS_{subjects}$, $df_{subjects} = n_{total} - 1$ and for $SS_{residual}$, $df_{residual} = df_{subjects} \times df_{between}$. The statistic used to test the hypothesis is $F = s^2_{between}/s^2_{within}$, with $df_{between}$ and $df_{residual}$.

Factorial ANOVAs

ANOVA involves the use of a single factor (or independent variable). To examine two or more independent variables (factors) simultaneously, a factorial analysis of variance procedure is used. **Factorial ANOVAs** are represented by numerous designs (e.g., fixed effects, random effects, mixed effects). A two-way ANOVA (e.g., 2×4 factorial design) has two independent variables, where one independent variable has two levels, and the other independent variable has four levels. For example, a professional school counselor may be interested in investigating type of therapy and length of treatment on the dependent variable motivation to decrease alcohol consumption for high school students who abuse alcohol. The independent variables would be type of therapy (two levels, individual and group) and treatment length (four levels: 2 weeks, 4 weeks, 6 weeks, and 8 weeks). To expand the two-factor design to a three-factor design, a third independent variable (e.g., $2 \times 4 \times 3$) can be added. The variable could represent type of external support (three levels: parental, peer, and mentor).

Important to these designs are the treatment effects, main effects, and interaction. The **treatment effect** represents a difference in the population means, whereas the **main effect** presents a difference in the population means for a factor collapsed over all other factors in the design. In the two-way ANOVA example, a treatment effect may be examined by looking at the effects of type of therapy (both types) for a specific length of treatment (e.g., 6 weeks). A main effect may be examined by looking at the overall influence of the type of therapy (across all four levels of treatment length). An **interaction effect** exists between two factors if the relationship among the effects associated with the levels of one factor differs according to the levels of the second factor. It represents an effect due to the joint influence of the two factors, over and above the effects of each factor considered separately. In the three-factor ANOVA example, an interaction effect could be examined by looking at individual therapy, treatment length of 2 weeks, and parental support. An F ratio can be used to test these effects.

Factorial ANOVAs with fixed effects focus on making statistical inferences about the main effects from a set of sample data (J groups of n persons) to the J groups in the population. The interest is in the J means in the population; specifically, the J main effects. The J levels in the population are fixed, requiring replications of the experiment to have the same J treatment levels. With a random effects model, the sample of J levels in each replication of the experiment is allowed to vary randomly across replications. For example, levels A, B, and C may be sampled this time and levels D, E, and F the next time. The mixed effects model is a combination of fixed effects and random effects.

MANOVA

MANOVA is an extension of ANOVA. The one-way ANOVA is used with one dependent variable, whereas MANOVA is used with two or more dependent variables. Participants are assigned randomly to levels of one or more independent variables and are measured on two or more dependent measures. Hotelling's T^2 is used to determine statistical significance when there is one dichotomous independent variable and multiple dependent variables. When the independent variable has more than two levels, Wilks's lambda may be used to test statistical significance.

When there are multiple independent and dependent variables, factorial MANOVA procedures are used to test statistical differences. The independent and dependent variables may be continuous or categorical. An example is a 2 × 3 factorial MANOVA design with two independent variables (one with two levels and one with three levels) and two dependent variables. An example would be a professional school counselor investigating whether gender and family status significantly affected the self-perception and self-motivation of fourth-grade students. The independent variables are gender (two levels: male, female) and family status (three levels: single parent never married, divorced parents, married parents). The two dependent variables are scores on a self-perception inventory and scores on a self-motivation scale.

ANCOVA and MANCOVA

ANCOVA is designed to enhance statistical precision or power when experimental control is not feasible. It is often the case that some characteristic correlates with the dependent variable. The characteristic can improve the accuracy in predicting the dependent variable and decrease error variance (residual). This characteristic is called a concomitant variable (also known as covariate and covariable). If measures of the concomitant variable are determined prior to the experiment and correlate with measures of the dependent variable, they can be used to reduce experimental error. They can also be used to remove the effects of an extraneous variable by removing the effects of the concomitant variable from the dependent variable. ANCOVA is used to test whether the population means of the dependent variables corresponding to the levels of the independent variable are equal. An example would be a researcher who investigated the effects of three different techniques on test anxiety among college students. The researcher might use ANOVA to examine the differences among the three techniques; however, if the researcher has each student's age, he or she could use ANCOVA to adjust the effects of the techniques to a particular age. MANCOVA is designed to enhance statistical precision or power with MANOVA procedures. Similar to ANCOVA, MANCOVA is used when there are two or more concomitant variables.

Post Hoc Comparisons

Post hoc comparisons (a posteriori) are tests used to make specific comparisons when the F ratio is rejected, indicating that differences exist among the means. A few of the most commonly used post hoc tests are Tukey's HSD, Newman–Keuls, Tukey–Kramer, Bonferroni, and Sheffé. These tests may be computed using SPSS. The common feature among these procedures is that they seek to control Type I error. In the Tukey HSD procedure, HSD stands for "honestly significant difference." It is limited to pair-wise comparisons based on equal sample sizes and involves a comparison of each mean with every other mean. The Newman–Keuls procedure, also limited to equal sample sizes, is based on a stepwise approach. The sample means are ordered from smallest to largest. Pair-wise comparisons begin with the largest difference. If significant, the next largest difference is tested. The procedure continues until a nonsignificant difference is found. Newman–Keuls increases the power of the Tukey HSD. It can find that a difference between two means is statistically significant in some cases where the Tukey HSD would conclude that the difference is not statistically significant; however, the increase in power may also increase Type I error. The Tukey–Kramer procedure addresses the equal sample size requirement of the Tukey HSD and Newman–Keuls procedures by identifying ways in which unequal sample sizes may be combined or averaged without completely risking control of Type I error. The Bonferroni procedure does not require equal sample sizes and considers all pair-wise comparisons. It controls Type I error by dividing the level of significance by the number of comparisons. The Sheffé procedure is used when the sample sizes are not equal or when comparisons other than simple pair-wise comparison between two means are of interest.

Contributed by Renée N. Jefferson,
The Citadel: The Military College of
South Carolina, Charleston, SC

Additional Resources

Glass, G. V., & Hopkins, K. D. (1995). *Statistical methods in education and psychology* (3rd ed.). New York: Allyn & Bacon.

Heiman, G. (2001). *Understanding research methods and statistics: An integrated introduction to psychology* (2nd ed.). Boston: Houghton Mifflin.

Minium, E. W., & King, B. M. (2002). *Statistical reasoning in psychology and education* (4th ed.). New York: Wiley.

Tatsuoka, M. M. (1988). *Multivariate analysis: Techniques for educational and psychological research* (2nd ed.). New York: Wiley.

Parent Disciplining Style

There has been much interest in the parent–child relationship, particularly the types of interactions that result in children who are happy, healthy, and well adjusted. Several major styles of disciplining by parents have been identified in the literature. Much of this research was conducted years ago, with little change to the core concepts. Although there is great variability in parental behavior, all parents teach, control, and influence their children. Each style of parent discipline is associated with various outcomes for the child in terms of social, emotional, and academic achievement.

Parenting style includes two important concepts: responsiveness and demandingness. **Parental responsiveness** refers to the degree to which a parent responds to a child's needs in an accepting and supportive manner as well as the degree to which parents foster independence and self-assertion in their children. There are two ends of the continuum: warm and nurturing versus hostile. The warm and nurturing parent is responsive to the child's needs and demands and provides a loving and supportive environment. There is parental involvement in the child's life through praise, frequent demonstrations of affection, and playtime with the child. These types of interactions tend to lead to prosocial behavior in children and low levels of aggressive behavior. In contrast, hostile parenting is characterized by harsh, coercive, and punitive discipline, including threats and frequent reprimands. These parents seem to be angry at their children most of the time. Long-term research has shown that children of parents who are hostile are at an increased risk for developing depression and conduct problems, including aggressive behavior. **Parental demandingness,** often referred to as parental control, is the attempts made by the parents to have the child obey and follow the rules of the family. The spectrum here ranges from restrictive to permissive. The restrictive parent clearly states rules and monitors behavior to ensure that it conforms to those rules. Furthermore, this parent consistently uses reinforcement when a child is compliant with the rules. The permissive parent does little to confront the child who has disobeyed. This parent is inconsistent and ineffectual in discipline. (Permissive parenting will be discussed in more detail later in this entry.) Some parents use punishment as a form of control in order to have a child conform to the rules, whereas others teach what to do instead of just teaching what not to do.

Diane Baumrind in the late 1960s and early 1970s conducted research with groups of nursery school children. She observed their behavior and obtained information on their parents' child-rearing practices. Then, she evaluated them again when the children were 8 or 9 years old and identified three patterns of child disciplining: authoritarian, permissive, and authoritative. Baumrind's (1989) research demonstrates that parenting styles have a significant bearing on children's current behavior and later development. Parenting style can influence the development of a child's personality and success in school.

Authoritarian parents tend to be controlling, punitive, rigid, and emotionally cold. They value strict, unquestioning adherence from their children and do not tolerate expressions of disagreement. When they establish rules at home, they often do so without regard for the child's developmental needs and do not expect these rules to be questioned by the children. They discourage debate and discussion, and there is almost no give-and-take in parent–child discussions. They have little tolerance for negotiating a compromise with children or letting children work toward their own solutions to problems. Authoritarian parents tend to shape and control their children's behavior and attitudes according to standards of conduct that are absolute, unbending, and often motivated by religious beliefs. They often rely on punitive and harsh (forceful) discipline. Violation of the rules is often punished without asking about purpose or reason for the transgression. Perceived as less warm toward their children than are other parents, authoritarian parents are detached and controlling.

Children of these parents tend to be withdrawn, lack sociability, and have difficulty interacting with their peers. They are unhappy, anxious, defiant, and low in self-confidence, and they lack initiative. These children are moody and easily annoyed. Children with authoritarian parents are less likely than others to have the chance to become autonomous. Because they are highly controlling and demanding, these parents do not allow children to make decisions on their own, resulting in children who are vulnerable to stress and who are often aimless. Girls raised in this environment tend to be dependent on their parents, whereas boys develop hostility. The result of this style of parenting is often children who are distrustful and discontent.

Permissive (e.g., indulgent, nondirective) parents provide a loving, supportive home environment; it just lacks limits or control on their child's behavior. These parents provide lax and inconsistent feedback and discipline and place few demands on their children for orderly behavior or responsibility. If there are rules, they are often very loose and not consistently enforced, leaving the child without a clear idea about expectations. Because there is so little structure, children in these environments are often struggling with what is and what is not acceptable behavior. These parents often act as peers rather than parents to their children.

Permissive parents are nondemanding and noncontrolling and avoid addressing problematic behaviors in their children. They rarely punish inappropriate behavior and allow the children to make many of their own decisions, for example about food and bedtimes; thus, the children become self-regulating. In some instances, these parents can be seen as indifferent or rejecting, because they require little of their children.

Although the styles of parenting are different, children of permissive parents tend to display many of the same negative qualities that children of authoritarian parents do. These children are prone to be dependent and moody and to lack social skills and self-control. They may be selfish, unmotivated, demanding of attention, disobedient, and impulsive. These children are expected to regulate their own behaviors and use the parent as a resource if they desire. Although these children may be intellectually capable, they tend to be low achievers. Permissive parents do not exert much control over their children, which is associated with negative emotions in the child. For example, when the child seeks attention, the parents respond negatively or inconsistently. This affects the child's interpersonal expectations; the child becomes reduced and does not feel worthy of others' love or attention. These children develop poor social skills and can be aggressive.

Authoritative parents fall somewhere between the authoritarian and permissive styles. Authoritative parents have sensible rules, which have been explained and agreed upon and can be flexibly changed as the child matures and develops. Often referred to as supportive parents, they set firm, clear, and consistent limits, but they try to reason with their children, giving explanations for why they should behave in a particular way. When these parents use discipline, they provide rules but explain why those rules make sense in language children can understand. Although the parents are in charge, the household is democratic in nature, and the children are allowed to provide input and are involved in the decision-making process. These parents are not flustered by a child's stubbornness or misbehavior but rather view it as something they can deal with constructively.

Although they are strict (similar to authoritarian parents), they are warm, loving, and emotionally supportive. These parents are involved in their children's lives and activities, they stay calm while disciplining, and they engage in proactive teaching. They hold high expectations and standards for their children's behaviors. They combine control with positive encouragement or autonomy and independence. They may direct their children's activities or actions but in a rational, reasoned manner. In respecting their children's interests and individual abilities, they encourage self-expression and a verbal give-and-take.

Being raised by authoritative parents seems to lead to the best outcome for children. These children are generally independent, possess good social skills, and are self-assertive and cooperative. They appear to be able to regulate their own emotions, handle stress, and have good relationships with others. They are usually likeable, independent, happy, and successful in school. Children with authoritative parents are likely to become independent individuals who are capable of making their own decisions. Children who are raised in this environment tend to show good adjustment later in life. These children have been found to be less likely to engage in risky adolescent behavior or experiment with drugs.

A fourth category of child discipline was noted in the 1980s by Maccoby and Martin (1983). This type is referred to as **uninvolved** or unengaged. Uninvolved parents show almost no interest in their children, are indifferent, and act in a rejecting way toward them. They are detached emotionally and see their role as parents as merely providing the basic necessities (e.g., clothing, food, shelter). They hold few expectations for their children and provide little emotional support. In extreme forms, uninvolved parenting dissolves into neglect, and the child's basic needs are not being met. These parents often appear overwhelmed by their own lives and seem not able to focus on their children. Uninvolved parents may abuse drugs or be too immature to meet the demands of parenting. A minimal amount of time and effort is spent with the child because uninvolved parents are, in general, unavailable to the child.

It is clear that children reared by uninvolved parents fare the worst. Their parents' lack of involvement disrupts their emotional development, often contributing to feelings of being unloved, not cared for, and emotionally detached from others. Their physical and cognitive development may be affected as well, resulting in poor academic performance and behavioral problems. They tend to be disobedient, demanding, low in self-control; lack tolerance for frustration; and lack long-term goals. They have low self-esteem and low levels of confidence. These children may have high levels of anxiety and depression. They tend to exhibit poor academic performance and many problem behaviors. Possessing little sense of responsibility, these children also lack respect for others.

Parental Style in a Cultural Context

The type of parenting style a parent adopts may be influenced by culture. Much of the research on these four types has been conducted solely in Western society. Cultural expectations, ethnic traditions, and religion may affect child-rearing styles. For example, in some cultures parents do not demonstrate excessive emotionality with their children, whereas others may condone physical punishment. Parenting styles change across time as well. For example, Benjamin Spock, a well-known pediatrician who was often thought to be an early authority on child rearing, initially advocated a lax parenting style that granted the child freedom and self-expression. As he revised his writings, he began to recognize the need for some parental control and strictness.

Although parenting style is fairly stable over time, parents do not always remain "true" to one style of parenting. Depending on demands or the situation, a parent may use a different style of parenting. For example, the generally permissive parent may yell or react in a harsh manner when her or his child places a hand near a hot stove. It is clear, however, that parents' early style of relating to and disciplining their children has lasting effects on the child's behavior and subsequent personality development.

Contribution by Maureen C. Kenny,
Florida International University,
Miami, FL

References

Baumrind, D. (1989). Rearing competent children. In W. Damon (Ed.), *Child development today and tomorrow* (pp. 349–378). San Francisco: Jossey-Bass.

Maccoby, E. E., & Martin, J. A. (1983). Socialization in the context of the family: Parent–child interaction. In P. H. Mussen (Ed.) & E. M. Hetherington (Vol. Ed.), *Handbook of child psychology: Vol. 4. Socialization, personality, and social development* (4th ed., pp. 1–101). New York: Wiley.

■ Peer Mediation

Mediation, a form of conflict resolution, is a voluntary negotiation process that helps to define and clarify issues and needs, create solutions, and reach mutually satisfactory agreements (Roush & Hall, 1993). **Peer mediation** is often used in school settings and involves the use of a third party, presumably an impartial person, to assist in resolving a dispute between two or more people (Sheperis, 2009). Sweeney and Carruthers (1996) defined peer mediation as a form of facilitated interpersonal communication requiring the application of problem-solving methods to achieve agreement between or among disputants. Peer-mediation programs are primarily based on social learning and modeling theory in that students are expected to develop better conflict resolution skills by observing the process modeled by the mediators and successful participants in the programs. School districts in the United States have increasingly adopted peer-mediation programs over the last decade, with more than 10,000 peer-mediation programs in existence (Ripley, 2003).

Implementing a Peer-Mediation Program

Typically, there are three stages in the implementation of a school-based peer-mediation program. The introductory stage involves (a) making operational decisions, (b) introducing the program to the school staff, and (c) gaining support for its implementation from a variety of interested parties. This process is followed by the training stage, which involves selecting and training the peer mediators. The final operational stage involves (a) operating the program, (b) evaluating its effectiveness, and (c) planning for its future (Lupton-Smith & Carruthers, 1996).

Peer-mediation programs can be implemented in either cadre or total-school approaches. The **cadre approach** (i.e., elective course or student club) involves training a limited number of students to serve as peer mediators who can defuse and constructively resolve interpersonal conflicts among students. This type of training program usually occurs in an intensive workshop or semester-long course. Some schools have established both **club** and **elective course models** simultaneously, whereas other schools have a **total-school program** that has evolved from a cadre approach . Although peer-mediation programs have been developed primarily for middle and high school populations, some programs have been developed for elementary schools. For example, the Peace Train program (Wittmer, Thompson, & Sheperis, 1999) was developed as a simplified peer-mediation program using train tracks to depict the steps of problem solving. In the Peace Train program, the mediators are conductors and walk disputants through the tracks toward conflict resolution. In general, peer-mediation programs for elementary school students should be a more simplified process that meets the developmental level of the participants.

Although there are several models of mediation, all tend to follow the same general process in which mediators (a) provide a nonthreatening environment where disputants can tell their side of the story, (b) focus disputants on mutually identified problems and identify any common ground, (c) help disputants develop a list of possible solutions and rationale for each solution, (d) assist disputants to take each other's perspective accurately and fully, and (e) guide disputants to mutually agreed-on resolutions and formalize each agreement.

Efficacy of Peer-Mediation Programs

Despite the widespread popularity and use of peer-mediation programs, there is a relatively small amount of evaluation literature on such programs. Furthermore, results have been inconsistent across research endeavors. Case study reports often indicate that peer-mediation programs improve the overall climate of the schools; however, there is a paucity of objective data to verify the impact of these programs (Smith & Daunic, 2002).

It appears that peer mediation can be a positive and significant resource for professional school counselors. The claims related to benefits of peer mediation are numerous, including that peer-mediation programs foster a cooperative and comfortable atmosphere in which students can learn more efficiently and teachers can spend more time teaching and can teach better. In addition, there is some evidence that students involved in peer-mediation programs develop feelings of empowerment, learn to take responsibility, and develop constructive solutions for interpersonal problems (Maxwell, 1989). Evidence also exists that peer-mediation programs offer potential reductions in violence, vandalism, chronic school absence, and student suspensions in schools (McCormick, 1988). Finally, some authors have asserted that peer mediation reduces the time teachers are involved in resolving conflicts in their classrooms, thus allowing them to focus more time on student learning (Johnson & Johnson, 1994). Although more research needs to be conducted in order to substantiate these claims, it appears that peer-mediation programs have an overall positive impact on school systems, mediators, and disputants.

Contributed by Carl J. Sheperis,
Mississippi State University, Starkville, MS

References

Johnson, D. W., & Johnson, R. T. (1994). *Teaching students to be peacemakers: Results of five years of research.* Minneapolis: University of Minnesota.

Lupton-Smith, H. S., & Carruthers, W. L. (1996). Conflict resolution as peer mediation: Programs for elementary, middle, and high school students. *School Counselor, 43,* 374–392.

Maxwell, J. P. (1989). Mediation in the schools: Self regulation, self-esteem, and self-discipline. *Mediation Quarterly, 7,* 149–155.

McCormick, M. (1988). *Mediation in the schools: An evaluation of the Wakefield Pilot Peer Mediation Program in Tucson, Arizona.* Washington, DC: American Bar Association.

Ripley, V. R. (2003). Conflict resolution and peer mediation in schools. In B. T. Erford (Ed.), *Transforming the school counseling profession.* Upper Saddle River, NJ: Merrill Prentice Hall.

Roush, G., & Hall, E. (1993). Teaching peaceful conflict resolution. *Mediation Quarterly, 11,* 185–191.

Sheperis, C. J. (2009). The evolution and application of peer mediation in schools. In B. T. Erford (Ed.), *Professional school counseling: A handbook of theories, programs and practices* (2nd ed.). Austin, TX: PRO-ED.

Smith, S. W., & Daunic, A. (2002). Using conflict resolution and peer mediation to support positive behavior. In P. Kay (Ed.), *Preventing problem behaviors: A handbook of successful prevention strategies* (pp. 142–161). Thousand Oaks, CA: Corwin Press.

Sweeney, B., & Carruthers, W. L. (1996). Conflict resolution: History, philosophy, theory, and educational applications. *School Counselor, 43,* 326–345.

Wittmer, J., Thompson, D. W., & Sheperis, C. J. (1999). *The Peace Train: A school-wide violence prevention program.* Minneapolis, MN: Educational Media.

Percentage Score

In a test where the raw score is the sum of the number of correct answers given to all the items on the test, the **percentage score** is the raw score divided by the total number of items on the test (i.e., correct ÷ total). A percentage score expresses the raw score on a "per 100" basis, so if the total test was 100 items, the percentage score would indicate how many questions the respondent answered correctly.

Although the percentage score is easily calculated, its usefulness may be marred by faulty interpretation. Achieving 80% on two or more separate tests does not mean that a student has done equally well across the test series. Thus, averaging student percentage scores across a series of tests may lead to faulty conclusions about student performance unless the tests are equated for overall test difficulty.

Furthermore, as is true with interpreting raw scores, the internal consistency (reliability) of the test or scale that leads to a percentage score is a function of the number of items on which the percentage score was based. Percentage scores mask the number of items making up the raw score from which the percentage score was calculated and, in the case of very short tests or scales, may lead to a false sense of confidence in the score. Finally, percentage scores (i.e., the percentage of items to which a person gave a correct answer) are sometimes confused with percentiles (i.e., the proportion of examinees who earned a score lower than the particular score value being considered).

Contributed by F. Robert Wilson,
University of Cincinnati, Cincinnati, OH

Percentile Rank

Percentile rank, a measure of relative performance that represents the percentage of cases falling below a given score, is a derived score that is closely related to the **percentile.** Because the percentile rank represents the percentage of cases below a given score, a percentile rank of 100 is not possible. Ebel and Frisbie (1991) have argued that defining the percentile rank as the percentage of scores that fall below the midpoint of the score interval of the given score gives greater precision. Many authors have defined a percentile, which is expressed in raw score units, as that point in a distribution of scores below which a certain percentage of the scores fall. For example, a person scoring at the 68th percentile has earned a score that is higher than 68% of the members of the comparison group. A percentile rank, however, is expressed in percentage terms and represents the percentage of cases falling below a given percentile. In common usage, however, statisticians differ in their definitions of these terms and, in fact, some use the terms *percentile* and *percentile rank* interchangeably (Ebel & Frisbie, 1991; Mehrens & Lehmann, 1991).

Percentile ranks are relatively easy to compute; however, care must be exercised in their interpretation. Because percentiles and percentile ranks are a measure of relative performance (how one individual's performance compares with others' performances), the examiner must take the population within which the set of scores was collected into account. For example, the interpretation of whether a runner's percentile rank of 95 is impressive depends on the strength of the field in which the runner was competing (e.g., local runners, Olympic-class runners). As Kaplan and Saccuzzo (2004) have said, "When interpreting a percentile rank, [one] should always ask the question, 'Relative to what?'" (p. 40). The examiner should also bear in mind that equal differences in percentiles do not imply equal differences in the raw scores that underpin them. Although raw scores and many other kinds of scores tend to be distributed normally, percentile ranks form a rectangular distribution. Mapping rectangularly distributed percentile ranks onto normally distributed raw scores magnifies raw-score differences in the midrange of the distribution and reduces raw-score differences at the extremes. In a set of normally distributed scores, the difference between the raw scores that bracket the 90th and 99th percentile is much larger than the difference between the raw scores that bracket the 50th and 59th percentiles (Ebel & Frisbie, 1991; Mehrens & Lehmann, 1991; Osterlind, 2006). Distortion may also be introduced when percentiles or percentile ranks are calculated from small samples or when there has been restriction of range. Osterlind (2006) recommended that percentile ranks should not be used with samples smaller than 70, when the score distribution is markedly skewed, or when a large number of raw score values are not observed. Furthermore, because percentile ranks are not equal interval scales, they should not be used in mathematical computations (e.g., addition, subtraction, multiplication) or for measuring change over time (i.e., posttest–pretest difference; Osterlind, 2006).

Contributed by F. Robert Wilson,
University of Cincinnati, Cincinnati, OH

References

Ebel, R. L., & Frisbie, D. A. (1991). *Essentials of educational measurement* (5th ed.). Englewood Cliffs, NJ: Prentice Hall.

Kaplan, R. M., & Saccuzzo, D. P. (2004). *Psychological testing: Principles, applications, and issues* (6th ed.). Belmont, CA: Wadsworth.

Mehrens, W. A., & Lehmann, I. J. (1991). *Measurement and evaluation in education and psychology* (4th ed.). Belmont, CA: Wadsworth.

Osterlind, S. J. (2006). *Modern measurement: Theory, principles, and applications of mental appraisal.* Upper Saddle River, NJ: Pearson.

■ Performance Assessment

Psychological **performance assessments,** also referred to as **nonverbal assessments,** are commonly defined as measurements requiring minimal verbal communication (Schofield, 1972). The individual is asked to perform tasks rather than answer questions using pencil-and-paper methods. Performance assessments measure broad attributes such as intelligence, development, and personality. Some tests incorporate multiple areas of study, such as intelligence and development (e.g., Bayley Scales, Gesell's Development Schedules). The benefits of performance assessments include the reduction of cultural bias, which is especially important with individuals who speak a foreign language. They are also beneficial for use with children who may be too young to understand elaborate directions and have not developed verbal cognitions. Furthermore, these tests may be used with individuals with physical and hearing disabilities.

Performance assessments are frequently used in training programs, especially in the counseling field. Supervision of counselor trainees during practicum and internship experience is an example of how performance assessments are used. Instructors observe the trainees live in session or on videotape and evaluate their counseling performance. Performance assessments do require a predetermined evaluative criterion for instructors to use when evaluating the trainee. The capacity to perform tasks in order to implement learning into actual real-world settings is an important contribution of performance assessments. Areas of study other than counseling rely heavily on this form of evaluation; for example, mechanical, technological, and medical fields require students to display learned skills under supervision for evaluative purposes.

Types of Performance Assessments

Performance assessments originated in response to criticisms of the Binet test of intelligence (later translated, adapted and referred to as the Stanford–Binet Intelligence Scale), an instrument that targeted children with special learning needs. The critics of the Binet test stated the intelligence test was culturally biased because it relied on social norms as a means to measure intelligence. This criticism served as a catalyst for the development of performance intelligence tests, which seek to measure intelligence through completion of tasks. Performance intelligence assessments may ask the individual to complete tasks that analyze and problem solve (e.g., Porteus Maze), repeat and find patterns (e.g., block exercises), or display depth in thought processes (e.g., Draw-a-Man Test). The Porteus Maze measures perceptual intelligence of children at the 8-, 10-, and 14-year-old levels by navigating through a paper maze. Tests that measure intelligence using pattern recognition include jigsaw blocks, in which individuals must copy a colorful pattern and shape using jigsaw pieces. Also, test takers may be asked to match different-shaped blocks with a corresponding shaped hole. To assess depth in thought processes, the Draw-a-Man Test involves a test administrator relaying simple instructions to a test taker to "draw a man, the best man you can." Individuals' responses are scored based on the details in the drawing. These intelligence performance tests are simple in nature and require minimal time for completion, therefore holding a child's attention. Performance assessments may also be more elaborate, combining basic tasks into a larger test.

There are a number of performance intelligence assessments that use a combination of these tasks as well as use classification and completion models specific to a particular test. The Bayley Scales of Infant Development assesses intelligence and development in children 2 months to 30 months in for three categories: mental, motor, and infant behavior. A child's intelligence is measured through sensory reactions and perceptions, body control and coordination, and orientation to the natural environment. The Cattell Culture Fair Intelligence Testis a series of performance tests for ages 4 years to adult. This test measures intelligence by assessing series completion, classification, pattern completion, and conditions. The Test of Nonverbal Intelligence (TONI) uses similar concepts in assessing intelligence by using pictures as a means to measure simple matching, analogies, classification, intersections, and progressions.

Perhaps the most popular of developmental performance tests is Gesell Developmental Schedules. This test surveys infant development based on the age at which the infant is ordinarily able to perform certain tasks (i.e., age norms); for example, at 3 months an infant ordinarily can reach for an object. The schedules assess children from ages 2 weeks to 36 months with tasks progressing from gross and fine motor skill to cognitive assessment. This test mirrors the age levels of the Binet test; thus, it could be used as a means of measuring intelligence as well as motor developmental progress.

In addition to assessing intelligence and development, performance assessments may also measure personality. Although the use for this purpose is less common, performance personality assessments establish a structured situation to observe a person's reaction. Intense stress is commonly induced in these situations, and a person is then tested for his or her response under this stress. This form of personality testing is more commonly used in military training, ensuring soldiers will respond appropriately in times of crisis.

Although performance assessments have a variety of functions in measuring nonverbal abilities, one criticism relates to difficulty assessing outcomes on a single score. For example, many of the performance assessments collect raw data that cannot be translated into standardized scores. Even when performance assessments use predetermined criterion scales to rate participants, subjectivity of the evaluator lowers interscorer reliability, which is an important issue to consider. Performance assessments such as the Bayley Scales of Infant Development, Cattell's Culture Fair Intelligence Test, and TONI have established standard scores. Although the findings of a performance assessment should not be the only findings used, they are a valuable component of an individual's total assessment and provide counselors with a multiculturally sensitive approach to testing (Samuda, 1998).

Contributed by Elizabeth A. Prosek,
Old Dominion University, Norfolk, VA

References

Samuda, R. J. (1998). *Psychological testing of American minorities.* Thousand Oaks, CA: Sage.

Schofield, H. (1972). *Assessment and testing: An introduction.* London: Allen & Unwin.

Additional Resource

Goldman, J., L'Engle Stein, C., & Guerry, S. (1983). *Psychological methods of child assessment.* New York: Brunner/Mazel.

■ Person–Environment Fit

Frank Parsons's (1909) book, *Choosing a Vocation,* introduced into the literature the idea of fitting a person's characteristics to an occupation. Parsons emphasized the advantage of examining abilities, interests, ambitions, resources, and limitations as part of the career decision-making process. In addition, he stressed that individuals should acquire knowledge of the requirements and conditions for successful work performance and the opportunities available in different lines of work. The **person–environment fit model (P–E fit model,** as it is now called) evolved from Parsons's early work.

Person–Environment Fit Theories

The **trait and factor theory** is one of the earliest applications of the P–E fit model. Made popular by psychologists such as D. G. Patterson, J. G. Darley, and E. G. Williamson at the University of Minnesota during the Great Depression prior to World War II, the trait–factor approach is an expansion of Parsons's (1909) ideas of personal analysis, job analysis, and careful matching of the two based on scientific evidence. Trait and factor theory's emphasis on using empirical data to measure individual differences to aid in career choice became known as the Minnesota Point of View.

Traits refer to latent characteristics of an individual, such as intelligence, personality, and interests. The term *factor* is borrowed from statistical terminology, and in the trait and factor theory, factors are the collection of different latent traits that form separate and unique dimensions. The underlying assumptions of the trait and factor theory are that (a) every person has a unique set of traits; (b) every occupation requires a person to have a specific set of traits to be successful in that occupation; (c) the choice of an occupation involves matching the traits of a person with those required of an occupation; and (d) the closer the match is between personal traits and job requirements, the more likely satisfaction and productivity are.

John Holland's (1997) **theory of vocational interest personality types,** an extension of the trait and factor theory, is one of the most popular P–E fit models. His model defines six work interest personalities that can be used to describe individuals: Realistic, Investigative, Artistic, Social, Enterprising, and Conventional (RIASEC). Each type captures different aspects of work; for example, those with Realistic interests prefer to work with their hands on concrete tasks. Personality characteristics of the other types involve solving problems (Investigative), aesthetics (Artistic), working around people (Social), managing and persuading others (Enterprising), and organizing data (Conventional). In addition, the RIASEC typology can be applied to work environments.

According to Holland's theory, people who have high congruence, or match, between their RIASEC work personality and the environment's RIASEC personality types are expected to be more satisfied and remain longer in their job. Given that vocational interest types are relatively stable across the life span, Holland's theory predicts that low congruence between an individual's interests and the activities required by the work will result in the person seeking a more congruent work environment (see Holland's Personality Types).

The **Theory of Work Adjustment (TWA;** Dawis & Lofquist, 1984**)** is another widely accepted P–E fit theory. In contrast to Holland's theory that focuses on P–E interest personality fit, TWA is concerned with the correspondence between an individual's abilities and needs with the skills required by a job and the reinforcement of specific needs in that job. Correspondence from the individual's perspective predicts job satisfaction for that individual. For the work organization, this correspondence predicts satisfactoriness or, in other words, the organization's satisfaction with the individual's performance. Job tenure, in turn, is predicted from correspondence.

According to TWA, the process of work adjustment is dynamic, and inevitably workers and environments change. When change occurs, either the person or environment or both adjust to maintain correspondence, or the relationship is terminated. Once discorrespondence occurs, the length of time before adjustment happens depends on the flexibility, or amount of tolerance for dissatisfaction, a person can maintain. Changes initiated by the person can be either active (i.e., the person attempts to change the environment) or reactive (i.e., the person tries to change skills to fit the environment). The work environment is also conceptualized as having active and reactive adjustment styles. A person's persistence in the process of adjustment is indicative of the person's level of perseverance.

Most models of P–E fit suggest that higher levels of similarity between an individual's characteristics and the characteristics of the work environment predict higher levels of job satisfaction and longer tenure for the individual. Negative outcomes are predicted when the characteristics of an individual and the work environment are incongruent. Research has shown that a poor fit between an individual's characteristics and those of the environment can lead to occupational stress, occupational strain, and the increased likelihood of changing careers (see, e.g., Dik & Hansen, in press).

Applications of P–E Fit Theories

P–E models have been applied in career counseling situations and organizational selection. Counseling that is driven by trait and factor theories focuses on helping clients with decision making by increasing their understanding of their own interests, personality, values, and abilities and the requirements of different environments. In addition, emphasis is placed on helping clients highlight areas for growth, such as skill development, as well as making adjustments in the workplace to increase their job satisfaction.

Holland's theory and the TWA are exemplars of the trait and factor approach. Both focus on understanding individual characteristics and how these relate to different occupational environments, with the goal of assisting in career decisions to increase an individual's job satisfaction. Holland's theory often focuses on finding a fit between interests and estimated abilities using measures that include the RIASEC types, such as the Self-Directed Search, the Vocational Preference Inventory, the Position Classification Inventory, the Career Attitudes and Strategies Inventory, and the Strong Interest Inventory. The TWA stimulated the development of several measures to operationalize the theory's constructs, including the Minnesota Importance Questionnaire, a measure of work needs and values; Minnesota Abilities Test Battery; Occupational Reinforcer Patterns, indices of job reinforcers; and the Minnesota Satisfaction Questionnaire.

From Parsons's seminal ideas about matching the characteristics of an individual with the characteristics of an environment to the expansion of these ideas in Holland's theory and TWA, P–E fit theories have been important in vocational psychology. The application of P–E fit theories has proved useful in helping individuals in the career decision-making process and in aiding organizations with employee selection.

Contributed by Melanie E. Leuty and
Jo-Ida C. Hansen,
University of Minnesota, Minneapolis, MN

References

Dawis, R. V., & Lofquist, L. H. (1984). *A psychological theory of work adjustment: An individual differences model and its applications.* Minneapolis: University of Minnesota Press.

Dik, B., & Hansen, J. C. (in press). Following passionate interests to well-being. *Journal of Career Assessment.*

Holland, J. L. (1997). *Making vocational choices: A theory of vocational personalities and work environments* (3rd ed.). Odessa, FL: Psychological Assessment Resources.

Parsons, F. (1909). *Choosing a vocation.* Boston: Houghton Mifflin.

Additional Resources

Brown, D., Brooks, L., & Associates (Eds.). (1996). *Career choice and development* (3rd ed.). San Francisco: Jossey-Bass.

Crites, J. O. (1981). *Career counseling: Models, methods, and materials.* New York: McGraw-Hill.

■ Personality Disorders

Personality consists of habitual and predictable patterns of human behavior, thinking, and feeling resulting from biological influences and life experiences. Although pliable in youth, personality solidifies as people age. When people exhibit consistent difficulties in relating with others in a variety of settings, it may be an indication of a personality disorder. If a **personality disorder** is present, the individual's maladaptive and inflexible interpersonal style is out of the ordinary for the person's age, gender, and culture, which results in a personal sense of distress or impairment in normal functioning in relationships.

Diagnostic criteria for personality disorders are discussed extensively in the *Diagnostic and Statistical Manual of Mental Disorders* (4th ed., text rev.; *DSM-IV-TR;* American Psychiatric Association [APA], 2000) that is used by professional counselors and other mental health professionals to guide diagnosis and treatment planning. In order for a personality disorder to be diagnosed, a qualified mental health professional must evaluate the individual's patterns of functioning over time, particularly those habitual patterns that are demonstrated by early adulthood as opposed to situational responses to stressful incidents or transient mental health issues, such as depression or anxiety. The *DSM-IV-TR* classifies personality disorders in three clusters: odd-eccentric, dramatic-emotional, and anxious-fearful.

Odd-Eccentric Cluster: Paranoid, Schizoid, and Schizotypal

Individuals in this cluster tend to be socially and emotionally distant, and this social and emotional distance is coupled with odd thought patterns not seen in social anxiety or shyness. **Paranoid personality disorder,** thought to occur in 2.5% of the general population or less (APA, 2000), is when an individual approaches the world with suspicion, believing other people intend him or her harm although there is no reason to believe this to be true. As children or adolescents, individuals with this diagnosis may appear odd and may experience teasing, poor peer relationships, and anxiety in social situations; this may lead to difficulties in school. Over time, they may become preoccupied with thoughts that others cannot be trusted, bearing grudges or exhibiting a quick temper. It is particularly important in determining the likelihood of paranoid personality disorder that the professional counselor determine whether the person's minority status, gender, ethnicity, or sociocultural background is the actual reason for his or her guarded or mistrustful approach to life.

Schizoid personality disorder, rare even in clinical settings, manifests as a pattern of detachment and an inability to experience a full range of emotions or understand social cues in interpersonal relationships. Often these individuals are referred to as loners, tending to spend time on hobbies or occupations that require little interpersonal interaction. A rare disorder, these people seem to garner little pleasure from sensory, bodily, or interpersonal stimulation.

Approximately 3% of the general population is thought to have **schizotypal personality disorder,** which tends to limit a person from forming close interpersonal relationships due, in part, to paranoid thinking (APA, 2000). Individuals who experience this disorder also tend to be superstitious or believe in paranormal activity, feel they have psychic powers or can magically control others, and speak in an idiosyncratic manner that is either overly abstract or overly concrete. Individuals with these symptoms will generally interact with others if necessary, but due to the anxiety it produces, particularly in unfamiliar situations, they prefer not to.

In determining whether a person has one of the personality disorders in this cluster, it is important that the professional counselor complete a thorough differential diagnosis to determine if the client is experiencing schizophrenia or some other disorder with psychotic features. In addition, an individual's behavior needs to be outside cultural norms to be considered a personality disorder. For instance, the professional counselor's culture may indicate a certain behavior is superstitious when the individual is simply carrying out a cultural or religious ritual. In these cases, the person is not exhibiting a personality disorder.

Dramatic-Emotional Cluster: Antisocial, Borderline, Histrionic, and Narcissistic

Individuals with personality disorders in this cluster manipulate their environment through erratic, dramatic, and demanding behavior or affect. Prevalence by gender is not specified in the *DSM-IV-TR* (APA, 2000) for borderline, narcissistic, or histrionic personality disorders, although it notes that women tend to be given these diagnoses more often than do men, likely because of gender role stereotyping. Caution should, therefore, be exercised when diagnosing these disorders.

People with **antisocial personality disorder** lack concern for others and exhibit aggressive behavior toward individuals or animals; destroy property; or display, beginning in childhood, serious disregard for the rules or law. Occurring in 3% of boys and men and 1% of girls and women in the general population (APA, 2000), individuals tend to be chronically irresponsible, impulsive, and reckless; lack empathy; and have an arrogant and inflated sense of self. This diagnosis may be associated with substance abuse and can be confused with aggressive behavior during a schizophrenic episode or impulsive or aggressive behavior as part of a manic episode.

Borderline personality disorder, occurring in 2% of the general population (APA, 2000), is characterized by unstable self-image and emotions as well as intense and unstable relationships with others. These individuals are hypersensitive to and fearful of potential abandonment, which results in episodes of intense anger when they believe the object of their affection (e.g., parent, child, friend, spouse) does not care about them and is withholding affection. In an attempt to master their perceived impending interpersonal failure, they often exhibit self-defeating behaviors that place them in control of the situation, acting in self-destructive ways to bring current happiness or satisfaction in relationships to an end prematurely, thus reinforcing their fears.

Individuals with **histrionic personality disorder** exhibit extreme emotionality and a need to be the center of attention. They may behave in provocative ways in order to gain the attention they desire. They often consider relationships to be more intimate than they actually are, and they are overly seductive, extreme in appearance, dramatic or exaggerated in their emotionality, or willing to change opinions to suit others. This disorder occurs in 2% to 3% of the general population (APA, 2000).

People with **narcissistic personality disorder** often have a very low self-esteem that motivates them to seek constant admiration from others, often exaggerating their own sense of importance. These individuals act as though they are entitled to special treatment, and they lack empathy because they take advantage of others to obtain the entitlements they believe they deserve. Although they may seem callous, they are extremely sensitive to criticism by others (narcissistic injury). Occurring in less than 1% of the general population (APA, 2000), care should be taken to distinguish this diagnosis from behavior associated specifically with substance abuse, manic episodes, or other personality disorders that may have some of the same features.

Anxious-Fearful Cluster: Avoidant, Dependent, Obsessive-Compulsive

Individuals in this cluster tend to be overly inhibited in their behavior and affect. Prevalence of these disorders by gender is not specified in the *DSM-IV-TR* (APA, 2000). Less than 1% of the population is thought to experience **avoidant personality disorder,** which is demonstrated through a chronic pattern of social inhibition because of fears that others will judge the individual to be inadequate. Behavior characterized as shy, quiet, and reserved begins in childhood and tends to become more extreme as individuals grow older, leading them to increasingly avoid new social situations or intimate relationships for fear of being criticized or embarrassed. It is important to distinguish this diagnosis from social phobia or another anxiety disorder; schizoid, schizotypal, or paranoid personality disorders; or a change in personality associated with a medical condition or substance use.

Dependent personality disorder manifests when individuals fear separation and strive for dependency and a sense of security from others. These individuals subjugate their own identities and opinions to other people in interpersonal relationships, fearing they will lose support or approval if they assert themselves. Feeling helpless and needing to sustain their need to be taken care of, they will seek out a new relationship if an existing one ends.

Finally, **obsessive-compulsive personality disorder** is characterized by extreme expectations that individuals should exhibit perfection in their activities and relationships. To ensure that they adhere to their rigid perception of perfection, they spend excessive amounts of time working on lists, organizing, and developing schedules to the exclusion of enjoyable activities, sometimes even missing important deadlines because of their attention to detail. Maintaining control in all contexts with all people is crucial to these individuals; thus, they appear quite formal and careful in the way they interact with others. They may appear morally rigid and overly conscientious. When they are unable to have control, their internal feelings of chaos may result in displays of anger or tears. Only 1% of the population is thought to have this disorder (APA, 2000).

Contributed by Leigh Falls,
Sam Houston State University,
Huntsville, TX

Reference

American Psychiatric Association. (2000). *Diagnostic and statistical manual of mental disorders* (4th ed., text rev.). Washington, DC: Author.

Additional Resources

Bleiberg, E. (2001). *Treating personality disorders in children and adolescents: A relational approach.* New York: Guilford Press.

Dobbert, D. L. (2007). *Understanding personality disorders: An introduction.* Westport, CT: Praeger.

Magnavita, J. J. (Ed.). (2004). *Handbook of personality disorders: Theory and practice.* Hoboken, NJ: Wiley.

■ Personality Tests

Professional counselors and other mental health professionals use results from **personality tests** to assess people's personality characteristics for the purposes of diagnosis, treatment planning, and structuring the therapeutic relationship with the client. Assessment of personality assists in the client's self-understanding as well as the counselor's understanding of the client's traits and needs. The two categories of personality tests or assessments are structured personality tests and unstructured or projective personality tests. **Structured personality tests** are standardized self-report tests that require the client to answer true or false (yes or no) to questions aimed at revealing aspects of personality, such as personality types, personality traits, personality states, and self-concept. **Projective personality tests** involve using ambiguous stimuli onto which the individual projects unconscious wants, needs, and personal characteristics.

Structured Personality Tests

Approaches to structured personality test construction include both deductive and empirical methods. Deductive methods are logical-content and theory-based strategies.

Empirical methods include criterion-group (often called criterion-keyed) and factor analysis strategies. The first personality test, the Woodworth Personal Data Sheet, developed during World War I to identify military recruits who might break down in combat, was constructed using the logical-content approach. This method consists of selecting test items based on face validity, or the belief that the item appeared to measure the construct under consideration.

Theory-based test construction involves developing test items to measure constructs of personality theories and then establishing construct validity. The Edwards Personal Preference Schedule (EPPS; Edwards, 1959) is an early example of a theoretically derived personality test. The EPPS was based on Henry Murray's theory of needs. Other theory-based tests include the Personality Research Form and the Jackson Personality Inventory–Revised, which were both based on Murray's theory of needs, and the Myers–Briggs Type Indicator, based on Carl Jung's theory of psychological types. Measures of self-concept have been developed based on the theoretical construct of the set of a person's self-assumptions. Examples of self-concept personality tests include the Piers–Harris Children's Self-Concept Scale–Second Edition, the Tennessee Self-Concept Scale–Second Edition, and the Coopersmith Self-Esteem Inventory.

In the **criterion-group method** of test construction, items are selected that are related to an external criterion. For example, the Minnesota Multiphasic Personality Inventory (MMPI) was originally developed by selecting items that distinguished between those individuals considered normal and people who had been diagnosed with psychopathology. The MMPI was used to assess psychopathology, or abnormal personality. A major advance in personality testing with the introduction of the MMPI was the addition of validity scales that provided an indication of the way in which people approached taking the test. These scales were the L scale, F scale, K scale, and Cannot Say (?) scale. The L, or "lie," scale was designed to detect individuals who attempted to show themselves in a favorable manner. The F, or "faking bad," scale indicated whether individuals were attempting to make themselves look worse, whereas the K, or "faking good," scale provided a measure of the person attempting to deny or minimize symptoms. The "cannot say" scale consists of the number of items to which the individual did not respond. If 10% or more items are omitted, the whole test is considered invalid. In 1989, a major revision of the MMPI resulted in the MMPI-2 (Butcher et al., 1989) with an improved norm sample and additional validity and content scales. The MMPI-2 consists of the original 10 clinical scales and additional validity scales, content scales, and special scales. The MMPI-A was developed for use with adolescents ages 14–18 years. The MMPI-2 continues to be the most widely used and researched personality test. The California Psychological Inventory–Revised (CPI-R) is another example of a personality test developed using the criterion-group method. The CPI-R is designed to measure aspects of normal personality as opposed to the MMPI-2, which is designed to measure abnormal aspects. The Millon Clinical Multiaxial Inventory–III (MCMI-III); Millon, Davis, & Millon, 1997) is the latest version of a structured inventory used to evaluate personality disorders. The MCMI-III is based on Millon's theory of personality disorders and is intended for use with clinical populations.

Factor analytic approaches to personality test construction use the statistical procedure of factor analysis to analyze interrelationships of test items to determine which items group together and are distinct from other groups. The NEO Personality Inventory–Revised (NEO-PI-R; Costa & McCrae, 1992) and the 16 Personality Factor Questionnaire (16PF; Cattell, Cattell, & Cattell, 1993) are the most commonly used tests constructed using the factor analysis method. The NEO-PI-R is based on the five-factor model of personality, which describes personality as comprising five factors: extroversion, agreeableness; conscientiousness, emotional stability or neuroticism, and intellect or openness to experience. The 16PF, a measure of normal personality, describes the individual on 16 primary factors and 5 global factors: extroversion, anxiety, tough-mindedness, independence, and self-control.

Projective Personality Tests

Projective personality tests are based on the **projective hypothesis,** the belief that when people are exposed to ambiguous or vague stimuli, their interpretation of the stimuli will reflect wants, needs, conflicts, thought processes, and motivations. Projective techniques, which can be divided into five categories (i.e., association, construction, completions, arrangement, and expression), have poor psychometric properties because of the subjective nature of interpretation of the client's responses. For most projective tests, scoring systems have been developed and require extensive training in proper use of the test. The most widely used and well-known projective test is an association technique, the Rorschach Inkblot Test. The test consists of 10 inkblots presented to the client in two phases: association and inquiry. In the association phase, the individual is asked what the card might be, and in the inquiry phase, the examiner goes through each card and asks the individual to explain what was seen in the card. Various scoring systems have been developed; the most widely used is Exner's (2003) Comprehensive System.

The Thematic Apperception Test (Murray, 1943) is an example of a construction technique in that the individual constructs a story from a picture shown by the person administering the test. The story is recorded verbatim and then interpreted using specific scoring criteria developed by the author. Examples of elements considered are the hero, needs or motives, presses or environmental factors, and recurring themes, among others. Examples of expressive techniques include tests that incorporate drawing or art. Draw-a-Person, House-Tree-Person, and Kinetic-Family-Drawing are examples of projective tests in which the client is asked to draw a person(s) or thing and the results are interpreted through various approaches.

The Rotter Incomplete Sentences Blank, Second Edition (Rotter, Lah, & Rafferty, 1992) consists of 40 sentence stems to which the individual responds by completing the sentence and is the most widely used completion projective technique. Responses are scored for conflict, positive response, and neutral response as well as an overall adjustment score. Arrangement projective techniques involve the individual selecting and arranging objects. Examples are the use of sand trays and projective play assessment. In comparison with other projective techniques, there has been much less empirical investigation into the validity of arrangement projective techniques in personality assessment.

Contributed by Nancy E. Sherman,
Bradley University, Peoria, IL

References

Butcher, J. N., Graham, J. R., Ben-Porath, Y. S., Tellegen, A., Dahlstrom, W. G., & Kaemmer, B. (1989). *The Minnesota Multiphasic Personality Inventory–Second Edition (MMPI-2).* Minneapolis: University of Minnesota Press.

Cattell, R. B., Cattell, A. K., & Cattell, H. E. (1993). *16PF* (5th ed.). Champaign, IL: Institute for Personality and Ability Testing.

Costa, P. T., & McCrae, R. R. (1992). *Revised NEO Personality Inventory (NEO-PI-R) and NEO Five-Factor Inventory (NEO-FFI) professional manual.* Odessa, FL: Psychological Assessment Resources.

Edwards, A. L. (1959). *Edwards Personal Preference Schedule.* New York: Psychological Corporation.

Exner, J. E. (2003). *The Rorschach: A comprehensive system: Vol. 1. Basic foundations and principles of interpretation* (4th ed.). Hoboken, NJ: Wiley.

Millon, T., Davis, R. D., & Millon, C. (1997). *MCMI-III manual* (2nd ed.). Minneapolis, MN: National Computer Systems.

Murray, H. A. (1943). *The Thematic Apperception Test.* Cambridge, MA: Harvard University Press.

Rotter, J. B., Lah, M. I., & Rafferty, J. E. (1992). *Rotter Incomplete Sentences Blank, second edition.* San Antonio, TX: The Psychology Corporation.

Additional Resources

Erford, B. T. (Ed.). (2007). *Assessment for counselors.* Boston: Lahaska/Houghton Mifflin.

Kaplan, R. M. (2005). *Psychological testing: Principles, applications, and issues.* Belmont, CA: Wadsworth.

Whiston, S. C. (2005). *Principles and applications of assessment in counseling.* Belmont, CA: Thomson Brooks/Cole.

■ Pervasive Developmental Disorders

Pervasive developmental disorders are identified in the *Diagnostic and Statistical Manual of Mental Disorders* (4th ed., text rev.; *DSM-IV-TR;* American Psychiatric Association [APA], 2000) as neurological conditions that are first diagnosed in infancy, childhood, and adolescence and typically manifest in qualitative delays in verbal and nonverbal communication; impairments in reciprocal social interaction; and stereotyped behaviors, interests, and activities. They include autistic disorder, Asperger's disorder, Rett's disorder, and childhood disintegrative disorder.

Autistic Disorder

In 1943, Leo Kanner identified three primary behavioral patterns in children that have become the criteria for diagnosing **autistic disorder,** or autism: the inability to relate to people, the psychological need for sameness, and significant impairment in communication. According to the *DSM-IV-TR* (APA, 2000), autistic disorder includes significant impairment in social interaction and communication with restricted, repetitive, and stereotyped patterns of behavior, interests, and activities. Individuals with autistic disorder may display poor use of nonverbal behaviors (e.g., eye contact, facial expression, gestures), fail to develop appropriate peer relationships, or show little interest in other people. They may prefer solitary activities and show an emotional indifference to the absence or presence of others.

Impairment in communication may include a delay in or lack of spoken language and poor comprehension. Individuals who do speak may be unable to initiate or sustain conversations or may simply have a stereotyped, repetitive use of language (e.g., a word or phrase may be repeated over and over with no contextual or functional meaning). Among children, imaginative or imitative play may be absent or significantly impaired.

Individuals with autistic disorder may display abnormal preoccupation with one narrow interest. Routines or rituals may be extremely important. Individuals may display stereotyped body movements, such as clapping, rocking, or swaying. Individuals may walk on tiptoes or have strange hand movements or body postures. Individuals may be fascinated with parts of objects or with movement.

Asperger's Disorder

Asperger's disorder was first described by Austrian physician Hans Asperger in 1944 but not identified as a disorder in the *DSM* until 1994 because of the lack of consensus regarding whether Asperger's disorder is the same as high-functioning autism. This is not surprising because Asperger's disorder and autistic disorder share similar characteristics, such as social impairments; communication difficulties; and the prevalence of a narrow range of behaviors, interests, and activities. Asperger's disorder is differentiated from autistic disorder in that there are no clinically significant delays in language development (e.g., use of single words by the age 2 years and phrases by the age 3 years) and cognitive development (e.g., self-help activities, adaptation, and curiosity about the environment). Asperger's disorder appears to be more common in boys and men and is a continuous, lifelong disorder.

According to the *DSM-IV-TR* (APA, 2000), the essential features of Asperger's disorder include severe and sustained impairments in social interaction and the development of restricted, repetitive patterns of behavior, interests, and activities. Individuals become intently focused on the parts of objects rather than the whole. A common feature among individuals diagnosed with Asperger's disorder is a preoccupation with a topic about which the individual accumulates extensive information and pursues with such intensity and vigor that other interests are excluded and there is little or no consideration for the conversational interests of others or their reactions are not recognized.

Because of their high degree of functioning, individuals with Asperger's disorder are often viewed as eccentric or odd. Children with Asperger's disorder may display difficulty using nonverbal social cues, be inflexible with routine change, display an inability to take another person's perspective, experience difficulty making friends, and have poor motor skills. Although language development seems, on the surface, normal, individuals with Asperger's disorder can be extremely literal and have difficulty using language in a social context.

Rett's Disorder

Rett's disorder is a rare neurodegenerative disorder that occurs in girls prior to the age of 4 years (with typical occurrence within the 1st or 2nd year of life). Rett's disorder is characterized by normal early development through the first 5 months of life followed by multiple specific deficits. Individuals lose previously acquired purposeful hand skills between the ages of 5 months and 30 months, followed by the development of characteristic stereotyped hand movements (similar to handwringing or hand washing). Between 5 months and 48 months, head growth decelerates. Coordination of gait or trunk movements becomes difficult. Communication is significantly affected due to severely impaired expressive and receptive language abilities, and these language impairments remain chronic throughout the life span. Another characteristic of Rett's disorder is the lack of interest in social interaction. The prognosis for recovery is generally poor, although there may be some modest developmental improvements and increased social interaction as the child advances through childhood and enters adolescence.

Childhood Disintegrative Disorder

Childhood disintegrative disorder, also known as Heller's syndrome, is characterized by normal development for the first 2 years in verbal and nonverbal communication, play, adaptive behavior, and social interactions. This distinguishes childhood disintegrative disorder from the other pervasive developmental disorders in that the onset and manifestation of symptoms in autistic, Asperger's, and Rett's disorders occur soon after birth or prior to age 2. When a child with childhood disintegrative disorder is between 2 years and 10 years old, there are clinically significant losses of previously acquired abilities, such as language skills, social skills, adaptive behavior, bowel or bladder control, play, and motor skills. Similar to autistic, Asperger's, and Rett's disorders, childhood disintegrative disorder is defined by qualitative impairments in social interaction; communication; and restricted repetitive patterns of interest, behaviors, and activities.

Socialization impairment includes poor eye contact and the inability to interpret or convey nonverbal gestures and facial expressions. The absence of social and emotional reciprocity contributes to the individual's inability to develop peer relationships. Verbal communication is significantly affected by either a total loss of, or a significant delay in, the development of spoken language. In the event that spoken language develops, it is characterized by repetitive, stereotypical, and idiosyncratic word usage. In addition, the individual may experience difficulty initiating and maintaining a conversation. Interests, behaviors, and activities tend to be repetitive and narrowly focused, adversely affecting communication and social interactions.

Contributed by Yegan Pillay,
Ohio University, Athens, OH,
and Kimberly R. Hall,
Mississippi State University, Starkville, MS

Reference

American Psychiatric Association. (2000). *Diagnostic and statistical manual of mental disorders* (4th ed., text rev.). Washington, DC: Author.

Additional Resources

Attwood, T. (2006). *The complete guide to Asperger's syndrome.* Philadelphia: Kingsley.

Cohen, D. J., & Volkmar, F. R. (1997). *Handbook of autism and pervasive developmental disorders* (2nd ed.). New York: Wiley.

Lindberg, B. (2006). *Understanding Rett syndrome: A practical guide for parents, teachers, and therapists.* New York: Hogrefe & Huber.

Murray-Slutsky, C., & Paris, B. A. (2000). *Exploring the spectrum of autism and pervasive developmental disorders: Intervention strategies.* San Antonio, TX: Therapy Skills Builders.

Sicile-Kira, C., & Grandin, T. (2004). *Autism spectrum disorders: The complete guide to understanding autism, Asperger's syndrome, pervasive developmental disorder, and other ASDs.* New York: Perigee Trade.

■ Pilot Study

A **pilot study** is often conducted in counseling research to test on a smaller scale various components of some aspect of research methodology, including sample selection procedures, instrumentation or evaluation protocols, and interventions. For example, the researcher who is interested in students' perspectives of a new teaching strategy could conduct a pilot study in various ways, including (a) collecting qualitative data on their perspectives through interviewing, observations, or document analysis; (b) administering a newly developed survey regarding the effectiveness of the teaching strategy and testing the items (e.g., item bias, ease of test use, reliability and validity estimates, response rate) before large-scale survey administration; or (c) comparing perspectives for students nested within two groups (e.g., one class that receives the strategy, one that does not). Any of these methods could provide an opportunity for the researcher to fine-tune the procedures and process of the study before performing the main study.

The value of a pilot study is that it allows the researcher to discover potential problems in research design before a main project or larger study is initiated. The pilot study might reveal the following potential problems, among many possibilities:

- The study takes longer than planned to gather the actual data due to study participants' inconsistent attendance and punctuality. This might lead the researcher to the realization that alternate participants need to be considered.
- The researcher needs to allow time for rapport building before the study even begins. Without the establishment of rapport, the participants might be less forthcoming with their reflections and revelations during focus group and individual interviews, for example. Thus, the researcher might need to schedule some time to get to know the participants and begin building a relationship of trust before conducting the research.
- Personal observations might be more time-consuming than expected and might be hard to document during the study, leading to the realization that a video camera might be necessary to film the sessions in order to record nonverbal behaviors accurately.
- Survey questions may not be worded effectively or may prove confusing to some of the participants, leading the researcher to omit or rewrite some of the survey items.
- The return rate for surveys may not be at the desired percentage, causing the researcher to adjust the incentive for completion, extend the deadline for return, or conduct a phone interview instead of written survey.

The pilot study may be used in lieu of a more formal study when there are limited resources, funding, and/or time. For example, the research institute may not be willing to help fund the research until the researcher can provide documentation demonstrating the possible success of the study. A pilot study could serve as a miniformal study to help gather such documentation. Another example would be when the researcher does not have time to conduct a lengthy, longitudinal study but could manage to perform research and gather data through a short-term pilot study. In addition, some pilot studies are appropriate to use in lieu of a formal study when the data sought are not generalizable. For example, a simple case study involving a participant with whom rapport has been established might prove more effective in gathering valid data than a large-scale study involving 50 participants with whom very little rapport has been established, and, therefore, participants may be less forthcoming with their responses.

Contributed by Leah Jean Alviar,
Our Lady of the Lake University,
San Antonio, TX

Additional Resources

Gall, M. D., Gall, J. P., & Borg, W. R. (2007). *Educational research: An introduction* (8th ed.). Boston: Pearson Education.

McMillan, J. H. (2004). *Educational research: Fundamentals for the consumer* (4th ed.). Boston: Pearson Education.

McMillan, J. H., & Schumacher, S. (2001). *Research in education: A conceptual introduction* (5th ed.). New York: Longman.

Play Therapy

Play therapy is a counseling medium used with individuals across the life span and in a variety of settings. In addition, play therapists can train parents (filial therapy) and teachers (kinder training) using the principles of play therapy. Play therapy is defined as "the systematic use of a theoretical model to establish an interpersonal process wherein trained play therapists use the therapeutic powers of play to help clients prevent or resolve psychosocial difficulties and achieve optimal growth and development" (Association for Play Therapy, 2007, p. 4). The use of play therapy is particularly optimal when assessing and counseling children and preadolescents, because they may have difficulty responding to traditional therapies due to language and other developmental concerns. Play therapy interventions can be used with individuals or groups to assist in establishing the counseling relationship, specifically by building rapport, finding meaning, unleashing the subconscious, increasing self-esteem, and decreasing defensiveness.

Purists in the field believe that it is in the selection of toys and actual play that therapy occurs. Others would include the use of music, dance, movement, art, poetry, drama, storytelling, literature, and sand along with toys because such activities and material allow clients to perform observable actions and, frequently, subsequently discuss these actions with the professional counselor. Counselors analyze themes and help clients communicate thoughts and emotions through the active play medium. Certain basic techniques specific to play therapy include tracking, restating content, reflecting feelings, setting limits, and returning responsibility (Kottman, 2001).

In an ever-changing, multiethnic society, it is imperative that play therapists demonstrate multicultural competence by being aware of their own biases and understanding cultural differences. The selection of toys and props should demonstrate cultural sensitivity and reflect the rich, diverse society. Some examples include dolls of different racial/ethnic backgrounds; family groups headed by a single mother or father or two mothers or fathers; and props such as a wheelchair, eyeglasses, Christian cross, and Star of David. These toys and props are used to represent a child's reality and evoke thinking, reflecting, and processing.

Contributed by Jolie Ziomek-Daigle,
The University of Georgia, Athens, GA

References

Association for Play Therapy. (2007). *Play therapy definition*. Retrieved March 19, 2007, from www.a4pt.org/ps.aboutapt.cfm?ID=1212

Kottman, T. (2001). *Play therapy: Basics and beyond*. Alexandria, VA: American Counseling Association.

Additional Resources

Axline, V. (1947). *Play therapy: The inner dynamics of childhood*. Boston: Houghton Mifflin.

Carmichael, K. (2006). *Play therapy: An introduction*. Upper Saddle River, NJ: Pearson.

Landreth, G. L. (1991). *Play therapy: The art of the relationship*. Bristol, PA: Accelerated Development.

Power

Power is the ability to reject a false null hypothesis, that is, the ability to find a statistically significant difference between groups when one exists. Sometimes, however, there are questions about the results of an experimental analysis. A **Type I error** means the researcher may have a "false alarm." This means that a difference was found between the two groups, but the difference is in fact nonsignificant. The researcher tries to prevent Type I errors when setting alpha (α) at .05 or lower. Related to the issue of power, if there is a difference between the two groups, but for some reason the researcher failed to detect that difference, this would be a **Type II error,** or a "miss." The probability of making a Type II error is referred to as beta (β). Power is referred to as $1-\beta$.

Power is affected by sample size, significance level, and the size of the treatment effect. (i.e., an estimate of the amount of overlap between the populations sampled in the experiment). Usually alpha is set at .05 or smaller in order to reduce the chance of a Type I error. The size of the treatment effect necessary to detect a difference decreases as sample size increases. If the researcher desires higher power and a smaller treatment effect to detect a difference, then much larger sample sizes are necessary. Power increases as the size of the treatment effect increases.

An example is a researcher who wants to demonstrate that a new type of cognitive therapy is beneficial in helping clients to quit smoking. A pool of 50 potential clients has been identified through a city public health center. The clients are ages 25 to 45 years, in general good health, have a high school education, and have a two-pack-a-day cigarette habit. These similarities are the controls. The clients are randomly assigned to two groups for the experiment. Group A is the **experimental group,** which means that the members will experience the new type of cognitive therapy. Group B is the **control group,** which means that the members are not receiving counseling of any type. The **independent variable** of the experiment is the two counseling-level groups, Group A and Group B, the researcher is using. The **dependent variable** is some type of data that is being collected, such as the number of cigarettes per day that each client is smoking 3 months after the intervention. The experimenter's hypothesis **(alternative hypothesis)** is that members of Group A will smoke less than members of Group B after counseling. The **null hypothesis** is that there will be no difference between Group A and Group B in terms of the average number of cigarettes per day that clients in each group smoke. If the experiment is designed well enough to be able to detect a difference between Group A and Group B, then the study has **power.** If results do not indicate a significant difference between these groups when there should be one (i.e., insufficient power), there are several factors that might contribute to this, including sample size, making sure the dependent variable scores are valid and reliable, watching for threats to internal validity (e.g., factors related to research participants, such as history, maturation, and practice effects; see Internal Validity), or external validity (e.g., factors that might effect the generalizability of the findings, such as the Hawthorne effect or the Rosenthal effect; see External Validity, Threats to). In the research example about counseling smokers, a researcher might tighten controls on the research participants by decreasing the age range of the sample and by controlling for education level.

When designing an experiment, a good rule of thumb is to have at least 20 observations in each group. Charts, however, are available to help researchers estimate how many observations are needed to obtain the power they desire for their research. Beyer's (1988) *CRC Handbook of Tables for Probability and Statistics* is a classic resource, which includes a table for the t test (p. 289) and for the F test (p. 321). In addition, Keppel (1991) has an excellent chart (p. 72) that shows the sample size necessary to obtain different levels of power given the desired effect size. If power is set at .50 and alpha at .05, then approximately 10 research participants are needed if the effect size desired is .15. If the researcher is more demanding, then it would require 232 research participants for the same power level, but with alpha at .01 and the effect size at .01. It is important to note, however, that excessive numbers of research participants might result in a very small difference between groups becoming statistically significant. Typically, as sample size increases, standard error decreases and power increases.

Another consideration is to look at the difference between using a one-tailed test and a two-tailed test. If the researcher is making a confident prediction (e.g., Group A will smoke less than Group B), then using a one-tailed test will put the whole region of rejection on one side, increasing the chance of finding a difference if it does, indeed, exist. The probability of a test statistic falling in the rejection region is alpha. One-tailed tests are more powerful because the whole rejection region alpha is in the same tail. For two-tailed tests, the probability of a test statistic falling in a single rejection region is only alpha/2. As alpha decreases, however, power also decreases. Setting alpha at .01 makes it more difficult to reject the null hypothesis.

Contributed by Bonnie M. Wright,
Gardner-Webb University,
Boiling Springs, NC

References

Beyer, W. H. (Ed). (1988). *CRC handbook of tables for probability and statistics* (2nd ed.). Boca Raton, FL: CRC Press.

Keppel, G. (1991). *Design and analysis: A researcher's handbook* (3rd ed.). Upper Saddle River, NJ: Prentice Hall.

Additional Resources

Bordens, K. S., & Abbott, B. B. (2005). *Research design and methods: A process approach* (6th ed.). Boston: McGraw-Hill.

LaFountain, R. M., & Bartos, R. B. (2002). *Research and statistics made meaningful in counseling and student affairs.* Pacific Grove, CA: Thomson Brooks/Cole.

■ Preexperimental Research Designs

Preexperimental research designs are those designs that do not control threats to internal validity or to the assurance that observed changes in participants' scores are best explained by whether the participants did or did not receive a particular treatment. Preexperimental designs are not considered true experimental designs because they do not use randomized assignment, a control group, or both pretesting and posttesting. Three classical preexperimental research designs include the one-group posttest-only design, the one-group pretest–posttest design, and the posttest-only nonequivalent group design.

One-Group Posttest-Only Design (X O)

The **one-group posttest-only design** is characterized as one group receiving an intervention (X) and then measured or observed (O). Although common in social science research, the one-group posttest-only design has, according to Campbell and Stanley (1963), "such a total absence of control as to be of almost no scientific value" (p. 5). With only posttest scores to examine, it is not possible to tell whether anyone was changed in any way by the treatment. Without a comparison group of persons who did not receive the treatment, it is impossible to assess the degree to which other rival factors may have caused the posttest scores to be of the magnitude assessed. The one-group posttest-only design should not be confused with the superficially similar "one-shot case-study," in which the measurement of multiple variables, the presence of rich contextual knowledge, and the plausibility of estimating what the group members would have been like if untreated elevate it to the status of a quasi-experimental design (Cook & Campbell, 1979).

One-Group Pretest–Posttest Design (O X O)

The **one-group pretest–posttest design** refers to a research strategy whereby one group is measured (O) before and after an intervention (X). Also common in social science research and especially common in program evaluation studies, the one-group pretest–posttest design offers weak control of threats to internal validity. Although the presence of pretesting and posttesting offers the opportunity to assess whether change occurred, the lack of an untreated comparison group makes it impossible to determine whether the changes occurred due to history (i.e., events other than the treatment that occurred during the time of the experiment); maturation (i.e., changes over time in the participants due to natural maturational factors); testing (i.e., changes in posttest scores due to having taken the pretest); and selection of participants because of their unusually low or high performance on the pretest, leading to statistical regression (i.e., expected improvement [or decline] in posttest scores when the sample is chosen from low-scoring [or high-scoring] individuals).

Posttest-Only Nonequivalent Groups Design (X O1 vs. O2)

In the **posttest-only nonequivalent groups design** (sometimes referred to as the static groups comparison design), posttreatment scores (O_1) for a treated group (X) are compared with those scores (O_2) of an untreated group; however, random assignment was not used to control for pretreatment differences between the groups. Because no pretest scores are available, it is not possible to tell whether posttest differences between the groups are a consequence of the treatment or better explained by selection (i.e., the initial differences between groups in their levels of performance on whatever is being measured by the posttest instruments). For similar reasons, effects of differential mortality (i.e., group member dropout) cannot be assessed.

Contributed by F. Robert Wilson,
University of Cincinnati, Cincinnati, OH

References

Campbell, D. T., & Stanley, J. C. (1963). *Experimental and quasi-experimental designs for research.* Boston: Houghton Mifflin.

Cook, T. D., & Campbell, D. T. (1979) *Quasi-experimentation: Design and analysis issues for field settings.* Chicago: Rand McNally.

■ Prejudice

The word **prejudice** is derived from the Latin word *praejudicium* and refers to prejudgment of someone or something without evidence. Allport (1954/1979) succinctly defined prejudice as "thinking ill of others without sufficient warrant" (p. 7). As a bias attitude, prejudice can either entail positive or negative feelings. Negative prejudice is considered a form of abuse that can cause emotional and physical violence and consistent denial and deprivation of opportunities for its victims. For this reason, it is in its negative form that prejudice is widely known and has received most of the attention of scholars, researchers, practitioners, and policy makers.

Manifestation and Pervasiveness of Prejudice

Unfortunately, prejudice is pervasive, and it seems that humans have a natural propensity toward negative prejudgment of others. Prejudice manifests itself in almost all demographic variables and personality attributes. From the name of a person to age, sex/gender, race/ethnicity, socioeconomic status, religion, relationship status, national origin, or language, prejudice manifests itself with a new label or insignia, generally called *isms*. For instance, prejudice is the core and permeating element in ethnocentrism, sexism, racism, ageism, ableism, and classism. *Phobia* is another word directly related to prejudice. For instance, **homophobia** concerning lesbian women and gay men and **xenophobia** against strangers are prompted by prejudice.

Racial prejudice regarding issues of color and culture continue to be pervasive and destructive in the United States,

resulting in interracial hate, fears, and violence. In the study of this perennial problem, two major sources of information are worth mentioning. W. E. B. DuBois's (1903/2006) *The Souls of Black Folk* and Gordon W. Allport's (1954/1979) *The Nature of Prejudice* are considered classic works on prejudice.

Stages of Prejudice

Allport (1954/1979) outlined five major stages of prejudice, ranging in intensity from benign to the most malevolent as follows:

1. **Antilocution** is the expression of antagonistic views shared among individuals, even strangers, who have a similar attitude. They simply share their concerns and negative feelings but never act on them.
2. **Avoidance** is a deliberate effort by prejudiced individuals to avoid those whom they dislike. They may not actively hurt the targeted individuals, but prejudiced people may exclude others from social organizations or avoid places such as restaurants or shopping malls to stay away from targeted individuals.
3. **Discrimination** is the deliberate effort to deny targeted individuals or groups special opportunities that can make a material difference in their lives, such as education, employment, or housing.
4. **Physical attack** is the violent or semiviolent action that is taken by prejudiced people against targeted individuals or groups in a tense or emotionally charged situation.
5. **Extermination,** the fifth stage of intensity, is the special and deliberate effort to destroy persons belonging to certain groups, such as the annihilation of people of Jewish descent in Hitler's concentration camps.

Types of Racial Prejudice

Negative prejudice is painful in all forms; however, the historical development of **racial prejudice** has received special attention in psychological and sociological literature. Ponterotto, Utsey, and Pedersen (2006) have described the following types of Whites' racial prejudice toward Blacks:

- **Dominative racism** is generally considered more overt and hostile in nature. The dominative racist strongly believes in the purity of Whites and considers Blacks and members of other ethnic groups inherently inferior.
- **Modern racism** holds that there is no racism in the United States; Blacks are to blame for their own economic and social conditions.
- **Laissez-faire racism,** compared with dominative racism, is subtler in nature. Generally, Whites possessing this type of racism do not believe that any structural or institutional barriers or roadblocks exist affecting the progress of Blacks and other minority groups. They also oppose any special efforts that are made to remedy the economic and social inequities.

- **Aversive racism** supports the racial superiority of Whites. According to this type of racism, Whites publicly advocate racial equality but privately avoid intimate contacts with Blacks due to fear, hate, or even disgust.
- **Color-blind racism** is based on the belief that the core of racial attitudes is attributed to ignorance or denial of the reality that race plays an important and undeniable role in people's lives. This type of racism also suggests that racism transcends the psychological attitudes of the individuals or ethnic groups and is deeply embedded in the social structures.

Some Psychological Theories of Prejudice

Why do people become prejudiced toward others or what are the underlying reasons that produce, perpetuate, and prolong prejudice? Following are some proposed theories, including ethnocentrism, frustration, belief congruence, defense mechanism, and cognitive categorizations, intended to explain the phenomenon of prejudice.

According to the theory of **ethnocentrism,** prejudice is considered an inevitable universal phenomenon. Ethnocentrism requires loyalty to an individual's own racial group and demands sacrifice for the group. In order to perpetuate the interests of an individual's own group and maintain its solidarity and superiority, members are mandated to reject and suppress out-groups, and this mandate results in prejudice. **Frustration theory** proposes that people who are unable to direct their aggression at the real source of frustration may displace their anger onto some other easily available target groups.

The theory of **belief congruence** explains the underlying causes of prejudice as a dissimilarity in cultural values, attitudes, and beliefs among various groups. Naturally, people belonging to out-groups, who do not share the same beliefs, are more susceptible to prejudice and discrimination than people belonging to in-groups, who have similar belief systems. **Defense mechanism** perspectives propose that prejudice can be explained as projection of the inner conflicts and unacceptable impulses of the prejudiced person directed at a targeted individual or group.

Finally, according to **cognitive categorizations theory,** people are categorized into discrete groups that play an important role in the development and perpetuation of prejudice through stereotyping. An outcome of cognitive categorization might be that persons classified into one special group tend to exaggerate their similarities with the members of their own group and dissimilarities with the members of the out-groups, resulting in prejudice and biased behaviors.

Psychological Impact of Prejudice on Mental Health

There is a general consensus that negative prejudice creates a hostile and stressful environment that causes severe mental health problems. Because prejudice is so demeaning, it can leave indelible scars of psychological wounds on its victims.

As a double-edged sword, prejudice injures not only the victim but also the victimizer—the former from anger, despair, and thoughts of revenge and the latter from guilt, shame, and remorse. Sadly, the victims of prejudice suffer from a psychological syndrome of pervasive anger, denial, loneliness, and isolation causing them depression and suicidal and homicidal ideations. They may also develop hypertension and problems related to alcoholism and substance abuse.

A society afflicted with racial prejudice is really a society without sound mental health. As human relations professionals, counselors can play a pivotal role in preventing, combating, and eliminating prejudice. For this reason, mental health counselors and other helping professionals must be equipped with necessary counseling skills and tools to deal with negative prejudice and racism.

According to Sandhu and Aspy (1997), prejudice is developed, maintained, and perpetuated by a combination of three major factors: individual personality, social traditions, and political systems. To eliminate or manage prejudice, it is important that deliberate, systematic, and proactive approaches be used at individual, social, cultural, and political levels. It is a daunting challenge to combat prejudice that manifests itself in many complex forms and *isms.* Although prejudice cannot be completely eliminated, it can be managed. Several resources are suggested at the end of this entry that can help professional counselors and other mental health professionals develop a constellation of practical and concrete strategies to intervene and to prevent the scourge of prejudice in the interest of maintaining and promoting the human dignity and decency of victims and perpetrators.

Contributed by Daya Singh Sandhu,
University of Louisville, Louisville, KY

References

Allport, G. W. (1979). *The nature of prejudice.* Cambridge, MA: Perseus Books. (Original work published 1954)

Du Bois, W. E. B. (2006). *The souls of Black folk.* West Valley City, UT: Waking Lion Press. (Original work published 1903)

Ponterotto, J. G., Utsey, S. O., & Pedersen, P. B. (2006). *Preventing prejudice: A guide for counselors* (2nd ed.). Thousand Oaks, CA: Sage.

Sandhu, D. S., & Aspy, C. B. (1997). *Counseling for prejudice prevention and reduction.* Alexandria, VA: American Counseling Association.

Additional Resources

Nelson, D. T. (2005). *Psychology of prejudice* (2nd ed.). Boston: Allyn & Bacon.

Parens, H., Mahfouz, A., Twemlow, S. W., & Scharff, D. E. (Eds.). (2007). *The future of prejudice: Psychoanalysis and the prevention of prejudice.* New York: Rowman & Littlefield.

Ridley, C. R. (2005). *Overcoming unintentional racism in counseling and therapy. A practitioner's guide to intentional intervention* (2nd ed.). Thousand Oaks, CA: Sage.

Trepagnier, B. (2007). *Silent racism: How well-meaning White people perpetuate the racial divide.* Boulder, CO: Paradigm.

■ Prevention Groups

Prevention is an approach that encompasses wellness and risk reduction, the enhancement of individual and community strengths, and the promotion of social justice (Hage et al., 2007). Evidence suggests that successful preventive programs are those that are of sufficient duration, targeted at several behaviors, theory driven, socially and culturally relevant, delivered across multiple contexts (e.g., individual, family, school, community), and connected within systems providing both primary and secondary preventive intervention services.

Prevention groups are a type of counseling that involves small groups of people meeting face-to-face with a trained group leader or leaders who assist them with gaining knowledge, attitudes, and behaviors that empower them to live their lives more meaningfully and effectively. The purpose of prevention groups is to enhance members' strengths and competencies while providing members with knowledge and skills to avoid harmful events and situations (Conyne & Wilson, 2000). Psychoeducational group processes, with their emphasis on competency development, are especially well suited for prevention groups. Examples of prevention groups are school-based groups to enhance social skills, reduce drug and alcohol use, and prevent bullying or eating disorders and groups for adults that focus on parenting skills, anger management, or relationship skills.

Prevention groups offer an alternative to the leading paradigm in mental health care that has largely focused on a remedial, individual, adaptation approach. This approach has been shown to be costly, time-consuming, culture bound, and largely inaccessible to lower income groups, including many children and older people. Prevention offers a means to bridge the disparity existing between the mental health needs in communities and the circumscribed availability of trained professionals. Early and focused group interventions have shown promise in limiting both the chronicity and severity of mental health symptoms and in enhancing the functioning of participants. They are also a major step in equalizing and enhancing mental health care.

History of Prevention Groups

Until the early 1990s, group work was used nearly exclusively as a remedial application in counseling and psychotherapy. With few exceptions (e.g., classroom guidance), group work was generally used to resolve, correct, and learn from existing dysfunctions and problems that group members were experiencing.

Beginning in the 1990s, prevention was identified as one major purpose of group work. Through its revised professional training standards, the Association for Specialists in Group Work (ASGW; 1990, 2000) expanded understanding regarding the variety of purposes and ways that groups could be used to include prevention. Since the release of the ASGW standards, interest in prevention groups, with their emphasis on protecting and promoting health and on forestalling dysfunction in individuals, organizations, and communities, has continued to expand. Division 49 of the American Psycho-

logical Association published a position paper in 2000 (Conyne & Wilson, 2000) that focused on recommendations for the use of groups for prevention. In addition, the *Journal for Specialists in Group Work* published a special issue devoted to the "The Use of Groups for Prevention" (Conyne & Horne, 2001).

Best Practice Steps for Leading Prevention Groups

A general set of 11 best practice guidelines exists to guide the conduct of prevention groups (Conyne & Wilson, 1999). These guidelines are adapted from the *ASGW Best Practice Guidelines for Group Workers* and are focused on the steps of planning, performing, and processing.

The planning process includes (a) conducting an ecological assessment, using various means (e.g., interviews, surveys, focus groups), to identify a target population, setting, and community needs; (b) collaborating with members of the target setting to coproduce a viable group plan; (c) identifying a generative body of knowledge from the professional literature that pertains to the emerging focal area; (d) setting goals collaboratively with members of the target population about what is to be prevented (e.g., sexually transmitted diseases, academic failure) and/or promoted (e.g., advocacy skills, life skills) through the group and how evaluation will be accomplished; (e) writing a detailed overall and session-by-session group plan that specifies group goals, group development model, recruitment, group setting, activities, strategies, resources, timelines, leader qualifications and responsibilities, and evaluation; and (f) attending to group length and structure while orienting the group toward goal accomplishment. Prevention groups are usually concise and focused, with an emphasis from the start on goals to be reached.

Performing steps include (a) balancing the attention group leaders give to information delivery, skill development, and group processes; (b) making sure sufficient consideration is devoted to promoting and learning from group interaction and processes; (c) promoting cohesion in the group by selecting members who share a similar problem or issue; and (d) considering the adoption of a systemic approach to enhancing members' skills development in the area of focus, as appropriate to the setting and population.

Finally, the first step in the processing of prevention groups is to give attention to the group process in and between each session in order to promote learning, make appropriate adaptations, and consider application to real-world settings and demand. In addition, leaders need to evaluate group process and outcomes (over time, if possible) to determine progress toward prevention goals.

Contributed by Robert K. Conyne, University of Cincinnati, Cincinnati, OH, and Sally M. Hage, Teachers College, Columbia University, New York, NY

References

Association for Specialists in Group Work. (1990). *Professional standards for the training of group workers* (2nd rev.). Alexandria, VA: Author.

Association for Specialists in Group Work. (2000). *Professional standards for the training of group workers* (3rd rev.). Retrieved May 25, 2007, from http://www.asgw.org/PDF/training_standards.pdf

Conyne, R., & Horne, A. (Eds.). (2001). The use of groups for prevention [Special issue]. *Journal for Specialists in Group Work, 26*(3).

Conyne, R., & Wilson, F. R. (1999). *Psychoeducation group training program* (Video No. 14Y1812). New York: Insight Media.

Conyne, R., & Wilson, F. R. (2000). Division 49 position paper: Recommendations of the task force for the use of groups for prevention. *The Group Psychologist, 11,* 10–11.

Hage, S. M., Romano, J., Conyne, R. K., Kenny, M. E., Matthews, C., Schwartz, J. P., et al. (2007). Best practice guidelines on prevention practice, research, training, and social advocacy. *The Counseling Psychologist, 35,* 493–566.

Additional Resources

Conyne, R. (2004). Prevention groups. In J. DeLucia-Waack, D. Gerrity, C. Kalodner, & M. Riva (Eds.), *Handbook of group counseling and psychotherapy* (pp. 621–629). Thousand Oaks, CA: Sage.

Conyne, R., & Horne, A. (2001). The current status of groups being used for prevention. *Journal for Specialists in Group Work, 26,* 289–292.

Gullotta, T., & Bloom, M. (Eds.). (2003). *The encyclopedia of primary prevention and health promotion.* New York: Kluwer.

■ Privilege

Many words come to mind when thinking about the construct of privilege. For example, the terms *advantage, prerogative, immunity, exemption, right, honor, status, power, choice, opportunity, access, favored, superior, benefit, promote, in-group,* and *freedom* may be equated with privilege. Privilege is a simple construct that has extremely powerful connotations, and it is particularly salient in the dialogue on racism, prejudice, and oppression in the United States. **Privilege** may be defined as benefits that an individual or group has over another individual or group. Moreover, privilege may or may not be deserved by or apparent to its beneficiaries. Privilege engenders power, oppression of others, and obliviousness. These concepts are intimately intertwined and represent varying manifestations of the same phenomenon. Privilege, whether accrued from primary (e.g., race, gender, age, physical ability, ethnicity, sexual identity) or secondary (e.g., income, education, religion, marital status, work experience) identities and whether earned or unearned may breed obliviousness and the systematic discrimination of others.

Peggy McIntosh's (1988) seminal article sparked voluminous scholarship and discussion about the notion of privilege. This discourse around privilege focuses primarily on skin color privilege—commonly referred to as **White privilege**—with its most visible recipients being White, middle-class, Christian, able-bodied, heterosexual men. Those who are not part of this in-group are summarily relegated to lesser rewards by virtue of their demographic identities. The beneficiaries of White skin privilege have this status ingrained so deeply into their psyche and entrenched in their lives that it becomes imperceptible to them but very obvious and recognizable to the nonrecipients of such privilege. Furthermore, White-skin privileged individuals adopt a worldview that assumes the ideals on which the United States was founded (e.g., freedom, liberty, equality, justice, the pursuit of happiness) are not only available to everyone and attainable by all but are also meted out equally and fairly. Therefore, those who do not reap the rewards have not worked hard enough, have an inherent character flaw, or are to be blamed for not being successful and "making it."

Believing otherwise for White-skin privileged individuals would mean several disturbing things. It would mean admitting that they are part of a social system that has oppressed, discriminated against, excluded, and denied certain freedoms and opportunities to specific segments of society and that still continues to do so. It would mean recognizing that they earned certain privileges unfairly or through the misfortunes of others. It would mean that they are not as virtuous and just as they believe, and the declaration that all men are created equal is simply a misstatement. The resulting cognitive dissonance may be extremely disconcerting for White-skin privileged individuals and can result in an array of uncomfortable emotions and behaviors such as anger and denial on one hand and shame and guilt on the other. Consequently, for White-skin privileged individuals, remaining oblivious to their privileged status, whether consciously or unconsciously, may provide a protective mechanism against confronting such a damaging reality. Unfortunately, the longer the obliviousness and lack of awareness are perpetuated, the longer inequities, injustice, and denial of human dignity are maintained.

Although White, unearned, skin-color privilege has stirred up significantly more discourse because of its interconnectedness with racism, prejudice, discrimination, and inequality, other kinds of privilege exist and are manifested in several ways. For example, there is heterosexual privilege, gender privilege, religious privilege, class privilege, educational privilege, able-bodied privilege, and age privilege, to name a few. **Heterosexual privilege** means being absolved from defending one's sexuality and having the freedom to marry another heterosexual without being subjected to societal condemnation, discrimination, sanctions, and violence. **Gender privilege** specifically refers to male privilege, that is, White, middle-class, Christian, able-bodied, heterosexual, men. Male privilege means being expected to earn more money than a woman while performing the same job. It means expecting to see primarily men dominate government and most positions of power, leadership, and influence in society. It also means that if men lose their jobs—or are never promoted, mismanage their finances, are poor drivers, make questionable decisions, and are too emotional—it will not be attributed to their gender. **Religious**

privilege means that Christians can count on their religious holidays being celebrated by the majority of the population, the laws and commandments of their religion being honored and obeyed, seeing pictures of their deity in public places, and not having their religious rituals questioned or held up to ridicule or scorn. **Social class privilege** means being able to possess many material possessions, live in more expensive neighborhoods, and feel financially comfortable. **Educational privilege** may mean being one of the select individuals in the United States with a terminal degree. Class privilege and educational privilege are interdependent because class privilege often pertains to socioeconomic and educational resources. **Able-bodied privilege** means having a body that will not be viewed as imperfect and deformed; not having to worry about the accessibility of places; and not being perceived as ignorant, childlike, dependent, physically weak, and always in need of special accommodations. **Age privilege** means being valued and appreciated for one's youth and ignored and devalued as one becomes elderly. The examples given here are only a few of the exhaustive list of privileges derived from demographic and other statuses.

The complex and emotional debate about White privilege will continue, given how deeply it is entrenched in the cultural/racial ethos of the United States. Although the existing empirical research on privilege has been scant, the topic has been examined in a variety of ways, such as students' awareness of their privilege (Chizhik & Chizhik, 2005); White privilege and oppression (Croteau, Talbot, Lance, & Evans, 2002; Hays, Chang, & Dean, 2004); attitudes in response to thoughts of White privilege (Branscombe, Schmitt, & Schiffhauer, 2007); definition, conceptualization, and experience of privilege among White counselor trainees (Hays et al., 2004); racial identity attitudes, White privilege, and awareness (Banaszynski, 2001; Chun, 2004); and White middle-class privilege and social class bias (Liu, Pickett, & Ivey, 2007). Suffice it to say that there is a need for much more empirical research surrounding the construct of skin color privilege as it relates to counseling.

Privilege, whether earned or unearned, is a double-edged sword, with benefits as well as detrimental consequences. Admitting unearned privilege and making a commitment to challenge the systems that perpetuate it may be the first step toward breaking the cycle of oppression and developing multicultural sensitivity.

Contributed by Eugenie Joan Looby,
Mississippi State University, Starkville, MS

References

Banaszynski, T. (2001). Beliefs about the existence of White privilege, race attitudes, and diversity-related behaviors. *Dissertation Abstracts International, 61*(10), 5619B. (UMI No. AA19991118)

Branscombe, N., Schmitt, M., & Schiffhauer, K. (2007). Racial attitudes in response to thoughts of White privilege. *European Journal of Social Psychology, 37,* 203–215.

Chizhik, E., & Chizhik, A. (2005). Are you privileged or oppressed: Students' conceptions of themselves and others. *Urban Education, 40,* 116–143.

Chun, K. (2004). The effect of White racial identity on awareness of privilege and color-blind racial attitudes. *Dissertation Abstracts International, 64*(10), 5273B. (UMI No. AA13108866)

Croteau, J., Talbot, D., Lance, T., & Evans, N. (2002). A qualitative study of the interplay between privilege and oppression. *Journal of Multicultural Counseling and Development, 30,* 239–258.

Hays, D., Chang, C., & Dean, J. (2004). White counselors' conceptualization of privilege and oppression: Implications for counselor training. *Counselor Education and Supervision, 43,* 242–257.

Liu, W., Pickett, T., Jr., & Ivey, A. (2007). White middle-class privilege: Social bias and implications for training and practice. *Journal of Multicultural Counseling and Development, 35,* 194–206.

McIntosh, P. (1988). *White privilege and male privilege: A personal account of coming to see correspondence through work in women's studies* (Working Paper Series No. 189.). Wellesley, MA: Wellesley College, Center for Research on Women.

Additional Resource

Anderson, S. K., & Middleton, V. (2005). *Explorations in privilege, oppression, and diversity.* Pacific Grove, CA: Brooks/Cole.

■ Privileged Communication

Communication that has been protected from disclosure in judicial court systems is usually referred to as **privileged communication.** Examples of privileged communication are communication between a physician and patient or a clergy member and parishioner. Recently, privileged communication generated in the course of a counseling relationship has also been afforded judicial protection from disclosure in many states. The counselor privilege laws enable professional counselors to maintain the confidentiality of information revealed to them by clients, even if they are called to testify as a witness in a trial or a court proceeding. This means that confidential communications may be disclosed by a person other than the client only with the prior written consent of the client. Both courts and legislatures in *Jaffee v. Redmond* (1996) acknowledged the importance of confidentiality in promoting an effective counseling relationship. In the *Jaffe v. Redmond* court case, a police officer shot and killed an individual and after the shooting sought counseling with a social worker. The decedent's family brought suit against the officer seeking damages for wrongful death and sought to obtain information regarding the contents of the counseling sessions. The defendant refused, citing psychotherapist–client privilege. The court found that the Federal Rules of Evidence did not provide for psychotherapist–client privilege. The Seventh Circuit Court reversed this decision, finding that the Federal Rules of Evidence did, indirectly, recognize a psychotherapist–client privilege; thus, the ruling acknowledges privileged communication for federal cases.

The U.S. Supreme Court found that effective counseling depends on an atmosphere of confidence and trust in which a client is willing to disclose thoughts, feelings, and emotions to a psychotherapist. Court systems have recognized that because of the sensitive nature of the problems for which individuals consult professional counselors, disclosure of confidential communications made during counseling sessions, or the mere possibility of disclosure, may impede development of the confidential counseling relationship. A major benefit provided by laws guaranteeing privilege is that counselors can assure clients that anything they discuss within the counseling relationship will be kept confidential, with the exception of the limits of confidentiality discussed later in this entry.

In addition to preventing professional counselors from testifying or being compelled to testify in court, many privilege laws extend protection to a counselor's written records, case notes, and working papers produced during counseling. As state laws have reasoned, the statutory privilege considered must extend to the subpoena of records and other documents developed throughout the counseling relationship. In such situations, the mere fact that a subpoena has been issued does not compel a professional counselor to testify or provide clients' records, only to appear in court. At that point, it is for the judge to decide whether the testimony or records in question are subject to a claim of privilege. Receipt of a subpoena should be a stimulus for a professional counselor to contact the lawyers involved to determine what information is being sought. If it is a case of privilege, the client or the client's lawyer should be notified. In this situation, a counselor may also want to contact his or her own attorney to clarify the professional counselor's rights and responsibilities.

There are conditions under which state laws may require a professional counselor to disclose what a client reveals. The American Counseling Association (2005) requires professional counselors to explain to their clients any limitations of confidentiality and to identify foreseeable situations in which confidential communications might be subject to disclosure. Most states specify exceptions to counselor privilege in their respective statutes and authorize disclosure in limited situations when disclosure of information is in the public interest. The most common exceptions involve reporting abuse or neglect of a child or vulnerable adult, evidence of a client's intent to harm self or others, evidence of a client's intent to commit a crime, or information collected in malpractice proceedings against the counselor. The exact conditions that trigger the duty to protect, as well as how the duty must be fulfilled, vary from state to state, depending on local statute and case law. Professional counselors need to be aware of special confidentiality considerations and state laws, because privileged communication may not apply in certain situations.

Contributed by Roxane L. Dufrene,
University of New Orleans,
New Orleans, LA

References

American Counseling Association. (2005). *ACA code of ethics.* Alexandria, VA: Author.

Jaffee v. Redmond, 518 U.S. 1 (1996).

■ Process Research

An underlying assumption of **process research** is that process is as important as content; how something is done is as important as what is done. In other words, how a professional counselor and client communicate and work together is as important as what they discuss in counseling. In addition, process research is distinguished from **outcome research,** in that outcome is often assessed as changes that occur between a pre- and postcounseling appraisal (see Outcome Research). Process research focuses on the behaviors and interactions between parts of a system, whether it is a dyadic (e.g., counselor and client), triadic (e.g., supervisor, counselor, and client), or multilevel (e.g., families, counseling groups, organization) system. Studies on the process of individual counseling began in the 1950s with naturalistic studies, and a large literature base has developed that includes analogue and qualitative research. There is less process research, however, in other areas of counseling, including in career counseling, group counseling, consultation, and counselor training.

The counseling process that has been most rigorously researched is the therapeutic alliance between a client and counselor in individual counseling. Research has shown that alliance is related to counseling outcome and higher ratings of the counseling alliance are associated with better counseling outcomes (Horvath & Symonds, 1991). A surprising finding is that neither counselors' experience nor competence was related to ratings of the counseling alliance (Dunkle & Friedlander, 1996; Svartberg & Stiles, 1992). Finally, it is important to note that counselors, clients, and outside observers tend to have very different perspectives on the counseling alliance. Group cohesiveness, the feeling of interconnectedness experienced by group members, is another counseling process that has received a good deal of research attention. Analogous to the alliance in individual counseling, group cohesiveness relates to the performance of group members during group counseling as well as treatment outcomes at the conclusion of group counseling. Furthermore, studies on counseling group processes indicate that group members value different counseling processes at different stages of the group (Shaughnessy & Kivlighan, 1995). When individuals first join a group, for example, the perception that other group members experience similar problems or feelings seems to be most important. Later in the life of a counseling group, members tend to value sharing feelings in a cathartic fashion.

The processes studied in process research may be overt or covert in nature. **Overt processes** include specific counselor techniques, client involvement, client resistance, and other behaviors that can be evaluated by external judges. The specific counselor technique of interpretation, for example, has been shown to be a helpful intervention when the interpretation is of moderate depth, is applied to a variety of situations, and is repeated often. **Covert processes** refer to internal reactions and thoughts that are not readily observed by outsiders but may influence the behaviors of counselors and clients, such as counselor intentions, counselor self-talk, client reactions, and client nondisclosures. Two common covert processes found in process research are clients' hiding negative reactions and keeping secrets from their counselors and counselors' ability in perceiving clients' positive reactions more so than their negative reactions.

Because of the inherent challenges in describing covert and overt interpersonal dynamics, researchers on process often use a variety of quantitative and qualitative methods, including interviews, observations, surveys, and videotaping or audiotaping to investigate processes within systems. Another challenge to process research is its relevance to counseling practice; historically, a typical researcher on process would measure an easily observed but inconsequential counseling process (e.g., head nods) that would yield few implications for counseling practice. However, advances in research methods, such as discovery-oriented and qualitative approaches, have enabled process research to become more applicable to, and hence beneficial for, counseling practice. Another benefit of process research is that through studying the interpersonal dynamics of a counseling situation, researchers begin to examine and develop more effective counseling interventions. Finally, findings from process research assist supervisors and counseling preparation programs in formulating training strategies for novice counselors.

Contributed by Rachel E. Crook Lyon,
Brigham Young University, Provo, UT

References

Dunkle, J. H., & Friedlander, M. L. (1996). Contribution of therapist experience and personal characteristics to the working alliance. *Journal of Counseling Psychology, 43,* 456–460.

Horvath, A. O., & Symonds, B. D. (1991). Relation between working alliance and outcome in psychotherapy: A meta-analysis. *Journal of Counseling Psychology, 38,* 139–149.

Shaughnessy, P., & Kivlighan, D., Jr. (1995). Using group participants' perceptions of therapeutic factors to form client typologies. *Small Group Research, 26,* 250–268.

Svartberg, M., & Stiles, T. C. (1992). Predicting patient change from therapist competence and patient therapist complementarity in short-term anxiety-provoking psychotherapy: A pilot study. *Journal of Consulting and Clinical Psychology, 60,* 304–307.

Additional Resources

Brown, S. D., & Lent, R. W. (Eds.). (2000). *Handbook of counseling psychology.* New York: Wiley.

Toukmanian, S. G., & Rennie, D. L. (Eds.). (1992). *Psychotherapy process research: Paradigmatic and narrative approaches.* Newbury Park, CA: Sage.

■ Professional Development

To keep up-to-date in the profession, counselors can learn both specific and general skills through continuing education and training. Because most people will have between five to seven careers and 10 or more jobs during their lifetime, people need to learn new skills continually. Job changes are the most dramatic since the Industrial Revolution. Over three fourths of the current workforce will need significant retraining. Over half of future jobs will require higher learning and training. Professional development offers professionals an opportunity to stay current by becoming lifelong learners. Specific reasons to expand skills include reorganization and changing needs in the workplace; desire to change positions in an organization; motivation to move out of a company to a more satisfying position; need to maintain an occupational level; desire to change careers or occupations; need to develop entry-level skills to enter a field; requirements to meet certification and licensing or continuing education requirements; family needs, including relocation and care giving; and personal enrichment.

An organizational development or human resources department often develops and implements a professional development program in a large corporation or institution. Four reasons for employers to provide professional development for employees are downsizing, reorganization, retention, and retirement. Education and training support services may include (a) policies and procedures (e.g., Equal Employment Opportunity or employee orientation), (b) systems (e.g., a job posting system), (c) classes and programs, and (d) resources (e.g., a career development center).

The following skills are required for successful job performance at all career levels: basic competency skills, communication skills, adaptability skills, developmental skills, self-management, group effectiveness skills, and influencing skills. The skills of most value to employers are knowledge and creative skills, especially those that highly motivate people, that engage both head and heart.

Acknowledgement of professional development may be in the form of a postsecondary or technical degree, a certificate or license, or continuing education credit. On-the-job professional development can address process skills (e.g., leadership, teamwork) or task skills (e.g., computer software application, health safety training).

In the United States, professional development for certain professions, such as state-licensed or national-certified counselors, is required within a specific time frame. The state or certifying body (such as the National Board for Certified Counselors [NBCC]) establishes standards of professional development that are mandated for national-certified counselors. State legislators set standards for licenses issued by the state and review them periodically to ensure that counselors meet certain standards.

Professional development is often available through an approved list of providers that includes organizations composed of members of a specific field. For example, the American Counseling Association, the American School Counselor Association, and the National Career Development Association offer a broad range of professional development opportunities for counselors who work in the general field of counseling or a specialty area, such as K–12 or career counseling. The authorizing institution, such as the International Association of Continuing Education or NBCC, requires providers to undergo a comprehensive authorization process.

Education and training resources can be found through one-stop centers, workforce investment centers, or employment development departments. Career centers at higher education institutions may provide resources for alumni. State-run community colleges often have career centers open to the public. Education and training may be in the form of formal education (e.g., through classes taken for credit, structured programs leading to diplomas, degrees, trade licenses, certificates, workshops and seminars), combinations of work and study (e.g., apprenticeships, internships, mentoring, and cooperative education), and personal enrichment and skill-building classes offered by adult education and continuing education services at a college. In addition, informal training may be gained on the job as part of marketing new products or attending professional meetings and conferences for continuing education units. Education and training can be delivered through a variety of systems, such as audiotape, live meeting or conference, DVD, teleseminar, Webinar, online course, mentoring, internship, and online forum.

Contributed by Sally Gelardin,
University of San Francisco,
San Francisco, CA

Additional Resources

American Counseling Association Web site: http://www.counseling.org/resources

National Career Development Association Web site: http://www.ncda.org

■ Professional Identity and Ethics, Key Historical Events In

Today, counselors have a unique belief system that is the foundation for their professional identity. For instance, counselors tend to (a) understand the importance of a wellness model in assisting individuals with their emotional and personal problems; (b) have a strong grounding in developmental theory and examine life's issues and problems from this perspective; (c) realize that preventative measures are likely to have more positive long-term benefits than remedial measures; and (d) understand the importance of empowering clients so that they can learn how to be autonomous, healthy, functioning individuals. The antecedents to this current professional identity have a long history that can be traced back to the 1800s and the beginning of vocational guidance in the United States.

At the end of the 19th century, a number of factors, including the social reform movement, the Industrial Revolution, an increase in immigration, and the development of assessment instruments, would be responsible for the beginning of vocational guidance. The individual who would be one of the first to offer a model of vocational guidance was **Frank Parsons** (1854–1908). Generally called the founder of guidance in America, Parsons established the Vocational Bureau, which assisted individuals in choosing and preparing themselves for an occupation. His book, *Choosing a Vocation*, was published posthumously in 1909 and, although focused on vocational counseling, demonstrated a number of principles that would be adopted widely by all kinds of counselors. Vocational guidance eventually became an important aspect of the public school curriculum, and individuals like Jesse Davis, Eli Weaver, and Anna Reed were some of the first to offer guidance services in major school systems. Soon after Parsons's untimely death, the **National Vocational Guidance Association (NVGA)** was founded in 1913 and is generally considered to be the distant predecessor of the American Counseling Association. In 1932, the Wagner O'Day Act strengthened the importance of vocational guidance by establishing the U.S. Employment Services, which provided vocational guidance for the unemployed.

Paralleling the rise of vocational guidance was the rise in the types of treatment approaches to mental illness. For instance, individuals like **Clifford Beers,** who had been hospitalized for schizophrenia, lobbied to improve the conditions of mental institutions and to offer clinics for individuals with mental disorders. As clinics spread, the need for psychological assistants, often with a bachelor's or master's degree, became evident. To fill this need, social workers and counselors began to work in these settings. As the role of the counselor expanded into agencies, others, like John Brewer, pushed for counselors to have an expanded role, one that also addressed mental health issues, in the schools.

The emergence of the counseling field as something more than vocational guidance continued during the 1930s as **E. G. Williamson** (1900–1979) developed one of the first comprehensive theories of counseling, known as the Minnesota Point of View, or trait and factor theory. Then, during the 1940s and 1950s, with influences by such individuals as Carl Rogers, the counseling profession began to take on an increasingly humanistic orientation. It was also around this time that developmental models that offered more of a wellness and preventative perspective began to become popular.

In 1957, the Russians launched **Sputnik,** and, fearing that the Russians would win the "space race," the U.S. Congress passed the **National Defense Education Act (NDEA)** in 1958, which allocated funds to increase the number of school counselors as a way to identify future scientists. The 1950s also saw the first full-time college counselors as well as counselors increasingly staffing vocational rehabilitation centers. Professional counselors also began working at community agencies as a result of increasing numbers of psychiatric inpatients being released from state hospitals due to the discovery of new psychotropic medications.

Increasing numbers and types of counselors led to an increased need for a professional identity, resulting in the establishment of many new professional associations. For instance, the **American Personnel and Guidance Association (APGA)**

was founded in 1952 by a merger of four counseling-related associations. A number of APGA divisions were soon formed, including the **American School Counselor Association,** the **Association for Counselor Education and Supervision,** the **National Career Development Association,** the **American Rehabilitation Counseling Association,** and the **Counseling Association for Humanistic Education and Development.**

During the 1960s, the need for counselors expanded as the result of legislative actions related to President Lyndon Johnson's Great Society initiatives such as the Community Mental Health Centers Act of 1963, which funded the establishment of mental health centers. With expansion and diversification came increased professionalism and the development, in 1961, of APGA's first ethics code as well as meetings to discuss accreditation of counseling programs. Finally, the 1960s saw the continued expansion of APGA with increased membership, the recommendation to have state branches, and the formation of the **Association for Assessment in Counseling** and the **National Employment Counseling Association.**

During the 1970s, a number of events occurred that increased the need for counselors. For instance, the 1975 Supreme Court decision in *Donaldson v. O'Connor* led to the deinstitutionalization of hundreds of thousands of state mental hospital patients who had been hospitalized against their will. In 1975, Congress passed an expansion of the original Community Mental Health Centers Act. The 1970s also saw legislation for individuals with disabilities that led to an increased need for rehabilitation counselors and expanded the role of school counselors. This decade also saw a focus on microcounseling skills training, which was based on many of the skills deemed critical by Carl Rogers and other humanistic psychologists. It was also during this decade that multicultural issues became popular, with important works by such individuals as Derald Sue, Paul Pedersen, William Cross, and Donald Atkinson.

The 1970s were also the decade of increased professionalization. It was then that the Association for Counselor Education and Supervision provided drafts of accreditation standards for master's-level counseling programs, which were adopted in 1981. National credentialing was offered by the **Council on Rehabilitation Education** in 1973 and by the **National Academy for Certified Mental Health Counselors** in 1979. Virginia became the first state to offer counselor licensing in 1976. New divisions of APGA were formed, including the **Association for Multicultural Counseling and Development,** the **Association for Spiritual, Ethical, and Religious Values in Counseling,** the **Association for Specialists in Group Work,** the **International Association of Addictions and Offender Counselors,** and the **American Mental Health Counselors Association.**

In 1982, APGA established the **National Board for Certified Counselors** and began to administer the first national certification exam. In 1983, APGA changed its name to the **American Association for Counseling and Development** and in 1992 changed its name again to the **American Counseling Association (ACA).** Also during the 1980s, more states offered licensure for counselors and new divisions arose, including the **Association for Counselors and Educators in Government,** the **Association for Adult Development and Aging,** the **International Association of Marriage and Family Counselors,** the **American College Counseling Association,** the **Association for Gay, Lesbian and Bisexual Issues in Counseling,** and **Counselors for Social Justice.**

During the 21st century, counselor certification and counselor licensing continued to expand. In 2008, there are more than 36,000 **National Certified Counselors,** and 49 states now offer licensure. In 2005, the sixth version of ACA's *ACA Code of Ethics* was adopted after a lengthy revision process. Also, in 2008, close to one half of all counseling programs were now accredited by the Council for Accreditation of Counseling and Related Programs, an accrediting organization established in the 1980s. This century has also brought a continued emphasis on multicultural issues, including a recent focus on multicultural counseling standards. Professionalism can be seen as being on a continuum, where legal standards are the lowest level of professionalism, codes of ethics and professional standards are at the midpoint of professionalism (and the minimum acceptable to professional counselors), and best practices are at the highest end of professionalism (and the goal of all professional counselors). As counselors continue to identify and refine codes and standards, there will hopefully be increased numbers of counselors offering best practices.

Finally, in recent years, the identity of the profession has been in some amount of transition, and, to some degree, this challenges counselors' ability to offer best practices. For instance, as the counseling profession has expanded, some of the divisions have threatened to disaffiliate or have developed a loose association with the founding organization, ACA. In addition to the most recent *ACA Code of Ethics*, a number of certification bodies, state licensing boards, divisions, and specialty groups have developed their own ethical codes. Multiple codes are difficult to enforce and can be confusing to professionals as well as consumers. This can make it difficult to understand what exactly best practices are. As the counseling profession has diversified and as counseling professionals decide which divisions or associations to join and which codes to follow, it is likely that counselors will continue to struggle to establish a professional identity.

Contributed by Ed Neukrug and
Theodore P. Remley Jr.,
Old Dominion University, Norfolk, VA

References

American Counseling Association. (2005). *ACA code of ethics.* Alexandria, VA: Author.

Parsons, F. (1909). *Choosing a vocation.* Boston: Houghton-Mifflin.

Additional Resources

Neukrug, E. (2007). *The world of the counselor* (3rd ed.). Belmont, CA: Brooks/Cole.

Remley, T. P., Jr., & Herlihy, B. (2005). *Ethical, legal, and professional issues in counseling* (2nd ed.). Upper Saddle River, NJ: Pearson Merrill Prentice Hall.

■ Professional Identity and Ethics, Key Legal Issues in

One common characteristic of professional identity in the counseling profession is evidenced by strict adherence to a professional code of ethics. The American Counseling Association's (ACA; 2005) *ACA Code of Ethics* presents guidelines for ethical professional behavior that primarily protects clients but also provides the profession with a way to monitor itself. Such codes, which must be interpreted and applied contextually, along with federal and state statutes guide counselors in appropriate professional behavior. Many federal statutes affect the work of a professional counselor, including the **Family Educational Rights and Privacy Act (FERPA), Individuals With Disabilities Education Improvement Act (IDEA), Section 504 of the U.S. Rehabilitation Act 1973, and the Health Insurance Portability and Accountability Act (HIPAA).** State statutes influencing professional counselors include those that address reporting child abuse and neglect, rights of parents and children when counseling minors, and professional decisions and actions related to a client who is in danger of harming himself or herself or another individual.

FERPA, IDEA, and Section 504 of the Rehabilitation Act

FERPA, IDEA, and Section 504 affect professional counselors working in schools and university settings. FERPA clearly states that parents control the privacy rights of educational records of students under the age of 18 years. Counselors in schools that receive federal funding are bound to adhere to the provisions in FERPA, usually with regard to students' educational records. Some states may consider counselor case notes involving personal counseling as accessible educational records under FERPA; one exception would include the counselor's right to withhold such notes if releasing them might endanger the child.

Full rights are available to minors upon their 18th birthday through Amendment XXVI; the U.S. Constitution established the right of 18-year-old citizens to vote. The age of 18 years is the generally accepted age at which minors are extended other adult rights, including the right to make educational decisions, provide consent to counseling, and so forth. However, in all educational institutions FERPA permits duty to warn if specific threats are made against specific people by their clients, as affirmed by *Jain v. State of Iowa* in 2000.

Federal legislation, including IDEA and Section 504, provides assurance of appropriate services in schools for students with disabilities. These civil rights laws state that no qualified person (of any age) who is disabled may be discriminated against in any federally assisted program. IDEA prohibits discrimination due to disability and requires schools to provide necessary services, including mental health services, to ensure that all students have equitable academic opportunities. Professional counselors in school settings often provide mental health services and may serve as members of multidisciplinary teams that make decisions about student placement and services. The rights and privileges of both students and their parents must be considered. In addition, through education and training, and in line with ethical standards of practice, school counselors must be knowledgeable about principles of psychological assessment, including proper interpretation and use of assessments. Section 504 provides accommodations for students with disabilities not covered under IDEA guidelines. Section 504 provides educational and disability-related services to clients with mild physical or mental disabilities that substantially limit a major life activity (e.g., learning, walking). Section 504 services, although different than IDEA, might likewise make provisions for meeting a student's mental health needs. Both IDEA and Section 504 require counselors to advocate for clients, both students and their families; formulate educational and transition plans; develop possible behavior intervention plans or behavior modification; and provide counseling services for students as needed. The confidentiality and privacy rights of students specified by IDEA and Section 504 are similar to those protected by FERPA. In a situation in which the codes of ethics may conflict with the law, the counselor is first and foremost required to try to resolve the dilemma using an accepted decision-making model. In the event that the conflict cannot be resolved, the counselor must comply with the law (ACA, 2005, H.1.b.).

HIPAA of 1996

HIPAA was passed to help protect and safeguard the security and confidentiality of individuals' health information, including mental health records. One part of HIPAA, the **privacy rule,** mandates the protection and privacy of all health information. This rule specifically defines authorized uses/disclosures of individually identifiable health information; it prevents unnecessary disclosures of protected health information. Professional counselors must provide prospective clients with a privacy policy, and they must ask clients for a signed form stating they have received this policy. Ethical standards of practice likewise ensure that professional counselors provide all clients with an informed consent. Statements of **informed consent,** in keeping with ethical standards, usually include information about the counselor's education and training, rights to privacy and confidentiality (including exceptions), procedures for protecting client privacy, and the process for release of information from client records. HIPAA gives clients in a counseling relationship access to their records (e.g., case notes, treatment plans) as well as the right to amend or disagree with the counselor's records. Clients may also request that counselors communicate with them in a confidential manner with regard to appointments, confirmation of services, and reports made to insurance companies. Professional counselors in private practice must be diligent to make sure clients' HIPAA rights are ensured. Similarly, counselors in schools need to work with other school personnel to ensure students' rights to privacy with regard to student records (e.g., health, psychological assessments, counseling notes). Contextual applications of laws regarding students' rights to privacy are often difficult; counselors in schools may have to educate other school personnel on the critical need to protect students' privacy rights.

Child Abuse and Neglect

All 50 U.S. states and the District of Columbia have laws requiring an individual to report suspected child abuse or neglect. When a client reveals that a child is being abused or neglected, a professional counselor regards both ethical standards as well as state statutes in reporting the alleged abuse to the proper authorities. Child abuse includes physical, emotional, sexual, and medical abuse; abandonment; and neglect (including neglectful supervision). Immunity is granted to the professional counselor or other reporter from any civil or criminal liability for breaking confidentiality.

Counseling Minors

When counseling minors, issues of concern include (a) to whom counselors owe the ethical obligation of confidentiality, (b) parental consent and legal rights, and (c) the competency level of a minor. Furthermore, these rights are greatly influenced by context. For example, professional counselors working with children and adolescents in community and private practice settings are sometimes bound by different standards than those working with students in schools.

In community counseling, a minor must have consent from a parent or guardian or a court order to receive counseling services. Further care must be taken when counseling children and adolescents in cases of divorce; counselors must ensure that the legal rights of both parents are protected. Exceptions in law requiring parental consent for counseling vary from state to state and may include reference to the following: mature minors (over the age of 16 years), emancipated minors, minors who may intend to harm themselves or someone else (most states require immediate parental notification), minors with sexually transmitted diseases, minors with drug and alcohol use/abuse issues, and minors over 12 years who have been sexually assaulted. Informing parents and/or guardians about the purpose of counseling and the limits of confidentiality is an ethical obligation of counselors when working with minors in any context (ACA, 2005).

In school settings, children and adolescents have a right to voluntary counseling and may agree to counseling without parental consent. Some districts or campuses may have policies requiring school counselors to obtain parental permission for counseling after a specific number of sessions. State statutes and school district policies may vary or even confound each other. Again, maintenance of ethical standards should override any decisions made by school counselors; the counselor is obligated to uphold parental rights as well as address the students' ethical rights to confidentiality and informed consent (ACA, 2005, B.5.b). Older minors (16- and 17-year-olds) are increasingly being granted more rights (e.g., informed consent, consent to counseling and

health services) because they are being held legally responsible for actions at an increasing rate by courts.

Contributed by Elsa Soto Leggett,
Texas Southern University,
Houston, TX,
and Gail K. Roaten,
Texas State University–San Marcos,
San Marcos, TX

Reference

American Counseling Association. (2005). *ACA code of ethics*. Alexandria, VA: Author.

Additional Resource

American School Counselor Association. (2004). *Ethical standards for school counselors*. Alexandria VA: Author

▮ Professional Identity and Ethics, Key People in

Many individuals at the national level have shaped the counseling profession over the past half century. West, Osborn, and Bubenzer (2003) highlighted 23 people who have contributed to the professional identity and ethics of the counseling profession. Individuals highlighted included Michael K. Altekruse, Roger F. Aubrey, Loretta Bradley, David K. Brooks Jr., Mary Thomas Burke, Harold F. Cottingham, Samuel T. Gladding, Harold L. Hackney, Edwin L. Herr, George E. Hill, Thomas Walsh Hosie, Kenneth B. Hoyt, Courtland C. Lee, Judith A. Lewis, Don C. Locke, John McFadden, Jane E. Myers, Merle M. Ohlsen, Theodore P. Remley Jr., Bruce Shertzer, Robert O. Stripling, Thomas J. Sweeney, and Joe Wittmer. These individuals have started counselor education programs, advocated for state licensure, created professional associations, developed codes of ethics, established accreditation standards, advanced social justice and multicultural principles, and dedicated themselves to advancing the identity of the counseling profession. Hundreds of individuals have had an impact on the professional identity and ethics of the counseling profession. This entry highlights a small selection of contemporary individuals whose contributions continue to affect the training of professional counselors: Thomas J. Sweeney, Samuel T. Gladding, Courtland C. Lee, Theodore P. Remley Jr., Carol A. Dahir, and Thomas E. Davis. All of the these individuals have advocated for the professional identity of counselors, provided service to counseling associations, and been recognized for their contributions.

Thomas J. Sweeney, emeritus professor of counselor education at Ohio University, created **Chi Sigma Iota (CSI),** a worldwide honor society recognizing the work of professional counselors, and serves as its executive director. Sweeney obtained his master's degree in school guidance from the University of Wisconsin and his doctorate in counselor education at The Ohio State University. He advocated for professional identity through advocacy for state licensure laws for counselors, standards for accreditation, and the creation of professional counseling associations. Sweeney held steadfast to the principle that eligibility for membership in CSI is for individuals who are or were students in counselor education programs and who hold their primary identity as professional counselors. In 2008, CSI has more than 250 chapters and has initiated more than 56,000 professional counselors around the world (CSI, 2008; see Chi Sigma Iota). Sweeney has served as the president of the Association for Counselor Education and Supervision (ACES) in 1976–1977 and of the American Counseling Association (ACA) in 1980–1981, the founding chairperson of the **Council for Accreditation of Counseling and Related Educational Programs (CACREP)** in 1981, and the founding president of the International Association for Marriage and Family Counseling in 1989. Sweeney has more than 75 publications and was recognized in the top 5% of contributors to the *Journal of Counseling & Development* from 1973 to 1998 (Witmer, 2003). Sweeney's contributions to the field of counseling were recognized when he received the ACA Distinguished Professional Service Award in 1983, the ACA Government Relations Award in 1986, ACA Fellow Award in 2005, and the ACA Distinguished Mentor Award in 2006 (ACA, 2007) and the ACES Distinguished Mentor Award in 2006.

Samuel T. Gladding, professor and chair of the Department of Counseling at Wake Forest University, served as the facilitator of the "20/20: A Vision for the Counseling Profession" initiative from 2006–2009. This initiative brought together leaders from 30 professional counseling entities to strengthen the identity of the counseling profession. Gladding served as president of ACA in 2004–2005, ACES in 1996–1997, Association for Specialist in Group Work in 1994–1995, and CSI in 1989–1990 (Henderson, 2003). Gladding obtained his master's degree in counseling from Wake Forest University and doctorate in counselor education from the University of North Carolina at Greensboro (Gladding, 2008). He has authored more than 75 publications and has served as the editor of the *Journal for Specialist in Group Work.* He has published books focusing on the professional identity of counselors, including *Counseling: A Comprehensive Profession* (Gladding, 2006) and *Community and Agency Counseling* (Gladding & Newsome, 2004). He has received numerous awards recognizing his services, including the Chi Sigma Iota Distinguished Service Award and the Thomas J. Sweeney Professional Leadership Award in 1997. He was recognized by ACES with the Outstanding Publication Award in 1993 and the Professional Leadership Award in 1999. In 2007, Gladding received the Bridgebuilder Award and the Gilbert and Kathleen Wrenn/ACA Counselor of the Year award, and was named an ACA Fellow.

Courtland C. Lee, professor and program director of counselor education at the University of Maryland, has worked to advance multicultural counseling within the professional identity of counseling. Lee obtained his doctorate in counseling from Michigan State University. He served as president of the Association for Multicultural Counseling and Development (AMCD) in 1988–1989, CSI in 1995–1996, and ACA in 1997–1998. During his ACA presidency,

Lee worked to build unity around the commonalities that all professional counselors share regardless of specialty or work setting (Herlihy & Brooks, 2003). Lee has worked to advance the profession of counseling on an international level. He established a connection with the British Association for Counselling (BAC) and served as president of the International Association for Counselling. Lee has authored more than 75 publications. He served as editor of the *Journal of Non-White Concerns in Personnel and Guidance* and provided leadership in changing the name to the *Journal of Multicultural Counseling and Development.* He also served as editor of the *Journal of African American Men.* His publication, *Multicultural Issues in Counseling: New Approaches to Diversity* (Lee, 2006), provided counselors practical techniques for working with diverse client populations. Lee was recognized for his contributions to the field of counseling in 1985 as the recipient of the AMCD Distinguished Professional Service Award, the BAC Fellow Award in 1999, and the ACA Fellow Award. The ACA Multicultural Excellence Scholarship Award was named in his honor in 2002 (Lee, 2008).

Theodore P. Remley Jr., professor and Batten Endowed Chair in the Department of Leadership and Counseling at Old Dominion University, has worked to advance the ethical understanding and practice of professional counselors. Remley obtained his juris doctorate from Catholic University and his master's degree and doctorate in counselor education from the University of Florida (Remley, 2008). Remley is licensed as a counselor in three states (Louisiana, Mississippi, and Virginia) and is licensed to practice law in both Virginia and Florida. Remley worked to help pass the first counselor licensure bill in the country in Virginia in 1976 (Hermann, 2003). He has served in several leadership positions, most notably as president of the Virginia Counseling Association and as the executive director of ACA from 1990 to 1993. Remley has combined his background as a lawyer and a professional counselor to write more than 50 publications, many on ethical and legal issues relevant to counselors. During his term as ACA executive director, he wrote monthly columns on the uniqueness of professional counselors compared with other mental health disciplines, and he served as the editor of the 12-volume *ACA Legal Series* (Hermann, 2003). His most recent books include *Ethical, Legal, and Professional Issues in Counseling* (Remley & Herlihy, 2005); *Ethical, Legal, and Professional Issues in the Practice of Marriage and Family Therapy* (Wilcoxon, Remley, Gladding, & Huber, 2006); and two book chapters in *Ethical and Legal Issues in School Counseling* (Remley, Hermann, & Huey, 2003). He has served as an expert witness for counseling-related cases and as keynote presenter on ethical and legal issues. He has received several awards recognizing his services, including the ACA Fellow Award in 2008, American Association of State Counseling Boards Leadership Award in 1992, and Southern ACES Individual Achievement Award in 1999. Remley has sought to present the counseling profession as a "unified profession that was stronger as a whole than it would be if fragmented by its many specialties" (Hermann, 2003, p. 255).

Carol A. Dahir, associate professor and coordinator of School Counselor Education at the New York Institute of Technology, has worked to advance the school counseling profession as the American School Counselor Association (ASCA) National Standards project director. Dahir has worked with state departments of education and school counselor associations to advance a set of national standards for the school counseling profession and coauthored the ASCA National Standards for School Counseling Programs (Campbell & Dahir, 1997). These standards strengthened the professional identity of school counselors through advocating for a national model that promotes structure and accountability. Dahir has authored or coauthored several publications that focused on the professional role of school counselors, including, *School Counselor Accountability* (Stone & Dahir, 2006), *The Transformed School Counselor* (Stone & Dahir, 2005), and *Vision Into Action: Implementing the National Standards for School Counseling Programs* (Dahir, Sheldon, & Valiga, 1998). She served as president of the New York State School Counselor Association and as an ASCA board member. Her contributions were recognized by the Association for Career and Technical Education as the 2001 recipient of the Friends of Guidance Award, which recognizes an individual who made a significant contribution to the advancement of career guidance and counseling (Petersen & Whitaker, 2002).

Thomas E. Davis, professor in the Department of Counseling and Higher Education at Ohio University, worked as the chair of the 2008 CACREP standards revision team. The revised CACREP accreditation standards will continue to shape the professional identity of counselors by providing guidelines for counselor education curricula and the hiring of counselor educators. One of the significant changes proposed in the new CACREP standards is requiring CACREP-accredited programs to hire individuals with doctorates in counselor education after 2013. This revision advanced the position that the professional identity of counselors should be shaped by counselor educators rather than by individuals from competing disciplines. On the national level, Davis has served as president of the **American Association of State Counseling Boards (AASCB)** and as an ACA Ethics Committee member. Davis exemplified strong leadership on the state level in the area of licensure for counselors. He served as president of the state branches of ACA and ACES. Davis's advocacy for professional identity was demonstrated as he worked with other state counseling leaders to change Ohio law to allow individuals with backgrounds in fields other than teacher education to become school counselors. Davis received his master's degree in counselor education from Marshall University and his doctorate in counselor education from The Ohio State University. His service to the counseling profession was recognized by receiving six state counseling association awards for his leadership. On a national level, he received the AASCB Presidential Achievement Award in 1998 and the ACES Distinguished Mentor award in 2004.

Numerous counselor educators, supervisors, and counseling leaders work to shape the professional identity of counselors and promote the goals of the profession. Counselor educators in university programs shape the professional identity and ethics of students through lecture, discussion, assigned reading, and individual mentorship. Program coordinators have advanced professional identity by hiring faculty who hold their professional identify as counselors, publish in ACA journals, and provide service to counseling associations. Internship and licensure supervisors shape professional identity and understanding of appropriate ethical behavior. Counselor supervisors model their professional identity by choosing to identify themselves as professional counselors instead of therapists or as school counselors instead of guidance counselors.

Most states have an ACA branch with leaders working to advance the professional identity of counselors in their states. State leaders often organize ways to educate the public about professional counselors, including advocacy efforts targeting state legislatures on issues of importance (e.g., scope of practice, state model for school counseling). State professional association leaders may also take action to protect the profession of counseling against other professions that may seek to limit or marginalize the professional privileges of counselors. For example, leaders in the Indiana Counseling Association recently worked to remove a restricted test list supported by psychologists that sought to prohibit Indiana professional counselors' ability to engage in psychological assessment. Leaders in the California Counseling Association are working to create and advocate for a counselor licensure law in their state, the final state without a licensure law for professional counselors.

Leaders of national counseling associations shape the professional identity and acceptable ethical practice through their publications, conferences, and resources. Leaders of counseling-related organizations continue to direct the future of the counseling profession through accreditation, certification, and state licensure. Some of these leaders are Carol L. Bobby, executive director of CACREP; Marv Kuehn, executive director of the Council on Rehabilitation Education; and Thomas W. Clawson, president and chief executive officer of the National Board for Certified Counselors.

Finally, editors of ACA and ACA affiliate counseling journals play a unique role in shaping the professional identity by selecting and editing the journal content for counseling professionals. Editors of counseling journals include Spencer G. (Skip) Niles *(Journal of Counseling & Development)*, Catherine B. Roland *(Adultspan Journal)*, Jerry Trusty *(The Career Development Quarterly)*, Richard Watts *(Counseling and Values)*, John D. West and Cynthia J. Osborn *(Counselor Education and Supervision)*, Kaye W. Nelson and Stephen Southern *(The Family Journal)*, Dimiter M. Dimitrov *(Measurement and Evaluation in Counseling and Development)*, W. Bryce Hagedorn *(Journal of Addictions & Offender Counseling)*, Alan M. "Woody" Schwitzer *(Journal of College Counseling)*, Thelma Duffey *(Journal of Creativity in Mental Health)*, Robert A. Neault *(Journal of Employment Counseling)*, Mark B. Scholl *(Journal of Humanistic Education, Counseling and*

Development), Ned Farley *(Journal of LGBT Issues in Counseling)*, James R. Rogers *(Journal of Mental Health Counseling)*, Gargi Roysircar-Sodowsky *(Journal of Multicultural Counseling and Development)*, Rebecca Toporek and Tod Solan *(Journal for Social Action in Counseling and Psychology)*, Sheri Bauman *(Journal for Specialists in Group Work)*, Richard W. Auger *(Professional School Counseling)*, and Douglas Strohmer *(Rehabilitation Counseling Bulletin)*.

The individuals discussed in this entry are only a small selection of the many professional counselors who are working to advance the professional identity of and shape the counseling profession. Many other key figures work diligently at local, state, and national levels to advance the profession of counseling.

Contributed by Jake J. Protivnak,
Youngstown State University,
Youngstown, OH

References

American Counseling Association. (2007). *National awards.* Retrieved January 20, 2008, from http://www.counseling.org/AboutUs/NationalAwards/TP/Home/CT2.aspx

Campbell, C. A., & Dahir, C. A. (1997). *Sharing the vision: The national standards for school counseling programs.* Alexandria, VA: American School Counselor Association.

Chi Sigma Iota. (2008). *What is CSI?* Retrieved January 20, 2008, from http://www.csi-net.org/displaycommon.cfm?an=1

Dahir, C. A., Sheldon, C. B., & Valiga, M. J. (1998). *Vision into action: Implementing the national standards for school counseling programs.* Alexandria, VA: Author.

Gladding, S. T. (2006). *Counseling: A comprehensive profession* (5th ed.). Upper Saddle River, NJ: Prentice Hall.

Gladding, S. T. (2008). *Brief curriculum vita.* Retrieved January 20, 2008, from http://www.wfu.edu/~stg/bio.htm

Gladding, S. T., & Newsome, D. W. (2004). *Community and agency counseling* (2nd ed.). Upper Saddle River, NJ: Prentice Hall.

Henderson, D. A. (2003). Samuel Templeman Gladding. In J. D. West, C. J. Osborn, & D. L. Bubenzer (Eds.), *Leaders and legacies: Contributions to the profession of counseling* (pp. 159–164). New York: Brunner-Routledge.

Herlihy, B., & Brooks, M. (2003). Courtland C. Lee. In J. D. West, C. J. Osborn, & D. L. Bubenzer (Eds.), *Leaders and legacies: Contributions to the profession of counseling* (pp. 205–211). New York: Brunner-Routledge.

Hermann, M. A. (2003). Theodore P. Remley, Jr. In J. D. West, C. J. Osborn, & D. L. Bubenzer (Eds.), *Leaders and legacies: Contributions to the profession of counseling* (pp. 253–258). New York: Brunner-Routledge.

Lee, C. C. (Ed.). (2006). *Multicultural issues in counseling: New approaches to diversity* (3rd ed.). Alexandria, VA: American Counseling Association.

Lee, C. C. (2008). *Vita Courtland C. Lee.* Retrieved January 20, 2008, from http://www.education.umd.edu/EDCP/facultystaff/Lee/lee.pdf

Petersen, J., & Whitaker, J. (2002). *Guidance division awards, 2001 convention.* Retrieved January 20, 2008, from http://goliath.ecnext.com/coms2/summary_0199-1504944_ITM

Remley, T. P., Jr. (2008). *Curriculum vitae Theodore P. Remley, Jr.* Retrieved January 20, 2008, from http://education.odu.edu/elc/docs/CVRemley.doc

Remley, T. P., Jr., & Herlihy, B. (2005). *Ethical, legal, and professional issues in counseling* (2nd ed.). Upper Saddle River, NJ: Prentice Hall.

Remley, T. P., Jr., Hermann, M. A., & Huey, W. C. (2003). *Ethical and legal issues in school counseling* (2nd ed.). Alexandria, VA: American School Counselor Association.

Stone, C. B., & Dahir, C. A. (2005). *The transformed school counselor.* Boston: Houghton Mifflin.

Stone, C. B., & Dahir, C. A. (2006). *School counselor accountability: A MEASURE of student success.* Upper Saddle River, NJ: Prentice Hall.

West, J. D., Osborn, C. J., & Bubenzer, D. L. (Eds.). (2003). *Leaders and legacies: Contributions to the profession of counseling.* New York: Brunner-Routledge.

Wilcoxon, S. A., Remley, T. P., Jr., Gladding, S. T., & Huber, C. H. (2006). *Ethical, legal and professional issues in the practice of marriage and family therapy* (4th ed.). Upper Saddle River, NJ: Prentice Hall.

Witmer, J. M. (2003). Thomas J. Sweeney. In J. D. West, C. J. Osborn, & D. L. Bubenzer (Eds.), *Leaders and legacies: Contributions to the profession of counseling* (pp. 273–281). New York: Brunner-Routledge.

Program Evaluation

Professional counselors are often called to evaluate the programs they manage or the programs of others. Adequate evaluation requires specific parameters and standard criteria to gauge the success of a program at various stages of development and implementation. Without these parameters and criteria, the door is open for disagreement about whether or not a program has been successful. For instance, proponents of peer mediation may decide that a specific peer-mediation program will be considered successful if it improves a school's climate. In such a case, evaluation is difficult because school climate is based on perception. Because perception has multiple facets, program evaluators would have to determine whose perception is important in this case. Evaluators would also have to determine how those perceptions would be measured. In other words, program evaluation is a complex process.

Benkofski and Heppner (1999) defined **program evaluation** as a process by which a "program's decision makers, recipients, funders, and/or managers want to determine whether a program is effective, to what degree, under what conditions, at what financial or social costs, and with what intentional or unintentional outcomes" (p. 490). According to Herman, Morris, and Fitz-Gibson (1987), there are four basic phases of program evaluation: (a) establishing boundaries for the evaluation, (b) determining methods of evaluation, (c) data collection and analysis, and (d) reporting the results.

Boundaries for Evaluation

Program evaluators must determine the overall objective of the evaluation process at the outset. Because many programs are funded by outside sources, measuring real success is essential for continuation of support. To begin this process, the evaluator must develop (a) an understanding of the history and current objectives of the program, (b) a strategic plan for the evaluation process, and (c) an agreement surrounding the range and cost of services provided with regard to the evaluation.

Methods of Evaluation

Best practices in program evaluation are well planned and focused. Comprehensive evaluation often involves examination of process and outcome. Aspects of **process evaluation** entail a focus on how programs are implemented and what factors affect the operation of the program. Process evaluation can be as simple as asking stakeholders open-ended questions in a structured interview format; however, development of effective questions is critical to the process. In an **outcome evaluation,** the overall effectiveness of the program is examined and a comparison is made to the program objectives.

Data Collection and Analysis

It is best if the data needed for a comprehensive program evaluation come from program participants, staff, and other stakeholders in the program; thus, evaluators often create separate questions to address the needs of the stakeholders and their relationship to the program. For example, an evaluation tool administered to program participants would likely contain questions related to the satisfaction with and perceived benefit from the program. Program staff may provide evaluation data relative to resource allocation, employee morale, and perceived benefit experienced by participants. In addition to collecting interview data, evaluators can learn a great deal from direct observation of program operations, review of program records, and any other materials the evaluator finds relevant. The program evaluator must consider all of these concerns in the development of data-collection procedures. Furthermore, the evaluator must have a plan for synthesizing the collected data and excluding extraneous and irrelevant information. A comprehensive plan for data analysis at the outset (e.g., frequency counts, mean scores, qualitative analysis, or parametric statistical analysis) helps guide the data-collection process.

Reporting the Results

Program evaluators have an ethical obligation to report accurate results, whether they are favorable or unfavorable to a specific program. It is important to note that although evaluations showing ineffective programs may create conflict, professional counselors should maintain a value-free approach toward providing results. Worthen, Sanders, and Fitzpatrick (1997) provided a guide for the development of a program evaluation report: The report should include (a) an executive summary, (b) an overview of the purpose and objectives of the evaluation as well as any limitations, (c) the specific focus of the evaluation, (d) procedures, (e) results, (f) conclusions and recommendations, (g) any responses to the report, and (h) appendixes.

Program evaluation is often needed to measure effectiveness and to validate ongoing financial support. More specifically, program evaluators are used to determine the usefulness and efficacy of a program in order to (a) adjust the program to meet the needs of the participants best and (b) secure or continue funding. Given these aims, program evaluators must consider who will benefit from the results of an evaluation and how such benefits will manifest.

Contributed by Carl J. Sheperis,
Mississippi State University, Starkville, MS,
and Donna S. Starkey,
Delta State University, Cleveland, MS

References

Benkofski, M., & Heppner, C. (1999). Program evaluation. In P. P. Heppner, D. M. Kivlighan Jr., & B. E. Wampold (Eds.), *Research design in counseling* (pp. 488–513). Belmont, CA: Wadsworth.

Herman, J., Morris, L., & Fitz-Gibbon, C. (1987). *Evaluator's handbook.* Newbury Park, CA: Sage.

Worthen, B., Sanders, J., & Fitzpatrick, J. (1997). *Program evaluation: Alternative approaches and practical guidelines.* White Plains, NY: Longman.

Additional Resources

Centers for Disease Control and Prevention. (n.d.). *Framework for program evaluation in public health*: Retrieved July 26, 2008, from http://www.cdc.gov/eval/framework.htm

Starkey, D. S., Nunnelly, R., & Sheperis, C. J. (2007). Program evaluations in peer helping: Essential steps. *Perspectives in Peer Programs, 20,* 116–121.

Wholey, J. S., Harty, H. P., & Newcomer, K. E. (2004). *Handbook of practical program evaluation.* San Francisco: Jossey-Bass.

■ Program Planning

Program planning focuses on the intentionality of the design and implementation of programs and/or services. Program planning addresses the appropriateness of the programs or services for the population being served and differs from strategic planning and long-range planning in that program planning is focused on articulating the details of how the program or service will be carried out and the expected outcomes.

Program planning is the process by which the need for the program, the conceptual model of the program, the processes, and the outcomes that the program is intended to have are used to document the impact and effects that the program has on the participants and larger community. It is through thoroughly clarifying why the program is needed, what type of activities are needed to accomplish the program goals, and what outcomes will be produced by the program that the program designers increase the likelihood that the programs or service will produce the specified outcomes and reach the goals set by the designers. In this process, the designer or designers use professional knowledge and skills, along with knowledge of the system in which the program will be embedded, to design a program that is contextually appropriate and is most likely to meet the needs of the target population. The designers of the program might include a variety of individuals, such as community members, who see the need for the program; however, usually the program designers are individuals such as mental health counselors, school guidance counselors, career counselors, or other individuals who are in the organization that is designing the program. Thus, a systematic approach to program planning produces the most effective planning process (Herr, Cramer, & Niles, 2004).

The program planning process (Herr et al., 2004; Rossi, Lipsey, & Freeman, 2004) consists of five stages: (a) the development of the program's rationale or mission statement, (b) statement of goals and objectives, (c) brainstorming potential program/service models and evaluating them for fit, (d) developing the method(s) for evaluating the program/service, and (e) developing an implementation plan.

Developing a program rationale/philosophy and mission statement (Stage 1) facilitates the grounding of the program appropriately within the context of the organization and community to be served. This process involves specifying the expectations and assumptions that the designer or designers have regarding "how things will be different" as a result of the implementation of the program. In addition to linking the program to the purpose of the larger institution, it provides the means for maintaining a similar direction among those engaged in providing and evaluating the program or service. The rationale or philosophy of the program is sometimes referred to as a conceptual framework for designing and implementing the program.

Often, activities such as conducting needs assessments, focus groups, or semistructured interviews with community leaders are used to obtain relevant information for developing or refining the program's philosophy and mission. In addition, research into available funding and resources can facilitate the development of a practical philosophy and mission.

Setting the goal for the program development activity helps to clarify the activities that need to be accomplished versus those that are beyond the scope of this project. If the boundaries of the program development activity are not clarified and agreed to, the project may veer off track. Is the goal of the program planning activity to refine an existing program, complement existing programs/services, or add a new direction to the larger organization? If the goal is to refine or complement, less consensus building within the organization or community is needed for successful development and implementation. If the goal is to add a new direction to the organization, consensus building among all stakeholders prior to and during the development will facilitate acceptance and utilization of the program. This work is facilitated through the use of an advisory board, which formally involves all relevant stakeholders in the design process.

Translating the philosophy and mission statements (Stage 2) into goals and objectives for the program or service involves specifying what it takes to achieve the mission statement and fulfill the philosophy specified in Stage 1. Once the designers have a clear picture of "how things will be different," it is possible to begin to identify the specific behaviors, attitudes, or knowledge that will change as a result of participation in the program/service. The application of theory and research on relevant interventions, programs, and outcomes is useful at this stage to identify appropriate and efficacious goals and objectives for the intended purpose. This is also the point at which boundaries of the program should be articulated. Because any organization has fiscal and other limits, programs should be designed with these in mind. Communities, likewise, have differing needs, goals, and limitations, which should be considered by the program designers in setting the boundaries for their program.

Specifically, goals are descriptions of midlevel changes that are to be expected from participation in the program. An example of a goal is "to improve the parenting skills of community members." On the other hand, behavioral objectives are statements about the expected behaviors that will occur as a result of participation in the program. Behavioral objectives are observable and, thus, can be described to others. An example of a behavioral objective is "the use of corporal punishment with 10-year-olds will be reduced by half within 2 weeks of completing the program." Behavioral objectives are used as the standard for measuring the success of the program and provide the basis for designing the evaluation of the program.

Once the conceptual framework is developed and goals and objectives are specified, selection of the process to be used to achieve the goals and objectives becomes the focus (Stage 3). The question being considered is, Given the specified goals and objectives, what processes or activities would best facilitate the successful attainment of the rationale, philosophy, and mission? This stage requires knowledge of the professional literature related to the program goals and knowledge of the context in which the program will be embedded. Once ideas have been generated, use of decision-making processes to evaluate the different options for efficiency, efficacy, appropriateness, and cost can facilitate the selection of the program process most likely to assist the organization in reaching its goals for the program.

The fourth stage, development of an evaluation design, builds on the previous work and enables the designers to know whether their program had the effect(s) intended. Evaluation of the activities and processes can assist in identifying why or how a program produced the results expected, or how it produced other, unexpected, results. Examples of methods for evaluating programs are rating forms, exit interviews, follow-up studies, observational studies, and opinion surveys. Five steps are involved in designing the evaluation: (a) clarify the identified goals and objectives; (b) select criterion measures; (c) establish expected performance levels; (d) identify program elements or goals/objectives that are to be evaluated by the specific evaluation process; (e) design the evaluation itself; and (f) collect, analyze, interpret, report, and use the data.

The fifth stage of the program planning process consists of developing a plan for implementing the program. This is often called setting milestones, because it facilitates the agreement among all parties involved regarding the effort and work it will take to implement the program or service. The milestones that are set remind the program designers to check to see that the program is functioning as intended. They are usually set at the points that certain tasks are accomplished or goals are met. For example, setting a date by which all arrangements for the program should be completed is a milestone that allows the designers to see if they allowed adequate planning time. Setting milestones can also be important in identifying situations that will alter the plans for implementing the program or service.

Contributed by Marie S. Hammond,
Tennessee State University, Nashville, TN

References

Herr, E. L., Cramer, S. H., & Niles, S. G. (2004). *Career guidance and counseling through the lifespan: Systematic approaches* (6th ed.). New York: Allyn & Bacon.

Rossi, P. H., Lipsey, M. W., & Freeman, H. E. (2004). *Evaluation: A systematic approach* (7th ed.). Thousand Oaks, CA: Sage.

■ Psychoanalysis

Psychoanalysis developed at the end of the 19th century as a result of the recognition that mental and emotional disorders may have psychological foundations. **Sigmund Freud** (1856–1939), considered to be the father of the psychoanalytical perspective, became familiar with August Liébeault's and Hippolyte Bernheim's work on hypnotism and hysteria under the tutelage of Jean Charcot. Freud, in collaboration with Josef Breuer, incorporated hypnosis into his clinical practice and hypothesized that powerful psychological processes that remain unconscious may manifest as mental and emotional disorders. Freud advanced his theory to include concepts that have become integral to the contemporary psychotherapy nomenclature. These include personality development; the Oedipal and Electra complexes; the preconscious, the conscious, and the unconscious; and transference and countertransference.

Personality Development: The Id, Ego, and Superego

Freud postulated that personality can be delineated into three major components, namely the id, ego, and superego. The interaction and integration of the components become manifest in the oral, anal, phallic, latency, and genital psychosexual stages (see Psychosexual Stages of Development).

The **id** is considered to be the genesis of personality and is an innate characteristic with which all babies are born. Freud postulated that the id is the structure from which the ego and superego later develop. The id operates entirely on the **pleasure principle.** The behavior is impulsive, selfish, and pleasure seeking and is directed toward the gratification of instinctual needs without morality or reality considerations. An example of the id's desire for instant gratification is a hungry infant who continues to cry even though it is evident that the caregiver is in the process of satisfying that need (e.g., preparing the feeding bottle).

The **ego** operates on the **reality principle.** As physical and cognitive development occurs, the rational and realistic aspect of personality begins to evolve. The ego mediates between the instinctual id drives and the demands of the external world and strives to meet the needs of the id by using reason and considering all aspects of a situation. A hungry child, under the direction of the ego, will stop throwing a tantrum when there is the cognition that the caregiver is in the process of preparing a meal to satisfy the instinctual drive. Through the mediation of the ego, the negative consequences of the demand for instant gratification are minimized and the realities of the external world recognized.

The Freudian perspective postulates that the superego is the final stage of personality development, operating on the **morality principle.** The **superego** (i.e., conscience) evolves through interactions with parents or caregivers who, in turn, are often the representatives of moral prescriptions of what is right and wrong in society. The superego is the inner control mechanism that monitors and addresses the unrestrained instinctual desires of the id. In essence, the id, ego, and superego, according to Freud, are the principle determinants of personality. The ego, also referred to as the executive branch of personality, mediates between the instinctual demands of the id, the realities of the external world, and the moral prescriptions of the superego.

Oedipus and Electra Complexes

According to Greek mythology, Oedipus kills his father and marries his mother. Freud hypothesized that during the phallic stage of development, the young boy becomes attracted to his mother and sees his father as a rival. This is referred to as the **Oedipus complex.** Because the father is in a more powerful position, the boy develops the fear that if his father discovers that the son has libidinal desires for his mother, the father will punish the son by excising his penis. The associated anxiety, also known as castration anxiety, causes the boy to suppress both his hostility toward his father and his sexual attraction toward his mother. Freud believed that if this stage of development is successfully completed, the child begins to identify with his father and develops a natural affection for his mother and directs his sexual energy toward other females.

In a similar vein, Freud formulated the **Electra complex** by using the Greek mythological character Electra, who wanted her brother to kill their mother Clytemnestra to avenge the death of her father. During the phallic stage of development, the daughter has a libidinal attraction toward her father and sees the mother as a rival. The hostility in this stage toward the mother develops as the result of physically identifying with her father and becoming envious of not having a penis. Penis envy, according to Freud, is resolved when the daughter begins to identify with the mother and realizes that someday she will become pregnant and the baby will become a penis substitute.

Unconscious, Preconscious, and Conscious

Freud proposed a model in which the mind is configured like an iceberg. The visible area is the conscious level of the mind, and the submerged area comprises the preconscious and the unconscious levels. Freud asserted that of the three levels of consciousness, a small percentage of experiences is at the conscious level, and most experiences are relegated to either the preconscious or unconscious levels.

The **conscious** level refers to the immediate awareness of emotions, thoughts, and behaviors that are easily and directly accessed thorough the sense perceptions. During a mental status examination, a professional counselor checks the conscious level of functioning by asking if the client is oriented to person, place, and time. If the client is well oriented, the client will be able to articulate without much thought his or her identity; the location; and the time, day, month, and year.

The **preconscious** level involves the information that is not conscious but is easily accessible and can be brought to the level of consciousness without much effort. This includes memories and individuals' general fund of knowledge. A professional counselor may prompt the client to reflect on what occurred since the last counseling session. If there is no cognitive impairment, the client can easily retrieve and share the information with the therapist. This is an example of information stored at the preconscious level.

The **unconscious** level refers to what is outside of people's conscious awareness and is the focus of psychoanalysis. The unconscious may be the repository for the thoughts and feelings that are too painful for an individual to endure. Freud asserted that the sublimation of fears, immoral desires, selfish needs, shame, traumatic experiences, dangerous impulses, and so forth did not cause them to disappear from the psyche but that they remained embedded in the unconscious. The material that is relegated to the unconscious may seek expression at the conscious level in the form of dreams, slips of the tongue, fantasies, and defense mechanisms. Defense mechanisms are considered to be the action of the ego to protect the individual from overwhelming anxiety and to create a manageable balance between the id and the superego. The primary function of ego defense mechanisms is to shift anxiety-provoking thoughts and emotions from the conscious to the unconscious. Some common ego defense mechanisms include denial, displacement, projection, rationalization, reaction formation, regression, repression, and sublimation. Freudian theorists posit that the unconscious material must be integrated at the conscious level through psychotherapy or else it will manifest as irrational or maladaptive behavior.

Transference and Countertransference

Transference refers to thoughts and feelings that are influenced by past relationships with parents and significant others and that the client projects onto the therapist. The client may reexperience positive or negative emotions from past relationships, such as love, rejection, criticism, hostility, and so forth, during therapy. Psychoanalysts identify issues of transference in the therapeutic relationship and work to address the emotions that may adversely affect the client's psychological functioning.

Countertransference refers to positive or negative thoughts and feelings that the therapist projects onto the client. It is recommended that therapists themselves undergo psychotherapy to work through "unfinished business" or work with a supervisor to identify and address issues of countertransference because it can affect the efficacy of the therapist and impede the therapeutic alliance.

Contributed by Yegan Pillay,
Ohio University, Athens, OH

Additional Resources

Craig, I. (2001). *Psychoanalysis: A critical introduction.* Oxford, United Kingdom: Blackwell.

Eidelberg, L. (1968). *Encyclopedia of psychoanalysis.* New York: Free Press.

Psychodrama

Psychodrama is an experiential psychotherapeutic intervention that uses action and role play in group settings to focus on the psychosocial concerns of participants. This method of group psychotherapy uses elements of theater to dramatize intrapersonal as well as interpersonal psychic dynamics. Psychodrama typically deals with the problems or concerns of an individual, whereas a related intervention, sociodrama, focuses on the problems or concerns of a group or society.

Psychodrama was conceptualized and developed by **Jacob Levy Moreno** (1889–1974) during the first half of the 20th century. Moreno was a psychiatrist and principal proponent of group psychotherapy in the earliest days of its development. He encouraged creativity and spontaneity, viewing them as essential sparks for successful group work (Blatner, 2000). The psychodrama method, considered by many as a type of group psychotherapy, was popularized in the second half of the 20th century and especially gained prominence in the 1980s.

The psychodrama event is composed of the following five elements: (a) the **stage** is the action area or physical space in which the drama is enacted; (b) the **protagonist** is the person or persons selected to represent the theme of enactment; (c) the **auxiliary egos** are the members of the group who assume the various significant roles in the drama; (d) the **audience** consists of the group members who witness the drama and also represent the larger world; and (e) the **director**, sometimes also referred to as the producer, is the trained psychodramatist who guides all actors, facilitates action, and adapts space to the needs of the players and their actions.

There are three distinct stages or phases of classical psychodrama. These are warm-up, action, and sharing. In more contemporary renditions of psychodrama, a fourth dynamic, processing, is often added. Processing is considered an extension of the sharing stage, but it contributes an interpretive or self-reflective dimension to the action.

In the **warm-up stage,** the group identifies a theme or problem area and selects a protagonist. The director typically uses these beginning-stage dynamics as a prelude for constructing the staged opportunity to externalize the internal psychodynamics of the problem. During this phase, the director stimulates and motivates participants toward dramatization of thematic concerns, with the eventual goal of identifying potential or alternative resolutions of the problem at hand.

During the **action stage,** the problem or concern is dramatized and acted out, the protagonist explores ways of resolving the core issue, and the director assigns roles to auxiliary egos to assist in the drama. At this time, the protagonist examines the identified issue through interaction with the director and the other actors. The director may use any of a number of dramatic techniques designed to focus deeper action on a particular dimension or dynamic of the articulated problem. These include **doubling** (i.e., an auxiliary ego is appointed by the director to stand with or behind the protagonist when the protagonist is having difficulty in the action or with the other actors), **role reversals** (i.e., the protagonist and an auxiliary ego play the role of one another), **mirrors** (i.e., the director has the protagonist stand aside or take a seat in the audience to observe an auxiliary ego assume the protagonist's role), **soliloquy** (i.e., the protagonist works through emotional difficulties and tension by airing inner thoughts and feelings), **empty chair** (i.e., the protagonist imagines the antagonist in an empty chair and interacts with the imaginary other), **magic shop** (i.e., either the director or an auxiliary ego takes on the role of proprietor of a magic shop, then confronts the protagonist with the offer of anything the protagonist may want in exchange for something highly valued by the protagonist), and **sociometry** (i.e., a research method for examining social relationships within groups).

The **sharing stage** occurs after the dramatization, when group members are invited to express the ways in which they have connected with the drama. Group sharing and subsequent processing offer opportunities for making meaning of the action, drawing insights about the situation and its context, discovering a new understanding of the problem, and illuminating multiple potential resolutions.

Psychodrama has been used throughout the world to focus on a variety of personal, interpersonal, and social problems, thus enabling exploration of past, present, and future life events. Common interventions have assisted individuals with exploring issues associated with trauma, grief, addictions, and relationships. Psychodrama recently has been used successfully in the treatment of depression.

Contributed by Lisa Lopez Levers,
Duquesne University, Pittsburgh, PA

Reference

Blatner, A. (2000). *Foundations of psychodrama: History, theory, and practice* (4th ed.). New York: Springer.

Additional Resources

Dayton, T. (2004). *The living stage: A step-by-step guide to psychodrama, sociometry and group psychotherapy.* Deerfield Beach, FL: HCI.

Karp, M., Holmes, P., & Tauvon, K. B. (Eds.). (1998). *The handbook of psychodrama.* New York: Routledge.

Wilkins, P. (1999). *Psychodrama.* Thousand Oaks, CA: Sage.

Yablonsky, L. (1981). *Psychodrama: Resolving emotional problems through role-playing.* New York: Gardner Press.

■ Psychosexual Stages of Development

One of **Sigmund Freud**'s contributions to the field of personality psychology was his theory of personality development. Freud believed that all children go through a series of biologically predetermined stages in the development of their personalities. Each stage is associated with an erogenous zone of the body. Stimulation of the erogenous zone allows for sexual gratification at a particular stage. Each stage also has a **psychosexual crisis** that must be satisfactorily resolved in order for the individual to go on to the next stage. If the individual is unable to resolve the crisis at a particular stage, he or she will become fixated at that stage.

Fixation occurs when a portion of the individual's libido remains behind in one of the psychosexual stages. Freud believed that all people have life instincts or Eros. The life instincts are people's instincts to grow and live. The psychic energy that comes from the life instincts is **libido.** When a portion of that energy is left behind in an earlier stage of development, the person is said to be fixated at that earlier stage. Fixation may occur because the child's needs are not satisfactorily met by the parents or because overindulgent parents have excessively gratified the child at a particular stage. Fixation at a particular stage results in the development of adult character types associated with that stage.

The first stage is the **oral stage,** which begins at birth and lasts until approximately age 2 years. The erogenous zone at this stage is the mouth. All pleasure is obtained through biting, sucking, and chewing. The conflict at this stage is the weaning of the child from the breast or the bottle. If children are weaned too early, they will be frustrated in terms of their need for oral satisfaction. If children are allowed to suckle too long at the breast or bottle, their need for oral satisfaction will be overindulged. In either case, the result will be fixation.

If the child becomes fixated at the oral stage, a portion of the libido remains in the oral stage of development. This will result in adult oral character types. The **oral-passive personality** occurs when the child is frustrated in attempts to suckle in the first 8 months of life. This adult character type is dependent and pursues oral gratification through eating, drinking, and smoking. The child is trying to make up for the gratification missed out on in infancy. The **oral-aggressive personality** is also due to the child being weaned too early. In this case though, the child is not allowed to chew and bite to satisfaction. This adult will usually want to chew on things (e.g., pencils, finger nails). Adults with oral-aggressive personality can also be sarcastic and verbally aggressive.

The second stage of psychosexual development is the **anal stage.** This stage lasts from approximately age 2 years to age 3 years. The erogenous zone now shifts from the mouth to the anus. The chief source of pleasure during this time is the retention or expulsion of feces. The primary conflict that must be dealt with is toilet training. If toilet training is too permissive and relaxed or, alternatively, too harsh and punitive, then a portion of the libido will be left in the anal stage, and the child will become fixated at this stage.

Fixation at the anal stage results in adult anal character types. If children are overindulged and parents have a permissive style of toilet training, the child will develop the **anal expulsive personality.** As adults, these individuals tend to be generous, messy, and disorganized. They can also be destructive and cruel. If the parents are punitive in their toilet training, the child may try to hold in his or her feces, thus, becoming constipated. This results in the **anal retentive personality.** The anal retentive personality tends to be a perfectionist, overly concerned with cleanliness, and stingy.

The third psychosexual stage is the **phallic stage.** During this stage, the erogenous zone shifts from the anus to the genitals. Children begin to explore their own genitals; they become aware of the physical differences between boys and girls. The conflict for little boys during this stage is the **Oedipus complex,** which is based on the Greek myth of Oedipus Rex who killed his father and unknowingly married his mother. The young boy during this stage unconsciously wishes to possess his mother as a sexual partner and to kill his father who is the primary rival for his mother's affections. Over time, the boy begins to worry that his father will figure out his intentions and will seek revenge. The boy develops **castration anxiety.** He believes that his father will punish him by cutting off his penis. Soon the castration anxiety becomes so great that the boy, out of fear, learns to repress his desires for his mother and identify with his father. This signals the successful resolution of the Oedipal complex.

Although the Oedipal complex is the conflict faced by boys in the phallic stage, girls must deal with the Electra complex. The **Electra complex** is named after the Greek myth of Electra who had her brother kill her mother and her mother's lover as revenge for the murder of her father. According to Freud, the young girl notices she does not have a penis and wonders why. She holds her mother responsible for her lack of a penis. Over time, she develops **penis envy;** that is, she wants her own penis. She grows to resent her mother who has deprived her of a penis, and she wants to possess her father sexually because he has a penis. Eventually, she comes to realize that the only way she can have a penis is to grow up and have a male baby. She represses her desires for her father and begins to identify with her mother.

Unresolved Oedipal and Electra complexes result in adult phallic character types that do not have names associated with them. Men with **phallic character types** tend to be boastful, brash, and hypermasculine. This behavior may be due to the man compensating for castration anxiety. Women with phallic character types tend to be vain, self-centered, and promiscuous. They may be trying to compensate for penis envy.

The **latency period** follows the phallic stage. This period lasts from about 5 years of age to puberty. During this period, sexuality is dormant. Freud believed that during this time the sexual drive is channeled into activities such as schoolwork, same-sex friendships, sports, and so forth.

The final stage is the **genital stage.** The genital stage starts at puberty and ends at death. During this stage, the individual stops sexual activity directed toward the self (i.e., masturbation) and begins to pursue sexual relationships with members of the opposite sex. The healthy adult is able to obtain satisfaction in both love and work, according to Freud.

Contributed by Wanda C. McCarthy,
University of Cincinnati–
Clermont College, Batavia, OH

Additional Resources

Feist, J., & Feist, G. J. (2006). *Theories of personality* (6th ed.). New York: McGraw-Hill.

Freud, S. (1925). An autobiographical study. In J. Strachey (Ed. and Trans.), *The standard edition of the complete psychological works of Sigmund Freud* (Vol. 20, pp. 3–70). London: Hogarth Press.

■ *Publication Manual of the American Psychological Association*

The *Publication Manual of the American Psychological Association* (American Psychological Association, 2001) had its beginnings in a 1928 meeting of anthropological and psychological editors and business managers who gathered under the sponsorship of the National Research Council to create instructions for authors writing journal manuscripts. These instructions were intended to provide a set of standards that authors could use as guidelines for easy reference rather than a set of obligatory rules. The seven-page report from that initial meeting was published in 1929 in the *Psychological Bulletin* and was the predecessor for the *Publication Manual.*

The first formal edition of the *Publication Manual* came in 1952 when the aforementioned instructions were revised and published as a 60-page supplement to the *Psychological Bulletin* and given the title *Publication Manual.* The *Publication Manual* has been revised and expanded five times, with the most recent revision in 2001 at 439 pages.

Information in the *Publication Manual* is useful for students writing papers for academic course work and for those writing manuscripts for publication. For students, the manual serves as a guide for academic writing. It provides information on a variety of topics, including writing style, grammar, punctuation, spelling, capitalization, abbreviations, quotations, and the creation of bibliographies and reference pages. For advanced students working on theses and dissertations, details about final manuscript preparation are included. For those students who have already completed a dissertation, the manual highlights methods that may be used to convert parts of a dissertation into an academic journal article.

The *Publication Manual* also includes instructions for writers preparing manuscripts for academic journals. These instructions include particulars about title pages, references, appendixes, indentation, page numbering, margins, and placement of tables and figures in a document. A checklist that authors can use to review their manuscripts one final time prior to final submission is also included in the manual. Once a manuscript is accepted for publication the manual may also be useful because it defines how to address copyrights, permissions, and reprints.

The American Counseling Association uses the *Publication Manual* as a guideline for its authors to review when creating manuscripts for its academic journals. Counseling programs in higher education institutions also use the *Publication Manual* as a guideline for students to follow when writing academic papers because the manual prepares students to write in the academic style used throughout the counseling profession.

Contributed by April K. Heiselt,
Mississippi State University, Starkville, MS

Reference

American Psychological Association. (2001). *Publication manual of the American Psychological Association* (5th ed.). Washington, DC: Author.

Qualitative Research

Qualitative researchers approach their questions of the human experience in an interpretive and naturalistic manner, providing counseling researchers with powerful tools of inquiry. Qualitative examinations of a problem are distinguished by their **inductive approach,** in which researchers immerse themselves in data in the process of allowing more general themes to emerge from the data. The researcher enters the **naturalistic setting** of the participants in order to capture the essence of their experiences. Table 1 provides basic characteristics of qualitative research.

Qualitative Research Traditions

Qualitative research approaches (e.g., grounded theory, ethnography, phenomenology, case study, biography, partici-

patory action research) have emerged from the disciplines of anthropology, linguistics, and sociology as a critical scientific inquiry focusing on social and human issues. The overarching goal of qualitative research is to understand a phenomenon within the context of a study, which makes qualitative work particularly applicable for multicultural and social justice research. Qualitative research is distinguished from quantitative studies by its emphasis on and value of the researcher's interpretation and description of a topic of inquiry rather than an emphasis on numerical data. Choosing a research tradition to guide a qualitative study is an important decision that should best fit the phenomenon under examination (Creswell, 2003).

Grounded theory is the rigorous approach to a scientific problem with the aim of identifying a theory of a phenomenon (Strauss & Corbin, 1998). For instance, the aim of a grounded theory study may be to generate a theory of how counselor trainees infuse multicultural counseling competencies into their work with clients in their clinical work. The primary investigator may choose to enter the field, or the site where counselor trainees are practicing, in order to gather data about this phenomenon. Data collection may include interviews with the counselor trainees, which are then transcribed in order to begin a coding process that would identify themes in the study. This type of grounded theory study may use constant comparison for data analysis, which involves checking new data collected against a codebook that lists categories of data previously collected. This process continues until the data reach a saturation point where there are no new categories of data identified in the data analysis. Constant comparison data analysis allows a grounded theory study to consolidate the essence of the emerging theory.

Ethnography differs from grounded theory in that the researcher interprets observations of a cultural group in order to document, understand, and convey their experience holistically. This research tradition typically involves immersion in the field, with the researcher having prolonged engagement with the culture studied. For example, a counselor researcher might participate in an immersion experience in a rural setting in the South with the aim of understanding how residents in this setting view mental health. With the goal of describing a Southern, rural framework of counseling services, the researcher might choose to interview key stakeholders or informants in a community mental health agency in addition to gathering data from people seeking mental health services. The goal of the data collection and analysis would be to give

Table 1. Basic Characteristics of Qualitative Research

Research Tradition	Data Collection	Data Analysis	Validity Issues
Grounded theory	Interviews	Constant comparison, saturation of data	Researcher bias, negative case analysis
Ethnography	Participant observation, prolonged engagement	Holistic description and interpretation of phenomenon	Interpretation of researcher, reflexivity
Phenomenology	Interviews	Horizontalization of data	Bracketing of researcher assumptions
Case study	Interviews with key stakeholders, participant observation, archival data	Description of phenomenon	Negative case analysis, triangulation of data sources
Biography/life history	Interviews, archival data, and stories	Holistic description of life stages and/or cultural context of individual(s)	Acknowledgement of how researcher worldview shapes story
Participatory action research	Interviews with key stakeholders, participant observation	Open coding, recursive research design with built-in evaluative process	Researcher bias, inclusion of key stakeholders, member checking, triangulation of data and researchers

a holistic view of the cultural components of Southern, rural mental health, which may also entail the researcher describing other sociopolitical factors (e.g., history of the region, politics, religion) that play a role in the cultural phenomenon. Ethnographies are often found in the form of narratives or books, describing the phenomenon and its related parts in detail so that an overall image emerges for readers.

Phenomenology is similar to ethnography in that there is an emphasis on understanding and describing a phenomenon; however, phenomenological approaches differ from ethnographical approaches in that the goal of the research is to describe the essence of the study participants' daily, lived experiences of a phenomenon from the participants' unique point of view. In order to detail the essence of the experience of a phenomenon, researchers must carefully select participants who have experienced the phenomenon in order to have information-rich cases to describe. For instance, a phenomenology seeking to understand the experiences of women in same-sex relationships who have survived intimate partner violence would entail researchers collecting data directly from this population. Researchers would continuously identify their assumptions about women in same-sex relationships who have experienced intimate partner violence in order to identify researcher bias, which is called **bracketing** in phenomenology (Moustakas, 1994). Data collection and analysis methods may be similar to grounded theory data collection in that data may be gathered in the form of interviews, and an open coding process is used to identify categories of meaning for those who have experienced the phenomenon. This process is called **horizontalization,** which is followed by a process of narrowing these categories further into a structural description of the phenomenon. Ultimately, the phenomenological researcher aims to describe the lived experiences of the population studied, while paying careful attention to how researcher bias affects this description.

In **case study** approaches, researchers use archival information, interviews, and other artifacts to obtain a holistic understanding of an individual, event, or program, and case study approaches may involve the examination of single or multiple cases. For instance, a researcher may examine how an Asian American family with a child with a learning disability navigates its way through the school system. In this case, the researcher may gather data through interviews with the individual student, family members, teachers, counselors, and/or school administrators in order to elucidate an overall understanding of the family's experience of using services. The researcher may choose to examine archival data regarding the student and family (e.g., grades, behavioral assessments, parent–teacher meetings) in order to portray a full description of the case. A common challenge to case study research is to decide what limits the researcher will place on the amount of data gathered, the time used to collect data, and the types of data required to describe the case in a meaningful manner (Stake, 1995).

Case study research differs from a **biography** in that a case study focuses on the experiences of one or more individuals (deceased or living). This research may be written by a person about his or her own life (autobiography) or by another person who documents the story of a person. A biography is called a "life history" when it examines the cultural context of a person's life in addition to the individual experiences (Creswell, 2003). In this case, the researchers would gather stories of an individual's life stages while simultaneously documenting the historical context of these accounts. It is common in biographical research for investigators to recognize the role they have in constructing the narrative. For instance, a biography in counseling might include historical accounts of the life stages of a major figure in the field of counseling, whereas a life history would not only gather the account of the milestones in the person's life but also describe the cultural context of the person's life (e.g., sociopolitical forces, race/ethnicity, gender).

Finally, **participatory action research (PAR)** is a qualitative approach in which the data collection and analysis stages guide decision making about interventions. In PAR, existing theory and research about a phenomenon guide the formation of a new theory that is specific to a certain study, location, population, or context, and PAR involves using key stakeholders as integral to the research process. PAR is designed not only to understand a system or phenomenon but also to use key stakeholders in the community throughout the research process. For instance, a PAR study may examine ways to increase community involvement in an urban area. The PAR researcher would initially identify the key stakeholders in this community, including leaders, counselors in the mental health system, and consumers, in order to define the course of the study. The researcher then creates intentional space for the key stakeholders to generate the research questions and plan for data collection and analysis. Because change of systems is the goal of PAR and the research process, it is critical for researchers to build in methods of evaluation and feedback throughout the research process and at the end of the inquiry.

Data Collection, Data Analysis, and Validity Issues

The qualitative research tradition that is selected guides data collection and analysis. Qualitative data are typically words, rather than numbers, and may be collected in the form of interviews, observations, and unobtrusive measures (see Qualitative Research: Data Collection Methods). **Field notes** are used to document a researcher's experience in the field and may include researcher observation, researcher bias, conversations with stakeholders, and other information gathered in the natural setting that contributes to the understanding of participants' experiences. The qualitative research process is often **recursive** in nature, with the research questions, data collection, and data analysis stages informing one another.

Qualitative data analysis focuses on allowing the essence of the human experience or problem to emerge from the words or participants through a process of consensus **coding,** in which overarching themes are identified using multiple researchers examining the same data (see Qualitative Research: Data Management and Analysis). Validity issues or limitations in establishing **trustworthiness** are particularly important in qualitative research (see Trustworthiness in Qualitative Research). For example, researchers use a variety of tools (e.g., reflexive journal, auditors, peer debriefing, member checking) to examine and identify researcher bias and how this subjectivity shapes the research process. In the presentation of the results of a qualitative study, researchers may include a thick description of the participants' words so that readers may gain a holistic understanding of participants' experiences.

Contributed by Anneliese A. Singh,
The University of Georgia, Athens, GA

References

Creswell, J. W. (2003). *Research design: Qualitative, quantitative, and mixed methods approaches* (2nd ed.). Thousand Oaks, CA: Sage.

Moustakas, C. (1994). *Phenomenological research methods.* Thousand Oaks, CA: Sage.

Stake, R. (1995). *The art of case study research.* Thousand Oaks, CA: Sage.

Strauss, A. L., & Corbin, J. (1998). *Basics of qualitative research: Techniques and procedures for developing grounded theory* (2nd ed.). Thousand Oaks, CA: Sage.

Additional Resource

Lincoln, Y., & Guba, E. (2006). Paradigmatic controversies, contradictions, and emerging confluences. In N. H. Denzin & Y. S. Lincoln (Eds.), *Handbook of qualitative research* (pp. 163–188). Thousand Oaks, CA: Sage.

■ Qualitative Research: Data Collection Methods

Applying **qualitative data collection methods** represents one phase of a larger research process, and methods should be concordant with the design of the study and its theoretical framework. Creswell (2007) emphasized that qualitative data collection is not a discrete and separate task but rather, "a series of interrelated activities aimed at gathering good information to answer emerging research questions" (p. 118). He described a data collection circle, illustrating a progression from earlier through later activities as points on a circle; these include locating the site or individual(s), gaining access and establishing rapport, purposeful sampling, collecting data, recording information, resolving field issues, and storing data. Each of these activities has inherent challenges associated with it, and each requires researchers to make context-related decisions. This is an area in which qualitative and quantitative paradigms differ greatly; the use of qualitative methods is not nearly as formulaic as quantitative methods and, therefore, necessitates many decisions on the part of the qualitative researcher and requires that the researcher be well-grounded in the theories that frame the inquiry.

Qualitative data collection methods cover a broad spectrum of research strategies or traditions, representing an array of theoretical perspectives across disciplines (see Qualitative Research). The same or similar data collection strategies may be used across various research designs, but they may be used very differently, depending on the methodological and theoretical framework of a particular study.

General challenges that exist across the continuum of qualitative data collection strategies include challenges pertaining to data interpretation and data management. The data collection methods most commonly used by qualitative researchers in the professional counseling field include various types of interviews, a continuum of observation strategies, and unobtrusive measures. These qualitative data collection methods are described briefly in this entry.

Interviews

One of the most widely used methods for collecting data in qualitative investigations is the **interview**. An interview may take the form of any of the following: the individual or key informant interview, the community interview, and the focus group interview. Interview protocols are structured to range from more close-ended to more open-ended questioning strategies. An **open interview** is one that is completely unstructured, having no standardized wording or order of questions or discussion points; it allows the interviewer maximum flexibility to engage interviewees conversationally, illuminating points of interest as they emerge. A semi-structured interview is more or less structured to follow a predetermined set of questions or probes, but wording can remain flexible; the interviewer may answer questions and may add or delete questions or probes between interviews. A **structured interview** is formal and adheres to the exact language and order of protocol questions and probes; the interviewer may not answer or clarify questions and may not add spontaneous points of discussion or change the order of questions or probes. Because interviews and focus groups are susceptible to personal bias, both on the part of the researcher and the participant, it behooves the qualitative researcher to undertake rigorous means for demonstrating trustworthiness, a construct that is parallel to the reliability and validity measures necessitated in statistical research. The following methods for capturing data are commonly used during interview or focus group sessions, depending on the setting: personal notes taken by the interviewer, formal interview data recording sheets, nonparticipant observer notes, "public" remarks taken on newsprint or white board by a selected recorder, audiorecorded materials, and videorecorded data. These data-capturing techniques may be used individually or in any methodologically appropriate combination. The use of reflexive personal memos and field notes, constructed by the researcher before, after, or between interviews or focus group sessions, is an enormously helpful way to capture data as well. Depending on the design of a particular inquiry, the interview may be the primary source for data collection, it may supplement another primary method for collecting data, or it may be used as one of several methods in a multimethod study.

Individual or Key Informant Interviews

In the case of the individual or **key informant interview,** persons who are knowledgeable about or have a unique perspective on the research topic are typically selected for an interview. In the designs of most qualitative investigations, individual interviews are planned as in-depth inquiries into the subject at hand; as such, it is not unusual for interviews to range from 1 to 2 hours or longer. Decisions regarding the number of interviews (from a sample of one for a case study, for example, to a small sample for an ethnographic or phenomenological study) and the selection process (e.g., purposeful vs. snowball sampling) are dependent on the research design. Interviewees are asked to respond to questions, probes, or discussion points presented by the interviewer. Questions tend to be less rigid or fixed; the degree to which the interview protocol is structured, semistructured, or open-ended depends largely on the theoretical design of the investigation. For the most part, qualitative interviews tend to be conversational in tone; after establishing rapport, the interviewer intends to elicit detailed information or greater elaboration from the interviewee about the interviewee's experience, perception, opinion, attitude, thinking, feeling, reaction, or recommendation regarding the topic or phenomenon.

Community Interviews

Sometimes the nature of a research question necessitates interviewing a group or community of people together. The community interview shares many elements with the individual interview. **Community interviews** are often used in community-based participatory research and other collaborative types of studies that involve higher levels of interactions between researchers and community stakeholders. A major aim is to engage community members in meaningful ways so that local knowledge can be used to address or resolve a specific problem, for example, one related to a health concern. Community interviews typically are held as public events that are open to all community members. The community interview is strategically similar to that of the individual or key informant interview; the researcher follows a predetermined protocol process, questioning and probing stakeholders regarding the problem at hand. Whereas the individual interview is defined typically in terms of one-to-one interaction, the community interview may, however, require multiple researchers and greater logistical management, due to potentially higher numbers of participants. A community interview can, at least theoretically, involve an entire community or selected segments of the community. Because community interviews are often conducted in naturalistic settings, they offer greater ecological validity.

Focus Groups

Although many people have associated focus groups primarily with research in marketing and advertising, some of the earliest uses of focus groups were among social scientists prior to and during World War II (Morgan, 1998). The use of **focus groups** for collecting qualitative data has reemerged in the social sciences and has recently become a more widely used methodology among counseling researchers. Typically, the qualitative researcher assembles a group of people for the purpose of directed or focused discussion about particular interests, knowledge, or experiences that are associated with the study. Focus groups commonly include 6 to 12 participants, although there are varying opinions about the ideal size of a focus group, and the size can be adjusted to match the nature and demands of the study. Focus groups are frequently held in more natural settings than individual interviews, thus often allowing for meaningful observation. As with individual and community interviews, the researcher has developed a protocol, which includes relevant questions and probes, in order to lay the groundwork for a well-planned focus group; however, the role of the researcher in a focus group is more that of a moderator or facilitator than that of an interviewer. Although the difference in roles may be subtle in some instances, the focus group researcher relies on the synergistic effects of group dynamics to obtain rich data from the members of the focus group. This latter point suggests that counseling researchers, who by virtue of their training in group work, already possess relevant skills for using this data collection strategy.

Observations

Observations, as performed in qualitative data collection, represent a continuum of activities, from complete nonparticipation by the researcher to full participation with the coresearcher(s). This form of data collection is also frequently referred to as **participant observation,** and the level of participation by the researcher is dependent on the design of the inquiry. Although one methodology might require the researcher to observe participants from behind a two-way mirror, other methodologies, such as participatory action research or dramaturgy, might require a much higher degree of involvement or participation with coresearchers. Some qualitative researchers prepare a protocol or observation rubric prior to the observation event. This is a printed form, with designated areas for anticipated information and space for both participant data and researcher notes. Other qualitative researchers may elect to rely on less formal mechanisms than a predesigned rubric to capture their observations by making copious field notes; these commonly include observer comments, analytic notes, reflections, field journals, photographs, audio or video recordings, drawings, and diagrams.

Unobtrusive Measures

Unobtrusive means of data collection are usually passive rather than dynamic, and they include all types of textual and archival data. Although textual data are often construed as exclusively meaning the written word, in qualitative paradigms, all types of written, visual, and audio formats can be considered as text; these may include traditional archival data, such as books and journal articles, but also may include films, videos, television programming, all types of artifacts, computer-generated texts and graphics, and Internet blogs (Web logs). Inquiries using unobtrusive measures frequently are of a historical nature and often involve public archives. An ethnographic content analysis of films may be used, for example, to investigate the cultural stereotypes associated with portrayals of psychiatric disabilities (e.g., Levers, 2001). Such an unobtrusive strategy is an inventive means of investigation and represents a legitimate method for counseling researchers to access socially and culturally relevant questions, as long as the strategy is congruent with the identified research design and the theoretical framework of the inquiry.

Contributed by Lisa Lopez Levers,
Duquesne University, Pittsburgh, PA

References

Creswell, J. W. (2007). *Qualitative inquiry and research design: Choosing among five approaches* (2nd ed.). Thousand Oaks, CA: Sage.

Levers, L. L. (2001). Representations of psychiatric disability in fifty years of Hollywood film: An ethnographic content analysis. *Theory and Science Pedagogy, 2*. Retrieved August 22, 2007, from http://theoryandscience.icaap.org/content/vol002.002/lopezlevers.html

Morgan, D. L. (1998). *The focus group guidebook.* Thousand Oaks, CA: Sage.

Additional Resources

Berg, B. L. (2006). *Qualitative research methods for the social sciences* (6th ed.). Boston: Allyn & Bacon.

Fischer, C. (Ed.). (2006). *Qualitative research methods for the psychological professions.* New York: Elsevier Press.

Glesne, C. (2006). *Becoming qualitative researchers: An introduction.* Boston: Allyn & Bacon.

Van Manen, M. (1997). *Researching lived experience: Human science for an action sensitive pedagogy.* New York: State University of New York Press.

Qualitative Research: Data Management and Analysis

Qualitative data are produced from various sources and produce a large volume of information for the counseling researcher to decipher in addressing a larger research question. One of the salient characteristics of qualitative research is that data are collected and analyzed concurrently. This process creates a need for thick description of incoming data, organization and management of the data, and continuous exploration of emerging themes and patterns. Often, textual documents are created and then analyzed through a process called content analysis.

Content Analysis

Content analysis is a systematic, objective, and theory-guided approach that researchers use to abstract and reduce the information collected. Through content analysis, the text of the documents is turned into the findings of the study. These findings are then used to construct theoretical or meaningful concepts. While collecting and analyzing data, qualitative analysts constantly compare emerging data and theory with data previously analyzed. This is known as **constant comparative analysis,** or constant comparison. The analysis is best maximized through the process of triangulation. **Triangulation,** the active search for codes that either build or refute theory, allows comparisons to be made among multiple data sources (i.e., participants), methods (e.g., interviews, observations), researchers, and theories.

Depending on the qualitative research practice (e.g., biography, phenomenology, grounded theory, ethnography, case study), content analysis is used to sort out, usually through a coding process or other means of delineation, the themes, patterns, categories, and/or meanings of both the apparent and hidden content of the text being analyzed.

Coding and Pattern Analysis of Qualitative Data

Qualitative methods produce a wealth of raw data. Two key analytic methods used in qualitative analysis for reducing raw data into broader themes and categories are **coding** and **pattern analysis. Coding** is a process that assists in the development of counselor theory by revealing and examining behaviors and emotions, psychosocial phenomena, and meanings that are given to events. This type of information can aid professional counselors in understanding the human experience. Generally, the coding process is driven by the research design and question or questions. A number of different types of coding can be done, and usually coding is a three-part process involving open, axial, and selective coding.

The first step in the coding process is **open coding.** Open coding breaks down the information collected into themes, categories, or units. Because open coding is unfocused, many categories will be identified during the open-coding process. In open coding, the data can be examined and compared line by line, sentence by sentence, paragraph by paragraph, or interview by interview.

The second step is **axial coding.** Axial coding builds connections among themes, categories, and subcategories that were identified during open coding. This process can lead to the establishment of a core category to which most or all of the data relate. During the axial coding process, the analyst looks for clues in the text that indicate connections and alliances between the data categories, units, or themes. These connections answer the who, what, where, and how of the phenomenon under study. Axial coding adds depth and structure to the analysis.

The finishing process is **selective coding.** Selective coding is the final analysis of the data. This is a process of evidencing those connecting relationships among data. The core category can be viewed as the "plot" or "storyline." Evidencing the relationship of the categories authenticates the story the researcher presents. These connecting relationships are substantiated through the existing data from the study and through triangulating the findings with similar studies found in the literature. This validation of relationships allows the analyst to develop and then state theory in the form of a proposition or hypothesis.

Pattern analysis focuses on identifying the repetition of ideas, actions, and emotional content as related to a specific phenomenon. For example, in Richards and Marquez's (2005) study of counseling clients with HIV, counselors reported feeling inadequate when counseling clients who were affected by or infected with HIV. To understand patterns of emotional experience and understand the phenomenon of counselor feelings of inadequacy with clients affected by or infected with HIV, data were examined for both concrete and abstract expressions of inadequacy related to counseling these clients.

Qualitative Data Management

Whether using coding, pattern analysis, or some other qualitative analytical process, there are ways of organizing and exploring information sources related to the study. This exploration and assembling of all information sources can assist in the analysis process and help to establish the **trustworthiness** of the data. For example, reviewing both contact summary sheets and document summary forms and displaying the data in various visual forms can assist in the analysis of the data.

Contact summary sheets contain information such as the date, time, and place of interview; context of occurrence; and summary of observations about the experience. Contact sheets can also be used to record flashes of insight, perceived ways forward, and any ideas that strike the researcher during the contact period. These sheets allow researchers to refresh their memories about a particular contact or thoughts about the contact. Such insights can later assist in the analysis of the data. Contact sheets can also provide information to others that will allow them to gain an understanding of the contact experience and preliminary impressions of the researcher.

Document summary forms summarize and synthesize the content of qualitative documents. These forms help the researcher to grasp content, themes, and meanings derived from analysis of the document. Document summary forms can also be used to compare and contrast data from documents from other projects and assist in constant comparative analysis.

Data displays are a way of organizing the data so that patterns and interrelationships between pieces of data can become more evident and core categories can be discerned. There are many forms of data displays, such as case comparison charts, diagrams, flowcharts, event mapping, tables, and matrices. These displays can be used to compare perceptions and responses to events; to identify both similarities and differences of cases under study; to see if, and understand how, two or more variables interact; and even to understand the analyst's reasoning process.

Qualitative Data Analysis Software

Qualitative data analysis (QDA) software is a tool for managing, coding, editing, and storing qualitative data. QDA programs allow the analyst either to prestructure the coding process, eliminating manual coding when appropriate to do so, or to code the data manually and then sort and group the data by using the data analysis software. QDA software does not interpret the data, but it can make the analysis process easier and possibly quicker. There are both advantages and disadvantages to using QDA software, and an analyst would need to become familiar with the qualities and abilities of various data analysis programs and decide whether to code manually or use a software program.

When choosing a QDA program, analysts need to consider a number of issues, including the type(s) of data they have and then decide the type of program they need. For example, EZ-text is a free QDA program produced by the Centers for Disease Control and Prevention (CDC). The program is used to analyze semistructured data and can be downloaded from the CDC Web site. The Qualitative Solutions and Research NVivo7 can manage most types of textual data so coding can be either structured or more flexible for data-rich documents. Multiple researchers at multiple sites can work on their own copies of the project and then merge their copies to create a final project document. The Atlas.ti program allows for more creativity in coding than most other software and can process text, audio, and visual data. It can also assist in visualized thinking and can be used with unstructured data. Multiple researchers can also use the program, but they have to work on the same copy. Most QDA software has a free trial version that can be downloaded from the maker's Web site.

Contributed by Kimberly A. M. Richards, HIV/AIDS Counseling Research Group, Centers for Disease Control, Zimbabwe

Reference

Richards, K. A., & Marquez, J. (2005). Experiences of HIV/AIDS counselors in Zimbabwe and their perceptions on the state of HIV/AIDS counseling in Zimbabwe. *International Journal for the Advancement of Counseling, 27,* 411–428.

Additional Resources

Centers for Disease Control and Prevention Web site: http://www.cdc.gov

Creswell, J. W. (1998). *Qualitative inquiry and research design: Choosing among five traditions.* Thousand Oaks, CA: Sage.

Denzin, N. K., & Lincoln, Y. S. (1998). *Strategies of qualitative inquiry.* Thousand Oaks, CA: Sage.

Qualitative Data Analysis Software: http://www.atlasti.com/ (Atlas.ti); http://www.cdc.gov/hiv/software/ez-text.htm (Ez Text); http://sophia.smith.edu/~jdrisko/qdasoftw.htm (QDA software); or http://www.qsr.com.au/ (QSR).

Strauss, A., & Corbin, J. (1998). *Basics of qualitative research* (2nd ed.). Thousand Oaks, CA: Sage.

◼ Quantitative Research

Quantitative research is a method of inquiry that answers questions or tests theories containing numerically measurable characteristics. Quantitative research's identifiable characteristics include variables, research design, hypotheses, and statistical significance. All quantitative studies are rule governed and deductive and use numerical representation of the data. A target population, sometimes known as the sampling frame, is a group of individuals with some common, definitive characteristic of interest to the researcher. Quantitative research's overarching goal is to measure results from a sample that can then be generalized to the target population, being able to do so also involves an appropriate sampling strategy. Meeting this goal requires the researcher to defend the believability of the sample from the population that was studied.

There are essentially two broad categories of sampling: probability and nonprobability. **Probability sampling** ensures that each individual in a known target population has an equal probability of being selected, and, therefore, the results of the study may be generalized to the population from which the sample was drawn. Probability sampling strategies include simple random, stratified random, systematic random, and multistage cluster sampling. **Nonprobability samples** have higher risk for sampling bias, thus inferences drawn from them are more questionable. The most common types of nonprobability sampling are convenience and snowball sampling.

Variables

Variables represent specific construct measures. The two "musts" for a variable are that it must be measurable and it must vary. A construct and one possible corresponding variable would be depression = score on the Beck Depression Inventory or student achievement = grade point average. These two examples represent variables that are **continuous variables** because they can occur along a continuum. The other major variable type is a **categorical variable,** which measures fit into one of several distinct categories. A construct and its corresponding categorical variable is gender = male or female. Here, the categorical variable has two levels, but depending on the nature of the researcher's categorical variables, there may be more. For example, researching transgender populations, the variable gender might include levels for male, female, male to female, and female to male, thus producing four categories or levels. Identifying whether research variables are continuous or categorical is important for selecting appropriate statistical analyses.

Variables are also categorized by whether the variables are status variables or are randomly assigned to treatment conditions. A variable that represents a trait or characteristic (e.g., gender, IQ, personality type) that is not manipulated or changed by the researcher is known as a status or an attribute variable. A variable that allows manipulation by a researcher (e.g., counseling treatment, training, hours of supervision) is known as an active variable.

Another major distinction between variables is their role in the study. **Independent variables** exert influence over **dependent variables.** Dependent variables are identified as the outcome or results variable. Independent variables generally, although not always, occur first, both in their occurrence and in their position in the hypothesis or research question. An example is the hypothesis "Eye movement desensitization and reprocessing (EMDR) will have a greater impact than stress inoculation training in the treatment of posttraumatic stress disorder (PTSD) on posttraumatic symptoms, as measured by the PTSD Symptom Scale (PTSD-SS)." In this hypothesis, the type of intervention is the independent variable, and the individual's score on the PTSD-SS is the dependent variable. More specifically, the type of treatment is a categorical independent variable on two levels, and the PTSD-SS score is a continuous dependent variable. Another hypothesis might be "There is a significant negative relationship between degree of parent–teacher collaboration and

student absenteeism." In this example, parent–teacher collaboration is the independent variable, and student absenteeism is the dependent variable. Both of these variables in this example are continuous. Independent and dependent variables are two of the primary distinctions; however, there are several additional types of variables (see Variables).

Research Design

Quantitative research can be classified as experimental, preexperimental, or nonexperimental. **Experimental research** involves manipulation by the researcher of the independent variable (active variable) through random assignment of participants to treatment and control groups. For instance, studying the effect of two different counseling approaches (with an additional wait list control group) on clients with PTSD is experimental in nature. The categories of true experimental and quasi-experimental, which are based on ability to assign participants to treatment groups randomly, fall under the term *experimental research*. **Preexperimental** research involves manipulation by the researcher of the independent variable but does not use a control group. **Nonexperimental** quantitative research does not manipulate the independent variable and is typically categorized as descriptive, relational, or comparative. Nonexperimental quantitative research that examines change over time is considered developmental. Figure 1 illustrates how these designs relate to each other.

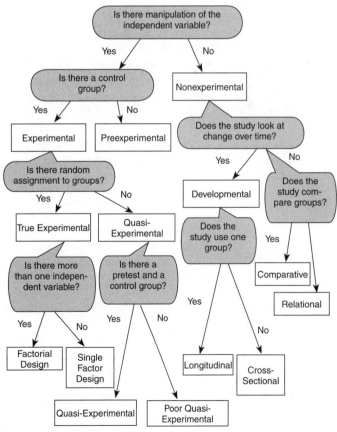

Figure 1. Quantitative Research Design

Hypothesis Testing and Statistical Significance

Hypothesis testing uses statistics to test whether an occurrence, relationship, effect, or difference is likely to occur by chance. That is, a test for significance determines the probability of obtaining a value as large as that which was observed. The process begins by identifying an appropriate degree of certainty. Basically, any result can occur anywhere within the normal curve, with most typical occurrences populating the inflated middle. Values or occurrences at the ends of the curve would represent results that are less usual. Most commonly, counseling researchers adopt a 95% confidence level, requiring results to occur 5% of the time or less to attain significance. Alpha represents the significance level, and in the previous explanation the alpha would be .05. In addition, counseling researchers are concerned with **power,** or the appropriateness of a sample size to detect a statistically significant relationship when one exists (see Power).

The statistical test chosen to evaluate significance varies depending on the number and type of variables as well as whether or not raw data are distributed normally (i.e., roughly conforms to the normal probability distribution or bell-shaped curve; see Nonparametric Statistics; Parametric Statistics). Each test yields its own statistic, but in all cases, significance is indicated by the likelihood (probability) of achieving that value due to mere chance. This likelihood is reported in analysis software and research reports as the **significance level** or p value. For a result to be considered statistically significant with an alpha of .05, the p value would typically need to be .05 or less.

In quantitative research, **practical significance** is as important as statistical significance. Practical significance is determined through the calculation of an **effect size.** An effect size calculation considers the sample's size and distribution characteristics. The most common effect size for comparative studies is the Cohen's $d,$ where .80 and above is considered to be a large effect.

Quantitative research is an extensive topic that does not lend itself to an easy or short explanation. Articulation of a research purpose, operationalization of variables, sampling strategies, measurement, selection of appropriate descriptive and inferential statistics, and accurate interpretation of results are all essential to conducting quantitative research.

Contributed by Laurie A. Carlson,
Colorado State University, Fort Collins, CO

Additional Resources

Creswell, J. W. (2007). *Educational research: Planning, conducting, and evaluating quantitative and qualitative research* (3rd ed.). Upper Saddle River, NJ: Pearson Education.

Gliner, J. A., & Morgan, G. A. (2000). *Research methods in applied settings: An integrated approach to design and analysis.* Mahwah, NJ: Erlbaum.

■ Quasi-Experimental Research Designs

Although some people believe the ideal quantitative research design is purely experimental, it is often the case, especially in the social sciences, that a true experimental design is neither possible nor feasible. Two of the necessary conditions of a true experiment include random assignment, which helps to ensure equivalent groups before any treatment is applied, and standardized treatments across participants. Often, participants already possess the characteristics necessary for study (e.g., extroverted or introverted, male or female, partnered or single), referred to as a subject characteristic, and therefore self-select to a particular group. A more elaborate example is the researcher who is interested in studying the effect of peer groups on the aggressive behavior of adolescents; this researcher would not randomly assign adolescents to particular peer groups but rather would select participants who already belonged to the peer groups of interest. If the outcome of the study shows a statistically significant difference in aggressive behavior by peer group affiliation, the researcher could say the two were related but could not say that affiliation with aggressive peers led to aggressive behavior. The researcher could suggest that being aggressive as an adolescent makes it more likely that he or she will choose peers who are also aggressive.

As can easily be seen in this example, it is not always possible to assign participants randomly to a particular group. Whenever the requirements of a true experiment cannot be met, a researcher may choose to use a **quasi-experimental research design.** Although the internal validity of this design is lower compared with a true experimental design, it still possesses many of the same characteristics of a true experiment, such as testing for significant differences between groups before and after treatments. Also, although quasi-experimental designs can offer answers to many questions pertinent to research, they cannot be used to draw causal conclusions, as evidenced by the previous example of the aggressive adolescent. The researcher, for instance, may glean an understanding of the relationship between variables, yet cannot say that one variable *caused* another. The two primary categories of quasi-experimental designs are nonequivalent groups designs and time-series designs. With nonequivalent groups designs, unequal groups are compared with one another to assess for differences possibly related to treatment. In time-series designs, the same group is measured repeatedly to detect differences related to treatment.

Nonequivalent Groups Designs

The **nonequivalent groups design** is more often used than the time-series design because it is easily interpreted and accounts for more threats to internal validity, such as history, maturation, and attrition. This design is used when the researcher cannot assume equivalent treatment groups because random assignment is not used. The researcher uses intact groups, engages each group in two observations or assessments, and administers treatment to one group between the observations or assessments.

An example would be a researcher wanting to study the effects of marital infidelity on the quality of a marital relationship. The researcher would certainly not randomly select married individuals to engage in extramarital behaviors and then assess the resulting impact it had on the quality of their relationships. Although this would enable the researcher to draw causal conclusions, it would hardly be ethical. Rather, the researcher is likely to place individuals in groups according to their history of marital infidelity and then make comparisons of each group's marital quality. This example shows how difficult it would be to draw causal conclusions because (a) marital quality could affect a person's likelihood to engage in extramarital relations, just as having engaged in extramarital relations is likely to affect the quality of a person's marital relationships, and thus it would be difficult to determine which variable was influencing the other and (b) there may be other variables not measured or controlled for that affect marital quality. A diagram of a nonequivalent groups design using a control group follows, where O = observation or assessment and X = treatment or intervention:

$$O \quad X \quad O$$
$$O \qquad\quad O$$

Some nonequivalent groups designs actually expose the participants to different treatments even though the participants are not randomly assigned. In this type, two common research techniques are used to increase the internal validity of the nonequivalent groups designs. In the first, **counterbalancing,** the researcher exposes both groups to all treatments but in a different order. An example of a counterbalanced design using three treatments is depicted in the following diagram:

Group A	X_1	O	X_2	O	X_3
Group B	X_2	O	X_3	O	X_1
Group C	X_3	O	X_1	O	X_2

In yet another attempt to equate the experimental and control groups, **matching,** which involves the researcher matching participants in the experimental and control group on certain variables to reduce differences where possible, is used. One popular example of matching is termed *cohort designs.* Cohort designs are typically stronger than other forms of nonequivalent groups designs because participants are likely to be more similar prior to beginning the study, especially with regard to certain demographic characteristics. In a cohort design, differences between cohorts are assessed at different points in time but at the same point in the progression of the cohort. For example, a researcher may

give a posttest to each cohort of 20 individuals as they near completion of an adolescent offender program. If the program spans 6 months, then every 6 months a different cohort group nearing completion is assessed and compared with the other cohorts who were assessed at the same point in the program. The shortcomings with the cohort design involve the passage of time between assessments as well as the nonrandom assignment of participants.

Time-Series Designs

Time-series designs include multiple observations with the same participants over time. Rather than comparing two groups of participants, the researcher typically compares the same group of participants before and after exposure to treatment, with repeated measurement of the dependent variable. When compared against the baseline, or the information collected prior to treatment, this design shows if there are treatment effects, if these effects are lasting, and if they are obvious soon after treatment. Regarded as a strong design, the time-series design is infrequently used because of the increased amount of data collection required. Threats to the validity of this design include the effects of history, testing practice, and attrition.

The single-group time series design may be depicted graphically as follows:

$$O_1 \quad O_2 \quad O_3 \quad O_4 \quad O_5 \quad X \quad O_1 \quad O_2 \quad O_3 \quad O_4 \quad O_5$$

The control group time series design may be depicted graphically as follows:

$$O_1 \quad O_2 \quad O_3 \quad O_4 \quad O_5 \quad X \quad O_1 \quad O_2 \quad O_3 \quad O_4 \quad O_5$$
$$O_1 \quad O_2 \quad O_3 \quad O_4 \quad O_5 \qquad\quad O_1 \quad O_2 \quad O_3 \quad O_4 \quad O_5$$

Contributed by Susan H. Eaves,
Mississippi State University, Starkville, MS

Additional Resources

Campbell, D. T., & Stanley, J. C. (1963). *Experimental and quasi-experimental designs for research.* Boston: Houghton Mifflin.

Cook, T. D., & Campbell, D. T. (1979). *Quasi-experimentation: Designs & analysis issues for field settings.* Boston: Houghton Mifflin.

Race

The construct of **race** has been used to describe biological characteristics, particularly differences and genetic variations (e.g., skin color, hair texture, eye shape). Researchers have noted, however, that there are few genetic differences between the various "racial" groups and that there are more genetic commonalities, resulting in the current belief that *race* is a nonscientific term and that racial designations are arbitrary and lack a meaningful definition. Thus, race has been defined more recently as a socially constructed term used to create segregation, exploitation, and other forms of racism. Racial classifications are often used to divide the population into identifiable groups for the allocation of resources.

Historically, there have been attempts to insert comments into this document classify humans on the basis of physical characteristics such as skin color, eye shape, and the form of a person's face. Race has been used to explain human diversity; to justify the ill treatment of groups of people who were viewed as inferior, such as Africans and the Chinese; and to create emotional and psychological distance between Europeans and those who were visibly different. In the 1700s, Linnaeus was the first scientist to develop a taxonomy of racial classifications, which was based on an individual's color, humor (e.g., a normal functioning bodily fluid, such as blood), and posture. The result of Linnaeus's work was the creation of four racial classifications: *homo sapiens Americanus* (Native American people), *homo sapiens Europaeus* (White people), *homo sapiens Asiaticus* (Asian people), and *homo sapiens Afer* (African people). In the late 1700s, Blumenbach developed a classification system of humans and divided them into five primary races: Caucasian or the White race, Ethiopian or the Black race, American or the Red race, Mongolian or the Yellow race, and Malay or the Brown race. Both of these racial taxonomies laid the foundation for the use of racial classifications that still affect the interactions of people today. Despite the lack of a scientific foundation, these racial classifications have remained in use with slight variations, as seen in U.S. census categories.

Race, as defined by the U.S. Census Bureau, reflects the self-identification of individuals according to the race or races with which they most closely identify. Racial classifications change from one census to another, and the racial categories include both racial and national origin groups. According to the U.S. census, racial classifications include White, Black, Asian, Alaskan Native, and Pacific Islander;

Hispanic/Latino/a is considered an ethnic designation and not a racial category. In the 2000 U.S. census, individuals identified with 165 racial group combinations. This resulted in the development of a new category ("Two or More Races Population"). The sociopolitical nature of race and its subsequent constructs have led to several issues, including color blindness, color consciousness, biracial identity, and multiracial identity.

Color Blindness

In 1896, Justice John Marshall Harlan of the United States Supreme Court wrote a dissenting opinion in the case of *Plessy v. Ferguson*. He stated that the U.S. Constitution is "color blind" and all people are equal under the law. This was the first time a reference was made to **color blindness** with respect to the racial classification of people. Since that time, this term has continued to be used in reference to African Americans. In the 1960s, the term *color blind society* referred to the desire to free society from prejudice and discrimination against African Americans. It was believed that if society no longer looked at skin color, the problems facing African Americans would go away. Martin Luther King Jr. suggested that society should no longer judge people "by the color of their skin but by the content of their character." He did not mean that people should not see color but instead meant that skin color should not form the basis of the judgments of a person's character. However, removing "color" from the way people were understood resulted in devaluing the contributions of racial and ethnic minorities.

The term *color blindness* has also been used to describe counselors who have chosen not to acknowledge the "racial" differences between client and counselor. It was believed that if these differences were not noticed, they would just go away. What this led to was a continuing distrust of White counselors. In addition, professional counselors who practice color blindness fail to focus on the culture of the client, which results in conceptualizations of the client's problems that are not consistent with the client's cultural belief system. With inconsistent cultural conceptualizations, professional counselors will also fail to develop methods for helping clients to resolve their problems within their cultural framework. Finally, professional counselors who practice color blindness frequently fail to establish counseling goals that are consistent with the cultural beliefs of the client, contributing to approximately 50% of ethnic minority clients failing to return for a second counseling session.

Color Consciousness

Color consciousness, or *colorism*, has traditionally focused on the manner in which African Americans define Blackness based on skin color. Currently, color consciousness has taken on a new meaning that focuses on an exaggerated look at race, resulting in an unintentional racism. In order to understand this concept, both meanings are presented.

Color consciousness has recently been defined as being the opposite of color blindness and is viewed as the result of White guilt for being previously color blind. It is the process of openly acknowledging the ethnic and cultural differences between counselor and client and the barriers that may exist as a result of these differences. It is also the idea that all of a minority individual's problems stem from the minority status of the individual. Emphasis is placed on the minority status of the client instead of on other contributing factors to the client's current difficulties. The result of color conscious behavior is often misdiagnosis and a failure to identify the severity of the problems experienced by the client. Through color consciousness, professional counselors are also able to demonstrate sensitivity to the history and socialization of ethnic minority group members and a willingness to address these issues in counseling. Color consciousness has also provided a means for understanding the issue of skin tone differences between African Americans, often referred to as colorism.

Colorism has been used by African Americans to differentiate between themselves and other African Americans on the basis of skin color. It is the idea that attractiveness is determined by how closely the physical characteristics of an African American resemble the physical attributes of Europeans, such as having lighter skin, which, in this view, makes the person more attractive than a person with darker skin. Because of the influence of European standards of beauty, colorism or race consciousness can also be defined as a caste system based on how closely skin color, hair texture, and facial features conform to a European ideal. For example, the more the African American resembles European definitions of beauty, the more attractive the African American. Colorism is basically the opposite of color blindness. With color blindness, a person seeks to avoid recognizing the color of the skin of another person and to focus on the other characteristics of the individual; however, colorism means the person focuses on the skin color of the person to determine the attractiveness of the individual.

Colorism (the judgment of African Americans based on skin color) dates to the sexual subjugation of Black women by slave owners and the preferential treatment their mixed-race children received during slavery. In other words, the mixed race children of Black–White unions were given preferential treatment because they had characteristics closer to European standards than African standards. The result of color consciousness has been greater economic success for lighter skinned African Americans and more difficult economic circumstances for darker skinned African Americans. Colorism also had an impact on the culture, art, and literature of the African American population.

Because many African Americans migrated to the North in the 1920s and 1930s seeking employment, Harlem in New York City grew in size and importance, which led to questioning the concept of colorism. The New Negro Movement and the Harlem Renaissance brought together many African Americans who rejected the colorism of the time. Much of the art and literature of the Harlem Renaissance focused on having pride in being Black and was an early projection of racial pride. Even though the Great Depression brought the Harlem Renaissance and the New Negro Movement to an end in the 1930s, it was the precursor of the Black Pride movement of the 1960s and helped to bring focus to the need for African Americans to unite for a common good regardless of skin complexion.

Biracial Identity

Biracial refers to individuals whose parents are from two different racial backgrounds, such as Asian and White. The concept, biracial, can be complex to understand because the definition of race is not clear and there are so many people who have parents of multiple racial backgrounds. The historical significance of the term *biracial* dates to slavery and the desire to keep the White race pure. In the 1880s and the 1890s, the belief that non-Anglo Saxon people were inferior led to beliefs that non-European Americans were the cause of corruption, alcoholism, poverty, and crime. This resulted in the U.S. Congress passing laws that limited or excluded undesirable people from entering the United States, which led to the American eugenics movement.

Eugenics is a science that deals with the improvement of the hereditary qualities of people by controlling the selection of mates. Sir Frances Galton led the eugenics movement in 1869 in England and spearheaded the passing of laws that forbade the marrying of White Anglo Saxons with non-White people and also forbade intermarrying with "inferior" White races. The eugenics movement took hold in the United States in 1875, resulting in the creation of miscegenation laws, which made marriage between Whites and non-Whites illegal, and laws that would keep those who were poor, uneducated, or had mental problems out of the gene pool. The purpose of the eugenics movement was to maintain the purity of White Anglo Saxons and to reduce the proportion of social ills in society. The outcome was the notion that biracial individuals were inferior and not accepted members of society.

The terms *multiracial* and *mixed-race* have also been used to describe people whose ancestors were not of a single racial category. Biracial strictly refers to those with ancestors from only two races, which is difficult to determine. One example might be a **mulatto,** a term of Spanish or Portuguese origin used in the United States during the colonial period to describe a person with one White parent and one African or slave parent. The term is also used in many Spanish- and Portuguese-speaking countries presently and has continued to be used in the United States, especially among young people. Another term used to describe biracial individuals is **mestizo.** These are individuals who descended from Caucasian and Native Indian ancestors. The origin of the term *mulatto* is from the Spanish word *mulato,* which means a small mule or a person of mixed race, from the word *mulo* for mule, from Old Spanish, and from the Latin *mulus.* The term was once a generic designation for any hybrid species, and as a result it may be considered offensive by those individuals who prefer terms like *biracial* or *multiracial.* Other biracial individuals, however, believe that the word *mulatto* maintains a sense of historical continuity or are comfortable with its use and are not offended.

Multiracial Identity

The term **multiracial** represents the idea that individuals or societies can be composed of, involve, or represent various racial groups. When talking about individuals or society, multiracial means individuals' having more than two racial backgrounds or there being more than two racial groups in the society. For example, the United States is considered a multiracial or a multicultural society because of the plurality of racial groups. The U.S. census lists multiple racial groups, such as African American, Asian American, White, and Native American, so that all of the racial groups in the country can be counted. In addition and more important, the word *multiracial* is used to describe individuals with multiple racial backgrounds. An individual could have parents whose backgrounds include Asian Americans, African Americans, and Whites. Multiracial individuals are often presumed to have struggles with identity crises because their sense of identity is different than the sense of identity of people who claim to be of a single racial group. Most multiracial people cannot or do not identify with just one racial or ethnic group. The first recognition of the multiple ways multiracial individuals identify themselves occurred in the 2000 U.S. census, which allowed individuals to identify all of the racial groups with which they identified.

Contributed by Richard C. Henriksen Jr.,
Sam Houston State University,
Huntsville, TX

Additional Resources

Cameron, S. C., & Wycoff, S. M. (1998). The destructive nature of the term *race:* Growing beyond a false paradigm. *Journal of Counseling & Development, 76,* 277–285.

Henriksen, R. C., Jr., & Paladino, D. A. (2009). *Counseling multiple heritage individuals, couples, and families.* Alexandria, VA: American Counseling Association.

Krogman, W. M. (1945). The concept of race. In R. Linton (Ed.), *The science of man in the world crisis* (pp. 38–62). New York: Columbia University Press.

Miller, J., & Garran, A. M. (2008). *Racism in the United States: Implications for the helping professions.* Belmont, CA: Thomson.

West, C. (2001). *Race matters* (Rev. ed.). Boston: Beacon Press.

■ Racial Identity Development Models, Minority

The origin of **minority racial identity development (MRID) models** is often associated with William Cross's (1991)

Black identity development model; however, the origin of the models dates to the early 1900s when the scientific community attempted to explain and justify the perceived racial differences between Blacks and Whites, with Whites being the dominant reference group. Social scientists, as products of their society and environments, believed race was biologically determined. Any physical, mental, intellectual, and social traits were associated and theorized as inherent biological or physiological characteristics of race. Thus, early cross-cultural research depicted Negroes (African Americans) as genetically deficient. Terms such as **culturally deficient** (e.g., poor, substandard environmental factors such as housing, education, nutrition) and **cultural deprived** (e.g., lack of political and economic power) were used to describe the social status of African Americans (Sue & Sue, 2003).

The **Black Power** and **civil rights movements** sparked a sociopolitical zeitgeist that shifted the general population's, particularly racial minority individuals' and researchers', views on race, self-definition, and meaning. Social researchers, especially researchers on people of color, turned their attention to the psychological development of Blacks and other racial minority individuals living in the social context of race relations in the United States. The term *people of color* or *minority* refers to individuals who identify as members of the racial groups of African American, Latino/a American, Asian American, Native American or Alaskan Native, or Pacific Islander. Membership in one of these racial groups also infers "minority" status compared with the racial group of White or European American, which holds the majority or dominant status in the United States.

William Cross's (1991) model, the psychology of **nigrescence** or the psychology of Blackness, became the seminal prototype of racial identity development models. Subsequently, other racial identity development models emerged that focused on specific minority populations such as Chicano/Latinos (Ruiz, 1990) and Asian Americans (Kim, 1981). MRID models contributed to human development theories by separating the domains of personality from group reference or social identity and acknowledging the impact of systemic oppression on reference group identity. MRID models provide a conceptual framework for understanding individual differences within specific racial minority populations. Consistent with traditional developmental models (e.g., Freud's psychosexual development, Erickson's psychosocial development, Piaget's cognitive development), MRID endorses progressive levels of racial development and describes an individual's self-perceptions in comparison with the perceptions of the dominant group and ascribed racial group. Early versions of MRID asserted mutually exclusive levels and linear progression through the levels.

MRID models generalized racial identity developmental processes for specific racial groups while ignoring within-group ethnic diversity (e.g., Mexican vs. Puerto Rican descent, Korean vs. Hmong descent, African vs. Caribbean descent). Prior to the 1990s, researchers viewed race and ethnicity as synonymous concepts. It was common to see the terms used interchangeably or referenced as "race/ethnicity" in the literature. Researchers debated the definition and usage of race and ethnicity that resulted in delineation of the terms. **Race** has no biological or physiological basis (see Race); it refers to the categorization of individuals who share similar visible physical characteristics (e.g., skin color, facial features, hair texture, and eye color). Its origins are historical and culturally based. **Ethnicity** refers to shared cultural heritage, customs, traditions, and rituals (see Ethnicity). Therefore, racial group members may have similar or diverse ethnic origins. The lack of biological origins of race, however, does not invalidate the historical and social implications on the personal development of racial minority individuals. For this reason, Helms (Helms, 1995; Helms & Talleyrand, 1997) asserted that the term **sociorace** best captured the role and dynamics of race in human development and relationships.

A complexity of MRID models was its specificity to designated minority racial groups and the labeling of each level. Yet, the models share common dynamics, processes, and assumptions. The following list collapses the stages of the MRID models by describing their shared dynamics, whereas Figure 1 provides a cross-referencing of the stages or statuses of each model associated with the descriptions from the list of levels in racial identity development.

General descriptions of minority racial identity development models' statuses, listed by level, follow:

Level 1. Possesses pro-White orientation; endorses dominant attitudes/beliefs of group; discounts or justifies prejudice/ discrimination directed toward group

Level 2. Experiences a shift in perspective resulting from an event that contradicts prior experiences; personalizes event that creates disorientation, confusion, and emotional and cognitive dissonance; propels movement toward proracial group

Level 3. Involves a two-step transitional process to eliminate the dissonance and confusion of the previous level, including a period of re-education about one's racial group; adopts behaviors, icons/symbols, labeling that represent racial group; increases racial pride and idealization of reference group; begins to internalize racial consciousness while rejecting dominant group; experiences drastic change in preferences for interpersonal relationships; possesses polarized views

of others—group members as all "good" and others are not; portrays cognitive rigidity

Level 4. Begins to understand race as a social and personal construction; understands historical and current racial dynamics and racial consciousness and pride; continues education; sees good/bad in all regardless of race

Level 5. (a level not reached by everyone). Reflects a deeper understanding of race relations and implications for all citizens; commits to improving life for others; advocates for social justice

The models' commonalities led to two unified MRID models: racial/cultural identity development model (Sue & Sue, 2003) and people of color model (Helms, 1995). These models subsume the basic assumptions of MRID models into one conceptual framework, highlighting the shared experiences of racial minorities living in oppressive, racialized society. The basic tenets of MRID models are the following:

1. The concept of race is socially constructed, not biological.
2. Race was constructed to establish and to maintain a sociopolitical hierarchy of dominance, oppression, and privilege.
3. Racial identity does not infer personality.
4. Self-concept is a function of the interaction of personal identity and reference group identity.
5. The social meaning of racial group membership is internalized into an individual's individual psyche, affecting his or her self-perceptions and interactions with other reference group members (**in-group members**) and individuals from other groups (**out-group members**).
6. Racial development is cyclical and dynamic, not linear and static.
7. Individuals start at a maladaptive level of pro-White/ anti–reference group orientation and move to a healthier orientation of social justice advocacy and the inclusion of the social values for biculturalism and social justice.

Model and Source

	Psychology of Black Identity (Cross, 1991)	Asian American Identity[a] (Kim, 1981)	Chicano/Latino Identity (Ruiz, 1990)	People of Color Model (Helms, 1995)	Racial/Cultural Identity Model (Atkinson, Morten, & Sue, 1998)
Level 1	Preencounter	White identification	Causal	Conformity	Conformity
Level 2	Encounter	Awakening to social and political consciousness	Cognitive	Dissonance	Dissonance
Level 3	Immersion–emersion	Redirection	Consequence	Immersion–emersion	Resistance and immersion
Level 4	Internalization	Incorporation	Working through	Internalization	Introspection
Level 5	Internalization–commitment		Successful resolution	Integrative awareness	Integrative awareness

Figure 1. Minority Racial Identity Models and Their Stages or Statuses by Level

Note. See text for definition of levels.
[a]Kim's (1981) research identified the first level of racial identity (ethnic awareness) as the childhood racial socialization provided by family and community. This socialization is credited with instilling a positive or neutral view of racial group.

As previously stated, the models acknowledge the impact of sociopolitical influences, specifically social injustices on minority individuals. Kim's (1981) and Ruiz's (1990) MRID models differ slightly from the remaining models mentioned. Their models present racial identity development starting in early childhood with the family, neighbors, and community as socializing agents of racial identity. One criticism of MRID models is their focus on adult development. Other limitations of MRID models are (a) limited empirically validated research, (b) overuse of traditional-age college students as research participants, and (c) lack of psychometrically sound assessments. Helms (1995) conducted the most empirically based research on racial identity development and the counseling process. Overall, the collective research on MRID validated the conceptualization of racial identity as a separate psychological construct from personal identity. MRID affects an individual intraphysically and interpersonally, because an individual's perceptions about self, group membership and esteem, and others, particularly members of the White dominant culture, are influenced by his or her racial identity. Research with African Americans, Asian Americans, Black Brazilian men, and Native Americans revealed, with few exceptions, consistent findings that the level of racial identity was significantly associated with collective esteem, trust of Whites, color-blind attitudes, cultural value conflicts, and race-related stress. The findings also showed slight variations in the characteristics of certain racial identity levels across the racial groups. This is extremely important, given that MRID theories characterize the shared (not identical) experiences of racial minorities living in a racialized America.

Even with the limitations listed earlier in this entry, MRID models greatly contributed to human development theories and counseling practices through their emphasis of within-group diversity (e.g., individual differences and preferences), role of racial identity in the counseling process, and acknowledgement of the impact of historical and contemporary sociopolitical environments on human development and relationships. MRID redirected the focus of the counseling relationship to include three simultaneous processes: (a) the client's cultural orientation, (b) the counselor's cultural orientation, and (c) the cultural dynamics within the counseling relationship. Thus, to understand the counseling process and, especially, to promote effective counseling, it was necessary to accept that both the client and counselor, regardless of their racial heritage, have been socialized and affected by race. MRID models assumed the counseling relationship reflected the perceptions and beliefs of the individuals and provided insights into how individuals at a certain level of racial identity interacted with people of not only of different racial backgrounds but also with people of a similar racial background who were at a different racial identity level. Research points to racial identity levels as significant factors in counselor preference, perceived cultural sensitivity and racial consciousness, and counseling effectiveness. Furthermore, the interaction theory (Helms, 1995, 2003) highlights the dynamics of counseling relationships when the counselor's level is (a) the same as the client's level (parallel rela-

tionship), (b) lower than the client's level (regressive relationship), or (c) higher than the client's level (progressive relationship) of racial identity. Of the three types of interactional relationships, the progressive relationship offers greater growth and satisfaction for clients, leading to greater counseling effectiveness. This information significantly contradicts the prior beliefs that same-race dyads yielded the most effective treatment for clients of color.

*Contributed by Cheryl B. Warner,
Clemson University, Clemson, SC*

References

Atkinson, D. R., Morten, G., & Sue, D. W. (1998). *Counseling American minorities,* (5th ed.). Boston: McGraw-Hill.

Cross, W. C. (1991). *Shades of Black: Diversity in African American identity.* Philadelphia: Temple University Press.

Helms, J. E. (1995). An update of Helms' White and people of color racial identity models. In J. G. Ponterotto, J. M. Casas, L. A. Suzuki, & C. M. Alexander (Eds.), *Handbook of multicultural counseling* (pp. 181–198). Thousand Oaks, CA: Sage.

Helms, J. E. (2003). Racial identity in the social environment. In P. B. Pedersen & J. C. Carey (Eds.), *Multicultural counseling in schools: A practical handbook* (2nd ed., pp. 44–58). Boston: Pearson Education.

Helms, J. E., & Talleyrand, R. M. (1997). Race is not ethnicity. *American Psychologist, 52,* 1246–1247.

Kim, J. (1981). The process of Asian American identity development: A study of Japanese-American women's perceptions of their struggle to achieve personal identities. *Dissertation Abstracts International, 42,* 155, 1A.

Ruiz, A. (1990). Ethnic identity: Crisis and resolution. *Journal of Multicultural Counseling and Development, 18,* 29–40.

Sue, D. W., & Sue, D. (2003). *Counseling the culturally diverse: Theory and practice* (4th ed.). New York: Wiley.

Additional Resources

Alvarez, A. N., & Helms, J. E. (2001). Racial identity and reflected appraisals as influences on Asian Americans' racial adjustment. *Cultural Diversity and Ethnic Minority Psychology, 7,* 217–231.

Bryant, A., & Baker, S. B. (2003). The feasibility of constructing profiles of Native Americans from the People of Color Racial Identity Scale: A brief report. *Measurement and Evaluation in Counseling and Development, 36,* 2–8.

Chen, G. A., LePhuoc, P., Guzman, M. R., Rude, S. S., & Dodd, B. G. (2006). Exploring Asian American racial identity. *Cultural Diversity and Ethnic Minority Psychology, 12,* 461–476.

Helms, J. E., & Cook, D. A. (1990). *Using race and culture in counseling and psychology: Theory and process.* Needham Heights, MA: Allyn & Bacon.

Ponterotto, J. G., Casas, J. M., Suzuki, L. A., & Alexander, C. M. (Eds.). (1995). *Handbook of multicultural counseling.* Thousand Oaks, CA: Sage.

Racism

Racism is generally defined as the belief that one race is superior to another. This belief in superiority can be based on many factors, including the notion that race is the primary determinant in a person's abilities, intelligence, or personality traits. Racism can be overt or covert, intentional or unintentional, and occurs at three main levels: individual, institutional, and cultural.

Covert racism describes racism that is not immediately visible and can be carried out consciously or unconsciously (i.e., intentionally or unintentionally). An example of covert intentional racism might be a professional counselor who consistently chooses not to work with clients of a certain racial/ethnic background. An example of covert unintentional racism would be a professional counselor who interprets a client's behavior as pathological or defensive due to lack of knowledge about the client's culture. **Overt racism** describes acts of oppression and discrimination that are more discernible and intentional. Overt racism is always intentional and conscious. A person exhibiting overt racism might make jokes about racial groups; make racial slurs; or in some cases, carry out acts of violence against members of other racial groups.

Racism may occur at the individual, institutional, and cultural levels and may even become internalized in the psyche and actions of the people who are oppressed. **Individual racism** refers to individuals' beliefs, attitudes, and actions that sustain or perpetuate racism. Individual racism may occur both at the conscious and unconscious levels and be either passive or active. Individual racism may take many forms, including the belief that members of other racial groups are dangerous, less intelligent, or less competent than one's own racial group. **Institutional racism,** a term coined by Stokely Carmichael in the late 1960s, refers to racial discrimination that is embedded in the culture of institutions (e.g., governments, companies, organizations). Examples of racist practices by institutions might be racial profiling by law enforcement officers, barriers to employment based on race, and racially motivated misrepresentation in the media (e.g., in the aftermath of hurricane Katrina, newspapers showed pictures of White people with headlines such as "People Search for Food," whereas similar pictures of African American people contained headlines about looting). Institutional racism can also be present in a system that creates advantages for Whites. **Cultural racism** (also referred to as **societal racism**) refers to an underrepresentation of nondominant groups' values in a range of cultural areas (e.g., education, humanities, the arts). One example of cultural racism in the world of art is the suggestion that certain types of art are superior (usually art created by Whites with advanced degrees), whereas other types of art (created by non-White groups with less education) are referred to as "folk art" or "outsider" art.

Costs of Racism

Racism of any type has a profound effect on all individuals involved. Professional counselors must be prepared to discuss racism openly and deal with it in session, whether counseling a client with racist beliefs or counseling a client who has been oppressed by racist actions. The costs of racism affect both Whites and oppressed groups. According to Spanierman, Armstrong, Poteat, and Beer (2006), documented costs for Whites include "guilt and shame, irrational fear of people of other races, distorted beliefs regarding race and racism, and limited exposure to different cultures" (p. 434). Racism causes Whites to have limited exposure to other racial/cultural groups, which prevents the development of a racial identity.

These costs pale in comparison to the costs of racism faced by members of underrepresented groups. The effects of racism on client mental health are extensive and include pervasive racism in institutions, which can result in limited access to necessary mental health services and resources for oppressed groups; reduced opportunity for education and training; and lower wages, resulting in inadequate living conditions and increased stress.

Cultural messages in the United States about the superiority of Whiteness and the devaluing of Blackness can lead to self-perceptions of worthlessness and powerlessness. Feelings such as sorrow, frustration, anger, guilt, and disgust are felt in response to racism and in turn may lead to internalized racism. **Internalized racism** occurs when members of an oppressed group begin to take on negative stereotypes perpetuated by the oppressive group. As a result of internalized racism, members of underrepresented groups may begin to believe and embrace the negative thoughts about themselves and others and exhibit decreased motivation, lowered self-esteem, and symptoms of depression. Williams and Williams-Morris (2000) found that members of underrepresented groups who had subjectively experienced discrimination were adversely affected in a variety of ways, including negative affects on their mental health. These authors cited several examples of experiments where exposure to racial discrimination was related to increased psychological distress (e.g., generalized anxiety, depression, and lower levels of life satisfaction).

In addition to interpersonal, cognitive, and affective costs, there are physical costs related to racism toward people of color (e.g., limited access to medical resources and institutional racism in the medical arena can severely affect the physical health of underrepresented group members). Williams and Williams-Morris (2000) discussed the physical consequences of discrimination and racist behaviors and cited several laboratory studies that found significant rates of cardiovascular and psychological reactivity (e.g., increases in blood pressure and other indicators of psychological distress) when African American participants were exposed to discrimination.

In another work addressing the affects of racism, Thompson and Neville (1999) discussed how the experiences of racism and discrimination could negatively affect the formation of a healthy personality. In addition, they provided information about treating the negative effects of racism through challenging irrational beliefs, encouraging moral self-development, and encouraging clients to engage in risk-taking behaviors.

Counseling Considerations

Professional counselors should prepare to deal with racism in the counseling relationship by engaging in an ongoing self-examination of personal values, assumptions, and biases. Arredondo (1999) provided counselors with information about addressing oppression and racism through the development of multicultural counseling competencies. Multicultural counseling competencies include counselor characteristics that fall into three categories: beliefs and attitudes, knowledge, and skills. Professional counselors should engage in an examination of their own beliefs, be self-aware, and monitor their sensitivity and comfort in working with those who are culturally different. In addition to examining beliefs, professional counselors should possess knowledge about working with clients from racially diverse backgrounds. An understanding of the history of racial classifications is also important (see Race). Knowledge is obtained through life experiences, and therefore counselors should seek opportunities to enhance their learning about cultures other than their own (e.g., attend a cultural event, take a tour of an ethnic community, continuing education). Developing multicultural counseling skills involves the attainment of professional development to increase competency in culturally relevant techniques and interventions. In an effort to be multiculturally competent, these three areas must be readily addressed by those in the helping professions.

Through constant attention to personal racial identity development, professional counselors can become more receptive to learning about worldviews different from their own. In addition, it is the professional counselor's responsibility to create a supportive, nurturing environment that is conducive to the discussion of sensitive issues such as racism and oppression. Professional counselors, through the use of appropriate techniques, should attempt to sensitize and alter the perspectives of oppressors, while aiding the oppressed.

In embracing the multicultural counseling competencies, professional counselors should possess knowledge about how racism, stereotyping, and oppression affect clients. In addition, professional counselors should strive to examine the role of racism in their lives and the lives of their clients, seek to learn about culturally relevant interventions, and take the necessary precautions to ensure that oppression and racism are not taking place in the institutions in which they are employed. All professional counselors should abide by the American Counseling Association's (ACA; 2005) *ACA Code of Ethics,* which compels counselors to respect the diverse opinions and beliefs of clients while advocating for social justice and directs counselors to seek consultation around these issues when necessary.

Contributed by Stephanie F. Hall,
Eastern Kentucky University,
Richmond, KY

References

American Counseling Association. (2005). *ACA code of ethics.* Alexandria, VA: Author.

Arredondo, P. (1999). Multicultural counseling competencies as tools to address oppression and racism. *Journal of Counseling & Development, 77,* 102–108.

Spanierman, L. B., Armstrong, P. I., Poteat, V. P., & Beer, A. M. (2006). Psychosocial costs of racism to Whites: Exploring patterns through cluster analysis. *Journal of Counseling Psychology, 53,* 434–441.

Thompson, C. E., & Neville, H. A. (1999). Racism, mental health, and mental health practice. *The Counseling Psychologist, 27,* 155–223.

Williams, D. R., & Williams-Morris, R. (2000). Racism and mental health: The African American experience. *Ethnicity and Health, 5,* 243–268.

Additional Resource

Ridley, C. R. (1995). *Overcoming unintentional racism in counseling and therapy: A practitioner's guide to intentional intervention.* Newbury Park, CA: Sage.

■ Randomization

Randomization of participants may involve both random selection and random assignment. A researcher can design a study in which the participants are both randomly selected for the study and randomly assigned to the study groups. Likewise, a study can be designed to use either random selection or random assignment or be designed so there is no randomization of participant selection.

The ideal method of selecting participants for a research study is random selection. Random selection does not mean a chaotic or unplanned selection of participants. **Random selection** is a procedure used to select participants from a population so that every member of the population has an equal chance of being selected. A random sample better represents the population than a nonrandom selection does. An example of a random selection would be to put the name of every member of a given population in a bag (e.g., every person in a multicultural counseling class) and then shake the bag up and have a blindfolded person select as many names as needed. Researchers, however, generally assign a number to each member of the population and then either use a **table of random digits** or computer to generate a list of random numbers that is then used to select the participants for the study.

Random assignment is a method used to assign participants to different groups, either an experimental or control group (or another experimental group). This randomization process assigns research participants to groups by chance rather than choice so that every participant has an equal chance of being assigned to every group in the study. Using random assignment helps to ensure that groups are equivalent and that differences between groups are due to chance.

A randomized, controlled study (i.e., using both randomization methods) is the most reliable and objective method of conducting research. It helps to reduce potential biases that can weaken a research study by making the findings unreliable. In addition, randomization allows for a greater generalization of the results to the population at large than a study that does not use random selection and random assignment. Random selection is related to external validity (i.e., the extent to which the results can be generalized to the population at large), and random assignment is related to internal validity (i.e., the degree to which the research design and methods eliminate potential bias).

Contributed by Kimberly A. M. Richards,
HIV/AIDS Counseling Research Group,
Centers for Disease Control, Zimbabwe

Additional Resources

Krathwohl, D. R. (2006). *Methods of educational and social science research*. Long Grove, IL: Waveland Press.

Lane, D. (2007). *HyperStat online statistics textbook*. Retrieved May 17, 2007, from http://davidmlane.com/hyperstat/

Leedy, P. D., & Ellis Ormrod, J. E. (2004). *Practical research: Planning and design*. Upper Saddle River, NJ: Prentice Hall.

Stata Trek. (2007). *Random number generator*. Retrieved May 17, 2007, from http://www.stattrek.com/Tables/Random.aspx

Web Center for Social Research Methods: http://www.socialresearchmethods.net/

■Rating Scales

Rating scales are indirect measures of behavior and, in general, do not involve directly observing the behavior of interest. Instead, rating scales rely on perceptions of the behavior according to self or others. Although all observation techniques have the potential to be biased or unreliable, the information obtained can be invaluable because it is a direct reflection of the behavior in the setting in which it is reported to occur. Thus, information obtained from rating scales is a valuable piece to the bigger picture but is best when used in conjunction with direct assessments (see Behavioral Assessment); however, when direct assessment cannot be obtained, rating scales are an excellent resource.

Characteristics of Rating Scales

Rating scales vary in scope. Some measure an array of behaviors while others measure specific behaviors and specific conditions in which the behaviors occur. Thus, the rating scale is designed either to provide a broad analysis of the individual's behavior or a more narrow analysis of a component or specific subset of behaviors as it relates to the overall clinical question. The specific design of the rating scales has lead to the nomenclature currently used: broad-band and narrow-band (Eckert, Dunn, Codding, & Guiney, 2000).

Types of Rating Scales

Broad-band behavior rating scales assess various behavioral domains, such as externalizing and internalizing behaviors (e.g., affect, family, social, academic areas). Broad-band rating scales are often administered first with the goal of gaining more insight into the problem behavior. Ideally, a broad-band scale would point to the most appropriate narrow-band scale that should be used for follow-up and clarification.

More specific behaviors are assessed with **narrow-band behavior rating scales.** Narrow-band scales should be administered after broad-band behavior rating scales have identified an area of concern or problematic behavior. The goal of narrow-band behavior rating scales is to provide detailed information regarding specific dimensions of the behaviors of interest. Table 1 presents information on some of the more commonly administered behavioral rating scales used with children and adolescents who display maladaptive behavior in educational settings and the behavioral rating scales most commonly used in research and practice

Table 1. Commonly Used Behavioral Rating Scales

Behavior Assessment System for Children (2nd ed.)
> *Purpose:* Comprehensive assessment of child and adolescent behavioral, emotional, and adaptive problems in various settings
> *Advantages:* Easy to use. Parent, teacher, and self-report versions available
> *Disadvantages:* Lengthy

Behavior Rating Profile (2nd ed.)
> *Purpose:* Identifies social, behavioral, emotional, and personal maladjustment in children
> *Advantages:* Evaluates behavior at home and school and from multiple perspectives
> *Disadvantages:* Manual scoring

Behavioral and Emotional Rating Scale
> *Purpose:* Assesses emotional and behavioral capacities of children across five areas
> *Advantages:* Contains target goals to be used for individual education plans and/or treatment plans
> *Disadvantages:* Lacks a means to record direct observational data

Burk's Behavior Rating Scale (2nd ed.)
> *Purpose:* Identifies the severity of 19 pathological symptoms occurring in children with emotional and behavioral problems
> *Advantages:* Provides suggestions for interventions in a companion handbook
> *Disadvantages:* Likert scale only, no open-ended questions

Achenbach System of Empirically Based Assessment
> *Purpose:* Assesses covert and overt behaviors of children and adolescents
> *Advantages:* Allows assessment from teacher, parent, or child
> *Disadvantages:* Difficult to assess thought disorders objectively; items may seem irrelevant for children displaying less severe behavioral and emotional problems

Revised Behavior Problem Checklist
> *Purpose:* Determine the extent of six categories of problem behavior exhibited by children and adolescents
> *Advantages:* Parent, teacher, or other rater may administer; designed for use with other assessments
> *Disadvantages:* Questions regarding its effectiveness in measuring internalizing symptoms

Social-Emotional Dimension Scale
> *Purpose:* Screens students for behavior problems that may be interfering with academic performance
> *Advantages:* Unique in that it looks at reactive behaviors in terms of escape and avoidance
> *Disadvantages:* Lacks updated normative data

Social Skills Rating System
> *Purpose:* Measures social skills at school and/or home
> *Advantages:* Parent, teacher, and self-report versions available
> *Disadvantages:* Underutilization of direct observation

Walker–McConnell Scale of Social Competence and School Adjustment
> *Purpose:* Identifies social skill deficits in students (K–6th grade, elementary version; 7th–12th grade, adolescent version)
> *Advantages:* Relies on estimates of frequency; quick to administer
> *Disadvantages:* Does not measure problem behavior; no recommendations regarding precise time period for observation on which the ratings are based

(i.e., cited in research journals within the past 5 years in a counseling, special education, or school psychology journal; Hosp, Howell, & Hosp, 2003).

In sum, rating scales are measures of an individual's functioning in terms of behavior, personality, social skills, and emotions. There are several advantages to using rating scales according to Hosp et al. (2003), including that they (a) provide quantifiable information with published data on reliability and validity, (b) provide a set of organized questions with scoring criteria, (c) provide normative data for comparison, and (d) make it possible to gather and compare ratings from different respondents. In addition, they are cost-effective and time effective, have a set of organized questions with normative data and scoring criteria, and may be used as pre- and postevaluations; however, reliance on self-report and other informants can sometimes yield biased and unreliable data because of subjectivity. Specifically, subjectivity occurs when the observer or informant records events erroneously, in a manner to satisfy a predetermined hypothesis regardless of what is actually occurring, or when the observer is not devoting the necessary amount of time or effort to completing the forms. In terms of unreliability, the main concerns are the behavior changing over time and the behavior varying according to the setting in which the observation occurred and the context of the behavior (Floyd, Phaneuf, & Wilczynski, 2005; Robbins & Merrill, 1998). Thus, data gathered from behavior rating scales may lack objectivity due to relying on individuals' perceptions of behavior and emotions rather than being gathered in a systematic means of time sampling in the natural setting.

Contributed by Laura Baylot Casey
and Sara Bicard,
University of Memphis, Memphis, TN

References

Eckert, T. L., Dunn, E. K., Codding, R. S., & Guiney, K. M. (2000). Self-report: Rating scale measures. In E. S. Shapiro & T. R. Kratochwill (Eds.), *Conducting school-based assessments of child and adolescent behavior* (pp. 150–169). New York: Guilford Press.

Floyd, R. G., Phaneuf, R. L., & Wilczynski, S. M. (2005). Measurement properties of indirect assessment methods for functional behavioral assessment: A review of research. *The School Psychology Review, 32,* 58–73.

Hosp, J., Howell, K., & Hosp, M. (2003). Characteristics of behavior rating scales: Implications for practice in assessment and behavioral support. *Journal of Positive Behavior Interventions, 5,* 201–208.

Robbins, R., & Merrill, K. (1998). Cross informant comparisons of the home and community social behavior scales and the school behavior scales. *Diagnostique, 23,* 204–218.

Additional Resources

Eckert, T. L., & DuPaul, G. J. (1996). Youth completed and narrow-band child behavior questionnaires. In M. Breen & C. Fiedler (Eds.), *Behavioral approach to the assessment of emotionally disturbed youth: A handbook for school-based practitioners* (pp. 289–357). Austin, TX: PRO-ED.

Heckaman, K., Conroy, M., East, J., & Chait, A. (2000). Functional assessment-based intervention research on students with or at risk for emotional and behavioral disorders in school settings. *Behavioral Disorders, 25,* 196–210.

McConaughy, S., & Ritter, D. (2002). Best practices in multidimensional assessment of emotional or behavioral disorders. In A. Thomas & J. Grimes (Eds.), *Best practices in school psychology* (Vol. 4, pp. 1303–1336). Bethesda, MD: National Association of School Psychologists.

■ Rational Emotive Behavior Therapy and Groups

Rational emotive behavior therapy (REBT), originally called rational emotive therapy (RET), was formally introduced by Albert Ellis in 1962 when he published *Reason and Emotion in Psychotherapy*. In this book, Ellis proposed that unhappiness, or emotional consequence, stemmed from 11 irrational beliefs that people associated with various adversities. Later, he categorized irrational beliefs into three major areas: a person *must* absolutely perform well and have the approval of significant others; a person *must* under all circumstances be treated kindly and lovingly by others, especially significant others; and a person *must* absolutely be comfortable in all conditions. In a humorous sense, he referred to these three categories of irrational beliefs as "musturbation." He cautioned clients against using other absolute terms such as *should, have to, ought to,* and *need to,* which invariably lead to making unreasonable demands and result in irrational thinking and unhappiness (Ellis, 1994).

One of the first cognitive–behavioral therapies, the basic premise behind REBT is that cognitions, emotions, and behaviors are not separate processes. Ellis often introduced this concept with a favorite quote by 1st-century stoic philosopher Epictetus, "Men feel disturbed not by things, but by the views which they take of them." REBT posits teaching the "A-B-C's" to clients, with A representing an activating (adversity) event, B an irrational belief, and C the emotional consequence. The therapeutic goal is for clients to dispute (D) the irrational belief, which is the real cause behind the emotional consequence—not the activating event that clients frequently associate with their unhappiness. After disputing the irrational belief the client should then adopt a new effective (E) philosophy leading to (F) new feelings (Ellis, 2004). An example is a presumption by someone that every vehicle driver should always abide by the rules of the road, and when they do not, the person becomes angry and reacts by honking the car horn, perhaps followed with a few choice words and gestures. The person attributes his or her anger (C: emotional consequence) to a bad driver (A: activating event). The real cause of the emotional response is linked to the person's irrational belief (B) that all drivers should be fully competent and must always follow traffic laws. The primary focus of REBT is for the person to dispute (D) this irrational belief, accept the fact that there are bad drivers on the road, and develop a more effective (E) philosophy. This leads to a change in the emotional response (new feelings: F) and the person not reacting to transgressions on the road.

REBT is used in both individual and group counseling and therapy. REBT groups focus on two major goals of assisting individuals with both unconditional self-acceptance and unconditional other-acceptance. If individual group members are capable of accepting themselves, they will also be more willing to accept others (Ellis, 2001). With REBT, group leaders use directive styles to challenge faulty assumptions and irrational beliefs that result in negative self-ratings and the blaming of others. Leaders assume roles as teachers to help members understand the importance of self-acceptance and develop the ability to discern the difference among cognitions, emotions, behaviors, and personal characteristics, faults and all. A number of techniques, such as questioning, challenging, giving homework, and role rehearsals, are used.

Therapeutic interventions with clients and group members include cognitive, emotive, and behavioral approaches. Cognitive approaches include the active disputing of irrational beliefs through the use of coping self-statements, psychoeducational presentations, and cognitive homework consisting of listing irrational beliefs and corresponding disputing statements. Emotive approaches include unconditional acceptance of self and others, **rational emotive imagery** (i.e., a process whereby clients are encouraged to imagine the worst outcome in a given situation and then change their reactant feelings of complete devastation to less destructive responses like disappointment or regret), humor, and shame-attacking exercises such as encouraging members to sing loudly in a crowded elevator or tying a ribbon around a banana and pretending it was a pet while out in public. Behavioral approaches are optimized with a combination of cognitive and emotive methods. Activities include homework assignments; in vivo desensitization involving repetitive encounters with what members fear most; role-playing; the use of reinforcements and penalties; and skills training, with the acquisition of new abilities influencing positive thoughts, feelings, and behaviors.

*Contributed by Phillip W. Barbee,
University of Texas at El Paso,
El Paso, TX*

References

Ellis, A. (1992). *Reason and emotion in psychotherapy.* New York: Stuart.

Ellis, A. (1994). *Reason and emotion in psychotherapy* (Rev. ed.). New York: Kensington.

Ellis, A. (2001). *Overcoming destructive beliefs, feelings and behaviors: New directions for rational emotive behavior therapy.* Amherst, NY: Prometheus Books.

Ellis, A. (2004). *Rational emotive behavior therapy: It works for me—It can work for you.* Amherst, NY: Prometheus Books.

Additional Resource

Ellis, A. (2000). *How to control your anxiety before it controls you.* New York: Citadel Press.

■Reality Therapy

William Glasser, a psychiatrist, developed reality therapy in the 1960s. **Reality therapy** can be classified under the cognitive–behavioral school of therapies due to its cognitive self-evaluation component and its emphasis on actions (Wubbolding, 2005). Over the years, Glasser has refined the theory, adding in elements of his control theory. Largely influenced by the work of William Powers (1973) in the area of perceptual control theory, Glasser's control theory emphasizes that behavior (e.g., thinking, feeling, doing) is chosen in reaction to a discrepancy between an inner vision of what people want and an inner vision of what people have. The chosen behavior is an effort to gain control over their lives (Glasser, 1984). Glasser later changed the focus from control theory to **choice theory,** to differentiate it, in part, from Power's theory and to help clarify that the theory concerns self-control rather than control over others (Sharf, 2008).

The primary emphasis in choice theory is that the majority of the behavior in people's lives is chosen to satisfy five genetically encoded needs: survival, love and belonging, power, freedom, and fun. According to the William Glasser Institute (n.d.), at present, reality therapy and choice theory are so intertwined in practice that they cannot be separated. The central premises of reality therapy and choice theory have been applied to therapy, education, management, relationships, and personality. Similar to rational emotive behavior therapy and Adlerian therapy, reality therapy emphasizes an internal control psychological system, which asserts that people's behavior originates within them and is influenced by physical and psychological needs (e.g., " I am choosing to depress because I am in an unhappy marriage") rather than being dictated by external events (e.g., "This marriage is causing me to be depressed").

These physical and psychological needs are manifested in wants and represented in reality therapy by the notion of a person's quality world. A person's **quality world** is a mental representation of the people and things that a person wants and values most. The motivation for behavior is the discrepancy that can exist between what a person wants and has.

The concept of behavior in reality therapy is broader than a focus on a person's specific actions. Behavior is viewed as "total behavior," consisting of actions, thoughts, feelings, and physiology. A key premise in reality therapy is that all behaviors are treated as if they are choices. A person's total behavior is viewed as purposeful choices aimed at obtaining from the outer world what a client perceives as satisfying needs and wants and communicating to the outer world messages of what the client needs.

In the practice of reality therapy, primary emphasis is given to the action component of total behavior, with a secondary emphasis on thoughts. This primary emphasis is on actions because if actions are changed, then the other components in a person's total behavior will change as well. Actions and thoughts are under the client's direct control, whereas feelings and physiology frequently are not. Professional counselors practicing reality therapy give less attention to feelings and physiology because these components of total behavior are viewed as difficult to change. Actions, in contrast, can be more readily influenced and modified. Feelings are attended to primarily as indicators that something is wrong in terms of a person being able to have one or more of her or his needs met effectively (Wubbolding, 2005).

As an aid to the practice of reality therapy, Wubbolding (2000) developed the acronym **WDEP** (see Reality Therapy: Underlying Principles and the WDEP System) to represent a general progression in the practice of reality therapy. WDEP stands for wants, doing, evaluation, and plan. Professional counselors initially seek to comprehend and help a client understand what it is he or she wants in relation to his or her needs. The counselor and client then explore what the client is doing, and willing to do, to obtain what the client wants. The counselor can then encourage the client to engage in a self-evaluation process to examine whether or not what the client is doing is helping obtain what is wanted. The counselor and client work together to develop a plan in which the client can choose more effective behaviors for achieving wants. In the course of working with a client, the counselor will teach the client the key concepts of choice theory, which offers an explanation for why people behave as they do. Once clients engage in a self-evaluation regarding their own behaviors, they can use the key concepts of choice theory in developing a plan that consists of more effective and satisfying behaviors to have needs met.

The incorporation of choice theory into reality therapy has resulted in some shifts in emphasis in the practice of reality therapy. A primary emphasis is given to the "love and belonging" need. Glasser (2001) contended that the source of virtually all clients' unhappiness was their failure to think and act in ways that helped them connect and get closer to the people they needed in their lives. Thus, a focus in reality therapy is helping clients find ways to reconnect with important people in their lives or to connect with new ones.

Beyond the emphasis on connection with significant persons, Glasser (2001) contended that knowledge of choice theory and external control psychology assists therapists in knowing additional characteristics about clients and their relationships: Clients tend to blame their problems on other people; clients tend to want to focus on their problems rather than on making changes to their behavior; clients want to blame their unhappiness on the past or potential future rather than focusing on the present; and clients tend to avoid the fact that they cannot control other people's behavior, only their own. This preknowledge regarding key client issues and considerations assists the counselor to focus the counseling process.

Through teaching choice theory and following the general WDEP process, a professional counselor can assist clients in understanding their wants, self-evaluating their current actions, and taking responsibility for making new and more effective choices to meet needs. The new behav-

ioral choices clients make emphasize reconnecting with important people in their lives or connecting with new ones and demonstrating self-control versus efforts to control other people.

Contributed by Robert I. Urofsky,
Clemson University, Clemson, SC

References

Glasser, W. (1984). *Control theory: A new explanation of how we control our lives.* New York: Harper & Row.

Glasser, W. (2001). *Counseling with choice theory: The new reality therapy.* New York: HarperCollins.

Powers, W. T. (1973). *Behavior: The control of perception.* Chicago: Aldine.

Sharf, R. S. (2008). *Theories of psychotherapy and counseling: Concepts and cases* (4th ed.). Belmont, CA: Thomson Brooks/Cole.

William Glasser Institute. (n.d.). *Reality therapy and choice theory.* Retrieved October 8, 2007, from http://wglasser.officewebsiteonline.com/images/articles/reality_choice.pdf

Wubbolding, R. (2000). *Reality therapy for the 21st century.* Philadelphia: Brunner-Routledge.

Wubbolding, R. (2005, October). *Teaching reality therapy.* Presentation at the conference of the Association for Counselor Education and Supervision, Pittsburgh, PA.

Additional Resources

Glasser, W. (1999). *Choice theory: A new psychology of personal freedom.* New York: HarperCollins.

Lennon, B. (2000). From "reality therapy" to "reality therapy in action." *International Journal of Reality Therapy, 20,* 41–46.

William Glasser Institute Web site: http://www.wglasser.com

■ Reality Therapy: Underlying Principles and the WDEP System

Developed in a mental hospital and a correctional institution, **reality therapy** has been applied to school, community, and family counseling; spirituality; aging; personal growth; management; and supervision (Glasser, 1965, 1998). It is widely used throughout North America and around the world. There are William Glasser Institutes in South America, Europe, Asia, Australia, and Africa. Current applications include parenting, self-help, and cross-cultural counseling.

Choice theory provides the theoretical basis for the delivery of reality therapy. As an internal control system, it is based on four psychological principles. First, human beings are not controlled by past behaviors or their environments; rather, they are motivated by current needs or genetic instructions: survival or self-preservation, belonging, power or inner control, freedom or independence, fun or enjoyment. Second, behavior is made up of actions, cognitions, feelings, and physiology. Choice plays a central role in counselor interventions, with emphasis on clients' ability to gain better control of their actions. The third principle is that behavior is purposeful. Behavior affects the external world and sends it a message. Finally, as a result of having an impact on and communicating with the world, human beings filter information through their perceptual system, which they use to recognize reality and put value on incoming information. In counseling, clients are asked how they fulfill their needs, what choices they are making and how they see their behavior (i.e., effective or ineffective), and how they perceive others as well as how others perceive their behavior.

The WDEP System

Wubbolding (1991, 2000, 2006) has formulated and developed an acronym for helping counselors and clients learn reality therapy. Each letter of the **WDEP system** represents a cluster of ideas and skills.

- **W:** Counselors explore clients' specific **wants** and desires related to each need: belonging, power or inner control, freedom or independence, and fun. Court-referred or involuntary clients manifesting resistant or hostile behavior often want people in authority or even their families to leave them alone. On the other hand, they want relationships that lead them toward more discord and torment rather than toward achievement, independence, and overall happiness. They want to satisfy their need for power and freedom by doing what pleases them, often without considering consequences or the impact of their behavior on others. Finally, their specific wants related to fun might challenge counselors' values and core beliefs.

- **D:** Counselors ask clients to **discuss** their actions, self-talk, and feelings. Emphasis rests on specific descriptions of current actions rather than on history. With involuntary and resistant clients, reality therapists ask, "What do other people think you're doing?" "What did they say to you when they sent you here?" "What changes do they want you to make?" The D includes a discussion of current behavior as well as clients' perceptions of how others view their behavior. Resistant clients sometimes deny responsibility for their own actions and are more willing to discuss others' perceptions of their behavior. They are not yet ready to take ownership of their own choices due to a perceived sense of external control. The reality therapist accepts this sense of external control and gradually leads them to a perceived inner locus of control.

- **E: Self-evaluation** is the cornerstone in the practice of reality therapy. Many clients who demonstrate difficult behaviors lack skill in examining the effectiveness of their behavior and the attainability of their wants. Consequently, after professional counselors have established the foundational relationship with clients, they assist them in evaluating their behavior by asking such questions as "Are your current actions getting you what you want?" "Are they helping you or the people around you?" "Is what you want attainable?"

Clients reared in substance abusing or dysfunctional families and families where inconsistency and lack of structure reign are often deficient in the skill of self-evaluation. They also lack skill in determining the efficacy of their choices and the attainability of their wants. The counselor, therefore, teaches these skills by asking appropriate and thoughtful questions.

- **P: Planning** for effective change follows self-evaluation. When clients decide their current choices are creating turmoil, trouble, and even their own unhappiness, they make plans for a more positive and productive life. Their plans can be strategic, but more often they are **s**imple, **a**ttainable, **m**easurable, **i**mmediate, **c**ontrolled by the planner, and **c**onsistent (SAMIC^2; i.e., repeated).

The WDEP system can facilitate inclusion, a sense of commonality among clients or group members, a willingness to work on issues, conflict resolution, and effective problem solving. By using creative inquiry skills and direct teaching, the professional counselor and group members promote the development and maturity of the group.

Choice theory provides foundational principles for the successful use of the WDEP system of reality therapy by emphasizing that human beings can control their own destinies by choosing to satisfy their five needs. When professional counselors incorporate effective questioning skills based on the WDEP system into the art of counseling, they assist clients to develop a sense of inner control, a skill in courageously examining and evaluating their behavior, and efficacious planning techniques aimed at productive living.

Contributed by Robert E. Wubbolding,
Xavier University, Cincinnati, OH

References

Glasser, W. (1965). *Reality therapy*. New York: HarperCollins.
Glasser, W. (1998). *Choice theory*. New York: HarperCollins.
Wubbolding, R. (1991). *Understanding reality therapy*. New York: HarperCollins.
Wubbolding, R. (2000). *Reality therapy for the 21st century*. Philadelphia: Brunner-Routledge.
Wubbolding, R. (2006). *Reality therapy training manual* (14th ed.). Cincinnati, OH: Center for Reality Therapy.

■ Rehabilitation Counseling

Rehabilitation counseling is a specialty within the counseling profession that has counseling at its core and has an emphasis on the emotional and psychological adjustment of clients with a disability. Rehabilitation counseling is defined as a systematic application of the counseling process that assists persons with a physical, mental, developmental, cognitive, and/or emotional disability to achieve his or her personal, career, and independent living goals in the most integrated setting possible (Commission on Rehabilitation Counselor Certification [CRCC], 2003). As with all counseling professions, the rehabilitation counseling process involves communication, goal setting, and beneficial growth or change through empowerment; self-advocacy; and psychological, vocational, social, and behavioral interventions.

What, perhaps, sets rehabilitation counseling apart from other forms of counseling is that rehabilitation counseling is actually the combination of two skill sets, counseling and rehabilitation, and includes an intersection of the knowledge and applications of counseling with the knowledge and applications of the medical and psychological needs of clients with a disability. Primary functions of the rehabilitation counselor are to work with clients who have a disability to help them develop or enhance their coping skills to achieve increased independence and self-actualization, to develop vocational skills to secure gainful employment (if applicable), and to develop other skills needed to increase or enhance their ability to function in the community.

Rehabilitation and related services that generally fall under the umbrella of rehabilitation counseling include assessment and appraisal; diagnosis and treatment planning; career (vocational) counseling; individual and group counseling focused on facilitating adjustment to the medical and psychosocial impact of disability; case management, referral, and service coordination; program evaluation and research; interventions to remove environmental, employment, and attitudinal barriers; consultation among multiple parties and regulatory systems; job analysis, job development, and job placement services, including assistance with employment and job accommodations; and consultation about and access to rehabilitation technology (CRCC, 2003). Another component includes postplacement services to ensure the client's successful transition to competitive or supported employment and to facilitate continued success on the job. Rehabilitation counseling is a holistic process that considers the whole person, including the nature of the client's medical condition, injury, or disability; his or her ability to adapt to the situation; his or her ability to live as independently as possible; and, where appropriate, his or her ability to function in a work setting.

History of the Rehabilitation Counseling Profession

Rehabilitation counseling history parallels society's attitudes toward and treatment of individuals with disabilities. Historically, this attitude has ranged from benign neglect and abuse (Rubin & Roessler, 2000) to present-day attitudes of empowerment and equality for all persons. The philosophy that forms contemporary rehabilitation counseling in the United States started in the early 1900s and is based on the progression of social movements that provided for the basic economic and health care needs of formerly marginalized groups of people. It can even be said that the evolution of rehabilitation counseling and rehabilitation service delivery mirrors the evolution of the industrial world to the point where self-determination and independence are a central component of rehabilitation counseling in present times (Neulicht & Berens, 2004).

The historical roots of rehabilitation counseling as a profession in the United States can be traced to 1920 with the passage of the Smith-Fess Act (i.e., the Vocational Rehabilitation Act of 1920), which established public vocational rehabilitation programs in all states for individuals with disabilities. The needs of individuals with disabilities became a major driving force for rehabilitation counseling after World War I due to the large numbers of veterans returning from war with disabling injuries from the war. These veterans, having survived their battle wounds, required rehabilitation counseling services to facilitate their and their family members' adjustment to their disability as well as their reintegration into society. This is a situation not at all unlike that of more recent veterans who have survived catastrophic and permanent disabilities and are returning to the United States to resume their lives. In this way, rehabilitation counseling is a profession that provides clients the tools for equal opportunity in society and emphasizes the normalization of disability through self-awareness, empowerment, and services that allow clients to attain and maintain their optimum functional ability. Current rehabilitation counseling practices include consumer choice and informed consent, empowerment, community reintegration, and the right of clients to contribute to society in a citizen capacity (Neulicht & Berens, 2004).

Opportunities in Rehabilitation Counseling

An important concept to bear in mind is that rehabilitation counseling, as one of the counseling professions, mandates that rehabilitation counselors be professional counselors first, although they also have education and training in the medical and psychological aspects of a variety of disabilities and/or disabling conditions (e.g., traumatic brain injury from a motor vehicle wreck, fall, or diving or hunting incident; acquired brain injury from a stroke, brain aneurysm, or tumor; amputation; severe burn; spinal cord injury; blindness; deafness; HIV/AIDS; mental illness; chronic and disabling back or other orthopedic injury; pain). As with most counseling professions, a master's degree in rehabilitation counseling is considered the requisite degree in order to practice as a rehabilitation counselor. In general, to be considered a qualified provider of rehabilitation counseling services, rehabilitation counselors must hold a master's degree in rehabilitation counseling or a related counseling discipline, be nationally certified as a rehabilitation counselor (i.e., hold the Certified Rehabilitation Counselor credential), and qualify for licensure (i.e., Licensed Professional Counselor) if they practice in a state where rehabilitation counselors are expected to be licensed in order to practice (CRCC, n.d.).

Even as recently as the early 1980s, there was limited opportunity for rehabilitation counselors to work in settings other than public vocational rehabilitation agencies, and most training programs placed a heavy emphasis on public sector practice (Weed & Field, 2001). However, with accelerating changes over the past 20 years, including advances in science, medicine, and technology, as well as an increase in the number of individuals living with a disability in U.S. society, rehabilitation counselors now work in a variety of employment settings ranging from the traditional public vocational rehabilitation agencies to Veterans Affairs programs, evaluation/training centers, specialty rehabilitation and psychiatric hospitals, community-based rehabilitation centers or programs, supported employment programs, workers' compensation and insurance rehabilitation agencies, disability management programs, employee assistance programs, schools, residential and independent living centers, mental health centers, drug treatment programs, case management, rehabilitation technology, student services and/or disability services departments at colleges and universities, jails and detention centers, career guidance and outplacement programs, private practice, and other public or private employment settings. Within the profession of rehabilitation counseling, rehabilitation counselors may work directly with clients or as counselor educators, counselor supervisors, or rehabilitation program administrators. Although the technical aspects of the rehabilitation counseling process may vary depending on the client population and the setting in which the services are provided, the essential elements of counseling are constant.

Rehabilitation counseling, as a profession, provides services to clients with a disability to enable them to address social, emotional, educational, vocational, and medically or psychologically related problems. As a holistic service-delivery system, rehabilitation counseling offers the opportunity to inform individuals with disabilities about educational, social, emotional, psychological, medical, or vocational planning as well as to guide them in identifying the supports they have and overcoming the barriers that continue to challenge individuals with a disability and their families in the 21st century.

Contributed by Debra E. Berens,
Georgia State University, Atlanta, GA

References

Commission on Rehabilitation Counselor Certification. (2003). *Scope of practice for rehabilitation counseling.* Retrieved June 7, 2007, from http://www.crccertification.com/pages/35scope.html

Commission on Rehabilitation Counselor Certification. (n.d.). *Rehabilitation counseling: The profession and standards of practice.* Rolling Meadows, IL: Author.

Neulicht, A. T., & Berens, D. E. (2004). The role of the vocational counselor in life care planning. In S. Riddick-Grisham (Ed.), *Pediatric life care planning and case management.* Boca Raton, FL: CRC Press.

Rubin, S. E., & Roessler, R. T. (2000). *Foundations of the vocational rehabilitation process* (5th ed.). Austin, TX: PRO-ED.

Weed, R. O., & Field. T. F. (2001). *Rehabilitation consultant's handbook* (Rev. ed.). Athens, GA: Elliott & Fitzpatrick.

Additional Resources

American Rehabilitation Counseling Association Web site: http://www.arcaweb.org/

Commission on Rehabilitation Counselor Certification Web site: www.crccertification.com

Online Resource for Americans With Disabilities Web site: http://www.disability.gov

Reinforcement Schedules

B. F. Skinner, one of the most influential and controversial figures in modern psychology, first described the concept of **reinforcement schedules,** which were based on experiments carried out initially on rats in his laboratory at Harvard University in the 1930s. From this basic research, Skinner and subsequent colleagues discovered that different schedules of reinforcement produced very predictable patterns of responding, even in humans.

The term **reinforcement** is used to describe any stimulus that strengthens one or more dimensions (i.e., duration, frequency, intensity, latency) of behavior in the future. Reinforcement is technically differentiated from the term **reward** in that a reward has no demonstrable effect on subsequent behavior, although laypersons frequently use the words *reinforcement* and *reward* interchangeably. It is also important to recognize that both positive reinforcement and negative reinforcement have the same effect on behavior; that is, they both increase the likelihood that a behavior will reoccur. The only difference is that **positive reinforcement** involves the contingent introduction of a stimulus, whereas **negative reinforcement** involves the contingent removal of a stimulus to strengthen behavior.

There are five basic reinforcement schedules: (a) continuous, (b) fixed ratio, (c) fixed interval, (d) variable ratio, and (e) variable interval. Each of these schedules produces different rates of responding in both human and nonhuman animals and is used in a variety of work, educational, and social settings. Sometimes reinforcement schedules occur naturally and are not programmed, whereas, in other instances, individuals make intentional use of one of these schedules to alter behavior or to change a pattern of responding.

A **continuous reinforcement (CRF) schedule** refers to situations in which every instance of a particular behavior is reinforced. Behaviors that are reinforced on a continuous schedule occur very rapidly until the organism becomes tired or satiated. One example of a naturally occurring continuous reinforcement schedule is parents who return a smile every time their infant smiles. The effect is an increase in the frequency, and perhaps duration, of the smiling by the infants. CRF schedules are preferred when teaching a new behavior or reinstating a behavior that an individual used to perform but no longer performs. To maximize effectiveness over the long term, continuous schedules should be gradually **thinned** to one of the other reinforcement schedules. One limitation of a CRF schedule is that it is very sensitive to the effects of **extinction,** defined as no longer reinforcing a previously reinforced response. From the smiling example above, if the parents stop returning smiles completely, the infant will evidence an initial increase in smiling, called an **extinction burst,** but then will rapidly decrease the frequency of smiling. This is a very predictable pattern of behavior and has been demonstrated across behaviors and organisms.

A **fixed ratio (FR)** schedule of reinforcement means that reinforcement is delivered after a fixed number of responses. That is, an FR 10 indicates that every 10th response will result in reinforcement. One example of a programmed FR schedule is a parent who allows his or her child to take a 5-minute break after correctly completing 10 math problems. The break from work is a negative reinforcer for completing 10 math problems. FR schedules, if gradually increased (e.g., from FR 5 to FR 300) produce high, steady rates of responding and a **postreinforcement pause** (i.e., a pause in responding after delivery of reinforcement). It is important to understand that the length of the postreinforcement pause depends on the number of responses required to earn reinforcement—the higher the FR value, the longer the pause (e.g., the individual stops responding for awhile); that is, a behavior that is programmed on an FR 500 schedule will result in a longer postreinforcement pause than the same behavior programmed on an FR 15 schedule. Behaviors that are on an FR schedule are moderately to highly resistant to extinction, especially when the ratio values are high.

Fixed interval (FI) schedules are similar to FR schedules in that they are both based on some type of fixed value and produce a postreinforcement pause. The primary differences are that an FI schedule is based on time rather than number of responses, and FI schedules result in gradually increasing responding as the interval increases, with a greater number of responses near the end of the interval instead of the characteristically steady responding of FR schedules. With FI schedules, a set amount of time must pass before a particular behavior will be reinforced. That is, an FI 4min means that four minutes must pass before an instance of the target behavior will be reinforced. Delivery of reinforcement resets the interval. During the interval, it is not unusual for the person to make **probe responses.** These are responses that occur infrequently to test whether or not reinforcement is available. An example of a naturally occurring FI schedule is seen at day care centers where food is provided on a structured schedule (e.g., snacks and meals occur at approximately 2-hour intervals). If a snack has just been provided at 10 a.m., children will sporadically ask for food a couple of times between 10 a.m. and lunchtime (probe responses), which is typically at noon. As time grows closer to noon, a greater amount of food-seeking behavior will occur, and the behaviors associated with eating will begin to occur (e.g., lining up to wash hands, sitting at the lunch table). At noon, food-seeking will be reinforced with lunch.

A **variable ratio (VR)** schedule is similar to the FR schedule except that a varied number of responses are required to earn reinforcement. For instance, a VR 10 means that, on average, every 10th response will be reinforced; actual reinforcement may occur after the 3rd, 9th, 5th, 16th, and so forth response. The VR schedule produces a high, steady rate of responding with very little or no postreinforcement pause. Behaviors that are on a VR schedule are also very resistant to the effects of extinction; that is, the behavior will persist for long periods of time without any immediate reinforcement. Perhaps the best example of a programmed VR schedule is a slot machine. The gambler is unsure of the exact schedule in effect but will play for long periods of time for infrequent reinforcement. Another example of a VR schedule is fishing. Typically, a fish is not caught every time (CRF) or every seventh time (FR 7) a cast is made. A fish

may be caught after the 20th cast, 14th, 32nd, 19th, and so on. The VR schedule explains why fisherman will persist for extended periods of time without actually catching any fish.

A **variable interval (VI)** schedule specifies that a variable amount of time must pass before an instance of the target behavior will be reinforced. A VI 20min schedule means that, on average, 20 minutes must elapse before the behavior will be reinforced. VI schedules produce moderate yet steady responding that is highly resistant to extinction. Everyday examples of VI schedules include the number of seconds a baby cries before an adult responds, the amount of time a person must wait in the checkout line of the supermarket, and the number of minutes it takes to drive from home to work. In fact, it can be safely said that many more daily events are on a VI schedule than an FI schedule.

Contributed by T. Steuart Watson and
Tonya S. Watson,
Miami University, Miami, OH

Additional Resources

Chance. P. (1998). *First course in applied behavior analysis.* Pacific Grove, CA: Brooks/Cole.

Pierce, W. D., & Epling, W. F. (1995). *Behavior analysis and learning.* Englewood Cliffs, NJ: Prentice Hall.

Skinner, B. F. (1953). *Science and human behavior.* New York: Macmillan.

■ Reliability

Reliability in measurement and assessment generally is concerned with the extent to which appraisal instruments produce similar results, and thus lead to similar inferences, as a function of their item composition, the elapsed time between successive administrations of the same instrument, and the equivalence of different forms of instruments designed to measure the same construct. The various types of reliability (e.g., internal consistency, split-half, interitem, Kuder–Richardson 20 [K-R 20], Kuder–Richardson 21 [K-R 21], test–retest, alternate-forms, and interrater reliability) make up one of the two most important psychometric characteristics of test instruments, the other being validity. Test developers use reliability information to select those items that are the most consistent with other items or that contribute to the overall test score stability for a chosen interval of time. Some psychometricians maintain that establishing the various forms of reliability, especially internal consistency and test–retest, is paramount and primary over validity. This reasoning is based on the fact that a measure cannot correlate with any other measure more than it correlates with itself. Hence, reliability limits validity.

An understanding of reliability is facilitated by considering the following equation from **classical true-score theory:** $X = T + E$, where X is the observed score on an individual test item, T is the **true score** that represents that level of trait or characteristic that the responder possesses, and E is the **error score** or error of measurement (Allen & Yen, 1979). A similar conceptualization (score = trait + error) can be used when considering how individual items in a measure function together in a population of respondents. Further assumptions of classical true-score theory include (a) the expected value (i.e., population mean) of observed scores (X) provides an estimate of the true scores (T), $\varepsilon(X) = T$; (b) the correlation of error (E) and true score trait (T) is zero in a population of examinees ($\rho_{ET} = 0$); (c) examinees' errors on two tests, E_1 and E_2, are uncorrelated ($\rho_{E_1 E_2} = 0$); and (d) examinees' errors on one test (E_1) are uncorrelated with their true scores on another test T_2 ($\rho_{E_1 T_2} = 0$). Two tests are considered parallel if they have observed scores X_1 and X_2 that satisfy the assumptions given earlier and, for the population of examinees, $T_1 = T_2$ and $E_1 = E_2$ (Allen & Yen, 1979, p. 57).

According to classical true-score theory, the reliability coefficient of two parallel tests is the proportion of variance among test scores that is due to true-score variance. Reliability = true variance / observed variance:

$$\rho_{X_1 X_2} = \frac{\sigma_T^2}{\sigma_{X_1}^2} = \rho_{X_1 T}^2,$$

where observed variance = true variance + error variance:

$$\sigma_{X_1}^2 = \sigma_T^2 + \sigma_E^2.$$

In addition, the reliability coefficient is equal to the square of the correlation between the observed and true scores. These equations can be rearranged to yield the standard error of measurement, which is the proportion of true score variability that is due to unreliability or error:

$$\sigma_{E_1}^2 = \sigma_X^2 (1 - \rho_{X_1 X_2}).$$

Internal consistency reliability is a measure of the extent to which the items in a measure consistently assess a single trait or construct. A measure is considered internally consistent if its items or items in respective subscales that are meant to measure different traits all exhibit high intercorrelations. Although inspection of such correlations provides good descriptive information, the procedure becomes cumbersome if there are a large number of test items. The need for a more parsimonious summary measure of item consistency gave rise to **split-half reliability,** which involves splitting a test into random, equal halves and then intercorrelating them. Because reliability will be attenuated when tests are shortened due to splitting, the **Spearman–Brown prophecy formula** is used to estimate the reliability of the whole test if the split tests are parallel:

$$\rho_{X_1 X_2} = \frac{N\rho_{YY'}}{1 + (N-1)\rho_{YY'}},$$

where N is the number of parallel tests and $\rho_{YY'}$ is the correlation between any two of the N parallel tests.

Because there are many possible ways to split a set of test items (e.g., even-odd, first and last halves), Cronbach (1951) developed a statistic (coefficient alpha [α]) that represents the degree of consistency among all possible ways of splitting a test. **Cronbach's alpha** ranges from 0 to 1; higher values indicate that the items function similarly in assessing T. Lower values of alpha suggest that one or more items may be assessing a different trait/characteristic than T. Such items may be discarded during the test-development phase or, in some cases, pooled with similar items to create a measure of another trait or characteristic, T_2. In the special case where items possess a dichotomous response format (i.e., true–false, yes–no), the internal consistency of a test is assessed using the **K-R 20 coefficient** (Kuder & Richardson, 1937). The **K-R 21 coefficient** makes the assumption that the difficulties of all items on the test are the same; this makes the K-R 21 easier to calculate. If all item difficulties are not the same, however, K-R 21 is not appropriate and will underestimate the internal consistency of the test (i.e., K-R 20 $\geq$ K-R 21).

Some testing purposes, such as intellectual assessment, require test authors to construct alternate or parallel forms of instruments because examinees can learn test items at one testing and, hence, the assessment will yield invalid results when used subsequently. As discussed earlier in this entry, the extent to which a second test form reproduces or repeats an ability or trait estimate that is consistent with the estimate on the first test form provides test users with an estimate of the extent to which a test possesses reliability across its alternate forms.

Test–retest reliability (r_{tt}) provides an indication of the extent to which scores on a test are reproducible over an interval of time. This reliability coefficient is calculated by administering a test to the same examinees over two different occasions and then intercorrelating each examinee's score on the first administration with his or her respective score on the second administration. Test developers must also examine the similarities of scores across the interval by using scatterplots or t tests to determine the degree of change in test scores over time that may be due to some systematic influence. Also, in evaluating test–retest reliability coefficients, test authors should specify the test–retest interval; the usefulness of test–retest reliability is limited without this information.

Interrater reliability should be evaluated for assessment procedures, such as behavioral checklists that require two or more observers to record the presence or absence (or the extent) of some phenomenon. A standardized interview or observation protocol would possess interrater reliability to the extent that two observers consistently agree in the results they produce in observing the same sample of behavior. Similarly, **interscorer reliability** pertains to the extent to which different evaluators can subjectively score the results from a multiple-choice exam or from a set of open-ended items of a personality or intellectual instrument, for example, in a consistent, reproducible manner. The **phi coefficient (r_ϕ)** may be used to indicate reliability when raters are evaluating the simple presence or absence of something. On other occasions, interrater or interscorer reliability is expressed simply as the percentage of agreement among raters. More typically, the reliability between different raters who are judging the degree or extent of some phenomena may be expressed as a Pearson product–moment correlation coefficient. Some test developers prefer to use **Cohen's κ coefficient** because it adjusts for the possibility that interrater or interscorer agreement occurs due to chance. Finally, some test developers also use intraclass correlation coefficients to evaluate this type of reliability.

Test users should also examine the various reliability coefficients to determine whether an instrument meets their requirements for a given purpose (e.g., research or individual appraisal). The *Standards for Educational and Psychological Testing* (American Educational Research Association, American Psychological Association, & National Council on Measurement in Education, 1999) provides guidelines on the manner in which the psychometric properties of appraisal instruments should be established and reported. Test users should also be aware of how the *Standards* are applied in counseling contexts (Association for Assessment in Counseling and Education, 2002).

Contributed by Alan E. Stewart,
The University of Georgia, Athens, GA

References

Allen, M. J., & Yen, W. M. (1979). *Introduction to measurement theory*. Monterey, CA: Brooks/Cole.

American Educational Research Association, American Psychological Association, & National Council on Measurement in Education. (1999). *Standards for educational and psychological testing*. Washington, DC: American Psychological Association.

Association for Assessment in Counseling and Education. (2002). *Applying the standards for educational and psychological testing—What a counselor needs to know*. Alexandria, VA: Author.

Cronbach, L. J. (1951). Coefficient alpha and the internal structure of tests. *Psychometrika, 16,* 297–334.

Kuder, G. F., & Richardson, M. W. (1937). The theory of the estimation of test reliability. *Psychometrika, 2,* 151–160.

Additional Resources

Anastasi, A., & Urbina, S. (1997). *Psychological testing* (7th ed.). Upper Saddle River, NJ: Prentice Hall.

Erford, B. T. (Ed.). (2006). *Assessment for counselors*. Boston: Houghton Mifflin.

■ Research and Evaluation, Key Ethical Issues in

Ethics are a system of moral principles or rules of conduct that are recognized by a particular group of individuals or professionals in respect to behaviors, decisions, or situations (see Ethical Principles). Ethics can be applied to research. Research is defined as a systematic or structured inquiry into a particular subject matter in order to discover or amend facts or theories. Thus, research ethics are principles or standards that are designed to guide an individual's judgment and decision-making process when it comes to designing, implementing, and completing research. Although ethics are not designed to provide an answer to a specific question, ethics can be used as a guide when making choices that pose ethical dilemmas.

The **Office of Research Integrity,** a federal organization that oversees, promotes, and directs research integrity for biomedical and behavioral research, and professional organizations such as the American Counseling Association (ACA) provide standards for conducting research in a responsible and ethical manner. These standards cover behaviors such as collecting, managing, and analyzing data; providing protection for human participants; respecting the rights of research participants; and reporting results. For example, ACA (2005) provides an ethical code that indicates that the researcher should not deviate from standard practices of counseling when conducting research. Thus, if a researcher attempts to examine the effects of a new intervention or treatment modality, the researcher needs to have a rationale for why the new method is appropriate and provide the client with informed consent that the treatment is not what is currently considered evidence-based practice. In addition, when using a new treatment method, the researcher must take precautions to avoid unnecessary risk or injury to the human participant.

Informed consent is a common method where the participant is provided with the purpose of the study, the procedures, what the direct risks and the benefits are, where the results would be made available, and how long and where data will be stored. Informed consent allows the participant to make an educated choice about whether or not to participate in the study (see Informed Consent).

Although protection of human participants and research ethics, in general, may seem commonplace, these guidelines were not always present or implemented. Most of the ethical standards today arose out of research experiments conducted on humans that did not respect or protect the rights of research participants. More specifically, one particular series of experiments, **the Nazi medical war crimes,** led to the development of ethical standards in research explicitly designed to protect human participants.

The Nazi medical war crimes, which were conducted during World War II by the German Nazi regime, were experiments conducted on thousands of prisoners in concentration camps. The purpose of these experiments was to ascertain how the human body would react to various situations. More specifically, multiple tests subjected the prisoners to horrendous situations that caused physical pain, disabilities, sterilization, mental and physical illnesses, and death. These experiments were conducted either through force or through deception. Thus, prisoners did not provide consent to participate in the studies, and injuries to participants were intentionally inflicted.

Because the victims of the Nazi medical war crimes were accorded no human rights protection and in response to the crimes committed then, the **Nuremberg Code** was created in 1947. The Nuremberg Code was one of the first sets of standards that required protection of human participants in research. The main tenets of the code include providing human participants with information so they have the ability to give informed consent and participate voluntarily in a study.

Regrettably, even after the Nuremberg Code was put into place to protect human participants, their rights were not always defended. Unethical experiments still occurred. Studies such as the **Tuskegee Syphilis Experiment,** in which physicians were interested in understanding how syphilis affected the human body, ran for 40 years (1932 to 1972) before it was publicly acknowledged as unethical. In this study, 400 Black men who had syphilis were informed they would have free medical treatment for their condition. Unfortunately, the patients were unaware of what their "condition" was and were never informed they actually had syphilis. After the initial 4 years of the experiment, physicians realized that those individuals with syphilis experienced problems that were more severe, including medical and mental symptoms from tumors, heart disease, paralysis, blindness, and insanity, than those patients without syphilis. Within 10 years, the death rate for the men with syphilis was double the rate of individuals without syphilis, yet the physicians did not provide any true treatment for syphilis besides a placebo of aspirin—even when penicillin was discovered as a cure in the 1940s (National Commission for the Protection of Human Subjects of Biomedical and Behavioral Research, 1979). Ultimately, what the doctors were interested in, unbeknownst to the research participants, was the data they would collect from the bodies of the deceased participants during autopsies. Thus, the goal was never to provide medical treatment but to provide placebo-based treatment until death. Extreme forms of deception were used with the patients and their families in this experiment.

Other unethical studies that went against the Nuremberg Code include the **Jewish Chronic Disease Hospital Study,** in which patients were injected with live cancer cells to determine if their bodies could reject cancer cells and if the ability to reject was related to a healthy or debilitated body. The patients were, however, never notified that cancer cells were injected into their bodies, nor was written informed consent provided to patients.

The **Willowbrook Study** (1960s) consisted of a school that housed children with mental disabilities. The purpose of the study was to examine the effects of hepatitis in a controlled setting; therefore, any parent who wanted to admit his or her child to Willowbrook was required to sign a consent form to allow the child to be injected with the hepatitis virus. Although parents knew the injection would take place, they were misinformed that the only way they could admit their child would be if they consented to the injection, and the parents were not informed of the later risks of hepatitis (e.g., chronic liver failure). In addition, none of the children were offered the ability to assent to the experiment.

In addition to medical studies and the impact of various diseases and foreign objects on the body, unethical behavioral and sociological studies were also conducted. Some of these studies are the **Milgram Obedience Study** in the 1960s, which used deception to understand the conditions under which people obey orders, and the **Tearoom Trade Study,** in which deception was used to collect data on why men had sex in public restrooms. In both instances, the participants had no idea what the study was truly about, nor were the participants debriefed afterward regarding the true nature of the study.

On the basis of the lack of protection of human participants in these and other studies, the Belmont Report was created in 1979. The **Belmont Report** added to the Nuremberg Code by formulating three main tenets for researchers. These tenets are (a) respect for persons (i.e., all human participants should be allowed autonomy to make their own choices, and when an individual has a diminished autonomy [e.g., children, mentally disabled, prisoners], additional protections will be provided); (b) beneficence (i.e., researchers will protect human participants from harm before, during, and after the study, and overall benefits should outweigh the risks); and (c) justice (i.e., that benefits and risks are fairly distributed among participants).

In addition to ethics related to the protection of human participants, as discussed by the Nuremberg Code and the Belmont Report, other areas of research ethics exist. Thus, although the 2005 *ACA Code of Ethics* in Section G: Research and Publication specifically covers human participants' rights in sections G.1. and G.2., it also includes many other references to research ethics. Another protection of human participants' rights is the prohibition against researchers engaging in non-research-related relationships with research participants. This prohibition includes sexual or intimate and nonprofessional relationships. When an interaction with a research participant seems to be beneficial in any way (e.g., the research participant could provide additional business for the agency; a future collegial relationship seems feasible), the researcher must document and rationalize the possible interaction prior to the study, if feasible.

Although the protection of human participants is a major concern in research ethics, ACA does address additional stages of the research process in its ethical code. One of the first stages of research after the completion of the study is reporting the results. It is ethical to report accurate results that are favorable and unfavorable, report errors that occurred during the research study if they are relevant to the findings, ensure that data are not falsified or distorted, ensure that all aspects of the study and variables are provided, and ensure that limitations of the study are discussed. An accurate and thorough reporting of the study and its findings helps others to replicate the study, eventually leading to evidence-based practices in counseling.

The results of research are typically published in journals or books or presented at workshops and conferences. When publishing results, it is important that researchers give credit to individuals who contributed to the study. This includes acknowledging any financial contributions or support as well as acknowledging other researchers who assisted in conducting the study. At a minimum, contributors should be recognized through acknowledgement statements at the beginning of a presentation or article, but if there was significant involvement by a contributor, that individual should be acknowledged through authorship. In order to avoid any later disputes, the ethical manner of determining authorship should actually be decided prior to the research study. These decisions include the order of authorship as well as the expected responsibilities to be carried out during the study. The order of authorship also involves respect for student-initiated and student-conducted research; thus, according to *ACA Code of Ethics* (ACA, 2005), when the research is based on a student's papers, thesis, or dissertation, then the student should be the first author. Finally, in reporting results, previous related research should be appropriately acknowledged and cited in the manuscript. Finally, it should be expected by authors—and the profession and general public—that a fair, confidential review will be given to of all manuscripts submitted for review, with the expectation that authors will not simultaneously submit the same or a similar article to more than one outlet.

Contributed by Kelly L. Wester,
The University of North Carolina at
Greensboro, Greensboro, NC

References

American Counseling Association. (2005). *ACA code of ethics.* Alexandria, VA: Author.
National Commission for the Protection of Human Subjects of Biomedical and Behavioral Research. (1979). *The Belmont Report: Ethical principles and guidelines for the protection of human subjects of research.* Retrieved June 17, 2006, from http://ohsr.od.nih.gov/guidelines/belmont.html#gob3

Additional Resources

Institute of Medicine. (2002). *Integrity in scientific research: Creating an environment that promotes responsible conduct.* Washington, DC: The National Academies Press.
Office of Research Integrity Web site: http;//ori.dhhs.gov
Steneck, N. (2004). *Introduction to the responsible conduct of research.* Rockville, MD: Office of Research Integrity. Retrieved May 17, 2007, from http://ori.hhs.gov/documents/rcrintro.pdf

■ Research and Evaluation, Key Historical Events

Many significant events in the development of research and evaluation practices have evolved in the context of major research paradigms. A **research paradigm** is the framework for organizing a study. The selection of a research paradigm is guided by how researchers view reality (e.g., is reality objective or subjective?), how and to what extent knowledge is acquired (e.g., is it limited or contextual?), the degree to which researchers perceive their values should bias the research, and researchers' perceptions on research design (i.e., how data are collected). There are numerous paradigms, including positivism, postpositivism, constructivism/interpretivism, and critical ideological positions. Positivism and postpositivism are the foundation of quantitative research, whereas constructivism/interpretivism and critical/ideologi-

cal paradigms are associated with qualitative research. In the discussion in this entry of each paradigm, key historical events and the individuals associated with the development of the paradigm are highlighted.

Positivism

Positivism is a hypothetical-deductive method (Ponterotto, 2005). It involves systematic observation and description of observations in the context of a model or theory, the presentation of an explanation for the observations, the execution of tightly controlled experimental study, the use of inferential statistics to test the explanations, and the interpretation of statistical results in light of the original theory. Positivism is based on the positivists' acknowledgement of an objective truth, that this truth can be captured, that this reality or truth is captured through data, and that large enough samples are the best way of getting to this truth because having large enough samples minimizes bias. The main focus of positivism is to corroborate a priori hypotheses, which are frequently stated in quantitative propositions, using a hypothetical-deductive method to achieve this purpose. The major objective of positivism is clarification that results in the calculation and direction of observable facts (Ponterotto, 2005).

Positivism developed during the Enlightenment period (17th–18th centuries) when philosophers moved away from the earlier Dark Ages acceptance, usually without question, of the totalitarian royal and religious order of the day. Positivism is based on Mill's book, *System of Logic* (Denzin & Lincoln, 2005). A summary of Mill's basic assumptions include (a) that natural and social sciences should lead to laws that lead to explanation and prediction, (b) the same sciences should include hypothetical-deductive methodology, (c) ideas should be classified by type, (d) there is consistency in nature of time and space, (e) the laws of nature can be obtained from statistical data, and (f) large samples show generalities or universal laws of nature (Ponterotto, 2005). Some prominent researchers who have used a positivist method include Philipp Frank (1884–1966) and Herbert Fiegl (1902–1988). Frank and Fiegl were attached to the Vienna circle of Logical Positivists (1920s) who campaigned for a systematic reduction of human knowledge to logical and scientific foundations.

Postpositivism

Although **postpositivism** shares many characteristics with positivism, the major difference between the two paradigms is that positivism stresses the confirmation of a theory and postpositivism stresses the disproving of a theory. In essence, postpositivists assert that a universal truth can only be approximated because reality cannot be measured without error. Theories are meant to be falsified in order to strengthen them (Ponterotto, 2005). Postpositivism developed because of discontent with some areas of positivism and asserted that truth can never be fully attained but only approximated. In essence, there will always be some error involved in arriving at truth. Concepts such as reliability and validity have been emphasized in research and evaluation based on these assumptions. One of the main supporters of postpositivism was the modern philosopher Karl Raimund Popper (1959–1994; Denzin & Lincoln, 2005). Popper is famous for his rejection of verification of knowledge used by positivists and promoting falsification of knowledge instead. John Dewey (1859–1952) is also a renowned psychologist mentioned in connection with postpositivism. Dewey believed that hypotheses should be tested against experience in order to survive. Dewey approached scientific inquiry in a tentative and fallible manner; this means that there is no absolute truth. Dewey's approach has created room for advancement in education and morality.

Constructivism/Interpretivism

Constructivism or **interpretivism** is an alternative research paradigm to positivism. This paradigm assumes that there are multiple truths versus the positivism assumption of a single, objective truth (Ponterotto, 2005). Constructivism assumes that the truth is created in the mind of an individual, whereas the positivism position is that truth is found outside the individual. Constructivism maintains that the truth is concealed and has to be arrived at through interaction between the researcher and the participant. The researcher and participant generate (i.e., construct) reality through this interaction. The objectives of constructivism are both individual and universal. The main underpinning of constructivism is that it is impossible for there to be an observable reality separate from the research participant.

Qualitative research and constructivism/interpretivism started in 1781 when Kant wrote *Critique of Pure Reason* (Kant, 1781/2007). Kant's argument is that knowledge emerges from what an individual perceives through the senses and mentally organizes (Sciarra, 1999). Another major figure in the development of constructivism is Dilthey, who tried to show that the difference between natural science and human science is that natural science attempts to give a scientific explanation and human science tries to understand the meaning of social experiences. Dilthey believed that experiences happened in the context of history; the individual may no longer have conscious memories of the happenings, but these memories can be brought back into his or her consciousness. Constructivism/interpretivism forms the foundation for qualitative research methods.

The Critical/Ideological Paradigm

The **critical/ideological paradigm** is researcher centered. The researcher has proactive values, which form the center of research (Ponterotto, 2005). The objective of critical/ideological research is to disturb and confront the social conditions of the day. The critical/ideological paradigm, or **critical theory,** began at the Institute of Social Research at the University of Frankfurt in the 1920s. Its originators include Max Horkimer, Herbert Marcuse, and Theodor Adorno. They believed that injustice and oppression shaped society. When the Nazis came to power, these originators of critical/ideological paradigm were forced to escape to the United States because they were Jews. They observed with shock the contradiction between the progressive expression of social equality and the reality of all forms of discrimination. Horkimer and Adorno returned to Frankfurt after World War II, but Marcuse remained in the United States. Marcuse's ideas influenced the 1960s student movement. Central tenets of critical theory include the belief in a constructed, lived experience that is influenced by power dynamics and historical framework. The objectives of the critical/ideological paradigm are freedom from repression for the oppressed; a freer society; and conceptualization of reality in the context of history, society, and power interaction. Critical theorists use research to free dominated groups. They involve these groups in research on oppression and privilege. The critical/ideological paradigm has both an individual and universal perspective. Some examples of critical/ideological paradigms are feminist, critical race, and queer theories. The critical/ideological paradigm forms the basis for qualitative multicultural research.

Contributed by Wangui Gathua,
University of Iowa, Iowa City, IA

References

Denzin, N. K., & Lincoln, Y. S. (2005). *Handbook of qualitative research* (3rd ed.). Thousand Oaks, CA: Sage.

Kant, I. (2007). *Critique of pure reason* (W. Weigelt, Ed. & Trans.). New York: Penguin. (Original work published 1781)

Ponterotto, J. G. (2005). Qualitative research in counseling psychology: A primer on research paradigms and philosophy of science. *Journal of Counseling Psychology, 52,* 126–136.

Sciarra, D. (1999). The role of the qualitative researcher. In M. Kopala & L. A. Suzuki (Eds.), *Using qualitative methods in psychology* (pp. 37–48). Thousand Oaks, CA: Sage.

Additional Resources

Dilthey, W. (1977). *Descriptive psychology and historical understanding* (R. M. Zaner & K. L. Heiges, Trans.). The Hague, Netherlands: Matinus Nijhoff. (Original work published 1894)

Posavac, E. J., & Carey, R. G. (1985). *Program evaluation: Methods and case studies.* Upper Saddle River, NJ: Prentice Hall.

■ Research and Evaluation, Key Legal Issues

Laws, statutes, and regulations related to research and evaluation are designed to protect the rights of participants in human biomedical and behavioral research. Specific regulations include directives about the selection and treatment of participants; the use, storage, and disclosure of personal information; and the processes of research and evaluation. Many of these protective legal mechanisms resulted from ethical violations in experiments on humans (e.g., The Tuskegee Study). As a result of such violations, the National Research Act of 1974 was passed, establishing a National Commission for the Protection of Human Subjects of Biomedical and Behavioral Research, and the Department of Health and Human Services (DHHS) implemented the federal policy for the protection of human subjects to protect human participants from potential harm or injustices in research and evaluation. This policy is contained in Title 45: Public Health Part 46: Protection of Human Subjects of the Code of Federal Regulations (45 CFR 46).

Subpart A of this policy, known as the **Common Rule,** describes policies that apply to all research that is conducted, supported, or regulated by a federal agency or department and involves human participants. It stipulates that this research must be reviewed and approved by an Institutional Review Board (IRB; see Institutional Review Board for the Protection of Human Subjects). Some research inquiries may be exempt from IRB approval or be allowed expedited review procedures if the level of risk to participants is minimal, if research is conducted in educational settings, if data are collected anonymously, or if the data are derived from archival or public record.

The IRB may only approve research if it meets the following criteria: (a) The risk to participants is minimized, (b) the risk to participants is reasonable in relation to the anticipated benefit to participants and/or to the importance of the knowledge gained, (c) selection of participants is equitable and takes into account the circumstances and setting in which the research will be conducted, (d) informed consent is sought, (e) informed consent is documented appropriately, (f) data are monitored to protect confidentiality and participant safety, and (g) the privacy of participants is respected.

Subparts B, C, and D of 45 CFR 46 contain additional regulations to prevent vulnerable populations, including pregnant women, human fetuses, newborns, prisoners, and children, from being harmed when participating in research or evaluation. Researchers soliciting participation of members of these vulnerable populations are subject to additional restrictions to reduce undue coercion and/or harm based on inability to give informed consent.

Similar to the Common Rule, DHHS also issued the **Privacy Rule,** establishing the Health Insurance Portability and Accountability Act of 1996 (HIPAA). HIPAA regulates the use and dissemination of protected health information, defined as information that is individually identifiable. Specific to research, the Privacy Rule stipulates that protected health information can be used or disclosed for research purposes without individual informed consent only when (a) there is documented approval of the waiver of consent by the IRB, (b) the use of the protected health information is necessary for the preparation of a research protocol but will not leave the possession of the individual or business that holds the information, or (c) the protected health information is about an individual who is deceased and is necessary for the research to take place. Under the Privacy Rule, a limited data set of protected health information may be used for research purposes without individual informed consent if identifying information, including name, contact information, Social Security number, insurance numbers, and other individually identifying details, is stripped from the information.

Contribution by Carrie A. Wachter,
Purdue University, West Lafayette, IN,
and Matthew Lemberger, University of
Missouri–St. Louis, St. Louis, MO

Additional Resources

National Research Act of 1974 Regulations, 45 Code of Federal Regulations 46. Retrieved August 28, 2007, from http://www.hhs.gov/ohrp/humansubjects/guidance/45cfr46.htm

Health Insurance Portability and Accountability Act of 1996, 45 C.F.R. 160 and 45 C.F.R. 164. Retrieved August 29, 2007, from http://www.hhs.gov/ocr/hipaa

Research and Evaluation, Key People in

Research is an essential component to counseling, important both in theory and practice. Research has grown from a scientific, statistical model focused on quantitative analysis to recent incorporations of a more naturalistic, qualitative method of inquiry. Evaluation differs from research in that it assesses the quality, worth, or merit of the object or program being considered. The evaluation process is often circular and feeds information back based on the outcomes of the initial process to inform practice more directly. Key people in quantitative research, qualitative research, action research, and program evaluation are discussed in this entry.

Quantitative Research

Two central figures in quantitative counseling research are **Thomas Cook** and **Donald Campbell** (1979). Their book *Quasi-Experimentation* builds on **Donald Campbell** and **Julian Stanley's** (1963) *Experimental and Quasi-Experimental Designs for Research.* These authors collectively outlined methods of experimental design and discussed validity, sampling methods, randomized experiments, and causal inference. Cook and Campbell are especially noteworthy for outlining various experimental designs for use with counseling research and their related threats to external validity. **Bruce Wampold** and **Clifford Drew** (1989) further developed the application of statistical methodology to psychological questions in their detailed text, *Theory and Application of Statistics.*

Stephen Issac and **William Michael** developed a detailed methodology for individuals interested in the various aspects of research design. They were instrumental in assisting those clinicians interested in developing key research questions and offered a rich variety of suggestions, from techniques for basic data collection to finalizing the written research reports. Their 1995 text, *Handbook in Research and Evaluation,* provides a detailed discussion of these key research concepts. **Ruth Ravid's** work continued to add a practical component for those looking to apply quantitative statistical methodology to everyday research questions. Her 2005 text, *Practical Statistics for Educators,* offers a straightforward, accessible style for those looking to apply the often-difficult language and structure of quantitative research models to real-world educational settings.

Qualitative Research

John Creswell (2002, 2006) advanced several core concepts in the area of naturalistic inquiry and qualitative research design. Previously, research design in psychology focused on statistical models borrowed from mathematics and the traditional sciences. Creswell argued for the application of subjective, flexible, inquiry models that took into account the full range of human experience. Creswell discussed the five qualitative inquiry traditions of biography, phenomenology, grounded theory, ethnography, and case study. Prior to his work, research design focused on reducing observable phenomena to numerical values to be compared through statistical methods. Creswell borrowed several key investigation techniques from anthropology and sociology to capture the richness and detail of the human experience.

Mary Kopala and **Lisa Suzuki** (1999) presented a collection of articles on qualitative methods in their text *Using Qualitative Methods in Psychology*. Their work expands both the philosophical and technical aspects of qualitative research. Other key writers in the field include **Matthew Miles** and **Michael Huberman** (1994) who provided straightforward and significant methods of conducting qualitative research in their text, *Qualitative Data Analysis: An Expanded Sourcebook*. **Michael Patton's** (2001) *Qualitative Research & Evaluation Methods* is another seminal work that deals with both themes and applications of qualitative research, offering 12 important standards to guide the work of the qualitative researcher.

Action Research

Ernest Stringer developed several key arguments that blended the traditional research model with a larger focus on practical application, that is, moving research into a more evaluative model. Stringer argued for research to become more action oriented in his 1999 book *Action Research*. The process is one in which the researcher is encouraged to look, think, and act in response to the research question at hand. Research occurs in a naturalistic framework, in which questions build on each other, and stakeholders are directly involved in the process and outcomes. Action research puts a primary focus on the practical utility of the research question at hand.

As research moved outside the laboratory and into real-world settings, the need for valid and reliable methods to assess participants' perceptions became increasingly important. In 2002, **Arlene Fink** developed a collection of books that are a useful one-stop-shop for researchers using surveys in research and assessment. The kit is helpful in determining question construction, analysis techniques, and sampling methods for those looking to build or critique the surveys that are often used to assess client satisfaction or make decisions about existing programs or allocation of funds.

Program Evaluation

Blaine Worthen, James Sanders, and **Jody Fitzpatrick** defined program evaluation as assessing the quality, worth, or merit of the program in question. Worthen, Sanders, and Fitzpatrick (1997) published *Program Evaluation,* which outlines several different methods of assessing and evaluating programs (i.e., objective-oriented, management-oriented, consumer-oriented approaches).

Counseling Outcome Research

Professional counselors are often concerned with applying program evaluation to answer questions regarding the efficacy and effectiveness of psychotherapy, counseling, and analysis (see Outcome Research). In efficacy studies of psychotherapy, the central question typically is, Can a particular treatment work under ideal circumstances? Two central studies include **Mary Smith** and **Gene Glass's** (1977) "Meta-Analysis of Psychotherapy Outcome Studies" and **Hans Eysenck's** (1952) "The Effects of Psychotherapy: An Evaluation." Eysenck initially concluded that the effects of therapy were insignificant and that most people improve on their own. He later revised his work, indicating that behavioral therapy was the most helpful form of therapy. In contrast, Smith and Glass's research concluded that psychotherapy was genuinely helpful to most clients regardless of the type of therapy. These researchers illustrated how the scientific method can be used to determine under what circumstances therapy works, with what particular population it works, and under which conditions it works.

Although efficacy studies are concerned with whether a particular treatment works in an ideal setting, effectiveness studies seek to understand whether a particular treatment works in a real-world clinic with a certain population. Two key research effectiveness summaries include "The Effectiveness of Psychotherapy: The Consumer Reports Study" by **Martin Seligman** (1995) and **Michael Lambert** and **Allen Bergin's** (1994) study, "The Effectiveness of Psychotherapy." These researchers measured client and patient satisfaction with their treatment and offered conclusions based on measurable satisfaction.

Contributed by Brian Van Brunt and
Eric D. Manley,
Western Kentucky University,
Bowling Green, KY

References

Campbell, D., & Stanley, J. (1963). *Experimental and quasi-experimental designs for research.* Boston: Houghton Mifflin.

Creswell, J. H. (2002). *Research design: Qualitative, quantitative, and mixed methods approaches* (2nd ed.). Thousand Oaks, CA: Sage.

Creswell, J. H. (2006). *Qualitative inquiry and research design: Choosing among five traditions* (2nd ed.). Thousand Oaks, CA: Sage.

Cook, T. D., & Campbell, D. T. (1979). *Quasi-experimentation: Design & analysis issues for field settings.* Boston: Houghton Mifflin.

Eysenck, H. J. (1952). The effects of psychotherapy: An evaluation. *Journal of Consulting and Clinical Psychology, 60,* 659–663.

Fink, A. (2002). *The survey kit* (2nd ed.). Thousand Oaks, CA: Sage.

Isaac, S., & Michael, W. B. (1995). *Handbook in research and evaluation* (3rd ed.). San Diego, CA: Educational and Industrial Testing Services.

Kopala, M., & Suzuki, L. A. (1999). *Using qualitative methods in psychology.* Thousand Oaks, CA: Sage.

Lambert, M. J., & Bergin, A. E. (1994). The effectiveness of psychotherapy. In A. E. Bergin & S. L. Garfield (Eds.), *Handbook of psychotherapy and behavioral change* (4th ed., pp. 143–189). New York: Wiley.

Miles, M. B., & Huberman, A. M. (1994). *Qualitative data analysis: An expanded sourcebook* (2nd ed.). Thousand Oaks, CA: Sage.

Patton, M. Q. (2001). *Qualitative research & evaluation methods* (3rd ed.). Thousand Oaks, CA: Sage.

Ravid, R. (2005). *Practical statistics for educators* (3rd ed.). Lanham, MD: The University Press of America.

Seligman, M. E. P. (1995). The effectiveness of psychotherapy: The Consumer Reports study. *American Psychologist, 50,* 965–974.

Smith, M. L., & Glass, G. V. (1977). Meta-analysis of psychotherapy outcome studies. *American Psychologist, 32,* 752–780.

Stringer, E. T. (1999). *Action research* (2nd ed.). Thousand Oaks, CA: Sage.

Wampold, B. E., & Drew, C. J. (1989). *Theory and application of statistics.* New York: McGraw-Hill College.

Worthen, B. R., Sanders, J. R., & Fitzpatrick, J. L. (1997). *Program evaluation: Alternative approaches and practical guidelines* (2nd ed.). New York: Longman.

Research Question

There are many steps involved in the process of conducting research. Before starting on research, a researcher must select a research topic on the basis of sufficient familiarity with the relevant theoretical and empirical literature. From this knowledge of previous literature, a set of research questions or hypotheses emerges, and these questions or hypotheses then define the constructs to be examined in the study as well as the research methodology to be used. Unlike a hypothesis that articulates what the researcher expects to find in the study on the basis of previous literature (see Hypothesis Testing), a **research question** explores the relationship between variables but does not state any specific expectations about the findings that may emerge in the study. The purpose of a research question is to articulate and operationalize a goal of a research study. Depending on what a researcher plans to study, there are three different ways to ask a research question: (a) A **descriptive research question** asks about a particular event or phenomenon and the specific characteristics of that event or phenomenon, (b) a **difference research question** examines the difference between groups or within a particular individual, and (c) a **relationship research question** asks if there is a relationship between two constructs (Heppner, Kivlighan, & Wampold, 2007).

A well-developed research question is important in any type of research because it is the cornerstone on which the research design and hypothesis are built. It is important that the research question match the intended research design used in a research study. The research question is the beginning point for a well-designed study.

The research question that drives a given study should both arise from knowledge of previous research related to the topic and inform the methodology (e.g., qualitative, quantitative, mixed methods) and design used during the study. According to Creswell (2006), "qualitative research questions are open-ended, evolving, and non-directional" (p. 107). Although a good qualitative research question allows the researcher to state the specific purpose of the study, a qualitative research study typically starts with a small number of research questions that are primarily descriptive in nature (i.e., asking what or how). In contrast, quantitative research questions facilitate the operationalization of the variables to be examined in the study and allow a researcher to develop testable statistical hypotheses.

Research Question Versus Research Hypothesis

Although a quantitative research question often leads to statistical hypotheses, it is important to note the difference between these terms. The term **hypothesis** is used in multiple ways in empirical research, describing both a general statement about a relationship a researcher believes will be found in a research study as well as statistical statements that inform the conduct and interpretation of statistical analyses. Researchers may or may not make **general hypothesis** statements in their research study, depending on whether or not there is sufficient reason to believe, based on previous research or a guiding theory, that a specific relationship may be found between variables. In contrast, **statistical hypotheses** are almost always used in analyses conducted in a quantitative study, although these statistical hypotheses are rarely directly stated in a research report. For each research question to be examined in a quantitative study, a corresponding set of null and alternative hypotheses is formulated in the process of conducting statistical analyses. The alternative hypothesis, sometimes referred to as the research hypothesis, is typically a mathematical statement of the research question, either in directional or nondirectional terms.

An example would be a researcher who was interested in examining the prevalence of posttraumatic stress disorder (PTSD) in male and female soldiers after they returned from a tour of duty. A quantitative research question for this study might be, "Do male and female soldiers differ in the number of PTSD symptoms they present with after returning home from a tour of duty?" A hypothesis for this study might be, "Male soldiers have a greater number of symptoms of PTSD after returning home from a tour of duty than female soldiers." Statistical hypotheses for this study would likely be stated to reflect a presence or absence of a significant difference (i.e., not likely due to chance) between the mean number of symptoms reported by male and female soldiers. For example, the null hypothesis might state that, in the population, there is no difference between the mean number of symptoms for men and women ($\mu_{men} - \mu_{women} = 0$). In contrast, the alternative or research hypothesis might state that a difference did exist in the population (i.e., $\mu_{men} - \mu_{women} \neq 0$ or $\mu_{men} - \mu_{women} </> 0$, depending on what the researcher expects on the basis of previous research and theory.

Alternatively, a number of parallel qualitative research questions could be posed by a researcher with an interest in PTSD symptoms and diagnosis in returning soldiers. Qualitative research questions might include "How do returning soldiers experience PTSD symptoms in their daily lives?" "How do returning soldiers experience the diagnostic and assessment process that they undergo prior to receiving a diagnosis of PTSD?" or "In the military culture, what does a diagnosis of PTSD mean to soldiers and how does it affect a soldier's identity?" These research questions would guide interviews, observations, and other means of gathering qualitative data.

Contributed by Eva D. Sloan and
Becky R. Davenport,
St. Mary's University, San Antonio, TX

References

Creswell, J. W. (2006). *Qualitative inquiry and research design: Choosing among five traditions* (2nd ed.). Thousand Oaks, CA: Sage.

Heppner, P. P., Kivlighan, D. M., Jr., & Wampold, B. E. (2007). *Research design in counseling* (3rd ed.). Belmont, CA: Wadsworth.

■ Resilience

The concept of resilience is growing increasingly prominent in professional literature and practice throughout all venues of counseling. A great deal of this attention is in direct response to recent traumatic and stressful events, which have left many people feeling damaged, hopeless, and helpless. There have been numerous attempts to define resilience empirically. Essentially, **resilience** is recognized as a person's ability to maintain equilibrium; adjust to distressful or disturbing circumstances; or to "bounce back" to a level of positive functioning in spite of, or often in response to, adverse situations. Resilience offers a positive and balanced view of all human beings as competent and capable, regardless of their background or experience. It is important to be cautious and culturally sensitive when identifying and defining resilient behaviors. Historically, resilient behaviors have been primarily defined from a White, Western perspective and may not take into account racial, ethnic, and cultural identities of participants who may be using resilience responses that are unrecognizable outside of the cultural context. Ultimately, resilience is a strength-based outcome or a developed response.

Researchers generally agree that people develop and demonstrate resilience by using one or more **protective factors** that span three major areas: (a) a person's positive attitudes and philosophies; (b) supportive family or other relationships with significant prosocial and competent people; and (c) involvement and attachment to a safe and supportive community, including schools, social organizations, and faith-based organizations. It has been suggested that using the concepts of capacity-building approaches (e.g., solution-focused brief therapy, positive psychology) can significantly increase resiliency. Currently, there are numerous empirical studies being conducted to determine how best to understand and use strategies that increase these positive outcomes. Resilience—and the parallel increase of protective factors—offers both practitioners and consumers of mental health services a more positive view of themselves, their circumstances, and their ability to create an environment in which they can not only survive but ultimately thrive.

Contributed by James R. "Jamey" Cheek,
University of Houston–Clear Lake,
Houston, TX

Additional Resources

Glicken, M. D. (2006). *Learning from resilient people: Lessons we can apply to counseling and psychotherapy.* Thousand Oaks, CA: Sage.

Thomsen, K. (2002). *Building resilient students: Integrating resiliency into what you already know and do.* Thousand Oaks, CA: Corwin Press.

Wolin, S., & Wolin. S. (n.d.) *Project resilience.* Retrieved April 15, 2007, from http://www.projectresilience.com

■ Resistance

It is not uncommon for professional counselors to encounter challenging clients. Regardless of theoretical orientation, all counselors are likely to have the disappointing and frustrating experience of opposition to counseling. Commonly referred to as **resistance,** these behaviors include avoidance of or minimizing the disclosure requested by the professional counselor because the client is uncomfortable. Simply, resistance is the client's avoidance of change in the counseling relationship. It is imperative that counselors remain culturally sensitive because some behaviors may appear resistant that are actually representative of cultural norms. For example, certain cultures view direct eye contact as disrespectful, and lack of eye contact could be viewed as resistance or avoidance when in fact it is a cultural norm. Thus, making an assumption too quickly about resistance may indicate disrespect for the counseling relationship.

Resistance is inevitable in the counseling process, although the frequency and duration of opposition vary from client to client. Because of the potential to influence the counseling dynamics, it is important for professional counselors to be aware of resistance and the potential effects on counseling process and outcome. Resistance has the potential to hinder the counselor's perceived effectiveness, interfere with client motivation, and threaten the change process (Watson, 2006). It may serve as a warning for the counselor that too much emphasis is being placed on the outcome and that more attention needs to be placed on the process of change.

Research suggests several causes for resistance, including anxiety, control, and noncompliance (Chen & Giblin, 2002; Otani, 1989; Watson, 2006). Early views of resistance suggest it exists as an individual defense mechanism. Psychoanalysts posit that resistance is an unconscious defense mechanism that clients use to repress anxiety-provoking material. Adlerian counselors maintain that resistance occurs at an unconscious level and define resistance as a self-protective mechanism that serves to defend views about the self, others, and life. Many behaviorists have disputed this theory, contending that the professional counselor induces resistance through faulty methodology or, alternatively, that resistance represents client noncompliance. Humanistic approaches consider resistance as avoidance of objectionable or unsafe feelings that impair functioning and suggest clients are reluctant to participate in any practice that might have a negative effect on their life scripts. Systems theorists view resistance as an attempt to protect family members by maintaining the status quo. Although change could be positive, clients place the family's welfare above their own, resulting in unwillingness to change beliefs or behaviors.

In spite of differing hypotheses regarding the causes of resistance, it is important for professional counselors to consider the position of a client seeking counseling. For some, counseling can seem intimidating and promote a sense of vulnerability. Whether a client's participation is voluntary or involuntary, clients are asked and expected to disclose intimate and personal details of their life experiences. This practice of making oneself known to another naturally leads to individuals' setting boundaries while evaluating the benefits and risks of disclosure. Indeed, most individuals tend to put up resistance in the presence of a threat or suggestion of a change. When professional counselors suggest incorporating change to clients who are hesitant, counselors potentially promote arguments for resistance. In other words, the more evidence counselors offer clients about the benefits of change, the more likely clients may be to disagree and resist change (Cade & O'Hanlon, 1993).

The characteristics may be expressed consciously or unconsciously, through passive indifference or active hostility. Clients may seem defensive in response to a professional counselor's request for information. Irritation or shame could manifest as resistance as clients struggle to discuss difficult topics. Clients may begin arriving late or missing appointments altogether. Regardless of the degree of resistance, counselors need to acknowledge that it is a natural reaction that can be dealt with once it is identified. Resistance that is openly verbalized is easier to deal with than resistance that is not even recognized. Once resistance is identified, professional counselors must consider possible causes for resistance and develop strategies for dealing with it.

It is important for professional counselors to resist the temptation to pass judgment and for them to consider that the resistant behavior is just one part of how the client is communicating. Individuals adjust to the demands of living by developing particular ways of behaving and thinking that meet needs and permit them to carry on. Efforts to change these patterns, regardless of how unhealthy the patterns may be, can be seen as a threat to be avoided. Professional counselors are best served by being honest, competent, and sensitive to what clients are saying. For example, if a professional counselor is not cognizant of the culture of the client, it is important to go slowly and be open to learning about the client's culture. Counselors must have respect for the client's rights, including the client's right to have and express negative feelings. Finally, the professional counselor should avoid being defensive and foster the ability to clarify goals and the means of reaching them.

Professional counselors must also realize how they contribute to resistance. If a professional counselor fails to establish rapport with a client or depends too heavily on questions as the basis of the relationship, it may put distance between the counselor and the client. Advice giving or flawed expectations of client behaviors can also alienate clients, and counselors may assume the client is being resistant. To minimize resistance, professional counselors are served best by being flexible with interactions and careful about choosing appropriate techniques. Professional counselors should work at the client's level and use interventions that are appropriate for the client at that particular time.

Finally, it is more likely that the counseling approach with the resistant client will be positive if a professional counselor views resistant behavior as an indication that the client is feeling scared or cautious than if the counselor views the client as difficult or uncooperative. Resistance can cause counselors to experience self-doubt about the ability to work with a particular client or to have empathy for the client. Viewing the resistant behavior as information the client is sharing with the counselor and as an opportunity rather than a problem can be the foundation of building a successful working relationship. When resistance is present, counselors should resist the urge to speed up the session (Mitchell, 2003). Counselors should maintain patience, be creative, and set a pace that allows the client to move through the change process. Resistant clients often fear embarrassment, reprimand, or sympathy. Regardless of how irrational, inappropriate, or illogical a counselor may feel the client's resistance is, the client has a perceived need for it. Not to respect the client's resistance is to reject the client. Demonstrating genuine respect and acceptance facilitates a therapeutic alliance that is one of the best predictors of a positive counseling outcome (Mitchell, 2003).

Contributed by Laura R. Simpson,
Delta State University, Cleveland, MS

References

Cade, B., & O'Hanlon, W. H. (1993). *A brief guide to brief therapy*. New York: Norton.

Chen, M., & Giblin, N. (2002). *Individual counseling: Skills and techniques*. Denver, CO: Love.

Mitchell, S. W. (2003). Tips for treating highly resistant clients. *Advocate, 26*(11), 10–11.

Otani, A. (1989). Client resistance in counseling: Its theoretical rationale and taxonomic classification. *Journal of Counseling & Development, 67,* 458–461.

Watson, J. (2006). Addressing client resistance: Recognizing and processing in-session occurrences. *VISTAS 2006 Online*. Retrieved July 28, 2008, from counselingoutfitters.com/Watson.htm

Additional Resource

Simpson, L. R., Helm, H., & Marbach, C. (2007). I don't know: Helping reluctant children tell their stories. In S. M. (Hobson) Dugger & L. A. Carlson (Eds.), Critical incidents in counseling children (pp. 93–101). Alexandria, VA: American Counseling Association.

■ Responsibilities of Users of Standardized Tests

The Association for Assessment in Counseling and Education (AACE; 2003) publishes **Responsibilities of Users of Standardized Tests (3rd ed.; RUST)**. AACE is a division of the American Counseling Association (ACA). The purpose of RUST is to promote the accurate, fair, and responsible use of standardized tests by counselors and educators. RUST has been developed and refined over 3 decades and three editions under the leadership of AACE in cooperation with ACA and its predecessors (i.e., the American Personnel & Guidance Association [APGA] and the American Association for Counseling and Development [AACD]). Work on the development of a statement focused on responsible use of standardized tests began in 1976 at the request of the board of directors of APGA. A committee comprising members of all APGA divisions and regions reviewed relevant professional literature as well as position papers, reports, articles, and monographs on the topic and then formulated RUST. This first edition of RUST was published in *Guidepost* on October 5, 1978. It was later published as a policy statement by APGA in 1980.

APGA changed its name to AACD in 1983, and AACD changed its name to ACA in 1992. Through these changes, the commitment of the premier professional counseling body to RUST continued. The 2003 third edition of RUST was prepared by a committee of AACE members. RUST serves as an important resource for both users and developers of standardized tests and assessment instruments. It is easily accessible via the AACE Web site.

In a climate of accountability and data-driven decisions, standardized tests are used in schools and other educational settings to make high-stakes evaluations of students and institutions. Standardized tests are also used by clinicians, counselors, and researchers as diagnostic tools and to enhance client self-assessment and understanding. The principles outlined in RUST help ensure that members of ACA and its divisions and branches, as well as teachers, administrators, and human service workers, use standardized tests with clients and students in a professional and ethical manner. Each section of RUST provides users of standardized tests with information that helps guide their decision making and processes. For example, counselors wishing to use standardized tests in their practice can obtain guidance on how to select a test in a responsible and ethical manner; processes recommended for administrations of standardized tests are also outlined.

RUST comprehensively addresses important and relevant issues applicable to written or computerized standardized tests administered to individuals and/or groups in seven sections. Salient points from each section are summarized in the following list:

1. *Qualifications of test users.* Professional counselors and educators are responsible for assessing that they are qualified and competent to select, administer, score, interpret, report, or communicate results on each standardized test used in their practice. Qualifications that test users should have before administering a test vary according to the test's complexity, usually according to four factors: (a) purposes of testing; (b) characteristics of tests; (c) settings and conditions for use of tests; and (d) roles of test selectors, administrators, scorers, and interpreters.

2. *Technical knowledge.* Test users should access training and professional development opportunities to become familiar with (a) validity of test results, (b) reliability, (c) errors of measurement, and (d) scores and norms.

3. *Test selection.* Test users must identify the specific purpose for testing and ensure that the test selected aligns with that purpose. Typical purposes for testing include (a) description, (b) accountability, (c) prediction, and (d) program evaluation. In addition, the following factors should be taken into consideration: (a) the test taker, (b) accuracy of scoring procedures, (c) norming and standardization procedures, (d) modifications, and (e) fairness.

4. *Test administration.* Standardized procedures ensure that the test is used in the manner specified by the test developers. Procedures to be followed before, during, and after the administration of standardized tests must all be given due consideration.

5. *Test scoring.* Scoring procedures should be consistently implemented, have methods for checking accuracy, and be audited regularly. Scoring that uses human judgment should have clearly specified criteria and rubrics to increase interrater reliability.

6. *Test interpretation.* Test interpretation must be conducted in a responsible manner and requires a thorough knowledge of the technical aspects of the test, the test results, and limitations. Factors that can affect the valid interpretation of tests include (a) psychometric factors, (b) test taker factors, and (c) contextual factors

7. *Communication of test results.* Counselors or educators using a test must have thorough knowledge of the test and its interpretation. Test results should be communicated in language that is easily understood by the test taker (e.g., client, student) as well as by parents and teachers. Information on how the test results can be interpreted, as well as ways that the results should not be interpreted, must be discussed.

The guidelines provided in RUST assist counselors and educators to use tests in responsible and ethical ways. RUST provides a useful list of references and additional resources for users of standardized tests.

Contributed by Christine Suniti Bhat,
Ohio University, Athens, OH

Reference

Association for Assessment in Counseling and Education. (2003). *Responsibilities of users of standardized tests* (3rd ed.). Retrieved July 1, 2007, from http://theaaceonline.com/rust.pdf

■ Retirement Counseling

Personal responses to the transition from working to retirement vary greatly among individuals. For some, the job "loss" at retirement may be no different than the personal responses a person experiences due to a job loss at any time during his or her working life. Preparing for and entering into retirement may be a crisis period because the transition is not only from working to not working, but it can involve perceived personal shifts in status, identity, and power. Other stressors such as financial constraints, medical problems, and psychological and emotional needs can also lead to crisis. For others, the transition involves a refocusing of energy from work to another personally rewarding activity or even from one occupation to another. Several theories can help understand retirement. Role theory is considered foundational to understanding retirement as life roles change and are redefined or expanded. **Retirement counseling,** then, is a counseling intervention undertaken to assist individuals in preparing for and adjusting to the transitions they experience as they enter retirement.

Several theories offer direction to these retirement counseling interventions. The roles individuals play in society continuously shape behavior, attitudes, and identity. When individuals shift from the worker role and make the transitions previously described in this entry to retiree role, adjustments must be made. For example, retirees may become social isolates, finding that they are suddenly disengaged from their usual activities and interpersonal interactions. One suggested remedy for such social isolation is for retirees to maintain activity levels similar to those they had while working by finding suitable substitute activities or increasing time spent in already familiar roles and activities.

Atchley (1975) was among the first to stress the need for career counselors who specialize in addressing retirement issues with retirees and workers facing imminent retirement. Richardson (1993) outlined preretirement and retirement adjustment counseling models. Her **preretirement counseling model** involves three phases: (a) listening, similar to bereavement counseling; (b) assessing the severity of the problem (symptoms can range from simple adjustment issues to depression and even suicide ideation); and (c) intervening, which involves assisting clients in developing an appropriate preretirement plan in anticipation of retirement. Richardson's **retirement adjustment counseling model** includes the same three phases but with a somewhat different paradigm shift on the part of the counselor. In the listening phase of retirement adjustment counseling, counselors help clients address the emotions associated with retirement. The assessment phase focuses on data collection regarding clients' occupational status, marital status, social supports, health, and financial status. Richardson then offered three specific intervention strategies (i.e., nondirective, collaborative, and directive), depending on the client's current capabilities.

Jensen-Scott (1993) suggested using Atchley's (1975) theory as a basis for retirement counseling interventions, noting that one or more of four major tasks may need to be addressed: (a) information need, (b) adjustment to change, (c) reprioritizing goals, and/or (d) seeking a new job or job substitute. Assessing a client's needs and feelings regarding these tasks should precede prioritizing the tasks, both leading to accurate conceptualization of the client's needs. Specific counseling interventions may range from simply providing assistance with information access to traditional in-depth, long-term personal counseling.

Simon and Osipow (1996) described the use of vocational scripts in retirement counseling and identified a vocational script as "a person's unique characterization of vocational identity independent of specific jobs, positions, and careers" (p. 153). Citing narrative psychology and constructivist theory, they recommended that clients be aided in focusing on a life review in order, first, to relate life changes to personality changes and then to consider work experience as a career, looking for themes among preferences and expertise, rewards, and behavioral responses. Finally, they encouraged future thinking by extending the vocational script into retirement.

Robinson and LaBauve (1999) delineated a **retirement-recycling model** of retirement adjustment counseling, which is a three-stage, three-phase intervention applicable "for any working or retired adult, regardless of age" (p. 44). This framework affords counselors much freedom in retirement adjustment and the application of counseling theories as they work with clients through the phases of assess, intervene, and evaluate within the preretirement, retirement, and postretirement stages. For example, in the assessment phase of the preretirement stage, the counselor's primary task is to gauge clients' planning for retirement, whereas the assessment phase of the retirement stage involves examining the clients' "retirement readiness." In the intervention phase of the retirement stage, the foundational goal "is to assist clients in experiencing and expressing positive emotions related to their pending retirement and consequent lifestyle adjustment, replacing any negative emotions revealed during the assessment phase" (Robinson & LaBauve, 1999, pp. 48–49). Similarly, the intervention phase in the postretirement stage also focuses on clients achieving positive emotional responses.

The **theory of work adjustment (TWA)** provided the foundation for Harper and Shoffner's (2004) contention that career development not only continues but should be enhanced well into retirement. They deemed TWA highly applicable, citing individual–environment correspondence, focus on adjustment and satisfaction, and flexibility in assessing personal and environmental needs and attributes. They emphasized that

> working with a retiree to identify and explore postretirement career and activity options that match the retiree's individual dimensions and that might provide

high levels of satisfaction and satisfactoriness can result in the development of a postretirement career plan that enables the retiree to retain (or gain) vital involvement in life. (p. 282)

Retirement counseling can have varied dimensions, be based on varied concepts of retirement adjustment, and be delivered via a variety of theories and models, all focusing on the successful transition from working to not working or to working differently.

Contributed by Chester R. Robinson,
Texas A&M University–Commerce,
Commerce, TX

References

Atchley, R. C. (1975). Adjustment to loss of job at retirement. *International Journal on Aging and Human Development, 6,* 17–27.

Harper, M. C., & Shoffner, M. F. (2004). Counseling for continued career development after retirement: An application of the theory of work adjustment. *The Career Development Quarterly, 52,* 272–284.

Jensen-Scott, R. L. (1993). Counseling to promote retirement adjustment. *The Career Development Quarterly, 41,* 257–267.

Richardson, V. (1993). *Retirement counseling: A handbook for gerontology practitioners.* New York: Springer.

Robinson, C. R., & LaBauve, B. J. (1999). Retirement-recycling: A model for retirement adjustment intervention. *Journal of Adult and Career Development, 15*(3), 41–53.

Simon, J., & Osipow, S. H. (1996). Continuity of career: The vocational script in counseling older workers. *The Career Development Quarterly, 45,* 152–162.

■ Roe's Theory of Personality Development and Occupational Classification

Anne Roe's theoretical orientation is an integration of personality theory and occupational classification. In developing her theory, Roe focused on the relationship between occupational choice and individual differences in terms of psychological, physical, and sociological variables and also incorporated Maslow's needs theory in order to explain the relevance of occupations to the satisfaction of basic needs. In addition, Roe placed an emphasis on early childhood experiences and occupational choice by hypothesizing that early child–parent relationships predispose children to either person-oriented or non-person-oriented careers. In this way, children with warm and accepting early parent–child relationships would be more inclined to enter a person-oriented career, whereas a child who encountered a cold and rejecting parent–child relationship would be more likely to choose a non-person-oriented or object-oriented career (Neff, 1985).

Roe also constructed a new occupational classification system in 1956 that was designed to classify logically a range of occupations and integrate her theory regarding person-oriented and non-person-oriented careers. Prior to the creation of her classification system, only the Minnesota Occupa-

tional Rating Scales (MORS) included a psychological basis in its framework (Roe & Lunneborg, 1990); however, the MORS contained 214 occupation groups, which Roe believed was too many to handle efficiently. Instead, Roe incorporated the content of the seven abilities and levels of ability of the MORS (Patterson, Gerken, & Milton, 1953) to create a two-dimensional classification system that comprised eight groups and six levels. The **groups,** which represent the horizontal set of categories, are divided in relation to the primary focus of activity involved in each occupation. The eight groups are also ordered along a continuum on the basis of the frequency and intensity of interpersonal relationships so that adjacent groups are more similar than those that are more distant (Roe, Hubbard, Hutchinson, & Bateman, 1966). The eight groups are described in the following list (Moser, Dubin, & Irving, 1956):

1. *Service.* This group contains occupations such as social work, guidance, and domestic and protective services that are focused on serving the needs and caring for the welfare of other people.

2. *Business Contact.* These occupations deal with interacting with and persuading people for the purpose of selling commodities such as services, real estate, and investments.

3. *Organization.* This group contains managerial and white-collar business, industry, and government occupations, and the main responsibility involves maintaining efficient functioning within those companies or organizations. These occupations have person contact, but the contact is usually at a formalized level.

4. *Technology.* The occupations in this group involve production, maintenance, and transportation of utilities and commodities. Because this group includes occupations such as engineering, crafts, transportation, and operating machinery, there is a heavy emphasis on working with objects rather than interpersonal interactions.

5. *Outdoor.* Included in this group are occupations dealing with preservation, cultivation, mineral and water resources, forestry, and animal care taking. Interpersonal relationships in these occupations are of little importance.

6. *Science.* This group is focused on the application of scientific theory, with the exception of technology. Non-person-oriented occupations, including physics as well as more person-oriented careers that also relate to Group 7 such as psychology and anthropology, are represented in this category.

7. *General cultural.* The primary orientation of this group is the preservation and transmission of general cultural heritage. Occupations in education, journalism, jurisprudence, humanities, linguistics, and the ministries are all included in this group. This group is most concerned with human activities rather than individual relationships.

8. *Arts and entertainment.* Included in this group are occupations using specialized skills in the creative arts

and entertainment industry such as art, music, and creative writing. Although interpersonal relations are important, there are not of the same nature or intensity as in Group 1 and focus more on the relationships between one person and small groups in addition to the more general public.

The **levels,** the vertical set of categories, are based on the degree of responsibility, capacity, and skill. The six levels are listed in the following order (Roe & Klos, 1969; Roe & Lunneborg, 1990):

1. *Professional and Managerial 1 (independent responsibility).* This level includes innovators, creators, and top managers and administrators with important, independent, and varied responsibilities. Education, when relevant, is usually at the doctoral level or equivalent.

2. *Professional and Managerial 2.* This level has a lower degree of autonomy with less significant responsibilities compared with Level 1, with medium-level responsibilities for self and others. Education is at or above the bachelor's level but below the doctoral level.

3. *Semiprofessional and small business.* These occupations contain a low level of responsibility for others and usually require a high school or technical school education.

4. *Skilled.* This level usually requires apprenticeships or other related experience and specialized training.

5. *Semiskilled.* The criteria in this level involve less training and experience than Level 4 with a greater reduction in autonomy and initiative.

6. *Unskilled.* Requirements of these occupations include no special training and mainly deal with following simple instructions and repetitive activities.

In terms of empirical evidence supporting the aspect of Roe's theory related to early childhood experiences, there appears to be no direct link between early parent–child relations and occupational choice (Neff, 1985); however, Roe's two-way occupational classification system has been used in numerous career development research studies, and her framework has been applied to several career choice and career exploration measures, including the Career Occupational Preference System and Vocational Interest Inventory (Roe & Lunneborg, 1990).

Contributed by Rebecca Christensen,
University of California, Berkeley,
Berkeley, CA

References

Moser, H. P., Dubin, W., & Irving, I. M. (1956). A proposed modification of the Roe occupational classification. *Journal of Counseling Psychology, 3,* 27–31.

Neff, W. S. (1985). *Work and human behavior.* New York: Aldine.

Patterson, D. G., Gerken, C., & Milton. M. E. (1953). *Revised Minnesota Occupational Rating Scales.* Minneapolis: University of Minnesota Press.

Roe, A., Hubbard, W. D., Hutchinson, T., & Bateman, T. (1966). Study of occupational history Part I: Job changes and the classification of occupation. *Journal of Counseling Psychology, 13,* 387–393.

Roe, A., & Klos, D. (1969). Occupational classification. *The Counseling Psychologist, 1*(3), 84–89.

Roe, A., & Lunneborg, P. (1990). Personality development and career choice. In D. Brown, L. Brooks, & Associates, *Career choice and development* (2nd ed., pp. 68–101). San Francisco: Jossey-Bass.

Additional Resources

Roe, A. (1956). *The psychology of occupations.* New York: Wiley.

Roe, A. (1957). Early determinants of vocational choice. *Journal of Counseling Psychology, 4,* 212–217.

■ Roles, Life and Work

The involvement of both husband and wife in the labor market requires a redefinition of traditional family roles and the division of labor in order for adults to compensate for work and family roles. A **role** is any set of behaviors that a person displays in social situations that have a socially agreed-on set of expectations, functions, and norms. Adults play many different roles. Some examples are the role of a parent, the role of a worker, the role of daughter or son, or the role of a friend, to name a few. Quite often, family and work roles compete and place incessant demands on individuals; thus, an individual's source of tension in adulthood is the competition of role demands. The many role demands often exert a great deal of pressure on adults to meet the expectations of both work and family. All too often, adults are pulled in many different directions in trying to meet the expectations that society places on the many roles they play. Trying to juggle family and work roles and attending to the commitments and responsibilities to spouse, children, parents, job, friends, and leisure can be difficult for many adults. Inevitably, the decisions a person must make to meet these demands affect the lives of the household or family members, friends, coworkers, and the person himself or herself.

In a traditional marriage, partners engage in complementary roles where one partner is primarily responsible for supporting the family financially and the other partner is responsible for nurturing the family. In traditional marriages involving a clear division of the husband's and wife's roles, the husband typically is the breadwinner of the family, engages in more paid work, focuses on advancing his career, and forms a sense of identity through his career. On the other hand, women engage in more housework, child care, and eldercare and focus on taking care of the family (Milkie & Peltola, 1999); however, with more women entering the labor market, the traditional, single-earner family has changed. More than 68% of U.S. families consisting of a married couple with children under 18 years are considered dual-earner couples, and both husband and wife participate in paid employment (U.S. Bureau of the Labor Statistics, 2005). Hence, dual-earner couples have replaced the traditional married-couple model of a breadwinner husband and home-maker wife. It is important to note that although men are participating more in child care than in the past, women still take responsibility for the majority of child-rearing and household tasks, such as cleaning, shopping, cooking, and laundry, to name a few (Milkie & Peltola, 1999). Thus, role complementarity still exists in many dual-career couples, with each partner adhering to or assuming the traditional role of the husband as the breadwinner and the wife as the nurturer.

Dual-earner marriages present both opportunities and challenges. On the positive side, a second income raises some families from poverty to middle-income status. A second income helps women become more independent and gives them a share of economic power, and it reduces the pressure on men to be the sole provider. Other benefits may include a more equal relationship between husband and wife, better health for both, greater self-esteem for the woman, and a closer relationship between a father and his children (Gilbert, 1994).

On the negative side, working couples face extra demands on time and energy, conflicts between work and family, possible rivalry between spouses, and anxiety and guilt about meeting children's needs (Perry-Jenkins, Repetti, & Crouter, 2000). Men and women are equally affected by the stress of a dual-earner lifestyle, but they may be affected in different ways. Because of their dual responsibilities to work and family, dual-earner couples are particularly vulnerable to the problems of role overload, role conflict, and role spillover.

Role overload exists when the total demands on time and energy associated with the prescribed activities of multiple roles are too great to perform these roles adequately. In other words, people have too much to do in the time available to them. For example, a working mother with three children ages 14, 8, and 6 years may find the demands of getting the children ready for school, attending Parent Teacher Association meetings at three schools, dropping children off at athletic events, and listening to their problems overwhelming and exhausting.

Role conflict refers to ways that the demands and expectations of various roles conflict with each other. A person is expected to play two incompatible roles. For example, work–family conflict occurs when a parent must leave work to attend to a sick child or when an employee brings work home to complete during family time.

Role spillover is the carryover of roles into the work and family setting, and it can interfere or complement one another. On the negative side of role spillover, the demands of work and family roles interfere with a person's ability to carry out another role. For example, an individual may be disrupted at work by worries of an ill child or parent or distracted at home by a homework assignment that is due the next day. On the positive side, role spillover can enrich work and family roles. For example, a math teacher could use mathematical skills to help his or her child with math homework.

Work–family conflict can arise from the stress originating in one role that spills over into the other role, detracting from the quality of life in that role. Unfortunately, many adults are placed in situations in which one role is given precedence over another role, which can lead to less satisfaction at work and in family roles (Milkie & Peltola, 1999). For example, an individual may struggle to meet the expectations of the boss, who requires work after hours to complete a project, whereas the family expects the dinner cooked, the children's homework done, and the muffins baked for the school's bake sale the next day.

To help manage work and family obligations, more and more dual-earner couples in the United States are embracing the ideal of **role-sharing** in housework and child care (Coltrane, 1989). As more egalitarian marriages emerge, the partners share power, authority, and household tasks equally. This means partners are trying to balance the time and energy they devote to their jobs, children, household, and relationships in order to meet life demands.

Managing multiple roles often leaves little time for leisure activities. Leisure, or free time, for many working families is scarce. In some occupations, the time schedule may leave little room for going to an aerobics class, taking the children to the playground, reading a book, or going to the movies. In other occupations, time that might have been spent in leisure activities is spent earning additional income to support the family. Family obligations, such as caring for aging parents, can leave little time for leisure activities. Nevertheless, couples who make time for and are able to enjoy leisure activities together found that it contributed to the strength of and satisfaction of their intimate relationship (Kalmijn & Bernasco, 2001).

Balancing work and life roles can be difficult. Yet, some adults have found creative ways to compensate for these conflicting roles. One or both partners may cut back on their working hours, refuse overtime, or turn down jobs that require excessive travel in order to increase family time and reduce stress (Becker & Moen, 1999). Furthermore, they may work at home, work nonstandard alternate shifts (e.g., not work Monday–Friday or work at night), have flexible job schedules, or work part-time. For example, a father of three works the morning shift so he can be home when his children return from school and take them to their extracurricular activities. A second example is a mother who works 3 days out of the 5-day workweek, leaving 2 days to attend to other personal, social, or leisure roles. Although role compensation assists adults in effectively balancing these roles, which can bring many benefits such as a better standard of living, improved work productivity, greater self-fulfillment, enhanced psychological well-being, and happier marriages, many adults may not be financially secure enough to consider the aforementioned alternative options.

Managing work and family life roles is challenging for many adults. Frequently, role conflicts put stress on the individual to meet the expectations and demands placed on the role. In the past, men tended to be more traditional than women in their expectations for work and family roles; however, with women making up at least half of the current workforce, dual-earner couples are beginning to redefine and share household responsibilities such as cleaning, taking care of the children, and time spent at work. Subsequently, the benefits and drawbacks of a dual-earner lifestyle affect both men and women equally. Finally, companies that have implemented family friendly, time-flexible workplace policies are helping dual-earner couples alleviate some of the stress placed on them by the competing work and family roles.

Contributed by Kimberly L. Mason,
Cleveland State University,
Cleveland, OH

References

Becker, P. E., & Moen, P. (1999). Scaling back: Dual-earner couples' work–family strategies. *Journal of Marriage and the Family, 61,* 995–1007.

Coltrane, S. (1989). Household labor and the routine production of gender. *Social Problems, 36,* 473–490.

Gilbert, L. A. (1994). Current perspectives in dual-career families. *Current Directions in Psychological Science, 3,* 101–105.

Kalmijn, M., & Bernasco, W. (2001). Joint and separated lifestyles in couple relationships. *Journal of Marriage and the Family, 63,* 639–654.

Milkie, M. A., & Peltola, P. (1999). Playing all the roles: Gender and the work–family balancing act. *Journal of Marriage and the Family, 61,* 476–490.

Perry-Jenkins, M., Repetti, R., & Crouter, A. (2000). Work and family in the 1990s. *Journal of Marriage and the Family, 62,* 981–998.

U.S. Bureau of Labor Statistics. (2005). *Table 6. Employment status of women by presence and age of youngest child, marital status, race, and Hispanic or Latino ethnicity, 2004.* Retrieved September 5, 2007, from http://www.bls.gov/cps/wlf-table6-2005.pdf

Additional Resources

Hansen, S. L. (1996). *Integrative life planning: Critical tasks for career development and changing life patterns.* San Francisco: Jossey-Bass.

Super, D. (1957). *The psychology of careers.* New York: Wiley.

Super, D., Sverko, B., & Super, C. (1995). *Life roles, values, and careers: International findings of the work importance study.* San Francisco: Jossey-Bass.

Sampling

A **sample** is a set of individuals or participants selected from a larger, inclusive group of individuals and used for either descriptive or inferential purposes. Researchers attempt to have the sample be "representative," that is, to have similar characteristics to the larger target population or to be used as information-rich cases of a phenomenon of interest. Samples are used in research to explain in more detail the population (descriptive) or to generalize the results of the study back to the target population (inferential). During the sampling process, it is imperative for the researcher to define the target population clearly. Once the researcher has defined the target population, the researcher must acquire a list of the members of that population. This member list, which is used in acquiring the sample, is commonly known as the sampling frame. With the defined target population in mind and the sampling frame in hand, the researcher can then begin to consider the multitude of sampling techniques available. Generally, sampling can be divided into two distinct types: random sampling and purposeful sampling. These types are also referred to as probability and nonprobability sampling, respectively. The central difference between these two types of sampling relies on the degree of importance placed on the theory of probability. Probability sampling, or random sampling, is rooted in the concept that for a sample to represent a population, there must be some type of probability that members in that population would be randomly selected for participation. Nonprobability sampling, or purposeful sampling, relies on the premise that probability is not required or desired to represent a population. Although quantitative research uses many methods from both types of sampling, qualitative research relies only on nonprobability sampling methods. The concepts of sample size, sampling error, and sampling bias are important considerations in selecting from various sampling methods.

Key Sampling Concepts

In general, **sample size** is the number of participants (n) in a given research study. The size required for a sample has a direct relationship with the target population size because researchers often seek to have samples that are representative of the target population. As the population size increases, so does the need for a larger sample. Sample size depends not only on the population size but also on the nature of the analysis used in the study, the researchers' desired precision of the statistical estimates, and the number of variables explored in the study. Deciding on the exact number of participants needed in a sample size is a complex process that consists of multiple factors, including the level of precision desired, the preferred confidence level, the homogeneity of the population, the sampling technique used, and the research question. One simple rule in selecting a sample size is the larger the population, the larger the sample size needed. If studying a smaller population, researchers should consider using a census, or the entire population, in the sample. When a population is substantial, researchers cannot explore all members in a population; therefore, they should consider using the existing literature in that area to help inform the decision about the number of participants needed in the sample. Another possible means for arriving at a sample size is to use published sampling tables. An adequate sample size will provide more precision and confidence in the representation of the population.

Sampling error can best be understood as the degree to which a researcher's sample differs from the target population. The sampling error gives the researcher some measure of how precise the sample is of the target population. Sample size is also related to sampling error. The larger the sample size, the less sampling error there is in the sample. Less sampling error is due to the fact that the larger the sample size, the closer the sample reflects the larger population being studied.

Chance and sampling bias are two distinct causes of sampling error in research. It is assumed that chance as the cause of sampling error can be eventually canceled out if samples are continually pulled from a target population. Researchers have little control over this type of sampling error. The other form of sampling error, sampling bias, is one that researchers can reduce but not eliminate.

Sampling bias is introduced into research when the probability of selecting a specific participant is not at all random. Simplistically stated, the introduction of bias, causing a sampling error that now favors some participants over others in a population, means that there is a risk that the sample deviates from being a representation of the target population. Sampling bias does not decrease with the increase in sample size and usually has little to do with population size. Sampling bias can occur for a number of reasons in the research process, including the inability of the researcher to adhere to random sampling procedures, the researcher forgetting to design the research to address subgroupings in the target population, faulty measuring by the researcher of constructs in a study, and nonresponsiveness of a specific subgroup in the target population.

Random Sampling Methods

Random sampling is the process of selecting a sample from a larger population, whereby each participant is chosen by chance, although the possibility of being selected for the sample may or may not be equal. A random sampling technique reduces sampling bias. The four types of random sampling are simple random, stratified, systematic, and cluster sampling.

Simple random sampling selects participants entirely by chance. This sampling technique differs from all other techniques in that all members of the population have the same probability of being chosen for the study. An example is if there were 1,000 students in a school district and if the names of all the students were placed in a container and 50 names were randomly chosen, each participant in the population (i.e., school district) would have an equal chance of being chosen for the study.

Simple random sampling ordinarily produces a sample that represents most parameters in a given population and, thus, distributes sources of sampling error across groupings of participants. This allows the results to be generalizable from the sample to the larger population. This type of sampling is rarely used in research; yet, it is the standard against which most sampling techniques are measured. Theoretically, this type of sampling has a low amount of sampling error and bias where only a moderate sample size is needed to represent the population. An apparent disadvantage to simple random sampling is the requirement for an accurate list of the whole population. If an accurate sampling frame is not available, sampling error begins to enter the design. In addition, simple random sampling can be extremely expensive and time-consuming if members of a population are spread out among geographic regions.

Stratified sampling is a form of random sampling that considers unique differences in a defined population. As a researcher defines the population that he or she desires to explore, the population may naturally divide into subpopulations that are not entirely homogenous (e.g., gender, geographical regions, age groups). Because these populations have dissimilar subpopulations, or strata, the researcher must isolate each subgroup in an attempt to re-create a sample that will be similar and generalizable to the larger population being studied. An example is because current exploratory research states that gender plays a significant role in the diagnosis of conduct disorder, with a 3:1 ratio (males: females), a researcher working with a stratified sample of 100 would divide the study on gender and randomly or systematically sample for 75 boys and 25 girls.

The advantages of using a stratified sampling technique include greater coverage of the differences in the population and the prevention of samples that do not represent the population on that specific strata or subgrouping. The disadvantages of stratified sampling are the difficulty in identifying an appropriate stratum or grouping and the difficulty with interpretation and organization of the results. Stratified sampling reduces the sampling error on a sampling size due to the concept of homogeneity. The more homogenous a

sample is, the smaller a sample size that is needed to represent the population accurately. The major consideration should be the accessibility of the subpopulations being studied.

Systematic Sampling

Cluster sampling uses preexisting groups or clusters to select a sample to study. This sampling technique randomly samples these groups or clusters, and all people in these clusters are included in a sample. Cluster sampling is effective when the researcher cannot obtain a complete listing of people yet can obtain a list of clusters in a given population. An example is if a researcher wishes to explore differences between fourth graders and fifth graders in public schools in Virginia, he or she can use a list of all the public schools in Virginia and randomly select schools to study the fourth and fifth graders of those schools (i.e., clusters). All students from the chosen schools will be part of the researcher's observations, and, therefore, participants in the study may be closer together on other variables not accounted for, such as socioeconomic status, race/ethnicity, and school-specific norms.

The advantage of using a cluster-sampling technique is primarily the convenience of conducting the study. The researcher decreases cost in time and resources because the population is not dispersed. The disadvantage to a cluster-sampling model is the larger chance of sampling error due to the participants possibly being too similar and less like the target population. The participants may be very similar on a number of variables that will confound or skew the results of the study. Cluster sampling is susceptible to a higher probability of sampling error than some of the other described means of sampling. This is because, in general, the more steps involved in a sampling process, the more chance sampling error will accidentally enter the design. In cluster sampling, if the clusters selected are relatively large and homogeneous, they run the risk of being unrepresentative of the target population. On the other hand, if there are more clusters consisting of smaller cases, allowing for more heterogeneity of clusters, the sample has a high probability of representing the target population. Thus, smaller sample size can be used to reduce sampling bias only if the clusters are heterogeneous in nature.

Purposeful Sampling Methods

In **purposeful sampling,** the researcher selects cases from the larger population to be in the sample to allow for more in-depth observation. The assumption behind purposeful sampling is that if "rich cases" are explored, then a fuller understanding of the area of interest is accomplished. This fuller understanding is then the justification for the use of a smaller number of participants. There are many differing forms of purposeful sampling, including convenience, maximal variation, and critical case sampling. In purposeful sampling, the major difference is that samples are not randomly selected but are selected with purpose or out of convenience. In purposeful sampling techniques, the researchers' control of selection is considered extremely important. Whether excluding or including certain members of a population, researchers using purposeful sampling stack the deck in order to say if something is true, false, apparent, or relevant to this population, then it may be generalized to a population that is similar. Although the following types of sampling (i.e., convenience, snowball, quota, maximal variation, and critical case sampling) are under the purposeful sampling umbrella, they differ on the amount of control the researcher assumes in selecting the members of a specific population as well as the degree to which cases or samples are considered information rich. The sampling size in these types of techniques generally ranges from extremely small to moderate, depending on the technique used.

Convenience sampling, or **opportunity sampling,** is the sampling technique of arbitrarily selecting participants based on proximity and/or availability. It is generally contended by most research texts that this form of sampling is most prevalent and popular in social science research. The major disadvantage to this form of sampling is that convenience sampling is not composed of a systematic selection process and, therefore, is not clearly representative of the target population. For example, a classic example of the use of convenience sampling is that of a professor who uses students in her or his Psychology 101 class to fill out a survey on memory acquisition.

Snowball sampling is the sampling technique that consists of a researcher starting with a few cases that represent the target population the researcher seeks to explore. The researcher then asks those participants to inform him or her of other individuals who are similar in that they have the desired characteristics of the study. This process allows the existent participants to become recruiters for the study. This process continues until the material becomes saturated or no new views emerge. This sampling technique is fruitful for acquiring populations that are not well defined (e.g., sex workers, drug users, homeless). For example, a researcher who desires to gain knowledge of how homeless individuals in a local community access services can attempt to contact and interview a few participants and then ask them to provide the names of additional individuals to interview to gain a fuller knowledge of those individuals' ability to access services.

Quota sampling is a sampling technique that involves dividing a population into categories and then setting a number (i.e., a quota) of participants needed in each category. This technique consists of establishing the categories and then filling those categories with participants. Once a quota is reached, no more participants from that category are included in the sample. Quota sampling is similar to stratified sampling without the random-selection component. For example, a researcher would like to interview 40 individuals (e.g., 30 women and 10 men) between the ages of 30 to 35 years concerning race, education, socioeconomic status, and their views on counseling. Quota sampling may appear similar to cluster sampling; however, quota sampling involves nonprobability samples.

Maximal variation sampling, a variant of quota sampling, is a sampling technique that consists of the purposeful selection of participants who appear to differ or have a great level of variance on an issue of interest. The researcher who uses this form of sampling attempts to present the differences that exist in the wide range of cases while also highlighting the commonalities that appear to cut across the extreme variations. These extreme variations are the researcher's central focus. For example, when exploring the level of comfort with accessing services to career counseling at a local university, a researcher selects individuals of different socioeconomic status, race, and religion and/or spirituality from the population at the university to capture the greatest variation on an individual's ability to access career counseling services.

Critical case sampling, a variant of expert sampling, is a sampling technique in which the sample consists of a set of cases (i.e., individuals) identified by others (i.e., experts in a particular field) as being significant in a particular way. These distinct cases (i.e., individuals) allow researchers to generalize to other populations or groups on the assumption that if something exists in this case, then it probably exists in all cases (Patton, 2002). Critical case sampling seeks to make a dramatic point by the use of the cases or individuals. An example of critical case sampling is interviewing a number of experts in the field of counseling who have written or addressed issues of integrating creativity into counseling practice. If the questions in the study seek to highlight ways to integrate creativity into counseling and if these nationally known counselors integrate creativity in certain ways, then it is reasonable to infer that all counselors, if made aware of these ways, could integrate creativity into practice.

Contributed by Matthew J. Paylo,
University of Virginia, Charlottesville, VA

Reference

Patton, M. Q. (2002). *Qualitative research & evaluation methods* (3rd ed.). Thousand Oaks, CA: Sage.

Additional Resource

Wilkinson, W. K., & McNeil, K. (1996). *Research and the helping professions*. New York: Brooks/Cole.

■ Sandwich Generation, Club Sandwich Generation

At least 20 million Americans, mostly female caregivers, are part of the **sandwich generation,** that is, sandwiched between parent care and child and/or grandchild care (Family Caregiver Alliance, 2005). There is a 3:1 ratio of daughter to son caregivers (not counting daughters-in-law) with 1 out of 5 women having a parent living in the home. The average American woman spends more time helping aging parents, including the husband's parents, than she spends raising children. Half of the women caring for aging parents also work outside the home. As women delay starting their own families, there is an increase in the number who become part of the sandwich generation. Although a spouse, children, or grandchildren may also be ill and require extraordinary care, the focus of this sandwich generation discussion is on adding the care of the aging-parent layer to the sandwich.

The fastest growing age group of the U.S. population is citizens over 80 years of age. This demographic change transforms the sandwich generation into the **club sandwich generation,** in which men and women in their 60s and 70s experience multiple layers of care giving, thus acting as caregivers to elderly parents, spouses, children, grandchildren, and even great-grandchildren. Communication and responsibilities become increasingly complex, depending on the number of relationships. Furthermore, caregivers may still have job responsibilities or, if retired, have to alter their plans because of these additional family responsibilities.

In addition, four, even five, generations may be separated by thousands of miles. Making decisions across long distances increases the tension because the caregiver must make difficult decisions without actually seeing the loved one. Fortunately, there are now more community organizations to help with the coordination of needed services. Some agencies give direct physical and emotional care, even doing shopping and helping in the household in addition to handling insurance and other finances. If these services are unavailable or insufficient, the family caregiver may need to move the parent(s) closer to the caregiver's home if assisted care or a nursing home care is needed. Other caregivers will move to where the parents live, especially if the parents want to remain in their own home. Still other caregivers will travel long distances several times a year to help with care giving and decision making.

Often the need for **elder care** occurs suddenly, and the person goes from being independent to needing 24-hour care. In such instances, family members have to make quick decisions. Most families have not prepared for such emergencies because it is difficult for them to talk to family members about illness and dying. It is helpful for professional counselors to advise families to have a will, a living will (advance directive), a durable power of attorney, and a health advocate (health care power of attorney or proxy). It is important to know what the family member wishes regarding living arrangements (when feasible) and medical care such as life support.

The increase in chronic disabling conditions (both physical and mental) increases the complexity of the situation. No matter how "high" the sandwich is, the caregivers usually assume their responsibilities because of love and loyalty; however, these responsibilities can become overwhelming, and life can become fragmented and chaotic. The stress resulting from this overload manifests itself in many ways. At work, productivity often decreases because the caregiver is frequently absent both physically and emotionally. At home, there is not enough time for family and household duties, and symptoms of stress, including anxiety, depression, exhaustion, helplessness, irritability, restlessness, headaches, stomachaches, and substance abuse, may appear. Stress can even lead to caregivers abusing the person for whom they are caring. The caregivers become burned out from prolonged stress and from ignoring their own needs. Because their stress level is high, caregivers need support and strategies for self-care, such as relaxation, meditation, prayer, and even humor. Respite care has become the most

urgent need for caregivers, and professional counselors should encourage clients to use these services. **Respite care** is a contracted care arrangement where someone else does the caring for several days, either in the aging parents' home or in a nursing or assisted-living facility. Adult day-care centers, companion programs, faith-based programs, and the Meals-on-Wheels program are also helpful.

Regardless of the methods used, it is essential for the family caregiver to have some time away from care-giving responsibilities. The caregiver needs to ask family or friends to help during a specific time each week (even for just a few hours) so the caregiver can be away to do something enjoyable. Professional counselors can help the caregiver become aware of and accept the feelings of sadness, anger, guilt, frustration, and discouragement as normal feelings under these circumstances. Helping caregivers understand that their own health will suffer unless they enlist others to help is important. Caregivers may be able to use the Family and Medical Leave Act, which was designed to promote family stability. The act allows employees of businesses with 50 or more employees to take 12 weeks of leave in a 12-month period for medical reasons, including the birth or adoption of a child or caring for a sick child, spouse, or parent.

Professional counselors can also help the caregiver to see the parent as the parent is now rather than dwell on what the parent was like in the past. The "child" within the caregiver often continues to expect the parent to be strong. When the caregiver decreases her or his expectations, it gives the parent the freedom to be who the parent is now. Although often emotionally and physically draining, with proper balance and perspective, care giving can be a rewarding experience for each generation.

Contributed by Beverly E. Eanes,
Loyola University Maryland,
Baltimore, MD

Reference

Family Caregiver Alliance. (2005). *Definitions*. Retrieved August 25, 2008, from http://www.caregiver.org/caregiver/jsp/content_node.jsp?nodeid=439

Additional Resources

Administration on Aging Web site: http://www.aoa.gov
Family Caregiver Alliance Web site: http://www.caregiver.org
National Association of Area Agencies on Aging Web site: http://www.n4a.org

■ Scales of Measurement

Scales of measurement are tools that provide a way for people to classify or measure qualities or characteristics of particular things via some comparison. Scales have different levels of detail, including nominal, ordinal, interval, or ratio scaling. Scales can measure variables that have an absolute identity, known as discrete; scales can also measure variables that can fluctuate, referred to as continuous. Scales also provide numerical descriptions of data, known as quantitative scales, but they can also be qualitative when they provide descriptions of data that are not numerical in nature. Understanding these interrelated concepts is key to illustrating how scales are used in the social sciences.

Nominal, interval, ordinal, and ratio scales have different purposes. The **nominal scale** (i.e., a scale that names) is the simplest level because it only serves the purpose of classifying or identifying an object. An example is locker numbers that are painted on high school hallway lockers. Each number that is painted on the side of the locker can be any value that is considered "acceptable" by the high school to use as a form of identification. Only one locker can have a number 23 on its side, another locker can have 71 painted on it, and yet another locker can have the number 3 affixed to its door. These numbers are there only to "name" the locker, that is, Locker 23, Locker 71, and Locker 3, respectively. Just because the number 23 is mathematically smaller than the number 71 does not mean that it is a locker of lesser value, nor does it mean that locker 71 is a better locker. The numbers exist because they have been assigned to each locker in order to tell them apart. This is the same reason why coded numbers are printed alongside disorders classified in the *Diagnostic and Statistical Manual of Mental Disorders* (American Psychiatric Association, 2000). The coded numbers do not imply that one disorder is of greater or lesser value, but they help distinguish one disorder from another. A nominal scale is considered to be the lowest level of scaling because the numbers that are derived from this scale are only used to give objects names, not imply greater or lesser value. Thus, no mathematical calculations (e.g., addition, subtraction, multiplication, division) can be performed.

The second level, ordinal scaling, goes one step beyond the nominal system of providing numbers for naming objects. **Ordinal scales** not only classify objects but they also help rank the position that each object has in comparison with other objects. For example, when constructing a genogram, a counselor often notes the birth order positions that exist among siblings in their family of origin. These positions represent the particular order in which they were born into the family system. The sibling that entered the family of origin first (before all other siblings) is identified as the firstborn, whereas the next sibling born into the family is the second born, followed by the third born. Unlike the numbers that are painted on the sides of the lockers, the numbers associated with birth order imply that one sibling entered the family system earlier than did another sibling. The firstborn is assumed to have been in the family system longer than the other siblings, whereas the second born has the next largest amount of time in the family system, followed by the third born. The ranked place numbers of first, second, and third also help to compare the behavioral tendencies each sibling displays in the family system; however, the order that is provided by ordinal scales is not guaranteed to be consistent from rank to rank. If one sibling is born in 1970, another sibling is born in 1974, and yet another sibling is born in 1981, they still are assigned first-, second-, and third-place positions. Even though the firstborn "beat" the second-born sibling's entry into the family system by 4 years, and the second-born sibling beat the third-born sibling's entry point

by 7 years, they still are assigned positions of first, second, and third born; the numbers associated with the ordinal scale do not imply a uniform distance between each sibling's year of birth. A similar phenomenon occurs when an individual completes a values inventory that requires ranking items from *least valuable* to *most valuable*. The item that receives a 1 *(least valuable)* is not necessarily 4 times less valuable than the item that receives a 4 *(more valuable)* or 10 times less valuable than an item that receives a 10 *(even more valuable)*. Ordinal scales both name and order, but they do not present equal intervals between place values. Some statistical tools can be used with ordinal quality data, but basic mathematical calculations are not possible because the scores are not equal intervals.

The third level, **interval scales,** goes one step beyond the ordinal scale level by providing an equal distance between each classified point on the scale. For example, temperature can be measured in degrees Celsius (C), which uses units of 1 degree between each temperature rating. There is an empirical meaning associated with this measurement, because it is possible to see that there is an equal distance between the degree markers on a thermometer; the distance between 15° and 16° is the same as between 100° and 101°. A tally sheet, such as one used by professional counselors to make naturalistic observations of students in a classroom, also illustrates this scale. There are also equal intervals between tally marks, because each mark represents one and only one occurrence of a particular observed behavior. There is, however, not an absolute zero point on the Celsius scale or on the tally sheet. The reading zero degrees Celsius is the point at which water freezes, but it does not mean there is no temperature. Likewise, the absence of tally marks on an observation sheet does not mean that the student never engages in the particular behavior being observed, but rather that it was not observed during the allotted observation period. Also, it is not logical to conclude that because it is 40° C today, it is twice as warm as yesterday when it was only 20° C; however, it is possible to state that a 40° C day is warmer than a 20° C day. It is also possible to take the averages of temperatures on previous days and make comparisons about current conditions that may have meaningful results. With rank and equidistance, addition and subtraction are possible, but because of the lack of an absolute zero, multiplication and division are not possible.

The most advanced scale measurement is the **ratio scale** because it contains all the qualities of the nominal, ordinal, and interval scales and has a true absolute zero point. In addition, subtraction, multiplication, and division are possible. This advantage serves the hard sciences, but in the social sciences, data do not generally meet this level of quality. An example is the amount of time that it takes for a client to complete a timed test of intelligence: A client who completes an intelligence test in 5 minutes and 0 seconds can be said to have taken half the time of another client who completes the test in 10 minutes and 0 seconds. The minutes and seconds are uniform measurements, and although it is not possible in reality to complete the test in 0 minutes and 0 seconds, all clients are measured from this universally understood starting point—the complete absence of time. This same principle is used when measuring height or distance; 0 inches literally means a complete lack of height or distance. The presence of this absolute zero starting point, coupled with the equally calibrated measurement points that exist along the scale, makes the ratio scale the most comprehensive and mathematically valuable level of measurement.

Discrete scales and continuous scales refer to the thing, concept, or object being measured. Some things can be easily classified into finite categories that contain absolute identities. These are **discrete variables.** A researcher who assigns a label of 1 to all individuals who were registered voters and a label of 2 to all individuals who were not registered voters is using discrete categories to classify these people. Because it is not theoretically or practically possible to partially register to vote, an individual cannot be anything other than a registered or nonregistered voter when classified by this scale. Discrete scales are particularly useful when attempting to classify research participants for a particular survey or study that a professional counselor may wish to conduct.

Some things cannot be classified into finite categories that contain absolute identities. These are **continuous variables.** For example, a person can obtain a score on the Beck Depression Inventory–Second Edition (BDI-II) that places him or her in a mild range of depression, but this numerical classification of 14–19 points does not reflect this person's level of depression for the rest of his or her life. Levels of depression can fluctuate on the basis of numerous factors, which means that this same person could complete the same inventory weeks later and obtain scores that place him or her in the minimal range of 0–13 points. These scores are not absolute identifications of depression because of the continuous nature of the variable. Many psychological tests are considered continuous scales. It is important to note that continuous scales can sometimes be converted into discrete categories, such as when participant categories on the BDI-II (i.e., minimal, mild, moderate, severe) are coded categorically (i.e., 1–4, respectively).

One other characteristic that scales possess is how they describe the data to the intended audience. Some scales provide **numerical classifications** only, which make them quantitative forms of assessment. The BDI-II, once again, serves as an example of this type of assessment, because numerical data are the only result obtained by administering this instrument. Some scales provide other forms of classification in addition to numbers, and these are **qualitative classifications.** The check engine light that flashes red and signals to the driver that the vehicle is in need of maintenance is a qualitative measurement because it is not providing a numerical output, although it does provide specific information to the driver based on quantifiable information. Both qualitative and quantitative scales provide useful information, and it largely depends on the person who constructed the scale to determine which version will be most helpful to the audience.

Contributed by Adam P. Zagelbaum,
Sonoma State University,
Rohnert Park, CA

Reference

American Psychiatric Association. (2000). *Diagnostic and statistical manual of mental disorders* (4th ed., text rev.). Washington, DC: Author.

Additional Resources

Anastasi, A. (1997). *Psychological testing* (7th ed.). Upper Saddle River, NJ: Prentice Hall.

Cohen, R., Swerdlik, M., & Phillips, S. (1998). *Psychological testing and assessment: An introduction to tests and measurement.* Mountain View, CA: Mayfield.

■ Scales, Types of

Scaling involves the assignment of numbers to observations in order to attribute meaning. It involves quantifying the psychological terrain of the client's subjective experience. If scaling is successful, the numerical score that is obtained from an assessment instrument can be used to attribute meaning of a person accurately.

A **scale** is a collection of items or questions that relate to a unitary dimension or single domain of cognition, behavior, or affect. They are often referred to as inventories, composites, schedules, or subtests. Personality, interest, ability, aptitude, attitude, and performance instruments are all assessment tools based on scales. A scale is always at the ordinal or interval level, but it is common for professional counselors to treat scales as being at the interval level or higher. Scales may be descriptive of outcomes (e.g., behavior, attitudes, affect) because they measure underlying traits (e.g., self-control, perfectionism, anger, verbal ability). Scales help professional counselors obtain information from parents, family members, teachers, and others about symptoms and functioning in various settings. The following three rating scales are discussed in this entry: Likert scales, Thurstone scales, and the semantic differential.

Likert Scales

A commonly used procedure for forming attitude or opinion measurements is the **Likert scale.** Developed by Rensis Likert in 1932, this procedure begins by assuming a natural variable with properties that can be ordered according to the magnitude of the trait possessed by the persons in each property set. The form of item used by the Likert procedure is a statement concerning the concept in question, followed by answer choices ranging from *strongly agree* to *strongly disagree* in most cases. The 5-point or 7-point varieties of Likert scales are commonly used today. It is assumed that the number of choices divides the natural variable into a particular number of classes that are ordered with respect to the attitude toward the concept. The respondent is asked to indicate the degree of agreement with the statement or any kind of subjective or objective evaluation of the statement. When a respondent gives his or her responses to a set of items, examiners often like to assign a single number that represents that person's overall attitude or belief. In the following example, examiners would like to give a single number that describes a person's attitude toward Acoholics Anonymous.

Alcoholics Anonymous is good for drinkers trying to recover: 1 *(strongly disagree)*, 2 *(disagree)*, 3 *(neutral)*, 4 *(agree)*, 5 *(strongly agree)*.

If the statement being rated has a negative connotation, the scoring can be reversed. Likert scaling measures either a positive or negative response to a statement. Some common Likert scale choices include the following:

- Regarding quality (5-point scale): *very good, good, barely acceptable, poor,* and *very poor*
- Regarding frequency (6-point scale): *very frequently, frequently, occasionally, rarely, very rarely,* and *never*
- Regarding likelihood (6-point scale): *definitely, very likely, probably, possibly, probably not,* and *not very likely*
- Regarding favorability (7-point scale): *very strongly unfavorable, unfavorable, neutral, favorable, strongly favorable,* and *very strongly favorable*

Sometimes, Likert scales are used in a forced-choice method where the middle option of *neither agree nor disagree* is not available. A *don't know* category is optional, and some counselors prefer not to use it because it is an odd response category. Examples using the optional response choice of *about 50/50, need more information,* or *a bit of both* are sometimes preferable. Examiners can increase the ends of the scale by adding additional points on a scale to increase reliability due to increased variability in scores. In some instances, it may be preferable to use a multipoint scale initially, because it always possible to collapse the responses into condensed categories later on for analysis.

There are a number of benefits to using Likert scales, including reducing lengthy delays between collecting data and interpreting the results, broadening the audience while improving the response rates, and allowing a participant to provide feedback that is more expansive than a simple close-ended question and much easier to quantify than a completely open-ended question. There are some rules of thumb for the appropriate selection of items that will give a range of scores. The scale contains several items. Response levels are arranged horizontally and are anchored with consecutive integers. Response levels are also anchored with verbal labels that connote approximately equal gradations. Verbal labels are bivalent and symmetrical around a neutral middle, and the scale always measures attitude in terms of level of agreement–disagreement to a target statement.

Likert scales may be subject to distortion from several causes, especially response bias. **Response bias** is a type of cognitive bias that can affect the results of a statistical survey if respondents answer questions in the way they think the questioner wants them to answer rather than according to their true beliefs. This may occur if the questioner is obviously angling for a particular answer or if the respondent wishes to please the questioner by answering what appears to be the "morally right" answer. Examples of the latter might be if a woman surveys a man on his attitudes to domestic violence or if someone who obviously cares about the environment asks people how much they value a wilderness

area. This occurs most often in the wording of the question. Response bias is present when a question contains a leading opinion. For example, saying "Even though at the age of 18 years, people are old enough to fight and die for their country, don't you think they should be able to drink alcohol as well?" could yield a response bias. To fix this, the question could be, "Do you think 18-year-olds should be able to drink alcohol?" Response bias also occurs in situations of voluntary response, such as phone-in polls, where the people who care enough to call are not necessarily a statistically representative sample of the actual population. Respondents may avoid using extreme response categories (i.e., central tendency bias), agree with statements as presented (i.e., acquiescence bias), or try to portray themselves or their organization in a more favorable light (i.e., social desirability bias).

A teacher who says "I never rate my students as excellent" provides an example of **central tendency bias.** This happens with a student rating scale with points on it that run from 1 *(poor)* to 7 *(excellent)*, with 4 being the average and a teacher who refuses to use the points at either ends of the scale. There is a tendency for most ratings to fall within the 3–5 range. This can cause problems because a very poor student may be rated slightly above average even though this rating is inaccurate, and, on the other end, a superior student may be rated in the same 3–5 range. Another problem that leads to incorrect answers is **acquiescence bias** or "yea-saying." This is a form of response bias in which participants in a survey have a tendency to agree with all the questions or to indicate a positive connotation. It implies that answers may depend on the wording of the question. For example, to a respondent who is asked a question on total family spending in the past month, the number of "yes" answers to the question "Was it $2,000 or more?" will be higher than the number of "no" answers to the question "Was it less than $2,000?" **Social desirability bias** is the inclination to present oneself in a manner that will be viewed favorably by others. Being social creatures by nature, people are generally inclined to seek some degree of social acceptance. Social desirability in its extreme, however, can cause difficulties in research, particularly in psychology. When research participants provide socially desirable answers, results can be inaccurate. One example of how social desirability can affect results involves administering a survey to a participant and asking, "Do you currently masturbate? If so, how often?" People, in general, are inclined to seek some degree of social acceptance.

When social desirability cannot be avoided in research, often the researcher will resort to a scale that measures socially desirable responding, with the assumption that if participants answer in a socially desirable manner on that scale, they are in all likelihood answering similarly throughout the study. Depending on the goals of the research, respondents who engage in significant amounts of socially desirable responding are discarded from statistical consideration; midrange scorers on a scale of social desirable responding may or may not be included in statistical consideration at the researcher's discretion, or their answers may be recalibrated commensurate with their perceived degree of skew, depending on the measures involved; the goal of the study; and the robustness of the measure used. A major problem with such scales, however, is that individuals actually differ in the degree to which they exhibit social desirability (e.g., nuns vs. criminals), and measures of social desirability may confuse true differences with social desirability bias.

Thurstone Scales

The **Thurstone scale** was developed by Louis Leon Thurstone in 1928 for measuring a core attitude when attitude involves multiple dimensions or concerns. In fact, this scale was the first formal technique used for the measurement of attitudes in psychology. In Thurstone scaling, the professional counselor would obtain a panel of judges and then dream up every conceivable question that can be asked about birth control (say 100 questions). By administering that questionnaire to the panel, the counselor can analyze inter-item agreement among the judges and then use a discrimination index to weed out what are called nonhomogenous items. Good scaling strives for *homogeneity,* a term sometimes synonymous with one-dimensional.

The Thurstone technique allows participants to express their beliefs or opinions by checking items that apply to them. It requires that a series of statements, usually 10 or 20, be created by experts in a specific area of interest. These statements are placed in order of intensity or rated in order of intensity by the experts. The participant is then asked to check all of the statements that apply to her or him, and a median score is computed based on which items she or he has checked. For example, if the participant checked three items that were rated an intensity of 4 and three items rated an intensity of 2, her or his median score would be 3. The participant who checked higher rated items would receive a higher median score, and the participant who checked lower level items would receive a lower median score.

The Thurstone scale consists of statements about a particular issue, and each statement has a numerical value indicating how favorable or unfavorable it is judged to be. People can check each of the statements with which they agree, and a mean score is computed, indicating their attitude at a point in time. An example of this type of scale is given here.

Check all of the statements below that apply to you at the present time:

_____ Decided on method of suicide

_____ Thoughts of death and suicide

_____ No longer interested in activities I used to enjoy

_____ Difficulty sleeping or falling asleep due to obsessive thoughts

_____ Isolating myself more than usual

_____ Negative thoughts are more common than positive

_____ Difficult time motivating self to do necessary things

_____ A little bit of difficulty concentrating

_____ Feel more blue than usual but otherwise Okay

_____ Occasionally down but overall I feel productive and happy

The steps involved in the Thurstone scale include the following: (a) Researchers should define the focus of the scale they are trying to develop, (b) they should have a clear understanding of what they are trying to measure, (c) they should generate statements that describe specific attitudes that people have toward a topic (e.g., AIDS), (d) they should create numerous statements, (e) they should have participants (i.e., judges) rate each statement on a 1 to 11 scale in terms of favorable attitudes (1 = *extremely unfavorable attitudes* and 11 = *extremely favorable attitudes*), (f) they should analyze the rating data, (g) they should select the final scale items, and (h) they should administer the scale to their population. There are advantages to using the Thurstone scale because many unidimensional scales measure people's attitudes along a single dimension by asking them to indicate that they agree or disagree with each of a large set of statements concerning that attitude. The statements are designed to be parallel in construction, but some should be toward one end of the scale and some toward the other end, and each should try to indicate the attitude in a slightly different way. This can be contrasted with a Likert scale, which asks a person to indicate her or his degree of agreement or disagreement with a single statement, For example, a Likert scale item would be "Please rate on a scale of 1 *(disagree)* to 7 *(agree)* the statement: 'This software was easy to use.'" The corresponding Thurstone scale would state this question in multiple ways, providing a richer assessment of responder attitudes (e.g.: "I had trouble finding what I wanted." "I liked how easy the software was." "The software has many convenient features." "The software was confusing.")

Semantic Differential

The **semantic differential** is a general technique that assesses affective responses. It is based on the idea that people think dichotomously or in terms of polar opposites such as good–bad, right–wrong, strong–weak, and so on. There are many varieties of the technique; the most popular variety asks respondents to place their own slash mark along a line between adjectives. The following is an example of a scale intending to measure feelings toward alcohol advertising as a cause of adolescent drinking:

On each line below and between each extreme, place a slash closest to your first impression.

How Do You Feel About The Argument That Alcohol Advertising Causes Adolescent Drinking?

Bad ————————————————	Good
Deep ————————————————	Shallow
Weak ————————————————	Strong
Unfair ————————————————	Fair
Quiet ————————————————	Loud
Dirty ————————————————	Clean

Professional counselors can use the semantic differential with any polarized adjectives. The point is to collect response patterns that can be analyzed. The technique has three features that distinguish it as a unique and effective scale. First, semantic differentials are easy to set up, administer, and code with demonstrated reliability and validity. Second, they possess an evaluation, potency, and activity structure that has an unprecedented amount of cross-cultural validation; they are interesting theoretically; and the measurements on all three dimensions yield a wealth of information about affective responses to a stimulus. Third, because the form of a semantic differential is basically the same whatever the stimulus, research using the semantic differential can cumulate. The semantic differential has been applied frequently as a procedure for the measurement of attitude, and its usefulness in this respect is indicated by the wide variety of meaningful results that have been obtained.

A number of challenges in the use of semantic differentials for the measurement of attitude still remain. When participants are highly invested in a topic and want to give socially desirable answers, it may be advisable to use an instrument that is less direct than the semantic differential. Social desirability ratings of semantic differential scales correlate very highly with the evaluation factor loadings of the scales. Thus, if participants choose to distort their responses toward social desirability, evaluation scores would be biased upward. If a researcher does use the semantic differential with especially sensitive topics, it is worth taking some precaution to guard against social desirability effects. The potency and activity measurements should be free of this problem because the typical scales for measuring these dimensions are essentially free of social desirability contamination. Perhaps the most important general contribution of the semantic differential is the provision of a single attitude space for all stimuli. This permits analyses, comparisons, and insights that are virtually impossible with traditional instruments.

Contributed by David J. Carter,
University of Nebraska, Omaha, NE

Additional Resources

Hand, D. J. (1996). Statistics and the theory of measurement, with discussion. *Journal of the Royal Statistical Society, Series A, 159,* 445–492.

Hood, A. B., & Johnson, R. W. (2007). *Assessment in counseling: A guide to the use of psychological assessment procedures* (4th ed.). Alexandria, VA: American Counseling Association.

Michell, J. (1986). Measurement scales and statistics: A clash of paradigms. *Psychological Bulletin, 100,* 398–407.

■ Schizophrenia and Other Psychotic Disorders

Schizophrenia is a psychiatric disorder defined most prominently by psychotic symptoms. Psychotic symptoms found in schizophrenia may include positive symptoms, such as delusions, hallucinations, disorganized speech, and grossly disorganized or catatonic behavior, as well as negative symptoms, which represent an absence of normal traits, including flat affect; avolition, where a person is unable to initiate and continue goal-directed behavior; and alogia, a problem with the thought process that manifests itself in problems with speech and language behavior. Some symptoms must be present for at least 6 months, with at least 1 month of active-phase symptoms, unless symptoms are successfully treated, in which case a period of less than 1 month of active-phase symptoms may be needed for diagnosis.

The *Diagnostic and Statistical Manual of Mental Disorders* (4th ed., text rev.; American Psychiatric Association [APA], 2000) presents subtypes for schizophrenia. Subtypes have been heavily debated because the course of the disorder and treatment response differ greatly in those diagnosed with the same subtype. Nevertheless, the subtypes include paranoid type, disorganized type, catatonic type, undifferentiated type, and residual type. A person with the **paranoid type** of schizophrenia presents with predominate symptoms of delusions or hallucinations. **Disorganized type** is defined by the prominent symptoms of disorganized speech, disorganized behavior, and flat or inappropriate affect. For those classified as **catatonic type,** the prominent feature is psychomotor disturbance. **Undifferentiated type** is used for classification of those for whom paranoid, disorganized, or catatonic criteria are not met. **Residual type** is assigned to those who have had at least one episode of schizophrenia yet who present at the time of diagnosis without prominent positive symptoms.

The course of schizophrenia may vary from individual to individual, and a diagnosis can only be applied after 1 year of active-phase symptoms. The courses schizophrenia may take include episodic with or without interepisode residual symptoms, continuous, single episode in partial or full remission, or unspecified. The onset of schizophrenia typically occurs between late adolescence and the mid-30s and often appears in boys and men earlier than in girls and women. Prevalence rates for schizophrenia are in the range of 0.5% to 1.5% in adults (APA, 2000), and schizophrenia has been found to affect people all over the world. Studies suggest individuals with first-degree relatives who have been diagnosed with schizophrenia have a risk of manifesting schizophrenia that is 10 times greater than those of the normal population. Studies with twins have shown that in addition to a biological predisposition, environmental factors also contribute to the development of schizophrenia. Treatment for schizophrenia and other psychotic disorders typically involves antipsychotic medication and psychotherapy.

Schizophreniform Disorder

Schizophreniform disorder is characterized as a psychiatric disorder whereby predominant psychotic symptoms similar to schizophrenia are present, yet an episode of the disorder lasts for at least 1 month but less than 6 months. Impaired social or occupational functioning, which is needed for the diagnosis of schizophrenia, is not required for a diagnosis of schizophreniform disorder. Approximately two thirds of those diagnosed with this disorder progress to a diagnosis of schizophrenia or schizoaffective disorder. It is believed prevalence rates for schizophreniform disorder may be as much as 5 times lower than rates for schizophrenia. Although few studies have focused on familial patterns in schizophreniform disorder, there is evidence to suggest that relatives of those diagnosed with schizophreniform disorder have an increased chance of being diagnosed with schizophrenia.

Schizoaffective Disorder

Schizoaffective disorder is a psychiatric diagnosis given to those who present with the predominant psychotic symptoms of schizophrenia concurrent with a mood episode that may be classified as major depressive, manic, or mixed. During this same period of illness, there must also be delusions or hallucinations for at least 2 weeks in the absence of predominant mood symptoms; however, prominent mood symptoms must be present for the majority of the duration of the disorder. Age of onset for schizoaffective disorder is typically early adulthood; however, the disorder may appear anywhere between adolescence and late adulthood. The incidence of schizoaffective disorder is higher in women than in men. Although no specific prevalence rates have been found, it appears that schizoaffective disorder is less common than schizophrenia. There is an increased risk of schizophrenia in those with first-degree relatives diagnosed with schizoaffective disorder.

Delusional Disorder

Delusional disorder involves the presence of nonbizarre delusions (i.e., delusions of things that could occur in real life) that last for at least 1 month. Aside from what occurs as a direct result of the delusions, functioning is not found to be markedly impaired, and behavior does not appear to be particularly bizarre. Prevalence rates for delusional disorder are around .03% for the general population (APA, 2000). The age of onset tends to range anywhere from adolescence to late adulthood. There does not seem to be a major gender difference in frequency of delusional disorder. Specific types, including erotomanic type, grandiose type, jealous type, persecutory type, somatic type, mixed type, and unspecified type, are assigned to individuals diagnosed with delusional disorder.

Erotomanic type is assigned to individuals who have delusions involving the belief that another person, often of higher status, is in love with them. **Grandiose type** is applied to those individuals who hold a sense of overarching self-worth, power, identity, or knowledge or who hold the belief in a special relationship to a deity or famous person. Individuals who hold the belief that their sexual partner is unfaithful are classified as the **jealous type. Persecutory type** is assigned to individuals who believe they or someone close to them are being malevolently treated. When individuals believe they have a physical defect or medical condition, **somatic type** is diagnosed. **Mixed type** is assigned to those whose delusions fit in more than one of the aforementioned types, but no type is predominant. **Unspecified type** is applied to those who have been diagnosed with delusional disorder but for whom no type fits (APA, 2000).

Brief Psychotic Disorder

Brief psychotic disorder is a psychiatric diagnosis given when a sudden onset of at least one of the following positive psychotic symptoms occurs: delusions, hallucinations, disorganized speech, or disorganized or catatonic behavior. The episode lasts for at least 1 day but less than 1 month, and the person returns to a normal level of functioning once the episode subsides. Brief psychotic disorder has an average age of onset between ages of the late 20s and the early 30s.

Shared Psychotic Disorder

Shared psychotic disorder (also know as *folie à deux*) is given as a psychiatric diagnosis when a person develops a delusion when involved with someone who already has a psychotic disorder with the prominent feature of delusions. The person develops delusions that are shared in whole or in part with the person who already has the psychotic disorder. Age of onset of shared psychotic disorder tends to vary; however, the disorder is usually chronic. There is some, though limited, evidence to suggest that it is more common in women than in men.

Contributed by Morgan Brooks Conway,
Niagara University, Niagara, NY

Reference

American Psychiatric Association. (2000). *Diagnostic and statistical manual of mental disorders* (4th ed., text rev.). Washington, DC: American Psychiatric Association.

Additional Resources

Green, M. F. (2001). *Schizophrenia revealed: From neurons to social interactions*. New York: Norton.

Noll, R. (2007). *The encyclopedia of schizophrenia and other psychotic disorders* (3rd ed.). New York: Facts on File.

◼ School Counseling

The scope of practice of a school counselor continues to evolve. The **American School Counselor Association (ASCA)** proactively defines school counselors as credentialed professionals with a master's degree or higher in school counseling, or the substantial equivalent, who are uniquely qualified to address the developmental needs of all students (ASCA, 2005). Professional school counselors deliver a comprehensive school counseling program that encourages all students' academic, career, and personal/social development and helps them maximize student achievement. Their work is differentiated by attention to developmental stages of student growth, including the needs, tasks, and student interests related to those stages.

ASCA, the professional association for school counselors, is a division of the American Counseling Association (ACA) and represents more than 21,000 school counselors from pre-K to the college campus. With a motto of "One Vision, One Voice," the ASCA mission is to promote professionalism and ethical practices while focusing on professional development and researching effective practices aimed at improving school counseling programs.

As recently as the early 1990s, school counseling programs were perceived as a collection of well-intentioned, responsive services based up professional orientation, the priorities of an individual school building, and administrative needs (Campbell & Dahir, 1997). Concerned that school counselors were being viewed as peripheral to the school reform agenda, leaders worked to include the school counseling program as an integral part of the total school program. The profession was charged to shift practice from the delivery of a menu of student services to providing a structured and programmatic approach to address the needs of all students (Gysbers & Henderson, 2006).

ASCA National Standards

In response to the GOALS 2000: Educate America Act, the **ASCA National Standards for School Counseling Programs** were developed to define what students should know and be able to do as the result of participating in a comprehensive, developmental K–12 school counseling program (Campbell & Dahir, 1997). The standards offered the school counseling community an opportunity to articulate the relationship of school counseling to student achievement and school improvement and served as the "single most legitimizing document in the school counseling profession" (Bowers, Hatch, & Schwallie-Giddis, 2001, p. 17).

The ASCA National Standards addressed the three domains of student development—academic, career, and personal/social development—and within each domain, three specific standards were supported with student competencies to identify specific knowledge, attitudes, or skills (see Figure 1). The ASCA National Standards provided the groundwork for the development of a national, comprehensive model for school counselor programs that evolved into the *ASCA National Model: A Framework for School Counseling Programs* (ASCA, 2005).

Transforming School Counseling Initiative

Concurrently, **The Education Trust** promoted the principle that school counselors are critical to closing the achievement gap for those students who have been traditionally underserved in their quest to graduate from high school and have access to higher education. To meet this goal, the **Transforming School Counseling Initiative** was designed to articulate the knowledge, attitudes, and skills that professional school counselors need to transition successfully from preservice to practice. The initial intent focused on the improvement of school counseling at the graduate level. In 1997, six universities were competitively selected to partner with The Education Trust to redesign counselor education programs and prepare school counselors as advocates, leaders, and systemic change agents in school improvement.

In 2003, The Education Trust and the MetLife Foundation established the National Center for Transforming School Counseling to call attention to the particular role school counselors play in increasing educational opportunities for all students and to emphasize advocacy, leadership, and contributions to the academic success of students. School counselors call attention to situations in schools that are defeating or frustrating students, thereby hindering the students' success. Measurable success from this effort can be documented by the increased number of students completing school with the academic preparation, the career awareness, and the personal/social growth essential to choose from a wide range of substantial postsecondary options, including college. Figure 2 summarizes these changes.

ASCA National Model

With the continued progression of school improvement due to the passage of the No Child Left Behind Act of 2001 and the widespread use of the ASCA National Standards, ASCA developed the *ASCA National Model: A Framework for School Counseling Programs*. The *ASCA National Model* integrated three widely accepted and respected approaches to developing school counseling programs: (a) comprehensive (Gysbers & Henderson, 2006), (b) developmental (Myrick, 2003), and (c) results based (Johnson & Johnson, 2003). ASCA's efforts produced a contemporary school counseling model that aligned the program with the expectations of 21st-century schools. The model has four components, or sections, and is intended to provide every student with the attitudes, knowledge, and skills to succeed in 21st-century schools:

1. The **foundation** component of the program addresses the belief and mission that every student will benefit from the school counseling program. It describes the

---

Academic Development

Standard A: Students will acquire the attitudes, knowledge, and skills that contribute to effective learning in school across the lifespan.
Standard B: Students will complete school with the academic preparation essential to choose from a wide range of substantial post-secondary options, including college.
Standard C: Students will understand the relationship of academics to the world of work and to life at home and in the community.

Career Development

Standard A: Students will acquire the skills to investigate the world of work in relation to knowledge of self and to make informed career decisions.
Standard B: Students will employ strategies to achieve future career success and satisfaction.
Standard C: Students will understand the relationship between personal qualities, education and training, and the world of work.

Personal/Social Development

Standard A: Students will acquire the attitudes, knowledge, and interpersonal skills to help them understand and respect self and others.
Standard B: Students will make decisions, set goals, and take necessary action to achieve goals.
Standard C: Students will understand safety and survival skills.

Figure 1. The National Standards for School Counseling Programs

Note. From *Sharing the Vision: The National Standards for School Counseling Programs*, by C. Campbell & C. Dahir, 1997, Alexandria, VA: American School Counselor Association. Copyright 1997 by the American School Counselor Association.

The Practice of the Traditional School Counselor (Service-driven model)	The Practice of the Transformed School Counselor (Data-driven and standards-based model)
• Counseling • Consultation • Coordination of services	• Counseling • Consultation • Coordination of services • Leadership • Advocacy • Collaboration and teaming • Managing resources • Use of data • Use of technology

Figure 2. Summary of Changes

"what" of the program, discussing what every student should know and be able to do based on the ASCA National Standards.

2. The **delivery** component defines the implementation process and the components of the comprehensive model (i.e., guidance curriculum, individual planning with students, responsive services, and system support).

3. The **management** component presents the organizational processes and tools needed to deliver a comprehensive school counseling program. These processes and tools include agreements about responsibility, use of data, action plans for guidance curriculum and closing the gap, and time and task analysis.

4. The **accountability** component of the *ASCA National Model* shows the relationship of the school counseling program to the instructional program. School counselors use their specialized training to demonstrate how the school counseling program moves school improvement data in a positive direction.

In addition, the *ASCA National Model* furthered the goals of Transforming School Counseling and the ASCA National Standards by doing the following things:

- Focusing counselors in the direction of improving academic achievement and eliminating the achievement gap;

- Connecting school counseling to each school district's mission and school improvement goals;

- Providing school counselors with the tools to develop school counseling programs that include student competencies and outcomes based on the ASCA National Standards;

- Encouraging school counselors to use school-based data to understand the current situation in their school building and district and to work collaboratively toward the goals of school improvement.

Professionalism for School Counselors

Voices, both internal and external to the profession, have called for an expansion in the role of the school counselor from the traditional emphasis on providing responsive services to one that also promotes optimal achievement for all students (Martin, 1998). ASCA has charged every professional school counselor to renew his or her practice and respond to the climate of school improvement.

Advocacy, leadership, collaboration and teaming, and use of data are essential components of the repertoire of skills that a contemporary school counselor uses in today's schools (ASCA, 2005). The school counseling profession has taken hold of the present and has transformed the future. No longer will the work of school counselors be defined by the perception of others. The comprehensive and systemic approach to program development, implementation, and evaluation is the way of work for 21st-century school counselors.

Contributed by Carol A. Dahir,
New York Institute of Technology,
New York, NY

References

American School Counselor Association. (2005). *ASCA National Model: A framework for school counseling programs* (2nd ed.). Alexandria, VA: Author.

Bowers, J., Hatch, T., & Schwallie-Giddis, P. (2001, September/October). The brain storm. *ASCA School Counselor, 42,* 17–18.

Campbell, C., & Dahir, C. (1997). *Sharing the vision: The national standards for school counseling programs.* Alexandria, VA: American School Counselor Association.

Gysbers, N. C., & Henderson, P. (2006). *Developing and managing your school guidance and counseling program* (4th ed.). Alexandria, VA: American Counseling Association.

Johnson, S., & Johnson, C. D. (2003). Results-based guidance: A systems approach to student support programs. *Professional School Counseling, 6,* 180–184.

Martin, P. (1998). *Transforming school counseling.* Washington, DC: The Education Trust.

Myrick, R. D. (2003). *Developmental guidance and counseling: A practical handbook.* Minneapolis, MN: Educational Media Corporation.

■ Section 504 of the U.S. Rehabilitation Act of 1973

Section 504 of the Rehabilitation Act of 1973 is a civil rights act designed to eliminate discrimination based on a person having a disability. This act ensures that individuals with disabilities can participate in and receive the benefits of any program or activity that receives federal funding. In the case of education, Section 504 is intended to guarantee that students with disabilities are able to participate fully in a school's educational and extracurricular activities to the same extent as students without disabilities. Through legal discovery, it was found that Section 504 plans were being written incorrectly, that they were not being completely enforced, and that some educators were losing their jobs due to federal lawsuits. After numerous presentations, the purpose became clear. Those working in schools must become knowledgeable about Section 504 plans in order to have a uniform method to serve students with a disability.

Who Is Protected by Section 504?

Any person who has physical or mental impairment that substantially limits one or more major life activities, has a record of such impairment, or is regarded as having such impairment is protected by Section 504. A physical or mental impairment is any physiological disorder condition; cosmetic disfiguration; and mental, psychological, or anatomical loss. Section 504 does not define specific impairments, but physical impairments include epilepsy, HIV/AIDS, allergies, arthritis, heart disease, Tourette syndrome, cerebral palsy, broken limbs, cancer, diabetes, hemophilia, temporary conditions due to accidents or illness, and visual impairment, among others. Mental impairments include attention-deficit/hyperactivity disorder (AD/HD), depression, eating disorders, bipolar disorders, conduct disorder, past alcohol or other drug abuse or addiction, and obsessive–compulsive disorder, among others.

Evaluation

Each school district establishes the requirements and procedures of a 504 evaluation. These procedures, which are similar to the processes and requirements of the Individuals With Disabilities Education Act (IDEA), include an initial referral to the multidisciplinary team and valid evaluations administered by professional personnel. At the initial referral meeting, the multidisciplinary team determines the problem or problems the student demonstrates, the student's grades/scores, if there have been any disciplinary referrals, if there are signs of a disability, if any interventions and/or accommodations had been attempted or implemented, and if there is a need for a 504 evaluation.

Section 504 Eligibility

Students who are considered for Section 504 eligibility have substantial limits, which mean they are unable to perform major life activities compared with the average student. Major life activities include, but are not limited to, learning, walking, talking, seeing, hearing, breathing, self-care, and performing manual tasks; however, educators are most concerned about the student's ability to learn. In order to determine if the student's learning is affected, several factors must be considered for eligibility. The multidisciplinary team, which should consist of representatives from special education, regular education, the student's family, and counseling, has to meet and examine multiple pieces of data.

If the team determines that there is a need for a 504 evaluation, a variety of sources of information are collected and should be used for the eligibility meeting. These sources include medical documentation, cumulative records, standardized tests, student work samples, report cards, parent and teacher input, disciplinary records, and prior special education testing results. Along with the school district's standards for qualifications, the team also explores the type of impairment, the educational impact, the disability's substantial limitation, and the appropriateness of a 504 finding. These sources not only contribute to determining eligibility under Section 504 but also provide documentation for the team's findings.

Poor academic performance or difficulties were not always due to a physical or mental impairment. The student must experience a physical or mental impairment at the present time. The student is not eligible based on the potential for impairment. Also, a student is not found eligible for a Section 504 plan as a consolation prize for not qualifying under IDEA. Students who are found eligible for IDEA are not eligible for a separate Section 504 plan.

A student's failure to meet parental expectations is not a factor when determining eligibility. According to case law, the Office of Civil Rights found that school officials had no duty to qualify a student for a Section 504 plan if the student had AD/HD, acceptable behavior, and passing grades. In the school setting, decisions about Section 504 plans are based on educational criteria, not medical criteria.

Planning and Development

Once the student qualifies under Section 504, the school appoints the student's case manager to initiate the development of the accommodation plan. This plan is developed with individuals who are familiar with the academic needs of the student. The plan should include the student's disability, major life activity affected, and the educational impact of the disability. The accommodations outlined in the plan should be clear, precise, and realistic. The need for a behavior management plan should be explored as well. Upon development, the plan should be distributed to all teachers, and a copy is placed in the cumulative folder. Once the plan is implemented, it should be evaluated on an ongoing basis to monitor for effectiveness. The school should review a student's 504 plan annually or upon any significant change in placement. A reevaluation for 504 qualifications should be conducted every 3 years.

Procedural Safeguards

Unlike IDEA, the Rehabilitation Act of 1973 does not contain numerous and specific procedural safeguards. It is basically the responsibility of the school systems to establish and implement a system of procedural safeguards. The Office for Civil Rights (OCR) identifies the basic rights of students and parents in Title 34 of the Code of Federal Regulations, Part 104. In this section, OCR goes so far as to state that conformity with IDEA's procedural safeguards would be a suitable means for a school system to satisfy the requirement for identifying and instituting appropriate procedural safeguards. Compliance with key components of IDEA's procedural safeguards, such as written notice, parental consent, access to records, placement, evaluations, and discipline, would certainly assist school systems in avoiding compliance issues. Parents have the right to file complaints with OCR, because compliance issues will possibly be viewed as discrimination in accordance with Title VII of the Civil Rights Act of 1964.

Regarding procedural safeguards, there are a few key things to remember when managing the Section 504 process. First, it is important to be familiar with the significant differences in students' and parents' rights between Section 504 and IDEA. IDEA is very specific about prior written notice, parental involvement in the decision making, and the receipt of parental permission. Section 504 is not as explicit. Second, it is important to understand and comply with the procedures for handling discipline issues of students covered by Section 504. As identified in IDEA's procedural safeguards, students protected by Section 504 may be disciplined like any student who is not disabled and may be unilaterally suspended for up to 10 school days. For future violations of the school's code of conduct or for violations that could result in the removal of the student for more than 10 school days, a manifestation determination must be held. It is critical for those responsible for managing the 504 plans to be especially familiar with this procedure and with conducting functional behavior analysis and behavior intervention plans. Review of case law regarding issues of students covered by Section 504 is highly recommended.

Contributed by Rivers S. Taylor Jr.,
J. Duncan Hubbell, Angela Williams,
and Denise Williams-Patterson,
Norfolk Public Schools, Norfolk, VA
and Fallon K. Dodson,
Charlottesville High School,
Charlottesville, VA

Additional Resources

Department of Education. (2006). *34 CFR Parts 300 and 301: Assistance to States for the Education of Children With Disabilities and Preschool Grants for Children With Disabilities; Final Rule.* Retrieved April 26, 2007, from http://www.wrightslaw.com/idea/law/FR.v71.n156.pdf

Electronic Code of Federal Regulations. (2007). *Title 34 Education.* Retrieved April 26, 2007, from http://www.access.gpo.gov/cgi-bin/cfrassemble.cgi?title=199934

LD OnLine Web site: http://www.ldonline.org/indepth/accommodations

U.S. Equal Employment Opportunity Commission. (1964). *Title VII of the Civil Rights Act of 1964.* Retrieved April 26, 2007, from http://www.eeoc.gov/policy/vii.html

Wrightslaw Web site: http://www.wrightslaw.com/info/sec504.index.htm

Self-Actualization

Self-actualization is a person's innate ability to grow and achieve full potential. This concept was originally identified by Kurt Goldstein and later elaborated on by Abraham Maslow. Maslow (1968) described self-actualization as a process in which a person developed "full use and exploitation of talents, capacities, and potentialities" (p. 153). The concept of self-actualization is a cornerstone in the development of his theory of motivation. In this theory, individuals strive to have their basic needs met on the way to becoming self-actualized individuals.

In order to illustrate this concept, Maslow identified a hierarchy of needs. The hierarchy includes five levels of needs: basic physiology, safety, love and belonging, esteem, and self-actualization. These needs are separated into deficiency needs and growth needs. The four lower levels of the hierarchy are considered deficiency needs, whereas the fifth level, or self-actualization, is a growth need. Deficiency needs are essential for survival and must be met for optimal growth and development to occur. Growth needs are considered psychological in nature and help a person to become a healthy, fully functioning person. As a person progresses upward on the hierarchy, the higher needs will emerge as the lower needs are met.

The first level of needs **(basic physiology needs)** established by Maslow (1947) includes such basics as food, water, and sleep. This category is the most potent and supersedes all higher level needs; without these needs being met, humans cannot function adequately. According to Maslow, an individual's thoughts and energies will be directed toward satisfying these very basic needs. Maslow's second level, **safety needs,** refers to a person's physical and emotional safety, which may include the security of property, resources, and employment. When clients are able to meet their basic needs as well as remain safe in their environment, they are able to advance to the next level **(love and belonging needs).** At the third level of Maslow's hierarchy, a person is motivated to find loving relationships and a sense of belonging. These relational needs can be fulfilled through one-on-one relationships or within groups of people. As a person proceeds up the hierarchy, **esteem needs** are seen as the fourth step toward self-actualization. Individuals possess a need for a stable, firm sense of self, which includes the ability to self-evaluate as well as have self-respect, self-confidence, and self-efficacy. Without a strong sense of self, it becomes very difficult for an individual to become self-actualized. Once people have met their deficiency needs, they are able to concentrate on their growth needs, which include self-actualization. At the final level, self-actualizing people are motivated by their own sense of purpose or mission in life rather than by others' opinions.

The concept of self-actualization and the hierarchy of needs are applicable in the field of counseling. By applying these principles to counseling and assessing a client's level of needs, a counselor's interventions may be more effective. Professional counselors may adapt their approach, depending on where their client is on the hierarchy. For example, a homeless client would benefit from counseling focusing on identifying local food pantries and affordable housing; however, if clients are attempting to meet their needs for love and belonging, they might benefit most from group treatment. Understanding the hierarchy is crucial for counselors and assists them to be more effective in their treatment planning.

Although the concept of self-actualization has been around for many years, researchers have not agreed on an operational definition. In an attempt to define self-actualization more clearly, Lecere, Lefrancois, Dube, Hebert, and Gaulin (1998) identified 36 self-actualization indicators. The authors then categorized these indicators into two essential characteristics of self-actualization: openness to experience and reference to self. **Openness to experience** refers to individuals' ability to be fully present and in contact with their "experiences of themselves, others, and the world" (Lecere et al., 1998, p. 78). **Reference to self** is individuals' ability to communicate honestly and openly with others; in other words, their behavior truly matches their thoughts and feelings and is not dependent on others' approval or demands. Thus, they defined self-actualization as "a process through which one's potential is developed in congruence with one's self-perceptions and one's experience" (Lecere et al., 1998, p. 78). These constructs, traits, and definitions will be helpful to advance research related to self-actualization.

Contributed by Darcie Davis-Gage,
University of Northern Iowa, Cedar
Falls, IA

References

Lecere, G., Lefrancois, R., Dube, M., Hebert, R., & Gaulin, P. (1998). The self-actualization concept: A content validation. *Journal of Social Behavior and Personality, 13,* 69–84.

Maslow, A. H. (1947). A theory of human motivation. *Psychological Review, 50,* 375–377.

Maslow, A. H. (1968). *Toward a psychology of being* (2nd ed.). Princeton, NJ: Van Nostrand.

Additional Resource

Koltko-Rivera, M. E. (2006). Rediscovering the later version of Maslow's hierarchy of needs: Self-transcendence and opportunities for theory, research, and unification. *Review of General Psychology, 10,* 302–317.

■ Self-Concept

Defining self-concept is a complex task. Historically, researchers have offered various operational constructs in an attempt to define the term. **Self-concept** can be understood as a person's overall assessment of the self (Bracken & Mills, 1994) or a hierarchically organized set of characteristics that relate to the self (Craine & Bracken, 1994; Shavelson, Hubner, & Stanton, 1976).

The term *self-concept* is frequently interchanged with other terms such as *self-worth, self-esteem,* and *self-identity,* further complicating the ability of investigators to arrive at a universally accepted definition (Wylie, 1961). **Self-esteem** is the global term most often used by professionals and lay people when attempting to describe the observable and measurable dimensions of an individual's view of his or her own life (e.g., academic ability, physical abilities and traits, vocational aptitude) as well as his or her personal characteristics (e.g., family satisfaction, health, social standing). Wylie (1961) moved away from a singular understanding of the self by examining critical variables that may constitute the self, such as parent–child dynamics, social environment, and gender role influences. In differentiating self-concept from self-esteem, it is necessary to define the variables that constitute the sources and inner workings of an individual's self-evaluation that is ultimately manifested in the outward expression of the self. Because self-esteem can be seen as a single phenomenon, self-concept underscores the need to evaluate a number of identifiable factors, understand their dynamics, and recognize how they produce an overall self-evaluation.

Shavelson et al. (1976), recognizing self-concept as a matter of cognition, investigated self-concept with adolescents. The authors' construct of self-concept underscores a self-perceptive quality, which provides for a self-evaluation formed by an individual's experiences through his or her environment as well as the degree of reinforcement from society or from significant relationships such as parents, siblings, or an individual's social network. This research initially saw self-concept defined by seven principles that stated self-concept was (a) organized around social networks (e.g., family, friends, school), (b) multifaceted, (c) hierarchical

according to an individual's sense of importance, (d) stable over time although degree of importance could change from time to time, (e) developmental, (f) evaluative against realistic or idealistic standards, and (g) differentiable from other situations. Shavelson et al.'s model of self-concept provided the launching pad for further research into defining self-concept (Ellis, 2000).

Craine and Bracken (1994) worked to validate the findings of Shavelson et al. (1976) and Wylie (1961). They reemphasized the need for a universal construct to streamline research in this area but moved away from the cognitive process proposed by Shavelson et al.; rather, they began to see self-concept as a behavioral construct. Their model proposed six subdimensions as reference points for each individual that constitute his or her global self-concept. Craine and Bracken's six subcomponents are (a) affect, (b) social, (c) physical, (d) competence, (e) academic, and (f) family. These six areas are specific to the person's behavioral responses to the world around him or her. The six subdimensions are arranged in the order of importance, as determined by the individual. Because the order of the subdimensions is interchangeable, depending on environmental and behavioral changes, the global self-concept can remain stable over time.

Self-Concept and Career Development

Career and vocational applications of self-concept are rooted in the work of Donald Super. Super's vocational application of self-concepts involves expressing self-concept through one's vocational choice. By declaring a vocational preference, individuals vocationally define the kind of person that they are by implementing a particular self-concept through their occupation. Super's initial thoughts of choosing a vocation as a means of implementing a person's self-concept gave way as Super evolved his theoretical perspectives of the interaction of the individual and society.

Super's belief in the application of self-concept in vocational/career work is rooted in his life-span theory. His sense of self-concept in vocational/career work indicates that (a) abilities vary among people; (b) these differences qualify each individual for a variety of occupations; (c) variance exists for each individual as it pertains to the model ability or trait for an occupation; (d) people's preferences and competence can change with time and experience; (e) preferences are adjusted as people go through a series of life stages; (f) people's career patterns are a product of their ecological environment as well as of their career maturity or adaptability in respect to their ability to manage the self and their environment effectively over the course of their lives; (g) proper development through life is a process of maintaining awareness of abilities and helping people make sound vocational choices by knowing their strengths and weaknesses; and (h) recognition that a person's self-concept has dynamic properties of vocational exposure, trial and error, approval of peers and superiors, feedback, and work satisfaction. Recent additions to Super's work involve coping with the environment based on an individual's life career stage; a greater emphasis on adaptability; recognition that work satisfaction is proportional to an individual's ability to implement high levels of his or her self-concept; and recognition that work preferences are also a part of society in the context of racial bias, gender bias, leisure activities, homemaking, and other life roles.

Super's use of self-concept is in direct relationship to an individual's view of self and society. The use of self-concept in Super's work, as with the Life Career Rainbow, recognizes the diversity of self-concepts that people hold regarding their lives as a child, student, husband/wife, or parent. The expanse of these life roles was depicted to help individuals identify previous life career roles or identify current life career roles (Herr, 1997). Super's (1990) archway model explicitly illustrates the interaction between individuals and society while tying in economic factors, family dynamics, and other ecological perspectives that influence the construction of a person's aptitudes, interests, and values across the life span. Work satisfaction, as well as life satisfaction, is dependent on a decision maker consolidating individual and ecological perspectives in order to weigh options and make informed career decisions. Super's integration of economic, familial, and environmental factors, along with individual aptitude, interests, and values at various developmental stages of life, underscores his desire to recognize the variety of self-concepts people have and how they are included in career decision making.

Contributed by Cyrus Marcellus Ellis,
Governors State University,
University Park, IL

References

Bracken, B., & Mills, B. (1994). School counselors' assessment of self-concept: A comprehensive review of 10 instruments. *The School Counselor, 42,* 14–31.

Craine, R., & Bracken, B. (1994). Age, race, and gender differences in child and adolescent self-concept: Evidence from a behavioral-acquisition, context-dependent model. *School Psychology Review, 23,* 496–511.

Ellis, C. M. (2000). Family strength patterns as a function of self-concept in low-income urban African American adolescents. *Dissertation Abstracts International 61*(06), 2194A.

Herr, E. L. (1997). Super's life-span, life-space approach and its outlook for refinement. *The Career Development Quarterly, 45,* 238–246.

Shavelson, R., Hubner, J., & Stanton, G. (1976). Self-concept: Validation of construct interpretations. *Review of Educational Research, 46,* 407–441.

Super, D. E. (1990). A life-span, life-space approach to career development. In D. Brown, L. Brooks, and Associates (Eds.), *Career choice and development* (pp. 197–261). San Francisco: Jossey-Bass.

Wylie, R. (1961). *The self concept: A critical survey of pertinent research literature.* Lincoln: University of Nebraska Press.

■ Self-Fulfilling Prophecy

Self-fulfilling prophecy occurs when an individual, the "self," creates a situation where her or his initial assumptions affect her or his behavior toward a target individual, which in turn causes the target individual to respond in a manner that fulfills the self's initial assumptions. There are three specific steps in this process. The process begins with a perceiver who has preexisting attitudes or expectations (either positive or negative) about a specific target. For example, a person might believe that a target is nice and extroverted or, alternatively, is unkind and aggressive. In the second step, these beliefs affect the perceiver's behavior toward the target. With the nice target, the perceiver interacts with the target, keeping this assumption in mind. With the perception being that nice, extroverted people tend to make good conversational partners, the perceiver is likely to approach the target and begin a conversation. On the other hand, if the perceiver is expecting unkindness or aggression and views a target as a threat, the perceiver will be very wary of the target and will be much more likely to interpret ambiguous actions by the target as signs of aggression or as a threat. In the third step, the target reacts to the behavior of the perceiver and, generally, supports the initial beliefs or expectancies held by the perceiver. If a target is treated in a nice, pleasant manner and is engaged in conversation, the target will probably respond in kind. The result is a good conversation between the perceiver and the target. The self now has evidence that her or his initial beliefs about the target were correct. The same pattern will occur in negative situations. If the target is being treated as though she or he is unkind or aggressive or a threat, the target will most likely respond in an unkind or aggressive manner and be prepared to defend herself or himself. Again, the result is the confirmation of the initial belief that the target is an unkind or aggressive individual who poses a potential threat. Thus, the self fulfilled her or his expectations of the target. Awareness of the self-fulfilling prophecy is essential for professional counselors, because it can have an impact on the counselors' relationship with clients by affecting how their clients behave. If a professional counselor has negative expectations regarding a particular client or a specific problem faced by clients, the counselor may inadvertently cause a reaction that affects the therapeutic relationship with the client. Equally important is the willingness to teach clients about the self-fulfilling prophecy, which may enable clients to alter their interpretations of others' behavior and realize that their initial expectations can produce a reaction in others.

Contributed by Peter J. Green,
Barton College,
Wilson, NC

Additional Resources

Madon, S., Willard, J., Guyll, M., Trudeau, L., & Spoth, R. (2006). Self-fulfilling prophecy effects of mothers' beliefs on children's alcohol use: Accumulation, dissipation, and stability over time. *Developmental Psychology, 42,* 950–961.

Weinstein, R. S., Gregory, A., & Strambler, M. J. (2004). Intractable self-fulfilling prophecies: Fifty years after *Brown v. Board of Education. American Psychologist, 59,* 511–520.

Sex and Gender

Although the terms *sex* and *gender* are commonly used interchangeably as distinctions between male and female, sex and gender are distinct concepts. Beginning in the 1950s and well established by the 1980s, **gender** refers to social categories (feminine vs. masculine) whereas **sex** refers to biological categories (female vs. male). Specifically, sex is determined by genetics and hormones and is reflected in an individual's anatomical structure and physiological characteristics. Gender, on the other hand, is socially constructed, with psychological and emotional characteristics, and may vary in response to experiences over a lifetime.

Related to gender are **gender roles,** which include society's expectations of how an individual should think, believe, and behave as well as how he or she should be treated on the basis of his or her biological sex. Gender roles may vary across cultures, time periods, and even throughout an individual's life (see Gender Roles). Although **sex role** is often used synonymously with gender role, distinct differences do exist between the two. Gender role is more likely to describe male–female behaviors determined by a particular culture, cohort, or developmental period; sex role is more likely to describe functions that are determined by biology (e.g., pregnancy).

Gender terms such as *femininity, masculinity,* and *androgyny* reflect socially constructed views of women and men. **Femininity** includes the stereotypical personality traits associated with being female, such as cooperation, nurturance, affection, and emotionality. **Masculinity** includes the stereotypical personality traits associated with being male, such as aggression, competitiveness, and independence. **Androgyny** reflects the blending of masculine and feminine personality traits.

Sandra Lipsitz Bem initially examined psychological androgyny. She believed that healthy functioning required both masculine and feminine psychological traits. Bem developed the Bem Sex Role Inventory, which contains questions related to 60 traits. Twenty items are stereotypically feminine, 20 are stereotypically masculine, and 20 are neutral. Scores classify an individual as being sex-typed (gender matches sex), sex-reversed (gender is opposite of sex), androgynous (possessing both masculine and feminine traits), or undifferentiated (below midpoint on both masculine and feminine traits). Bem applied the instrument experimentally and concluded that psychological androgyny was healthiest for men and women. This finding is in contrast to Broverman and colleagues (Broverman, Broverman, Clarkson, Rosenkrantz, & Vogel, 1970) who concluded that psychologically healthy adults display more stereotypically masculine traits. Broverman and colleagues believed that society desired more stereotypically masculine traits, whereas Bem concluded that society valued both feminine and masculine traits.

Bem (1994) also proposed **gender schema theory** to explain reasons that individuals use gender to categorize aspects in their lives. Gender schema theory contends that children learn conceptions of appropriate gender behavior and gender-related associations from their culture. Children then apply these associations as they learn new information. Therefore, a child's preexisting views about gender will affect how new information is understood. On the basis of her work, Bem concluded that individuals who had a gender schema tended to fulfill stereotypical gender roles (e.g., males may exhibit more dominant, aggressive behavior, whereas females may exhibit more passive behaviors); therefore, she suggested that individuals should work to remove cultural associations regarding appropriate behaviors for males and females, which would allow individuals greater freedom in expressing their individuality.

Contributed by Kimberly R. Hall,
Mississippi State University,
Starkville, MS

References

Bem, S. L. (1994). *The lenses of gender: Transforming the debate on sexual inequality*. New Haven, CT: Yale University Press.

Broverman, I. K., Broverman, D. M., Clarkson, F. E., Rosenkrantz, P. S., & Vogel, S. R. (1970). Sex-role stereotypes and clinical judgments of mental health. *Journal of Consulting and Clinical Psychology, 34,* 1–7.

Additional Resources

Connell, R. W. (2002). *Gender (short introductions)*. Malden, MA: Blackwell.

Ivy, D. K., & Backlund, P. (2004). *Gender speak: Personal effectiveness in gender communication* (3rd ed.). New York: McGraw-Hill.

Sexual and Gender Identity Disorders

The primary characteristic of **sexual dysfunctions** is the impairment in normal sexual functioning. According to the *Diagnostic and Statistical Manual of Mental Disorders* (4th ed., text rev.; American Psychiatric Association [APA], 2000), sexual dysfunctions can refer to an inability to perform or reach an orgasm, pain during sexual intercourse, repulsion regarding intercourse or any kind of sexual activity, or an exaggerated sexual response cycle or sexual interest. A medical cause must be ruled out prior to making any sexual dysfunction diagnosis, and the symptoms must hinder the person's daily functioning. Some of the disorders characterized as sexual dysfunctions are sexual desire disorders, sexual pain disorders, and gender identity disorder. Relationship issues or childhood sexual trauma may play a role in the development of many of these disorders.

Sexual Desire Disorders

The normal sexual response cycle is desire, arousal, orgasm, and resolution. This cycle unfolds naturally in a sexually healthy person and can be disrupted at any point during the cycle. If the problems become chronic, then the client is said to have sexual desire disorder. Within the domain of **sexual desire disorders** are categories related to desire, orgasm, arousal, and pain. The major sexual desire disorders are hypoactive sexual desire disorder, sexual aversion disorder, sexual arousal disorder, and orgasmic disorder.

Hypoactive sexual desire disorder, or **sexual anhedonia,** refers to the ongoing lack of sexual fantasies or thoughts (APA, 2000). This disorder can occur in men or women. A woman with hypoactive sexual desire disorder does not have a desire for sex and is not interested in the sexual advances of her partner (i.e., a lack of libido). A man with the disorder may have difficulty achieving an erection or have a delay in ejaculation. The lack of desire must result in significant distress for the individual and is not better accounted for by another disorder or physical diagnosis. This disorder can be present in adolescents and can persist throughout a person's life. Many times, however, the lowered sexual desire occurs during adulthood, often times following a period of stress.

Sexual aversion disorder is an ongoing, severe fear or phobia of any sexual activity with a partner. There is persistent or recurring aversion to or avoidance of sexual activity, which must result in significant distress for the individual and is not better accounted for by another disorder or physical diagnosis. When presented with a sexual opportunity, the individual may experience panic attacks or extreme anxiety.

Sexual arousal disorder is an ongoing problem of staying sexually excited and can occur in either men or women. Men may have an inability to attain or maintain arousal until completion of sexual activity in response to sexual excitement. Initially, women may want to have sex, but they experience minimal pleasure during intercourse; this may be due to decreased genital sensitivity, lack of vaginal lubrication, or decreased blood flow to the vagina or clitoris.

Orgasmic disorder refers to a difficulty in reaching orgasm (i.e., persistently or repeatedly delayed or absent). Orgasmic disorder can occur in both men and women. It may be diagnosed even if a man or woman is sexually stimulated and aroused. Orgasmic disorder may begin in adolescence or early adulthood and may result from relationship issues or a negative life event.

Sexual Pain Disorders

Sexual pain disorders include dyspareunia, which both men and women can experience, and vaginismus and vulvodinia, which are disorders that exclusively affect women. There is a special type of recurrent and persistent pain associated with sexual activity that is different from other types of pain because it limits sexual activity. These conditions are different from the inability to achieve orgasm, as is the case with **orgasmic disorder** previously described in this entry. **Dyspareunia** involves pain in the pelvic area during or after sexual intercourse. **Vaginismus** refers to an involuntary spasm of the musculature surrounding the vagina so that it closes, causing penetration to be difficult and painful or impossible. **Vulvodinia** refers to lasting pain around the opening of the vagina, the vulva. Symptoms can include burning, itching, and continuous pain around the vulva.

Paraphilias

Paraphilias all have in common distressing and repetitive sexual fantasies, urges, or behaviors. In order for the diagnosis to be made, these fantasies, urges, or behaviors must occur for a significant period of time and must interfere with either satisfactory sexual relations or everyday functioning (APA, 2000). There is also often a sense of distress in these individuals. In other words, they typically recognize the symptoms as negatively affecting their life but feel as if they are unable to control them. Some paraphilias are **exhibitionism** (i.e., exposing genitals to an unsuspecting person), **fetishism** (i.e., having intense and repetitive sexual fantasies or urges for at least 6 months or engaging in the act of using nonliving objects or a nongenital body part in a sexual manner), **frotteurism** (i.e., having intense and repetitive sexual fantasies or urges for at least 6 months or engaging in the act of touching or rubbing against a nonconsenting person in a sexual manner), **pedophilia** (i.e., having intense and repetitive sexual fantasies or urges for at least 6 months regarding sexual activity with a prepubescent child), **sexual masochism** (i.e., engaging in or frequently fantasizing about being beaten, bound, or otherwise made to suffer, resulting in sexual satisfaction that may involve self-infliction of pain or infliction of pain by a partner), **sexual sadism** (i.e., having intense and repetitive sexual fantasies or urges for 6 months or engaging in the act of causing humiliation or physical suffering of another person without the person's consent), **transvestic fetishism** (i.e., heterosexual men having fantasies, urges, and desires about cross-dressing), and **voyeurism** (i.e., having intense and repetitive sexual fantasies or urges for 6 months or engaging in the act of observing an unsuspecting stranger who is naked, disrobing, or engaging in sexual activity).

Gender Identity Disorder

Gender identity disorder (GID) is a rare condition that features a strong and persistent identification with the opposite gender, a strong and intense discomfort with one's own gender, and a feeling of being "born the wrong sex" (APA, 2000). According to Morrison (1995), GID is a rare disorder affecting about 3 of every 100,000 men and 1 of every 100,000 women. GID has been confused with transvestic fetishism, but both are distinct diagnoses. In order to be clinically diagnosed with GID, a person must persistently and strongly identify with the opposite gender (aside from desiring perceived cultural advantages of being another gender) in any of the following: stated wish to be another gender, frequently passing as another gender, desiring to live or be treated as another gender, or belief that client's feelings and reactions are typical of a person of another gender (APA, 2000). The client must have strong discomfort with his or her own gender and may express any of the following: preoccupation with hormones, surgery, and so on as a means to change gender physically; belief that he or she was born the wrong gender; absence of a physical intersex condition; or symptoms significantly impairing occupational, social, or personal functioning. In sexually mature patients, the disorder includes the following subtypes: sexually attracted to men, sexually attracted to women, sexually attracted to both men and women, and sexually attracted to neither men nor women.

There has been controversy over the diagnosis of GID. Some clients who are lesbian, gay, bisexual, transgender, or questioning (LGBTQ) have been diagnosed as "gender non-conforming" because of sexual attractions and/or dress or manner. Some have proposed that psychiatrists created the GID diagnosis to replace homosexuality, which was removed as a mental disorder from the *Diagnostic and Statistical Manual of Mental Disorders* (3rd ed.; APA, 1980). The focus of GID has shifted from the assumed deviant sexual desire for a member of the same sex to the assumed subversive identity (e.g., the belief/desire for membership of the opposite sex/gender; Rudacille, 2005). Furthermore, the implication of GID criteria is that being a person with GID is mentally ill, if left untreated.

Contributed by Bianca M. Gregory,
Cambridge College, Chesapeake, VA

References

American Psychiatric Association. (1980). *Diagnostic and statistical manual of mental disorders* (3rd ed.). Washington, DC: Author.

American Psychiatric Association. (2000). *Diagnostic and statistical manual of mental disorders* (4th ed., text rev.). Washington, DC: Author.

Morrison, J. (1995). *The first interview: Revised for DSM-IV.* New York: Guilford Press.

Rudacille, D. (2005). *The riddle of gender: Science, activism, and transgender rights.* New York: Pantheon.

Additional Resources

Davis, H., & Reissing, E. (2007). Relationship adjustment and dyadic interaction in couples with sexual pain disorders: A critical review of the literature. *Sexual & Relationship Therapy, 22,* 245–254.

Rekers, G., & Mead, S. (1980). Female sex-role deviance: Early identification and developmental intervention. *Journal of Clinical Child Psychology, 9,* 199–203.

Zucker, K., Bradley, S., Sullivan, C., Kuksis, M., Birkenfeld-Adams, A., & Mitchell, J. (1993). A gender identity interview for children. *Journal of Personality Assessment, 61,* 443–457.

■ Sexual Identity Development

A wide variety of theories for understanding sexual identity development, which is the process by which individuals incorporate sexual orientation into their identity, can be traced to the early 1970s, with initial contributions primarily generated from the psychology literature and focused largely on gay male identities. More recently, theorists from other fields, including queer and gender studies as well as higher education, have contributed to a more nuanced understanding of sexual identity development and related processes. One such process is the concept of **coming out,** wherein an individual discloses his or her sexual identity publicly; depending on the model, this may or may not be a significant part of identity development. In addition, internalized homophobia (i.e., acceptance/incorporation of negative views of

nonheterosexual identities) and sexual identity management (i.e., decision-making strategies about disclosing sexual identity) are also constructs that have been theorized to influence the sexual identity development process. Sexual identity development, however, is a more complicated process, with theories outlining development for both individual and group-related identities. Thus, although initial models presented a linear process of sexual identity development, recent models stress the nonlinear and contextual nature of sexual identity development, identifying parallels between individual and group identities as well as their interrelatedness with other aspects of identity development. Several models of nonheterosexual identity development, a model of heterosexual development, review-related critiques, and recommendations for using these models in practice are highlighted.

Stage and Phase Models of Nonheterosexual Identity Development

Cass (1979) presented the original **lesbian and gay (LG) identity development** model, laying the groundwork for many future stage models. This approach assumed a linear progression through each stage and introduced many of the concepts commonly used in discussing identity development today. This model consists of six stages: (a) identity confusion (e.g., a person begins to consider he or she may be homosexual), (b) identity comparison (e.g., tentatively commit to a homosexual identity), (c) identity tolerance (e.g., see self as probably homosexual, begins to seek out the gay community), (d) identity acceptance (e.g., homosexual identification becomes a normalized part of life, gay community becomes increasingly important), (e) identity pride (e.g., dichotomizing the world as either homosexual and heterosexual, developing an "us-versus-them" mentality), and (f) identity synthesis (e.g., homosexual identity becomes one part of the individual's identity, and there is an integration of both public and private self).

Troiden (1989) presented an alternative yet similar model of LG identity development, which differed from Cass's model because it conceptualized identity development as nonlinear and placed emphasis on social context. Changes in self-concept distinguished its stages, which consisted of (a) sensitization (e.g., sees self as sexually different from peers), (b) identity confusion (e.g., uncertainty about sexual orientation), (c) identity assumption (e.g., homosexual identity becomes self-identity and presented identity, exploration of the gay community), and (d) commitment (e.g., homosexuality becomes a way of life, and there is fusion of both sexual and emotional self).

Coleman (1982) also offered an early model of identity development. Similar to Cass's model, this model assumed a linear, though not always distinct, progression through stages; however, Coleman placed more emphasis on developmental tasks, specifically those interpersonal and behavioral in nature. In the first stage, pre–coming out, individuals deny, repress, and suppress homosexual feelings while internalizing indirect societal rejection of homosexuality and generalizing this rejection to all aspects of self. The accompanying task is to come out to oneself. The next stage is coming out, during which the developmental task is to disclose sexual identity to others. In the exploration stage, individuals experiment socially and sexually to retrace adolescent development. Once individuals see themselves as capable of being loved, they enter the first relationships stage, a time marked by intense, insecurely attached relationships with high expectations, and they return to the exploration stage after failed relationships. By better understanding the components of mature relationships, individuals enter the integration stage, where maintaining a long-term and committed relationship is possible.

With a similar emphasis on developmental tasks and in an effort to address concerns regarding the pathologizing of nonheterosexual identities in earlier models, D'Augelli and Garnets (1995) offered a contextual, life-span approach, identifying six interactive processes present throughout development. Individual processes may co-occur and reoccur and are thought to influence and be influenced by one another and the environment. The first process is exiting heterosexuality and hinges upon realizing that one is not heterosexual and telling others of this. Developing a personal lesbian, gay, bisexual (LGB) identity status occurs in context with other LGB people who confirm ideas about nonheterosexuality. Developing a social LGB identity status consists of creating a network of supportive people who know an individual's LGB identity status. Process 4, becoming an LGB offspring, redefines family relationships within the context of a person's LGB identity status. The fifth process, developing an LGB intimacy status, refers to the building of physical and emotional relationships, whereas entering an LGB community involves a commitment to sociopolitical action.

In response to theories largely based on the experiences of White men, McCarn and Fassinger (1996) offered a model of lesbian identity development with parallel, but distinct, individual sexual and oppressed group membership branches. In their model, progress occurs in a continuous, circular, and reciprocal manner in four shared phases marked by attitudes toward self, other lesbians/gays, and people who are not gays. The first phase is awareness, and, for individual identity, this phase consists of an awareness of sexual feelings outside the heterosexual norm. For group membership, it consists of an awareness that a group of nonheterosexuals exists. Exploration is marked by strong relationships and feelings for other women; regarding group membership, this phase is marked by a desire to define oneself in relation to a lesbian reference group. The deepening/commitment phase consists of increased self-knowledge and commitment to self-fulfillment as a sexual being; regarding group membership, this phase consists of an awareness of the value and oppression of the lesbian/gay community. Internalization/synthesis consists of a fuller individual clarification and self-acceptance of same-sex desire/love. For group membership, it is identification as a minority group member, including a redefinition of that group and an internalization of this new identity.

Although some prior models purport to be inclusive of bisexuality, they do not raise bisexual-specific concerns;

however, Weinberg, Williams, and Pryor (1994) introduced a model of bisexual identity involving four stages. In the first stage, initial confusion, individuals may experience anxiety or inhibition about their identity. In the second stage, finding and applying a label, through a discovery process individuals adopt the *bisexual* label. The third stage, settling into the identity, involves seeking relationships and questioning if bisexuality is a phase. Finally, in the fourth stage, individuals may experience continued uncertainty, or intermittent periods of doubt, about their identity. Brown (2002) updated this model, changing the final phase to identity maintenance, wherein individuals may engage in a variety of activities to maintain their identity. Furthermore, he identified several differences between bisexual women's and men's experiences. For example, for women, the feminist community may play an important role in their development, with feelings toward both sexes varying over time. Men, on the other hand, may experience conflicts between sexual identity and gender role and may also experience more behaviorally based definitions of identity.

Stage Model of Heterosexual Identity Development

Worthington, Bielstein-Savoy, Dillion, and Vernaglia (2002) have developed a model of heterosexual identity development in which both individual identity and social identity processes are recognized, similar to some nonheterosexual models. Individual heterosexual identity is conceptualized as perceived sexual needs, preferred sexual activities, preferred characteristics of sexual partners, sexual values, sexual orientation identity, and preferred modes of sexual expression. Social identity is conceptualized as group membership identity and attitudes toward sexual minorities. For both these individual and group identity processes, there are five identity statuses, which can be revisited throughout an individual's life. During the first status, unexplored commitment, an individual accepts compulsory heterosexuality and culturally prescribed group norms without exploring them. The second status, active exploration, consists of purposeful exploration and evaluation of the components of heterosexual identity and either a questioning or a more consistent assertion of privilege. Next, the diffusion status is characterized by an absence of exploration or commitment in either individual or group identity. The fourth status, deepening and commitment, occurs when an individual shows a greater commitment to all components of his or her heterosexual identity and experiences a crystallization of perspectives on dominant/nondominant group relations, privilege, and oppression. The final status, synthesis, is characterized by congruence between individual sexual identity, group membership identity, and attitudes toward sexual minorities, which creates an overall sexual self-concept.

Critiques and Alternative Approaches

Savin-Williams (2005) presented a number of concerns about these stage and phase models, arguing that many offer a simplistic, universal explanation of sexual identity development and are often insensitive to differences based on cohort, gender, or ethnicity. In addition, many models do not distinguish between sexual orientation, sexual behavior, and sexual identity and ignore individuals who have homoerotic attraction or behavior but do not identify as LGB or who may have fluid identities. Others, for example, queer theorists like Judith Butler (1990) have critiqued the binary (either/or) nature of sexuality as socially constructed, and, thus, Butler has contended that sexuality is fluid and can only be understood in context.

In an attempt to address some of these contemporary concerns, Dilley (2005) conducted qualitative interviews. The findings from these interviews suggest that self-identity for nonheterosexual individuals is not a process of unbecoming straight or becoming gay but a continuous negotiation of self and other and the implications one's sexuality has for "normality." Findings reveal six different identity types present during men's college years: homosexual (share homosexual feelings/attraction privately and identify publicly as heterosexual), gay (share homosexual feelings/attraction publicly and identify publicly as gay), queer (share homosexual feelings/attraction publicly but reject normative sexuality identities), closeted (do not share homosexual feelings/attraction at all and identify publicly as heterosexual), normal (do not consider homosexual feelings/attraction as a meaningful identifier of sexuality), and parallel (identify publicly as heterosexual in heterosexual company and as nonheterosexual in nonheterosexual company). Although some of these types might be explained by prior models as steps in the process of integrating a positive, nonheterosexual identity into an individual's view of "normal," queer and normal identities, in particular, challenge the fit of stage models because these two identities imply an integrated individual identity without an expected group identity and question the binary assumptions inherent in other models.

Furthermore, conceptualizing sexual identity as something without context diminishes the influence of multiple cultures (e.g., ethnic, socioeconomic, gendered) in identity development. Thus, inclusive of issues related to membership in multiple marginalized groups, some models highlight parallel processes of cultural identity development or describe the negotiation of oppressed and privileged statuses based in multiple identities. For instance, Chung and Katayama (1998) developed a dual identity model for sexual minority individuals who are members of an ethnic minority group. This approach identifies parallels between both sexual and ethnic identity development processes and introduces the notion that a double minority identity presents many challenges. It is proposed that in order to achieve a positive ethnic-minority sexual identity, dealing with the parallel psychological process of integrating both ethnic and sexual identity is essential. Other theories have addressed the intersection of an individual's sexual identity and racial identity and have described identity development as a navigation of an individual's oppressed (e.g., being nonheterosexual) and privileged status (e.g., being White) leading to an understanding of systemic oppression and commitment to social activism. Although empirical research on sexual identity development is sparse, Parks, Hughes, and Matthews (2004) found that lesbians of color encountered developmental milestones earlier than did their White counterparts.

Although this largely theoretical progression has just begun to explore the complexity of sexual identity development in the context of other identities and environment, there are currently a number of approaches to help professional counselors understand this process, ranging from stage models to phases and identity types. Given the current knowledge of sexual identity development, it is important for professional counselors to consider clients' individual and group identities. For example, clients who are at earlier stages of identity development may benefit from increased social support of same-group communities, whereas individuals in later stages of identity development may not feel this desire or need for formal community membership. Also, it is relevant to keep in mind that a cohort effect may influence differences in client conceptualizations of sexual identity (e.g., recent increase in acceptance of queer or fluid identities) and processes. For example, coming out may be less salient in sexual identity development for some individuals and may look very different for bisexual individuals compared with those identifying as gay. Similarly, as Pachankis and Goldfried (2004) suggested in their in-depth review of clinically relevant issues for LGB clients, the pros and cons of coming out may be completely different depending on a client's age and resources. As such, contextual and cultural factors relevant to client identity development, such as diverse cultural norms and pressures, must also be considered when conceptualizing clients and developing therapeutic goals and tasks related to identity development. As an evolving body of research, influenced by multiple disciplines and changing social conditions surrounding these identities, ongoing empirical exploration will play a pivotal role in the understanding of these models and of these identities.

Contributed by Matthew A. Malouf,
Lindsey M. Brooks, and
Arpana G. Inman,
Lehigh University, Bethlehem, PA

References

Brown, T. (2002). A proposed model of bisexual identity development that elaborates on experiential differences of men and women. *Journal of Bisexuality, 2,* 67–91.

Butler, J. (1990). *Gender trouble: Feminism and the subversion of identity.* New York: Routledge.

Cass, V. C. (1979). Homosexual identity formation: A theoretical model. *Journal of Homosexuality, 4,* 219–235.

Chung, Y. B., & Katayama, M. (1998). Ethnic and sexual identity development of Asian American lesbian and gay adolescents. *Professional School Counseling, 1,* 21–25.

Coleman, E. (1982). Developmental stages of the coming-out process. *American Behavioral Scientist, 25,* 469–482.

D'Augelli, A. R., & Garnets, L. D. (1995). Lesbian, gay, and bisexual communities. In A. R. D'Augelli & C. J. Patterson (Eds.), *Lesbian, gay, and bisexual identities over the lifespan: Psychological perspectives* (pp. 293–320). New York: Oxford University Press.

Dilley, P. (2005). Which way out? A typology of non-heterosexual male collegiate identities. *Journal of Higher Education, 76*, 56–88.

McCarn, S. R., & Fassinger, R. E. (1996). Revisioning sexual minority identity formation: A new model of lesbian identity and its implications for counseling research. *The Counseling Psychologist, 24*, 508–534.

Pachankis, J. E., & Goldfried, M. R. (2004). Clinical issues in working with lesbian, gay, and bisexual clients. *Psychotherapy Theory, Research, Practice, Training, 41*, 227–246.

Parks, C. A., Hughes, T. L., & Matthews, A. K. (2004). Race/ethnicity and sexual orientation: Intersecting identities. *Cultural Diversity and Ethnic Minority Psychology, 10*, 241–254.

Savin-Williams, R. (2005). *The new gay teenager.* Cambridge, MA: Harvard University Press.

Troiden, R. R. (1989). The formation of homosexual identities. *Journal of Homosexuality, 17*, 43–73.

Weinberg, M. S., Williams, C. J., & Pryor, D. W. (1994). *Dual attraction: Understanding bisexuality.* New York: Oxford University Press.

Worthington, R. L., Bielstein-Savoy, H., Dillion, F. R., & Vernaglia, E. R., (2002). Heterosexual identity development: A multidimensional model of individual and social identity. *The Counseling Psychologist, 30*, 496–531.

■ Sexual Minority Clients, Counseling

Counseling **sexual minority clients** refers to providing counseling to clients who identify as a sexual minority in American society. Specifically, *sexual minority* is an inclusive term to describe all the various aspects of sexuality and gender, including gay, lesbian, bisexual, transgender, intersex, queer, and questioning.

Sexual minority individuals seek counseling for all of the reasons that any other client seeks counseling: relationships, career choice, substance abuse and other addictions, grief, parenting, aging, health, and their own personal growth and development as a human being. There are, however, some special considerations that are part of providing counseling to such individuals. These include the lack of civil rights, secret or semisecret lives, oppression, rejection or ostracism by their family of origin, societal censure, lowered self-esteem due to internalized homophobia, fear and reality of physical violence, and being the object of political and religious campaigns.

Definitions

Sexual orientation describes a person's sexual or affectional attraction to another person, specifically identified by gender, and this attraction can be opposite sex (heterosexually oriented), same sex (homosexually oriented), or both sexes (bisexually oriented). Sexual orientation can be categorized in several ways. The term **gay** can be used broadly to include men or women who are sexually and/or affectionally attracted to members of their same gender. Some women identify as gay, others as **lesbian**, usually for political reasons. In the mental health literature the term *lesbian women*, although redundant, is being used more and contrasted with the term *gay men*. Here, the term *gay* is used exclusively to refer to gay men and *lesbian* to refer to lesbian women. **Bisexual** is a term that refers to a person of one gender who is sexually attracted to individuals of both genders.

Gender identity describes a person's internal identification as male or female or both. **Transgender** refers to individuals who identify as one gender but who have the physiology of the opposite gender; this refers to gender identity not sexual orientation. **Intersex** refers to individuals who are born with physiological attributes of both genders, including sexual organs and/or hormones.

Queer, although not generally used in the United States, is a political statement of difference from the majority culture. A person does not have to be self-identified as gay or lesbian to self-identify as queer. **Questioning** is a broad transitional category that refers to any `person who has questions about his or her sexual orientation or gender identity.

Sexual Minorities and Counseling

Providing counseling for sexual minority clients is a complicated process that requires a person to have strong cultural counseling competence. Three important seminal documents inform the competence of individuals who provide counseling to lesbian, gay, or bisexual people: the *Multicultural Counseling Competencies* (Sue, Arredondo, & McDavis, 1992; see Cultural Competence); the Association for Lesbian, Gay, Bisexual and Transgender Issues in Counseling's (ALGBTIC) *Competencies for Counseling Gay, Lesbian, Bisexual and Transgendered Clients* (Terndrup, Ritter, Barret, Logan, & Mate, 1997); and the American Psychological Association's (2000) *Guidelines for Psychotherapy With Lesbian, Gay, and Bisexual Clients.*

Because they live in communities that routinely discriminate against sexual minorities, it is virtually impossible, however, for professional counselors to avoid internalizing negative stereotypes or attitudes about these sexual minority cultures. Misinformation or misunderstanding will quickly be evident to sexual minority clients and may cause them to seek help elsewhere or not to get help at all. Professional counselors, however, must be familiar with these cultures so they are credible and congruent in their attitudes. Counselors should become aware of sociopolitical issues, specific knowledge, and necessary information concerning counseling members of sexual minority cultures and of the institutional barriers that confront sexual minority clients who are seeking counseling. Counselors must also be aware of the history, language, rituals, traditions, and sense of community that define the sexual minority cultures. Counselors who want to work with sexual minority clients must first take a personal inventory of the ways that their own often subtle or unconscious biases may influence the counseling process. Attending workshops, reading the literature, and participating in sexual minority cultural events are effective ways to acquire knowledge about such individuals. Former clients and friends who are members of sexual minority groups are an invaluable source of information.

Finally, professional counselors need explicit awareness of their own religious and spiritual nature and beliefs because the professional counselors' role in providing counseling to sexual minorities in almost all national and tribal cultures is important. Professional counselors never impose their own belief systems on their clients, but many sexual minority clients have been hurt deeply by religious organizations. Professional counselors do not have to study religion to have respect for the role that such beliefs play in many people's lives or to help clients discover positive alternatives to a fundamentalist religious approach. When and if professional counselors decide they cannot be affirming in their attitudes, they are ethically required to refer the client to a professional counselor who has positive attitudes and experience with members of sexual minority groups.

Coming Out

A central developmental task for gay, lesbian, and bisexual persons is coming out. **Coming out** is a process in which a person comes to identify as gay, lesbian, bisexual, transgender, or intersex and recognizes this position as part of a stigmatized and semihidden minority. Coming out is also of critical importance to the mental health of an individual, because it allows sexual minorities to build a positive self-identity in a world that is not always supportive of their sexual orientation or gender identity. There are two different types of coming out: coming out to self and coming out to others. The former involves a self-acceptance of the individual's own sexual orientation. The latter involves disclosing to others that orientation through verbal or written, private or public statements.

Although this process is most developmentally appropriate during adolescence, many individuals manage to hide into their 20s or even later a full realization that they are not like the dominant cultural groups—those with an opposite-sex sexual orientation or congruent gender identity and physiology. Researchers have identified inherent problems in delayed mastery of the developmental task of accepting one's sexual orientation (i.e., coming out to self) along with the concomitant development of appropriate dating and relationship strategies with same-sex partners. This delayed coming out may cause a "developmental domino effect" in which the inadequate completion of a particular task causes the next important developmental task to be delayed, missed, or inadequately completed.

Furthermore, many gays, lesbians, and bisexuals can hide their sexual orientation and pass for having an opposite-sex sexual orientation; this is, however, not a very effective method of creating a positive self-identity and, therefore, good mental health. In fact "passing" behavior is antithetical to creating this positive self-identity. According to researchers, the consequences of passing include lower self-esteem, along with feelings of inferiority and the internalization of negative self-concepts. The cumulative effect of this devaluing of self and similar others is emotionally unhealthy.

The traditional stages of coming out to self are awareness of attraction to and feelings for individuals of the same sex; then experiences of sex; followed by explorations of the gay and lesbian cultural community; then self-labeling as *lesbian, gay,* or *bisexual*; and, finally, the disclosure of one's identity to others (coming out to others). Cass (1979) was one of the first to offer such an identity development model and identified the specific developmental stages that gays and lesbians must accomplish (see Sexual Identity Development).

Social, Cultural, and Historical Context

For professional counselors and other mental health professionals, the first step in counseling gay, lesbian, or bisexual clients is to gain access to the information that will help them understand the social, cultural, and historical context in which lesbian women and gay men operate. It is of critical importance that they have an appreciation of this context because so much of what makes counseling lesbian and gay people different from counseling others is a direct result of this. A legal, political, and professional chronology follows:

Legal and Political Chronology

- In 1995 in the United States, there were only 90 state and local governments that provided domestic partner benefits to their gay and lesbian employees. In 2004, there were 185 state and local governments that provided these benefits, with 2,867 employers including sexual orientation in their nondiscrimination policies and 8,250 offering domestic partners benefits (Perez, DeBord, & Bieschke, 2007).
- On June 26, 2003, in *Lawrence and Garner v. Texas,* the U.S. Supreme Court struck down Texas's sodomy law, which had criminalized oral and anal sex by consenting gay couples and was used widely to justify discrimination against lesbians and gay men. This effectively overturned all the remaining 13 state sodomy laws in the United States.
- On May 17, 2004, Massachusetts became the first state in the United States to grant marriage licenses to same-sex couples.

Professional Chronology

- Gay, lesbian, and bisexual people were labeled as "diseased" by the psychological community until 1973 and the seventh printing of the *Diagnostic and Statistical Manual of Mental Disorders* (2nd ed.; American Psychiatric Association, 1980, p. 380).
- In 2003, the first openly gay man was elected president of a major mental health professional association, the American Counseling Association (ACA).

Changing Sexual Orientations

Sexual orientation is not amenable to change. Repeated studies by top mental health researchers (see Money, 1990) confirmed it is virtually impossible to change someone's sexual orientation, even through behavioral therapy measures such as electric shock treatments and pain therapy (aversive conditioning), hypnosis, psychotropic medications, clinical/religious individual and group therapy, and others had been used. In 1997, the American Psychological Association passed a resolution stating that "that there is no sound evidence on the efficacy of '**reparative therapy**,' [boldface added] which seeks to 'cure' homosexuals." The American Psychiatric Association (1998) also stated that "[t]he potential risks of 'reparative therapy' are great, including depression, anxiety and self-destructive behavior, since therapist alignment with societal prejudices against homosexuality may reinforce self-hatred already experienced by the patient."

The claims of "ex-gay" religious ministries that state that they can "cure" individuals of same-sex attractions have been repeatedly repudiated by authoritative and credible scientific groups. Not one professional society supports their work. ACA, the American Psychiatric Association, American Psychological Association, American Medical Association, National Association of Social Workers, National Association of School Psychologists, American School Health Association, American Federation of Teachers, National Education Association, and American Academy of Pediatrics have all issued strongly worded admonitions combating the idea that homosexuality (a) is a disease, (b) can be effectively treated, and (c) even needs to be treated. The main approach to counseling with gay and lesbian people is to help them accept and love themselves.

Shidlo and Schroeder (2002) surveyed 202 individuals who had participated in interventions designed to change their sexual orientation from a same-sex sexual orientation to an opposite-sex sexual orientation. They found that only 4% of those individuals were able to "manage" their same-sex sexual behavior successfully, with over 74% of the group experiencing significant long-term (psychological) damage from the "conversion" therapy. They blamed themselves for not being able to change and reported feeling worse than when they had originally sought conversion therapy. Such therapies were not only ineffective in changing same-sex attractions, but in many cases, these therapies did considerable harm to the clients' mental and emotional health.

Providing counseling to sexual minority individuals is similar to, yet different from, providing counseling to other clients. It is important to know the special considerations that are part of providing counseling to such individuals. Professional counselors must be familiar with the history and culture of sexual minority communities, with the ways that oppression manifests itself with these groups, and with the special developmental tasks (e.g., coming out as acceptance of self), and professional counselors must be aware of their own biases. Finally, efforts by professional counselors to change a client's sexual orientation from a same-sex focus to an opposite-sex focus are, at best, suspect and, at worst, harmful to the client and certainly unethical if the client is not fully informed of the potential hazards of such interventions (ACA, 2005).

Contributed by Mark Pope,
University of Missouri–Saint Louis,
St. Louis, MO

References

American Counseling Association. (2005). *ACA code of ethics*. Alexandria, VA: Author.

American Psychiatric Association. (1980). *Diagnostic and statistical manual of mental disorders* (3rd ed.). Washington, DC: Author.

American Psychiatric Association. (1998). *"Reparative" therapy* [Position statement]. Washington, DC: Author.

American Psychological Association. (2000). *Guidelines for psychotherapy with lesbian, gay, and bisexual clients*. Washington, DC: Author.

Cass, V. (1979). Homosexual identity formation: A theoretical model. *Journal of Homosexuality, 4,* 219–235.

Money, J. (1990). Agenda and credenda of the Kinsey scale. In D. P. McWhirter, S. A. Sanders, & J. M. Reinisch (Eds.), *Homosexuality/heterosexuality: Concepts of sexual orientation* (pp. 41–60). New York: Oxford University Press.

Perez, R. M., DeBord, K. A., & Bieschke, K. J. (Eds.). (2007). *Handbook of counseling and psychotherapy with lesbian, gay, and bisexual clients* (2nd ed.). Washington, DC: American Psychological Association.

Shidlo, A., & Schroeder, M. (2002). Changing sexual orientation: A consumers' report. *Professional Psychology: Research and Practice, 33,* 249–259.

Sue, D. W., Arredondo, P., & McDavis, R. J. (1992). Multicultural counseling competencies and standards: A call to the profession. *Journal of Counseling & Development, 70,* 477–486.

Terndrup, A., Ritter, K., Barret, B., Logan, C., & Mate, R. (1997). *Competencies in counseling gay, lesbian, bisexual, and transgendered clients*. Retrieved January 15, 2004, from http://www.aglbic.org/competencies.html

Additional Resources

Barret, B., & Logan, C. (2002). *Counseling gay men and lesbians: A practice primer*. Belmont, CA: Brooks/Cole.

Dworkin, S., & Gutierrez, F. (Eds.). (1992). *Counseling gay men and lesbians: Journey to the end of the rainbow*. Alexandria, VA: American Counseling Association.

■ Sexual Orientation

Sexual orientation remains a topic of intriguing research, speculation, and gossip in society. In some circles, it is almost passé, and in others, it is a topic charged with emotion and values. This requires counseling professionals to navigate carefully with their clients as they honor values while creating a safe environment for expression and exploration of sexuality. In this entry, the beginning points of sexual orientation, from the prospective of keeping both clients and professional counselors safe and productive during such explorations, are highlighted.

There is a consensus among social scientists that sexual orientation is not only a construction of an individual's biological and psychosocial identity but also a social construct created by the attitudes, needs, beliefs, and traditions of the culture surrounding the individual. This bidirectional source of sexual orientation requires the counseling profession to define **sexual orientation** as the client's identified means of sexual expression. The basis of sexual expression is sexual attraction. Sexual attraction can be defined as a person's interests and activities that stimulate sexual arousal. Sexual orientation is usually categorized with three terms: *heterosexual, homosexual,* and *bisexual*. **Heterosexual orientation** implies that a person is predominantly attracted to the opposite sex and that the person's sexual fantasies and desires are focused largely on the opposite sex. **Homosexual orientation** implies that a person is predominately attracted to individuals of the same sex and the person's sexual fantasies and desires are focused largely on the same sex. **Bisexual orientation** implies that a person is aware of sexual attraction to both sexes and has both opposite-sex and same-sex sexual fantasies and desires. These categories should not be considered discrete; rather they exist on a continuum.

Sexual orientation is the primary part of the wider concept of sexual identity. Sexual identity involves a person's awareness of his or her sexual identity and being personally and socially comfortable with that identity. Healthy sexual identity involves the expression of and satisfaction with a person's sexual orientation. Sexual orientation and identity may simply be a relevant piece of information in the profile of the client, or a client might seek help in clarification of sexual orientation as a goal during the counseling relationship. The professional counselor must remember that sexual orientation is the client's expression and should be identified by the client. The professional counselor should not make assumptions about specific behaviors from stereotypical or traditional perspectives.

The basis of sexual orientation is a person's sexual and romantic attractions. Understanding one's sexual orientation requires becoming aware of one's common sexual and romantic fantasies and attractions. The awareness of an individual's sexual attractions occurs in the cultural settings of the individual. The individual must compare his or her sexual orientation to the sexual practices and climate of the environment. Sexual orientation is the result of a synthesis between an individual's internal sexuality and the cultural environment of the individual. This may be an unconscious process for some people or a very deliberate, conscious process for others. The age at which sexual orientation is understood or adopted can vary greatly from person to person.

People who identify as heterosexual or straight are persons who have attractions to and romantic interests in persons of the opposite sex. The social environment supports heterosexual behavior, and, thus, a person who enjoys opposite-sex attractions might unconsciously adapt to a heterosexual orientation; however, the professional counselor should not assume an unconscious process. Many persons who may have same-sex attractions may express with a heterosexual orientation because they judge the outside environment to be unsupportive of a different choice. Another example of the need for a deliberate process might be a person with bisexual inclinations that are not strong enough to warrant in-depth exploration.

People who identify as either gay men or lesbian women are those who have attractions that focus predominately on same-sex romantic and sexual experiences. The social environment of such an individual may not be conducive to forming a gay or lesbian identity, and as a result, most people with same-sex attractions enter a lengthy and lifelong process of expressing their sexual orientation. This more deliberate process of expressing a gay or lesbian identity is called *coming out*. There are numerous coming-out models in the counseling literature that theorize how this process works for most gay men and lesbians. These models are predominantly an explanation of how people who have made an internal acknowledgement of their same-sex attractions begin and continue to adopt an identity based on their gay or lesbian orientation (see Sexual Identity Development).

People who identify as bisexual are those who have strong sexual and romantic attractions for both genders. As with the environment for gay men and lesbians, the environment may or may not be conducive to a person adapting to a bisexual orientation. A further complication for bisexuals is that often they are not validated by either the straight community or the gay and lesbian communities. The reason that some gay and lesbian people may resist the notion of bisexuality is because they went through a bisexual behavioral phase during their own coming-out process. In the counseling literature, there is less written about bisexual identity and issues specific to bisexual persons. They are often included in the literature for gay men and lesbians, but the profession needs to create more specific research and insight into this population.

Counseling considerations for people who are out as gays, lesbians, and bisexuals include the coming-out process, professional barriers, (e.g., potential for job discrimination and glass ceiling effects in some professions), social barriers (e.g., integrating into the larger community systems such as religious affiliation or school affiliation for their children), and family issues. Professional counselors should not assume that people who identify as gay, lesbian, or bisexual are asking for specific help around their status; however, professional counselors should use this knowledge to help clients identify strengths and aptitudes that the process of coming-out may have helped them acquire. There is only fledgling research on the issues of youth who identify as gay, lesbian, or bisexual. The primary counseling considerations are keeping them safe; helping them with appropriate disclosure of their concerns, questions, and identity formation; family counseling; and school counseling interventions and school policy considerations. For young people exploring same-sex attractions, it is particularly important for the professional counselor to consider the local atmosphere for gay, lesbian, and bisexual persons.

The term **queer** is a once-pejorative term that has been reclaimed and is used primarily but not exclusively to refer to gay, lesbian, bisexual, and transgender persons. The history of this reclamation stems to the early 1980s when more universities were adding feminism as a specific focus in academic programs. As women's studies became more prevalent, the interest in gender issues, transgender issues, and sexual orientation became more acceptable as areas of research in the social sciences. Today there are Queer Studies and GLBT Studies programs on many campuses. It was these social scientists and social philosophers who began to use the term **queer theory** to refer to a body of academic literature focusing on sexual and gender behaviors and attitudes—especially those that fall outside the mainstream social norms. Queer theory asserts that the concepts of heterosexual, gay, lesbian, and bisexual are social constructs. It also asserts that social construct defines gender descriptions and gender roles. In addition, the term *queer* has been used to include gay or straight persons who practice sexual and gender behaviors that lie outside of social norms. Examples of such practices are leather, cross-dressing, sadomasochism, or bondage and domination. The term *queer* also includes intersexed and transsexual issues. *Queer* is a much broader term than sexual orientation or the terms typically associated with sexual orientation.

The importance of queer in counseling is that it speaks specifically to the unconditional positive regard that most of professional counselors value so much in the counseling relationship. It reminds professional counselors to be nonjudgmental of a person's sexual or gender expression and to look beyond such expression to the needs of the individual client. It reminds professional counselors that a person can suffer at the hands of greater society and local community or learn to thrive in spite of the barriers. This potential for suffering or thriving includes gender and sexual expression, but it is certainly not limited to them. If taken in its truest spirit, the term *queer* reminds professional counselors of the multidirectional nature of their development, problems, and successes.

Contributed by George R. Beals,
Mississippi State University,
Starkville, MS

Additional Resources

Ritter, K., & Terndrup, A. (2002). *Handbook of affirmative psychotherapy with lesbians and gay men.* New York: Guildford Press.

Seidman, S. (Ed.). (1996). *Queer theory/sociology.* Cambridge, MA: Blackwell.

Single-Subject Research Design

Using **single-subject research design (SSRD)** methodology, professional counselors can evaluate, document, and communicate their work with clients. This research methodology allows professional counselors to examine the effectiveness of specific counseling interventions with individual clients or a small group of clients. SSRD methods offer counselors a way to explore characteristics of the therapeutic process carefully (Heppner, Wampold, & Kivlighan, 2008). They give professional counselors a means to document treatment outcomes and conduct research with an individualized focus. In addition, the use of SSRD is increasingly being recognized and used by many professionals (e.g., school counselors, special education teachers, school psychologists, therapeutic recreation therapists) because of its low data-collection costs, lack of complicated statistics, and ability to assess individualized interventions.

Types of SSRDs

SSRD involves the study of one individual or one group that is treated as a single entity. The study of individual participants or clients has a long history in the field of psychology and behaviorism. Professional counselors can establish the effects of an intervention through repeated observations or repeated assessment over time. The counselor/researcher repeatedly measures behaviors (including both overt and covert) of an individual client during baseline and treatment phases. Comparison of these observations is used to determine whether an intervention is effective in helping the client meet some agreed-on goal. This comparison may consist of a visual examination of the graphic representation of the two phases. Observations may take the form of assessing cognitive, behavioral, and affective process or outcome data. Professional counselors can gain insight into aspects of the client's functioning prior to therapy, and data are collected after the implementation of interventions to compare the levels of functioning.

The initial counseling period, when the professional counselor is forming a relationship and gathering information from the client to determine the problem, can be used to assess the **baseline (A) phase.** The basic sequence of who, what, where, when, how, and why helps evaluate the client's function and determine baseline behavior. The professional counselor collects baseline data through assessment of the client's issues or concerns (e.g., measuring the frequency, intensity, and/or duration of the client's distress). This data collection occurs before the working stage, which moves the client toward exploring alternatives, generating solutions, and providing interventions to alleviate the client's concern or issue. The **treatment (B) phase** occurs during the working stage. Assessment of the client's functioning would occur again after the B phase to compare with information collected during the A phase.

If interventions were successful, as demonstrated by significant changes from the A phase, teaching the client to generalize these interventions to other situations would be supportive and help move the client toward termination of counseling. This example might be considered a basic **A–B design** (i.e., baseline phase followed by a treatment phase). If interventions were not successful, implementing other strategies or interventions may indicate additional B phases; therefore, the basic A–B design would be repeated by another period of baseline data gathering (A_2) and a second treatment phase (B_2). A repeated A–B design becomes an **A–B–A–B design,** which includes two or more baseline phases and two or more treatment phases. Figure 1, a graphic representation of an A–B design, shows the measurement of the effectiveness of cognitive–behavioral therapy with a client who exhibits harmful behaviors resulting from high stress. As an example, the counselor would collect data or information regarding the client's behaviors, the antecedents to the behaviors, and the consequences of the harmful behaviors. The counselor would gather information about the frequency, intensity, and duration of the harmful behaviors and plot this information on a graph. This represents the A phase. The counselor would then teach the client new replacement

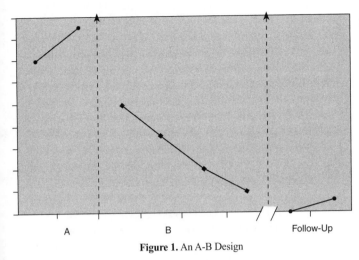

Figure 1. An A-B Design

behaviors through role plays, rehearsal, modeling, and feedback. The new replacement behaviors resulted in a decrease of the problematic behaviors as shown in the B phase (the treatment phase). A follow-up several days later again indicated decreased problematic behaviors.

Another design that may have applicability for professional counselors is the **multiple-baseline design.** A multiple baseline design is essentially a series of A–B designs that are replicated in one of three ways: (a) with the same individual across different behaviors, (b) with the same individual across different settings, or (c) with the same behavior across different individuals. A multiple-baseline design supports the hypothesis that an intervention is associated with behavior change but still does not allow for statements of causality. The multiple-baseline design may be helpful to a professional counselor when a target behavior is exhibited by multiple clients (e.g., several students in the same classroom), when more than one problematic behavior is exhibited by an individual client (e.g., talking loudly in class, not completing work, and physical aggression), or when a behavior is demonstrated by a client in more than one setting such as in the workplace and at home (Miltenberger, 2008).

Another type of single subject research design is the **changing criterion design.** The changing criterion design is different from the A–B design because the criterion for success is changed. The client's behavior is expected to change each time the goal or expectation level is changed. A changing criterion design is simply an A–B design wherein the intervention remains the same but the criterion for success is sequentially changed. For example, a changing criterion design might be used in a situation in which a student (with adequate skills) is experiencing difficulty completing course work. If during baseline, only 30% of course work is being completed, the goal is to increase the amount of course work to a reasonable level. A changing criterion would be implemented, in which the amount of work is increased over a period of time. Positive reinforcers are offered for increasing percentages of completed work. Realistic goals should be considered to ensure a successful outcome.

Another type of research design is **alternating treatment design** in which the baseline and treatment phases are alternated, perhaps as frequently as on a daily basis. This method

may be used to assess the effectiveness of two or more treatments, such as using client self-talk during one treatment and client journal as another treatment option. The client may use self-talk on one day to eliminate fear of failure and another day may use journal writing to eliminate fear. Comparison of two different treatments would rely on the client's self-report to determine which might be the more effective or beneficial method to alleviate fear of failure.

Cautions When Using SSRDs

In the world of researchers, it is necessary to demonstrate a functional relationship to "prove" an intervention was solely responsible for a behavior change. If a client has achieved success due to the interventions implemented, it could be considered unethical to "remove" the intervention just to prove a functional relationship. Single subject research methods are not usually considered generalizable, but they may be extremely useful and are considered clinically significant by helping individual clients achieve success. Researchers' motivation for empirical data cannot overshadow the welfare of clients and researchers' ethical responsibility to clients

Contributed by Linda H. Foster,
University of Alabama at Birmingham,
Birmingham, AL

References

Heppner, P. P., Wampold, B. E., & Kivlighan, D. M. (2008). *Research design in counseling* (3rd ed.). Belmont, CA: Brooks/Cole.

Miltenberger, R. G. (2008). *Behavior modification: Principles and procedures.* Belmont, CA: Brooks/Cole.

■ Skewness

Frequency distributions occur in various shapes. In understanding a distribution, it is important to describe both the shape of the data as well as the actual numerical data. The shape of the data refers to the manner in which the data are distributed. In considering the shape of a distribution, three terms are important: *uniform* (rectangular), *symmetric,* or *skewed* distributions. In a **uniform distribution,** scores are evenly distributed. In a **symmetrical distribution,** the curve is symmetrical; that is, the lower half of the distribution is a "mirror image" of the upper half of the distribution. This symmetrical distribution is commonly referred to as a **bell-shaped curve,** or a normal distribution in which there are many scores in the middle with progressively fewer scores toward both ends. If a curve is not a symmetrical distribution, then it is **asymmetrical** or **skewed.**

In some distributions, the most frequently occurring scores do not congregate in the middle but instead congregate at the lower or higher end of the distribution. These distributions are called skewed distributions. They are positively or negatively skewed, depending on whether the scores "tail off" toward the high or low end. Specifically, the scores accumulate (pile up) at one end of the distribution and decrease at the other end.

As Figure 1 indicates, in a **positively skewed distribution,** the tail of the distribution extends toward the higher end (positive) of the distribution, and the scores "pile up" at the lower end of the distribution. In contrast, in a **negatively skewed distribution** (see Figure 2), the tail extends toward the lower end (negative) of the distribution. Specifically, in a negatively skewed distribution, most of the scores occur at higher values, and the curve "tails off" at the lower end. For example, consider the distribution of test scores when a professor administers an exam to 15 students. In this case, the students' scores were as follows: 1 student obtained a perfect score of 100, 2 students scored 95, 6 students scored 90, 1 student scored 85, 4 students scored 40, and 1 student scored 35. If these scores were plotted on a distribution graph, most of the scores would accumulate at the high end of the graph, thus indicating high test performance. Because the tail of the distribution points to the lower end, this distribution is negatively skewed. In contrast is the distribution of the salaries of faculty and administrators. The salaries are the following: 4 faculty earned $50,000, 6 faculty earned $55,000, 2 faculty earned $65,000, 1 faculty earned $70,000, and 2 administrators earned $200,000 and $250,000. If these salaries were plotted on a graph, more scores would accumulate at the lower end, and the curve of the tail of the distribution would tail off at the upper end. This distribution would be positively skewed.

Another way to describe skewness is to consider the measures of **central tendency** (mean, median, mode). Specifically, skewness can be identified if the values of the mean and median are known. Because the mean is influenced by extremely high or low scores, the mean is "pulled" toward the part of the distribution in which the extreme scores are found. The median, on the other hand, is not influenced by the size of the extreme scores but instead is influenced by the position of scores. Therefore, the extreme scores have less impact on the median than on the mean. The other measure of central tendency, the mode, is not influenced by extreme scores, nor is it influenced by either end of the distribution. When the distribution is symmetrical (bell-shaped), the mean, median, and mode are equal. When the distribution is

asymmetrical (skewed), the mean, median, and mode do not have the same value. In a negatively skewed distribution, the mean is pulled toward that part of the distribution in which the extreme scores are found. In contrast, the median is influenced by the position of scores and not by the size of the extreme scores; therefore, the extreme scores have less impact on the median than on the mean. The mode is not influenced by extreme scores, and, in fact, the mode is not influenced by either end of the distribution.

In skewed distributions, when the mean is increased by very low scores, negative skewness occurs. In a negatively skewed distribution, the mean is always smaller than the median. Usually the median is smaller than the mode. When the mean is influenced by very high scores, positive skewness occurs. In a positively skewed distribution, the mean is greater than the median and is usually greater than the mode. Thus, skewness can be determined by the following principles:

Negatively Skewed	Mean < Median < Mode
Positively Skewed	Mean > Median > Mode
Symmetrical	Mean = Median = Mode

The relationship between the measures of central tendency and skewness is illustrated in Figures 1 and 2. As they show, the numerical values of the mean and median indicate whether the distribution is skewed and in which direction (positively or negatively).

In summary, if a distribution is not symmetrical, then it is asymmetrical, or skewed. A skewed distribution is either positively or negatively skewed, depending on the distribution of the scores. If the tail of the distribution points to the higher end, then the distribution is positively skewed. If, on the other hand, the tail of the distribution points to the lower end, then the distribution is negatively skewed.

Contributed by Loretta J. Bradley,
Texas Tech University, Lubbock, TX

Additional Resources

Creswell, J. W. (2002). *Educational research: Planning, conducting, and evaluating quantitative and qualitative research.* Upper Saddle River, NJ: Merrill Prentice Hall.

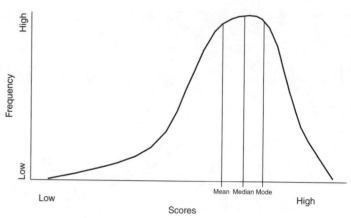

Figure 2. Example of a Negatively Skewed Distribution

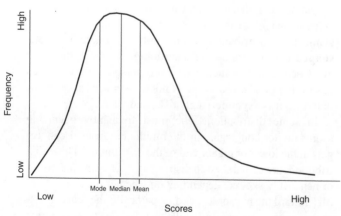

Figure 1. Example of a Positively Skewed Distribution

Rosenthal, J. A. (2001). *Statistics and data interpretation for the helping professions.* Belmont, CA: Brooks/Cole.

Thorndike, R. M., & Dinnel, D. L. (2001). *Basic statistics for the behavioral sciences.* Upper Saddle River, NJ: Merrill Prentice Hall.

Sleep Disorders

The *Diagnostic and Statistical Manual of Mental Disorders* (4th ed., text rev.; *DSM-IV-TR;* American Psychiatric Association [APA], 2000) delineates **sleep disorders** into four major categories: primary sleep disorders, sleep disorder related to another mental disorder, sleep disorder due to a general medical condition, and substance-induced sleep disorder. The influences of mental disorders, medical conditions, or substances are excluded from the diagnostic criteria for primary sleep disorders. Primary sleep disorders are further subdivided into dyssomnias and parasomnias.

Dyssomnias

Dyssomnias are sleep disorders that can be described as alterations in the quality, quantity, and timing of sleep. They include primary insomnia, primary hypersomnia, narcolepsy, breathing-related sleep disorder, and circadian rhythm disorder.

Primary Insomnia

Primary Insomnia is the inability to fall asleep or sleep that is interrupted by periods of wakefulness during which the individual has difficulty returning to the sleep state. This experience must last for a period of at least 1 month to be classified as a disorder. A common consequence of insomnia is excessive daytime sleepiness, which may adversely affect cognitive functioning, levels of alertness, work productivity, social activities, and family relationships.

Primary Hypersomnia

Individuals diagnosed with **primary hypersomnia** have a heightened need for daytime sleep despite having 8–12 hours of nocturnal sleep. They tend to have difficulty awakening in the morning and have a strong urge to take naps during the day although this provides little respite from the sleepiness. The symptoms must be prevalent for at least 1 month to meet the *DSM-IV-TR* (APA, 2000) diagnostic criteria. The sleep episodes are intentional and usually occur during periods of low-level stimulation or inactivity such as watching television or listening to a lecture.

Narcolepsy

Narcolepsy is unintended sleep that occurs spontaneously. Most individuals with narcolepsy experience cataplexy, which manifests as drooping eyelids, sagging jaw, or loss of muscle tone in the neck or arms. The loss of muscle tone in some individuals is more overt and may result in the temporary inability to speak, dropping objects, or suddenly falling to the ground. Cataplexy is typically preceded by a heightened emotional state such as elation or anger. The loss of muscle tone is brief, and the return to full functioning occurs immediately after the episode. Another feature of narcolepsy is the intrusion of rapid eye movement (REM) sleep into the waking state, which is accompanied by paralysis of the voluntary muscles and/or hallucinations. The hallucinations are usually visual but may also be auditory or kinetic.

Breathing-Related Sleep Disorder

There are three types of breathing-related sleep disorders: obstructive sleep apnea syndrome, central sleep apnea syndrome, and central alveolar hypoventilation syndrome. **Obstructive sleep apnea syndrome,** the most common of the three syndromes, occurs when there is a complete obstruction of the upper airway passage due to the collapse of the soft tissue at the back of the throat, which causes a cessation of breathing. Although the complete cessation of breathing typically lasts for 20–40 seconds, the instinctual effort to restore breathing, such as shifting body position or gasping, results in the interruption of sleep. Obesity appears to play a role in obstructive sleep apnea syndrome. **Central sleep apnea,** on the other hand, occurs as a result of neurological or cardiac irregularities that affect breathing, resulting in sleep interruptions. People who are elderly appear to be afflicted to a greater extent, and insomnia is the major complaint. **Central alveolar hypoventilation** occurs as a result of inadequate levels of oxygen in the bloodstream, which is believed to be caused by defects in the central nervous system that control breathing. Obesity is known to exacerbate central alveolar hypoventilation. Breathing-related sleep disorders interrupt the sleep cycle and cause daytime sleepiness or nocturnal insomnia.

Circadian Rhythm Sleep Disorder

Circadian rhythm sleep disorder occurs when there is a mismatch between the internal circadian timing (the body's biological clock) and the external 24-hour clock of the environment. This mismatch results in recurrent and persistent disruptions in the sleep patterns, which manifest as insomnia or sleepiness. Individuals who move regularly between time zones (e.g. airline staff) or those who need to be awake during the night because of occupational responsibilities run the risk of circadian rhythm sleep disorder.

Parasomnias

Parasomnias are distinct from dyssomnias in that they are unusual behaviors that occur during sleep or sleep–wake transitions. Parasomnias such as nightmare disorder, sleep terror disorder, and sleepwalking disorder activate the motor system, the autonomic nervous system, and affective and cognitive processes.

Nightmare Disorder

Nightmare disorder is the repeated awakening from sleep because of terrifying dreams, which the individual recalls in vivid detail. The recollection causes severe distress and threatens security, self-esteem, or survival. The nightmares occur during the second half of the night, usually during REM sleep. The nightmares end upon awakening with a full return to alertness, although there may be remnants of autonomic responses, such as hyperventilation or increased pulse rate.

Sleep Terror Disorder

Sleep terror disorder is differentiated from nightmare disorder in that it is difficult to comfort or awaken the individual during the sleep terror episode. The episode begins with screaming and crying, which is followed by autonomic, affective, and behavioral responses that typically accompany intense fear. Sleep terror episodes usually occur during non-REM sleep and individuals have no recollection of the dream immediately after the episode.

Sleepwalking Disorder

Sleepwalking disorder is the activation of complex motor behaviors during the first third of the sleep cycle during which the individual may sit up in bed or get out of bed and walk about. The sleepwalker has a blank stare, is unresponsive to communication, and cannot be easily awakened. If the individual awakens shortly after the episode, there is initial confusion and disorientation, but the return to full alertness happens within a few minutes. The sleepwalker has no recollection of the sleepwalking episode.

Treatment Options for Sleep Disorders

The etiology for sleep disorders may be neurological, psychological, or environmental. Treatment is guided by an accurate diagnosis of the disorder, and, in some cases, psychotropic medication or medical devices (e.g., an oxygen pressure mask for sleep apnea) may be the only effective intervention. Excessive sleepiness (narcolepsy or hypersomnia) may respond to stimulant medications, such as methylphenidate, antidepressants, or amphetamines, and insomnia is typically treated with sedatives.

Psychotherapy is recommended if a psychological condition (e.g., depression or anxiety) impedes the quantity and quality of sleep. Psychotherapy may also be used in conjunction with pharmacological interventions and environmental modifications. Cognitive–behavioral therapy, systematic desensitization, guided imagery, and relaxation strategies are known to be efficacious in reducing arousal levels and, therefore, enhancing the quantity and quality of sleep. Eliminating distractions from the sleep environment (e.g., television or computer) and behavioral strategies such as going to bed only when sleepy, avoiding caffeine prior to bedtime, allowing enough time for digestion, and so forth have proven to be reduce symptoms of insomnia.

The treatment for parasomnias (i.e., nightmare disorder, sleep terror disorder and sleepwalking disorder) remains inconclusive because the etiology is unknown; however, the symptoms appear to reduce in frequency or abate altogether as individuals afflicted with parasomnias grow older.

Contributed by Yegan Pillay,
Ohio University, Athens, OH

Reference

American Psychiatric Association. (2000). *Diagnostic and statistical manual of mental disorders* (4th ed., text rev.). Washington, DC: Author.

Additional Resources

Bayer, L. N. (2001). *Sleep disorders*. Philadelphia: Chelsea House.

Pressman, M. R., & Orr, W. C. (1997). *Understanding sleep: The evaluation and treatment of sleep disorders*. Washington, DC: American Psychological Association.

■ Social and Cultural Foundations, Key Ethical Issues in

In light of the increasing diversification in American society, the importance of social and cultural foundations in ethical counseling cannot be overstated. Nondiscrimination and multiculturalism have been codified in the American Counseling Association's (ACA; 2005) *ACA Code of Ethics*, all ACA divisional codes of ethics, the accreditation standards for counselor education programs (Council for Accreditation of Counseling and Related Educational Programs [CACREP], 2001), and the certification requirements of the National Board for Certified Counselors (2007). ACA has endorsed the Association for Multicultural Counseling and Development's Multicultural Counseling Competency Standards, which detail 31 competencies requisite for culturally competent professional counselor practice (Arredondo et al., 1996; Sue, Arredondo, & McDavis, 1992).

The 2005 revision to the *ACA Code of Ethics* reaffirms a commitment to social and cultural issues by recognizing the uniqueness of people within their social and cultural contexts, referencing multiculturalism and diversity throughout subsections of the *Code,* and reducing explicit and implicit reliance on Western European values in the Preamble. Although the 2005 *ACA Code of Ethics* gives extensive attention to social and cultural issues specific to multicultural counseling, many ethical challenges continue to emerge, from code formation through implementation. The following issues highlight these challenges.

Ethical Foundations

Professional counselors need to be aware of and avoid majority culture encapsulation (i.e., viewing the world through only one, traditionally White, cultural lens) and cultural bias in the formation of ethics committees and codes and in decision making. They also need to learn about and practice multiculturalism in the ethical decision-making process. Ethical principles, including autonomy, the duty to maximize the individual's right to make decisions; beneficence, the duty to do good both individually and for all; nonmaleficence, the duty to do no harm; fidelity, the duty to respect trust by keeping commitments and being honest with clients; and justice, the duty to treat all fairly, must also be viewed in a cultural context. For example, in resolution of cultural conflicts inherent in the ethical principles (e.g., autonomy vs. nonmaleficence when a person refuses allopathic medical treatment), counselors need to be aware that the foundational principles in the *ACA Code of Ethics* are not consonant with all cultures (e.g., autonomy and right to privacy vs. collectivist orientation where family is more apt to be party to health care decisions).

Should counselors focus on universal values that transcend all cultures (etic perspective), values unique to a given culture (emic perspective), or a combination of the two?

Definition

Is multiculturalism an exclusive or an inclusive concept? Exclusive definitions focus only on race and ethnicity and prevent addressing the broader context, such as social class or spirituality issues. Inclusive definitions recognize discrimination and unequal treatment based on cultural differences, including, but not limited to, race, ethnicity, age, sexual identity, social class, spirituality, and disability. Inclusive definitions are likely to increase ethical conflicts surrounding cultural differences, and counselors need to explore how to honor and affirm diversity in the face of clashes of values. An example is the way that respect for spiritual and religious diversity may conflict with a client's right to treatment when a student who opposes homosexuality on the basis of religious convictions refuses to counsel a homosexual client.

Developing and Maintaining Multicultural Competence

Counselors have an ethical obligation to gain personal awareness, sensitivity, and skills to work with diverse client populations (Section C.2.a. of the *ACA Code of Ethics*), but developing and maintaining that competence are complex, lifelong challenges, especially when training is limited and the range of cultural groups is expanding. This competency requires counselors to understand their own cultural roots and values and actively challenge internalized beliefs and prejudices. Professional counselors must increase their sensitivity to cultural differences, expand their knowledge of diverse cultures and their influence on human development, and avoid imposing their own values onto clients. To overcome cultural encapsulation in the therapeutic relationship, assessment, and intervention, professional counselors must use treatment modalities and define counseling goals consistent with the ways diverse clients define concerns and the values they deem relevant.

Knowledge and Skills

To become more culturally sensitive, counselors need new awareness, knowledge, and skills, but what knowledge and skills are needed and who will determine their selection? Traditional counseling approaches were developed by White European men for persons of European cultural origins. Counselors need to decide whether their focus should be on modifying traditional counseling approaches, studying indigenous healing practices and working with traditional healers to integrate these practices into traditional counseling, and/or using indigenous healing practices to develop more culturally relevant healing approaches.

Bounds of Competence

Professional counselors have an ethical responsibility to practice only within bounds of their competence (*ACA Code of Ethics* C.2.a.), but the definition and boundaries of such competence still need to be determined and the quality of training required to achieve competence can prove elusive. Counselors cannot possess training or experience relevant to every culture, but if counselors restrict themselves to treating only those populations with whom they have experience, they fail to stretch the boundaries of their competence by gaining new knowledge and skills for working with diverse populations (*ACA Code of Ethics* C.2.a.).

Boundaries Within Counseling Relationships

Defining and maintaining professional boundaries when working with culturally diverse, often oppressed, clients are difficult. Professional counselors are called on to affect change at the individual, group, institutional, and societal levels (*ACA Code of Ethics* A.6.a.-b.; C.), necessitating multiple, often overlapping, roles so clients may know counselors in other capacities. The 2005 *Code* responded to this issue through a more fluid and culturally sensitive discussion of dual relationships, including roles/relationships that could be beneficial (A.5.d.). These multiple roles need to be reframed in ways that are consonant with boundary considerations in the *Code*.

Supporting the Status Quo

The 2005 ACA *Code* advises professional counselors to respect approaches to professional counseling that differ from their own and the traditions and practices of other professional groups with which they work (D.1.a.), but this standard could be construed as supportive of the status quo. When counselors work within a system based on majority culture values, they need to be sensitive to cultural differences and find ways to reconcile their acceptance of employment with the ethical mandates to be aware of discriminatory practices and cultural biases and to advocate for the removal of the systemic barriers that inhibit client access and development (*ACA Code of Ethics* A.6.a.-b., C., C.5.). When clients are referred because of differences in values (e.g., with regard to sexual orientation; *ACA Code of Ethics* A.11.b.) or because the fee structure is inappropriate for the client (e.g., refugee client unable to pay for services; *ACA Code of Ethics* A.10.b.), professional counselors need be aware of their professional responsibility when no comparable services exist, especially at an acceptable cost, and must determine whether such referrals constitute cultural discrimination or cause emotional harm.

Counselor Education

To infuse multiculturalism and diversity into curriculum (*ACA Code of Ethics* F.6.b.), counselor education (CE) programs need faculty with appropriate training to design the curriculum as well as faculty representative of the diverse groups they serve. CACREP Standards and the *ACA Code of Ethics* exhort counselor education programs to recruit and retain a diverse faculty (*ACA Code of Ethics* F.11.a.) and a diverse student body (*ACA Code of Ethics* F.11.b.), but culturally diverse role models (e.g., persons of color, persons with disabilities, lesbian/gay/bisexual) remain underrepresented.

In faculty and student recruitment, CE programs need to incorporate culturally affirming and discerning screening and selection processes. Questions addressing cultural diversity issues need to be raised, eliciting information indicating interest in working with diversity or discriminatory attitudes toward diverse populations. Programs committed to diversity proactively seek representation of diverse populations and make accommodations for persons with differing abilities.

CE programs need to determine whether traditional counseling theories and techniques still have value or whether they require augmentation or replacement with new training models, theories, and techniques that enhance and support diverse students' well-being and academic performance (*ACA Code of Ethics* F.11.b) and their work with clients from differing cultural backgrounds.

Assessment, Diagnosis, and the *Diagnostic and Statistical Manual of Mental Disorders*

Assessment procedures establish the direction of counseling. To assess clients of differing cultural backgrounds effectively, counselors must take into account the personal and cultural context of the client (*ACA Code of Ethics* Introduction to E) and incorporate assessment measurements that are valid and reliable in either comparative or absolute terms (*ACA Code of Ethics* E.1.a.). Assessment measurements must address difficulties in establishing equivalence across cultures, lack of appropriate cultural norms, differing attitudes across cultures with regard to testing, and the appropriateness of test items.

Counselors are required to consider socioeconomic and cultural experiences when diagnosing mental disorders (*ACA Code of Ethics* E.5.b.), but interpretation of this standard is unclear, and more specific guidelines for implementing this standard need to be developed. As the counseling profession expands its role into broader mental health areas and the desire for professional parity in health insurance reimbursement increases, use of the *Diagnostic and Statistical Manual of Mental Disorders* (4th ed., text rev.; *DSM-IV-TR;* American Psychiatric Association, 2000) has become a more accepted part of counseling assessment. But the *DSM-IV-TR* is based on a medical model of mental illness that defines problems as residing in the individual and minimizes contextual factors. This system pathologizes the problems of cultural minorities by not recognizing how oppression, discrimination, and poverty can lead to feelings of worthlessness, powerlessness, and depression. Historical and social prejudices in the misdiagnosis and pathologizing of certain individuals and groups, the role of mental health in perpetuating these prejudices (*ACA Code of Ethics* E.5.c.), and the underlying reasons for embracing this diagnostic system all need to be examined. Counselors also need to consider how this system fosters cultural oppression and decide if they should advocate for its removal and should use alternate assessment methods that do not inhibit client access and growth (*ACA Code of Ethics* A.6.b.).

Research

Professional counselors are advised to use research procedures that take into account cultural considerations (*ACA Code of Ethics* G.1.g.). More attention must be given to the influence of cultural elements in study conceptualization, data collection methods and instrumentation, and assessment and interpretation of findings. Researchers must expand their methods of data collection and research designs to incorporate culturally diverse populations who may be reluctant to participate in research supported and/or conducted by majority culture agencies they mistrust. Researchers need to avoid overreliance on populations who are easily accessible (e.g., college students) but not representative of the cultural populations to which they want to generalize their findings. In addition, empirical research is needed to investigate the relationship between culture and group-specific treatment modalities as well as the efficacy of culture-specific techniques in counseling.

In summary, ethical challenges surrounding the social and cultural foundations of counseling are ever present, complex, inextricably linked to multiculturalism, and continually evolving in the face of increasing diversification worldwide. This entry highlights issues central to these challenges, including multiculturalism in the ethical decision-making process; how to define multiculturalism; developing and maintaining multicultural competency; multicultural considerations in counselor education and training; multicultural assessment, diagnosis, and the *DSM-IV-TR;* and culturally sensitive research.

Contributed by MaryLou Ramsey,
The College of New Jersey, Ewing, NJ

References

American Counseling Association. (2005). *ACA code of ethics*. Alexandria, VA: Author.

American Psychiatric Association. *Diagnostic and statistical manual of mental disorders* (4th ed., text rev.). Washington, DC: Author.

Arredondo, P., Toporek, R., Brown, S., Jones, J., Locke, D. C., Sanchez, J., et al. (1996). Operationalization of the multicultural counseling competencies. *Journal of Multicultural Counseling and Development, 24,* 42–78.

Council for Accreditation of Counseling and Related Educational Programs. (2001). *CACREP accreditation manual: 2001 standards*. Alexandria, VA: Author.

National Board for Certified Counselors. (2007). *National Certified Counselor 2007 application packet*. Retrieved May 26, 2007, from www.nbcc.org

Sue, D. W., Arredondo, P., & McDavis, R. J. (1992). Multicultural counseling competencies and standards: A call to the profession. *Journal of Counseling & Development, 70,* 477–486.

Additional Resources

Herlihy, B., & Corey, G. (Eds.). (2006). *ACA ethical standards casebook* (6th ed.). Alexandria, VA: American Counseling Association.

Herlihy, B., & Watson, Z. E. (2003). Ethical issues and multicultural competence in counseling. In F. D. Harper & J. McFadden (Eds.), *Culture and counseling: New approaches* (pp. 363–393). Boston: Allyn & Bacon.

Schmidt, J. J. (2006). *Social and cultural foundations of counseling and human services: Multiple influences on self-concept development* Boston: Allyn & Bacon.

Social and Cultural Foundations of Counseling, Key Historical Events in

Changes in U.S. diversity have required the counseling profession to meet the needs of a changing society. Foundations in counseling theories had previously focused on the three forces of psychodynamic, humanistic, and behavioral theories. Newer theoretical forces—multiculturalism—emphasize the need for an increased awareness of cultural and social foundations in assessing and counseling human behavior. Social justice is also emphasized, advocating for change of the status quo for individuals who experience a substantial lack of social and financial resources. The descriptor of these forces indicates that a theoretical concept has had a substantial and distinguishable impact on the field of counseling equivalent to the three preexisting forces of psychodynamic, humanism, and behaviorism (see Multiculturalism as a Fourth Force in Counseling; Social Justice in Counseling).

Developing new models for addressing the needs of all persons in counseling has received increased recognition in the last several decades (Sue, 1996). One of the pivotal occurrences on the national scene that led to the rise of multicultural thinking was the passage of the **civil rights acts.** Events leading up to this legislation made Americans increasingly aware of the social, educational, and political inequities that existed for African Americans. Later civil rights acts included provisions for the protection of human rights regardless of color, religion, gender, sexual orientation, and national origin. The National Organization of Personnel Workers was formed in the 1950s to support African American professionals, who frequently were not permitted to join the all-White organizations. This organization is currently called the National Association of Student Affairs Professionals.

Cultural terminology that appeared in the literature during the 1960s reflected the societal changes that were occurring. **Gilbert Wrenn** (1962) published "The Culturally Encapsulated Counselor" and defined *cultural encapsulation* as the notion that a counselor's cultural value system creates a biased lens through which he or she examines client issues. Wrenn warned counselors not to give absolute credit to the effectiveness of their counseling techniques and to take into account cultural differences and how those differences might affect the counseling relationship and outcomes. In other words, the counseling techniques and skills, which are often based on a counselor's worldview, are not more important than clients' values and worldviews. **Clemmont Vontress** introduced the term *culturally different* to offset the negative effects of terms such as *culturally deprived* and *culturally disadvantaged.*

At the American Personnel and Guidance Association (APGA; currently called the American Counseling Association [ACA]) Conference, African Americans held a Black caucus petitioning for the establishment of a National Office for Non-White Concerns in APGA. **Richard Kelsey** served as the first director. The name of this group was changed in 1985 to the Association for Multicultural Counseling and Development.

Culture became a prominent topic in the professional counseling literature during the 1970s. Special issues of *The Personnel and Guidance Journal* (currently named the *Journal of Counseling & Development [JCD]*) emerged, including "Culture as a Reason for Being," "Women and Counselors," "Asian Americans: The Neglected Minority," "Counseling Across Cultures," and "What Guidance for Blacks?" In 1972, a new journal, *The Journal of Non-White Concerns in Personnel and Guidance,* was created; the journal is currently known as the *Journal of Multicultural Counseling and Development (JMCD).* In addition, during this decade, **William Cross** developed one of the first racial identity development models focusing on psychological nigrescence or resocialization experiences. Thomas Parham described a model of racial identity development that is a lifelong and continuous experience, and Janet E. Helms developed one of the first White racial identity models that focuses on interracial exposure as critical to racial identity development.

In 1975, **Thelma Daley** became the first African American president of the APGA. Later in the 1970s, the *International Journal for the Advancement of Counseling* was published to address cross-cultural issues and to create a venue for exchange of ideas about counseling throughout the world. During the late 1970s and in the 1980s, theories were developed about acculturation. Various assessment tools measuring ethnic identity, acculturation levels, and acculturative stress were developed as the inherent bias in many assessment instruments was acknowledged. In the 1980s, a special issue of *The Counseling Psychologist* titled "Cross-Cultural Counseling" was also printed.

The 1990s brought large advances in multicultural emphasis. In 1990, **Janet E. Helms** edited *Black and White Racial Identity: Theory, Research, and Practice,* which was the first comprehensive work on racial identity and counseling.

In 1991, the American Association of Counseling and Development (the successor to APGA and now known as ACA) approved new standards for counselors. These standards, **The Thirty-One Multiculturalism Counseling Competencies,** were developed by the Professional Standards Committee to meet the growing need for multicultural competency. This work emphasized a rationale for competencies based on awareness, knowledge, and skills. During this same year, Ponterotto and Casas's (1991) *Handbook of Racial/Ethnic Minority Counseling Research* was published, and **Paul Pedersen** described multiculturalism as a "fourth force in counseling" in a special issue of *JCD.* Several other special issues of *JMCD* were published, with titles including, "Gender and Relationships," "Native American Indians," "Asian and Pacific Islander Americans," and "Counseling Mexican American/Chicano."

In 1992, the first Multicultural Counseling Summit met at the ACA annual conference in Baltimore. That same year, an article titled "Multicultural Counseling Competencies and Standards: A Call to the Profession" by Sue, Arredondo, and McDavis (1992) was published in both *JMCD* and *JCD*. Publishing the article in two prominent journals allowed the competencies and standards endorsed by ACA to reach a larger audience in the profession. Advancements in multicultural emphasis and awareness continued both in ACA and on the international scene. **Courtland Lee** became the first African American man to be elected president of the ACA in 1997. He was later elected secretary of the International Association for Counselling, and another African American, Frederick Harper, became the managing editor of the *Journal for the Advancement of Counselling*.

At the ACA conference in Washington, DC, in 2000, invited speakers debated issues related to multicultural counseling. In 2001, the Council for Accreditation of Counseling and Related Educational Programs included social and cultural diversity in its standards. In 2002, the African Conference on Guidance and Counseling was held in Kenya, which resulted in the African Association for Guidance and Counseling. The ACA 2005 *ACA Code of Ethics* included greater emphasis on cultural issues. In 2006, ACA evidenced further acknowledgment of the need for emphasis in multiculturalism and the need to connect the globalization of ideas when the organization joined with the Canadian Counseling Association in holding its annual conference in Montreal, Canada, and opened the ceremonies with a multicultural exercise.

Recent emphasis has expanded the concept of multicultural counseling. This has prompted research and interest in the areas of age, gender, sexual identity, socioeconomic status, and religious and spiritual issues in counseling. Significant events resulting from this interest include the establishment of the Association for Lesbian, Gay, Bisexual and Transgender Issues in Counseling; the establishment of Counselors for Social Justice; and the election of an openly gay president and an openly lesbian president of ACA. These new interest areas and research studies that focus on social justice have provided momentum for the social advocacy movement and have resulted in the fifth force, social justice, which is an expansion of multicultural issues in the counseling field.

Contributed by Donna Eckstein,
Capella University,
and Judith A. Nelson,
Sam Houston State University,
Huntsville, TX

References

American Counseling Association. (2005) *ACA code of ethics.* Alexandria, VA: Author.

Helms, J. E. (Ed.). (1990). *Black and White racial identity: Theory, research, and practice.* New York: Greenwood Press.

Ponterotto, J. G., & Casas, J. M. (1991). *Handbook of racial/ethnic minority counseling research.* Springfield, IL: Thomas.

Sue, D. W. (1996). Multicultural counseling: Models, methods, and actions. *The Counseling Psychologist, 24,* 279–284.

Sue, D. W., Arredondo, P., & McDavis, R. J. (1992). Multicultural counseling competencies and standards: A call to the profession. *Journal of Counseling & Development, 70,* 477–486.

Wrenn, C. G. (1962). The culturally encapsulated counselor. *Harvard Educational Review, 32,* 444–449.

Additional Resources

Harper, F. D., & McFadden, J. (2003). *Culture and counseling: New approaches.* Boston: Pearson Education.

Pedersen, P. B. (Ed.). (1999). *Multiculturalism as a fourth force.* Philadelphia: Taylor & Francis.

■ Social and Cultural Foundations, Legal Issues in

The United States has gradually become a pluralistic and racially, culturally, and ethnically diverse society. It is predicted that in the year 2050, combined racial ethnic minorities such as Hispanic Americans and African Americans will become the majority of the U.S. population. The rapid diversification and the changing complexion of U.S. society, spurred by the Immigration and Naturalization Act 1965, have brought many challenges to the counseling profession. Since the 1965 act, individual visas have been granted, with priority given to reunification of families, individuals with skills needed in the United States, and political refugees. This has directly led to an enormous influx of immigrants from Latin America and Asia. Professional counselors are certain to encounter clients who are different ethnically or culturally from the counselors' own ethnic or cultural background. A review of U.S. history shows that many legal cases and laws have had an impact on the development of multicultural counseling. Some of them are *Brown v. Board of Education of Topeka*, the Civil Rights Act of 1964, affirmative action policies and initiatives, Immigration and Naturalization Act of 1965, and the Americans With Disabilities Act (ADA) of 1990.

Brown v. Board of Education of Topeka

In the early 1950s, racial segregation in public schools was enforced across the United States. Linda Brown, a Black third-grader in Topeka, Kansas, had to walk 1 mile to get to her elementary school because she was denied admission to a nearby Whites-only elementary school. Oliver Brown, Linda's father, and the **National Association for the Advancement of Colored People (NAACP)** protested that segregation in public schools had a detrimental effect on the Black children and that it deprived them of equal protection under the law.

In 1951, Brown and the NAACP brought the appeal to the U.S. Supreme Court, and their case was combined with other cases that challenged school segregation in several states. In 1954, the Supreme Court declared that the establishment of separate public schools for Black and White students was inherently unequal. The court further concluded that segregation of public schools was a violation of the Fourteenth Amendment and was therefore unconstitutional. This historic decision overturned the separate but equal ruling 60 years earlier in the case of *Plessy v. Ferguson.*

Brown v. Board of Education was not just about children and education. By declaring the discriminatory nature of segregation, the legal ruling pointed out the human tendencies to prejudge, discriminate against, and stereotype other people by their race and their ethnic, religious, physical, or cultural characteristics. The *Brown* decision influenced educational and social reform throughout the United States and prepared the path for integration and the Civil Rights Movement.

The 1964 Civil Rights Act

The Civil Rights Act, proposed by President John F. Kennedy to ensure equal treatment of every American regardless of race, was signed into law by President Lyndon Johnson on July 2, 1964. The Civil Rights Act made racial discrimination illegal in businesses such as theaters, restaurants, and hotels. It also required employers to provide equal employment opportunities. Federally funded projects could now be cut off if there was evidence of discrimination based on color, race, or national origin. Segregation in public places such as swimming pools, libraries, and public schools was outlawed.

The landmark Civil Rights Act passed in 1964 also attempted to resolve the issue of African Americans who were denied the right to vote. The act forbade discrimination on the basis of gender as well as race in hiring, promoting, and firing. The attorney general of the United States was given the power to take legal action in any area where discrimination occurred. The original 1964 Civil Rights Act, which confronted issues of racial discrimination and upheld human rights and equality, was the most important piece of civil rights legislation in U.S. history. A series of very important laws, also referred to civil rights acts, have been passed since 1964.

Affirmative Action

Affirmative action refers to policies that help women and people of color obtain equal opportunities to education and employment. The motivation of affirmative action policies is to address historical discrimination problems in the United States. Affirmative action policies encourage public institutions to hire more underrepresented minority groups and aim to help women and people of color overcome sexism and racism.

In June 1965, President Johnson outlined the major principles of affirmative action and used the actual phrase "affirmative action" in Executive Order 11246, which requires government contractors to "take affirmative action" toward prospective minority employees in all aspects of hiring and employment. Contractors need to take specific measures to ensure equality in hiring and they need to document their efforts. In 1967, the Executive Order was expanded to ensure that women would benefit. The policies were made mostly race sensitive and have opened many doors for minorities, especially in higher education. Recruiting people from sociopolitically disadvantaged groups, through the use of quotas, has also resulted.

ADA of 1990

Signed into law on July 26, 1990, the **ADA** was the world's first comprehensive civil rights law addressing the needs of people with disabilities and was intended to make it possible for them to have the same access to buildings and so on as any other member of American society. *Disability* is defined as "a physical or mental impairment that substantially limits a major life activity" (ADA, 1990, § 12102 [2] [A]). ADA establishes a clear and comprehensive prohibition of discrimination on the basis of disability and it forbids private employers, state and local governments, employment agencies, and labor unions from discriminating against qualified individuals with disabilities in job application procedures; hiring; firing; advancement; compensation; job training; and other terms, conditions, and privileges of employment.

ADA also prohibits discrimination in public services, public accommodations, or telecommunications against people who are disabled. ADA provides similar protections against discrimination to Americans with disabilities as does the *Civil Rights Act of 1964*, which made discrimination based on race, religion, sex, national origin, and other characteristics illegal. ADA has been described as the Emancipation Proclamation for the disability community.

Implications for Professional Counselors

The growing recognition of racial or other forms of discrimination resulted in minority and ethnic groups becoming a major focus in the field of counseling. The American Counseling Association's (ACA; 2005) *ACA Code of Ethics* requires counselors to make an active effort to understand the diverse cultural backgrounds of their clients and to be sensitive to the needs of the client when establishing a counseling relationship. Professional counselors are also asked not to engage in discrimination based on age, religion/spirituality, gender, gender identity, sexual orientation, marital status/partnership, language preference, socioeconomic status, or any basis proscribed by law.

To be culturally competent, professional counselors are urged to become aware of their racial/cultural biases and are not to assume that their values are universally shared. Professional counselors are also encouraged to reach out and gain understanding of the cultural values and worldviews of various groups in the society, such as African Americans, Asian Americans, and Hispanic Americans. Finally, professional counselors are asked to develop culturally appropriate intervention strategies in working with a diverse population. In other words, professional counselors must reexamine whether the traditional forms of counseling, strategies, and techniques are equally applicable across all populations. Professional counselors must move to a systemic intervention approach to become advisers, consultants, and social change agents.

Contributed by Chi-Sing Li
and Yu-Fen Lin,
Sam Houston State University,
Huntsville, TX

References

American Counseling Association. (2005). *ACA code of ethics*. Alexandria, VA: Author.

American With Disabilities Act of 1990, 42 U.S.C.A. § 12101 *et seq.* (West, 1993).

Additional Resource

Sue, D. W., & Sue, D. (2003). *Counseling the culturally diverse: Theory and practice* (4th ed.). New York: Wiley.

■ Social and Cultural Foundations of Counseling, Key People in

The following key figures, whose names appear in alphabetical order, have made a considerable impact on the social and cultural foundations of counseling. Although this list is not meant to be exhaustive, the significant contributions of these individuals to the counseling field have changed the way professional counselors think about their profession and how they integrate diversity into their work with clients, students, and other professionals.

Patricia Arredondo is a professor specializing in teaching and research in the areas of multicultural competency development; organizational development in higher education; and counseling with women, Latinas/os, and immigrants. She has written extensively on counseling Latinas/os, multicultural counseling competencies, and multicultural issues for women. She is recognized as a living legend by the American Counseling Association (ACA). Her major contributions include her research with immigrant populations, particularly the grief and loss associated with immigration. She has offered guidelines on how to think about the immigrant experience and she has also been instrumental in contributing to the multicultural competencies adopted by ACA, which have led to a personal identity model and have served as a guide for the counseling profession.

Madonna Constantine, a professor of psychology and education, has been the director of the Winter Roundtable, which is the longest running continuing professional education program in the United States devoted solely to cultural issues in psychology and education. Her interests include cultural competence in counseling, training, and supervision; the mental health issues of people of color in the United States and immigrants; and vocational issues of adolescents and college students of color. She believes in the significance of applying cultural competencies in counseling, and she has been a proponent of looking at all aspects of identity, including racial and sexual identity. ACA presented her with the Association's 2001 Research Award. She is noted for embarking on a systematic research program to isolate and measure aspects of multicultural counseling competence.

Michael D'Andrea is a counselor educator whose focus over the past 20 years has been looking at health, well-being, and development from a culturally diverse perspective. More specifically, he is interested in how issues of social justice compliment or conflict with the ways that people from different groups construct meaning of wellness and psychological development. His contributions include the RESPECTFUL counseling model as it relates to the complexity of cultural diversity, including religion, economic status, sexual and psychological maturity, ethnicity and racial identity, chronological differences, family history, threats to well-being, physical characteristics, location of residence, and language. A second contribution is the community counseling model that embraces traditional counseling theory but takes an ecological approach to promoting mental health by emphasizing prevention as well as addressing remediation. His third contribution focuses on the psychology of White racism.

Janet E. Helms is a professor and director of the Institute for the Study and Promotion of Race and Culture at Boston College. The institute hosts a conference on racial identity each year. She has served on the editorial boards of the *Journal of Psychological Assessment* and the *Journal of Multicultural Counseling and Development*. She has written more than 60 empirical and theoretical articles and numerous books on the topics of racial identity and cultural influences on assessment and counseling practice and has been acknowledged for her work in Iowa State University's Plaza of Heroines and the Distinguished Career Contributions to Research award from the Society for the Psychological Study of Ethnic Minority Issues, awarded at the convention of the American Psychological Association. In 1991, she was the first annual recipient of the Janet E. Helms Award for Mentoring and Scholarship in Professional Psychology. This award was inaugurated in her honor by Columbia University Teachers College.

Courtland C. Lee, past president of ACA, is a nationally recognized scholar in the field of multicultural counseling. He is the author, editor, or coeditor of many books on multicultural counseling and counseling African American males. He has also published numerous book chapters and articles on adolescent development and counseling across cultures. He believes that a scholarly analysis of the challenges that African American men face is necessary and that the *Journal of African American Men* can provide an appropriate forum for that analysis, and he was instrumental in challenging the membership of the Association for Multicultural Counseling and Development (AMCD) to outline the competencies necessary for multicultural counseling, resulting in the 31 competencies that now are a part of ACA and AMCD. As a researcher, he is particularly interested in studying how counseling and education are affected by race, disability, gender, sexual orientation, and other cultural factors. Recently, Lee has written about the experience of marginalized communities, the perpetration of oppression in schools, and empowerment theory as it relates to professional school counselors.

Thomas Parham is a psychologist and educator, a past president of the Association of Black Psychologists, and a past president of AMCD. He has written or edited several books, including *Counseling Persons of African Descent: Raising the Bar of Practitioner Competence* (2002). For the past 20 years, he has focused his research efforts in the area of psychological nigrescence and has authored many articles in this area. Research in the area of racial identity development remains his primary focus.

Derald Wing Sue assumed a leadership role in writing about counseling Chinese and other Asian clients during the 1970s when journal articles on counseling focused on specific ethnicities. Sue referred to Asian Americans as the neglected minority. In 1973, Sue was a guest editor for a special issue of *The Personnel and Guidance Journal*, titled "Asian-Americans: The Neglected Minority." Sue (Sue, Arredondo, & McDavis, 1992) was also the first author of a hallmark article titled "Multicultural Counseling Competencies and Standards: A Call to the Profession," which appeared in the *Journal of Multicultural Counseling and Development* and was also published during the same year in the *Journal of Counseling & Development* in order to reach a broader audience. The article outlined 31 competencies for multicultural counselors, which were approved by AMCD and ACA as necessary to counsel diverse clients effectively. These competencies have served as a template for counselors and their understanding of the whole person in counseling relationships. His Asian American Acculturation Scale is one of the most widely used acculturation scales in the field. Recent publications include *Overcoming Our Racism: The Journey to Liberation* (2003) and the classic text *Counseling the Culturally Diverse: Theory and Practice* (2002).

Stanley Sue is a distinguished professor of psychology and Asian American Studies Program at the University of California, Davis. He has been a national pioneer in helping ethnic minority groups and service providers overcome ignorance about adequate mental health services for minorities. For this accomplishment, he was awarded the 2001 Academic Senate Distinguished Public Service Award. He was the first recipient of the Stanley Sue Award for Distinguished Contributions to Diversity in Clinical Psychology. This award was established in 2003 to recognize a psychologist who has made remarkable contributions to the understanding of human diversity. In 2005, he was the recipient of the Distinguished Research Contributions to Ethnic Minorities awarded by the American Psychological Association. He has been the director of the National Research Center on Asian American Mental Health from 1988 to 2001.

Clemmont Vontress, a counselor educator, is a pioneer author on diversity issues shaping the development of multicultural studies and counseling. He has been instrumental in making multicultural counseling into a major discipline. His writings on Black–White, cross-cultural counseling in the 1960s focused on assisting White counselors' understanding of the special challenges of working with Black clients. In 1967, Vontress was the first author to use the term *culturally different* in an article titled "The Culturally Different" published in the *Employment Service Review*. Making a distinction between culturally different and culturally deprived or disadvantaged was groundbreaking and significantly affected the counseling profession's thinking about the notion of differences. Perplexed by his personal experience of racial oppression, Vontress has devoted his professional career to studying culture and how it affects counseling.

Contributed by Judith A. Nelson,
Sam Houston State University,
Huntsville, TX

References

Parham, T. (2002) *Counseling persons of African descent: Raising the bar of practitioner competence.* Thousand Oaks, CA: Sage.

Sue, D. W. (Ed.). (1973). Asian Americans: The neglected minority [Special issue]. *The Personnel and Guidance Journal, 51*(6).

Sue, D. W. (2002). *Counseling the culturally diverse. Theory and practice* (4th ed.). New York: Wiley.

Sue, D. W. (2003). *Overcoming our racism: The journey to liberation.* San Francisco: Jossey-Bass.

Sue, D. W., Arredondo, P., & McDavis, R. J. (1992). Multicultural counseling competencies: A call to the profession. *Journal of Counseling & Development, 70,* 477–486.

Vontress, C. (1967, October). The culturally different. *Employment Service Review, 4,* 35–36.

■ Social Identity Theory

Social identity theory has its roots in European social psychology. It was developed by Henri Tajfel and John Turner in 1979 in order to understand the psychological basis for intergroup discrimination. With social identity theory, the self is defined in intergroup contexts. The central tenets of social identity theory include categorization, identification, and comparison. Through the process of categorization, social groups are defined and evaluated based on the attributes of the group members. The social value, or the status and importance of belonging to a particular group, is defined through social comparison between groups. Through identification, individuals look to identify and belong to groups that they consider to be superior to other groups. This group identification enhances a person's self-esteem.

Social identity theory relies heavily on a process called **self-categorization.** Through this process, the self is viewed as an object and can categorize, classify, or name itself in particular ways. Individuals develop a social identity that signifies to them their membership in particular social groups. These social groups function to evaluate appropriate behaviors associated with the identity and assign a societal worth to the identity. Although individuals are born into a structured society in which many of their social categories are defined for them (e.g., ethnic groups, gender), individuals become members of many more social categories (e.g., friends, occupation) through their personal development. The combination of social groups to which each individual belongs is unique to that individual and develops into a person's own self-concept.

Social groups are evaluated on the basis of numerous factors (e.g., power, prestige, status), and the value of the group can only be determined in relation to that of other groups. Through social comparison, others who are evaluated as being similar to the self are categorized as the **in-group** and those who differ from the self make up the **out-group.** Accentuation of perceived similarities between the self and other in-group members is desirable, as is accentuating the perceived differences between the self and the out-group.

The in-group is evaluated on characteristics that are judged to be positive, and the out-group is evaluated on areas considered to be negative. This process of evaluation allows individuals to pursue positive distinctions for their group, thereby also elevating themselves and increasing self-esteem. The theory posits that people will often rely on their group identity rather than their personal identity to achieve status and esteem. Discrimination and bias toward out-group members can develop as individuals respond favorably to in-group members and less favorably to out-group members.

Social identity theory continues to grow and develop. Some related theories that have developed from social identity theory are self-categorization theory, optimal distinctiveness theory, social identity theory of leadership, and the social identity model of deindividuation. Social identity research is being conducted in many fields, including group processes, intergroup relations, social cognitions, organization and management science, and psychological and social psychology (Hogg & Ridgeway, 2003). Research continues to look at how individuals' group identification can affect their level of satisfaction with their lives and their own self-perceptions. Professional counselors can use this theory, along with current research trends, to work with clients who are dealing with racism, sexism, and other group identification stressors. The research indicates that these clients benefit from working on coping strategies as well as issues related to self-esteem.

Contributed by Karen M. Decker,
William Paterson University, Wayne, NJ

Reference

Hogg, M., & Ridgeway, C. (2003). Social identity: Sociological and social psychological perspectives. *Social Psychology Quarterly, 66,* 97–100.

Additional Resources

Hogg, M., & Williams, K. (2000). From I to we: Social identity and the collective self. *Group Dynamics: Theory, Research, and Practice, 4,* 81–97.

Stets, J., & Burke, P. (2000). Identity theory and social identity theory. *Social Psychology Quarterly, 63,* 224–237.

Social Influence Model

Stanley Strong (1968) proposed a **social influence model** with two counselor dimensions: (a) **credibility** (i.e., counselor expertness and trustworthiness) and (b) **interpersonal attractiveness** (i.e., counselor behavior that conveys to clients that they are liked and that they share meaningful similarities). Drawing on findings from social psychology, Strong postulated that professional counselors who are perceived by their clients as possessing more credibility and attractiveness would be able to exert greater influence in the counseling process. Counselors would then use this greater influence to assist clients in reaching their goals.

Professional counselors increase their perceived expertness by (a) providing verification of their competency by displaying evidence of training (e.g., certificates, diplomas), (b) offering behavioral indication of competency (e.g., being competent, organized, interested), and (c) building a positive reputation (e.g., having current or former clients willing to refer new clients). Professional counselors increase their perceived trustworthiness by being sincere, open, and honest. Finally, counselors increase their attractiveness by being perceived as similar to their clients and by having clients feel that the counselor likes them. Counselors who share similar values and styles of behaving as their clients are perceived as being more attractive. One way this can be accomplished is by counselors offering a moderate amount of self-disclosure because this lets clients know more about how the counselors and clients share some similarities.

Contributed by John M. Littrell,
Colorado State University,
Fort Collins, CO

Reference

Strong, S. R. (1968). Counseling: An interpersonal influence process. *Journal of Counseling Psychology, 15,* 215–224.

Additional Resource

Corrigan, J. D., Dell, D. M., Lewis, K. N., & Schmidt, L. D. (1980). Counseling as a social influence process: A review. *Journal of Counseling Psychology, 27,* 395–441.

Social Justice in Counseling

The social justice perspective in counseling is an approach wherein professional counselors focus on simultaneously promoting individual needs and development as well as the common good through addressing challenges related to individual and distributive justice. **Social justice** in the context of counseling includes the empowerment of clients as well as active confrontation of injustices and inequities as they affect clients and other people within their clients' systemic contexts. Professional counselors who work from a social justice perspective focus on cultural, contextual, and individual needs of those served in the context of four key principles: equity, access, participation, and harmony.

Equity

Equity can be defined as the fair distribution of resources, rights, and responsibilities to all members of society. Professional counselors who work from a social justice perspective are aware of historical, contextual, and environmental factors that create systemic and systematic inequities in the lives of their clientele. Furthermore, they are aware of the impact that living under systemic and systematic oppressions has on human development. These professional counselors strive to educate, empower, and advocate for their clients with an eye to diminishing the inequities they experience.

Access

In a social justice perspective in counseling, **access** refers to notions of fairness for both the individual and the common good based on the ability of all people to access the resources, services, power, information, and understanding crucial to realizing a standard of living that allows for self-determination and human development. This value was a basis for the Bill of Rights, which was drafted based on the assumption that all human beings have certain inalienable rights, such as the right to life, liberty, and the pursuit of happiness. Professional counselors working from a social justice perspective realize that there are people who are marginalized (e.g., people of color, people who are differently abled, women, people who are gay or lesbian) to the point that they experience environmental barriers that systematically undermine their ability to access what they need to prosper. Marginalized people cannot be expected to function as effectively as people who are not marginalized in society (e.g., people who are heterosexual, men, people who are able-bodied) who experience privileges that give them greater access to these forms of social capital.

Participation

Participation refers to the right for every person in society to partake in and be consulted on decisions that have an impact on their lives as well as the lives of other people in their contexts and systems. Social justice–oriented professional counselors are aware that the experience of not being permitted to participate in processes that influence the options and opportunities that their clients have results in deleterious effects on their clients. When people are not allowed to and not invited to participate in processes that influence them, they lose a sense of control that can result in a loss of hope, decreased motivation to change, and increased feelings of nihilism, as well as an increased sense of personal and collective disenfranchisement. Social justice–minded professional counselors work from this awareness to support clients' empowerment by educating them on issues related to their participatory rights as well as helping them develop practical strategies to implement in situations where they are adversely affected. These professional counselors also strive to help clients connect with resources and other people in their communities who might be useful in further enhancing their clients' sense of empowerment.

Harmony

In the context of social justice within counseling, **harmony** is defined as a principle of social adjustment wherein the actions revolving around the self-interests of any individual or group ultimately produce results that afford the best possible outcomes for the community as a whole. A key assumption in this principle is that social justice exists only under conditions that take into account the needs and rights of all the people in society in a balanced fashion. From this perspective, individual rights are considered in the context of the needs of society at large. Therefore, individuals are generally willing to make short-term sacrifices with the faith and understanding that such choices will ultimately address and maintain the best interests of all persons concerned. Professional counselors operating from a social justice perspective constantly strive to update their understanding of the interplay of various environmental systems, contexts, and groups on their clients' mental well-ness and physical well-being. This is done with a goal to expand understanding of competing interests that might be addressed in a manner that results in more equitable and harmonious outcomes.

Social justice has developed into an increasingly influential theme in counseling over the past few decades. Evidence includes social justice being increasingly referred to as the fifth force in counseling; the creation of Counselors for Social Justice, a division of the American Counseling Association (ACA); and the development of the ACA advocacy competencies. The advocacy competencies provide counselors a framework for addressing issues of oppression both with and on behalf of clients and include clear articulation of the concepts of client advocacy and client empowerment. As experts in the field continue to develop awareness and understanding of the relationship between social injustice/oppression and mental health outcomes, social justice will continue to be a force that shapes counseling.

Contributed by Hugh C. Crethar,
University of Arizona, Tucson, AZ

Additional Resources

Constantine, M. G., Hage, S. M., Kindaichi, R., & Bryant, R. M. (2007). Social justice and multicultural issues: Implications for the practice and training of counselors and psychologists. *Journal of Counseling & Development, 85,* 24–29.

Toporek, R. L., Gerstein, L., Fouad, N. A., Roysircar, G., & Israel, T. (Eds.). (2006). *Handbook for social justice in counseling psychology: Leadership, vision and action.* Thousand Oaks, CA: Sage.

Toporek, R. L., Lewis, J., & Crethar, H. C. (2009). Promoting systemic change through the advocacy competencies. *Journal of Counseling & Development, 87*(3).

■ Social Learning Theory

Albert Bandura is the originator of **social learning theory,** a theory closely related to behaviorism that incorporates modeling and vicarious learning. Many people learn through imitation of others and through interaction and observation. Social learning theory explains human behavior in terms of continuous reciprocal interaction among cognitive, behavioral, and environmental influences (Bandura, 1977). According to this theory, attitudes, behaviors, and skills may be acquired through modeling.

Bandura obtained his doctorate from the University of Iowa in 1952. In 1953, he accepted a teaching position at Stanford University, where he continues to teach. He wrote *Social Foundations of Thought and Action* in 1986, which provides a framework of this social cognitive theory today. In his long and influential career, Bandura has written many books and articles on various topics in psychology.

Bandura is known for his work with children and aggression. He believed that television is a source of aggressive behavior modeling and testified in the U.S. Congress regarding the effects of televised violence on youth. According to Bandura, films and television shows illustrate violence graphically and as being acceptable behavior, especially for heroes who are never punished. Because aggression is a prominent feature of many shows, children who have a high degree of exposure to the media may exhibit a relatively high incidence of hostility themselves in imitation of the aggression they have witnessed.

In order to test his theory, Bandura (1973, 1977) conducted one of psychology's most well-known studies, the Bobo Doll experiment. He presented three aspects of children and aggressive behavior: (a) how patterns of aggression are developed; (b) what provokes aggression; and (c) what determines whether children will resort to aggressive behavior in the future. In this experiment, children witnessed a model aggressively attacking a plastic blow-up clown called a **Bobo Doll.** After children viewed the video, they were placed in a room with attractive toys, but they could not touch the toys. Process of retention occurred, and the children then became angry and frustrated. Next, the children were led to another room where there were toys identical to the ones that had been used in the Bobo Doll video. Motivation occurred, and as a result, Bandura found that 88% of the children imitated the aggressive behavior. Eight months later, 40% of the same children reproduced violent behavior observed in the Bobo Doll experiment. In addition, the children changed their behavior without reward connected to the behavior.

Observational Learning and the Modeling Process

Bandura (1977) outlined four primary steps to the modeling process: **attention** (e.g., modeled events, observer characteristics), **retention** (e.g., symbolic coding, cognitive organization, symbolic rehearsal, motor rehearsal), **motor reproduction** (e.g., physical capabilities, self-observation of reproduction, accuracy of feedback), and **motivation** (e.g., external, vicarious, and self-reinforcing). Modeled observations serve as guides for individuals' chosen behavior and performances. In essence, in order to learn a modeled behavior accurately, an individual must pay attention to, or attend to, the observed behavior. The more rewarding the modeled behavior is perceived to be, the more likely it will hold the observer's attention. Observers must remember, or retain, the modeled behavior. This is represented in people's memory by symbols. Symbols can be encoded as visual images, words, or concise labels. Individuals then convert the symbolic representations to appropriate actions. This begins by imagining oneself performing the act. Behavioral enactment is organized by cognitive responses, initiation, monitoring, and refinement based on feedback. Social learning theory maintains that individuals are more likely to adopt a modeled behavior if they value the outcome and are less likely if the outcome is not perceived as rewarding or has an undesired effect (Bandura, 1977).

An example of observational learning occurs when there is a dispute between two 11-year-old students over the time spent on a favored activity during a recess break. The students react with anger and aggression. The behaviors of the students are to seek revenge through force or intimidation and dominance, no doubt behaviors that have been modeled

for them at times throughout their lives. The school counselor invites the students to participate in a peer-mediation process. In this process, two other students, also age 11, attempt to assist the disputants in settling their differences and achieve a win–win resolution for both of them.

An early step in the peer-mediation process is to have the students agree to participate. In essence, the students agree to cooperate, and they must pay close attention to the process. The students are observing the social skills of the student mediators because they are also looking forward to the rewards of having both of them come to a win–win agreement, thereby obtaining the **attention** part of the process.

The student mediator asks for a concrete description of how the conflict developed and what steps each student would be willing to take to resolve this and future conflicts. The cognitive acknowledgement of the steps involved in the dispute and the potential solutions helps to make the situation real, understandable, and thus manageable and increases the likelihood of **retention** of steps learned to obtain the desired outcome. Next, peer mediators ask that the disputants sign an agreement or contract indicating that they will abide by the principles of the resolution that they coauthored. The disputants agree to prosocial behaviors and to reconvene at a specific date in the near future to report on progress. These steps put the disputants in the role of taking concrete action to back up the symbolic gestures of the easing of tension, thereby taking the step of **motor reproduction.** The fact that the disputants authored the solution to the problem and they agreed that the solution met their needs both now and in the future contributes to their high **motivation** level for following through with the behaviors, because this following through has high reward potential.

Self-Efficacy

Self-efficacy plays a central role in Bandura's social learning theory and in the observational learning process. Self-efficacy is the individual's belief in his or her ability to produce an effect through personal actions. This belief may or may not be accurate; however, in either case, it may influence the outcome of the individual's attempt. Bandura differentiated between outcome expectancy and efficacy expectation. **Outcome expectancy** is an individual's estimate that a specific behavior will result in a desired outcome. **Efficacy expectation** is the individual's belief that he or she can successfully perform the needed behavior to result in the desired outcome (Bandura, 1977). The concept of self-efficacy plays a role in the preceding example in that the disputants—having been treated respectfully and fairly, having coauthored a win–win resolution to their dispute, and having witnessed prosocial modeling—will likely have an increased belief in their ability to promote a positive change through their actions. Outcome expectations have been bolstered by modeling from student mediators, who have demonstrated concrete steps to take and how these steps lead to a desired outcome.

Contributed by Edward J. Hanna,
University of Pittsburgh,
and Mark Lepore,
Chatham University, Pittsburgh, PA

References

Bandura, A. (1973). *Aggression: A social learning analysis.* Englewood Cliffs, NJ: Prentice Hall.

Bandura, A. (1977). *Social learning theory.* Englewood Cliffs, NJ: Prentice Hall.

Bandura, A. (1986). *Social foundations of thought and action.* Englewood Cliffs, NJ: Prentice Hall.

■ Social Learning Theory of Career Decision Making

The social learning theory of career decision making comprises three theoretical statements articulated by John Krumboltz in 1976, 1996, and 1999. **John Krumboltz** first published his **social learning theory of career decision making** (Krumboltz, Mitchell, & Jones, 1976) as a supplement to traditional trait–factor models of career decision making. Trait–factor approaches presume that stable personal traits (e.g., interests, values, personality) can be objectively measured and logically matched with existing career opportunities. The added focus of social learning career theory has been on learning processes that result in career-relevant beliefs and behaviors. Krumboltz's social learning theory of career choice is composed of four factors that influence career decision making and three outcomes of interactions among those four factors. The four factors are described in the following list:

1. **Genetic endowment and special abilities.** Genetic endowment includes race, sex, and physical appearance and characteristics. Special abilities consist of such abilities as intelligence, musical talent, muscular coordination, and artistic ability.

2. **Environmental conditions and events.** Environmental conditions and events are influences in the life of an individual that may affect his or her educational and career decisions. Environmental conditions are characteristics of an individual's circumstances, such as geographic location, education opportunities, and government policies. Events in a person's life may include such unplanned occurrences as natural disasters, economic trends, and technological developments.

3. **Instrumental and associative learning experiences.** Instrumental learning experiences occur when an individual engages in a behavior and produces certain consequences such as rewards or punishers. Associative learning may take place when a person reacts to his or her surroundings by either connecting two events (e.g., shying away from a career as an air traffic controller after President Ronald Reagan fired striking workers who sought a pay increase and better working conditions) or emulating the behavior of a model (e.g., admiring the field of forensics after watching *Crime Scene Investigation* on television).

4. **Task approach skills.** Task approach skills are skills people use to cope with any task, problem, or challenge in their environment. Task approach skills include decision making, problem solving, and work habits. The outcome of tasks in a person's life (e.g., seeking a job) is affected by his or her task approach skills (e.g., sending out résumés), and those same task approach skills may be altered by the results of the task (i.e., a person might decide to contact an employer personally if sending out résumés in the past failed to obtain employment).

The complex interactions of the four factors previously described in this entry result in self-observation and world-view generalizations, task approach skills, and action. **Self-observation generalizations** are self-assessments (overt or covert) about one's own performance (e.g., "I earned an *A* on a school writing assignment so I must be a good writer"), whereas worldview beliefs concern evaluation of the surrounding environment (e.g., "I see a lot of verbal abuse on TV; therefore, I think raising my voice is an appropriate response to workplace conflict"). These personal beliefs may or may not be accurate and realistic, but they shape the way in which individuals cope with the challenges of everyday life. Task approach skills, as mentioned in the section on factors, are personalized coping mechanisms. These methods of dealing with tasks in the environment may be shaped every time they are used, depending on their efficacy in obtaining desired results (e.g., "I may try a new method of conflict resolution if my past verbal attacks got me into trouble"). Action or behavior by an individual (e.g., college application, job change) completes the dynamic process of learning described in the social learning theory of career decision making. Behavior produces certain consequences (i.e., degrees of success or failure), and once again individuals' task approach skills and self-observation/worldview generalizations are affected by the learning opportunity that their actions have created.

The social learning theory of career decision making was updated by Krumboltz in 1996. His new theory, titled **learning theory of career counseling (LTCC),** added explanations to help career counselors facilitate the career development of their clients. Unlike the focus of trait–factor counseling on decision making based on current knowledge, LTCC promotes the acquisition of additional career-relevant knowledge and skills. Four guidelines to assist career clients follow:

1. Encourage clients to explore new interests and activities.
2. Prepare clients to expect and adapt to changing work tasks.
3. Encourage, support, and empower clients to develop coping skills and to take action in response to the stressors of an ever-changing world.
4. Recognize that the significant overlap of work and a person's general lifestyle cannot be separated. Professional counselors should extend their role to incorporate lifestyle issues such as family reactions to work, burnout, peer relationships, and retirement.

Finally, Krumboltz, along with Kathleen Mitchell and Al Levin, articulated a third component of social learning theory of career decision making that is called **planned happenstance theory** (Mitchell et al., 1999). Planned happenstance is an expansion of the role of the career counselor that acknowledges the role of chance in career development, reframes client indecision as open-mindedness, and promotes exploratory activities that increase the probability that they will be exposed to unexpected opportunities. Counselors are encouraged to implement planned happenstance with their clients by (a) making clients aware of the role of chance in career development and thus normalize the happenstance experience, (b) helping clients see curiosity as an opportunity for additional learning and exploration, (c) teaching clients to produce and encourage desirable chance events, and (d) teaching clients to overcome obstacles to action.

Krumboltz indicated that planned happenstance is an integral component of his theory (Feller, Honaker, & Zagzebski, 2001). Chance events are special examples of environmental conditions and events that create learning opportunities for individuals regarding their career development (e.g., "being at the right place at the right time"). Furthermore, planned happenstance theory suggests that individuals can act in ways that create unexpected events. For example, a person mentioning to someone else that she or he is looking for a job can lead the second person to offer encouragement or direction in the job search.

Contributed by S. Alan Silliker,
St. Bonaventure University,
St. Bonaventure, NY

References

Feller, R. W., Honaker, S. L., & Zagzebski, L. M. (2001). Theoretical voices directing the career development journey: Holland, Harris-Bowlsbey, and Krumboltz. *Career Development Quarterly, 49,* 212–224.

Krumboltz, J. D. (1996). A learning theory of career counseling. In M. Savickas & B. Walsh (Eds.), *Integrating career theory and practice* (pp. 233–280). Palo Alto, CA: CPP Books.

Krumboltz, J. D., Mitchell, A. M., & Jones, G. B. (1976). A social learning theory of career selection. *The Counseling Psychologist, 6,* 71–81.

Mitchell, K. E., Levin, A. S., & Krumboltz, J. D. (1999) Planned happenstance: Constructing unexpected career opportunities. *Journal of Counseling & Development, 77,* 115–124.

Additional Resource

Bandura, A. (1986). *Social foundations of thought and action: A social-cognitive theory.* Upper Saddle River, NJ: Prentice Hall.

■ Socioeconomic Status, Socioeconomic Class

Many professional counselors inherently understand that variables such as gender, age, and ethnicity can fundamentally affect the counseling relationship; however, the one factor that can be most critical for counselors to consider when conceptualizing and intervening with clients is socioeconomic status. **Socioeconomic status** is a complex description that is based on access to resources such as money, occupations, and education. Socioeconomic status also describes people's relative rank in society, or their socioeconomic class.

Socioeconomic class can be categorized in various ways in the United States. It is most commonly divided into the four positions of upper, middle, working, and under classes. People who have **upper-class status** usually have inherited wealth, or they may have generated wealth through their ownership of corporations or industries. Those in the **middle-class status** usually have professional or technical occupations, are self-employed, or are employed as supervisors or managers. People in the middle class typically have sufficient income and resources to provide for not only immediate but also longer term needs. People who have **working-class status** are often those who provide manual labor or work in service industries. These people earn low wages and may have pressing concerns regarding their livelihood, ranging from managing unstable working conditions to struggling to afford health insurance or child care. Many professional counselors also frequently work with people who have **underclass status.** These people are often unemployed or underemployed and may have to rely on temporary and substandard housing. Some are or will become **homeless.** These people live in **poverty;** they do not have the minimum resources, such as access to health care, food, or shelter, to meet their regular physical, mental, and emotional needs. The U.S. Department of Health and Human Services establishes poverty thresholds and guidelines that identify eligibility for numerous government-sponsored aid programs. Professional counselors working with clients who are homeless or live in poverty usually consult and collaborate regularly with representatives from these aid programs.

Socioeconomic status and class are vitally important considerations for professional counselors because these factors reflect aspects of people's culture. Someone who has working-class status, for instance, has distinctly different perceptions, concerns, and resources than someone who has upper-class status. These views and concerns combine to create a worldview that reflects the reality of the individual's socioeconomic status and may become a primary aspect of that person's identity. Furthermore, individuals who have working-class or underclass status usually face numerous environmental stressors, such as inadequate housing, as well as ongoing anxiety about resources that can exacerbate their mental health concerns.

The specific mental health concerns of people from working and underclasses vary widely, but counselors should keep in mind that some clients may have limited access to health care and may experience complications such as depression and anxiety as a result of medical conditions that are untreated or inadequately treated. Furthermore, clients who have working-class and underclass status and who are undereducated may not have sufficient information and education regarding topics such as stress management, parenting, and holistic wellness. As a result, these clients may feel helpless and hopeless in their efforts to improve their life situations. Clients who have struggled to meet their basic needs may present with hostility, suspicion, and confusion, and clients who have faced instability regarding their living situations may exhibit posttraumatic stress symptoms. The prevalence of alcohol and other substance abuse disorders, in particular methamphetamine addiction, may be of particular concern among people from the working and under classes.

People who have working-class or underclass status may also experience **classism,** a type of prejudice or mistreatment on the basis of a person's social class. Classism can include individual actions such as social snubs, in which people are excluded from gatherings, or making jokes at the expense of people who are poor or undereducated. When applied at the structural or institutional level, classism is often passive and works to support the status quo. **Structural classism,** for instance, is often at work when jobs are given to family and friends, colleges reserve admission offers for children of alumni, and politicians allow well-financed lobbying efforts to influence their legislative decision making. Individual and structural classism can cause people to feel **marginalized** in society, and both forms of classism have the potential to create real emotional pain or hardship.

The sense of being marginalized, or not valued in society, can generate an array of reactions among people who have working-class or underclass status. Some may draw away from middle- and upper-class structures of society, such as higher education or certain white-collar types of jobs, believing that the goals of these institutions are inconsistent with the working-class or underclass lifestyle and needs. Others may strive to be accepted into these institutions in the hopes that they can attain a higher socioeconomic status for themselves and their families. Just as not all people of a specific ethnic group are alike, not all people who share a socioeconomic status are alike.

Counseling Implications

In order to be most responsive to their clients' needs, professional counselors are encouraged to consider several important points regarding socioeconomic status. First, although socioeconomic status is determined in part by access to resources and relative societal rank, clients' perceptions of themselves and their socioeconomic status are more important than their actual income. For example, first-generation college students who were born in poverty but who later obtain high-status positions in society may retain the lower class perceptions and attitudes of their youth. They may feel out of place in situations that reflect higher class customs, such as cocktail parties, and may feel their current work lacks the integrity of manual labor. Similarly, a secretary who has middle-class status but who works closely for people with higher class status and feels excluded from their lifestyles may feel more anger regarding the situation than someone who has spent his or her life in poverty. Furthermore, clients who experience **generational poverty,** meaning that their family has been in poverty for several generations, may have much more restricted views of their options than those who

experience **situational poverty.** Situational poverty occurs when people become temporarily poor due to life circumstances such as divorce or sudden job loss. Conceptualizing clients' perceptions regarding their socioeconomic status is therefore imperative.

Second, professional counselors need to be responsive to the array of emotions their clients may exhibit related to their socioeconomic class and status. For instance, clients who have experienced classism may feel anger and helplessness regarding their life situations. Furthermore, clients who have working-class or underclass status may have begun to believe the negative stereotypes they have heard about their class. In these cases, they may be experiencing **internalized classism,** in which they feel shame and worthlessness because of their socioeconomic status. Professional counselors often represent middle-class values as a result of their education and experience, regardless of their own socioeconomic status. Therefore, the anger, shame, and potential mistrust clients may feel as a result of their working-class or underclass status may present significant obstacles to the therapeutic relationship. Counselors need to listen to, understand, and validate the various emotions and reactions their clients express.

Third, in order to ensure that their interventions are relevant, professional counselors must assess their clients holistically, taking into consideration the reality of their clients' daily lives. Maslow's (1954) hierarchy of needs suggested that people must first meet their deficiency needs prior to addressing their growth needs. The most basic deficiency needs are physiological needs and safety. In some cases, those who have underclass or working-class status may be forced to spend most of their time attending to these fundamental concerns. Professional counselors who push for self-awareness and insight with these clients, rather than acknowledging and attending to their clients' basic struggles, are providing ineffective service that fails to respect their clients' lives. Similarly, counselors have a responsibility to ensure the services they provide are accessible and affordable. Some counselors offer evening and weekend hours to meet the needs of clients who have inflexible work schedules. Many offer pro bono services or charge based on a sliding scale to serve clients who do not have adequate mental health insurance.

Finally, professional counselors have a responsibility to understand their own social class background and to investigate the stereotypes and beliefs they hold regarding socioeconomic class. Although many believe that the United States is a land of opportunity in which all people can overcome obstacles and succeed, the fact remains that social class divisions exist in all aspects of society. Professional counselors are not immune to societal messages regarding the relative worth of people. Taking time to reflect on their own privileges and economic hardships will enable counselors to understand and respect their clients' experiences better.

The reality of socioeconomic status influences not only the options people have but also the perceptions they have of the world. People's lifestyles, the dreams they have for the future, and their ability to find respite from stress through leisure are all linked to socioeconomic status. Socioeconomic status is, therefore, a critical variable for professional counselors to consider when conceptualizing their clients.

Contributed by A. Renee Staton,
James Madison University,
Harrisonburg, VA

Reference

Maslow, A. (1954). *Motivation and personality.* New York: HarperCollins.

Additional Resources

Constantine, M. (2002). The intersection of race, ethnicity, gender, and social class in counseling: Examining selves in cultural contexts. *Journal of Multicultural Counseling and Development, 30,* 210–215.

Pope-Davis, D. B., & Coleman, H. L. K. (Eds.). (2001). *The intersection of race, class, and gender in multicultural counseling.* Thousand Oaks, CA: Sage.

Solution-Focused Brief Counseling

Solution-focused brief counseling (SFBC) grew in the 1970s out of the strategic therapy orientation at the Mental Research Institute (MRI) in Palo Alto, California. It is a social constructionist approach to counseling, a view that emphasizes that people make their own meaning out of life events. In the solution-focused approach, narratives and language processes are emphasized in understanding clients and helping them change. Clients are the "experts" in their life narratives, and the solution-focused brief counselor enters the relationship as a collaborator and listens with empathy and curiosity and from a perspective of not knowing and not understanding too quickly. Clients construct meaning in life through their interpretive stories. This can be done individually or socially, with socially constructed narratives having greater power.

Steve de Shazer is credited with developing this approach to counseling. He was originally trained at the MRI and then collaborated with Michelle Weiner-Davis on the solution-focused brief approach. Weiner-Davis and Bill O'Hanlon, who was trained by Milton Erickson, also collaborated to expand the solution-focused counseling model. They built on the foundation developed by de Shazer and articulated various solution-focused beliefs. For example, they maintained that change was inevitable and that people could be guided in a self-determined direction. They believed that clients were capable of doing the necessary work and of assuming responsibility for change. In addition, they noticed that counselors and clients got more of whatever was emphasized in counseling, such as problems or solutions.

Walter and Peller (1992) identified five assumptions to guide solution-focused counselors. The first of these assumptions states that constructive change occurs when counselors concentrate on successes. The solution-focused counselor needs to help the client focus on what is already working for the client. The second assumption contends that every problem has exceptions that can lead to solutions. The solution-focused counselor can help clients to realize that their problems do not always occur and to pay attention to what happens when the problems are not present. The third assumption is that small changes can lead to larger changes. A small change in behavior in the right direction leads to changes in others in the clients' environment, as well as in clients. The fourth assumption states that all clients have the ability to solve their problems. Through a process of exposing, detailing, and emphasizing clients' successes, clients are empowered to implement the changes needed to accomplish their goals. The fifth assumption asserts that clients' goals should be stated in positive, active terms, describing what clients want to accomplish. A goal stated in positive and active terms can be measured, allowing clients and solution-focused counselors to identify clearly when it occurs.

De Shazer (1988) and Berg and Miller (1992) proposed three basic rules of SFBC. The rules are "If it ain't broke, don't fix it," "Once you know what works, do more of it," and "If it doesn't work, don't do it again. Do something different" (Berg & Miller, 1992, p. 17). These three practical rules reflect the core beliefs of the solution-focused counseling approach and guide the application of the model.

De Shazer believed that professional counselors do not need to know a problem to help a client solve it. Furthermore, there does not have to be a relationship between the problem and its solution or solutions. Multiple solutions can be considered for a problem. Clients choose their own goals while engaged in counseling. They typically come for counseling focused on problems and on the past or present. The emphasis of solution-focused counseling is on facilitating the discovery of solutions for the future with optimism and hope. Solution-focused counselors engage clients in conversations that facilitate clients' progress toward their goals. Actions are emphasized rather than insight.

Sklare (2005) identified some additional guiding concepts for solution-focused counselors. He recommended that solution-focused counselors avoid analysis of problems and seek information on when the problem does not occur. He advised solution-focused counselors to be efficient with interventions. The counselor should get the most accomplished in the shortest amount of time, seeking solutions that work for the client. Sklare suggested that solution-focused counselors should help their clients to focus on the present and future. The counselor should help clients to identify what has to happen so that they will no longer need counseling. The solution-focused counselor needs to focus on client action rather than client insights, because insights do not offer solutions.

The skills associated with SFBC include listening with empathy, supporting, open-ended questioning, solution-focused questioning including the miracle question, helping clients identify goals, cheerleading, and scaling. Solution-focused counselors use language that emphasizes the discovery of practical and achievable goals. They use language similar to the client's and also use a similar pace and tone as they communicate in an effort to "join" with the client. They ask solution-focused questions that presuppose change and the possibility of multiple solutions. In addition, they ask exception questions, inquiring about times when the problem did not exist or was much less a problem, reminding clients that the problems were not always there.

Solution-focused counselors look for untapped strengths or resources available to clients. They ask scaling questions to help clients gauge change when it occurs, even to a slight degree. When change occurs in the right direction, solution-focused counselors assign positive blame to clients and ask how clients accomplished the desired changes. Solution-focused counselors cheerlead clients' progress and challenge them to continue to move in the direction of desired change. An important tool of SFBC is the miracle question, which is used to help clients change how they view the problem and how they act in response to it.

There has been documented support for use of SFBC with diverse populations. The approach focuses on the client's own frame of reference and on solutions that fit within that frame of reference. The client's own language is used, and the client is viewed as the expert on self and encouraged to build on strengths.

Contributed by Joyce A. DeVoss,
Northern Arizona University at Tucson,
Tucson, AZ

References

Berg, I. K., & Miller, S. (1992). *Working with the problem drinker*. New York: Norton.

de Shazer, S. (1988). *Clues: Investigating solutions in brief therapy*. New York: Norton.

Sklare, G. B. (2005). *Brief counseling that works*. Thousand Oaks, CA: Corwin Press.

Walter, J. L., & Peller, J. E. (1992). *Becoming solution-focused in brief therapy*. New York: Brunner/Mazel.

Additional Resources

de Shazer, S. (1991). *Putting difference to work*. New York: Norton

O'Hanlon, W. H., & Weiner-Davis, M. (1989). *In search of solutions: A new direction in psychotherapy*. New York: Norton.

■ Solution-Focused Brief Counseling Techniques

The basic premise of the **solution-focused brief counseling** approach is that clients prefer to talk and work on solutions in counseling rather than an in-depth exploration and discussion of their problems (de Shazer, 1985, 1988, 1991; O'Hanlon & Weiner-Davis, 2006). When clients express emotions, solution-focused counselors do not highlight them. Instead, they listen carefully to the language clients use and pay attention to the context and behavior associated with their emotions. In addition, solution-focused counselors discourage the use of diagnosis. If they must diagnose, they think about criteria and symptoms in terms of maladaptive solutions (see Solution-Focused Brief Counseling).

Through the use of solution-focused brief counseling techniques, the professional counselor raises two important questions: "How will you know your problem is solved?" "And, how will you know that counseling is finished?" The answers to these questions represent the goals the clients establish for counseling. Solution-focused counselors believe clients are always enacting solutions that vary in degree of effectiveness. Given this assumption, solution-focused counselors strive to use **isomorphic interventions.** De Shazer (1985) introduced this concept as a way to help clients recognize and implement positive solutions to their concerns that fit, or were isomorphic, with their experiences. An example of an isomorphic intervention would be increasing the frequency of a positive solution, such as when a couple reports they tend to "get along" when they eat dinner out as compared with when they eat at home and cook their own food. They claim to eat out once per month. The solution-focused counselor might suggest to them that they consider eating out every other week or that one of them order food from a restaurant and bring it home for both of them to eat. By using such interventions, solution-focused counselors build on their clients' current and previous successes and their strengths in relation to the solution. In addition, solution-focused counselors focus on small steps or incremental steps, as opposed to big steps, in the enactment of the solution. When working with clients to strengthen their solutions, solution-focused counselors want their clients to make slight modifications in what they were already doing well. There are several techniques associated with solution-focused brief counseling, including the yes set, use of questions, exception rule, miracle question, and scaling questions.

Yes Set

For solution-focused counselors, it is critical from the moment they begin to speak with clients that they discern how to communicate effectively an understanding of clients' language and situations (De Jong & Berg, 2001a, 2001b; de Shazer, 1994). What they want to see happen is that clients are nodding their heads in agreement when the counselor speaks. When this occurs, the solution-focused counselor has successfully established what is called a "yes set." Often the **yes set** develops as a result of the counselor focusing on the client's positive behaviors. For example, the counselor might state "that's great" when a client reports she often compliments her husband when he expresses his emotions about their relationship. It is essential the yes set continue during the entire course of counseling (Berg & Reuss, 1998).

Use of Questions

Solution-focused counselors ask what, who, where, when, which, and how questions, not why questions (De Jong & Berg, 2002), to obtain detailed descriptive information about clients' behavior to help with the formulation of clients' strengths and solutions. Why questions are not asked because they often result in explanations rather than descriptions of behavior and situations. Here are some typical questions: (a) What needs to come out of this meeting so that you can say this is helpful? (b) Tell me about the times when the solution is present? What is different then? (c) What has changed, even a little bit, since you made this appointment? and (d) What would your best friend or manager or mother say you are like when you are enacting the solution?

The Exception Rule

The **exception rule** is one of the most important components of the solution-focused approach (De Jong & Berg, 2001a, 2001b; de Shazer, 1991). It states there are always exceptions to the clients' problems and also exceptions to their beliefs that they have never enacted an effective solution. For example, a client wants to stop smoking and says he cannot quit. A solution-focused counselor would ask the client to share his history of not smoking, when he does not smoke, where he is when he is not smoking, whom he is with when he is not smoking, and what he is doing when he is not smoking. These are the exceptions to the problem. Obtaining answers to these questions also provides the client and solution-focused counselor with many rich potential solutions that will help the client understand his problems are not always present.

The Miracle Question

The **miracle question** is also a fundamental component of solution-focused counseling (de Shazer, 1991; Metcalf, 2004; Miller & Berg, 1995). Solution-focused counselors use the miracle question to help clients change how they view the problem and how they act in response to it. Solution-focused counselors introduce this question different ways. In general terms, here is how it is introduced:

> You have told me you have been experiencing some problem. I want you to try something with me. I have a very strange question for you, one you have probably never thought about. Suppose you leave here today and do everything else you need to do. Let's also suppose you get ready for bed and go to sleep. You have a very comfortable sleep. During the night something really amazing happens in your life. While you are sleeping, a miracle happens and the problem you talked with me about today is gone. It is solved! OK, now here is the tricky part. Because the miracle happens while you are sleeping, there is no way for you to know that the miracle did indeed happen. But, when you wake up tomorrow and open your eyes, you realize this miracle did happen. What will be the first small signs you notice in the morning telling you something is different and that a miracle has occurred? What else will you notice?

As the client shares the miracle, the solution-focused counselor responds with genuine excitement and appreciation and seeks additional details about the miracle, as appropriate. Once the client has finished describing all aspects of the behavioral evidence surrounding the miracle, the counselor then moves on to another question: "Are there times when

pieces of the miracle are happening already?" The solution-focused counselor continues to ask the client to elaborate on the situations when parts of the miracle are actually occurring in his or her life. Also, the counselor asks the client to share how it happens that these pieces occur.

Scaling Questions

Following the miracle question, the solution-focused counselor typically asks **scaling questions.** These questions are designed to help the client assess the current situation and also instill hope for change and success in counseling. Here is an example:

> Let's say I have given you a scale. On a scale of 1 to 10, where 1 is *perhaps the worst things have been for you* and 10 is *considering where you would like your life to be,* where do you see yourself today?

The solution-focused counselor would then encourage the client to share a number with him or her between 1 and 10 and to operationalize what that number means to the client. In this model, the scaling question is used to facilitate the client's movement, identify successive steps or goals the clients can take, and motivate and encourage the client.

Once the client shares where she or he is on the scale, then the solution-focused counselor asks some follow-up questions, such as the following:

> You see yourself or your family at a 4. OK, this is good. What will be different as you begin to see yourself or your family at a 5? What small step can you take to get to a 5? As you leave here today, what small things will you or your family be doing differently when you are at the next step on the scale? How willing are you to take this small step?

Focusing on Strengths

Solution-focused counselors frequently point out the things their clients are doing well. They compile a list of all their client's successes, strengths, and solutions in relation to the client's stated concern. Also, they construct a theme or pattern that captures different items on this list. Solution-focused counselors share highlights of this list and the themes with their client. This information is presented to the client in a positive and genuine way.

Use of Clues

Sometimes solution-focused counselors offer their clients clues about how they might modify their solution and use solutions more frequently (de Shazer, 1988). Clues are used when the client is not completely able to identify successes, strengths, or solutions. An example might be telling a couple who reports difficulty communicating to think about times in their lives when they were able to communicate effectively with other people such as their teenage friends or coworkers.

Use of Metaphors

There are also times that solution-focused counselors use metaphors. A **metaphor** takes the client's information and places it into some meaningful story to which the client can relate. For example, a client might tell a solution-focused counselor he cannot seem to understand why he is depressed. He shares with the counselor many different reasons, but he cannot put all the pieces together. The client also tells the counselor he is an architect. One metaphor the solution-focused counselor could use is a blueprint. This is sort of a map an architect develops when designing something. The solution-focused counselor might tell the client that

> he has many pieces of a blueprint concerning his depression, but he has not found the right picture as yet that captures the design. Just like developing a blueprint, the pieces will slowly come together. It is just a matter of time.

Homework

Typically, the solution-focused counselor gives the client **homework** at the end of each session. Often, the homework is an extension of what the client is already doing well. The homework task is isomorphic with the client's reported solutions. In other words, the homework represents something slightly different than what the client is already doing. For example, if a client reported that when he was depressed during the week, he sometimes took a walk and this seemed to help, the counselor would encourage the client either to think about other times he could go for a walk or to take a walk at least one more time during the week when feeling depressed.

There are other strategies that solution-focused counselors use; however, the strategies discussed in this entry represent the major techniques used by counselors who are guided by de Shazer and Berg's solution-focused brief counseling model. Regardless of the solution-focused model, solution-focused counselors strive to implement strategies that empower clients and help them to implement effective solutions.

Contributed by Lawrence H. Gerstein,
Ball State University, Muncie, IN

References

Berg, I. K., & Reuss, N. (1998). *Solutions step-by-step.* New York: Norton.

De Jong, P., & Berg, I. K. (2001a). *Instructor's resource manual for interviewing for solutions.* Pacific Grove, CA: Brooks/Cole.

De Jong, P., & Berg, I. K. (2001b). *Learner's workbook for interviewing for solutions.* Pacific Grove, CA: Brooks/Cole.

De Jong, P., & Berg, I. K. (2002). *Interviewing for solutions* (2nd ed.). Pacific Grove, CA: Brooks/Cole.

de Shazer, S. (1985). *Keys to solution in brief therapy.* New York: Norton.

de Shazer, S. (1988). *Clues: Investigating solutions in brief therapy.* New York: Norton.

de Shazer, S. (1991). *Putting difference to work.* New York: Norton.

de Shazer, S. (1994). *Words were originally magic.* New York: Norton.

Metcalf, L. (2004). *The miracle question: Answer it and change your life.* Bethel, CT: Crown House.

Miller, S., & Berg, I. K. (1995). *The miracle method: A radically new approach to problem drinking.* New York: Norton.

O'Hanlon, W. H., & Weiner-Davis, M. (2006). *In search of solutions: A new direction in psychotherapy* (2nd ed.). New York: Norton.

Additional Resources

Berg, I. K., & Szabo, P. (2005). *Brief coaching for lasting solutions.* New York: Norton.

Guterman, J. T. (2006). *Mastering the art of solution-focused counseling.* Alexandria, VA: American Counseling Association.

■ Somatoform Disorders

The **somatoform disorders** are a group of mental disturbances characterized by physical complaints not otherwise accounted for by a general medical condition, the effects of a substance, or another mental disorder. In these disorders, psychological distress is often manifested through physical symptomatology (e.g., pain, aches, nausea, dizziness, soreness, or other physical complaints/impairments).

Recognizing somatoform disorders and treating them prove challenging because patients often have long histories of physical complaints with unsuccessful medical treatments authorized by multiple providers. Patients who have somatoform disorders often create significant problems for health care systems due to overuse of medical services and resources. Misdiagnosis of this disorder also creates concerns for patients whose genuine maladies may remain undiagnosed and untreated.

In order to meet diagnostic criteria for a somatoform disorder, physical symptoms must be serious enough to cause significant emotional distress and create disruption in social and/or occupational functioning. A diagnosis of a somatoform disorder implies that psychological factors contribute to symptom onset, severity, and duration. It is important to note that the unexplained symptoms in somatoform disorders are not intentionally produced or feigned by the patient. Somatoform disorders classified in the *Diagnostic and Statistical Manual of Mental Disorders* (4th ed., text rev.; American Psychiatric Association [APA], 2000) include somatization disorder, conversion disorder, pain disorder, hypochondriasis, and body dysmorphic disorder.

Somatization disorder, historically known as hysteria or Briquet's syndrome (after the French physician Paul Briquet), is a psychiatric condition applied to individuals who persistently complain of recurring, multiple-site physical ailments that have no identifiable physical origin. Symptoms include combinations of the following somatic complaints:

pain, gastrointestinal symptoms other than pain, nausea and abdominal bloating, at least one sexual or reproductive symptom other than pain, and at least one nonpain symptom suggestive of a neurological condition (APA, 2000). The complaints, which begin before age 30 years, extend over the course of several years and lack full explanation by the person's medical history. Although somatization disorders rarely remit completely, antidepressants and cognitive–behavioral therapy have shown to be helpful treatments.

Conversion disorder, once referred to as hysterical neurosis or wandering uterus, is a condition in which physical symptoms occur in the absence of an identifiable medical condition and are thought to stem from underlying emotional conflicts or severe stressors (e.g., stress, trauma). The symptoms of conversion disorder include paralysis, loss of neurological function, and loss of motor or sensory function (e.g., inability to walk, difficulty swallowing, double vision, blindness, deafness, pseudo-seizures, inability to speak, and hallucinations; APA, 2000). Typical onset occurs between adolescence and early adulthood but may appear at any age. Phillips (2001) stated that the best course of treatment includes collaboration between the primary care physician, internist, neurologist, and professional counselor using the following effective therapeutic techniques: hypnosis, biofeedback, neurofeedback, and relaxation training.

Pain disorder, defined by the presence of severe pain as the focal point of the patient's concern, is characterized by the following essential features: (a) significant distress or impairment; (b) associated with psychological factors; (c) not intentionally produced or contrived; and (d) not better accounted for by another medical or psychological explanation. Physical ailments (e.g., chronic headaches, back problems, arthritis, muscle aches and cramps, or pelvic pain) result in a variety of impairments, including inability to work or attend school, relational problems, increased need for medical attention, and substantial use of medication. Pain disorder seems to be more common in older adults, and the gender ratio is a female-to-male ratio of 2:1 (APA, 2000).

In some cases, the patient's pain appears to be largely due to underlying psychological factors, but in other cases, the pain is derived from a medical condition as well as the patient's mental status. Pain disorder does not mean that the individual lacks a biological reason for pain; it suggests that there are psychological factors that most likely contributed to the onset, severity, maintenance, or exacerbation of the pain. In addition, the individual's pain may be worse in association with life events, stress, or internal emotional conflicts. Effective interventions for individuals with pain disorder include group therapy; support groups; cognitive–behavioral therapy; or even the use of alternative therapies, including acupuncture, hydrotherapy, therapeutic massage, meditation, botanical medicine, and homeopathic treatment.

Hypochondriasis, otherwise known as health anxiety/health phobia, refers to an excessive preoccupation or worry about having a serious illness or disease when an illness or disease is nonexistent. The condition persists even after a physician has provided medical evaluation and reassurance

that there is no underlying medical basis for the patient's concerns about the symptoms. This occurs because the individual doubts and questions the medical advice sought from medical professionals. Hypochondriasis is often characterized by fears that minor bodily symptoms may indicate a serious illness, thus warranting constant self-examination and diagnosis, as well as a preoccupation with one's body (APA, 2000). Impairment to quality of life occurs because hypochondriacs often require continual reassurances from doctors, family members, or friends and often become preoccupied with the scheduling of multiple medical appointments ("doctor shopping"), consulting medical books, and researching the Internet to find a medical diagnosis. Previously thought to be untreatable, recent studies show that cognitive–behavioral therapy and serotonin reuptake inhibitors provide a means for effective treatment of hypochondriasis.

Body dysmorphic disorder (BDD) is extremely common in clinical populations, especially those in dermatology (12%) or cosmetic surgery (15%) settings (Phillips, 2005). Also known as beauty hypochondria or an intense fear of being ugly, BDD, called dysmorphophobia by European psychiatrist Enrico Morselli more than 100 years ago, is characterized by a preoccupation with an imagined or slight defect in appearance that causes mild to severe distress in all areas of functioning.

The onset of the disorder usually occurs in adolescence or early adulthood, which are developmental stages when appearance plays a major role. Although preoccupations with appearance usually involve facial features (e.g., skin, nose, acne, or scarring) or hair concerns (e.g., excessive, thinning, baldness), any body part or even multiple body parts can be involved in the obsession. Common behaviors associated with BDD include skin picking, excessive grooming, camouflaging (e.g., hiding the flaw with clothing, makeup, hair), excessive checking of the perceived flaw, reassurance-seeking behaviors, self-surgery, or the seeking of multiple dermatologic or cosmetic surgery treatments to "fix" the flaw (APA, 2000). Individuals with BDD often seek treatment for secondary symptoms (e.g., depression, anxiety, insomnia, social phobia) instead of the BDD due to an intense fear of being labeled vain or of having a trivial concern. People with BDD experience the disorder as a physical problem (e.g., "My nose is large and crooked, I can get a rhinoplasty") that can be fixed through exhaustive surgeries and cosmetic treatments rather than viewing it as a psychiatric condition. Research confirms that prevalence rates and appearance concerns are similar across all cultures, and the disorder is not limited to Western cultures.

Contributed by Ashlea R. Worrell,
St. Mary's University, San Antonio, TX,
and Suzanne D. Mudge,
Our Lady of the Lake University,
San Antonio, TX

References

American Psychiatric Association. (2000). *Diagnostic and statistical manual of mental disorders* (4th ed., text rev.). Washington, DC: Author.

Phillips, K. A. (2001). *Somatoform and factitious disorders.* Washington, DC: American Psychiatric Publishing.

Phillips, K. A. (2005). *The broken mirror.* New York: Oxford University Press.

■ Special Education

Special education is instruction that is designed to provide students who have disabilities with an education in a format that recognizes the learning needs of the student and the approach or format that will make instruction accessible to the student. In the United States, the standards for the provision of special education are established by federal law. The **Education for All Handicapped Children Act** (Public Law 94-142), which was enacted in 1975 and became effective in 1977, provided for the first time a national guarantee of a free and appropriate public education for all eligible school-age students with disabilities whose disability affects educational performance. This law, now called the **Individuals With Disabilities Education Improvement Act (IDEA),** was most recently amended in 2004. This set of amendments was the sixth time the act has been amended since its initial passage. Each of these enactments added particular requirements to the law, but IDEA has six major requirements that are the foundation for special education policy and practice and that have remained consistent since the law was passed: identification, evaluation, individualized education, education in the least restrictive environment, parental participation, and due process.

Identification

IDEA requires that public agencies identify all eligible children in their jurisdictions. This is known as **child find.** All eligible children, including those who have the most severe disabilities such as children who are hospitalized or institutionalized, are to be identified and receive special education programs and services. This is often referred to as the **"zero reject principle."**

Evaluation

IDEA requires that each child identified as potentially eligible for special education programs and services receive a multidisciplinary, nondiscriminatory evaluation. This **evaluation** consists of a series of assessments that are selected by an evaluation team and that are based on the individually identified strengths and needs of the child. The child's parents or guardians are part of the evaluation team, participate in designing the evaluation, and must consent to the particular assessments. If the parents or guardians do not consent, the public agency may seek an order from a hearing officer allowing it to conduct the assessments. The assessments include an educational assessment and may include assessments in related-services areas. IDEA identifies 16 specific **related services:** audiology, counseling services, early identification and assessment of disabilities in children, interpreting services, medical services, occupational therapy, orientation and mobility services, parent counseling and training, physical therapy, psychological services, recreation, rehabilitation counseling, school nurse services, social work

services, speech pathology, and transportation. The evaluation team can request other assessments, such as a psychiatric assessment, if the members of the team think additional assessments are necessary for determining the educational needs of the child.

Evaluation team members review the assessments and decide whether the child has a disability that affects educational performance. If they decide the child's disability affects educational performance, the student is found eligible for special education and related services. IDEA defines special education as instruction, instruction in physical education, speech–language pathology or any other related service if the service is considered special education under state standards, travel, training, and vocational education. The child must have a disability that affects educational performance to meet the IDEA requirements. Related services alone are not sufficient to meet the requirements.

An eligible child is placed in one of 13 disability categories: autism, deaf–blindness, deafness, developmental delay (for children ages 3 to 9), hearing impairment, mental retardation, multiple disabilities, orthopedic impairment, other health impairment (including attention-deficit/hyperactivity disorder), specific learning disability, speech or language impairment, traumatic brain injury, and visual impairment. IDEA requires a reevaluation be conducted every 3 years to determine whether the student remains eligible for special education unless a team determines it is not necessary to conduct the reevaluation.

Individualized Education

IDEA requires that all eligible children with disabilities between the ages of 3 and 21 years receive a **free, appropriate, public education,** commonly referred to as a **FAPE.** Each eligible child is entitled to special education and related services selected to address individual educational needs. A team, including the child' parent or parents, develops an **individualized education program (IEP)** designed to address the child's identified needs. The IEP defines FAPE for that particular child. The team is composed of the child's parent or parents, at least one regular education teacher of the child, at least one special education teacher of the child, a representative of the school system who has supervisory authority and knows about curriculum and resources, an individual who can interpret evaluation results, others who have knowledge of the child, and the child with a disability, whenever appropriate. Children ages 16 years and older are to receive transition services designed to address their post–high goals and must be invited to the IEP meeting along with representatives of agencies that will be providing services after the child exits the school system, if consent is obtained. The team that develops the IEP is often the same team that determines the student's eligibility for special education and related services. Each IEP must include the following points according to the reauthorization statute of the IDEA (34 C.F.R. §300.320):

1. A statement of the child's present levels of academic and functional performance;

2. A statement of measurable annual academic and functional goals;

3. A description of how the child's progress toward meeting the goals will be measured and when periodic reports on the child's progress will be provided;

4. A statement of the special education and related services and supplementary aids and services, based on peer-reviewed research, to be provided the child or on the child's behalf and a statement of the program modifications or supports for school personnel. Both these statements are to address how these factors will enable the child to advance toward attaining the goals, make progress in the general education curriculum, participate in extracurricular and nonacademic activities, and be educated and participate in activities with other children, including those who do not have disabilities;

5. A statement of the extent, if any, the child will not participate with children without disabilities in regular classes and in activities;

6. A statement of any individual accommodations necessary to measure the academic achievement and functional performance of the child on state and district assessments, including whether the child must take an alternate assessment, and if so, why;

7. Beginning date of the identified programs and services, as well as the frequency, location, and duration of the services;

8. Beginning with the first IEP in effect when the child turns 16 years, postsecondary goals based on assessments related to training; education; employment; and, if appropriate, independent living skills as well as the services needed to assist the child in reaching those goals;

9. Beginning 1 year prior to the child's reaching the age of majority under state law, a statement that the child has been informed of the rights that will transfer to the student upon reaching the age of majority, if any.

Once the child's parent or parents consent to the initial provision of IEP programs and services, the services must be initiated. Unlike consent for evaluation, public agencies may not seek permission to initiate special education services from a hearing officer if a parent fails to consent. In each ensuing year, an IEP team meets, reviews the student's progress, and develops a new IEP, unless the team determines the child is no longer eligible for services and dismisses the child from special education using the required process.

Education in the Least Restrictive Environment

Once an IEP is developed, a team must determine the student's placement. The team making the placement decision is usually the same team that develops the child's IEP. The placement decision is to be based on the child's IEP and is to be in the school the child would attend if the student did not have a disability, unless the IEP requires some alternative placement. A child is not to be removed from the regular education classroom solely because of the need for modifications in the general education curriculum.

IDEA requires placement in the **least restrictive environment** appropriate to the particular child. IDEA supports education in the regular education classroom whenever possible. Children with disabilities are to be educated with children who are not disabled to the maximum extent appropriate and are to participate in extracurricular and noneducational activities with children who do not have disabilities whenever possible. Each public agency must provide a continuum of placements ranging from the least restrictive to the most restrictive (e.g., regular classes, special classes, special schools, home instruction, and instruction in hospitals and institutions). Supplementary services such as resource rooms and itinerant services must be provided to support instruction in regular classes.

Parental Participation

IDEA conceptualizes parents as equal participants in the special education process. They are members of the evaluation team, the IEP team, and the placement team. IDEA includes requirements designed to encourage parent participation in the process, including providing the parent or parents with advance, written notice of meetings; scheduling meetings at mutually convenient times and locations; requiring the public agency to provide interpreters, if needed; requiring teams to make multiple efforts to obtain parent participation before they can meet without a parent; and allowing parents to participate in team meetings through alternative means such as conference calls.

Due Process

IDEA contains multiple procedural safeguards that protect students' and parents' rights and thereby provide **due process,** the protection of the legal rights of students and parents. Due process rights include the following:

1. Parents must be provided the opportunity to inspect all education records.

2. Parents must be provided the opportunity to participate in meetings regarding the child's identification, evaluation, and educational placement as well as the provision of a FAPE to the child.

3. Parents are entitled to participate in any group making placement decisions regarding the child.

4. Parents have the right to obtain an independent educational evaluation at public expense if they disagree with an evaluation obtained by the public agency.

5. Parent-initiated evaluations that are not at public expense must be considered by the public agency.

6. Parents must be provided written notice any time the public agency proposes to or refuses to initiate or change the identification, evaluation, educational placement, or provision of a FAPE.

7. Parents must receive a copy of the procedural safeguards upon initial referral or parent request for evaluation, upon receipt of the first state complaint, upon receipt of the first due process complaint, in accordance with discipline requirements and annually.

8. Mediation must be available to resolve disputes.

9. Parents may file a state complaint. The state educational agency must have procedures for resolving a complaint that a public agency has violated a requirement of Part B within the preceding year. The complaint must include the related facts and a proposed resolution.

10. Parents may file a due process complaint. A **due process complaint** is the initiation of a hearing-based process designed to resolve issues regarding identification, evaluation, educational placement, and provision of FAPE to a child. The complaint must be filed within 2 years and must state the description of the problem and a proposed resolution. Prior to the actual hearing, the parent or parents and relevant members of the IEP team are to participate in a resolution meeting in an effort to resolve the dispute. If they have not resolved the dispute through the resolution meeting, the parties also may choose to participate in mediation prior to the hearing.

Preschool Requirements of IDEA

IDEA includes two sets of educational program requirements for the education of students with disabilities. The first set, Part B, addresses students ages 3 through 21 years. The second set of program requirements, Part C, applies to children from birth through age 2 years. Not all of these program requirements are mandatory unless the state accepts funds for the program. All states currently have accepted these funds so the program requirements apply. Resources for obtaining additional information about both Part B and Part C are provided in the additional resources section.

Contributed by Erin H. Leff,
Baltimore, MD

Additional Resources

Council for Exceptional Children Web site: http://www.cec.sped.org

National Dissemination Center for Children With Disabilities Web site: http://www.nichcy.org

Office of Special Education and Rehabilitative Services, U.S. Department of Education Web site: http://www.ed.gov/about/offices/list/osers/index.html

■ Spiritual Bypass

Spiritual bypass refers to the unhealthy misuse of the spiritual life to avoid dealing with psychological difficulties (Welwood, 2000; Whitfield, 2003). Originally used in the recovery literature by Whitfield, the term became popular in the transpersonal psychology literature and has only recently been discussed in the counseling field (Cashwell, Bentley, & Yarborough, 2007). The premise of spiritual bypass suggests that life difficulties occur at the emotional, cognitive, interpersonal, behavioral, or physical levels or at any combination of these. Spiritual bypass occurs when an individual attempts to bypass the difficulty by misusing his or her spiritual beliefs, practices, or experiences rather than address the struggle at the level at which it occurs. In essence, then, spir-

itual bypass serves an avoidance function; it allows the individual to avoid the often painful and difficult psychological work of healing old wounds.

In the short-term, spiritual bypass might be an adaptive coping strategy. When it becomes a long-term and chronic strategy, however, it is problematic. For example, two people may be highly involved in service to others, behaviors that on the surface seem motivated by compassion and may be grounded in the teachings of their religion. For one of the people, though, these behaviors might be motivated by a pervasive sense of inadequacy and need for approval from others, issues that cannot be resolved solely through service to others. In such a case, these behaviors are a part of spiritual bypass.

An example of spiritual bypass would be a person who has a history of childhood abuse, struggles with anxiety, and self-medicates with alcohol, yet is only willing to consider the substance abuse problem as a lack of faith and relies solely on prayer and involvement in a faith community. Although recognizing powerlessness and surrendering are aspects of many substance abuse treatment programs, it is the failure to look at the self beyond "lack of faith" and address the abuse history and anxiety that makes this scenario an example of spiritual bypass. People in spiritual bypass may approach a professional counselor requesting a psychospiritual intervention process. It is critical that the counselor consider how the counselor might inadvertently support the client's avoidance and work with intention to support the client in working with the underlying issues. In this example, it might be necessary to support the client's perspective at the outset of counseling, but at some point the counselor may need to gently challenge the notion that the only problem is a lack of faith. This might include an assessment of family history, including abuse, and an assessment of current mood states, including anxiety. With the additional information from a more thorough assessment and knowledge of the phenomenon of spiritual bypass, the counselor is more readily equipped to support the client in working at both the spiritual and psychological levels to address these complex issues.

Contributed by Craig S. Cashwell,
The University of North Carolina
at Greensboro, Greensboro, NC

References

Cashwell, C. S., Bentley, D. P., & Yarborough, P. (2007). The only way out is through: The peril of spiritual bypass. *Counseling and Values, 51,* 139–148.

Welwood, J. (2000). *Toward a psychology of awakening: Buddhism, psychotherapy, and the path of personal and spiritual transformation.* Boston: Shambhala.

Whitfield, C. (2003). *My recovery: A personal plan for healing.* Deerfield Beach, FL: Health Communications.

Additional Resource

Cashwell, C. S., Myers, J. E., & Shurts, W. M. (2004). Using the development counseling and therapy model to work with a client in spiritual bypass: Some preliminary considerations. *Journal of Counseling & Development, 82,* 403–409.

Spiritual Identity

Spiritual identity is a multidimensional concept that refers to an integrated sense of self in relation to the contexts and meaning of life. Kiesling, Sorrell, Montgomery, and Colwell (2006) defined spiritual identity more precisely as "a persistent sense of self that addresses ultimate questions about the nature, purpose, and meaning of life resulting in behaviors that are consistent with the individual's core values" (p. 1269). Although identity development has long been a topic of interest among psychologists and professional counselors, spiritual identity is emerging as a vital aspect of human development and personal well-being.

Personal identity development is a process through which an individual seeks answers to questions like "Who am I?" "How did I get here?" and "Where am I going?" Many theorists (e.g., Erik Erikson, James Marcia) posit that adolescence is a crucial time for exploring and developing identity. The cognitive and neuropsychological changes that emerge at this time are likely a major factor in young peoples' search for self-understanding. Additional questions often posed during adolescence are "Why am I here?" and "What does my life mean?" These latter questions are reflective of the active attempt of individuals to understand the meaning and purpose in life. This search for meaning often continues throughout adulthood as the individual negotiates his or her own developmental changes, including ways of knowing. Quite frequently, it is in the realm of spirituality that a person finds answers to these intangible life questions.

Spirituality is not a new topic in counseling and psychology (see Spirituality in Counseling). In the late 1800s, William James (1902/1999) noted that states of mind included aspects of the spiritual, the material, and the social, thus suggesting that spirituality is an intricate part of an individual's sense of self. Erik Erikson wove spirituality throughout the eight stages of life that make up a part of his psychosocial theory of development. In particular, Erikson's stage of identity development, which occurs during adolescence, includes a search for religious/spiritual ideology that complements, and provides a sense of coherence to, one's inner self. The successful resolution of this "identity crisis" allows the individual to continue on a positive developmental pathway. Expanding on Erikson's theory, James Marcia focused on what he termed *statuses* of identity development. These statuses are very relevant to spiritual identity in that they highlight the need to explore spiritual and religious beliefs and values in order to fully understand and commit to a personal, core set of beliefs that are evident in a person's expression of being. In a stage-structural approach, James Fowler's theory of faith development focuses on the cognitive developmental aspects of meaning-making. Spiritual identity emerges after the individual has consistently organized and reorganized his or her knowledge and understanding of relationships of self to others, to self, and to the ultimate (God).

Also focused on the cognitive developmental aspects of identity, intellectual, and ethical development, **William Perry** (1999) addressed the transformational processes in thinking and metathinking that occur as an individual progresses through a developmental sequence of "positions," beginning with a dualistic understanding of right and wrong to a more relativistic contextual view of the world and eventually emerging in a commitment to a way of life that is consistent with one's worldview. In Perry's scheme, this commitment to relativism is essential to identity development and very salient to an individual's spirituality. Finally, presenting a more theistic view of spiritual identity, Poll and Smith (2003) emphasized the centrality of the divine in an individual's experiences and the uniqueness of the spiritual in the identity process. In their model, spiritual identity necessarily implies a belief in God or a transcendent being. They suggested a developmental progression through several stages of spirituality (preawareness, awakening, recognition, integration) that culminates in spiritual identity evidenced in a relationship with God and others as spiritual beings.

Although each theory focuses on slightly different aspects of spirituality and identity processes, there are common themes across theories and models. All tend to agree that humans actively seek answers to questions of self, self in relation to others, and self in relation to time and context. All refer to making meaning of life in general and personal experience in particular. They imply a universal need for humans to know who they are and why they exist. Spiritual identity, then, is not simply the sum of what is considered spiritual and an individual's current identity status; rather, it is a unique synthesis and integration of an individual's belief in and/or relation to what is held to be sacred, as in a transcendent or ultimate being, and that individual's personal search for meaning in life. Spiritual identity also encompasses the life and religious/spiritual experiences of the individual, which in turn relate to how the individual views the world and the individual's place in it across time and context, a triadic connection with self, others, and the supernatural.

Spiritual identity can be viewed as an aspect of diversity and a natural part of development. It is individually constructed and based on the beliefs and experiences of an individual's own life history. It provides a framework for how a person deals with ultimate life questions and how he or she views the world. Like other facets of diversity, spirituality may be the focal point of an individual's life. Spiritual identity insinuates a level of commitment that may act as a barrier to or a facilitator of effective communication and treatment. Assessment of the spiritual condition of a client can be beneficial to the professional counselor in diagnosing the client's needs and concerns and developing a treatment plan that effectively addresses them.

Much contemporary research has revealed a link between spirituality and health. Health care professionals are becoming more and more aware of the strong influence that spirituality has on personal well-being. With this in mind, it is only prudent for professional counselors and other health care providers to seek a more thorough understanding of the role that spiritual identity plays in a particular individual's life and to integrate that into a holistic treatment plan. Such a plan would acknowledge spirituality as an integral part of human development and psychological well-being and facilitate the individual's ability to recognize and clarify his or her spiritual identity.

Contributed by Mary D. Hancock,
University of West Georgia,
Carrollton, GA

References

James, W. (1999). *The varieties of religious experience.* New York: Random House. (Original work published 1909)

Kiesling, C., Sorrell, G. T., Montgomery, M. J., & Colwell, R. K. (2006). Identity and spirituality: A psychosocial exploration of the sense of spiritual self. *Developmental Psychology, 42,* 1269–1277.

Perry, W. G. (1999). *Forms of intellectual and ethical development in the college years.* San Francisco: Jossey-Bass.

Poll, J. B., & Smith, T. B. (2003). The spiritual self: Toward a conceptualization of spiritual identity development. *Journal of Psychology and Theology, 31,* 129–142.

Additional Resource

Roehlkepartain, E. C., King, P. E., Wagener, L., & Benson, P. L. (Eds.). (2006). *The handbook of spiritual development in childhood and adolescence.* Thousand Oaks, CA: Sage.

■ Spirituality in Counseling

Spirituality has become a major focus in counseling. Theologians suggest this is due to the emptiness experienced when individuals try to evaluate meaning in life through counseling that does not access the individual's spiritual dimension. Using spirituality in counseling can help the individual develop a higher purpose and personal meaning in life. In addition, spirituality helps clients to emphasize meaningfulness in their day-to-day experiences and personal development. Through the integration of various elements, including psychological and biological, the spiritual focus rounds out the possibility for individual development and the transcendence of the daily-life experiences. In addition, the relationship between health and spirituality has been well documented and indicates that individuals who hold spirituality and religious beliefs are healthier than those who do not.

The definition of spirituality varies but is distinct from religion. Spirituality encompasses the meaningful experiences that may or may not involve a religion and may or may not include transcendence of the material world. It may include a relationship to God or a divine being as well as a relationship to nature, other individuals, or the infinite. It contributes to a sense of completeness and openness to higher levels or infinite realities. As such, it may be considered an essential element of humanness. On the other hand, **religion** is the practice of faith individually or with an organized group and usually includes authority figures, sometimes a hierarchical structure, moral concepts and values, and specific forms of rituals or behaviors. Religion can be an element of spirituality.

Encountering and understanding different worldviews help to broaden the scope of accepted spiritual dimensions. Although most religions focus on a polytheistic (i.e., belief in many gods) or monotheistic (i.e., belief in only one God) component, nontheistic individuals may also experience spirituality. Their nonacceptance of a particular religion does not preclude spiritual meaning from life experiences. Some specific elements of spirituality in religious expression follow. This brief examination touches on practices and beliefs and provides a basis for understanding the counselor's need for perspective when working with various spiritualities.

Buddhism

Buddhism is focused on the attainment of nirvana, a condition in which an individual experiences deep awareness and comprehension of the human experience or dilemma, reducing the stressful components of life. Through meditative practices, elements of individual self-knowledge are found. Buddhism focuses on the meditative practice and the idea that individuals are illusions. Incorporating the ideas of karma and reincarnation, individuals who practice this faith seem to be nonviolent and have deep patience. Achieving nirvana through meditation, an individual strives to overcome the self and find the spiritual being that the individual is. Parallels and similarities have been noted between Buddhism and counseling and psychology. Similar to Buddhism, Christianity focuses on self-knowledge but also incorporates forgiveness and the promise of grace from God for self-development.

Christianity

Christianity embraces the sovereignty of God and the role of forgiveness in its beliefs. Consequently, sin and forgiveness must be incorporated in the counseling process. Grace, a transforming gift from God, allows individuals to know God and discover the mysteries of God. Creation is also important to Christian believers because God is considered the source and maintainer of existence as well as all truth. Basing counseling on Scripture, especially the New Testament, would help the Christian client to acknowledge God's power to change life and grow in love of others and God. Finding this truth in the midst of problems, the Christian client would seek to understand the message of God and use grace and forgiveness to change and develop solutions and intentions for possible growth. This encourages the development of self-knowledge in relation to God. Confucianism also incorporates the development of the self but accomplishes this through finding self-fulfillment and increasing self-knowledge.

Confucianism

Confucianism is based on perfecting the self through learning. Confucianism is based on perfecting the self through learning, which can encompass many dimensions of development, including moral and cognitive development. Personal interaction with others is the focus of this understanding of harmony and fulfillment. The continual development of self is lifelong and is considered an individual strength. A focus on the power of the person helps to develop self-fulfillment found in the concept of self-cultivation. The enhancement of the morals of an individual becomes a constant effort. This is exemplified in an individual's behaviors and is practiced through a humble stance in life. Similarly, Hinduism focuses on self-development through giving to others.

Hinduism

Hinduism is the oldest of the larger religious affiliations. Although most Hindus live in India, Hinduism is also practiced in other parts of the world. This pantheistic religion states that Brahman, the ultimate reality, is the creator; however, the focus of this religion is not on the deity, but on **karma,** which can be interpreted as "action." Good actions to others will ensure that good will return to the giver here or in the next world. Including reincarnation, this system believes all living creatures are manifestations of Brahman. The basis of the spirituality is that the individual is to strive to transcend the ego and experience the reality of self-identity. Thus, the struggle is to attain unity with Brahman in existence. Focusing on the union, an individual hopes to reach the highest level of development through enlightenment. Meditative practices are considered elemental. Islam expands the meditative element to include fasting and almsgiving.

Islam

Islam, which is considered by Muslims to be the universal expression of the word of God, focuses on surrender to God. Muslims believe that the Prophet Muhammed was God's messenger, and through him God revealed the Qur'un. Included in the practice of this faith are believing that there is only one God, praying daily, sharing wealth because it is considered an act of loaning money to God, fasting, and making a pilgrimage to Mecca during one's life. This pilgrimage involves ritualistic commemorations of the lessons of Abraham. It is worth noting that collectivism is the operant relationship and that personal problems are discussed only within the hierarchical structure of the family. Following prescribed rules promises happiness on earth. Islam advocates forgiveness, kindness, and self-knowledge. Although incorporating political elements, all understanding of the self emerges from the spirituality of Islam. Distress in a client would indicate a tension in the heart or a soul that has been lost and separated from its creator; the individual seeks balance to cure the psychological distress. Knowing that an individual is able to perform evil, he or she must master it and find balance in the self. The same collectivistic element found in Islam is also found in Judaism and contributes to the integration of self-knowledge and union with God.

Judaism

The Jewish religion, or **Judaism,** includes the internalization of the Torah and the Kabbalah, or the force of the Creator. Individuals seek the selflessness of behaviors that maintain a stance of humility. The understanding and wisdom discovered through living in this world, is meant to prepare the individual for life after death. Stigmas may still exist when a person of the Jewish faith, especially an Orthodox Jew, seeks advice. Complexities involved with diverse groups of Jewish faith may arise, although most Jewish clients would seek help from a rabbi. Because the family and community systems are close-knit, seeking help outside the community is not encouraged. In this faith system, counseling would provide restoration for the soul and the self, a union of understanding that yields wholeness. Counseling may serve as a means of self-integration through faith, the source of wholeness. Formerly focusing on the medical model of psychotherapy, the Jewish community now tends toward the spiritual dimension and outside resources. By using the Jewish Bible and other literary elements of Jewish history, the professional counselor is aided in providing treatment. Spiritual distress may be explained by religious ideology. With Frankl's understanding of meaning as a primary motivating force, an individual counseling in the Jewish faith could maintain this break from a psychoanalytic tradition to focus on including the spirituality of the individual who is attempting to make meaning of life experiences to create change—physical, emotional, and spiritual.

Taoism

Unlike the Jewish spirituality, Taoist spirituality seeks self-fulfillment in the humble union of individuals with nature instead of with God. **Taoism** embraces three meanings: the way of ultimate reality, the way of human life, and the way of the universe. It can also be regarded as a pathway and an element that includes all existence—a type of mysterious behavior creating all elements in the world. It is also the power accessed through Doa. The Tao implies that people's actions should be united with nature, the flowing of an individual in a harmonious relationship through openness and humility in the world. There is a great respect for mothers and peaceful existence. Maslow, Jung, and Rogers focused on Tao elements in counseling. Tao is self-transcendent and self-existent. Through great self-discipline and work, an individual is able to transcend mankind. Tao is considered to lie within all mankind and focuses on a morality that is within all. To achieve it, a person must use intense contemplative practice and the knowledge gained through life. Because the Tao is infinite, the interpretation of any experience of Taoism is impossible. Taoism believes that the way an individual acts should be in union with Earth, which is in harmony with heaven and the Tao.

Spirituality and Counseling

Historically, Freud discounted religion, but it is possible to find elements of the spiritual dimension in Jung, Frankl, Erikson, Adler, and Rogers. Jung emphasized the psychological dimension found in spirituality. This relationship to a higher power or higher being addresses the concept of **soul,** or the essence of the individual. Many refer to the relationship as one of authenticity, and in this relationship the true self is envisioned. Spirituality is a natural outgrowth of counseling. Psychology is the study of the soul. The meaning of soul or psyche refers to the existence of the spiritual dimension of individuals. This connection between the body and mind is found in cultures worldwide. Because the search for one's meaning in life and the search for the truth of one's existence (existential meaning) are components of counseling, the need for the incorporation and acceptance of spirituality as a component of counseling can be seen.

The relationship between professional counselor and client is one of care and concern—helping to nurture the development of the individual and the soul. Incorporating spiritual influences in counseling allows the therapist and client to focus on the integration of psychological and spiritual elements of life, enabling the client to define the meaning of life as well as accessing the self. Through recognizing that spirituality transcends a subjective element, the counselor is able to enhance clients' awareness of their spirituality and not limit their experience to only their beliefs or behaviors that are observable. Research is replete with the importance of including spirituality in counseling. Jung (1933), for example, expressed the understanding that individuals were ill due to a loss of religious focus. In recent times, Corey (2006) cited the relevance of integrating spirituality and counseling:

> Spiritual and religious matters are therapeutically relevant, ethically appropriate, and potentially significant topics for the practice of counseling in secular settings. Counselors must be prepared to deal with their clients' issues of the human spirit. Religion and spirituality are often part of the client's problem, but can also be part of the client's solution. Because spiritual and religious values can play a major part in human life, spiritual values should be viewed as a potential resource in therapy rather than as something to be ignored. (p. 117)

Faiver, Ingersoll, O'Brien, and McNally (2001) provided support for the integration of spirituality and counseling based on multicultural concerns, existential components, the mind–body connection, the reality of evil, and the movement of transpersonal psychology that focuses on individual development. The authors indicated that "spirituality is innate to the human experience" (p. 4). Their focus on the use of spiritual rudiments throughout the counseling process helps to illustrate the importance of various spiritual components. "True spirituality results in making people calmer, happier, and more peaceful, and it is a mental attitude that can be practiced at any time" (Corey, 2006, p. 118).

Frame (2003) also focused on the evidence linking spirituality as a strength in the individual that may aid in integrating wholeness. Hall, Dixon, and Mauzey (2004) provided evidence of the benefits of incorporating spirituality in counseling for children in schools and in health care settings as well.

Dimensions of spiritual wellness include hope and experience, freedom of spiritual expression, connectedness, and meaning, among others. The acceptance of suffering and pain, as well as evil, is another factor that manifests in different ways

in various spiritualities. A person should not ignore the relationship of spirituality to improved health of mind and body. The spiritual element is necessary for self-understanding and exploration of values and meaning in life in the transformation of the individual.

Although most counseling approaches include a trusting relationship, collaboration, and encouragement for individual growth, hope is an important element in spirituality. Its presence provides meaning for suffering or sorrow. It is the existence of a possibility and a future that encourages a person to continue pursuing self-fulfillment and meaning in life (Faiver et al., 2001). For some, the existence of hope fortifies their faith.

As counselors attempt to aid clients in integrating their encounters into meaningful experiences, the recognition of the need for incorporating another dimension into the counseling relationship, that of spirituality, is in concert with therapeutic goals. Many different methods of incorporating spirituality are related to the use of specific therapies and, thus, should be examined within the goals and methods of individual therapeutic traditions. Some common techniques may involve the incorporation of prayer and meditation, forgiveness, actions leading to self-fulfillment through giving to others, the explanation of spiritual rituals by the client, and the confession of personal failures or concerns by the client. Recognizing that the common element of self-understanding exists in the spiritual traditions examined, counselors can use the goals and meanings of spiritual practices to enhance client self-understanding.

Contributed by Jocelyn Sherman,
Capella University, Minneapolis, MN

References

Corey, G. (2006). *Integrating spirituality in counseling practice*. Retrieved Aug. 4, 2007, from http://counselingoutfitters. com/vistas/vistas06/vistas06.25.pdf

Faiver, C., Ingersoll, R. E., O'Brien, E., & McNally, C. (2001). *Explorations in counseling and spirituality*. Toronto, Ontario, Canada: Brooks/Cole.

Frame, M. W. (2003) *Integrating religion and spirituality into counseling: A comprehensive approach*. Pacific Grove, CA: Brooks/Cole.

Hall, C. R., Dixon, W. A., & Mauzey, E. D. (2004). Spirituality and religion: Implications for counselors. *Journal of Counseling & Development, 82,* 504–507.

Jung, C. G. (1933). *Modern man in search of a soul*. New York: Harcourt Brace.

Additional Resource

Kollar, C. A. (1997). *Solution-focused pastoral counseling*. Grand Rapids: Zondervan.

■ Split-Plot Design

A **split-plot design** is used in an experiment in which one or more factors or treatments are randomly applied to the whole plot, and then another set of one or more factors or treatments is also applied to random subplots within the whole plot. The design was first developed for use in the field of agriculture, where a large section of land (the whole plot) received a treatment (Factor 1), and a second treatment would be introduced to the smaller subplots within the whole plot (Factor 2).

Although developed in the field of agriculture, split-plot designs can be applied readily to the counseling research process. For example, during the summer vacation, a school offers a free course on SAT preparation to students who will be in the 12th grade in the coming academic term. After reading the literature, the counselor decides the best SAT program for her school would be the Do Well SAT preparation program. Having never had this course before at the school, the counselor wants to know if length of time of the preparation classes affects the outcome of the students' SAT scores. The counselor randomly selects from all students who have signed up for the 5-week SAT preparation course (the whole plot) and assigns the participants to either 45-, 60-, or 90-minute class sessions (the subplots). The counselor trains the three instructors who will teach the SAT course in the use of the Do Well SAT preparation program.

The students take the SAT in October, and the counselor compares the SAT scores of the students who were in each subplot (i.e., the 45-, 60-, or 90-minute classes) to see which class time produced the highest SAT scores. The counselor noticed that the group of students who had 60-minute classes did significantly better than the students in the 45- or 90-minute classes. She also noticed that, in general, the students who had the Do Well SAT preparation course did better than the other students at the school who took the SAT. The counselor may want to repeat the experiment several times to see if the same results occur. This repetition will help to ensure the results are not just by chance.

Split-plot designs are useful in identifying what factors work together to produce the best results. As a general rule, when making decisions about what factors to use in either the whole plot or subplots, variables that are expected to show larger differences are usually best assigned to the whole group. For example, although the teachers used the same SAT preparation program (Do Well) and were all taught how to use the program, variables such as teacher personality, number of years of teaching experience, teaching style, and the teacher's beliefs about how young adults learn best show greater differences than the variable of time, which is a set amount. Therefore, the SAT preparation program would be assigned to the whole plot and class time to the subplots.

Contributed by Kimberly A. M. Richards, HIV/AIDS Counseling Research Group, Centers for Disease Control, Zimbabwe

Additional Resources

Goos, P. (2002). *The optimal design of blocked and split-plot experiments*. New York: Springer.

Polhemus, N. W. (2005). *How to: Analyze a split-plot design using STATGRAPHICS Centurion*. Retrieved June 11, 2007, from www.statgraphics.com/How To Analyze a Split-Plot Design.pdf

Sports Counseling

During the past 2 decades, many efforts have been devoted to sports counseling and the developmental needs and concerns of youth, adolescent, young adult, and adult athletes who may require professional assistance. The professional literature has called increased attention to the counseling needs of athletes, with most articles focusing on college athletes and others focusing on youth sports programs, high school athletes, professional athletes, or recreational and leisure athletes. Sports counseling has emerged as a specialization in the fields of counseling and psychology. The terms *sports counseling* and *athletic counseling* are used interchangeably in this entry to describe this emerging field.

History of Sports Counseling

Counseling athletes, counseling models, and initiatives identifying the needs of athletes preceded the development of preparation programs and has yet to be fully integrated into counselor education programs. It was not until 1985 that competencies for athletic counselors were first outlined in the Association for Counselor Education and Supervision's project Counselors of Tomorrow (Nejedlo, Arredondo, & Benjamin, 1985). The purpose of the project was to develop a visionary model for future counselor educators, supervisors, and counselors to "insure that we were not only maintaining pace with society's development, but also anticipating probable changing needs of our clientele in a society characterized by change" (p. iv).

Athletic counseling (sports counseling) is defined as

> a process which attempts to assist individuals in maximizing their personal, academic, and athletic potential. This [athletic counseling] is accomplished through a proactive, growth-oriented approach that incorporates the principles of counseling, career development, movement science, psychology, and human development. (Nejedlo et al., 1985, p. 9)

Both sports counseling and sports psychology are concerned with the developmental needs of the athlete population and their athletic performance; however, sports counseling focuses on an athlete's psychoemotional needs and difficulties as well as his or her development as an individual, including personal and clinical issues, whereas sports psychology focuses on an athlete's performance enhancement and mental skills training.

Athlete Culture

Although there is not one categorical definition of what is meant by the term *culture,* the athlete population is a subgroup of people with their own culture. "We may still be discussing the same people: those with cultural experiences different from those of White middle-class men of European descent, those with less power to control their lives, and those who experience discrimination in the United States" (Sedlacek, 1996, p. 200). Athletes have faced prejudice and are a group that has been oppressed and discriminated against, much like groups thought of as minority cultures. The athlete population is a group of people who appear to have a unique culture in which norms of behavior and values are well-defined. They spend a great deal of time together, often have common goals generated by their experiences together as athletes, and have a set of experiences in life that differentiate them from others (Cole, 2006; Sedlacek, 1996; Tinsley, 2005).

Moreover, there are subgroups and diversity within groups, as well as diversity between individuals who participate and compete. Racial, ethnic, and religious minorities as well as women differ in their goals and objectives for engaging in sports, and these goals and objectives reflect individual developmental needs. Some athletes from specific cultural groups face racism, sexism, heterosexism, or other types of isms in their sport. Professional, collegiate, high school, and leisure athletes also differ in their developmental needs. Overall, athletes may require assistance from counselors in dealing with career development; psychosocial development; retirement from sport; athletic competition; and, for some, personal clinical issues.

Clinical Issues

Although athletes may face similar developmental challenges encountered by nonathletes, many athletes' difficulties may be manifested by athletic transitions (e.g., sport retirement; coping with injury, or role changes); public scrutiny (e.g., criticism from media and/or fans); athletic achievement (e.g., skill mastery or performance challenges); identity formation and conflict (e.g., athletic identity development or role foreclosure); alcohol and substance abuse (e.g., using performance enhancing drugs/illegal street drugs or abusing alcohol); interpersonal relationships (e.g., maintaining relationships with teammates, coaches, and peers); career-related concerns (e.g., transitioning from high school to college and college to professional ranks; identifying career interests outside of sports); and/or intellectual, physical, or interpersonal competence (e.g., navigating negative stereotypes regarding athletes). The psychological and social implications of the aforementioned may result in failure to attend to daily responsibilities and difficulties while working through developmental tasks, such as making major life decisions, cultivating lasting and meaningful relationships, and identifying and modifying personal values (Ferrante, Etzel, & Lantz, 1996). Although these concerns may vary from athlete to athlete, many may experience the negative consequences of athletic competition on their overall development; hence, the need for sports counseling services. Specialized counseling for the athlete population is imperative but becomes even more critical when discussing the differences existing between subgroups. In addition, there is a critical need for specialized training for counselors who work with the athlete population.

Multicultural Sports Counseling Competencies

Because athletes are confronted with a myriad of complex demands, stressors, and challenges as a consequence of their involvement in sports, those who work with this population must acquire knowledge and skills beyond basic counselor preparation as well as an acute awareness regarding any perceptions or preconceived notions about this group (Cole, 2006; Nejedlo et al., 1985). Training counselors who are able to address the unique needs of the athlete population, a group not always thought of as a specific and diverse culture, presents major challenges. Like many cultural groups, athletes may be underserved by counseling services.

By extending the principles of multicultural counseling to include the athlete population, counselor educators and supervisors, as well as professional counselors, may be in a better position to receive formalized training, respond to the developmental needs of athletes, and enhance the quality of counseling services they provide to a specific and diverse culture. Thus, multicultural sports counseling competencies have been developed that use language and statements that have been adapted from the Multicultural Counseling Inventory (Sodowsky, Taffe, Gutkin, & Wise, 1994). Multicultural sports counseling competencies, consisting of four dimensions, are defined as the extent to which the counselor has developed and integrated awareness, knowledge, and skills while maintaining a positive counseling relationship necessary to work with the athlete population. (Sodowsky et al., 1994; Tinsley, 2005).

Ethical Issues

Ethical codes for professional organizations have been developed to serve as a guide for helping professionals' practice with clients and to assist in garnering the public's trust by increasing the probability that counselors will not harm their clients and will provide quality service (Kocet, 2006). Currently, there are no specific ethical guidelines for sports counselors or counselors who work with the athlete population; however, those who provide counseling services to the athlete population can use the American Counseling Association's (ACA; 2005) *ACA Code of Ethics,* the Multicultural Counseling Competencies (Arredondo et al., 1996), and the Council for Accreditation of Counseling and Related Educational Programs (2009) Standards to guide professional practice.

Members of the athlete population may experience a number of external and internal stressors and pressures that can affect their ability to perform on and off the playing field, maintain equilibrium between daily functioning and athletics, and transition successfully out of sport competition. Multicultural competent sports counselors recognize these challenges and work with athletes to identify areas of stress and conflict, assess strengths and challenges, and manage multiple relationships. More important, they understand that because the athlete population is a unique and diverse group, members of the population may require additional assistance with obtaining practical life skills.

Contributed by
Karesha (Kaye) Williams Cole,
The Cole Group, LLC,
and Taunya Marie Tinsley,
California University of Pennsylvania,
California, PA

References

American Counseling Association. (2005). *ACA code of ethics*. Alexandria, VA: Author.

Arredondo, P., Toporek, R., Brown, S. P., Jones, J., Locke, D. C., Sanchez, J., et al. (1996). Operationalization of the multicultural counseling competencies. *Journal of Multicultural Counseling and Development, 24,* 42–78.

Cole, K. W. (2006). An examination of school counselors' knowledge and perceptions of recruited student-athletes (Doctoral dissertation, University of Iowa, 2006). *Dissertation Abstracts International, 67,* 2891.

Council for Accreditation of Counseling and Related Educational Programs. (2009). *CACREP accreditation manual: 2009 standards.* Alexandria, VA: Author.

Ferrante, A. P., Etzel, E. F., & Lantz, C. (Eds.). (1996). *Counseling college student-athletes: Issues and interventions.* Morgantown, WV: Fitness Information Technology.

Kocet, M. M. (2006). Ethical challenges in a complex world: Highlights of the 2005 *ACA code of ethics. Journal of Counseling & Development, 84,* 228–234.

Nejedlo, R. J., Arredondo, P., & Benjamin, L. (1985). *Imagine: A visionary model for the counselors of tomorrow.* DeKalb, IL: George's Printing.

Sedlacek, W. E. (1996). An empirical method of determining nontraditional group status. *Measurement and Evaluation in Counseling and Development, 28,* 200–210.

Sodowsky, G. R., Taffe, R. C., Gutkin, T. B., & Wise, S. L. (1994). Development of the Multicultural Counseling Inventory: A self-report measure of multicultural competencies. *Journal of Counseling Psychology, 41,* 137–148.

Tinsley, T. (2005). The self-reported multicultural sports counseling competencies among professional school counselors and Play It Smart academic coaches (Doctoral dissertation, Duquesne University, 2005). *Dissertation Abstracts International, 66,* 3942.

Additional Resources

Goldberg, A., & Chandler, T. (1995). Sports counseling: Enhancing the development of the high school student athlete. *Journal of Counseling & Development, 74,* 39–44.

Miller, G., & Wooten, R. (1995). Sports counseling: A new counseling specialty area. *Journal of Counseling & Development, 74,* 172–173.

Standard Error of Estimate

A **regression line** is commonly used in attempting to predict the value of a variable based on another known variable or group of variables. For example, if a professional counselor knows how a client or student performs on a test or group of tests, the counselor might be able to make some predictions, based on a regression line, about how the client or student might perform in some other activity, such as a course, work behavior, an academic program, or a certain type of job. The ability to predict performance and other behaviors is clearly important to the work of all counselors. One of the most common tests used for prediction is the SAT. On the basis of a student's performance on the SAT, a professional counselor can make a reasonably good guess about how the student will perform in college. This prediction is based on a regression equation that can be used to create a regression line.

The more accurate the regression line, the greater the confidence in its prediction of performance. The **standard error of estimate** is a statistic that gives a sense of how accurate regression equations are in predicting performance or other kinds of variables. It is computed by subtracting the predicted scores of a regression equation from the actual scores on an outcome variable. By computing the standard deviation of these difference scores, the standard error of estimate is derived. The formula is

$$\sigma_{est} = \sqrt{\frac{\sum (Y-Y')^2}{N}},$$

where Y is the actual score, Y' is the predicted score, and N is the number of scores that were used.

The smaller the standard error of estimate, the more confidence in the accuracy of the regression equation, the regression line, and in any decision that might be based on these predictors. In contrast to the standard error of measurement, which is a measure of confidence in a score on a single test, the standard error of estimate is a measure of confidence in the *prediction* of a score on a test or measure based on a *known* score on a separate test.

The key to understanding the standard error of estimate to think about it as an indicator of the degree of confidence a person can have in a prediction based on a test score or a combination of test scores. An example is a school counselor who is trying to predict how a student will perform in an advanced math course. The counselor knows that the math aptitude test that has been used in the school system has been only marginally successful in predicting grades in the advanced course. In doing some research on math aptitude tests, the counselor discovers that there is a new math aptitude test that has a much lower standard error of estimate for advanced math courses than the one that is currently being used. Armed with knowledge about the standard error of estimates, the counselor correctly decides that it is in the student's best interest to use the new aptitude test because it has been shown to be the better predictor.

Contribution by Charles F. Gressard,
College of William & Mary,
Williamsburg, VA

Additional Resources

Howell, D. C. (2007). *Fundamental statistics for the behavioral sciences* (6th ed.). Belmont, CA: Wadsworth.

Rosenthal, J. A. (2001). *Statistics and data analysis for the helping professions.* Belmont, CA: Wadsworth.

Standard Error of Measurement

The **standard error of measurement (*SEM*)** is a measure of the deviation of an individual's measured score on a particular scale or instrument. *SEM* is an estimate of error in an individual's test score as determined by the reliability of a set of scores. $SEM = SD\sqrt{1 - r_{tt}}$, where *SD* equals standard deviation and r_{tt} equals the reliability of the scores of the group.

Conceptually, repeated scores of an individual are assumed to be normally distributed. The probability that the individual's true score falls between specific scores, called a **confidence interval,** can be estimated by using the properties of the normal curve. There is a 68% probability that the individual's true score lies between +1 *SEM* and –1 *SEM* of the measured score and a 95% chance that the individual's true score lies between +2 *SEM* and –2 *SEM* of the measured score. For example, if Pete's measured IQ score is 85 and the *SEM* of the instrument is 2.5, then an IQ score of 87.5 corresponds to +1 *SEM,* 90 corresponds to +2 *SEM,* 82.5 correspond to –1 *SEM,* and 80 corresponds to –2 *SEM.* Thus, there is a 68% likelihood that Pete's true score falls between 82.5–87.5 (i.e., 85±2.5) and a 95% likelihood that Pete's true score falls between 80–90 (i.e., 85±5).

By using the *SEM* and the properties of the normal distribution, professional counselors can report a score band within which the individual's true score is likely to fall as well as make a statement about the likelihood that it does so. For example, the score band shown here for Pete's score illustrates a 95% confidence interval.

$$80 \rule{2cm}{0.4pt} 85 \rule{2cm}{0.4pt} 90$$

The professional counselor can be 95% confident that Pete's true IQ score lies between an IQ of 80 and an IQ of 90. This approach to reporting an individual's score is more accurate than reporting a single score point because it presents the individual's score in a context that reflects the error in the measurement of the individual's observed score.

Contributed by Betsy J. Page,
Kent State University, Kent, OH

Additional Resources

Anastasi, A., & Urbina, S. (1997). *Psychological testing* (7th ed.). Upper Saddle River, NJ: Prentice Hall.

Drummond, R. J., & Jones, K. D. (2006). *Assessment procedures for counselors and helping professionals* (6th ed.). Upper Saddle River, NJ: Pearson Prentice Hall.

Gregory, R. J. (2007). *Psychological testing: History, principles, and applications* (5th ed.). Boston: Allyn & Bacon.

■Standardization

Standardized tests are designed so that the items, administration, scoring, and interpretations are consistent. The administration and the scoring procedures are predetermined "to ensure that all test takers are given a comparable opportunity to demonstrate" (Joint Committee on Testing Practices, 2004, p. 1) their knowledge and performance in the area being tested As a part of administration procedure, test users should be informed about testing materials, format of questions, and confidentiality of scores.

Standardization, sometimes called **normalizing,** also refers to the conversion of the distribution of scores so that the mean equals zero and the standard deviation equals 1.0 for a particular sample or population (i.e., a *z* score distribution). A number of procedures can be used to standardize the scores on psychological and educational tests, including simple random sampling, stratified sampling, the equipercentile method, anchor norming, and item response theory. The effectiveness of standardization depends on selection of the sample from the sampling frame intended to yield some knowledge about a population of concern, especially for the purposes of statistical inference. Sampling frame has the property that every single element can be identified and be included in the sample. In a **simple random sampling,** each element of the sampling frame has an equal probability of selection. Simple random sampling is rarely used in test standardization because total populations are difficult to identify and to select from randomly; thus, stratified samples are more frequently used in test standardization. A **stratified sampling** process is appropriate if the population is divided into distinct categories. The sampling frame is organized by dividing these categories into separate strata. A sample is then selected from each stratum separately, producing a stratified sample. Stratified sampling methods can be either proportionate or disproportionate. In proportionate sampling, the strata sample sizes are made proportional to the strata population sizes; for example, the male strata needs to represent around 50% of the total sample. In disproportionate sampling, the strata are not sampled according to the population sizes; for example, the cost of data collection may result in disproportionate samples from subgroups.

Equipercentile equating is a common classical procedure and can be used when equivalent groups of students take two forms of the test. Ordinarily, one of the versions is standardized and accepted as a reasonable standard of comparison (Anastasi & Urbina, 1997). In this method, the cumulative distributions of both the forms are plotted, and scores are transformed based on the percentile ranks.

A final method of standardization is **item response theory (IRT).** IRT supposes that examinees' performances can be predicted by their latent trait or ability (Lord, 1980) and operates at the item level. Characteristics of each item, such as item difficulty index and item discrimination index, are usually computed (see Item Analysis).

Procedures for standardization of test questions, directions, conditions of testing, and scoring are needed to make test scores comparable and to ensure, as much as possible, that tests are fair to all test takers.

Contributed by Sachin Jain,
University of Idaho, Coeur D'Alene, ID

References

Anastasi, A., & Urbina, S. (1997). *Psychological testing.* Upper Saddle River, NJ: Prentice Hall.

Joint Committee on Testing Practices. (2004). *Code of fair testing practices in education.* Washington, DC: Author.

Lord, F. M. (1980). *Applications of item response theory to practical testing problems.* Hillsdale, NJ: Erlbaum.

Additional Resources

Gronlund, N. E. (1988). *How to construct achievement tests* (4th ed.). Englewood Cliffs, NJ: Prentice Hall.

Oosterhof, A. (2001). *Classroom applications of educational measurement* (3rd ed.). Columbus, OH: Merrill Prentice Hall.

Standardized Scores

The most widely used grading system applied to scoring classroom tests in schools in the United States is based on the percentage of correct responses (percentage scores), so the scores vary from 0 to 100, where 0 means the student got all the answers wrong, and 100 means the student got all the answers right. Percentage scores are interpreted as criterion-referenced scores because an examiner compares the client's scores to some criterion or standard in order to determine the meaning of the client's score. When others (e.g., parent, a teacher in a different school) not familiar with the specific test look at the score, they still may not know how to judge the student's ability or performance. For example a 10-year-old who earned a 50 on a calculus test may be gifted in mathematics, whereas a 20-year-old who earned a 50 on a simple addition test may be cognitively impaired. The solution to this problem is to create standardized scores.

Standardized scores are norm-referenced scores created by using formulas that take into account the scores obtained by other people in a sample who also took the same test. There are many types of standardized scores, several of which are described later in this entry. If the type of standardized score is known and the population upon which the score is based is known, then a specific numerical value for the standardized score will yield a specific meaning in terms of how the score compares with all the other scores. Four definitions of related concepts help in understanding the various types of standardized scores:

1. The **norm group** or **standardization sample** is a group of people who are given a newly developed test. Their scores are used as a standard for evaluating the performance of future test takers.
2. The **raw score** is a score based on the number of correct responses before any standardization process takes place.
3. The **mean score** is the average of all the scores in a particular set of scores and is, thus, a measure of central tendency.
4. The **standard deviation** is a more complex statistic that measures how widely spread out a particular set of scores is (i.e., a measure of dispersion).

Perhaps the most basic standardized score is the z score. A z **score** can be created by subtracting the mean of the raw score distribution from a specific raw score (the client's raw score) and dividing the result by the standard deviation of the raw scores. A z score distribution has a mean of 0 and a standard deviation of 1. Tables of scores can be found in most statistics textbooks. These tables can be useful in finding what percentage of the population scored in a specific z score range. For example, 68% of the population will have a z score between -1 and $+1$, over 95% will have a z score between -2 and $+2$, and over 99% will have a z score between -3 and $+3$. The z score tables are also used by researchers for testing hypotheses.

T scores are standardized scores that are adjusted to have a mean of 50 and a standard deviation of 10. T scores are easily obtained from z scores by multiplying the z score by 10 and adding 50 to the result. A person whose raw score is equal to the average raw score of the people in the norm group will have a T score of 50 (equivalent to a z score of 0). A person with a T score of 70 (equivalent to a z score of $+2$) scored higher than almost 98% of the norm group, and a person who has a T score of 30 (equivalent to a z score of -2) scored lower than over 97% of the norm group. The Minnesota Multiphasic Personality Inventory–Second Edition (MMPI-2) uses T scores. Whether a given T score is interpreted to be clinically relevant or not is a practical and empirical question. For example, examiners who used the original MMPI were taught that a T score over 70 was clinically significant. For the current test, the MMPI-2, a T score of 65 is considered clinically significant.

In addition to T scores, countless other kinds of standard scores can be constructed from z scores by multiplying the z score by a desired standard deviation and then adding the desired mean. For example, the Wechsler Adult Intelligence Scale–Third Edition (WAIS-III) uses a standardized score called a **deviation IQ score** with a mean of 100 and a standard deviation of 15, which is commonly referred to simply as a "standard score." A score on an IQ test of 100 is average. An IQ score of 130 would be higher than almost 98% of the people of that age.

Another standardized score is the score on the SAT. SAT scores have a mean of 500 and a standard deviation of 100. Of course, a person with an average IQ score of 100 will probably score below 500 on the SAT because the SAT norm group is composed of college-bound high school students as opposed to the norm group for the WAIS-III, which spans the general population and includes some people who are mentally retarded.

A **normal curve equivalent** (NCE) score is a standard score with a mean of 50 and a standard deviation of 21.06, with the lowest possible score being 0 and the highest score being 99. This range of scores looks a great deal like the grades children get on school tests yet means something very different because the NCE scores tell how well a specific person did compared with the norm group.

A **scaled score** is a score that has been standardized to fit a specific numerical range. Scaled scores are found in a variety of fields with a variety of ranges and a variety of norm groups. An example in the field of psychology is the age-adjusted scaled scores that combine to form the IQ scores already described on the WAIS-III. The total IQ score is obtained by combining 11 age-adjusted scaled scores. The age-adjusted scores are converted by the examiner who looks up the raw scores for each of the 11 subtests (e.g., vocabulary, arithmetic, block design, matrix reasoning) in a norm conversion table corresponding to the age of the person who was tested. The age-adjusted scaled scores range from 1 to 19 with a mean of 10 and a standard deviation of 3.

Any type of standard score can be converted to any other type of standard score by using simple arithmetic. The different types are rather arbitrary, being chosen by convention or for the comfort that certain people have with the particular numbers used. All standardized scores have the same meaning relative to their respective means and standard deviations because all are based on the normal curve. Professional counselors, however, need to be very careful not to be lulled into thinking that they know what standardized scores mean about a specific person. In each instance where these scores are used, professional counselors need to know a great deal about the characteristics of the norm group (e.g., age, culture, educational level, race) to ensure that the comparison with the person taking the test is an appropriate one.

Contributed by David P. Sarnoff,
Capella University, Charleston, SC

Additional Resources

Erford, B. T. (Ed.). (2007). *Assessment for counselors*. Boston: Houghton Mifflin/Lahaska Press.

Erford, B. T. (Ed.). (2008). *Research and evaluation in counseling*. Boston: Houghton Mifflin/Lahaska Press.

■ *Standards of Educational and Psychological Testing*

The *Standards for Educational and Psychological Testing* (the *Standards;* American Educational Research Association [AERA], American Psychological Association [APA], & National Council on Measurement in Education [NCME], 1999) is the fourth collaboration in test information among AERA, APA, and NCME. Written for professionals in education, psychology, and employment, the *Standards* provide guidelines for developing, evaluating, and using test instruments and promoting ethical testing practice.

In 1954, APA published *Technical Recommendations for Psychological Tests and Diagnostic Techniques*, a document that focused on technical construction and documentation of psychological tests. The National Education Association published *Technical Recommendations for Achievement Tests* in 1955, written by AERA and the National Council on Measurement Used in Education (NCMUE). The three associations (APA, AERA, & NCME) collaborated on four revisions: *Standards for Educational and Psychological Tests and Manuals* in 1966; *Standards for Educational and Psychological Tests* in 1974; and *Standards for Educational and Psychological Testing* in 1985 and 1999. During the 1985 revision process, which spanned 8 years, the committee reviewed nearly 8,000 pages of comments submitted by 200 individuals and organizations and developed three drafts for review before publishing the 1999 *Standards*. The next revision process began in 2007, with an anticipated publication date of 2013.

Evolving Standards

Each revision reflects expanded knowledge and evolving issues in test development and use. In 1954, each standard was designated as essential, very desirable, or desirable. In 1985, the labels were changed to primary, secondary, and conditional. The practice was discontinued in 1999 with a shift toward compliance as an ethical issue. Although the assignment of levels for test user qualifications (A, B, and C) was discontinued in 1974, these levels continue to be required by some test publishers.

The 1985 *Standards* addressed legal, ethical, and professional areas of assessment that reflected evolving societal issues for both test users and test takers. In 1999, the *Standards* defined fairness in testing in four ways: lack of bias, equitable treatment in the testing process, equality in outcome of testing, and opportunity to learn. The current *Standards* address choice of predictors as a fairness issue, reflecting the growing importance of high-stakes testing.

As early as 1966, the *Standards* considered that types of validity evidence were interrelated. Content validity was reframed as content-related evidence in 1974, reflecting a unitary concept of validity. The 1985 *Standards* supported the concept of the unitary validity concept and defined the traditional tripartite content, criterion-related, and construct validity as convenient labels for kinds of validity evidence rather than different types of validity.

The 1999 *Standards* reflect significant changes that strengthen the unitary concept of validity, and traditional validity terms were omitted from the standards. The *Standards* defined five sources of evidence for validity based on test content, response processes, internal structure, relations to other variables, and consequences of testing. The 1999 *Standards* place a stronger emphasis on the impact of technology on test taking; issues with culture, language, and disabilities; and the use of multiple measures.

Contents

With extensive conceptual changes, the 1999 *Standards* nearly doubled in size to 194 pages with the addition of 103 new standards and expanded background material. Fifteen chapters are organized into three key areas of test development, fairness, and applications. Each chapter begins with an introduction and background material, and comments follow each standard. The *Standards* provide an index and glossary.

In Part 1: Test Construction, Evaluation and Development, six chapters address validity; reliability and errors in measurement; test development and revision; scales, norms, and score comparability; test administration, scoring, and reporting; and supporting documentation for tests. Current issues addressed are measurement error, limitations of test scores, consequential validity for assessment and accountability, and the use of technology in assessment as both an access and a delivery issue.

Four chapters in Part II: Fairness in Testing address fairness in tests and test use, the rights and responsibilities of test takers, testing individuals of diverse linguistic backgrounds, and testing individuals with disabilities. This section was extensively revised, and greater attention given to assessment for subgroups, appropriate accommodations, differential item functioning, and the use of multiple measures to demonstrate competencies.

In Part III: Test Applications, five chapters address the responsibilities of test users, psychological testing and assessment, educational testing and assessment, testing in employment and credentialing, and testing in program evaluation and public policy. Ethical issues focus on the secondary test analysis of test data leading to inappropriate interpretations about students or programs and the use of multiple measures in making educational placement decisions. This section reflects the growing interest in ethical issues in assessment and focuses on the rights and responsibilities of both the test user and taker.

The Future *Standards* Revision Process

A three-member Management Committee comprising one representative from each of the three organizations (i.e., AERA, APA, and NCME) is responsible for overseeing the next revision, appointing committee members, and developing rules for the process. Evolving issues that may be addressed in the next revision process are compliance by test publishers, protection of test takers from inappropriate use of tests, use of test information by secondary test users with inadequate training, use of tests in policy and accountability in federal and state assessments, evolving applications of educational assessments, and cross-referencing standards.

Contributed by Jane Webber,
Seton Hall University, South Orange, NJ

Reference

American Educational Research Association, American Psychological Association, & National Council on Measurement in Education. (1999). *Standards for educational and psychological testing*. Washington, DC: American Psychological Association.

Additional Resources

Camara, W. J. (2006). A historical perspective and current views on the *Standards for Educational and Psychological Testing*. *Educational Measurement, Issues, and Practice, 25,* 35–42.

Eigner, D. R. (2001). Standards for the development and use of tests: The *Standards for Educational and Psychological Testing. European Journal of Psychological Assessment, 17,* 157–163.

Goodwin, L. D., & Leech, N. L. (2003). The meaning of validity in the new *Standards for Educational and Psychological Testing*: Implications for measurement courses. *Measurement and Evaluation in Counseling and Development, 36,* 181–191.

■ Strategic Family Therapy

Strategic family therapy is one of the original systemic approaches established in the 1950s, then developed over the subsequent 3 decades. The name emerged from the work of **Milton Erickson,** in which he proposed that the professional counselor create a subtle alteration in the communication, relational, or behavior processes for the client that would change, thwart, or redirect established and undesirable patterns of action. The term was adapted and the approach developed for family contexts by Gregory Bateson, Jay Haley, Don Jackson, and their colleagues at the Mental Research Institute, Palo Alto, California.

Strategic family therapy views family symptoms and dysfunction as a metaphor, in which errant communication processes become fixed in the family patterns of behavior. The hallmark of the approach involves a series of therapist-initiated directives, termed **paradoxical interventions,** in which the professional counselor instructs the family to increase the symptomatic or dysfunctional behavior. If family members defy the directive and intentionally do not continue in the dysfunctional behavior, they gain control over their problematic patterns. If they comply with the directive and intentionally increase the frequency or degree of family symptoms, they demonstrate that they have control over it and could redirect their foci to reduce it if they choose. Essentially, the professional counselor creates an impasse in which the family has no choice but to change toward more satisfactory relationships.

Strategic family therapy can be understood as evolving through three phases. The first phase involved work at the **Mental Research Institute,** Palo Alto, California, through the leadership of Gregory Bateson, Jay Haley, and Don Jackson. This phase occurred between 1952 and 1967. This era focused on communication research, initially with patients diagnosed with schizophrenia and their families. The dysfunctional family pattern labeled by Gregory Bateson as *double-bind communication* became an important conceptual and therapeutic construct. **Double-bind communication** was believed to be a causal component of schizophrenia. It is the delivery of two incompatible messages such that the receiver has no option except to be wrong. An example could be "Come to dinner right now! . . . with your hands washed!" If a boy, with dirty hands, obeys the first command to come to dinner immediately, he will disobey the second command, and vice versa. Later, another form of a double bind was identified. It was to deliver an impossible message, such as "Good children never disobey their parents." Such conflicting messages create confusion, self-doubt, exasperation, and a dysfunctional response that become integrated into the family system.

The second phase of strategic family therapy is most closely associated with the clinical work and writings of **Jay Haley** and **Cloe Madanes.** Haley's work first came to prominence in Palo Alto, then later with Madanes in Philadelphia and in Washington, DC, starting in the late 1960s through the mid-1990s. During this era, strategic therapy emerged as a major force in therapeutic work with families. Haley and

Madanes focused on the usefulness of a symptom in the family pattern against which strategies, including paradoxical interventions, could be created to shift relational symptoms to functional patterns. Haley emphasized the use of symptoms to maintain power within the system. Madanes emphasized four unmet categories of needs and desires: to control, to love, to be loved, and to reconcile and forgive as the origin of family dysfunction that therapist-directed strategies are intended to rectify.

The third phase was exemplified by the work of clinicians in Milan, Italy, under the leadership of **Maria Selvini Palazzoli** and her associates from 1967 until the early 1980s. The **Milan group** learned from and collaborated with the Palo Alto group in developing strategic ideas and interventions. Their contributions were the emphasis on a therapeutic team of observing and participating therapists and a greater emphasis on gathering history and asking questions. The Milan emphasis was less prescriptive than the strategic approaches developed in the United States, and it often recommended extending the sessions over many months (e.g., one session a month for a year) to institute change more effectively.

The strategic therapist plays a central role in helping family members alter symptoms/problems that bring them to therapy. Families are seen as stuck and lacking the knowledge or resources to start moving again. The therapist, by the use of an intentional intervention or strategy, guides and directs the family toward the desired goal or to the next stage in family life. The specific roles of strategic therapists differ among the Mental Research Institute, Washington, and Milan schools; however, they share a belief in being active and flexible with their family clients. The professional counselor plays an active and directive role, even inserting himself or herself into the family. Because family dysfunction is seen as a communication problem, the solution is the insertion of an intentional, strategic directive that alters the established pattern of discourse and behavior.

Strategic family therapy continues to have a significant presence because it is associated theoretically with many second-generation individual and family therapies currently practiced, such as solution-focused therapy, brief family therapy, and solution-oriented therapy, particularly because of the common theoretical influence of Milton Erickson and the brief short-term model developed and advocated at the Mental Research Institute. Strategic family therapy's chief contributions to family therapy were an emphasis on human psychological functioning as a product of miscommunication within family units and a belief that repair of the problems, initially assumed to be individually based, can be addressed by a reorganization of the communication patterns within the family system. Finally, the strategic family therapy approach emphasized an active role for the professional counselor to initiate change by overcoming homeostatic resistance with creative circuitous paradox or by direct challenge and encouragement.

Contributed by James N. Sells,
Regents University, Virginia Beach, VA

Stress

Coping with **stress** is a fundamental concept in theory, research, and clinical practice in counseling. There are various definitions of stress used in the literature, but the best known was offered by the pioneer researcher on stress, **Hans Selye** (1993), who conceptualized his theory in the 1930s. Selye was one of the first researchers to tie together the idea that stress can have a direct impact on physical and mental illness in the theory called **general adaptation syndrome.** This theory describes a person's short-term and long-term physiological responses to stress. He described three stages of the general adaptation syndrome: the alarm reaction, the stage of resistance, and the stage of exhaustion.

The initial **alarm reaction stage** was seen as an autonomic response of an organism to a demand. **Walter Cannon** (1939) called this stage the flight or fight response. The **flight or fight reaction** is an animal's physiological response of the sympathetic nervous system to a threat, priming the animal for fight or flight. This alarm reaction is not the organism's entire response though, because this state of alarm cannot be maintained indefinitely. The stage of **resistance,** or more aptly the stage of **adaptation,** is characterized by ongoing physiological and psychological attempts to adapt to exposure to the stressor. This stage requires the organism to expend substantial levels of energy. Changes at many levels occur in order to reduce the stressor. If there is not a resolution to the stressor in the resistance stage, the third stage of exhaustion may occur. The stage of **exhaustion** occurs when there is prolonged and severe exposure to the stressor, and the organism has been unable to achieve relief. After exhaustion from an excessively stressful activity, sleep and rest can restore resistance and adaptability very close to previous levels; however, according to the general adaptation syndrome, complete restoration is probably not possible. In addition, because of innate problems within an organism, such as understress, overstress, or psychological mismanagement, the adaptive response can break down or go wrong and lead to potential illness. The most common stress diseases, the so-called **diseases of adaptation,** are peptic ulcers, high blood pressure, and nervous disturbances.

Selye did not regard stress in a purely negative fashion. In fact, he often emphasized that stress was inevitable and a part of life even during joyful moments; however, regardless of whether the demand (i.e., **stressor**) was experienced as negative or positive, the physiology of the organism responds to it. Later researchers distinguished between **eustress** (good) and **distress** (bad).

Seyle's general adaptation syndrome was developed primarily on the basis of physiological models. Later, the notion of cognitive and affective components of stress was added. Stress was further refined to include anticipated events as well as situations that require an individual to engage in adaptation. According to Lazarus and Folkman (1984), stress requires a person to engage in an appraisal process that may result in efforts toward coping with the situation or anticipated event. The word **stressor** is used to represent the cause.

Stress then usually refers to the psychological and physiological responses that result from the stressor. The impact of a stressor may be physiological, such as increased heart rate, increased rate of respiration, clammy hands, and/or perspiration. The impact of the stressor may also be psychological, with various cognitions and affective responses. This definition of stress refers to the responses an individual may make when confronted with a stressor and does not characterize the responses as positive or negative; it is simply the physiological or psychological reaction to the real or anticipated event or situation.

Further conceptualizations of stress resulted in the exploration of the stressors and the effects of the stressors on the individual. These stressors are often categorized into broadband groupings such as daily hassles, daily uplifts, or major life events. Although research on life events has focused attention on the relationship between life changes and their impact on the individual, this relationship is often oversimplified. What are missing from this definition and conceptualization of stress are the coping skills of the individual and the variables moderating the impact of a life event.

Lazarus and Folkman (1991) conceptualized stress in terms of a **person–environment interaction.** Their **theory of transactional stress and coping** has generated many lines of inquiry since its conceptualization and is one of the most comprehensive theories developed explaining the stress process. According to this theory, the impact of a stressor is mediated by the individual's appraisal of the stressor in terms of risk to the person and his or her ability to cope with the situation. The pivotal postulate of their theory is that stress is not inherent either to the environment or to the person but that it results from the ongoing relationship between the environment and the person, in a process they termed *transaction.* "**Transaction** implies a newly created level of abstraction in which the separate person and situation elements are joined together to form a new relational meaning" (Lazarus & Folkman, 1984, p. 294). Transaction is a distinct construct that departs from the construct of interaction. **Interaction** means that the interacting variables—the person and the environment—retain their separate identities.

There are two important implications to be drawn from the concept of transaction. First, the same environment may be interpreted as stressful by one person but not by another. This indicates that most external stimuli cannot be defined in any absolute sense as stressful. What makes the event stressful or not depends on some type of cognitive appraisal by an individual. Second, the same person may interpret the event as stressful on one occasion but not on another. This may be due to changes in physical conditions or changes in psychological states.

A person's efforts to manage the stressor and his or her response to the stressor are called the coping process. Coping is an important mediator of experience that shapes personality development and influences adaptability and resilience in difficult or stressful situations. Lazarus and Folkman (1984) provided a fundamental definition of coping that has met with widespread adoption. **Coping** is continually changing behavioral or cognitive efforts to manage external and internal demands that are perceived as taxing or exceeding an individual's resources. Coping may consist of behaviors and intrapsychic responses designed to overcome, reduce, or tolerate these demands.

The literature on coping theory has further defined specific types of coping responses, or coping dispositions, that vary according to a person's method of dealing with stress. Although researchers differ in their use of the terms, the terms for these popular coping dispositions are *problem-focused* or *task-oriented, emotion-focused,* and *avoidance* coping (Folkman & Moskowitz, 2004). **Problem-focused coping,** also named **task-focused coping,** aims to lessen the effect of the original trigger. **Emotion-focused coping** or **response-directed coping** aims to lessen the heavy impact of the stress response. **Avoidance-directed coping** aims to alter the perception of the stressor cognitively.

The **theory of transactional stress and coping** takes into account preexisting individual factors or mediators that influence cognitive appraisal and subsequent coping responses (Lazarus & Folkman, 1991). The appraisal process can involve such considerations as what individuals think about the situation or themselves, the type of stress, the level of experience with the stressful situation, and the uncertainty about the situation. Folkman and Moskowitz (2004) noted coping strategies are intricately related to an individual's approach to stressful life events. Emotions are an integral part of the coping process. If a stressful encounter has had a successful resolution, positive emotions will predominate, and, conversely if a resolution has had a negative resolution, negative emotions will predominate. Coping styles and strategies mediate between antecedent stressful events and such consequences as anxiety, psychological distress, and somatic complaints. Folkman and Moskowitz emphasized that the changing aspects of individuals' coping behavior are dependent upon their situations. The psychological response to the interplay of the stressor, cognitive appraisal, coping, and mediating factors can be either positive or negative and may be measured in terms of a normal range of affect states or moods.

Initially, conceptualizations of children's and adolescents' coping were derived mainly from adult theories and empirical studies in which the focus was primarily on adult samples; however, growing evidence suggests that coping abilities in children and adolescents may differ from those of adults in some very important ways. Children may be limited in their coping repertoire by cognitive, affective, expressive, or social facets of development and by lack of experience (Skinner & Zimmer-Gembeck, 2007). Children's and adolescents' environments are quite different from adults' environments, particularly because children have less control over circumstances. Children and adolescents are limited by realistic constraints, such as restricted freedom to actively avoid stressors and personal and financial dependence on adults.

Contributed by Carol Klose Smith,
Winona State University,
Winona, MN

References

Cannon, W. B. (1939). *The wisdom of the body.* New York: Norton.

Folkman, S., & Moskowitz, J. T. (2004). Coping: Pitfalls and promise. *Annual Review of Psychology, 55,* 745–774.

Lazarus, R. S., & Folkman, S. (1984). *Stress, appraisal, and coping.* New York: Springer.

Lazarus, R. S., & Folkman, S. (1991). The concept of coping. In A. Monat & R. S. Lazarus (Eds.), *Stress and coping: An anthology* (pp. 189–206). New York: Columbia University Press.

Selye, H. (1993). History of the stress concept. In L. Goldberger & S. Brenznitz (Eds.), *Handbook of stress: Theoretical and clinical aspects* (2nd ed., pp. 7–17). New York: Free Press.

Skinner, E. A., & Zimmer-Gembeck, M. J. (2007). The development of coping. *Annual Review of Psychology, 58,* 119–144.

Additional Resources

de Minzi, M. C. R. (2006). Stress and coping in adolescence. In A. Columbus (Ed.), *Advances in psychology research* (Vol. 45, pp. 67–84). Hauppauge, NY: Nova Science.

Pedersen, P. B. (2006). Knowledge gaps about stress and coping in a multicultural context. In P. T. P. Wong & L. C. J. Wong (Eds.), *Handbook of multicultural perspectives on stress and coping* (pp. 579–595). Dallas, TX: Spring.

■ Structural Family Counseling

Structural family therapy was founded by **Salvador Minuchin,** a child psychiatrist who worked with families in the slums of Wiltwyck, New York. He was convinced that to help persons with mental disorders or families in poverty, the ecosystemic factors surrounding the family and community must be addressed. With Minuchin as the director of the **Philadelphia Child Guidance Clinic** from 1965–1975, family therapy training became a significant counseling discipline. Structural family therapy became a buzzword of family counseling when his classic book *Families and Family Therapy* was published in 1974.

Major Concepts

Structural family therapy is based on systems theory and the cybernetic theory of the 1950s. The **structure** of the family refers to the invisible organized pattern of both verbal and nonverbal interactions and behaviors of a family. In order to ascertain the structure of the family, the counselor must understand the concepts of subsystem and boundary. The family **subsystems** are the subgroup alignments within the family. In a well-functioning family, there are definitive spousal, parental, and sibling subsystems. Each subsystem is shaped by the way family members interact with each other. A well-functioning parental subsystem exercises executive leadership in the family and supports the developmental and individuation needs of its members, especially the sibling subsystem. Subsystems go beyond the nuclear family to encompass multigenerational and societal levels.

To assess the functioning of subsystems, the professional counselor needs to observe the transactional demarcation—or **boundary**—delineating each subsystem. Boundaries are defined by family roles, rules, and communication patterns. A **clear** is semipermeable and allows for feedback loops to take place. Family interaction is not rigid and allows for changes as the family negotiates through life transitions and crises. A family with a clear boundary promotes both autonomy and interdependence among its members. A maladaptive family has a **rigid boundary** that is fused or enmeshed. There is overinvolvement between subsystems, and there are inflexible rules and roles limiting the adaptability of the family in times of stress and crisis. At the other extreme, a family with a **diffused boundary** is often disengaged, with severe emotional cutoffs. The family interaction is often chaotic, and rules and roles are often nebulous.

Assessment

The family counselor needs to make an assessment of the family structure as determined by its subsystems and boundaries. A well-functioning family has boundaries that are clear, with both parents taking the lead as the executive subsystem. In a dysfunctional subsystem, however, there are often cross-generational coalitions and alliances that hinder the normal development of the family members through life transitions and crises. For instance, a mother may align with her son against an absentee father, creating a situation where the father is dethroned from his role and the son becomes "parentified."

Structural family counseling assesses here-and-now interactions through a technique known as **enactment.** The counselor initiates discussion among the family members about the presenting problem or facilitates the family's speaking to each other about the problem. During an enactment, the counselor often disengages from the family and observes family members' behavior as dysfunctional sequences become apparent. The counselor reflects on how long two family members talk without being interrupted. This provides information about boundary issues. Also, do parents triangulate children into their disagreements? This assesses the level of cross-generational coalitions in the family.

A **structural map** enables the professional counselor to see the family dynamics that maintain maladaptive family transactions. The structural map has lines that represent inappropriate boundaries and positioning of the members that represent maladaptive alliances in the subsystem. In Figure 1, Johnnie, a 10th grader, is presented as the identified patient who acts out in school and has been receiving poor grades recently. During an enactment, the mother, Melody, keeps speaking for Johnnie, and together they seemed to present a covert coalition against Mickey, the father. The diffused boundary between mother and son (denoted by the dotted line) and the rigid boundary (denoted by the solid line) of this unhealthy coalition against the father create a dysfunctional family structure.

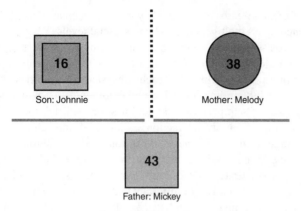

Figure 1. A Structural Map

Key Interventions

Joining is a key therapeutic technique that is significant for the outcome of counseling. Joining refers to the different intensity of the counselor's engagement throughout the counseling process. Close joining describes the way the professional counselor tracks and mirrors the behaviors of the family. The counselor may be in cahoots with the family and become a member of the family system by accommodating to existing styles of interactions. This is important at the initial stages of counseling when trust is being built. At other times, the counselor distances from the family and becomes an observer of the family process and a commentator on it. Often, the counselor may even challenge the family's dysfunctional patterns.

The art of **reframing** relabels a family's description of behaviors and provides a different context in which an equally plausible explanation is made. An escalation of anger can be reframed as a choice made by the members to engage with each other rather than to abandon the family. A difficult child may be reframed as a high-need child. Reframing encourages the family to depathologize any current dysfunctional attitudes or behaviors.

Enactment is an assessment tool, but it is also a platform used to reorganize the structure of the family, called **restructuring.** The counselor may ask family members to explore alternative behaviors to change a rigid boundary. The parental and spousal subsystems may be strengthened by spatial restructuring. For instance, the son is asked to sit next to the professional counselor rather than between the parents. Part of restructuring may include unbalancing a stuck interactional subsystem. The counselor temporarily aligns with a weaker member of the family by blocking the dominating member of the family. Some **microskills techniques** include focusing the task by asking a series of pointed questions, increasing intensity through repetition, changing affect, confirming the family's responses, and strengthening the competencies in the family.

Role of the Professional Counselor

Structural family counselors are experts in family dynamics and process. They take the lead in negotiating change in the family; however, they do it through a gradual process of joining and building therapeutic alliance by carefully listening to the views of every family member. Structural family counselors prefer to see problematic interactions as opposed to simply hearing about them. After making careful assessment of the family structure, the counselors proceed to intervene by restructuring the dysfunctional pattern through empowering the executive parental subsystem.

In the family depicted in Figure 1, the goal of counseling is to disentangle the structural impasse that prevents the family from mobilizing its resources to meet the developmental needs of the son. The professional counselor breaks up the inappropriate mother–child coalition by asking the son to speak for himself rather than have his mother be his voice. The counselor may also use spatial restructuring by inviting the son to move his chair closer to the counselor rather than sitting between his parents. The counselor reestablishes the authority of the parental executive subsystem by asking Mickey to sit closer to his wife, Melody, so that together they can discuss and find ways to resolve the problem presented by their son. The two-step process of strengthening the parental subsystem and empowering the parents to deal with the presenting problem constitutes the essence of structural family counseling.

Contributed by Ben K. Lim, Bethel Seminary San Diego, Bethel University, San Diego, CA

Reference

Minuchin, S. (1974). *Families and family therapy.* Cambridge, MA: Harvard University Press.

Additional Resources

Minuchin, S., & Fishman, H. C. (1981). *Family therapy techniques.* Cambridge, MA: Harvard University Press.

Minuchin, S., Montalvo, B., Guerney, B., Rosman, B., & Schumer, F. (1967). *Families of the slums.* New York: Basic Books.

Minuchin, S., Rosman, B., & Baker, L. (1978). *Psychosomatic families: Anorexia nervosa in context.* Cambridge, MA: Harvard University Press.

■ Substance-Related Disorders

Substance-related disorders represent an inclusive category of the *Diagnostic and Statistical Manual of Mental Disorders* (4th ed., text rev.; *DSM-IV-TR;* American Psychiatric Association [APA], 2000) that describes both physiological and psychological effects of a variety of mood-altering substances and toxins. Such substances include central nervous system (CNS) depressants (e.g., alcohol, antianxiety medications, sleeping medications, narcotic painkillers), CNS stimulants (e.g., amphetamines, caffeine, cocaine, nicotine), hallucinogenic substances (e.g., lysergic acid diethylamide, marijuana, phencyclidine, psilocybin mushrooms), and inhalants (e.g., gasoline, glue, spray paint). A variety of other medications (e.g., antihistamines, antiparkinsonian medications, cardiovascular medications, corticosteroids, antidepressant medications), both prescription and over-the-counter medications, may also lead to substance-related disorders. The substance-related disorder category of the *DSM-IV-TR* does not, however, include problematic behaviors (e.g., pathological gambling, Internet addiction, sex addiction), which share many symptom patterns and features with this category.

Substance use falls on a six-level continuum ranging from abstinence to addiction (Inaba & Cohen, 2000). The first level of use, **abstinence,** refers to the individual who does not consensually use psychoactive substances. The second level, **experimentation,** involves a level of curiosity wherein an individual intentionally exposes herself or himself to a substance with limited negative consequences. **Social or recreational use** is the third level in which an individual seeks out a substance for a desired effect without an established pattern of usage. The fourth level, **habituation,** involves a clearly definable pattern of use that does not affect an individual's life in a negative way. The fifth level, referred to as **drug abuse,** involves problematic, patterned use of a substance despite negative life consequences (e.g., relationship problems, loss of employment related to drug use). The sixth and final level, **addiction,** has the hallmark feature of loss of control. At this level, the individual can no longer control substance usage, and the substance has become the most important thing.

Regarding the clinical treatment of substance-related disorders, primary focus is placed on Levels 5 and 6 of Inaba and Cohen's (2000) continuum. The *DSM-IV-TR* (APA, 2000) refers to these levels collectively as **substance-use disorders.** The first such disorder, **substance abuse,** involves patterned and maladaptive use of a substance that causes clinically significant impairment or distress as demonstrated in one or more of the following avenues: (a) interference with work, school, or household obligations; (b) usage in conjunction with physically hazardous situations (e.g., while driving); (c) recurrent legal problems related to substance use (e.g., public intoxication, driving under the influence); or (d) use of a substance despite having interpersonal problems directly related to the effects of the substance. Individuals meeting the *DSM-IV-TR* criteria for substance abuse, by definition, have not crossed the threshold of addiction. Nonetheless, such individuals often benefit from mental health interventions designed to interrupt the progressive and destructive nature of substance-use disorders.

The second substance-use disorder presented in the *DSM-IV-TR* is **substance dependence.** This category correlates directly with Inaba and Cohen's (2000) sixth and most problematic level, addiction. Symptoms of substance dependence include three or more of the following: (a) tolerance, as demonstrated by a need for increasing amounts of the substance or decreased effects in conjunction with the same amount of a substance; (b) a withdrawal syndrome correlating with substance-use cessation; (c) use of increasing amounts of the substance or use for longer periods of time; (d) unsuccessful attempts at quitting use of the substance despite a genuine desire to quit; (e) a great deal of time spent on securing, using, or recovering from use or effects of the substance; (f) neglect of social, occupational, or recreational activities

and responsibilities due to substance usage; and (g) continued use of the substance despite knowledge that such usage is problematic.

The substance-related disorders section of the *DSM-IV-TR* also includes a section describing **substance-induced disorders.** This section provides typical symptom patterns in conjunction with intoxication and withdrawal from a variety of substances (e.g., alcohol, nicotine, amphetamines). It also provides information designed to assist professional counselors in deducing whether or not symptoms related to delirium, dementia, amnesia, psychosis, mood disorders, anxiety disorders, sexual dysfunction, or sleep disorders are caused by substance usage rather than by other psychological or physiological factors. Such distinctions are crucial in establishing effective treatment interventions for disorders that may be primary or secondary to substance usage.

Contributed by Daniel J. Weigel,
Southeastern Oklahoma State University,
Durant, OK

References

American Psychiatric Association. (2000). *Diagnostic and statistical manual of mental disorders* (4th ed., text rev.) . Washington, DC: Author.

Inaba, D. S., & Cohen, W. E. (2000). *Uppers, downers, all arounders: Physical and mental effects of psychoactive drugs* (5th ed.). Ashland, OR: CNS.

Additional Resource

Lewis, J. A., Dana, R. Q., & Blevins, G. A. (2001). *Substance abuse counseling* (3rd ed.). Pacific Grove, CA: Brooks/Cole.

■ Suicide Assessment

When assessing a client's potential for suicide, clinicians must establish the severity of a client's **suicide lethality;** in other words, how likely is the client to die as a result of suicidal thoughts and behaviors? In a lethality assessment, clinicians place clients on a continuum of suicide lethality ranging from low lethality to high lethality. **Low lethality** is when clients are not suicidal at the time of the assessment or counseling session. Low-to-moderate lethality is when clients are somewhat suicidal but do not possess many risk factors of suicide. **Moderate lethality** is when clients are suicidal and possess several suicide risk factors, such as access to weapons or a previous history of suicide attempts. Moderate-to-high lethality is when clients are determined to commit suicide and may die within 72 hours unless there is an intervention. **High lethality** is when clients are currently in the process of attempting suicide (e.g., have already overdosed on pills, have a gun in hand). High lethality clients will die without intervention and require immediate intervention or hospitalization.

The **clinical interview** is typically seen as the most effective way to assess suicide lethality. Clinicians begin this interview with questions pertaining to suicidal intent (e.g., "Are you thinking of suicide?") and suicide ideation (e.g., "On a scale from 1 to 10, with 1 being *not likely at all* and 10 being *definite,* how likely are you to commit suicide within the next 72 hours?"). Clinicians would also inquire about the method of suicide (e.g., "How are you going to kill yourself?" "How are you thinking of killing yourself?" and "Are the means available?"). Other components of a thorough suicide assessment include the following:

- The degree of emotional pain a person is experiencing, also known as perturbation
- Experienced or perceived loss
- Previous suicide attempts
- Current alcohol or drug use or lack of prescription medication compliance
- Lack of problem-solving abilities
- Inability to see options other than suicide, also known as cognitive constriction
- Five key suicidal emotions: hopelessness, helplessness, worthlessness, loneliness, and depression
- A diagnosis associated with increased risk of suicide (e.g., mood disorders, anxiety disorders, schizophrenia, substance abuse disorders, borderline personality disorders, antisocial personality disorders, and narcissistic personality disorder)
- A history and prevalence of suicide and mental illness in the family
- Significant or accumulative stressors

Clinicians may consider using assessment acronyms to help focus or guide their clinical interview to ensure they are covering all areas of a suicide assessment. For example, in a triage situation or during an intake, clinicians could use the PIMP acronym that stands for assessing the client's suicide Plan, Intent, Means, and Prior attempts. In all other situations, a more thorough suicide assessment acronym is SIMPLE STEPS. The SIMPLE STEPS model assesses the client's:

- **S**uicidality
- **I**deation
- **M**ethod
- **P**ain (Perturbation)
- **L**oss (both perceived and experienced)
- **E**arlier attempts
- **S**ubstance use and misuse
- **T**roubleshooting and problem-solving abilities
- **E**motions and diagnosis
- **P**arental and family history
- **S**tressors

Beyond the clinical interview, standardized paper–pencil tests can also be used for assessing suicide lethality. Such assessments come in four versions. First, specific suicide assessments (e.g., Beck Scale for Suicide Ideation, the Suicidal Ideation Scale, Suicidal Ideation Questionnaire) only assess suicide lethality and ideation. Second, reasons-for-living inventories (e.g., Reasons for Living Inventory, College Student Reasons for Living Inventory, or Brief Reasons for Living Inventory) assess reasons people stay alive and

what is meaningful in their lives. Third, standardized personality tests (e.g., Minnesota Multiphasic Personality Inventory, Millon Clinical Multiaxial Inventory-III) typically have subscales or other indicators related to suicidal ideation. Last, projective techniques (e.g., Thematic Apperception Test, Rotter Incomplete Sentence Blank, Rorschach Inkblot Method, projective drawings) can reveal unconscious or overt feelings of suicide. Prior to using the instruments mentioned in this entry, clinicians must receive appropriate training on administration and interpretation of these instruments.

Before using a clinical interview or another form of suicide assessment tool, it is critical to keep in mind the different warning signs of suicide. A thorough knowledge of how people present with signs of suicide at different developmental levels and stages in life (especially in adolescents and older adulthood) is critical for proper suicide assessment practices. It is also important to remember that comprehensive follow-up measures must take place. Depending on the client's level of lethality, varying levels of care or supervision need to be established (e.g., hospitalization, partial hospitalization, monitoring). Treatment planning, short- and long-term goal development, and the inclusion of additional personnel must also be maintained. No matter if clinicians are just finishing their master's program or are considered to be a seasoned clinician, when assessing suicidal clients, it is always wise to receive supervision or seek consultation.

Contributed by Jason M. McGlothlin
and Rachel M. Hoffman,
Kent State University, Kent, OH

Additional Resources

McGlothlin, J. (2008). *Developing clinical skills in suicide assessment, prevention, and treatment.* Alexandria, VA: American Counseling Association.

McGlothlin, J., Jencius, M., & Baker, S. (2008). *Working with suicidal clients: Skills for counselors and supervisors* [DVD]. Alexandria, VA: American Counseling Association.

■ Suicide Intervention

Suicide is the act of killing oneself. It can either be intentional or unintentional. **Intentional suicides** occur when clients purposefully act to kill themselves via the use of deadly instruments (e.g., guns, hanging) or behaviors (e.g., walking in front of fast-moving, oncoming traffic). **Unintentional suicides** most often occur when clients feign suicide but mistakenly kill themselves. An example of such an unintentional suicide would be a client who intentionally ingests a container of Tylenol in front of a group of friends but expects that help will be summoned; however, if help is significantly delayed or never occurs, the client may ultimately die due to significant organ damage.

Approximately 32,000 individuals in the United States committed suicide in 2002 (National Center for Health Statistics, 2004). This equates to roughly one suicide every 17 minutes. Overall, suicide is the 11th leading cause of U.S. deaths (Centers for Disease Control and Prevention [CDC],

2004). Suicide is the 3rd leading cause of death for persons ages 10 to 24 years (CDC, 2004) and the 2nd leading cause of death for persons ages 25 to 34 years (CDC, 2007).

Although suicides can occur at almost any age, suicide frequency rates are bimodal, and suicides occur in greater numbers toward both ends of the life span; therefore, the highest number of suicides occur in persons 35 years of age and younger and persons 65 years of age and older (CDC, 2006a). Regarding ethnic groups, non-Hispanic Whites (12.9 suicides per 100,000) and American Indian and Alaska Natives (12.4 suicides per 100,000) have the highest U.S. suicide rates (National Institute of Mental Health [NIMH], 2007). The lowest U.S. suicide rates are for non-Hispanic Blacks (5.3 suicides per 100,000), Asian and Pacific Islanders (5.8 suicides per 100,000), and Hispanics (5.9 suicides per 100,000; NIMH, 2007). In regard to sex, males are 4 times more likely to die as a result of suicide than females. Yet, women attempt suicide more frequently than do men (CDC, 2006b).

Many life circumstances may contribute to clients' decisions to attempt and complete suicide. The leading comorbid suicide-related life circumstances include current depressed mood (45%), mental health problems (42%), intimate partner conflict (27%), physical health problems (22%), history of suicide attempts (19%), and alcohol dependence (18%; NIMH, 2007). Usually, no single life event causes clients to end their lives.

Given the frequency of suicides and the number of persons who annually commit suicide, professional counselors should have a general understanding of how to respond to clients presenting with immediate, imminent, and severe suicide risk. What follows is a general description of how to intervene with clients assessed as posing imminent danger to themselves. Professional counselors must adapt this general suicide intervention description so that it meets the immediate needs of suicidal clients and complies with the counselor's state ethical codes and laws.

Involuntary Hospitalization

Clients assessed for suicide risk (see Suicide Assessment) and presenting as an imminent danger require immediate clinical intervention within a least restrictive environment (e.g., psychiatric hospital, respite care, intensive outpatient treatment). Most often persons perceived as an imminent suicide risk will present with focused and sustained suicide intent, active suicidal ideation, and a highly lethal suicide plan. However, each of these factors is not required for imminent risk, and it should be remembered that suicide risk can greatly fluctuate even within a short period of time. Thus, the immediate goal for professional counselors treating clients presenting with imminent suicide risk is to eliminate access to the intended suicide method (e.g., asphyxiation, hanging) or reported suicide instrument (e.g., handgun, prescribed medications) and provide a place of safety until the client's imminent suicide risk has passed or significantly diminished.

Most often, imminent suicide risk requires either voluntary or **involuntary hospitalization.** In cases where clients are assessed as presenting an imminent danger to themselves and are unwilling to enter the hospital voluntarily, the professional counselor must take immediate steps to protect the client. For example, should a client indicate immediate intent to harm himself or herself and leave the counseling session, the professional counselor should contact 911 or the local emergency telephone number. Here, the professional counselor would report her or his professional perceptions that the client is an immediate threat to himself or herself, provide a description of the client, indicate the direction the client was going when last seen, and provide any information related to the suspected suicide plan. Should the 911 operator be unwilling or unable to assist, the operator should be able to direct the professional counselor to the appropriate court or agency charged with authorizing involuntary hospitalization petitions. Depending on the local mental health practice protocols and state laws, this typically requires the professional counselor to go to a local community mental health agency or the county district attorney's office and petition the court for an assessment of the client who is perceived to be suicidal.

Voluntary Hospitalization

Voluntary hospitalization occurs when clients agree to enter a hospital setting to ensure their safety. In the case of a suicidal adult, the professional counselor may say something like the following:

> Jane, I am very concerned about your safety. You report that you have a gun in your car and that you intend to shoot yourself immediately upon leaving my office. Based upon your suicidal statements, your current state of depression, and your previous two serious suicide attempts during the past month, it is my professional opinion that we need to get you to a place of safety for a few days. I know the folks at Restful Mission Hospital. Some of my clients have entered into their Safe and Secure Program and found it quite helpful. Let's call them and get you over there.

Should the client agree, the professional counselor will gather the necessary confidential releases of information, contact the hospital's admissions representative, and provide the referral.

This, however, does not mean that the professional counselor's obligations are complete. Given the client's suicide risk, the professional counselor should not allow the client to be alone or leave the office. Either the professional counselor or another professional should remain with the client until the client is transported to the hospital. During this time, it may be helpful to have the adult client contact two trusted family members, friends, or clergy for hospital transport. Given that the client has voluntarily agreed to enter the hospital, such transportation generally goes smoothly; however, the professional counselor should have the client sign confidential releases of information allowing the professional counselor to speak to the persons making the transfer to the hospital. Specifically, the professional counselor should instruct the transporting persons to ensure that the client is taken directly to the hospital and not left alone. This means that the client is even accompanied to the restroom. Furthermore, the professional counselor will request that the transporting persons contact the counselor once they arrive at the hospital to ensure that the transport has been successful.

In the case of a minor or nonadult student, the situation is slightly different and depends on a number of factors related to state laws and the school district's standardized policies. Again, if the client is assessed as an imminent suicide risk, the minor client should never be left alone or allowed to leave the school counseling office. The parents or legal guardian should be immediately contacted, informed of the professional counselor's perceptions based upon the suicide risk assessment, and asked to meet with the professional counselor and student client. At that meeting, the parents should be informed of the professional counselor's perceptions of imminent suicide risk based on the clinical assessment and the immediate need for hospitalization or treatment referral.

In most cases, parents will appropriately respond and take the child for further psychiatric evaluation or hospitalization. Should the parents be unwilling to do so, however, the professional counselor should inform the parents that (a) the professional counselor continues to perceive the student as an imminent suicide risk and in need of immediate hospitalization, (b) the school district's legal counsel will be contacted to ensure that all is done to protect the child, and (c) Child Protective Services will be contacted to ensure the student's safety.

When there is no imminent suicide risk and the client presents only mild and fleeting suicidal ideation, professional counselors can quickly implement two precautionary safety interventions. First, the professional counselor can help the client create a schedule that ensures daily social interactions with trusted others between scheduled counseling sessions. The intent is to protect against potential isolation, which often can lead to increased suicidal ruminations. In addition, professional counselors can use a **"no-suicide contract."** In this contract, the client agrees to contact a 24-hour helpline or the professional counselor if thoughts of suicide or feelings of intense emotional pain occur. Because a no-suicide contract cannot stop clients from committing suicide, it should only be used when clients are assessed as being lucid and willing to follow through with the agreement.

Contributed by Gerald A. Juhnke,
and Pei-Hsuan Hsieh,
The University of Texas at San Antonio,
San Antonio, TX

References

Centers for Disease Control and Prevention. (2004). Suicide and attempted suicide, *MMWR Weekly, 53*(22), 47. Retrieved June, 1, 2007, from http://www.cdc.gov/mmwr/preview/mmwrhtml/mm5322al.htm

Centers for Disease Control and Prevention. (2006a). Homicides and suicides: National violent death reporting system, United States, 2003–2004. *MMWR Weekly, 55*(26), 721724.

Centers for Disease Control and Prevention. (2006b). *Welcome to WISQARS.* Retrieved September 14, 2007, from http://www.cdc.gov/ncipc/wisqars

Centers for Disease Control and Prevention. (2007). *Health, United States, 2007.* Retrieved August 25, 2008, from http://www.cdc.gov/nchs/hus07.pdf

National Center for Health Statistics. (2004). *Deaths: Final data for 2002* [National Vital Statistics Reports 53(5) October 12, 2004]. Rockville, MD: Author.

National Institute for Mental Health. (2007). *Suicide in the U.S.: Statistics and prevention.* Retrieved December 12, 2007, from www.nimh.nih.gov/health/publications/suicide-in-the-us-statistics-and-prevention.shtml#races

■Supervision

Clinical supervision is widely viewed as a pivotal experience in counselor training. While under supervision, professional counselors apply the skills and theory they learned in didactic courses. Through being supervised, they learn how and when to adapt their approaches to meet the unique needs of diverse clients. Supervision, then, is essentially an educational process. Supervisors use a variety of instructional and experiential methods (e.g., review of audiotapes and videotapes, role plays, modeling, live observation, live supervision, reflection teams) during individual and group sessions with professional counselors. Notably, direct observation of the counselor's work through these methods is critical. Regardless of method and setting, the supervisory relationship is key to supervisor effectiveness and counselor growth.

Prominent models of supervision include Bernard's (1979) discrimination model and developmental models (e.g., Blocher, 1983; Loganbill, Hardy, & Delworth, 1982; Skovholt & Rønnestad, 1992; Stoltenberg, 1981). The **discrimination model** is depicted as a matrix of three **supervisor roles** (i.e., teacher, counselor, and consultant) and four areas of **focus during supervision** (i.e., clinical skills, conceptualization skills, self-awareness, and professional behaviors). Throughout a session, supervisors determine what role and focus area are needed to meet the counselor's learning needs; these may shift several times during one session. The **developmental models,** based in psychosocial and cognitive developmental theories, provide descriptions of how professional counselors learn and behave across the professional life span. Beginning counselors, for example, are characterized by black-and-white thinking and a preoccupation with performing skills correctly; in this situation, more instructional supervision strategies are needed. More advanced counselors are able to recognize the complexity of their clients' lives as well as the counseling process, including dynamics such as transference and countertransference and cultural influences; here, more process-oriented supervision strategies are appropriate.

Although supervisors clearly use their counseling knowledge and skills, clinical supervision is a distinct professional activity with its own standards of practice and ethical guidelines. In contrast to clinical work, supervision also involves evaluation of the counselor, including grades for internship and recommendations for employment and licensure. Given the complexity of supervision practice and the significant ethical and professional responsibilities of the supervisor, supervision training, including supervised supervision, is critical to effective practice, and a supervisor credential (e.g., Approved Clinical Supervisor, National Board for Certified Counselors) is highly recommended.

Contributed by L. DiAnne Borders,
The University of North Carolina at
Greensboro, Greensboro, NC

References

Bernard, J. M. (1979). Supervisor training: A discrimination model. *Counselor Education and Supervision, 19,* 60–68.

Blocher, D. H. (1983). Toward a cognitive developmental approach to counseling supervision. *The Counseling Psychologist, 11*(1), 27–34.

Loganbill, C., Hardy, E., & Delworth, U. (1982). Supervision: A conceptual model. *The Counseling Psychologist, 10*(1), 3–42.

Skovholt, T. M., & Rønnestad, M. H. (1992). Themes in therapist and counselor development. *Journal of Counseling & Development, 70,* 505–515.

Stoltenberg, C. (1981). Approaching supervision from a developmental perspective: The counselor complexity model. *Journal of Counseling Psychology, 28,* 59–65.

Additional Resources

Bernard, J. M., & Goodyear, R. K. (2004). *Fundamentals of clinical supervision* (3rd ed.). Needham Heights, MA: Allyn & Bacon.

Borders, L. D., & Benshoff, J. M. (1999). *Learning to think like a supervisor* [Instructional videotape]. Alexandria, VA: American Counseling Association.

Borders, L. D., & Brown, L. L. (2005). *The new handbook of counseling supervision.* Mahwah, NJ: Lahaska/Erlbaum.

■ Survey Research in Counseling

Survey is a method in which an investigator asks questions of respondents relating to some topic and is one of the most widely used forms of research in counseling. The purpose of surveys or survey questions is to describe attitudes, beliefs, and behaviors of a population. The term *survey research* may be used interchangeably with the terms *surveys, questionnaires, polls, interviews, telephone surveys, Internet surveys,* and *school surveys,* to name a few. Over the past half century, investigators have developed the theory and techniques of survey research. Because it is difficult to construct a survey instrument that yields valid and reliable results, many counseling researchers use questionnaires that either they or others have already used successfully.

Methods for Survey Research

There are many methods of collecting data through surveys, for example, telephone surveys, including computer-assisted telephone interviewing surveys; personal interviews; school evaluation surveys; e-mailed and traditionally mailed questionnaires; and Internet surveys. The definitions, advantages, and disadvantages of each of these methods are presented in Table 1.

Survey Construction

In survey research, variables are often operationalized. The questions may be asked by an interviewer or written down and given to participants for completion. The construction of surveys involves the nature and wording of the questions asked. This may include using questions or statements and choosing open-ended or closed-ended questions and may involve three domains: memory and behavior, attitudes, and demographics.

An **open-ended question** requires respondents to provide their own responses to the question, much like an essay-type question. For example, the respondent may be asked, "What do you feel is the most important contribution of online courses in counseling?" and be provided with a space to write in the answer or request to report it to an interviewer verbally. They are appropriate in an exploratory study in which the lack of theoretical development suggests that the researcher should place few restrictions on respondents' answers. In addition, when researchers cannot predict all the possible answers to a question in advance or when too many possible answers exist to list them all practically, then open-ended questions are appropriate. In a **closed-ended question,** the respondent is asked to select an answer from among a list provided by the researcher. Researchers use closed-ended questions when they can determine all possible, theoretically relevant responses to a question in advance, and the number of possible responses is limited. Closed-ended surveys are very popular because they provide a greater uniformity of responses and are more readily processed than open-ended surveys (Babbie, 2004).

Memory and behavior questions require the respondents to remember something. People may not be lying when they misreport their behaviors. They may not know the answer to the question, but they give it their best guess, trying to be helpful. The same is probably true regarding answers to a questionnaire. This pattern is true for responses to surveys. When people are asked to tell how often they have engaged in mundane behaviors that do not stand out in memory, they are prone to significant error. There are four problems associated with memory questions: (a) Respondents use different strategies to recall events from the recent past and distant past in some cases; (b) when a question involves a time span (e.g., "How many times in the last year have you," respondents may engage in a memory phenomenon called telescoping (i.e., a phenomenon of memory in which events that occurred in the distant past are remembered as having occurred more recently than they actually did); (c) the nature of previous questions affects the responses

Table 1. Methods of Survey Research

Computer-Assisted Telephone Interviewing (CATI) Surveys

Method: A central computer has been programmed to select a telephone number at random and dials it. When the respondent answers the phone, the interviewer introduces the study and asks the first question displayed on the screen. When the respondent answers the question, the interviewer types that answer into the computer terminal. CATIs are increasingly used in academic, counseling, government, and commercial survey studies.

Advantages: High response rate; allow for faster data collection across a broad range of locations and respondents; automatically prepare data for analysis, allowing the researcher to begin analyzing data before the interviewing is complete.

Disadvantages: Limited access to computers for potential respondents; potential difficulty in obtaining telephone numbers; sampling bias among respondents, limiting generalizability of findings; competency of administrator not guaranteed; lack of multilingual interviewers for non-English-speaking respondents may occur; difficulty in obtaining in-depth data due to time constraints; and lack of visual contact eliminates several desirable features characteristic of personal interviews.

E-Mailed Surveys

Method: The researcher sends the survey to respondents via e-mail. Method consists of collecting data through individuals using computer and the Internet.

Advantages: E-mail surveys are fairly straightforward, requiring only that one have access to the e-mail address of all the respondents. It is inexpensive, can be confidential or anonymous, easy to score, standardized items and procedures, rapid access to large numbers of people, and a detailed rich text database for qualitative analysis.

Disadvantages: Researcher needs e-mail lists and addresses. Not everyone has e-mail; response rate may be low; cannot probe, explain, or follow up items; limited to respondents who can read; ethical issues, such as whether there is permission from respondents and whether confidentiality can be protected; may be difficult to obtain a good list of e-mail addresses that are current or well-suited for the survey; possibility of multiple replies from single participant; and sampling bias.

Internet Surveys

Method: The Internet and World Wide Web may be used to collect information and resources on many topics related to education, finances, politics, community issues, and other topics.

Advantages: May be faster, better, cheaper, and easier to conduct than surveys using more traditional telephone or mail methods. Internet surveys have the ability to reach people anywhere in the world. Researchers can access respondents instantly, collect data from respondents on the Internet, create and distribute surveys, collect response data, produce and analyze real-time reports in a fast online environment, create custom Web-based surveys and get rapid results, create surveys using just a Web browser. Web surveys incur virtually no coding or data-entry costs because the data are captured electronically.

Disadvantages: A list of e-mail addresses for the target population should be available. One of the disadvantages is sampling and representativeness. Generally, people who use the Internet tend to be skewed toward those who are more affluent, better educated, and young (e.g., online survey of faculty members in a college). Another problem with online surveys is formatting: Different computer systems can change formatting in unpredictable ways. This problem may discourage people from taking part in Internet surveys; potentially high labor costs for design and programming; and limited access to a computer for some individuals.

Mailed Questionnaires

Method: Questionnaires are designed so that they can be answered without assistance. To be effective, questionnaire items must be clear and unambiguous. Questions should be relevant, short, and direct.

Advantages: Require less time, are less expensive, and permit collection of data from a much larger sample; can be anonymous or confidential; easy to score; typically standardized; and may provide more accurate answers than interviews by minimizing interviewer bias.

Disadvantages: Require the respondents to have a minimal degree of literacy in English that some respondents may not possess; researcher has no opportunity to investigate for more information or evaluate the body language of the respondents; lack of guarantee that the person who should answer the questionnaire is the one who actually does so; and low response rate.

Personal (Face-to-Face) Interviews

Method: The investigator or an assistant reads the questions directly to the respondents and records their answers.

Advantages: Can probe, follow up, and explain questions; high return rate; may be recorded and analyzed.

Disadvantages: Expensive and time consuming; no anonymity; quality of data collection depends heavily on the interviewer; and interviewer falsification can result in the contamination of data.

School Evaluation Surveys

Method: In education, surveys are most commonly used for the collection of data by schools or about schools. Schools conduct surveys to collect certain kinds of information related to the instruction, facilities, or student population. For example, school surveys may examine such variables as public attitudes toward schools, school personnel, curriculum and instruction, physical facilities, and finances.

Advantages: High response rate; allow for faster data collection across a broad range of locations and respondents. They are inexpensive and confidential. Can create custom Web-based surveys and get faster results. School surveys can be used with clients in both public and private sectors to collect data on needs assessment and technical assistance and to assess program outcomes.

Disadvantages: Labor costs for design and programming can be high. Non-English speakers may not be able to complete the survey.

Telephone Surveys

Method: The researcher interviews the respondents by telephone.

Advantages: High response rates, quick data collection; can reach a range of locations and respondents without traveling, saving time and money. The supervisor can control interviewer bias by being present and monitoring from an extension or just listening to the interviewer's question. Non-English-speaking respondents can be handled fairly easily with telephone surveys by using a few multilingual interviewers.

Disadvantages: Respondents may refuse to be interviewed; people may hang up and refuse to answer; problems of answering machines and caller ID; potential language barriers; and sampling bias. All of the visual clues used by the interviewer to assess the respondent's attitudes are missing. Certain visual question materials cannot be used. The telephone interview may result in a sampling bias because some people do not have a telephone or have an unlisted number.

---

to later ones (i.e., people want to appear consistent in their responses so they may use previous answers to help them form responses to new questions); and (d) the nature of alternatives presented in a closed-ended question.

Attitude questions may pose some problems in their development. Generally, respondents have attitudes on many different issues, and they are often willing to share their attitudes with others. There are seven major concerns that researchers should consider: (a) wording of the question (emotionally laden terms can result in answers that are likely to be responses to the wording than to the meaning of the question); (b) order of the questions (the order may affect the responses; the attitudes expressed are highly context dependent); (c) perceptions of the purpose of the interview or questionnaire; (d) sensitivity of the issue being investigated (people may be reluctant to admit to illegal drug use or other behaviors, people may simply ignore the question); (e) nature of the person doing the questioning (e.g., race/ethnicity); (f) distinguishing between attitudes and opinions that respondents already have, as opposed to attitudes that they create when a researcher asks them a question; (g) respondents' positive or negative attitudes about some topic (although it is not always clear how deeply they hold that attitude). Thus, a lot of people may favor gun control laws, but they might not hold that conviction deeply enough to write a letter to their political representatives (Beins, 2004). In addition to the nature of survey questions, it is imperative to take care in the wording of items in order to obtain an accurate assessment of a variable of interest. The following list presents strategies for writing effective survey items:

1. Know what information is needed.
2. Know why each item is needed.
3. Write items that make sense.
4. Define or explain ambiguous terms.
5. Include only items respondents can answer.
6. Focus items on a single topic or idea.
7. Use short questions; do not require a great deal of reading.
8. Word questions as briefly and clearly as possible.
9. Word questions in positive, not negative, terms.
10. Avoid leading questions.
11. Organize items from general to specific.
12. Use examples if item format is unusual.
13. Try to keep items that are clustered on a single page; if a second page is needed, put the response options at the top of that page.
14. If using open-ended items, leave sufficient space for respondents to write their responses.
15. Avoid or carefully word items that are potentially controversial or embarrassing.
16. Subject items to a pretest review of the questionnaire.

Additional Considerations in Survey Research

There are additional considerations in the use of surveys in counseling research. These include development of directions, design and implementation of pilot studies, and response rate concerns and follow-up procedures.

Use of Directions

One of the most important tasks of the researcher is to construct a questionnaire and include precise directions for completing the questionnaire. Precise directions improve the quality of data that questionnaires generate. Some questionnaires may contain questions requiring different kinds of answers. Whenever the format changes, include additional directions.

Pilot Studies

No matter how carefully researchers design a survey instrument such as a questionnaire, there is always a possibility of error, such as an ambiguous question that people cannot answer. A degree of protection against such error is to pretest the questionnaire in a pilot study. Pretesting the questionnaire provides useful information about problems and suggestions for improvement. The participants should be similar to the research participants and possess the ability to critique the questionnaire and make suggestions for improvement. Reviewers can determine the content validity by examining the completeness of the questionnaire (Gay, Mills, & Airasian, 2006).

Response Rate and Follow-Up

One of the problems associated with survey research is **response rate,** the proportion of a sample that completes and returns a questionnaire or agrees to an interview. With mailed questionnaires, there is typically no personal pressure, and people may feel freer to refuse. This can result in many nonreturns, or people who refuse to complete and return the questionnaires. Response rates for mailed questionnaires vary considerably, from an unacceptable 20% to levels of 60% to 75%. With interviews, response rates are very high, up to 90%, because people are reluctant to refuse a face-to-face request for cooperation. A response rate of 50% is adequate for analysis and reporting, a response rate of 60% is good, and a response rate of 70% is very good. These percentages are only rough guides. A properly constructed cover letter can increase the response rate. Every mailed questionnaire must be accompanied by a cover letter that explains what is being asked of the respondents and why. The letter should be neat, brief, and addressed specifically to the individual person. Recipients want to know who is seeking the information they are asked to provide; research indicates that knowledge of the sponsoring organization influences the response rate (Rea & Parker, 1992).

Not everyone to whom a questionnaire is sent is going to return it. Some recipients will have no intention of returning it. Follow-up activities can improve response rates and can include sending out a reminder postcard or letter encouraging the participants to take part in the survey or sending a new copy of the survey questionnaire with the follow-up letter. In addition, phone calls may be used in conjunction with any other method of written, verbal, or personal communication that might encourage additional recipients to respond.

Contributed by Kananur V. Chandras,
Fort Valley State University,
Fort Valley, GA;
Sunil V. Chandras,
Macon State College, Macon, GA;
and David A. DeLambo,
University of Wisconsin–Stout,
Menomonie, WI

References

Babbie, E. (2004). *The practice of social research* (10th ed.). Belmont, CA: Thomson Wadsworth.

Beins, B. C. (2004). *Research methods: A tool for life.* New York: Pearson Education.

Gay, L. R., Mills, G. E., & Airasian, P. (2006). *Educational research: Competencies for analysis and applications.* Upper Saddle River, NJ: Pearson Prentice Hall.

Rea, L., & Parker, R. (1992). *Designing and conducting survey research.* San Francisco: Jossey-Bass.

Test Adaptation and Test Translation

Test adaptation refers to a process through which a test originally developed for one population is altered for use with another population that has a different culture or language, or both. The process includes forward and backward language translation as well as empirical validation to evaluate the level of linguistic and cultural equivalence of the adapted test. The goal of test adaptation, then, is to develop two or more versions of an instrument that stimulate the same responses from test takers if they have equal amounts of a trait, regardless of the language in which the test is presented. Language translation of a test by itself, without empirical validation, has been criticized for assuming equivalent psychological properties and cultural values across cultures. Some examples of successful large-scale, cross-cultural test adaptations are the adaptations of the Minnesota Multiphasic Personality Inventory and the Wechsler Adult Intelligence Scale.

The increasing recognition that test adaptation is an important component of testing and assessment is reflected in the *Standards for Multicultural Assessment* (Association for Assessment in Counseling and Education, 2003) and the *Standards for Educational and Psychological Assessment* (American Educational Research Association, American Psychological Association, & National Council on Measurement in Education, 1999). In addition, the International Test Commission (ITC) has outlined guidelines for adapting psychological and educational tests that address key areas such as cultural context, technicalities of test development and adaptation, test administration, documentation, and interpretation. According to the *Guidelines for Test Adaptation* (International Test Commission, 2001), steps of test adaptation include the following.

The first step is reparation, which involves selecting appropriate tests for adaptation that have established, sound psychometric properties in the source culture or country and will be of valuable use in the target culture or country. This step includes conducting comprehensive literature reviews and obtaining copyright permission to make sure that no similar work has been done previously.

An important step is to use both forward translation and backward translation, which are two of the most widely used translation methods. **Forward translation** is the process of translating the test from the source language to the target language by a group of bilingual translators. Then, experts discuss the linguistic (i.e., word-for-word compatibility) and cultural (i.e., definition and meaning) equivalence of the two versions. Multiple revisions usually are made to ensure the accuracy of the language of the target version. The main advantage of forward translation is that the equivalence between source and target language can be directly evaluated and adjustments can be made quickly by a group of experts; however, the accuracy and equivalency of the translation depend on the language and cultural expertise of the bilingual translators. Therefore, it is recommended to use **backward translation** sequentially with forward translation. After the test is translated from the source language to the target language, independent bilingual translators translate the target-language version of the test back to the source language. Then, groups of experts compare the version of the test in the original language and the back-translated version of the test to evaluate equivalency. The process of translating and back-translating is repeated until all the items meet the equivalence standard. Although forward translation addresses the linguistic equivalence of the source and translated instruments, the backward translation method provides an opportunity to address cultural equivalence; using forward and back translation sequentially and iteratively enhances the probability of linguistic and cultural equivalence.

Making judgments about linguistic equivalence cross-culturally is usually easier than making judgments about cultural equivalence. On occasion, items that appear to be linguistically equivalent do not exhibit cultural equivalence after the back translation has been completed. In such cases, items are modified in the target language to better approximate cultural equivalence.

If time and resources permit, a pilot bilingual test–retest study can be conducted. This procedure involves administering both the source and target language versions of the test to a group of bilingual test takers over a certain period of time to ensure the equivalence between the two versions of the tests.

Test validation, which is a continuous empirical process, usually starts with administration of the translated test to a sample representing the target population. Factor analytical methods can then be used to ensure the structural equivalence (i.e., that the same factors emerge) between the target and source tests. Other statistical analyses, such as internal consistency of items and test–retest stability of scores, can also be conducted to establish the psychometric properties of the target test. In addition, norms developed in the source culture or country may not be appropriate for use in the target culture or country. In those cases, developing new norms based on the target population is necessary. Construct and criterion-related validity studies are also conducted to show evidence that the scores on the target test are consistent with its original purpose.

Test adaptation is an evolving process that takes substantial resources, time, and effort. Despite all the difficulties, cross-cultural adaptation of psychological and educational tests is a fast-growing area that is receiving more and more attention from researchers and practitioners. Globalization and the ease of communication through modern technology increase the opportunities for counselors to incorporate instruments developed in other countries and in other languages into their practice and research. The advantage, of course, is that counselors and researchers have a larger array of instruments from which to choose. Best practices in assessment, however, require that careful attention be paid to test translation and adaptation prior to using instruments in a cross-cultural context to increase fairness in assessment and to allow comparative research across countries and cultures.

Contributed by
Shuangmei Zhou (Christine) and
Jo-Ida C. Hansen,
University of Minnesota, Twin Cities, MN

References

American Educational Research Association, American Psychological Association, & National Council on Measurement in Education. (1999). *Standards for educational and psychological testing*. Washington, DC: American Psychological Association.

Association for Assessment in Counseling and Education. (2003). *Standards for multicultural assessment*. Retrieved August 1, 2008, from http://aac.ncat.edu/Resources/documents/STANDARDS%20FOR%20MULTICULTURAL%20ASSESSMENT%20FINAL.pdf

International Test Commission. (2001). Guidelines for test adaptation. Retrieved August 25, 2008, from http://www.intestcom.org/test_adaptation.htm

Additional Resources

Butcher, J. N., & Han, K. (1996). *International adaptations of the MMPI-2: Research and clinical applications*. Minneapolis: University of Minnesota Press.

Hambleton, R. K. (1994). Guidelines for adapting educational and psychological tests: A progress report. *European Journal of Psychological Assessment, 10*, 229–244.

Hambleton, R. K., Merenda, P. F., & Spielberger, C. D. (2005). *Adapting educational and psychological tests for cross-cultural assessment*. Mahwah, NJ: Erlbaum.

■ Test Theory

In 1904, the first treatise on test theory, titled *An Introduction to the Theory of Mental and Social Measurements,* was published by E. L. Thorndike. **Test theory** states that what empirically "exists" must involve knowing or measuring some construct's quality and quantity to some amount or degree, as operationalized (Crocker & Algina, 1986). In measuring some construct, a test or its variables contain error. In short, test theory seeks to reduce errors in a test or boost its constructs' consistency (reliability) and accuracy (validity). In practice, tests developed under this model keep or lose their operationalized, measurable characteristics based on the amount of variance they explain or do not explain in a consistent, predicted relationship to what is being tested (Crocker & Algina, 1986; Hansen, 2006). Professional counselors should be familiar with three models of test theory: classical test theory, generalizability theory, and modern test theory.

Classical Test Theory

Simply put, **classical test theory** and its algebraic equation, $X = T + E$, note that any obtained score or distribution of scores (X) consists of true (T) and error (E) variance. **True variance** refers to what the test really tests, whereas **error variance** refers to the random error that interferes with true measurement. Not surprisingly, classical test theory's reliability-based precursor, called "the true score model," was tested and proposed vigorously by Charles Spearman between 1904 and 1913 and no doubt stems from his zeal and commitment to the many applied uses for correlation. Trying to identify and eliminate fallible measures from true objective values or scores through simple matrix algebra, Spearman (1907) published a number of theoretical pieces and mathematical proofs showing that to the degree that tests are fallible measures, the correlation of these fallible parts will always be lower than the correlation coefficient for the true (r) objective values. Many key test theorists have expanded on Spearman's work and refined the notion that all obtained scores (X) are combined of two hypothetical components: a true, error free score (T) and recurrent random error term (E; Crocker & Algina, 1986). This notion is applied when measuring or estimating a test or construct's reliability and validity according to variance estimation statistics, but this model uses only a single term (E) for the multiple sources of error that can be anticipated in a validation or cross-validation study.

Generalizability Theory in a Classical Test Theory Context

In response to classical test theory, Cronbach, Gleser, and Rajaratnam (1963) thought that if classical test theory provides a way to generalize true and error variance from observed scores from a parallel test, item, or its constructs with a single correlation, then the model may also be adapted to handle multiple, parallel observations, raters, or ratings with multiple reliability coefficients. Indeed, this adapted model would "fix" the lower correlations that occur when unidimensional-assumption-based methods are misapplied to multidimensional measures (Matt, 2007). Thus, **generalizability theory (G theory)** was born.

G theory ranks individuals and their score levels in the multidimensional context, which allows a generalization made using G theory sample statistics into the universe of admissible observations (Matt, 2007). This cleverly presupposes that an individual's estimated "universe" score is the average score based on all admissible observations, not just one set. G theory "error reduction" not only boosts reliability but validity as well, by proactively identifying and measuring multiple variances by explicitly "analyzing" them in the model a priori. Indeed, single- and multiple-facet generalizability studies are undertaken using analysis of variance (ANOVA) features to address and interpret the significance and effect size of a score/distribution to determine whether a decision study is warranted (the next confirmatory step) to establish a relative or absolute ranking and a confidence interval derived from error variance (Matt, 2007).

What is presented here is a description of classical G theory within parametric, quantitative inferential design, and bivariate statistics. The G theory model can also be applied using more complex designs with multiple random and assigned factors (nested or crossed), the analysis of score profiles, composite scores, Bayesian estimates, or covariance matrices to study the dependability (reliability and validity) of any facet or variable of interest (Matt, 2007).

Modern Test Theory

Unmeasured variance nonuniformly occurs within and across the constructs created to measure abstract human traits, and measurement specialists have engaged in multiple, sustained attempts to reduce this error (Crocker & Algina, 1986). A calculus equation that is based on hundreds if not thousands of slopes and intercepts mathematically allows for group differences to be "smoothed out." This is how **modern test theory** (MTT) indices are created. One index is a "non-norm norm," which "shows" what a perfectly reliable and content-valid item or test should look like: a perfect S-shaped curve (Camilli & Shepherd, 1994; Matt, 2007). To the extent that any derived Raschian curve or function differs from perfect, its reliability and validity are said to be "marred" by group and not individual differences, and MTT numeric indices reflect these nonuniform differences in function and variance accordingly (Camilli & Shepherd, 1994).

Again, shared variance in an item or test and its strength and direction (controlled or otherwise) can also be explained by examining the MTT statistical indices. A few of these include (a) signed proportional differences that do and do not control for total observed scores; (b) log odds ratio analyses, such as the Beta Mantel Haenszel Log-Odds Ratio, that stratify individuals according to their observed total score(s) on the control variable(s); and (c) logistic or other forms of regression on the differential item or test functioning indices used as population parameter estimates (Camilli & Shepherd, 1994). The math is different between classic and MTT, but G theory's method of estimating true variance from ANOVA remains in use for better estimating "true" reliability, reducing multiple error sources beforehand, and thus improving a measure's generalizability.

MTT or Raschian-Based G Theory

First, Raschian-based G theory has no pilot or G studies, nor are the statistical findings of the D studies as done in classical test-based G theory applications tremendously helpful, assuming the test ratings are neither too hard nor too easy, too exclusive nor too inclusive, and so on (Rasch Organization, 2007). The **Rasch model** requires three basic assumptions or steps, which take place using a nomograph or logit chart with a person's true standard deviation on axis Y and average standard error on axis X.

First, precision of measurement or validity is operationalized by the average standard error (SE), while true standard deviation (SD) to the average standard error is its reliability, usually within 1–2 logits, as measured in the upper part of any MTT-based G theory nomograph (Rasch Organization, 2007). Below that, or in what is called the "separation" of the nomograph, the ratio of SD to SE tells how many distinct levels each test has and how many ratings must be collected for each examinee to meet the a priori reliability coefficient selected or desired. All test indices constitute a profile of generalizability for MTT, Raschian-based assessment.

Contributed by Jesus (Jesse) Aros,
Texas A&M International University,
Laredo, TX

References

Camilli, G., & Shepherd, L. (1994). *Methods for identifying biased test items.* Thousand Oaks, CA: Sage.

Crocker, L., & Algina, J. (1986). *Introduction to classical and modern test theory.* New York: Holt, Rinehart & Winston.

Cronbach, L, Gleser, G., & Rajaratnam, N. (1963). Theory of generalizability: A liberalization of reliability theory. *British Journal of Mathematical and Statistical Psychology, 16,* 137–173.

Hansen, J. (2006). Counseling theories within a postmodern epistemology: New roles for theories in counseling practice. *Journal of Counseling & Development, 84,* 291–297.

Matt, G. (2007). *Generalizability theory.* Retrieved October 15, 2007, from http/www.psychology.sdsu.edu/faculty/matt/Pubs/GThtml/GTheory_GEMatt.html

Rasch Organization. (2007). *Rasch-based generalizability theory.* Retrieved October 15, 2007, from http:/www.rasch.org/rmt/rmt71h.htm

Spearman, C. (1907). Demonstration of formulae for true measurement of correlation. *American Journal of Psychology, 18,* 161–169.

Thorndike, E. L. (1904). *An introduction to the theory of mental and social measurements.* New York: Science Press.

■ Therapeutic Alliance

Although studies indicate that treatment methods do affect outcome and that individuals who participate in some form of therapy do better than those who do not, all methods are fairly similar in effectiveness. The therapeutic alliance, however, when compared to method, has a far greater impact on treatment retention and outcome. Carl Rogers asserted that without a therapeutic alliance (i.e., two people in therapeutic contact), there could be no significant psychological change. Rogers called the **therapeutic alliance** a "common" factor because it is endemic to all psychotherapies. On the basis of his work, researchers have defined, in a variety of studies, the therapeutic alliance as having three fundamental features: a collaborative relationship, an affective bond, and an agreement on goals and tasks. These facets of the alliance form early in treatment, usually within the first three to five sessions.

Ratings of the alliance have been conducted from the perspectives of the client, professional counselor, and independent observers, but most studies rely on clients' perceptions. Findings consistently indicate that a client rates the alliance more favorably than do counselors and observers. Researchers postulate that this reflects a client's unique but limited experience in therapeutic relationships, whereas the professional counselor experiences multiple alliances from which to form a comparison. The wise, skilled counselor does well to honor the client's experience as paramount, because it ultimately affects outcome.

Client characteristics also have an impact on alliance formation and utilization. Those clients high on motivational readiness, for example, more easily establish a therapeutic alliance, but they place less reliance on it as treatment progresses. In contrast, research shows that highly anxious, severely psychiatrically ill, and cognitively impaired clients are slow to develop an alliance, but that once it develops, the therapeutic alliance becomes increasingly important for treatment retention and outcome. The demographics of clients do not generally predict alliance formation, retention in treatment, or more favorable outcome. A modicum of evidence suggests that men may prefer a more practical, utilitarian approach, whereas women may benefit from a more empathic and caring approach, but more research is needed in this area.

Client characteristics predict response to treatment and treatment outcome more than either the alliance or method of treatment. Characteristics include the client's neighborhood and family, peer and social relationships, workplace, and spirituality. The client's intelligence, motivation, trust, and resiliency also affect response to, and progress after, treatment. Of course, the client's disorder or predicament, which is usually determined by the number of symptoms, severity of problems, capacity to relate, and ability to identify a focal problem, has an impact as well on posttreatment functioning.

To whatever extent client characteristics affect the alliance and treatment outcome, the professional counselor's interpersonal attributes and interventions also have a significant effect on building a positive, therapeutic relationship and, ultimately, more favorable outcome. Counselor warmth, empathy, acceptance, and encouragement have been linked to alliance formation as have been honesty, professional expertise and experience, and respect for the client. Productive interventions consist of accurate interpretation, active participation, affirmation, facilitation of affect expression,

goal directedness, exploration, recognition of past therapy successes, and attention to the client's experience.

Helpful and effective counselors also use confrontation as a selective, context-driven intervention rather than as a style of interaction. These clinicians monitor the alliance and repair ruptures as they occur, dealing with them directly and honestly, admitting their mistakes, because they see the therapeutic experience as a joint, collaborative enterprise. Although they remain aware of the power advantage they hold in the alliance, these professional counselors recognize their shared humanity with the client.

The therapeutic alliance happens by conscious intent. Professional counselors may more naturally "connect" with some clients than with others, but even in those cases, the alliance can never be taken for granted. Clients stand a greater chance of therapeutic gain if the alliance is managed and modified in their best interests. To confuse the alliance with a friendly, easy, or laissez-faire relationship would be to undermine the not so "common" factor of healing in counseling.

Contributed by Daniel C. Frigo,
Hazelden Graduate School of
Addiction Studies,
Center City, MN

Additional Resources

Johnson, J. L. (2004). *Fundamentals of substance abuse practice*. Belmont, CA: Thomson Brooks/Cole.

Lambert, M. J., & Bradley, D. E. (2001). Research summary on the therapeutic relationship and psychotherapy outcome. *Psychotherapy Theory Research Practice and Training, 38,* 357–361.

Martin, D. J., Garske, J. P., & David, M. K. (2000). Relation of the therapeutic alliance with outcome and other variables: A meta-analytic review. *Journal of Consulting and Clinical Psychology, 68,* 438–450.

Rogers, C. R. (1957). The necessary and sufficient conditions of therapeutic personality change. *Journal of Consulting and Clinical Psychology, 21,* 95–103.

■ Tic Disorders

Tic disorders include Tourette's disorder, chronic motor or vocal tic disorder, transient tic disorder, and tic disorder not otherwise specified (American Psychiatric Association [APA], 2000). **Tics** are rapid, sudden, repetitive motor or vocal movements believed to be involuntary in nature. **Motor tics** include repeated movement of one or more muscle groups, whereas **vocal tics** are utterances of one or more vocal sounds, words, or phrases.

Tics are categorized as simple or complex. **Simple tics** involve a single muscle group or individual vocal utterance. A **complex tic** entails more than one muscle group (motor tic) or repetition of a word, phrases, or complete sentences. A simple motor tic may include behaviors such as an eye twitch, head jerk, or clearing one's throat. A complex motor tic may include repeatedly retracing one's steps. Tics may begin as simple tics and over time develop into complex tics.

In addition, the developmental trajectory of tics is typically head to toe.

Diagnosis of Tic Disorders

Tourette's disorder is a presentation of a combination of multiple motor tics as well as one or more vocal tics. The tics must have been present for a minimum of 12 months and must occur many times during a day without an absence in symptoms for more than 3 consecutive months. Onset of the tics must occur before the individual is 18 years of age. Last, the tics cannot be due to a medical condition or be induced through substance use (APA, 2000).

Chronic tic disorder (motor or vocal) is diagnosed when there is a display of single or multiple motor or vocal tics; however, both motor and vocal tics cannot be present. Like Tourette's disorder, the symptoms must have been present for a minimum of 1 year, with symptoms occurring at least every 3 months. The onset must be before age 18 years and not due to substance use or a medical condition. Last, chronic tic disorder can only be diagnosed in an individual who has not previously been diagnosed with Tourette's disorder (APA, 2000).

Transient tic disorder diagnosis is specified as either a single episode or recurrent in nature. The diagnostic criteria require single or multiple motor and/or vocal tics. The symptoms cannot have lasted for more than 1 year but must have been present for a minimum of 1 month, occurring nearly every day. Furthermore, onset of symptoms must have occurred before 18 years of age, symptoms must not be due to effects of substance use or a medical condition, and criteria for Tourette's disorder or chronic tic disorder (APA, 2000) are not met. Tic disorder not otherwise specified is used as a diagnosis when criteria for one of the other tic disorders are not met.

Etiology

The exact etiology and mode of transmission of tic disorders are unknown; however, genetic factors and neurobiological factors may play a role in vulnerability to tic disorders. Researchers have identified many neurochemical systems that may be involved in tic disorders; however, this area still has many unanswered questions.

Tourette's disorder is estimated to occur twice as often in males than in females in the general population, but clinical samples have shown rates of Tourette's disorder in males to be 5 times the rate in females. In addition, prevalence in children is 5 to 30 per 10,000, and it is 1 to 2 per 10,000 for adults (APA, 2000). Prevalence rates for transient tic disorder in children were reported to occur in up to 18% of the population, decreasing in midadolescence to approximately 2% (Peterson, Pine, Cohen, & Brook, 2001); whereas the rate of chronic tic disorder is estimated to be between the rate for transient tic disorder and Tourette's disorder (Peterson, Campose, & Azrin, 1994).

Treatment of Tic Disorders

The most common pharmacological treatment for tic disorders is neuroleptics. **Neuroleptic medications** block the reuptake of dopamine, which may decrease the frequency and intensity of the behaviors associated with tic disorders. Neuroleptics are divided into two types: typical neuroleptics and atypical neuroleptics. Atypical neuroleptics have been found to be nearly as effective as typical neuroleptics but have less dangerous side effects.

Simplified habit reversal (SHR) is the most common behavioral treatment for tic disorders. The original habit reversal protocol included 13 steps and was highly effective; however, after much research, the original 13-step procedure was reduced to an equally effective 3-step procedure (Woods & Miltenberger, 2006). The 3 steps of SHR are awareness training, competing response training, and social support training.

Awareness training is segmented into two components, response description and response detection. Response description includes teaching the client to describe the tic as well as the sensations that occur directly before and after the tic. Response description is then followed by multiple opportunities for the client to detect self-exhibition of a tic (i.e., response detection). Awareness training may be achieved in one to two clinic sessions, with additional practice by the client at home.

Competing response training includes having the client identify a competing response and replacing the tic behavior with the competing response. The competing response should be incompatible with the tic (e.g., if the tic is a shoulder shrug, then an appropriate competing response would be to push the hands toward the floor). Anytime the client exhibits the tic, the client is taught to demonstrate the competing response for 1 minute. Prompts by the counselor may be necessary at first, but prompts may be reduced over time as the client becomes more independent.

Social support training is the last component of SHR and includes recruiting and training individuals to aid the client in implementation of SHR. An individual who spends substantial time with the client is usually chosen. This individual is then trained to provide verbal praise for the client each time the client exhibits the competing response. Last, the individual is taught to prompt the client to display the competing response anytime the client exhibits the tic (Woods & Miltenberger, 2006).

Contributed by Brad Dufrene
and Amy E. Baranek,
The University of Southern Mississippi,
Hattiesburg, MS

References

American Psychiatric Association. (2000). *Diagnostic and statistical manual of mental disorders* (4th ed., text rev.). Washington, DC: Author.

Peterson, A. L., Campose, R. L., & Azrin, N. H. (1994). Behavioral and pharmacological treatments for tic and habit disorders: A review. *Journal of Developmental and Behavioral Pediatrics, 15,* 430–441.

Peterson, B. S., Pine, D. S., Cohen, P., & Brook, J. S. (2001). Prospective, longitudinal study of tic, obsessive-compulsive, and attention-deficit/hyperactivity disorders in an epidemiological sample. *Journal of the American Academy of Child & Adolescent Psychiatry, 40,* 685–695.

Woods, D. W., & Miltenberger, R. G. (Eds.). (2006). *Tic disorders, trichotillomania, and other repetitive behavior disorders: Behavioral approaches to analysis and treatment.* New York: Springer.

■ Tiedeman and O'Hara Career Development Model

Tiedeman and O'Hara (1963) developed a vocational decision-making model, and they explained vocational decision making as a process of differentiation and integration when an individual attempts to make rational decisions regarding the problems experienced in vocational matters. This model emphasized the complexity of the decision-making process for each unique individual and provided a framework for the integration of self-concept formation and career development.

Tiedeman and O'Hara stressed the aspects of self-exploration and self-renewal. Their approach to career decision making revolved around the individual's life processes of choice and growth and the motivation and ability to change and adapt. This individual, lifelong process was their focus in career decisions, not narrowing the focus to a chosen occupation or job. The vocational aspect referred to how people intentionally occupied their time.

The metaphor of a sailing vessel was used to explain the decision-making process (Miller-Tiedeman & Tiedeman, 1990). The theorists encouraged the process to be viewed as an exciting journey during which the individual adapts to changing natural circumstances and remains flexible, just as a captain navigating the open seas. Growth and change are limitless, just as the horizons at sea are. This journey was referred to as the **lifecareer process.**

A central idea of this decision-making model is that careers satisfy needs. Also, experience and maturity in school, work, and life are considered to be important factors as individuals experience vocational problems and must rationally evaluate and decide what actions to take. These problems may be external in nature, involving social or environmental factors, or they may be derived from internal dissonance. This decision-making process is considered to be ongoing throughout the life span, and individuals may move forward or backward in the sequence of career development stages.

According to this model, there are two periods in the process: the anticipation period and the implementation period. The **anticipation period** is divided into four stages: (a) **exploration stage** (accentuates exposure to a wide variety of vocational possibilities and consideration of goals), (b) **crystallization stage** (stresses the emergence of patterns, the evaluation of alternatives, and the rank ordering of remaining options), (c) **choice stage** (emphasizes the selection of a particular option and preparation to act on the decision), and (d) **clarification stage** (stresses the questioning and reexamining of the choice, then dispelling the doubts and incorporating the image of self in relation to the vocational goal).

The **implementation period** has three stages: (a) **induction stage** (the individual begins the chosen job, school, cur-

riculum, and so forth and is required to fulfill the requirements of the position and assume a friendly, cooperative attitude), (b) **reformation stage** (the person becomes assertive and tries to change or restructure the group); and (c) **integration stage** (the individual compromises with the social faction and becomes accepted as a group member). The growth and learning that occur as the person moves through these ongoing periods and stages are central in the construction of the self-concept.

Tiedeman and O'Hara used their career model of differentiation and subsequent reintegration in explaining the organization of self and environment, which is the process of ego identity development. This is the process whereby an individual experiences dissonance between self and environment and searches for an integration of experiences at more comprehensive levels. The reintegrations in personality occur when the individual can identify, accept, and reconfigure continuously differentiated elements of his or her experience. Although Tiedeman and colleagues continued to develop elements that specified personal use of decision making and others later revised the model, the paradigm remains basically intact.

Contributed by Rochelle C. Moss,
University of Arkansas at Little Rock,
Little Rock, AR

References

Miller-Tiedeman, A., & Tiedeman, D. V. (1990). Career decision making: An individualistic perspective. In D. Brown, L. Brooks, & Associates (Eds.), *Career choice and development* (pp. 308–337). San Francisco: Jossey-Bass.

Tiedeman, D. V., & O'Hara, R. P. (1963). *Career development: Choice and adjustment.* New York: College Entrance Examination Board.

■ Token Economy

Token economy is a behavioral intervention associated with behavior modification. Token economy involves establishing a systematic reward system in which concrete rewards are used to reinforce positive behavior and thereby reduce or extinguish negative behavior. Rewards are given in the form of privileges, material rewards, or tokens that can be exchanged for desired items or activities. Token economy is typically used in classroom settings with individuals and groups. Implementing a token economy involves the following steps:

1. Identify the negative behavior to be extinguished and/or the desired behavior to be increased.
2. Establish a short-term goal (e.g., student will raise hand to get teacher's attention without calling out).
3. Design a reinforcement schedule and reinforce with behavioral praise.
4. Begin the intervention and keep track of progress.
5. Allow the client to trade in earned tokens for items or activities.

6. Modify the goal and begin on intermittent reinforcement schedule as the client increases desired behavior, continuing to praise correct behavior.

7. Replace token reinforcement with intermittent praise as desired behavior increases.

For example, a teacher asks the professional school counselor for help with a male 2nd-grade student who is disruptive in class and shouts out for the teacher's attention. The school counselor identifies the shouting-out behavior as the first behavior to be targeted and by observation determines that this behavior occurs on average 20 times during the morning. A short-term goal is established; the student will reduce shouting-out behavior by half. Each time the student raises his hand, he will be given a chip and praised by the teacher for raising his hand. The plan and the reward system are explained to the student. He is told that if he earns 10 chips, he will be allowed to trade them in at the end of the school day for free-time privileges (a reward the student chose). The teacher keeps track of how many chips are earned each day. At the end of the first week, if the student has met his goal, his reward schedule will be revised. The student will continue to earn chips; however, praise will increase and earning chips will decrease until the student is regularly raising his hand to get the teacher's attention.

Token economy is most often used when working with young children and children with disabilities. It is an effective way to increase desired behavior because the emphasis is on practicing and rewarding desired behavior rather than punishing negative behavior. Although the token economy requires a considerable amount of planning, when implemented effectively, children perform desired behaviors without needing a reward and take pride in their accomplishments.

Contributed by Carol J. Kaffenberger,
George Mason University, Fairfax, VA

Additional Resources

Ayllon, T. (1999). *How to use token economy and point system*. Austin, TX: PRO-ED.

DuPaul, G. J., & Weyandt, L. L. (2006). School-based interventions for children with attention deficit hyperactivity disorder: Effects on academic, social, and behavioural functioning. *International Journal of Disability, Development & Education, 53,* 161–176.

Token Economy Checklist Web site: http://www.usu.edu/teachall/text/behavior/LRBIpdfs/Token.pdf

Token Economy Facts Web site: http://www.polyxo.com/visualsupport/tokeneconomies.html

■ Transactional Analysis

Transactional analysis (TA) is a theory of personality, communication, and child development that has been applied to individual counseling, couples counseling, counseling children, group work, and a number of other settings including education and organizational development. TA was the brainchild of **Eric Berne** who wrote six books about the theory and steered its emergence as a new theoretical position until his death in 1970. Subsequently, disciples **Claude Steiner** (radical psychiatry) and **Mary and Robert Goulding** (redecision therapy) pushed TA in new directions. In 1999, the International Transactional Analysis Association (ITAA) identified the core concepts of the theory and five key premises: ego states, transactions, strokes, existential position, and contracts.

When people interact, they do so from one of three **ego states:** Parent, Adult, or Child. When a person is in one of these ego states, the person thinks, feels, and behaves like that state. The **Parent** in all people is a reflection of their own parents and is composed of prerecorded tapes about how they should behave, not based on logic but injunctions. The Parent is judging and can either be a **critical Parent** or **nurturing Parent.** When people operate out of their **Adult ego state,** they use logic, and like Mr. Spock on *Star Trek,* the Adult bases behavior on facts. Finally, the **Child** ego state is the natural, impulsive, fun-loving, or just nasty kid in everyone. This ego state can be spontaneous **(natural child),** creative **(little professor),** or plagued by negative emotions such as fear and guilt **(adapted child).** To understand this better, it is useful to imagine members of a group counseling session where each one of these three ego states is represented by a different person and how they might interact with each other. Of course, most people do not operate solely out of one ego state all the time; they vacillate between states. As they do so, they "hook" or activate ego states in others.

Transactions are communications from one of an individual's ego states to that of another person. Each transaction has a stimulus, something that triggers it, and a response from the ego state of the other person. Transactions are of three types: complementary, crossed, and covert. **Complimentary transactions** allow communication exchange because the line from one person's ego state parallels that of the other, as when two business people talk Adult to Adult about a problem. **Crossed transactions** occur when lines intersect and communication is disrupted. An example is when a boss compliments you on your performance (Parent ego state) and you respond by discounting your own abilities (Child ego state). **Covert transactions** occur when words and intentions do not match. Covert transactions are the basis of **games,** which are a series of transactions designed to obtain a payoff. One of the most well-known games is WDYYB ("Why don't you. . . . Yes, but . . . "). This game is often played early in group counseling. One client will present her or his woes each week, and the other members try to solve the problem by giving suggestions only to meet with "Yes, but . . . " on the part of the sufferer. The aim of the game is to receive attention (strokes or the payoff) and not to solve the problem as it appears overtly. That is why it is a covert transaction. TA writers have identified hundreds of games, but good relationships should be free of games according to TA. People in good relationships can ask and receive without manipulation.

Strokes are units of recognition that people give to each other. Strokes can be physical or verbal. They can be positive (warm fuzzies) like hugs, encouragement, or praise, or they can be negative (cold pricklies) like putdowns. The exchange of strokes is an activity that human beings engage in during their transactions. TA believes that most people suffer from a lack of strokes from others and from themselves. People function best when they have an ample supply of strokes and freely stroke others and openly receive strokes.

According to TA, all people are born OK, but they can come to think of themselves and others as not OK; thus, there are four potential bases (referred to as **existential position**) for their life script: (a) "I'm OK, You're OK"; (b) "I'm OK, You're Not OK"; (c) "I'm Not OK, You're OK"; and the worst (e) "I'm Not OK, You're Not OK." TA asserts that people decide on their life position early and that each of these four positions has distinct consequences about how they envision and script their lives. Although not identical, the idea of existential position is similar to the Adlerian concept of lifestyle, which is a crystallized version of how people envision life, themselves, and others.

TA therapists insist that clients develop **contracts,** such as "developing better communication in our relationship," "stop putting myself down," "asking for what I want," or some other simple agreement with the counselor about how they want to change. The client must agree to a contract for help; it cannot be imposed. Contracts keep counseling focused on what the client wants, not what some third party or the counselor wants.

Eric Berne and the Current Status of TA

Eric Berne was a psychiatrist and was trained as a psychoanalyst. Even though he was analyzed and supervised by Federn and Erik Erikson, he was rejected when he applied to be a psychoanalyst in 1956. This incident precipitated an irreparable break with traditional psychoanalysis for him, and in 1957 he began writing the first seminal papers establishing the theoretical basis for transactional analysis. Berne founded the International Transactional Analysis Association in 1964 about the time his most popular book, *Games People Play* (1964) was published. He died in 1970 just after authoring his masterpiece, *What Do You Say After You Say Hello?* (1972). Other books about TA by Eric Berne include *Transactional Analysis in Psychotherapy* (1961), *Structure and Dynamics of Organizations and Groups* (1963), *Principles of Group Treatment* (1966), and *Sex in Human Loving* (1970).

TA reached its zenith of popularity by the mid-1970s and has been in decline ever since. At its height, nearly 10,000 people belonged to the ITAA, and membership has dwindled to about 10% of the previous high in recent years. A survey by the author of this entry revealed that fewer than 1% of counselors and counselor educators describe themselves as primarily grounded in TA. Most major textbooks that teach counselors basic theories no longer include TA as a primary focus. During the past 5 years, the number of research articles and books on transactional analysis has not grown. Approximately 30 articles per year appear on the topic of TA, mostly in TA's *Journal of Transactional Analysis.* Still, TA has strong adherents worldwide and has large followings in South America, India, Japan, and the United Kingdom.

ITAA certifies transactional analysts, a process that takes 3 to 5 years.

One of the reasons that TA lost popularity was the untimely death of its founder, Eric Berne (1910–1970). Although he compiled a canon of literature, he was unable to inspire its critical later development. Both Berne's (1964) book, *Games People Play,* and Thomas Harris's (1969) book, *I'm OK, You're OK,* became well-known. TA's image as a pop psychology may have seemed to trivialize the counseling process in the eyes of professional counselors and therapists, but Eric Berne believed that simplicity was important, both when constructing theories and in dealings with clients. He advised professional counselors never to accept a client's contract that an eight-year-old could not understand.

Contributed by Mark E. Young,
University of Central Florida,
Orlando, FL

References

Berne, E. (1961). *Transactional analysis in psychotherapy: A systematic individual and social psychiatry.* New York: Grove Press.

Berne, E. (1963). *Structure and dynamics of organizations and groups.* Philadelphia: Lippincott.

Berne, E. (1964). *Games people play: The psychology of human relationships.* New York: Watts.

Berne, E. (1966). *Principles of group treatment.* New York: Oxford University Press.

Berne, E. (1970). *Sex in human loving.* New York: Simon & Schuster.

Berne, E. (1972). *What do you say after you say hello?* New York: Grove Press.

Harris, T. A. (1969). *I'm OK—You're OK: A practical guide to transactional analysis.* New York: Harper & Row.

Additional Resources

International Transactional Analysis Association Web site: http://www.itaa-net.org

James, M., & Jongeward, D. (1996). *Born to win.* Boston: Addison-Wesley.

Steiner, C. (1976). *Beyond scripts and games.* New York: Grove Press.

Stewart, I., & Joines, V. (1987). *TA today: A new introduction to transactional analysis.* Kegworth, Derbyshire, United Kingdom: Lifespace.

■ Transgendered and Trans-Individuals

The term **transgender** was originally created by Virginia Prince in the 1970s to describe men who lived their lives as women and who were believed not to want sex reassignment surgery. Today, *transgender* is a general term that describes individuals whose anatomy and/or appearance may not conform to traditional gender roles. In addition, some individuals whose behaviors and attitudes cross traditional boundaries of gender identity may also identify themselves as transgendered. Although often confused with sexual orientation, which is related to a person's affectual and/or sexual attractions, transgenderism pertains to gender identity, which is an individual's sense of femaleness, maleness, or neither; therefore, transgendered individuals may or may not identify as lesbian, gay, or bisexual.

Frequently described as an umbrella term, *transgender* includes all who self-identify as transsexuals, cross-dressers, drag kings and queens, transgenderists, intersexed individuals, genderqueers, or two-spirited individuals. In general, **transsexuals** are individuals who feel such a disparity between their body and gender that many often seek medical intervention to eliminate the incongruity (i.e., sex reassignment, hormone treatments). Formerly called transvestites, **cross-dressers** are individuals who enjoy wearing clothing of the opposite sex periodically and often for sexual gratification. Cross-dressers tend to be heterosexual men who enjoy dressing in women's clothing. Individuals who cross-dress for purposes of entertainment and/or public performance are called **drag kings** (women who dress as men) or **drag queens** (typically gay men who dress as women). **Transgenderists** are individuals who live full-time as the opposite gender but may or may not feel the need to have medical interventions to alter their appearance. Historically referred to as hermaphrodites, **intersexed** people often possess biological and/or genetic characteristics at birth that cause ambiguous male/female anatomy. Use of the term *hermaphrodite* is considered offensive. The term **genderqueer** is a fairly new term used to describe those individuals who step outside of the boundaries of the dominant culture's notions of gender identity and sexual orientation. Last, because gender is often rooted in a cultural context, variations of gender identity have been identified in other cultures. For example, **two-spirited** is a term used by some members of Native American cultures to describe individuals with both a male and a female spirit. Spirit may pertain to sexual orientation, gender identity, or other personal characteristics. It is often considered rude when individuals from the dominant culture use the term *two-spirited* to describe members of Native American communities.

Assessing accurate prevalence rates of transgenderism is difficult because of the diverse categories of individuals who fall under the transgender umbrella. Accessing these populations is often difficult because of the shame and fear associated with being identified as transgendered. Furthermore, many individuals may not yet realize they are in fact transgendered. Finally, identifying actual numbers of transgendered individuals is also difficult because epidemiological research among transgendered persons is scarce. As a result, there are discrepancies in the reported numbers of transgendered persons, and the true number of transgendered persons is likely greater than the reported numbers.

The Harry Benjamin International Gender Dysphoria Association (2001) estimated that transsexualism affects approximately 1 in 11,900 men and 1 in 30,400 women. Ettner (1999) estimated that individuals with gender dysphoria range from 3% to 10% of the population. **Gender dysphoria**

is a syndrome in which an individual is determined to be one gender at birth but may identify as belonging to another gender category and, as a result, experiences clinically significant discomfort. Conway (2002) estimated that approximately 1 out of 50 people are cross-dressers, 1 out of 200 people have strong transgendered feelings, 1 out of 500 people have intense transgendered feelings, 1 out of 1,000 individuals are transgendered transitioners (without sex reassignment surgery [SRS]), and 1 out of 2,500 individuals are transsexual transitioners (with SRS). Regardless of the numbers, it seems likely that most professional counselors will counsel at least one transgender client at some point. Professional counselors should therefore be aware of some of the issues with which transgendered clients might present.

Although transgendered clients may present with issues common to other populations, problems such as depression, low self-esteem, substance abuse disorders, and HIV/AIDS seem to affect transgendered individuals disproportionately. Competent professional counselors should not attribute these problems to clients' transgendered identities; rather, clinicians should explore how transphobia in the contextual environments of transgendered clients contributes to the high rates of mood and substance use disorders and HIV infection rates. **Transphobia** is discrimination toward and oppression of individuals who do not conform to traditional gender roles and/or societal expectations of sex assignment. By directly asking transgendered clients about their experiences with transphobia, professional counselors will be better able to assess the mental and physical consequences of transphobia in the lives of transgendered clients. This is a first step to professional counselors embracing a trans-affirmative counseling style. A **trans-affirmative approach** to counseling involves professional counselors advocating for transgendered clients both at the microlevel and the macrolevel. At the microlevel, professional counselors should give transgendered clients time to tell their stories. When exploring clients' narratives, professional counselors should use transgendered clients' strengths and resources to teach self-advocacy and self-empowerment skills. At the macrolevel, professional counselors should collaborate with clients to advocate for political, legal, and economic rights for the transgendered communities, including equal access to social, medical, and mental health resources.

Contributed by Michael P. Chaney,
Oakland University, Rochester, MI

References

Conway, L. (2002). *How frequently does transsexualism occur?* Retrieved June 18, 2007, from http://ai.eecs.umich.edu/people/conway/TS/TSprevalence.html

Ettner, R. (1999). *Gender loving care: A guide to counseling gender-variant clients.* New York: Norton.

Harry Benjamin International Gender Dysphoria Association. (2001). *Standards of care for gender identity disorders* (6th ver.). Retrieved June 16, 2007, from http://www.symposion.com/ijt/soc_2001/index.htm

Additional Resources

Goethals, S. C., & Schwiebert, V. L. (2005). Counseling as a critique of gender: On the ethics of counseling transgendered clients. *International Journal for the Advancement of Counselling, 27,* 457–469.

World Professional Association for Transgender Health Web site: http://www.wpath.org

◼ Transpersonal Counseling

Transpersonal counseling refers to the application of transpersonal psychology to the field of counseling. The term *transpersonal* means "beyond the personal." The field of **transpersonal psychology** addresses experiences that transcend the usual personal limits of space and/or time and the usual sense of identity as a separate person. It also addresses levels of human development beyond the levels that involve the surviving and thriving of the individual person in the material world. Early Western transpersonal psychotherapy approaches included Carl Jung's analytical psychotherapy and Roberto Assagioli's psychosynthesis. Some major contemporary figures in the field are psychiatrists Stanislav Grof and Roger Walsh and psychologist Frances Vaughan.

Probably the term in the professional health care literature that approximates most closely the domain of transpersonal psychology is *spiritual;* however, the term *spiritual* carries different meanings and values for different people and often conjures up association with the human social institution of religion. The term *transpersonal* is intended to be broader and more neutral by virtue of its definition. Transpersonal psychology addresses all phenomena that involve the transcendence of space/time and separate individual identity, whether or not some people might consider those phenomena spiritual and/or religious. The application of transpersonal psychology to counseling seems quite natural in that, like the philosophical foundations of counseling, transpersonal psychology is inherently developmental, multicultural, and holistic.

Transpersonal experiences include the intuitive, paranormal, and mystical. **Intuitive experiences** involve a holistic knowing about some aspect of the material world that cannot be attributed to experience or reason, such as encountering a complete stranger for the first time and having an immediate, strong positive or negative reaction that later proves accurate. Further along the transpersonal continuum are **paranormal experiences.** Examples are precognition, telepathy, clairvoyance, telekinesis, and mystical experiences. **Precognition** involves knowing beforehand that something is going to happen, such as feeling a sense of powerful excitement in the hours preceding the surprise notification of having won an award for which a person did not even know that he or she had been nominated. **Telepathy** involves apparently direct mind-to-mind communication, such as thinking suddenly of a long-forgotten friend just as the phone rings and that friend is on the line. **Clairvoyance** involves seeing distant events, such as having a vivid dream that is qualitatively different than typical dreams of a specific public disaster and, the following day, seeing the exact image from the dream in a newspaper front-page photograph. **Telekinesis** involves influence of the physical world through the mind alone, such as in the case of some individuals who have had near-death experiences (NDEs) and who report that their mere proximity to electrical devices often seems to cause the devices to malfunction. Even further along the transpersonal continuum are **mystical experiences** that involve a sense of communion or union with a perceived real power beyond the usual material world. Examples are the vacationing hiker who suddenly feels overcome with a sense of union with the natural world around her or him or an individual communing with a being of light during an NDE.

Transpersonal experiences can perhaps best be understood in the context of a developmental framework. For example, Ken Wilber (2000), although not self-identified as a transpersonal theorist, has described in his integral psychology a model whereby people are understood to have the potential to move through three broad phases of development. During the prepersonal phase, roughly ages 0 to 7 years, the child is in the process of developing a sense of individual self, and mental functioning is primarily prerational. During the personal phase, roughly ages 8 years to at least 21 years, the individual consolidates and elaborates a sense of individual self, and mental functioning is predominantly rational. During the transpersonal phase, roughly beginning any time after age 21, if at all, the individual transcends a sense of individual self, and mental functioning is predominantly transrational, involving increasing identification with all of humanity, all of nature, and/or perceived realities beyond the material world. In each phase of development, the functioning of the previous phase is retained yet expanded. Thus, the individual in a transpersonal phase of development retains yet also transcends the sense of an individual self in the material world.

In Wilber's (2000) model, anyone has the potential to experience briefly the transient state of any developmental level, such as an adolescent or adult (personal phase of development) who recalls a typical dream (prerational phenomenon) or who has a paranormal or mystical experience (transrational phenomenon). Emergence into a phase of development, however, involves the manifestation of a permanent trait of that level, such as a widow who, after an experience of communication with her deceased husband, experiences a comforting sense of sustained connection with him that facilitates her healthy reengagement in life, or the individual who, in the aftermath of an NDE, has a subtle, yet stable, sense of ongoing connection with the omniscient, omnibenevolent force with which he communed in the NDE, a connection that results in his relating to others in an increasingly compassionate way.

Transpersonal counseling consists of theory and practice that prepare a professional counselor to address a client's manifestation or pursuit of transpersonal experiences and/or development constructively. Thus, the transpersonal counselor holds a theoretical perspective that includes transpersonal experience and development and techniques that facilitate clients' integration of their spontaneous and overall transpersonal experiences into a system of healthy functioning. Examples of the latter are the counselor using meditation or a Course in Miracles as an adjunct to counseling (Boorstein, 1996) or using Induced After-Death Communication (Botkin, 2005) to facilitate a client's healthy grieving process.

Like transpersonal psychology, transpersonal counseling includes attention to several unique and critical issues. These issues include differential diagnosis between prepersonal and transpersonal experiences—experiences that usually call for very different therapeutic responses—such as clinical depression versus spiritual Dark Night of the Soul. These issues also include **spiritual bypass,** in which a person seeks refuge in transpersonal phenomena as a way to avoid facing challenging personal issues (see Spiritual Bypass).

In summary, most of the well-known theories of counseling are, from a transpersonal perspective, limited to personal development: surviving and thriving in the material world. Transpersonal counselors affirm the necessity and value of personal development and also endorse a perspective that includes an inherent potential in humans for experiences and development beyond the personal. Thus, they strive to develop the competence to address what they perceive to be the full range of human consciousness and developmental potential.

Contributed by Janice Miner Holden,
University of North Texas, Denton, TX

References

Boorstein, S. (1996). *Transpersonal psychotherapy* (2nd ed.). Albany: State University of New York Press.

Botkin, A. L. (2005). *Induced after-death communication: A new therapy for healing grief and trauma.* Charlottesville, VA: Hampton Roads.

Wilber, K. (2000). Integral psychology: Consciousness, spirit, psychology, therapy. In K. Wilber (Ed.), *The collected works of Ken Wilber* (Vol. 4, pp. 423–742). Boston: Shambhala.

Additional Resources

Braud, W., & Anderson, R. (1998). *Transpersonal research methods for the social sciences: Honoring human experience.* Thousand Oaks, CA: Sage.

Cardeña, E., Lynn, S. J., & Krippner, S. (Eds.). (2000). *Varieties of anomalous experience: Examining the scientific evidence.* Washington, DC: American Psychological Association.

Scotton, B. W., Chinen, A. B., & Battista, J. R. (Eds.). (2005). *Textbook of transpersonal psychiatry and psychology.* Boulder, CO: Westview Press.

Walsh, R., & Vaughan, F. (1992). *Paths beyond ego: A transpersonal vision.* Los Angeles: Tarcher.

■ Trauma Counseling

Psychological **trauma** can result from a single exposure to a devastating experience (e.g., genocide, torture, a life-threatening accident), a catastrophic natural event like Hurricane Katrina, acts of terror (e.g., attacks on September 11, 2001; kidnapping or rape; interpersonal violence and combat), or even experiences that are part of everyday life (e.g., illnesses, "routine" medical procedures, bullying). Traumatic stress symptoms can develop in direct victims, in bystanders who are in some way a witness to the victimization or event, and even in those who are not directly involved. It is important to note that working with survivors of the Holocaust, sexual abuse, and political terror can create a significant risk of vicarious trauma for professional counselors and other professional helpers.

Initial response to trauma usually comes in the form of disturbing and intrusive images, thoughts and dreams, and flashbacks. These experiences are common with traumatic events and will often resolve after a few days or a week or two. If they do not, a cycle of avoidance can arise in a conscious and/or subconscious attempt to ward off these persistent stimuli, leading to feelings of detachment, numbness, restricted affect, memory loss, and avoidance of people and places reminiscent of the trauma. Physical reactions that accompany the body's fight–flight response can develop into hyperarousal, which includes sleep disturbance, anger, and irritability, and hypervigilance, which includes exaggerated startle responses and difficulty concentrating. These three symptom dimensions (i.e., intrusion, avoidance, and hyperarousal) form the diagnostic criteria for posttraumatic stress disorder (PTSD). Whether a response to a traumatic event develops into PTSD depends not only on the nature of the stressor but also on an individual's resiliency and degree of vulnerability.

In her landmark book, *Trauma and Recovery,* **Judith Herman** (1992) described recovery from psychological trauma as a three-stage process: establishment of safety, remembrance and mourning, and reconnection with ordinary life. The stages are not linear and discrete but are part of an ongoing process that is characterized by different survivor needs and treatment interventions at each stage. Severe trauma is never completely resolved but resonates throughout a survivor's life as the meaning of the experience continues to be integrated and reinterpreted in the context of daily living. Stages are often revisited throughout recovery or when developmental challenges arise that link back to the trauma. For example, a survivor of childhood sexual abuse may revisit her traumatic experiences when her daughter becomes the age at which she was first abused.

Stage 1: The Establishment of Safety

The key task of Stage 1 is establishing safety by returning power and control to the survivor. Choice is critical. The survivor must remain the arbiter of therapeutic progress and the decision maker at every phase. Accurate diagnosis is a crucial first step. When trauma is acute and stems from a single incident, diagnosis is often straightforward. Preventative education can prepare the survivor and reduce the impact of symptoms, which can be treated immediately. With chronic or prolonged trauma, or what Herman (1992) described as "complex" PTSD, the trauma may be buried in the past, appearing in the present as a collection of symptoms: substance abuse, sleeplessness, eating disorders, a history of broken relationships, depression, or anxiety. Uncovering the source of the symptoms and naming the trauma start the process of ending isolation, secrecy, and silence. Through sharing the story, the survivor begins to realize that he or she is not alone.

Creating safety can be a complex process lasting days, weeks, or longer. It begins with ensuring the physical safety of the survivor, then focuses on the environment. The heart of this stage's work is crisis intervention, education, and reduction of symptoms. Traumatic stress affects human functioning in every area: physical, cognitive, social, emotional, and spiritual, all of which must be addressed. Physically, the neurochemical fight–flight response of the body becomes overstimulated, no longer able to discriminate between genuine threats and ordinary stimuli and flooding the body with hormones and creating fear, panic, anger, hypervigilance, and sleep disturbances. Cognitively, trauma disrupts an individual's entire belief system about self, others, and the world, destroying trust, relationships, and social networks. Emotional numbness, depression, and anxiety isolate the individual. Spiritually, the victim is left in a void, searching for meaning. None of these issues can be treated without first establishing a refuge to ensure physical safety from harm. Without this haven, suicidal behaviors, eating disorders, substance abuse, and other self-injurious behaviors cannot be effectively addressed. Safety in this context also relates to living conditions and potentially dangerous relationships. Is the abuse still ongoing? Is action against the abuser necessary? Is there a plan for future protection? During this phase, survivors may have fantasies of a cathartic cure and may rush into "putting it all behind them." The professional counselor helps survivors understand that recovery from trauma is more like a marathon, requiring endurance, preparation, and practice. Groups at this stage should be psychoeducational in nature and complement the therapeutic focus on crisis management, cognitive understanding of stress disorders, and self-care. What the survivor most needs at this stage is not the ventilation of strong feelings or storytelling but relief from symptoms and fear.

Stage 2: Remembrance and Mourning

By its nature, trauma is unspeakable, and it is in the telling of the story that the memories are transformed and begin to lose their power. This is where the professional counselor serves as "witness and ally" as the survivor reconstructs the trauma and begins to restore continuity with the past. During the beginning of this phase, the trauma is explored: What was the event? How did the survivor and the important people in his or her life respond? All the details must be included. What the survivor was hearing, smelling, feeling, thinking. What were the bodily sensations? This approach helps to reduce the depersonalized "surreal" or "dreamlike" quality of many traumatic experiences and to ground the survivor's understanding in reality.

Remembrance is an overwhelming experience. Techniques such as flooding and testimony may help remove intrusive thoughts and images and reduce hyperarousal, but they do not seem effective with emotional numbing, improved

relationships, or adjustment to the world-of-work. These issues must be addressed separately. Whatever the technique and tempo of therapeutic progress, the locus of control must remain with the survivor, and treatment must include the physiological aspects of the trauma: disturbances in sleep, eating, endocrine cycles, perceptions of pain, arousal, bodily sensations, and physical ailments. Medication may help with symptoms (e.g. depression, anxiety, sleep disorders), and regular physical exercise can burn off the excess adrenaline and glucose that accompany stress disorders. Massage and practices such as meditation can counter the physical and psychological symptoms of stress and help restore calm.

As survivors struggle to empower themselves during Stage 2, mourning and grief follow remembrance. In the case of natural disasters, victims may have to struggle with the most basic spiritual questions of meaning and the seemingly random unfairness, cruelty, and brevity of life. What was once comfortable and predictable and safe must be reconciled with sudden chaos and destruction and loss. When the source of the trauma is another person, symptoms may be more personal and severe, and recovery may necessitate facing the question of human evil. Survivors may seek empowerment through revenge on their abuser or by gaining compensation. They may seek to escape the hard work of mourning and grief by "forgiving" the perpetrator or by refusing to grieve because they believe grieving gives the abuser a victory. None of these, however, will produce the desired result because they all hinge on the abuser and keep the survivor's fate linked to the perpetrator. What was lost or stolen from the survivor can never be restored; there is no "getting even." These losses can only be grieved. There may also be the need to grieve for the loss of moral integrity if the survivor in some way harmed others in the struggle to survive. Participation in group therapy at this stage can advance the survivor's empowerment and connection to others, but participation should be highly structured, time limited, and focused on personal goals in order to prevent retraumatization. As survivors regain a sense of self, there may not be a corresponding improvement in relationships or capacity for intimacy because they are now able to articulate their own wants and needs, creating potential conflict with others.

Stage 3: Reconnection

During Stage 3, reconnection, survivors reconcile with themselves, learning how to appreciate their struggles with a sense of compassion and respect. They begin to focus on the person they want to be, reconnecting with others and risking deeper, more intimate relationships. Groups in this stage should be aimed at reintegrating the survivor into the community of ordinary people. Groups should be diverse and open-ended and focused on interpersonal relationships, aspects of life and living, and sexual function. Finally, there may be a desire to achieve broader meaning by connecting to others by choosing public truth telling to raise awareness. This is the ultimate defiance of the abuser's demand for silence and secrecy. Through this experience, survivors find new allies and transcend their trauma by making a gift of it to others. In the case of natural disasters, these needs may be met by participating in the rebuilding of the community, which can help in restoring a sense of connection and purpose.

As Herman (1992) pointed out, regardless of the nature of the traumatic event, "psychological trauma is an affliction of the powerless. At the moment of trauma, the victim is rendered helpless by overwhelming force. Traumatic events overwhelm the ordinary symptoms of care that give people a sense of control, connection, and meaning" (p. 33). Recovery from trauma is a process through which disempowerment, isolation, and disconnection must be transformed into empowerment and reconnection. It is only through the hard task of making meaning of their experiences that individuals are able to regain their sense of self and their lives.

Contributed by Gregory R. Janson,
Ohio University, Athens, OH

Reference

Herman, J. L. (1992). *Trauma and recovery.* New York: Basic Books.

Additional Resources

Briere, J. N., & Scott, C. (2006). *Principles of trauma therapy and treatment: A guide to symptoms, evaluation, and treatment.* Washington, DC: American Psychiatric Association.

Van der Kolk, B. A., McFarlane, A. C., & Weisaeth, L. (Eds.). (1996). *Traumatic stress: The effects of overwhelming experience on mind, body, and society.* New York: Guilford Press.

Yehuda, R. (Ed.). (2006). *Psychobiology of posttraumatic stress disorder: A decade of progress.* New York: Annals of the New York Academy of Sciences.

■ Triad Model of Multicultural Counselor Training

The **triad model for multicultural counselor training** was developed by Paul B. Pedersen in 1977. This view of multicultural counseling grew out of his 6 years of counseling experience and teaching in various countries. The triad model encourages professional counselors to evaluate the messages, both positive and negative, that a culturally different client might be thinking but not saying (Irvin & Pedersen, 1995).

"The Triad Model consists of simulated cross-cultural counseling role plays among three persons" (Neimeyer, Fukuyama, Bingham, Hall, & Mussenden, 1986, p. 437). One of the individuals plays the role of the counselor, another plays the role of the client from a different culture, and the third person plays the "role of the problem" from the client's worldview (e.g., the third person makes comments or displays actions that bring the client's problem into the here and now). This third person acts as either an encouraging, facilitative helper (pro-counselor) or an antagonistic, rebellious agent (anti-counselor), depending on which role is needed more to accentuate the role that the problem is playing in the client's here-and-now existence.

The **pro-counselor** focuses more on the positive messages from both the professional counselor and the client and helps articulate the internal dialogue and the successful strategies used. According to Pedersen (1997), having the pro-counselor offers the following advantages:

- Provides a resource person to consult when the professional counselor is confused or in need of support,
- Gives explicit information about the client that might facilitate the professional counselor's success,
- Provides a partner for the professional counselor to work with on the problem rather than the counselor having to work alone,
- Helps the professional counselor stay on track and avoid sensitive issues in ways that might increase client resistance, and
- Provides beneficial feedback to the professional counselor to avoid mistakes and build on successful strategies. (pp. 187–188).

The **anti-counselor** focuses more on the mistakes made by the professional counselor and is contrary to the professional counselor; the client decides which person is more accurate. According to Pedersen (1997), the anti-counselor provides the following advantages:

- Forces the professional counselor to be more aware of the client's perspective;
- Articulates the negative, embarrassing, and impolite comments that a client might not otherwise say;
- Forces the professional counselor to examine personal defensiveness;
- Points out a professional counselor's inappropriate interventions immediately while the counselor still has time to recover;
- Attempts to distract the professional counselor, thus training the professional counselor to focus more intently on the client. (p. 186).

Regardless of the third party's focus (i.e., pro-counselor or anti-counselor), the issues relevant to the cross-cultural relationship are highlighted by revealing unique cultural values and their influence on the counseling relationship. Both the pro-counselor and the anti-counselor increase consciousness of cultural differences, create knowledge about the culture at hand, and increase skills in negotiating therapeutic cross-cultural interaction. This problem, personified in the third person, is ever changing and obtains its identity from the client's surrounding relationships. This problem is concrete and defined by its own pressures and assurances in the perceptual worldview of the client (Neimeyer et al., 1986). This model is ultimately designed to help make external the client's internal dialogue by using the pro-counselor and anti-counselor (Pedersen, 1997).

According to Pedersen (1997), the triad model seems to work best when the following conditions are present:

- The counselor receives both positive and negative feedback during the interview.
- The simulated interview reflects actual events in realistic ways.
- The simulated interview occurs under conditions that the professional counselor considers "safe."
- Pro-counselors and anti-counselors must be carefully trained to be effective.
- Feedback to the professional counselor and client is immediate and explicit during the actual interview.
- The resource person is both articulate and authentic to the client's background.
- The professional counselor learns how to focus on the client while listening to the anti-counselor or the pro-counselor at the same time.
- The interview is spontaneous and not scripted.
- The interaction is videotaped.
- The interview is brief (8–10 minutes) to avoid overwhelming the counselor with information during or after the interview. (p. 186)

The triad model of counselor training can be used in a variety of training venues. It may be used for prepracticum students who are early in their training experiences and for more experienced professional counselors through various types of workshops. Researchers have found evidence that this model promotes the following features of professional counselor growth: (a) increased skill in identifying client resistance, (b) greater empathy, (c) more respect and congruence, (d) less defensiveness in therapy, (e) less threatened in counseling, and (f) more realistic views of themselves as counselors. The triad model provides training for professional counselors at any level dealing with barriers due to cross-cultural counseling (Pedersen, 1997).

Contributed by
Susanna Capri Posey Brooks
and Carl J. Sheperis,
Mississippi State University,
Starkville, MS

References

Irvin, R., & Pedersen, P. (1995). The internal dialogue of culturally different clients: An application of the triad training model. *Journal of Multicultural Counseling and Development, 23,* 4–10.

Neimeyer, G. J., Fukuyama, M. A., Bingham, R. P., Hall, L. E., & Mussenden, M. E. (1986). Training cross-cultural counselors: A comparison of the pro-counselor and anti-counselor triad models. *Journal of Counseling & Development, 64,* 437–439.

Pedersen, P. B. (1997). *Culture-centered counseling interventions: Striving for accuracy.* Thousand Oaks, CA: Sage.

Additional Resources

Pedersen, P. (2000). *Handbook for developing multicultural awareness* (3rd ed.). Alexandria, VA: American Counseling Association.

Pedersen, P., Draguns, J., Lonner W., & Trimble, J. (2002). *Counseling across cultures* (5th ed.). Thousand Oaks, CA: Sage.

■ True Experimental Design

A **true experimental design** is used when the researcher wants to test a causal relationship between the independent and dependent variables through controlled observational methods. The essential ingredients for a true or classic experimental design are **randomization** (i.e., random assignment; see Randomization), manipulation and control of variables and conditions, and standardized observational methods. When used correctly, a true experimental design will control for most threats to internal validity and for some threats to external validity, thus making this design the "gold standard" for understanding causal relationships between variables of interest.

The three major forms of true experimental designs are pretest–posttest control (or comparative) group design (the most commonly used true experimental research design), Solomon four-group design, and posttest-only control group design. The **posttest-only control group** design is used rarely in research and has been criticized because many question the ability of randomization to control for differences between groups that are not being measured by a pretest. The design is identical to the last two groups of the Solomon four-group design (Campbell & Stanley, 1963).

The steps for a **pretest–posttest control group design** are (a) randomized assignment of participants to experimental or control conditions, (b) pretesting all participants on a standardized measure of the dependent variable, (c) administering the experimental stimulus only to the experimental condition and not to the control condition, (d) posttesting all participants on a standardized measure of the dependent variable, and (e) analyzing values of the dependent variable to determine whether the independent variable (experimental stimulus) produced variation in the dependent variable compared with the control condition.

The pretest–posttest control group design is graphically displayed as follows, where R = randomization, O = measurement of the dependent variable, and X = exposure to the independent variable (experimental stimulus):

Experimental Group	R	O	X	O
Control Group	R	O		O

In a **pretest–posttest comparative group design,** the second group in the previous graphic would be another experimental group.

The other true experimental designs are the Solomon four-group design and the posttest-only control group design. The **Solomon four-group design,** as its name implies, requires four groups in order to control for both the main and interactive effects of testing on the observations. The second set of observations is conducted at posttest to control for testing effects. The Solomon four-group design is graphically displayed as follows:

$$R \quad O_1 \quad X \quad O_2$$
$$R \quad O_3 \quad \quad O_4$$
$$R \quad \quad X \quad O_5$$
$$R \quad \quad \quad O_6$$

The **posttest-only control group design** is graphically displayed as follows:

$$R \quad X \quad O_1$$
$$R \quad \quad O_2$$

Contributed by Michael J. Mason,
Villanova University, Villanova, PA

Reference

Campbell, D., & Stanley, J. (1963). *Experimental and quasi-experimental designs for research.* Boston: Houghton Mifflin.

Additional Resource

Heppner, P. P., Kivlighan, D. M., Jr., & Wampold, B. E. (2008). *Research design in counseling* (3rd ed.). Pacific Grove, CA: Brooks/Cole.

■ Trustworthiness in Qualitative Research

The rigor of qualitative research design is evaluated by its **trustworthiness,** or the degree to which a study presents data that genuinely reflect the participants and settings under study; that is, do conclusions accurately represent information received from participants? If a study was replicated, would other researchers find consistent results? The terms *trustworthiness* and *strategies for maximizing trustworthiness* are similar to the quantitative research terms *validity* and *reliability;* however, because qualitative data collection and analysis are often subjective and, thus, open to more scrutiny, researchers actively reflect on how their data collection and data analysis methods might be inaccurate.

Two threats to qualitative research design that can affect trustworthiness are researcher bias and reactivity. **Researcher bias** refers to a qualitative researcher's preexisting theories, conceptions, and assumptions about a study that influence design. This bias is evident in the selection of research topics, research questions, data collection methods, participants, interview questions, observation rubrics, and coding manuals. **Reactivity** is similar to researcher bias and refers to the influence a researcher has on the setting or individuals studied. These components can both positively and negatively influence a study. A general rule of thumb is for qualitative researchers to articulate how researcher bias and reactivity affected research design, what the threats to trustworthiness were, and ways in which the researchers minimized any negative effects.

Several strategies for strengthening a study's trustworthiness have been proposed and are categorized under components of credibility, transferability, dependability, and confirmability. **Credibility** refers to the "believability" of a study's conclusions. There are several major techniques that help ensure the credibility of findings: prolonged engagement, persistent observation, triangulation, negative case analysis, referential adequacy, peer debriefing, and member checking. Many of these methods are also used to maximize the remaining three components of trustworthiness. **Prolonged engagement** represents an appropriate extent of time a researcher spends in a setting to establish trust with participants. **Persistent observation** refers to a deepening focus in a setting to uncover data relevant to the research question(s). Often, increased prolonged engagement allows for persistent observation. **Triangulation** is the use of multiple and different sources; these sources can be researchers, participants, data collection methods, and theoretical perspectives. The purpose of triangulation is to gather information that can support earlier findings and interpretations and strengthen a developing theory or understanding of a phenomenon. An additional benefit of triangulation involves searching for data or interpretations through multiple and different sources that may not support initial findings. This active search refers to the strategy of **negative case analysis.** In essence, the researcher asks, "What else might be going on?" or "How could current data not represent what is really going on?" with respect to a phenomenon. **Referential adequacy** also strengthens a study's credibility because it involves checking preliminary findings and interpretations against archived raw data and existing research to explore alternative explanations for findings as they emerge. Two final methods are peer debriefing and member checking, which are similar in that they involve the researcher or researchers consulting with others about the findings. **Peer debriefing** refers to seeking consultation with a professional outside the study, whereas **member checking** involves an ongoing dialogue with participants of the study to test the accuracy of data and subsequent interpretations.

Transferability, the second component of trustworthiness, refers to the degree to which results may be generalized to other contexts and settings. Although this strategy may seem similar to the quantitative research term *external validity,* it differs because the goal of most qualitative research is not to generalize to other samples and settings but instead to provide potential researchers interested in developing a similar design with enough information to do so. This process refers to providing **thick description,** and it involves the researcher providing substantial detail about the study's context, participants, data collection process, and data analysis steps. This allows other researchers to have enough information about how data were collected, interpreted, and reported to extrapolate a study's findings and better understand a larger phenomenon.

Dependability involves the consistency of results over time and across researchers, a concept similar to reliability. Although dependability and credibility overlap in scope, dependability is an extension of credibility, with the unique focus that multiple researchers provide evidence of the believability of the study and report its rigor. Thus, triangulation of multiple researchers or research teams is necessary to ensure consistency of findings. Furthermore, including additional peer debriefers increases a study's dependability. Another strategy for demonstrating dependability involves using an external investigator **(auditor)** to review data sources and their documentation specifically as well as the final report (i.e., **audit trail**).

Confirmability is the component of trustworthiness that specifically focuses on the degree to which a study's findings accurately reflect the participants' perspectives. This is assessed primarily through the degree to which the researcher thickly describes any biases or assumptions that potentially influence the study. This thick description may involve a discussion of the ways that the personal and professional motives for conducting the study; personal and professional affiliations with participants and the phenomenon under investigation; initial expectations related to the study's findings; and the researcher's initial and ongoing thoughts, feelings, and behaviors can interfere with the research process. In order to provide the most accurate description of the role of the researcher in qualitative design, researchers are encouraged to keep a reflexive journal and audit trail throughout the study.

Contributed by Danica G. Hays,
Old Dominion University, Norfolk, VA

Additional Resources

Creswell, J. W. (2006). *Qualitative inquiry and research design: Choosing among five traditions* (2nd ed.). Thousand Oaks, CA: Sage.

Maxwell, J. A. (2005). *Qualitative research design: An interactive approach* (2nd ed.). Thousand Oaks, CA: Sage.

Patton, M. Q. (2002). *Qualitative research and evaluation methods* (3rd ed.). Thousand Oaks, CA: Sage.

Validity

Validity is an important concept in the field of assessment. Validity is determined by estimating if scores from a measure assess what they are supposed to assess. There are a number of ways that validity of the scores on a measure can be established. There are many good discussions of techniques to determine validity (e.g., Anastasi & Urbina, 1997; Linn & Gronlund, 2000). Validity should always be stated in terms of a specific purpose for a specific group, and validity is a characteristic of the results, or scores, on a measure rather than of the measure itself (American Educational Research Association, American Psychological Association, & National Council on Measurement in Education, 1999). For example, do the scores on a measure show validity and reliability in predicting grades for Asian American students at a certain secondary school? Validity is not a general characteristic of an assessment method; it is a characteristic of the scores from a particular sample in a specific context.

There are several ways validity can be estimated, depending on the type of test, the test's intended purpose, and the construction of the test. The scores on a measure have **face validity** if they look like they are measuring topics of interest, with no further evidence. An example is group of people who are evaluating a questionnaire, or other measure, by looking over the items. With little more than personal hunches, the group picks the measure that looks as if it will best measure the concept. **Content validity** requires more documentation than face validity. The logic here is that the content of the items on a test, questions in an interview, themes in a focus group, and so on should contain the content that a researcher is seeking to measure or evaluate. As opposed to face validity, content validity requires collection of some empirical information or expert judgments and should have a scholarly foundation. In **construct validity**, a number of items are written to cover certain abstract constructs or dimensions of interest, or the items are from the literature on a topic. Often, use is made of statistical techniques that group items together empirically, such as factor analysis or cluster analysis (Merenda, 1997).

Convergent validity is demonstrated when several assessments are shown to achieve the same result using different measures, whereas **discriminant validity** is achieved when one measure is differentiated from another. For example, if two personality assessments give the same profile, there is evidence for convergent validity, whereas if the two measures show markedly different results, there is evidence for discriminant validity.

As the name suggests, in **predictive validity,** the test developer is trying to predict scores on some future criterion measure. A common example in higher education is in admissions. Scores from a given test are said to have validity in admissions decisions if they can predict future student success (e.g., grades, retention, graduation) for certain groups in certain contexts (e.g., Latino students at college X). In the pure form of demonstrating predictive validity, all applicants would be admitted, criterion measures on each student would be obtained, and the most accurate prediction equations possible would be developed. A variety of statistical techniques can be used, including multiple regression, multiple discriminant analysis, logistic regression, and LISREL (Cizek & Fitzgerald, 1999). In practice, however, the test developer rarely, if ever, has the opportunity to obtain criterion scores on an unselected sample, even though this is required for the best estimate of predictive validity. If the range of possible scores is restricted on the predictors or criteria, the size of the statistic representing the extent of the relationship (e.g., correlation coefficient) is artificially reduced.

In **concurrent validity,** the test developer identifies those people who are successful (or unsuccessful) on a criterion measure, and a measure is developed that reflects the characteristics of the successful group, ideally contrasted with the unsuccessful group. In developing the Minnesota Multiphasic Personality Inventory, Hathaway and McKinley (1943) compared people with certain clinical symptoms with a "normal" group on their responses to many items. Items that differentiated between the two groups were retained in the instrument. **Congruent validity** is estimated by correlating scores from a new measure with scores from an existing measure against a specific criterion (Fuertes, Miville, Mohr, Sedlacek, & Gretchen, 2000). It is an easy way to check the validity of scores on a new measure.

Contributed by Alan Basham,
Eastern Washington University,
Spokane, WA,
and William E. Sedlacek,
University of Maryland,
College Park, MD

References

American Educational Research Association, American Psychological Association, & National Council on Measurement in Education. (1999). *Standards for educational and psychological testing* (3rd ed.). Washington, DC: American Psychological Association.

Anastasi, A., & Urbina, S. (1997). *Psychological testing* (7th ed.). Upper Saddle River, NJ: Prentice Hall.

Cizek, G. J., & Fitzgerald, S. M. (1999). An introduction to logistic regression. *Measurement and Evaluation in Counseling and Development, 31,* 223–241.

Fuertes, J. N., Miville, M. L., Mohr, J. J., Sedlacek, W. E., & Gretchen, D. (2000). Factor structure and short form of the Miville-Guzman Universality-Diversity Scale. *Measurement and Evaluation in Counseling and Development, 33,* 157–169.

Hathaway, S. R., & McKinley, J. C. (1943). *The Minnesota Multiphasic Personality Inventory (Rev. ed.).* Minneapolis: University of Minnesota Press.

Linn, R. L., & Gronlund, N. E. (2000). *Measurement and assessment in teaching.* Upper Saddle River, NJ: Prentice Hall.

Merenda, P. F. (1997). A guide to the proper use of factor analysis in the conduct and reporting of research: Pitfalls to avoid. *Measurement and Evaluation in Counseling and Development, 30,* 156–164.

Validity Scales

Validity scales are included in test instruments to ensure the accuracy of the test taker's answers and scores. A clinician interpreting validity scales looks for response distortions that can occur in three main areas where the test taker (a) attempts to make it appear that he or she has some disorder or problem (faking bad); (b) responds in a defensive or socially desirable manner in an attempt to put himself or herself in a favorable light or hide symptoms or problems (faking good); or (c) responds randomly to questions either through carelessness, lack of understanding, or confusion. Several commercially available inventories make use of validity scales in order to ensure that the respondent is answering questions in an open and honest manner.

The most straightforward validity scales consist of a few questions whose answers are infrequently endorsed by the population for whom the test was created. The Millon Clinical Multiaxial Inventory–III (MCMI-III; Millon, Davis, & Millon, 1997) personality test includes three questions in its 175-question test that are infrequently endorsed. A contrived example is "I have not been in a building in the last 10 years." The Substance Abuse Subtle Screening Inventory–3 (SASSI-3; Miller, 2003) includes six questions such as "I have never felt happy about anything." False answers to two or more of these six questions invalidate a client's test scores.

In more sophisticated testing instruments, validity scales indicate the level of defensiveness, lying, inconsistent responses, and responding in a random or socially desirable manner. The questions used in validity scales are scattered throughout the testing booklet. The most comprehensive set of validity scales is included in the Minnesota Multiphasic Personality Inventory–2 (MMPI-2; Butcher, Graham, Ben-Porath, Tellegen, & Dahlstrom, 2001); the MMPI-2's validity scales are presented in this entry as an illustration of potential validity scales. The original version of the MMPI was developed in the late 1930s and had just three validity scales. The current version of the MMPI-2 has 10 validity scales. It is important to note that the MMPI-2 validity scales work on the theory of large numbers. Single (or even a few) infrequent or inconsistent answers do not cause a scale to be endorsed. A pattern of infrequent and inconsistent responding is needed to elevate a scale's score. Some other inventories use some scales similar to those found on the MMPI-2, but the actual MMPI-2 validity scales are described throughout the remainder of this entry. It is important to review a client's scores on MMPI-2 validity scales in context with each other. They provide a better picture of the client when taken as a whole.

The first validity scale on the MMPI-2 is the **cannot say** or "**?,**" which is simply the number of answers on the 567 question MMPI-2 left blank. If the test taker leaves more than 30 items blank, the profile is considered invalid and not interpreted.

The **Variable Response Inconsistency (VRIN)** validity scale looks at a test taker's tendency to respond inconsistently. The scale couples 67 item pairs that contain either similar or opposite items. One point is given for each pair that was scored inconsistently. Scores greater than 13 suggest inconsistent responding, and the profile is treated as invalid. An example of items that contribute to the VRIN would be responding true to both "I wake up tired every morning" and "My sleep is restful." It would be unlikely both of these situations would occur, leading the clinician to surmise the test taker was responding randomly or inconsistently. Although these questions are paired on the hand-scoring sheet, they are spread throughout the test booklet.

The **True Response Inconsistency (TRIN)** scale is made up of 23 paired items of opposite content. Unlike the VRIN, the TRIN is made up only of item pairs that have the opposite content. The TRIN measures the potential for **acquiescence,** a response style in which the test taker displays a tendency to mark all answers as true. In contrast, a nonacquiescence response style occurs when a test taker displays a tendency to mark all answers as false. Two true responses or two false responses for item pairs would indicate a pattern of inconsistent responding throughout the MMPI-2. Raw scores of 13 or more or 5 or fewer indicate a greater potential of an invalid protocol. A test taker who responds true to both "I like to tell dirty stories" and "I am embarrassed about sex" would likely be responding in an inconsistent, illogical, or random manner. As with the questions on the VRIN, although these TRIN questions are paired on the hand-scoring sheet, they are spread throughout the test booklet.

The **Lie scale (L)** consists of 11 items and is useful in detecting profiles where clients answer questions in a deliberate and unsophisticated attempt to put themselves in a favorable light or are unwilling to admit even minor shortcomings. High scorers on this scale are often said to be responding in a **socially desirable** way by denying minor faults or character flaws that most people would be willing to admit. Those who answer false to questions such as "I never eat candy" and "Once in a while I have a sexual thought about a friend or coworker" are likely making an attempt to put themselves in a more favorable light. Conversely, they may have a highly exaggerated set of moral ethics.

The **Correction (K)** scale is similar to the L scale but is better at detecting more subtle attempts by respondents at either denying psychopathology by trying to put themselves in a better light or exaggerating psychopathology by trying to put themselves in a very unfavorable light. It is expected that certain groups of people (e.g., college-educated persons, those with lower socioeconomic status, those in certain professions such as police officers) will have naturally elevated K levels. Those who respond false to a question like "Sometimes I feel useless" and true to a question like "I hardly ever argue with friends and family" may be responding in a way that attempts to deny pathology and put themselves in a better light.

The **Infrequency (F)** scale was designed to detect odd or atypical ways that a respondent may answer 60 test items. Once the test administrator is able to rule out the respondent's attempts at faking good or faking bad in a pattern of responses, high F scores indicate the presence of psychopathology, because these types of questions on the test would also be seen as odd or atypical. Those who respond true to "I hate my father, or (if your father is dead) I hated my father" would be responding in an atypical way.

The **Infrequency (Fb)** scale consists of 40 items that are found exclusively in the second half (b for back) of the MMPI-2 questions. A large (30-point) difference between F and Fb indicates that respondents have changed their test-taking strategy on the second half of the test. This may indicate they became tired, began to randomly respond, or were making a new attempt to fake good or fake bad.

The **Infrequency Psychopathology (Fp)** scale was developed by Arbisi and Ben-Porath (1995) and consists of 27 items that are unlikely to be endorsed by respondents, regardless of their potential psychopathology (high F/Fb scores). High scores on Fp indicate potential fabrication and exaggeration of clinical symptoms. Those who respond with false to "I find myself worrying sometimes" and true to a question like "Sometimes when I have a headache I am short-tempered" are responding in an unlikely manner, even considering they may be experiencing psychopathology.

The **Fake Bad Scale (FBS)** was created by Less-Haley, English, and Glenn (1991) to provide information about the reporting of noncredible symptoms, particularly in personal injury litigants. The scale contains 43 items, with respondents endorsing more than 20 of these items classified as exaggerating or fabricating somatic complaints. Respondents who answer true to "Everything smells similar to me" and "I wake up in a cold sweat every few nights" are likely reporting somatic or noncredible symptoms.

The **Superlative Self-Presentation Scale (S)** was designed by Butcher and Han (1995) to detect response styles where respondents create an overly favorable image of themselves, exaggerating and highlighting their positive aspects while concealing symptoms or problems. The 52-item scale is further broken down into subscales (S1: Belief in Human Goodness, S2: Serenity, S3: Contentment With Life, S4: Patience/Denial of Irritability, S5: Denial of Moral Flaws). Test takers who respond false to questions such as "I've had to do things the way my boss said even

though I knew how to do it better" and "I have had trouble making up my mind about a really complicated decision" are likely trying to put themselves in a more favorable light.

Whether validity scales are straightforward (as with the MCMI-III or the SASSI-3) or more sophisticated and covert (as with the MMPI-2), they provide clinical information regarding the test taker's response style. A recent set of scales, the Paulhus Deception Scales (Paulhus, 1998), was developed as a stand-alone test to measure a test taker's tendency to give socially acceptable or desirable responses. This test can be paired with other measures to provide information regarding the method in which the test taker approaches subsequent tests.

Contributed by Brian Van Brunt,
New England College, Henniker, NH

References

Arbisi, P. A., & Ben-Porath, Y. S. (1995). On MMPI-2 Infrequent Response Scale for use with psychopathological populations: The Infrequent Psychopathology Scale F(p). *Psychological Assessment, 7,* 424–431.

Butcher, J. N., Graham, J. R., Ben-Porath, Y. S, Tellegen, A., & Dahlstrom, W. G. (2001). *Manual for administration scoring and interpretation of the MMPI-2.* Minneapolis: University of Minnesota Press.

Butcher, J. N., & Han, K. (1995). Development of a MMPI-2 scale to assess the presentation of self in a superlative manner: The S scale. In J. N. Butcher & C. D. Spielberger (Eds.), *Advances in personality assessment* (Vol. 10, pp. 25–50). Hillsdale, NJ: Erlbaum.

Less-Haley, P. R., English, L. T., & Glenn, W. J. (1991). A Fake Bad Scale on the MMPI-2 for personal-injury claimants. *Psychological Reports, 68,* 203–210.

Miller, G. A. (2003). *Adult SASSI-3 user's guide.* Springfield, IN: The SASSI Institute.

Millon, T., Davis, R., & Millon, C. (1997). *Millon Clinical Multiaxial Inventory—III manual.* Minneapolis, MN: NCS Pearson.

Paulhus, D. L. (1998). *Paulhus Deception Scales: User manual.* North Tonawanda, NY: Multi-Health Systems.

Variability

Variability is one of several terms used to describe a research sample and is considered a descriptive statistic concept. **Variability** refers to the amount of spread in a distribution of scores or data points. For instance, in the case of a normal distribution, the scores from a test given to participants would approximate a bell-shaped or normal curve. In this example, the variability, or amount of dispersion of scores about a central value, is neither low nor high, and scores are said to be normally distributed. In another distribution, scores may be quite spread out, in which case the variability would be high. If scores were to cluster around the mean score for the sample, then the variability would be low.

There are three main statistics associated with variability: range, standard deviation, and variance. The **range** is the most basic indicator of variability, and it is calculated by simply subtracting the lowest score from the highest score, although it is becoming more common for researchers to compute the range as H (high score) – L (low score) + 1. The range does not tell the researcher much, and it is greatly influenced by one unusually high or low score, called an outlier. The most frequently reported measure of variability is called the **standard deviation** (*sd, s,* or *SD*), which represents the typical distance from any point in a data set to the center, or average score. Standard deviation is the square root of the variance, so standard deviation and variance are both measuring variability in a distribution of scores, but standard deviation is preferred because it is reported in the original units from which it was derived. **Variance,** on the other hand, is also a measure of the variability of scores about a mean, but it is stated in units that are squared. Researchers use the standard deviation statistic to represent variability within a distribution of scores to determine the average amount a score deviates from the mean score for the sample. For instance, a normal distribution can be divided into equal sections, each of which represents a proportion of participants in the sample, or 1 standard deviation. In a normal distribution, 68% of the sample lies within 1 standard deviation below and 1 standard deviation above the mean. Researchers can also calculate a standardized score based on the standard deviation measure, called a *z* score, to compare distributions.

Contributed by Edward P. Cannon,
Marymount University, Arlington, VA

Additional Resources

McLeod, J. (2003). *Doing counseling research* (2nd ed.). Thousand Oaks, CA: Sage.

Salkind, N. (2007). *Statistics for people who (think they) hate statistics* (3rd ed.). Thousand Oaks, CA: Sage.

■ Variables

In quantitative research, a **variable** refers to an attribute or characteristic of the data related to the phenomenon under study. Several different variable nomenclatures exist, and which nomenclature is used depends on whether a variable is being discussed and defined by its nature or by its use in research. Several types of variables are commonly described in research, including independent or dependent, organismic, extraneous, and confounding.

Independent and Dependent Variables

Variables are distinguished as independent or dependent depending on how they are used in research. An **independent variable** is a variable that is manipulated, whereas a **dependent variable** is a variable that is affected by the independent variable. Both experimental and nonexperimental research involves the study of independent and dependent variables.

In nonexperimental research, preexisting differences in the attribute or characteristic under study are used to define the independent variable, and the researcher looks for any effects on the dependent variable. In this case, the independent variable is presumed to cause, affect, or influence the outcome or response variable. For example, the relationship between the session content and client satisfaction at termination could be examined, in which case the preexisting differences in session content is the independent variable and satisfaction the dependent variable.

In experimental research, the independent variable is systematically manipulated while everything else is held constant so that the results of the manipulation can be measured in the dependent variable. In such research, there must be at least two different treatments or levels of the independent variable being measured. For example, session content could be used to establish two or more groups that would become the independent variable, in which satisfaction at termination was measured. An independent variable is also sometimes referred to as an input, predictor, manipulated, or exogenous variable, and a dependent variable can be called an outcome or endogenous variable.

Organismic Variables

Organismic variables include physical and psychological characteristics inherent in the participants and are one example of preexisting individual differences. Such preexisting differences can exist in either an independent or dependent variable. When an organismic variable is the independent variable, it can be held constant or randomized to neutralize its effects on the dependent variable. In these instances, the organismic variable is also known as the **blocking variable** or **control variable.** For example, in a study examining the relationship between session content and the counselor's case conceptualization, possible organismic variables include factors such as client and counselor age, sex, or educational level. In this instance, it is possible that such preexisting differences may influence the independent or dependent variable; however, it is also possible for an organismic variable to be used to define the levels of the independent variable. For example, organismic variables such as age, sex, and educational level can each be an independent variable and their effects on case conceptualization examined in a study. It is problematic when an organismic variable is also the dependent variable because, by definition, it is possible for the preexisting differences existent in the dependent variable to contribute to the over- or undermeasurement of the relationship between the independent and dependent variables.

Extraneous and Confounding Variables

Any variable that is not related to the study itself but thought to plausibly affect the outcome is deemed an **extraneous variable.** An extraneous variable is undesirable because, although it can influence the research outcome by affecting the relationship between the independent and dependent variables, it is not a variable under study. Therefore, both independent and dependent variables differ from an extraneous variable because they, by definition, are under study in the specific research. Said another way, in a research study, the independent and dependent variables can never be extraneous. For example, in a study concerned with the relationship between session content and case conceptualization, a possible extraneous variable might be the counselor's theoretical orientation. If theoretical orientation was not being examined in the study and it influenced the relationship between session content and case conceptualization, as an extraneous variable it would contribute error to the experiment and therefore be undesirable. Although an extraneous variable can be an organismic variable, an extraneous variable does not necessarily have to be an individual difference inherent in participants. In an example of a study examining the relationship between session content and case conceptualization, an extraneous variable external to participants could be the counseling context, in that the setting of the counseling sessions was not a variable of interest but influenced the relationship between the independent and dependent variables.

An extraneous variable can also be a **confounding variable.** This can occur whenever the extraneous variable covaries, or changes systematically with the level of the independent variable. There is increased likelihood of this occurring in research designs that do not use random assignment. For example, in the study examining the relationship between session content and case conceptualization, there could be an extraneous confounding variable of the time of day of the counseling sessions such that the session content covaries with the time the counseling sessions are held. When there is a confounding variable, the researcher is unable to determine whether the observed influence on the dependent variable is a result of the independent variable, the confounding variable, or an interaction between them both. Researchers attempt to minimize the confounding or contaminating influence of extraneous variables in order to strengthen the knowledge claim of a study. In this case, participants could be randomly assigned to one of two treatment groups (e.g., counselor operating from interpersonal framework, counselor operating from a cognitive–behavioral perspective) or the counselor's theoretical orientation could be held constant statistically.

Contributed by Melissa Luke,
Syracuse University, Syracuse, NY

Additional Resources

Afifi, A., Clark, V. A., & May, S. (2004). *Computer-aided multivariate analysis* (4th ed.). Boca Raton, FL: Chapman & Hall.

Ary, D., Jacobs, L. C., Razvieh, A., & Sprensen, C. (2006). *Introduction to research in education.* Belmont, CA: Thomson Wadsworth.

Trochim, W. M. (2006). *The research methods knowledge base* (2nd ed.). Retrieved May 25, 2007, from http://www.socialresearchmethods.net/kb/

Vygotsky's Cognitive Developmental Theory

Lev Vygotsky was a Russian psychologist who developed theories about the cognitive development of children that differed significantly from other theories of the day. Vygotsky wrote about the importance of social development as a means to promote the cognitive growth and development of children. He believed culture greatly influenced how cognitive development unfolded and emphasized the importance of language in how a child learned to think. Children learn how to think and solve problems within the context of a culture, especially when they have the support and guidance of adults and older (or more skillful) peers in their society or culture. Vygotsky believed that social learning could lead and shape cognitive development.

Vygotsky believed children could only learn so much information on their own. An individual child, working alone, can make some significant cognitive strides; however, that same child with the support and instruction of a skillful teacher can learn more. The difference between what a child can actually learn or do on her or his own and what that child can learn or do with the help of a teacher or guide is called the **zone of proximal development.** It is the gap between what a child can achieve through independent problem solving and what that child's potential level of development is with guidance and support.

When a child is given the correct assistance, this support serves as a way to promote learning to the next level. A skillful teacher can gear the level of support and teaching needed to promote the most growth and change, which Vygotsky referred to as **scaffolding.** Once a child is independent and capable of doing a task on his or her own, the scaffolding, or support, can be removed.

Finally, another concept promoted by Vygotsky was the **private speech** of children. Preschool children often talk to themselves and seem to be working out plans and strategies through this self-talk. In time, that private speech is internalized and becomes a foundation of thought. Thus, language can be thought of as fundamental to the process of thinking.

Contributed by Mardi Kay Fallon,
University of Cincinnati, Cincinnati, OH

Additional Resources

Vygotsky, L. S. (1978). *Mind in society: The development of higher psychological processes.* Cambridge, MA: Harvard University Press.

Vygotsky, L. S. (1997). *The collected works of L. S. Vygotsky: Vol. 4. The history of the development of higher mental functions* (R. W. Rieber, Ed., & M. Hall, Trans.). New York: Plenum Press.

Wellness Counseling

The roots of the modern wellness movement began more than 2,000 years ago in ancient Greece. According to the Greek myth, Asclepius, the ancient Greek god of healing, had two daughters who established separate ways of approaching health and illness. One daughter, Panacea, promoted the idea that healing meant approaching people to treat existing illness. Hygeia, his other daughter, believed that the best way to approach healing would be to teach people ways of living so that they would not become sick. Panacea was the forerunner of modern medicine, whereas Hygeia may be credited with initiating the wellness movement.

The Greek philosopher Aristotle, writing in the 5th century BCE, is credited with being the first to write about wellness. His scientific attempts to explain health and illness resulted in a model of good health as avoidance of the extremes of excess and deficiency. Stated succinctly, this philosophy is expressed as "nothing in excess." More recently, wellness has been defined as something more than health, which the World Health Organization has stated is simply a neutral state in which people experience the absence of disease. **Wellness** refers to a state of positive well-being, one in which body, mind, and spirit are integrated.

Virtually all definitions of wellness emphasize that wellness is a choice. Individuals make decisions on a daily basis that move them either toward greater wellness or a lowered state of health. Although nutrition and exercise stand out as the most visible markers of health, in holistic wellness models, the physical aspects of wellness constitute only a piece of the whole. People make choices concerning who they will spend their time with, how they will relate and respond to others, how they will practice their faith beliefs, and where they will work and live and in the myriads of little things they do as they live out their lives each day.

Wellness Counseling Models

Given the vast array of often conflicting information available on virtually every topic, a person wanting to learn more about wellness may well ask what factors are truly important for a healthy lifestyle. Reviews of research studies in multiple disciplines, including medicine, psychology, anthropology, psychoneuroimmunology, and others, have revealed a number of factors that contribute to a better quality of life. People who have positive amounts of these qualities may expect to live longer and to live well. The main qualities defined by the ancient Greeks remain the hallmarks of wellness today. To live long and live well, individuals need to attend to their physical, cognitive, emotional, and spiritual selves. Each of these areas, in turn, comprises multiple components and characteristics; hence, models that demonstrate the factors and relationships among the factors are helpful in understanding the complexity of what makes people well rather than ill.

In counseling, one of the earliest wellness models was based in the individual psychology theory of Alfred Adler, a contemporary of Sigmund Freud. Adler emphasized the indivisibility of the self and taught that all components of wellness are interrelated. Hence, change in any one area both causes and contributes to changes in other areas. Of course, change works in both directions and can be for better or for worse.

The **wheel of wellness model** is a theoretical model that includes five interrelated life tasks defined by Adler: spirituality, self-direction, work and leisure, friendship, and love. The task of self-direction is further defined as including 12 subtasks: sense of worth, sense of control, realistic beliefs, emotional awareness and management, problem solving and creativity, sense of humor, nutrition, exercise, self-care, stress management, gender identity, and cultural identity. Each of these components of wellness is important for creating a greater quality of life and better health.

Data collection and structural equation modeling analysis over more than 12 years led to the development of a new evidence-based model of wellness, the indivisible self (IS-Wel; Myers & Sweeney, 2005), which provides an alternative perspective for viewing wellness across the life span, incorporating the 17 separate wellness dimensions of the Wheel as third-order factors, grouped according to five second-order factors, and one higher order Wellness factor. Adler proposed that the self was indivisible and that purposiveness was central to understanding human behavior. This philosophy provided a structure for making sense of studies in which wellness emerged both as a higher order and seemingly indivisible factor and as a factor made up of identifiable subcomponents, as originally hypothesized.

The five second-order factors in the IS-Wel model were named the Creative Self, Coping Self, Social Self, Essential Self, and Physical Self. These factors constitute the indivisible self, which in turn exists in the context of a variety of interacting systems. These systems include an individual's local influences such as family and community; institutional contexts such as the government and media; global contexts including culture and world events; and chronometrical contexts, or the effects of changes over time. This final context helps people understand that wellness involves the acute and chronic effects of lifestyle behaviors and choices throughout an individual's life span.

Counseling for Wellness

Wellness provides a philosophy for incorporating a strength-based approach in counseling. From this perspective, counselors seek to determine how "well" an individual is in the various areas of wellness previously defined. Areas of high wellness constitute strengths that people can draw on to enhance their functioning in areas where they might experience lower wellness. Given the interactive nature of the wellness areas, a focus on strengths facilitates more rapid change than looking only at individuals' deficits.

When using the wellness models in counseling, professional counselors should adopt a four-step, or four-phase, process: Step 1: introduction of the model, including a life-span focus; Step 2: formal and/or informal assessment based on the model; Step 3: intentional interventions to enhance wellness in selected areas of the model; and Step 4: evaluation, follow-up, and continuation of Steps 2 through 4. These same steps can be applied to the development of a personal wellness plan. Outside intervention is not required, although it is often a helpful means of furthering people's plans for greater wellness in a more efficient and rapid manner.

The steps in wellness counseling are to define wellness, choose a model to follow, introduce the model, and explain how a focus on healthy living can contribute to overall well-being. A depiction of the model is provided in Figure 1, and each characteristic of wellness is briefly described. The interaction of the components of the model is emphasized. The model emphasizes the point that wellness is a choice and that each choice made toward wellness empowers people toward even greater happiness and life satisfaction by enhancing overall well-being. Choices for wellness can be made in any area, at any time people choose. Typically, choices are made daily.

It is important when presenting the model to emphasize the three, or even four-dimensional, nature of wellness. When presenting the Wheel, for example, it is important to encourage individuals to view the model as a round sphere or globe, with spirituality in the center. If a person's sense of spirituality is healthy, the middle of the sphere is round and full and provides a firm foundation or core for the rest of the components of wellness. If a person's sense of spirituality is somehow flat, the rest of the sphere cannot be firm and round. Similarly, the tasks of self-direction function metaphorically like the spokes in a wheel. So long as they are strong, the wheel can roll along solidly through time and space. If one or more spokes are defective, as in the broken spokes of a bicycle, the wheel is unable to move smoothly through time and space. It is, in effect, similar to a wheel that is out of balance as it travels roughly along the continua of time and space.

Similarly, the IS-Wel should be considered a three-dimensional model, which ideally will roll smoothly through space and time. In contrast to the Wheel model, when using

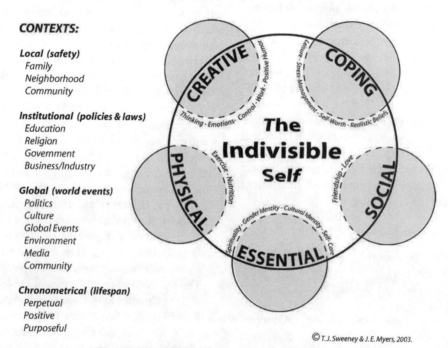

© T. J. Sweeney & J. E. Myers, 2003.

Figure 1. The Indivisible Self: An Evidence-Based Model of Wellness

Note. Creative = Creative Self; Coping = Coping Self; Social = Social Self; Essential = Essential Self; Physical = Physical Self. From *The Indivisible Self: An Evidence-Based Model of Wellness,* by T. J. Sweeney and J. E. Myers, 2003, Greensboro, NC: Author. Copyright 2003 by T. J. Sweeney and J. E. Myers. Reprinted with permission.

the IS-Wel model, it should be recognized that life is not always smooth. There are numerous forces, including the contextual factors, that cause people to move from their set course. The "bumps" on the circle in this model, represented by the five factors of the self, create "course corrections" as people bounce through life.

The models represent the components of wellness over the life span, and attention to each component has consequences that multiply over time. For those who make wellness choices, the cumulative effect over the life span is one of increasing wellness in all dimensions, thereby contributing to quality of life and longevity. Each person should take a life-span perspective on his or her total wellness, reviewing the impact of prior choices in each dimension of wellness and projecting the future impact of choices made at this time.

Finally, individuals should review the model and reflect on the personal meaning of wellness. Clients are encouraged first to seek to achieve a personal definition of wellness, then to reflect on wellness as a process rather than an outcome. Next, to personalize their view of wellness even further, clients are encouraged to partake of informal and sometimes formal assessments of the dimensions of wellness. Following assessment, people should recognize and build on their strengths to help construct a personal wellness plan to increase wellness in areas that are not as strong. Wellness plans may focus on any of the areas of wellness described in the model and are personalized depending on an individual's strengths, limitations, resources, and goals.

Contributed by Jane E. Myers,
The University of North Carolina
at Greensboro,
Greensboro, NC

Reference

Myers, J. E., & Sweeney, T. J. (2005). The indivisible self: An evidence-based model of wellness. *Journal of Individual Psychology, 60,* 234–244.

Sweeney, T. J., & Myers, J. E. (2003). *The indivisible self: An evidence-based model of wellness.* Greensboro, NC: Author.

Additional Resources

Healthy People 2010 Web site: http://www.healthypeople.gov/

Myers, J. E., & Sweeney, T. J. (2005). *Counseling for wellness: Theory, research, and practice.* Alexandria, VA: American Counseling Association.

Myers, J. E., Sweeney, T. J., & Witmer, J. M. (2000). The Wheel of Wellness counseling for wellness: A holistic model for treatment planning. *Journal of Counseling & Development, 78,* 251–266.

National Center for Complementary and Alternative Medicine Web site: http://nccam.nih.gov/

SparkPeople: Make Your Life an Adventure Web site: http://www.sparkpeople.com/

■ White Racial Identity Models

According to Janet Helms (1993), **racial identity** is a social construction related to a sense of group identity (i.e., collective identity) that is based on the perception of common heritage with a particular racial group. Racial identity, however, can be a frame to categorize others based on skin color (O'Hearn, 1998). As an example, the term *White* has always been used by the U.S. Census Bureau as a demographic label. Caucasian, European American, and Anglo typically have been used to describe racial group membership based on demographics for other purposes (McDermott & Samson, 2005).

Several theorists (e.g., Helms, Carter, Hardiman, and Poston) have authored **White racial identity development models.** The essential idea among these models is that a White person goes through several stages or statuses in which he or she may accept or reject positive and negative self-attitudes related to race. The person may not go through all the stages/statuses and could be in several stages/statuses at the same time. Two of the leading theorists in White racial development are Janet Helms and Rita Hardiman. The models developed by Helms and Hardiman are similar in that a White individual progresses away from a racist frame before moving to the next stages/statuses (an individual can be in more than one stage/status at a time) in which they discover a nonracist White identity. These models presuppose that White racial identity in the United States is linked with racism (e.g., individual, cultural, and institutional) and that White individuals are socialized to develop stereotypes and racist attitudes. It then follows that White individuals who develop socialized racial stereotypes and racist attitudes would have skewed interactions with individuals from other races. Because racial issues permeate all facets of life in the United States, it is important to understand the development of racial identity among the dominant culture.

Models of White Racial Identity Development

Helms's and Hardiman's models differ within individual stages/statuses. **Helms's (1993) White racial identity model** focuses on the movement away from racist attitudes and movement toward acceptance of other cultures. As individuals move into higher order statuses, they begin to develop a nonracist identity. Helms's model:

Stage 1. Contact—Obliviousness to own racial identity. In this status, individuals are unaware of the impact of their cultural/racial background. They do not consider the role of race in their daily lives.

Stage 2. Disintegration—First acknowledgement of White identity. In this status, individuals become aware that being White has an impact on their personal development, but they do not have full understanding of the implications.

Stage 3. Reintegration—Idealizes Whites/denigrates Blacks. Individuals who are predominantly in this status tend to self-segregate and idealize the White dominant cultural attitudes and beliefs.

Stage 4. Pseudo-Independence—Intellectualized acceptance of own and others' race. Individuals in this status develop a cognitive awareness of the benefits and affect of being White and also become aware of the affect of other race issues.

Stage 5. Immersion/Emersion—In this stage, there is honest appraisal of racism and significance of Whiteness.

Stage 6. Autonomy—An individual internalizes a multicultural identity with nonracist Whiteness at its core.

Hardiman's (1994) White racial identity model was developed from a qualitative study of six White autobiographies. Hardiman evaluated each of the biographies for themes and developed a four-stage model as a result:

Stage 1. Acceptance—Active or passive acceptance of White superiority. In this stage, Whites are socialized to accept their superiority. According to Hardiman's analysis, this conditioning begins between birth and age 5 years.

Stage 2. Resistance—Person's awareness of own racial identity for the first time. This awareness occurs among interactions with parents, extended family, the church, the surrounding community, and school.

Stage 3. Redefinition—An individual attempts to redefine Whiteness from a nonracist perspective.

Stage 4. Internalization—An individual internalizes a nonracist perspective.

Theorists like Helms (19993) and Hardiman (1994) have developed models to explain White individuals' development of identity around their racial/cultural being. These models are based on the assumption that White individuals begin with some sense of racist indoctrination and that, through learning about and exposure to other races and cultures, they develop and internalize a nonracist perspective. The models are somewhat controversial because they are primarily focused on Black and White relations and the presupposition of White supremacy by individuals going through the stages of development. The majority of White racial identity models are criticized because they are based on minority models, focus on attitudes toward other races, neglect self-awareness of White cultural attitudes, and are stage oriented, but put in the proper context, these models are the first attempts to explain racial attitudes of White, majority-culture members.

Contributed by Robika Modak and
Carl J. Sheperis,
Mississippi State University,
Starkville, MS

References

Hardiman, R. (1994). White racial identity development in the United States. In E. P. Salett & D. R. Koslow (Eds.), *Race, ethnicity, and self: Identity in multicultural perspective* (pp. 117–140). Washington, DC: National Multicultural Institute.

Helms, J. E. (1993). Introduction: Review of racial identity terminology. In J. E. Helms (Ed.), *Black and White racial identity: Theory, research and practice.* Westport, CT: Praeger.

McDermott, M., & Samson, F. L. (2005). White racial and ethnic identity in the United States. *Annual Review of Sociology, 31,* 245–261.

O'Hearn, C. C. (1998). *Half and half: Writers growing up biracial and bicultural.* New York: Pantheon Books.

■ Within-Subjects Design

A **within-subjects design** is used when a change in the dependent variable in a group is measured across time or when participants in a group are exposed to two or more treatments sequentially and the outcomes of the treatments are evaluated across time. Random assignment may be used in some within-subjects designs; however, it is the different sequences of a treatment or series of treatments that are highlighted in this type of design.

In a within-subjects design, the researcher is interested in identifying changes over time in one or more groups. In this type of study, a group receives a pretest in order to establish a baseline for a particular topic of interest (e.g., depression, wellness). The pretest is typically followed by a treatment or intervention. A posttest is administered in order to see if there is any change in the baseline after the treatment or intervention. Statistical tests may be conducted to determine whether there are differences between the pretest and posttest scores. From the results of the tests, inferences may be made as to the effectiveness of the treatment or intervention. For example, a counselor may wish to determine the extent of progress made in depressive symptoms for clients from a group counseling experience. The counselor administers an instrument measuring depression (baseline or pretest), provides the intervention over a preestablished period, and then administers the instrument again at the end of the intervention (posttest). Comparisons can be made between the pretest and posttest scores.

When comparing scores across time, measurement of an initial score (baseline) is compared with subsequent scores of the same measure for the same participants. Usually, subsequent scores can be compared to the baseline scores, or even to the latter scores. This type of design is also known as a **repeated measures design.** Common models include pretest–posttest designs, with additional follow-up measures often used. For example, if a professional school counselor wants to track progress of students in a career development class, the counselor may wish to administer students a career decision-making instrument at the beginning of the school year (the baseline measure) and track progress at midyear and then again at the end of the year. The school counselor could ascertain whether students in the class are making significant progress in career decision making.

Multiple treatments may also be addressed in a within-subjects design. For example, a professional counselor may wish to know the effect of a substance abuse program that uses psychoeducation, group counseling, and individual counseling as interventions. The counselor may obtain a baseline before any intervention and then provide measures after each component is offered (i.e., psychoeducation, group counseling, individual counseling) and see how the clients change over time. One issue to consider is whether or not the sequence of the treatments has an effect. Thus, the counselor may wish to divide the clients into separate groups, with each group experiencing the same interventions but offered in a different sequence.

Contributed by Richard S. Balkin,
Texas A&M University–Commerce,
Commerce, TX

Additional Resources

Creswell, J. W. (2007). *Educational research: Planning, conducting, and evaluating quantitative and qualitative research* (3rd ed.). Upper Saddle River, NJ: Pearson Merrill Prentice Hall.

Gall, M. D., Gall, J. P., & Borg, W. R. (2007). *Educational research: An introduction* (8th ed.). Boston: Allyn & Bacon.

Vogt, W. P. (2007). *Quantitative research methods for professionals*. Boston: Allyn & Bacon.

Women's Development, Counseling Women

Women's development is best understood as the confluence of the experience of gender and many other identity markers, such as immigration status, physical ability, race, sexual orientation, and social class, to name just a few. Multiple and overlapping identity markers guide women's development and have an impact on their experiences, which include sexism and other forms of oppression and subordination over the life span. These identity markers can be experienced as oppressive or empowering at different times and in various contexts in women's lives, and they are central considerations in addressing women's counseling needs.

Sexism consists of institutional and relational systems of inequality that are based on biological sex. As a prevalent developmental theme in the lives of women, sexism may be secondary to the experience of racism in the lives of women of color. Women marginalized by race and sexual orientation, for example, may also struggle with internalized racism or internalized heterosexism, whereas for privileged women, internalized domination may be central to their gender identity.

Oppression and abuse are ways of actively reinforcing inequity and subordination (see Oppression). One in 4 women experiences sexual abuse (Liang et al., 2002), whereas countless others experience domestic and sexual violence, sexual harassment, or other forms of emotional abuse. The source and impact of these experiences, which in large part involve feelings of shame, need to be named in order for counseling to empower and heal women effectively.

Developmental Models for Women

Participating in activities that foster the development of others is essential to the survival of the human species. These activities, which are indicative of women's traditional roles and professions, are paradoxically devalued, misunderstood,

and misrepresented in traditional theories of counseling and development. Such theories (i.e., Rogerian therapy, psychoanalysis, Abraham Maslow's theory of self-actualization, and object relations theory) emphasize personal (individual) growth, self-awareness, self-actualization, and individuation as indicators of emotional well-being and mature psychological growth development. Although Carl Rogers, Alfred Adler, and Erik Erikson emphasized relational development to some degree in their theories of counseling and development (it should also be noted that they were all highly criticized by their psychoanalytic peers for doing so), their therapeutic outcomes were all based on the traditional Western ideology of individualism. Such ideology is in clear contrast to the notion of becoming better able to create and participate in mutually empathic growth-fostering relationships as a goal of human development that was first proposed by Jordan, Kaplan, Miller, Stiver, and Surrey (1991).

Jordan et al. (1991) proposed an alternative developmental theory, initially referred to as self-in-relation theory, that suggested the process of psychological growth and relational development over the life span involves the ideas that (a) people grow through and toward relationship throughout the life span; (b) movement toward mutuality and deepening connections characterizes mature functioning; (c) participating in increasingly complex and diversified relational networks characterizes psychological growth; (d) mutual empathy and mutual empowerment are at the core of growth-fostering relationships; (e) authenticity is necessary for real engagement in growth-fostering relationships; (f) all people grow and change in growth-fostering relationships; and (g) the goal of development involves a gradual increase in a person's ability to name and resist disconnections, sources of oppression, and obstacles to mutuality.

The strengths of self-in-relation theory, which has evolved into a model of psychotherapy that is now known as relational-cultural theory (RCT; Jordan, 2000), include the ideas (a) that taking a contextual approach, recognizing that disconnections not only occur in interpersonal relationships but are experienced on a broader sociopolitical level, is essential for healing and (b) that understanding developmental experiences, such as trauma, neglect, internalized dominance, and oppression, affect a person's relational capacities in any number of ways that may vary depending on the particular relational context. The limitations of this model are that it is often marginalized in lieu of traditional approaches and that it is still evolving in that there is much work to be done in understanding culture-specific disconnections between individuals and within groups of people from diverse backgrounds.

Lawrence Kohlberg's model of moral decision making had elevated the nonrelational focus on enforcing justice as the highest state "man" could achieve. Women, whose decision-making patterns did not fit neatly into Kohlberg's model, were portrayed as being less morally developed than their male counterparts. Carol Gilligan, recognizing that Kohlberg had only studied college-age men, set out to explore moral decision making in women. She discovered that women make moral decisions based primarily out of the care and concern for others. Gilligan's work resulted in a deeper understanding of the role of relationships in the moral decision-making process for both women and men. Her research was published in the book, *In a Different Voice* (Gilligan, 1993).

Gilligan's model of moral development was structured like Kohlberg's in that she found levels of moral reasoning that somewhat mirrored Kohlberg's stages of preconventional, conventional, and postconventional. The main difference, however, was that at each level, the struggle for women reflected an ongoing tension between a responsibility to one's self and the responsibility to another—or ultimately negotiating a balance between both (Qin & Comstock, 2005). Kohlberg's stages of moral development are most often characterized as men's struggle with "an ethic of rights," whereas Gilligan found women struggle with "an ethic of care." At Level 1 of Gilligan's model, women are concerned with survival and feelings of being alone and powerless. Transition to the next level occurs once they understand that a selfish concern for oneself is at odds with their responsibility to others. Level 2 is characterized by a preoccupation with only others' needs. Transition to the next stage typically occurs following experiences of ambivalence and/or conflict resulting from a lack of self-care. Last, Level 3 is characterized by the ability to negotiate one's own needs with the needs of others to create mutuality, in that caring is extended between the self and others.

Mental Health Issues for Women

Women's relational skill is often devalued and pathologized in the professional and popular literature, often by describing the skill as dependent or enmeshed. As a result, women are vulnerable to devaluing aspects of themselves, just as they are devalued in the larger culture. This dynamic sometimes results in internalized misogyny. **Internalized misogyny** is the result of sexism and patriarchy and operates in the same way as internalized racism does in people of color. The cultural context in which women are devalued, yet challenged to develop and thrive, is often an ongoing, yet unnamed dilemma and a source of stress in women's lives.

Gilligan clearly indicated that a developmental challenge for women is the ongoing struggle to balance the need for self-care with the care for others. Studies have consistently shown that women are diagnosed twice as often as men with depression and that 1 in 10 women can expect to have a serious depressive episode in her life (Stiver & Miller, 1997). Stiver and Miller also suggested that depression was often misunderstood in women and that sadness, as a result of subordination and a lack of mutuality in women's relationships, needed to be understood as a normative experience reinforced by cultural mandates that women were to make others a priority. Gilligan (1993) also suggested that cultural mandates related to women as the primary caretakers of relationships played a role in a woman's difficulty in reaching Level 3 in Gilligan's model of moral development.

Other mental health issues for women include ongoing feelings of devaluation, which can have detrimental effects on a woman's mental health. Chronic dieting, eating disorders, poor body image, substance abuse, and various forms

of self-mutilation may be the result of low self-worth stemming from the effects of internalized misogyny and other forms of oppression. Frequently, this results in what is becoming more commonly referred to as "dual-traumatization" (e.g., a combination of racism and sexual abuse; Walker, 1999). Women experience the effects of chronic stress or distress from various forms of oppression and abuse such as shame, self-blame, and disempowerment.

In an effort to negotiate potential conflicts in relationships and to preserve a sense of connection, women will paradoxically hide their true hurt feelings, particularly anger, and relate in a style known as "silencing the self," a pattern of engagement that begins in early adolescence (Witte & Sherman, 2002). This style of relating involves the acceptance of sex role stereotypes, which is correlated with depression in White middle-class adolescent girls and women (Gilligan, 1993). Implications for counseling women need to be understood in the context of women's mental health as related to sex role socialization, oppression, subordination, shame, and relational ethics (to name just a few), all of which are demonstrated in how women respond to stress. The remainder of this entry addresses cutting-edge research on women's responses to stress and concludes with recommendations for how professional counselors might best facilitate and promote women's psychological growth and well-being.

Implications for Counseling Women

Women and men have very different behavioral and physiological responses to stress. Women respond to stress in a way that has been coined "tend and befriend," in stark contrast to the fight or flight paradigm, which has been accepted for decades as the way "mankind" responds to stress, although it may misrepresent women's experiences. The differences are due to the hormone oxytocin, which is secreted by both men and women, but in significantly higher levels in women (Taylor, 2002).

The effects of oxytocin on women during times of stress prompt them to nurture and tend to others, including their own and others' offspring. They affiliate and befriend others in an effort to expand and reinforce supportive relational networks necessary for the survival of humankind. Hormonal responses in women serve as a calming mechanism, which is very different from hormones that incite violent or aggressive behavior. This is not to suggest that women are never physically aggressive or that all women respond to various forms of stress in the same way. Female aggression most regularly occurs as an acute means of self-defense or for the protection of those in their care.

In general, women are more likely to incite and participate in indirect forms of aggression such as gossiping, spreading rumors, isolating other women from peer groups, and other behaviors referred to as **relational aggression** (Brown, 2003). This is due, in part, to cultural prohibitions regarding the direct expression of anger by women, which is seen as unnatural and inconsistent with maternal behavior and care giving and is generally not well received. Overall, female relational aggression (and aggression in general) is more prevalent in patriarchal cultures wherein individuals work to attain status and power and to preserve and promote their individual interests.

It is crucial that professional counselors understand the roles of relationships in women's lives because they are key to their (a) psychological well-being and emotional resilience over the life span (Jordan et al., 1991), (b) moral development (Gilligan, 1993), and (c) responses to stress (Taylor, 2002). A growing body of empirical data suggests that a contextual and a relational approach to counseling women is optimal in promoting their mental health and psychological adjustment (Liang et al., 2002). In practical terms, goals such as becoming increasingly independent or autonomous may not be as effective as working with women to expand their relational networks and evaluate the level of mutuality in their current relationships so that they might make better choices about whom they become involved with in any number of relational contexts.

As previously emphasized in this entry, the abilities to create, maintain, and participate in healthy relationships are central guiding features in women's lives. Relationship, affiliation, and befriending are the means women use to cope with normative and nonnormative stressors in their lives. Egalitarian and mutually empowering counseling relationships (i.e., feminist approaches) are very helpful in working with women. Counseling women involves the challenges of helping them (a) identify and express a range of feelings in relationships while negotiating cultural expectations regarding the care of others; (b) cope with the effects of sexism, subordination, oppression, and various forms of violence; and (c) create and participate in mutually empowering relationships in which they can discover and assert their authentic relational needs and desires. For women who have been enculturated to accept traditional sex role stereotypes, counseling can involve a consciousness-raising process that can be very painful. Yet, increased levels of mutuality in all women's relational networks lead to women's psychological growth and emotional well-being (Liang et al., 2002).

Contributed by Dana L. Comstock,
St. Mary's University, San Antonio, TX

References

Brown, L. M. (2003). *Girlfighting: Betrayal and rejection among girls*. New York: New York University Press.

Gilligan, C. (1993). *In a different voice: Psychological theory and women's development*. Cambridge, MA: Harvard University Press.

Jordan, J. V. (2000). The role of mutual empathy in relational-cultural therapy. *In Session: Psychotherapy in Practice, 55,* 1005–1016.

Jordan, J. V., Kaplan, A., Miller, J. B., Stiver, I., & Surrey, J. (1991). *Women's growth in connection: Writings from the Stone Center*. New York: Guilford Press.

Liang, B., Tracy, A., Taylor, C. A., Williams, L. M., Jordan, J. V., & Miller, J. B. (2002). The relational health indices: A study of women's relationships. *Psychology of Women Quarterly, 26,* 25–35.

Qin, D., & Comstock, D. (2005). Traditional models of development: Appreciating context and relationship. In D. Comstock (Ed.), *Diversity and development: Critical contexts that shape our lives and relationships* (pp. 1–23). Belmont, CA: Thomson Brooks/Cole.

Stiver, I. P., & Miller, J. B. (1997). From depression to sadness in women's psychotherapy. In J. V. Jordan (Ed.), *Women's growth in diversity: More writings from the Stone Center* (pp. 217–237). New York: Guilford Press.

Taylor, S. E. (2002). *The tending instinct: How nurturing is essential to who we are and how we live*. New York: Times Books.

Walker, M. (1999). Dual traumatization: A sociocultural perspective. In Y. Jenkins (Ed.), *Diversity in college settings: Directives for helping professionals* (pp. 51–66). New York: Routledge.

Witte, T. H., & Sherman, M. F. (2002). Silencing the self and feminist identity development. *Psychological Reports, 90,* 1075–1080.

Additional Resources

Herman, J. L. (1997). *Trauma and recovery*. New York: Basic Books:

Miller, J. B. (1986). *Toward a new psychology of women* (2nd ed.). Boston: Beacon Press.

Miller, J. B., & Stiver, I. P. (1997*). The healing connection: How women form relationships in therapy and in life*. Boston: Beacon Press.

Slater, L., Daniels, J. H., & Banks, A. E. (Eds.). (2003). *The complete guide to mental health for women*. Boston: Beacon Press.

Tolman, D. (2002). *Dilemmas of desire*. Cambridge, MA: Harvard University Press.

■ Work Values

Originally, career development theory centered on the two primary variables of abilities and interests until Donald Super introduced a third important variable, work values. Super initially conceptualized work values as "qualities desired by people in their activities, life situations, and acquisitions" (Zytowski, 1994, p. 26). Super's early conceptualization of work values could be equated to work preferences as "qualities desired" in the workplace. In contrast, Dawis and Lofquist (1984) defined work values as needs, rather than work preferences, that work environments must reinforce to result in a person's work satisfaction. In the theory of work adjustment (TWA), a person's needs (work values) are conceptualized through the construct of "reinforcer requirements" (e.g., flexible work schedule) that a work environment must address for the worker to be satisfied in that work setting (Dawis, 2005). To understand the concept of work values further, however, counselors need to understand the context in which work values make sense. Brown's (2002) value-based theory, which includes the concepts of values, lifestyle values, cultural values, and work values (i.e., the intrinsic vs. extrinsic work values and taxonomy of work values introduced by Ginzberg, Ginsburg, Axelrad, & Herma, 1951), is a helpful starting point.

Brown (2002) defined **values** as individual beliefs that are experienced as standards that guide individual behavior as well as associated emotional experiences. Brown's definition of values would be consistent with Dose's (1997) dimension of moral versus preference values, aligning more with moral values that reflect ethical standards that must be present rather than with preferred values that are operative when an individual chooses a course of action. For example, an individual who has the value of marital fidelity would choose to confront a friend who self-discloses an extramarital affair. Thus, the individual's value (e.g., marital fidelity) is an ethical/moral standard that guides behavior (e.g., confronting a friend to end the affair or choosing not to continue the friendship with a friend who continues the affair). Conversely, in this example, an individual who has a preference-oriented definition of values would prefer that a friend not have extramarital affairs but would not confront the friend or end the friendship.

Individuals have many different values that can be sorted into three basic types: lifestyle values, cultural values, and work values. **Lifestyle values** can be defined as individual values that guide behavior in roles outside of work, such as family, friendships, and other important social relationships and leisure and community activities (Brown, 2002). For example, an individual may have the lifestyle value that it is important to spend significant time with family, and this value influences the individual to limit commitments that interfere with family social plans (e.g., bringing work home, going out with friends). Similarly, a person who values leisure activities (e.g., golf) will actively protect this activity from competing demands of family and will also work to protect the resources (e.g., golfing money or membership) necessary to continue to engage regularly in the leisure activity.

Cultural values are the cultural beliefs that guide the behavior of the culture group's members. Kluckhorn and Strotbeck (1961) identified several broad cultural values that include human nature beliefs (e.g., people are basically trustworthy, people cannot be trusted), person–nature relationship (e.g., Native American cultural value of living in harmony with nature), time orientation (e.g., Native Americans tend to be present oriented and focus less on future planning), activity (e.g., German Americans tend to have a doing-action-oriented self-expression, whereby they express themselves through deed and attention to detail, workmanship, and order of their homes and yards), rules of emotional expression (e.g., Irish men tend to be more expressive to strangers than to family members), and value of social relationships (e.g., individualistic cultures emphasize the needs of the individual, whereas collectivistic cultures reflect that the needs of the group supersede the needs of the individual).

Work values are the values that should be satisfied as a result of the individual's participation in the work role (Brown, 2002). The key phrase "should be satisfied" in Brown's definition of work values further establishes that work values reflect a moral dimension (i.e., work role should/

ought to satisfy my work values) rather than merely reflect preferences in the work role (i.e., "I would prefer that my work role satisfied my work values but it is not required"; Dose, 1997). Brown's definition of work values implies that an individual's work values become required criteria in searching for potentially satisfying work as well as criteria for self-evaluating work satisfaction and work role success. Brown's definition of work values would be consistent with Dawis and Lofquist's (1984) definition of work values as needs or requirements that must be reinforced by work environments. If work values were mere work role preferences, the work selection process (e.g., wider pool of potential work), self-evaluations of work satisfaction (e.g., an individual could still be satisfied in a work role that did not reflect key work values because the work role might satisfy the individual's other lifestyle values and/or cultural values), and work success (e.g., individuals might place more emphasis on self-evaluating their work role success based on the extent that they are able to meet the work role demands and less on the congruence between their work values and values reinforced in the work role) would be less difficult. Furthermore, to understand work values, it is useful to relate work values (as defined as needs or requirements) to work outcome preferences. The Minnesota theory of work adjustment (TWA; Dawis, 2005) focuses on two types of work outcome preferences, the first being the work outcome preference of the person (worker) and the second being the work outcome preference of the work environment (workplace). Dawis's basic TWA model explains that both the worker and the work environment have the same primary goal, or work outcome preference, of tenure or remaining on the job; however, tenure requires that both the worker and the work environment be satisfied. The work environment has certain work requirements (work demands), and the extent to which the worker has the necessary abilities and meets the work demands will influence the work environment's satisfactoriness and the decision to retain or dismiss the worker (work outcome preference). Similarly, the worker's decision of whether to continue to work or quit the job (work outcome preference) is primarily related to his or her work satisfaction, which is the correspondence between a person's work values and the work environment's ability to reinforce those values. Stated differently, because the TWA model is a worker–work environment interactional model that allows for different ways of as sequencing interactions, the work outcome preference of the employee can be thought of as satisfaction of his or her needs or work values rather than just work tenure. Ideally, workers would choose work environments that reasonably satisfied their needs or work values (both intrinsic and extrinsic), and such a fit between worker and work environment would result in worker job satisfaction and tenure.

The two basic types of work values are intrinsic and extrinsic. Rosenberg (1957) distinguished between the terms *self-expression rewards* and *extrinsic rewards* in regard to the occupational choice process. Self-expression rewards **(intrinsic work values)** are the rewards received or values satisfied as a result of performing the work itself. Examples of intrinsic work values (self-expression rewards) are opportunities to express creativity, to help others, to help society, to compete with others, to work for an important cause, to experience excitement, or to interact socially with the public. Extrinsic rewards (**extrinsic work values**) are the rewards received or values satisfied in exchange for completing work. Examples of extrinsic work values (i.e., extrinsic rewards) are financial compensation, opportunity to set own work schedule (e.g., flexibility), travel opportunities, job security (e.g., permanent employment), social status, intellectual status, or work recognition rewards or honors.

The major underlying assumption of Brown's (2002) value-based theory is that cultural and work values are the primary variables that influence the occupational choice-making process, the occupation chosen, and the resulting satisfaction with and success in the occupation chosen. Although Brown focused on several cultural values, social value (individualistic vs. collectivistic culture) is the focus of this discussion because several of the main propositions of Brown's theory hinge on the interaction between work values and social value in explaining occupational choice, satisfaction, and success.

In terms of occupational choice, Brown's (2002) value-based theory proposes that persons with an **individualistic social value** will use their prioritized work values as the most important determinant of occupational choice; however, Brown's theory also proposes that persons with a **collectivistic social value** will be most influenced in their occupational choice not by their own work values but rather by the work values of their group or family members. Brown's theory proposes that there are three primary bases for job satisfaction, although the order of importance of the primary bases was influenced by the cultural social value (e.g., individualistic vs. collectivistic). The three primary bases for job satisfaction are (a) congruence between work values reinforced on the job and individuals' work values; (b) conflicts that occur between the career role and other life roles; and (c) approval of the work role by others such as parents, spouses, and friends (Brown, 2002). Persons with an individualistic social value will order the primary bases of job satisfaction differently (i.e., work value congruence, career/life role conflicts, and work role approval by others) than persons with a collectivistic social value (i.e., work role approval by others, career/life role conflicts, and work value congruence). In terms of occupational success, Brown proposed that being successful in an occupation was influenced by the degree of congruence between estimates of a person's abilities and values and the skills, abilities, and values necessary to be successful in that occupation. For persons who are individualistic (cultural value), the estimates of abilities and values are derived from the individual in the work role, whereas for collectivistic persons (cultural value), the estimates are derived by the group decision makers (e.g., individual, spouse, extended family members).

Lifestyle values, cultural values, and intrinsic and extrinsic work values guide people's behavior and help them to live meaningful lives. To have a meaningful work life, work and cultural values interact to influence people's occupational choice, satisfaction, and success.

Contributed by Darren A. Wozny,
Mississippi State University–
Meridian Campus,
Meridian, MS

References

Brown, D. (2002). The role of work and cultural values in occupational choice, satisfaction, and success: A theoretical statement. *Journal of Counseling & Development, 80,* 48–56.

Dawis, R. V. (2005). The Minnesota theory of work adjustment. In S. D. Brown & R. W. Lent (Eds.), *Career development and counseling: Putting theory and research to work* (pp. 3–23). New York: Wiley.

Dawis, R. V., & Lofquist, L. H. (1984). *A psychological theory of work adjustment.* Minneapolis: University of Minnesota Press.

Dose, J. (1997). Work values: An integrative framework and illustrative application to organizational socialization. *Journal of Occupational and Organizational Psychology, 70,* 219–240.

Ginzberg, E., Ginsburg, S. W., Axelrad, S., & Herma, J. L. (1951). *Occupational choice: An approach to general theory.* New York: Columbia University Press.

Kluckhorn, F. R., & Strotbeck, F. L. (1961). *Values in values orientations.* Evanston, IL: Row Paterson.

Rosenberg, M. (1957). *Occupations and values.* New York: Free Press.

Zytowski, D. G. (1994). A Super contribution to vocational theory: Work values. *The Career Development Quarterly, 43,* 25–31.

Additional Resource

Johnson, M. K., Mortimer, J. T., Lee, J. C., & Stern, M. J. (2007). Judgments about work: Dimensionality revisited. *Work and Occupations, 34,* 290–317.

■ Worldview

Worldview is defined as a person's relationship with the world; it is the mediating variable or the core of assumptions a person uses to understand, relate to, and act on the world. Worldview is used in counseling to refer to core assumptions that people, families, and groups hold about the world. A result of the socialization process, worldview mediates all human perceptions and helps categorize and define reality. Until the professional counselor understands the client's values, beliefs, assumptions, and life experiences (i.e., worldview), appropriate and ethical counseling cannot take place. Understanding worldview is considered an important component in ethical, culture-specific counseling (American Counseling Association, 2005).

The construct of worldview was introduced in the counseling literature by Sue (1978) to help counselors understand clients who were culturally different from the counselor. He articulated an ethical format for establishing process and goals in counseling using worldview information. His articulation of worldview juxtaposed two psychological concepts: **locus of control** and **locus of responsibility.** These two psychological constructs can be used to understand how cultures socialize people to rely on each other as members of a group (i.e., **collectivism**) and to accept the underlying belief that the good, or survival, of the group results in the good, or survival, of the individual, as opposed to how cultures socialize people to rely on themselves. **Individualism** refers to the notion that individual freedom leads to the good, or survival, of the individual and, ultimately, society; thus, it is a negative to rely on others. This approach encourages the counselor to understand the client's socialization assumptions and to structure counseling interventions both in terms of goals and process on the basis of the client's cultural identification.

The simplest way to understand the concept of worldview is to understand worldview in terms of basic or core values that people hold about their world that are acquired within a cultural and social context and to recognize that these core values and beliefs guide behavior, thoughts, feelings, and emotions. An **etic** worldview refers to something universally accepted by all cultures. An **emic** worldview refers to a worldview specific to a person or a specific culture, but this specific worldview may not resonate with others. Because culture is a major socializing variable that is primarily responsible for influencing beliefs, values, and assumptions—worldview—understanding a client's worldview is a critical requirement for counselors. In addition, as awareness of culture and its affect on counseling process and outcome increased, it became clear that counseling theories and skills derived in a certain environment were usually from an emic (i.e., culture-specific) perspective and might not be relevant to all clients, depending on their socialization; however, each culture that generates counseling theories, strategies, and skills assumes that theirs are etic (i.e., universal assumptions), leading to charges of cultural encapsulation and cultural malpractice. This knowledge and the awareness of it in the profession led to the development of guidelines for cultural competence by all leading psychological and counseling associations.

Anthropologist Clyde Kluckhohn (1965) originally articulated the following universal value orientations that pertain to five dimensions relevant to human experiences over the life span:

1. **Human nature.** The emic articulations of this value can be that human nature is good, bad, or a combination of good and bad. Also, human nature is either mutable (changeable) or immutable.
2. **Social relationships.** Emic articulations include lineal hierarchical (e.g., highly structured, traditional culture with clear lines of authority and power figures, father as head of household), collateral mutual (a mutually supportive and caring society), and individualistic (e.g., relationships are secondary and the person's needs, desires are primary).
3. **Nature.** Nature has the following emic articulations: accepting the power of nature, living in harmony with nature, and humans having control over nature.
4. **Time.** Time focuses on the past, present, or the future.
5. **Activity.** In culture-specific terms, activity operates as being (i.e., a spontaneous way of living), being-in-becoming (i.e., living in a manner that is focused on both inner [spiritual-moral development] and material achievement), or doing (i.e., a life focused on external achievements on culturally valued dimensions). It is accepted that humans at some time over the life span will confront dilemmas around these value orientations. Each category may not be relevant at any given moment but over time will be relevant in the human experience.

Ibrahim (1991) proposed using the universal and the culture-specific value orientations and values to understand worldview and has empirically derived the four worldviews that incorporate elements of etic and emic values: optimistic, traditional, pessimistic, and here and now. Each of these worldviews has specific emic elements incorporating some of the five universal value orientations:

1. **Optimistic worldview.** This worldview primarily accepts that human nature is basically good. There is a strong belief in achievement and success that incorporates spiritual growth with external success. Success is as important as spontaneity in life. There is also a strong identification with nature, living in harmony with nature, and acceptance of the power of nature.
2. **Traditional worldview.** This worldview is focused on lineal-hierarchical and, to a certain extent, collateral-mutual social relationships. The traditional worldview is very future oriented, with little emphasis on the past. There is also a belief that nature can be controlled.
3. **Pessimistic worldview.** This worldview perceives human nature as basically bad. Nature is perceived as a powerful force, and there is an acceptance of human vulnerability. Finally, social dimension is perceived as collateral mutual (i.e., do unto others as they do unto you)
4. **Here and now worldview.** This worldview has two major elements from the universal value orientations (i.e., time and activity). This worldview only operates from a present-time focus and may allow the past to influence the present. A clear identification is made with being, spontaneous work, and personal-life focus, with no set schedule, goals, or commitments.

Ibrahim (1991) contended that everyone has a primary worldview and a secondary worldview, and both of these sets of values and assumptions help people negotiate their relationships with people, nature, institutions, and the world. People come to counseling with dilemmas that are usually very difficult to resolve because the issues involve coming to terms with conflicting values and the decisions made can affect the course of a person's life. A relevant example would be an unwed Catholic teenager coming to terms with a pregnancy. In this example, the client's primary worldview derives from a traditional and mostly religious worldview regarding the sanctity of human life and the injunction against taking life (in this case of a fetus). The secondary worldview, given the client's developmental stage, is primarily here and now. In a culturally competent counseling intervention, the counselor will respect the client's worldviews and help the client find a solution that she can live with for the rest of her life. Given this caveat, it is critical to understand the client's worldview in order for the professional counselor to conduct culturally relevant and ethical counseling. Without this information, counseling can be misleading, harmful, and based only on the counselor's worldview or reality. To make counseling relevant to the client as a cultural entity, it is important to understand the client's core assumptions or worldview.

Implications for Counseling

Worldview is a mediating variable that helps professional counselors access the inner world of clients and understand the client's core values, beliefs, and assumptions. To use worldview successfully, it must be placed within the context of the client's cultural identity. Cultural socialization affects how people understand and accept their gender, age, sexual orientation, social class, religion, and ability or disability status. Given that worldview is such an important construct, especially in counseling clients who are culturally different from the counselor, and given the reality of a diverse society, it is important to know how to use worldview in counseling.

The first step is to assess the client's worldview according to either locus of control and locus of responsibility theory or the four value-based empirically derived worldviews. Clients can be involved in identifying their worldviews by using either the Scale to Assess Worldview© (Ibrahim & Kahn, 1984), a paper–pencil empirically derived inventory, or using the four worldviews and their composite parts in the scale to help the client identify the worldview prior to deciding on the goals and treatment plans for counseling (Ibrahim, 1991). Once the client's values, beliefs, assumptions, and cultural socialization have been identified, the next step is to identify the best communication strategy or process to use (e.g., nondirective, action-oriented [directive], or a collaborative process) to arrive at the goals and outcomes for counseling. The counseling literature indicates clients from traditional, col-lateral-mutual, or interdependent socializing systems value a more action-oriented and directive style of counseling. Clients from individualistic sociocultural systems value a nondirective, reflective mode of counseling.

According to Sue's (1978) worldview paradigm, the higher the external locus of control and responsibility, the more directive the style should be. The higher the internal locus of control and responsibility, the more nondirective the communication strategy should be. In Ibrahim's (1991) worldview paradigm, people with traditional and here and now worldviews prefer a directive style.

Contributed by Farah A. Ibrahim,
University of Colorado at Denver and
Health Sciences Center, Denver, CO

References

American Counseling Association. (2005). *ACA code of ethics.* Alexandria, VA: Author.

Ibrahim, F. A. (1991). Contribution of cultural worldview to generic counseling and development. *Journal of Counseling & Development, 70,* 13–19.

Ibrahim, F. A., & Kahn, L. (1984). *Scale to Assess World View©.* Unpublished scale.

Kluckhohn, C. (1965). *Mirror for man: Survey of human behavior and social attitudes.* Greenwich, CT: Premier Books.

Sue, D. W. (1978). Worldviews and counseling. *Personnel & Guidance Journal, 56,* 458–462.

Additional Resources

Ibrahim, F. A. (2003). Existential worldview counseling theory: Inception to applications. In F. D. Harper & J. McFadden (Eds.), *Culture and counseling: New approaches* (pp. 196–208). Boston: Allyn & Bacon.

Ibrahim, F. A., & Kahn, H. (1987). Assessment of world views. *Psychological Reports, 60,* 163–176.

Ibrahim, F. A., Roysircar-Sodowsky, G. R., & Ohnishi, H. (2001). Worldview: Recent developments and needed directions. In J. G. Ponterotto, M. Casas, L. Suzuki, & C. Alexander (Eds.), *Handbook of multicultural counseling* (2nd ed., pp. 425–456). Thousand Oaks, CA: Sage.

Koltko-Rivera, M. E. (2004). The psychology of worldviews. *Review of General Psychology, 8,* 3–58.

Lonner, J., & Ibrahim, F. A. (in press). Appraisal and assessment in cross-cultural counseling. In P. Pedersen, J. Lonner, J. Trimble, & J. Draguns (Eds.), *Counseling across cultures* (6th ed.). Thousand Oaks, CA: Sage.

Page numbers in bold indicate primary topics. Figures and tables are indicated by "f" and "t" following the page number. Alphabetization is word-by-word (e.g., "ACA Legal Series" precedes "Academic achievement). Note that there is a separate Names Index.

(Continued)

Compassion, 218
Compensation, 15–16, 146t
Compensatory equalization of treatments, 293–294
Compensatory rivalry by participants receiving less desirable treatments, 293
Competence, 174, 259–260
Competencies for Counseling Gay, Lesbian, Bisexual and Transgendered Clients (ALGBTIC), 488
Competencies testing, 3
Complementarity, 340–341
Complex, 305
Complex tics, 544
Complimentary transactions (TA), 547
Componential analysis, 318
Componential subtheory, 318
Comprehensive Personality Profile, 85
Compromise process, 98
Compton, W., 384
Computer-adaptive testing, 113
Computer-assisted career guidance systems (CACGS), **110–113**
Computer-based testing, **113–114**
Computer Occupational Information System, 111
Computer Sciences Corporation, 174
Computerized Heuristic Occupational Information, 111
Conant, James Bryant, 35
Concordance, ecological niche, 172
Concrete operations stage, 317
Concreteness, 121
Concurrent designs, 339–340
Concurrent validity, 557
Conditioned response (CR), 99
Conditions of worth, 100–101
Conduct disorder (CD) disruptive behavior disorder, 51–52
Confianza (mutual generosity), 314
Confidence interval, 525
Confidentiality, **114**
    child abuse and, 414
    fidelity and, 179
    group work and, 232, 235–236
    legal issues, 260
    privileged communication and, 235, 261, 408–409
    technology and, 112
Confirmability, 556
Confirmatory factor analysis, 194
Conflict
    in group process, 230
    intergenerational, 276
Conflict resolution, **115–116**
Confluence, 212
Confounding variables, 188, 561
Confrontation
    as counseling skill, 128
    decision-making and, 338
    Roger's core condition and, 121
Confucianism, 519–520
Congruence
    in client-centered counseling, 101
    in Holland's career typology, 91
    in Satir's conjoint family therapy, 116
Congruent validity, 557
Conjoint family therapy, **116–117**
Conjoint Family Therapy (Satir), 116
Conjoint sexual therapy, **117–118**
Connolly, Colleen, 45
Conscientizacào (critical consciousness), 382
Conscious, 421
Consciousness-raising groups, 252
Consciousness revolution, 208
Consequences, 55
Conservation, 105t
Consistency (Holland's career typology), 91
Consolidating stage, 323
Constant comparative analysis, 429
Constantine, Madonna, 502
Constructive development theory (Kegan), 271–272
Constructive norms, 224, 225t
Constructive strategy, 384

Constructivism
    Bronfenbrenner and, 171
    discovery learning, 318
    research, 454
    scaffolding, 318
    social development theory, 318
    zone of proximal development, 318
Constructivist learning theory, 10
Consultant, 118
Consultation and collaborative consultation, **118–119**
Contact summary sheets, 430
Contagion, 246
Contagious, life-threatening diseases, duty to warn and protect, 165, 261
Content bias, 140
Content learning models, 10
Content validity, 557
Contextual subtheory, intelligence theory, 318
Contiguity, 317
Continuous development and discontinuous development, **119–120**
Continuous reinforcement (CRF) schedule, 448
Continuous variables, 431, 472
Contreras v. City of Los Angeles (1981), 38
Control/comparison groups, 187
Control group, **120**, 402
Control variables, 560
Controllable attribution, 52
Convenience sampling, 469
Conventional career preference, 91
Convergence, 340
Convergent validity, 557
Conversion disorder, 514
Conversion therapy, sexual, 490
Conway, L., 549
Conyne, Robert, 239
Cook, Thomas, 455
Cook-Greuter, Susanne, 175–176
Cooley, Fannie R., 48
Cooperative interactive work, 228
Coopersmith Self-Esteem Inventory, 398
Coping
    patterns, 70
    stress and, 530
CORE (Council on Rehabilitation Education), **126**, 359, 412
Core conditions, **120–121**, 262
Core Group Work Skills Inventory, 225
Core schemas, 107
Core training standards, 250, 251t
Corey, Gerald, 170, 236, 239, 281, 521
Corey, Marianne, 170
Correction (K) validity scales, 559
Corrective Feedback Self-Efficacy Instrument, 225
Corrective Feedback Self-Efficacy Instrument–Revised, 239
Corrective recapitulation of the primary family group, 141
Correlation and regression, **121–123**
Correlation coefficient, **123–124**
Correlational research, 365
Correlational studies, 149
Corroboration, 340
Corsini, R. J., 170, 233, 234
Cott, C., 16
Couch, R. D., 219
Council for Accreditation of Counseling and Related Educational Programs (CACREP), **125–126**
    ACA collaboration with, 19
    accreditation, 2, 17, 412, 416
    ACES collaboration with, 44
    addiction counseling, 295
    counselor education standards, 1
    CSI collaboration with, 95
    founding of, 415
    leaders, 416
    mental health counselor standards, 22, 102
    multicultural awareness, 346, 496, 497, 500
    NCE and, 357, 357t
    program evaluations, 363
    rehabilitation counselors, 359
Council for Higher Education Accreditation (CHEA), 2, 125

Discontinuous development, 119–120
Discordance, 172
DISCOVER, 111–112
Discovery learning (Bruner), 318
Discrete variables, 472
Discriminant validity, 557
Discrimination
    See also Cultural bias; Racism
    against GLBTQ individuals, 267–268
    against international students, 297
    against persons with HIV/AIDS, 265, 478
    counseling of minorities and, 11, 12, 29
    out-group members and, 504
    as stage of prejudice, 404
    transphobia, 549
Discrimination index, 301
Discrimination model of supervision, 536
Discuss (WDEP system), 446
Diseases of adaptation, 529
Disengagement stage, 118, 324
Disengagement theory, 14–15, 16
Disequilibrating experiences, 176
Dismantling strategy, 384
Disorders. *See specific types*
Disorganized type schizophrenia, 475
Displacement, 146*t*
Displacement stories, 63
Disruptive behavior disorders, 50–52
Dissociation, 145*t*
Dissociative amnesia, 157
Dissociative disorders, **157–158**
Dissociative fugue, 157–158
Dissociative identity disorder (DID), 158
Dissonance, 176
Distal level of ecosystems, 171
Distance career services, 79–80
Distracters, 116
Distractors or foils in item analysis, 301
Distress, 529
Disturbance of conduct, 7
Disulfuram, 6
Diversity, 33–34, 140
    See also Multicultural counseling; *specific minorities*
    ASGW Best Practice Guidelines on, 233
    in group intervention strategies, 241
Diversity-competent group work, 240–242
Division 49—Group Psychology and Group Psychotherapy (APA), 234, 235, 406
Divorce and separation, **158–160**
Dixon, W. A., 521
Dr. Lesley Jones Creativity in Psychotherapy Conference, 45
Document summary forms, 430
Doers personality type, 266–267
DOL. *See* Labor Department, U.S.
Domains, defined, 104
Domestic, defined, 160
Domestic disturbances euphemism, 161
Domestic partner benefits, 489
Domestic violence, **160–162**
    substance abuse and, 5
Domestic Violence Office (DHS), 161
Dominative racism, 404
Donaldson v. O'Connor (1975), 412
Doroslateral prefrontal cortex, 9
Dose, J., 570
DOT (Dictionary of Occupational Titles), 77, 112, **155–156**
Double-bind communication, 528
Double blind, **162–163**, 190
Double jeopardy, 382
Doubt, 177
Downing, N. E., 199–200
Doyle, Robert, 48
DPE (Deliberate psychological education), 105–106
Drag kings, 549
Drag queens, 549
Draw-a-Person Test, 394, 399

Drawing out, 244
Drew, Clifford, 455
Driver, Helen, 239
Dropout rates, high school, 315, 361
Drug abuse and addiction, 533
    See also Substance abuse
Drummond, R. J., 114
DSM-IV-TR. *See Diagnostic and Statistical Manual of Mental Disorders*
Dual diagnosis, 5
Dual-earner couples, 463–465
Dual relationship, ethical issues, 258
Dual-traumatization, 568
Dubler, N., 379
DuBois, W. E. B., 404
Due process and special education, 516–517
Duffey, Thelma, 45
Duhl, Bunny, 199
Duhl, Fred, 199
Duncan, Jack A., 48, 239
Dunn, R., 10
Dunn, T., 136
Duty to warn and protect, **163–165**, 260–261
Dvoskin, J. A., 379
Dysfunctional Thought Record, 108
Dysmorphophobia, 514
Dyspareunia, 484
Dyssomnias, 495
Dysthumic disorder, 342

◼ E

E-BASS (Ecological Behavioral Assessment System), 55, 56*t*
EAGALA (Equine Assisted Growth and Learning Association), 25
Eagan, G., 128
Early adult transition, 327
Early adulthood, 327
Early recollections, 282
Eating Attitudes Test (EAT), 340
Eating disorders, **167–169**
    among adolescents, 8
Eating disorders not otherwise specified (NOS), 168–169
Ebel, R. L., 393
Eclecticism to integration in counseling, **169–171**
Eco-map, **172–173**
    sample, 172*f*
Ecofeminism, 201
Ecological Behavioral Assessment System (E-BASS), 55, 56*t*
Ecological bias, 59–60
Ecological counseling, 139, **171–172**, 270–271
Ecological culture. *See* Ecological counseling
Ecological factors in leadership, 221
Ecological niche, 171–172
Ecological validity, 189
The Ecology of Human Development (Bronfenbrenner), 271
Ecosytem, 171
Education Department, U.S., 2, 78, 125
Education for Handicapped Children Act Amendment of 1975, 36
Education of all Handicapped Children Act of 1975, 36, 515
Education of the Handicapped Act of 1990, 36–37
Education Resources Information Center (ERIC), 47, **174**
The Education Trust, 477
Educational planning, 109
Educational privilege, 408
Educational Testing Service, 35, 111
Edwards Personal Preference Schedule (EPPS), 398
Effect size (ES), 285, 335, 432
Effectance motivation, **174–175**
"The Effectiveness of Psychotherapy" (Lambert & Bergin), 456
"The Effectiveness of Psychotherapy" (Seligman), 456
"The Effects of Psychotherapy" (Eysenck), 456
Efficacy, 174–175
Efficacy expectation, 506
Efficiency, 143, 143*f*
Egalitarian structures, 181
Egan, Gerard, 262–263
Ego, 175, 305, 420

Ego development, Loevinger's theory of, **175–176**
Ego identity, 176–178, 364
Ego psychology (Erikson's psychosocial stage theory), **176–178**, 363
    career construction theory and, 72
    critique, 178
    developmental counseling and, 152
    discontinuous development and, 119
    ego identity, 364
    spirituality and, 518, 520
    stage 1: basic trust vs. basic mistrust, 177
    stage 2: autonomy vs. shame and doubt, 177
    stage 3: initiative vs. guilt, 177
    stage 4: industry vs. inferiority, 8, 177
    stage 5: identity vs. role confusion, 8, 177, 275
    stage 6: intimacy vs. isolation, 177
    stage 7: generativity vs. stagnation, 177–178
    stage 8: integrity vs. despair, 177–178
Ego states, 547
Egocentrism, 105*t*
Egotism, 212
Eigenvalues, 195
Eisel v. Board of Education of Montgomery County (1991), 260
Elaborative rehearsal, 286
Elder abuse, 260
Elder care, 470
    gerontological counseling, 210–211
Elective course model, 392
Electra complex, 420–421, 423
ELL (English language learner), 311, 312
Elliot, Hellen, 100
Ellis, Albert, 107, 170, 249, 281
    See also Rational emotive behavior therapy and groups
Emancipated minor, 319
Embedded analysis, 93
Embeddedness–emanation, 200
EMDR (eye movement desensitization and reprocessing), **191**
Emic
    defined, 348
    perspective, 497
    worldview, 572
Eminent Career Award (ASGW), 239, 240
Eminent Career Award (NCDA), 80
Emotion-focused coping, 530
Emotional abuse, 96
Emotional cutoff, 62
Emotional distance, 62
Emotional stimulation by group leader, 219, 221
Empathic understanding, 101
Empathy
    group leader communication of, 218
    Roger's core condition, 120–121
    self-psychology and, 249
Employment Service Review, 503
Employment Service, U.S., 77, 411
Empowerment, 115
Empty chair
    dialogue technique, 212
    psychodrama, 422
Enablers, 203
Encoding, 286
Encounter group movement, 100, 234
Encounter groups, 252
Encouragement, 283, 338
Enculturation, 139
Endorsement, 321
Energizers, 218
England, G. W., 66
English, L. T., 559
English language learner (ELL), 311, 312
Enterprising career preference, 91
Enterprising/persuader personality type, 267
Enthusiasm, 218
Entrance (Jungian psychotherapy), 306
Entry in client system, 118
Environment factors (behaviorism), 317
Environmental conditions and events, 507
Environmental crises, 132

Epictetus, 443
Episodic memory, 286–287
EPPS (Edwards Personal Preference Schedule), 398
Epston, David, 130, 353
Equal Employment Act of 1966, Tower Amendment, 36
Equine Assisted Growth and Learning Association (EAGALA), 25
Equipercentile, 525
Equity, 504
Erectile disorder, 117–118
ERIC (Education Resources Information Center), 47, **174**
Erickson, Milton, 510, 528, 529
Erikson, Erik, 119, 270, 548, 567
    See also Ego psychology (Erikson's psychosocial stage theory)
Erotomanic type delusional disorder, 476
Error score, 449–450
Error variance, 542
ES (effect size), 285, 335, 432
ES index, 335
Esalen Institute, 234, 238
Espanek, L., 130
Espiritismo (spiritism), 315
Esquirol, Jean, 34
Establishment stage, 323
Esteem needs, 480
Eta coefficient (η), 124
Ethical Guidelines for Counseling Supervisors (ACES), 44
Ethical, Legal, and Professional Issues in Counseling (Remley), 415
Ethical, Legal, and Professional Issues in the Practice of Marriage and Family Therapy (Remley), 415
Ethical principles, **178–180**
    See also Belmont Report; *specific codes*
Ethical Standards for School Counselors (ASCA), 232, 236
"Ethics and Clinical Research" (Beecher), 287–288
Ethnic identity, 31, 138, 180
Ethnicity, **180**
    See also Multicultural counseling
    defined, 139–140, 438
    ethnocentrism, 180
    race, 180
Ethnocentric cross-cultural communications, 134
Ethnocentrism, 180, 405
Ethnography, 425–426
Ethnorelative cross-cultural communications, 134
Etic
    defined, 348
    perspective, 497
    worldview, 572
Eubanks, R., 185
Eugenics, 436
European Agency for Safety and Health at Work (EU), 378
European Americans
    communication styles, 182
    counseling, **180–183**
    counseling attitudes, 182
    cultural values, 181–182
    demographics, 181
    family structures, 181
    individualistic vs. collectivistic cultures, 181
Eustress, 377, 529
Evaluation
    AACE and, 43–44
    in assessment, 39
    consultation stage, 118
    of counselor effectiveness, 1
    IDEA mandated, 515
Evaluation apprehension, 190, 292–293
Evaluation—The International Journal of Theory, Research and Practice (Tavistock Institute), 238
Evaluative hypotheses, 273
Evidenced interests, 84
The Evolving Self (Kegan), 272
Ewing v. Goldstein (2004), 261
Ex post facto research design, **185**, 365
Examiner bias, 59
Examplar (CSI), 95
Exception rule, 512
Exchange theory, **183**

Harry Benjamin International Gender Dysphoria Association, 549
Hartling, L., 14
Hartmann, Heinz, 363
Hate crimes, 30
Hathaway, S. R., 35, 557
Havighurst, Robert J., 15, 255–257
Havighurst's developmental tasks, **255–257**
Hawking, Stephen, 157
Hawthorne effect, 163, 189, 403
Hayslip, Jo, 129
Hazan, Cindy, 50
Head Start, 146
Health and Human Services Department (DHHS), 161, 454–455, 508
Health anxiety/health phobia, 514
Health care professionals, 518
Health Insurance Portability and Accountability Act of 1996 (HIPAA), 37, 260, 261, 413–414, 455
Health management organizations (HMOs), **257**
Healthcare Providers Service Organization, 320
Hedlund v. Superior Court (1983), 261
Hegel, G. W. F., 184
Heidegger, Martin, 183, 184
Heider, Fritz, 52
Heiros gamos (union of polarities), 306
Heller's syndrome, 400–401
Helms, Janet E., 438, 438*f*, 439, 499, 502
Helms's White racial identity model, 565–566
Helper group member role, 222
HELPING model, 350–351
Helping others and contributing to group goals, 228
Helping relationships
ethical issues in, **257–259**
key people in, **262–263**. *See also specific individuals*
legal issues in, **259–261**
Henderson, Patricia, 80
Heppner, C., 417
Heppner, P., 384
Here and now worldview, 572
Herligh, B., 163
Herma, John L., 78, 87, 214
Herman, Joan, 417
Herman, Judith, 551–553
Hermaphrodite terminology, 549
Herr, Edwin L., 80, 81
Heterogeneous group members, 242–243
Heterosexism, **267–268**, 383
Heterosexual, 491
Heterosexual identity development, 486
Heterosexual privilege, 407
Hexagonal Model (Holland), 91*f*, 266*f*
Hierarchy, cultural value, 30
Hierarchy of needs (Maslow), 480, 509
Hiett, Jim, 21–22
High-context communication, 367
High lethality in suicide assessment, 533
High School Readjustment Scale, 322
High-stakes testing, **263–264**
achievement tests, 3, 3*t*
Advanced Placement examinations, 263
state proficiency tests, 263
Hill, C. L., 348
Hill Interaction Matrix, 225, 226
Hinduism, 520
HIPAA. *See* Health Insurance Portability and Accountability Act of 1996
Hispanics, 161, 378
Histograms, 151, 151*f*
Historical research, 149
History effects, 190
internal validity, 293
Histrionic personality disorder, 397
HIV/AIDS, counseling clients with, **264–266**
confidentiality, 261, 265
counselors' feelings of inadequacy, 429–430
dementia and, 313
transgendered individuals, 549
HMOs (health management organizations), **257**
H$_o$ (null hypotheses), 273, 402, 403

Holding environment, 364, 373
Holding in maintenance stage, 323–324
Holland, John, 71, 78, 80, 81
See also Career typology; Holland's personality types
Holland's Hexagonal Model, 91*f*, 266*f*
Holland's personality types, **266–267**, 395, 396
Holmes, S. E., 226
Holmes, Thomas, 321–322
Holmes–Rahe Scale, 321–322
Holocaust, 303
Homans, George C., 183
Homelanders generation, 208, 209
Homeless, 508
Homeopathic treatment methodology, 212
Homeostasis, 196, 198
Homework, 513
Homo sapiens Afer (African people), 435
Homo sapiens Americanus (Native American people), 435
Homo sapiens Asiaticus (Asian people), 435
Homo sapiens Europaeus (White people), 435
Homogeneity, 474
Homogeneous group members, 242–243
Homophobia and heterosexism, 207, **267–268**, 383, 404
Homoprejudice, 268
Homoscedasticity, 123
Homosexuality, 118, 490, 491
Honesty, 217
Honigsfeld, A., 10
Hoppock's Job Satisfaction Measure, 304
Horizontalization, 426
Horkimer, Max, 454
Horn, John, 289
Horne, Arthur M., 239
Horne, S. G., 206
Hosp, J., 443
Hotelling's T^2, 389
Hotseat dialogue technique, 212
House, Reese, 129
House-Tree-Person test, 35, 399
How the Way We Talk Can Change the Way We Work (Kegan), 272
How to Counsel Students (Williamson), 77–78
Howe, N., 208
Hoyt, Kenneth B., 80, 81
Huberman, Michael, 456
Hull, C., 317
Hull House, 201
Hulse-Killacky, Diana, 239
Human agency, 272
Human growth and development
ethical issues in, **268–269**
historical events in, **269–270**
key people in, **270–272**
Human immunodeficiency virus. *See* HIV/AIDS, counseling clients with
Human nature, universal value orientation, 572
Human potential movement, 234
Human Process Validation Model, 116–117
Human Relations (Tavistock Institute), 238
Humanism, 272
Humanistic theories, 10, **272–273**
See also specific theorists
Humanitarian Assistance Programs (EMDR-HAP), 191
Humiliation, 13, 14
Humor, 218
Hunter, C. C., 281
Hyde, J. S., 200
Hyperactive delirium, 147
Hypervigilance coping pattern, 70, 75
Hypoactive delirium, 147
Hypoactive sexual desire disorder, 484
Hypochondriasis, 514
Hypomanic episode, 342
Hypothesis, 457
Hypothesis interpretation, 284
Hypothesis testing, **273–274**
null hypotheses, 273, 402, 403
quantitative research, 432
testing model, 274*f*

Hypothesized sequential cues, 278–279
Hypothesizing, 338
Hysteria syndrome, 513–514

I

I & Thou (Buber), 184
I-position, 61, 63
I-statements, 245, 246
I-thou relationship, 184, 211–212
IAAOC. *See* International Association of Addiction and Offender Counselors
IAAOC News, 295
IAAOC Web site, 295
IAMFC (International Association of Marriage and Family Counselors), **296**, 412, 415
Ibrahim, F. A., 572–573
ICC (item characteristic curve), 302, 302*f*
Id, 420
IDEA. *See* Individuals With Disabilities Education Act of 1975
Identification, 118
    with the aggressor, 145*t*
Identity achievement, 275
Identity formation, **275**
Identity status concept (Marcia), 275, 275*f*
IEP (individualized education program), 515–516
Illegal aliens, 276
I'm OK, You're OK (Harris), 548
Imitative behavior, 141
Immediacy, 121
Immigrants and refugees, **275–278**
    See also Multicultural counseling
Immigrants, defined, 275–276
Immigration, 28–29, 180–181, 276–277, 500
Immigration and Naturalization Act of 1965, 500
Immigrationism, 383
Imminent justice, 105*t*
Imparting information, 141
Impelleteri, Joseph, 110–111
Imperato-McGinley, J., 205
Impersonals, 218
Implementation period (Tiedeman & O'Hara), 546
Implicit memory, 287
Implosive therapy, **278–279**
Impulse control disorders, 279–280
Impulse control disorders not elsewhere classified, 279
In a Different Voice (Gilligan), 568
In Over Our Heads (Kegan), 272
In-group, 503–504
    racial identity development models, 438
Inaba, D. S., 533
Inappropriate standardization sample, 140
Incorporation (indirect), 145*t*
Incorporation (physical), 145*t*
Incremental validity, 143, 143*f*
Indecisiveness, 85
Independent means, *t* test, 387–388
Independent variables, 402, 431, 560
Index of discrimination (*D*), 301–302
Indexes of item validity, 302
Indigenous healers, 280
Indigenous healing approaches, **280–281**
Indigenous perspective, 280
Indigenous societies, 280
Indirect methods (behavioral assessment), 55
The Individual and His Religion (Allport), 262
Individual Group Member Interpersonal Process Scale, 226
Individual interviews, 427–428
Individual or special aptitude tests, 28
Individual psychology (Adler), **281–283**
    wellness models and, 563–565, 564*f*
Individual psychology counseling techniques (Adler), **283–285**
Individual racism, 440
Individual roles of group members, 224
Individual tests, defined, 39
Individualism, 567, 572
Individualistic social value, 571

Individualistic vs. collectivistic cultures, 181
Individualized education program (IEP), 515–516
Individuals With Disabilities Education Act of 1975 (IDEA)
    assessment methods, 34, 515
    career counseling, 80
    due process rights, 516–517
    individualized education, 515–516, 517
    least restrictive environment, 516
    scope of, 36–37, 156, 413, 479, 515
Individuation, 373
Individuum (indivisible), 281
Indivisible Self, 563–565, 564*f*
Induced After-Death Communication, 551
Inductive approach, 26
Inferential statistics, 150, **285–286**
Inferiority complex, 282
Inferiority, sense of, 177, 282
Influencing skills, decision-making, 338
Infochange (C-AHEAD), 127
Informal group member role, 221–222
Information, group content, 229
Information-processing model, **286–287**
Information-processing theory, 317
Information theory, 196
Informed consent, **287**
    ACA Code of Ethics and, 268–269
    Belmont Report and, 288
    ethical issues, 33, 257, 287, 451
    fidelity and, 179
    group work and, 232, 235–236
    HIPAA and, 413
    legal issues, 259, 287, 319
Infrequency (F) validity scales, 559
Infrequency (Fb) validity scales, 559
Infrequency Psychopathology (Fp) validity scales, 559
Ingersoll, R. E., 521
Ingham, Harry, 304
Initiation, mixed method designs, 341
Initiative, 177
Innovating in maintenance stage, 324
Input hypothesis, language acquisition, 312
Instillation of hope, 141
Institute of Education Sciences, 174
Institute of International Education's Open Doors Report 2007, 296
Institutional racism, 440
Institutional Review Board for the Protection of Human Subjects, **287–288**, 455
Institutional review boards (IRBs), 288
Institutionalized accreditation, 2
Instructional events in learning theory, 317–318
Instrumental and associative learning experiences, 507
Instrumental case study, 92
Instrumentation, 294
Insurance
    liability, 164, 260, 320
    mental health coverage, 330
Integral psychology, 550
Integrated Life Planning (Hansen), 80
Integration, 170
    acculturation model, 297
    of self, 61
    stage in lifecareer process, 546
Integrative approach, 170
Integrity, 178
Intellectual functioning, 332, 334
Intellectualizers, 116
Intelligence, **289–290**
    crystallized, 9–10, 289
    fluid, 9–10, 289
Intelligence quotient (IQ), 34–35
Intelligence testing, 27, **290–292**, 290*f*
Intelligences. *See specific types*
Intentional suicides, 534
Interaction, 530
Interaction (ASERVIC), 49
Interaction Process Analysis, 226
Intercept bias, 140–141

Intercultural communications, 133
Intercultural sensitivity development model (Bennett), 134
Interest autobiography, 84
Interest-based negotiations, 115
Interests in career assessment, 68, 323
Intergenerational conflict, 276
Intermittent explosive disorder, 279
Internal attributions, 52
Internal consistency reliability, 450
Internal locus of control, 324–325
Internal objects, 373–374
Internal validity, **292–294**
Internalized anti-semitism, 303
Internalized classism, 509
Internalized homophobia, 268, 485
Internalized misogyny, 568
Internalized oppression, 382
Internalized racism, 440
International Association for Analytical Psychology, 305
International Association for Counseling, 415
International Association of Addiction and Offender Counselors (IAAOC), **294–296**, 412
International Association of Continuing Education, 411
International Association of Marriage and Family Counselors (IAMFC), **296**, 412, 415
International Association of Rehabilitation Professionals, 126
International Business Machines Corporation, 110
International Journal for the Advancement of Counseling, 499
International Statistical Classification of Diseases and Related Health Problems (WHO), 147
International students, counseling, **296–299**
International Transactional Analysis Association, 548
Internet
    CACGS online services, 110–113
    career Web sites, 86, 375–376
    ERIC digital library, 174
    ethical issues and guidelines, 75–76, 112
    unobtrusive data collection, 428
Interpersonal attractiveness, 504
Interpersonal learning, 141
Interpersonal mattering, 329
Interpersonal psychoanalysis, 364
Interpersonal psychotherapy, 249
Interpretation of assessment, 39, **299–300**
Interpreting, 128, 219
Interpretive bias, 59
Interpretive phase (behavioral assessment), 55
Interpretivism, 454
Interracial families, 60
Interrater reliability, 450–451
Interscorer reliability, 450–451
Intersexed, 488, 549
Interval scales, 471
Interviewing, **300–301**
    career assessment, 67
    clinical, 300
    community, 428
    focus groups, 428
    key informant, 427–428
    open, 427
    semistructured, 300
    structured, 300, 427
    unstructured, 300–301
Intimacy, 177
Intimate distance, 368
Intimate partner abuse or violence, 160
Intrinsic case study, 92
Intrinsic motivation, 344
Intrinsic values, 68
Intrinsic work values, 570–571
An Introduction to the Theory of Mental and Social Measurements (Thorndike), 542
Introjection, 145*t*, 212
Introverts, 306
Intuition, 306
Intuitive experiences, 550
Inventiveness, 218

Inventoried interests, 84
Investigative/analyzer personality type, 267
Investigative career preference, 90–91
Invisible disabilities, 156
Invitational skills, 262
Involuntary hospitalization as suicide intervention, 535
Iowa Test of Basic Skills, 35
Ipsative assessment, 368
IQ (intelligence quotient), 34–35
IRBs (institutional review boards), 288
Irish Americans, 181–182
    See also European Americans
Irrational beliefs, 443
IRT (item response theory), 302, 525
IS-Wel model, 563–565, 564*f*
Islam, 520
Isms, 404
Isolation, 144*t*, 177, 184
Isomorphic interventions, 511
Issac, Stephen, 455
Italian Americans, 181–182
    See also European Americans
Item analysis, **301–302**
Item characteristic curve (ICC), 302, 302*f*
Item difficulty, 301
Item discrimination, 301
Item response theory (IRT), 302, 525
Ivey, Allen E., 170, 244, 263, 337–338
Ivey, Mary Bradford, 170, 263, 337–338

▪ J

Jackson, Anita, 129
Jackson, Don, 116, 528
Jackson Personalty Inventory–Revised, 398
Jackson Vocational Interest Survey, 84
Jacobsen, Edith, 363
Jaffee v. Redmond (1996), 261, 408
Jain v. State of Iowa (2000), 413
Jamais vu (familiar place or feeling), 333
James, R. K., 132
James, William, 518
Janis, I. L., 70–71
Japanese Americans, 30
Jealous type delusional disorder, 476
Jenkins, Yvonne, 14
Jensen, A. R., 289
Jensen, M. A. C., 227–229
Jensen-Scott, R. L., 461
Jewish Chronic Disease Hospital Study, 452
Jewish culture, 206
Jews, counseling, **303–304**
Jindal, S., 193
Job Descriptive Index, 304
Job Diagnostic Survey, 304
Job loss, 276, 461, 509
Job satisfaction/dissatisfaction, **304**
Job Satisfaction Survey, 304
Job Training and Partnership Act of 1982, 70
Johari Window, **304–305**, 304*f*
Johnson, Lyndon, 412, 501
Johnson, Samuel H., 46
Johnson, Virginia, 117–118
Joint Commission on Mental Illness and Health, 102
Jones, K. D., 114
Jordan, J. V., 567
Journal for Specialists in Group Work (ASGW), 47, 216, 234, 237, 406, 415
Journal of Addictions & Offender Counseling (*JAOC*), 295
Journal of African American Men, 415, 502
Journal of Applied Rehabilitation Counseling (NRCA), 359
Journal of College Counseling (ACCA), 18
Journal of Counseling & Development (*JCD*), 415, 499–500
Journal of Creativity in Mental Health (ACC), 45
Journal of Employment Counseling (*JEC*), 295, 358
Journal of Group Psychotherapy, Psychodrama, and Sociometry (ASGPP), 238

(Continued)

Marsh, E. J., 55
Marshall v. Georgia (1985), 37
Martin, J. A., 391
Mary Smith Arnold Anti-Oppression Award (CSJ), 129
Masculinity, 483
Maslow, Abraham, 462, 480, 509, 520
Massachusetts, same-sex marriage, 489
Master Addictions Counselor (NBCC), 295, 354
MasterFILE FullTEXT, 47
Masters, William, 117–118
Masters and Johnson treatment model, 117–118
Matching, 433
Matriarchal family structures, 181
Mattering to others in counseling, **329**
Matthews, A. K., 487
Maturation, internal validity, 293
Mature minor, 319
Mauzey, E. D., 521
Maximal performance tests, 40
Maximal variation sampling, 469
May, Rollo, 184
MBTI. *See* Myers–Briggs Type Indicator
McCants, T. R., 322
McCarn, S. R., 486
McCarthy, E., 185
McCaughey, T. J., 340
McDavis, R. J., 47, 500
McDonough, Joe, 48
McIntosh, Peggy, 407
McKinley, J. C., 35, 557
MCMI-III (Millon Clinical Multiaxial Inventory–III), 398–399, 558
McMillan, Jan, 17
McNally, C., 521
Meadows, Mark E. "Gene," 18
Mean, 93, 151
Mean score, 526
Mean square error, 388
Mean square within, 388
Meaning attribution, 219, 221
Meaninglessness, 184
Measurement
    AACE and, 43–44
    defined, 39
Measurement and Evaluation in Counseling and Development (AACE), 44
Measures of central tendency, 93, 151
Measures of group climate, 225
Measures of variability, 151–152, 151*t*
Med-arb, conflict resolution, 116
Median, 93, 151
Mediation, conflict resolution, 115
Medicaid, 23
Medical College Admission Test, 28
Medicare, 23, 354
Meichenbaum, Donald, 103–104
Melting pot concept, 40
Member checking, 555
Member satisfaction and group work evaluation, 231
Memory, 9, 286–287, 334
Memory and behavior questions, 537–538
Mental energy, 289
Mental health counseling, 102
Mental health practitioners, **330–331**
Mental Measurements Yearbook (*MMY*), 67, **331–332**
Mental Research Institute (MRI), 116, 338, 510, 528, 529
Mental retardation, **332**
Mental status examination (MSE), **332–334**
Mental test, defined, 34
Mentoring, 86
Merchant, N. M., 241
Merriam, S., 10
Mesokurtic distributions, 309, 309*f*
Messe, L. A., 42
Messina, James, 21, 22
Mestizo, 436
Meta-analysis, **334–337**

"Meta-Analysis of Experimental Research Based on the Dunn and Dunn Model" (Lovelace), 10
"Meta-Analysis of Psychotherapy Outcome Studies" (Smith & Glass), 456
Metaphors, use of, 131, 513
Metatheory, 171
Methadone, 6
MetLife Foundation, 477
Metropolitan Achievement Test, 35
Mexican Americans, 42
MI (motivational interviewing), 344–345
Michael, William, 455
Michaels, D., 379
Microaggression, 14
Microculture, 140
Microskills counseling, **337–338**, 338*f*
    Frank's theory on, 262
    Ivey's theory on, 263
    structural family counseling and, 532
Microsystems, 139, 171, 270
Microtraining Associates, 263
Middle adulthood, 328
Middle-class status, 508
Milan group, 338–339, 529
Milan systemic family therapy, **338–339**
Mild mental retardation, 332
Miles, Matthew B., 221, 234, 456
Milgram Obedience Study, 452
Mill, John Stuart, 453
Millennials generation, 208, 209
Miller, George, 317
Miller, J. B., 567, 568
Miller, John Stuart, 161
Miller, S., 510
Miller, William R., 344–345
Miller Analogy Test, 28
Millon Clinical Multiaxial Inventory, 35
Millon Clinical Multiaxial Inventory–III (MCMI-III), 398–399, 558
Millon, T., 399
Miner, J. B., 35
Mini-mental state examination (MMSE), 332, 334
Minimum competency-based assessment, 133
Minimum level of skills, 3
Minnesota Abilities Test Battery, 396
Minnesota Importance Questionnaire, 68
Minnesota model (MM), 344
Minnesota Multiphasic Personality Inventory (MMPI), 35, 398, 557, 558
Minnesota Multiphasic Personality Inventory–2 (MMPI-2)
    clinical symptoms and, 69
    degree of characteristic prominence, 370
    development of, 398
    diverse norm-group, 369
    T scores, 526
    validity scales, 558, 559
Minnesota Occupational Rating Scales (MORS), 462
Minnesota Satisfaction Questionnaire, 304
Minor consent, 259, 319
Minorities
    See also Biracial/multiracial clients; Multicultural counseling; Race; Racial identity; *specific groups*
    discrimination and racism against, 11, 12–13, 29, 30
    employment opportunities for, 78
    racial identity development (MRID) models, 437–439
    suicide rates among, 361, 535
Minority group, 140
Minority-Majority Relations Scale, 42
Minors. *See* Children
Minuchin, Salvador, 531–532
Miracle question, 512
Miranti, Judy, 49
Mirrors, 422
Miscegnation laws, 436
Misogyny, 568
Mistrust, 177
Mitchell, Kathleen, 79, 507–508
Mixed delirium, 147
Mixed method designs, **339–340**, 339*f*
Mixed-race persons, 436–437

Mixed type delusional disorder, 476
MM (Minnesota model), 344
MMPI. *See* Minnesota Multiphasic Personality Inventory
MMSE (Mini-mental state examination), 332, 334
MMY (Mental Measurements Yearbook), 67, **331–332**
Moccoby, E. E., 391
Mode, 93, 151
Model group member role, 222
Model minority myth, 30
Model of second language acquisition (Lambert), 311
Modeling
    cultural respect and sensitivity, 241
    by group leader, 219
    group work technique, 245
Moderate lethality in suicide assessment, 533
Moderate mental retardation, 332
Moderation design strategy, 384
Modern test theory (MTT), 543
Mollen, D., 348
Monitor hypothesis, 312
Monochromic time, 368
Monster (Web site), 86
Montgomery, M. J., 518
Montoya, J., 136
Mood (MSE), 333
Mood disorders, **341–343**
    medical condition causing, 203, 342
Mood disorders NOS, 342–343
Moore, Lawrence, 163
Moore, Virginia, 22
Moradi, B., 200
Moral development, **343–344**
    model (Gilligan), 343–344, 567–568
    model (Kohlberg), 343, 567–568
Morality principle, 233, 420
Moratorium, 275
Moreno, Jacob Levy, 234, 253, 421–422
Morgan v. Fairfield Family Counseling Center (1997), 261
Morphological systems, 313
Morris, L., 417
Morrison, J., 484
MORS (Minnesota Occupational Rating Scales), 462
Morselli, Enrico, 514
Morten, G., 438, 438*f*
Moskowitz, J. T., 530
Motivation, **344**
    modeling process, 506
Motivational interviewing (MI), **344–345**
Motor reproduction, modeling process, 506
Motor tics, 544
Mourning, 229
Movement and behavior (MSE), 333
MRI. *See* Mental Research Institute
MRID (Minority racial identity development models), 437–439
MSE. *See* Mental status examination
MTT (modern test theory), 543
Muhammed (Prophet), 29, 520
Mulatto, 436–437
Multiaxial assessment system, 155
Multicolinearity, 123
Multicultural assessment standards, **345–347**
Multicultural Center (Antioch University), 42
Multicultural competence, **136–138**, 499
Multicultural counseling, **347–349**
    communication, **133–134**
    competencies, 348, 499
    cultural traits, 347
    genograms and, 210
    multiculturalism as fourth force, 136, 347–348, 499
    multidimensional model for developing culture competence, 348
    sports counseling competencies, 523
    stereotyping and, 382
    tripartite model of competencies, 348
Multicultural Counseling Competencies and Standards (AMCD), 47, 240, 382, 488, 499
"Multicultural Counseling Competencies and Standards" (Sue, Arredondo, & McDavis), 500

Multicultural Counseling Inventory, 523
The Multicultural Counselor (AMCD), 47
Multicultural Issues in Counseling, 415
Multicultural supervision, **134–136**
Multiculturalism, 139, **349–350**, 497
Multidimensional Aptitude Battery–Second Edition (MAB-II), 292
Multidimensional model for developing culture competence, 348
Multigenerational transmission process, 62
Multimodal approach, 283
Multimodal Handbook for a Mental Hospital (Brunnell & Young), 351
Multimodal therapy, 170, **350–351**
Multiple aptitude tests, 28
Multiple-baseline design (SSRD), 493
Multiple correlation coefficient, 123
Multiple family therapy, 63
Multiple intelligences theory (Gardner), 291, 318
Multiple personality disorder. *See now* Dissociative identity disorder
Multiple regression, 122–123
Multiracial identity, 437
Multiracial persons, 60
Multivalent logic, 212
Munchausen by proxy, 193
Munchausen syndrome, 193
Munson, M., 158
Murphy, Michael, 238
Murphy, V. M., 322
Murray, D. W., 379
Murray, Henry, 35, 398
Muslims, 520
Musturbation (Ellis), 443
My Vocational Situation (inventory), 69
Myers, Jane, 18, 43
Myers–Briggs Type Indicator (MBTI), 35, 68, 305, 370, 398
Mystical experiences, 550

N

NA (Narcotics Anonymous), 5, 6, 172
NAACP (National Association for the Advancement of Colored People), 500–501
NACCMHC (National Academy for Certified Clinical Mental Health Counselors), 17, 22, 412
Naltrexone, 6
Narcissistic personality disorder, 397
Narcolepsy, 495
Narcotics Anonymous (NA), 5, 6, 172
Narrative letters, 353–354
Narrative Means to Therapeutic Ends (White & Epston), 353
Narrative therapy, 130, **353–354**
Narratives, 82, 353–354, 364
Narrow-band behavior rating scales, 442–443
National Academy for Certified Clinical Mental Health Counselors (NACCMHC), 17, 22, 412
National Association for the Advancement of Colored People (NAACP), 500–501
National Association of Alcohol and Drug Abuse Counselors, 238, 320
National Association of Guidance and Counselor Trainers. *See now* Association for Counselor Education and Supervision
National Association of Multi-Cultural Rehabilitation Concerns, 126
National Association of Non-White Rehabilitation Workers, 126
National Association of Student Affairs Professionals, 499
National Board for Certified Counselors (NBCC), **354**
    ACA collaboration with, 19
    accreditation, 17, 22, 76, 354, 496
    ASGPP continuing education, 238
    Code of Ethics, **355**, 356
    CSI collaboration with, 95
    founding of, 412
    mental health counselor certification, 102
    multicultural awareness and, 496
    professional development, 411
    Standards for the Ethical Practice of Internet Counseling, 112, **355–356**
National Career Counseling and Development Guidelines (NOICC), 78
National Career Development Association (NCDA), **356–357**
    career counseling guidelines, 85
    Code of Ethics, 75–77, 79, 112, 356

history of, 80–82, 356, 412
professional development, 410–411
National Catholic Guidance Conference (NCGC), 48–49
National Center for Transforming School Counseling, 477
National Certified Career Counselor (NCCC) credential, 76, 79, 412
National Certified Counselor (NCC), 102, 354
National Certified School Counselor (NCSC), 354
National Clinical Mental Health Counselor Examination (NCMHE), 17
National Coalition Against Domestic Violence (NCADV), 161, 162
National Commission for Certifying Agencies, 109
National Commission for Protection of Human Subjects of Biomedical and Behavioral Research, 288, 454
National Conference of Guidance Councils, 48
National Council of Rehabilitation Education (NCRE), 126
National Council of State Agencies for the Blind, 126
National Council on Measurement in Education (NCME), 527
National Council on Measurement Used in Education (NCMUE), 527
National Counselor Examination for Licensure and Certification (NCE), 17, **357–358**
National Credentials Registry (NCR), 17
National Crime Victimization Survey (BJS), 160
National culture, 139
National Defense Education Act of 1958 (NDEA), 78
National Domestic Violence Hotline (NDVH), 160, 162
National Education Association, 527
National Education Goals Panel, 37, 133
National Employment Counseling Association (NECA), 295, **358**, 412
National Institute for Occupational Safety and Health, 378
National Institute of Justice
intimate partner violence, 160
violence and racial groups, 160–161
National Institute of Mental Health, 22, 61
National leadership (ACA), 20
National Occupational Information Coordinating Committee (NOICC), 78, 111
National Organization for Women, 68, 161
National Organization of Personnel Workers, 499
See also now National Association of Student Affairs Professionals
National Registry of Group Psychotherapists, 238
National Rehabilitation Association, 359
National Rehabilitation Counseling Association (NRCA), 23, 126, **359**
National Research Act of 1974, 288, 454
National Research Center on Asian American Mental Health, 503
National Research Council, 423
National Training Laboratory (NTL), 234, 238
National Vocational Guidance Association (NVGA), 80, 411
See also now National Career Development Association
Native Americans
counseling, **360–362**
Homo sapiens Americanus, 435
Natural child, 547
Natural order hypothesis, 312
Naturalistic generalizations, 93
Naturalistic setting in qualitative research, 26
Nature
nurture vs., **362–363**
universal value orientation, 572
The Nature of Prejudice (Allport), 262, 404
Nazi medical war crimes, 451–452
NBCC. *See* National Board for Certified Counselors
NCC (National Certified Counselor), 102, 354
NCDA. *See* National Career Development Association
NCE (National Counselor Examination for Licensure and Certification), 17, **357–358**
NCE (normal curve equivalent), 526
NCGC (National Catholic Guidance Conference), 48–49
NCME (National Council on Measurement in Education), 527
NCMHE (National Clinical Mental Health Counselor Examination), 17
NCMUE (National Council on Measurement Used in Education), 527
NCR (National Credentials Registry), 17
NCRE (National Council of Rehabilitation Education), 126
NCSC (National Certified School Counselor), 354
NDEA (National Defense Education Act of 1958), 78
NDVH (National Domestic Violence Hotline), 160, 162
Near-death experiences (NDEs), 550
NECA (National Employment Counseling Association), 295, **358**, 412
NECA Newsletter, 358

Needs assessment, 1, **363**
Negative case analysis, 555
Negative correlation, 123
Negative punishment, 381
Negative reinforcement, 380–381, 448
Negatively skewed distribution, 494, 494*f*
Neglect, child, 96–97
Negligence, 319
See also Malpractice
Negligence suits, 236
Negotiation, conflict resolution, 115
Neo-Freudian approaches, **363–364**
NEO Personality Inventory–Revised (NEO-PI-R), 203, 370, 399
Nepomuceno, C. A., 136
Nested designs, 340
Neuroleptic medications, 545
Neutrality, 339
Neville, H. A., 440
New Deal, 78
New England Journal of Medicine, 287
New Negro Movement, 436
New silent generation, 208, 209
New York Times on the year of the group, 234
Newsbytes (AACE), 44
NewsNotes (AACE), 44
Nguyen, H. H., 42
Nietzsche, Friedrich, 183
Nightmare disorder, 495
Nigrescence, psychology of, 437
Nihilism, 183
Niles, S. G., 77, 78, 87
No Child Left Behind Act of 2001, 37, 133, 146, 263–264, 477
No-suicide contract, 536
No-treatment control groups, 120
Nominal group technique, 247
Nominal scales, 471
Nondirective client growth, 100
Nonequivalent group designs, 432–433
Nonexclusionary time-out, 57
Nonexperimental research, **364–365**, 431
Nonheterosexual identity development, 485–486, 487
Nonmaleficence, 178–180, 257–258
Nonparametric statistics, **365–366**
Nonparametric tests, 285–286, 365
Nonprobability sampling, 431
Nonstandardized tests, defined, 39
Nonverbal assessments, 394–395
Nonverbal communications, **367–368**
cross-cultural, 134, 367
Norcross, J. C., 170
Norm, aggregated data, 369
Norm group, 526
Norm-referenced assessment, 3, **368–369**
Norm-referenced tests, 370
Normal curve, **369–370**, 370*f*
Normal curve equivalent (NCE), 526
Normal distribution, 369–370
Normalizing, 525
Norming
diversity-competent group work, 241
group work stage, 227, 228
Norms, **370–371**
developmental scores, 153–154
group content, 219, 229
North American Riding for the Handicapped Association, 25
Norton, Joe, 46
Nothing in excess health model, 563
Novelty/disruption effects, 190
Novice phase, 328
NRCA (National Rehabilitation Counseling Association), 23, 126, **359**
NTL Institute, 234, 238
Nuclear conflicts, 248
Nuclear family emotional process, 62
Null hypotheses (H_o), 273, 402, 403
Numerical classifications, 472
Nuremberg Code, 451–452
Nurture, 362

Qualitative data analysis (QDA) software, 430
Qualitative research, **425–427**
    basic characteristics of, 425*t*
    case study approaches, 426
    coding, 429
    content analysis, 429
    data analysis, 425*t*, 426–427
    data analysis software, 430
    data collection methods, 425*t*, **427–429**
    data management and analysis, **429–430**
    ethnography, 425–426
    grounded theory, 425
    inductive approach, 426
    interviews, 427–428
    naturalistic setting, 426
    observations, 428
    participatory action research, 426
    pattern analysis, 429–430
    phenomenology, 426
    recursive nature of, 426
    research traditions, 425
    unobtrusive measures, 428–429
    validity issues, 425*t*, 426–427
Qualitative Research & Evaluation Methods (Patton), 456
Qualitative Solutions software, 430
Quality world, 444
Quantitative research, **430–432**
    research design, 431, 431*f*
Quasi-experimental research designs, 188, **432–433**
Quasi-Experimentation (Cook & Campbell), 455
Queer, 488, 491–492
Queer Studies curriculum, 492
Queer theory, 492
The question, Adlerian technique, 283–284
Questioning of sexual identity, 488
Questions, use of, 511–512
    in surveys, 537–539
Quinceañera (Latino celebration), 206
Quota sampling, 469
Qur'an, 29, 520

▉R

R (coefficient of multiple determination), 122
r^s (Spearman rank correlation coefficient), 124
r_u (test–retest reliability), 450
Race, **435–437**
    See also Biracial/multiracial clients; Minorities; Multicultural
        counseling
    defined, 437–438
    ethnicity vs., 180
Racial/Cultural Identity Model, 438, 438*f*
Racial identity, 138, 565–566
    development models, 135, **437–439**, 438*f*
Racial prejudice, 404–405
Racial profiling, 30
Racial socialization, 12
Racio-ethnic culture, 139
Racism, **440–441**
    See also Cultural bias; Racial prejudice
    costs of, 440
    counseling considerations, 11, 12–13, 440
    microaggression and, 14
    model minority myth and, 30
    multiculturalism and, 349
    as oppression, 383
    subtle forms of, 12
Radical feminism, 201
Rahe, Richard, 321–322
Rahe's Stress and Coping Inventory (SCI), 322
Rajaratnam, N., 542
Random assignment, 187–188, 441–442
Random sampling, 467, 468
Random selection, 441
Randomization, **441–442**
    true experimental design and, 554
Range, 559–560

Rank, Otto, 100, 363
Rasch model, 543
Rating scales, **442–443**
    behavioral assessment, 55
    commonly used scales, 442*t*
Ratio IQ, 35, 289
Ratio scales, 471–472
Rational emotive behavior therapy (REBT), 119, 220, **443–444**
    group counseling, 249, 443–444
Rational emotive imagery, 444
Ravid, Ruth, 455
Raw score, 526
Rawlings, John, 234
RCE (rehabilitation counselor education) programs, 126
RCT (relational-cultural theory), 567
Reaction formation, 144*t*
Reactivity, 189
    qualitative research, 555
Reading Recovery, 146
Realistic period (Ginzberg), 214
Realistic personality type, 90–91, 266–267
Reality check group member role, 222
Reality principle, 420
Reality therapy, **444–445**
    scope of, 249
    WDEP system, **445–446**
Reason and Emotion in Psychotherapy (Ellis), 443
REBT. *See* Rational emotive behavior therapy
Receptive language difficulties, 313
Recidivism prevention, adult offenders, 379–380
Reciprocal inhibition, 57
Reciprocity in licensure, 321
Recursive, qualitative research, 426
Reed, Anna, 411
Reeve, Christopher, 157
Reference to self, 480
Referential adequacy, 555
Referral, ethical issues of, 258
Reflecting, 128
Reflecting skills, 262
Reflection of meaning, 338
Reformation stage of lifecareer process, 546
Reframing, 532
Refugees, defined, 276
Regehr, C., 80
Regional culture, 139
Regression (statistics), 122–123
Regression as defense mechanism, 145*t*
Regression equation, 122
Regression line, 122, 524
Regression to the mean, 294
Rehabilitation Act of 1973, 80, 156, 413, 478–480
Rehabilitation counseling, **446–448**
    ARCA services, 23–24
    defined by NRCA, 359
    history of, 447
    opportunities in, 447–448
    services provided, 447, 448
Rehabilitation Counseling Bulletin (ARCA), 23
Rehabilitation counselor education (RCE) programs, 126
Rehabilitation counselors, 359
Rehearsal, 57
Reinforcement
    behaviorism, 317
    defined, 448
    schedules, **448–449**
Relapse prevention, 6
Relational aggression, 13, 568–569
Relational-cultural theory (RCT), 567
Relational hypotheses, 273
Relationship building, 126
Relationship, efficacy, practicing, lowering, activating, new (REPLAN), 170
Relationship experiments, 63
Relationship groups, 253
Relationship mattering, 329
Relationship research question, 457

Shenson, D., 379
Shidlo, A., 490
Shiffrin, R., 287–288
Shin v. M. I. T., 260–261
Shoah (Holocaust), 303
Shoffner, M. F., 461–462
Short-term memory, 9–10, 286
SHR (simplified habit reversal), 545
Shutz, William, 234
Sibling position, 62
SIGI, 111
Significance level
    correlation coefficient, 124
    hypothesis testing, 273, 432
Silencing the self, 568
Silent generation, 208
Simmons, Richard, 45
Simon, J., 461
Simon, Theodore, 289, 290
Simple random sampling, 468, 525
Simple regression, 122
SIMPLE STEPS model, 534
Simple tics, 544
Simplified habit reversal (SHR), 545
Single-blind studies, 162
Single-parent-headed households, 197
Single-subject research design (SSRD), **492–493**
    A–B type, 492, 493*f*
    A–B–A–B type, 492–493
    scope of, 188
SIT (stress inoculation training), 103–104
SIT-R (Slosson Intelligence Test–Revised), 291
Situational bias, 59
Situational crises, 132
Situational factors in language acquisition, 311
Situational poverty, 509
Six orders of interracial contact, 41
16 Personality Factor Questionnaire (16PF), 68, 399
Skewed curve, 493
Skewness, **493–495**, 494*f*
The Skilled Helper (Egan), 262
Skilleg Group Counseling Scale, 225
Skin picking, 280
Skinner, B. F., 56, 317, 448–449
    See also Operant conditioning
Sklare, G. B., 510
SL-ASIA (Suinn–Lew Asian Self-Identity Acculturation) scale, 42
Slander, 319
Slavson, Samuel, 234
Sleep apnea, 495
Sleep disorders, **495–496**
Sleep terror disorder, 496
Sleepwalking disorder, 496
Sloan, Ted, 129
Slope bias, 140
Slosson Intelligence Test–Revised (SIT-R), 291
Smith, Mary, 456
Smith, Robert, 296
Smith, T. B., 136, 336, 518
Smith, W., 384
Smith–Fess Act of 1920, 447
Smith–Hughes Act of 1917, 77
SMMSE (standardized mini-mental state examination), 332–333, 334
Snowball sampling, 469
SOC (Standard Occupational Classification), 375
Social activism, 202
Social advocacy groups, 252
Social and cultural foundations
    ethical issues in, **496–499**
    historical issues in, **499–500**
    key people in, **502–503**. *See also specific individuals*
    legal issues in, **500–502**
Social career preference, 90–91
Social class privilege, 408
Social cognitive learning theory, 10
Social desirability bias, 473–474
Social development theory (Vygotsky), 318

Social/discusser personality type, 267
Social distance, 368
Social engineers, 218
Social exchange theory, 183
Social feminism, 201
Social identity theory, **503–504**
Social influence model, **504**
Social isolation, 461
Social justice, 504
    See also Counselors for Social Justice
Social justice in counseling, **504–505**
Social learning theory (Bandura), 318, **505–507**
Social learning theory of career counseling (LTCC), 81–82, 507–508
Social learning theory of career decision making (Krumboltz), **507–508**
Social narratives, 353
Social or recreational substance use, 533
Social phobia, 26
Social Readjustment Rating Scale (SRRS), 321–322
Social relationships, 572
Social systems and eco-map, 172–173
Social workers, 320
Socialization, 139
Socializing techniques, 141
Socially desirable responses, 558
Societal emotional process, 62
Societal racism, 440
Socioeconomic status or class, **508–510**
Sociometry, 422
Sociorace, 438
Socratic dialogue, 249
SOLER attending skills, 128
Soliloquy, psychodrama, 422
Solomon four-group design, 554–555
Solution-focused brief counseling (SFBC), **510–511**
Solution-focused brief counseling techniques, **511–513**
Somatic type delusional disorder, 476
Somatization disorder, 513–514
Somatoform disorders, **513–515**
    defined, 193
Somatogenic symptom, 284
Sorrell, G. T., 518
Soul, Jung's concept of, 520
The Souls of Black Folk (DuBois), 404
Soviet Union (USSR), 78
Space race, 78
Spanierman, L. B., 440
Spanish language tests, 3*t*, 291
SPATE (Student Personnel Association for Teacher Education), 127
    See also now American Counseling Association
Spearman, Charles, 27, 124, 194, 289, 450, 542
Spearman rank correlation coefficient (r^s), 124
Spearman–Brown prophecy formula, 450
Special education, **515–517**
Specialized accreditation, 2
Specific phobia, 26
Specification, 323
Specificity/true negative rate, 143
The Spectrum (ACES), 44
Speed test, defined, 39
Spiers, E. M., 379
Spiritual and religious support systems, 202–203, 241
Spiritual bypass, **517–518**
    transpersonal counseling and, 551
Spiritual identity, **518–519**
Spirituality in counseling, **519–521**
Spisso, Nancy, 21
Split-half reliability, 450
Split-plot design, **521–522**
Splitting
    as defense mechanism, 145*t*
    object relations, 374
Spock, Benjamin, 391
Spontaneity, 218
Spontaneous recovery, 99
Spontaneous-content groups, 242
Sports counseling, **522–524**
Spranger, E., 71

Spurious correlation, 124
Sputnik, 411
SRE (Schedule of Recent Events). *See now* Holmes–Rahe Scale
SRRS (Social Readjustment Rating Scale), 321–322
SRS (sex reassignment surgery), 549
SSRD. *See* Single-subject research design
Stabilizing, 323
Stable causes (attribution theory), 52
Stage theories, 104
 See also specific theories
Stagnation, 178
Stakeholders, 1, 363
Stampfl, Thomas G., 278–279
Standard deviation, 526, 560
Standard error of estimate, **524**
Standard error of measurement (SEM), **524–525**
Standard Occupational Classification (SOC), 375
Standardization, **525–526**
Standardization sample, 526
Standardized mini-mental state examination (SMMSE), 332–333, 334
Standardized scores, **526–527**
Standardized testing
 comparable opportunity to demonstrate, 525
 defined, 39
 for high-stakes decisions, 263–264
Standards-based assessment, 133
Standards for Counseling Supervisors (ACES), 17
Standards for Educational and Psychological Assessment (AERA, APA, NCME), 541
Standards for Educational and Psychological Testing (AERA, APA, NCME), **527–528**
 career-related formal testing, 67
 multicultural awareness, 346
 reliability coefficients and, 451
Standards for Educational and Psychological Tests and Manuals (AERA, APA, NCME), 527
Standards for Multicultural Assessment (AACE), 346, 541
Standards for the Ethical Practice of Internet Counseling (NBCC), 355–356
Stanford Achievement Test, 35, 68
Stanford–Binet Intelligence Scales
 achievement testing, 68
 aptitude testing, 28, 69
 Army use of, 291
 criticisms of, 394
 development of, 34–35, 290
 raw scores and, 289
Stanines, 3
Stanley, Julian, 455
Stanton, Elizabeth, 161
State-Event Classroom Observation Code (SECOS), 55, 56*t*
The State of Americans (Bronfenbrenner), 271
State-Trait Anxiety Inventory, 69
States
 licensure laws, 20, 102, 235, 259
 proficiency tests, 263
Statistical hypotheses, 457
Statistical power, 274
Statistical significance level, 273, 285
Status concept, 275
Status of identity development, 518
Status offenders, 307
Stealing, 279
Steiner, Claude, 547
Stereotypes
 cultural relativism vs., 139
 hidden gender role, 206
 negative sexual, 488
 socioeconomic, 509
Stern, G. S., 322
Stern, William, 289, 290
Sternberg, Robert, 27, 291, 318
Stimulus-response chain, 57
Stiver, I., 567, 568
Stockton, Rex, 240
Stollak, G. E., 42
Storming, 227, 228

Strategic family therapy, **528–529**
Strategies variable, Schlossberg's 4S model, 90
Stratified sampling, 468, 525
Strauss, W., 208
Strength-based model, 146
Stress, **529–531**
Stress inoculation training (SIT), 103–104
Stressors, 529
 occupational, 377
Stringer, Ernest, 456
Stripling, Robert, 22
Striving for superiority, 282
Strohmer, D. C., 340
Strokes (TA), 547–548
Strong, Edward K., 35, 71
Strong Interest Inventory, 35, 81, 84, 92, 112
Strong Interest Inventory-II, 68
Strong, Stanley, 504
Strong Vocational Interest Blank, 35
Strotbeck, F. L., 570
Structural assimilation, 40
Structural classism, 509
Structural components, group content, 229
Structural family counseling, **531–532**
Structural map, 531, 532*f*
Structure, 219
 in family counseling, 531
Structure and Dynamics of Organizations and Groups (Berne), 548
Structured interviews, 427
Structured personality tests, 398–399
Structuring
 diversity-competent group work, 241
 as group work technique, 244
Struggle (Jungian psychotherapy), 306
Student Personnel Association for Teacher Education (SPATE), 127
 See also now American Counseling Association
Students, international, **296–299**
Stuttering, 313
Style of life analysis, 282, 283
Style of life, personality, 282
Subculture, 140
Subich, L. M., 200
The Subjection of Women (Mill), 161
Subjective tests, defined, 40
Sublimation, 144*t*
Substance abuse
 addiction counseling, 4–7, 220, 344
 adolescents, 8
 adult offenders, 378
 enablers, 203
 Native Americans, 361
Substance Abuse Subtle Screening Inventory–3 (SASSI-3), 69, 558
Substance dependence, 4–5, 533
Substance-induced disorders, 533
 anxiety disorders, 26
 mood disorders, 342
Substance-related disorders, **532–533**
Substitution, 145*t*
Subsumption theory, 317
Subsystems in family counseling, 531
Subtractive perspectives in second language acquisition, 311
Sue, David, 280–281, 438, 438*f*
Sue, Derald W.
 on indigenous healing, 280–281
 on multicultural counseling competencies, 47, 136, 412, 500
 profile, 503
 racial identity models, 438, 438*f*
 worldview paradigm, 571–572, 573
Sue, Stanley, 503
Suicide
 assessment, **533–534**
 duty to warn and protect, 163, 164, 260–261
 incidence of, 534–535
 intervention, **534–536**
 lethality, 533, 534
 minorities and, 361, 535
Suinn–Lew Asian Self-Identity Acculturation (SL-ASIA) scale, 42

Suinn–Lew Asian self-identity measurement model, 41
Sullivan, Harry Stack, 175, 364
Sum of squares, 388
Summarizing, 128, 338
Summative evaluation, 38–39
Summit on Spirituality (ASERVIC), 49
Super, Donald E.
    See also Life span, life-space career theory
    establishes ACA ethics code, 20
    NCDA Eminent Career Award recipient, 80
    profile, 82
    publications, 82, 83
    technology and, 110
    work values, 569
Superego, 420
Superiority complex, 282
Superlative Self-Presentation Scale (S), 559
Superman symbology, 208
Supervision, **536–537**
    cross-cultural supervision, 134–136
Supervisor roles, 536
Supreme Court, U.S.
    on color blindness, 435
    on involuntary commitment to state mental hospitals, 412
    on privileged communication, 261, 408–409
    on school segregation, 500–501
    on state sodomy law, 489
Surrey, J., 567
Survey achievement tests, 3
Survey construction, 537–539
Survey, defined, 537
Survey of Personal Values, 68
Survey research, 148–149, 365
    in counseling, **537–539**
Survival language, 311
Sutton, P., 158
Suzuki, Lisa, 456
Sweeney, B., 392
Sweeney, Thomas J., 296, 414–415
Switching, 158
Symbols of Transformation (Jung), 305
Symmetrical distribution, 493
Symptom Checklist–90–Revised, 231
Symptom-contingent cues, 278–279
Syncretism, 170
Syntactical systems, 313
Synthesis in feminist identify development model, 200
System of Logic (Mill), 453
Systematic desensitization, 57, 99
Systematic Training for Effective Parenting (Dinkmeyer), 239
Systems for Multiple Level Observation of Groups, 226
Systems theory, 195–196, 531

◼ T

T scores, 3, 526
t test, 387–388
T-groups, 252
TA (transactional analysis), 547–548
Table of random digits, 441
Taijin kyofusho (culture-bound syndrome), 155
Tail off, scores, 493
Tajfel, Henri, 503–504
Talk therapies, 130
Talley, W. B., 381
Tang, M., 185
Taoism, 520
Tarasoff v. Regents of the University of California (1976), 163–164, 261
Task accomplishment, 228
Task approach skills, 507
Task-focused coping, 530
Task Force on Family Violence, 161
Task group consultation, 251–252
Tavistock Clinic, 234
Tavistock Group. *See now* Tavistock Institute of Human Relations
Tavistock Institute of Human Relations, 222, 234, 238, 239

Teachers College Personnel Association, 127
    See also now American Counseling Association
Team-building, 252
Tearoom Trade Study, 452
Technical eclecticism, 170
Technical Recommendations for Achievement Tests (AERA, NCMUE), 527
Technical Recommendations for Psychological Tests and Diagnostic Techniques (APA), 527
Technology
    assistive, 157
    CACGS assessment instruments, 110–113
    career Web sites, 86
    ethical issues and, 258–259
    ethical issues in career counseling and, 75–76, 112, 113–114
    legal issues and, 75–76, 261
    security and confidentiality, 112
Telekinesis, 550
Telepathy, 550
Tend and befriend, 568
Tennessee Self-Concept Scale–Second Edition, 398
Tentative phase (Ginzberg), 214
Terdal, L. G., 55
Terman, Lewis, 34–35, 289
Terminally ill clients
    counseling ethics, 163, 258
    grief stages, 215–216
Termination
    counseling stage, 126–127
    ethical issues, 258
    legal issues, 259
Tertiary oppression, 381–382
Tertiary prevention, domestic violence, 162
Test adaptation and test translation, **541–542**
Test bias, 59
Test of Nonverbal Intelligence (TONI), 394, 395
Test theory, **542–543**
Test-operate-test-exit (TOTE), 317
Tested interests, 84
Testing, defined, 368
Testing effects of internal validity, 294
Test–retest reliability (r_{tt}), 450
Tests. *See* Achievement tests; Assessment; *specific types*
Tests in Print (*TIP*), 331
Theft, 51
Thematic Apperception Test, 35, 399
Theme-oriented groups, 242
Themes in group work, 227–229
Theoretical integration, 170
Theory and Application of Statistics (Wampold & Drew), 455
The Theory and Practice of Group Psychotherapy (Yalom), 184, 240
Theory-based career stages, 69
Theory of multiple intelligences (Gardner), 291, 318
Theory of work adjustment (TWA), 66, 395–396, 461–462, 569, 570
    See also now Person-environment-correspondence theory
Theory X group leadership, 220
Theory Y group leadership, 220–221
Theory Z group leadership, 221
Therapeutic alliance, **543–544**
Therapeutic factors, **141–142**
Therapeutic Factors Scale, 226
Therapist's View of Psychotherapy (Rogers), 262
Therapy Dogs International, 25
Therapy triangles, 63
Thibaut, John, 183
Thick description, transferability, 555
Thinking (Jungian personality typology), 306
Thinned, CRF schedule, 448
Thirty-One Multiculturalism Counseling Competencies (ACA), 499
Thompson, C. E., 440
Thompson, Clara, 364
Thorndike, Edward L., 35, 255, 316, 317, 542
    See also Operant conditioning
Thorne, Frederick, 169–170
Thought content (MSE), 333
Thought process (MSE), 333
Thurstone, Louis Leon, 289, 474

World Health Organization
    on traditional healing approaches, 280
    on wellness, 563
World War I veterans
    intelligence testing of, 290
    personality testing of, 398
    rehabilitation counseling, 447
World War II veterans
    college counseling for, 109
    focus groups and, 428
    German Nazi medical war crimes against, 451
    mental health counseling for, 23, 78, 100, 234
    occupational information, 376
Worldview, **571–573**
    Ibrahim model, 572–573
    Sue model, 571–572, 573
Worthen, Blaine, 418, 456
Worthington, R. L., 486
Wrenn, Gilbert, 499
Wu, J. T., 136
Wubbolding, Robert, 249, 445, 446
Wundt, Wilhelm, 34
WUSCT (Washington University Sentence Completion Test), 176

 X

Xenophobia, 404
Xers, 208–209

Y

Yalom, Irvin D., 141–142, 184–185, 220, 221, 240
Yalom's ultimate concerns, 184–185
Yeh, C. J., 281
Yerkes, Robert, 35, 290
Yes set, 511
Young, W., 351

Z

z score, 526
Zangwill, Israel, 40
Zero reject principle, IDEA, 515
Zimpfer, David G., 240
Zone of proximal development, 318, 561
Zytowski, Donald, 71

NAMES INDEX

Names of contributors are flagged with an asterisk and the page numbers of their articles are in italics.

A

ACA Insurance Trust, Inc., 19
ACT Educational Technology Center, 81
*Adams, A. J., *60*
Addams, J., 202, 233
Addison, K. D., 185
Adler, A., 71, 130, 169, 170, 239, 272, 281, 282, 363, 520, 563, 567
Administration of Children and Families, 96
Adorno, T., 454
Adrian, G., 185
Advisory Committee on Education, 376
Aguilar-Gaxiola, S., 315
Ahuna, C., 41
*Ainbinder, D. L., *44*
Ainsworth, M., 49
Airasian, P., 539
Al-Anon, 254
Al-a-teen, 254
Al-Timimi, N., 296
Albertson, R., 82
Albin, D., 45
Alcántara, A., 361
Alcoholics Anonymous, 5, 6, 254
Alegria, M., 315, 316
Alemaychu, E., 332, 334
*Alessi, H. D., *280*
*Alexander-Albritton, C., *286*
Algina, J., 542
Allen, C. H., 127
Allen, M. J., 449, 450
Allen, R. D., 239
Alleyne, V., 378, 379
Allgood, S. M., 379
Allport, G., 262, 272, 404
Altekruse, M. K., 414
*Alviar, L. J., *401*
American Academy of Pediatrics, 490
American Association for Counseling and Development (AACD), 17, 19, 77, 412, 460
American Association for Marriage and Family Therapy, 196, 321
American Association of Counseling and Development (AACD), 294, 296
American Association of State Counseling Boards (AASCB), 16, 17, 321, 416
American Association of Teachers Colleges, 127
American College Counseling Association (ACCA), 18, 19, 109, 412
American College Personnel Association (ACPA), 18, 19
American Counseling Association (ACA), 1, 11, 17, 18, 19, 20, 21, 33, 34, 38, 43, 44, 45, 46, 47, 48, 77, 80, 81, 82, 102, 112, 113, 114, 127, 129, 130, 134, 137, 163, 164, 165, 179, 219, 232, 233, 235, 236, 243, 257, 258, 259, 260, 261, 264, 265, 272, 291, 294, 296, 320, 321, 346, 349, 356, 357, 358, 359, 382, 409, 410, 411, 412, 413, 414, 415, 416, 424, 441, 451, 452, 460, 476, 489, 490, 496, 497, 498, 499, 500, 501, 502, 505, 523, 571

American Counseling Association Foundation, 19
American Educational Research Association, 67, 264, 346, 451, 527, 541, 557
American Federation of Teachers, 490
American Group Psychotherapy Association (AGPA), 232, 234, 235, 237, 238
American Medical Association, 490
American Mental Health Association, 232
American Mental Health Counselors Association (AMHCA), 19, 21, 22, 23, 101, 102, 320, 412
American Personnel and Guidance Association (APGA), 19, 20, 46, 48, 49, 77, 127, 294, 321, 411, 412, 460, 499
American Psychiatric Association (APA), 8, 25, 26, 46, 51, 52, 147, 148, 167, 169, 193, 203, 234, 279, 300, 313, 332, 333, 341, 342, 362, 371, 396, 397, 399, 471, 475, 476, 483, 484, 485, 490, 495, 498, 513, 514, 532, 544, 545
American Psychological Association, 35, 67, 100, 320, 321, 346, 349, 382, 406, 423, 451, 488, 490, 503, 527, 541, 557
American Rehabilitation Counseling Association (ARCA), 19, 23, 126, 359, 412
American School Counselor Association (ASCA), 1, 19, 24, 44, 236, 264, 410, 412, 416, 476, 478
American School Health Association, 490
American Society of Group Psychotherapy and Psychodrama (ASGPP), 234, 237, 238
American University School of Public Affairs, 238
Amundson, N. E., 85, 358
Anastasi, A., 525, 557
*Ancis, J. R., *349, 383*
Anderson, E., 22
Anderson, J., 22
Anderson, M. L., 89
Anderson, R., 82
Anderson, W. T., 198
Andrés-Hyman, R. C., 314, 315
Andrews, J. A., 8
Añez, L. M., 314, 315
Anthony, S. B., 161
Antioch University New England Online Multicultural Center, 42
*Aponte, L., *316*
Arab American Institute, 28
Arbisi, P. A., 559
Archer, J., 381
Aristotle, 269, 362, 563
*Armeniox, L. F., *144*
Armstrong, A. H., 379
Armstrong, P. I., 440
Arnold, D., 239
Arnold, M. S., 129, 383
*Aros, J., *543*
Arredondo, P., 47, 129, 136, 240, 382, 441, 488, 496, 500, 502, 503, 522, 523
Arthur, N., 297, 298
*Ascolese, J., *316*
Ashlock, G., 45
Askenasy, A. R., 322

Asmus, C. L., 247
Asperger, H., 400
Aspy, C. B., 405
Asrabadi, B. R., 296, 298
Assagioli, R., 550
Association for Adult Development and Aging (AADA), 19, 43, 210, 412
Association for Assessment in Counseling and Education (AACE), 19, 43, 44, 67, 346, 347, 412, 451, 460, 541
Association for Career and Techical Education, 416
Association for Counselor Education and Supervision (ACES), 17, 19, 22, 44, 81, 321, 412, 415, 416, 522
Association for Counselors and Educators in Government (ACEG), 19, 45, 412
Association for Creativity in Counseling, 19, 45
Association for Gay, Lesbian and Bisexual Issues in Counseling, 412
Association for Humanistic Psychology, 272
Association for Lesbian, Gay, Bisexual, and Transgender Issues in Counseling (ALGBTIC), 19, 46, 268, 488, 500
Association for Measurement and Evaluation in Guidance, 43
Association for Multicultural Counseling and Development (AMCD), 19, 46, 47, 240, 346, 382, 412, 415, 496, 499, 502
Association for Non-White Concerns, 46
Association for Play Therapy, 402
Association for Religious and Values Issues in Counseling, 49
Association for Specialists in Group Work (ASGW), 19, 47, 48, 220, 225, 230, 231, 232, 233, 234, 235, 236, 237, 239, 240, 241, 243, 250, 251, 253, 406, 412, 415
Association for Spiritual, Ethical, and Religious Values in Counseling (ASERVIC), 19, 48, 49, 412
Association of Black Psychologists, 502
Association of Specialized and Professional Accreditors (ASPA), 125
Astramovich, R. L., 1
Atchley, R. C., 461
Atherton, J. S., 106
Atkinson, D., 412
Atkinson, R., 286
Aubrey, R. F., 414
Auger, R. W., 417
Austin, K. M., 163, 164
Austin, R., 137
Ausubel, D., 317
Avanta Network, 116
Axelrad, S., 78, 87, 214, 569
Axline, 130
Azrin, N. H., 545

B

Babbie, E., 537
Badley, E. M., 16

611

Cass, V. C., 485, 489
Castaneda, C., 207
*Castro, V., 263
Cattell, A. K., 399
Cattell, H. E., 399
Cattell, J. M., 34
Cattell, R. B., 9, 27, 195, 289, 399
*Cavallaro, M. L., 98, 104
Cavanagh, M. E., 170
Cavanaugh, J. C., 9, 10
Cecchin, G., 338, 339
Census Bureau. See U.S. Bureau of the Census
Center for Advanced Study in the Behavioral
    Sciences, 81
Center for Credentialing Education, 17
Center for Public Education, 264
Center for the Study of Technology in
    Counseling and Career Development, 111
Centers for Disease Control and Prevention
    (CDC), 264, 265, 430, 534
Chan, F., 334
*Chandler, C. K., 25
*Chandras, K. V., 539
*Chandrus, S. V., 539
*Chaney, M. P., 549
Chang, C., 408
*Chang, C. Y., 135, 141
Chapman, A., 129
Charcot, J., 420
Charkow, W. B., 295
Charkow-Bordeau, W. B., 295
Charles, R., 157
*Cheek, J. R., 458
Cheldelin, S. I., 115, 116
Chen, M., 458
*Chen-Hayes, S. F., 129, 384
Chi Sigma Iota (CSI), 19, 94, 95, 414, 415
Chiang, L., 281
*Chibbaro, J. S., 11, 128
Chickering, A., 153
Child Protective Services, 536
Chizhik, A., 408
Chizhik, E., 408
Choate, L., 109
Chomsky, N., 153, 311
*Christensen, R., 463
*Christensen, T. M., 174
Chun, K., 408
Chung, Y. B., 487
*Cigrand, D. L., 80
Cisler, R., 385
Cizek, G. J., 557
Clarkson, F. E., 483
Clawson, T. W., 416
Clayton, J., 322
Cluse-Tolar, T., 235
Cochran, A. W., 198
Codding, R. S., 55, 442
Cohen, A. M., 227
*Cohen, D., 326
Cohen, J., 336
Cohen, P., 545
Cohen, R., 235
Cohen, S. P., 226
Cohen, W. E., 533
*Coker, A. D., 243
Coker, J. K., 1
Colah, J., 250
*Colangelo, J., 23
*Cole, K. W., 523
Cole, N. S., 266
Coleman, E., 485
Coleman, H., 137
Coles, A., 129
Coltrane, S., 464
Columbia University, 316
Columbia University Teachers College, 502

Colwell, R. K., 518
*Combs, D. C., 225
Commission on Rehabilitation Counselor
    Certification (CRCC), 94, 110, 126, 359, 446,
    447
Commission on Standards and Accreditation,
    126
Compton, W., 384
*Comstock, D. L., 14, 344, 568, 569
Conant, J. B., 35
Connolly, C., 45
Constantine, M. G., 135, 336, 502
Conway, L., 549
*Conway, M. B., 476
*Conyne, R. K., 220, 225, 239, 241, 250, 406
Cook, D., 135
Cook, D. A., 135
Cook, P., 8
Cook, T. D., 403, 455
Cook-Greuter, S., 175, 176
*Cooke, P., 32
Cooley, F. R., 48
Cooney, N. L., 226
Corbin, J., 425
Corcoran, K., 231
Corey, G., 164, 170, 179, 223, 225, 227, 235,
    236, 239, 248, 281, 521
Corey, M. S., 164, 170, 179, 225
Corsini, R. J., 170, 233, 234
Costa, P. T., 203, 399
Costantino, G., 281
Cott, C., 16
Cottingham, H. F., 414
Couch, R. D., 219
Council for Accreditation of Counseling and
    Related Educational Programs (CACREP), 1,
    2, 17, 19, 22, 44, 95, 102, 125, 137, 295, 346,
    357, 359, 363, 412, 415, 416, 496, 500, 523
Council for Higher Education Accreditation
    (CHEA), 125
Council of State Administrators of Vocational
    Rehabilitation, 126
Council on Rehabilitation Education (CORE),
    126, 412, 416
Counseling Association for Humanistic
    Education and Development (C-AHEAD), 19,
    127, 272, 412
Counselors for Social Justice (CSJ), 19, 129,
    130, 412, 500, 505
*Cowger, E., 170
Craine, R., 481
Cramer, S. H., 419
Crane, D. R., 196
Creswell, J. H., 455, 456
Creswell, J. W., 93, 425, 426, 427, 458
*Crethar, H. C., 505
Crites, J. O., 65, 66, 82
Crocker, L., 542
Cronbach, L. J., 450, 542
Cross, W., 199, 412, 437, 499
Croteau, J., 408
Crouter, A., 464
*Crowell, J. L., 223
Cullari, S., 247
Cumming, E., 14, 15
Curry, M. A., 16

D

*Dahir, C. A., 414, 416, 476, 477, 478
*Daidone, E. W., 157
Daiger, D. C., 92
Daley, T., 499
Damianopoulos, W., 14, 15
D'Andrea, M., 129, 137, 502
*Daneker, D., 206, 325
Daniels, J., 129, 137

Darley, J. G., 395
Darwin, C., 34
D'Augelli, A. R., 486
*Daughhetee, C., 339
Daunic, A., 392
*Davenport, B. R., 458
Davidson, L., 314, 315
Davidson, T., 161
Davis, D. C., 18
Davis, J., 411
Davis, J. B., 80, 233, 234
Davis, M., 226
Davis, R. D., 398, 558
Davis, T., 232
*Davis, T. A., 349, 383
*Davis, T. E., 357, 414, 416
*Davis-Gage, D., 480
Davison-Aviles, R., 129
Dawis, R. V., 66, 67, 78, 395, 569, 570
*Dawson, G. A., 10
de Beauvoir, S., 183
De Jong, P., 511, 512
de Ridder, D. T. D., 16
de Shazer, S., 510, 511, 512, 513
Dean, B., 109
Dean, J., 408
*Dean, L. A., 18
DeBord, K. A., 489
*Decker, K. M., 504
*Decker, S. L., 290
Deemer, H. N., 193
Defense Department, 35, 81
*Degges-White, S., 43
*DeLambo, D. A., 539
Delta Society, 25
*DeLucia-Waack, J. L., 225, 226
Delworth, U., 536
*Demask, M. P., 21
Demby, A., 226
Demming, W. E., 234
Denzin, N. K., 453, 454
Department of ___. See specific name of
    department
*Deroche-Philpot, M., 158
Derogatis, L. R., 231
Descartes, 183
Dettmer, P. A., 119
Deutsch, M., 229
*Deveaux, F., 129, 198
*Devlin, J. M., 123
*DeVoss, J. A., 511
Dewey, J., 454
Dewey, T., 189
*Dickson, G. L., 268
Dickson, M. W., 16
DiClemente, C., 385
Dies, R. R., 219
*Dik, B. J., 84, 396
Dilley, P., 487
Dillion, F. R., 486
Dilthey, W., 454
Dimitrov, D. M., 416
Dinehart, J. M., 336
DiNitto, D., 8
Dinkmeyer, D., 239
Dinsmore, J., 129
Dise-Lewis, J. E, 322
*Dixon, A., 329, 368
Dixon, W. A., 521
*Dodson, F. K., 480
Dohrenwend, B. P., 322
Dohrenwend, B. S., 322
*Dollarhide, C. T., 127, 272
*Domene, J. F., 366
*Dooley, K., 147
Dose, J., 570
Dougherty, A. M., 118